M000239701

SAP®
BusinessObjects

Web Intelligence BI 4.1 Training Course

A Practical Step-by-Step Guide to Creating Queries and Reports for Data Analysis

ISBN 978-1-291-86734-3

ISBN [illegible]

Trademarks

SAP, BusinessObjects, [illegible] Crystal Reports, [illegible] and other Business Objects products and services mentioned herein as well as their respective logos are trademarks or registered trademarks of SAP AG [illegible] Germany. Business Objects is an SAP company.

Screenshots and graphics reproduced in this book for SAP BusinessObjects products are subject to copyright [illegible]

Microsoft Windows, Microsoft Access, Microsoft SQL Server, Microsoft Excel, Microsoft Word, Microsoft PowerPoint, [illegible] are trademarks of Microsoft Corporation.

Oracle is a registered trademark of Oracle Corporation.

Java is a registered trademark of Oracle Corporation and/or its affiliates.

Adobe, the Adobe logo, Acrobat, [illegible] are either trademarks or registered trademarks of Adobe Systems Incorporated in the United States and/or other countries.

All other products mentioned are registered or unregistered trademarks of their respective companies.

Limits of Liability and Disclaimer of Warranty

The Author and Publisher of this book have used their best endeavours in providing examples used in this book and any accompanying sample data.

The Author and Publisher make no warranty of any kind, expressed or implied, with regards to the examples, sample data and documentation in this book. The Author and Publisher shall not be liable in any event for incidental or consequential damages in connection with, or arising out of the use of, examples contained in this book and any accompanying sample data.

CONTENTS

A Few Words

بِسۡمِ ٱللَّهِ ٱلرَّحۡمَٰنِ ٱلرَّحِيمِ

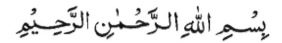

Bismillah ir-Rahman ir-Rahim

In the name of Allah (God), most Gracious, most Compassionate

I would like to begin by thanking Allah for making it possible for me to write this book by giving me the time, energy and dedication to share the knowledge and experience I have gained over many years of my working life.

Thank you for purchasing the SAP BusinessObjects Web Intelligence BI 4.1 Training Course.

This is probably the most comprehensive step-by-step training guide available for Web Intelligence in a book format. The aim of this book is to introduce you to the basics of Web Intelligence and then take you through to advanced topics by using practical examples at every step.

Each session covers a different area of functionality and as you work through the sessions, I hope it will become evident that Web Intelligence is a great tool for creating queries, developing reports and analysing data. I believe the course will help to gradually build your confidence in using Web Intelligence by covering concepts and techniques in a sequence that have been tried and tested in delivering classroom based training.

I have tried to ensure the material presented in this book is accurate but please do get in touch if you come across errors of any sort, or to give feedback on the course by emailing **feedback@webiworx.com**.

Accompanying the book is a dedicated website (**www.webiworx.com**). Please visit the website to download sample files and to learn more about using Web Intelligence.

I hope you enjoy the book and using Web Intelligence.

Shakil Ahmed

April 2014

1 Overview of Web Intelligence

SAP BusinessObjects Enterprise (also known as SAP BusinessObjects Business Intelligence Platform) is a suite of products designed to deliver business intelligence solutions for making informed decisions.

Some components run on servers but other applications can be installed locally to run on PCs and laptops (usually connected to the server components).

To use Web Intelligence you log into the SAP BusinessObjects Enterprise portal (known as BI Launch Pad) via your internet browser. Then, depending on your role, you can interact with the documents using BI Launch Pad, or build/edit your own documents using Web Intelligence.

1.1 What is a Repository?

The SAP BusinessObjects Repository stores information about documents, user IDs, privileges, etc.

The Central Management Console (CMC) is the administration module for SAP BusinessObjects Enterprise and it is used to manage the repository and its contents.

In a secured environment, only users with valid IDs can access the various components of SAP BusinessObjects Enterprise.

The CMS (Central Management Server) is the centralised software providing communication and interaction functionality for users of SAP BusinessObjects Enterprise products (such as enabling you to login). The CMS is effectively the repository.

NOTE – There can be many repositories and you simply use a different hyperlink to access each one (for example, organisations typically have separate repositories for Development, Testing and Production environments).

1.2 What is BI Launch Pad?

BI Launch Pad is web based software that allows you to log into a SAP BusinessObjects Repository and then perform a number of actions depending on your security profile.

SAP BusinessObjects Enterprise BI 4.x is a suite of many products and BI Launch Pad lets you access some of these products depending on the security applied to your user account and the licensing agreement (i.e. what products have been purchased by your organisation).

In relation to Web Intelligence (the query and reporting tool covered in this course), BI Launch Pad is used to:

Navigate, organise, refresh, schedule, share and print documents previously created in Web Intelligence (including Web Intelligence Rich Client), and also to view other types of documents such as Microsoft Word, Excel, and Adobe PDF.

With BI Launch Pad you can securely share documents in a corporate setting. User identification and privileges are tied to folders, groups, or even individual documents so only authorised users may view sensitive data. Documents may be organised, categorised, shared and scheduled under the secure environment managed using the CMC.

1.3 What is Web Intelligence?

Web Intelligence is a module within BI Launch Pad providing an interactive user interface for building reports and analysing data.

Web Intelligence is used to create, edit, and format documents (known as Web Intelligence documents or WID files). Web Intelligence documents are commonly referred to as 'reports' by users.

An intuitive interface is available to interact with data providers (sources of data). This interface is designed for end-users to drag and drop objects, or click on a few items in order to create a database/file request for retrieving a specified set of data.

There is built-in drag-and-drop functionality to provide speed and accuracy in report building and formatting. Web Intelligence also provides analysis functionality, allowing you to drill into and across data.

Data is retrieved into a 'microcube' giving the user multi-dimensional access to the information. This functionality resides within the reporting tool, making it possible to switch into drill mode at the click of a button in order to see any slice of data.

1.4 What is Web Intelligence Rich Client?

Web Intelligence Rich Client is a Java based application that has to be installed locally on every machine that you want to use it on. It offers the same functionality as the Java based Web Intelligence interface except you can run it without connecting to a repository (for example when you are travelling).

Web Intelligence Rich Client can be used:

1. With an open connection to a repository (known as Connected Mode).
2. With an offline connection to a repository (known as Offline Mode), i.e. you previously logged into a repository and saved documents for local processing.
3. With no connection to a repository (known as Standalone Mode), i.e. you do not have a repository but want to use and create Web Intelligence documents in your organisation.

This course mainly focuses on:

1. Creating and editing documents using Web Intelligence.
2. Using Web Intelligence Rich Client in Connected and Offline Modes to create and edit documents.
3. Using BI Launch Pad to navigate, refresh, schedule, share and print Web Intelligence documents.

NOTE

This course focuses first and foremost on creating and editing documents using the Web Intelligence interface (browser based), but Web Intelligence Rich Client is also covered.

Except for the connection methods, both of the tools (Web Intelligence and Web Intelligence Rich Client) offer the same functionality, therefore learning to use one of the tools should make you proficient in both tools.

2 Introduction to BI Launch Pad

This session introduces SAP BusinessObjects BI Launch Pad by describing how to log into the environment, navigating around, and managing areas where you save your work.

2.1 Logging On

Your BI Launch Pad Log On screen is accessed through a browser using a dedicated URL pointing to your repository location. Contact your SAP BusinessObjects Administrator or Web Server Administrator to determine your site's URL.

http://localhost:8085/BOE/BI
BI launch pad

Getting to this page requires that the web server is active and that you have rights to view this page. Security rights to this page are handled through the web server and not through the SAP BusinessObjects repository.

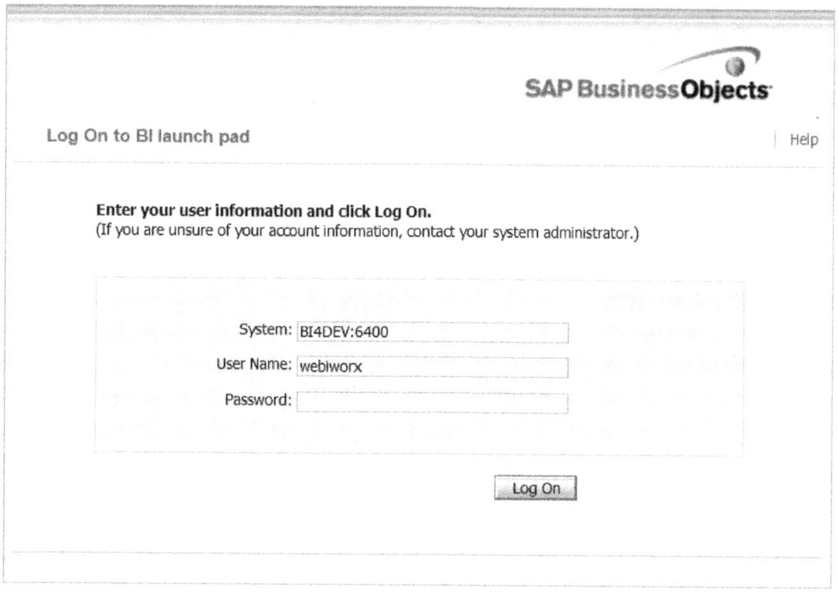
SAP BusinessObjects
Log On to BI launch pad
Help
Enter your user information and click Log On.
(If you are unsure of your account information, contact your system administrator.)
System: BI4DEV:6400
User Name: webiworx
Password:
Log On

Type in your User Name and Password provided by your administrator.

In 'Single Sign-On' implementations there is no need to provide User Name and Password as your Windows ID is automatically used to Log On to BI Launch Pad.

2.2 BI Launch Pad Home Page

When you first log on to BI Launch Pad, you retrieve the home page but you can select a different page to be your homepage by customising BI Launch Pad (see session on 'Setting BI Launch Pad and Web Intelligence Preferences'). This page might also appear differently depending on how your administrator has configured BI Launch Pad and your privileges.

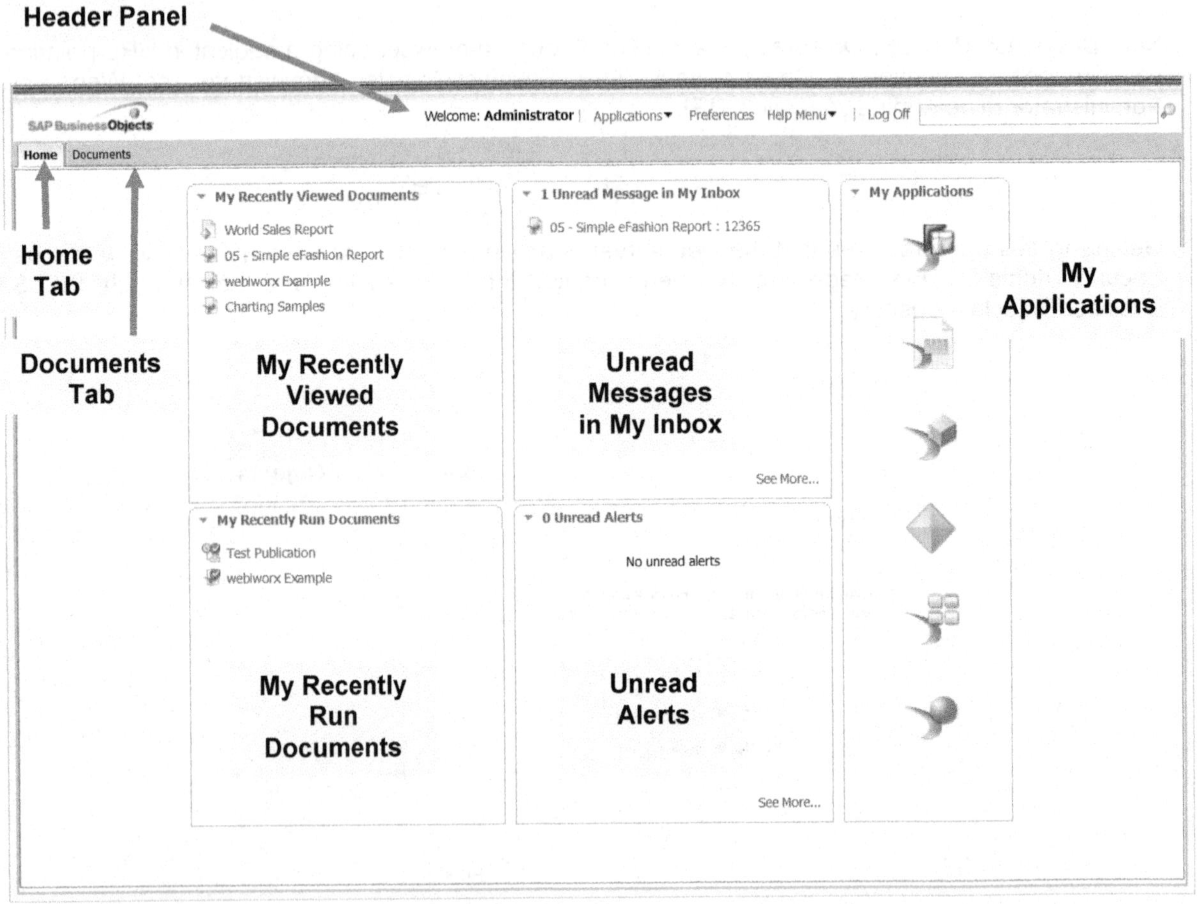
Header Panel
SAP BusinessObjects
Welcome: Administrator | Applications | Preferences | Help Menu | Log Off
Home | Documents
Home Tab
Documents Tab
My Recently Viewed Documents
World Sales Report
05 - Simple eFashion Report
webiworx Example
Charting Samples
My Recently Viewed Documents
1 Unread Message in My Inbox
05 - Simple eFashion Report : 12365
Unread Messages in My Inbox
See More...
My Applications
My Applications
My Recently Run Documents
Test Publication
webiworx Example
My Recently Run Documents
0 Unread Alerts
No unread alerts
Unread Alerts
See More...

The BI Launch Pad default view is made up of:

- Header Panel
- Home Tab
    - My Recently Viewed Documents panel
    - My Recently Run Documents panel
    - Unread Messages in My Inbox panel
    - Unread Alerts panel
    - My Applications panel
- Documents Tab

2.2.1 Header Panel

The Header Panel displays the logo and the user name of the account that you used to log on to BI Launch Pad. It also has a few menu items that you can use to perform the following actions:

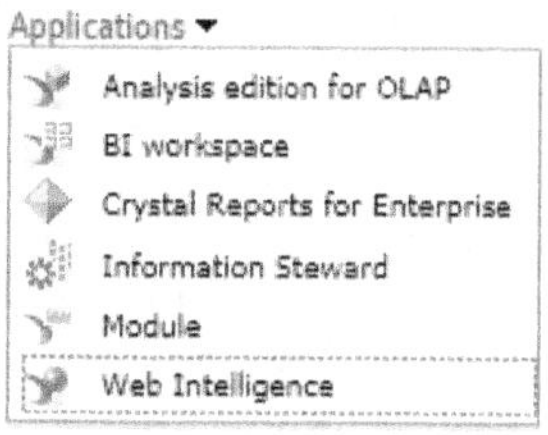
Applications
Analysis edition for OLAP
BI workspace
Crystal Reports for Enterprise
Information Steward
Module
Web Intelligence

Applications – You can launch the BusinessObjects applications you have access to use from here.

Preferences

Preferences – Determine how you log on to BI Launch Pad and what view is displayed when you do. Preferences also control specific settings for the various objects that you view, such as viewers for Crystal Reports and view formats for Web Intelligence documents.

As a best practice, you should set your preferences before you begin to work with objects in BI Launch Pad. However, depending on your deployment, your SAP BusinessObjects Enterprise Administrator may configure your system to use predetermined settings by default.

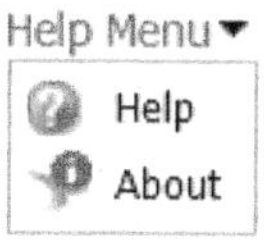
Help Menu
Help
About

Help – Displays the online help for BI Launch Pad.

About – Displays information about the version of SAP BusinessObjects Enterprise being used.

Log Off

Log Off – Click to Log Off and return to Log On screen

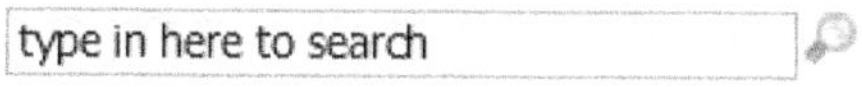
type in here to search

Search box – Provides search functionality for objects stored in the repository. Search is performed on object names, descriptions, keywords, etc.

2.2.2 Home Tab

The default Home tab is designed to offer quick access to the features you will probably work with most in SAP BusinessObjects. The tab contains 5 panels:

My Recently Viewed Documents

Displays a list of the last ten documents that you have viewed. The most recently viewed document will be at the top of the list.

My Recently Run Documents

Displays a list of the latest documents that you have run/scheduled. The status of the document instance is also shown (i.e. success/failure).

If the schedule has been successful then clicking the document name will open the relevant instance.

If the document has failed to run then clicking the document name will show more details related to the failure.

Unread Messages in My Inbox

Documents can be sent to your SAP BusinessObjects BI 4.x inbox by other users, schedules or publications.

Displays a list of the latest documents sent to your inbox. Click on a document name to view the document contents.

If you have more unread documents in your inbox then click on 'See More…'

Unread Alerts

You can subscribe to Alerts, for example values in reports exceeding specified limits, or system alerts for monitoring the SAP BusinessObjects Enterprise environment.

Displays a list of the latest alerts. Click on the alert name to view more details of the alert.

If you have more unread alerts then click on 'See More…'

Applications

You can launch the BusinessObjects applications you have access to use from here.

2.2.3 Documents Tab

The Documents tab is designed for you to interact with all types of objects in the SAP BusinessObjects Enterprise environment (such as folders, categories, documents, dashboards, etc).

The Document tab:

- Contains a Toolbar with the options View, New, Organize, Send, More Actions, and Details. The toolbar options are context sensitive depending on what is selected in the three panels.

- Is made of three panels acting in a hierarchical manner to display content (Navigation \ List \ Details):

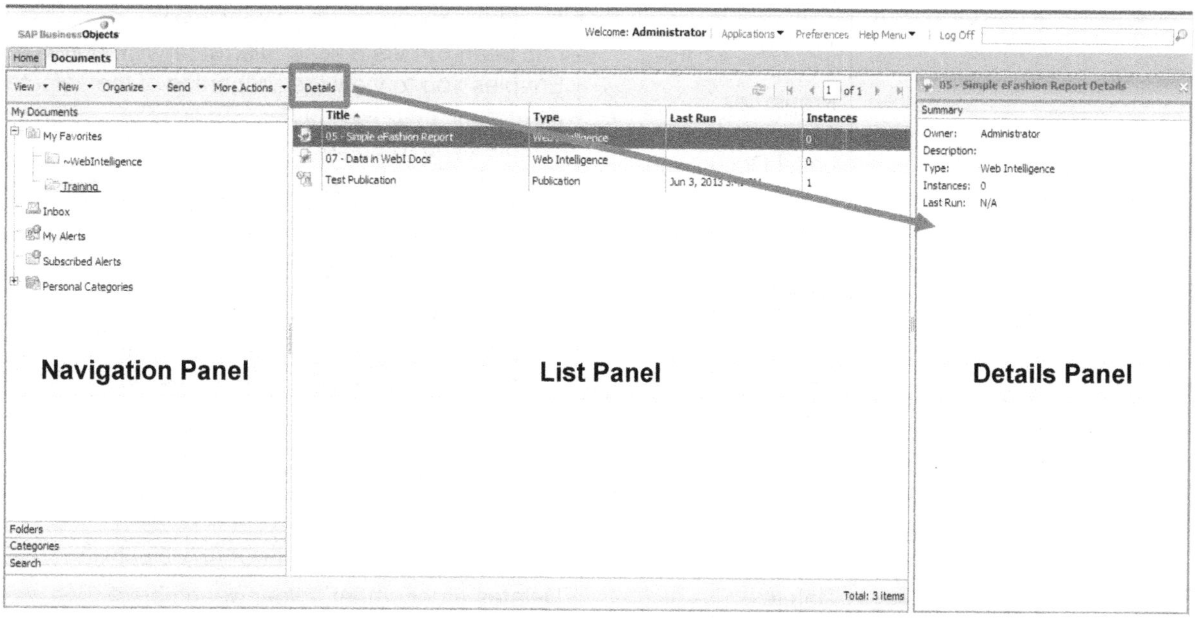
Welcome: Administrator
Applications
Preferences
Help Menu
Log Off
Home
Documents
View
New
Organize
Send
More Actions
Details
My Documents
My Favorites
~WebIntelligence
Training
Inbox
My Alerts
Subscribed Alerts
Personal Categories
Title
Type
Last Run
Instances
05 - Simple eFashion Report
07 - Data in WebI Docs
Web Intelligence
Test Publication
Publication
05 - Simple eFashion Report Details
Summary
Owner: Administrator
Description:
Type: Web Intelligence
Instances: 0
Last Run: N/A
Navigation Panel
List Panel
Details Panel
Folders
Categories
Search
Total: 3 items

NOTE – By default the 'Details Panel' maybe be visible, so click on 'Detail' button to toggle the panel off/on.

A brief description of each of the panels is given below:

Navigation Panel This panel is designed for you to manage and locate your documents within the SAP BusinessObjects Enterprise environment.

To enable this, the panel is organised into four drawers called My Documents, Folders, Categories, and Search.

List Panel Displays a list of objects belonging to the currently selected folder or category (in the Navigation Panel).

Details Panel Displays the details associated to the object/item currently selected in either the Navigation Panel, or the List Panel.

2.2.3.1 Documents Tab Toolbar

The Documents Tab Toolbar contains the following options:

Home
Documents
View
New
Organize
Send
More Actions
Details

These toolbar options are context sensitive in that they are made active/inactive depending on what is selected in the Navigation / List panels.

Functionality of toolbar options are described in more detail below:

Toolbar Option	Menu Option	Functionality
View	View	Enables you to view the object or document
	View Latest Instance	Enables you to view the latest instance of a document that has been run via a schedule (otherwise option is disabled)
	Properties	Enables you to view the properties of the selected object, document, instance, etc
New	Local Document	Enables you to upload local documents such as Word, Excel, PDF, JPG, etc into the repository
	Publication	Create an advanced type of schedule for batch processing using one or more documents, dynamic recipients, etc
	Hyperlink	Creates a hyperlink within the repository for internal or external URLs
	Folder	Creates a new folder within an existing folder
	Category	Creates a new category within an existing category
Organize	Create Shortcut in My Favorites	Creates a shortcut in My Favorites folder for the currently selected object / document
	Cut	Cuts a document, folder or an object
	Copy	Copies a document, folder or an object
	Paste	Pastes a document, folder or an object
	Delete	Deletes a document, folder or an object
	Copy Shortcut	Creates a copy of a shortcut
	Paste Shortcut	Pastes a copy of a shortcut
Send	BI Inbox	Sends a document to user's BusinessObjects inbox(es)
More Actions	View Lineage	For use with SAP Information Steward
	View Metapedia Terms	For use with SAP Information Steward
	Modify	Enables you to modify the document
	Schedule	Enables you to schedule a document to run
	Mobile Properties	Enables you to specify properties for when document is accessed by the SAP BI Mobile App
	History	Enables you to view the historical instances of the document (if it has been scheduled and run at least once)
	Categories	Adds a document or object to a category
	Document Link	Enables you to copy a link for the object or document so you can share it externally
Detail		Displays the Details Panel which opens up on the right-hand side

The toolbar also has the following options on the right hand side:

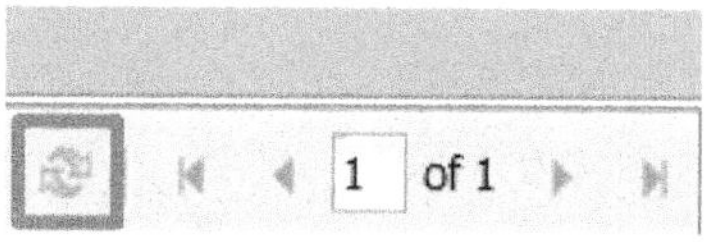
1
of 1

Contents of panels should auto refresh, but you can manually refresh using the circled icon.

The page navigation buttons are to cycle through the content list because you might have lost of documents. The number of items listed on a page can be changed in 'Preferences'.

2.2.3.2 Documents Tab – My Documents Drawer

The Documents Tab Toolbar contains the following options:

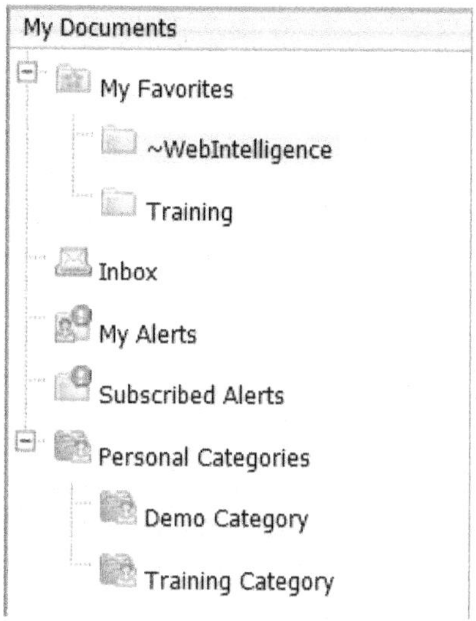
My Documents
My Favorites
~WebIntelligence
Training
Inbox
My Alerts
Subscribed Alerts
Personal Categories
Demo Category
Training Category

My Documents Drawer is typically available to each user to store their own documents and objects.

The folder ***~WebIntelligence*** is created automatically as Web Intelligence uses this folder to save temporary copies of documents you are working on.

Inbox is also auto-generated and is used to store documents that have been sent to you by other users or schedules/publications.

My Alerts are alerts that you have defined.

Subscribed Alerts are alerts that you have subscribed to.

Personal Categories are categories you define for your personal use.

We will now create the Training folder within My Favorites, and the two categories listed under Personal Categories.

1. Within My Favorites you can create Folders by clicking on 'My Favorites' and then using right-click for 'New – Folder':

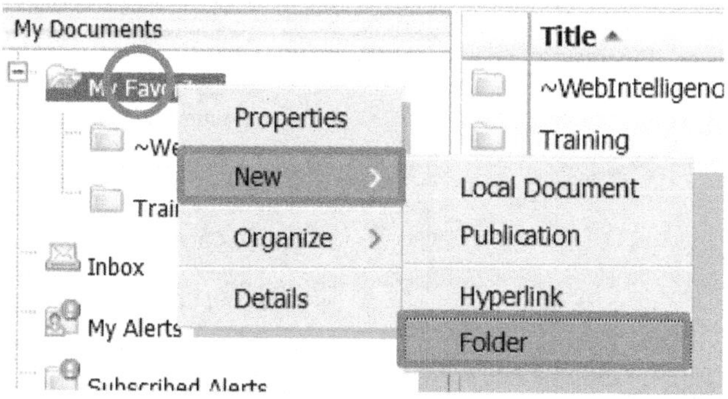
My Documents
Title
~WebIntelligenc
Training
Properties
New
Organize
Details
Local Document
Publication
Hyperlink
Folder
Inbox
My Alerts

Or you can click on 'My Favorites' and then select 'New – Folder' from the toolbar options:

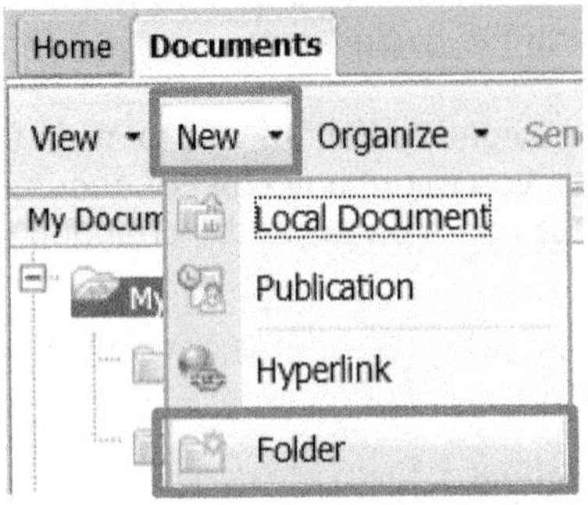
Home
Documents
View
New
Organize
My Docum
Local Document
Publication
Hyperlink
Folder

2. Give the folder a name, e.g. 'Training' and then click OK:

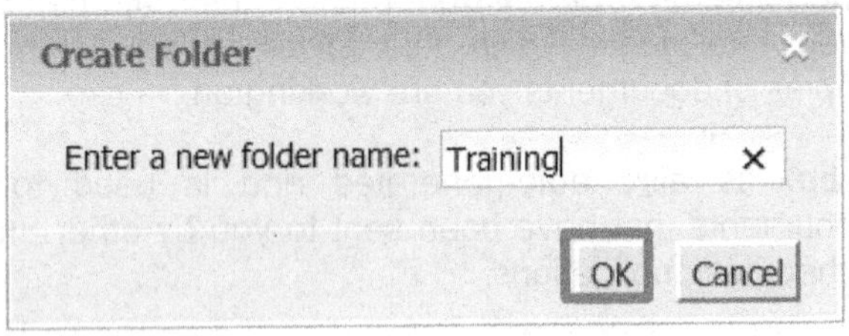
Create Folder
Enter a new folder name:
Training
OK
Cancel

3. Likewise, for the categories, you can first click on 'Personal Categories' and then create the 2 new categories using 'New – Category' menu from the toolbar, or right-click and 'New – Category':

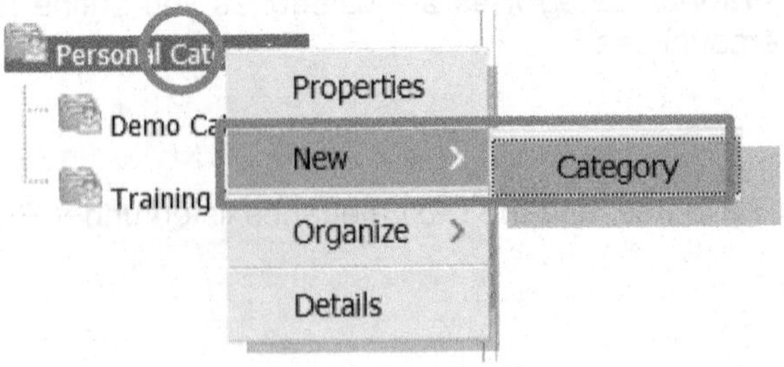
Properties
New
Category
Organize
Details

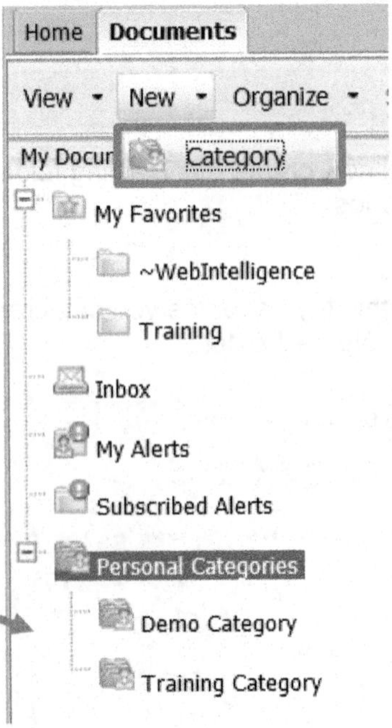
Home
Documents
View
New
Organize
Category
My Favorites
~WebIntelligence
Training
Inbox
My Alerts
Subscribed Alerts
Personal Categories
Demo Category
Training Category

Create the two Personal Categories; 'Demo Category' and 'Training Category'.

2.2.3.3 Documents Tab – Folders Drawer

Folders Drawer contains Public Folders.

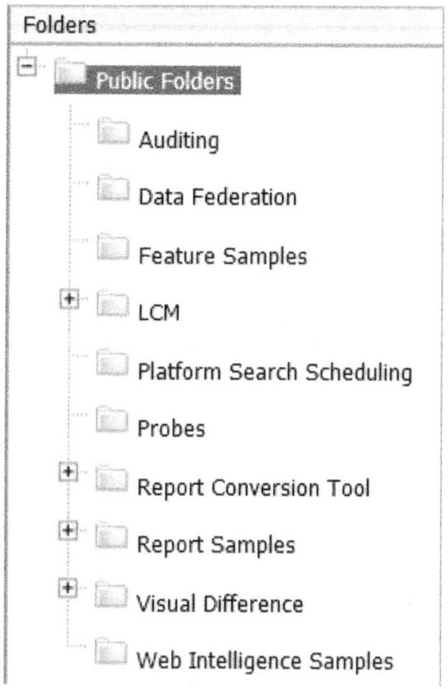
Folders
Public Folders
Auditing
Data Federation
Feature Samples
LCM
Platform Search Scheduling
Probes
Report Conversion Tool
Report Samples
Visual Difference
Web Intelligence Samples

These are shared folders within SAP BusinessObjects Enterprise that have been defined by your Administrators.

For example, each department might have their own folder(s) and only relevant users within your organisation would have access to certain folders depending on their roles.

Group security would then be applied to folders to allow only the correct users to view the folders and their content.

2.2.3.4 Documents Tab – Categories Drawer

Categories Drawer contains Corporate Categories.

Categories
Corporate Categories
Web Intelligence Examples

These are shared categories within SAP BusinessObjects Enterprise that have been defined by your Administrators.

For example, you can have categories that span organisational departments.

A document can be saved in one physical folder, but can have multiple categories assigned to it.

This enables cross-departmental documents to be shared using category based security, rather than having multiple copies of documents in different folders.

NOTE – Navigating the Folders or Categories drawers will show relevant objects/documents in the List Panel.

2.2.3.5 Documents Tab – Search Drawer

Search Drawer enables you to search across the SAP BusinessObjects Enterprise environment using the term you type into the Search box:

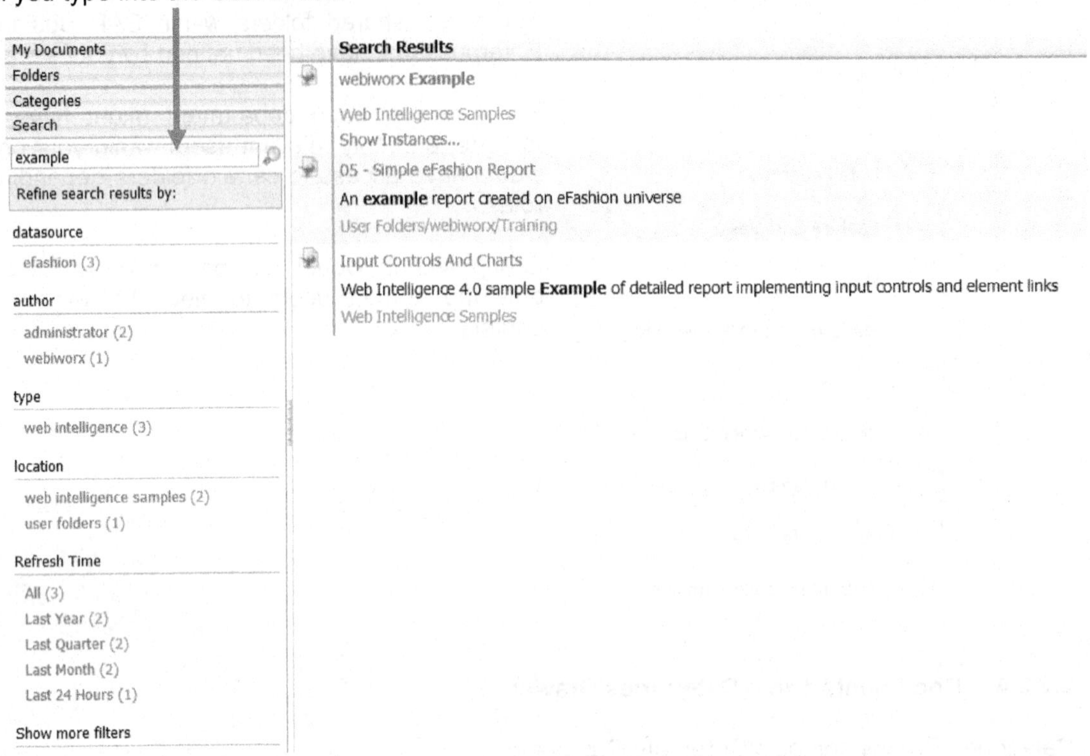
My Documents
Folders
Categories
Search
example
Refine search results by:
datasource
efashion (3)
author
administrator (2)
webiworx (1)
type
web intelligence (3)
location
web intelligence samples (2)
user folders (1)
Refresh Time
All (3)
Last Year (2)
Last Quarter (2)
Last Month (2)
Last 24 Hours (1)
Show more filters
Search Results
webiworx Example
Web Intelligence Samples
Show Instances...
05 - Simple eFashion Report
An example report created on eFashion universe
User Folders/webiworx/Training
Input Controls And Charts
Web Intelligence 4.0 sample Example of detailed report implementing input controls and element links
Web Intelligence Samples

2.3 Logging Off from BI Launch Pad

Click on **Log Off** at any time (saving any work first if necessary).

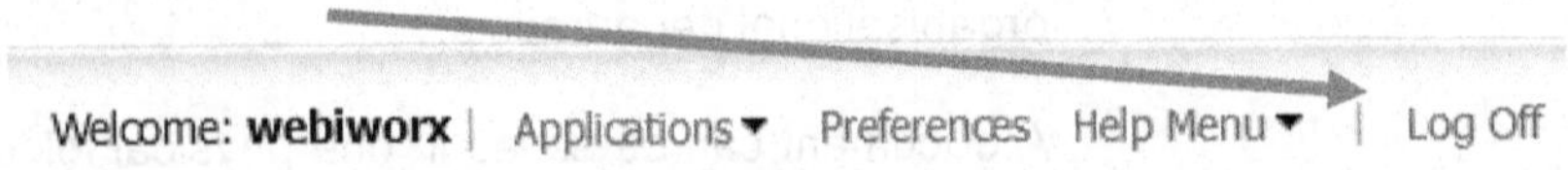
Welcome: webiworx
Applications
Preferences
Help Menu
Log Off

The server will try and log you out when you close the window, it is however recommended that you log out rather than close the browser window.

3 Setting BI Launch Pad and Web Intelligence Preferences

This session describes the various settings and preferences you can change (depending on permissions) to personalise your BI Launch Pad and Web Intelligence environment.

Preferences determine what view is displayed after you log in as there are specific settings for the various objects that you view, such as viewers for Web Intelligence and other BusinessObjects documents (such as Crystal Reports).

As a best practice, you should set your preferences before you begin to work with objects in BI Launch Pad. However, depending on your deployment, your SAP BusinessObjects Enterprise Administrator may have configured your system to use some predetermined settings by default.

There a number of different preferences that can be set depending on your installation (in terms of your licensing agreement). We will only discuss the settings for BI Launch Pad and Web Intelligence.

3.1 General Preferences

This section describes how to set your general viewing preferences for BI Launch Pad. These 'General' settings are used by BI Launch Pad and not Web Intelligence.

1. Log on to BI Launch Pad.

2. On the Header Panel, click on 'Preferences' :

Welcome: webiworx
Applications
Preferences

3. Make any changes to settings (discussed on next page).

4. Click on 'Save' or 'Save and Close' to apply changes.

   NOTE – These buttons are at the bottom of the screen.

General
Use Default Settings (Administrator defined)

Uncheck this setting to set your own preferences.

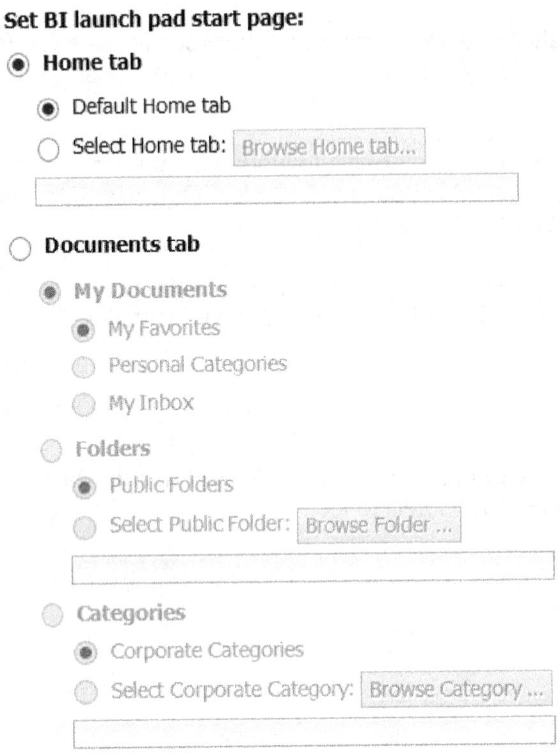
Set BI launch pad start page:
Home tab
Default Home tab
Select Home tab:
Browse Home tab...
Documents tab
My Documents
My Favorites
Personal Categories
My Inbox
Folders
Public Folders
Select Public Folder:
Browse Folder ...
Categories
Corporate Categories
Select Corporate Category:
Browse Category ...

If you want your Home tab to show a different view then use the 'Select Home tab' preference to do that.

If you prefer you can set your launch page to be the Documents tab rather than the Home tab.

And you can decide what you default folders and categories you would like to display within the Drawers of the Documents tab.

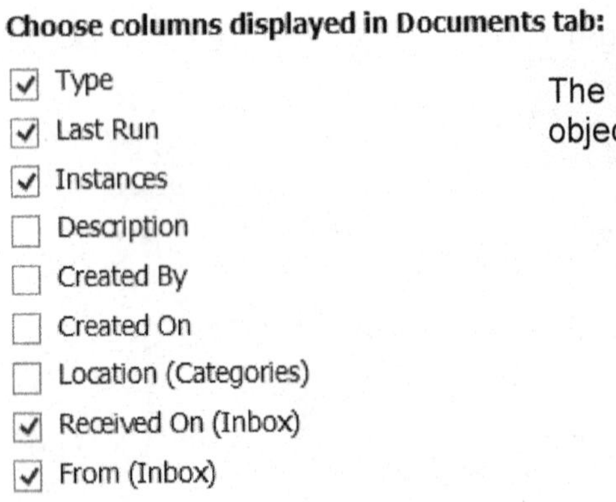
Choose columns displayed in Documents tab:
Type
Last Run
Instances
Description
Created By
Created On
Location (Categories)
Received On (Inbox)
From (Inbox)

The summary information you want to see displayed (per object) in the List panel within the Documents tab.

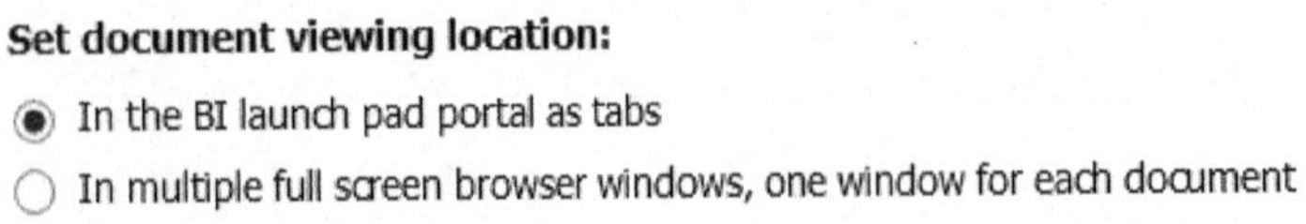
Set document viewing location:
In the BI launch pad portal as tabs
In multiple full screen browser windows, one window for each document

Number of windows you would like BI Launch Pad to use. See next page 'Document Viewing' for more details.

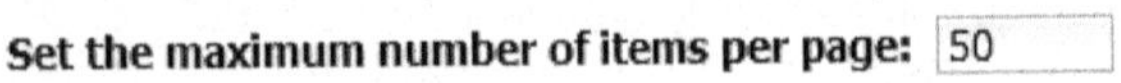
Set the maximum number of items per page:
50

Documents (or objects) are listed in alphanumeric order based on their names. This setting controls how many objects are displayed per page.

In **Document Viewing** select how you want to view your documents.

'In the BI Launch Pad portal as tabs' displays each document on a new tab within a single browser window.

'In multiple full screen browser windows, one window for each document' mode you will have one window for BI Launch Pad portal and then individual windows for each document you have open. You then close each window individually by clicking on the Close button ('X' in top right corner of window).

3.2 Changing Password for BI Launch Pad

Use the 'Change Password' settings to modify the password you use to Log On to BI Launch Pad.

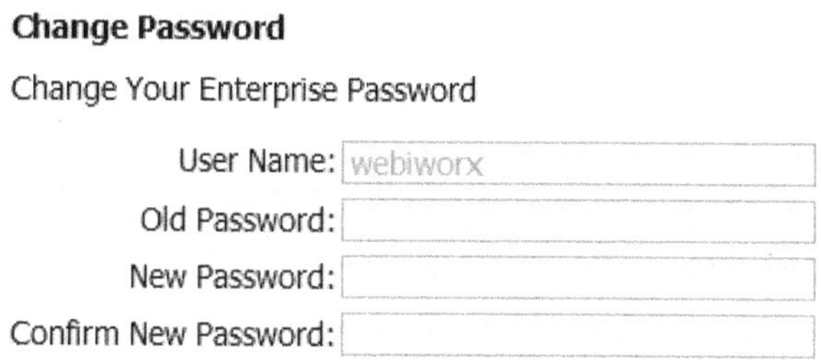
Change Password
Change Your Enterprise Password
User Name:
webiworx
Old Password:
New Password:
Confirm New Password:

To change your password:

1. Provide your existing password.
2. Type a new password.
3. Type the new password again for validation purposes.

Click 'Save and Close' to confirm the changes.

3.3 Locales and Time Zone Preferences

You can specify the language and time zone to use for BI Launch Pad sessions.

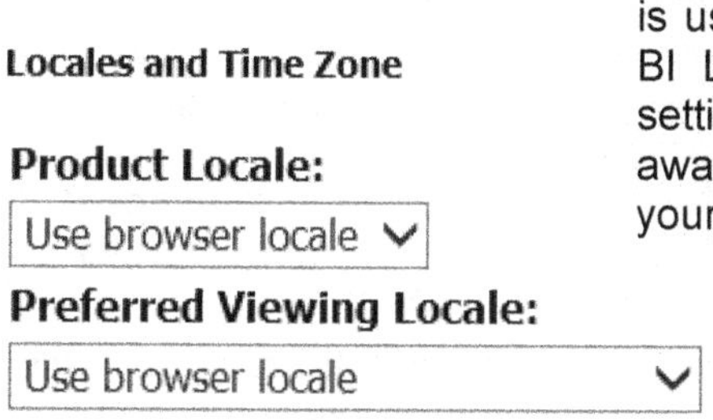
Locales and Time Zone
Product Locale:
Use browser locale
Preferred Viewing Locale:
Use browser locale

This setting determines the language set and date format that is used by BI Launch Pad, i.e. the language used to display BI Launch Pad menus, data in documents, etc. Default setting **Use browser locale** is recommended, unless you are away from home and need to change the settings to reflect your language, etc.

See next page for more details.

Current Time Zone:
Local to web server

See next page for more details.

Preferred Viewing Locale:

Data in documents is displayed and saved using the 'Product Locale' by default, but you can override this choosing a different locale here. This then becomes the default viewing/saving locale for all your documents, unless a document has been saved with a permanent locale applied to it (to enforce a particular locale).

For **Current Time-Zone** select the appropriate time zone.

It is important that you check this setting before you schedule any objects to run. The default time zone is local to the web server that is running SAP BusinessObjects Enterprise, not the Central Management Server (CMS) machine(s) to which each user connects. By properly setting your time zone, you ensure that your scheduled objects are processed in accordance with the time zone in which you are working.

3.4 Web Intelligence Preferences

Before you work with Web Intelligence documents in BI Launch Pad, it is recommended that you set the Web Intelligence preferences to suit your query and reporting needs.

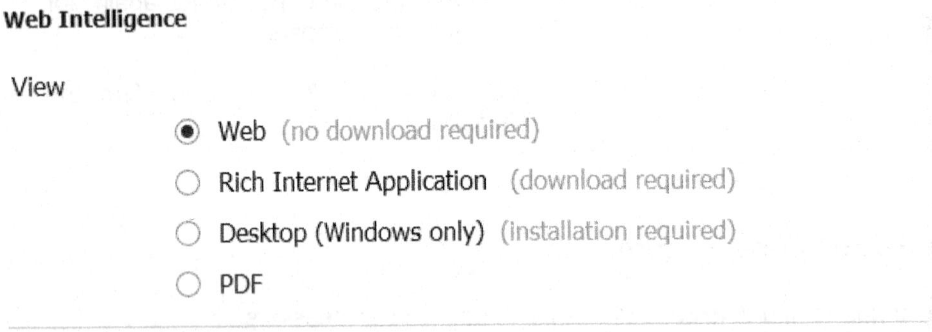
Web Intelligence
View
Web (no download required)
Rich Internet Application (download required)
Desktop (Windows only) (installation required)
PDF
Modify (creating, editing and analyzing documents):
This is also the interface launched from the Go To list or My Applications shortcut.
Web (no download required)
Rich Internet Application (download required)
Desktop (installation required)

Web is browser based HTML interface.

Rich Internet Application is browser based Java interface.

Desktop is Java based Windows application.

PDF offers no interactivity.

See overleaf for more details.

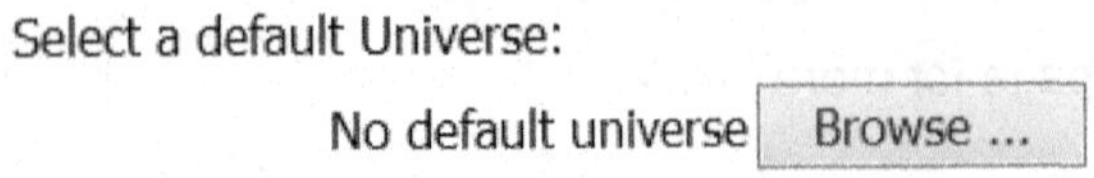
Select a default Universe:
No default universe
Browse ...

Best to leave as '**No default universe**', unless you only have access to a single universe.

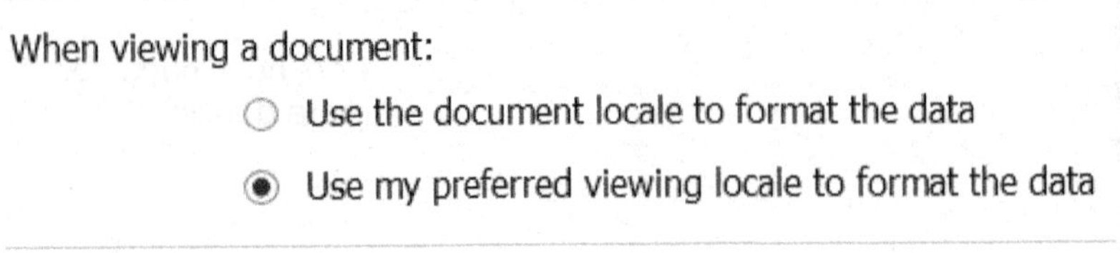
When viewing a document:
Use the document locale to format the data
Use my preferred viewing locale to format the data

Documents can be viewed using the 'Product Locale' by default, or in your preferred locale that was specified in '**Locales and Time Zone – Preferred Viewing Locale**'.

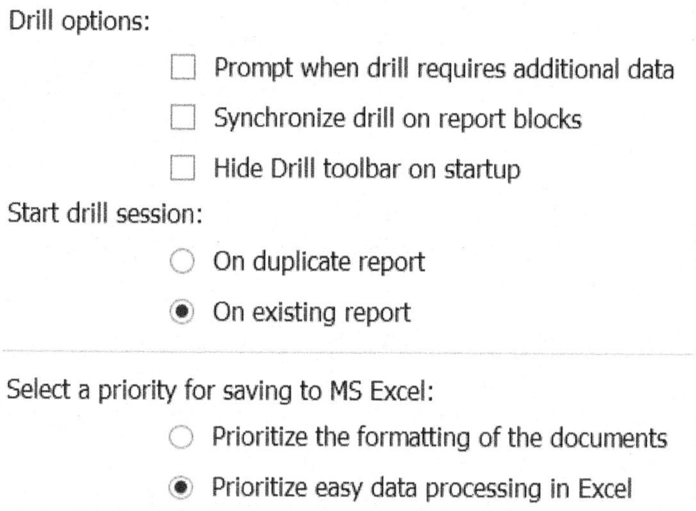
Drill options:
Prompt when drill requires additional data
Synchronize drill on report blocks
Hide Drill toolbar on startup
Start drill session:
On duplicate report
On existing report
Select a priority for saving to MS Excel:
Prioritize the formatting of the documents
Prioritize easy data processing in Excel

'**Drill options**' and '**Start drill session**' are discussed in more detail Section 1.4.1 using some examples.

When saving to MS Excel format:

- If you want to display the data in a format that is similar to working in Web Intelligence, then select '**Prioritize the formatting of the documents**'.
- If you want to display the data in a text format then select '**Prioritize easy data processing in Excel**'.

For Web Intelligence View and Modify preferences:

1. **'Web'** is HTML based interface that allows you to develop Web Intelligence reports and also enables users to interact with the reports in view mode.

   This interactivity is in view mode, therefore you can develop 'basic' reports and other users with this setting can then modify the reports (but not the queries) to suit their requirements.

2. '**Rich Internet Application**' format offers the most functionality enabling you to perform all aspects of Web Intelligence.
3. '**Desktop**' offers the same Java based functionality as '**Advanced**' but requires an application to be installed on local machine(s).

   Discussed in detail later in the session on '**Web Intelligence Rich Client**'.

4. '**PDF**' offers very little (or no) interactivity and should only be selected if the documents are very static, i.e. require no interaction.

3.4.1 Selecting your Drill Options

Before you begin a drill session, you must specify how your Web Intelligence documents change when you perform a drill.

To set your drill options

1. Ensure '**Select a default view format**' is either '**Web**' or '**Rich Internet Application**' (ideally the latter).
2. For '**Start drill session**' select the option that you want to apply to your drill sessions:

   - If you want to retain a copy of the original report tab so you can compare the drilled results to the data in the original report tab then choose '**On duplicate report**'.

     BI Launch Pad / Web Intelligence will create a duplicate of the original report tab. When you end drill mode, both the original report and the drilled report remain in the document for you to view.

   - If you want to drill on the report so that the original report tab is modified by your drill actions, then choose '**On existing report**'.

     When you end drill mode, the report displays the drilled values.

3. For '**Drill options**' select the general options that you want to apply to your drill sessions:

   - If you want Web Intelligence to prompt you whenever a drill action requires a new query to add more data to the document, then select '**Prompt when drill requires additional data**'.

     For example, when you drill on the results that are displayed in a Web Intelligence document, you may want to drill to higher or lower-level information that is not included in the scope of analysis for the document. In this situation, Web Intelligence needs to run a new query to retrieve additional data from the data source.

     You can choose to be prompted with a message whenever a new query is needed. The prompt message asks you to decide whether or not you want to run the additional query.

   - If you want Web Intelligence to synchronise drilling on all report blocks, then select '**Synchronize drill on report block**'.

     There are two ways to drill on a report with multiple report blocks:

     - Synchronise drill on report blocks (Recommended).
     - Drill only on the selected block.

The following examples show how each synchronise option affects a report as you drill down on a table to analyse detailed results per service line.

In this first example, '**Synchronize drill on report blocks**' is selected, so both the table and the chart display the drilled values:

The [Quarter] column was previously [Year] but the drill action forced the data to go one level down from [Year] = '2005' down to each [Quarter] in '2005'.

The chart then synchronises itself to the table to also display [Quarter].

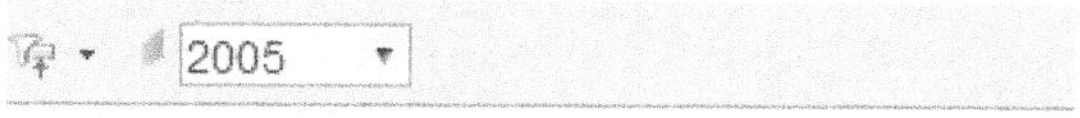
2005

Quarter	Quantity sold
Q1	21,135
Q2	17,152
Q3	19,224
Q4	22,344

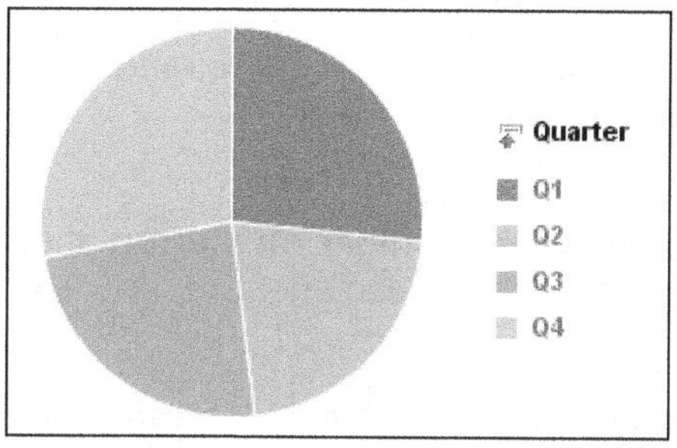
Quarter
Q1
Q2
Q3
Q4

In the second example below, '**Synchronize drill on report blocks**' is not selected, so only the table displays the drilled values:

The [Quarter] column was previously [Year] but the drill action forced the data to go one level down from [Year] = '2005' down to each [Quarter] in '2005'.

The chart does not synchronise itself to the table therefore it continues to display data at [Year] level, but has gone from showing 3 years to a single year.

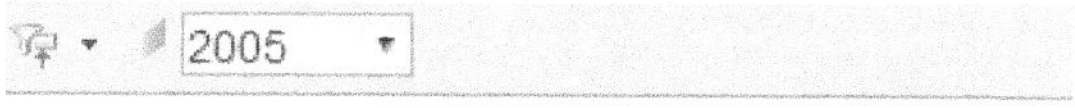
2005

Quarter	Quantity sold
Q1	21,135
Q2	17,152
Q3	19,224
Q4	22,344

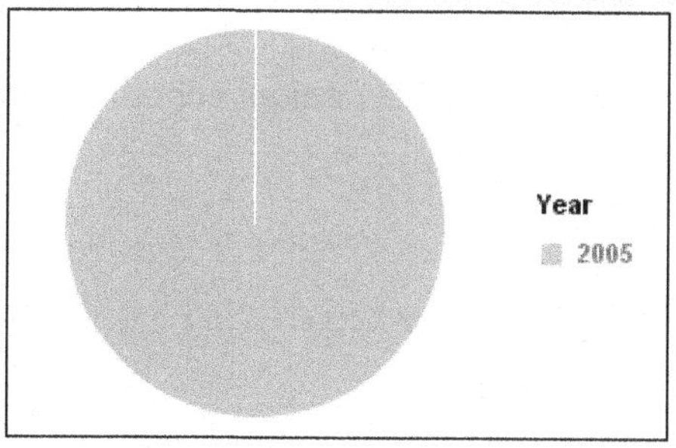
Year
2005

- If you want Web Intelligence to hide the Drill Bar when you switch to drill mode, then select '**Hide Drill toolbar on startup**'.

When you start drill mode, the Report Filters Bar (i.e. the 'Drill Bar' automatically appears at the top of the drilled report). The bar displays the value(s) on which you drilled. These values filter the results that are displayed on the drilled report.

For example, if you drill on [State] = 'Florida' and [Year] = '2005' then the Report Filters Bar shows:

2005
Florida

This means that the quarterly values to which you drilled to are filtered for 'Florida' and '2005'.

If you do '**Hide Drill toolbar on startup**' then you still have the option of showing the drill toolbar when using the document.

Recommended to not '**Hide Drill toolbar on startup**'.

The Report Filters Bar allows you to select other values to filter the results differently. For example, if you use the Report Filters Bar to select [Year] = '2006', then the results that are displayed in the drilled table will change to Q1, Q2, Q3, and Q4 for Year 2006.

If the drilled report includes dimensions from multiple queries, a tooltip appears when you rest your cursor on the value that is displayed in the filter. The tooltip displays the name of the query and the dimension for the value, for example, '**Dimension: Year (Query 2)**'.

3.5 BI Workspaces Preferences

You can select the style (look and feel / colour scheme) to use for your BI Workspaces:

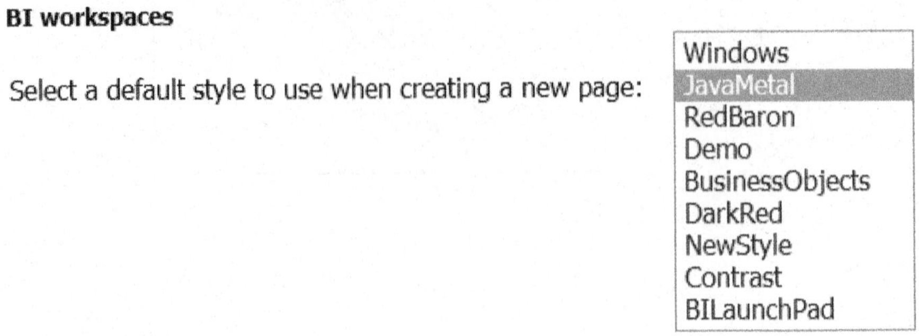
BI workspaces
Select a default style to use when creating a new page:
Windows
JavaMetal
RedBaron
Demo
BusinessObjects
DarkRed
NewStyle
Contrast
BILaunchPad

You can also use a background image and a color of your choice:

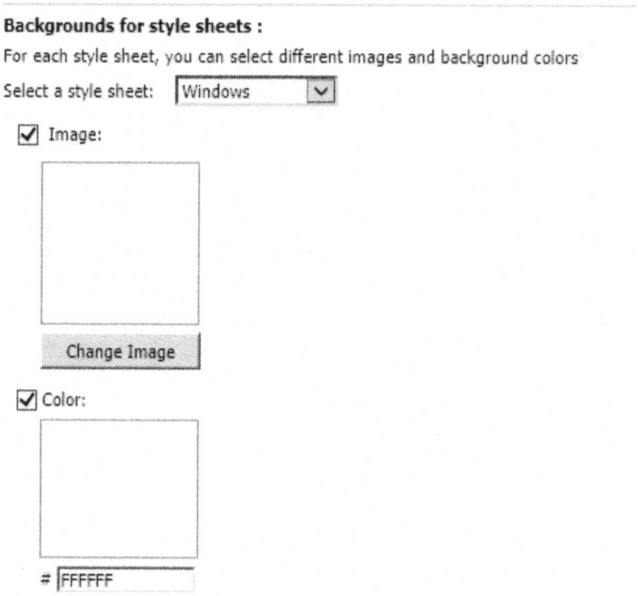
Backgrounds for style sheets :
For each style sheet, you can select different images and background colors
Select a style sheet:
Windows
Image:
Change Image
Color:
#
FFFFFF

Click on 'Save and Close' to apply changes after setting your style.

4 Introduction to Web Intelligence

Web Intelligence enables you to create documents for reporting, data analysis, and sharing with other users using the BI Launch Pad environment.

Querying

The required data is fetch from the database by using the universe, BEx or Analysis Views. Web Services and Excel/Text Files can also be used. The Query Panel within Web Intelligence uses the universe layer to assist the end user in querying the underlying database.

Data is returned from the database(s) for the queries generated by the Query Panel.

Reporting

The data returned by the database is then stored within the Web Intelligence document itself (as a 'microcube') and can be formatted in a variety of ways depending on presentation requirements.

Analysing

The microcube within the Web Intelligence document enables end users to drag and drop data, create formulas and calculations, and drill into the data for detailed analysis using different perspectives in design mode.

The analysis can also be performed using 'HTML' or 'Applet' modes when viewing.

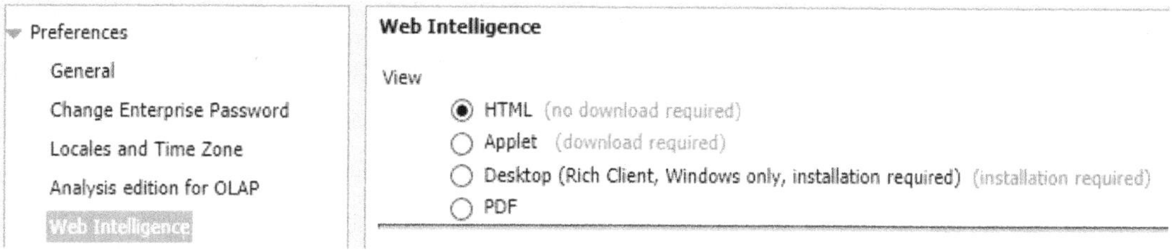
Preferences
General
Change Enterprise Password
Locales and Time Zone
Analysis edition for OLAP
Web Intelligence
Web Intelligence
View
HTML (no download required)
Applet (download required)
Desktop (Rich Client, Windows only, installation required) (installation required)
PDF

Sharing

Web Intelligence documents can be shared within the SAP BusinessObjects Enterprise environment by sending them to other users or by placing them in the central shared area known as 'Public Folders'.

Documents can be scheduled and distributed at specified times using the scheduling/publishing functionality within BI Launch Pad.

Web Intelligence documents can also be saved in Excel, Adobe PDF, and Text files for sharing with non-BusinessObjects users.

NOTE – We will be using the 'Applet' version of Web Intelligence for both Modify and View modes.

4.1 Universes and Objects

Web Intelligence queries and documents are created using different types of objects from universes. This session discusses universes, objects and also introduces the two sample universes provided by the SAP BusinessObjects Enterprise BI 4.x installation.

4.1.1 Universes

Universes are developed by universe designers using the SAP BusinessObjects product called Information Design Tool (previously known as Designer). The universes are then made available for creating reports.

The universe layer in SAP BusinessObjects acts as the interface between the database and the end user. The universe is used to map data in the database using everyday business terminology, therefore making it simpler for the end user when creating reports.

A universe translates business terms into database query language. The business terms are presented as objects such as 'Margin' or 'Store name'. The query statements are written according to the universe design into SQL (Structured Query Language) in order for the database to fulfil the request (such as 'Revenue per Customer').

UNIVERSES ENABLE END USERS TO CREATE MEANINGFUL REPORTS BY PRESENTING COMPLEX DATA STRUCTURES INTO BUSINESS TERMINOLOGY.

Universes contain a number of different objects.

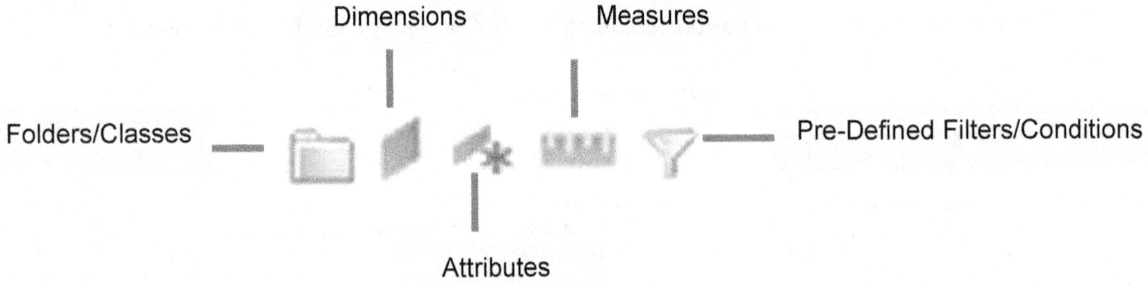
Dimensions
Measures
Folders/Classes
Pre-Defined Filters/Conditions
Attributes

4.1.2 Folders/Classes

These are similar to folders (or directories) in Microsoft Windows. Folders are used to logically group objects (e.g. the Product folder would contain objects related to Product; the Customer folder would contain objects related to Customer, etc).

Shown opposite are **folders** in the 'eFashion' universe (sample universe provided in the SAP BusinessObjects Enterprise BI 4.x installation).

Objects within a folder are typically related to the folder, e.g. the **Time period** folder has been expanded to show the objects it contains (all time related).

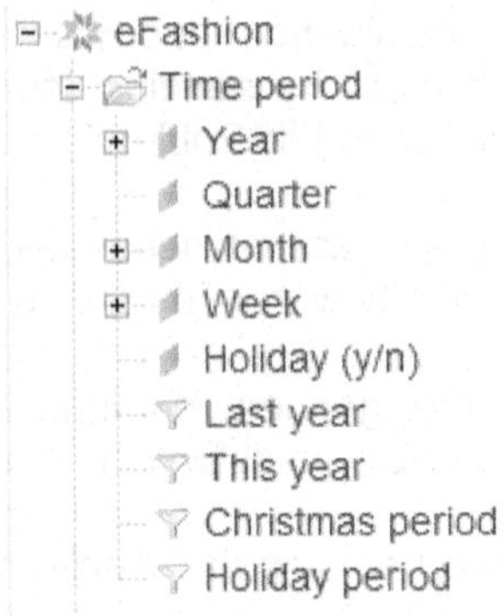
eFashion
Time period
Year
Quarter
Month
Week
Holiday (y/n)
Last year
This year
Christmas period
Holiday period

4.1.3 Objects

These are the individual elements of a universe that are used when creating reports. There are four types of objects:

DIMENSION objects are represented in Web Intelligence by a blue parallelogram. A typical dimension object might be Country, City, Year, Month, Product Category, Product Item, etc. Dimensions objects represent the framework for analysing numerical facts.

Let us say we have four types of dimensions - Product, Customer, Region and Time. These describe the What, Who, Where and When of the business facts. For example, if you have a measure of a thousand pieces of sales, by asking the questions what did you sell (which Product), who bought it (Customer), where it was sold (Region) and when did you sell it (Year or Month)? You can determine the context within which the sale was made, and what the sale of the thousand pieces actually means to the business.

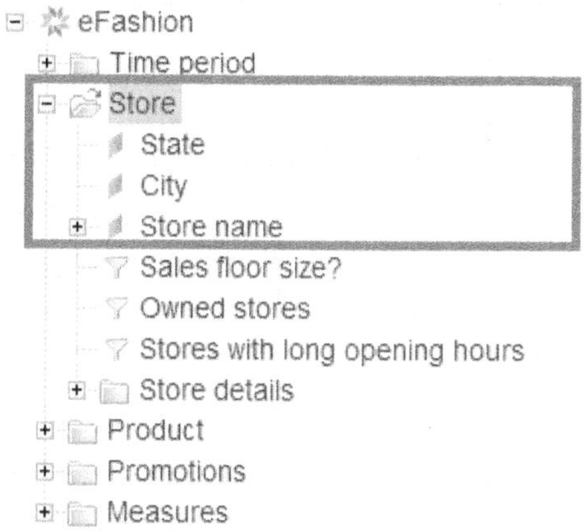
eFashion
Time period
Store
State
City
Store name
Sales floor size?
Owned stores
Stores with long opening hours
Store details
Product
Promotions
Measures

Example of **dimensions** in **Store** and **Product** folders of the eFashion universe.

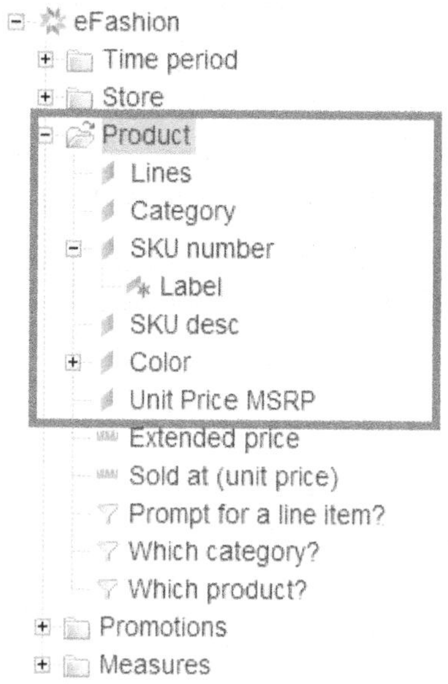
eFashion
Time period
Store
Product
Lines
Category
SKU number
Label
SKU desc
Color
Unit Price MSRP
Extended price
Sold at (unit price)
Prompt for a line item?
Which category?
Which product?
Promotions
Measures

ATTRIBUTE objects are represented by blue parallelogram with a green asterisk. An attribute object is directly mapped to a dimension object and is used to provide more information about the dimension object it is associated with.

Attribute objects are typically used less frequently than dimensions (i.e. you might have a dimension called Product Item Description and an attribute called Product Item Code). For most users the Product Item Description is sufficient in reports, but some users might want to use the Product Item Code so it is made available as an attribute object.

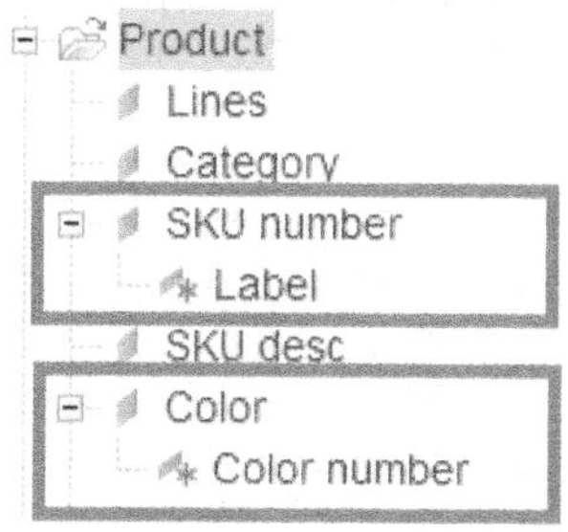
Product
Lines
Category
SKU number
Label
SKU desc
Color
Color number

In the eFashion universe:

Label is an attribute of **SKU number** and

Color number is an attribute of **Color**

NOTE – Attributes can only be defined against dimension objects.

MEASURE objects are the numerical data that determine business performance. They are represented in Web Intelligence by orange rectangles. Typical measure objects might be Sales quantity, Sales revenue, Margin, Discount, Promotion Cost USD, etc.

Promotions
Promotion (y/n)
Duration
Promotion Cost USD
Measures
Sales revenue
Quantity sold
Margin
Discount

Usually, measure objects behave dynamically within reports in that they aggregate ('roll up' or 'break down') depending on the number of dimensions and details they are being displayed against.

1 – Block of data showing **[Year]**, **[Quarter]** and **[Sales revenue]**.

Year	Quarter	Sales revenue
2004	Q1	$2,660,700
2004	Q2	$2,278,693
2004	Q3	$1,367,841
2004	Q4	$1,788,580
2005	Q1	$3,326,172
2005	Q2	$2,840,651
2005	Q3	$2,879,303
2005	Q4	$4,186,120
2006	Q1	$3,742,989
2006	Q2	$4,006,718
2006	Q3	$3,953,395
2006	Q4	$3,356,041
	Sum:	**$36,387,203**

Year	Sales revenue
2004	$8,095,814
2005	$13,232,246
2006	$15,059,143
	$36,387,203

2 – **[Quarter]** removed leaves 3 unique values for **[Year]**. All the quarters in each year have been added together.

Quarter	Sales revenue
Q1	$9,729,861
Q2	$9,126,062
Q3	$8,200,539
Q4	$9,330,742
	$36,387,203

3 – **[Year]** removed leaves 4 unique values for **[Quarter]**. All the 'Q1' values have been added together and similarly all the 'Q2' values have been added together, etc.

Sales revenue
$36,387,203
$36,387,203

4 – **[Year]** and **[Quarter]** removed leaves no dimensions to be broken down by, therefore the measure rolls up to its total value.

In the example above we have **[Sales revenue]** broken down per **[Quarter]** per **[Year]**. Three years with four quarters gives us 12 unique combinations of the dimension values, therefore we get 12 rows of data.

By removing a dimension, Web Intelligence will automatically aggregate the figures to the unique combinations of the remaining dimensions. In this case we have shown what happens when we remove the **[Year]** object, or the **[Quarter]** object, or both objects.

The total in each case remains the same showing correct aggregation behaviour.

PRE-DEFINED FILTER/CONDITION objects restrict the data returned from the database (i.e. narrow/concentrate/filter the query), usually by an associated dimension. They can be fixed conditions (Current Month, Next Quarter, etc) or they can be dynamic conditions requiring user input (via Prompts) to specify value(s) when the document is refreshed. Pre-Defined Filter/Condition objects are yellow funnels.

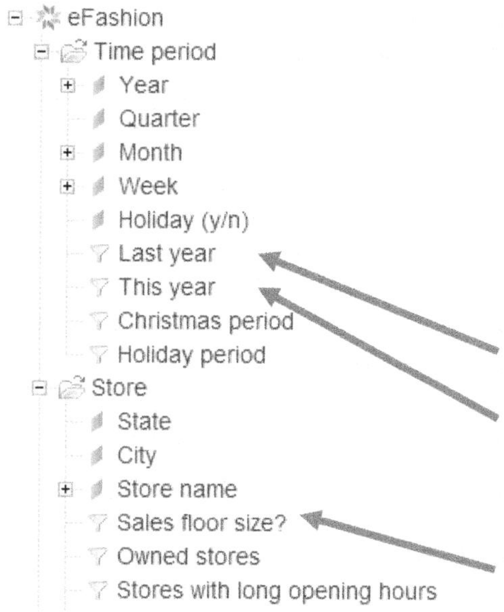
eFashion
Time period
Year
Quarter
Month
Week
Holiday (y/n)
Last year
This year
Christmas period
Holiday period
Store
State
City
Store name
Sales floor size?
Owned stores
Stores with long opening hours

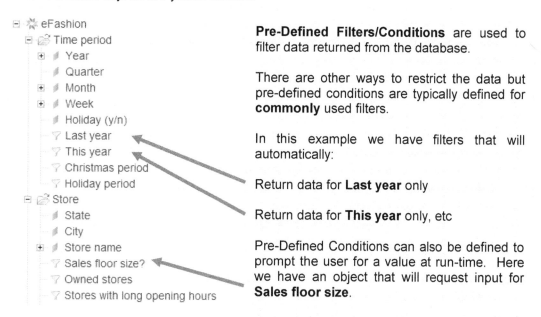

Pre-Defined Filters/Conditions are used to filter data returned from the database.

There are other ways to restrict the data but pre-defined conditions are typically defined for **commonly** used filters.

In this example we have filters that will automatically:

Return data for **Last year** only

Return data for **This year** only, etc

Pre-Defined Conditions can also be defined to prompt the user for a value at run-time. Here we have an object that will request input for **Sales floor size**.

4.1.4 eFashion Universe

The eFashion universe is provided by the installation of SAP BusinessObjects Enterprise BI 4.x. It is based on a Microsoft Access database in order to provide sample data for examples, help text, etc. We have already used this universe in this session to describe Universes, Classes and Objects but an overview is given below:

The database is based on sales data for fashion clothing and the universe has been designed to report:

[Sales revenue], [Quantity sold], [Margin] and [Discount] by any combination of:

Time dimension (e.g. [Year], [Quarter], [Month], etc)

Store dimension (e.g. [State], [City], [Store name], etc)

Product dimension (e.g. [Lines], [Category], [SKU number], etc)

There are also objects specifically to analyse Promotions data:

Promotions dimension (e.g. [Promotion (y/n)], [Duration], [Promotion cost USD], etc)

NOTE – 'eFashion' data exists for the years 2004, 2005 and 2006

4.1.5 Island Resort Marketing Universe

The Island Resorts Marketing universe is also provided by the installation of SAP BusinessObjects Enterprise BI 4.x. It is also based on a Microsoft Access database.

An overview of this universe and its database is given below:

The database is based on sales and reservations data for holiday resorts used by customers.

Island Resorts Marketing
Resort
Sales
Customer
Reservations
Measures

The universe has been designed to report:

Customers making Reservations at a Resort

Customers taking part in Sales at a Resort

NOTE

Sales data exists for the years 2004, 2005 and 2006

Reservations data exists for the years 2007, 2008 and 2009

4.1.6 eFashion Oracle Universe

Certain Web Intelligence functionality cannot be demonstrated using universes that are based on underlying Microsoft Access databases, therefore in some examples we will be using a modified universe based on an Oracle database.

Further details and instructions can be found at www.webiworx.com. Look for information on 'SAP BusinessObjects Web Intelligence Training Course' on the 'Downloads' page.

If your company uses Oracle and the 'eFashion Oracle' universe is made available to you in your environment then it can be used in all examples, whereas the 'eFashion' universe cannot be used in examples that explicitly reference the use of 'eFashion Oracle' universe.

4.1.7 Other Sample Data

Some other sample data is also required in certain parts of the training course.

Further details and instructions can be found at www.webiworx.com. Look for information on 'SAP BusinessObjects Web Intelligence Training Course' on the 'Downloads' page.

5 Creating and Saving a Web Intelligence Document

This session introduces how to create a new document in Web Intelligence (in Applet mode) using a universe as the data source.

You can create Web Intelligence documents by selecting a universe and building one or more queries to define the data content of the documents. When you connect to a universe, Web Intelligence automatically launches the document editor that is selected as the 'default creation/editing tool' in BI Launch Pad preferences.

5.1 Create a New Document

1. Within BI Launch Pad we have the option to create a new Web Intelligence document.

Web Intelligence

You can click on the Web Intelligence Application icon in the BI Launch Pad.

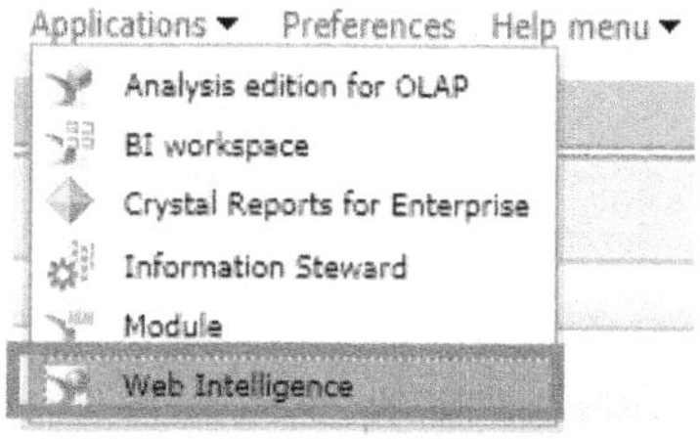
Applications
Preferences
Help menu
Analysis edition for OLAP
BI workspace
Crystal Reports for Enterprise
Information Steward
Module
Web Intelligence

You can select 'Web Intelligence' from the Applications menu.

If you are unable to select 'Web Intelligence' then contact your SAP BusinessObjects Enterprise Administrator.

NOTE – If you have specified '**Desktop**' as the '**Modify**' tool then Web Intelligence Rich Client will be launched instead.

2. BI Launch Pad will now contain an extra tab labelled as 'Web Intelligence'.

Home
Documents
Web Intelligence
Web Intelligence

If you prefer, you can use a new window for the document. If you do then the new document will be placed in a separate window and not on an extra tab.

3. You can create a new document or open an existing document.

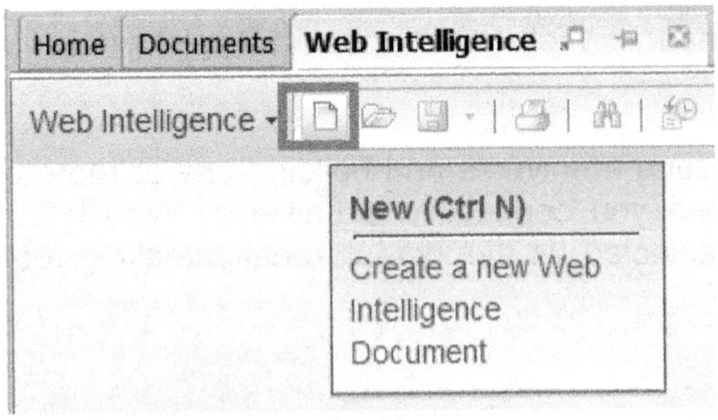
Home
Documents
Web Intelligence
Web Intelligence
New (Ctrl N)
Create a new Web Intelligence Document

You need to select 'New' to create a new document.

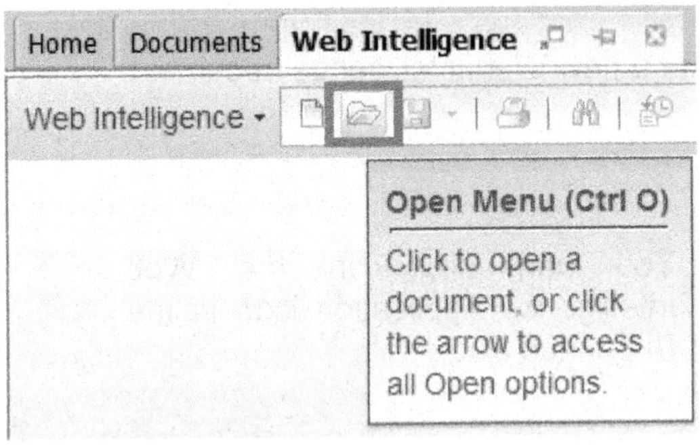
Home
Documents
Web Intelligence
Web Intelligence
Open Menu (Ctrl O)
Click to open a document, or click the arrow to access all Open options.

You can open an existing document using 'Open'.

4. Click on 'New' to create a new document.

5. Choose a Data Source.

   The first step in creating a document is to choose the data source.

   For Web Intelligence the data source can be a Universe, BEx or an Analysis View, Text and Microsoft Excel files, and Web Services can also be used.

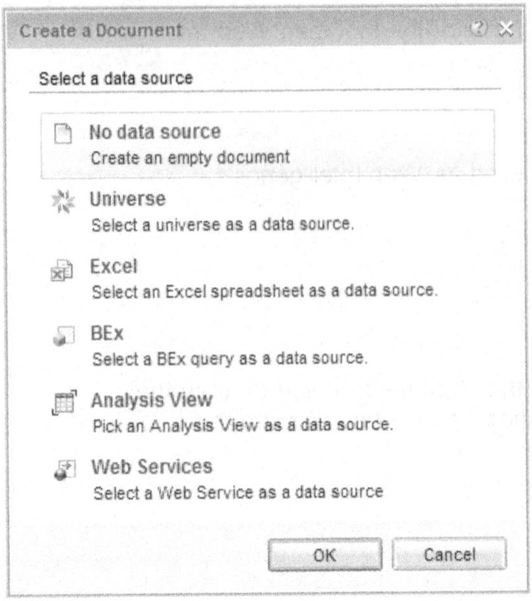
Create a Document
Select a data source
No data source
Create an empty document
Universe
Select a universe as a data source.
Excel
Select an Excel spreadsheet as a data source.
BEx
Select a BEx query as a data source.
Analysis View
Pick an Analysis View as a data source.
Web Services
Select a Web Service as a data source
OK
Cancel

NOTE

In this course, when using Web Intelligence we will primarily use Universe, but we will also explore Excel files as data sources.

We will not cover Web Services, BEx and Analysis View as data sources for Web Intelligence reports in this course.

6. Select 'Universe' and then click 'OK'.

   Many universes may be available depending on the complexity of the underlying data sources, business requirements, technical design, etc. Typically, separate universes are created for each set of similar users. For instance, you might have an Accounting universe, a Human Resources universe, a Customer Sales universe and an Inventory universe all accessing the same database or separate databases.

   For this reason, the first step in creating a universe based Web Intelligence document is to first select a universe.

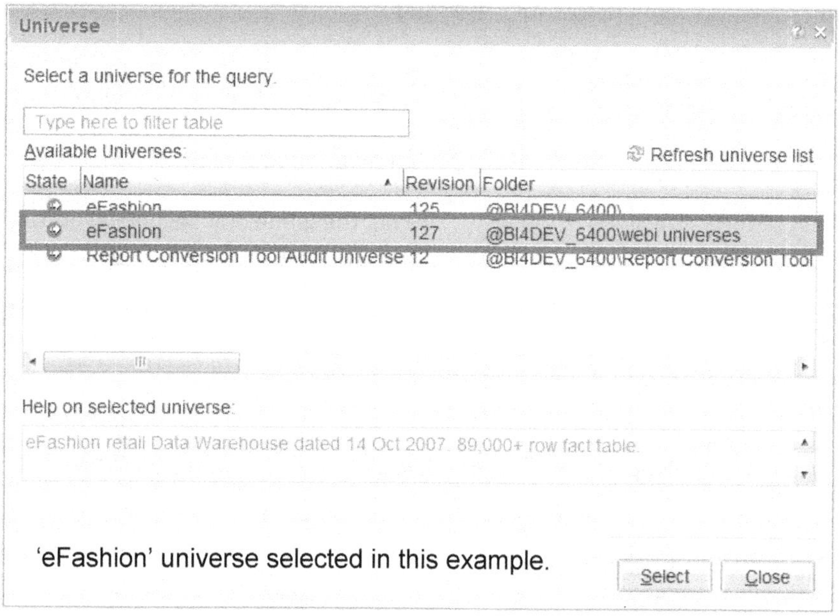
Universe
Select a universe for the query
Type here to filter table
Available Universes:
Refresh universe list
State
Name
Revision
Folder
eFashion
127
@BI4DEV_6400\webi universes
Help on selected universe:
eFashion retail Data Warehouse dated 14 Oct 2007. 89,000+ row fact table.
'eFashion' universe selected in this example.
Select
Close

Once selected, the universe is loaded into a Query Panel.

7. Drag-and-drop or double-click on objects to add them into the relevant panes.

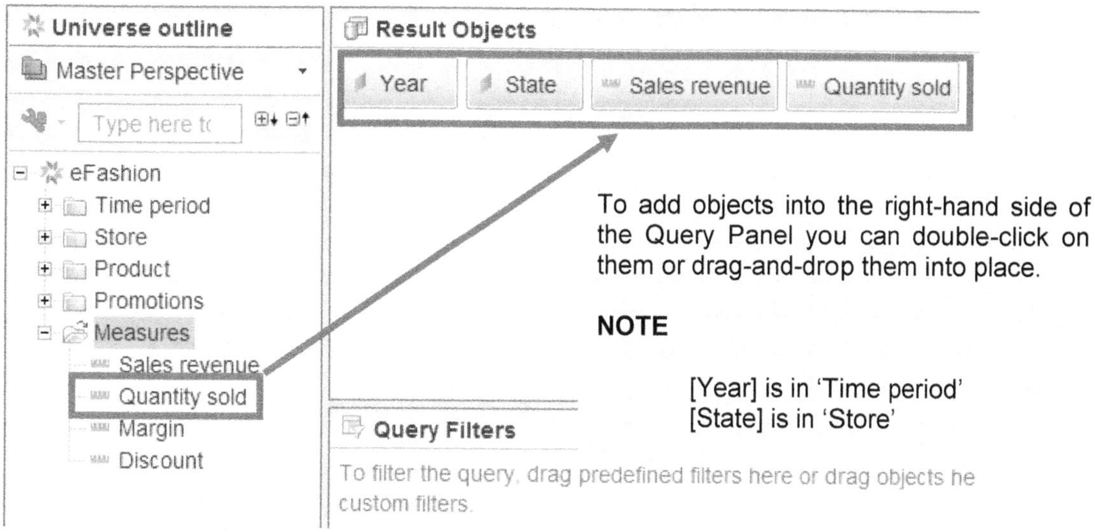
Universe outline
Master Perspective
eFashion
Time period
Store
Product
Promotions
Measures
Sales revenue
Quantity sold
Margin
Discount
Result Objects
Year
State
Sales revenue
Quantity sold
To add objects into the right-hand side of the Query Panel you can double-click on them or drag-and-drop them into place.
NOTE
[Year] is in 'Time period'
[State] is in 'Store'
Query Filters
To filter the query, drag predefined filters here or drag objects he
custom filters.

8. Add the objects shown above into the 'Result Objects' pane and then click on '**Run Query**'.

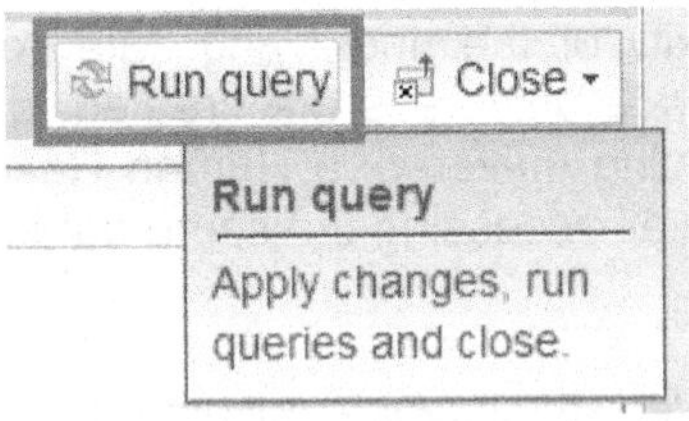
Run query
Close
Run query
Apply changes, run queries and close.

9. You might be presented with the following message:

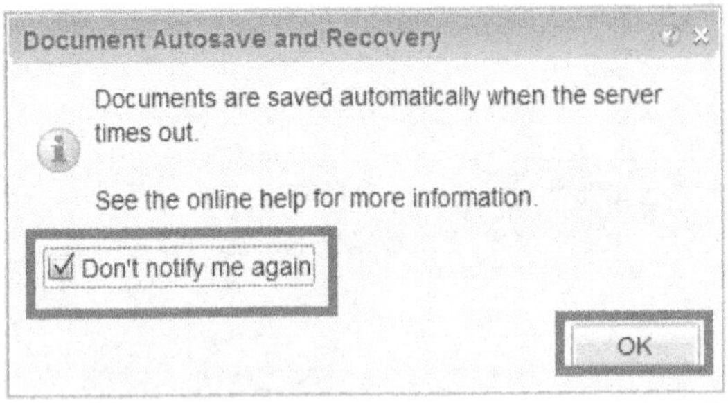
Document Autosave and Recovery
Documents are saved automatically when the server times out.
See the online help for more information.
Don't notify me again
OK

In some earlier versions of Web Intelligence, unsaved work was lost when timeouts occurred, e.g. being away from your desk without saving the latest changes, etc.

This message will be displayed after your very first query has finished running.

Tick the box '**Don't notify me again'** and then click 'OK'.

10. You will be taken into the Report Panel with a default block appearing as follows:

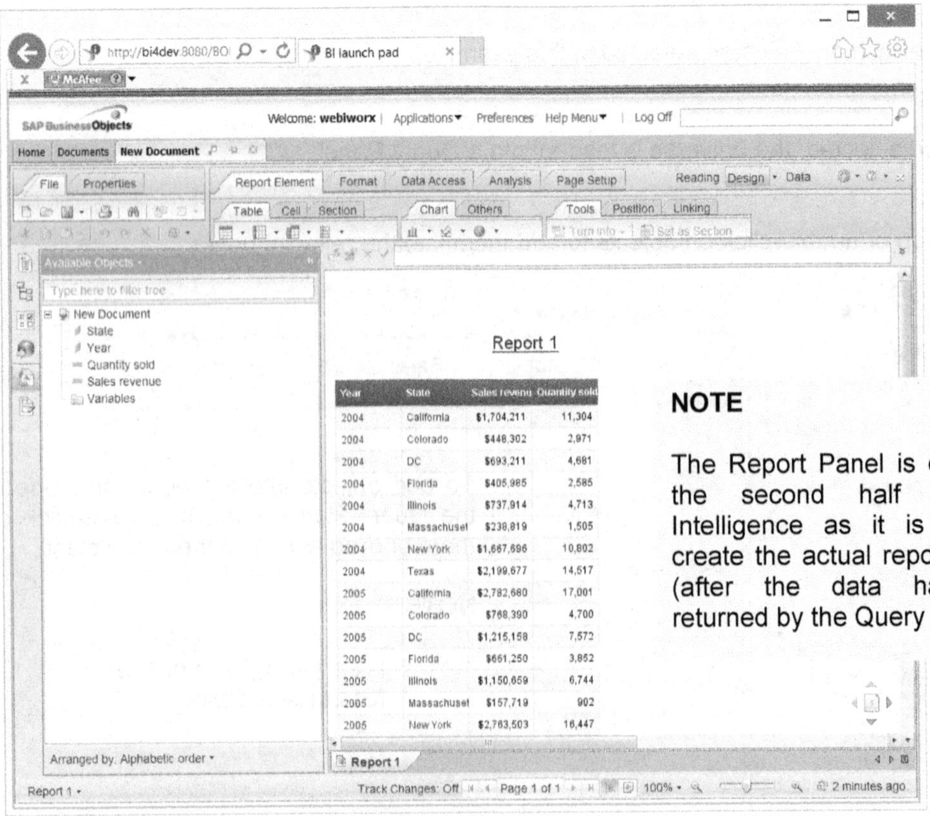
Report 1

NOTE

The Report Panel is effectively the second half of Web Intelligence as it is used to create the actual report layouts (after the data has been returned by the Query Panel).

11. We will now save the document (described next) and then we will return back to the query panel to describe the interface in more detail.

5.2 Saving a Web Intelligence Document

Web Intelligence allows you to save documents to a variety of locations such as local folders (on your machine), network folders or within the BusinessObjects repository.

In most cases you will save documents to the BusinessObjects repository.

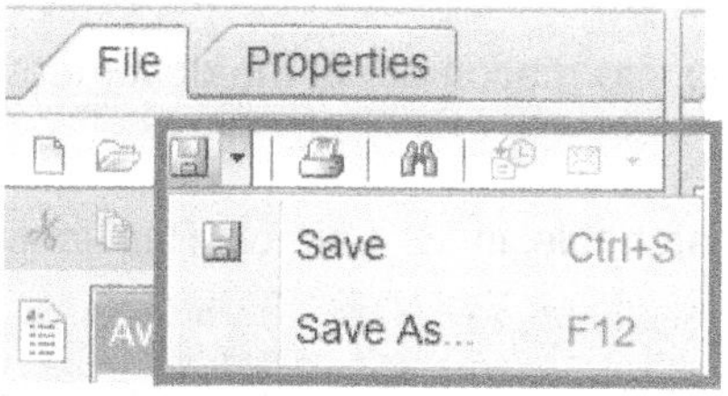
File
Properties
Save
Ctrl+S
Save As...
F12

'Save' will save the Web Intelligence document to the repository.

'Save As...' will enable you to save the document as a Web Intelligence document to the repository, or in other formats such as PDF, Text, Excel, and Excel 2007.

We will look at saving to different formats later in the course.

1. Click on 'Save' or 'Save As...' and then give your document a name.

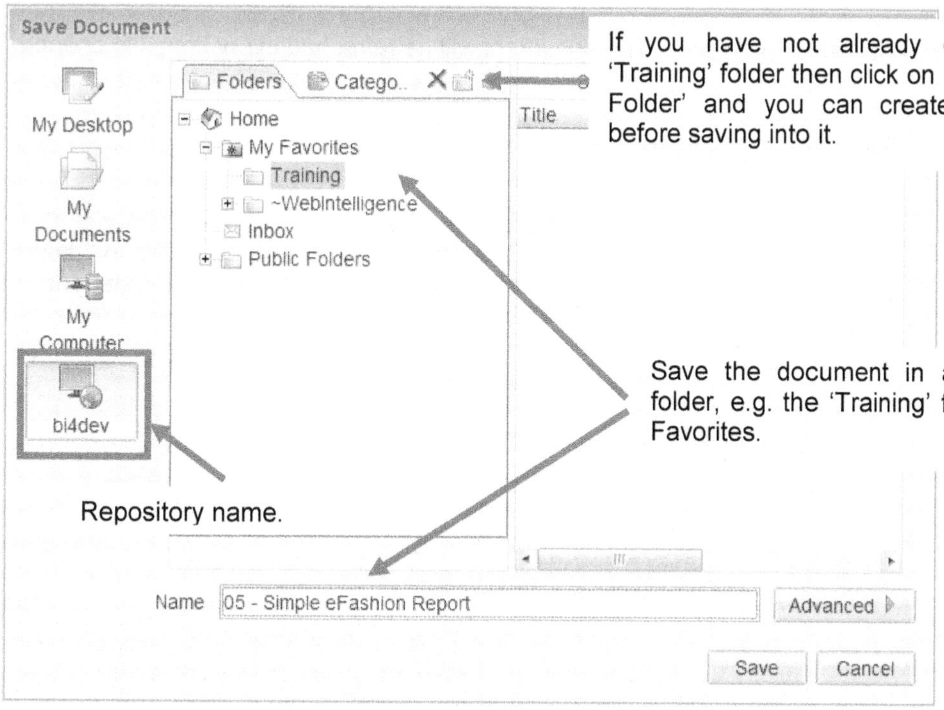
Save Document
Folders
Catego..
Title
My Desktop
My Documents
My Computer
bi4dev
Home
My Favorites
Training
~WebIntelligence
Inbox
Public Folders
Name
05 - Simple eFashion Report
Advanced
Save
Cancel
If you have not already created the 'Training' folder then click on 'Create New Folder' and you can create the folder before saving into it.
Save the document in a repository folder, e.g. the 'Training' folder in 'My Favorites.
Repository name.

When saving to the repository you can save documents as personal documents (in My Favorites), or for shared use (in Public Folders), however, your permissions might prevent you from saving to certain locations (such as Public Folders).

Remember, **Folders** are physical **Locations** into which documents are saved. When saving a document it can only be saved in one folder (in a single Save action), but it can be saved again in a different folder.

Saving a document to 2 different folders results in 2 documents being stored in the repository with the same name, but in different folders. Making changes to one document will not be reflected in the other documents of the same name.

2. Click on the 'Advanced' button:

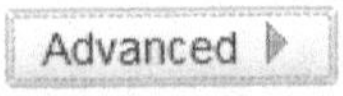
Advanced

Advanced options enable you to:

a) Give the document a '**Description**'. Useful to give more information about the document to potential users.

b) Assign '**Keywords**' to the document. These are searchable in BI Launch Pad to find documents with similar assigned keywords to them.

c) Apply '**Permanent regional formatting**' to the document. If you tick this box and you are in the UK then the document will be saved with UK regional formatting. All users (global) of this document will then view the data in UK regional formatting. If you do not tick this box then users with different regional formatting will view the data in their own regional formatting.

d) Force a '**Refresh on open**'. The document will be refreshed every time it is opened.

3. Click on the 'Categories' tab within the 'Save Document' interface:

If you have not already created the Personal Categories called 'Demo Category' and 'Training Category' then click on 'Create New Category' to create the categories before assigning them to the document.

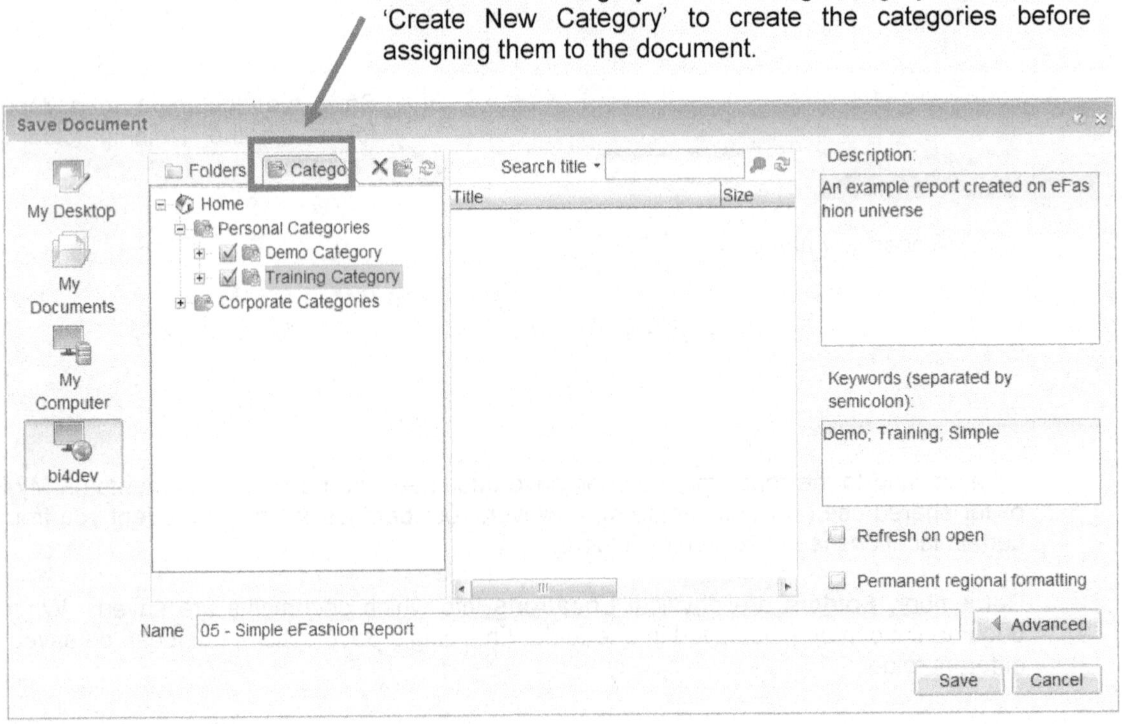
Save Document
My Desktop
My Documents
My Computer
bi4dev
Folders
Catego
Home
Personal Categories
Demo Category
Training Category
Corporate Categories
Search title
Title
Size
Description:
An example report created on eFashion universe
Keywords (separated by semicolon):
Demo; Training; Simple
Refresh on open
Permanent regional formatting
Name
05 - Simple eFashion Report
Advanced
Save
Cancel

Categories are logical associations to documents. When a document is saved it can have more than one Category assigned to it.

In our example, after saving the document it will be visible in **Demo Category** and **Training Category**, but the physical location of the document will be the **Training** folder.

We have also given a Description to the document as 'An example report created on eFashion universe' and assigned the Keywords 'Demo; Training; Simple'. **NOTE** – You must use semicolon (;) to separate keywords.

When saving to the repository it is recommended that documents be saved to at least one **Category**. New categories can be created in Personal Categories and in Corporate Categories (if you have sufficient privileges or ask your Administrator to create them).

It is also good practice to give the document a '**Description**' and '**Keywords**' (optional).

4. Click 'Save' to save the document.

5.3 The Java Query Panel

Let us return to the Query Panel and have a look at it in more detail. The Query Panel is the interface to a universe and allows you to drag and drop objects to create a request for data.

To return back to the Query Panel from the Report Panel:

1. Click on 'Data' icon (towards top right hand corner of the window).

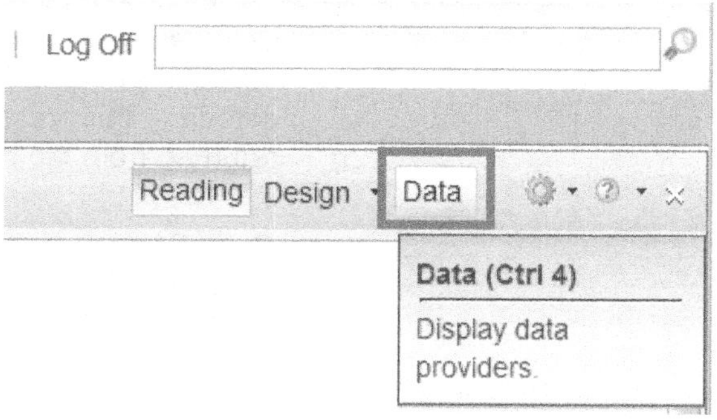

Log Off
Reading
Design
Data
Data (Ctrl 4)
Display data providers.

2. Then select the query (data provider) you want to view/edit and click 'Edit'.

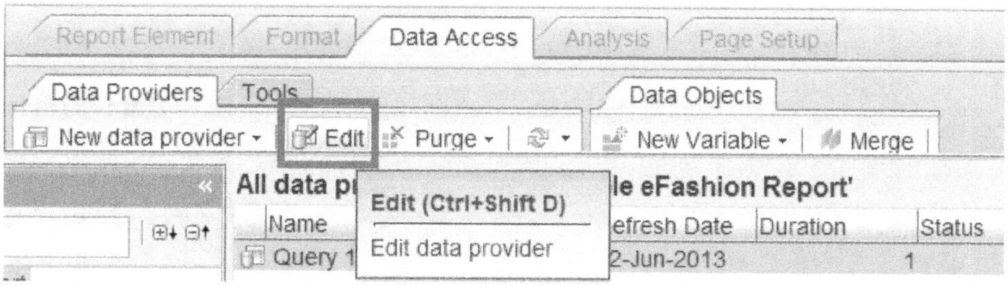

Report Element
Format
Data Access
Analysis
Page Setup
Data Providers
Tools
Data Objects
New data provider
Edit
Purge
New Variable
Merge
All data p
Edit (Ctrl+Shift D)
Edit data provider
le eFashion Report'
Name
efresh Date
Duration
Status
Query 1
2-Jun-2013
1

If you are in 'Design' mode then simply click on 'Data Access' and then 'Edit':

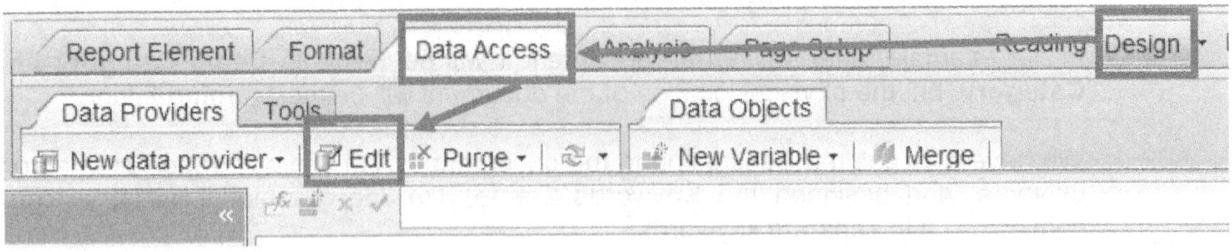
Report Element
Format
Data Access
Analysis
Page Setup
Reading
Design
Data Providers
Tools
Data Objects
New data provider
Edit
Purge
New Variable
Merge

The Java Query interface has 5 panels.

A. Universe outline
B. Result Objects
C. Query Filters - Conditions
D. Scope of analysis
E. Data Preview

NOTE – Scope of analysis and Data Preview cannot be displayed at the same time, therefore a maximum of 4 panels can be visible at any one given time.

A – **Universe outline** contains all objects available to the user for creating queries.

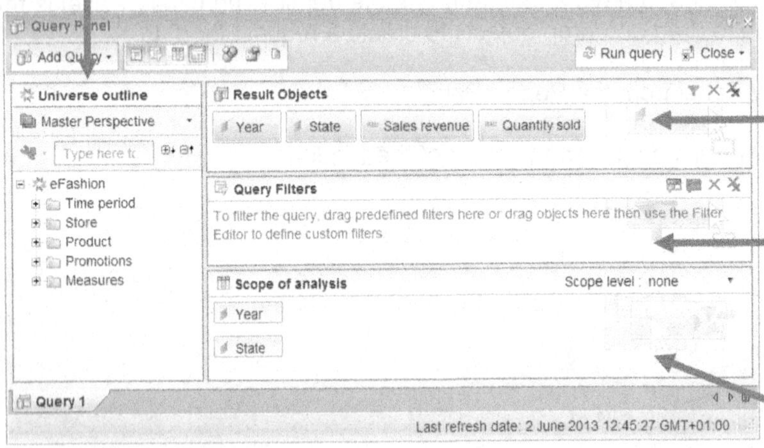
Query Panel
Add Query
Run query
Close
Universe outline
Master Perspective
eFashion
Time period
Store
Product
Promotions
Measures
Result Objects
Year
State
Sales revenue
Quantity sold
Query Filters
To filter the query, drag predefined filters here or drag objects here then use the Filter Editor to define custom filters
Scope of analysis
Scope level : none
Query 1
Last refresh date: 2 June 2013 12:45:27 GMT+01:00

B – **Result Objects**. Place objects in here to make them available for use within the document (e.g. for displaying, creating formulas, etc).

C – **Query Filters**. Place objects in here to define criteria to restrict data returned from the database.

D – **Scope of analysis** is used to define drill levels. This is described in detail later in the course.

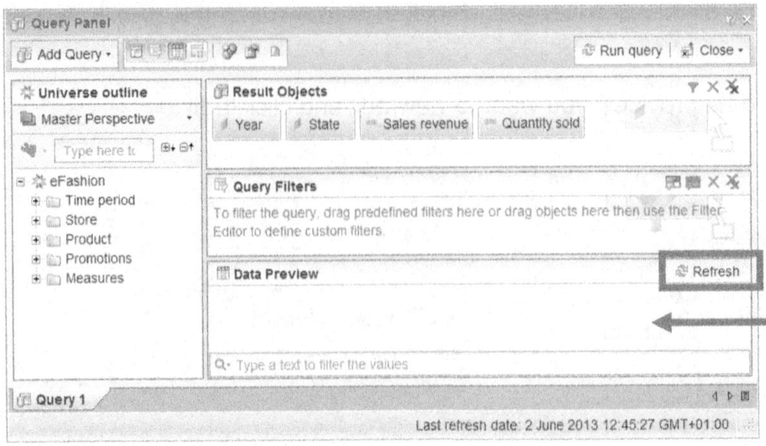
Query Panel
Add Query
Run query
Close
Universe outline
Master Perspective
eFashion
Time period
Store
Product
Promotions
Measures
Result Objects
Year
State
Sales revenue
Quantity sold
Query Filters
To filter the query, drag predefined filters here or drag objects here then use the Filter Editor to define custom filters
Data Preview
Refresh
Type a text to filter the values
Query 1
Last refresh date: 2 June 2013 12:45:27 GMT+01:00

E – **Data Preview** can be used to preview the results of the query within the Query Panel using the 'Refresh' icon.

A. Universe outline panel

The display of the available universe objects can be switched between the standard Folders view (Master Perspective) and hierarchical view of dimensions (Navigation Paths).

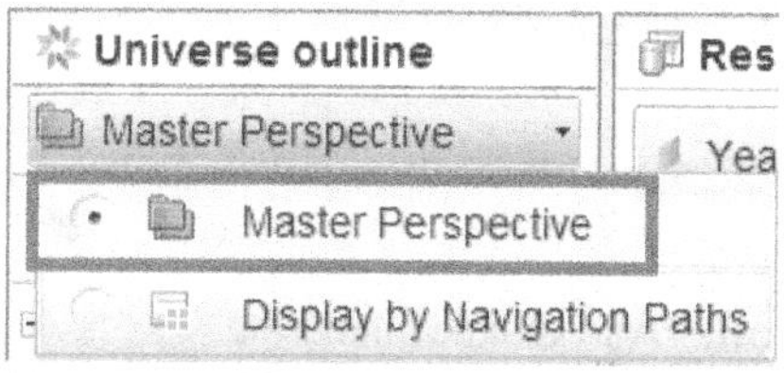
Universe outline
Res
Master Perspective
Yea
Master Perspective
Display by Navigation Paths

Objects can be searched by typing in characters into the search box.

NOTE

Master Perspective is the most widely used.

View of Navigation Paths can be useful when defining queries for drill purposes and you are unfamiliar with the hierarchy of your data.

Universe outline
Master Perspective
sa
eFashion
Store
Sales floor size?
Store details
Sales floor size gr
Sales floor size
Extended sales flc
Measures
Sales revenue

Folders can be expanded with a single action.

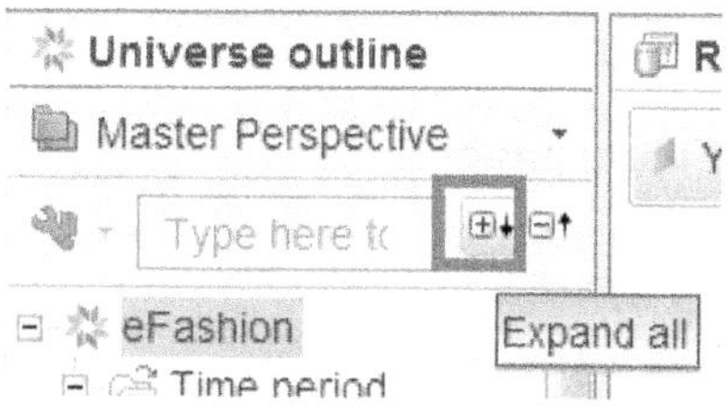
Universe outline
R
Master Perspective
Type here tc
eFashion
Expand all

Folders can be collapsed with a single action.

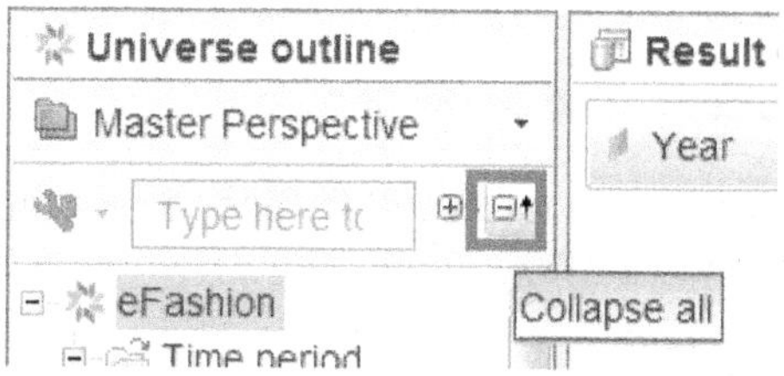
Universe outline
Result
Master Perspective
Year
Type here tc
eFashion
Collapse all

Hovering over an object reveals descriptions that have been added to the object by the Universe Designer.

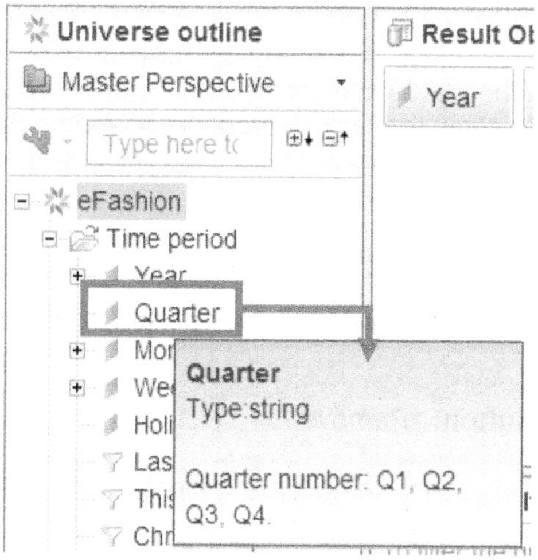
Universe outline
Result Ol
Master Perspective
Year
Type here tc
eFashion
Time period
Quarter
Quarter
Type:string
Quarter number: Q1, Q2, Q3, Q4.

B. Result Objects panel

Result Objects
Year
State
Sales revenue
Quantity sold

Button: 'Add Quick Filter' 

This button becomes active once an object is selected in the Results Objects pane.

When active  it enables you to select value(s) in order to restrict the data to these values for the selected object in the Results Object pane.

Button: 'Remove' 

This button removes a single pre-selected object from the Results Objects pane.

Button: 'Remove All' 

This button removes all objects from the Results Objects pane.

C. Query Filters panel

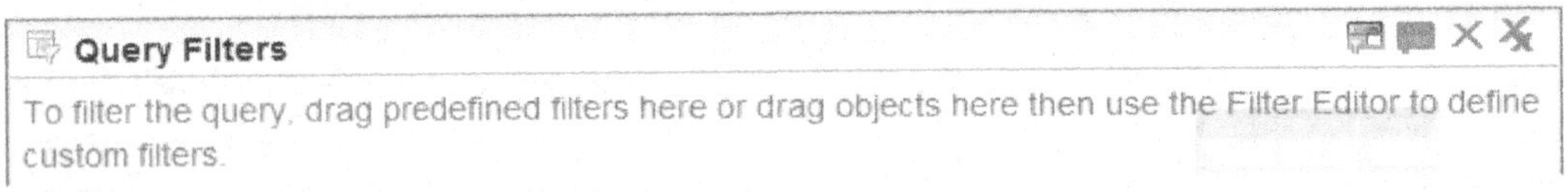
Query Filters
To filter the query, drag predefined filters here or drag objects here then use the Filter Editor to define custom filters.

Button: 'Add a subquery' 

Enables you to create an outer-query that is filtered using the results of an inner-query (known as a subquery).

Button: 'Add a database ranking' 

This button is only enabled if your database platform (and version) supports database ranking. When available for use, this button enables you to create queries to ask questions such as '...show the Top 10 products based on Sales Revenue in Last Year...', etc.

Button: 'Remove' 

This button removes a single pre-selected object from the Query Filters pane.

Button: 'Remove All' 

This button removes all objects from the Query Filters pane.

D. Scope of analysis panel

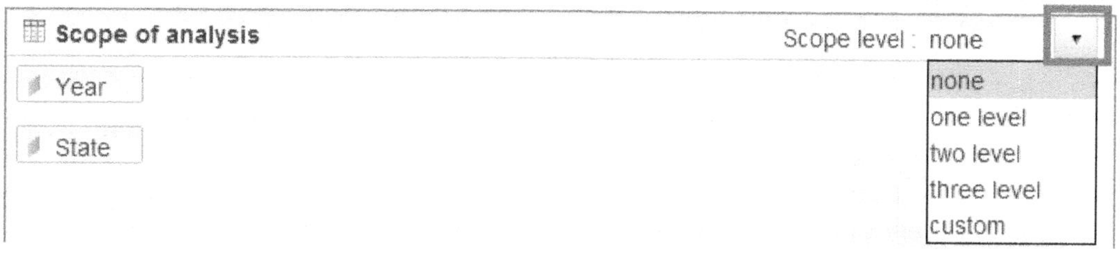
Scope of analysis
Scope level : none
Year
State
none
one level
two level
three level
custom

The 'Scope level' drop down is used when creating queries that will be used for drill analysis within reports. Discussed in detail in session on 'Exploring Report Data using Drill Mode'.

E. Data Preview panel

You can preview the type of data that will be returned by the query (for use within the report) by clicking on the 'Refresh' icon on the Data Preview panel.

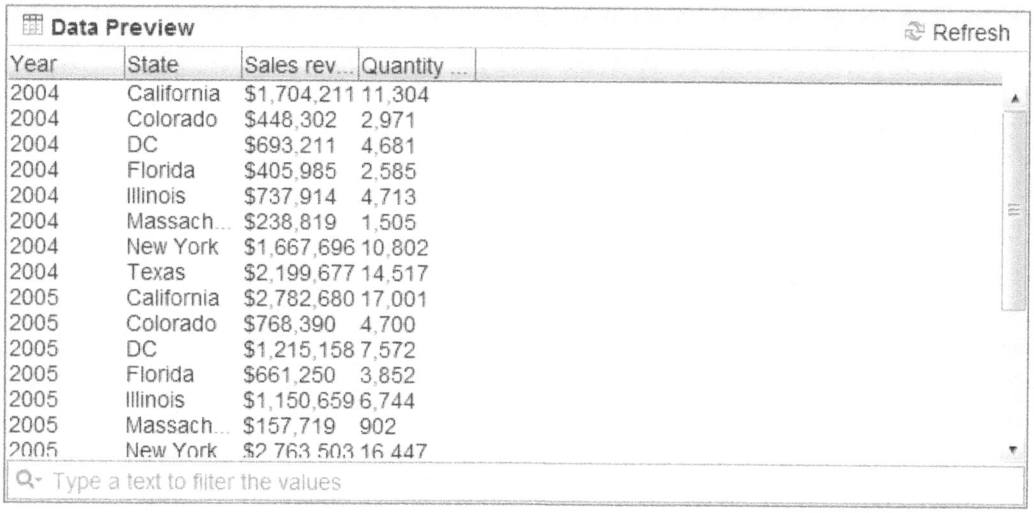
Data Preview
Refresh
Type a text to filter the values

Year	State	Sales rev...	Quantity ...
2004	California	$1,704,211	11,304
2004	Colorado	$448,302	2,971
2004	DC	$693,211	4,681
2004	Florida	$405,985	2,585
2004	Illinois	$737,914	4,713
2004	Massach...	$238,819	1,505
2004	New York	$1,667,696	10,802
2004	Texas	$2,199,677	14,517
2005	California	$2,782,680	17,001
2005	Colorado	$768,390	4,700
2005	DC	$1,215,158	7,572
2005	Florida	$661,250	3,852
2005	Illinois	$1,150,659	6,744
2005	Massach...	$157,719	902
2005	New York	$2,763,503	16,447

Data returned by the query can be filtered (for preview purposes) using the search box.

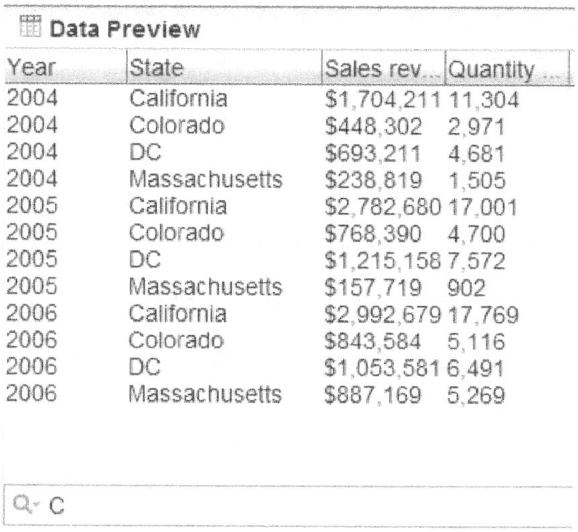
Data Preview
C

Year	State	Sales rev...	Quantity ...
2004	California	$1,704,211	11,304
2004	Colorado	$448,302	2,971
2004	DC	$693,211	4,681
2004	Massachusetts	$238,819	1,505
2005	California	$2,782,680	17,001
2005	Colorado	$768,390	4,700
2005	DC	$1,215,158	7,572
2005	Massachusetts	$157,719	902
2006	California	$2,992,679	17,769
2006	Colorado	$843,584	5,116
2006	DC	$1,053,581	6,491
2006	Massachusetts	$887,169	5,269

Query Toolbar

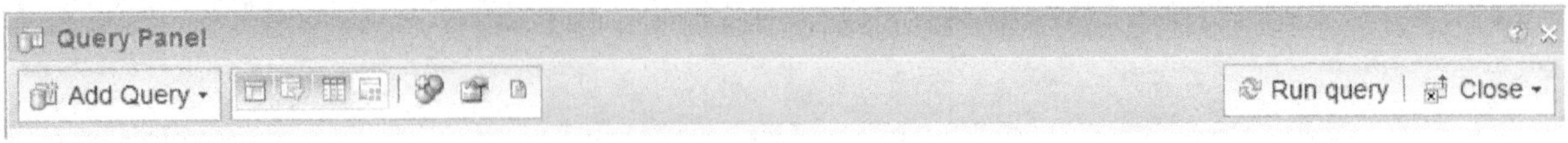
Query Panel
Add Query
Run query
Close

Multiple queries can be added to the document using the 'Add Query' button.

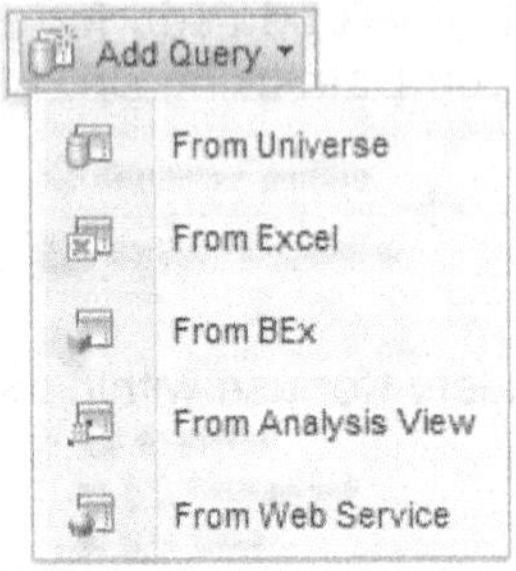
Add Query
From Universe
From Excel
From BEx
From Analysis View
From Web Service

Multiple queries are discussed later in the course, excluding BEx and Analysis View.

All panes (except for Results Objects) can be toggled open or closed by the first three buttons on the Query toolbar.

From left to right:

'Show/Hide Data Outline Panel'	Shows or Hides the All Objects and Hierarchies pane, i.e. the Universe outline panel
'Show/Hide Filters Panel'	Shows or Hides the Query Filters panel
'Show Hide Data Preview Panel'	Shows or Hides the Data Preview panel
'Show/Hide Scope of Analysis Panel'	Shows or Hides the panel for specifying query drill levels

Button: 'Add a combined query' 

Enables you to create queries such as:

1. List all customers who purchased Product X and also purchase Product Y
2. List all customers who purchased Product X but did not purchase Product Y
3. List all customers who purchased Product X, or Product Y, or both.

Button: 'Query Properties' 

Enables you to view (and modify) the query properties (as shown below).

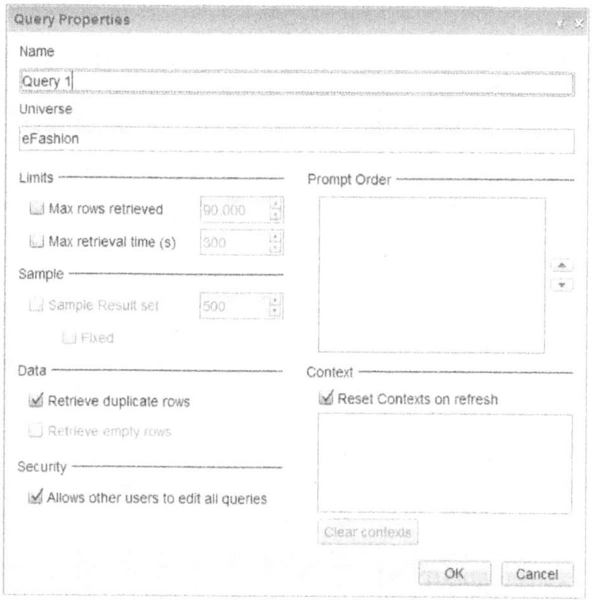
Query Properties
Name
Query 1
Universe
eFashion
Limits
Max rows retrieved
90,000
Max retrieval time (s)
300
Sample
Sample Result set
500
Fixed
Prompt Order
Data
Retrieve duplicate rows
Retrieve empty rows
Security
Allows other users to edit all queries
Context
Reset Contexts on refresh
Clear contexts
OK
Cancel

Query Property	Description/Usage
Name	Queries can be given meaningful names as there might be multiple queries within the document.
Universe	The universe being used for the query.
Max rows retrieved **Max retrieval time (s)** **Sample Result set** **Fixed**	To bring back a limited amount of rows, perhaps to test a query, you can set a limit to the amount of rows retrieved or limit the query execution time. Partial, or incomplete, results are indicated in the comment section at the bottom of the report. If your database supports random record sampling then you can specify how many records to randomly sample. Further to this if your database supports fixed sampling then ticking the '**Fixed**' property ensures the same rows are returned on each refresh.
	'**Sample Result set**' is more efficient than the '**Max rows retrieved**' property, which discards rows beyond the maximum limit only after retrieving all the rows in the query. 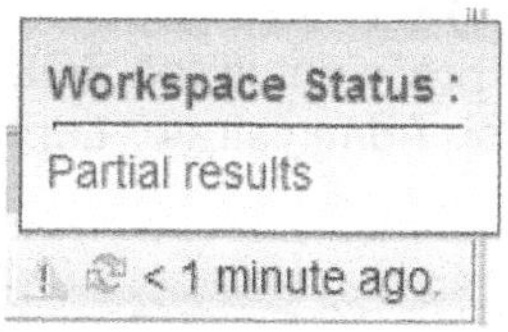 If a query has been run with '**Limits**' or '**Sample**' then the '**Partial results**' message will be displayed within the Report Panel (in the bottom right corner).

Workspace Status :
Partial results
< 1 minute ago

Query Property	Description/Usage
Retrieve duplicate rows	The default setting is to retrieve duplicate rows. Duplicate rows are aggregated into a single row for display in the report. Most queries will want to retrieve the duplicate rows when you include measures in the Result Objects pane. Un-checking this property is useful when **querying dimension values only** as it ensures only one row is returned by the database per DISTINCT combination of dimension values. Querying a table for a distinct list of months (i.e. time periods) in which there are 120,000 rows with only 36 distinct month values. Without a measure object in the query and with this property checked the database would return all 120,000 records, but with the property unchecked only 36 records would be returned as the SQL is modified to use 'SELECT DISTINCT'. **NOTE** – For more complex queries, un-checking this property can have a serious performance impact on the query run time (as the database has to sort and retrieve unique rows).
Retrieve empty rows	
Allows other users to edit all queries	Default setting to allow other users to edit all queries within the document (relevant privileges are required). This setting applies to all queries in a multiple query document.
Prompt Order	Prompts used within a Web Intelligence query can be ordered in the Query Panel Properties tab.
Reset Contexts on refresh	If multiple paths are available in the universe between two tables of data (when the query definition is ambiguous) then the user will be presented with a choice of which path to navigate. If you do not want the choice to appear then uncheck this setting after specifying default paths. '**Clear Contexts**' will clear any selected paths you have specified as defaults when overriding '**Reset contexts on refresh**'.

Button: 'View Script'

Enables you to view (and modify) the SQL generated by Web Intelligence, but this is usually only available for users who are proficient in the SQL database language, i.e. enabled/disabled by the BusinessObjects Enterprise Administrator depending on your role.

Button: 'Run Query' 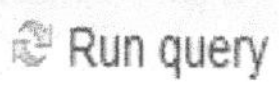
Run query

Runs the query and exits the Query Panel.

Button: 'Close' 
Close
Apply Changes and Close
Revert Changes and Close

'Apply Changes and Close' – Closes the query (without running it) and returns back to the Report Panel. If the query has been modified then all data will be 'purged' but the new definition of the query will be kept. Save the document to make the query changes permanent.

'Revert Changes and Close' – Closes the query and keeps the previous definition. The previous definition refers to the latest run of a query, i.e. if you have made modifications to a query and run it, then that becomes the previous definition.

You will be prompted with the following to confirm you want to proceed with this action:

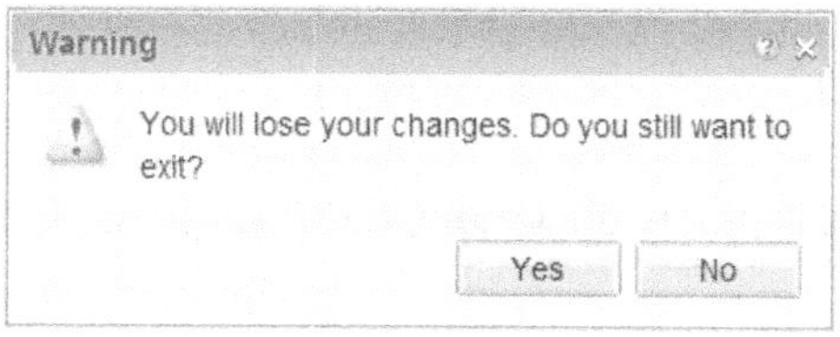
Warning
You will lose your changes. Do you still want to exit?
Yes
No

Button: 'Help' 

The Help button links to HTML based help pages.

NOTE – Panels can be resized horizontally or vertically by hovering near the perimeter of a panel and then resizing (with the left mouse button held down) when the resizing bars appear:

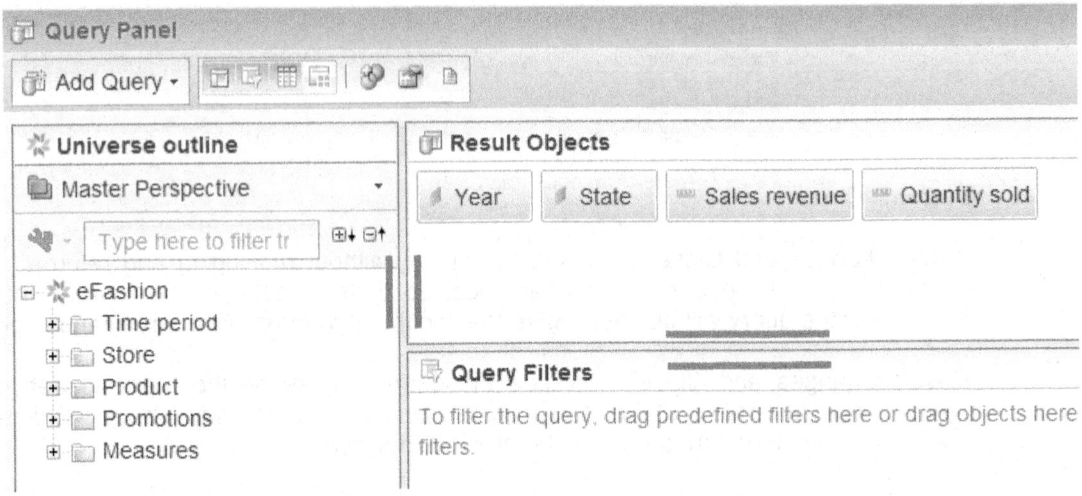
Query Panel
Add Query
Universe outline
Master Perspective
Type here to filter tr
eFashion
Time period
Store
Product
Promotions
Measures
Result Objects
Year
State
Sales revenue
Quantity sold
Query Filters
To filter the query, drag predefined filters here or drag objects here
filters.

5.4 Closing a Web Intelligence Document

When you have finished working with your Web Intelligence document then you can exit using the 'Close' button

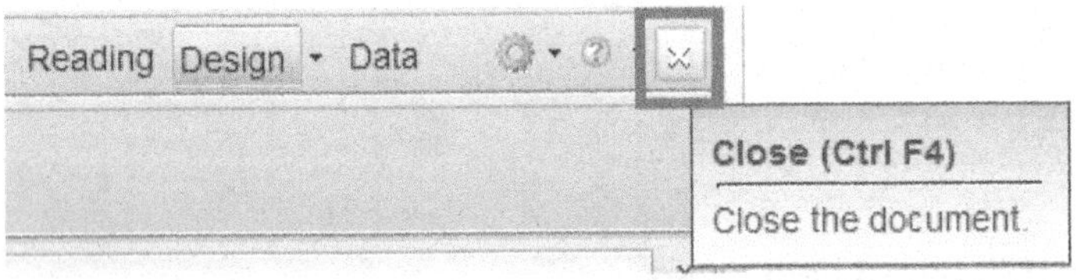
Reading
Design
Data
Close (Ctrl F4)
Close the document.

Or the 'Close this Tab' button.

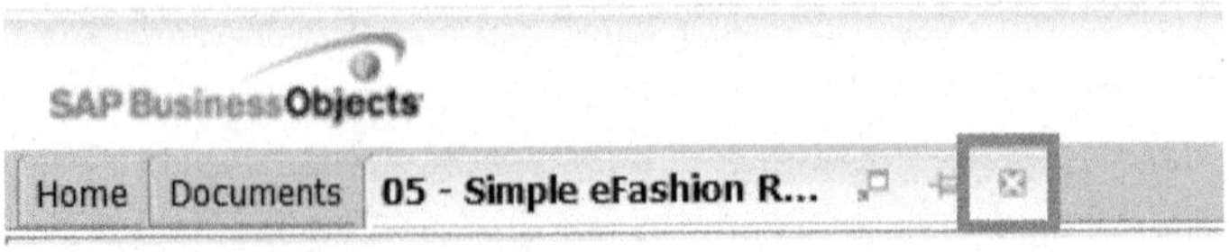
SAP BusinessObjects
Home
Documents
05 - Simple eFashion R...

6 Viewing and Editing Web Intelligence Documents

It is very important to understand that once created, Web Intelligence documents are mostly viewed, refreshed, analysed and distributed in BI Launch Pad. When you decide to modify the document then Web Intelligence is initiated in order to allow changes to be made. Formatting changes can be made in BI Launch Pad 'Interactive' mode, but query changes can only be made in Web Intelligence.

6.1 Viewing Web Intelligence Documents

Documents can be accessed using Folders (My Favorites or Public Folders) or Categories (Personal Categories and Corporate Categories). Simply navigate to these locations using the relevant links.

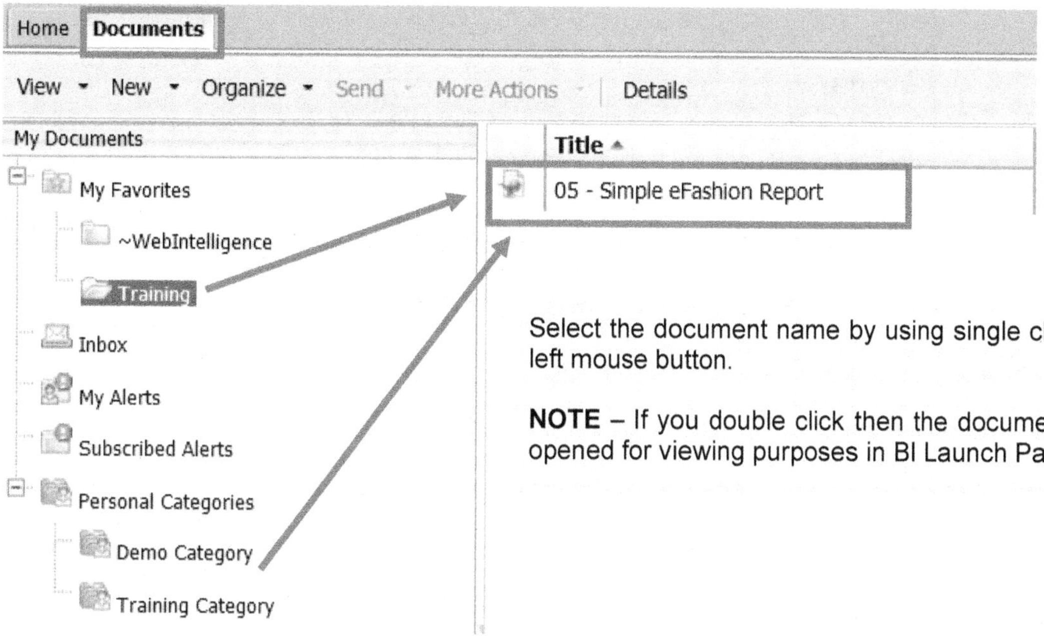
Home
Documents
View
New
Organize
Send
More Actions
Details
My Documents
Title
05 - Simple eFashion Report
My Favorites
~WebIntelligence
Training
Inbox
My Alerts
Subscribed Alerts
Personal Categories
Demo Category
Training Category

Select the document name by using single click of the left mouse button.

NOTE – If you double click then the document will be opened for viewing purposes in BI Launch Pad.

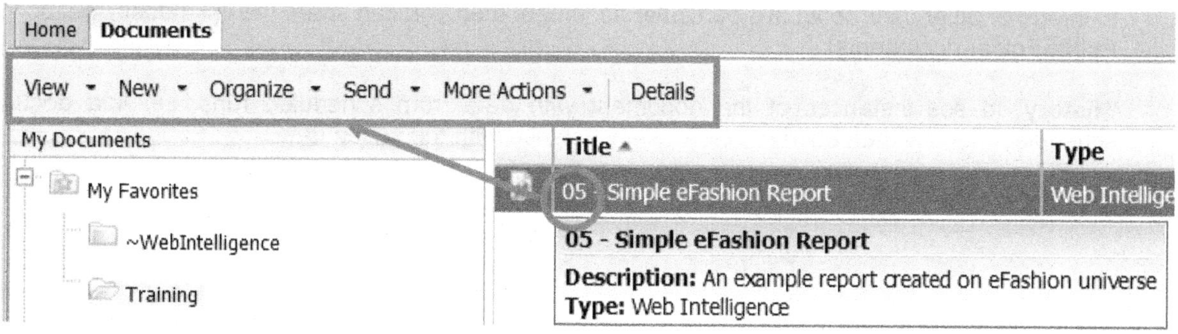
Home
Documents
View
New
Organize
Send
More Actions
Details
My Documents
Title
Type
05 - Simple eFashion Report
My Favorites
~WebIntelligence
Training
05 - Simple eFashion Report
Description: An example report created on eFashion universe
Type: Web Intelligence

Once the document has been selected then the various menus can be used to work with the document.

Alternatively, the same menus are available using right-click on the document name (shown on next page).

Title
05 - Simple eFashion R
View
Properties
View Lineage
View Metapedia Terms
Modify
Schedule
Mobile Properties
History
Categories
Document Link
New
Organize
Send
Details

NOTE – Right click on a document name to use shortcut menus.

'**View**' to open the document in BI Launch Pad for viewing only.

'**Properties**' to view and modify document properties (such as the Title and Description).

'**View Lineage**' and '**View Metapedia Terms**' are used with SAP Information Steward.

'**Modify**' to open the document in Web Intelligence for editing.

'**Schedule**' to define a schedule for automated refreshing and distribution.

'**Mobile Properties**' to define properties on how document should be displayed on mobile devices.

'**Categories**' to view/edit assigned categories to this document.

'**Document Link**' enables you to copy and share the link to this document, for example if you would like to inform another user about this particular document then you can share the link (ideally needs to be for Public Folder documents).

'**History**' to see instances of the document with data from scheduled runs, i.e. if a document is scheduled monthly then each run creates an instance with the saved data.

'**Details**' to view summary details about the document:

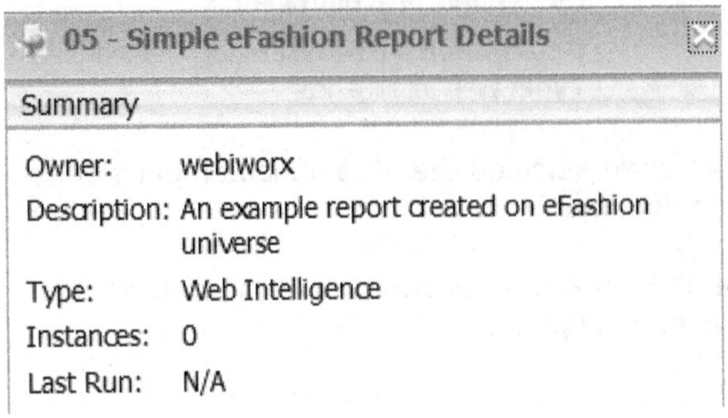
05 - Simple eFashion Report Details
Summary
Owner: webiworx
Description: An example report created on eFashion universe
Type: Web Intelligence
Instances: 0
Last Run: N/A

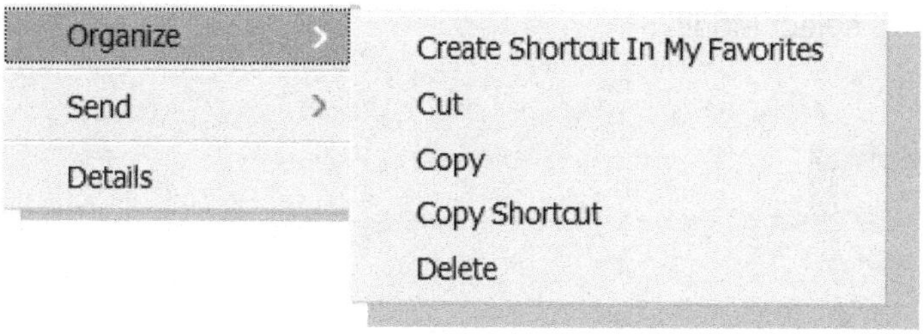
Organize
Send
Details
Create Shortcut In My Favorites
Cut
Copy
Copy Shortcut
Delete

'**Organize**' enables you to perform tasks such as:

- Copy (and then Paste)
- create and copy shortcut to the document
- Delete the document
- Cut (and then Paste) if you would like to move the document to another folder

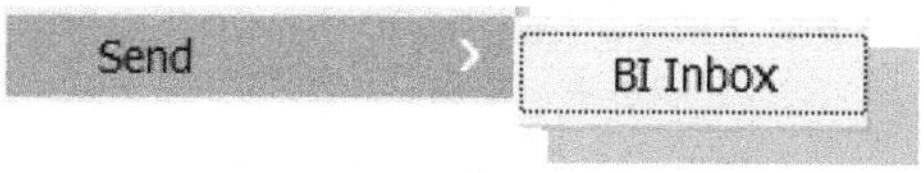
Send
BI Inbox

'**Send**' to send the document to other users within the BusinessObjects Enterprise environment using the Inbox.

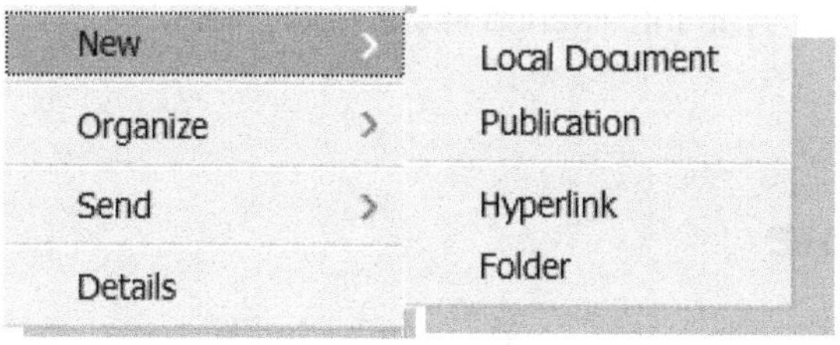
New
Organize
Send
Details
Local Document
Publication
Hyperlink
Folder

'**New**' is a general right-click menu and not specifically for documents.

- It can be used to add a Local Document into the repository (such as an Excel file).
- Set up a Publication (an advanced type of refresh schedule).
- Add a Hyperlink into the repository, e.g. maybe to a site showing latest exchange rates, etc.
- Create a new Folder.

6.2 Editing an Existing Web Intelligence Document

Web Intelligence documents can be edited by initiating the document to be opened using Web Intelligence rather than within BI Launch Pad. There are number of ways to open the document for editing:

1. Select the document and then apply the action 'Modify' as shown here.

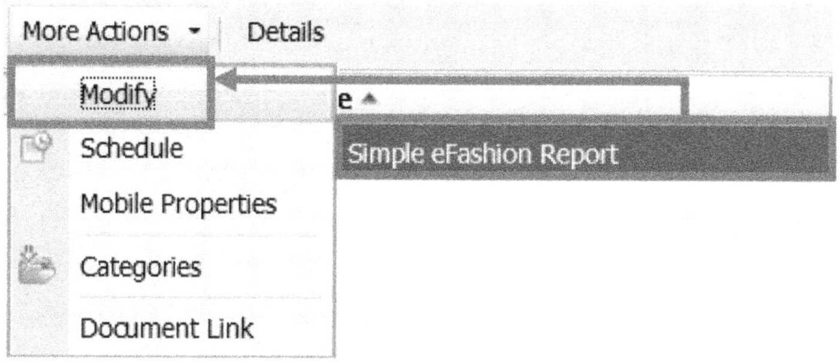
More Actions
Details
Modify
Schedule
Mobile Properties
Categories
Document Link
Simple eFashion Report

2. Or right click on the document name and select Modify:

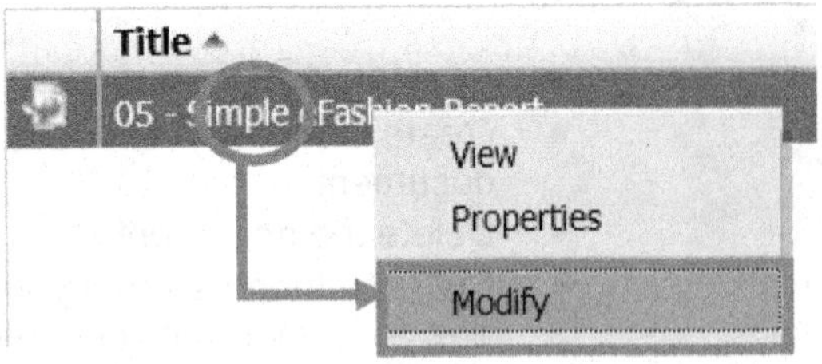
Title
View
Properties
Modify

3. Or open the document after first launching Web Intelligence and then browsing to the document:

Open Web Intelligence from BI Launch Pad and then browse to the document. The document will be opened in Web Intelligence in view/edit mode.

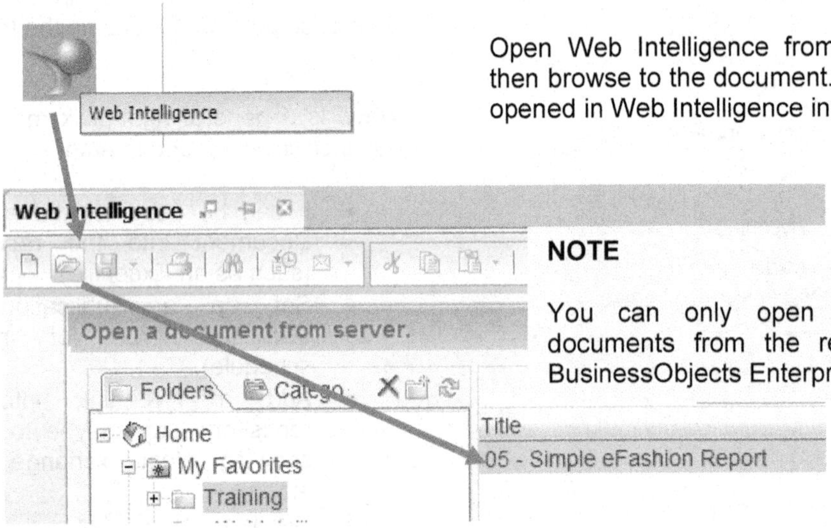
Web Intelligence
Open a document from server.
Folders
Home
My Favorites
Training
Title
05 - Simple eFashion Report

NOTE

You can only open Web Intelligence documents from the repository (i.e. the BusinessObjects Enterprise server).

6.3 Edit Query / Edit Report within Document

A Web Intelligence document can be edited in two modes ('Query' and 'Report').

It is important to recognise that the document contains a set of data attached to it.

- When **editing the data provider(s)** you are editing the attached set of data.
- When **editing the document/report** you are editing the display or use of the data in the document/report.

1. To edit a data provider, first open the Web Intelligence document and then you can use 'Edit' under the 'Data Access' ribbon.

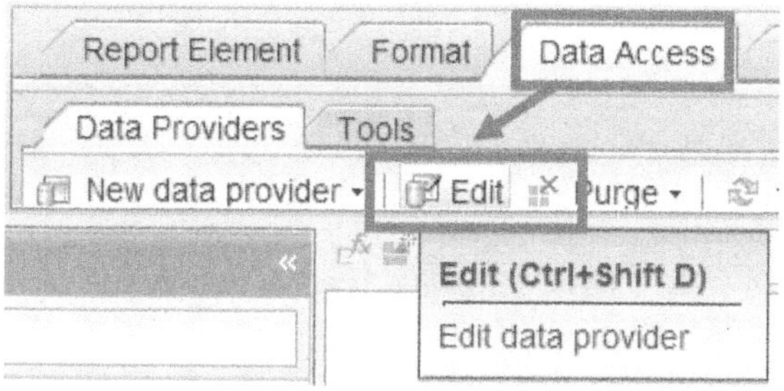
Report Element
Format
Data Access
Data Providers
Tools
New data provider
Edit
Purge
Edit (Ctrl+Shift D)
Edit data provider

2. Or click on the 'Data' button and Web Intelligence will automatically take you to the 'Data Access' ribbon, showing all data providers within the document.

Report Element
Format
Data Access
Analysis
Page Setup
Reading
Design
Data
Data Providers
Tools
Data Objects
New data provider
Edit
Purge
New Variable
Merge
All data providers of '05 - Simple eFashion Report'
Name
Data Source
Refresh Date
Duration
Status
Data
Query 1
eFashion
02-Jun-2013
1
24 rows

3. You can then select the data provider and click on 'Edit'.

Editing the query is effectively redesigning the query, meaning you will need to re-run any change in the Query Panel to 'modify' the attached query. The revised request is sent back to the database and then the old set of data is dropped and the new set of data is attached to the document.

6.4 Editing an Existing Query

As explained above, a query attached to a document can be edited after a document has been opened for modify purposes and 'edit data provider' mode selected. The following steps will introduce how a query is typically modified.

1. From BI Launch Pad, open the 'Simple eFashion Report' for modify purposes:

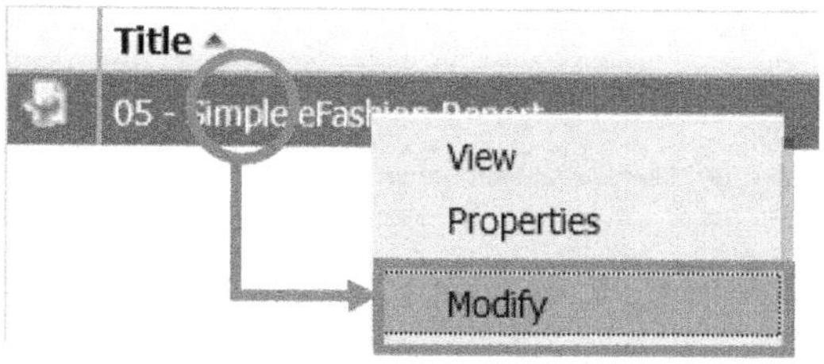
Title
View
Properties
Modify

2. In the Report Panel select 'Data Access – Edit' to switch to the Query Panel:

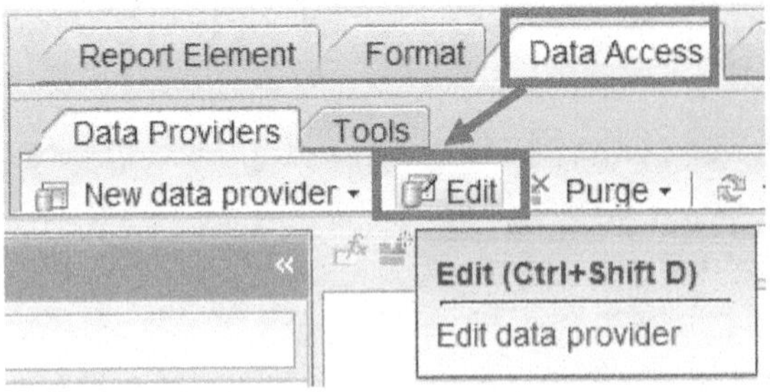
Report Element
Format
Data Access
Data Providers
Tools
New data provider
Edit
Purge
Edit (Ctrl+Shift D)
Edit data provider

3. Drag the [Quarter] object from the Data tab and drop into the Result Objects pane in between [State] and [Sales revenue]:

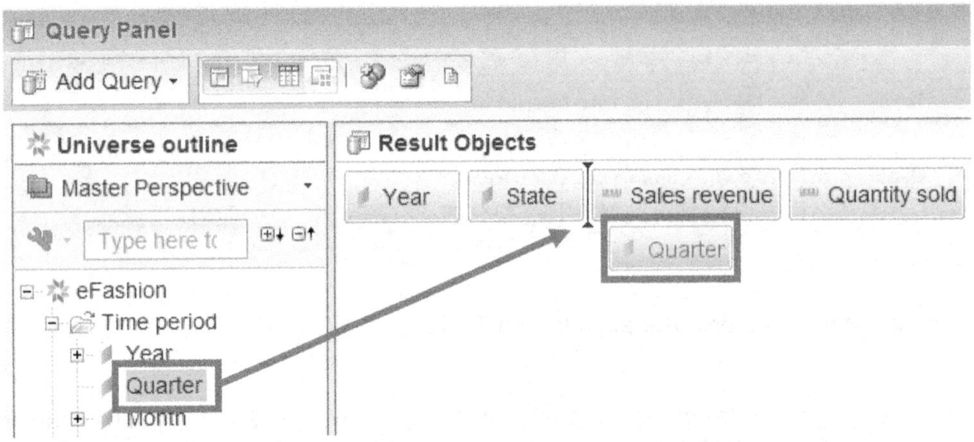
Query Panel
Add Query
Universe outline
Master Perspective
Type here tc
eFashion
Time period
Year
Quarter
Month
Result Objects
Year
State
Sales revenue
Quantity sold
Quarter

NOTE – Within the Query panel, objects can be placed in the Results Objects panel in any order. You have total control of re-arranging the display of data in the Report Panel.

4. Run the query 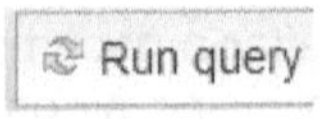 :
Run query

5. Web Intelligence displays:

File
Properties
Report Element
Format
Data Access
Analysis
Page Setup
Reading
Design
Data
Data Providers
Tools
Data Objects
New data provider
Edit
Purge
New Variable
Merge
Data
Type here to filter tree
05 - Simple eFashion Report
eFashion
Query 1
Quarter
State
Year
Quantity sold
Sales revenue
Variables
All data providers of '05 - Simple eFashion Report'
Name
Data Source
Refresh Date
Duration
Status
Data
Query 1
eFashion
03-Jun-2013
1
93 rows

The [Quarter] object has been added into the Data tab within the Report Panel and we now have 93 rows of data compared to 24 rows previously.

6. Click on 'Design' – 'With Data':

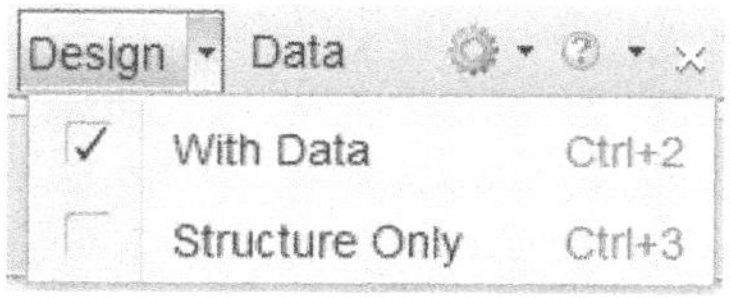
Design
Data
With Data
Ctrl+2
Structure Only
Ctrl+3

7. Web Intelligence displays:

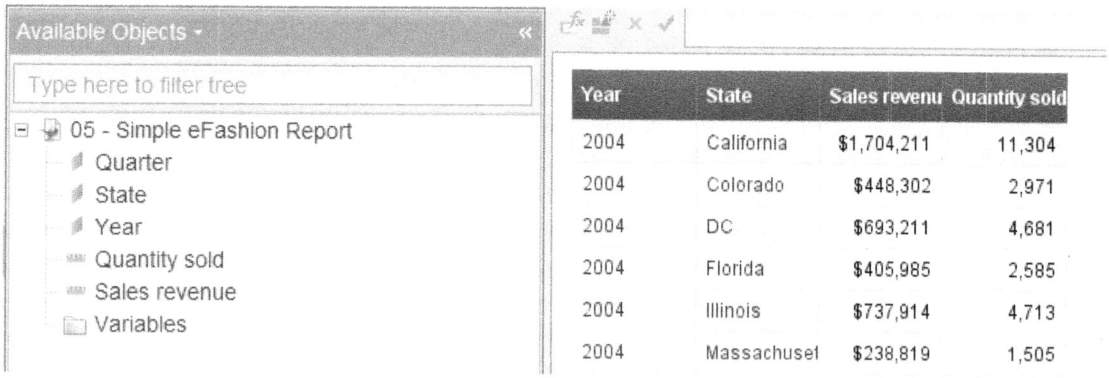
Available Objects
Type here to filter tree
05 - Simple eFashion Report
Quarter
State
Year
Quantity sold
Sales revenue
Variables
Year
State
Sales revenu
Quantity sold
2004
California
$1,704,211
11,304
2004
Colorado
$448,302
2,971
2004
DC
$693,211
4,681
2004
Florida
$405,985
2,585
2004
Illinois
$737,914
4,713
2004
Massachuset
$238,819
1,505

Web Intelligence has included the [Quarter] object in 'Available Objects' but it has not been inserted into the table. We will look at adding and removing objects from the display area in the session on 'Introducing Drag and Drop Techniques'.

NOTE – If an object is removed from the Results Objects panel in the Query Panel then it will automatically be removed from any report element (table, chart, cell, etc) that was using it.

An object can be removed from a Query Panel pane in a number of ways:

1. In the Report Panel return back to query edit mode:

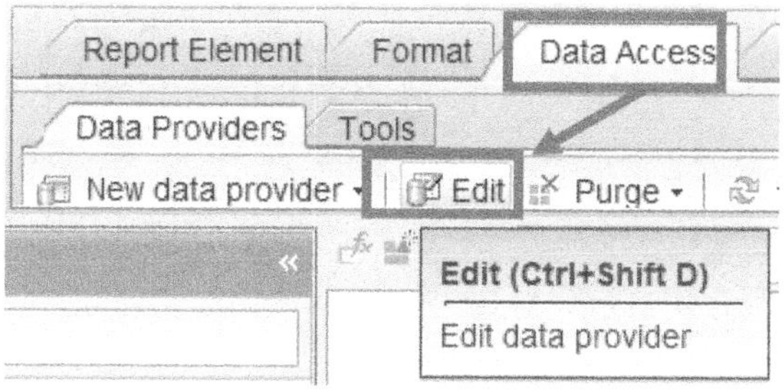
Report Element
Format
Data Access
Data Providers
Tools
New data provider
Edit
Purge
Edit (Ctrl+Shift D)
Edit data provider

2. Select the object and then use the 'Remove' button in the relevant pane.

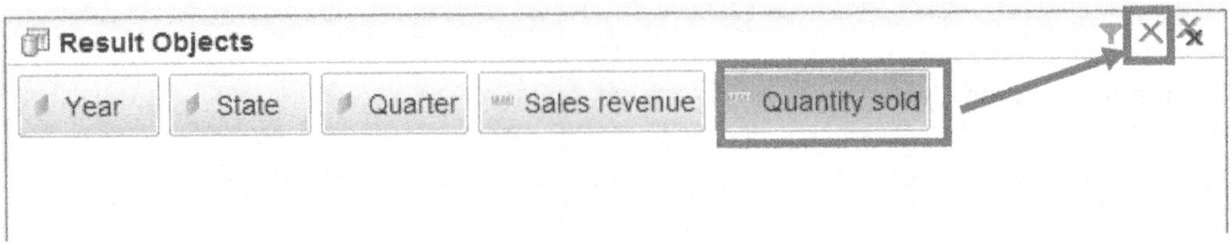
Result Objects
Year
State
Quarter
Sales revenue
Quantity sold

Or select the object and then press the <Del> or <Delete> key on your keyboard.

Or select the object and drag it out of the pane back into the 'Universe outline' panel.

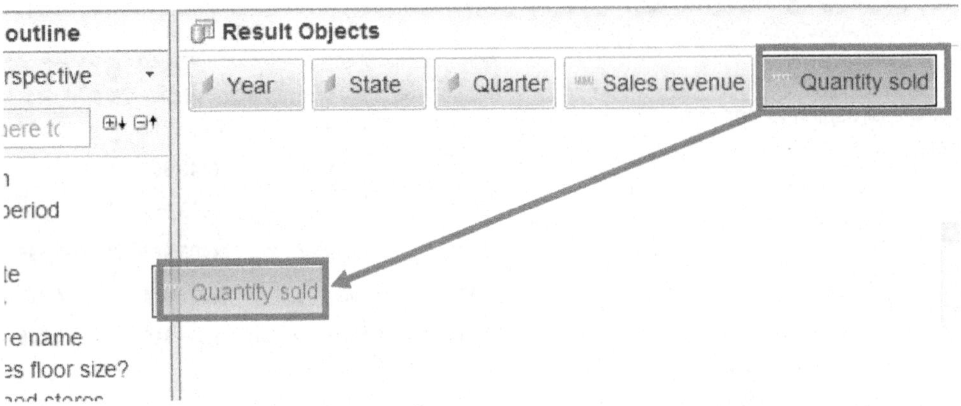
outline
rspective
Result Objects
Year
State
Quarter
Sales revenue
Quantity sold
period
re name
Quantity sold

3. Run the query 
Run query

4. Save the document 
File
Properties

7 Data in Web Intelligence Documents

The set of data that is attached to a document is often referred to as a 'microcube'. You can see the objects within a document's microcube in the 'Available Objects' tab that is displayed to the left of the report area. The microcube is a multi-dimensional cube of data, from which you can select any part to view in a report, and it also enables you to perform analysis on your data.

The concept of a 'cube of data' implies that the results may be in a multi-dimensional relationship (e.g. multiple queries) that is flattened for display of all the possible unique rows. You may not see each distinct row retrieved because the data is summarised as much as possible, (e.g., measure objects are aggregated for duplicate rows of data).

7.1 Duplicate Rows

By default, Web Intelligence queries will retrieve all of the possible results according to the query request for data, often returning duplicate rows of data when flattened out. Duplicate rows are handled by Web Intelligence depending upon the type of objects present because dimensions and attributes in a duplicate row are not repeated, but the measure values are rolled up according to their aggregation property.

1. For example if we have the following query from the 'eFashion' universe:

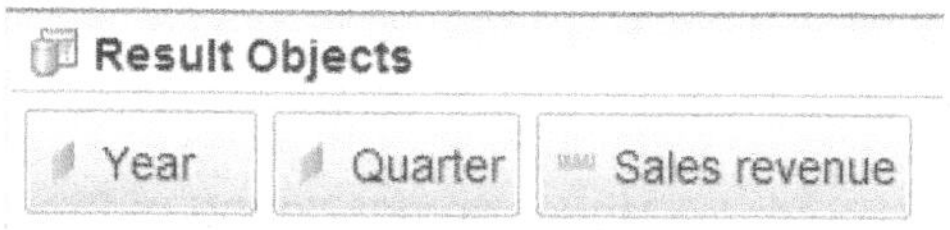
Result Objects
Year
Quarter
Sales revenue

2. The data returned would be as follows:

Year	Quarter	Sales revenu
2004	Q1	$2,660,700
2004	Q2	$2,279,003
2004	Q3	$1,367,841
2004	Q4	$1,788,580
2005	Q1	$3,326,172
2005	Q2	$2,840,651
2005	Q3	$2,879,303
2005	Q4	$4,186,120
2006	Q1	$3,742,989
2006	Q2	$4,006,718
2006	Q3	$3,953,395
2006	Q4	$3,356,041

We have one row per year per quarter, making 12 rows in total (3 years with 4 quarters).

3. If we were to remove [Quarter] from the block (i.e. the table and not the query):

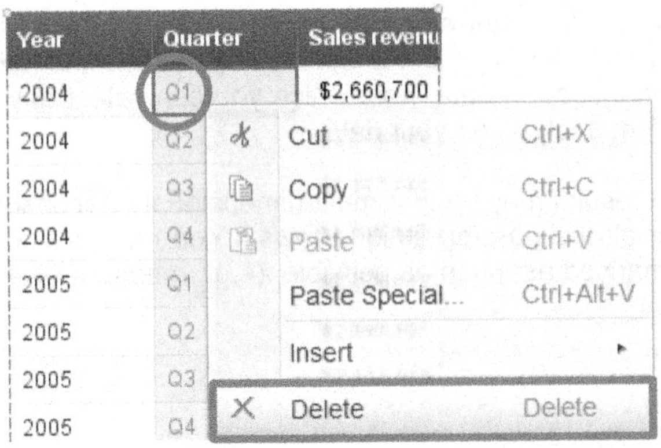
Year
Quarter
Sales revenu
2004
Q1
$2,660,700
2004
Q2
2004
Q3
2004
Q4
2005
Q1
2005
Q2
2005
Q3
2005
Q4
Cut
Ctrl+X
Copy
Ctrl+C
Paste
Ctrl+V
Paste Special...
Ctrl+Alt+V
Insert
Delete
Delete

Right-click in any cell of the [Quarter] column and then select 'Delete'.

4. Then the default presentation of the data by Web Intelligence would result in:

Year	Sales revenue
2004	$8,096,124
2005	$13,232,246
2006	$15,059,143

If you cannot see all of the values in the [Sales revenue] column then you can resize the column by hovering on the right edge and dragging towards the right (as shown below).

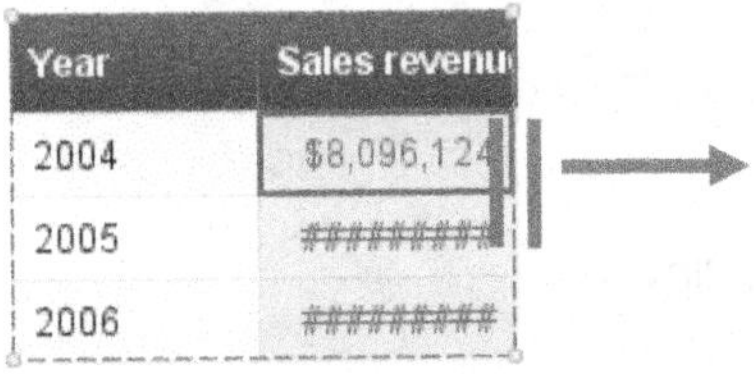
Year
Sales revenu
2004
$8,096,124
2005
#########
2006
#########

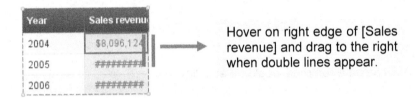

Hover on right edge of [Sales revenue] and drag to the right when double lines appear.

Web Intelligence has reduced the 12 records into 3 because we have 3 unique values for [Year]. The measure object [Sales revenue] has been aggregated to the level (or context) of the single dimension.

This can be overridden to display all 12 rows by turning on the **block** property '**Avoid duplicate row aggregation**'.

5. Right-click on the perimeter of the table (any side) and select ‘Format Table’.

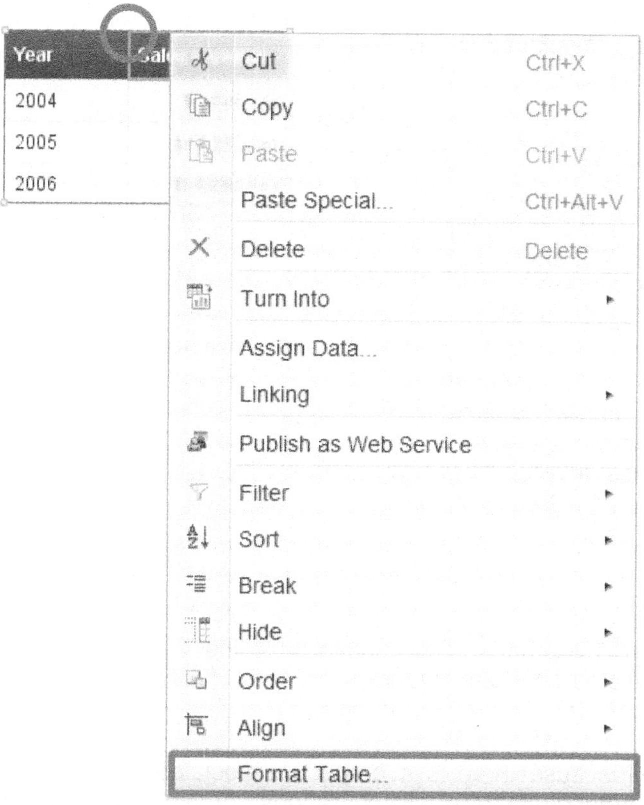
Year
2004
2005
2006
Cut Ctrl+X
Copy Ctrl+C
Paste Ctrl+V
Paste Special... Ctrl+Alt+V
Delete Delete
Turn Into
Assign Data...
Linking
Publish as Web Service
Filter
Sort
Break
Hide
Order
Align
Format Table...

6. In the ‘Format Table’ interface, select ‘Avoid duplicate row aggregation’ and click ‘OK’.

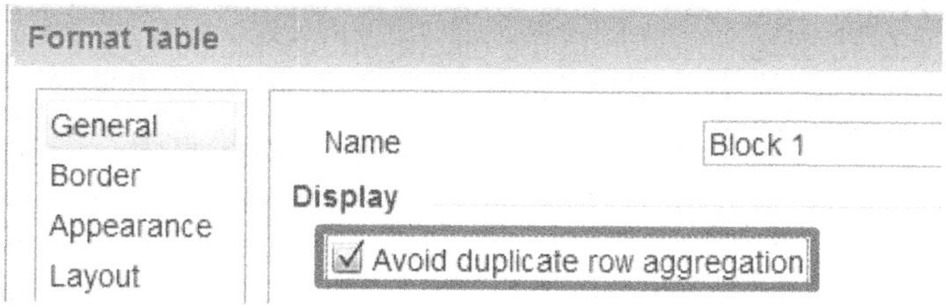
Format Table
General
Border
Appearance
Layout
Name
Block 1
Display
Avoid duplicate row aggregation

7. Web Intelligence displays:

Year	Sales revenue
2004	$2,660,700
2004	$2,279,003
2004	$1,367,841
2004	$1,788,580
2005	$3,326,172
2005	$2,840,651
2005	$2,879,303
2005	$4,186,120
2006	$3,742,989
2006	$4,006,718
2006	$3,953,395
2006	$3,356,041

The data displayed in this block is somewhat confusing as we have 4 values per [Year], but what are they? In this case we know them to be the [Sales revenue] for each [Quarter], but no breakdown is shown.

Example, we would have a similar looking display if the query was for [Sales revenue] for the Top 4 [States] in each [Year].

We now have all 12 rows but without [Quarter]. In the above table the 4 rows per year do not inform the viewer which row is associated with which [Quarter], so it is much better to present the data as 1 row per year.

The reason the data aggregates is because there is a property associated with each measure object that controls its projection/aggregation behaviour within reports. In this case [Sales revenue] has been set to aggregate using the 'SUM' function when dimensions are removed from the report block.

NOTE – The microcube still holds the 'raw data' at the lower level but the measures behave dynamically when dimensions are added or removed from the displayed block.

8 The Java Report Panel

The Java Report Panel is the most feature rich of the interfaces available for creating, editing and analysing Web Intelligence documents. With the Web Intelligence Java Report Panel, you can:

- connect to databases, files and web services (using the Java Query Panel) to fetch data for your documents
- present the data in one or more report tabs using tables, crosstabs and charts
- use drag and drop functionality to visually construct and format the report layouts
- filter the data
- rank the data
- apply sorts
- create formulas and variables to perform calculations
- apply other formatting such as Sections, Breaks, and Conditional Formatting
- use Drill Mode for analysing data
- merge data from multiple data sources
- refresh the document for latest data
- track data changes
- save and print the document in various formats

We have already briefly used the Java Report Panel and all of the above will be discussed in detail throughout this course.

Please make sure you have set the following **Preference** (as described previously):

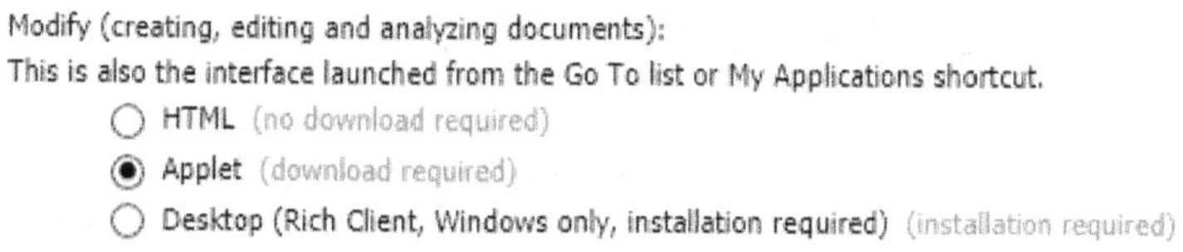
Modify (creating, editing and analyzing documents):
This is also the interface launched from the Go To list or My Applications shortcut.
HTML (no download required)
Applet (download required)
Desktop (Rich Client, Windows only, installation required) (installation required)

After setting this preference, when Web Intelligence is launched, it will use the Java Report and Query Panels.

Remember, you can launch Web Intelligence from the BI Launch Pad in a variety of ways:

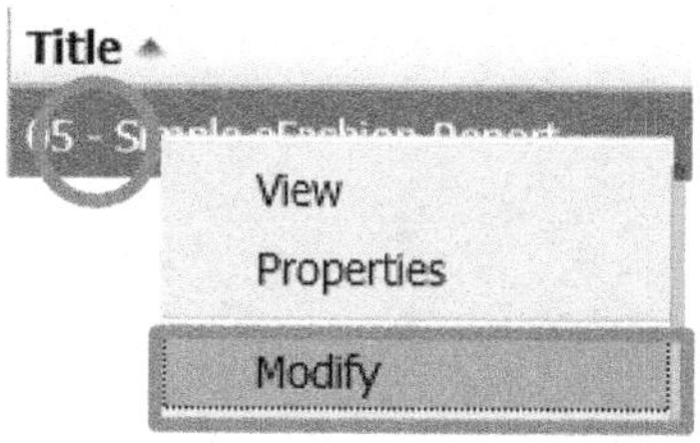
Title
View
Properties
Modify

In the Documents Tab, right-click on a document and select 'Modify'.

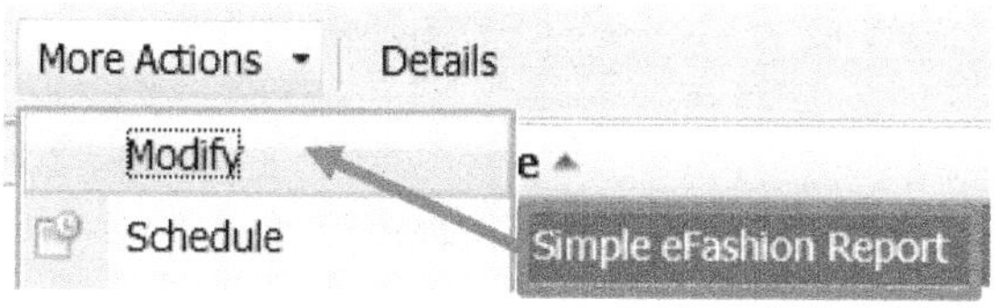
More Actions
Details
Modify
Schedule
Simple eFashion Report

In the Documents Tab, select a document and then select 'More Actions – Modify'

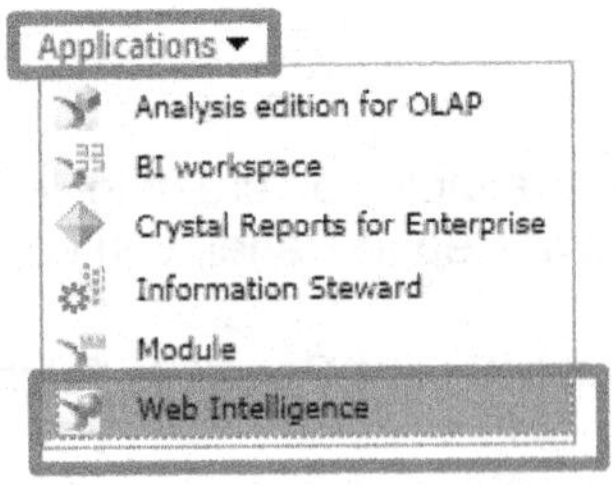
Applications
Analysis edition for OLAP
BI workspace
Crystal Reports for Enterprise
Information Steward
Module
Web Intelligence

Select Web Intelligence Application from 'Applications' menu.

Or click on 'Web Intelligence Application' icon on the Home Tab.

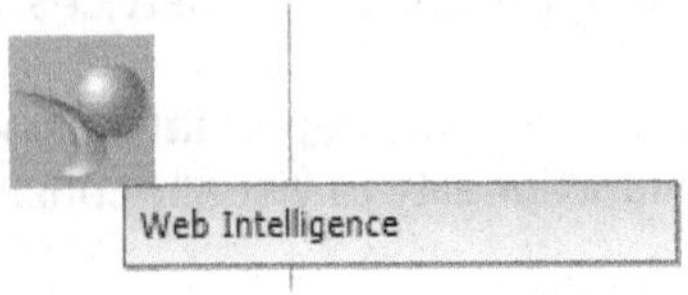
Web Intelligence

8.1 Layout of the Java Report Panel

The general layout of the Java Report Interface is as follows:

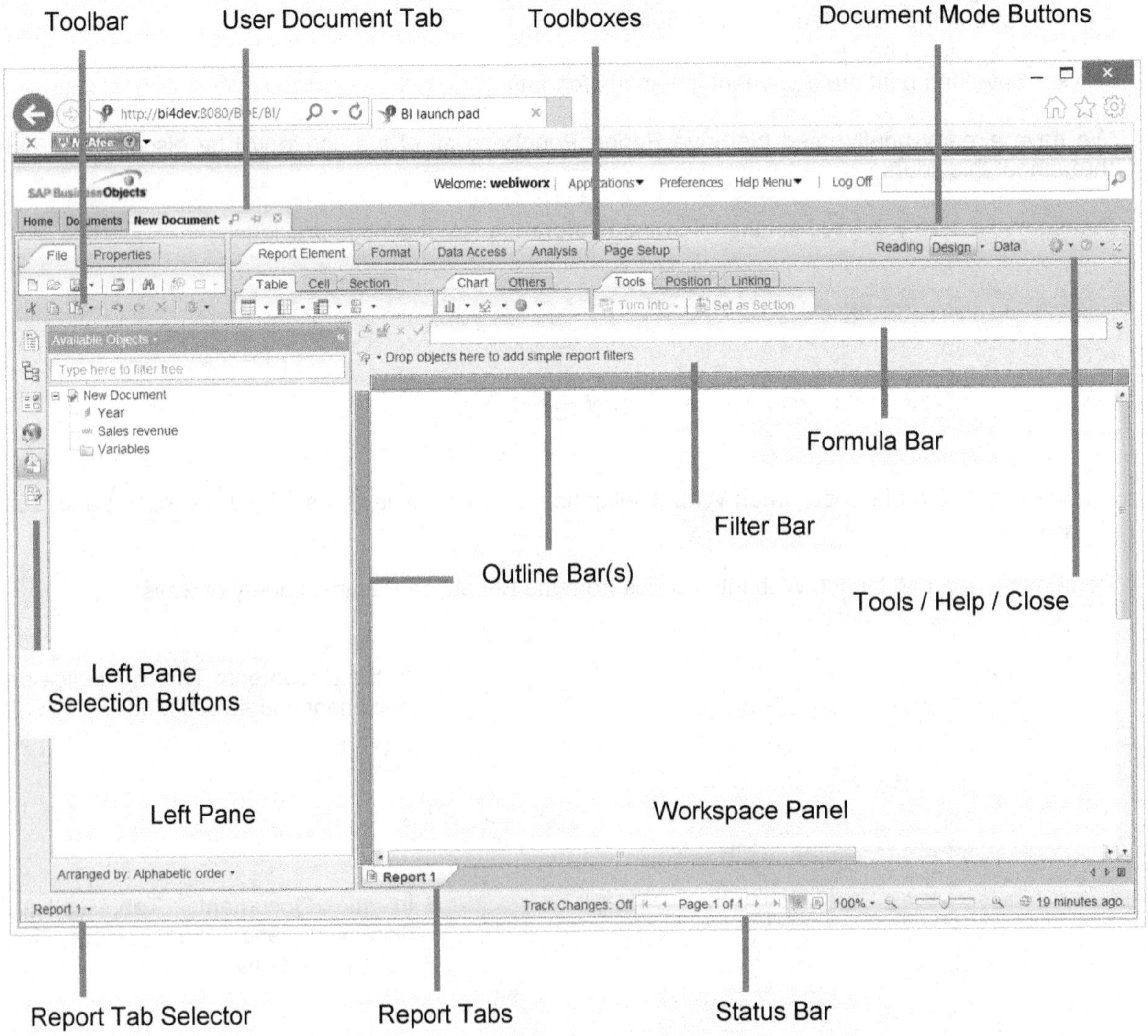
Toolbar
User Document Tab
Toolboxes
Document Mode Buttons
Formula Bar
Filter Bar
Outline Bar(s)
Tools / Help / Close
Left Pane Selection Buttons
Left Pane
Workspace Panel
Report Tab Selector
Report Tabs
Status Bar

We will cover all the various panels, toolboxes, tabs, etc. throughout the course and there are lots of buttons to describe, so here we will give a brief introduction the Java Report Panel functionality (in terms of layout).

8.1.1 User Document Tab

Web Intelligence documents are displayed in tabs, so you can have multiple documents open for editing/analysing purposes.

NOTE – If you have selected the following **Preference** (as previously described):

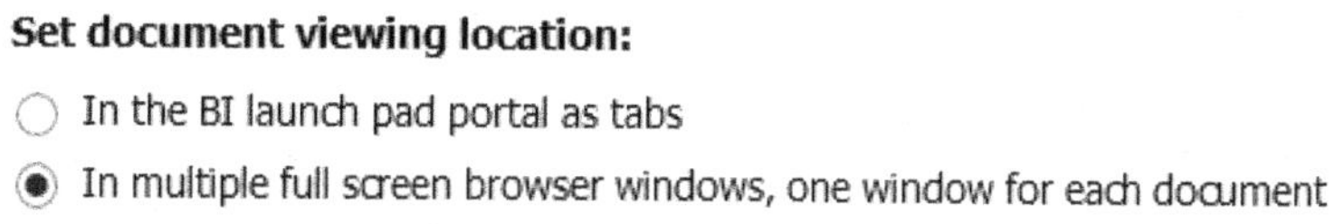
Set document viewing location:
In the BI launch pad portal as tabs
In multiple full screen browser windows, one window for each document

Then your documents will be opened in multiple windows rather than tabs.

8.1.2 Toolboxes

There are seven Toolboxes are similar to using Ribbons in Microsoft Office applications.

File
Properties
Report Element
Format
Data Access
Analysis
Page Setup

Using the analogy of Toolboxes, most of the Toolboxes are broken into smaller 'trays' or 'compartments', for example the 'Report Element' toolbox contains trays for Table, Cell, Section, Chart, etc. (as shown below):

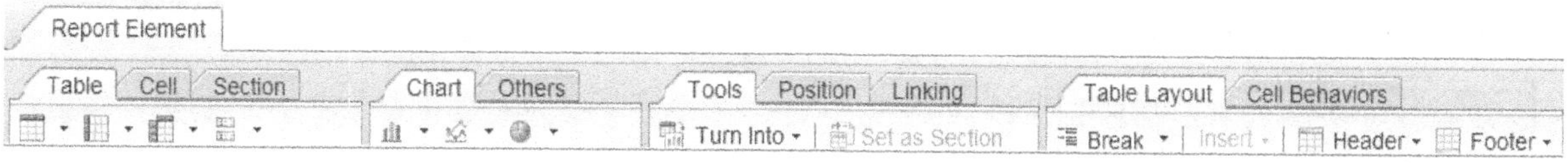
Report Element
Table
Cell
Section
Chart
Others
Tools
Position
Linking
Table Layout
Cell Behaviors
Turn Into
Set as Section
Break
Insert
Header
Footer

The trays are context sensitive (i.e. auto enable/disable depending on what you have selected in the Workspace Panel), for example the 'Report Element' toolbox will show only the trays that contain buttons for working with the table, cell, chart, etc. that you are working with in the Workspace Panel (the Report Element Toolbox shown below contains fewer trays).

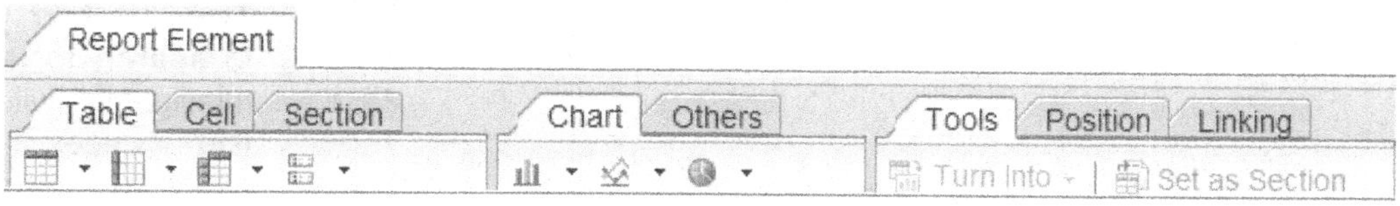
Report Element
Table
Cell
Section
Chart
Others
Tools
Position
Linking
Turn Into
Set as Section

We will be using the various Toolboxes in detail throughout the course, so here we will describe the use of each Toolbox and its trays.

8.1.2.1 File Toolbox

Most of the buttons on this toolbox are similar to other applications you will typically use.

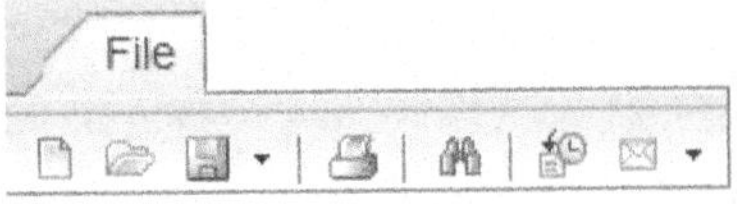
File

The purpose of this toolbox is to enable you to perform actions such as:

 Create new documents

 Open existing documents

 Save documents in various formats

 Print documents

 Find/Search values on current document (i.e. can search displayed data)

 View details of historical scheduled instances of documents

 Send the document to BusinessObjects Inbox, email, or FTP

Button: 'Find' 

Use this button to find text and values on the current page.

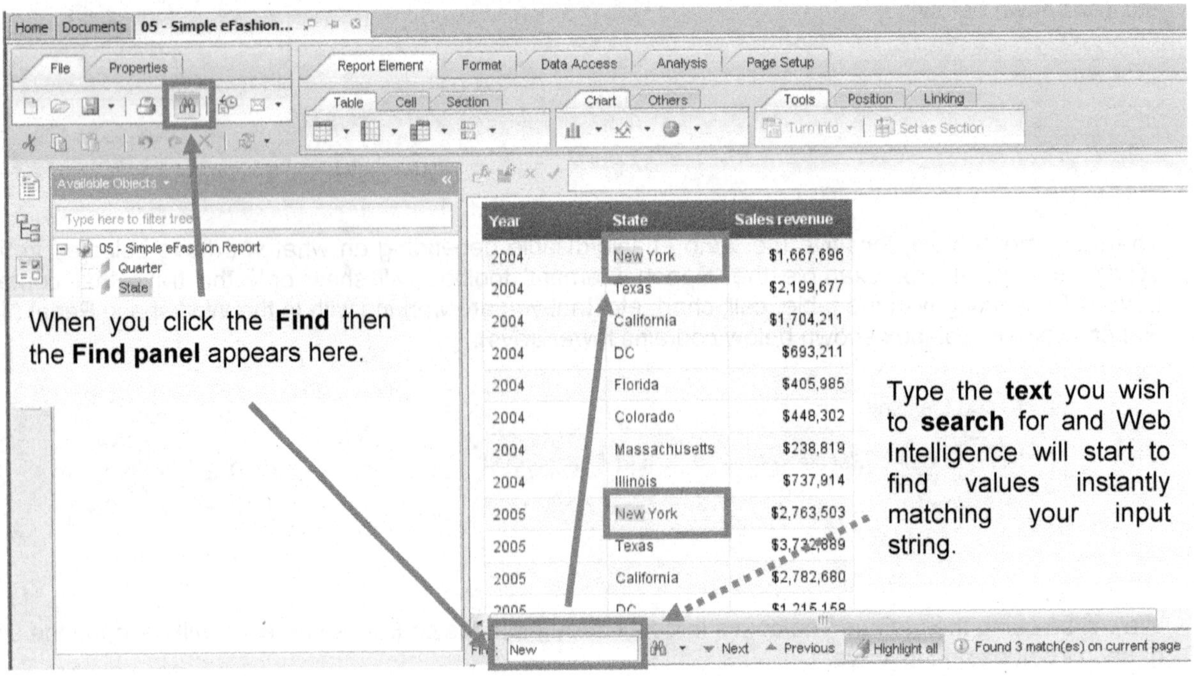
When you click the **Find** then the **Find panel** appears here.
Type the **text** you wish to **search** for and Web Intelligence will start to find values instantly matching your input string.

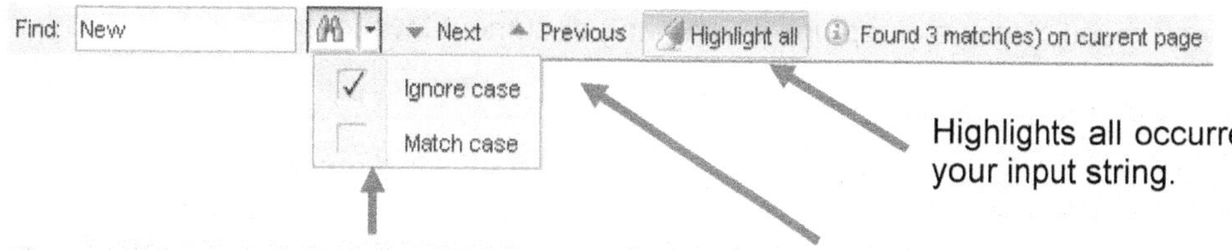
Find: New
Next
Previous
Highlight all
Found 3 match(es) on current page
Ignore case
Match case

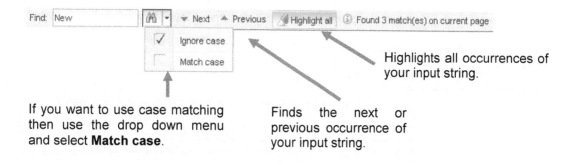

Highlights all occurrences of your input string.

If you want to use case matching then use the drop down menu and select **Match case**.

Finds the next or previous occurrence of your input string.

When finished using this feature, click again on the '**Find**' button to close the '**Find panel**' or click on the '**Close the Find panel**' button (on the right hand side of the panel).

8.1.2.2 Properties Toolbox

This toolbox enables you to work with properties relating to the document and the Java Report Panel itself.

You can switch parts of the Java Report Panel on or off using the 'View' menu.

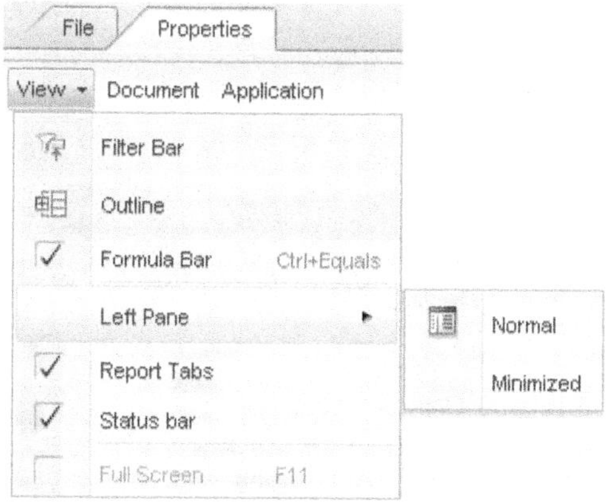
File
Properties
View
Document
Application
Filter Bar
Outline
Formula Bar
Ctrl+Equals
Left Pane
Normal
Minimized
Report Tabs
Status bar
Full Screen
F11

Filter Bar is used to interactively filter the data in a report tab.

Outline Bars are used to expand rows/columns of data when using totals/sub-totals.

Formula Bar can be used to view or create calculations and expressions.

Left Pane can be minimized to make more space available when working.

Report Tabs toggles the Report Tab selector (shown on bottom left corner) when activated.

Status bar toggles the Status Bar (shown on bottom right corner when activated).

The ‘Document’ menu displays a pop up box showing document level properties.

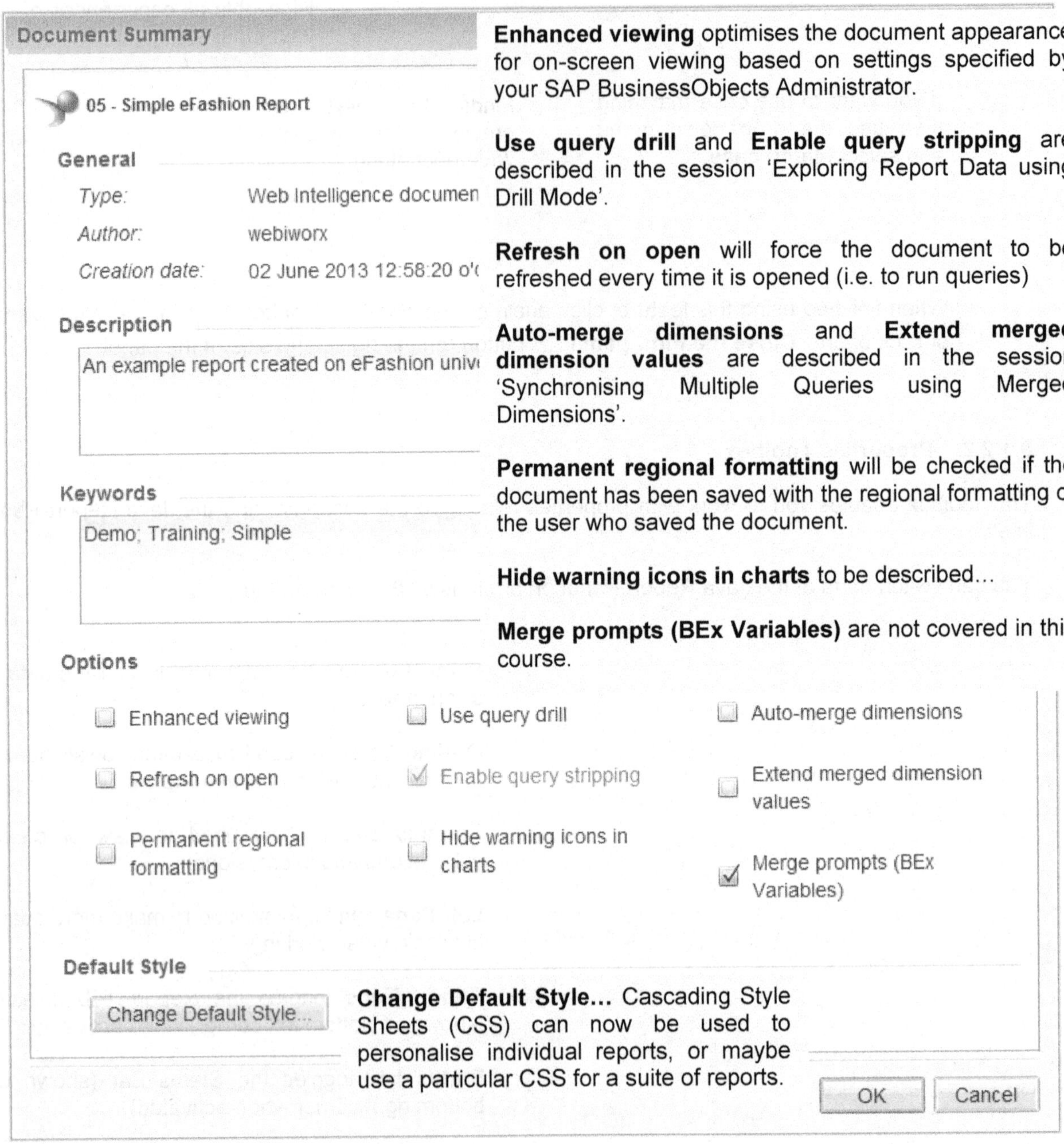
Document Summary
05 - Simple eFashion Report
General
Type:
Web Intelligence documen
Author:
webiworx
Creation date:
02 June 2013 12:58:20 o'
Description
An example report created on eFashion univ
Keywords
Demo; Training; Simple
Options
Enhanced viewing
Use query drill
Auto-merge dimensions
Refresh on open
Enable query stripping
Extend merged dimension values
Permanent regional formatting
Hide warning icons in charts
Merge prompts (BEx Variables)
Default Style
Change Default Style...
OK
Cancel

Enhanced viewing optimises the document appearance for on-screen viewing based on settings specified by your SAP BusinessObjects Administrator.

Use query drill and **Enable query stripping** are described in the session ‘Exploring Report Data using Drill Mode’.

Refresh on open will force the document to be refreshed every time it is opened (i.e. to run queries)

Auto-merge dimensions and **Extend merged dimension values** are described in the session ‘Synchronising Multiple Queries using Merged Dimensions’.

Permanent regional formatting will be checked if the document has been saved with the regional formatting of the user who saved the document.

Hide warning icons in charts to be described…

Merge prompts (BEx Variables) are not covered in this course.

Change Default Style… Cascading Style Sheets (CSS) can now be used to personalise individual reports, or maybe use a particular CSS for a suite of reports.

Use the 'Application' menu to personalise display settings of the Web Intelligence Java Report Panel to help you position tables, charts, and other blocks on report pages.

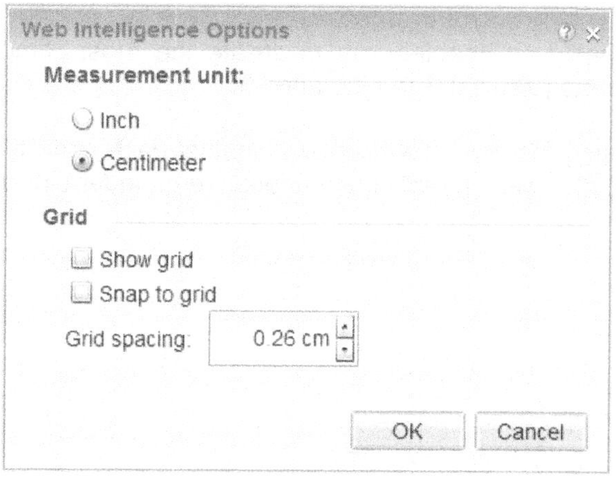
Web Intelligence Options
Measurement unit:
Inch
Centimeter
Grid
Show grid
Snap to grid
Grid spacing:
0.26 cm
OK
Cancel

- Define the unit for measurement
- Display a grid to help align page elements
- Use snap to grid to reposition page elements accurately

8.1.2.3 Report Element Toolbox

This toolbox enables you to work with the various 'Report Elements' such as Tables, Cross Tables, Charts, Cells, Sections, Breaks, etc.

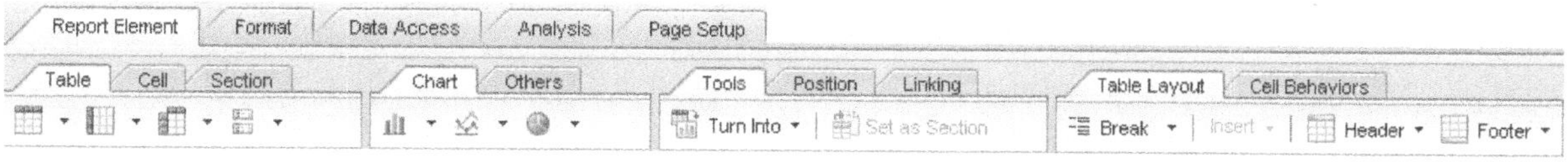
Report Element
Format
Data Access
Analysis
Page Setup
Table
Cell
Section
Chart
Others
Tools
Position
Linking
Turn Into
Set as Section
Table Layout
Cell Behaviors
Break
Insert
Header
Footer

The trays within this toolbox are as follows:

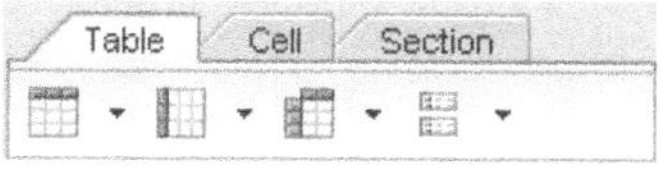
Table
Cell
Section

Using the **Table** tray you can create Vertical Tables, Horizontal Tables, Cross Tables and Forms.

See session on 'Formatting Cells, Tables and Cross Tables'.

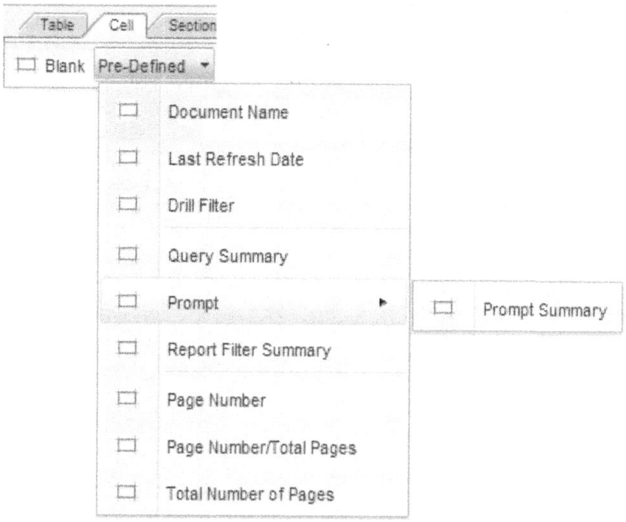
Table
Cell
Section
Blank
Pre-Defined
Document Name
Last Refresh Date
Drill Filter
Query Summary
Prompt
Prompt Summary
Report Filter Summary
Page Number
Page Number/Total Pages
Total Number of Pages

Cell tray allows you to insert a Blank cell or select from the Pre-Defined cells.

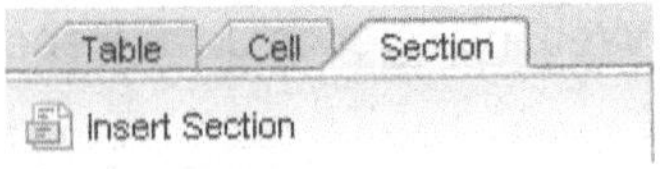
Table
Cell
Section
Insert Section

Using the **Section** tray you can create a section.

Explained in session on 'Sections'.

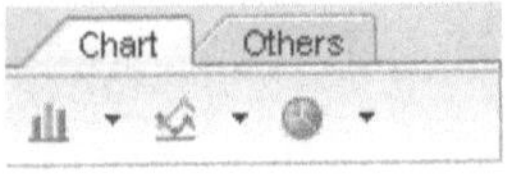
Chart
Others

Chart tray enables you to create the most commonly used charts (Vertical Bar, Line and Pie).

Using the drop down arrows against each chart type enables you to select a particular variation, e.g. under Line we have:

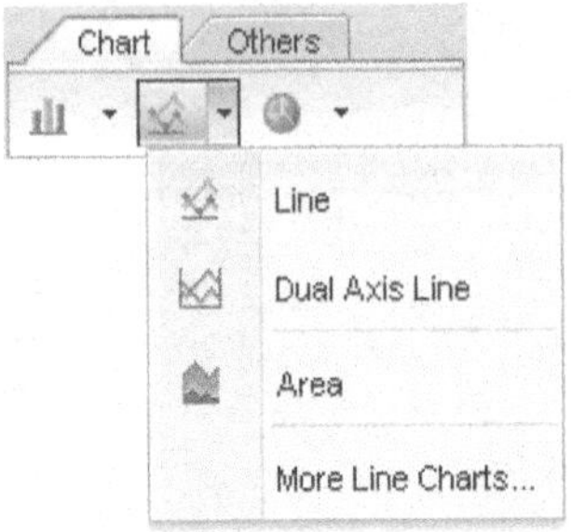
Chart
Others
Line
Dual Axis Line
Area
More Line Charts...

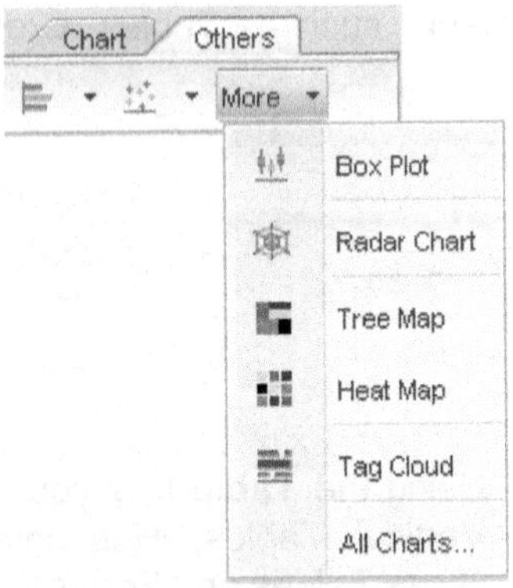
Chart
Others
More
Box Plot
Radar Chart
Tree Map
Heat Map
Tag Cloud
All Charts...

Others tray contains chart types such as Horizontal Bar, Scatter, Bubble and various others as shown opposite (under 'More').

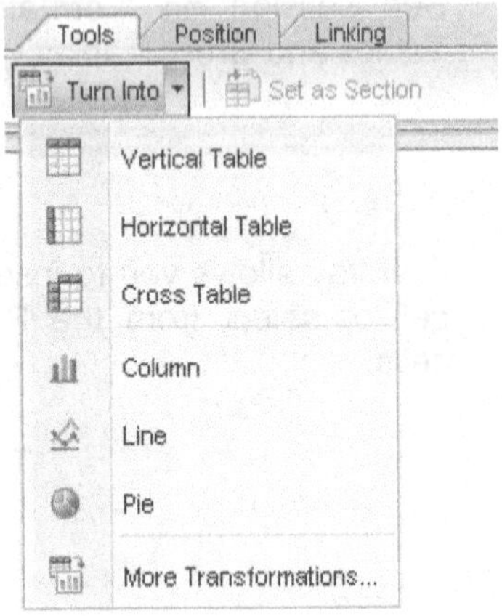
Tools
Position
Linking
Turn Into
Set as Section
Vertical Table
Horizontal Table
Cross Table
Column
Line
Pie
More Transformations...

Tools tray – By selecting an existing report element (such as a Vertical Table) you can quickly turn it into another type of report element by using 'Tool – Turn Into'.

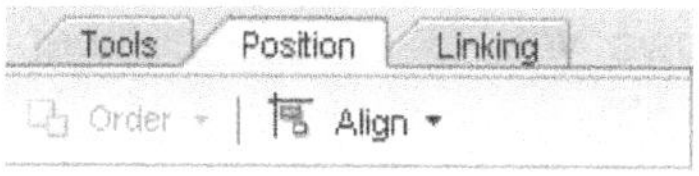
Tools
Position
Linking
Order
Align

Position tray enables you to use Alignment and Order on report elements to arrange the display of objects to your liking.

Tools
Position
Linking
Element

Linking tray enables you to insert Hyperlinks or to use Element Links to link together report elements, for example selecting a value in one table could filter a related chart.

Table Layout
Cell Behaviors
Break
Insert
Header
Footer

Table Layout tray is only enabled when a whole table, or a cell within a table is selected.

It enables you to insert new columns/rows and work with table Headers/Footers.

It also allows you to insert Breaks which are discussed in more detail in the session 'Breaks'.

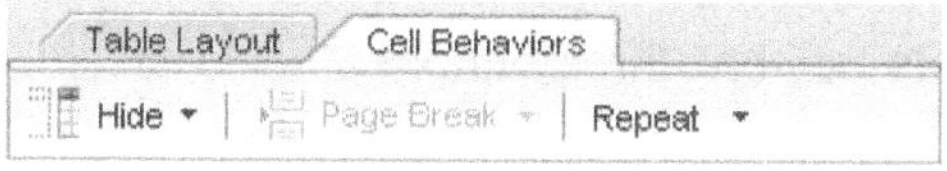
Table Layout
Cell Behaviors
Hide
Page Break
Repeat

Cell Behaviors tray enables you to work with cell properties (whether they are cells within tables or free-standing cells).

8.1.2.4 Format Toolbox

This toolbox enables you to apply formatting to report elements.

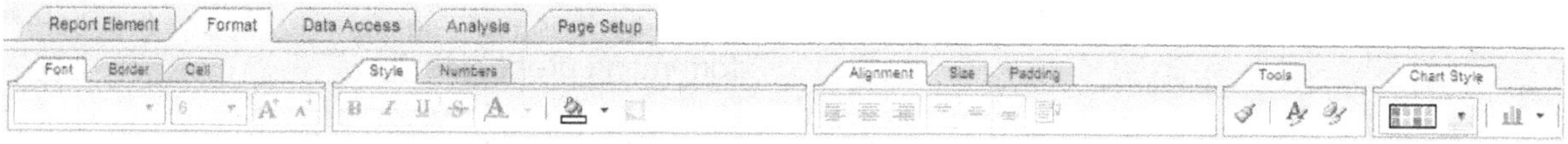
Report Element
Format
Data Access
Analysis
Page Setup
Font
Border
Cell
Style
Numbers
Alignment
Size
Padding
Tools
Chart Style

The trays within this toolbox are as follows:

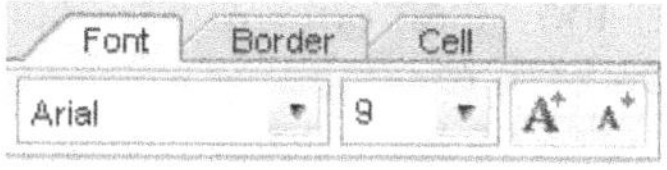
Font
Border
Cell
Arial
9

Font tray enables you to select a font and font size for the selected report element. These can be applied at individual cell level.

Font
Border
Cell

Border tray enables you to specify a border type for the selected report element and also a border color.

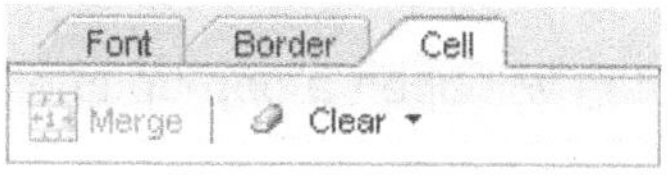
Font
Border
Cell
Merge
Clear

Cell tray enables you to merge multiple cells (where possible) and also clear formatting already applied to the selected cell(s).

Style
Numbers

Style tray enables you to apply font styles, font color, background color and insert background images.

Style
Numbers
DEFAULT
Custom

Numbers tray allows you to specify number formatting from the drop down list.

You can click on 'Custom' to select from a larger range of number format types, or you can specify a custom number format.

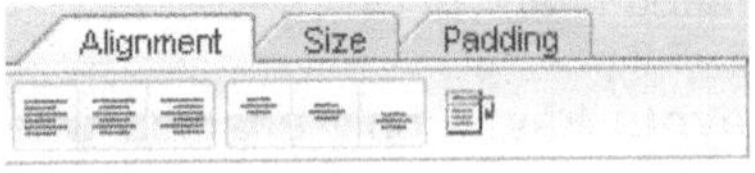
Alignment
Size
Padding

Use the **Alignment** tray to specify alignment within an individual cell, including Wrap Text.

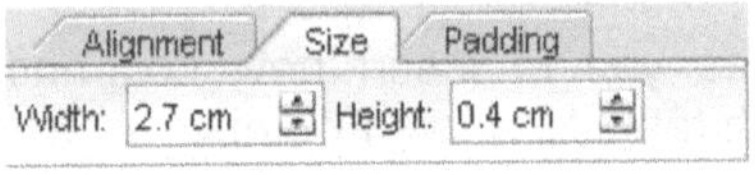
Alignment
Size
Padding
Width: 2.7 cm
Height: 0.4 cm

Use the **Size** tray to specify Width and Height dimensions for selected cell.

Alignment
Size
Padding
Horizontal: 0.18 cm
Vertical: 0.16 cm

The **Padding** tray enables you to specify Horizontal and Vertical padding to use within selected cell.

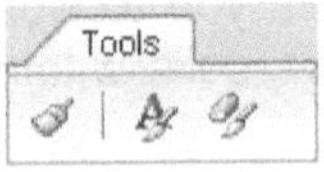
Tools

The **Tools** tray has three buttons:

The **Format Painter**  button enables you to take the formatting from the currently selected report element and apply it to another report element.

1. Select the element that contains the formatting you wish to copy
2. Single click on the Format Painter button
3. Click on another element to apply the selected formatting properties

If you want to apply the formatting to multiple report elements then:

1. First select the element which contains the formatting you wish to copy
2. Then double click on the Format Painter button
3. Click in turn on individual items you want to apply the formatting to
4. Press <ESC> when finished

The **Format**  button will open a pop-up interface which contains all the properties that can be formatted for the selected report element.

The **Clear Format**  button will clear all existing formatting applied to the selected report element.

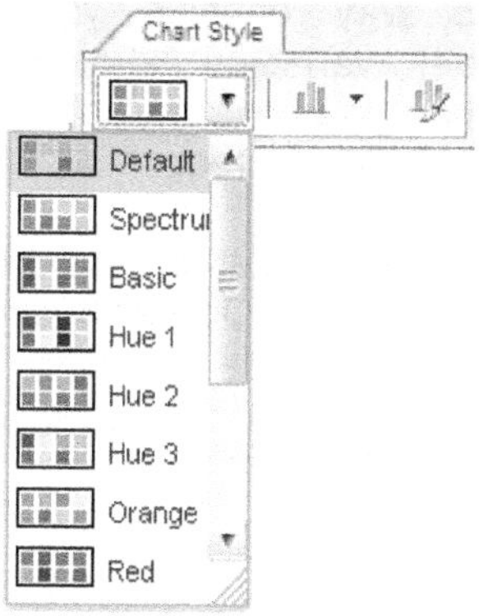
Chart Style
Default
Spectrum
Basic
Hue 1
Hue 2
Hue 3
Orange
Red

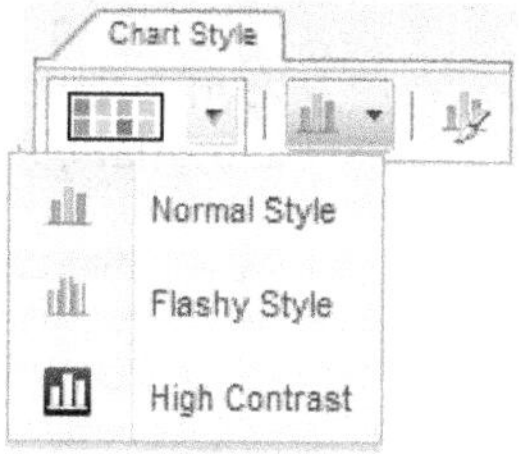
Chart Style
Normal Style
Flashy Style
High Contrast

If you are working with charts then the 'Chart Style' tray will appear with 3 buttons.

Left to right:

- It enables you to quickly apply a color palette
- Select one of three appearances
- Activate the detailed 'Format Chart…' interface.

8.1.2.5 Data Access Toolbox

This toolbox enables you to work with Data Providers (queries) and document level variables.

Report Element
Format
Data Access
Analysis
Page Setup
Data Providers
Tools
Data Objects
New data provider
Edit
Purge
New Variable
Merge

The trays within this toolbox are as follows:

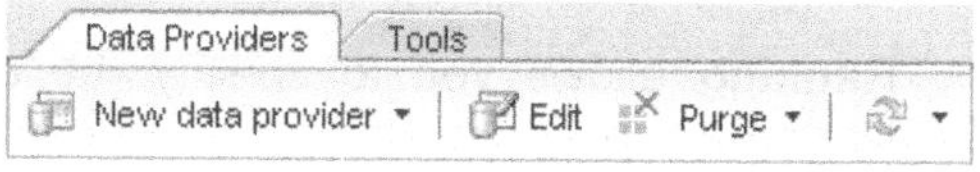
Data Providers
Tools
New data provider
Edit
Purge

Data Providers tray enables you to see a list of all queries within the document.

You can Add new queries, Edit existing queries, Purge queries and Refresh queries.

NOTE – To Purge means keeping the query definition and all report layouts, and simply deleting data from the document. You can purge individual queries or all queries within a document.

Data Providers
Tools
Change Source
Export Data

Tools tray enables you to change the source of a query and also export query data into CSV format.

Change Source means you can point an existing query to a different universe, for example you might have a new version of a universe and want existing reports to use the new universe.

Export Data enables you to export the raw data returned by the database for the selected query, i.e. no document level calculations, formatting, filtering, etc. are exported

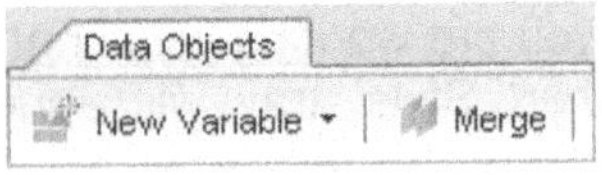
Data Objects
New Variable
Merge

Data Objects tray enables you to create document level variables and also Merge dimensions when you have multiple queries in a document that can be related.

Discussed in more detail in the session 'Synchronising Multiple Queries using Merged Dimensions'.

8.1.2.6 Analysis Toolbox

This toolbox enables you analyse and interact with your data.

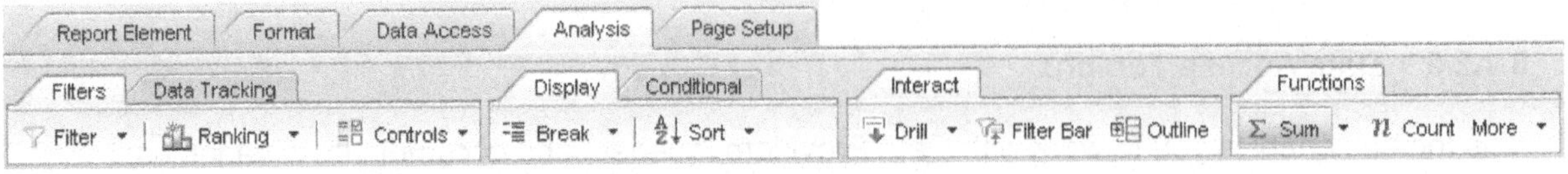
Report Element
Format
Data Access
Analysis
Page Setup
Filters
Data Tracking
Filter
Ranking
Controls
Display
Conditional
Break
Sort
Interact
Drill
Filter Bar
Outline
Functions
Sum
Count
More

The trays within this toolbox are as follows:

Filters
Data Tracking
Filter
Ranking
Controls

Filters tray enables apply filtering to data within report tabs using Filters, Ranking and Input Controls.

Filter is used to apply simple filters to a selected object by selecting from a list of values.

Ranking allows you to specify the data to be filtered using Top n, Bottom n values based on a measure.

Controls enables you add Input Controls to report tabs allowing users to dynamically interact with the data using boxes, sliders, spinners, etc.

All of these are covered later in dedicated sessions.

Filters
Data Tracking
Track
Show Changes

Data Tracking tray enables you track changes in data when a report is refreshed.

For example, you might want to see which regions have increased or decreased in sales revenue since last month.

Data Tracking enables you to do this and is covered in more detail in the session 'Tracking Changes in Data'.

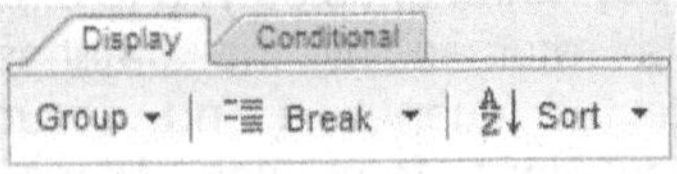
Display
Conditional
Group
Break
Sort

Display tray enables you to:

Group values within the document (for example, cities into regions, products into categories, etc). This is covered in the session 'Formulas and Variables'.

Group within tables using Breaks, covered in the session

'Breaks'.

Sort data in almost all report elements (tables, charts, etc), covered in the session 'Sorting Data in Tables and Cross Tables'.

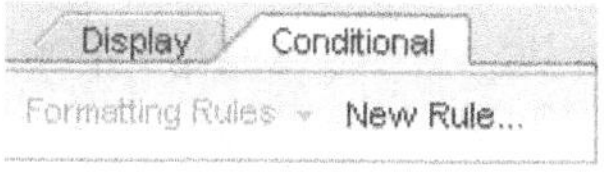
Display
Conditional
Formatting Rules
New Rule...

Conditional tray enables you to define rules and apply conditional formatting based on those rules.

Covered in more detail in the session on 'Conditional Formatting'.

Interact
Drill
Filter Bar
Outline

Interact tray enables you to toggle Drill, Filter Bar and Outline.

These are all covered in detail in later sessions.

Functions
Sum
Count
More

Functions tray contains the more commonly used Standard Calculations such as Sum, Count, Min, Max, Average and Percentage.

These will be covered in more detail in the session on 'Using Standard Calculations'.

8.1.2.7 Page Setup Toolbox

This toolbox enables specify the page settings to use (per report tab) in the document.

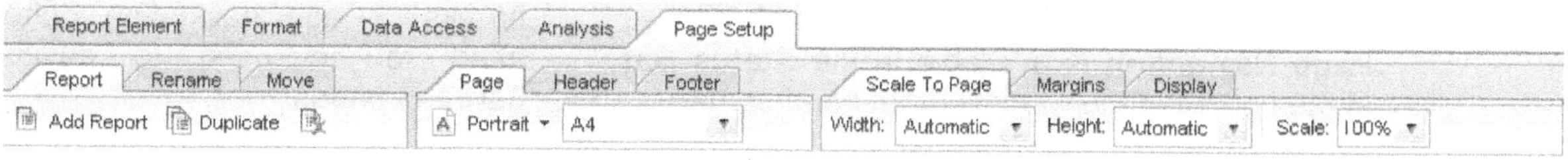
Report Element
Format
Data Access
Analysis
Page Setup
Report
Rename
Move
Add Report
Duplicate
Page
Header
Footer
Portrait
A4
Scale To Page
Margins
Display
Width:
Automatic
Height:
Automatic
Scale:
100%

The trays within this toolbox are as follows:

Report
Rename
Move
Add Report
Duplicate

Report tray enables you to add a new report tab to the document, duplicate an existing tab or delete the current tab you are working on.

Report
Rename
Move
Data

Rename tray allows you to rename the current report tab you are working on.

Report
Rename
Move
Move Left
Move Right

Move tray enables you to move the current tab you are working on to the left or to the right (depending on where the tab is currently) within the document.

Page
Header
Footer
Portrait
A4

Page tray enables you to select the page orientation and page size for a report tab.

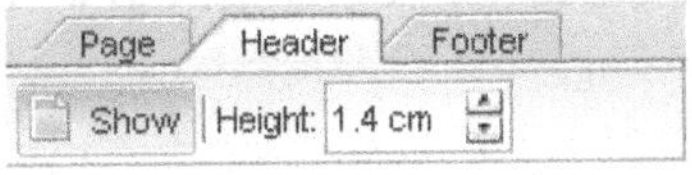
Page
Header
Footer
Show
Height: 1.4 cm

Header tray enables you to specify a page header height or you can click on 'Show' to not hide the page header.

Page
Header
Footer
Show
Height: 1.2 cm

Footer tray enables you to specify a page footer height or you can click on 'Show' to not hide the page footer.

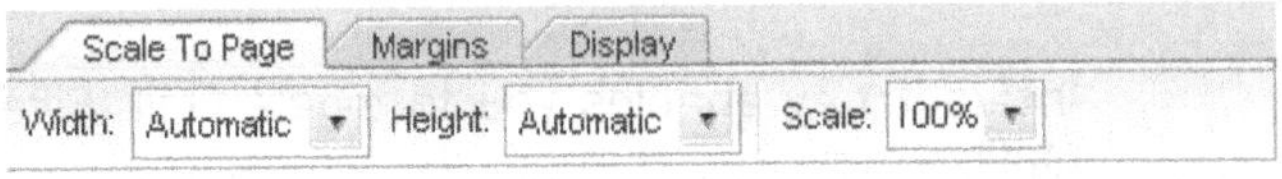
Scale To Page
Margins
Display
Width: Automatic
Height: Automatic
Scale: 100%

Scale To Page tray enables you to specify how you would like the report tab content to fit on a page.

For example, you might want to keep the report 2 pages in Width.

Scale To Page
Margins
Display
2 cm
2 cm
2 cm
2 cm

Margin tray enables you to specify heights of Top, Bottom, Left and Right margins.

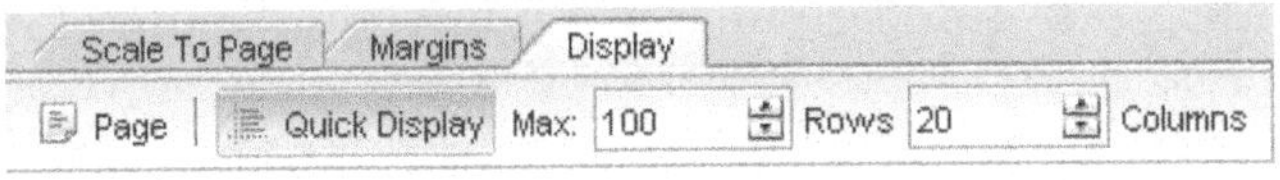
Scale To Page
Margins
Display
Page
Quick Display
Max: 100
Rows 20
Columns

Display tray has a toggle button for Page and Quick Display.

Page mode will display the report as it would appear when printed. You are able to see page headers, footers, page margins and page breaks. Page navigation buttons need to be used to navigate between pages.

Quick Display does not display as a printed report and you can scroll through the report with fewer pages to navigate because you can specify the number of rows to display on the 'on screen' page.

Page 1 of 1+

Page Navigation is available in the **Status Bar** at the bottom of the window (right hand corner).

8.1.3 Document Mode Buttons

These buttons are located on the top right hand corner of the window.

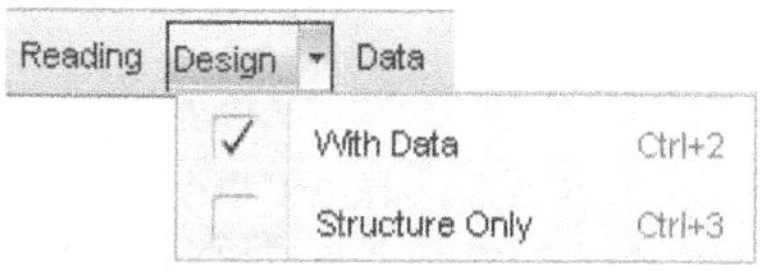
Reading
Design
Data
With Data Ctrl+2
Structure Only Ctrl+3

Reading Mode switches Web Intelligence to a 'view' only mode, i.e. effectively this is what your report will look like to users who do not have privileges to modify documents.

Data Mode automatically shifts the focus of Web Intelligence to the Data Access Toolbox, however there is slight difference in that all other toolboxes (except File and Properties) are disabled when in Data Mode.

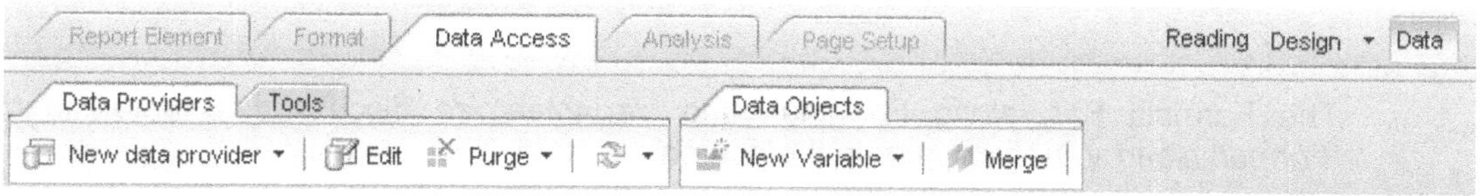
Report Element
Format
Data Access
Analysis
Page Setup
Reading
Design
Data
Data Providers
Tools
Data Objects
New data provider
Edit
Purge
New Variable
Merge

Design Mode has two options:

- **With Data** shows the report elements displaying data, for example:

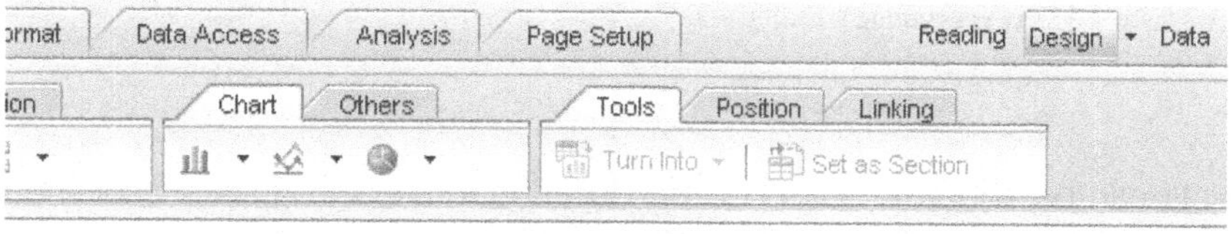
Data Access
Analysis
Page Setup
Reading
Design
Data
Chart
Others
Tools
Position
Linking
Turn Into
Set as Section

Year	Quarter	Sales revenue
2004	Q1	$2,660,699
2004	Q2	$2,278,693
2004	Q3	$1,367,841

- **Structure Only** shows the report elements without any data, for example the table above is displayed as:

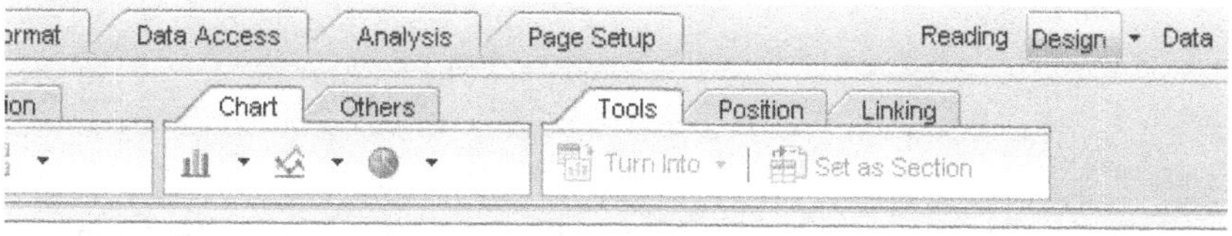
Data Access
Analysis
Page Setup
Reading
Design
Data
Chart
Others
Tools
Position
Linking
Turn Into
Set as Section

=NameOf([Year])	=NameOf([Quarte	=NameOf([Sales r
=[Year]	=[Quarter]	=[Sales revenue]
		=Sum([Sales reve

8.1.4 Formula Bar

The **Formula Bar** is displayed underneath the Toolboxes.

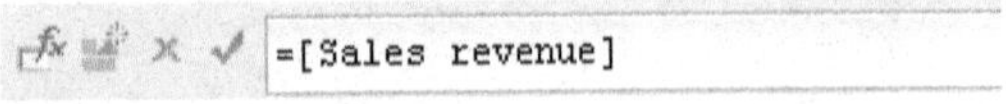
=[Sales revenue]

When the Formula Bar is being displayed then clicking into cells shows the expression being used within that cell, for example here we can see the selected cell is displaying the value of [Sales revenue].

- The Formula Bar can be used to type in expressions directly.
- You can click on the Formula Editor  button to initiate an interface that helps with creating expressions/calculations.
- You can also click on Create Variable  button to create re-usable expressions.

The Formula Bar, along Formulas and Variables are discussed in detail in the section '*Formulas and Variables*' later in the course.

8.1.5 Filter Bar

The **Filter Bar** is displayed underneath the Formula Bar.

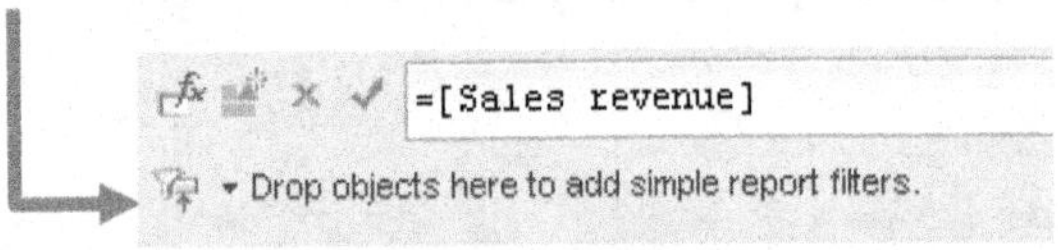
=[Sales revenue]
Drop objects here to add simple report filters.

Objects can be added to the Filter Bar to enable users to quickly filter the data within the tab (similar to using column filters in Microsoft Excel).

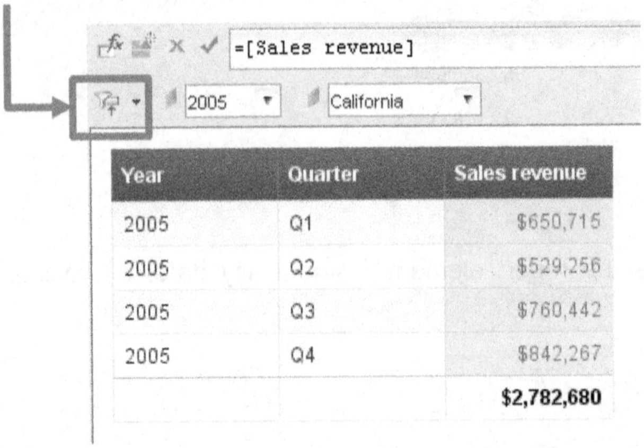
=[Sales revenue]
2005
California

Year	Quarter	Sales revenue
2005	Q1	$650,715
2005	Q2	$529,256
2005	Q3	$760,442
2005	Q4	$842,267
		$2,782,680

Discussed in more detail in the session 'Filtering Data in Reports'.

8.1.6 Outline Bars

Outline Bars are displayed on the left hand side and at the top of the Workspace Panel.

They are used with Breaks to expand/collapse rows of data within table type report elements.

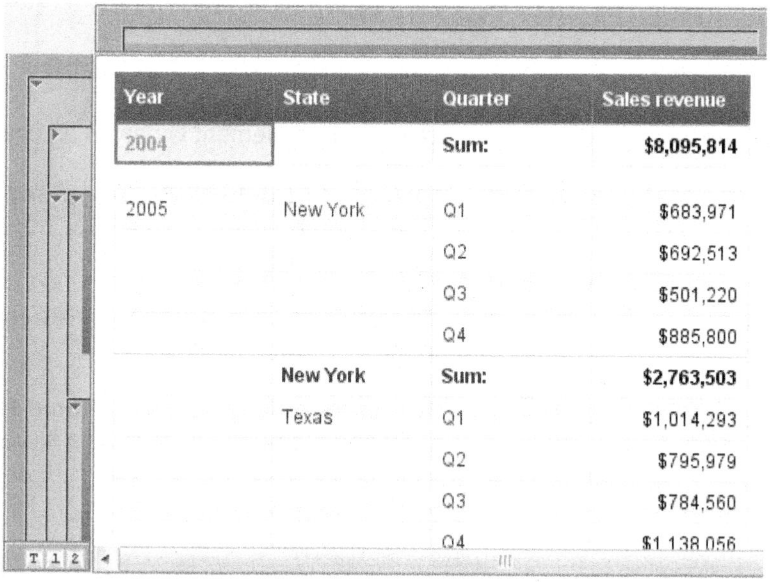
Year
State
Quarter
Sales revenue
2004
Sum:
$8,095,814
2005
New York
Q1
$683,971
Q2
$692,513
Q3
$501,220
Q4
$885,800
New York
Sum:
$2,763,503
Texas
Q1
$1,014,293
Q2
$795,979
Q3
$784,560
Q4
T
1
2

Here, we have collapsed row for Year = 2004, but Year = 2005 is expanded to show data for each Quarter per State.

Outline Bars are discussed in more detail later in the course in the session 'Breaks'.

8.1.7 Toolbar

The Toolbar sits just below the File and Properties toolboxes.

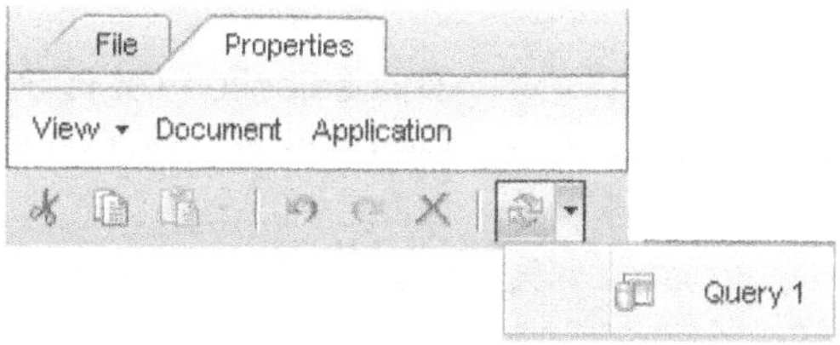
File
Properties
View
Document
Application
Query 1

It is static, but its buttons are context sensitive in that they become disabled if they cannot be used with the report element that is currently selected.

It contains some standard but very useful buttons for Cut, Copy, Paste, Paste Special (see below), Undo, Redo, and Refresh (for queries).

When using Paste Special you are given options as to how you want the copied report element to be pasted:

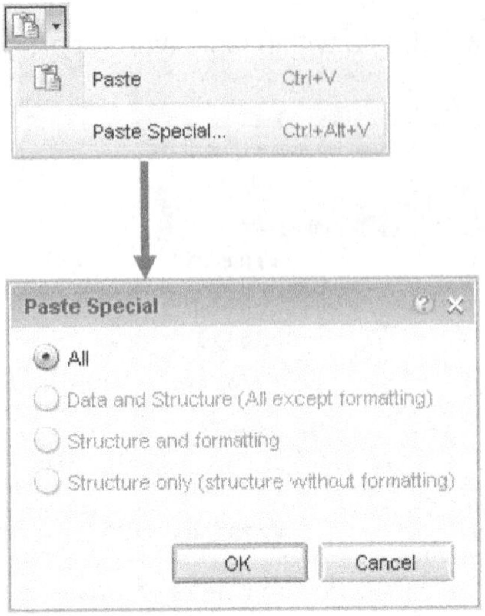
Paste Ctrl+V
Paste Special... Ctrl+Alt+V
Paste Special
All
Data and Structure (All except formatting)
Structure and formatting
Structure only (structure without formatting)
OK
Cancel

All – Report element is pasted as copied.

Data and Structure (All except formatting) – The report element is pasted as copied, except the formatting is not pasted.

Structure and formatting – Report element pasted but with no data.

Structure only (structure without formatting) – Report element is pasted as a structure only.

8.1.8 Left Pane

The **Left Pane** is displayed vertically on the left hand side of the window and its contents change depending on what has been selected using the **Left Pane Selection Buttons**.

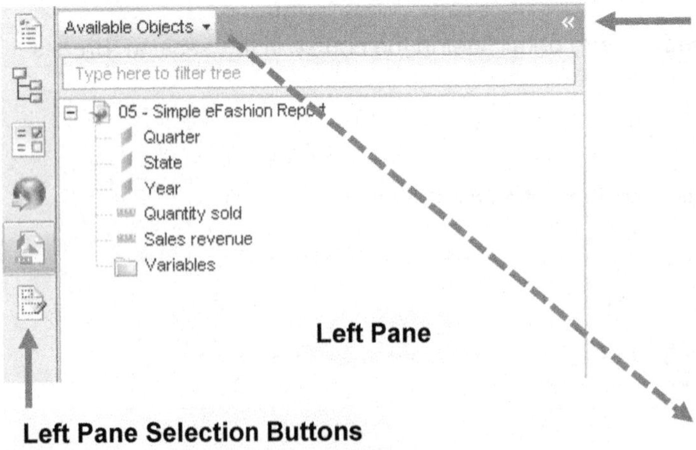
Available Objects
Type here to filter tree
05 - Simple eFashion Report
Quarter
State
Year
Quantity sold
Sales revenue
Variables
Left Pane
Left Pane Selection Buttons

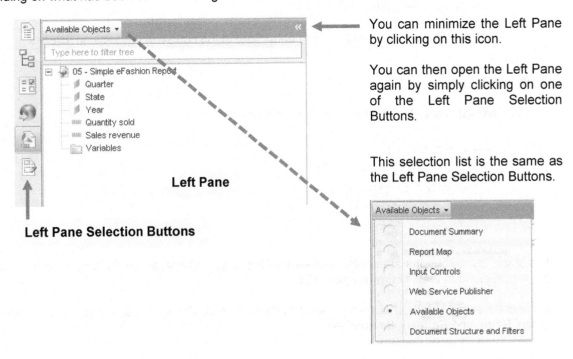

You can minimize the Left Pane by clicking on this icon.

You can then open the Left Pane again by simply clicking on one of the Left Pane Selection Buttons.

This selection list is the same as the Left Pane Selection Buttons.

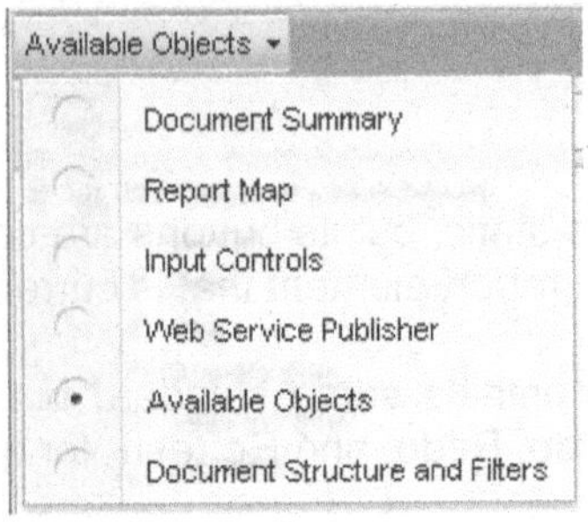
Available Objects
Document Summary
Report Map
Input Controls
Web Service Publisher
Available Objects
Document Structure and Filters

8.1.8.1 Left Pane – Document Summary Tab

This lists a summary of the document properties and can be printed.

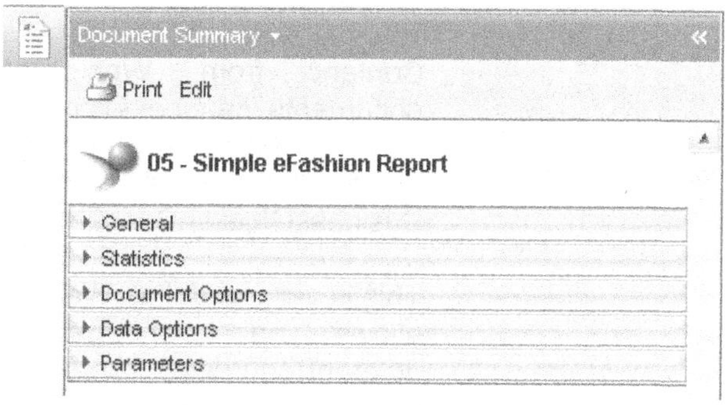
Document Summary
Print Edit
05 - Simple eFashion Report
General
Statistics
Document Options
Data Options
Parameters

If you click on 'Edit' then the Document Summary properties editor is initiated (as described earlier in this session).

8.1.8.2 Left Pane – Report Map Tab

This lists all the report tabs in the document.

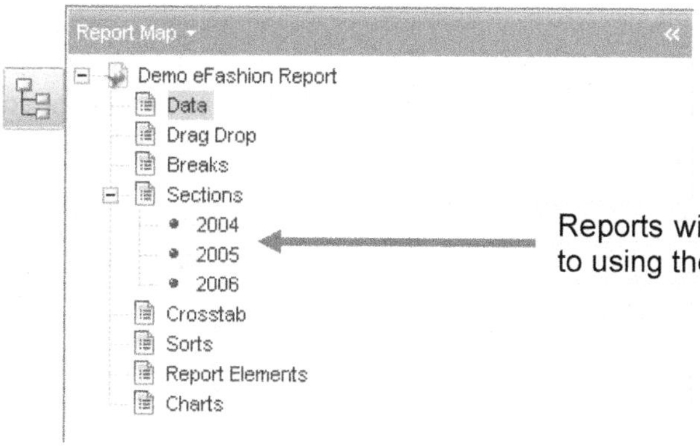
Report Map
Demo eFashion Report
Data
Drag Drop
Breaks
Sections
2004
2005
2006
Crosstab
Sorts
Report Elements
Charts

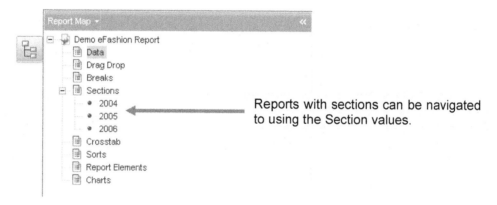

Reports with sections can be navigated to using the Section values.

8.1.8.3 Left Pane – Input Controls Tab

This purpose of this tab is to display any Input Controls that have been defined for use in the report.

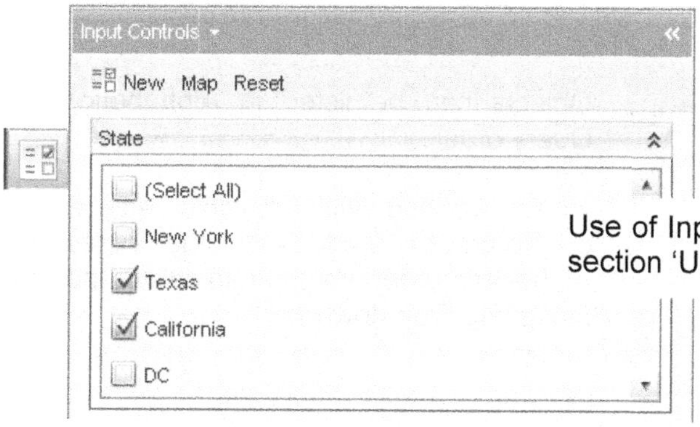
Input Controls
New Map Reset
State
(Select All)
New York
Texas
California
DC

Use of Input Controls is discussed later in the section 'Using Input Controls to Filter Data'.

8.1.8.4 Left Pane – Web Service Publisher Tab

This purpose of this tab is to view, edit and manage Web Services that have been created/published in the SAP BusinessObjects environment.

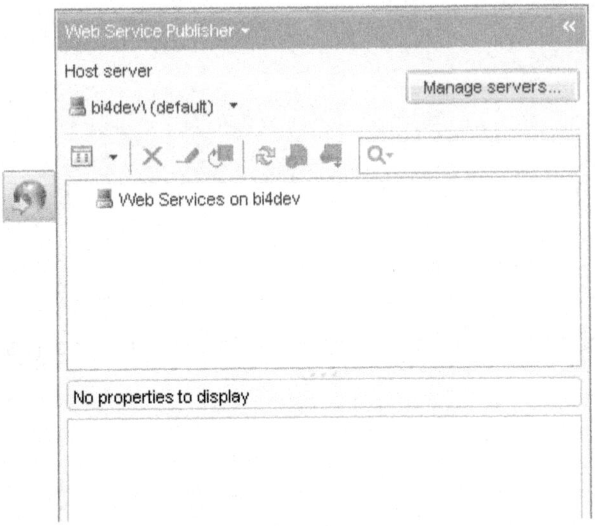
Web Service Publisher
Host server
bi4dev\ (default)
Manage servers...
Web Services on bi4dev
No properties to display

Content from Web Intelligence documents can be exposed as Web Services which can then be used by other applications, such as SAP BusinessObjects Dashboards.

This is very useful as Web Intelligence allows you to merge data from different sources. Therefore you can create a consolidated Table or Cross Table of data and make it available to Dashboards.

8.1.8.5 Left Pane – Available Object Tab

This purpose of this tab is to list all the queries, objects and variables that are available for you to use in your Web Intelligence document. This is the tab you will use most often from the Left Pane.

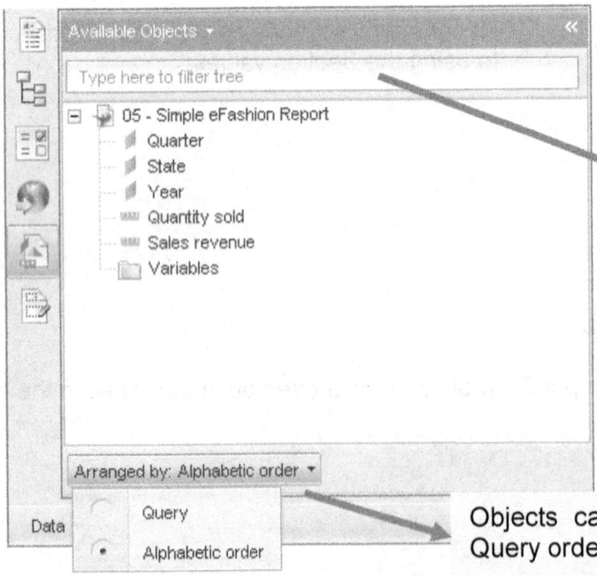
Available Objects
Type here to filter tree
05 - Simple eFashion Report
Quarter
State
Year
Quantity sold
Sales revenue
Variables
Arranged by: Alphabetic order
Data
Query
Alphabetic order

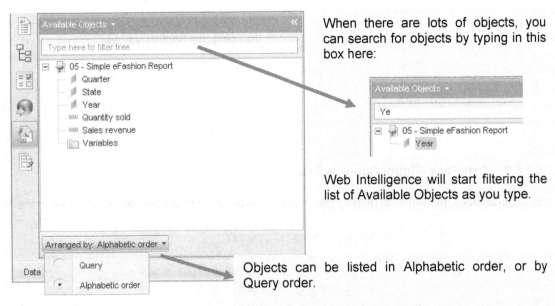

When there are lots of objects, you can search for objects by typing in this box here:

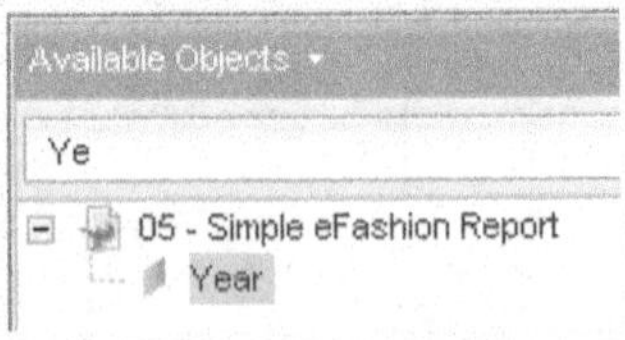
Available Objects
Ye
05 - Simple eFashion Report
Year

Web Intelligence will start filtering the list of Available Objects as you type.

Objects can be listed in Alphabetic order, or by Query order.

When working with multiple queries it can be confusing to work with the object names in Alphabetic order, so you can switch the arrangement using this drop down.

8.1.8.6 Left Pane – Document Structure and Filters Tab

This purpose of this tab is to list all the report tabs in your document along with all report elements and how they are structured / filtered.

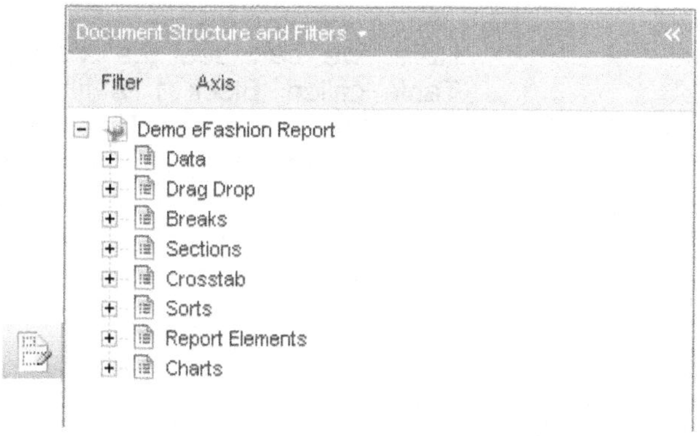
Document Structure and Filters
Filter
Axis
Demo eFashion Report
Data
Drag Drop
Breaks
Sections
Crosstab
Sorts
Report Elements
Charts

Here we can see our document is called 'Demo eFashion Report' and it contains a number of report tabs.

We can click on a report tab and see what report elements it contains:

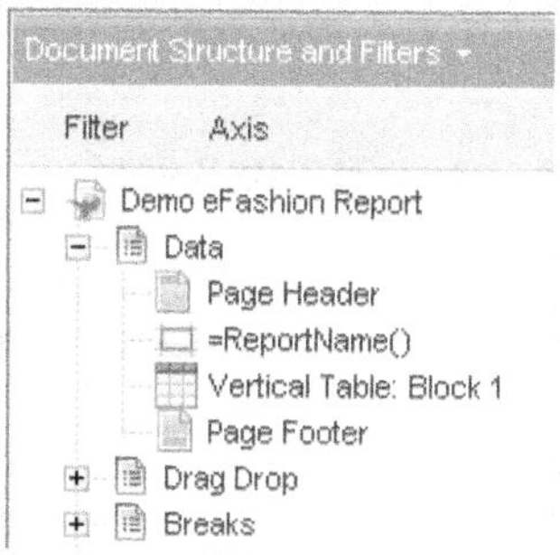
Document Structure and Filters
Filter
Axis
Demo eFashion Report
Data
Page Header
=ReportName()
Vertical Table: Block 1
Page Footer
Drag Drop
Breaks

Using this view is very useful to get an overview of your document because some functionality could have been applied that is not visible to the viewer (such as filters).

Click on a report element and Web Intelligence will shift the focus onto that element in the Workspace Panel.

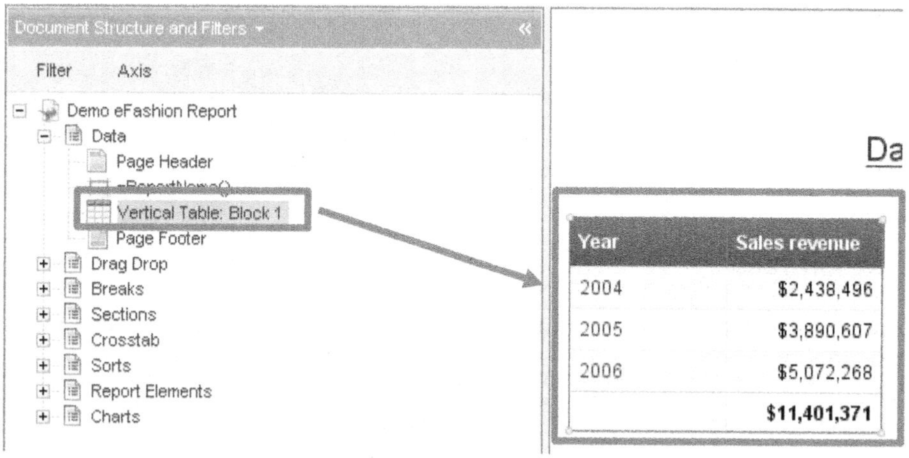
Document Structure and Filters
Filter
Axis
Demo eFashion Report
Data
Page Header
Vertical Table: Block 1
Page Footer
Drag Drop
Breaks
Sections
Crosstab
Sorts
Report Elements
Charts
Year
Sales revenue
2004
$2,438,496
2005
$3,890,607
2006
$5,072,268
$11,401,371

You can go view columns / axis used in tables and charts by enabling the 'Axis' button:

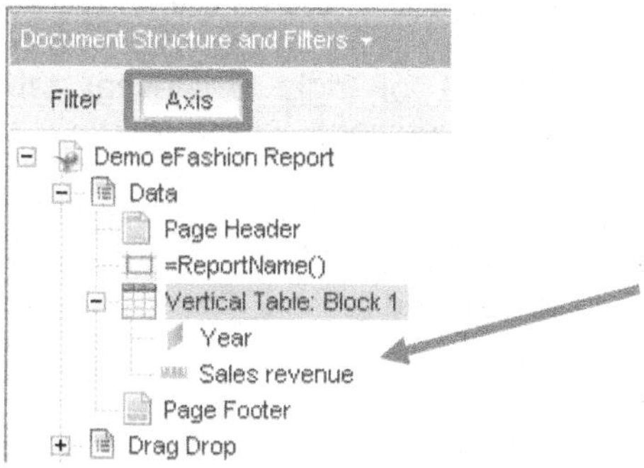
Document Structure and Filters
Filter
Axis
Demo eFashion Report
Data
Page Header
=ReportName()
Vertical Table: Block 1
Year
Sales revenue
Page Footer
Drag Drop

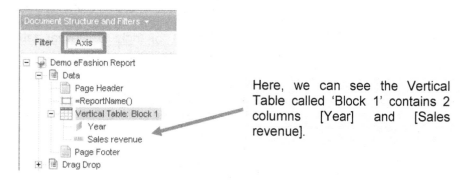

Here, we can see the Vertical Table called 'Block 1' contains 2 columns [Year] and [Sales revenue].

You can also view filters applied to the report elements using the 'Filters' button:

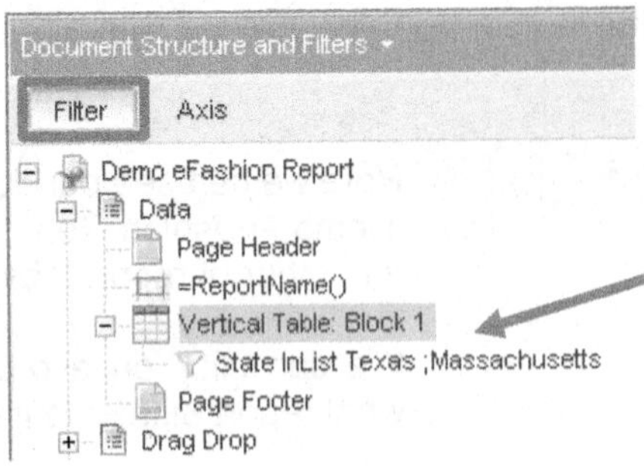
Document Structure and Filters
Filter
Axis
Demo eFashion Report
Data
Page Header
=ReportName()
Vertical Table: Block 1
State InList Texas ;Massachusetts
Page Footer
Drag Drop

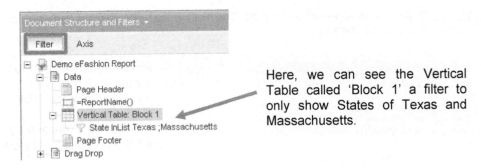

Here, we can see the Vertical Table called 'Block 1' a filter to only show States of Texas and Massachusetts.

8.1.9 Report Tab Selector

The **Report Tab Selector** is situated in the bottom left hand corner of the window and can be used to shift focus to a particular tab in a multi-report tab document.

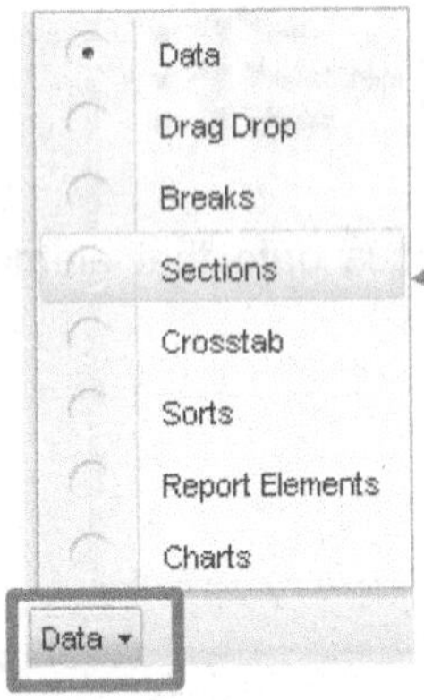
Data
Drag Drop
Breaks
Sections
Crosstab
Sorts
Report Elements
Charts
Data

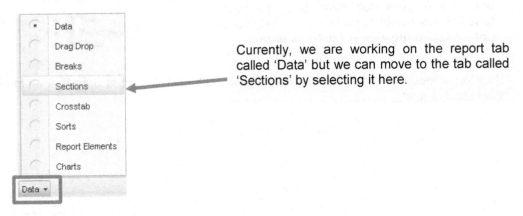

Currently, we are working on the report tab called 'Data' but we can move to the tab called 'Sections' by selecting it here.

8.1.10 Report Tabs

The **Report Tabs** are located along the bottom of the window and can also be navigated by simply clicking on the tab name.

Data
Drag Drop
Breaks
Sections
Crosstab
Sorts
Report Elements

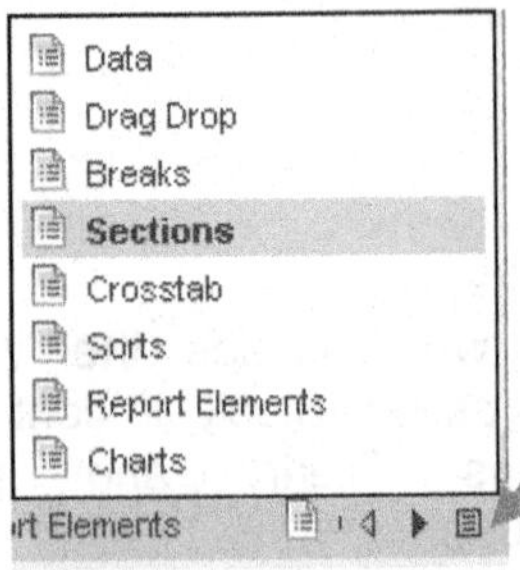
Data
Drag Drop
Breaks
Sections
Crosstab
Sorts
Report Elements
Charts
rt Elements

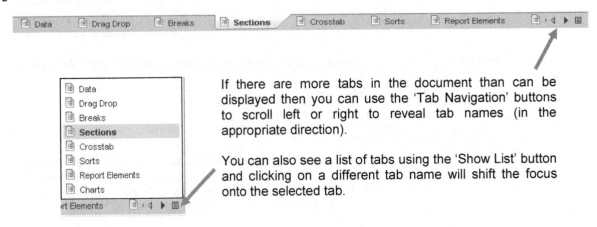

If there are more tabs in the document than can be displayed then you can use the 'Tab Navigation' buttons to scroll left or right to reveal tab names (in the appropriate direction).

You can also see a list of tabs using the 'Show List' button and clicking on a different tab name will shift the focus onto the selected tab.

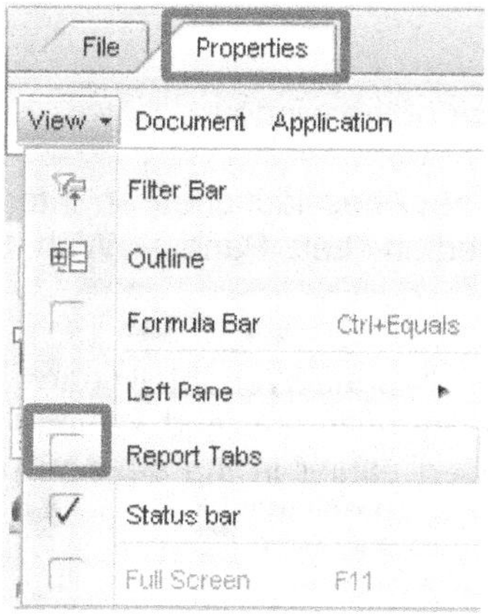
File
Properties
View
Document
Application
Filter Bar
Outline
Formula Bar
Ctrl+Equals
Left Pane
Report Tabs
Status bar
Full Screen
F11

You can hide the Report Tab Selector by unticking the toolbox menu option 'Properties – View – Report Tabs'.

This will then hide the Report Tabs, the Tab Navigation buttons and the Show List button.

8.1.11 Status Bar

The **Status Bar** is located along the bottom of the window.

Track Changes: Off
Page 1 of 1
100%
1 day ago.

8.1.12 Workspace Panel

The **Workspace Panel** takes up most of the screen and is the 'canvas' for creating your report layouts.

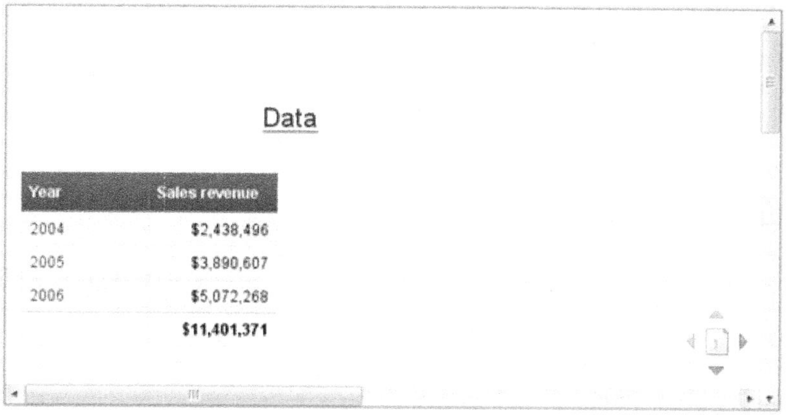
Data
Year
Sales revenue
2004
$2,438,496
2005
$3,890,607
2006
$5,072,268
$11,401,371

8.1.13 Tools / Help / Close Web Intelligence

These buttons are located in the very top right hand corner of the window.

Manage BI services
Options...

Manage BI services launches an interface similar to the one described in 'Left Pane – Web Services Publisher Tab'.

Options launches the Web Intelligence Options box where you can specify units and grid settings. This has already been described earlier in the session under 'Properties – Application' menu.

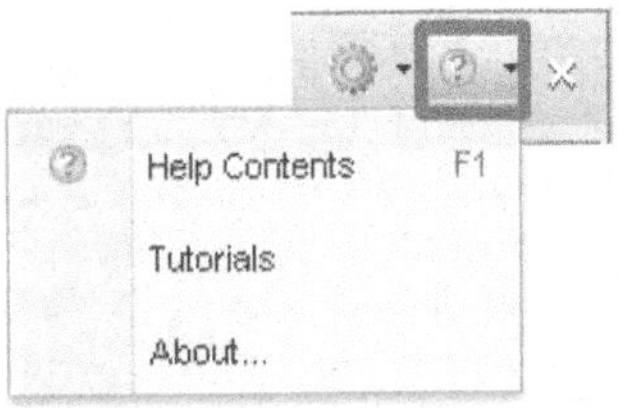
Help Contents
F1
Tutorials
About...

Help Contents launches browser based help for Web Intelligence.

Tutorials launches browser based tutorials from the SAP website.

About displays information about the version of Web Intelligence you are using.

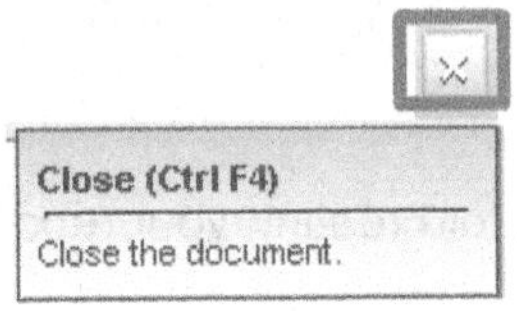
Close (Ctrl F4)
Close the document.

Close will close the current document but keep Web Intelligence tab open.

If you want to end your Web Intelligence session then you do this by closing the actual tab.

Demo eFashion Report
Close this tab

8.1.14 Right-Click Menus in Web Intelligence

Most of the menus and options available via the various Toolboxes are available using right-click on report elements.

Using right-click can be more convenient as all available options will become apparent rather than looking across the various Toolboxes, etc.

It all comes down to personal preference and during the course we will use a combination of right-click and Toolbox menus.

9 Introducing Drag and Drop Techniques

The general technique for dragging and dropping involves:

1. Clicking once to first select an object.
2. Holding the left mouse button down to grab the object for dragging.
3. Dragging the object into position.
4. Dropping the object in the desired position.

Web Intelligence uses indicators such as highlights and tooltips telling you what action will be performed if the selection is dropped at that position.

> **NOTE - We will use the existing document saved as '05 - Simple eFashion Report'. Open the saved document for editing.**

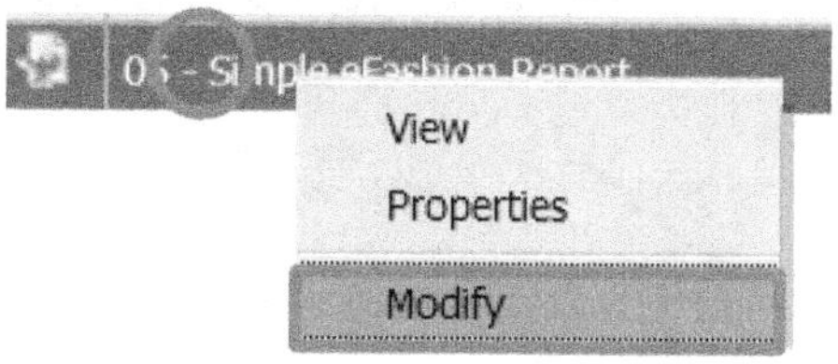
View
Properties
Modify

9.1 Inserting an Object

To insert an object into a table type block, drag and drop the object to the side of another column.

In the following example, [Quarter] values will be inserted to the right of [Year] values.

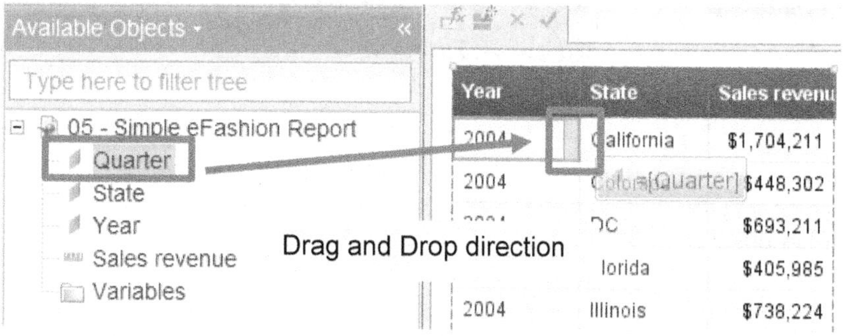
Available Objects
Type here to filter tree
05 - Simple eFashion Report
Quarter
State
Year
Sales revenue
Variables
Drag and Drop direction
Year
State
Sales revenu
2004
2004
2004
Illinois
$1,704,211
$448,302
$693,211
$405,985
$738,224

NOTE – When you insert an object then you can drop the object in four positions (as shown next):

Year
State
Sales revenu
2004
California
$1,704,211
2004
Colorado
2004
DC
$693,211

1 – In this case it will be a column to the **right** of [State] because we are dropping into the right hand side of the [State] cell.

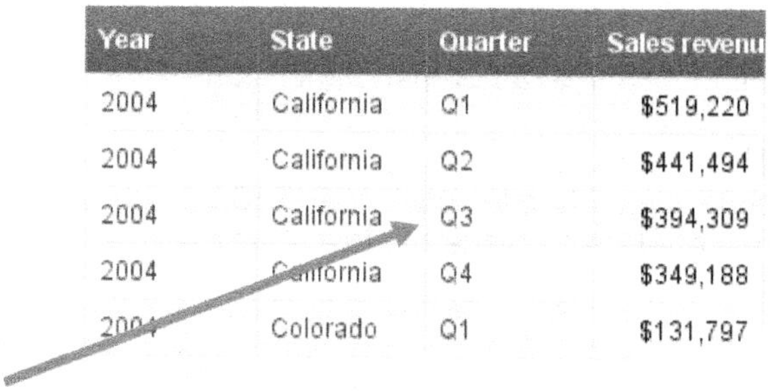
Year
State
Quarter
Sales revenu
2004
California
Q1
$519,220
2004
California
Q2
$441,494
2004
California
Q3
$394,309
2004
Q4
$349,188
Colorado
Q1
$131,797

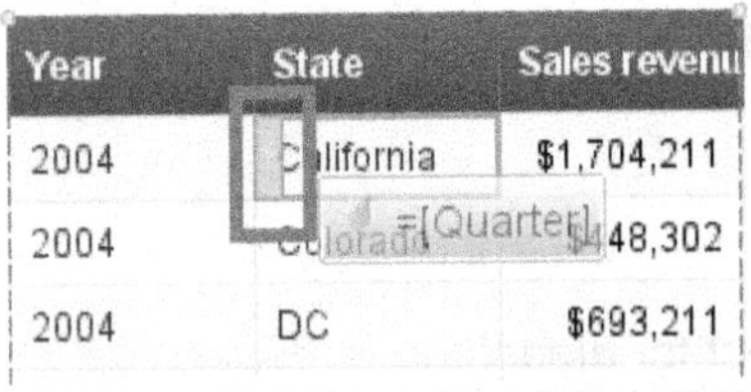

Year
State
Sales revenu
2004
California
$1,704,211
2004
Colorado
$448,302
2004
DC
$693,211
=[Quarter]

2 – In this case it will be a column to the **left** of [State] because we are inserting into the left hand side of the [State] cell.

Year	Quarter	State	Sales revenu
2004	Q1	California	$519,220
2004	Q1	Colorado	$131,797
2004	Q1	DC	$208,324
2004	Q1	Florida	$137,530
2004	Q1	Illinois	$256,454

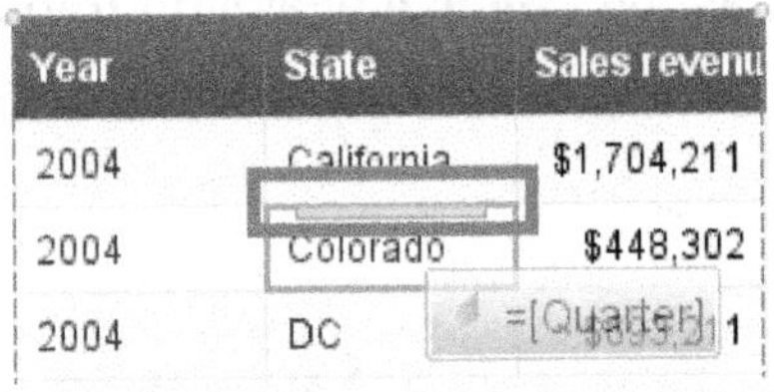

Year
State
Sales revenu
2004
California
$1,704,211
2004
Colorado
$448,302
2004
DC
=[Quarter]

3 – In this case it will be a **new row** and the value will be inserted into the **cell above** the [State] cell because we are inserting into the top part of a [State] cell.

	Quarter	
Year	State	Sales revenu
	Q1	
2004	California	$519,220
	Q1	
2004	Colorado	$131,797
	Q1	
2004	DC	$208,324

Year
State
Sales revenu
2004
California
$1,704,211
2004
Colorado
$448,302
2004
DC
$693,211
=[Quarter]

4 – In this case it will be a **new row** and the value will be inserted into the **cell below** the [State] cell because we are inserting into the bottom part of a [State] cell.

Year	State	Sales revenu
	Quarter	
2004	California	$519,220
	Q1	
2004	California	$441,494
	Q2	
2004	California	$394,309
	Q3	

NOTE – Multiple rows are better used with measures rather than dimensions.

This example shows data for each state over multiple rows due to [Sales revenue] being placed below [Quantity sold].

Year	State	Quantity sold
		Sales revenue
2004	California	11,304
		$1,704,211
2004	Colorado	2,971
		$448,302
2004	DC	4,681
		$693,211

9.2 Replacing an Object

To replace the results for a given object with the results of another object, drag and drop the replacing object on top of the values for the object being replaced.

In the following example, [Quarter] will replace [Year].

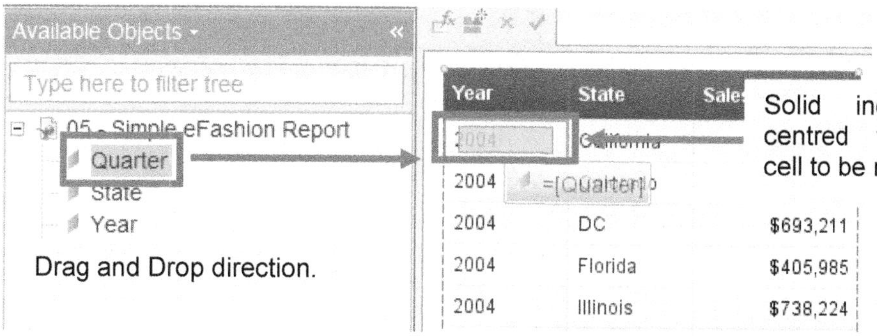
Available Objects
Type here to filter tree
05 - Simple eFashion Report
Quarter
State
Year
Drag and Drop direction.
Year
State
2004
=[Quarter]
DC
Florida
Illinois
$693,211
$405,985
$738,224

Solid indicator is centred within the cell to be replaced.

[Year] has been replaced by [Quarter].

Quarter
State
Sales revenue
Q1
California
$1,899,680
Q1
Colorado
$525,682
Q1
DC
$766,822

9.3 Removing an Object

To remove an object from a block, drag and drop the object from the block into the Left Pane.

In the following example, dragging and dropping [Quarter] from the displayed results into the Report Manager will remove [Quarter] object from the table.

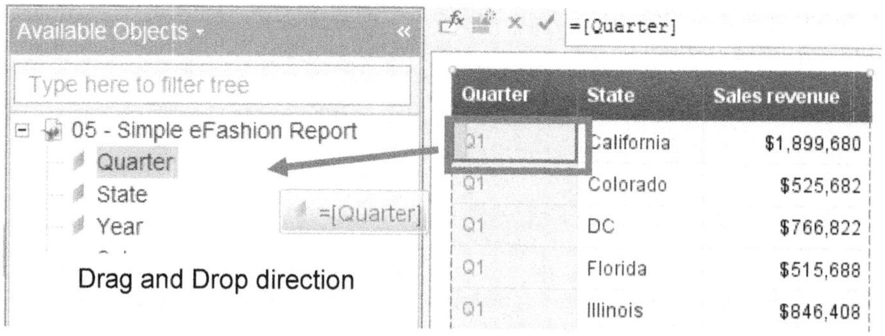
Available Objects
Type here to filter tree
05 - Simple eFashion Report
Quarter
State
Year
=[Quarter]
Drag and Drop direction
=[Quarter]
Quarter
State
Sales revenue
California
$1,899,680
Colorado
$525,682
DC
$766,822
Florida
$515,688
Illinois
$846,408

Columns can also be removed using right-click menu and then selecting 'Delete'.

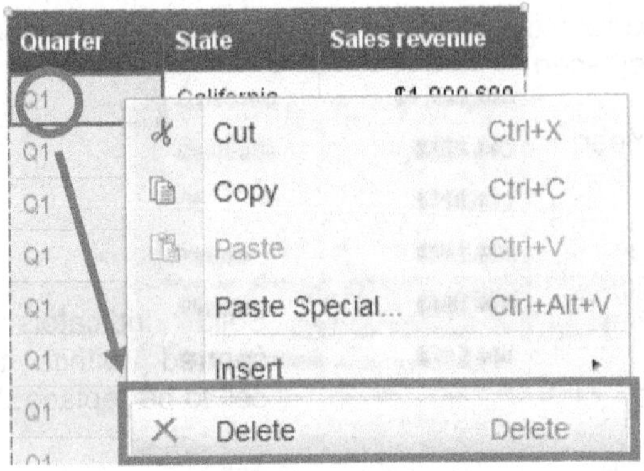
Quarter
State
Sales revenue
Q1
Cut Ctrl+X
Copy Ctrl+C
Paste Ctrl+V
Paste Special... Ctrl+Alt+V
Insert
Delete Delete

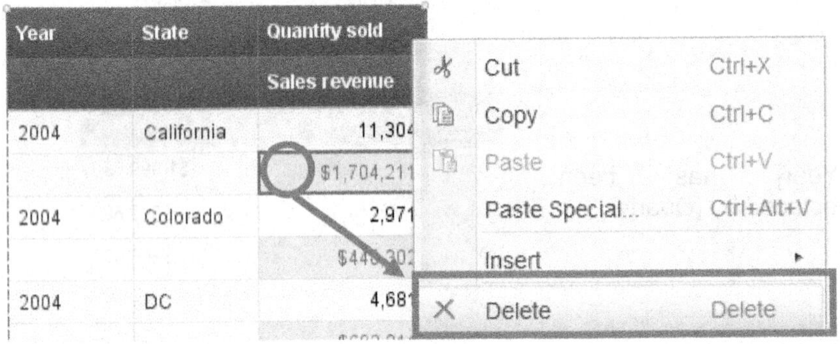
Year
State
Quantity sold
Sales revenue
2004
California
Colorado
DC
Cut Ctrl+X
Copy Ctrl+C
Paste Ctrl+V
Paste Special... Ctrl+Alt+V
Insert
Delete Delete

If Web Intelligence is unsure of whether you are wanting to delete a row or a column, then you will be prompted.

You can then specify whether a column or a row should be deleted.

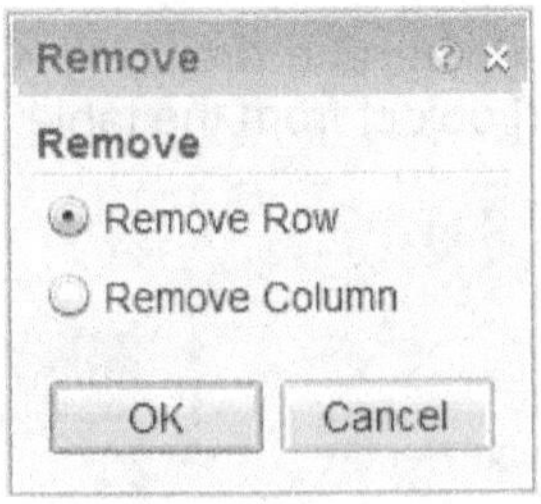
Remove
Remove
Remove Row
Remove Column
OK
Cancel

9.4 Auto-Resizing Cells

To auto-resize cells horizontally within a block, double-click on the line to the right of the column or to the bottom of the row you wish to resize.

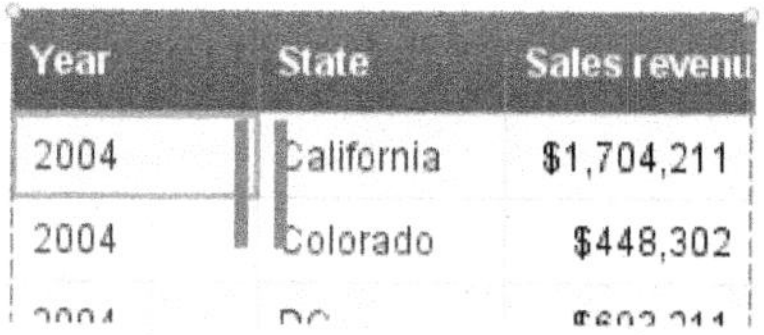
Year
State
Sales revenu
2004
California
$1,704,211
2004
Colorado
$448,302

Double click when markers appear for column width or row height.

Year
State
Sales revenu
2004
California
$1,704,211
2004
Colorado
$448,302
2004
DC
$693,211
2004
Florida
$405,985

You may also manually resize a column or row by dragging and dropping the line to the desired width or height.

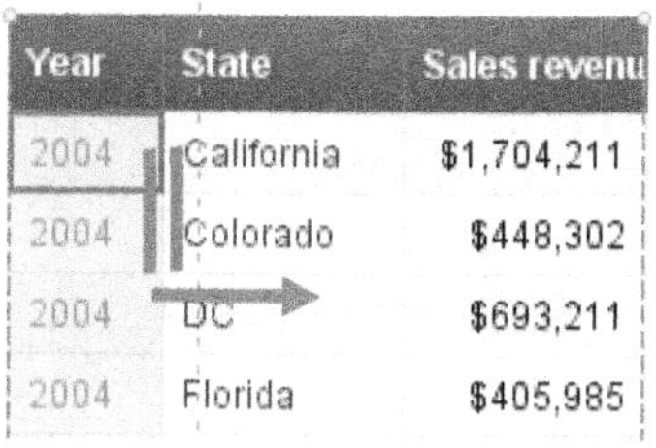
Year
State
Sales revenu
2004
California
$1,704,211
2004
Colorado
$448,302
2004
DC
$693,211
2004
Florida
$405,985

Select markers for column width or row height and then drag to set the required size.

NOTE:

Be careful when auto-sizing all columns for reports as it could lead to pagination problems. Fixing the column widths manually enables you to ensure report layouts fit your page dimensions.

9.5 Copying a Block

Making a copy of a block within a report is simple via Drag and Drop:

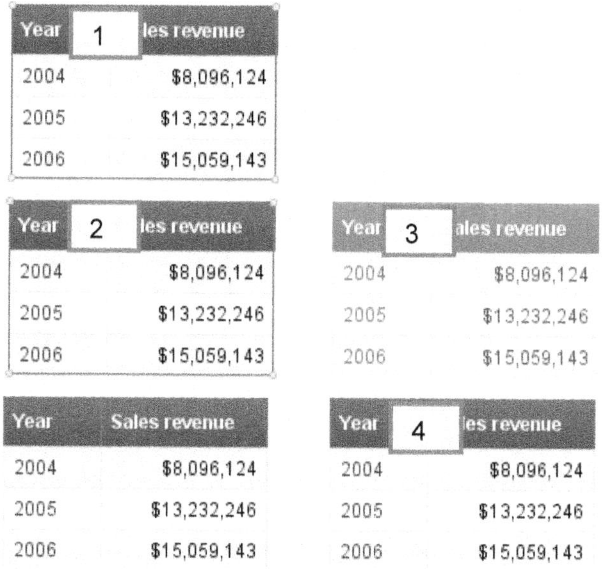
1
2
3
4
Year
Sales revenue
2004
$8,096,124
2005
$13,232,246
2006
$15,059,143

1 – Select the block by clicking on the perimeter of the block (the block will become highlighted with a border).

2 – Hold down <Ctrl> key and drag the block with left mouse button pressed.

3 – With the <Ctrl> key held down, let go of the left mouse button when block is in the desired position.

4 – Web Intelligence creates a copy of the original block (table, chart, crosstab).

NOTE – Use the same actions for copying other blocks (charts, etc).

You can also copy a block within a report using right-click menu:

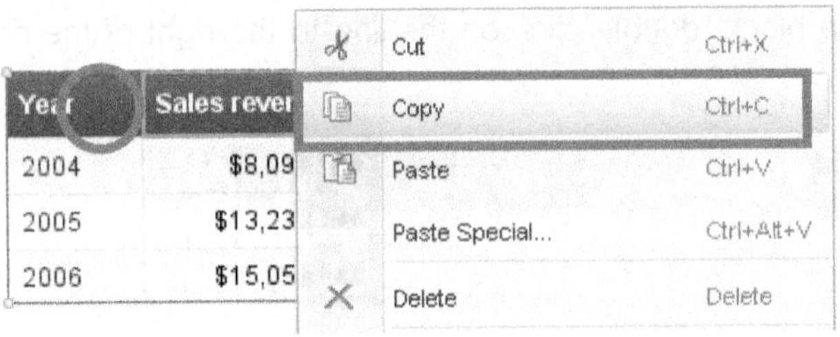
Year
Sales rever
2004
$8,09
2005
$13,23
2006
$15,05
Cut
Ctrl+X
Copy
Ctrl+C
Paste
Ctrl+V
Paste Special...
Ctrl+Alt+V
Delete
Delete

1 – Select the block by clicking near the perimeter.

2 – Right-click and select ‘Copy’.

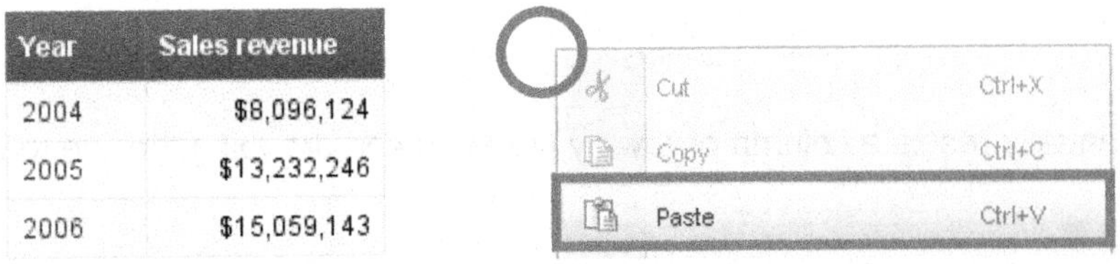
Year
Sales revenue
2004
$8,096,124
2005
$13,232,246
2006
$15,059,143
Cut
Ctrl+X
Copy
Ctrl+C
Paste
Ctrl+V

3 – Left-click where you would like to paste the copied block (e.g. circled area).

4 – Right-click and select ‘Paste’.

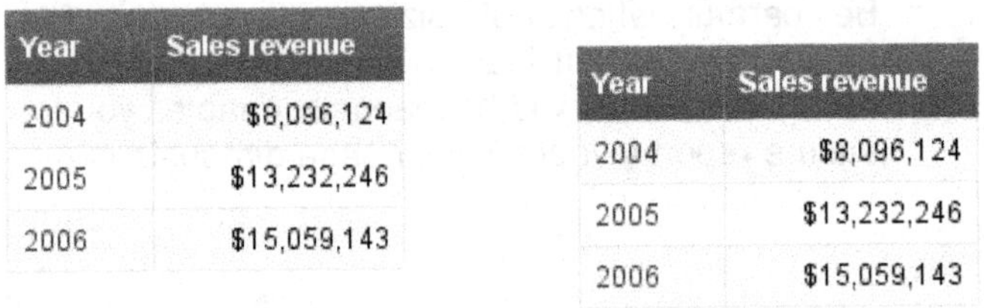
Year
Sales revenue
2004
$8,096,124
2005
$13,232,246
2006
$15,059,143
Year
Sales revenue
2004
$8,096,124
2005
$13,232,246
2006
$15,059,143

5 – Pasted block appears at selected spot.

9.6 Inserting a Table using Multiple Data Objects

A vertical table is the default report element style. If you hold the <Ctrl> key down and select multiple objects, you can drag all of those objects together into the report to create a table of those objects.

1. Select the objects from the Available Objects tab of the Left Pane and drag into the report.

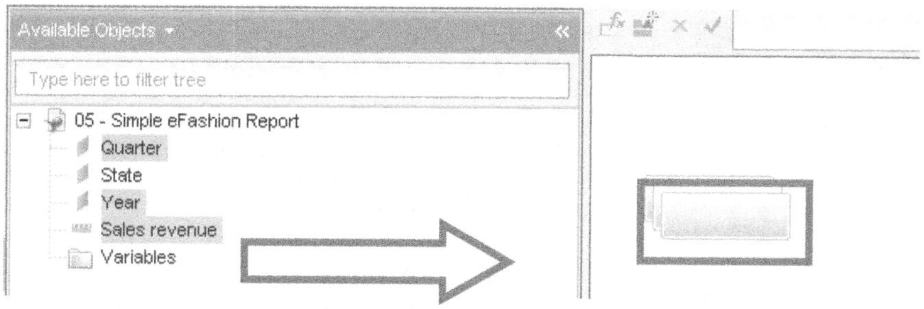
Available Objects
Type here to filter tree
05 - Simple eFashion Report
Quarter
State
Year
Sales revenue
Variables

HINT – Select the objects in the order you want them to appear in the block to save re-arranging columns within the block.

2. Drop the objects in the report to produce the table.

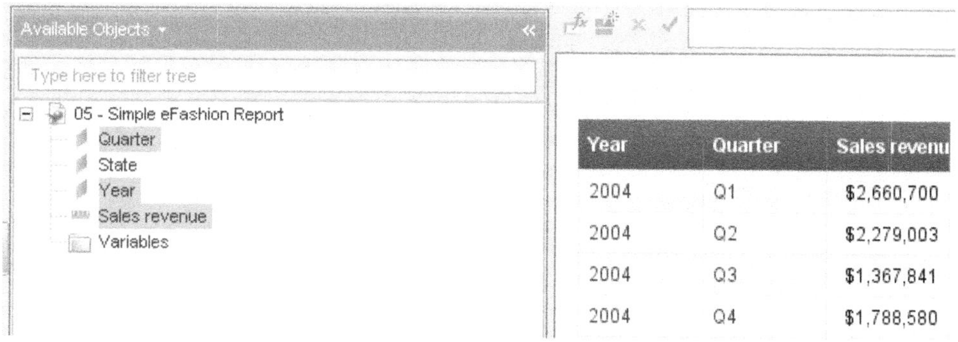
Available Objects
Type here to filter tree
05 - Simple eFashion Report
Quarter
State
Year
Sales revenue
Variables
Year
Quarter
Sales revenu
2004
Q1
$2,660,700
2004
Q2
$2,279,003
2004
Q3
$1,367,841
2004
Q4
$1,788,580

9.7 Right-Click Menus

Web Intelligence offers context sensitive right-click menus that are shortcuts (in most cases) to toolbar buttons. Some examples are shown below (red circle indicates source of right-click).

Use of these and other right-click menus will be explained in later sessions.

Year
State
Sales revenu
Cut Ctrl+X
Copy Ctrl+C
Paste Ctrl+V
Paste Special... Ctrl+Alt+V
Insert
Delete Delete
Clear Contents
Set as Section
Turn Into
Edit Formula...
Linking
Start Drill
Filter
Ranking
Sort
Break
Hide
Text
Format Cell...

Options available when right-click is initiated inside a **cell within a block**.

Year
State
2004 California
2004 Colorado
2004 DC
2004 Florida
2004 Illinois
2004 Massachi
2004 New York
2004 Texas
2005 California
2005 Colorado
2005 DC
2005 Florida
2005 Illinois
2005 Massachi
2005 New York
2005 Texas
2006 California
Cut Ctrl+X
Copy Ctrl+C
Paste Ctrl+V
Paste Special... Ctrl+Alt+V
Delete Delete
Turn Into
Assign Data...
Linking
Publish as Web Service
Filter
Sort
Break
Hide
Order
Align
Format Table...

Options available when right-click is initiated after selecting the block first.

NOTE – The block is selected by clicking on the perimeter of the block.

Options available when right-click is initiated in a blank area of the page (i.e. the page background).

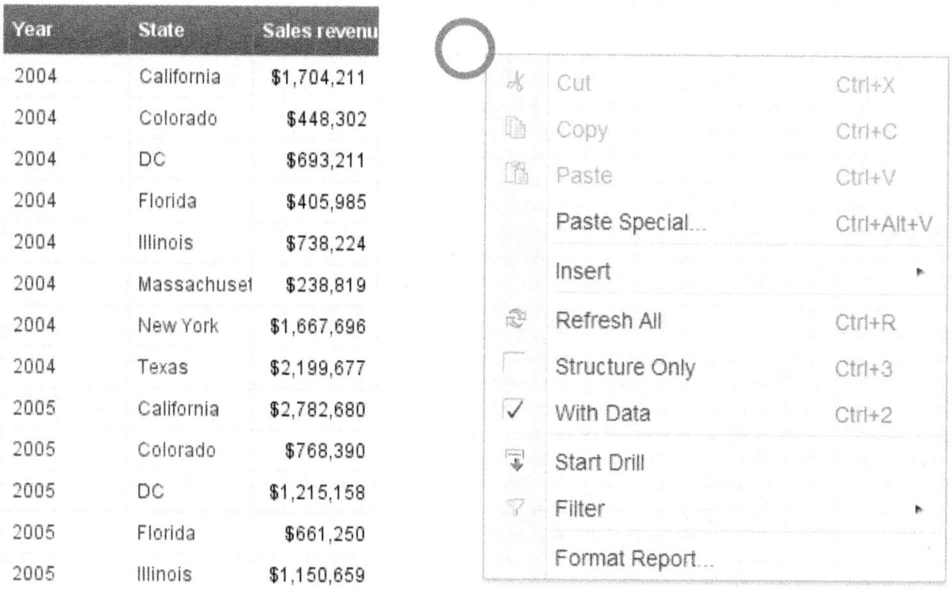
Year
State
Sales revenu
2004 California $1,704,211
2004 Colorado $448,302
2004 DC $693,211
2004 Florida $405,985
2004 Illinois $738,224
2004 Massachuset $238,819
2004 New York $1,667,696
2004 Texas $2,199,677
2005 California $2,782,680
2005 Colorado $768,390
2005 DC $1,215,158
2005 Florida $661,250
2005 Illinois $1,150,659
Cut Ctrl+X
Copy Ctrl+C
Paste Ctrl+V
Paste Special... Ctrl+Alt+V
Insert
Refresh All Ctrl+R
Structure Only Ctrl+3
With Data Ctrl+2
Start Drill
Filter
Format Report...

10 Formatting Cells, Tables and Cross Tables

This session describes how to apply formatting to cells, tables, and cross tables.

Let us start with a new document containing the following query using the 'eFashion' universe:

Result Objects
Year
Quarter
State
Quantity sold
Sales revenue
Margin
Discount

We will use objects from this query in examples during this session.

Run the query and Web Intelligence will display the above objects in a default vertical table.

To describe the construct of tables, we have removed some objects from the block and added a footer row (more on this in later sessions).

Year	Quantity sold	Sales revenue	Margin	Discount	Header Cells
2004	53,078	$8,095,814	$3,731,971	$1,824,510	
Body Rows comprising of Body Cells			$5,187,886	$1,021,257	
2006	90,296	$15,059,143	$5,667,084	$2,128,330	
	223,229	**$36,387,203**	**$14,586,940**	**$4,974,097**	Footer Cells

1. The cells in the first row are the Header cells for the block.
2. The cells of the last row are Footer cells.
3. The rows in between the header and footer rows are the 'Body Rows' made up of Body Cells.

Block can be formatted as a whole, or individual cells within a block can be formatted.

NOTES:

1. Unlike spreadsheet formatting, Web Intelligence will group cells for formatting according to their type, i.e. making changes to a body cell will cause all body cells within that column to be formatted.

2. The term '**Block**' is generic in that it is used for tables, cross tables, charts, and forms.

   However, Web Intelligence will automatically recognise what type of block has been used and offer the relevant properties and right-click menus.

We will use the above query in a few examples within this session.

You can create a new report tab within the document by using right-click on a report name and then selecting 'Add Report'.

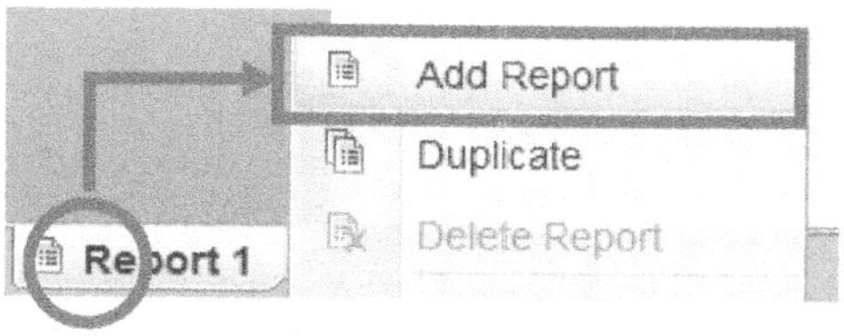
Add Report
Duplicate
Delete Report
Report 1

10.1 Formatting Free-Standing Cells

Free-Standing Cells are cells that are not part of a block (i.e. not in a table or cross table), for example the default title cell placed in the report is a free-standing cell.

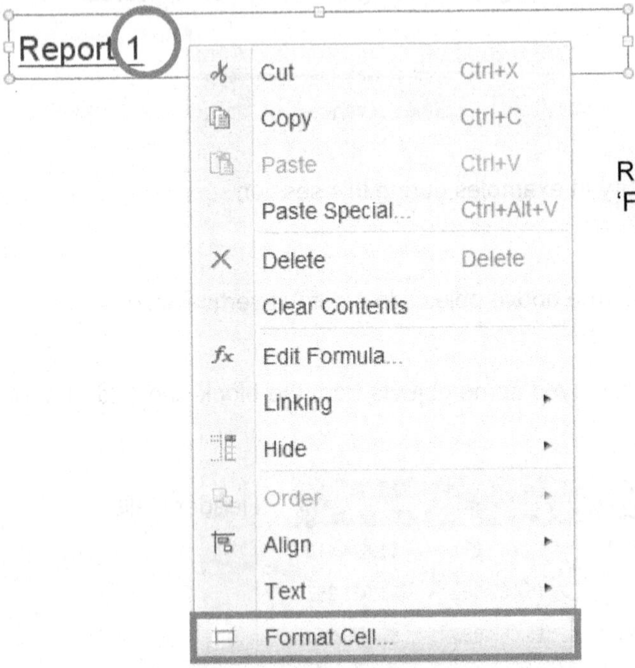
Report 1
Cut Ctrl+X
Copy Ctrl+C
Paste Ctrl+V
Paste Special... Ctrl+Alt+V
Delete Delete
Clear Contents
Edit Formula...
Linking
Hide
Order
Align
Text
Format Cell...

Right-click on a free-standing cell and select 'Format Cell...'

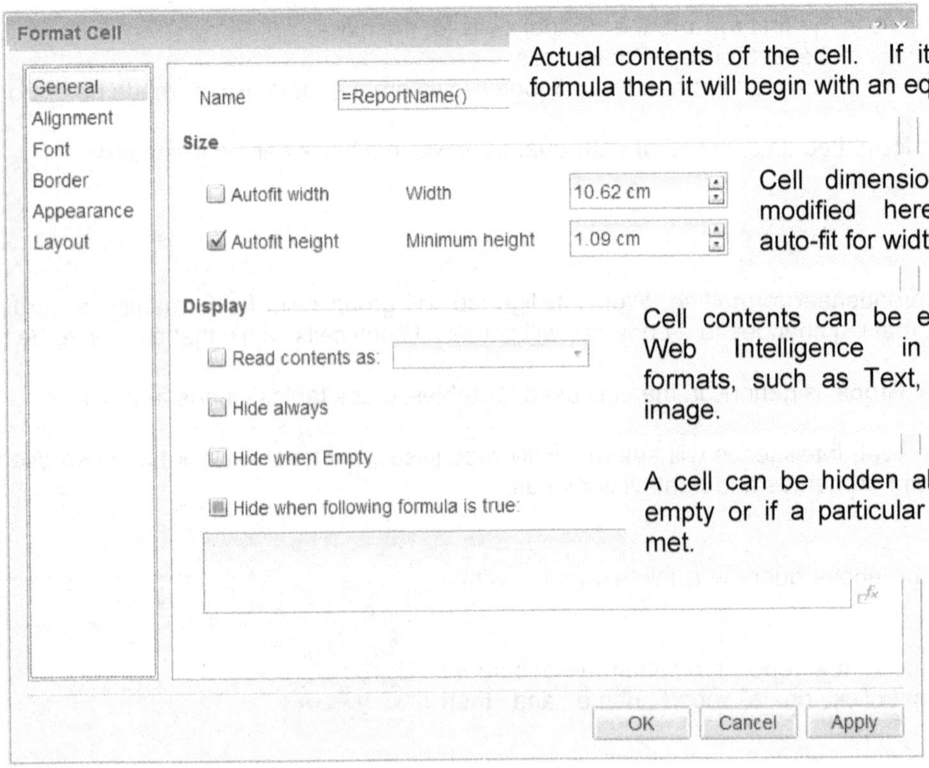
Format Cell
General
Alignment
Font
Border
Appearance
Layout
Name =ReportName()
Size
Autofit width Width 10.62 cm
Autofit height Minimum height 1.09 cm
Display
Read contents as:
Hide always
Hide when Empty
Hide when following formula is true:
OK Cancel Apply

Actual contents of the cell. If it contains a formula then it will begin with an equal sign '='.

Cell dimensions can be modified here, including auto-fit for width / height.

Cell contents can be evaluated by Web Intelligence in difference formats, such as Text, HTML, and image.

A cell can be hidden always, when empty or if a particular condition is met.

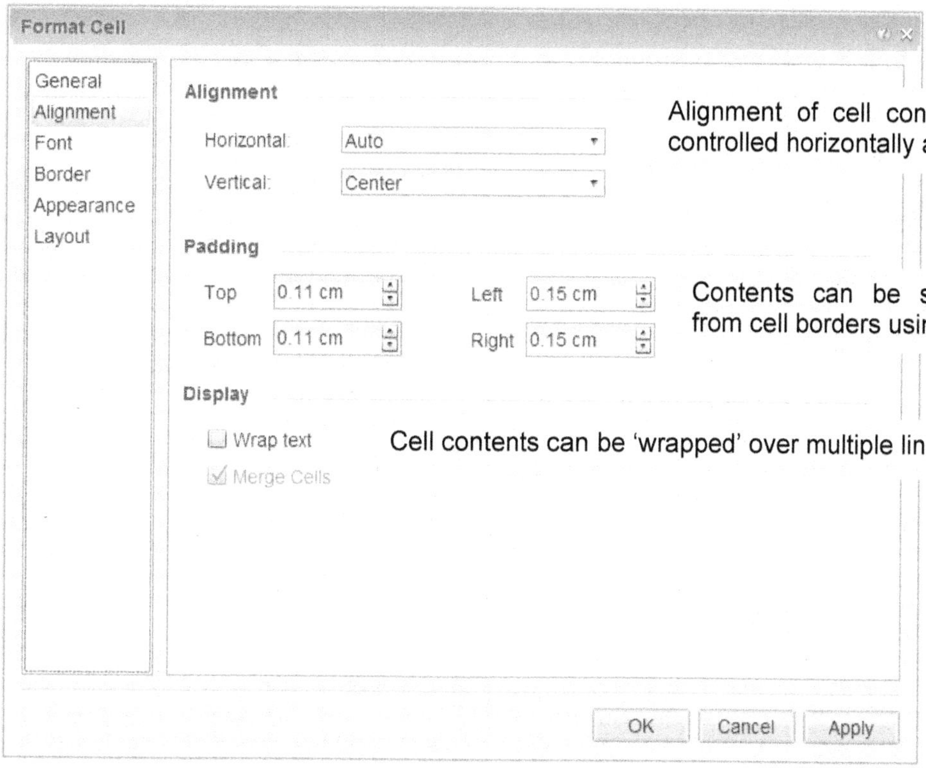
Format Cell
General
Alignment
Font
Border
Appearance
Layout
Alignment
Horizontal: Auto
Vertical: Center
Padding
Top 0.11 cm
Bottom 0.11 cm
Left 0.15 cm
Right 0.15 cm
Display
Wrap text
Merge Cells
OK
Cancel
Apply

Alignment of cell contents can be controlled horizontally and vertically.

Contents can be spaced away from cell borders using Padding.

Cell contents can be 'wrapped' over multiple lines.

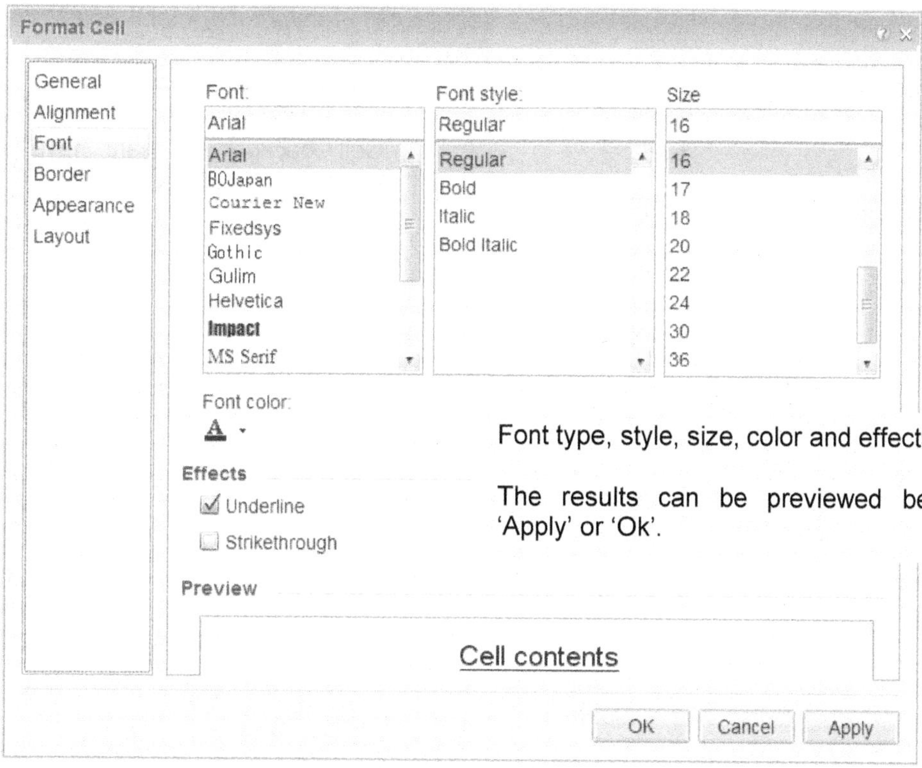
Format Cell
General
Alignment
Font
Border
Appearance
Layout
Font: Arial
Arial
BOJapan
Courier New
Fixedsys
Gothic
Gulim
Helvetica
Impact
MS Serif
Font style: Regular
Regular
Bold
Italic
Bold Italic
Size: 16
16
17
18
20
22
24
30
36
Font color:
Effects
Underline
Strikethrough
Preview
Cell contents
OK
Cancel
Apply

Font type, style, size, color and effects can be set.

The results can be previewed before clicking 'Apply' or 'Ok'.

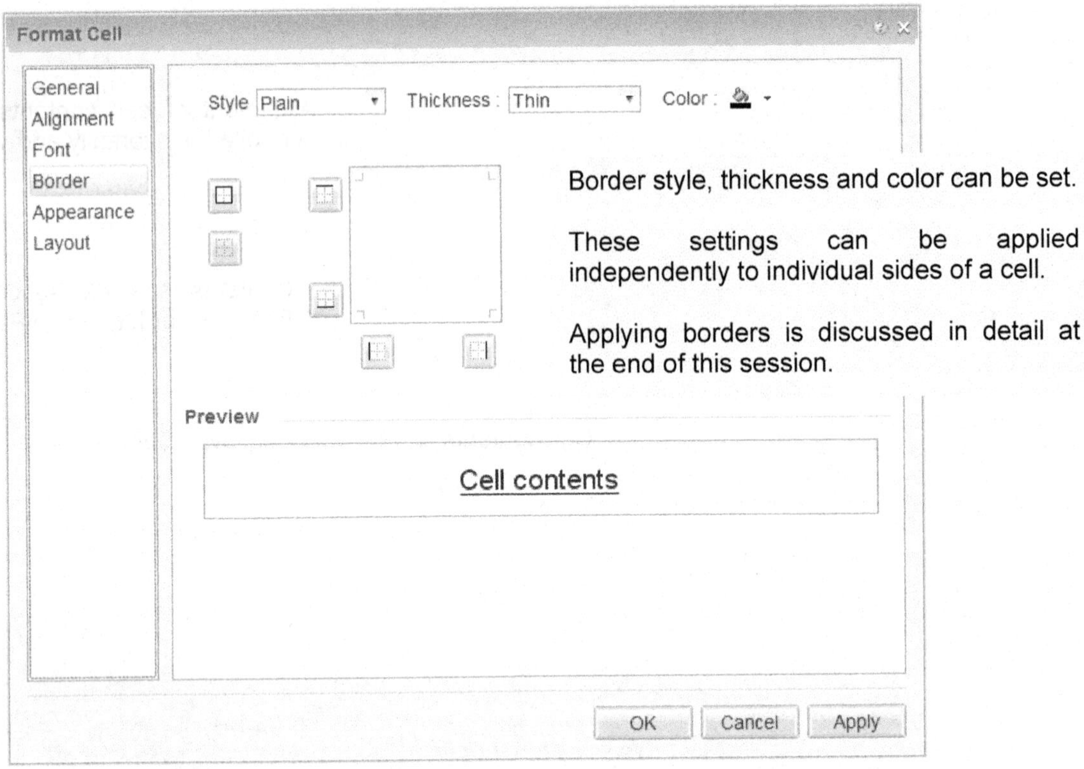
Format Cell
General
Alignment
Font
Border
Appearance
Layout
Style Plain
Thickness : Thin
Color :
Border style, thickness and color can be set.
These settings can be applied independently to individual sides of a cell.
Applying borders is discussed in detail at the end of this session.
Preview
Cell contents
OK
Cancel
Apply

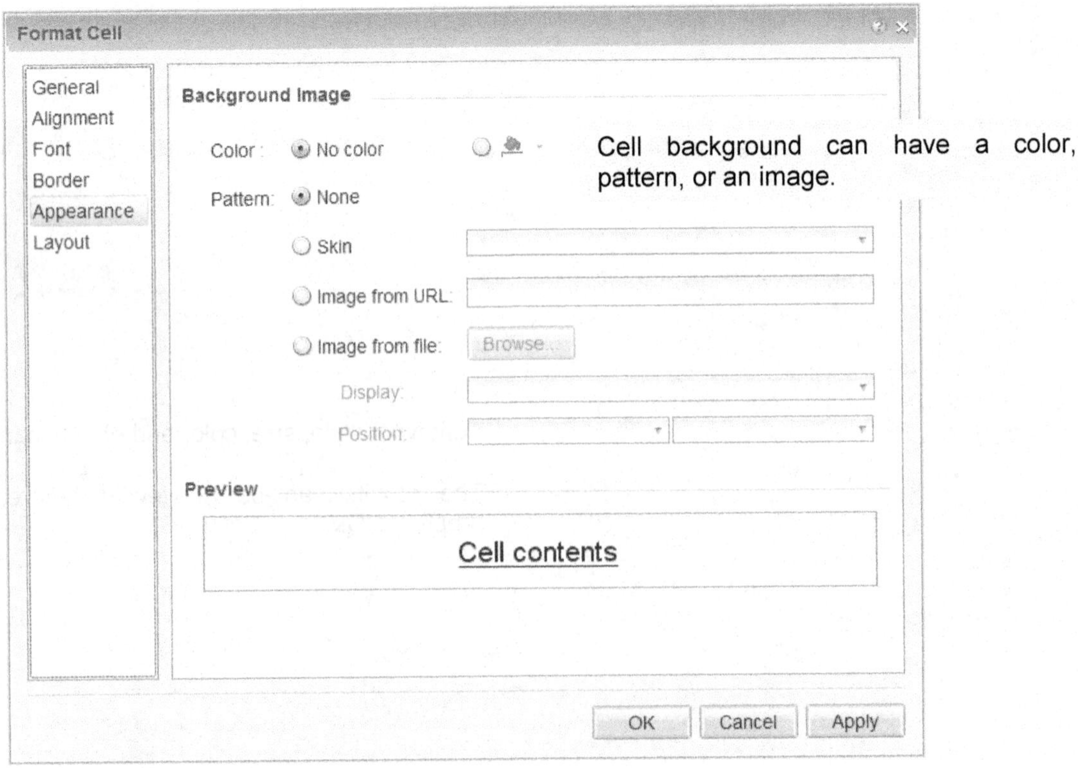
Format Cell
General
Alignment
Font
Border
Appearance
Layout
Background Image
Color : No color
Cell background can have a color, pattern, or an image.
Pattern: None
Skin
Image from URL:
Image from file: Browse...
Display:
Position:
Preview
Cell contents
OK
Cancel
Apply

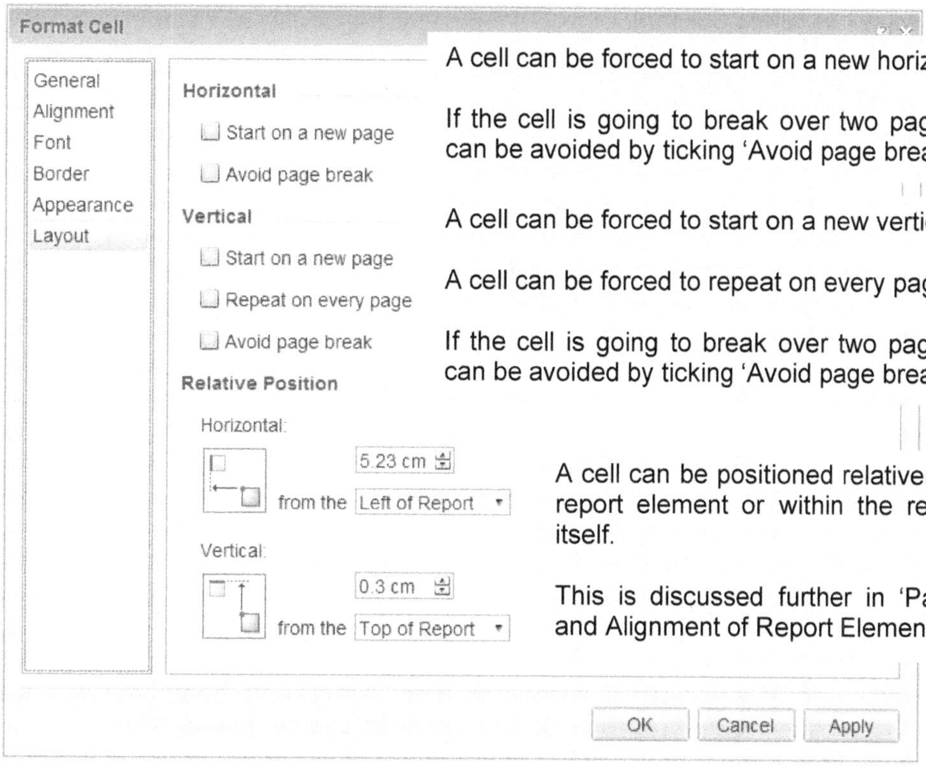
Format Cell
General
Alignment
Font
Border
Appearance
Layout
Horizontal
Start on a new page
Avoid page break
Vertical
Start on a new page
Repeat on every page
Avoid page break
Relative Position
Horizontal:
5.23 cm
from the Left of Report
Vertical:
0.3 cm
from the Top of Report
OK
Cancel
Apply

A cell can be forced to start on a new horizontal page.

If the cell is going to break over two pages then this can be avoided by ticking 'Avoid page break'.

A cell can be forced to start on a new vertical page.

A cell can be forced to repeat on every page.

If the cell is going to break over two pages then this can be avoided by ticking 'Avoid page break'.

A cell can be positioned relatively to another report element or within the report canvas itself.

This is discussed further in 'Page Layouts and Alignment of Report Elements'.

10.2 Formatting Cells within Blocks

Cells within blocks can be formatted in the same was as free-standing cells and have very similar formatting options.

Firstly, let us look at how we can select cells in a table:

1. We have a vertical table block with four columns and we have clicked on the body cell displaying the value 'California'.

Year	State	Sales revenu	Quantity sold
2004	California	$1,704,211	11,304
2004	Colorado	$448,302	2,971
2004	DC	$693,211	4,681
2004	Florida	$405,985	2,585

Web Intelligence treats this as if we have selected all the body cells in the [State] column, hence the column takes on a shaded appearance (as shown).

If we then right-click and select 'Format Cell...' then we are able to apply formatting to the body cells within the [State Column].

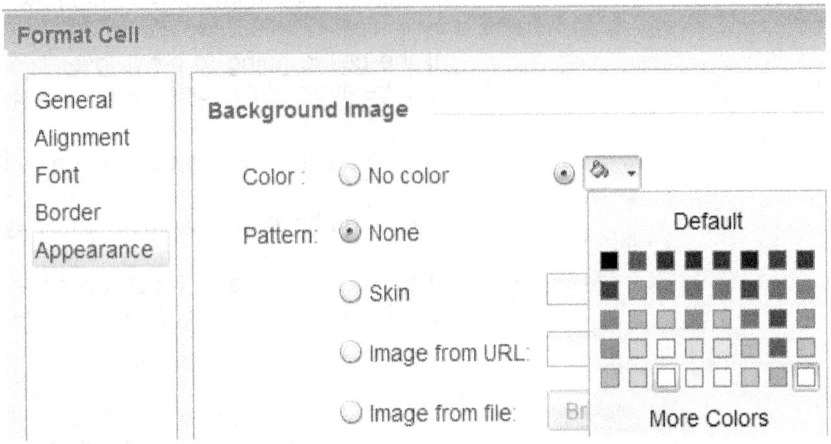
Format Cell
General
Alignment
Font
Border
Appearance
Background Image
Color :
No color
Pattern:
None
Skin
Image from URL:
Image from file:
Default
More Colors

2. We have now clicked on the header cell displaying the value 'State'.

Year	State	Sales revenu	Quantity sold
2004	California	$1,704,211	11,304
2004	Colorado	$448,302	2,971
2004	DC	$693,211	4,681
2004	Florida	$405,985	2,585

Web Intelligence treats this as we have selected a single header cell.

The same applies to footer cells (which we will look at in later sessions).

3. We have now clicked on the first cell in the [Sales revenue] column and Web Intelligence selects all the body cells in this column.

Year	State	Sales revenu	Quantity sold
2004	California	$1,704,211	11,304
2004	Colorado	$448,302	2,971
2004	DC	$693,211	4,681
2004	Florida	$405,985	2,585

We can hold down the <CTRL> key and then click in another column (or header/footer cells) to select multiple cells/columns.

Year	State	Sales revenu	Quantity sold
2004	California	$1,704,211	11,304
2004	Colorado	$448,302	2,971
2004	DC	$693,211	4,681
2004	Florida	$405,985	2,585

NOTE – After selecting the cell(s) use right-click 'Format Cell...' for formatting options.

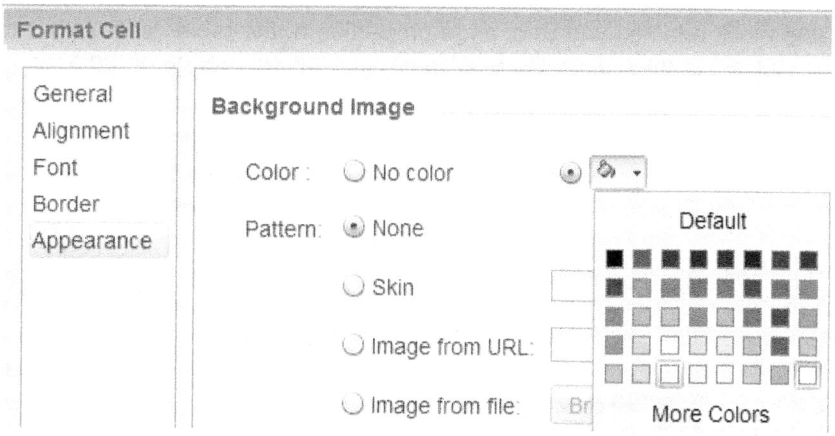
Format Cell
General
Alignment
Font
Border
Appearance
Background Image
Color :
No color
Pattern:
None
Skin
Image from URL:
Image from file:
Default
More Colors

Secondly, the formatting properties available for cells within blocks are almost the same as previously described for free-standing cells.

The differences are:

1. Changes applied to a single body cell in a column will apply the formatting to all of the body cells in that column.

2. If you have selected body cells in multiple columns then the formatting will be applied to all of the body cells in the selected columns.

3. '**Layout**' properties do not exist as cells within a block are automatically positioned, but we have other properties like '**Merge Cells**' (for use in Headers and Footers).

10.3 Formatting Tables

Selecting a table block enables you to change properties of the table itself (rather than the cells within it), for example you can show or hide the block's header row (at the top of the block) or its footer row (at the bottom of the block).

Right-click on any edge and select 'Format Table...'

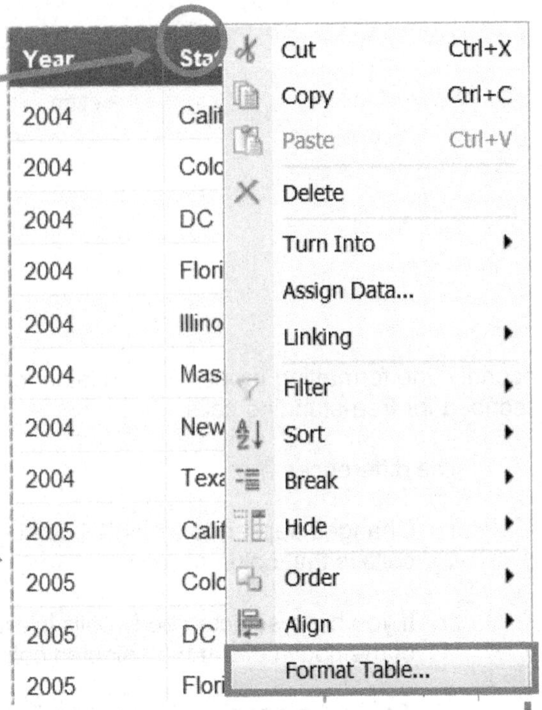

Year
Sta
2004
Calif
2004
Colo
2004
DC
2004
Flori
2004
Illino
2004
Mas
2004
New
2004
Texa
2005
Calif
2005
Colo
2005
DC
2005
Flori
Cut Ctrl+X
Copy Ctrl+C
Paste Ctrl+V
Delete
Turn Into
Assign Data...
Linking
Filter
Sort
Break
Hide
Order
Align
Format Table...

NOTE

Generally, to select a table, move the cursor to any edge of the table and an outline will appear around the table.

Click onto the outline and then you can work with the table (for example to move it).

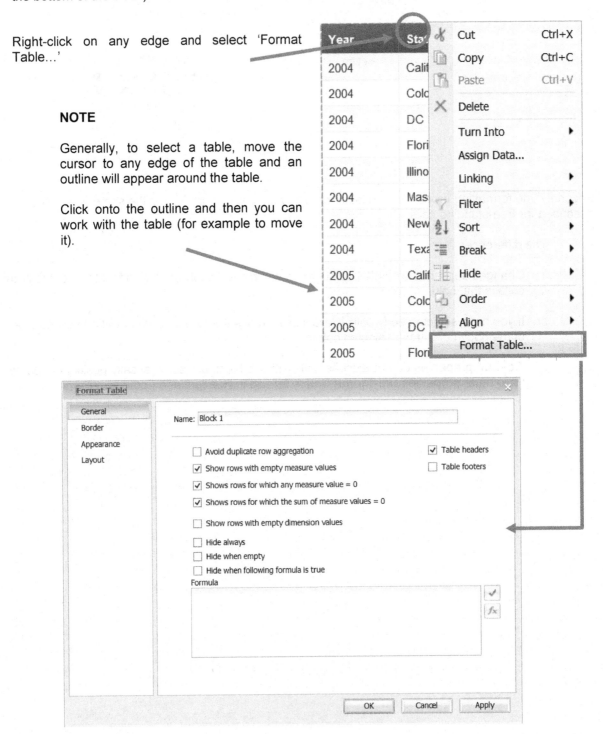

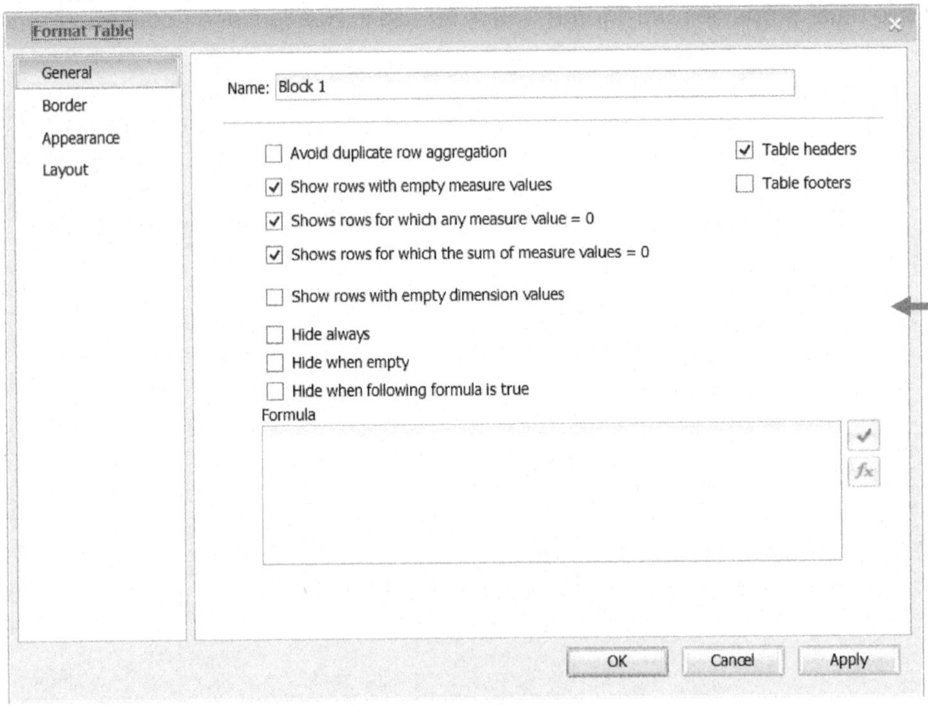

Format Table
General
Border
Appearance
Layout
Name: Block 1
Avoid duplicate row aggregation
Show rows with empty measure values
Shows rows for which any measure value = 0
Shows rows for which the sum of measure values = 0
Show rows with empty dimension values
Hide always
Hide when empty
Hide when following formula is true
Formula
Table headers
Table footers
OK
Cancel
Apply

Format Table – General Tab	Description
Name	You can change the name for the block. Use meaningful names for table blocks, especially when you have a few on the same page.
Avoid duplicate row aggregation	To display duplicate rows in their raw form, rather than rolled up into one row with their measure values aggregated (typically summed), check the '**Avoid duplicate row aggregation**' property. We have demonstrated this in the session on 'Data in Web Intelligence Documents'.
Show rows with empty measure values	Uncheck this property if you do not want to show rows where all measure values are empty.
Show rows for which any measure value = 0	
Show rows for which the sum of measure values = 0	
Show row with empty dimension values	Uncheck this property if you do not want to show rows where all dimension values are empty.
Hide always	Check this property if you want to hide the table block.
Hide when empty	Check this property if you want to hide the table block only when it is empty of data.
Hide when following formula is true	Check this property if you want to hide the table block based on evaluation of a formula, then specify the formula in the Formula box.
Table headers	By default, table headers are shown when a table block is created, but you can show/hide the table header(s) using this property.
Table footers	By default, table footers are not shown (unless a calculation is applied which we will discuss in later sessions of the course). You can manually show/hide the table footer(s) using this property.

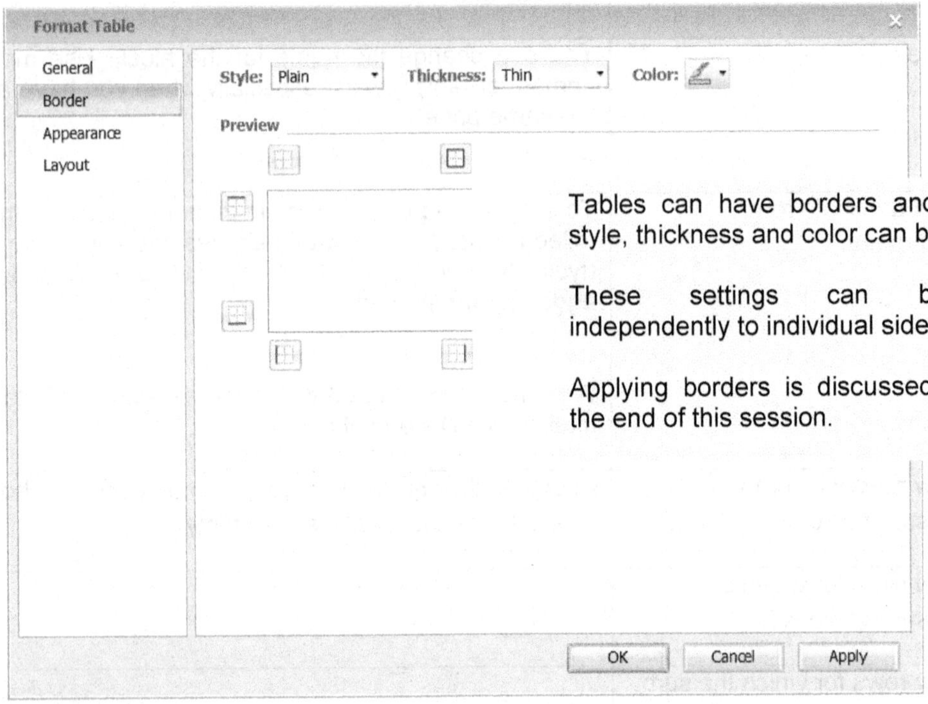
Format Table
General
Border
Appearance
Layout
Style: Plain
Thickness: Thin
Color:
Preview
OK
Cancel
Apply

Tables can have borders and the border style, thickness and color can be set.

These settings can be applied independently to individual sides of a table.

Applying borders is discussed in detail at the end of this session.

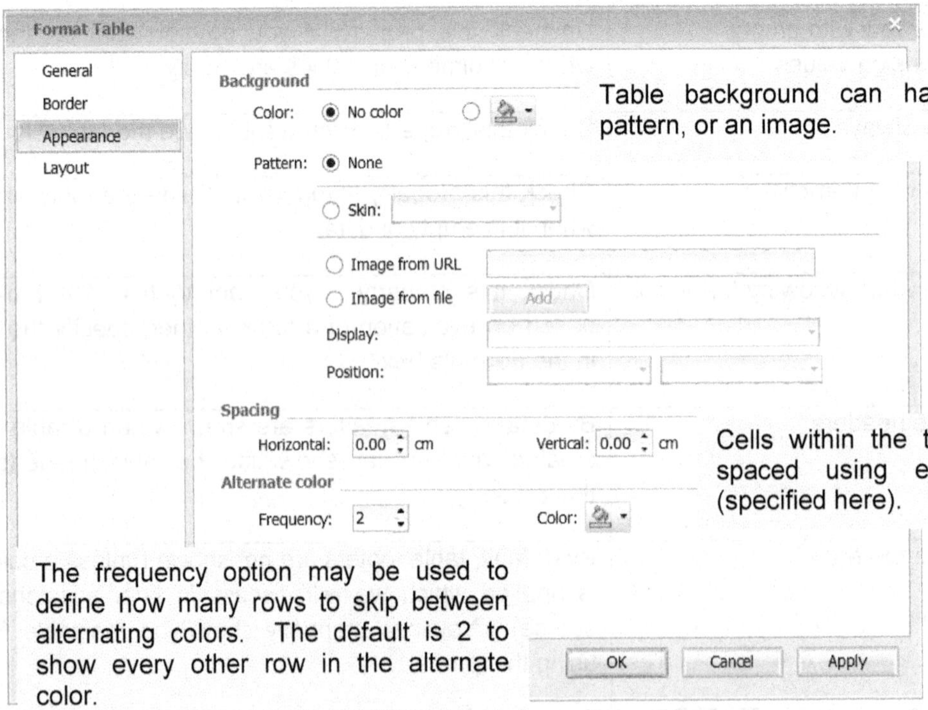
Format Table
General
Border
Appearance
Layout
Background
Color: No color
Pattern: None
Skin:
Image from URL
Image from file
Add
Display:
Position:
Spacing
Horizontal: 0.00 cm
Vertical: 0.00 cm
Alternate color
Frequency: 2
Color:
OK
Cancel
Apply

Table background can have a color, pattern, or an image.

Cells within the table can be spaced using empty space (specified here).

The frequency option may be used to define how many rows to skip between alternating colors. The default is 2 to show every other row in the alternate color.

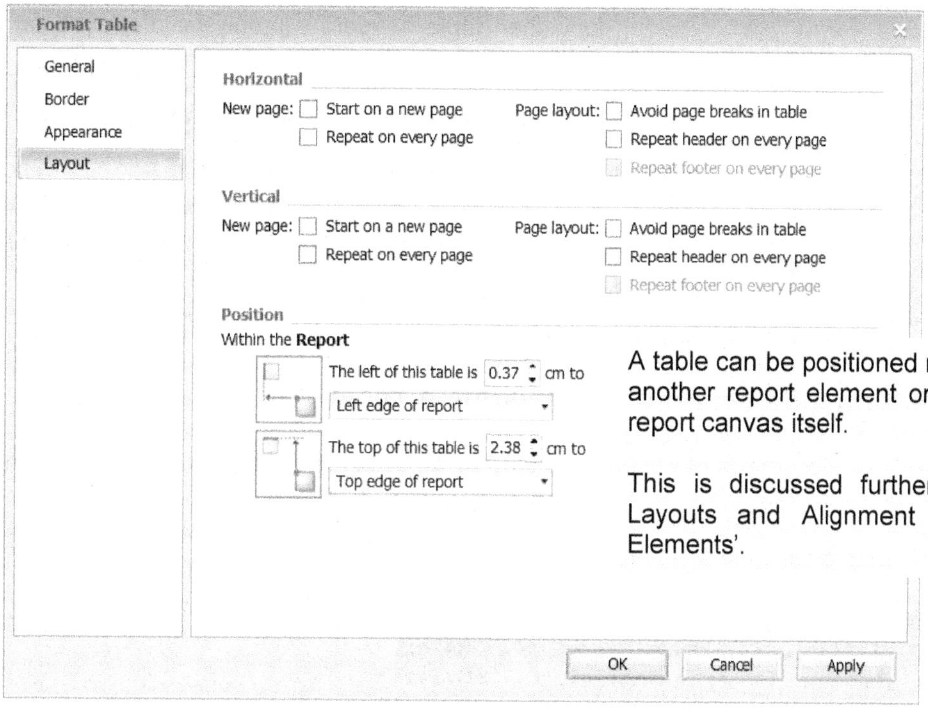
Format Table
General
Border
Appearance
Layout
Horizontal
New page: Start on a new page
Repeat on every page
Page layout: Avoid page breaks in table
Repeat header on every page
Repeat footer on every page
Vertical
New page: Start on a new page
Repeat on every page
Page layout: Avoid page breaks in table
Repeat header on every page
Repeat footer on every page
Position
Within the Report
The left of this table is 0.37 cm to
Left edge of report
The top of this table is 2.38 cm to
Top edge of report
OK
Cancel
Apply

A table can be positioned relatively to another report element or within the report canvas itself.

This is discussed further in 'Page Layouts and Alignment of Report Elements'.

Format Table – Layout Tab	**Description**
Horizontal *(going left to right when printed)*	A table can be forced to start on a new horizontal page. The table can be repeated on every horizontal page. If the table is going to break over two pages then this can be avoided by ticking 'Avoid page breaks in table'. The table header can be repeated on every horizontal page, i.e. if you have a report that is 2 pages wide and 10 pages long then table headers will only be displayed on pages 1 and 2, but you can have the header repeat on every page. If footers are being displayed then the same can be specified for the footers. *Note – When exporting data (say to Excel) the headers/footers will only be exported once per table block.*
Vertical *(going top to bottom when printed)*	A table can be forced to start on a new vertical page. The table can be repeated on every vertical page. If the table is going to break over two pages then this can be avoided by ticking 'Avoid page breaks in table'. The table header can be repeated on every vertical page, i.e. if you have a report that is 1 page wide and 10 pages

	long then table headers will only be displayed on page 1, but you can have the header repeat on every page. If footers are being displayed then the same can be specified for the footers. *Note – When exporting data (say to Excel) the headers/footers will only be exported once per table block.*

10.4 Formatting a Selection of Cells within a Table Block

A range of cells can be formatted simultaneously by selecting them first and then changing required properties.

Create the following block in new report tab within your document.

Year	State	Quantity sold	Sales revenu	Margin
2004	California	11,304	$1,704,211	$774,893
2004	Colorado	2,971	$448,302	$203,701
2004	DC	4,681	$693,211	$310,356
2004	Florida	2,585	$405,985	$192,479

Now, we would like to modify the background color of the columns **[Quantity sold]** and **[Margin]**.

1. Click in any body cell of **[Quantity sold]** column to select the cells in this column.

Year	State	Quantity sold	Sales revenu	Margin
2004	California	11,304	$1,704,211	$774,893
2004	Colorado	2,971	$448,302	$203,701
2004	DC	4,681	$693,211	$310,356
2004	Florida	2,585	$405,985	$192,479

2. Hold down the **<Ctrl>** key and then click in any body cell of the **[Margin]** column. We now have both columns selected.

Year	State	Quantity sold	Sales revenu	Margin
2004	California	11,304	$1,704,211	$774,893
2004	Colorado	2,971	$448,302	$203,701
2004	DC	4,681	$693,211	$310,356
2004	Florida	2,585	$405,985	$192,479

NOTE – **<Ctrl>** key is used to select a discontinuous range of cells (as shown above).

If you want to select a continuous range of columns then you can use the **<Shift>** key.

Example

1. Click in [Quantity sold] body cell
2. Hold down <Shift> key
3. Click in [Margin] body cell
4. Web Intelligence will select [Quantity sold], [Sales revenue] and [Margin] columns

3. Now select a color for the cell background.

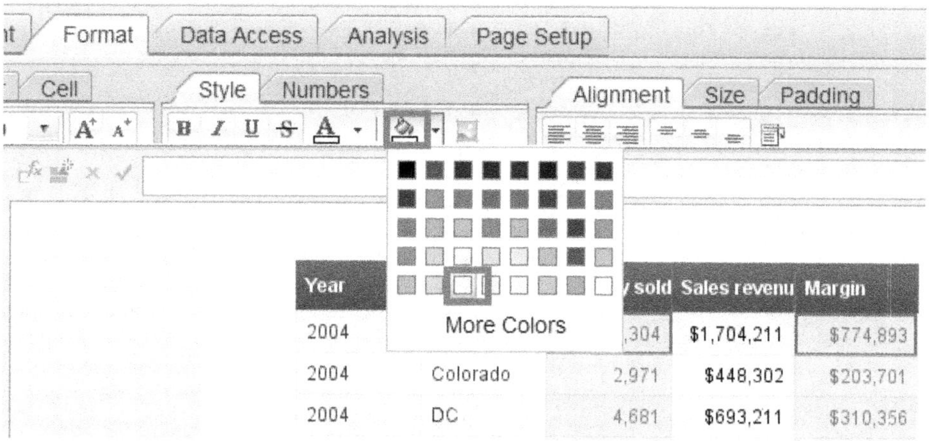
Format
Data Access
Analysis
Page Setup
Cell
Style
Numbers
Alignment
Size
Padding
More Colors
Year
sold
Sales revenu
Margin
2004
,304
$1,704,211
$774,893
2004
Colorado
2,971
$448,302
$203,701
2004
DC
4,681
$693,211
$310,356

4. Background color has been changed for the selected cells.

Year	State	Quantity sold	Sales revenu	Margin
2004	California	11,304	$1,704,211	$774,893
2004	Colorado	2,971	$448,302	$203,701
2004	DC	4,681	$693,211	$310,356
2004	Florida	2,585	$405,985	$192,479

10.5 Using Turn Into

It only takes a few clicks to change a block from one type to another (e.g. turning a vertical table into a cross table or a chart).

1. Right-click anywhere on the existing block and then select the block type you want to change to:

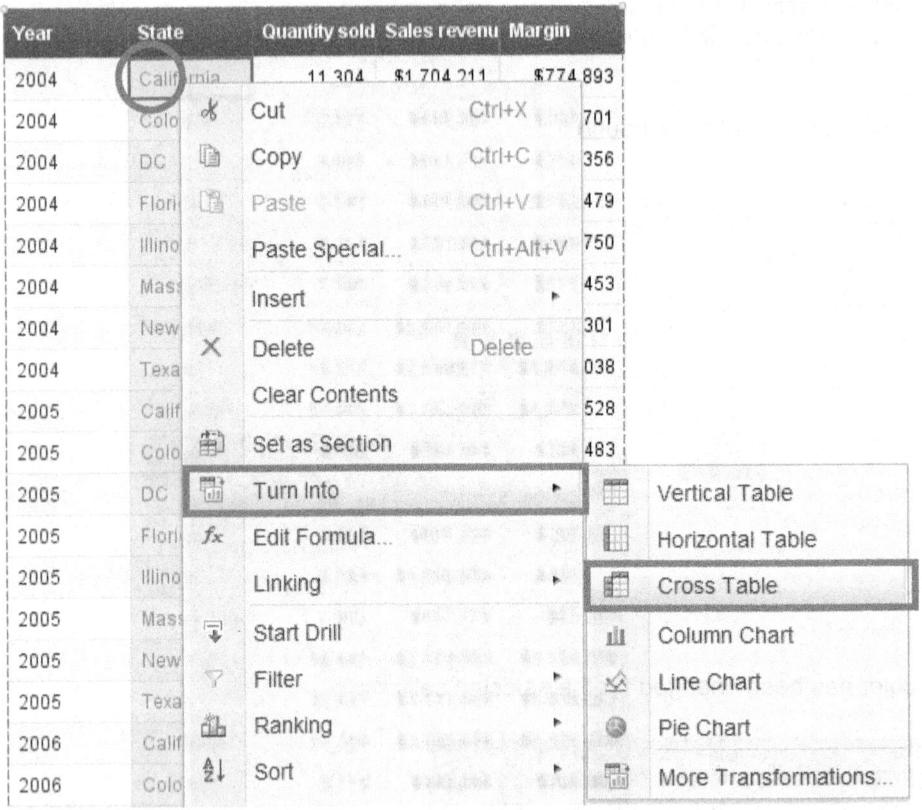
Year
State
Quantity sold
Sales revenu
Margin
Cut Ctrl+X
Copy Ctrl+C
Paste Ctrl+V
Paste Special... Ctrl+Alt+V
Insert
Delete Delete
Clear Contents
Set as Section
Turn Into
Edit Formula...
Linking
Start Drill
Filter
Ranking
Sort
Vertical Table
Horizontal Table
Cross Table
Column Chart
Line Chart
Pie Chart
More Transformations...

2. The vertical table has been turned into a cross table.

	2004			2005		
California	11,304	$1,704,211	$774,893	17,001	$2,782,680	$1,076,528
Colorado	2,971	$448,302	$203,701	4,700	$768,390	$294,483
DC	4,681	$693,211	$310,356	7,572	$1,215,158	$457,231
Florida	2,585	$405,985	$192,479	3,852	$661,250	$266,670
Illinois	4,713	$737,914	$348,750	6,744	$1,150,659	$465,478
Massachuse	1,505	$238,819	$111,453	902	$157,719	$63,657
New York	10,802	$1,667,696	$779,301	16,447	$2,763,503	$1,104,278
Texas	14,517	$2,199,677	$1,011,038	22,637	$3,732,889	$1,459,562

10.6 Insert a Block from a Template

Another way to insert a new table block is to drag a template into the report area. The template will appear in the report ready for objects to be dropped on to it in order to be display relevant data.

1. Insert a new report tab into your document for this example.

   From the Report Element toolbox select 'Define Cross Table'

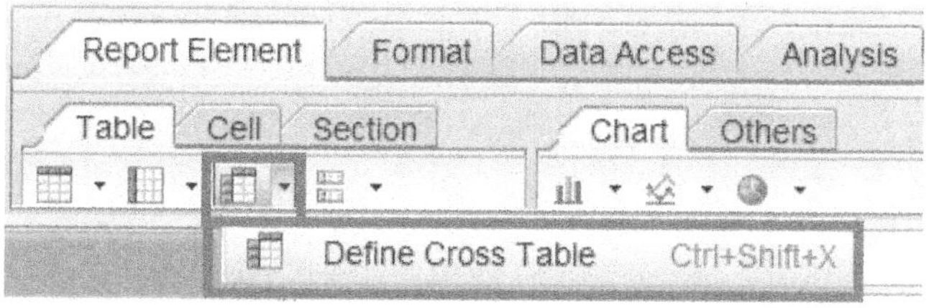
Report Element
Format
Data Access
Analysis
Table
Cell
Section
Chart
Others
Define Cross Table
Ctrl+Shift+X

   Or right-click on any part of the report and select 'Insert – Cross Table'.

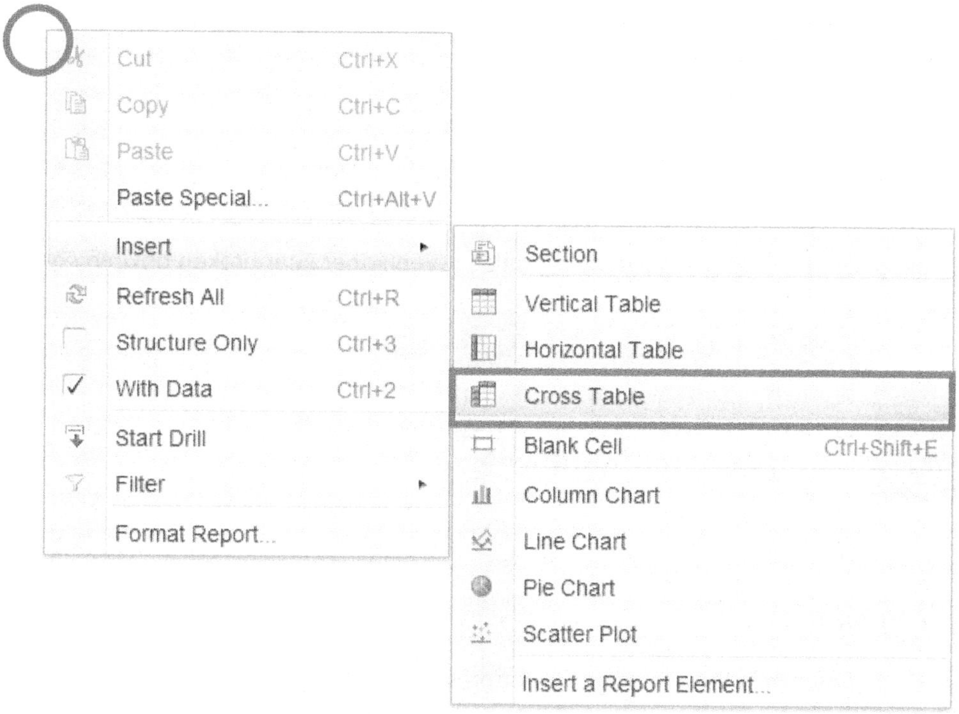
Cut Ctrl+X
Copy Ctrl+C
Paste Ctrl+V
Paste Special... Ctrl+Alt+V
Insert
Refresh All Ctrl+R
Structure Only Ctrl+3
With Data Ctrl+2
Start Drill
Filter
Format Report...
Section
Vertical Table
Horizontal Table
Cross Table
Blank Cell Ctrl+Shift+E
Column Chart
Line Chart
Pie Chart
Scatter Plot
Insert a Report Element...

2. Drag and drop the template onto the report page.

Click to insert the table here or Esc to cancel.

3. Drag and drop [Year] into the left part of the template (as shown below).

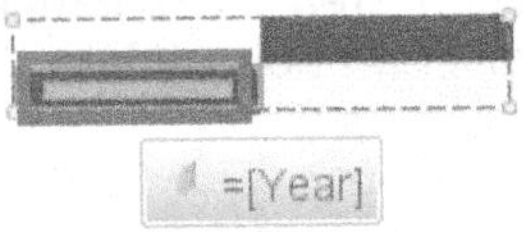
=[Year]

4. Drag and drop [Quarter] into the top part of the template (as shown below).

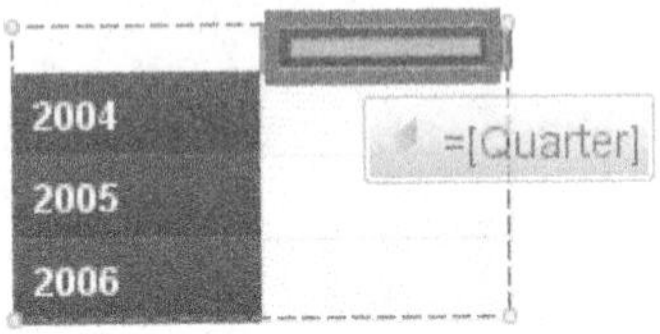
2004
2005
2006
=[Quarter]

5. Drag and drop [Sales revenue] into the centre part of the template (as shown below).

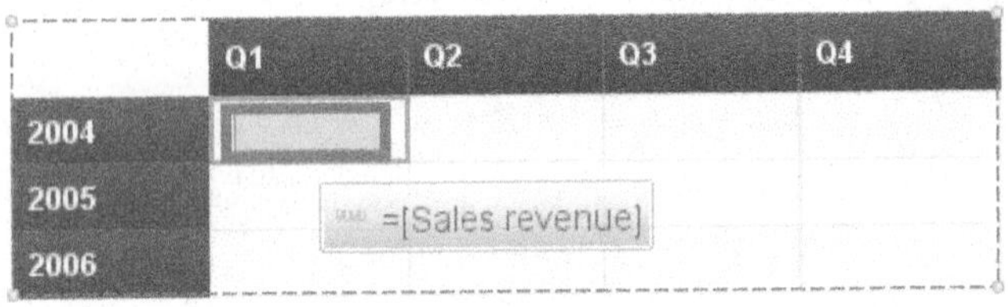
Q1
Q2
Q3
Q4
2004
2005
2006
=[Sales revenue]

We have now created a Cross Table showing sales revenue per year broken down by quarters.

	Q1	Q2	Q3	Q4
2004	$2,660,700	$2,278,693	$1,367,841	$1,788,580
2005	$3,326,172	$2,840,651	$2,879,303	$4,186,120
2006	$3,742,989	$4,006,718	$3,953,395	$3,356,041

10.7 Table Templates

Four table types are provided in Web Intelligence for presenting data in tabular format.

10.7.1 Vertical Table

Year	State	Quantity sold
2004	California	11,304
2004	Colorado	2,971
2004	DC	4,681
2004	Florida	2,585
2004	Illinois	4,713
2004	Massachusetts	1,505

Vertical Table is the default table template used by Web Intelligence.

A row represents a record (or line) of data.

From this template we can convert to any other format (as described previously).

10.7.2 Horizontal Table

Year	2004	2004	2004	2004	2004	2004
State	California	Colorado	DC	Florida	Illinois	Massachusetts
Quantity sold	11,304	2,971	4,681	2,585	4,713	1,505

Horizontal Tables are opposite to Vertical Tables in that a row of data (in a vertical table) is presented as a column of data instead. The header column is on the left-hand side and the footer column is on the right-hand side.

10.7.3 Cross Table

	2004	2005	2006
California	11,304	17,001	17,769
Colorado	2,971	4,700	5,116
DC	4,681	7,572	6,491
Florida	2,585	3,852	4,830
Illinois	4,713	6,744	6,519
Massachusetts	1,505	902	5,269
New York	10,802	16,447	19,109
Texas	14,517	22,637	25,193

Pivot tables are known as 'Cross Tables'.

Cross Tables are typically used with two dimensions and one measure (as shown here), but multiple dimensions can be used on both axes as well as multiple measures in the cross table body.

10.7.4 Form

Year	2004
State	California
Quantity sold	11,304

Year	2004
State	Colorado
Quantity sold	2,971

Year	2004
State	DC
Quantity sold	4,681

Forms present the data from a single row of data into a record like structure.

Possibly useful for information such as employee details, product detail and other 'record' type data.

However, the fields in the form cannot be laid out individually across the page, therefore limiting the presentation (as shown here).

Not friendly for large volumes of data that is to be navigated online.

But forms can be used to display data in layouts which are different to Vertical, Horizontal and Cross Tables (as shown below):

Year	2004	Quantity sold	11,304	Margin	$774,893
State	California	Sales revenue	$1,704,211	Discount	$495,472

Year	2004	Quantity sold	2,971	Margin	$203,701
State	Colorado	Sales revenue	$448,302	Discount	$104,654

Year	2004	Quantity sold	4,681	Margin	$310,356
State	DC	Sales revenue	$693,211	Discount	$195,644

10.8 Formatting Cross Tables

For spreadsheet users, Cross Tables are similar to pivot tables.

Cross Tables have a few extra formatting properties compared to Vertical and Horizontal Tables.

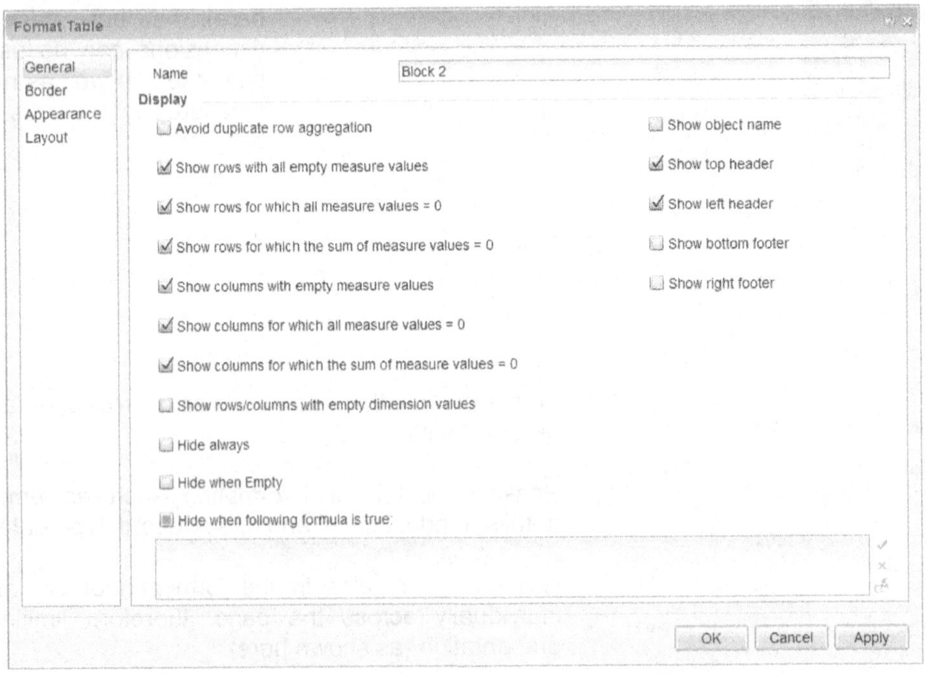
Format Table
General
Border
Appearance
Layout
Name
Block 2
Display
Avoid duplicate row aggregation
Show rows with all empty measure values
Show rows for which all measure values = 0
Show rows for which the sum of measure values = 0
Show columns with empty measure values
Show columns for which all measure values = 0
Show columns for which the sum of measure values = 0
Show rows/columns with empty dimension values
Hide always
Hide when Empty
Hide when following formula is true:
Show object name
Show top header
Show left header
Show bottom footer
Show right footer
OK
Cancel
Apply

Format Cross Table – General Tab	Description
Show object name	The default view for Cross Tables is to not display the object names (i.e. the row and column headings). Check this property to show the object names.
Show rows/columns with empty dimension values	Uncheck this property if you do not want to show rows or columns where all dimension values are empty.

Format Cross Table – General Tab	Description
Show top header	Check this property to display the top header, uncheck to hide.
Show left header	Check this property to display the left header, uncheck to hide.
Show bottom footer	Check this property to display the bottom footer (i.e. column totals), uncheck to hide.
Show right footer	Check this property to display the right footer (i.e. row totals), uncheck to hide.

10.9 Inserting Free Standing Template Cells

Some formulas that are commonly used in Free Standing Cells are available to drag and drop straight onto the report canvas.

1. Click on 'Last Refresh Date' as shown below:

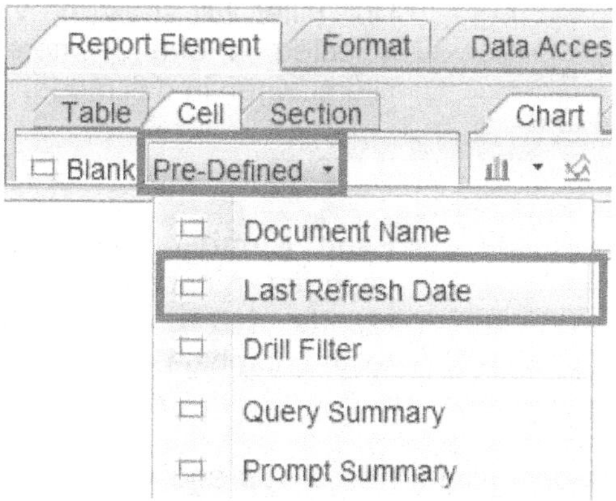
Report Element
Format
Data Acces
Table
Cell
Section
Chart
Blank
Pre-Defined
Document Name
Last Refresh Date
Drill Filter
Query Summary
Prompt Summary

2. Drag and drop the template cell onto the report canvas.

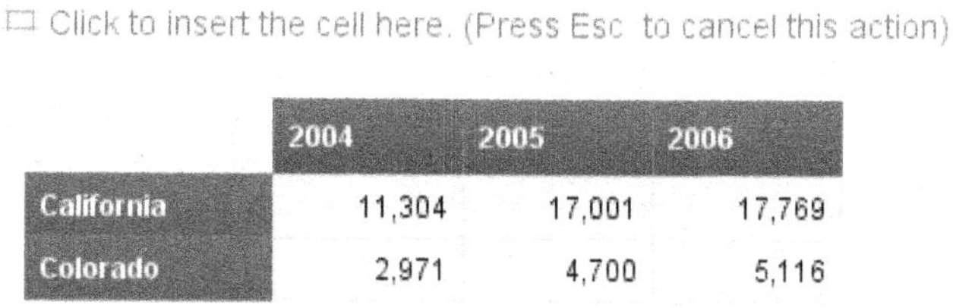
Click to insert the cell here. (Press Esc to cancel this action)
2004
2005
2006
California
11,304
17,001
17,769
Colorado
2,971
4,700
5,116

3. Web Intelligence will display the relevant content in the cell.

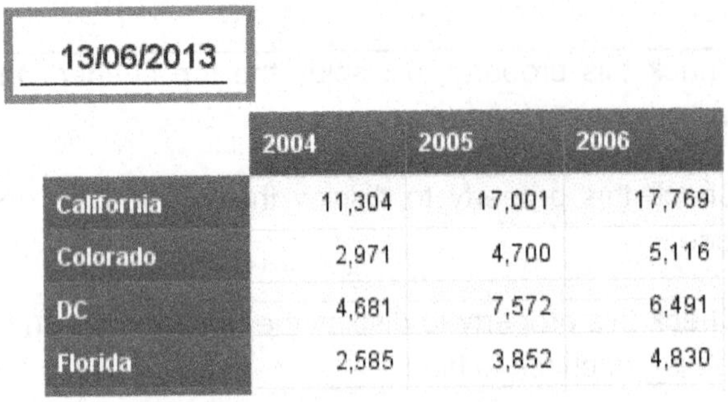
13/06/2013

	2004	2005	2006
California	11,304	17,001	17,769
Colorado	2,971	4,700	5,116
DC	4,681	7,572	6,491
Florida	2,585	3,852	4,830

Free-Standing Cells use functions provided in Web Intelligence (e.g. **Last Refresh Date**).

Formulas and functions are discussed in later sessions.

The following Free-Standing Cells are available (we will use them in later sessions):

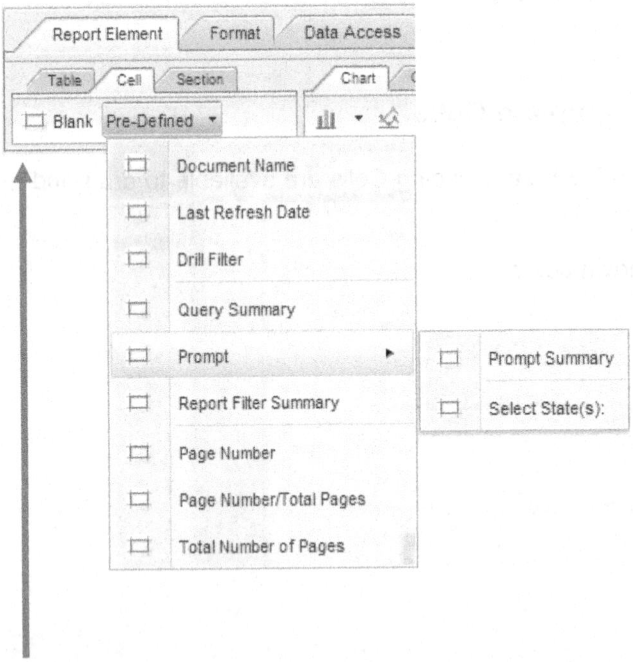
Report Element
Format
Data Access
Table
Cell
Section
Chart
Blank
Pre-Defined
Document Name
Last Refresh Date
Drill Filter
Query Summary
Prompt
Prompt Summary
Select State(s):
Report Filter Summary
Page Number
Page Number/Total Pages
Total Number of Pages

Document Name will show the name of the overall Web Intelligence document (not the name of an individual report tab).

Last Refresh Date will show the last time the report was refreshed.

Drill Filter will show the values selected in one or more drill filters (when in drill mode).

Page Number Cells can be used for numbering pages in reports. **NOTE** – Each tab will restart numbering from 1.

Blank Cell is an empty cell that can be dropped onto the canvas and then used to display results of manually defined/formulas, or to display an image as a logo, etc.

The other cells are useful for displaying information about the document, as described below:

Query Summary gives details of every query within the document and associated information:

Report Filter Summary gives details of any filters applied throughout the Web Intelligence document, i.e. on every report tab. Very useful but it can show a lot of information if a document contains many tabs and blocks, etc.

Prompt Summary provides information about user supplied values to query prompts.

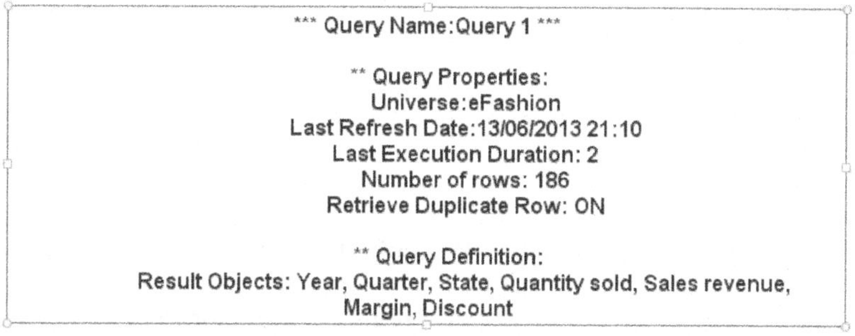
*** Query Name:Query 1 ***
** Query Properties:
Universe:eFashion
Last Refresh Date:13/06/2013 21:10
Last Execution Duration: 2
Number of rows: 186
Retrieve Duplicate Row: ON
** Query Definition:
Result Objects: Year, Quarter, State, Quantity sold, Sales revenue, Margin, Discount

If you have other prompts then they will be listed underneath 'Prompt Summary', for example we have shown one below:

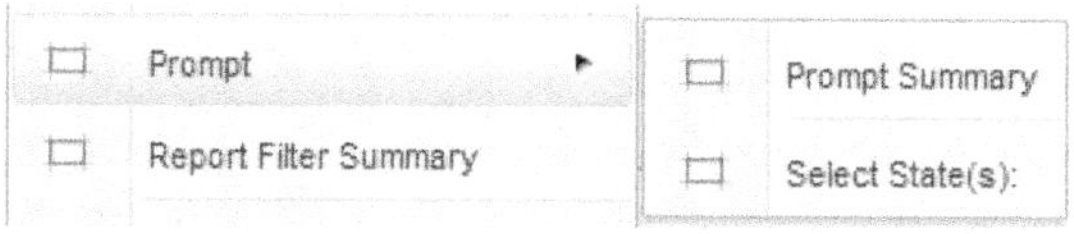
Prompt
Report Filter Summary
Prompt Summary
Select State(s):

NOTE – Apart from the Blank Cell, all of the other Template Cells use standard Web Intelligence functions. These cells can be used 'as-is' or the formulas in these cells can be modified to suit individual requirements.

10.10 Formatting Borders

Borders can applied to lots of different types of report elements and the general concept is the same irrespective of the element being formatted.

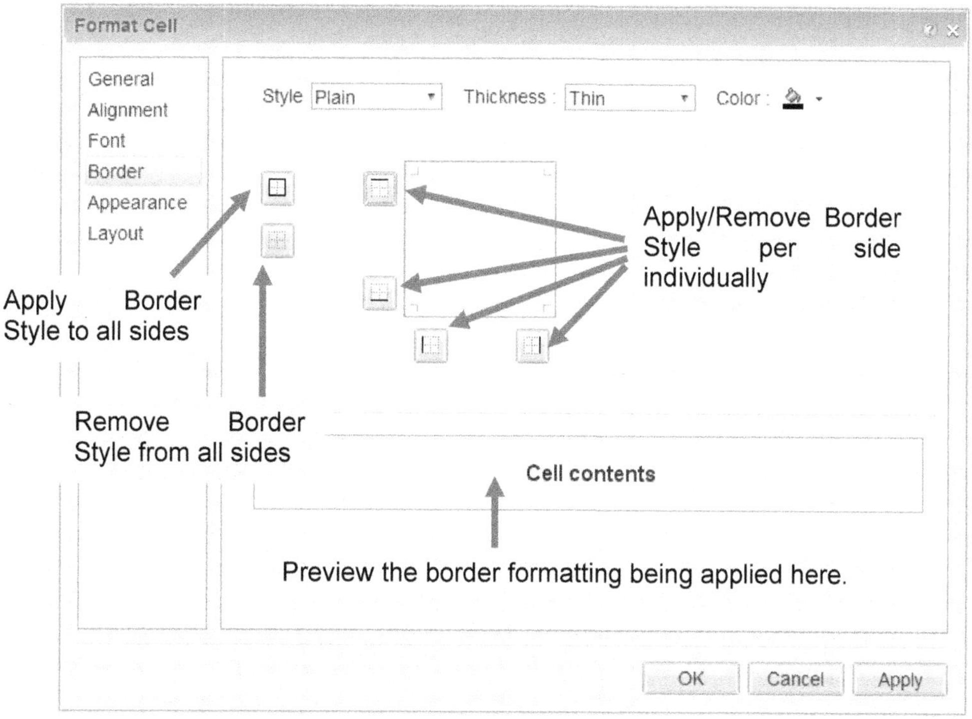
Format Cell
General
Alignment
Font
Border
Appearance
Layout
Style Plain
Thickness : Thin
Color :
Apply/Remove Border Style per side individually
Apply Border Style to all sides
Remove Border Style from all sides
Cell contents
Preview the border formatting being applied here.
OK
Cancel
Apply

To apply a border:

1. Select the Style
2. Select the Thickness
3. Select the Color
4. Click on individual side buttons or on all sides button
5. Click on 'Apply'
6. Close box by clicking on 'OK'

You can also turn on/off individual border lines (left, right, top, bottom).

To remove border select Style of 'None' or click on Preview button showing no border.

11 Using Standard Calculations

The Standard Calculations list on the Analysis toolbox enables you to use quick calculations in tables and cross tables within Web Intelligence reports.

This session demonstrates Standard Calculation functions and their use within documents.

Let us start with a new document containing the following query using the 'eFashion' universe:

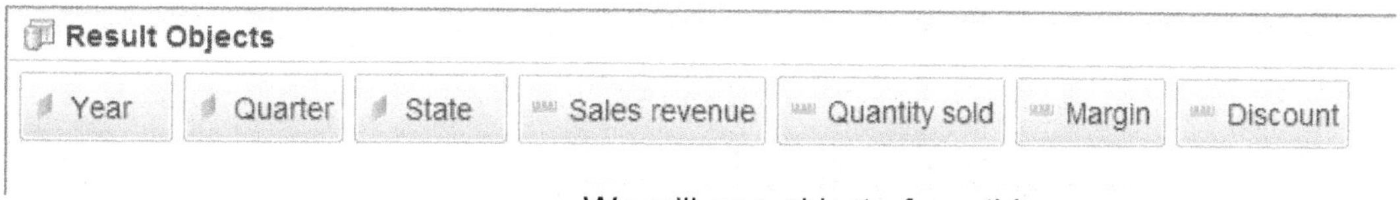
Result Objects
Year
Quarter
State
Sales revenue
Quantity sold
Margin
Discount

We will use objects from this query in examples during this session.

11.1 What are Standard Calculations?

Standard Calculations are the functions available from the Calculations list shown below. They are located in the Analysis toolbox.

Calculate the **Sum** of the selected number object.

Count all rows for a measure object or count distinct rows for a dimension (or detail) object.

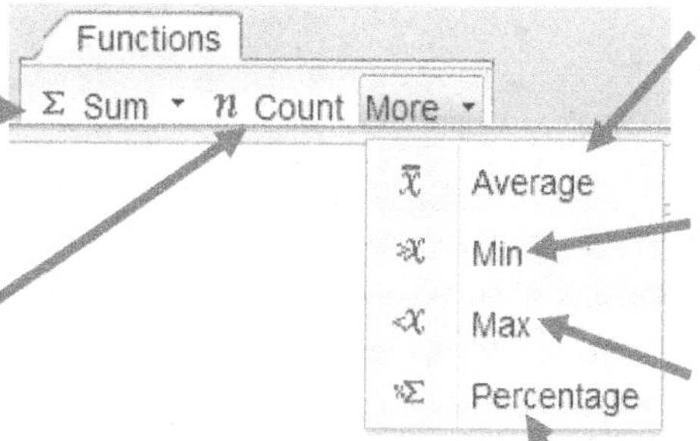
Functions
Σ Sum
Count
More
Average
Min
Max
Percentage

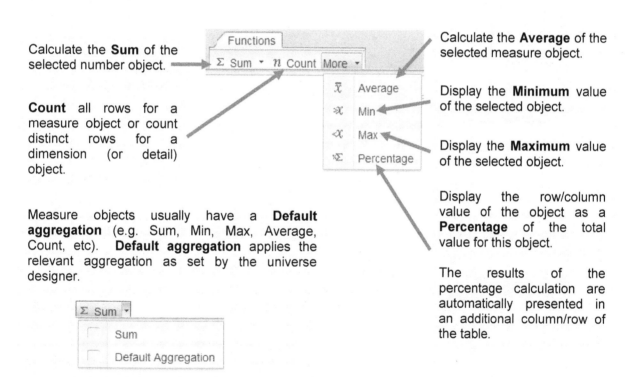

Calculate the **Average** of the selected measure object.

Display the **Minimum** value of the selected object.

Display the **Maximum** value of the selected object.

Display the row/column value of the object as a **Percentage** of the total value for this object.

The results of the percentage calculation are automatically presented in an additional column/row of the table.

Measure objects usually have a **Default aggregation** (e.g. Sum, Min, Max, Average, Count, etc). **Default aggregation** applies the relevant aggregation as set by the universe designer.

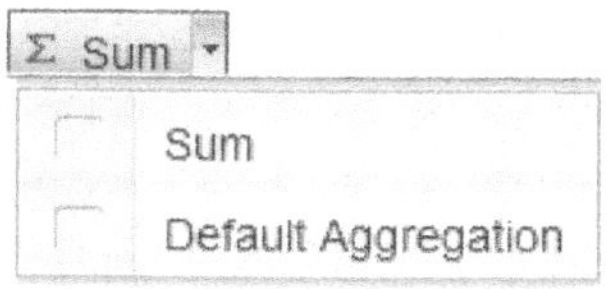
Σ Sum
Sum
Default Aggregation

Depending on the object type (i.e. text, date, or number) some of the above calculations cannot be applied (e.g. Sum cannot be applied to an object containing text values).

When a text object is selected then the Standard Calculations available are Count, Min and Max.

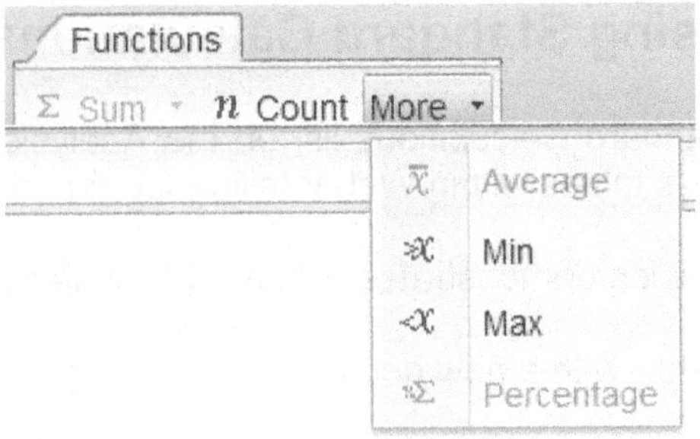
Functions
Sum
Count
More
Average
Min
Max
Percentage

11.2 Applying Standard Calculations

Standard Calculations are applied by first selecting the object of interest (i.e. the column/row in a table/cross table) and then selecting one of the available calculation functions to use.

1. Select the object of interest in table (or cross table) and then the Standard Calculation function to apply.

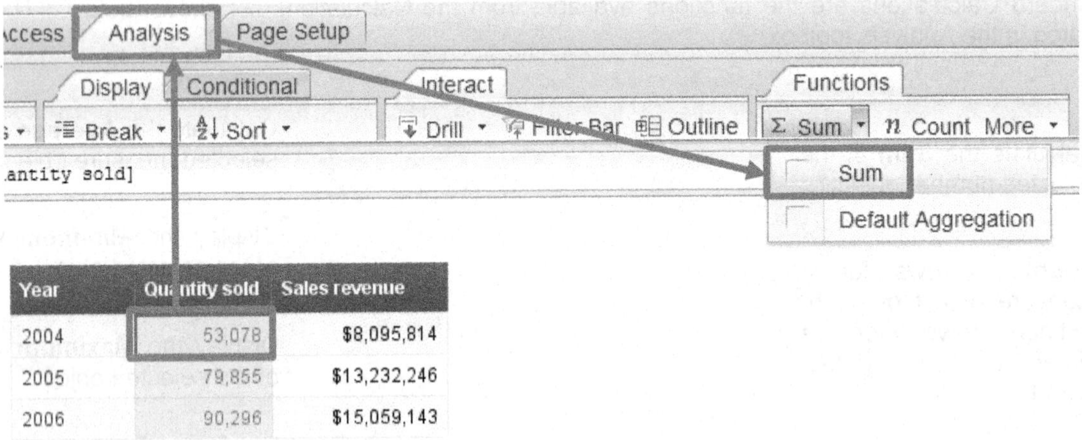
Analysis
Page Setup
Display
Conditional
Interact
Functions
Break
Sort
Drill
Outline
Sum
Count
More
Sum
Default Aggregation
Year
Sales revenue
2004
53,078
$8,095,814
2005
79,855
$13,232,246
2006
90,296
$15,059,143

2. New row is added showing the result of the applied calculation with a default label, in this case 'Sum:'

Year	Quantity sold	Sales revenue
2004	53,078	$8,095,814
2005	79,855	$13,232,246
2006	90,296	$15,059,143
Sum:	**223,229**	

3. Formatting can be applied to the new row if required.

Year	Quantity sold	Sales revenue
2004	53,078	$8,095,814
2005	79,855	$13,232,246
2006	90,296	$15,059,143
Total:	223,229	

To type in a table cell simply double click in the cell and then type.

e.g. Double click in the cell containing 'Sum:' and type 'Total:' and then press <Enter>.

11.3 Applying Multiple Standard Calculations

Multiple Standard Calculations can be applied to the same object if required. Simply select the object of interest, apply first calculation, apply second calculation, etc.

Year	Quantity sold	Sales revenue
2004	53,078	$8,095,814
2005	79,855	$13,232,246
2006	90,296	$15,059,143
Total:	223,229	
Count:	3	
Average:	74,410	
Min:	53,078	
Max:	90,296	

Example shows multiple Standard Calculations applied to [Quantity sold] column in a vertical table.

11.4 Applying the Percentage Standard Calculation

When the Percentage calculation is applied it results in a new column being created to show the value of each row (for the selected object) as a percentage of the total (for the selected object).

Year	Quantity sold	Percentage:	Sales revenue
2004	53,078	23.78%	$8,095,814
2005	79,855	35.77%	$13,232,246
2006	90,296	40.45%	$15,059,143
Total:	223,229		
Count:	3		
Average:	74,410		
Min:	53,078		
Max:	90,296		
	Percentage:	100.00%	

Applying the **Percentage** Standard Calculation on [Quantity sold] results in a new column being added called Percentage.

The value in each row of the Percentage column is based on the row value of the object as a percentage of the total for the object, i.e.

53,078 / 223,229 = 23.78%
79,855 / 223,229 = 35.77%
90,296 / 223,229 = 40.45%

11.5 Applying Standard Calculations to Cross Tables

When Standard Calculations are applied to cross tables then by default you get the calculations applied in both directions (columns and rows).

1. We have a simple cross table (create this on a new report tab).

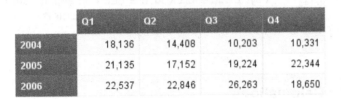

	Q1	Q2	Q3	Q4
2004	18,136	14,408	10,203	10,331
2005	21,135	17,152	19,224	22,344
2006	22,537	22,846	26,263	18,650

2. Select an object from the body (here we have [Quantity sold]) and apply a Standard Calculation, such as Sum.

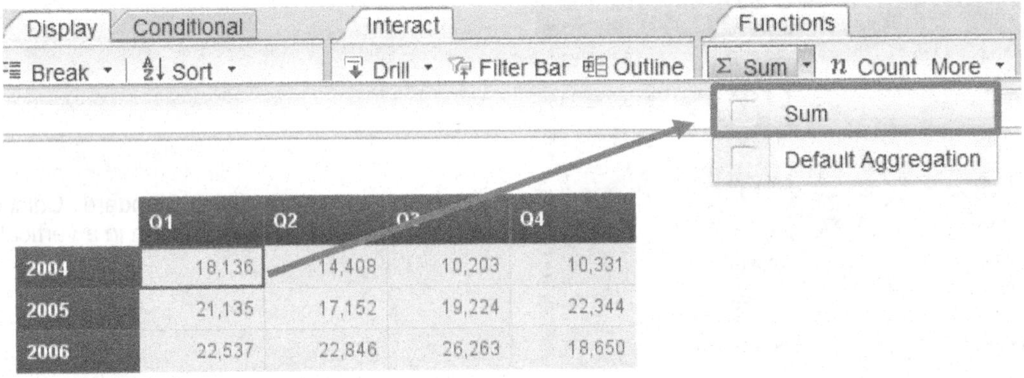
Display
Conditional
Interact
Functions
Break
Sort
Drill
Filter Bar
Outline
Σ Sum
Count
More
Sum
Default Aggregation
Q1
Q2
Q4
2004
2005
2006
18,136
14,408
10,203
10,331
21,135
17,152
19,224
22,344
22,537
22,846
26,263
18,650

3. A dialog box will appear requesting in which direction you want to apply the calculation. Select 'In both directions'.

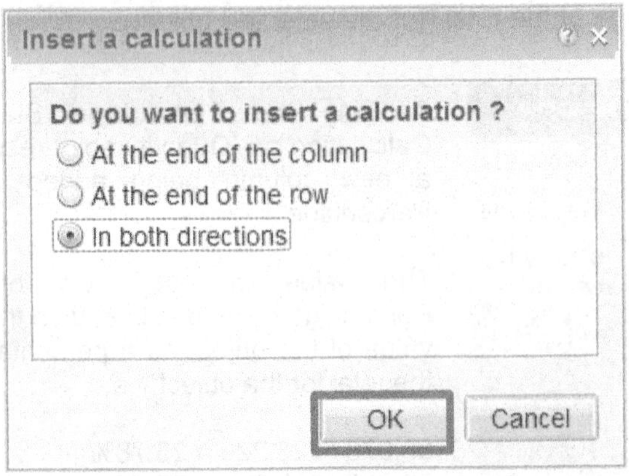
Insert a calculation
Do you want to insert a calculation ?
At the end of the column
At the end of the row
In both directions
OK
Cancel

4. The calculation will be applied in both directions:

	Q1	Q2	Q3	Q4	Sum:
2004	18,136	14,408	10,203	10,331	**53,078**
2005	21,135	17,152	19,224	22,344	**79,855**
2006	22,537	22,846	26,263	18,650	**90,296**
Sum:	**61,808**	**54,406**	**55,690**	**51,325**	**223,229**

A grand total for rows and columns will also be shown when 'In both directions' is selected.

11.6 Applying the Percentage Standard Calculation to Cross Tables

When the Percentage Standard Calculation is applied to a cross table (in both directions) then it results in new columns and new rows being created to show:

1. The values of each row cell (for selected object) as a percentage of the row total (for selected object).

2. The values of each column cell (for selected object) as a percentage of the column total (for selected object).

Using the previous example, we have now used the Percentage Standard Calculation on the [Quantity Sold] measure. The results are as follows:

	Q1	Percentage:	Q2	Percentage:	Q3	Percentage:	Q4	Percentage:	Sum:	
2004	18,136	29.34%	14,408	26.48%	10,203	18.32%	10,331	20.13%	**53,078**	**Percentage:**
Percentage:	34.17%		27.14%		19.22%		19.46%			**100.00%**
2005	21,135	34.19%	17,152	31.53%	19,224	34.52%	22,344	43.53%	**79,855**	**Percentage:**
Percentage:	26.47%		21.48%		24.07%		27.98%			**100.00%**
2006	22,537	36.46%	22,846	41.99%	26,263	47.16%	18,650	36.34%	**90,296**	**Percentage:**
Percentage:	24.96%		25.30%		29.09%		20.65%			**100.00%**
Sum:	**61,808**		**54,406**		**55,690**		**51,325**		**223,229**	
		100.00%		**100.00%**		**100.00%**		**100.00%**		

If we take the column for Q1 then its Percentage column is the one immediately next to it on the right hand side.

The total for column Q1 is 61,808 and therefore we have its percentages calculated as:

[Year 2004] = 18,136 / 61,808 = 29.34 %
[Year 2005] = 21,135 / 61,808 = 34.19 %
[Year 2006] = 22,537 / 61,808 = 36.46 %

The total of these percentages = 29.34 % + 34.19 % + 36.46 % = 99.99 % (with the 0.01 % being a rounding issue due to 2 decimal places being used for display purposes).

Likewise, if we take the row for 2004 then its Percentage row is the one immediately below it.

The total for the row for 2004 is 53,078 and therefore we have its percentages calculated as:

[Quarter Q1] = 18,136 / 53,078 = 34.17 %
[Quarter Q2] = 14,408 / 53,078 = 27.14 %
[Quarter Q3] = 10,203 / 53,078 = 19.22 %
[Quarter Q4] = 10,331 / 53,078 = 19.46 %

The total of these percentages = 34.17 % + 27.14 % + 19.22 % + 19.46 % = 99.99 % (with the 0.01 % being a rounding issue due to 2 decimal places being used for display purposes).

11.7 Folding/Unfolding Data in Tables and Cross Tables

The 'Outline' mode enables you to collapse and expand tables to show or hide rows/columns (within a vertical table or a cross table).

Let us first try this with the existing vertical table we have in our document (on Report 1 tab).

1. First activate the 'Outline' mode by clicking on the Outline button on the Analysis toolbox.

Interact
Drill
Filter Bar
Outline

This will activate the Outline mode to the left of the report:

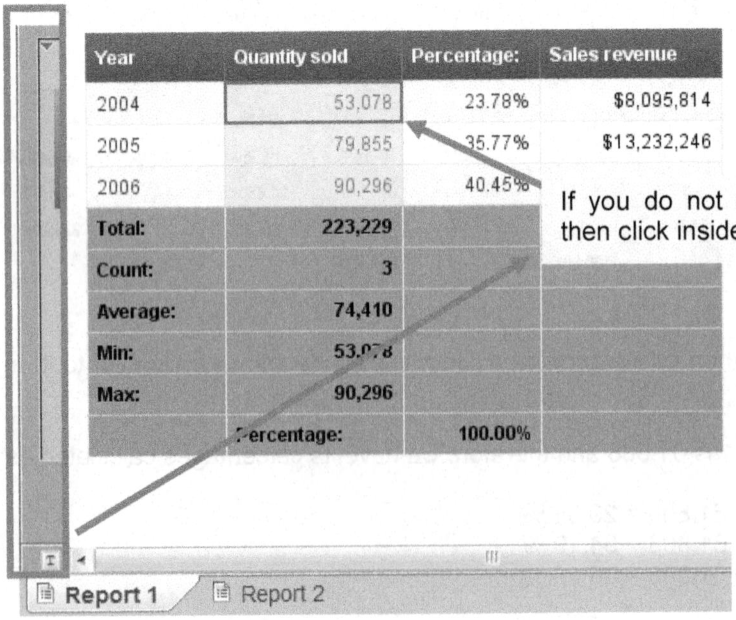
Year
Quantity sold
Percentage:
Sales revenue
2004
53,078
23.78%
$8,095,814
2005
79,855
35.77%
$13,232,246
2006
90,296
40.45%
Total:
223,229
Count:
3
Average:
74,410
Min:
Max:
90,296
100.00%
Report 1
Report 2

If you do not see 'T' in Outline mode then click inside any cell within the table.

2. Click on 'T' or the arrow to fold the table rows:

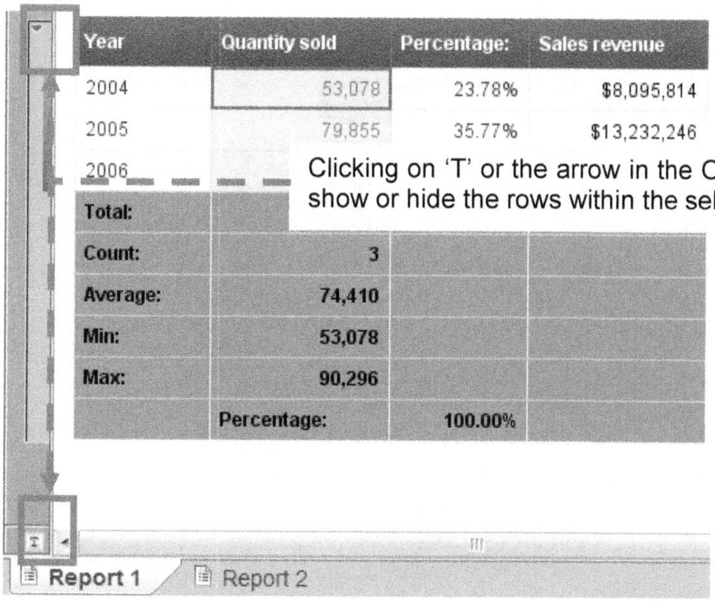
Year
Quantity sold
Percentage:
Sales revenue
2004
53,078
23.78%
$8,095,814
2005
79,855
35.77%
$13,232,246
2006
Clicking on 'T' or the arrow in the Outline bar will show or hide the rows within the selected table.
Total:
Count:
3
Average:
74,410
Min:
53,078
Max:
90,296
Percentage:
100.00%
Report 1
Report 2

NOTE – 'T' signifies the 'Top' level fold, i.e. folds everything within the table.

3. Web Intelligence will fold the body rows in the table and display only the footer rows showing totals.

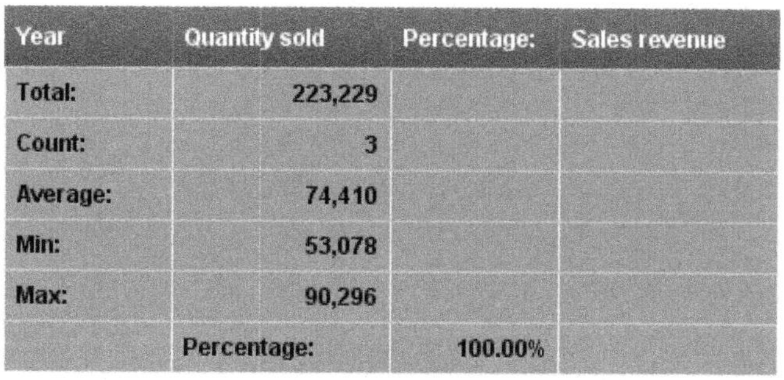

Year	Quantity sold	Percentage:	Sales revenue
Total:	223,229		
Count:	3		
Average:	74,410		
Min:	53,078		
Max:	90,296		
	Percentage:	100.00%	

4. The table can then be unfolded to display detail rows again (as shown below):

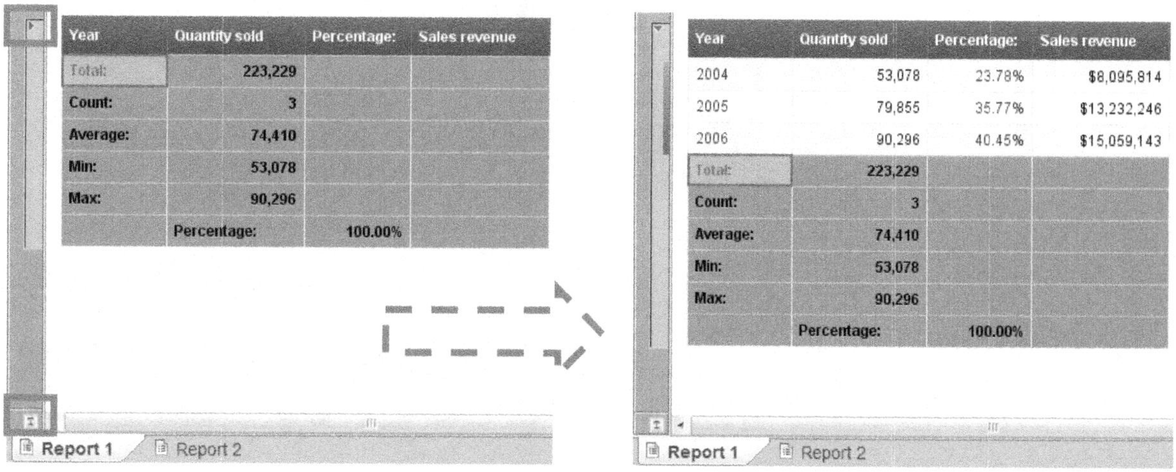
Year
Quantity sold
Percentage:
Sales revenue
Total:
223,229
Count:
3
Average:
74,410
Min:
53,078
Max:
90,296
Percentage:
100.00%
Report 1
Report 2
Year
Quantity sold
Percentage:
Sales revenue
2004
53,078
23.78%
$8,095,814
2005
79,855
35.77%
$13,232,246
2006
90,296
40.45%
$15,059,143
Total:
223,229
Count:
3
Average:
74,410
Min:
53,078
Max:
90,296
Percentage:
100.00%
Report 1
Report 2

Let us now try Outline mode with a cross table.

1. Create a new cross table as shown below:

	Q1	Q2	Q3	Q4	Sum:
2004	18,136	14,408	10,203	10,331	**53,078**
2005	21,135	17,152	19,224	22,344	**79,855**
2006	22,537	22,846	26,263	18,650	**90,296**
Sum:	**61,808**	**54,406**	**55,690**	**51,325**	**223,229**

2. Switch to Outline mode:

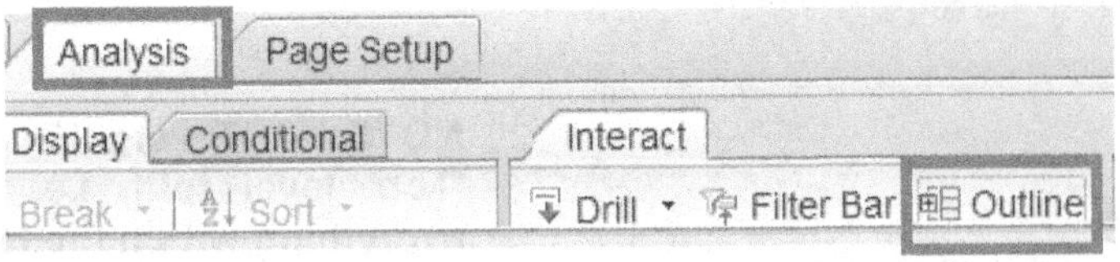
Analysis
Page Setup
Display
Conditional
Interact
Break
Sort
Drill
Filter Bar
Outline

3. Cross tables can be folded in both directions:

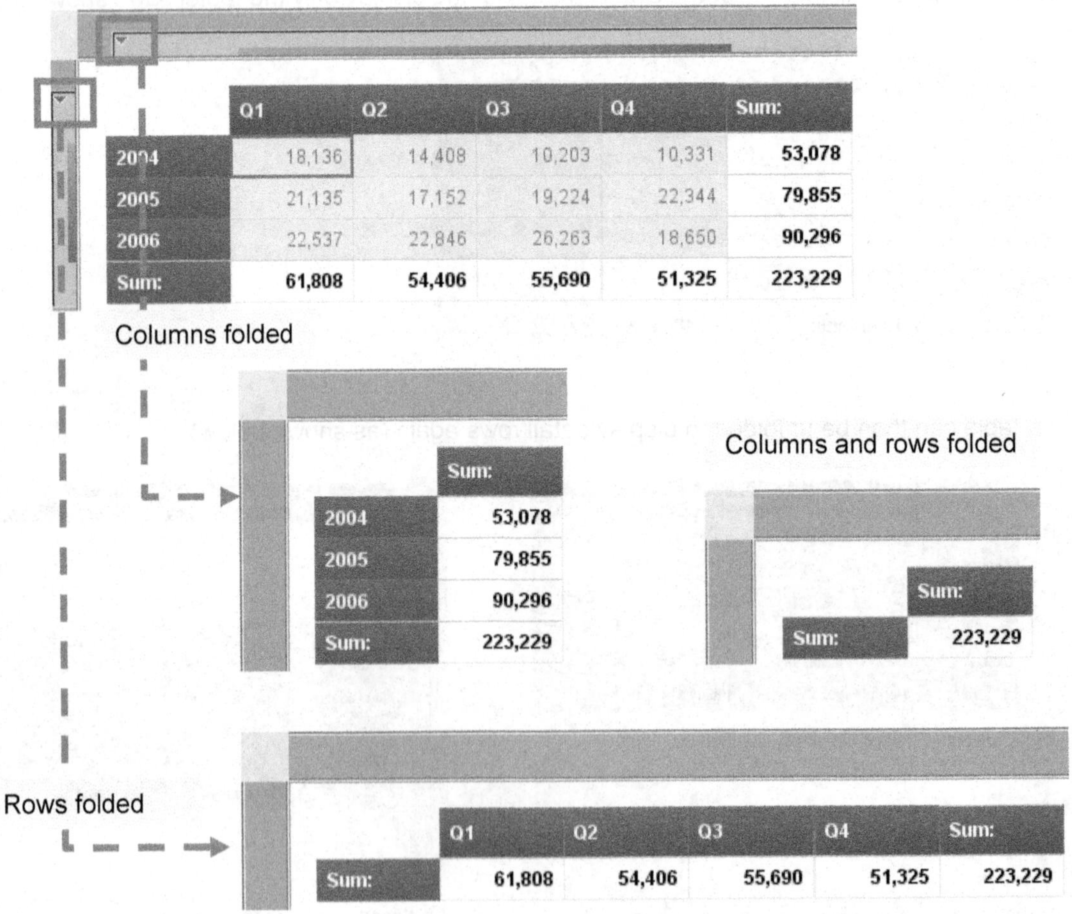
Q1
Q2
Q3
Q4
Sum:
2004
18,136
14,408
10,203
10,331
53,078
2005
21,135
17,152
19,224
22,344
79,855
2006
22,537
22,846
26,263
18,650
90,296
Sum:
61,808
54,406
55,690
51,325
223,229
Columns folded
Columns and rows folded
Rows folded

12 Sorting and Hiding Data in Tables and Cross Tables

Web Intelligence by default displays dimension values sorted in ascending order (i.e. data appears to be sorted but there are no sorts defined). The default sort order for the table is from the leftmost dimension column to the rightmost dimension column.

To override this sort order, you can set the primary (and secondary, tertiary, etc) sorts according to the order in which you require by applying explicit sorts.

Let us start with a new document containing the following query using the 'eFashion' universe:

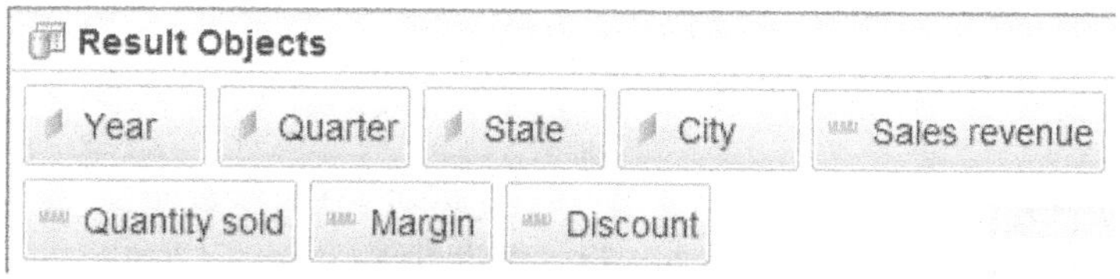
Result Objects
Year
Quarter
State
City
Sales revenue
Quantity sold
Margin
Discount

We will use objects from this query in examples during this session.

12.1 Applying Standard Sorts

Sorts can be easily applied by selecting the column values and clicking on the sort button. The drop arrow to the right of the sort button reveals the sort setting options of ascending (A to Z and 1 to 10) or descending (Z to A and 10 to 1).

1. Make the table in the report appear as follows:

Year	Sales revenue	Quantity sold
2004	$8,095,814	53,078
2005	$13,232,246	79,855
2006	$15,059,143	90,296

2. Click into any cell within the year column and then apply a Descending sort using the Analysis toolbox.

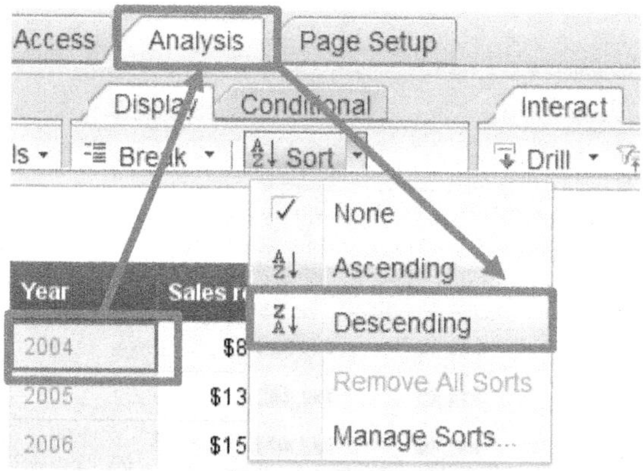
Access
Analysis
Page Setup
Display
Conditional
Interact
Break
Sort
Drill
None
Ascending
Descending
Remove All Sorts
Manage Sorts...
Year
2004
2005
2006

3. Data in the table block is now displayed in Descending sort order on [Year]. The Sort button indicates a Descending sort has been applied as it changes to 
Sort
.

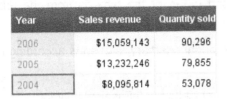

Year	Sales revenue	Quantity sold
2006	$15,059,143	90,296
2005	$13,232,246	79,855
2004	$8,095,814	53,078

NOTE – Sorts can also be applied using right-click menus:

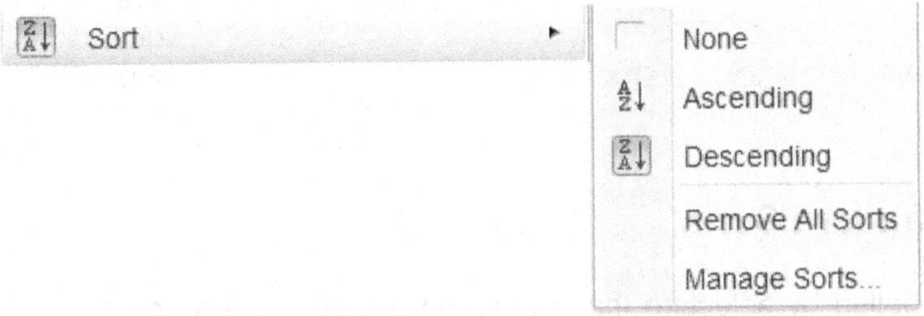
Sort
None
Ascending
Descending
Remove All Sorts
Manage Sorts...

12.2 Removing Standard Sorts

Standard Sorts may be removed using the cell properties or they can be easily removed by selecting 'None' from the Sort menu button.

To remove the sort, first click into any cell of the column on which the sort is applied and then select 'None' from the Sort menu button.

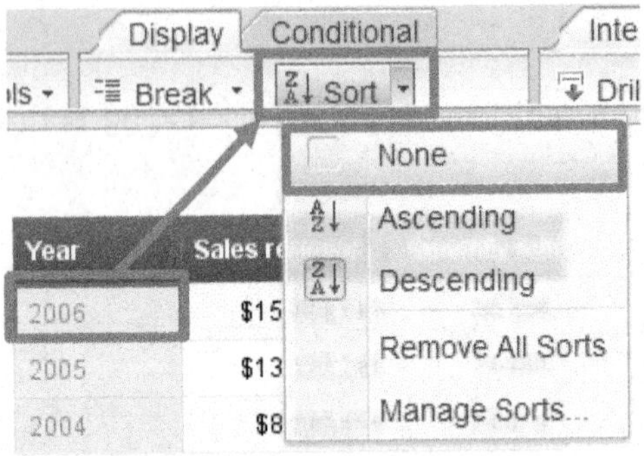
Display
Conditional
Inte
Break
Sort
Dril
None
Ascending
Descending
Remove All Sorts
Manage Sorts...
Year
2006
2005
2004

NOTE – You can also remove a sort by using the right-click menu after clicking in the column that contains the sorted data.

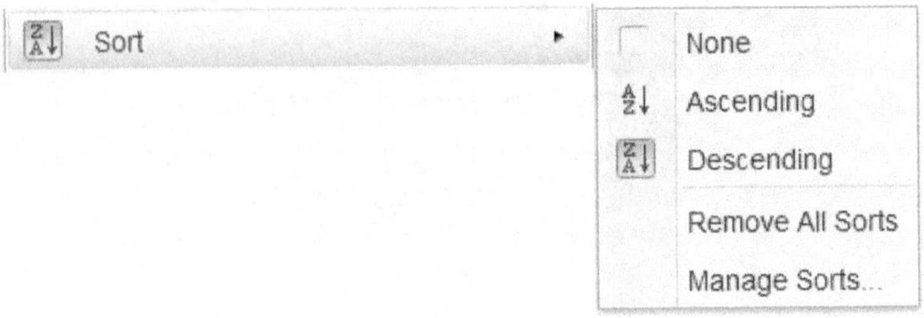
Sort
None
Ascending
Descending
Remove All Sorts
Manage Sorts...

12.3 Applying Custom Sorts

Custom Sorts enable you to specify a sort order that is different to using standard Ascending or Descending sorts. Custom Sorts are global, therefore, once created they are automatically applied across the document wherever the particular object is used.

1. Create the following vertical table:

Year	State	Sales revenue	Quantity sold
2004	California	$1,704,211	11,304
2004	Colorado	$448,302	2,971
2004	DC	$693,211	4,681
2004	Florida	$405,985	2,585
2004	Illinois	$737,914	4,713
2004	Massachuset	$238,819	1,505

2. First select any cell in the [State] column and then select 'Manage Sorts…' using the Sort button.

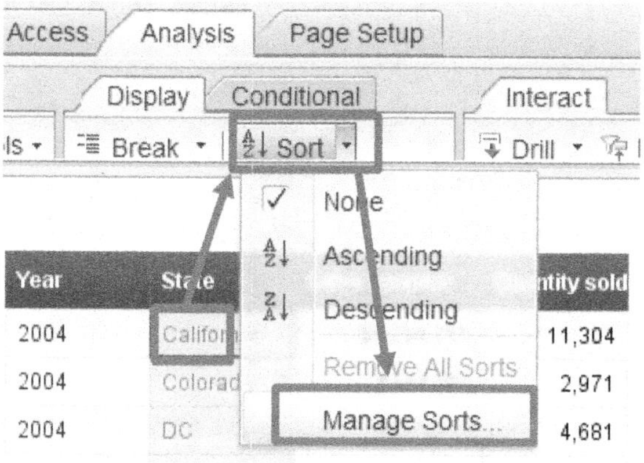
Access
Analysis
Page Setup
Display
Conditional
Interact
Break
Sort
Drill
None
Ascending
Descending
Remove All Sorts
Manage Sorts...
Year
State
ntity sold
2004
Califor
11,304
2004
Colorad
2,971
2004
DC
4,681

3. Click on 'Add' in the 'Manage Sorts' interface.

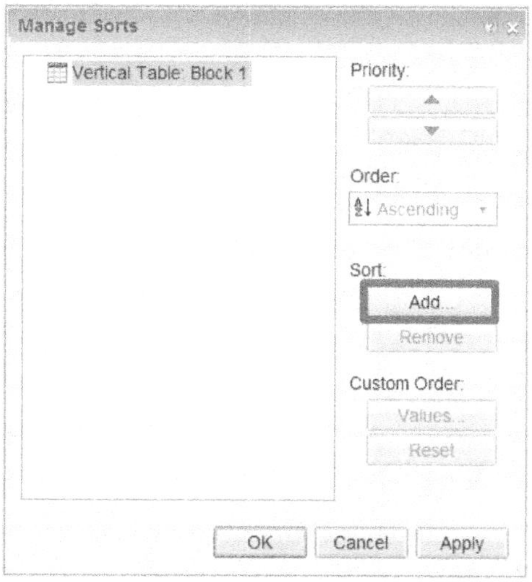
Manage Sorts
Vertical Table: Block 1
Priority:
Order:
Ascending
Sort:
Add...
Remove
Custom Order:
Values...
Reset
OK
Cancel
Apply

4. Select [State] in the 'Add Sort' interface and click 'OK'.

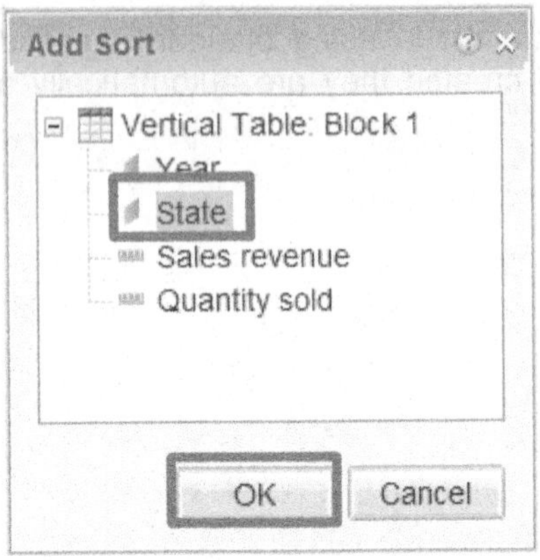
Add Sort
Vertical Table: Block 1
Year
State
Sales revenue
Quantity sold
OK
Cancel

5. Click on 'Values' to specify a 'Custom Order'

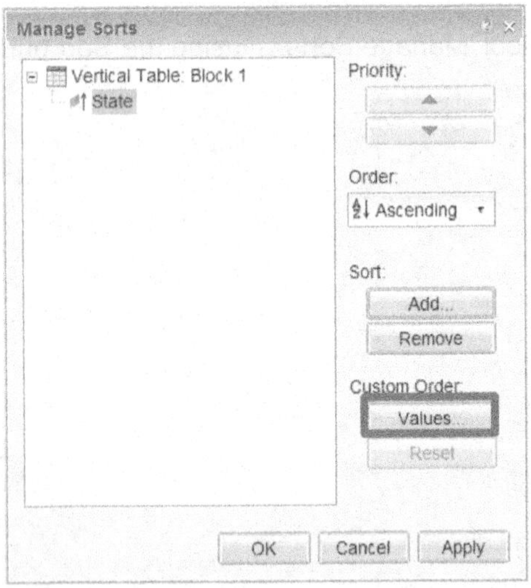
Manage Sorts
Vertical Table: Block 1
State
Priority:
Order:
Ascending
Sort:
Add...
Remove
Custom Order:
Values...
Reset
OK
Cancel
Apply

6. The Custom Sort interface allows you to specify a sort order that is different to the values being sorted alphanumerically in ascending or descending order

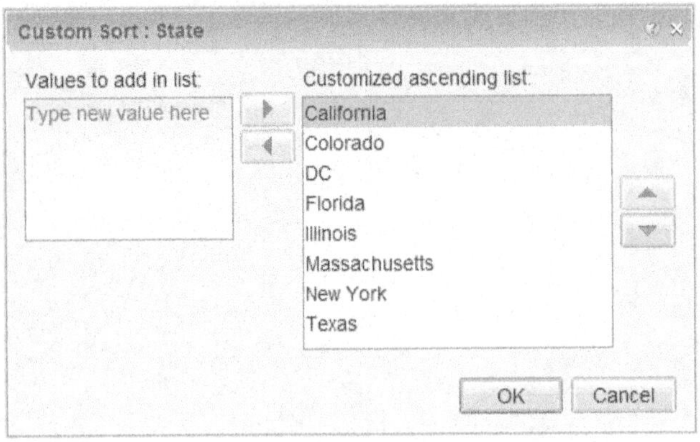
Custom Sort : State
Values to add in list:
Type new value here
Customized ascending list:
California
Colorado
DC
Florida
Illinois
Massachusetts
New York
Texas
OK
Cancel

7. Move the values into the desired order.

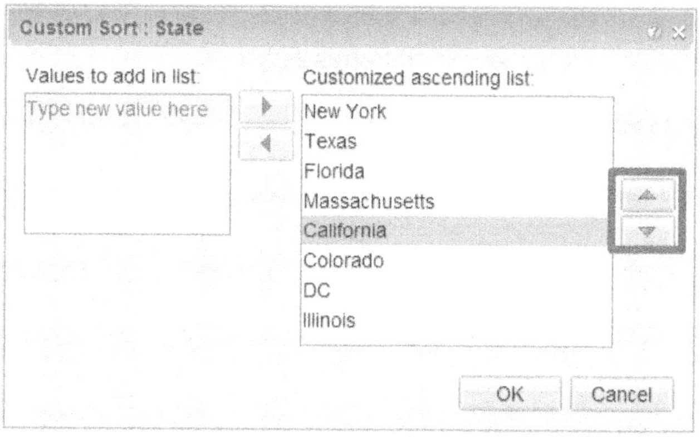
Custom Sort : State
Values to add in list:
Type new value here
Customized ascending list:
New York
Texas
Florida
Massachusetts
California
Colorado
DC
Illinois
OK
Cancel

8. If required you can also specify values that might be occur in the future but are not present in the current data set

   In this example '**Arizona**' will be sorted to fourth position when data is available for it.

   Type 'Arizona' in the 'Values to add in list' box and then click on the right arrow to move it into the customised list.

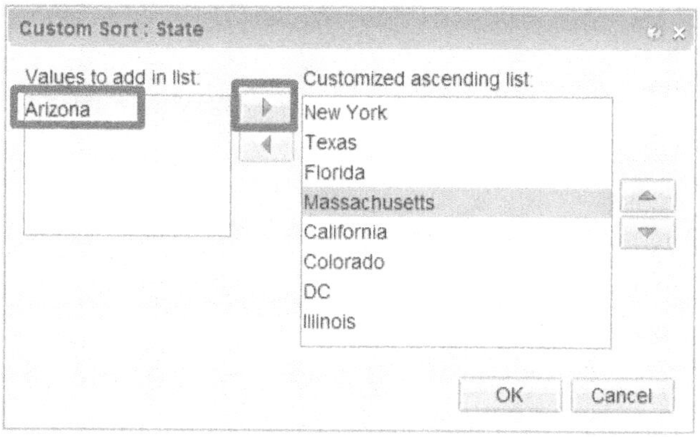
Custom Sort : State
Values to add in list:
Arizona
Customized ascending list:
New York
Texas
Florida
Massachusetts
California
Colorado
DC
Illinois
OK
Cancel

9. Move 'Arizona' into fourth position in the customised list.

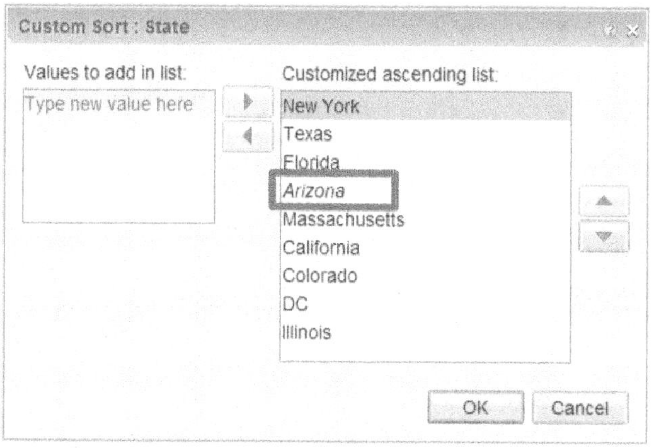
Custom Sort : State
Values to add in list:
Type new value here
Customized ascending list:
New York
Texas
Florida
Arizona
Massachusetts
California
Colorado
DC
Illinois
OK
Cancel

The order shown opposite is effectively the ascending custom sort order.

Descending order would be based on this definition but will be reversed.

NOTE – Custom Sort cannot be applied to Measure objects.

10. Click ‘OK’ twice to close the Custom Sort and Manage Sorts interfaces.

11. The data is now displayed with an Ascending sort using our customised list.

Year	State	Sales revenue	Quantity sold
2004	New York	$1,667,696	10,802
2005	New York	$2,763,503	16,447
2006	New York	$3,151,022	19,109
2004	Texas	$2,199,677	14,517
2005	Texas	$3,732,889	22,637
2006	Texas	$4,185,098	25,193
2004	Florida	$405,985	2,585
2005	Florida	$661,250	3,852
2006	Florida	$811,924	4,830
2004	Massachuset	$238,819	1,505

12. If we change the sort order to Descending:

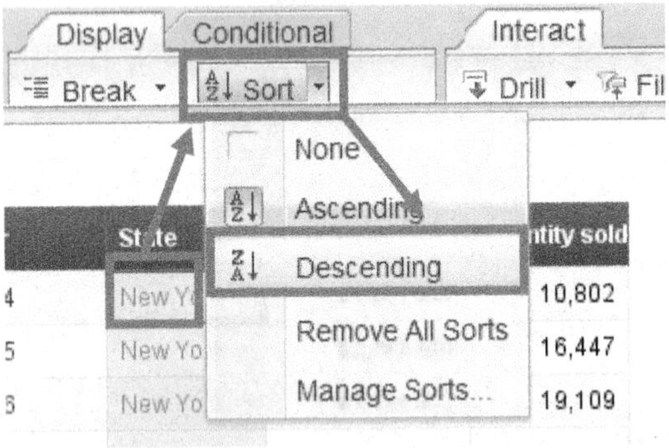
Display
Conditional
Interact
Break
Sort
Drill
None
Ascending
Descending
Remove All Sorts
Manage Sorts...
State
New Yo
New Yo
New Yo
ntity sold
10,802
16,447
19,109

The order of the Custom Sort is reversed as shown below:

Year	State	Sales revenue	Quantity sold
2004	Illinois	$737,914	4,713
2005	Illinois	$1,150,659	6,744
2006	Illinois	$1,134,085	6,519
2004	DC	$693,211	4,681
2005	DC	$1,215,158	7,572
2006	DC	$1,053,581	6,491
2004	Colorado	$448,302	2,971

NOTES ON CUSTOM SORTS

We have seen that the default behaviour of dimensions in Web Intelligence is to be implicitly sorted (in ascending order), although no sort is actually applied.

When a Custom Sort has been created for a dimension then the implicit sort for the dimension (across the whole document) will become the Custom Sort order definition.

In our example wherever [State] is used in this document then its default sort order will be that of the Custom Sort definition (existing report tabs, tables, cross tables, charts, etc will also be affected).

Original	Custom
California	New York
Colorado	Texas
DC	Florida
Florida	*Arizona*
Illinois	Massachusetts
Massachusetts	California
New York	Colorado
Texas	DC
	Illinois

Therefore, if you create a Custom Sort for an object and then select to apply 'None', the data will be sorted for that object in the default Custom Sort order.

Also, you cannot have more than one Custom Sort defined for an object.

12.4 Deleting Custom Sorts

Deleting a Custom Sort on an object will cause the object's default sort behaviour to revert to standard ascending order.

To delete a Custom Sort requires the use of the 'Manage Sorts...' interface.

1. Click in any cell of the table and then select 'Manage Sorts...' from the Sort button.

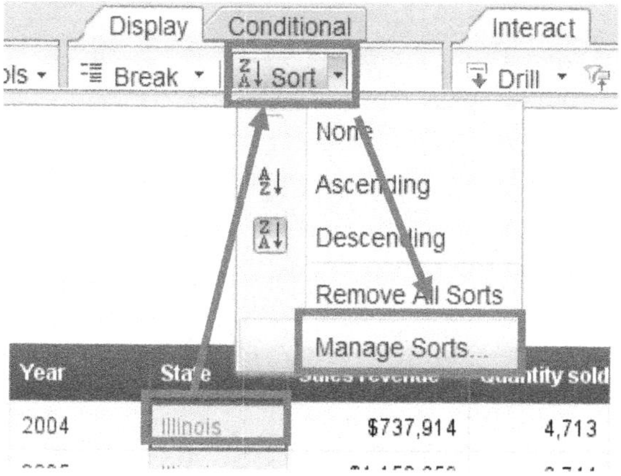
Display
Conditional
Interact
Break
Sort
Drill
Remove All Sorts
Manage Sorts...
Year
2004
Illinois
$737,914
4,713

2. Click on 'Reset' for 'Custom Order' and then on 'Apply' or 'OK'.

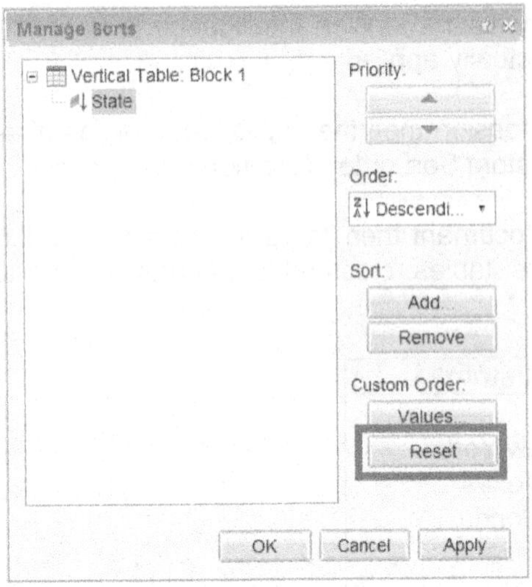
Manage Sorts
Vertical Table: Block 1
State
Priority:
Order:
Descendi...
Sort:
Add...
Remove
Custom Order:
Values...
Reset
OK
Cancel
Apply

NOTE – The custom order has been removed and the data is now being displayed in standard Descending order (because we still have the Descending Sort applied, i.e. we only reset the Custom Order and not Remove the sort).

Year	State	Sales revenue	Quantity sold
2004	Texas	$2,199,677	14,517
2005	Texas	$3,732,889	22,637
2006	Texas	$4,185,098	25,193
2004	New York	$1,667,696	10,802
2005	New York	$2,763,503	16,447
2006	New York	$3,151,022	19,109
2004	Massachuset	$238,819	1,505
2005	Massachuset	$157,719	902
2006	Massachuset	$887,169	5,269
2004	Illinois	$737,914	4,713

12.5 Sort Priorities

Sort priorities are created when multiple sorts are applied. Multiple sorts can be re-prioritised if required.

12.5.1 Sort Priorities on a Vertical Table

1. We have the following block:

Year	State	Quantity sold
2006	Florida	4,830
2006	Colorado	5,116
2006	Massachuset	5,269
2006	DC	6,491
2006	Illinois	6,519

Two sorts have been applied.

- Firstly apply a Descending Sort on [Year]
- Then apply an Ascending Sort on [Quantity Sold]

2. Click in any cell of the table and then select 'Manage Sorts…' or you can do the same using right-click menus.

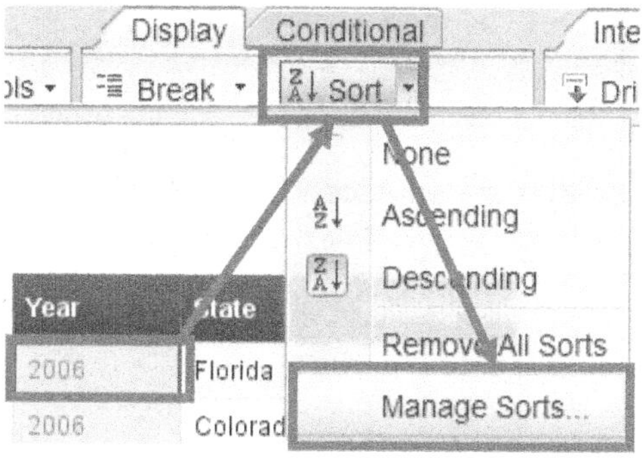
Display
Conditional
Break
Sort
Ascending
Descending
Manage Sorts...
Year
Florida
2006

3. In this block, the data has been sorted in priority [Year] and then [Quantity sold] because [Year] appears above [Quantity sold] in the 'Manage Sorts' interface. Click on [Year] and then the down arrow.

Manage Sorts
Year
Priority
Order
Descendi...
Sort
Add...
Remove
Custom Order
Values...
Reset
OK
Cancel
Apply

4. The Sort Priority now changes so that [Quantity sold] is before [Year].

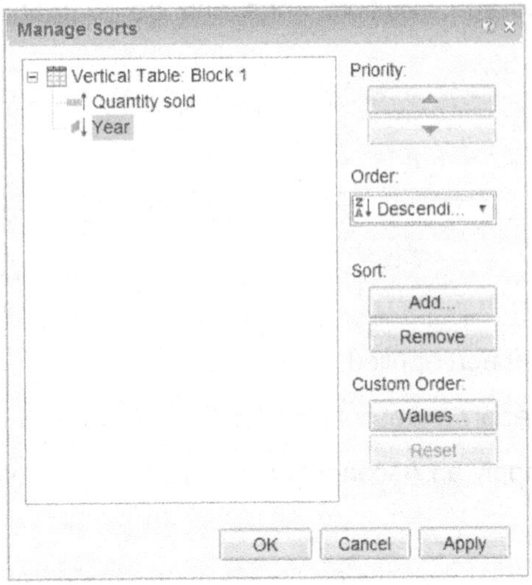
Manage Sorts
Vertical Table: Block 1
Quantity sold
Year
Priority:
Order:
Descendi...
Sort:
Add...
Remove
Custom Order:
Values...
Reset
OK
Cancel
Apply

5. Click 'OK' or 'Apply' and the results now reflect the new Sort Priority:

Year	State	Quantity sold
2005	Massachuset	902
2004	Massachuset	1,505
2004	Florida	2,585
2004	Colorado	2,971
2005	Florida	3,852
2004	DC	4,681
2005	Colorado	4,700
2004	Illinois	4,713
2006	Florida	4,830

i.e. [Quantity sold] is sorted Ascending first.

NOTE – We can change the Sort Order of any object independently without affecting the Sort Priority because the order is how the data should be sorted (ascending, descending or custom) and the priority is which sort should be applied first, second, third, etc.

12.5.2 Sort Priorities on a Cross Tables

Cross Tables can be sorted in 2 directions for dimensions (vertically in columns and horizontally in rows).

Measures can be also sorted but only vertically, i.e. in a column.

1. Create the following cross table:

	Year	2004	2004	2004	2004
	Quarter	Q1	Q2	Q3	Q4
State	City	Quantity sold	Quantity sold	Quantity sold	Quantity sold
California	Los Angeles	2,094	1,615	1,821	1,053
California	San Francisco	1,415	1,173	1,214	919
Colorado	Colorado Springs	921	828	628	594
DC	Washington	1,467	1,149	1,012	1,053
Florida	Miami	924	747	353	561
Illinois	Chicago	1,711	1,526	725	751

Cross Table (below) showing [Year] and [Quarter] (**horizontally**) with [State] and [City] (**vertically**).

2. Now apply the following sorts.

   [State] *descending*
   [City] *ascending*
   [Year] *ascending*
   [Quarter] *descending*

   The cross table should now look like this...

	Year	2004	2004	2004	2004	2005	2005
	Quarter	Q4	Q3	Q2	Q1	Q4	Q3
State	City	Quantity sold	Quantity sold	Quantity sold	Quantity sold	Quantity sold	Quantity sold
Texas	Austin	741	679	986	1,418	1,595	1,482
Texas	Dallas	525	546	764	1,053	1,180	1,268
Texas	Houston	1,607	1,254	2,137	2,807	3,286	2,468
New York	New York	2,134	1,887	3,064	3,717	4,717	3,288
Massachusetts	Boston	393	84	419	609	902	Discontinued
Illinois	Chicago	751	725	1,526	1,711	1,722	1,398

3. Select the 'Manage Sorts…' interface using right-click or from the Sort button.

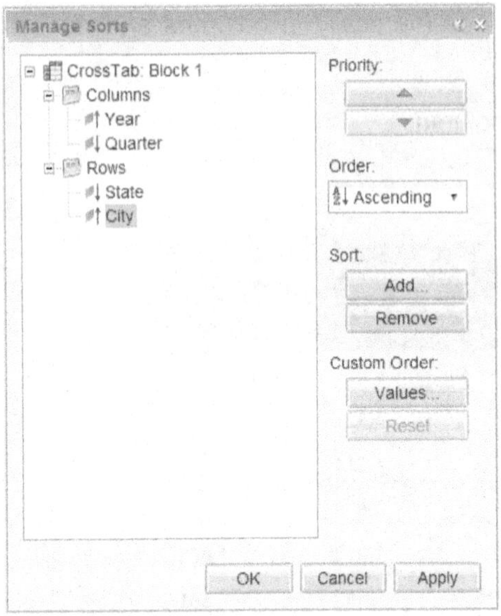
Manage Sorts
CrossTab: Block 1
Columns
Year
Quarter
Rows
State
City
Priority:
Order:
Ascending
Sort:
Add...
Remove
Custom Order:
Values...
Reset
OK
Cancel
Apply

We can see there are:

- Two column sorts, in the priority [Year] and [Quarter]
- Two row sorts, in the priority [State] and [City]

We can also see the order of each sort due to the arrows next to each object:

- [Year] = Ascending, [Quarter] = Descending
- [State] = Descending, [City] = Ascending

Also when you click on an object name then Order will indicate Ascending or Descending.

12.5.3 Changing Sort Priorities on a Cross Tables

1. We can change the Sort Priorities for rows and/or columns by simply selecting an object and then using the arrows to demote or promote its priority.

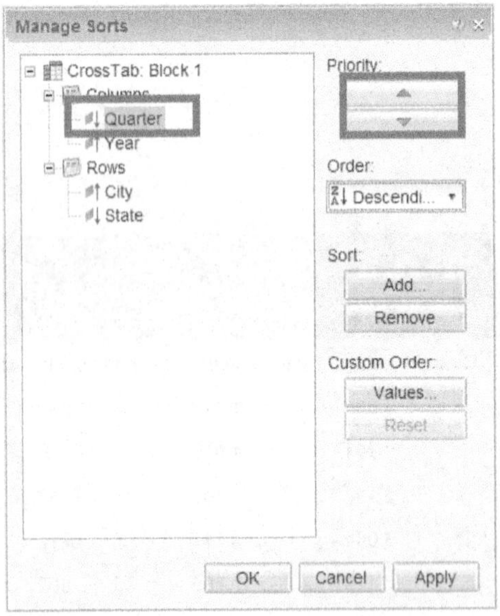
Manage Sorts
CrossTab: Block 1
Quarter
Year
Rows
City
State
Priority:
Order:
Descendi...
Sort:
Add...
Remove
Custom Order:
Values...
Reset
OK
Cancel
Apply

- Select [Quarter] and move it to be above [Year]
- Select [State] and move it to be below [City]

The end result should look as shown opposite.

Click 'OK' or 'Apply'.

The data will now be sorted using the new priorities.

	Year	2004	2005	2006	2004
	Quarter	Q4	Q4	Q4	Q3
State	City	Quantity sold	Quantity sold	Quantity sold	Quantity sold
Texas	Austin	741	1,595	1,440	679
Massachusetts	Boston	393	902	1,175	84
Illinois	Chicago	751	1,722	1,288	725
Colorado	Colorado Springs	594	1,248	1,073	628
Texas	Dallas	525	1,180	1,062	546
Texas	Houston	1,607	3,286	2,854	1,254
California	Los Angeles	1,053	2,238	2,096	1,821
Florida	Miami	561	1,153	950	353
New York	New York	2,134	4,717	3,607	1,887
California	San Francisco	919	2,154	1,751	1,214
DC	Washington	1,053	2,149	1,354	1,012

Results show the sort priorities have now changed to:

Row sorts = **[City]** and then **[State]** *([City] is sorted first, i.e. Austin to Washington)*
Column sorts = **[Quarter]** and then **[Year]** *(descending [Quarter] followed by [Year] ascending)*

Reminder

Changing the priority of the sorts does not affect the order of each sort, i.e. if a sort is descending and has a priority of 2, then moving it to priority 1 will cause it to be applied first but still in descending order.

12.6 Hiding Data

Dimensions can be hidden in table type blocks.

1. Create a new document with the following query (from 'eFashion' universe).

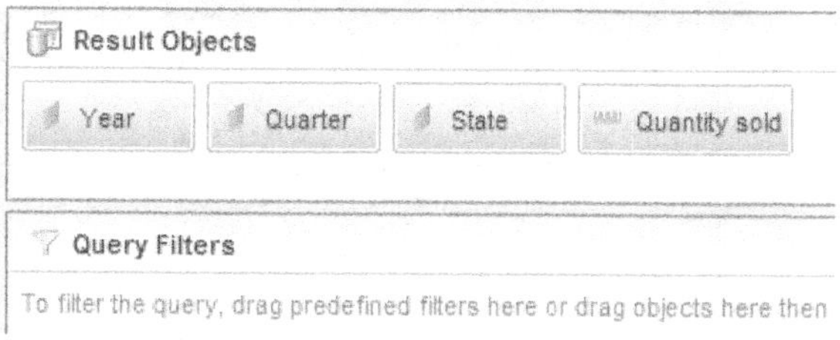
Result Objects
Year
Quarter
State
Quantity sold
Query Filters
To filter the query, drag predefined filters here or drag objects here then

2. Run the query and we will have the default Vertical Table displayed as:

Year	Quarter	State	Quantity sold
2004	Q1	California	3,509
2004	Q1	Colorado	921
2004	Q1	DC	1,467
2004	Q1	Florida	924
2004	Q1	Illinois	1,711
2004	Q1	Massachusetts	609
2004	Q1	New York	3,717
2004	Q1	Texas	5,278
2004	Q2	California	2,788
2004	Q2	Colorado	828
2004	Q2	DC	1,149

i.e. we have one row per [State] per [Quarter] per [Year]

3. Right-click in any cell of the [State] column and select 'Hide – Hide Dimension'.

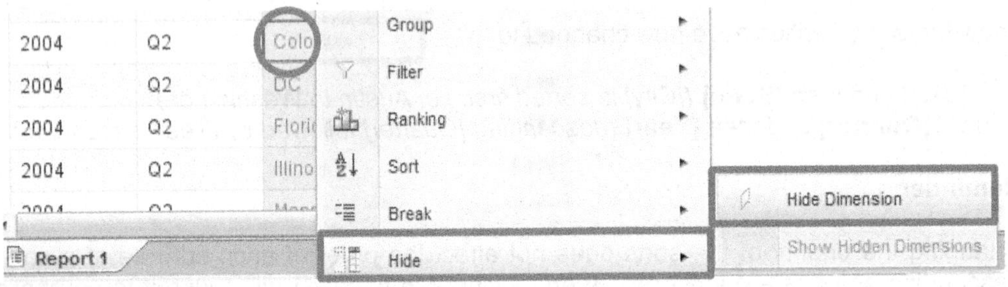
Group
Filter
Ranking
Sort
Break
Hide
Hide Dimension
Show Hidden Dimensions
Report 1

4. The [State] column will become hidden.

Year	Quarter	Quantity sold
2004	Q1	3,509
2004	Q1	921
2004	Q1	1,467
2004	Q1	924
2004	Q1	1,711
2004	Q1	609
2004	Q1	3,717
2004	Q1	5,278
2004	Q2	2,788
2004	Q2	828
2004	Q2	1,149

However, the number of rows have remained the same, i.e. hiding a column does not cause the data to aggregate in the same way as removing a column.

If we had removed the [State] column then we would have one row per [Quarter] per [Year], i.e.

Year	Quarter	Quantity sold
2004	Q1	18,136
2004	Q2	14,408
2004	Q3	10,203
2004	Q4	10,331
2005	Q1	21,135
2005	Q2	17,152

5. To unhide dimensions, simply right-click on any column of data and select 'Hide – Show Hidden Dimensions'.

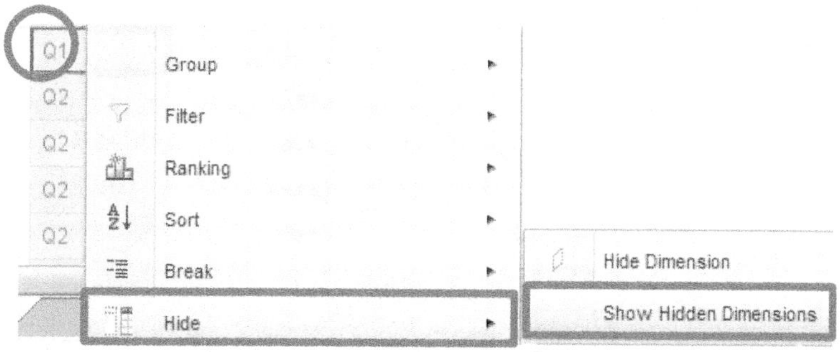
Q1
Q2
Q2
Q2
Q2
Group
Filter
Ranking
Sort
Break
Hide
Hide Dimension
Show Hidden Dimensions

NOTE

You can also hide/unhide dimensions in other types of blocks (Cross Tables, Horizontal Tables and Forms).

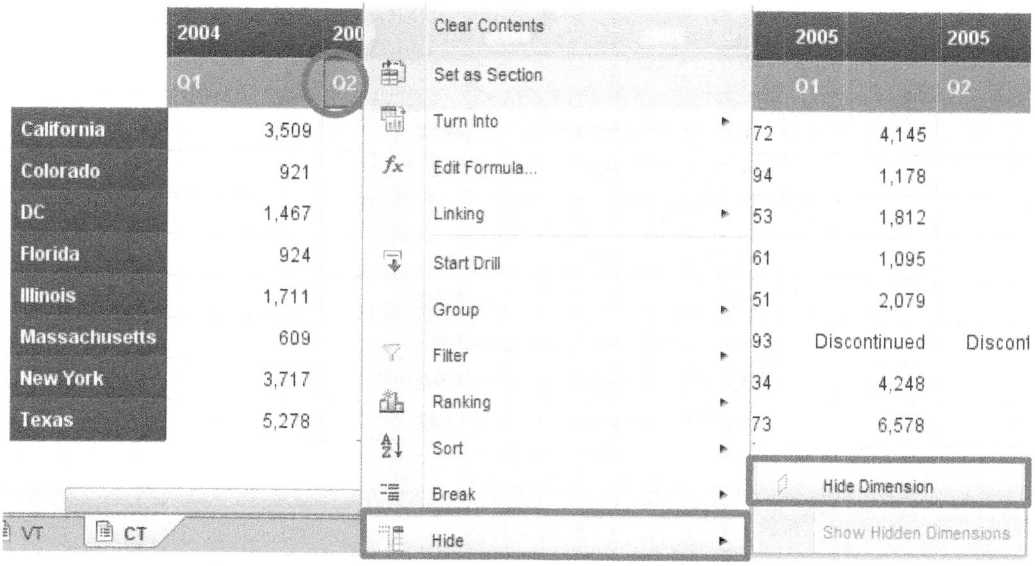
2004
Q1
Q2
2005
2005
Q1
Q2
California
Colorado
DC
Florida
Illinois
Massachusetts
New York
Texas
3,509
921
1,467
924
1,711
609
3,717
5,278
Clear Contents
Set as Section
Turn Into
Edit Formula...
Linking
Start Drill
Group
Filter
Ranking
Sort
Break
Hide
4,145
1,178
1,812
1,095
2,079
Discontinued
4,248
6,578
Hide Dimension
Show Hidden Dimensions
VT
CT

The example above shows the [Quarter] dimension being selected to be hidden.

We will look at hiding dimensions in charts in a later session.

6. Save and close your document.

13 Breaks

So far we have looked at applying calculations at table level, i.e. showing totals for the whole of the table or cross table. But what if we want to use sub-totals, for example we might want to show something like the following:

		California	Colorado	DC
2004	Q1	$519,220	$131,797	$208,324
	Q2	$441,494	$129,076	$179,863
	Q3	$394,309	$85,621	$131,687
	Q4	$349,188	$101,807	$173,336
2004	Sum:	**$1,704,211**	**$448,302**	**$693,211**
2005	Q1	$650,715	$189,131	$279,490
	Q2	$529,256	$157,337	$263,486
	Q3	$760,442	$192,267	$288,926
	Q4	$842,267	$229,654	$383,257
2005	Sum:	**$2,782,680**	**$768,390**	**$1,215,158**
2006	Q1	$729,745	$204,754	$279,008
	Q2	$789,398	$213,663	$263,098
	Q3	$775,766	$232,889	$271,645
	Q4	$697,770	$192,279	$239,831
2006	Sum:	**$2,992,679**	**$843,584**	**$1,053,581**
	Sum:	**$7,479,569**	**$2,060,275**	**$2,961,950**

This cross table uses sub-totals to show [Sales revenue] per [State] per [Year].

We then have a total for all 3 years at the bottom.

We can achieve this type of output using 'Breaks' in Web Intelligence as Breaks are a way of grouping data within tables and cross tables.

When a break is applied:

1. The data is separated into groups based on unique values of the selected object, i.e. if we applied a break in a vertical table on [State] then all rows for each [State] value will be grouped together.

2. A header row is created for each break value.

3. A footer row is inserted after each break value. This can be used to insert sub-totals for the break.

4. An implicit sort is automatically applied to the break column in order to bring the rows together for grouping purposes. This implicit sort is ascending but you can explicitly apply a sort (Ascending, Descending or Custom).

Let us start with a new document containing the following query using the 'eFashion' universe:

Result Objects
Year
Quarter
State
City
Lines
Quantity sold
Sales revenue

We will use objects from this query in examples during this session.

After the query has run, strip out the objects from the table so it contains only the following three columns.

State	Year	Sales revenue
California	2004	$1,704,211
California	2005	$2,782,680
California	2006	$2,992,679
Colorado	2004	$448,302
Colorado	2005	$768,390
Colorado	2006	$843,584
DC	2004	$693,211
DC	2005	$1,215,158
DC	2006	$1,053,581

13.1 Applying Breaks

1. Click in any cell of the [State] column and then apply a break by clicking on the 'Break' icon.

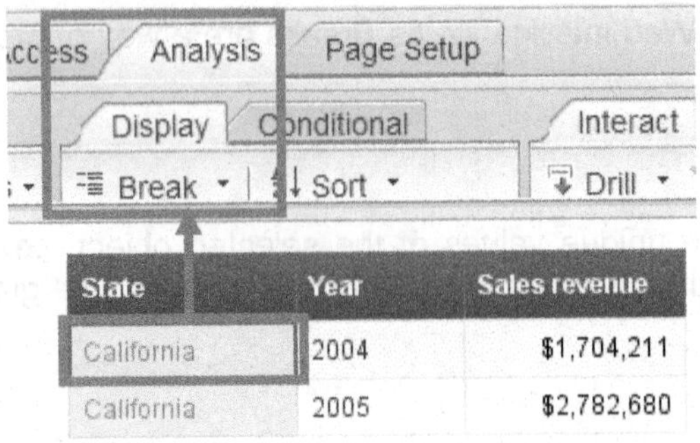
Analysis
Page Setup
Display
Conditional
Interact
Break
Sort
Drill
State
Year
Sales revenue
California
2004
$1,704,211
California
2005
$2,782,680

Web Intelligence will now break the table into parts (based on how many distinct values it sees for [State], because we have applied a break on [State]).

The net result of applying a break is that we still have a single block, but it appears to be split into sub-blocks based on the number of distinct values for the object used in the break.

State
Year
Sales revenue
California
2004
$1,704,211
2005
$2,782,680
2006
$2,992,679
California
State
Year
Sales revenue
Colorado
2004
$448,302
2005
$768,390
2006
$843,584
Colorado

The 4 points mentioned earlier can be seen here on the left:

a) Data has been separated into groups based on [State] values.

b) A header row exists for each break value.

c) A footer row exists for each break value.

d) An implicit ascending sort has been applied to the [State] column as data is sorted 'California, Colorado, ..., Texas'.

13.2 Formatting Breaks

Formatting properties are available for an object that has a break applied to it (using the 'Manage Breaks' interface).

1. Click in any cell of the [State] column and then select 'Manage Breaks':

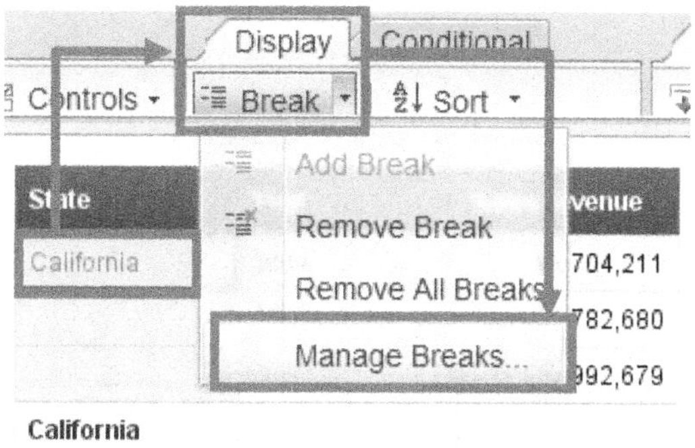
Display
Conditional
Controls
Break
Sort
State
California
Add Break
Remove Break
Remove All Breaks
Manage Breaks...
venue
704,211
782,680
992,679
California

This will initiate the 'Manage Breaks' interface.

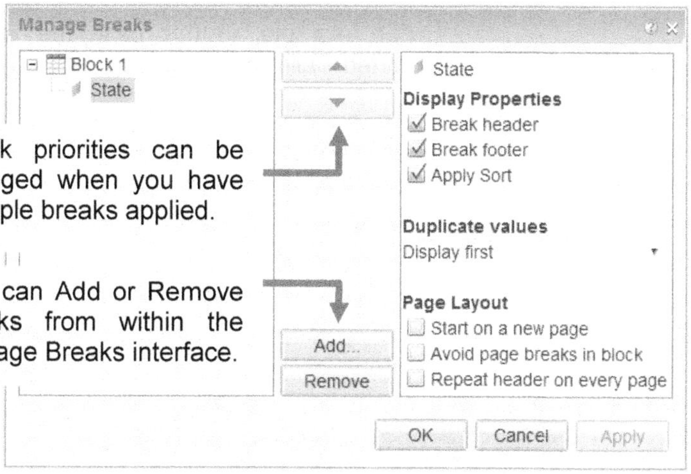
Manage Breaks
Block 1
State
State
Display Properties
Break header
Break footer
Apply Sort
Duplicate values
Display first
Page Layout
Start on a new page
Avoid page breaks in block
Repeat header on every page
Add...
Remove
OK
Cancel
Apply

Break priorities can be changed when you have multiple breaks applied.

You can Add or Remove breaks from within the Manage Breaks interface.

Break properties are discussed in detail next.

13.2.1 Break Properties

The following properties can be used to control the display or structure of the block (in which the break is a part of).

Display Properties

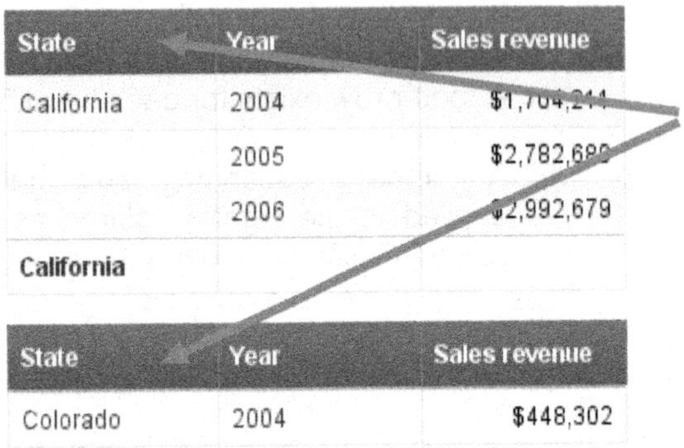
State
Year
Sales revenue
California
2004
2005
$2,782,68
2006
2,992,679
California
State
Year
Sales revenue
Colorado
2004
$448,302

Break header

If this is ticked then a header is shown (per break value).

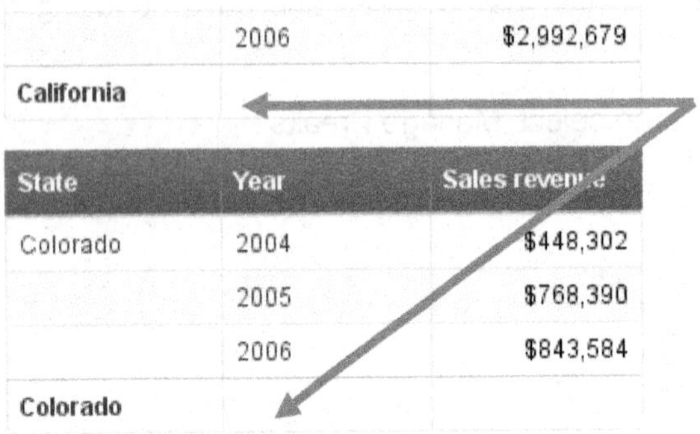
2006
$2,992,679
California
State
Year
Colorado
2004
448,302
2005
$768,390
2006
$843,584
Colorado

Break footer

If this is ticked then a footer is shown (per break value).

State
Year
Sales revenue
California
2004
$1,704,211
2005
$2,782,680
2006
$2,992,679
California
State
Year
Sales revenue
Colorado
2004
$448,302
2005
$768,390
2006
$843,584
Colorado

Apply Sort

If this is ticked then the data is automatically sorted in ascending order (based on the values in the object to which the break has been applied).

For example, in this case the values are sorted California, Colorado, DC... Texas.

NOTE on Apply Sort

Sorts on other objects will cause the display of data to vary depending on whether you decide to use Apply Sort on the break or not.

Apply Sort (ticked)

State	Year	Sales revenue
California	2006	$2,992,679
	2005	$2,782,680
	2004	$1,704,211
California		

State	Year	Sales revenue
Colorado	2006	$843,584
	2005	$768,390
	2004	$448,302
Colorado		

The [Sales revenue] is sorted within each break when Apply Sort is selected.

Typically your users will want to see the data grouped together as above.

Apply Sort (unticked)

State	Year	Sales revenue
Texas	2006	$4,185,098
	2005	$3,732,889
Texas		

State	Year	Sales revenue
New York	2006	$3,151,022
New York		

State	Year	Sales revenue
California	2006	$2,992,679
	2005	$2,782,680
California		

When Apply Sort is not selected, then the sort on [Sales revenue] takes precedence.

If 2 or more rows successively belong to the same break value then they are grouped together.

Duplicate Values

When a break is applied, the default behaviour is for the break value to be shown only once on the first row of each break group.

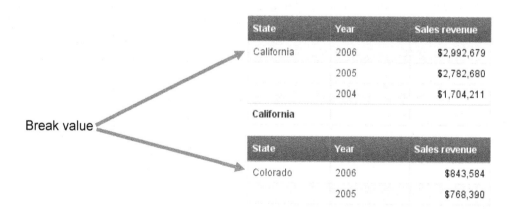

Break value

State	Year	Sales revenue
California	2006	$2,992,679
	2005	$2,782,680
	2004	$1,704,211
California		

State	Year	Sales revenue
Colorado	2006	$843,584
	2005	$768,390

The Duplicate values property can be used to control the display of the break value.

Duplicate values
Display first

This is the default setting whereby the break value is displayed once at the start of each break group.

If the break group spreads over multiple pages then with this setting you will only see the break value appear once (on the first row).

State	Year	Sales revenue
California	2006	$2,992,679
	2005	$2,782,680
	2004	$1,704,211
California		

State	Year	Sales revenue
Colorado	2006	$843,584
	2005	$768,390
	2004	$448,302
Colorado		

Duplicate values
Merge

With this setting the break value is centred vertically depending on the number of rows within the break group.

If the break group spreads over multiple pages then with this setting you will only see the break value appear once (on the middle row).

State	Year	Sales revenue
	2004	$1,704,211
California	2005	$2,782,680
	2006	$2,992,679
California		

State	Year	Sales revenue
	2004	$448,302
Colorado	2005	$768,390
	2006	$843,584
Colorado		

Duplicate values
Repeat first on new page

If the break group rows span over multiple pages then with this setting you will see the break value appear on the first row for the break group and then the first row of every new page.

State	Year	Sales revenue
California	2006	$2,992,679
	2005	$2,782,680
	2004	$1,704,211
California		

State	Year	Sales revenue
Colorado	2006	$843,584
	2005	$768,390
	2004	$448,302
Colorado		

Page Layout

When a break is applied, the default behaviour is for the break value to be shown only once on the first row of each break group.

Start on a new page	Forces a new page to be started when the break value changes.
Avoid page breaks in block	If a break is spread over multiple pages then this will force the break to start on a new page.
Repeat header on every page	Repeats the header at the top of the table on every new page when a table goes over onto a new page.

13.3 Sorting on Breaks

Data is sorted within a block that has break(s) based on the hierarchical order in which the break(s) are applied.

If there are existing sorts on a block and a break is applied, then the break will automatically override the existing sorts and take priority by becoming the primary sort (due to the Apply Sort property).

Applying a second break (and further breaks) will cause the data to be sorted in a hierarchical manner starting from the first break, second break, etc. The break hierarchy becomes the priority for the sorts but you can change the sort type for each break independently (i.e. Ascending, Descending, Custom).

Let us have a look at a few examples of combining Breaks and Sorts.

13.3.1 Changing Sort Order on a Single Break

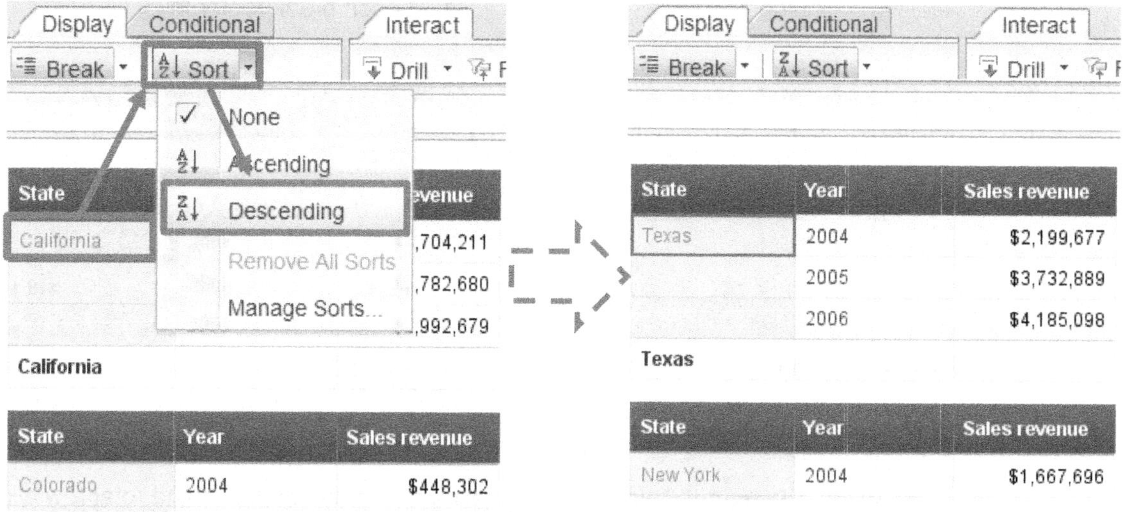
Display
Conditional
Interact
Break
Sort
Drill
None
Ascending
Descending
Remove All Sorts
Manage Sorts...
State
California
,704,211
,782,680
,992,679
California
State
Year
Sales revenue
Colorado
2004
$448,302
Display
Conditional
Interact
Break
Sort
Drill
State
Year
Sales revenue
Texas
2004
$2,199,677
2005
$3,732,889
2006
$4,185,098
Texas
State
Year
Sales revenue
New York
2004
$1,667,696

In this example, the default break on [State] is shown as having no sort applied, but it will be implicitly sorted (due to the Apply Sort property).

We can apply a Descending sort to the break and the data will be displayed in reverse order.

Custom Sorts can also be used with breaks. It does not matter whether you define the Custom Sort before or after applying the break because Custom Sorts automatically get applied when created.

13.4 Using Subtotals and Grand Totals on Breaks

Breaks are often used to set up the formatting for creating subtotals and grand totals. To get subtotals and grand totals, first apply the break, then select the measure value and apply a calculation function.

We already have our break defined on [State], so if we now apply a Standard Calculation to [Sales revenue]...

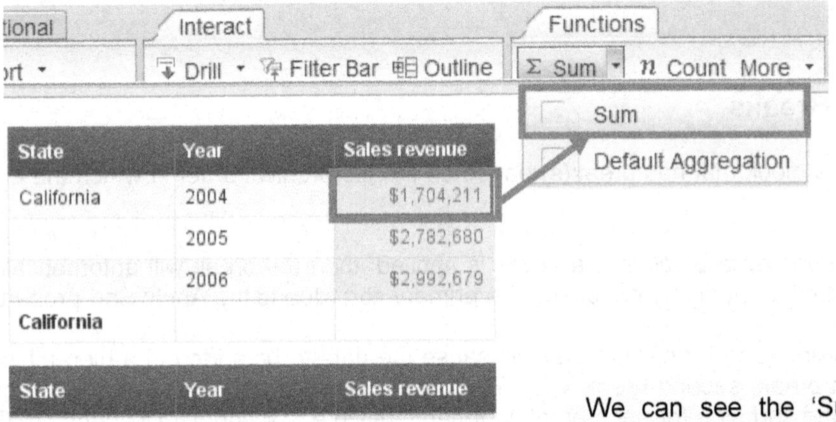
tional
Interact
Functions
Drill
Filter Bar
Outline
Σ Sum
n Count
More
Sum
Default Aggregation
State
Year
Sales revenue
California
2004
$1,704,211
2005
$2,782,680
2006
$2,992,679
California
State
Year
Sales revenue

We can see the 'Sum' calculation has been applied to all break footers, i.e. for California, Colorado, etc.

We will get the following display:

Scrolling down to the bottom, you should see a grand total appear in addition to the subtotals appearing at each break footer level.

State
Year
Sales revenue
California
2004
$1,704,211
2005
$2,782,680
2006
$2,992,679
California
Sum:
$7,479,569
State
Year
Sales revenue
Colorado
2004
$448,302
2005
$768,390
2006
$843,583
Colorado
Sum:
$2,060,275

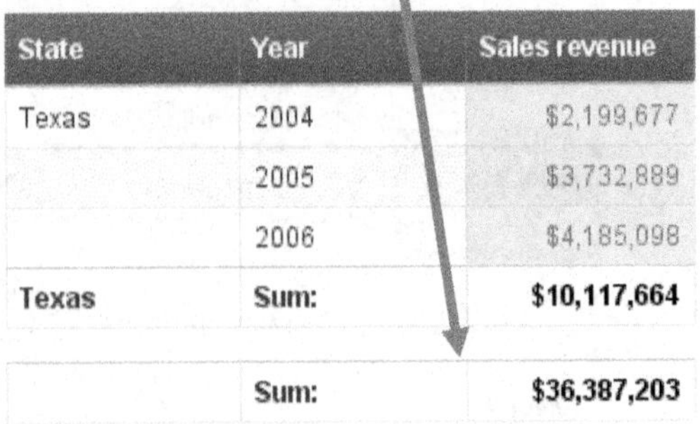
State
Year
Sales revenue
Texas
2004
$2,199,677
2005
$3,732,889
2006
$4,185,098
Texas
Sum:
$10,117,664
Sum:
$36,387,203

NOTE

When a Standard Calculation is applied to a break then a grand total row will appear in the block. If you do not want to show the grand total then simply right-click and select delete to remove the grand total row from the block.

13.5 Nested Breaks

Nested breaks (or multi-level breaks) are a result of applying a first break on one object then applying second break on another object, etc.

You can have sub-totals at each break level plus an overall grand total (if required).

1. Create a new vertical table (as below) and apply a break on [Year].

Year	Quarter	State	Sales revenue
2004	Q1	California	$519,220
	Q1	Colorado	$131,797
	Q1	DC	$208,324
	Q1	Florida	$137,530
	Q1	Illinois	$256,454

2. Then apply a break on [Quarter]... simply click in any cell of [Quarter] column and then apply a break.

Year	Quarter	State	Sales revenue
2004	Q1	California	$519,220
		Colorado	$131,797
		DC	$208,324
		Florida	$137,530
		Illinois	$256,454
		Massachusetts	$92,596
		New York	$555,983
		Texas	$758,796
	Q1		
Year	**Quarter**	**State**	**Sales revenue**
	Q2	California	$441,494
		Colorado	$129,076

Therefore, we now have a nested break with a break priority of [Year] followed by [Quarter].

NOTE:

If required you can still apply sorts on individual levels within a nested break.

3. Apply the 'Sum' Standard Calculation to [Sales revenue] as shown here.

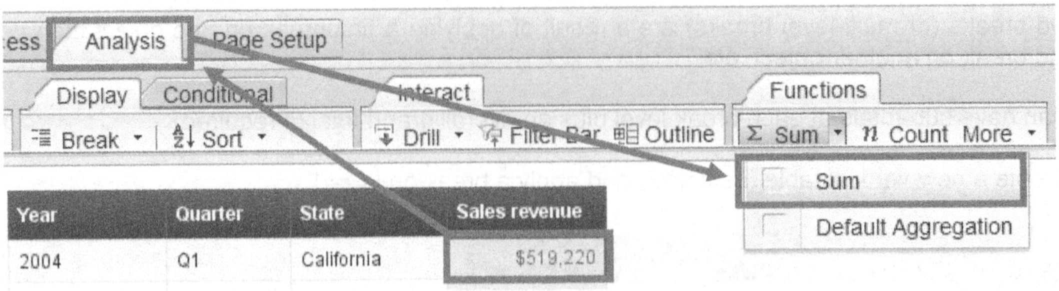
Analysis
Page Setup
Display
Conditional
Interact
Functions
Break
Sort
Drill
Filter Bar
Outline
Σ Sum
Count
More
Sum
Default Aggregation
Year
Quarter
State
Sales revenue
2004
Q1
California
$519,220

This will apply sub-totals in every [Quarter] and [Year] footer, plus an overall grand total at the bottom of the table.

		New York	$914,247
		Texas	$1,032,629
	Q3	**Sum:**	**$3,953,395**
Year	**Quarter**	**State**	**Sales revenue**
	Q4	California	$697,770
		Colorado	$192,279
		DC	$239,831
		Florida	$171,003
		Illinois	$250,517
		Massachusetts	$208,877
		New York	$633,998
		Texas	$961,768
	Q4	**Sum:**	**$3,356,041**
2006		**Sum:**	**$15,059,143**
		Sum:	**$36,387,203**

Scroll down and you will see the subtotal has been added to both [Quarter] and [Year] breaks.

Scroll down further and you will also see a Grand Total for the block.

With nested breaks it is recommended that you apply all required breaks first and then apply Standard Calculations. The reason for this is that the calculation will then be applied at all levels (child levels, parent levels, and table level grand total).

If a child-break is added after an existing parent-break has had calculations applied then the calculations will need to be applied again.

13.6 Break Priorities

You can change the order of breaks that are already in place on a block (we can use the table from previous example on nested breaks).

1. Click in any cell of the table and then open the 'Manage Breaks' interface.

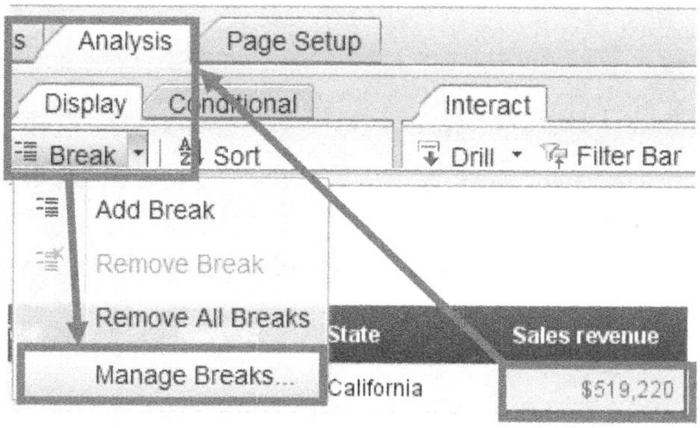

Analysis
Page Setup
Display
Conditional
Interact
Break
Sort
Drill
Filter Bar
Add Break
Remove Break
Remove All Breaks
Manage Breaks...
State
Sales revenue
California
$519,220

2. The 'Manage Breaks' interface shows the break priority as [Year] and then [Quarter].

   Click on [Quarter], then on the 'up' arrow as shown below.

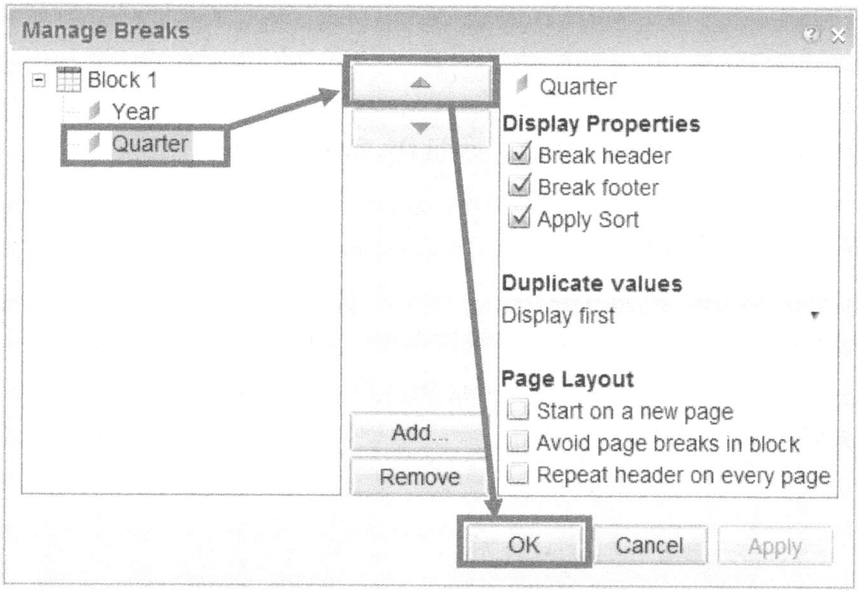

Manage Breaks
Block 1
Year
Quarter
Quarter
Display Properties
Break header
Break footer
Apply Sort
Duplicate values
Display first
Page Layout
Start on a new page
Avoid page breaks in block
Repeat header on every page
Add...
Remove
OK
Cancel
Apply

Click 'OK'.

3. We now see the block has a break priority of [Quarter] and then [Year] because we have Q1 2004, Q1 2005, Q1 2006, Q2 2004, Q2 2005, etc.

Year	Quarter	State	Sales revenue
2004	Q1	California	$519,220
		Colorado	$131,797
		DC	$208,324
		Florida	$137,530
		Illinois	$256,454
		Massachusetts	$92,596
		New York	$555,983
		Texas	$758,796
2004		**Sum:**	**$2,660,700**
2005		California	$650,715
		Colorado	$189,131
		DC	$279,490
		Florida	$174,276
		Illinois	$334,297
		New York	$683,971
		Texas	$1,014,293
2005		**Sum:**	**$3,326,172**

Previously it was [Year] and then [Quarter], i.e. 2004 Q1, 2004 Q2, etc.

13.7 Breaks on Cross Tables

With cross tables you are able to apply Vertical and Horizontal breaks and prioritise the breaks within each type. In the following example we have a cross table showing:

- Vertical axis (columns) = [State], [Lines], [City]
- Horizontal axis (rows) = [Year], [Quarter]
- Body axis = [Sales revenue]

			2004 Q1	2004 Q2	2004 Q3	2004 Q4	2004 Sum:	2005 Q1	2005 Q2	2005 Q3	2005 Q4	2005 Sum:
California	Accessories	Los Angeles	$135,150	$106,560	$36,994	$6,567	$285,270	$330,058	$216,818	$62,654	$13,715	$623,244
		San Francisco	$84,616	$88,737	$26,305	$4,737	$204,396	$198,115	$168,206	$48,923	$15,048	$430,293
	Accessories	Sum:	$219,766	$195,297	$63,298	$11,304	$489,666	$528,173	$385,024	$111,577	$28,763	$1,053,537
	City Skirts	Los Angeles	$1,722	$91	$118	$3,339	$5,271	Discontinued	$129	$249	$10,816	$11,194
		San Francisco	$912	Discontinued	Discontinued	$4,890	$5,802	Discontinued	Discontinued	$1,245	$10,338	$11,583
	City Skirts	Sum:	$2,634	$91	$118	$8,230	$11,072	Discontinued	$129	$1,494	$21,153	$22,776
	City Trousers	Los Angeles	$2,403	$252	$236	$2,363	$5,254	$207	$294	$1,593	$10,356	$12,451
		San Francisco	$603	$180	$684	$4,215	$5,681	Discontinued	$245	$2,116	$8,121	$10,482
	City Trousers	Sum:	$3,006	$432	$921	$6,577	$10,935	$207	$539	$3,710	$18,477	$22,932
	[illegible]	[illegible]	[illegible]	[illegible]	[illegible]	[illegible]	$55,295	[illegible]	[illegible]	[illegible]	[illegible]	$101,002

- The cross table has 2 vertical breaks applied ([State], [Lines]) and these can be seen on the left hand side of the cross table.

- The cross table also has 1 horizontal break applied ([Year]) and this can be seen at the top of the crosstab.

- We can also see sub-totals running in both directions.

Let us create this cross table to learn about working with breaks and cross tables.

1. Using our existing query, create the cross table as shown below, you can do this on a new report tab:

			2004	2004	2004	2004	2005
			Q1	Q2	Q3	Q4	Q1
California	Accessories	Los Angeles	$135,150	$106,560	$36,994	$6,567	$330,058
California	Accessories	San Francisco	$84,616	$88,737	$26,305	$4,737	$198,115
California	City Skirts	Los Angeles	$1,722	$91	$118	$3,339	Discontinued
California	City Skirts	San Francisco	$912	Discontinued	Discontinued	$4,890	Discontinued
California	City Trousers	Los Angeles	$2,403	$252	$236	$2,363	$207

Note – You can add in [Quarter] underneath [Year] by dropping [Quarter] into the cross table as shown below, or use right-click and select the 'Assign Data…' interface.

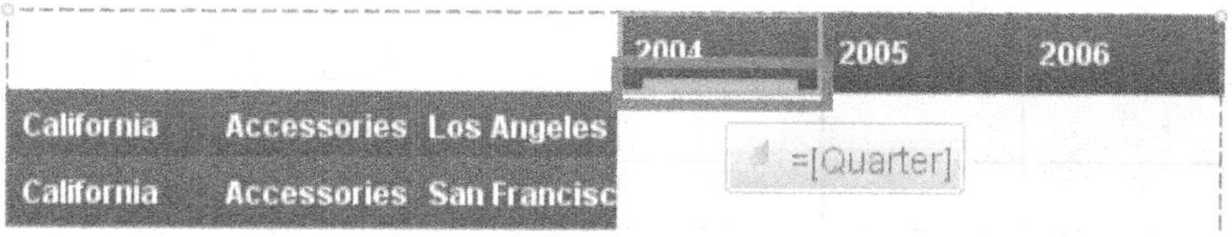
2004
2005
2006
California
Accessories
Los Angeles
California
Accessories
San Francisc
=[Quarter]

2. Click into any cell on [State] and then apply a break, we get:

			2004	2004	2004	2004	2005
			Q1	Q2	Q3	Q4	Q1
California	Accessories	Los Angeles	$135,150	$106,560	$36,994	$6,567	$330,058
	Accessories	San Francisco	$84,616	$88,737	$26,305	$4,737	$198,115
	City Skirts	Los Angeles	$1,722	$91	$118	$3,339	Discontinued
	City Skirts	San Francisco	$912	Discontinued	Discontinued	$4,890	Discontinued

3. Click into any cell on [Lines] and then apply a break, we get:

			2004	2004	2004	2004	2005
			Q1	Q2	Q3	Q4	Q1
California	Accessories	Los Angeles	$135,150	$106,560	$36,994	$6,567	$330,058
		San Francisco	$84,616	$88,737	$26,305	$4,737	$198,115
	Accessories						
	City Skirts	Los Angeles	$1,722	$91	$118	$3,339	Discontinued
		San Francisco	$912	Discontinued	Discontinued	$4,890	Discontinued
	City Skirts						

4. Click into any cell on [Year] and then apply a break, we get:

			2004				2004
			Q1	Q2	Q3	Q4	
California	Accessories	Los Angeles	$135,150	$106,560	$36,994	$6,567	
		San Francisco	$84,616	$88,737	$26,305	$4,737	
	Accessories						
	City Skirts	Los Angeles	$1,722	$91	$118	$3,339	
		San Francisco	$912	Discontinued	Discontinued	$4,890	
	City Skirts						
	City Trousers	Los Angeles	$2,403	$252	$236	$2,363	
		San Francisco	$603	$180	$684	$4,215	

5. Click into any cell on [Sales revenue] and then apply the Standard Calculation of Sum (in both directions), we get:

			2004				2004
			Q1	Q2	Q3	Q4	Sum:
California	Accessories	Los Angeles	$135,150	$106,560	$36,994	$6,567	**$285,270**
		San Francisco	$84,616	$88,737	$26,305	$4,737	**$204,396**
	Accessories	Sum:	**$219,766**	**$195,297**	**$63,298**	**$11,304**	**$489,666**
	City Skirts	Los Angeles	$1,722	$91	$118	$3,339	**$5,271**
		San Francisco	$912	Discontinued	Discontinued	$4,890	**$5,802**

We now have the cross table set up as per the example shown at the start of this topic.

6. Click into any cell of the cross table and select 'Manage Breaks…':

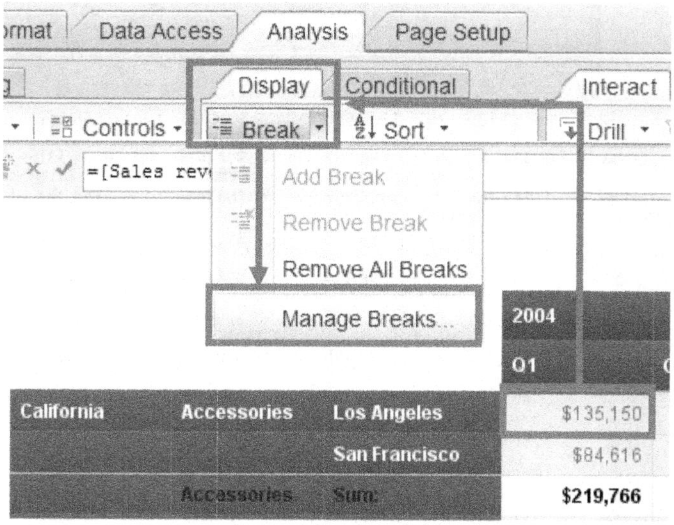

rmat
Data Access
Analysis
Page Setup
Display
Conditional
Interact
Controls
Break
Sort
Drill
=[Sales rev
Add Break
Remove Break
Remove All Breaks
Manage Breaks...
2004
Q1
California
Accessories
Los Angeles
$135,150
San Francisco
$84,616
Accessories
Sum:
$219,766

7. Change the priority of row breaks by moving [Lines] above [State] and click 'OK'.

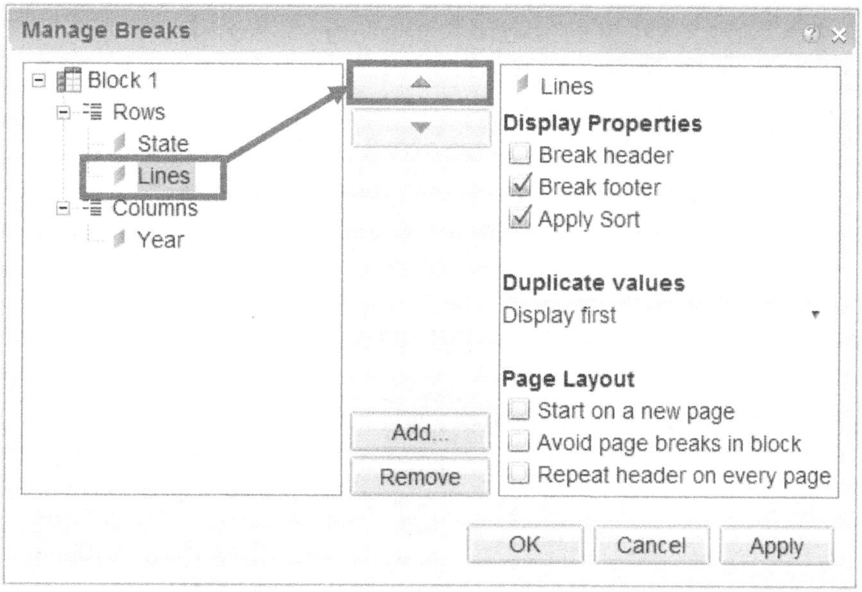

Manage Breaks
Block 1
Rows
State
Lines
Columns
Year
Add...
Remove
Lines
Display Properties
Break header
Break footer
Apply Sort
Duplicate values
Display first
Page Layout
Start on a new page
Avoid page breaks in block
Repeat header on every page
OK
Cancel
Apply

8. The break priorities in the cross table will now change to [Lines] then [State].

			2004				2004
			Q1	Q2	Q3	Q4	Sum:
California	Accessories	Los Angeles	$135,150	$106,560	$36,994	$6,567	**$285,270**
		San Francisco	$84,616	$88,737	$26,305	$4,737	**$204,396**
California		Sum:	**$219,766**	**$195,297**	**$63,298**	**$11,304**	**$489,666**
Colorado		Colorado Springs	$61,609	$58,434	$19,441	$5,609	**$145,093**
Colorado		Sum:	**$61,609**	**$58,434**	**$19,441**	**$5,609**	**$145,093**
DC		Washington	$105,411	$89,485	$30,163	$5,483	**$230,541**
DC		Sum:	**$105,411**	**$89,485**	**$30,163**	**$5,483**	**$230,541**
Florida		Miami	$61,678	$50,135	$15,325	$2,315	**$129,452**
Florida		Sum:	**$61,678**	**$50,135**	**$15,325**	**$2,315**	**$129,452**
Illinois		Chicago	$110,717	$107,389	$20,567	$6,915	**$245,590**
Illinois		Sum:	**$110,717**	**$107,389**	**$20,567**	**$6,915**	**$245,590**
Massachusetts		Boston	$6,094	$4,074	$709	$1,779	**$12,655**
Massachusetts		Sum:	**$6,094**	**$4,074**	**$709**	**$1,779**	**$12,655**
New York		New York	$243,514	$241,611	$71,242	$11,356	**$567,722**
New York		Sum:	**$243,514**	**$241,611**	**$71,242**	**$11,356**	**$567,722**
Texas		Austin	$92,604	$77,151	$26,145	$4,079	**$199,978**
		Dallas	$65,203	$54,519	$12,064	$3,258	**$135,044**
		Houston	$171,532	$156,979	$48,150	$13,820	**$390,482**
Texas		Sum:	**$329,339**	**$288,649**	**$86,359**	**$21,157**	**$725,503**
	Accessories	Sum:	**$1,138,127**	**$1,035,073**	**$307,103**	**$65,919**	**$2,546,222**

9. The current display looks confusing, so swap the [Lines] and [State] objects around by...

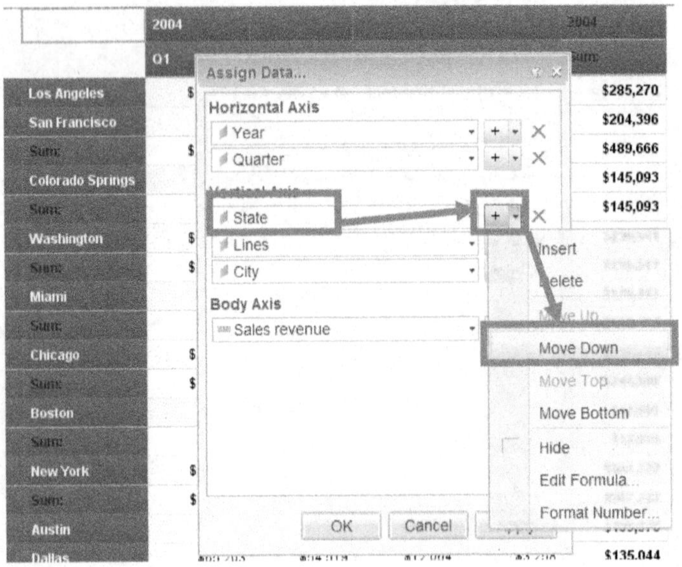
Assign Data...
Horizontal Axis
Year
Quarter
State
Lines
City
Body Axis
Sales revenue
Insert
Move Down
Move Bottom
Hide
Edit Formula...
Format Number...
OK
Cancel

- Right-clicking on any edge of the cross table and selecting ‘Assign Data...’
- Then moving [State] down one place.

You can also achieve the same by dragging the [Lines] object into the centre of the [State object].

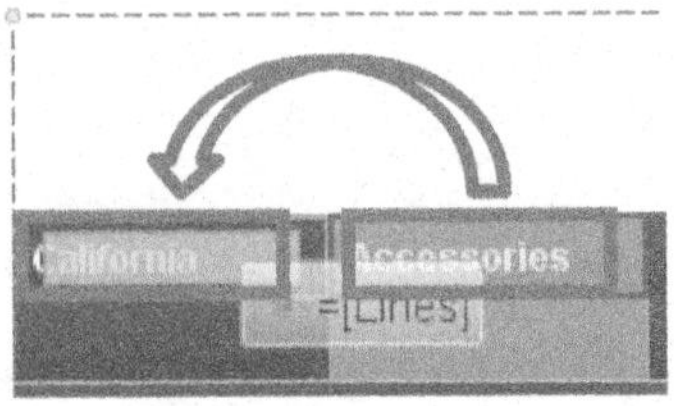
California
Accessories
=[Lines]

10. The display now reflects the break priorities and is easier to understand:

			2004				2004
			Q1	Q2	Q3	Q4	Sum:
Accessories	California	Los Angeles	$135,150	$106,560	$36,994	$6,567	**$285,270**
		San Francisco	$84,616	$88,737	$26,305	$4,737	**$204,396**
	California	Sum:	**$219,766**	**$195,297**	**$63,298**	**$11,304**	**$489,666**
	Colorado	Colorado Springs	$61,609	$58,434	$19,441	$5,609	**$145,093**
	Colorado	Sum:	**$61,609**	**$58,434**	**$19,441**	**$5,609**	**$145,093**
	DC	Washington	$105,411	$89,485	$30,163	$5,483	**$230,541**
	DC	Sum:	**$105,411**	**$89,485**	**$30,163**	**$5,483**	**$230,541**
	Florida	Miami	$61,678	$50,135	$15,325	$2,315	**$129,452**
	Florida	Sum:	**$61,678**	**$50,135**	**$15,325**	**$2,315**	**$129,452**
	Illinois	Chicago	$110,717	$107,389	$20,567	$6,915	**$245,590**
	Illinois	Sum:	**$110,717**	**$107,389**	**$20,567**	**$6,915**	**$245,590**
	Massachusetts	Boston	$6,094	$4,074	$709	$1,779	**$12,655**
	Massachusetts	Sum:	**$6,094**	**$4,074**	**$709**	**$1,779**	**$12,655**
	New York	New York	$243,514	$241,611	$71,242	$11,356	**$567,722**
	New York	Sum:	**$243,514**	**$241,611**	**$71,242**	**$11,356**	**$567,722**
	Texas	Austin	$92,604	$77,151	$26,145	$4,079	**$199,978**
		Dallas	$65,203	$54,519	$12,064	$3,258	**$135,044**
		Houston	$171,532	$156,979	$48,150	$13,820	**$390,482**
	Texas	Sum:	**$329,339**	**$288,649**	**$86,359**	**$21,157**	**$725,503**
Accessories		Sum:	**$1,138,127**	**$1,035,073**	**$307,103**	**$65,919**	**$2,546,222**

13.8 Formatting Hints and Tips on Breaks

Here are some hints and tips to make presentation of breaks better by using formatting properties.

13.8.1 Displaying a single block header instead of multiple break headers

Vertical table with no breaks shows a single table header row

Year	Quarter	Sales revenue
2004	Q1	$2,660,700
2004	Q2	$2,278,693
2004	Q3	$1,367,841
2004	Q4	$1,788,580
2005	Q1	$3,326,172
2005	Q2	$2,840,651
2005	Q3	$2,879,303
2005	Q4	$4,186,120
2006	Q1	$3,742,989
2006	Q2	$4,006,718
2006	Q3	$3,953,395
2006	Q4	$3,356,041

Vertical table with a break on [Year] shows multiple break header rows

Year	Quarter	Sales revenue
2004	Q1	$2,660,700
	Q2	$2,278,693
	Q3	$1,367,841
	Q4	$1,788,580
2004		

Year	Quarter	Sales revenue
2005	Q1	$3,326,172
	Q2	$2,840,651
	Q3	$2,879,303
	Q4	$4,186,120
2005		

Year	Quarter	Sales revenue
2006	Q1	$3,742,989
	Q2	$4,006,718
	Q3	$3,953,395
	Q4	$3,356,041
2006		

When breaks are applied we lose the table header and it is replaced by a break header. In the above example we had a single table header row that got replaced by 3 break header rows (due to 3 values for [Year]).

> **NOTE** – If you applied a second break then you will lose the break headers of the first break and have them replaced by headers of the second break.

We would like to only show a single header row at the top of the table so we do not get the repeated break header rows on the page.

To do this we need to show the table header and hide the break headers as shown overleaf.

1. Right-click on any edge of the table and select 'Format table…'

2. Tick 'Show table headers' and click 'OK'.

3. We will now get an extra header row appear at the top of the table:

Year	Quarter	Sales revenue
Year	Quarter	Sales revenue
2004	Q1	$2,660,700
	Q2	$2,278,693
	Q3	$1,367,841
	Q4	$1,788,580
2004		

4. Right-click on any of the 'break header' rows (not the top of the row of the table as that is the 'table header') and then select 'Delete'.

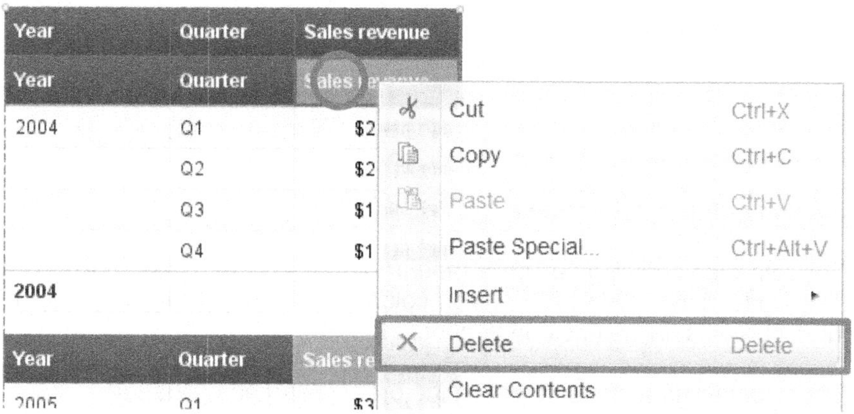
Year
Quarter
Sales revenue
Cut
Ctrl+X
Copy
Ctrl+C
Paste
Ctrl+V
Paste Special...
Ctrl+Alt+V
Insert
Delete
Delete
Clear Contents

5. Select 'Remove Row' and click 'OK'.

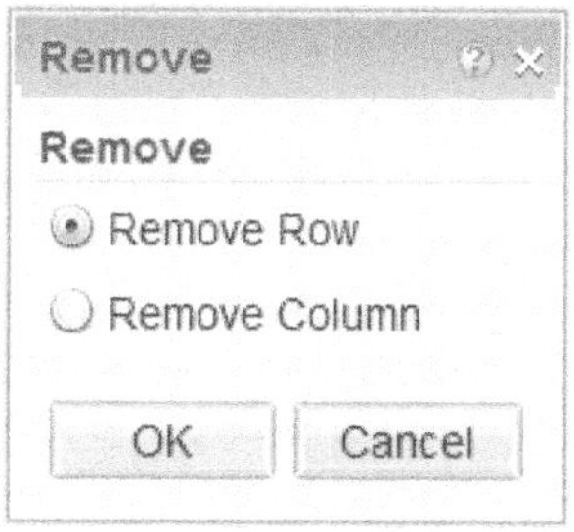
Remove
Remove
Remove Row
Remove Column
OK
Cancel

NOTE

You can also remove the break header by using the 'Manage Breaks…' interface:

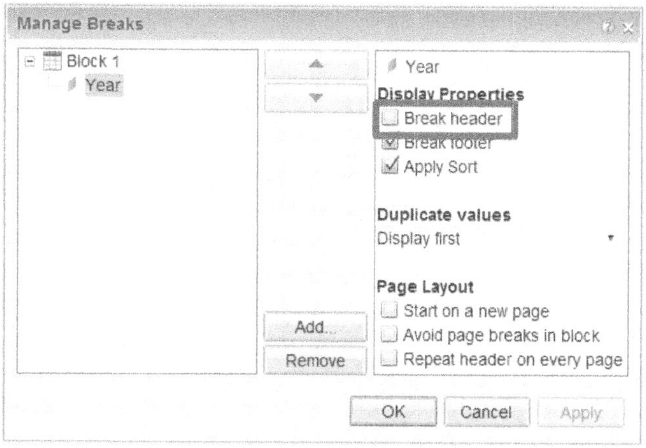
Manage Breaks
Block 1
Year
Year
Display Properties
Break header
Break footer
Apply Sort
Duplicate values
Display first
Page Layout
Start on a new page
Avoid page breaks in block
Repeat header on every page
Add...
Remove
OK
Cancel
Apply

6. We will now have only one header row for a table containing break(s):

Year	Quarter	Sales revenue
2004	Q1	$2,660,700
	Q2	$2,278,693
	Q3	$1,367,841
	Q4	$1,788,580
2004		
2005	Q1	$3,326,172
	Q2	$2,840,651
	Q3	$2,879,303
	Q4	$4,186,120
2005		
2006	Q1	$3,742,989
	Q2	$4,006,718
	Q3	$3,953,395
	Q4	$3,356,041
2006		

13.8.2 Using text labels and colours with breaks

If a block contains a lot of data then scrolling vertically (and/or horizontally for cross tables) is required for online viewing (in draft mode view). Use of colour on columns/rows with breaks can be helpful to users who are using your documents online (instead of printed format).

1. We have a vertical table containing a nested break in the order [Year] and [Quarter].

Year	Quarter	State	Sales revenue
2004	Q1	California	$519,220
		Colorado	$131,797
		DC	$208,324
		Florida	$137,530
		Illinois	$256,454
		Massachusetts	$92,596
		New York	$555,983
		Texas	$758,796
	Q1	**Sum:**	**$2,660,700**
	Q2	California	$441,494
		Colorado	$129,076
		DC	$179,863

2. We have added an extra column using the [Lines] object and placed a third level break on [State].

   The Standard Calculation 'Sum' has been re-applied after adding the break on [State].

Year	Quarter	State	Lines	Sales revenue
2004	Q1	California	Accessories	$219,766
			City Skirts	$2,634
			City Trousers	$3,006
			Dresses	$23,357
			Jackets	$13,802
			Leather	$3,089
			Outerwear	$8,612
			Overcoats	$3,980
			Shirt Waist	$46,524
			Sweaters	$29,460
			Sweat-T-Shirts	$156,783
			Trousers	$8,209
		California	**Sum:**	**$519,220**
		Colorado	Accessories	$61,609
			City Skirts	$124
			City Trousers	$427

3. Scroll to the very last page of the report using the Last Page button on the Page Navigation toolbar (located at the bottom of your working window).

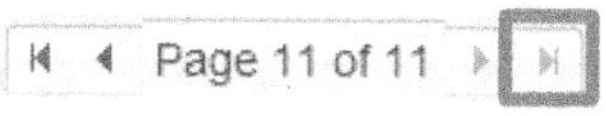
Page 11 of 11

			Outerwear	$878
			Overcoats	$2,997
			Shirt Waist	$106,555
			Sweaters	$116,468
			Sweat-T-Shirts	$525,501
			Trousers	$18,669
		Texas	**Sum:**	**$961,768**
	Q4		**Sum:**	**$3,356,041**
2006			**Sum:**	**$15,059,143**
			Sum:	**$36,387,203**

This area of the report showing subtotals at all the break levels looks very cluttered.

4. Select each cell displaying the text 'Sum:' and use right-click 'Clear Contents' to remove some of the clutter.

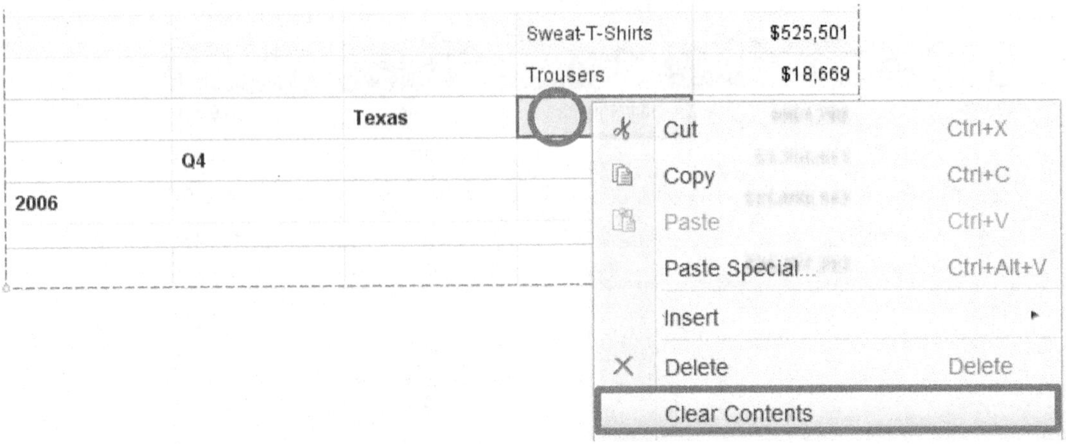
Sweat-T-Shirts
$525,501
Trousers
$18,669
Texas
Q4
2006
Cut
Ctrl+X
Copy
Ctrl+C
Paste
Ctrl+V
Paste Special...
Ctrl+Alt+V
Insert
Delete
Delete
Clear Contents

5. Drag-and-drop the break footer text for [State] into the [Lines] column as shown.

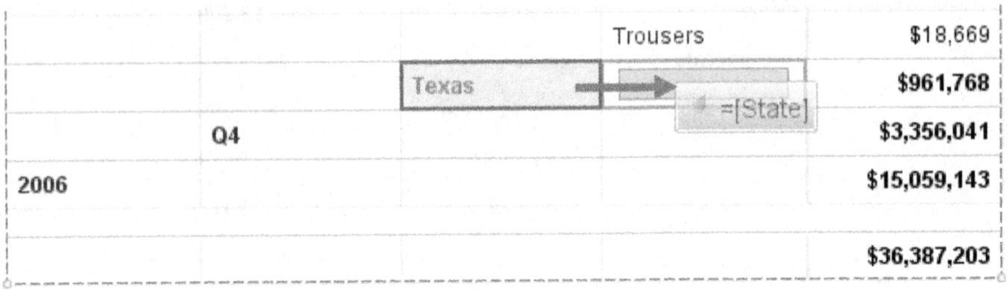
Trousers
$18,669
Texas
$961,768
=[State]
Q4
$3,356,041
2006
$15,059,143
$36,387,203

6. Do the same for [Quarter] and [Year] footer rows:

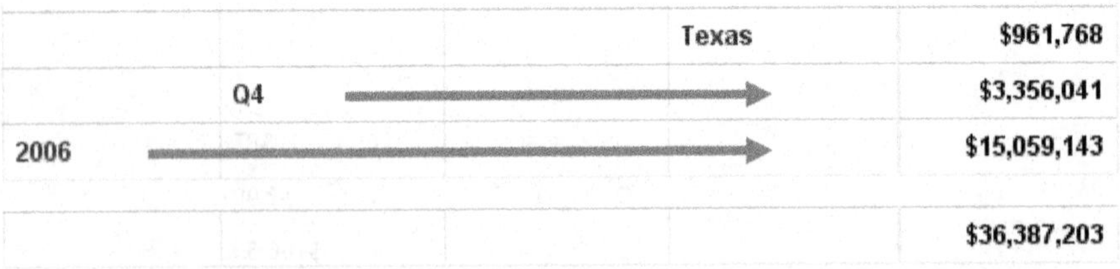
Texas
$961,768
Q4
$3,356,041
2006
$15,059,143
$36,387,203

7. Double-click in the following cell and type 'Report Total' and then click the 'green tick' icon to validate the formula:

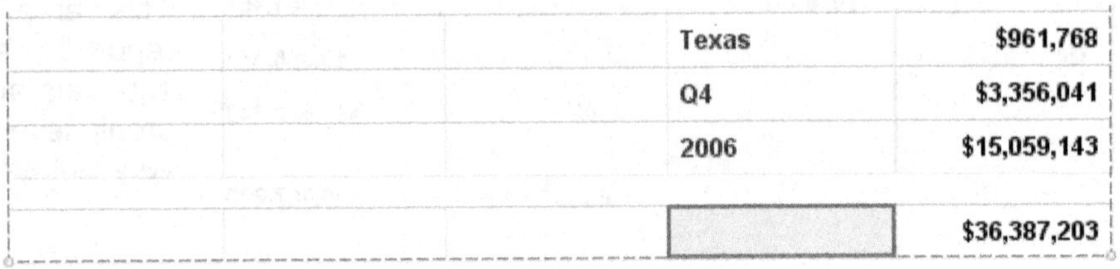
Texas
$961,768
Q4
$3,356,041
2006
$15,059,143
$36,387,203

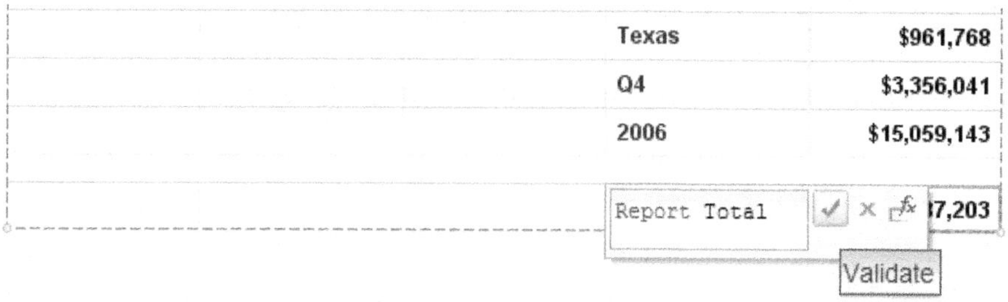
Texas
$961,768
Q4
$3,356,041
2006
$15,059,143
Report Total
7,203
Validate

8. The bottom of the block will now appear as:

Texas
$961,768
Q4
$3,356,041
2006
$15,059,143
Report Total
$36,387,203

9. With the <Ctrl> key held down select cells to form the outline shown here.

   Essentially, we have selected the cells in the [Year] column and the cells in the break footer row for [Year].

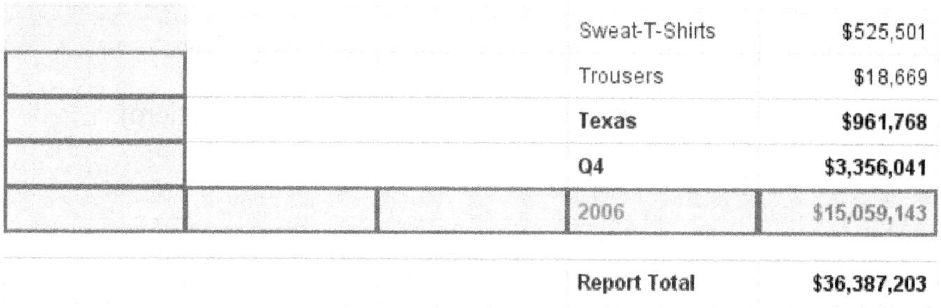
Sweat-T-Shirts
$525,501
Trousers
$18,669
Texas
$961,768
Q4
$3,356,041
2006
$15,059,143
Report Total
$36,387,203

10. Apply a background colour to these cells (Pale Blue has been selected here).

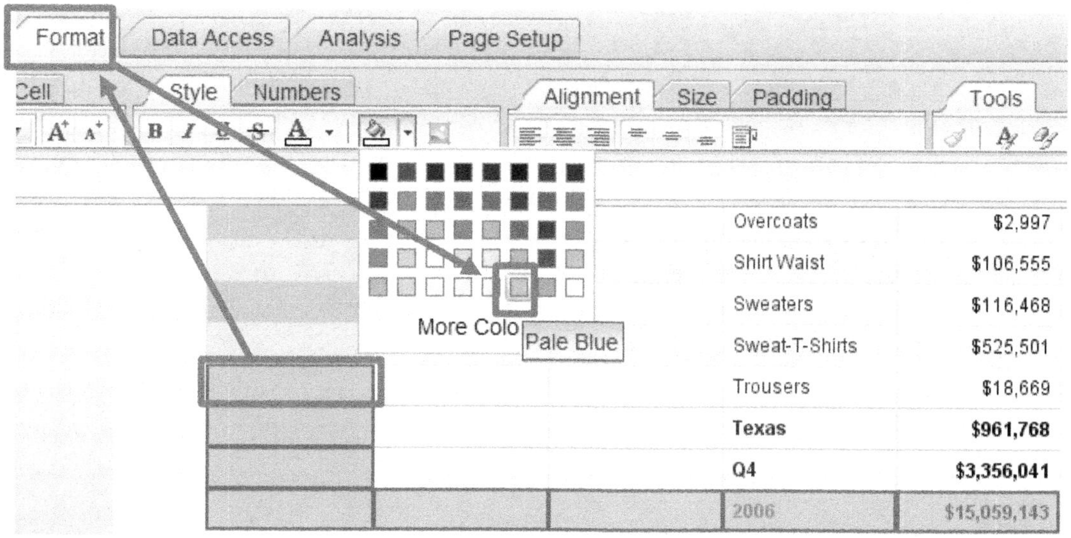
Format
Data Access
Analysis
Page Setup
Cell
Style
Numbers
Alignment
Size
Padding
Tools
More Colo
Pale Blue
Overcoats
$2,997
Shirt Waist
$106,555
Sweaters
$116,468
Sweat-T-Shirts
$525,501
Trousers
$18,669
Texas
$961,768
Q4
$3,356,041
2006
$15,059,143

11. Similarly, select the cells in the [Quarter] column and [Quarter] break footer row.

    Apply a background colour to these cells (Light Green has been selected here).

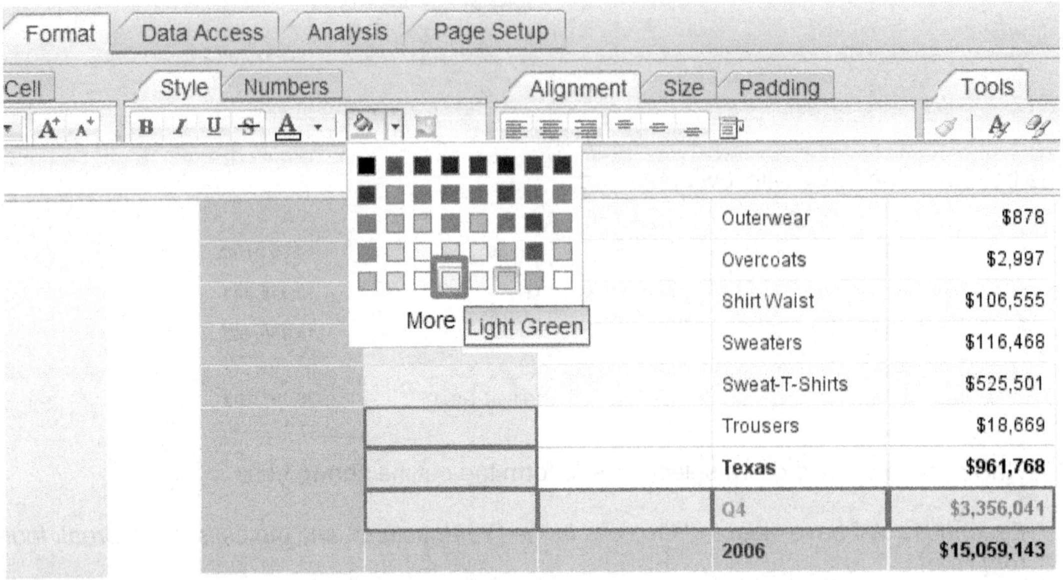
Format
Data Access
Analysis
Page Setup
Cell
Style
Numbers
Alignment
Size
Padding
Tools
More
Light Green
Outerwear
$878
Overcoats
$2,997
Shirt Waist
$106,555
Sweaters
$116,468
Sweat-T-Shirts
$525,501
Trousers
$18,669
Texas
$961,768
Q4
$3,356,041
2006
$15,059,143

12. Likewise, select the cells in the [State] column and [State] break footer row.

    Apply a background colour to these cells (Light Yellow has been selected here).

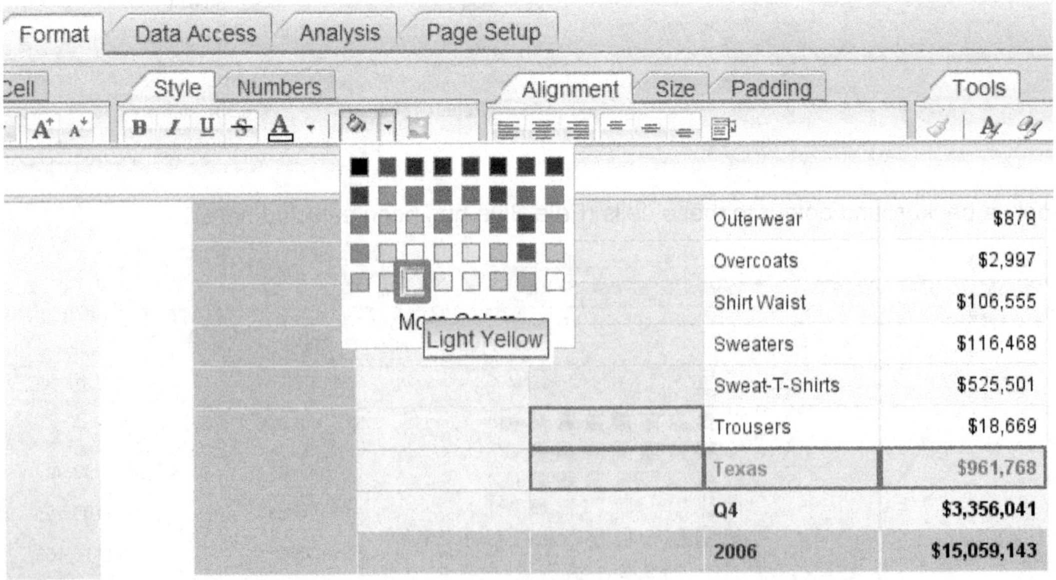
Format
Data Access
Analysis
Page Setup
Cell
Style
Numbers
Alignment
Size
Padding
Tools
Light Yellow
Outerwear
$878
Overcoats
$2,997
Shirt Waist
$106,555
Sweaters
$116,468
Sweat-T-Shirts
$525,501
Trousers
$18,669
Texas
$961,768
Q4
$3,356,041
2006
$15,059,143

13. Navigate to other pages of the report to see how the use of colour makes the report appear less cluttered.

New break and subtotals rows are now easily identified using the coloured formatting.

	New York	**$885,800**
Texas	Accessories	$51,263
	City Skirts	$21,361
	City Trousers	$32,523
	Dresses	$190,391
	Jackets	$20,286
	Leather	$8,226
	Outerwear	$5,686
	Overcoats	$58,889
	Shirt Waist	$278,112
	Sweaters	$51,348
	Sweat-T-Shirts	$388,843
	Trousers	$31,130
	Texas	**$1,138,056**
	Q4	**$4,186,120**
	2005	**$13,232,246**

13.9 Using the Percentage Standard Calculation with Breaks

When the Standard Calculation of Percentage is used with Breaks then the percentage values are calculated at various levels (depending on the number of breaks).

Year	Quarter	Quantity sold	Percentage:
2004	Q1	18,136	8.12%
2004	Q2	14,408	6.45%
2004	Q3	10,203	4.57%
2004	Q4	10,331	4.63%
2005	Q1	21,135	9.47%
2005	Q2	17,152	7.68%
2005	Q3	19,224	8.61%
2005	Q4	22,344	10.01%
2006	Q1	22,537	10.10%
2006	Q2	22,846	10.23%
2006	Q3	26,263	11.77%
2006	Q4	18,650	8.35%
		Percentage:	**100.00%**

Here we have a vertical table block with no breaks showing how each row contributes to the total as a percentage.

We have described this in the earlier session on 'Using Standard Calculations'.

1. Create the following vertical table block (you can use the use the same document and add a new report tab for this).

   Apply a break on the [Year] column.

Year	Quarter	Quantity sold
2004	Q1	18,136
	Q2	14,408
	Q3	10,203
	Q4	10,331
2004		

Year	Quarter	Quantity sold
2005	Q1	21,135
	Q2	17,152
	Q3	19,224
	Q4	22,344
2005		

Year	Quarter	Quantity sold
2006	Q1	22,537
	Q2	22,846
	Q3	26,263
	Q4	18,650
2006		

2. Apply the Percentage (Standard Calculation) to [Quantity sold].

   'Functions' are located on the 'Analysis' toolbox.

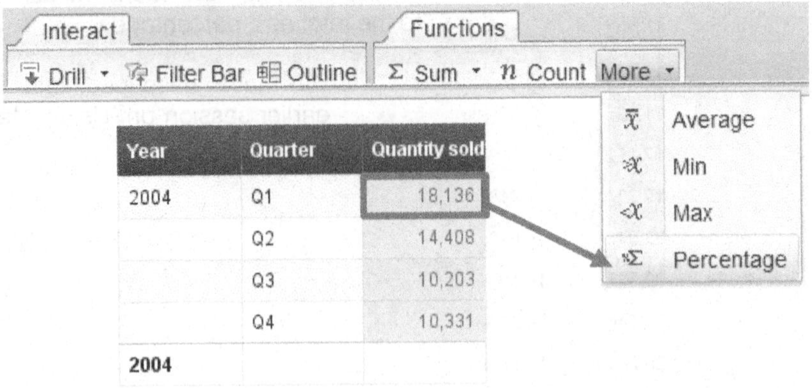
Interact
Functions
Drill
Filter Bar
Outline
Σ Sum
n Count
More
Average
Min
Max
Percentage
Year
Quarter
Quantity sold
2004
Q1
18,136
Q2
14,408
Q3
10,203
Q4
10,331
2004

3. Web Intelligence displays:

Year	Quarter	Quantity sold	
2004	Q1	18,136	34.17%
	Q2	14,408	27.14%
	Q3	10,203	19.22%
	Q4	10,331	19.46%
2004		**Percentage:**	**23.78%**

Year	Quarter	Quantity sold	
2005	Q1	21,135	26.47%
	Q2	17,152	21.48%
	Q3	19,224	24.07%
	Q4	22,344	27.98%
2005		**Percentage:**	**35.77%**

Year	Quarter	Quantity sold	
2006	Q1	22,537	24.96%
	Q2	22,846	25.30%
	Q3	26,263	29.09%
	Q4	18,650	20.65%
2006		**Percentage:**	**40.45%**
		Percentage:	**100.00%**

Block with a break on [Year] shows how each row contributes as a percentage within the break.

Total within the break value:

34.17 + 27.14 + 19.22 + 19.46 = 99.99 (100%)

Percentages are also calculated at the break summary level as shown here.

Total across all break values:

23.78 + 35.77 + 40.45 = 100%

13.10 Hiding/Showing Data in Blocks with Breaks

The 'Outline Toolbar' enables you to collapse and expand breaks to show or hide rows of data.

We will take the earlier example used to demonstrate the use of text labels and colours for formatting of breaks and use it to show 'Outline Toolbar'.

1. Switch to the tab containing the following report:

Year	Quarter	State	Lines	Sales revenue
2004	Q1	California	Accessories	$219,766
			City Skirts	$2,634
			City Trousers	$3,006

2. Activate the 'Outline Toolbar' from the 'Properties' toolbox:

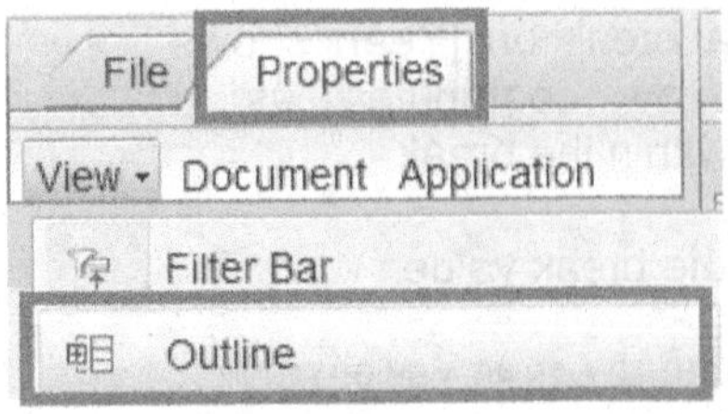
File
Properties
View
Document
Application
Filter Bar
Outline

This will show the Outline Toolbar to the left and above the report:

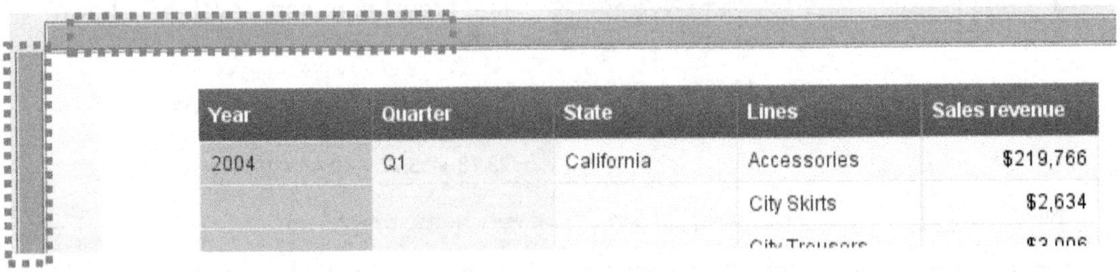
Year
Quarter
State
Lines
Sales revenue
2004
Q1
California
Accessories
$219,766
City Skirts
$2,634

3. Click into any cell within the table and the left outline bar changes to show:

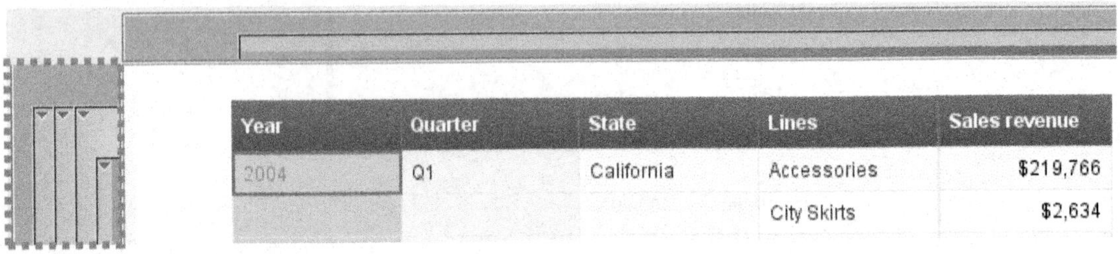
Year
Quarter
State
Lines
Sales revenue
2004
Q1
California
Accessories
$219,766
City Skirts
$2,634

4. At the bottom of the left outline bar we have:

The left outline bar is indicating we have 3 breaks due to the 1, 2, and 3 appearing at the bottom.

Hovering over the labels or the arrows indicates the break level/value being displayed:

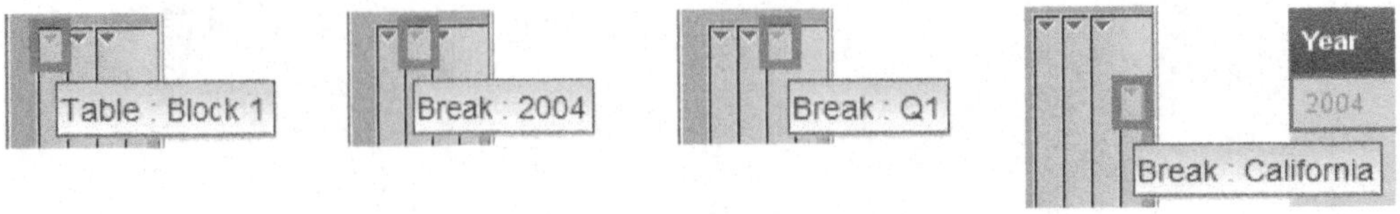
Table : Block 1
Break : 2004
Break : Q1
Year
2004
Break : California

5. Clicking on ‘T’ (i.e. 'Top' or 'Table') or its associated navigation arrow

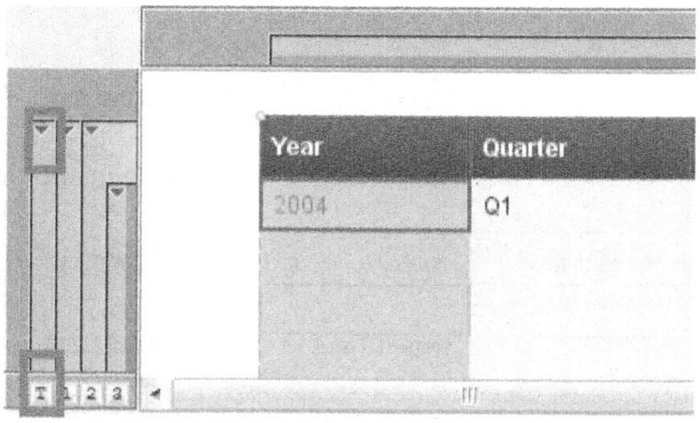
Year
Quarter
2004
Q1

...will collapse all the breaks (i.e. ‘Fold’ the table completely) as shown below:

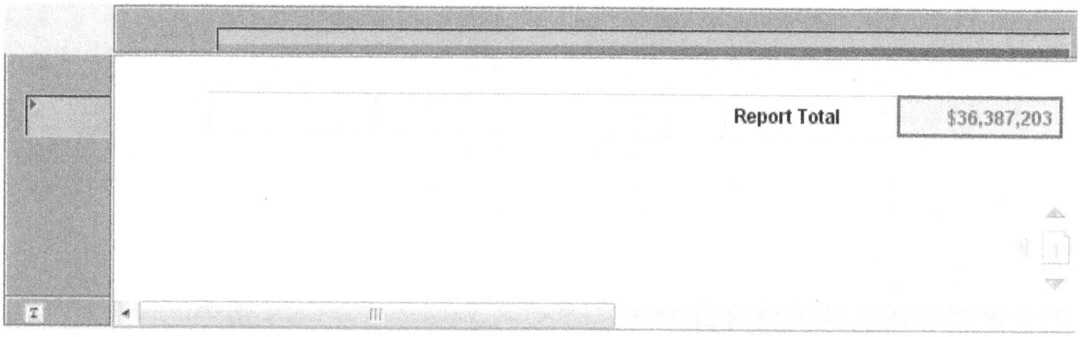
Report Total
$36,387,203

You can click on ‘T’ again or its associated navigation arrow to Unfold all the breaks.

6. Click on ‘1’ to Unfold the level 1 break (as shown below):

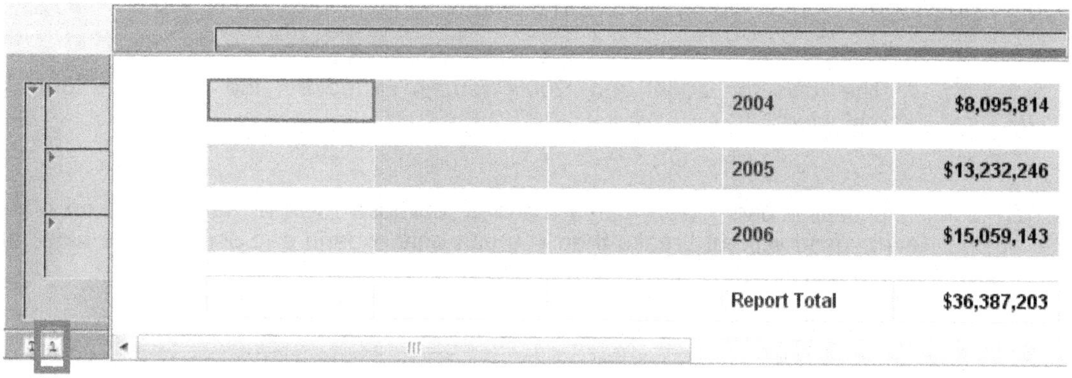
2004
$8,095,814
2005
$13,232,246
2006
$15,059,143
Report Total
$36,387,203

7. If we now want to expand (i.e. 'Unfold') the rows just for '2005' then we use the arrow for the '2005' data:

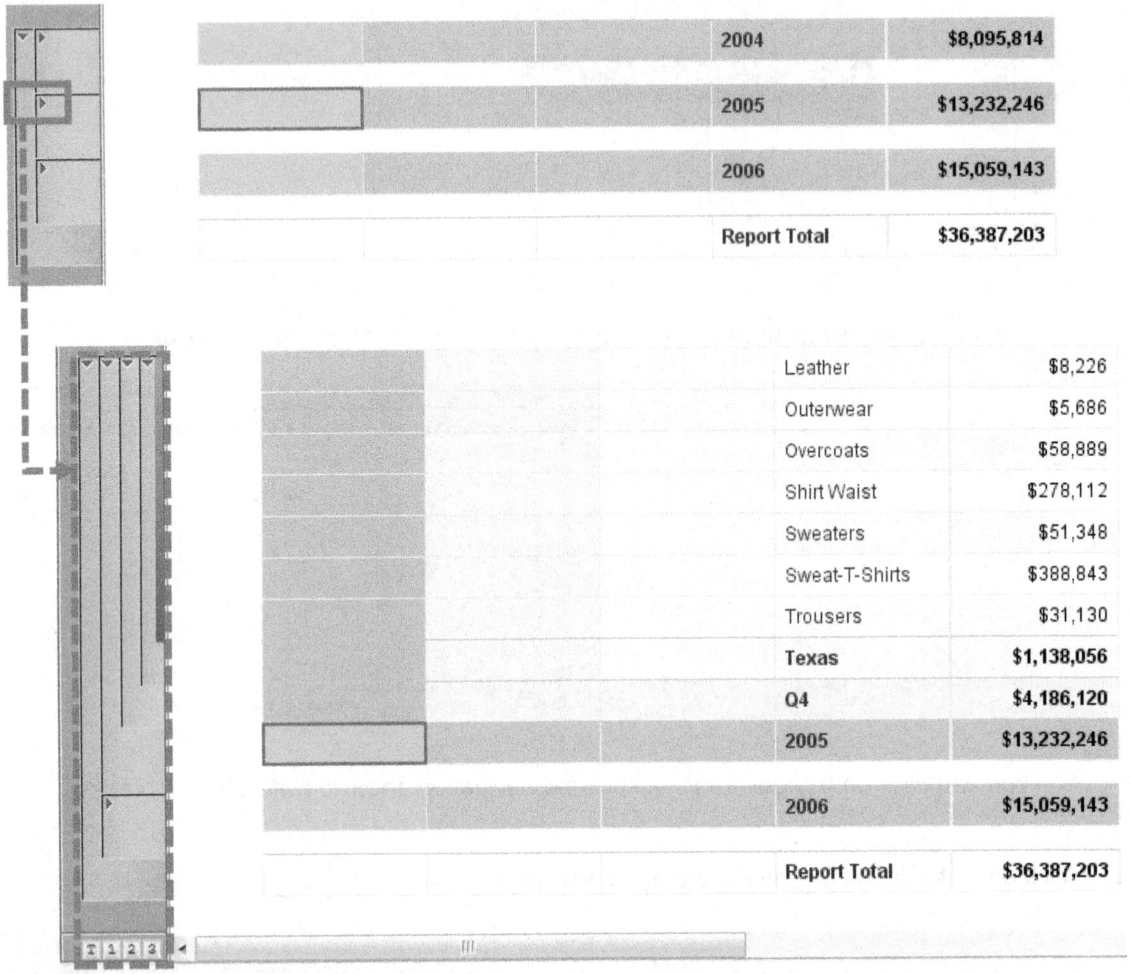
2004
$8,095,814
2005
$13,232,246
2006
$15,059,143
Report Total
$36,387,203
Leather
$8,226
Outerwear
$5,686
Overcoats
$58,889
Shirt Waist
$278,112
Sweaters
$51,348
Sweat-T-Shirts
$388,843
Trousers
$31,130
Texas
$1,138,056
Q4
$4,186,120
2005
$13,232,246
2006
$15,059,143
Report Total
$36,387,203

The rows for '2004' and '2006' remain folded but the rows for '2005' have been 'unfolded'.

8. By using the outline bars, users can expand or collapse rows of data based on breaks. If the outline view is used without breaks then you can only expand and collapse the block at one level (because the breaks give you the different levels).

NOTES / TIPS for OUTLINE VIEW

1. It is best to include a Table Header as well as (or to replace Break Headers) because as you have seen above without a Table Header when breaks are collapsed, you lose the column headers.

   Using the Table Headers will always give you the column headers:

Year	Quarter	State	Lines	Sales revenue
			2004	$8,095,814
2005	Q1	California	Accessories	$528,173
			City Trousers	$207

2. It is best to prepare the block for fold/un-fold analysis by folding all the breaks first.

   In this example with all the breaks unfolded first, we would first click on '3', then on '2' and finally on '1' to display the following:

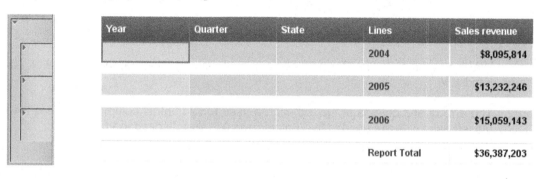

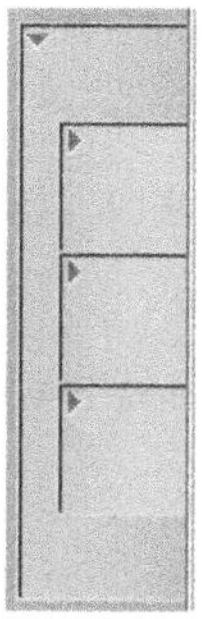

Year	Quarter	State	Lines	Sales revenue
			2004	$8,095,814
			2005	$13,232,246
			2006	$15,059,143
			Report Total	$36,387,203

The above table is now showing totals for each year and a Grand Total.

Users can then fold/unfold the data from this point depending on how they want to analyse the data.

REMEMBER

- To fold/unfold a break completely then click on the relevant **LABEL** (e.g. '1', '2', '3', etc).
- To fold/unfold an individual break value then click on the **ARROW** to the left of the relevant break value (e.g. '2005', 'Q1', Q2', etc).

3. In cross tables, you can fold/unfold columns as well as rows:

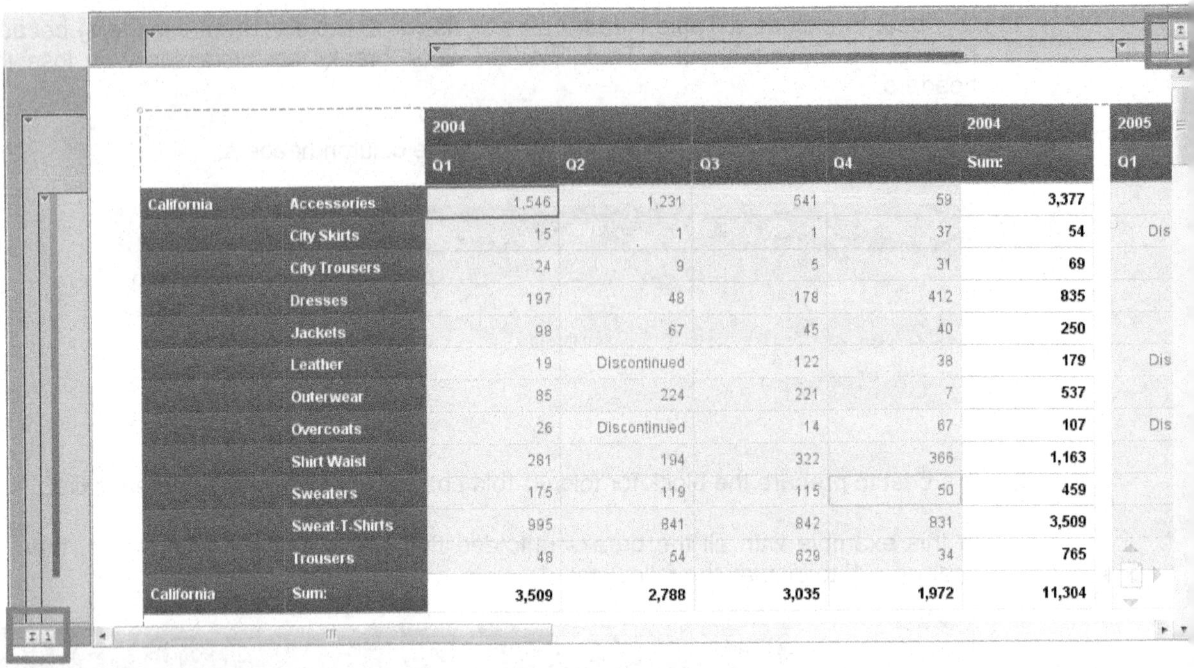

		2004				2004	2005
		Q1	Q2	Q3	Q4	Sum:	Q1
California	Accessories	1,546	1,231	541	59	3,377	
	City Skirts	15	1	1	37	54	Dis
	City Trousers	24	9	5	31	69	
	Dresses	197	48	178	412	835	
	Jackets	98	67	45	40	250	
	Leather	19	Discontinued	122	38	179	Dis
	Outerwear	85	224	221	7	537	
	Overcoats	26	Discontinued	14	67	107	Dis
	Shirt Waist	281	194	322	366	1,163	
	Sweaters	175	119	115	50	459	
	Sweat-T-Shirts	995	841	842	831	3,509	
	Trousers	48	54	629	34	765	
California	Sum:	3,509	2,788	3,035	1,972	11,304	

We can see the Outline Bar now contains buttons and labels at the top as well as on the left hand side.

The arrows and buttons at the top can be used to fold/unfold columns, whereas the buttons on the left hand side are used to fold/unfold rows (as already described).

Clicking on '1' within the top Outline Bar, we can fold the break applied to the [Year] object:

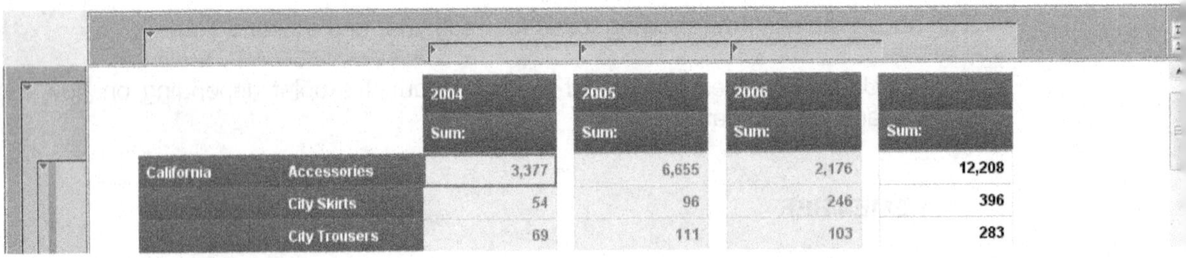

		2004	2005	2006	
		Sum:	Sum:	Sum:	Sum:
California	Accessories	3,377	6,655	2,176	12,208
	City Skirts	54	96	246	396
	City Trousers	69	111	103	283

The buttons and arrows in the top Outline Bar work in the same way as the ones in the left Outline Bar, so users can collapse/expand rows and columns based on their analysis requirements.

14 Sections

Sections enable you to create Master-Detail reports:

- A section is created for every value of the object (dimension or detail) chosen as the section master. This value is shown in a cell called the Section Header Cell.
- You cannot create a section using a measure object.
- Any blocks (tables, charts) inserted into one section are displayed in all sections.
- Sections can be navigated so users can 'jump' to the section that is of interest to them.

Let us start with a new document containing the following query using the 'eFashion' universe:

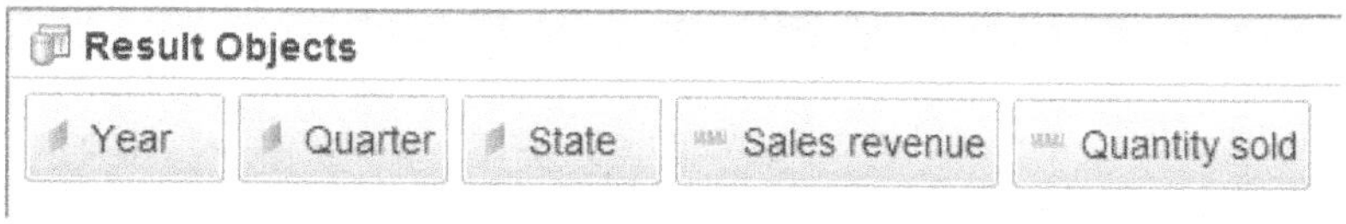
Result Objects
Year
Quarter
State
Sales revenue
Quantity sold

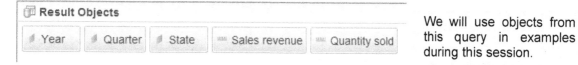

We will use objects from this query in examples during this session.

14.1 Creating Sections

There are a number of ways to create a section.

1. Select the object in a table and choose the 'Set as Section' command from the right-click menu.

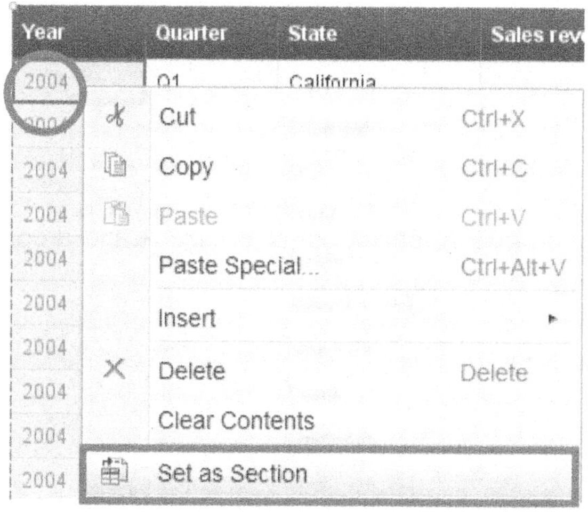
Year
Quarter
State
Sales rev
2004
Q1
California
Cut
Ctrl+X
Copy
Ctrl+C
Paste
Ctrl+V
Paste Special...
Ctrl+Alt+V
Insert
Delete
Delete
Clear Contents
Set as Section

2. You can also create a section using 'Insert Section' within the 'Report Element – Section' toolbox.

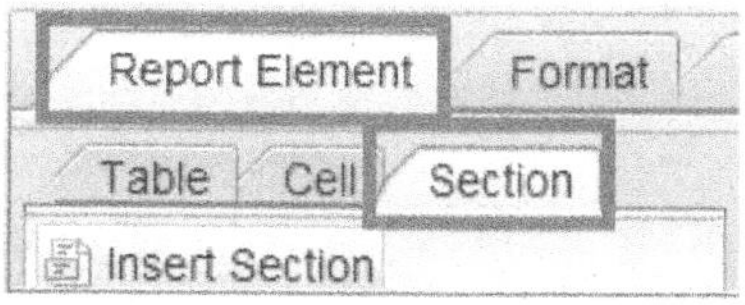
Report Element
Format
Table
Cell
Section
Insert Section

Drag and Drop the template onto the report canvas as shown here.

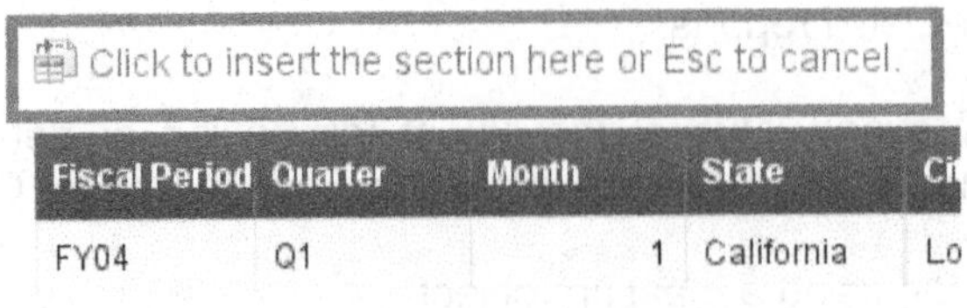
Click to insert the section here or Esc to cancel.
Fiscal Period
Quarter
Month
State
FY04
Q1
1
California
Lo

You can always move and reposition the section, cells, and blocks after creating the section.

Select the object you want to use for the section and click 'OK'.

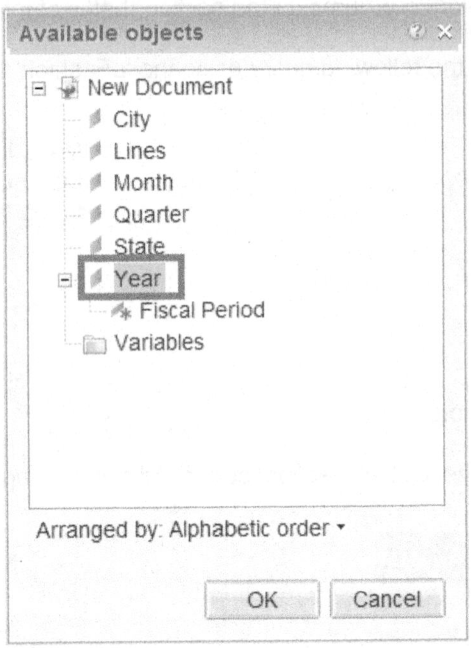
Available objects
New Document
City
Lines
Month
Quarter
State
Year
Fiscal Period
Variables
Arranged by: Alphabetic order
OK
Cancel

3. You may also use drag and drop techniques to pull an object out of the block and drop it in the blank report area to create a section.

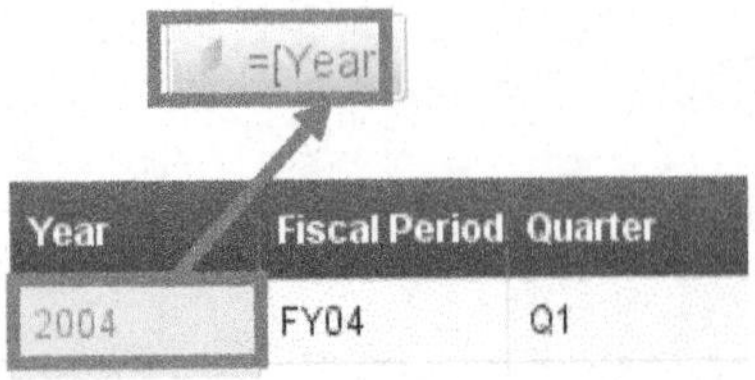
=[Year
Year
Fiscal Period
Quarter
2004
FY04
Q1

Whichever technique you use, a sectioned report (by default) will appear with a Section Master Cell containing the Section Value.

Any blocks within a section will only show rows that are associated with that section's value.

For example, if before creating a section on [Year] we have:

State	Quantity sold	Sales revenue
California	46,074	$7,479,569
Colorado	12,787	$2,060,275
DC	18,744	$2,961,950
Florida	11,267	$1,879,159
Illinois	17,976	$3,022,658
Massachusetts	7,676	$1,283,707
New York	46,358	$7,582,221
Texas	62,347	$10,117,664

[Quantity sold] and [Sales revenue] have been aggregated [State] for all 3 years (2004, 2005 and 2006) in this single block.

After creating the section on [Year] we get a Master-Detail presentation:

2004

State	Quantity sold	Sales revenue
California	11,304	$1,704,211
Colorado	2,974	$448,302
DC	4,681	$693,211
Florida	2,585	$40[illegible],985
Illinois	4,713	$737,914
Massachusetts	1,505	$238,819
New York	10,802	$1,667,696
Texas	14,517	$2,199,677

2005

State	Quantity sold	Sales revenue
California	17,001	$2,782,680
Colorado	4,700	$768,390
DC	7,572	$1,215,158
Florida	3,852	$661,250
Illinois	6,744	$1,150,659
Massachusetts	902	$157,719
New York	16,447	$2,763,503
Texas	22,637	$3,732,889

Creating a section on [Year] creates 3 sections (as we have 3 values for year) and the block is repeated in each section.

However, in each section, the block will only contain data that is related to the Section Header.

Section Header Cell acting as the **Master**.

Everything else within a section is affectively the **Detail**.

14.2 Formatting Sections

The best way to format a section is to use the **right-click** menu 'Format Section…' because all the available formatting options are available within the 'Format Section' interface.

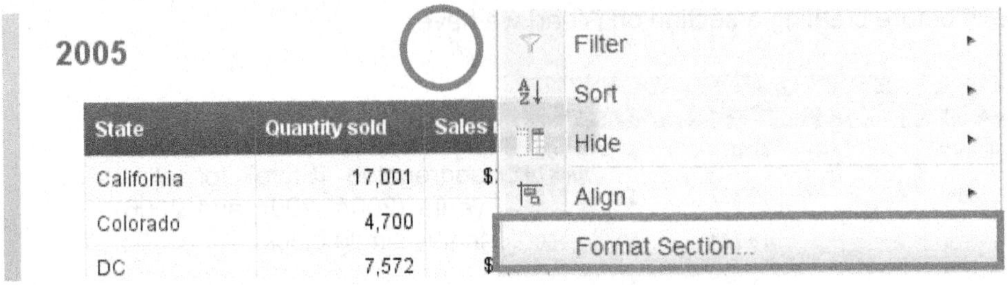
2005
State
Quantity sold
Sales
California
17,001
Colorado
4,700
DC
7,572
Filter
Sort
Hide
Align
Format Section...

Formatting options for sections are:

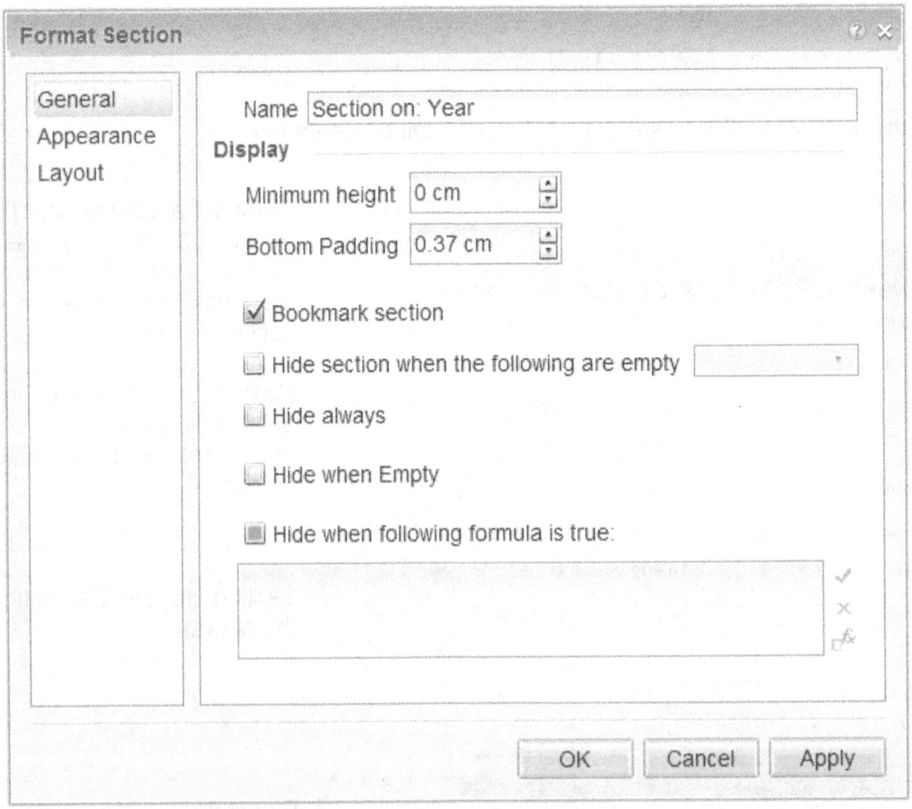
Format Section
General
Appearance
Layout
Name
Section on: Year
Display
Minimum height
0 cm
Bottom Padding
0.37 cm
Bookmark section
Hide section when the following are empty
Hide always
Hide when Empty
Hide when following formula is true:
OK
Cancel
Apply

Section Property	Usage
Name	You can change the name of the section other than the default name used by Web Intelligence. Typically the default name will suffice.
Minimum height	The minimum height of the section within the report. This height will dynamically change based on number of rows in the block (or other report elements within the section, e.g. such as charts). You can fix the minimum height if you wish so you always get a certain minimum section size.

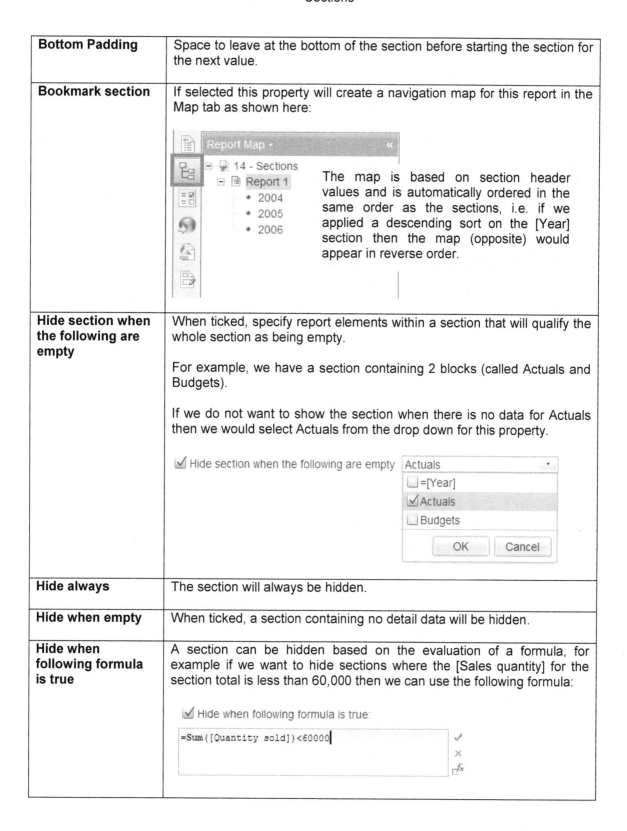

<table>
<tr><td>Bottom Padding</td><td>Space to leave at the bottom of the section before starting the section for the next value.</td></tr>
<tr><td>Bookmark section</td><td>If selected this property will create a navigation map for this report in the Map tab as shown here:
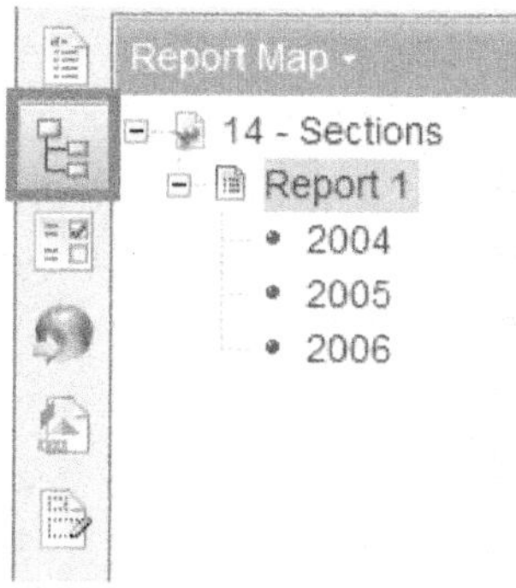
Report Map
14 - Sections
Report 1
2004
2005
2006
The map is based on section header values and is automatically ordered in the same order as the sections, i.e. if we applied a descending sort on the [Year] section then the map (opposite) would appear in reverse order.</td></tr>
<tr><td>Hide section when the following are empty</td><td>When ticked, specify report elements within a section that will qualify the whole section as being empty.

For example, we have a section containing 2 blocks (called Actuals and Budgets).

If we do not want to show the section when there is no data for Actuals then we would select Actuals from the drop down for this property.
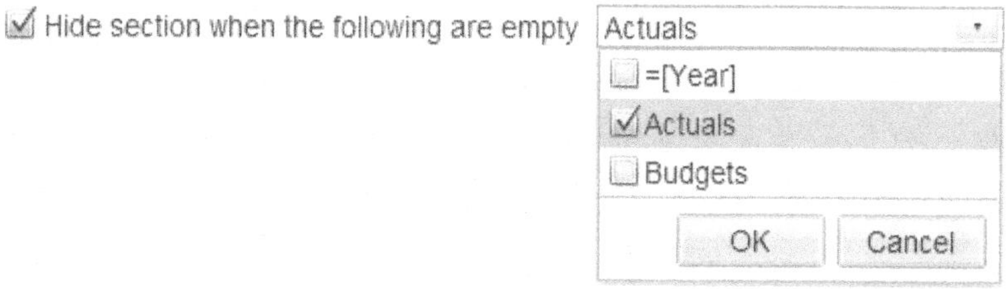
Hide section when the following are empty
Actuals
=[Year]
Actuals
Budgets
OK
Cancel</td></tr>
<tr><td>Hide always</td><td>The section will always be hidden.</td></tr>
<tr><td>Hide when empty</td><td>When ticked, a section containing no detail data will be hidden.</td></tr>
<tr><td>Hide when following formula is true</td><td>A section can be hidden based on the evaluation of a formula, for example if we want to hide sections where the [Sales quantity] for the section total is less than 60,000 then we can use the following formula:
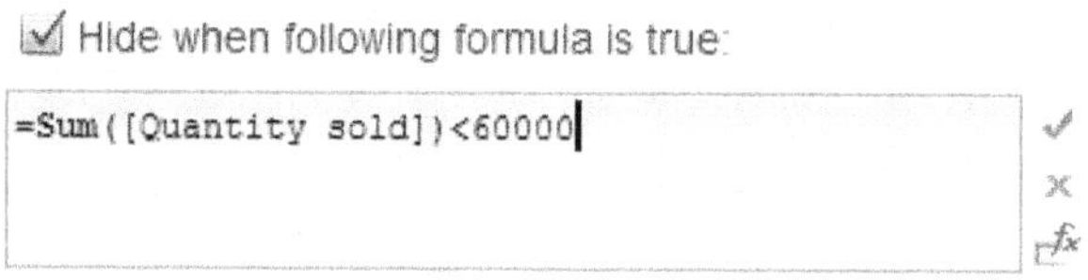
Hide when following formula is true:
=Sum([Quantity sold])<60000</td></tr>
</table>

You can also use colour, patterns and images for the section background. This is the same as previously described in earlier sessions.

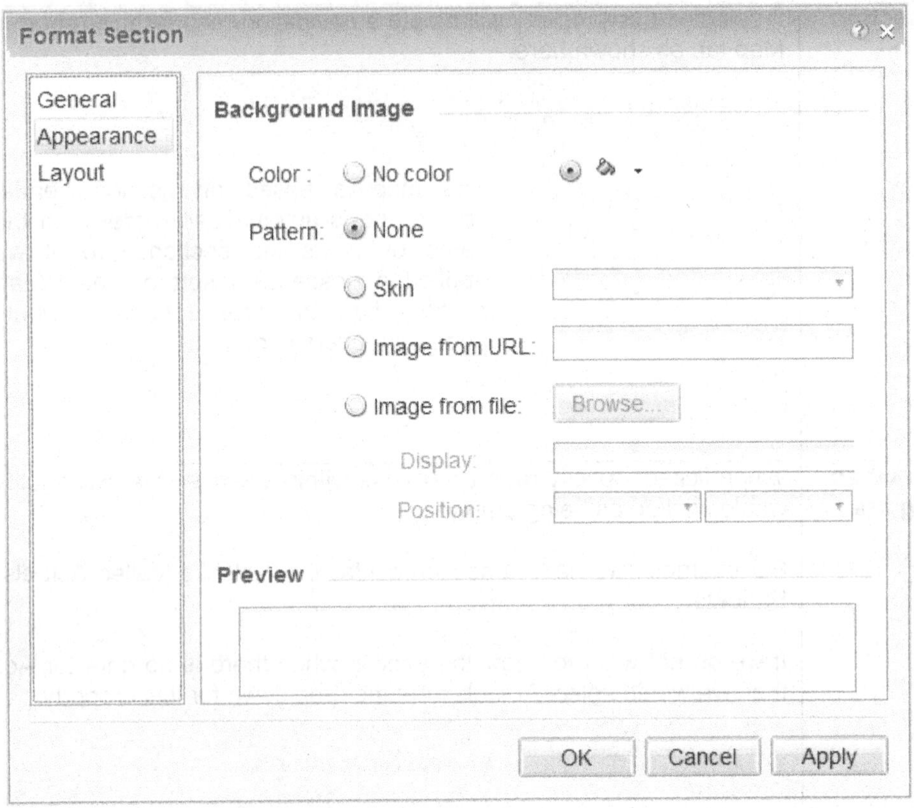
Format Section
General
Appearance
Layout
Background Image
Color :
No color
Pattern:
None
Skin
Image from URL:
Image from file:
Browse...
Display:
Position:
Preview
OK
Cancel
Apply

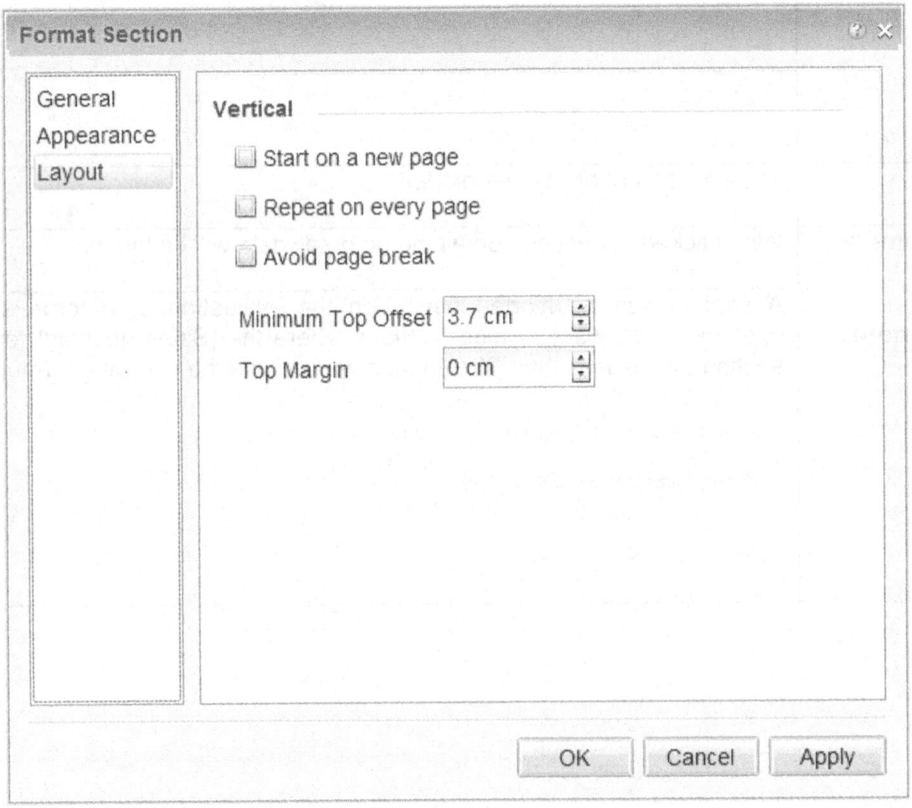
Format Section
General
Appearance
Layout
Vertical
Start on a new page
Repeat on every page
Avoid page break
Minimum Top Offset
3.7 cm
Top Margin
0 cm
OK
Cancel
Apply

Section Property	Usage
Start on a new page	You can force a section to start on a new page, i.e. when the section master value changes then the section will be forced to start on a new page.
Repeat on every page	The section will be repeated on every page.
Avoid page break	If a section starts part way on a page (vertically) and is going to be spread over two or more pages (vertically) then the section will be forced to start on a new page.
Minimum Top Offset	Space to leave between top of page and start of the first section value.
Top Margin	Margin for the first section value.

14.3 Section Calculation Contexts

All values within a section are related to the section's value. For measure values, the section defines a default calculation level (referred to as a calculation context).

2004

State	Quantity sold	Sales revenue
California	11,304	$1,704,211
Colorado	2,971	$448,302
DC	4,681	$693,211
Florida	2,585	$405,985
Illinois	4,713	$737,914
Massachusetts	1,505	$238,819
New York	10,802	$1,667,696
Texas	14,517	$2,199,677
Sum:	**53,078**	**$8,095,814**

Section on [Year] containing a block of data with subtotals for measures.

If you want to use the existing report tab then remove the [Quarter] object from the block.

2004

State	Quantity sold	Sales revenue
California	11,304	$1,704,211
Colorado	2,971	$448,302
DC	4,681	$693,211
Florida	2,585	$405,985
Illinois	4,713	$737,914
Massachusetts	1,505	$238,819
New York	10,802	$1,667,696
Texas	14,517	$2,199,677
Sum:	**53,078**	**$8,095,814**

=[Quantity sold]

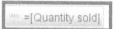

If we drag [Quantity sold] and drop it into the section on [Year] then Web Intelligence will display it in a Free-Standing Cell (as shown below).

The projection function for the measure (set in the universe) will then aggregate the measure values for that section.

If the measure is set to sum, then the rows will sum up to a subtotal for the section.

Here we have shown the measure [Quantity sold] at section level has a value of 53,078 and this is the same as the subtotal for the block because both are related to [Year] = 2004.

2004

53,078

State	Quantity sold	Sales revenue
California	11,304	$1,704,211
Colorado	2,971	$448,302
DC	4,681	$693,211
Florida	2,585	$405,985
Illinois	4,713	$737,914
Massachusetts	1,505	$238,819
New York	10,802	$1,667,696
Texas	14,517	$2,199,677
Sum:	**53,078**	**$8,095,814**

Similarly, the calculation context for the area above the outer most section (or below the bottom of the outer most section) is the entire report.

=[Quantity sold]

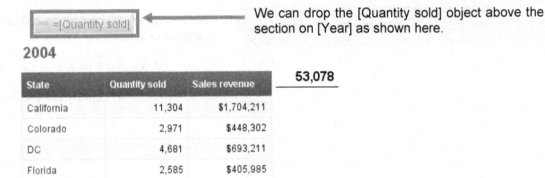

We can drop the [Quantity sold] object above the section on [Year] as shown here.

2004

53,078

State	Quantity sold	Sales revenue
California	11,304	$1,704,211
Colorado	2,971	$448,302
DC	4,681	$693,211
Florida	2,585	$405,985

There are no dependencies associated with this context for this area, so the measure aggregates to become the report level total.

223,229 Report Total

2004

53,078 Section Total

State	Quantity sold	Sales revenue
California	11,304	$1,704,211
Colorado	2,971	$448,302

14.4 Nested Sections

Sub-sections can be inserted into sections, i.e. Parent/Child sections or Inner/Outer sections.

1. We have a section on [Year] containing a vertical table with [Quarter], [State], [Sales revenue] and [Quantity sold].

   Right-click in any cell of the [Quarter] column and then select 'Set as Section'.

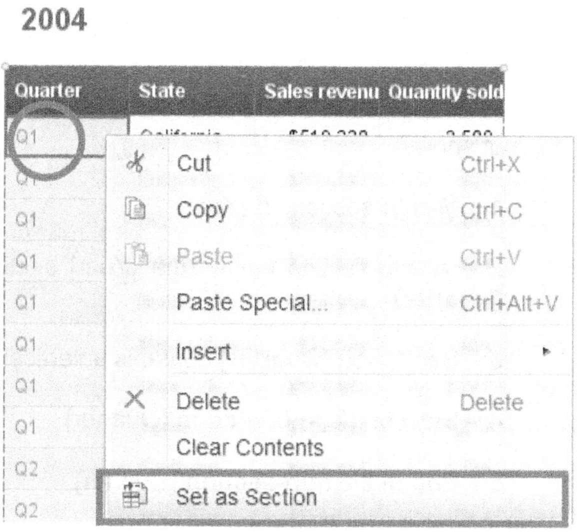
2004
Quarter
State
Sales revenu
Quantity sold
Q1
Cut Ctrl+X
Copy Ctrl+C
Paste Ctrl+V
Paste Special... Ctrl+Alt+V
Insert
Delete Delete
Clear Contents
Set as Section
Q2

2. Web Intelligence will now display the [Quarter] sections within each [Year] section:

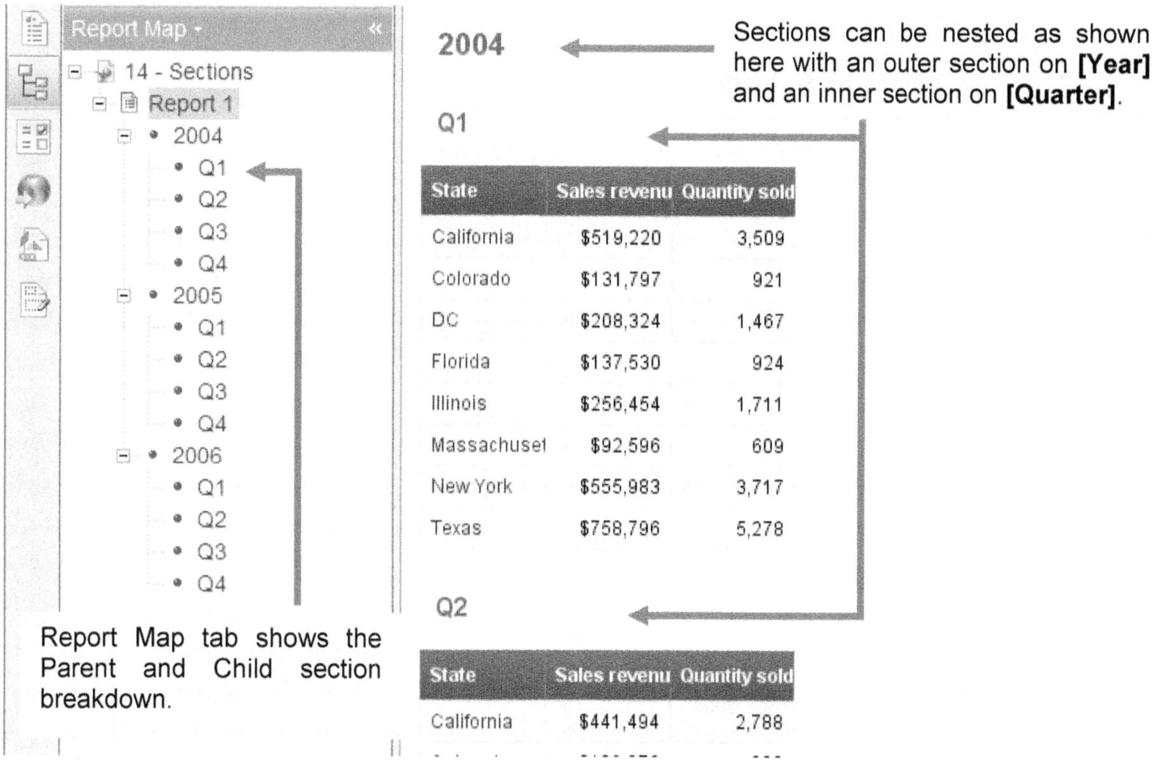
Report Map
14 - Sections
Report 1
2004
Q1
Q2
Q3
Q4
2005
Q1
Q2
Q3
Q4
2006
Q1
Q2
Q3
Q4
Report Map tab shows the Parent and Child section breakdown.
2004
Sections can be nested as shown here with an outer section on **[Year]** and an inner section on **[Quarter]**.
Q1
State | Sales revenu | Quantity sold
California | $519,220 | 3,509
Colorado | $131,797 | 921
DC | $208,324 | 1,467
Florida | $137,530 | 924
Illinois | $256,454 | 1,711
Massachuset | $92,596 | 609
New York | $555,983 | 3,717
Texas | $758,796 | 5,278
Q2
State | Sales revenu | Quantity sold
California | $441,494 | 2,788

3. Switching to 'Design – Structure Only' mode makes it easier to view the layout of the sections, cells and block.

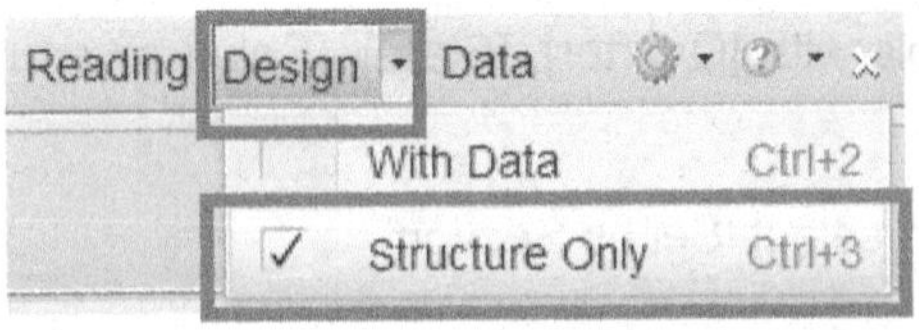
Reading
Design
Data
With Data Ctrl+2
Structure Only Ctrl+3

In 'Structure Only' mode the layout is displayed as follows

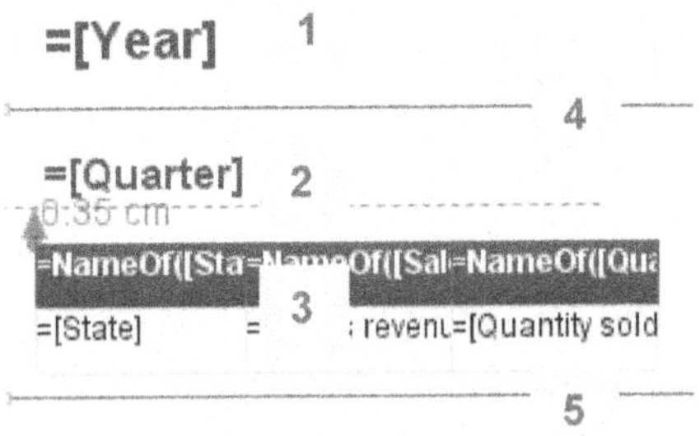
=[Year] 1
4
=[Quarter] 2
3
=[State]
5

Layout shows:

1 – Master section on **[Year]**

2 – A sub-section (within the [Year] section) on **[Quarter]**

3 – Section on **[Quarter]** contains a vertical table

4 – **Start** of the **sub-section** [Quarter]

5 – **End** of the **sub-section** [Quarter]

We can work in 'Structure Only' mode very much like in 'With Data' Mode, except we will not see any data until we switch back to 'With Data' mode. More details about structure mode will be discussed in the session on 'Working in Structure Mode'.

14.5 Sorting Data in Sections

Sort orders on sections can be viewed and changed if required.

1. Click in the Section Master cell for [Quarter] and then apply a Descending sort.

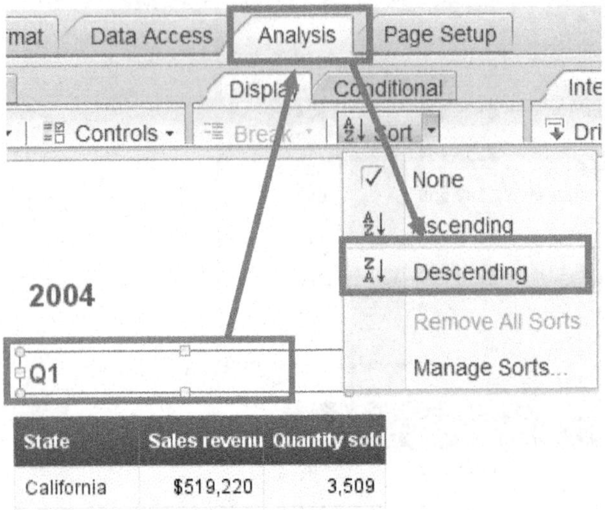
Data Access
Analysis
Page Setup
Conditional
Controls
None
Descending
Remove All Sorts
Manage Sorts...
2004
Q1
State
Sales revenu
Quantity sold
California
$519,220
3,509

2. Web Intelligence will display the [Quarter] values in descending order within each year (as shown below):

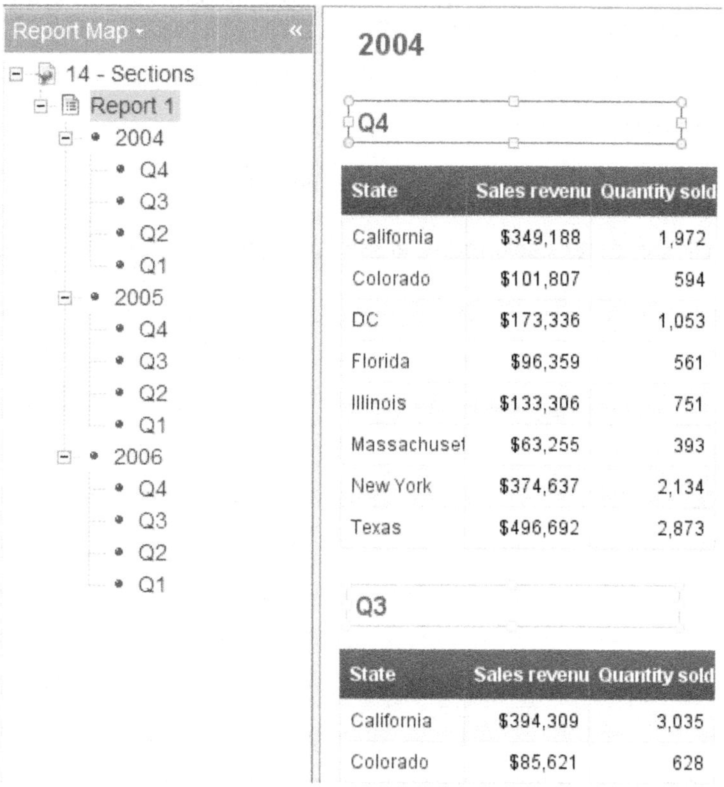
Report Map
14 - Sections
Report 1
2004
Q4
Q3
Q2
Q1
2005
Q4
Q3
Q2
Q1
2006
Q4
Q3
Q2
Q1
2004
Q4
State
Sales revenu
Quantity sold
California
$349,188
1,972
Colorado
$101,807
594
DC
$173,336
1,053
Florida
$96,359
561
Illinois
$133,306
751
Massachuset
$63,255
393
New York
$374,637
2,134
Texas
$496,692
2,873
Q3
State
Sales revenu
Quantity sold
California
$394,309
3,035
Colorado
$85,621
628

3. You can use the 'Manage Sorts' Interface to edit/delete the sorts on sections (as previously described in sorting data in tables and cross tables).

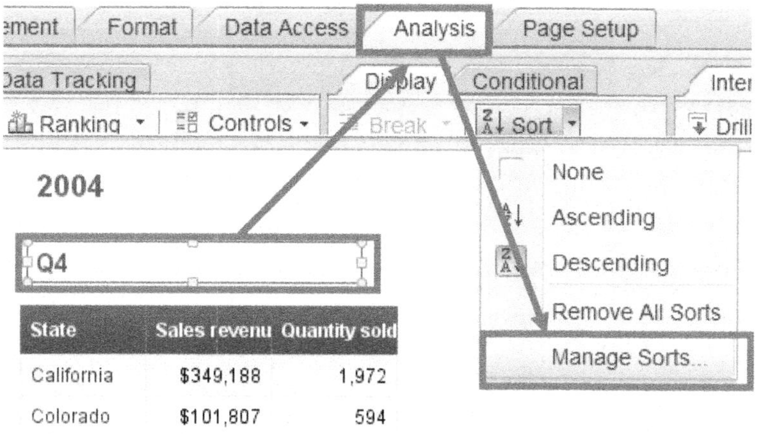
Format
Data Access
Analysis
Page Setup
Data Tracking
Display
Conditional
Ranking
Controls
Break
Sort
Drill
2004
Q4
State
Sales revenu
Quantity sold
California
$349,188
1,972
Colorado
$101,807
594
None
Ascending
Descending
Remove All Sorts
Manage Sorts...

14.6 Section Sort Priorities

Section sort priorities cannot be changed, i.e. a child section cannot be sorted before a parent section. By default parent sections will always take priority over child sections.

14.7 Removing / Deleting Sections

Sections can be deleted (or removed) simply by using a right-click menu option.

1. In '**View Report**' mode simply click into the background area of a section and then select 'Delete' from right-click menu options.

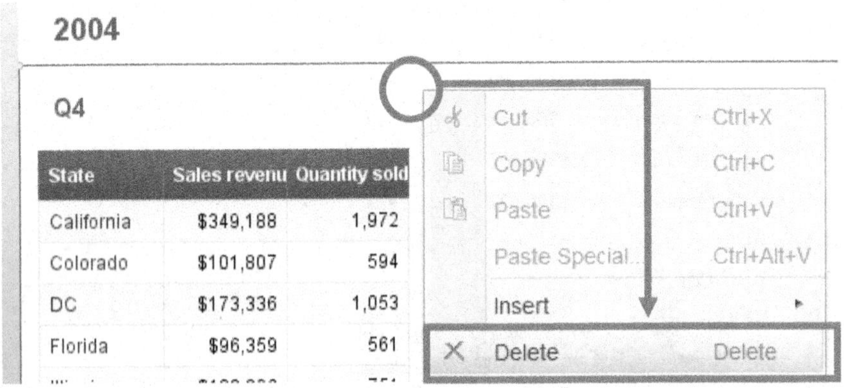
2004
Q4
State
Sales revenu
Quantity sold
California
$349,188
1,972
Colorado
$101,807
594
DC
$173,336
1,053
Florida
$96,359
561
Cut
Ctrl+X
Copy
Ctrl+C
Paste
Ctrl+V
Paste Special...
Ctrl+Alt+V
Insert
Delete
Delete

Or in '**View Structure**' mode simply click into the background area of a section and then select 'Delete' from right-click menu options.

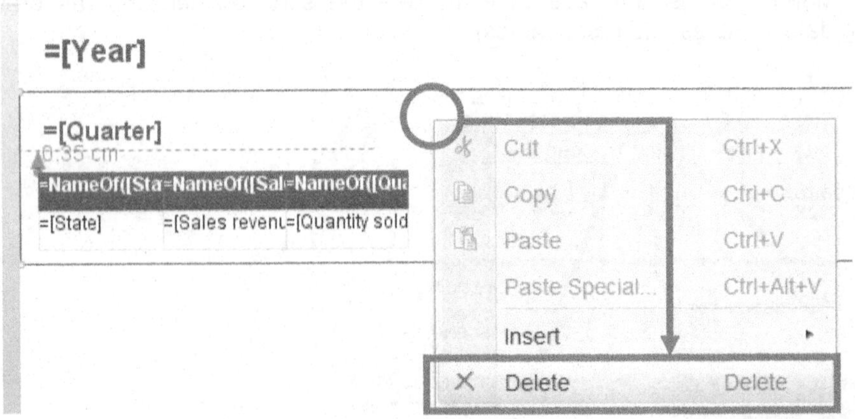
=[Year]
=[Quarter]
0.35 cm
=NameOf([Sta
=NameOf([Sal
=NameOf([Qu
=[State]
=[Sales revenu
=[Quantity sold
Cut
Ctrl+X
Copy
Ctrl+C
Paste
Ctrl+V
Paste Special...
Ctrl+Alt+V
Insert
Delete
Delete

2. Confirm you want to delete the section:

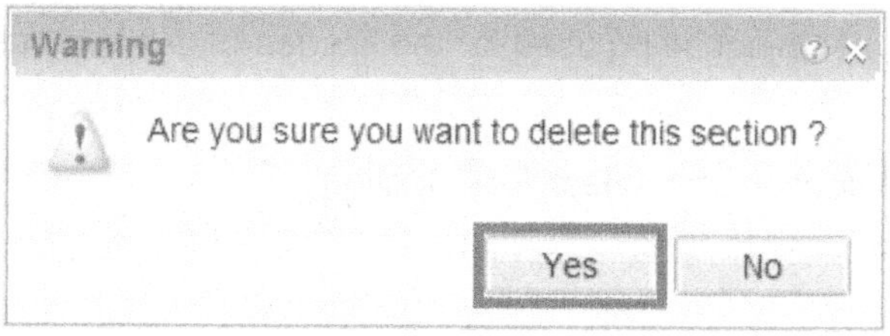
Warning
Are you sure you want to delete this section ?
Yes
No

3. Section will be deleted:

2004

Q4

State	Sales revenu	Quantity sold
California	$349,188	1,972
Colorado	$101,807	594
DC	$173,336	1,053
Florida	$96,359	561
Illinois	$133,306	751
Massachuset	$63,255	393
New York	$374,637	2,134
Texas	$496,692	2,873

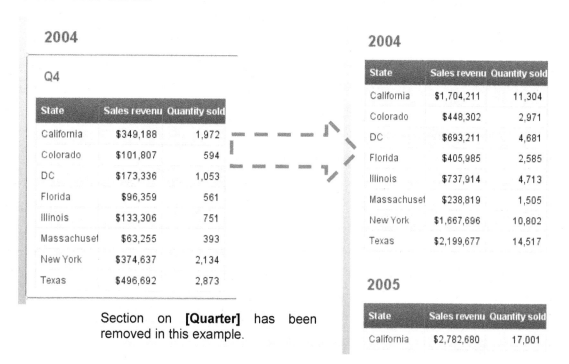

Section on **[Quarter]** has been removed in this example.

2004

State	Sales revenu	Quantity sold
California	$1,704,211	11,304
Colorado	$448,302	2,971
DC	$693,211	4,681
Florida	$405,985	2,585
Illinois	$737,914	4,713
Massachuset	$238,819	1,505
New York	$1,667,696	10,802
Texas	$2,199,677	14,517

2005

State	Sales revenu	Quantity sold
California	$2,782,680	17,001

14.8 Editing Sections

The 'Edit Section' option allows you to change the object being used for the section (as shown below):

1. We have a section on [Year]. Right-click in section and select 'Edit Section':

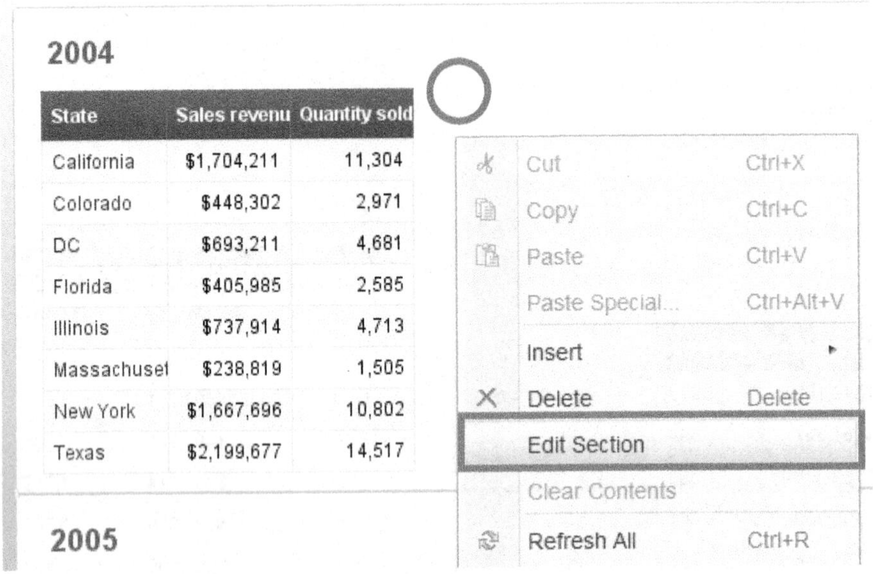
2004
State
Sales revenu
Quantity sold
California $1,704,211 11,304
Colorado $448,302 2,971
DC $693,211 4,681
Florida $405,985 2,585
Illinois $737,914 4,713
Massachuset $238,819 1,505
New York $1,667,696 10,802
Texas $2,199,677 14,517
2005
Cut Ctrl+X
Copy Ctrl+C
Paste Ctrl+V
Paste Special... Ctrl+Alt+V
Insert
Delete Delete
Edit Section
Clear Contents
Refresh All Ctrl+R

2. Click on [Quarter] and then 'OK'.

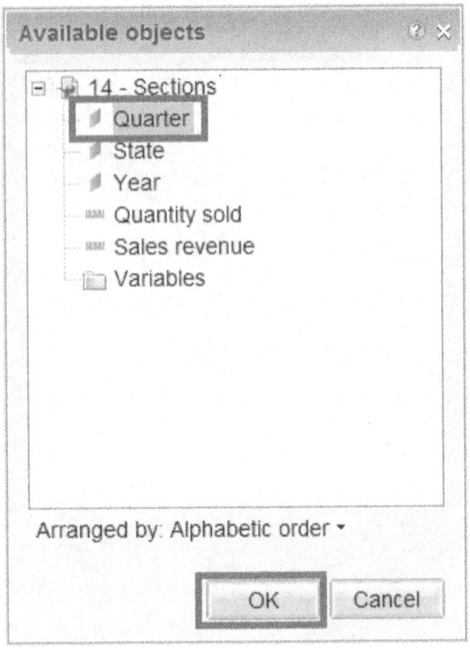
Available objects
14 - Sections
Quarter
State
Year
Quantity sold
Sales revenue
Variables
Arranged by: Alphabetic order
OK
Cancel

3. Section changes from [Year] to [Quarter]:

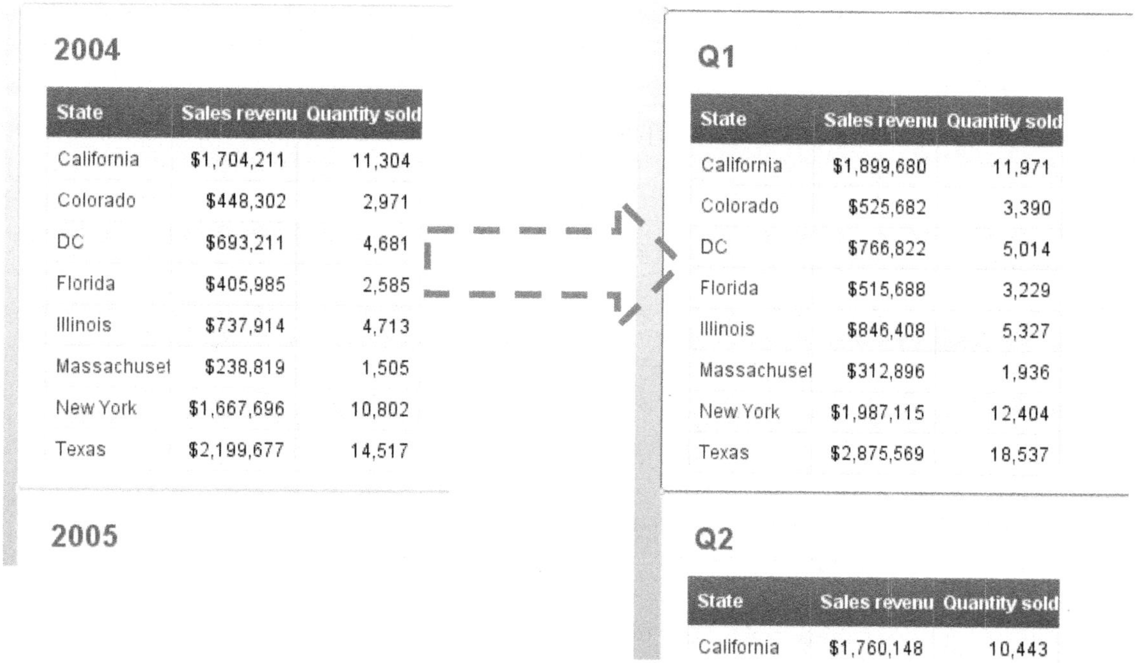

2004

State	Sales revenu	Quantity sold
California	$1,704,211	11,304
Colorado	$448,302	2,971
DC	$693,211	4,681
Florida	$405,985	2,585
Illinois	$737,914	4,713
Massachuset	$238,819	1,505
New York	$1,667,696	10,802
Texas	$2,199,677	14,517

2005

Q1

State	Sales revenu	Quantity sold
California	$1,899,680	11,971
Colorado	$525,682	3,390
DC	$766,822	5,014
Florida	$515,688	3,229
Illinois	$846,408	5,327
Massachuset	$312,896	1,936
New York	$1,987,115	12,404
Texas	$2,875,569	18,537

Q2

State	Sales revenu	Quantity sold
California	$1,760,148	10,443

14.9 Use of Charts in Sections

Sections are often used to display tabular data along with charts as shown below. The table and chart are defined once, but repeated in every section by Web Intelligence.

2004

State	Sales revenu	Quantity sold
California	$1,704,211	11,304
Colorado	$448,302	2,971
DC	$693,211	4,681
Florida	$405,985	2,585
Illinois	$737,914	4,713
Massachuset	$238,819	1,505
New York	$1,667,696	10,802
Texas	$2,199,677	14,517

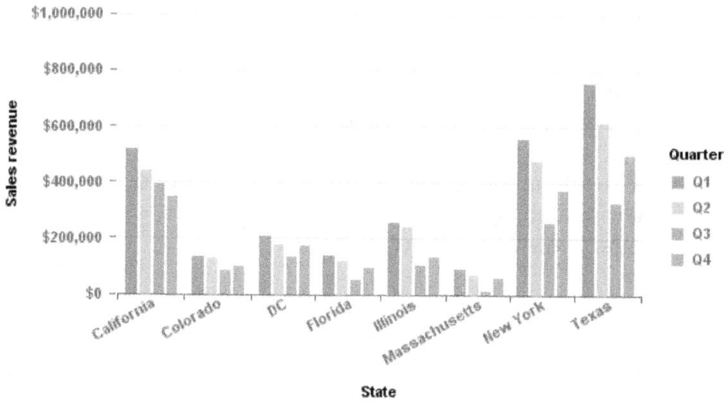

$1,000,000
$800,000
$600,000
$400,000
$200,000
$0
Sales revenue
California
Colorado
DC
Florida
Illinois
Massachusetts
New York
Texas
State
Quarter
Q1
Q2
Q3
Q4

Creating and using charts is covered in the next session.

14.10 Hiding/Showing Data in Sections

The ‘Outline Toolbar’ enables you to collapse and expand sections so users can hide or show details within a section. We will take the above example to demonstrate the Outline Toolbar functionality with sections.

1. We have a sectioned report on [Year] and [Quarter], as used in earlier examples in this session.

2004

Q1

State	Sales revenu	Quantity sold
California	$519,220	3,509
Colorado	$131,797	921
DC	$208,324	1,467
Florida	$137,530	924
Illinois	$256,454	1,711
Massachuset	$92,596	609
New York	$555,983	3,717
Texas	$758,796	5,278

2. Activate the ‘Outline Toolbar’ by clicking on the button ‘Analysis – Outline’:

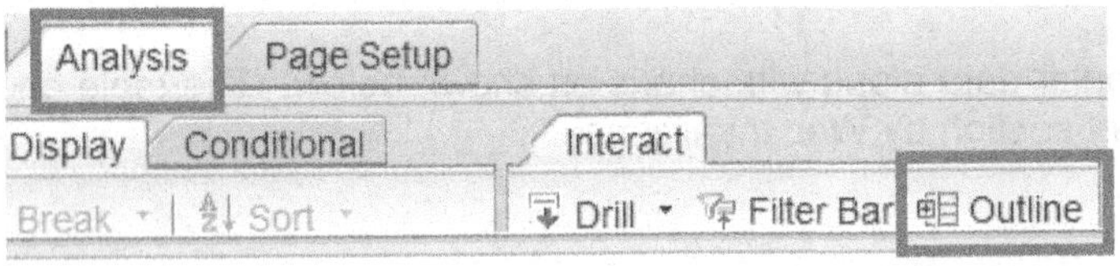
Analysis
Page Setup
Display
Conditional
Interact
Break
Sort
Drill
Filter Bar
Outline

This will activate the Outline Toolbars (on the left and above the report).

The left hand Outline Toolbar can be used to expand/collapse sections because sections effectively only run ‘top to bottom’.

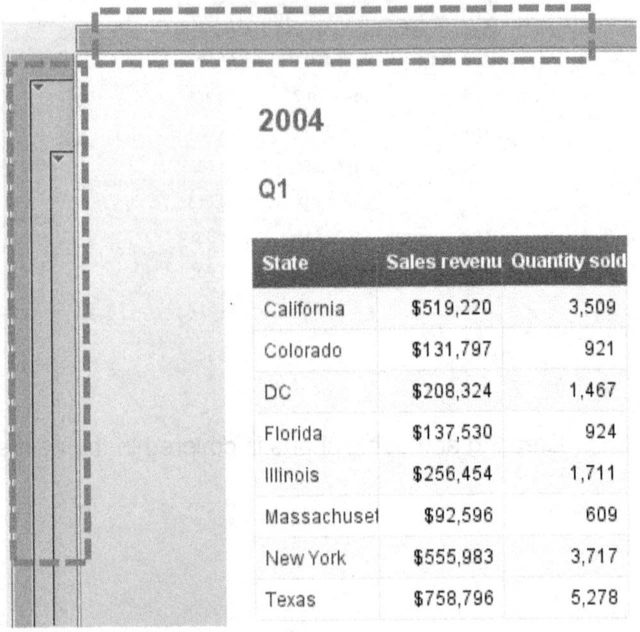

2004

Q1

State	Sales revenu	Quantity sold
California	$519,220	3,509
Colorado	$131,797	921
DC	$208,324	1,467
Florida	$137,530	924
Illinois	$256,454	1,711
Massachuset	$92,596	609
New York	$555,983	3,717
Texas	$758,796	5,278

In this example the Outline Toolbar is indicating we have 2 sections due to the '1' and '2' appearing at the bottom.

1 2

But if you click into the table then you will also see 'T' appear for the 'Table'.

1 2 T

3. Drag in the [Sales revenue] object and drop it next to the [Quarter] object, so we can see a total for each [Quarter], as shown below:

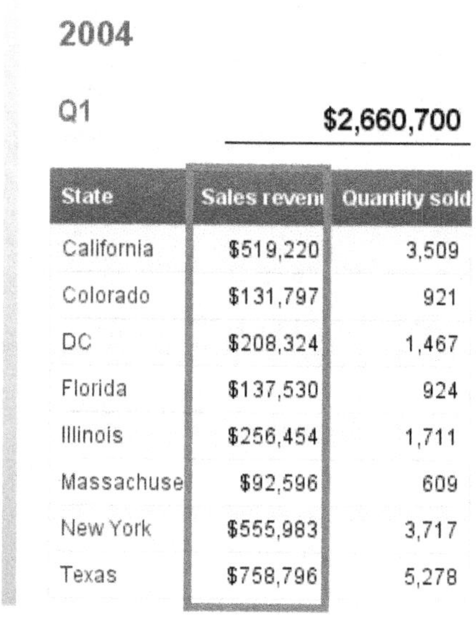

2004

Q1 $2,660,700

State	Sales reven	Quantity sold
California	$519,220	3,509
Colorado	$131,797	921
DC	$208,324	1,467
Florida	$137,530	924
Illinois	$256,454	1,711
Massachuse	$92,596	609
New York	$555,983	3,717
Texas	$758,796	5,278

4. Clicking on '2' (i.e. Section 2) will collapse all the sections (i.e. 'Fold' the section on [Quarter] completely) as shown below:

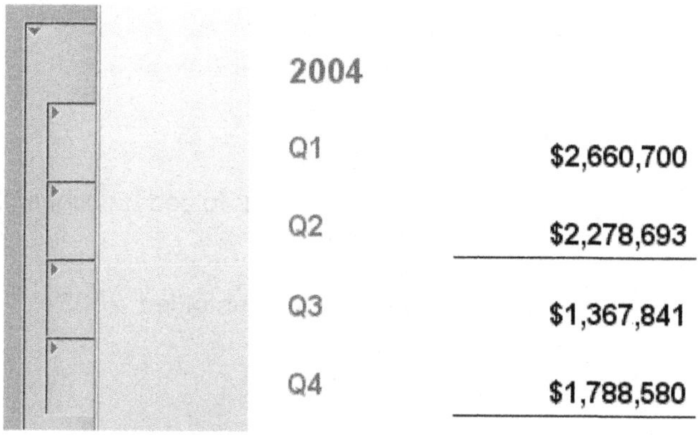
2004
Q1 $2,660,700
Q2 $2,278,693
Q3 $1,367,841
Q4 $1,788,580

When a section is folded the details within the section are hidden (i.e. tables and charts) but the free standing cells are shown.

5. If we want to just expand (i.e. 'Unfold') a single section, for example '2004 / Q3' then we use the arrow for the 'Q3' section within '2004' section:

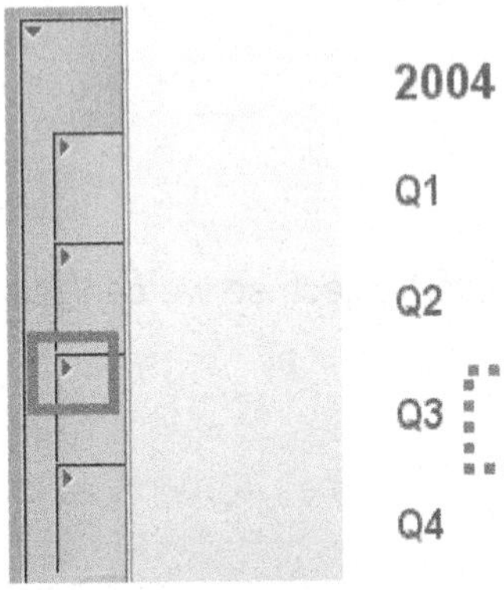
2004
Q1
Q2
Q3
Q4

Clicking the arrow next to a section value will fold or unfold that individual section only.

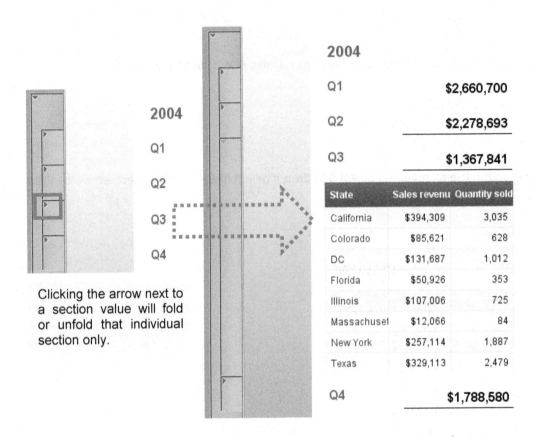

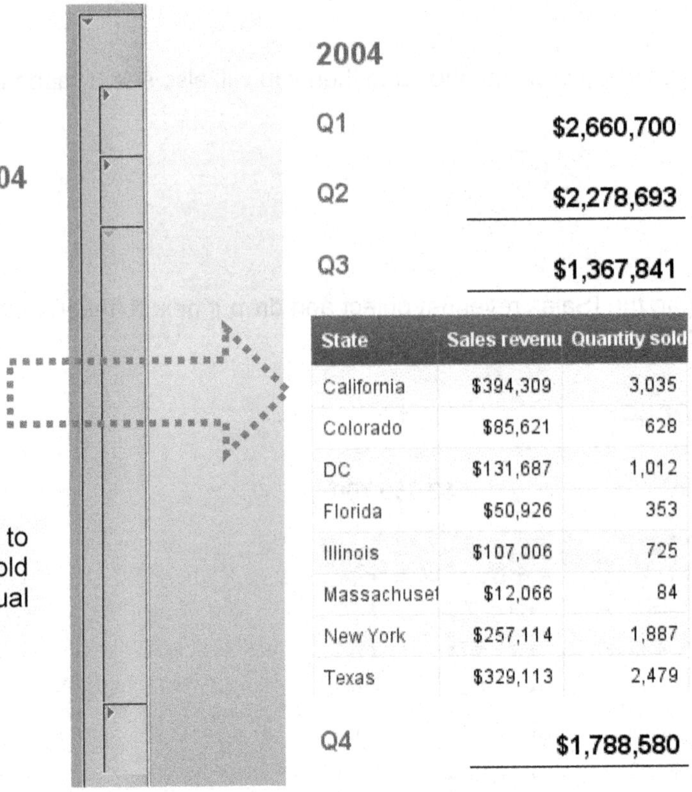
2004
Q1 $2,660,700
Q2 $2,278,693
Q3 $1,367,841
Q4 $1,788,580

State	Sales revenu	Quantity sold
California	$394,309	3,035
Colorado	$85,621	628
DC	$131,687	1,012
Florida	$50,926	353
Illinois	$107,006	725
Massachuset	$12,066	84
New York	$257,114	1,887
Texas	$329,113	2,479

6. Nested sections can be folded or unfolded individually.

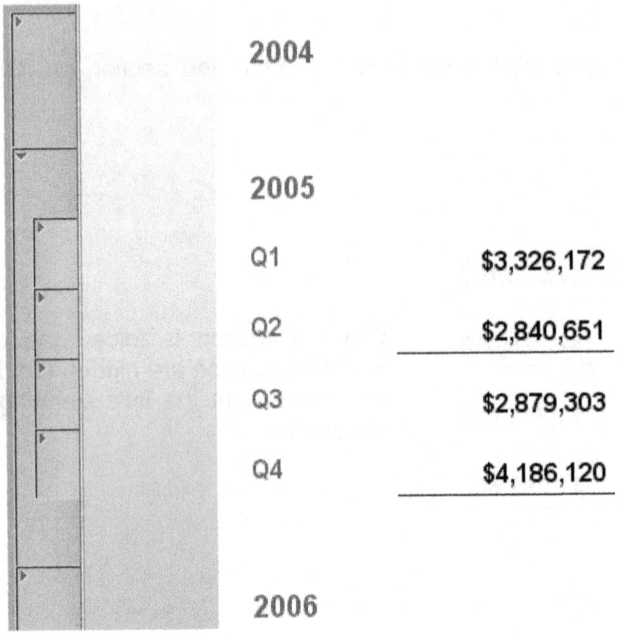
2004
2005
Q1 $3,326,172
Q2 $2,840,651
Q3 $2,879,303
Q4 $4,186,120
2006

Here we have folded sections '2' and then '1'.

Then we have unfolded '2005'.

NOTE – If a parent section is folded then unfolding its child sections will not cause the parent section to unfold.

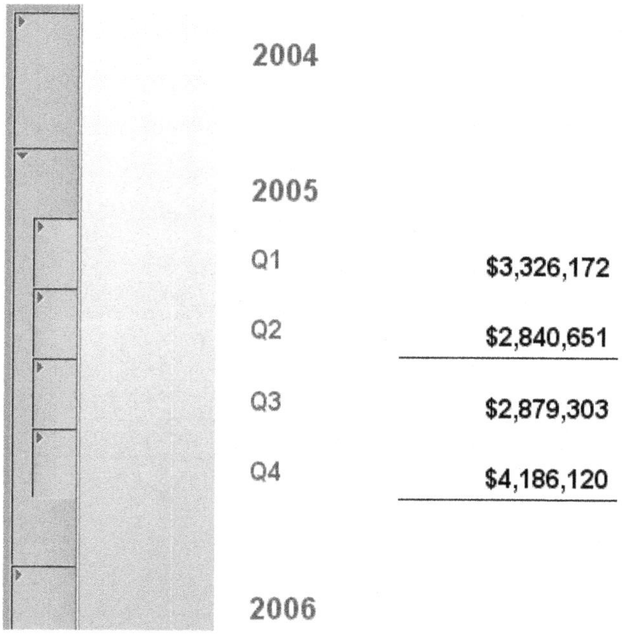
2004
2005
Q1 $3,326,172
Q2 $2,840,651
Q3 $2,879,303
Q4 $4,186,120
2006

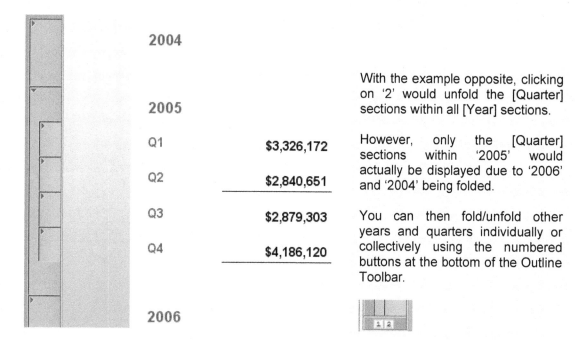

With the example opposite, clicking on '2' would unfold the [Quarter] sections within all [Year] sections.

However, only the [Quarter] sections within '2005' would actually be displayed due to '2006' and '2004' being folded.

You can then fold/unfold other years and quarters individually or collectively using the numbered buttons at the bottom of the Outline Toolbar.

1 2

15 Creating and Formatting Charts

This session describes how to create and format charts from tables and from chart templates.

Let us start with a new document containing the following query using the 'eFashion' universe:

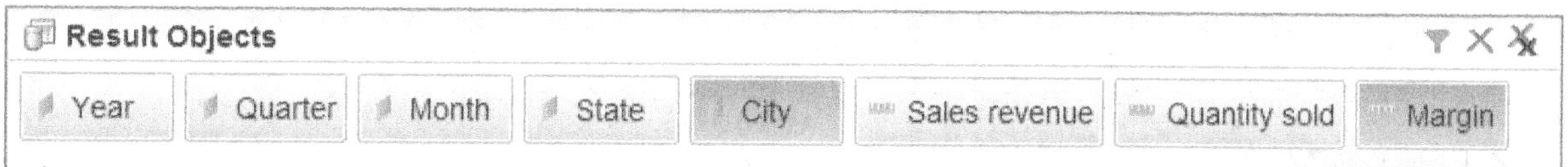
Result Objects
Year
Quarter
Month
State
City
Sales revenue
Quantity sold
Margin

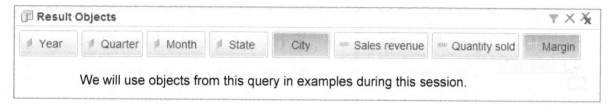

We will use objects from this query in examples during this session.

15.1 Creating Charts using 'Turn Into'

Tables can easily be converted into charts by using the right click menu 'Turn Into'.

1. Create the following vertical table block first:

Year	Quarter	Sales revenu	Quantity sold
2004	Q1	$2,660,700	18,136
2004	Q2	$2,278,693	14,408
2004	Q3	$1,367,841	10,203
2004	Q4	$1,788,580	10,331
2005	Q1	$3,326,172	21,135
2005	Q2	$2,840,651	17,152

2. Then right-click on the vertical table and select 'Turn Into – Column Chart'

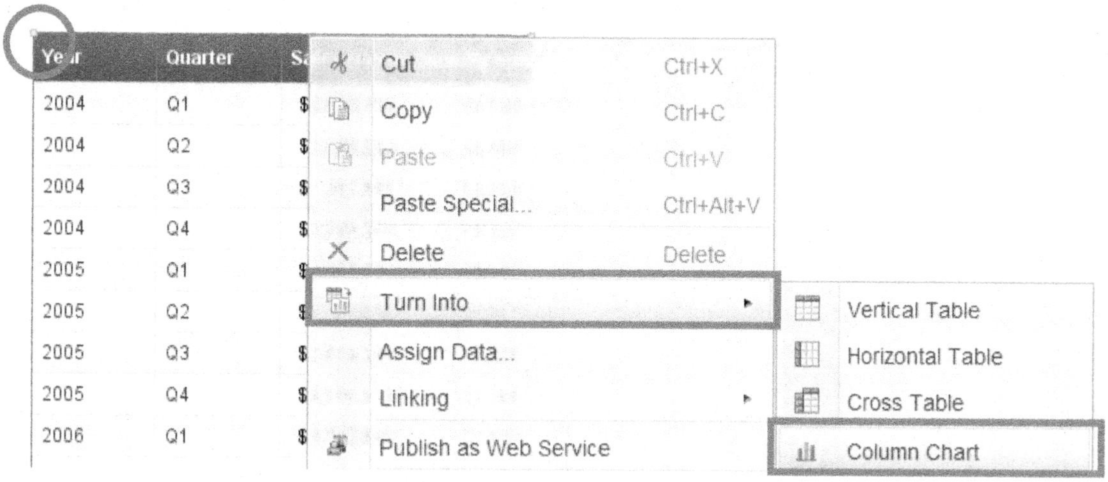
Year
Quarter
2004 Q1
2004 Q2
2004 Q3
2004 Q4
2005 Q1
2005 Q2
2005 Q3
2005 Q4
2006 Q1
Cut Ctrl+X
Copy Ctrl+C
Paste Ctrl+V
Paste Special... Ctrl+Alt+V
Delete Delete
Turn Into
Assign Data...
Linking
Publish as Web Service
Vertical Table
Horizontal Table
Cross Table
Column Chart

When using 'Turn Into' you can change tables into charts, charts into tables, and from one chart type to another.

Web Intelligence will turn the vertical table into a chart (a column chart in this case).

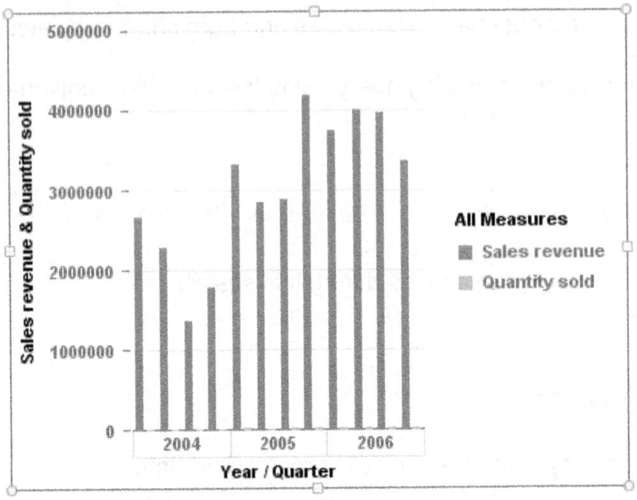
5000000
4000000
3000000
2000000
1000000
0
Sales revenue & Quantity sold
2004
2005
2006
Year / Quarter
All Measures
Sales revenue
Quantity sold

Further resizing and formatting will be required to make the chart more presentable (*described next*).

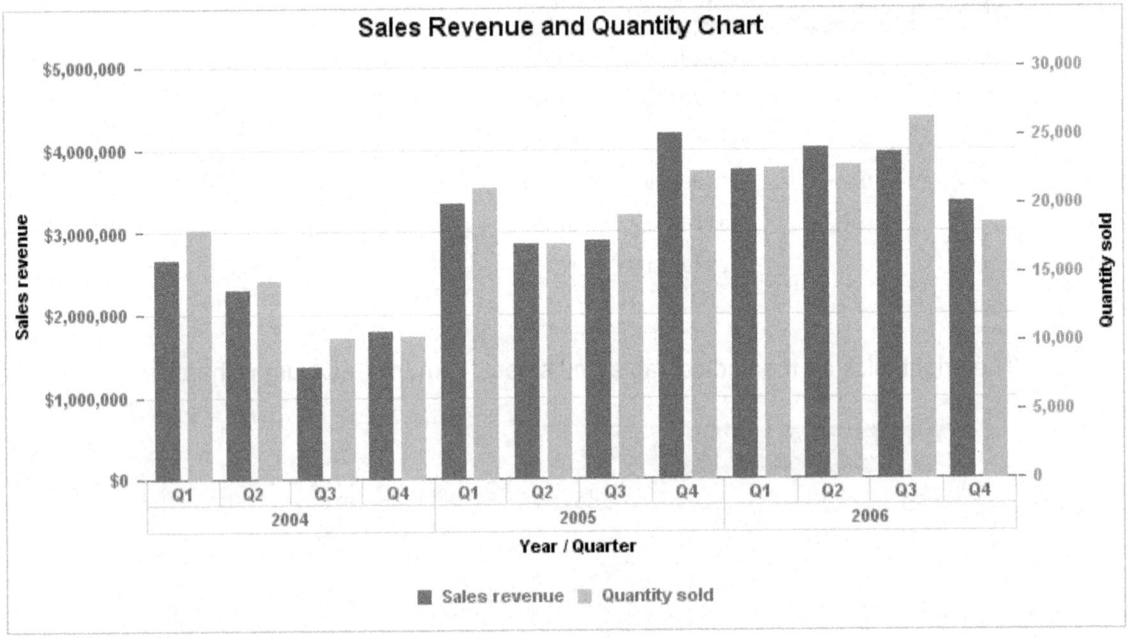
Sales Revenue and Quantity Chart
$5,000,000
$4,000,000
$3,000,000
$2,000,000
$1,000,000
$0
Sales revenue
30,000
25,000
20,000
15,000
10,000
5,000
0
Quantity sold
Q1
Q2
Q3
Q4
2004
2005
2006
Year / Quarter
Sales revenue
Quantity sold

15.2 Formatting Charts

There are many different chart types and associated formatting properties. We will describe how you can generally format charts to make them more presentable using the various different properties.

1. Charts can be formatted using right-click 'Format Chart…'

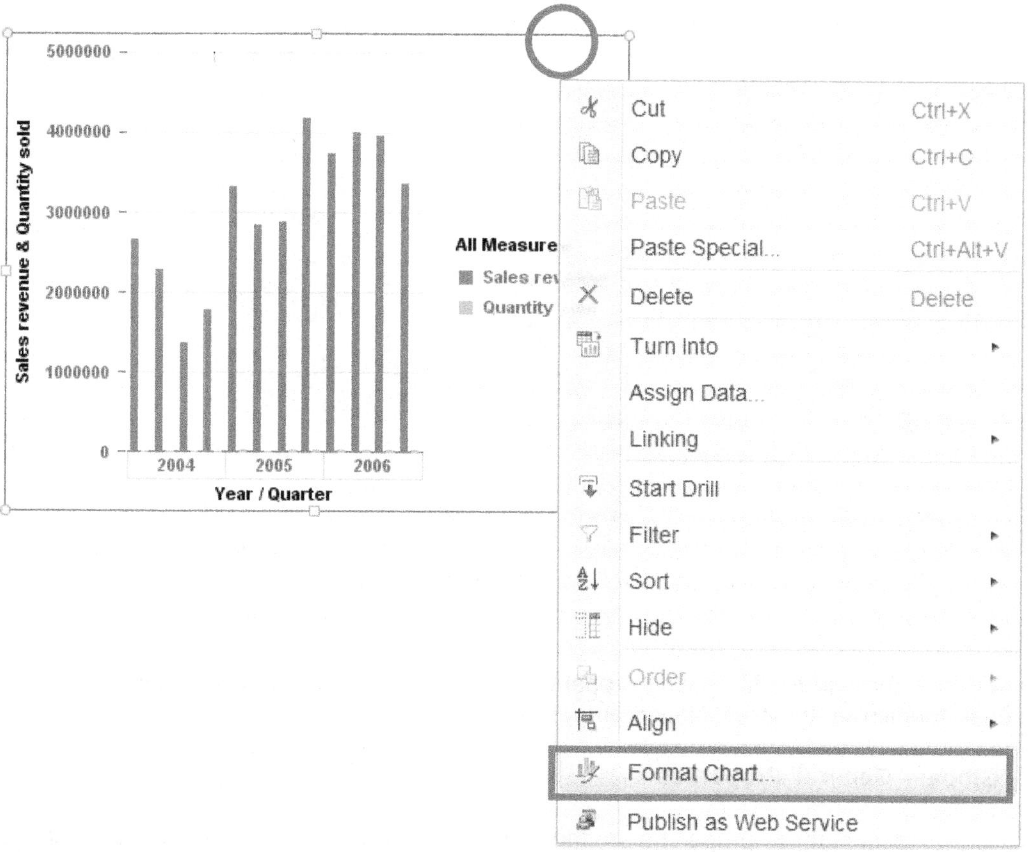

5000000
4000000
3000000
2000000
1000000
0
Sales revenue & Quantity sold
2004
2005
2006
Year / Quarter
All Measure
Sales rev
Quantity
Cut Ctrl+X
Copy Ctrl+C
Paste Ctrl+V
Paste Special... Ctrl+Alt+V
Delete Delete
Turn Into
Assign Data...
Linking
Start Drill
Filter
Sort
Hide
Order
Align
Format Chart...
Publish as Web Service

2. The 'Format chart' interface will appear to enable you to work with the presentation and formatting properties relevant to the chart type.

NOTE

There are lots of properties available for formatting charts, some of them are the same as table properties, but others are more specific to charts.

3. The properties have been grouped (examples shown below):

Global
General
Area Display
Region Type
Data Values
Palette and Style
Background
Border
Layout
Title
Legend
Category Axis
Value Axis
Plot Area
Global
General
Area Display
Region Type
Data Values
Palette and Style
Background
Border
Layout
Title
Legend
Category Axis
Value Axis
Value Axis 2
Plot Area

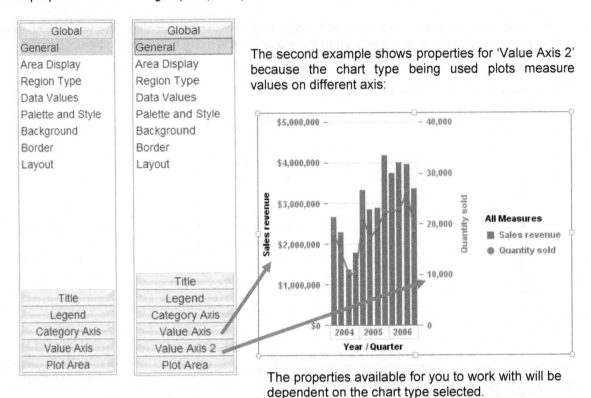

The second example shows properties for 'Value Axis 2' because the chart type being used plots measure values on different axis:

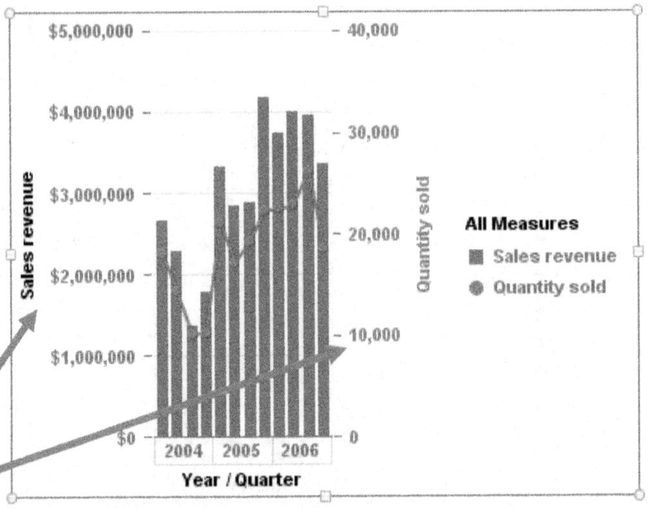
$5,000,000
$4,000,000
$3,000,000
$2,000,000
$1,000,000
$0
Sales revenue
40,000
30,000
20,000
10,000
0
Quantity sold
2004
2005
2006
Year / Quarter
All Measures
Sales revenue
Quantity sold

The properties available for you to work with will be dependent on the chart type selected.

4. We will work through the formatting properties to try and describe how they can be used to format the chart for display and presentation purposes.

'Global – General' Properties

- Most of these properties are the same as ones previously described for table blocks.
- If you tick the 'Horizontal Orientation' property then the chart will switch to display values on the horizontal axes instead of the vertical axes.

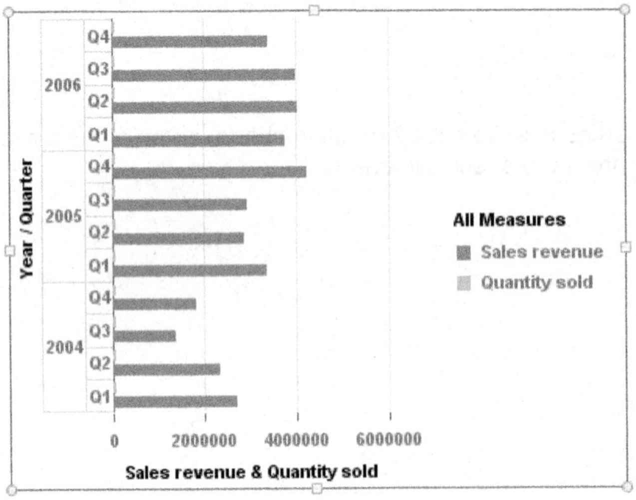
Q4
Q3
Q2
Q1
2006
2005
2004
Year / Quarter
0
2000000
4000000
6000000
Sales revenue & Quantity sold
All Measures
Sales revenue
Quantity sold

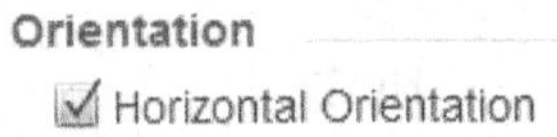
Orientation
Horizontal Orientation

'Global – Area Display' Properties

- Use these properties to show or hide the labels for the axes, title and legend.
- You can also change the actual text displayed for the Title.

'Global – Region Type' Properties

- Use these properties to specify how each measure should be presented (in terms of lines, bars, etc).

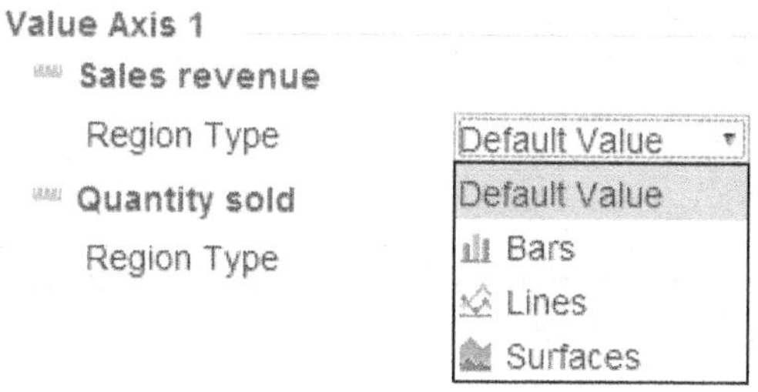
Value Axis 1
Sales revenue
Region Type
Quantity sold
Region Type
Default Value
Default Value
Bars
Lines
Surfaces

If the measures have been plotted on multiple axes then you will get options similar to the following:

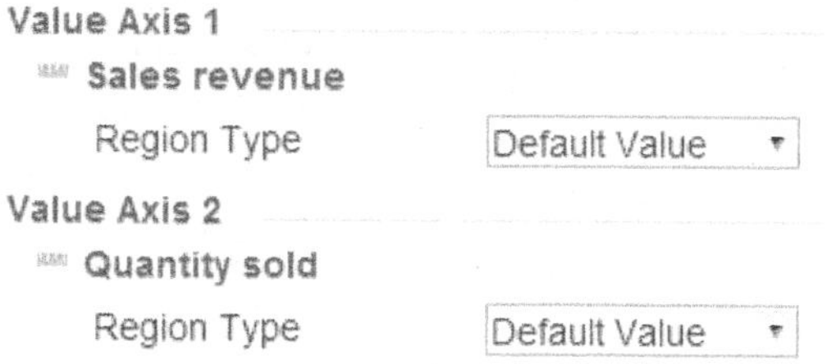
Value Axis 1
Sales revenue
Region Type
Default Value
Value Axis 2
Quantity sold
Region Type
Default Value

'Global – Data Values' Properties

- Tick this property to display the data values on the chart as well as the lines, bars, etc.

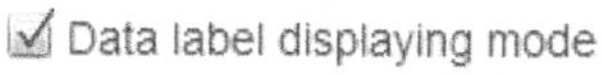
Data label displaying mode

- You can display the actual data Value, a Percentage or the label (dimension value). Typically, you will want to display the value so you can leave the setting as 'Automatic' or select 'Value'.

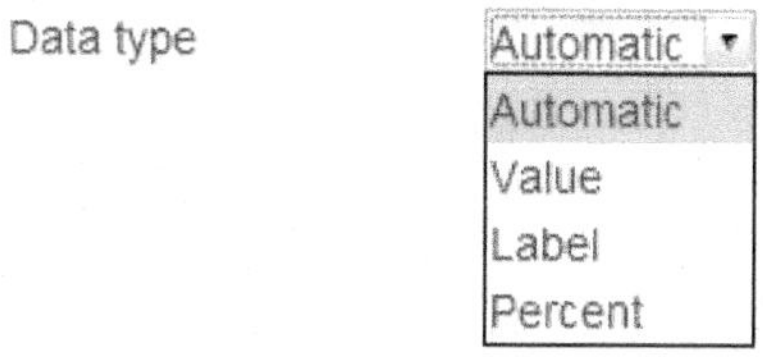
Data type
Automatic
Automatic
Value
Label
Percent

- You can display the values explicitly inside or outside the regions, or both inside and outside the bars (depending on the space available).

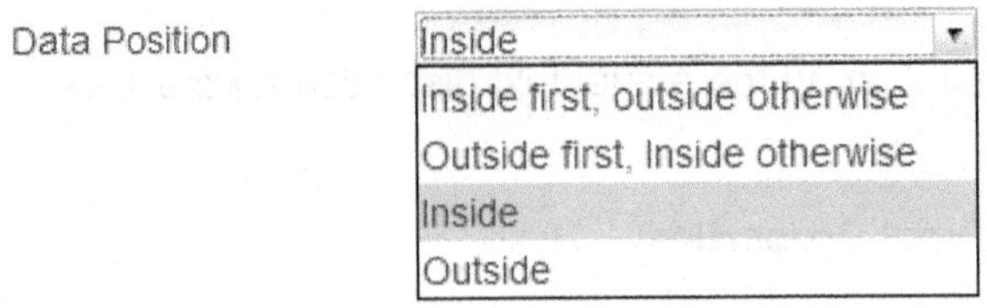
Data Position
Inside
Inside first, outside otherwise
Outside first, Inside otherwise
Inside
Outside

- If you leave 'Automatic Hiding Mode' ticked then any values that cannot be displayed due to lack of space will be hidden.

Automatic Hiding Mode

- There are various other properties you can use for the presentation of the data values (such as font, font size, borders, etc).

'Global – Palette and Style' Properties

This group of properties is used to control the presentation of the chart in terms of the color scheme, symbols, bar types, etc.

- The chart can be presented with a 2D or 3D look using the 'Depth' property.

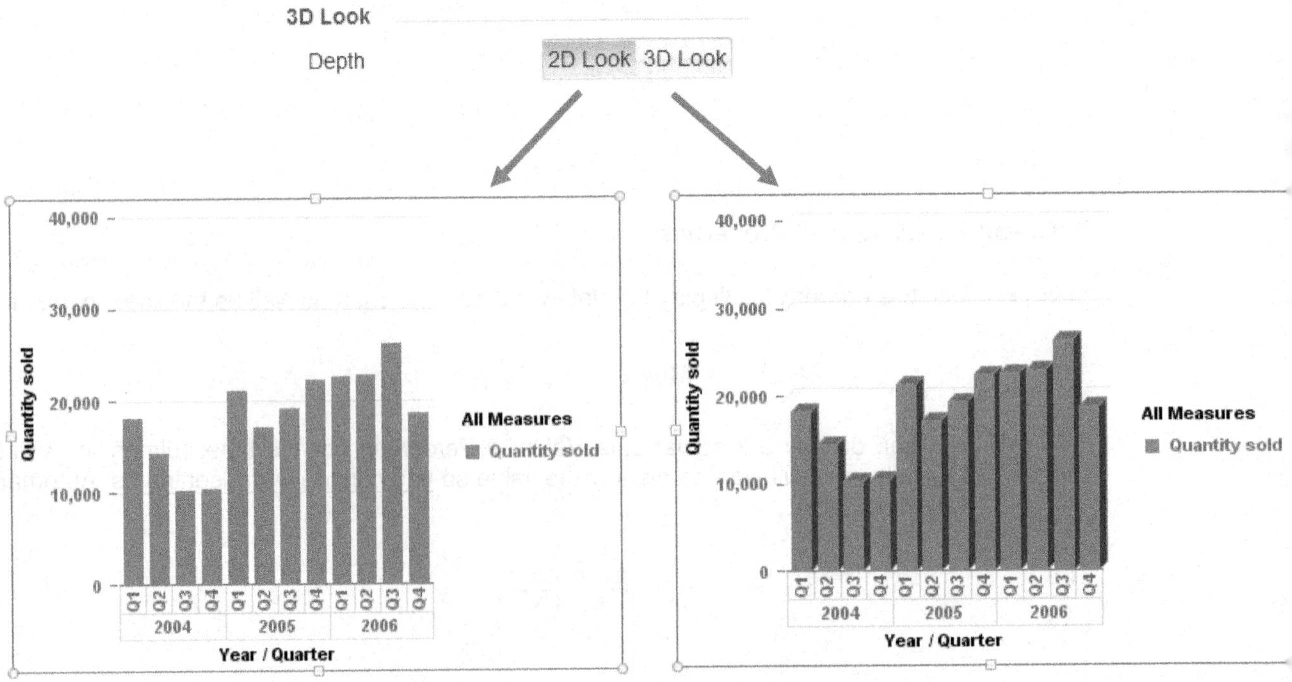
3D Look
Depth
2D Look
3D Look
40,000
30,000
20,000
10,000
0
Quantity sold
Q1 Q2 Q3 Q4 Q1 Q2 Q3 Q4 Q1 Q2 Q3 Q4
2004 2005 2006
Year / Quarter
All Measures
Quantity sold

- A color scheme (palette) can be applied to the bars, lines, areas, etc and a transparency level can also be used, where 0 = Transparent and 100 = Solid.

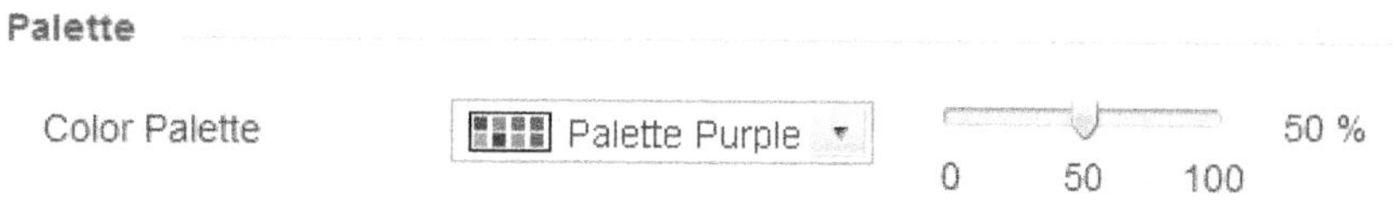
Palette
Color Palette
Palette Purple
50 %
0
50
100

A column chart example using the Palette Purple color scheme with 50% Opacity.

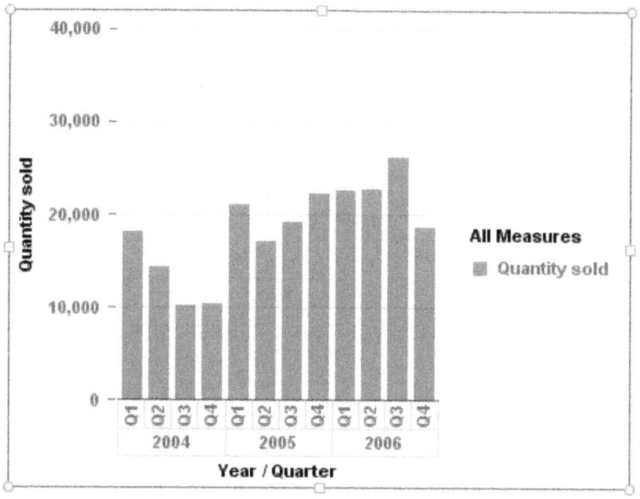
40,000
30,000
20,000
10,000
0
Quantity sold
Q1
Q2
Q3
Q4
2004
2005
2006
Year / Quarter
All Measures
Quantity sold

- For charts containing lines you can use markers on data points by ticking the 'Line Symbol' property and then applying the required formatting.

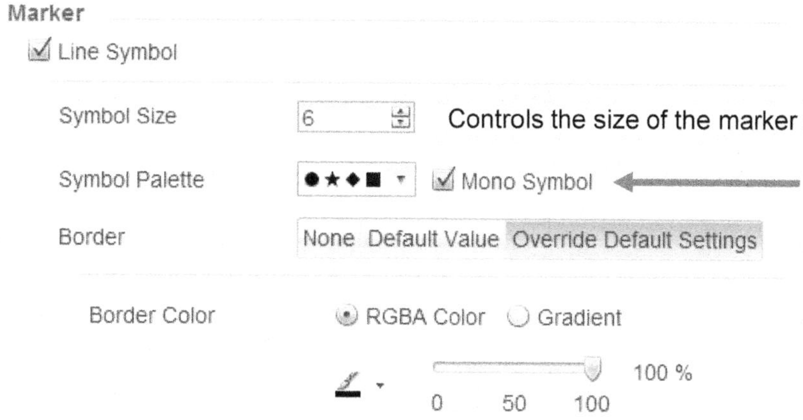
Marker
Line Symbol
Symbol Size
6
Symbol Palette
Mono Symbol
Border
None
Default Value
Override Default Settings
Border Color
RGBA Color
Gradient
100 %
0
50
100

Controls the size of the marker symbol.

For charts displaying multiple measures you can un-tick the 'Mono Symbol' property if you want each line to use a different symbol.

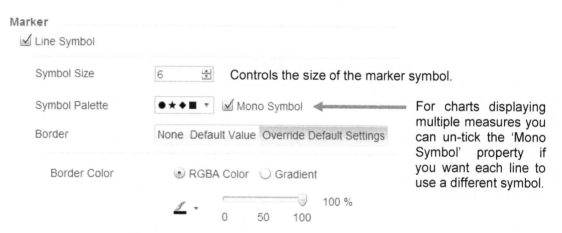

You can also apply a border around the marker symbol itself.

A line chart example using a marker symbol of size 6 and a black border around the symbol.

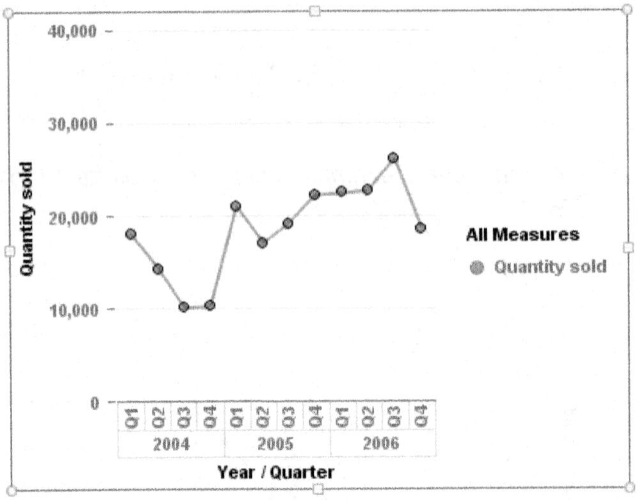
40,000
30,000
20,000
10,000
0
Quantity sold
Q1 Q2 Q3 Q4 Q1 Q2 Q3 Q4 Q1 Q2 Q3 Q4
2004
2005
2006
Year / Quarter
All Measures
Quantity sold

- For charts containing lines you can use extra effects on the lines.

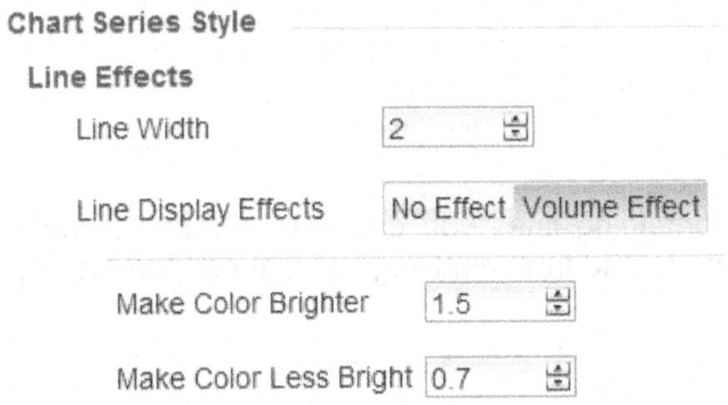
Chart Series Style
Line Effects
Line Width
2
Line Display Effects
No Effect
Volume Effect
Make Color Brighter
1.5
Make Color Less Bright
0.7

☑ Spline Line   Spline Line plots a curved line between the data points.

Line Width = 2, No Effect, Spline Line

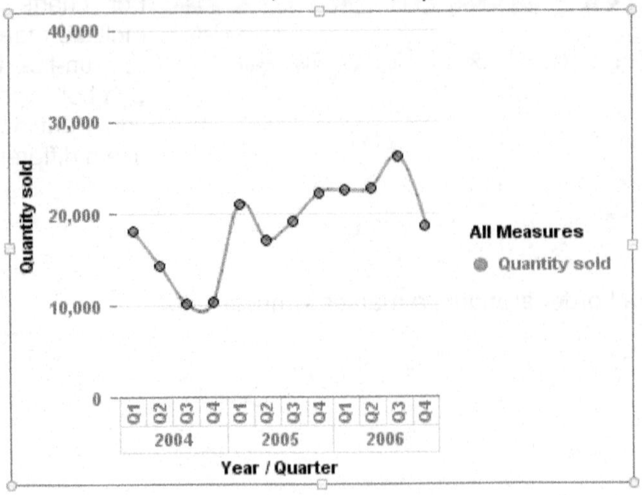
40,000
30,000
20,000
10,000
0
Quantity sold
Q1 Q2 Q3 Q4 Q1 Q2 Q3 Q4 Q1 Q2 Q3 Q4
2004
2005
2006
Year / Quarter
All Measures
Quantity sold

Line Width = 2, Volume Effect, Spline Line

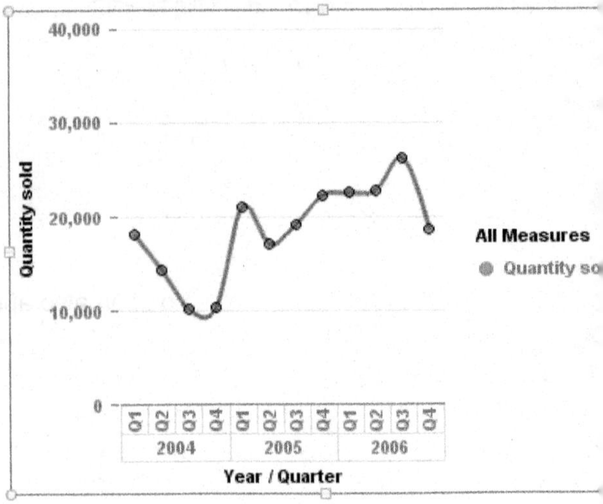
40,000
30,000
20,000
10,000
0
Quantity sold
Q1 Q2 Q3 Q4 Q1 Q2 Q3 Q4 Q1 Q2 Q3 Q4
2004
2005
2006
Year / Quarter
All Measures

- For charts containing bars/columns you can use extra effects on the bars.

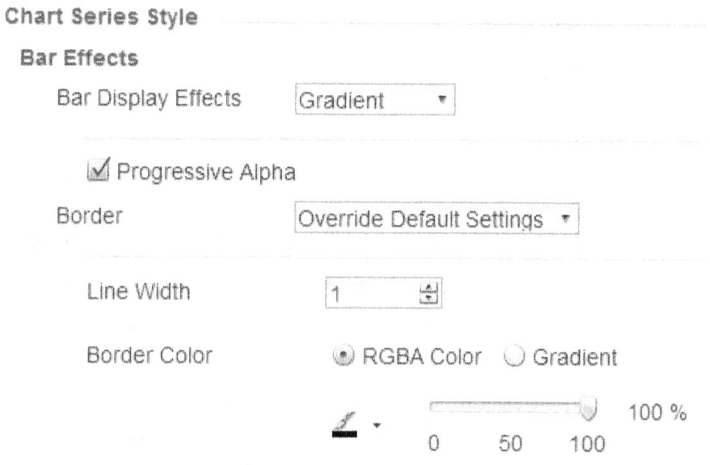
Chart Series Style
Bar Effects
Bar Display Effects
Gradient
Progressive Alpha
Border
Override Default Settings
Line Width
1
Border Color
RGBA Color
Gradient
100 %
0
50
100

Bar Display Effects = None, Border Line Width = 1, Border Color = Black 100%

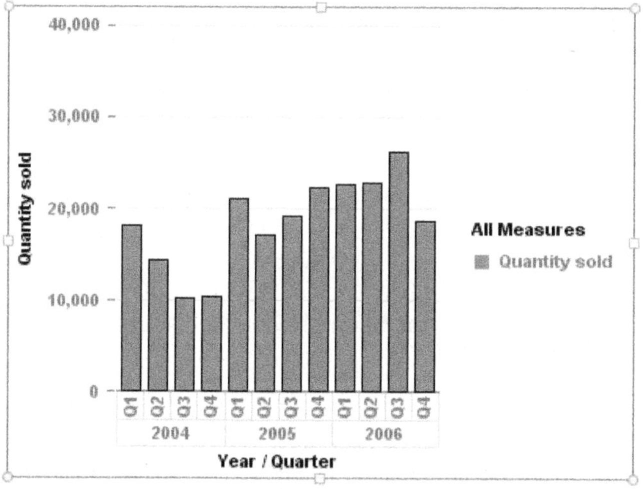
40,000
30,000
20,000
10,000
0
Quantity sold
Q1
Q2
Q3
Q4
2004
2005
2006
Year / Quarter
All Measures
Quantity sold

Bar Display Effects = Gradient, Border Line Width = 1, Border Color = Black 100%

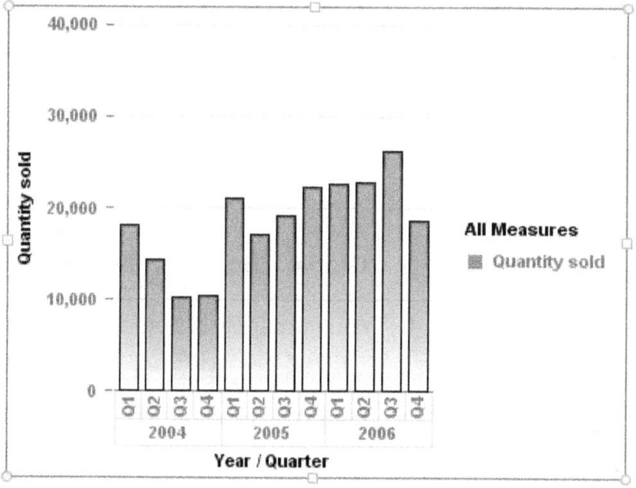
40,000
30,000
20,000
10,000
0
Quantity sold
Q1
Q2
Q3
Q4
2004
2005
2006
Year / Quarter
All Measures
Quantity sold

'Global – Background' Properties

You can apply a background colour to the chart.

Background Color
RGBA Color
Gradient
Diagonal up

Background color using a gradient of 'Diagonal Up' from Light Yellow to White.

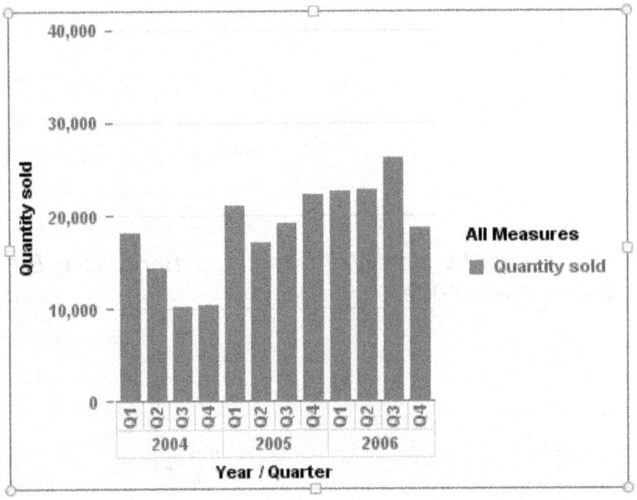
40,000
30,000
20,000
10,000
0
Quantity sold
Q1
Q2
Q3
Q4
2004
2005
2006
Year / Quarter
All Measures
Quantity sold

'Global – Border' Properties

You can apply a border to the chart. Applying borders has been previously discussed in detail.

'Global – Layout' Properties

You can specify how the chart should be positioned in relation to other report elements, repeat it on every page, etc. These properties have been previously described in detail for tables and cells.

'Title – Design' Properties

- These properties control the display of the Chart Title in terms of caption/label, position, font and borders.

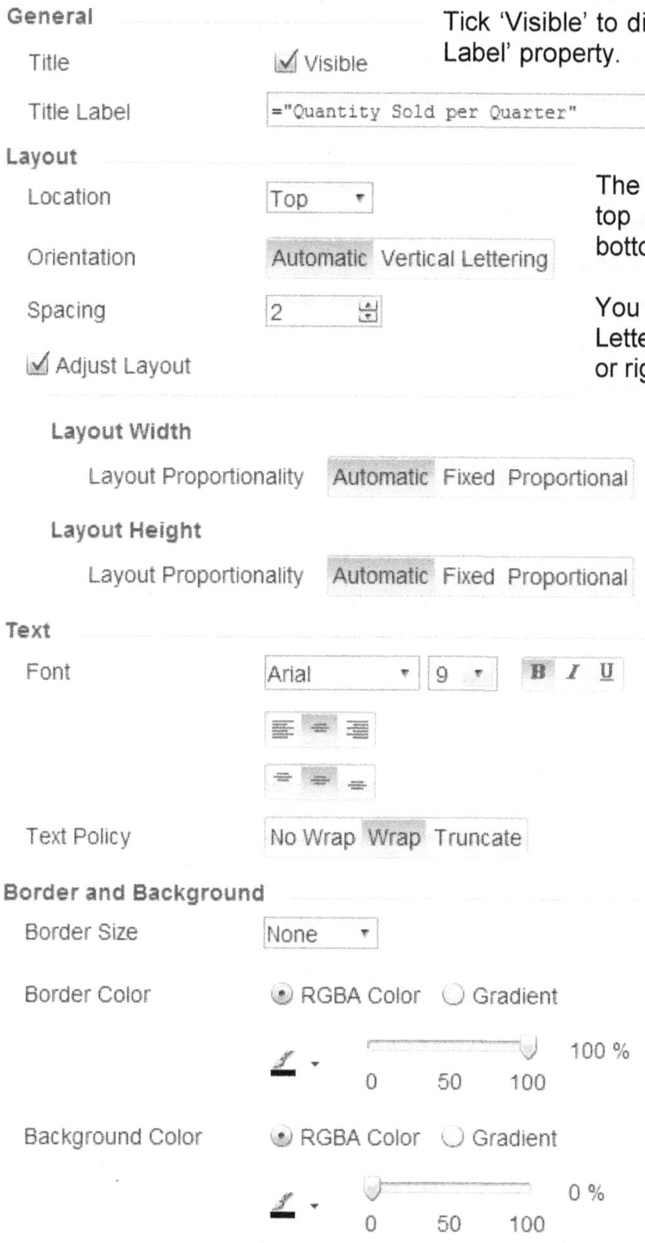
General
Title
Visible
Title Label
="Quantity Sold per Quarter"
Layout
Location
Top
Orientation
Automatic
Vertical Lettering
Spacing
2
Adjust Layout
Layout Width
Layout Proportionality
Automatic
Fixed
Proportional
Layout Height
Layout Proportionality
Automatic
Fixed
Proportional
Text
Font
Arial
9
B I U
Text Policy
No Wrap
Wrap
Truncate
Border and Background
Border Size
None
Border Color
RGBA Color
Gradient
100 %
0
50
100
Background Color
RGBA Color
Gradient
0 %
0
50
100

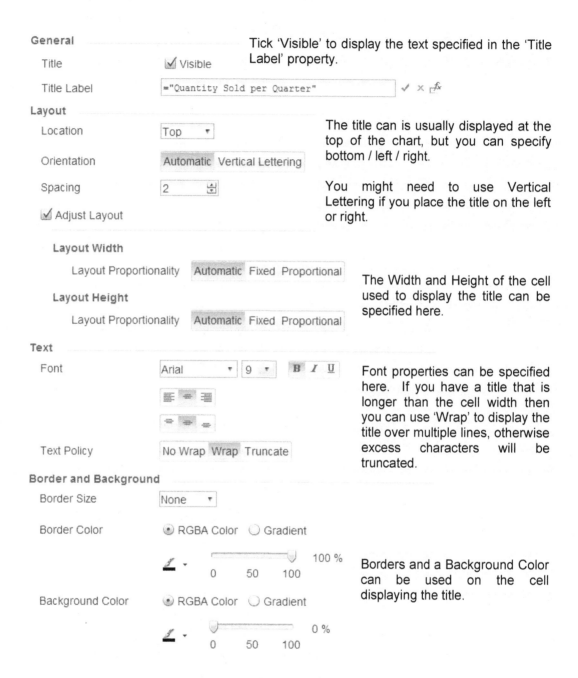

Tick 'Visible' to display the text specified in the 'Title Label' property.

The title can is usually displayed at the top of the chart, but you can specify bottom / left / right.

You might need to use Vertical Lettering if you place the title on the left or right.

The Width and Height of the cell used to display the title can be specified here.

Font properties can be specified here. If you have a title that is longer than the cell width then you can use 'Wrap' to display the title over multiple lines, otherwise excess characters will be truncated.

Borders and a Background Color can be used on the cell displaying the title.

Title Label = "Quantity Sold per Quarter",
Layout Location = Top,
Text Font = Arial / 12 / Bold,
Background Color = Light Blue / 50% Opacity

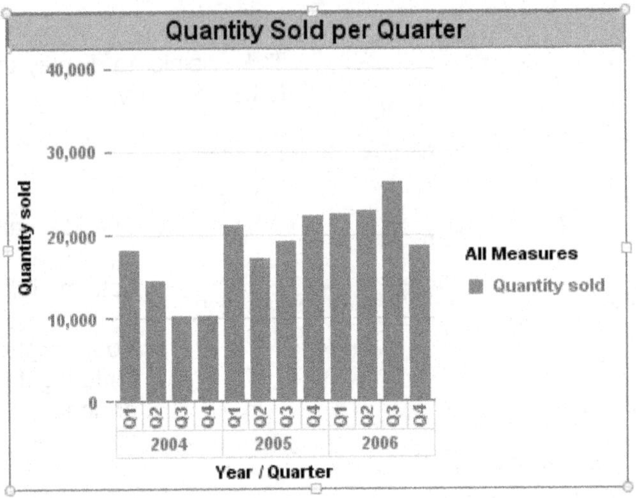
Quantity Sold per Quarter
40,000
30,000
20,000
10,000
0
Quantity sold
Q1
Q2
Q3
Q4
2004
2005
2006
Year / Quarter
All Measures
Quantity sold

'Legend – Design' Properties

- These properties control the display of the Legend in terms of visibility, position, font, symbol size, background and border colors.

'Legend – Title' Properties

- These properties control the display of the Legend Title in terms of visibility, font, background and border colors.

Legend = Visible, Location = Bottom, Symbol Size = 4
Title = not Visible (unticked)

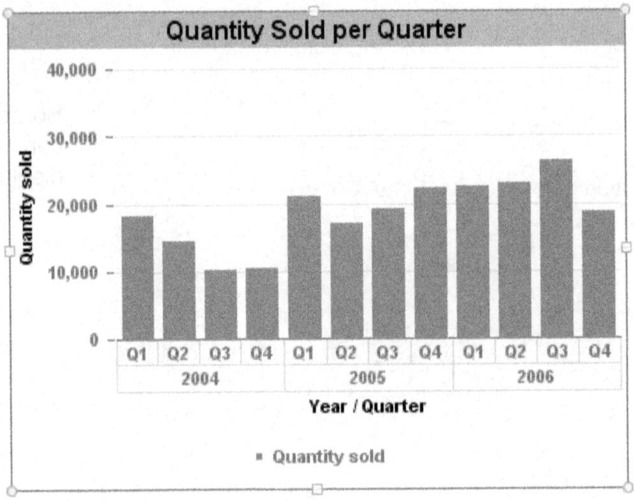
Quantity Sold per Quarter
40,000
30,000
20,000
10,000
0
Quantity sold
Q1
Q2
Q3
Q4
2004
2005
2006
Year / Quarter
Quantity sold

'Category Axis – Design' Properties

- These properties control the display of the Category Axis (i.e. dimension values) and its labels in terms of visibility, font, grid lines, and grid background color.

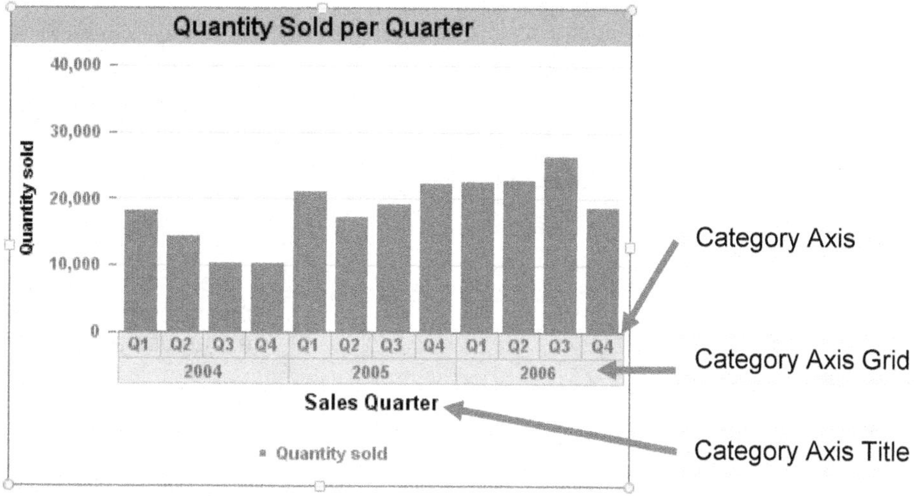
Quantity Sold per Quarter
40,000
30,000
20,000
10,000
0
Quantity sold
Q1 Q2 Q3 Q4 Q1 Q2 Q3 Q4 Q1 Q2 Q3 Q4
2004
2005
2006
Sales Quarter
Quantity sold
Category Axis
Category Axis Grid
Category Axis Title

'Category Axis – Title' Properties

- These properties control the display of the Title on the Category Axis in terms of visibility, font, background and border colors. You can also provide a custom label, i.e. text to display for the category axis.

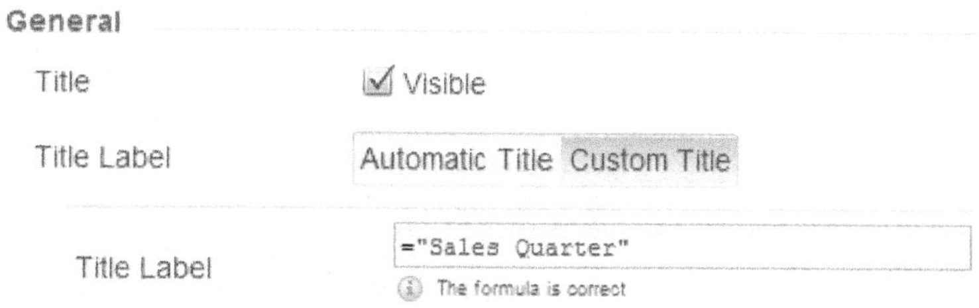
General
Title
Visible
Title Label
Automatic Title
Custom Title
Title Label
="Sales Quarter"
The formula is correct

As used in above example.

NOTE

Category Axis refers to the axis that will be displaying the dimension (or attribute) values such as Year, Quarter, Product, Region, etc.

'Value Axis – Design' Properties

- These properties control the display of the value axis (i.e. the axis on which measure values are plotted against) and its labels in terms of visibility, font, grid lines, and grid background color.

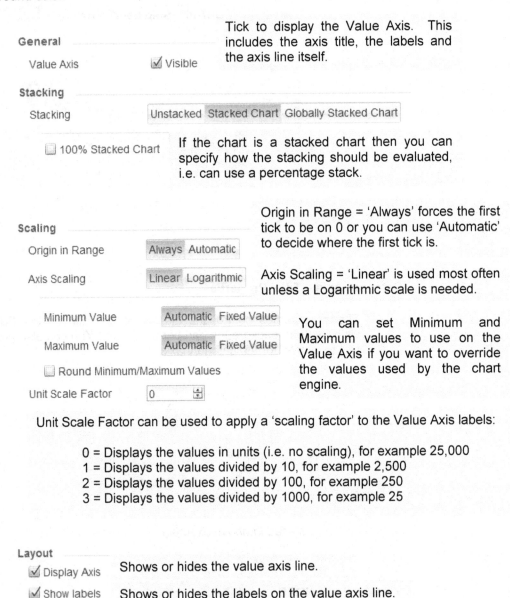

General
Value Axis
Visible

Tick to display the Value Axis. This includes the axis title, the labels and the axis line itself.

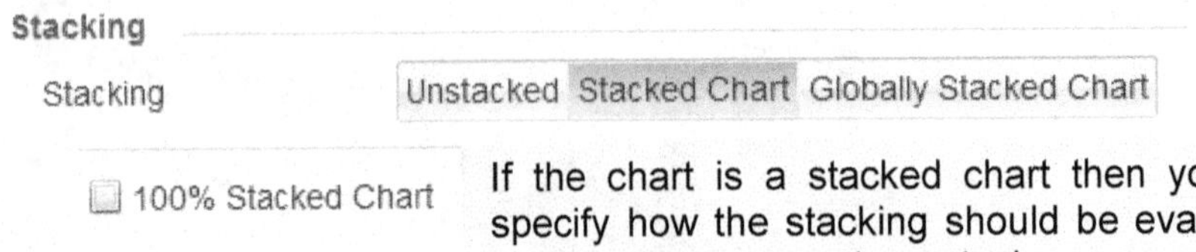
Stacking
Stacking
Unstacked
Stacked Chart
Globally Stacked Chart
100% Stacked Chart

If the chart is a stacked chart then you can specify how the stacking should be evaluated, i.e. can use a percentage stack.

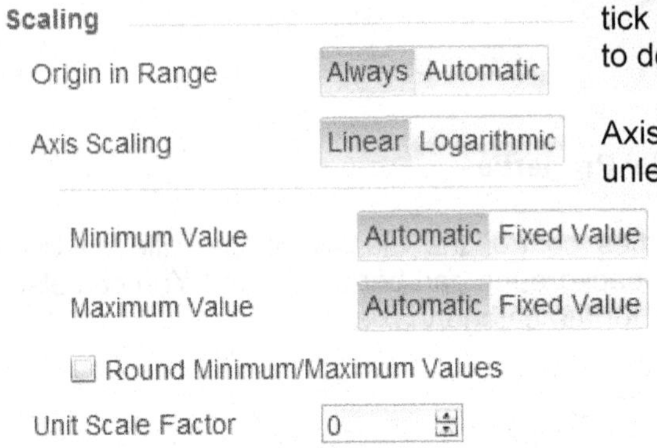
Scaling
Origin in Range
Always
Automatic
Axis Scaling
Linear
Logarithmic
Minimum Value
Automatic
Fixed Value
Maximum Value
Automatic
Fixed Value
Round Minimum/Maximum Values
Unit Scale Factor
0

Origin in Range = 'Always' forces the first tick to be on 0 or you can use 'Automatic' to decide where the first tick is.

Axis Scaling = 'Linear' is used most often unless a Logarithmic scale is needed.

You can set Minimum and Maximum values to use on the Value Axis if you want to override the values used by the chart engine.

Unit Scale Factor can be used to apply a 'scaling factor' to the Value Axis labels:

0 = Displays the values in units (i.e. no scaling), for example 25,000
1 = Displays the values divided by 10, for example 2,500
2 = Displays the values divided by 100, for example 250
3 = Displays the values divided by 1000, for example 25

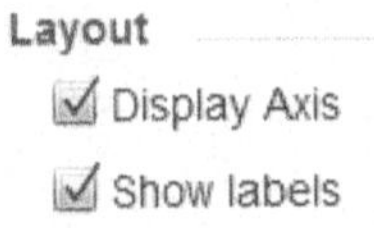
Layout
Display Axis
Show labels

Shows or hides the value axis line.

Shows or hides the labels on the value axis line.

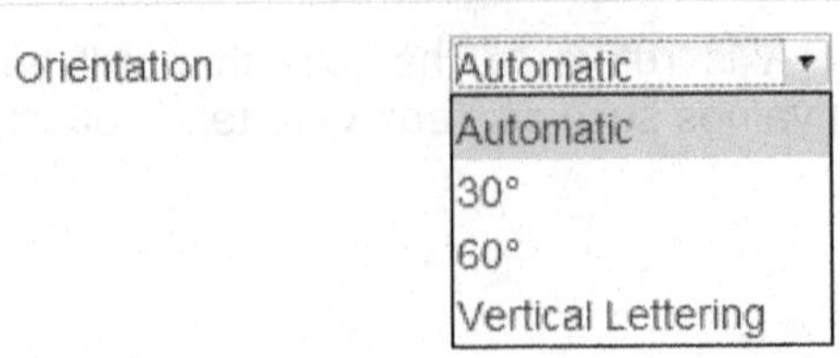
Orientation
Automatic
Automatic
30°
60°
Vertical Lettering

Adjusts the angle of the value axis labels.

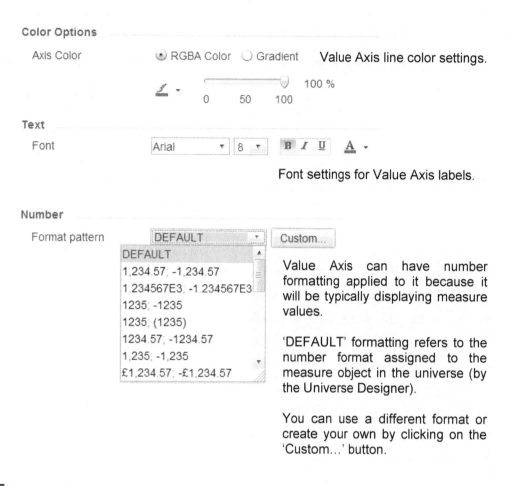

Color Options
Axis Color
RGBA Color
Gradient
100 %
0
50
100

Value Axis line color settings.

Text
Font
Arial
8

Font settings for Value Axis labels.

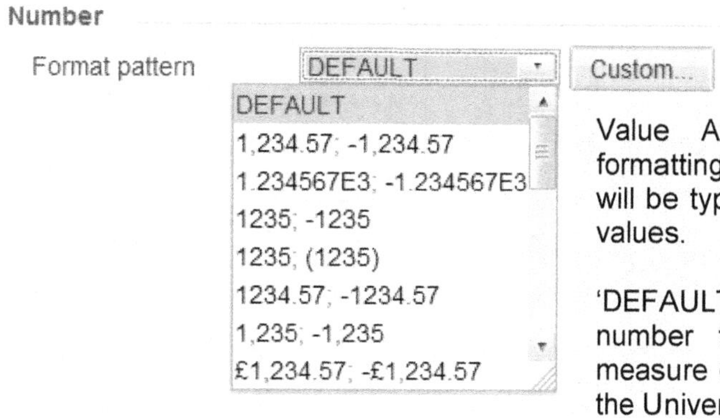
Number
Format pattern
DEFAULT
Custom...
DEFAULT
1,234.57; -1,234.57
1.234567E3; -1.234567E3
1235; -1235
1235; (1235)
1234.57; -1234.57
1,235; -1,235
£1,234.57; -£1,234.57

Value Axis can have number formatting applied to it because it will be typically displaying measure values.

'DEFAULT' formatting refers to the number format assigned to the measure object in the universe (by the Universe Designer).

You can use a different format or create your own by clicking on the 'Custom...' button.

NOTE

If the chart contains 2 Value Axes then you will be able to format Value Axis 2 independently from Value Axis.

'Plot Area – Design' Properties

- Plot Area refers to the region of the chart that contains the bars and lines, etc.
- 'Spacing within Groups' varies the amount of empty space left between bars/columns within a dimension group (i.e. in the example below the space between the two bars within Q1, or within Q2, etc).

Spacing within Groups 0.2

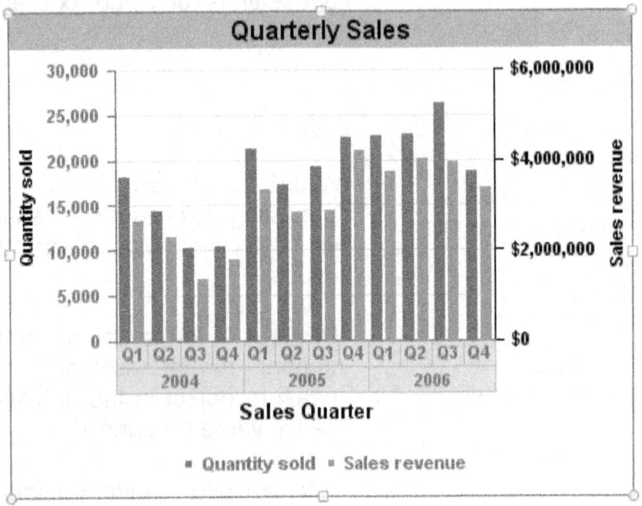
Quarterly Sales
Quantity sold
Sales revenue
30,000
25,000
20,000
15,000
10,000
5,000
0
$6,000,000
$4,000,000
$2,000,000
$0
Q1 Q2 Q3 Q4 Q1 Q2 Q3 Q4 Q1 Q2 Q3 Q4
2004 2005 2006
Sales Quarter
Quantity sold Sales revenue

Spacing within Groups 0

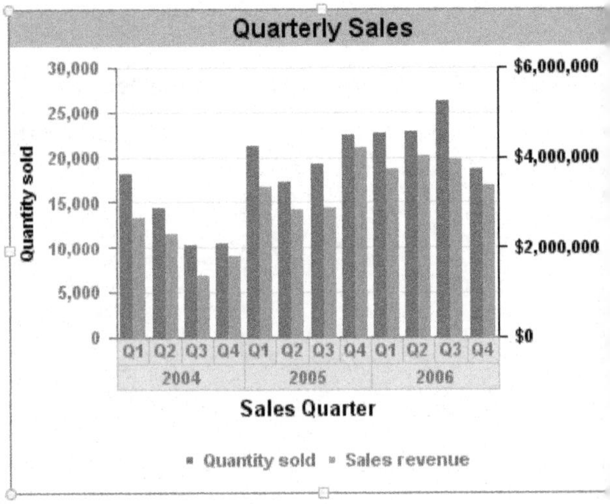
Quarterly Sales
Quantity sold
30,000
25,000
20,000
15,000
10,000
5,000
0
$6,000,000
$4,000,000
$2,000,000
$0
Q1 Q2 Q3 Q4 Q1 Q2 Q3 Q4 Q1 Q2 Q3 Q4
2004 2005 2006
Sales Quarter
Quantity sold Sales revenue

- 'Spacing between Groups' varies the amount of empty space left between different dimension values (i.e. in the example below it would be the space between Q1 and Q2, Q2 and Q3, etc).

Spacing between Groups 0.2

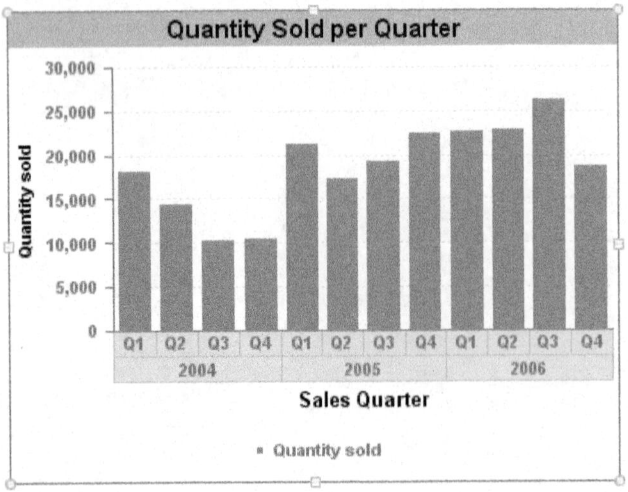
Quantity Sold per Quarter
Quantity sold
30,000
25,000
20,000
15,000
10,000
5,000
0
Q1 Q2 Q3 Q4 Q1 Q2 Q3 Q4 Q1 Q2 Q3 Q4
2004 2005 2006
Sales Quarter
Quantity sold

Spacing between Groups 0.4

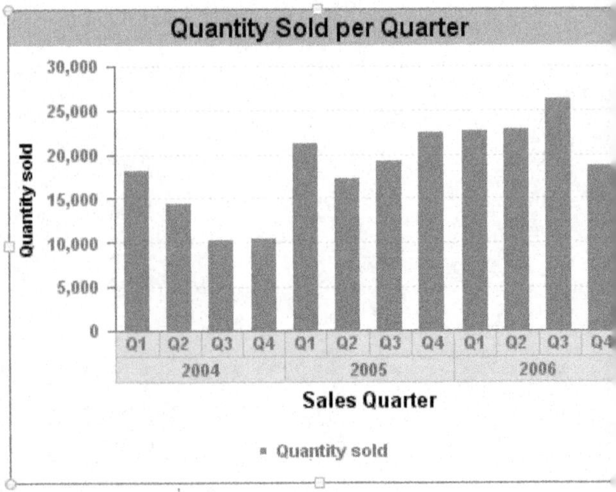
Quantity Sold per Quarter
Quantity sold
30,000
25,000
20,000
15,000
10,000
5,000
0
Q1 Q2 Q3 Q4 Q1 Q2 Q3 Q4 Q1 Q2 Q3 Q4
2004 2005 2006
Sales Quarter
Quantity sold

'Plot Area – Background' Properties

- The background of the Plot Area can be colored using a single color, a gradient effect or a striped effect (alternate colors).

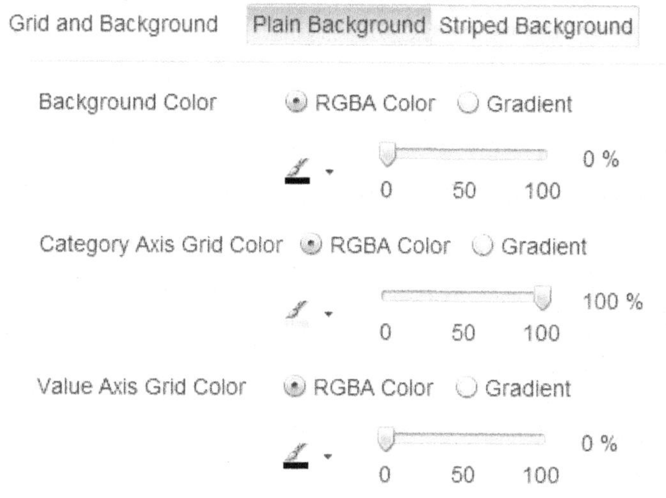
Grid and Background
Plain Background
Striped Background
Background Color
RGBA Color
Gradient
0 %
0
50
100
Category Axis Grid Color
RGBA Color
Gradient
100 %
0
50
100
Value Axis Grid Color
RGBA Color
Gradient
0 %
0
50
100

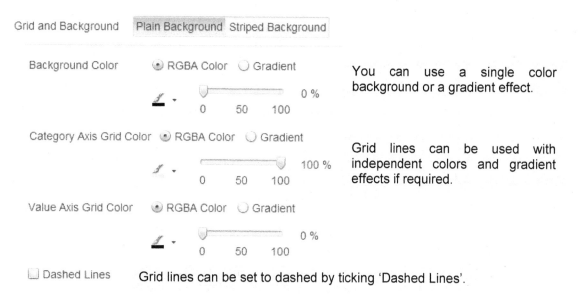

You can use a single color background or a gradient effect.

Grid lines can be used with independent colors and gradient effects if required.

Dashed Lines

Grid lines can be set to dashed by ticking 'Dashed Lines'.

Grid and Background
Plain Background
Striped Background
Background Color 1
RGBA Color
Gradient
100 %
0
50
100
Background Color 2
RGBA Color
Gradient
100 %
0
50
100

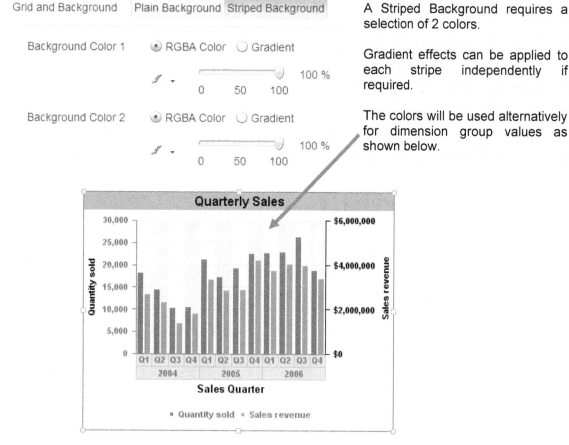

A Striped Background requires a selection of 2 colors.

Gradient effects can be applied to each stripe independently if required.

The colors will be used alternatively for dimension group values as shown below.

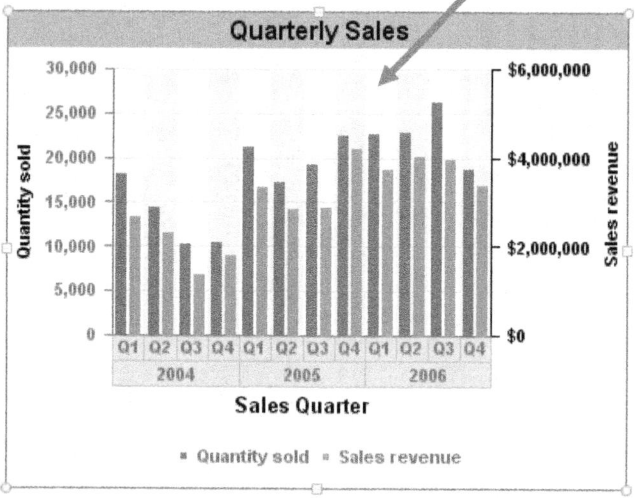
Quarterly Sales
30,000
25,000
20,000
15,000
10,000
5,000
0
Quantity sold
$6,000,000
$4,000,000
$2,000,000
$0
Sales revenue
Q1 Q2 Q3 Q4 Q1 Q2 Q3 Q4 Q1 Q2 Q3 Q4
2004
2005
2006
Sales Quarter
Quantity sold
Sales revenue

15.2.1 Example Use of Chart Properties

The chart we created at the start of this session looks as follows:

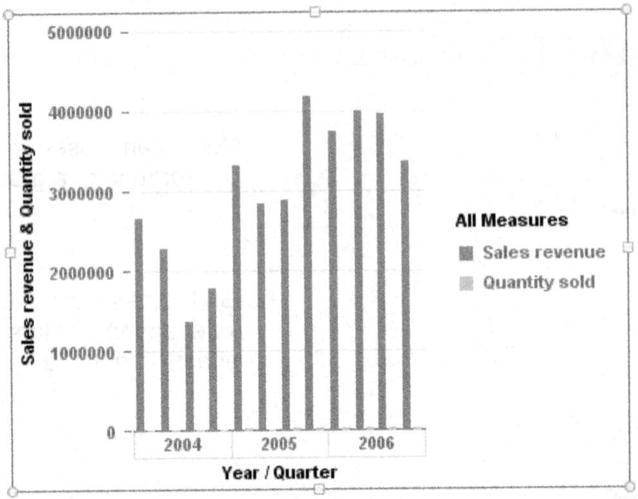

5000000
4000000
3000000
2000000
1000000
0
Sales revenue & Quantity sold
2004
2005
2006
Year / Quarter
All Measures
Sales revenue
Quantity sold

The values for [Sales revenue] and [Quantity sold] are both being plotted on a single Value Axis and it is almost impossible to see the [Quantity sold] columns.

If you do not have the above chart then please go to the start of this session, recreate the chart and return to this point.

1. Right-click on chart and select 'Turn Into – More Transformations'.

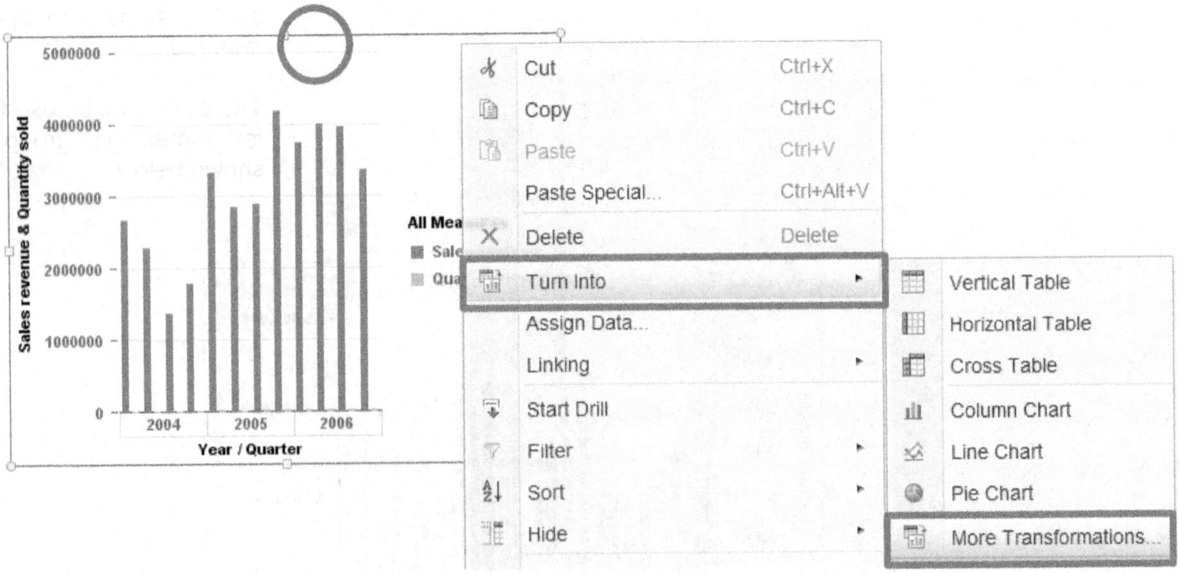

Cut Ctrl+X
Copy Ctrl+C
Paste Ctrl+V
Paste Special... Ctrl+Alt+V
Delete Delete
Turn Into
Assign Data...
Linking
Start Drill
Filter
Sort
Hide
Vertical Table
Horizontal Table
Cross Table
Column Chart
Line Chart
Pie Chart
More Transformations...

2. Select 'Column Chart with Dual Value Axes' and click 'OK'.

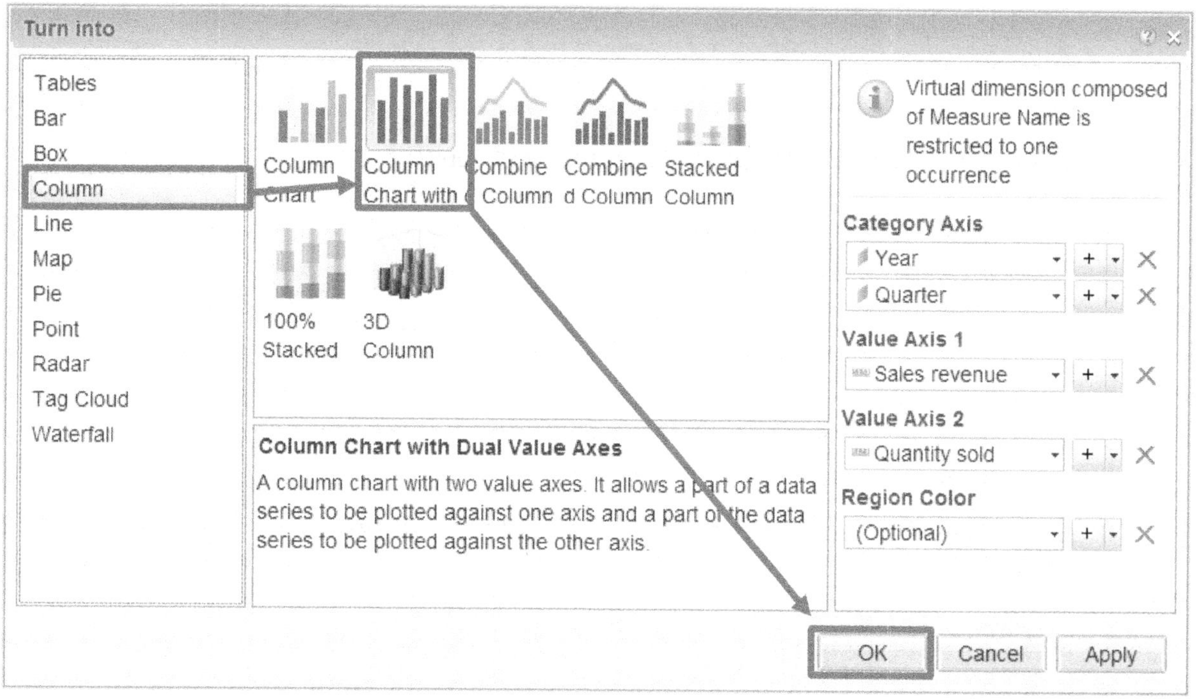
Turn into
Tables
Bar
Box
Column
Line
Map
Pie
Point
Radar
Tag Cloud
Waterfall
Column Chart
Column Chart with
Combine Column
Combine d Column
Stacked Column
100% Stacked
3D Column
Column Chart with Dual Value Axes
A column chart with two value axes. It allows a part of a data series to be plotted against one axis and a part of the data series to be plotted against the other axis.
Virtual dimension composed of Measure Name is restricted to one occurrence
Category Axis
Year
Quarter
Value Axis 1
Sales revenue
Value Axis 2
Quantity sold
Region Color
(Optional)
OK
Cancel
Apply

NOTE – Hovering over the chart icons will display more information:

We will now have a column chart with 2 axes plotting [Sales revenue] on the left hand side and [Quantity sold] on the right hand side.

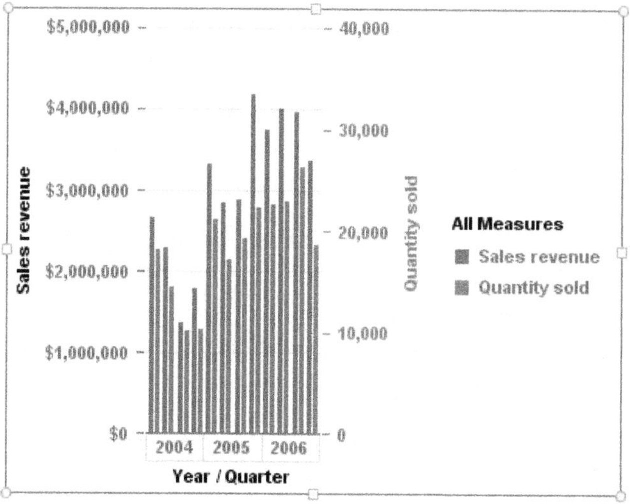
$5,000,000
$4,000,000
$3,000,000
$2,000,000
$1,000,000
$0
Sales revenue
40,000
30,000
20,000
10,000
0
Quantity sold
2004
2005
2006
Year / Quarter
All Measures
Sales revenue
Quantity sold

3. Right-click on chart and select 'Format Chart...'

4. Give the chart a name, 'cht Example' and click 'Apply'.

Global
General
Name
cht Example

5. Give the chart a Title of 'Quarterly Sales' and click 'Apply'.

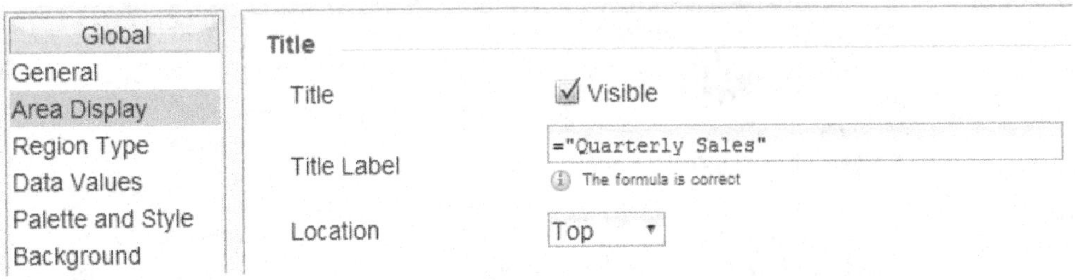
Global
General
Area Display
Region Type
Data Values
Palette and Style
Background
Title
Title
Visible
Title Label
="Quarterly Sales"
The formula is correct
Location
Top

6. Within the 'Area Display' group of properties, untick the 'Visible' property for the Legend Title and click 'Apply'.

Legend
Legend
Visible
Title
Visible

7. Select 'Single Color Palette' with the 'Palette default' color scheme, and click 'Apply.

Global
General
Area Display
Region Type
Data Values
Palette and Style
Background
Border
Layout
3D Look
Depth
2D Look
3D Look
Color Options
Color Palette
Single Color Palette
Dual Color Palette
Palette
Color Palette
Palette default
10...
0
50
100

8. Apply a border to the chart by following the arrows below and then click 'Apply'.

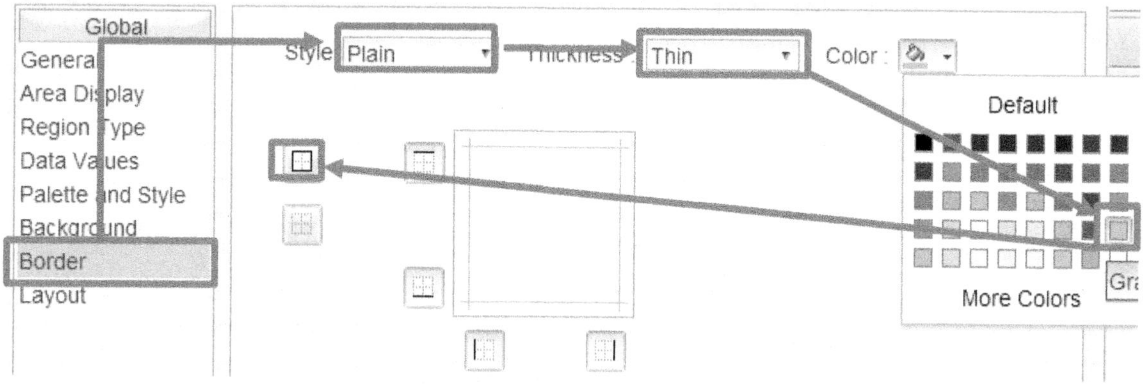
Global
General
Area Display
Region Type
Data Values
Palette and Style
Background
Border
Layout
Style
Plain
Thickness
Thin
Color :
Default
More Colors

Our chart should now appear as:

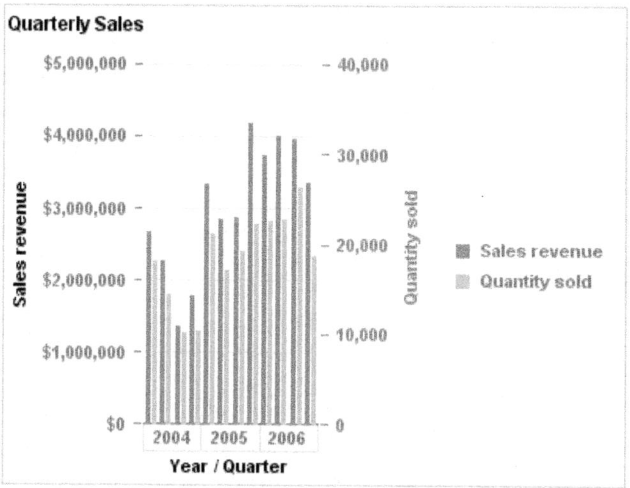
Quarterly Sales
$5,000,000
$4,000,000
$3,000,000
$2,000,000
$1,000,000
$0
40,000
30,000
20,000
10,000
0
Sales revenue
Quantity sold
2004
2005
2006
Year / Quarter
Sales revenue
Quantity sold

9. Make the title font size 14 and centre the title on the chart. Click 'Apply'.

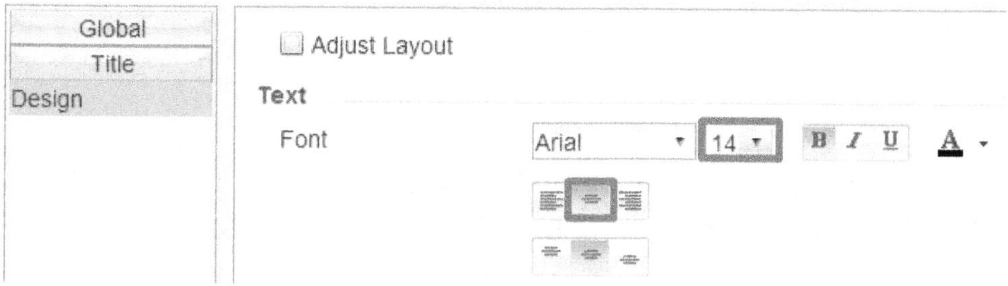
Global
Title
Design
Adjust Layout
Text
Font
Arial
14

10. Place the legend at the bottom of the chart using a symbol size of 6, label font size of 8 and regular font (i.e. not bold). Click 'Apply'.

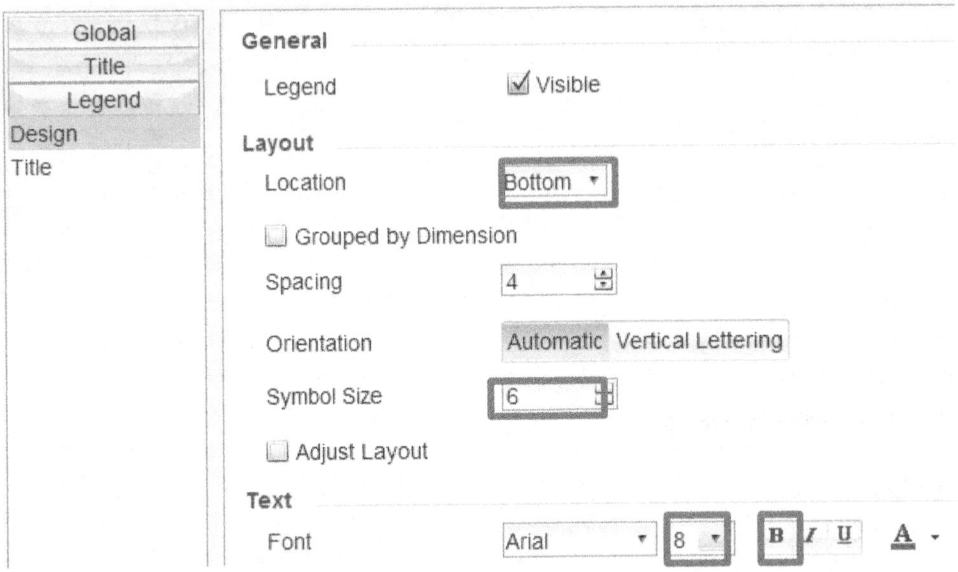
Global
Title
Legend
Design
Title
General
Legend
Visible
Layout
Location
Bottom
Grouped by Dimension
Spacing
4
Orientation
Automatic
Vertical Lettering
Symbol Size
6
Adjust Layout
Text
Font
Arial
8

Our chart should now appear as:

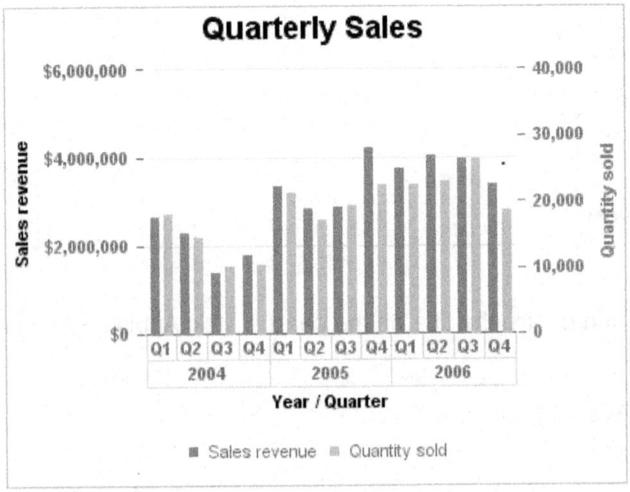
Quarterly Sales
$6,000,000
$4,000,000
$2,000,000
$0
Sales revenue
40,000
30,000
20,000
10,000
0
Quantity sold
Q1 Q2 Q3 Q4 Q1 Q2 Q3 Q4 Q1 Q2 Q3 Q4
2004
2005
2006
Year / Quarter
Sales revenue
Quantity sold

By moving the legend to the bottom, the charting engine now has more space available to display the quarters on the category axis as well as the years.

11. It is obvious the category axis is displaying [Year] and [Quarter] so we do not need a Title for it. We can hide it by unticking the 'Visible property and clicking 'Apply'.

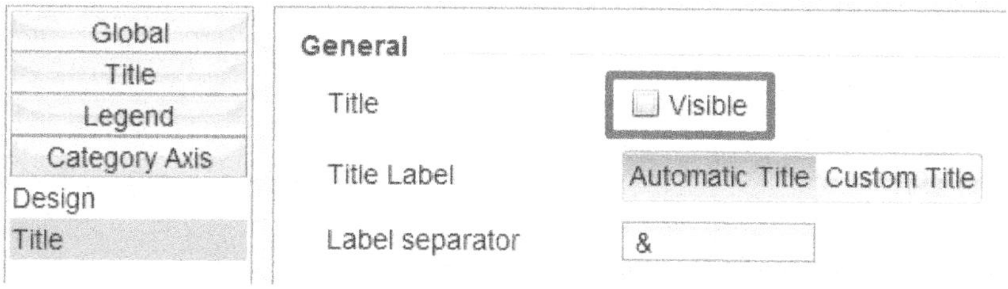
Global
Title
Legend
Category Axis
Design
Title
General
Title
Visible
Title Label
Automatic Title
Custom Title
Label separator
&

12. Value Axis is being used to display [Sales revenue] containing values in the 'millions'. We can apply a 'Unit Scale Factor' of 6 to reduce the number of zeros displayed on the Value Axis, i.e. 2,000,000 will be displayed as 2.

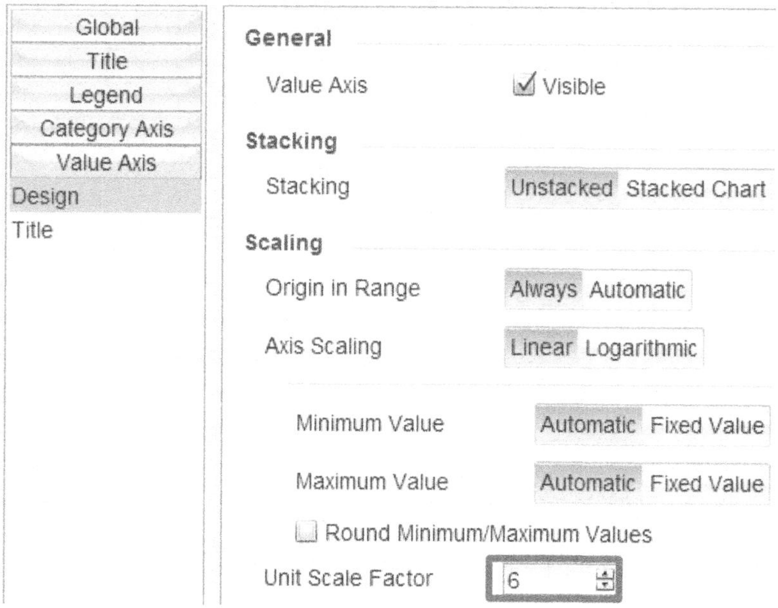
Global
Title
Legend
Category Axis
Value Axis
Design
Title
General
Value Axis
Visible
Stacking
Stacking
Unstacked
Stacked Chart
Scaling
Origin in Range
Always
Automatic
Axis Scaling
Linear
Logarithmic
Minimum Value
Automatic
Fixed Value
Maximum Value
Automatic
Fixed Value
Round Minimum/Maximum Values
Unit Scale Factor
6

13. We should then change the Value Axis title to make it clear we have applied a scaling factor to the values.

Global
Title
Legend
Category Axis
Value Axis
Design
Title
General
Title
Visible
Title Label
Automatic Title
Custom Title
Title Label
="Sales Revenue ($m)"
The formula is correct

14. Tick 'Display Axis' and click 'Apply'.

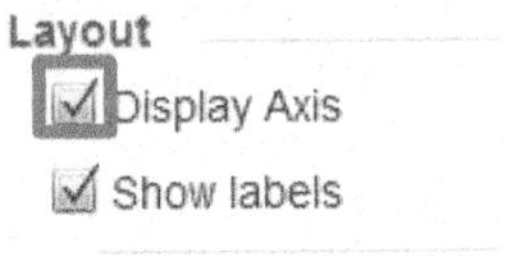
Layout
Display Axis
Show labels

Our chart should now appear as:

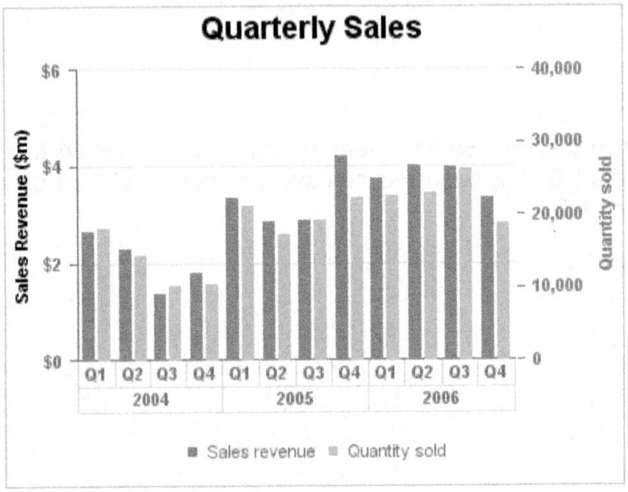
Quarterly Sales
$6
$4
$2
$0
Sales Revenue ($m)
40,000
30,000
20,000
10,000
0
Quantity sold
Q1
Q2
Q3
Q4
2004
2005
2006
Sales revenue
Quantity sold

15. For Value Axis 2, tick 'Display Axis'.

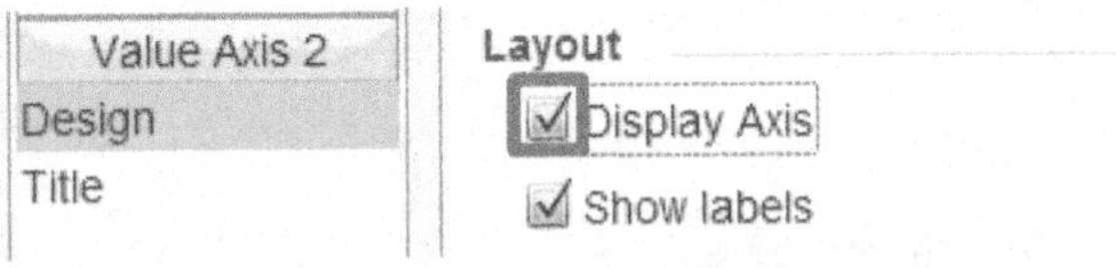
Value Axis 2
Design
Title
Layout
Display Axis
Show labels

16. Set the Value Axis 2 color to 'Black', this will change the color of the axis line.

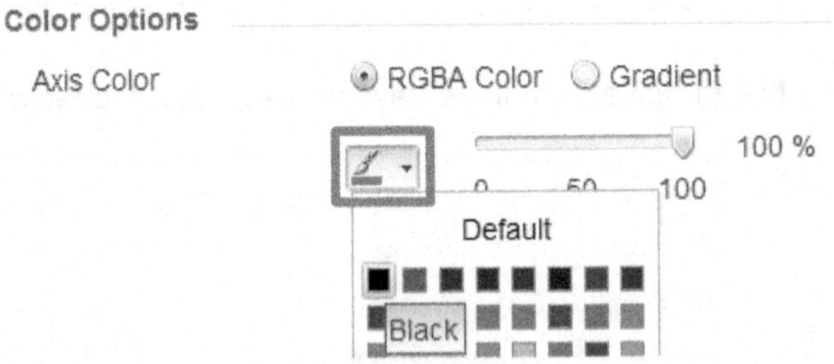
Color Options
Axis Color
RGBA Color
Gradient
100 %
100
Default
Black

17. Set the Value Axis 2 Font color to 'Black', this will change the color of the values displayed on the axis to black.

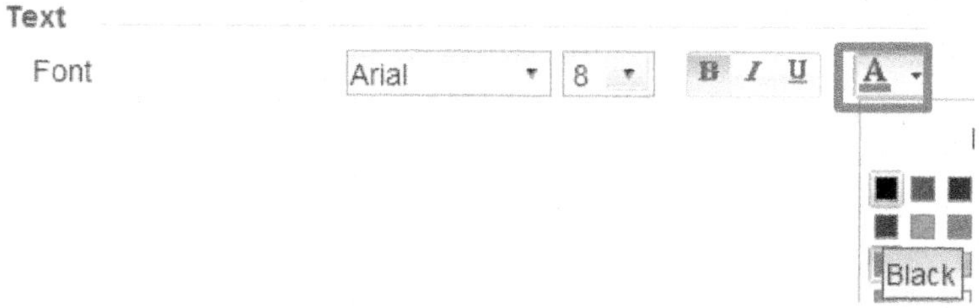
Text
Font
Arial
8
Black

18. Set the scaling factor for Value Axis 2 as '3'.

Unit Scale Factor
3

19. Set the Value Axis 2 Title = 'Quantity Sold (k)'.

Title Label
Automatic Title
Custom Title
Title Label
="Quantity Sold (k)"

20. Set the Value Axis 2 Title color to 'Black', this will change the color of the title 'Quantity sold' to black.

Value Axis 2
Design
Title
Text
Font
Arial
8
Black

21. Click 'Apply'.

Our chart should now appear as:

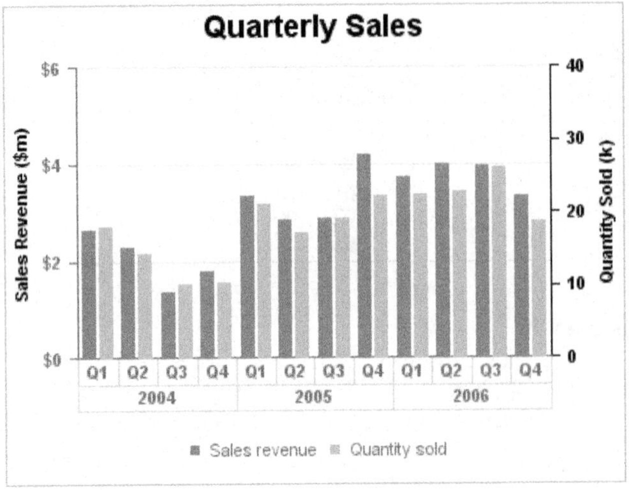
Quarterly Sales
$6
$4
$2
$0
Sales Revenue ($m)
40
30
20
10
0
Quantity Sold (k)
Q1 Q2 Q3 Q4 Q1 Q2 Q3 Q4 Q1 Q2 Q3 Q4
2004
2005
2006
Sales revenue
Quantity sold

22. Let us now resize the chart.

    Set Width = 20cm and Height = 10cm and click 'Apply'.

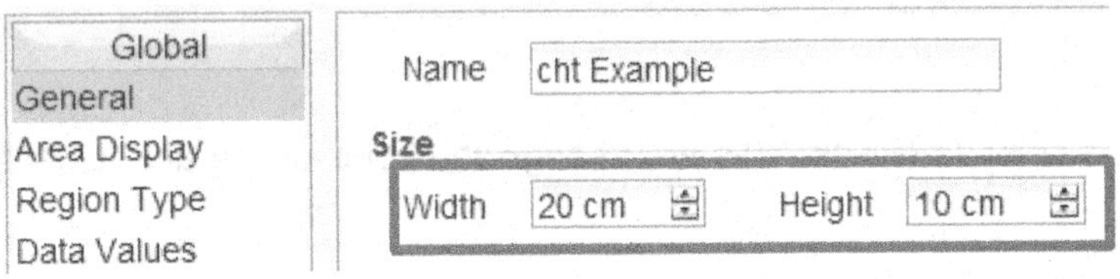
Global
General
Area Display
Region Type
Data Values
Name
cht Example
Size
Width
20 cm
Height
10 cm

NOTE - You can do also this by dragging the on the chart borders (highlighted points below).

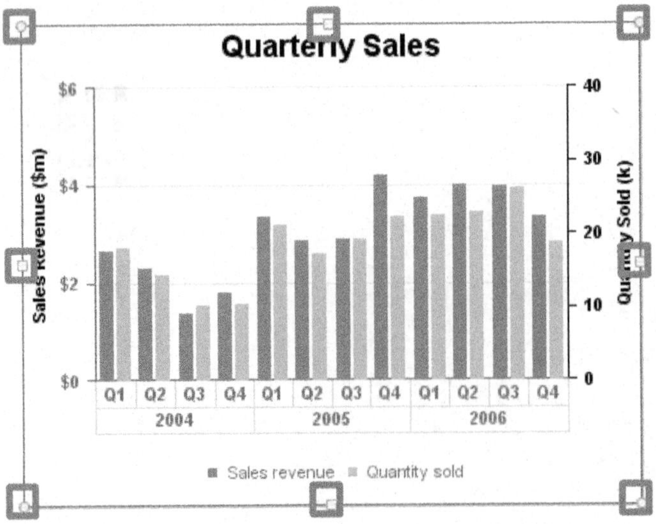
Quarterly Sales
$6
$4
$2
$0
Sales Revenue ($m)
40
30
20
10
0
Q1 Q2 Q3 Q4 Q1 Q2 Q3 Q4 Q1 Q2 Q3 Q4
2004
2005
2006
Sales revenue
Quantity sold

23. Set the ‘Spacing within Groups’ = 0 and click ‘OK’ to close the ‘Format Chart’ interface.

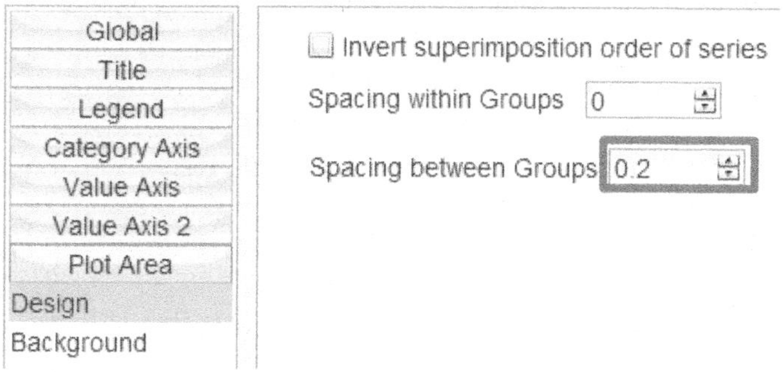
Global
Title
Legend
Category Axis
Value Axis
Value Axis 2
Plot Area
Design
Background
Invert superimposition order of series
Spacing within Groups 0
Spacing between Groups 0.2

Our chart should now appear as:

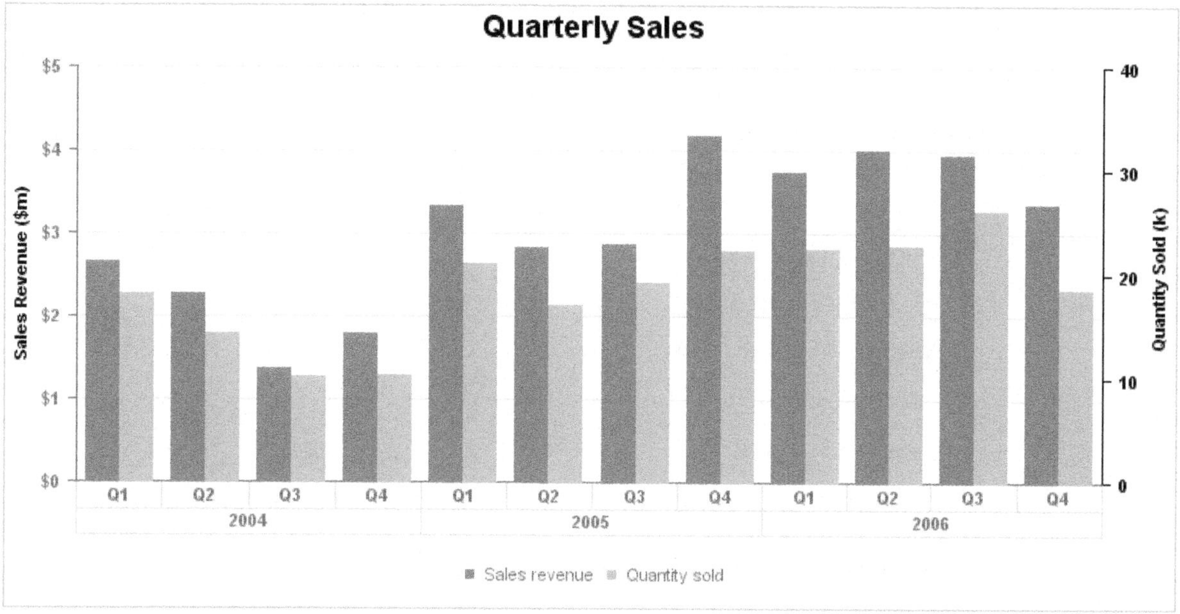
Quarterly Sales
$5
$4
$3
$2
$1
$0
Sales Revenue ($m)
40
30
20
10
0
Quantity Sold (k)
Q1
Q2
Q3
Q4
2004
2005
2006
Sales revenue
Quantity sold

We have worked through most of the formatting properties of charts to create the above example.

15.3 Creating Charts using Chart Templates

Charts can be created using Chart Templates.

1. Add a new tab to the document.

   You can do this by right-clicking on an existing report tab and selecting 'Add Report'.

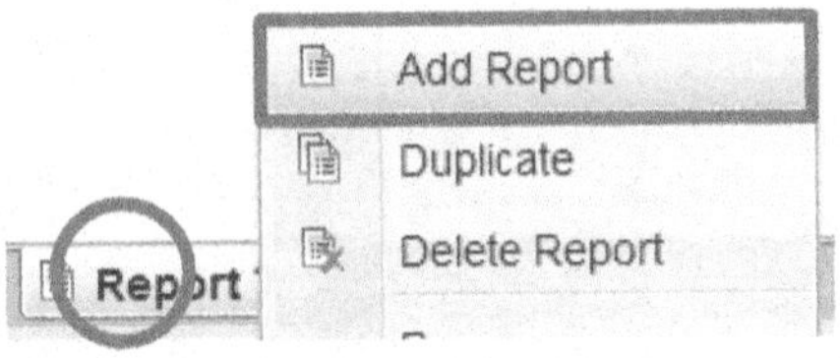
Add Report
Duplicate
Delete Report
Report

2. Select 'Stacked Column' from the 'Report Element' toolbar.

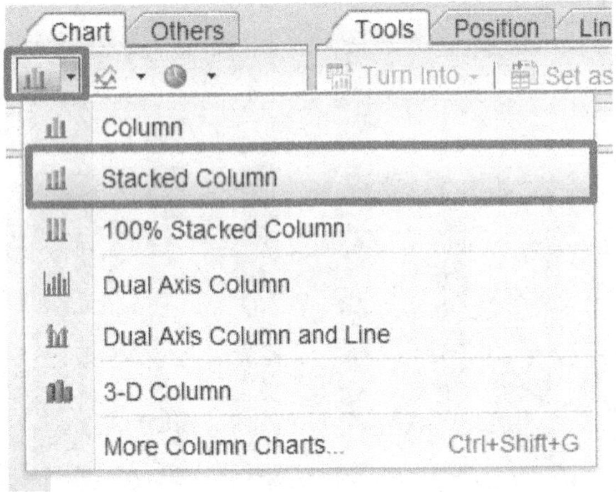
Chart
Others
Tools
Position
Turn Into
Set as
Column
Stacked Column
100% Stacked Column
Dual Axis Column
Dual Axis Column and Line
3-D Column
More Column Charts...
Ctrl+Shift+G

3. Drop the template onto the report canvas.

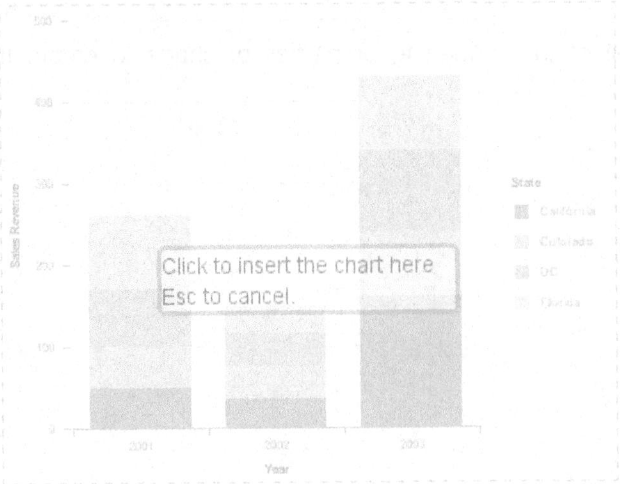
Click to insert the chart here
Esc to cancel.

4. We can now drop objects onto the template to create the chart.

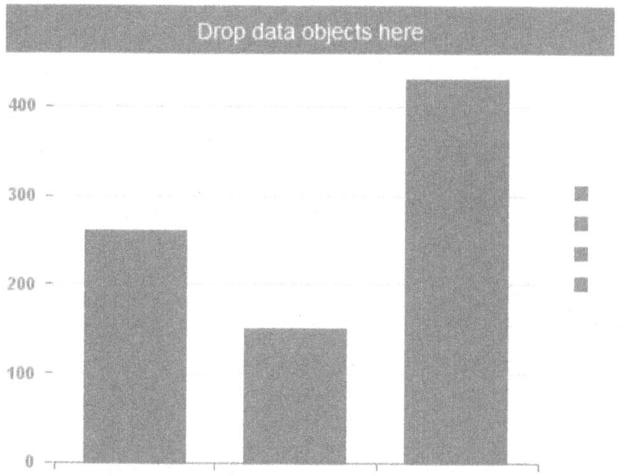
Drop data objects here
400
300
200
100
0

However it is simpler to do this using the 'Assign Data…' interface (discussed next).

15.4 Assigning Data Objects to Charts

Charts can be assigned objects using the 'Assign Data…' interface.

1. Right-click on the new chart (or existing chart) and select 'Assign Data…'

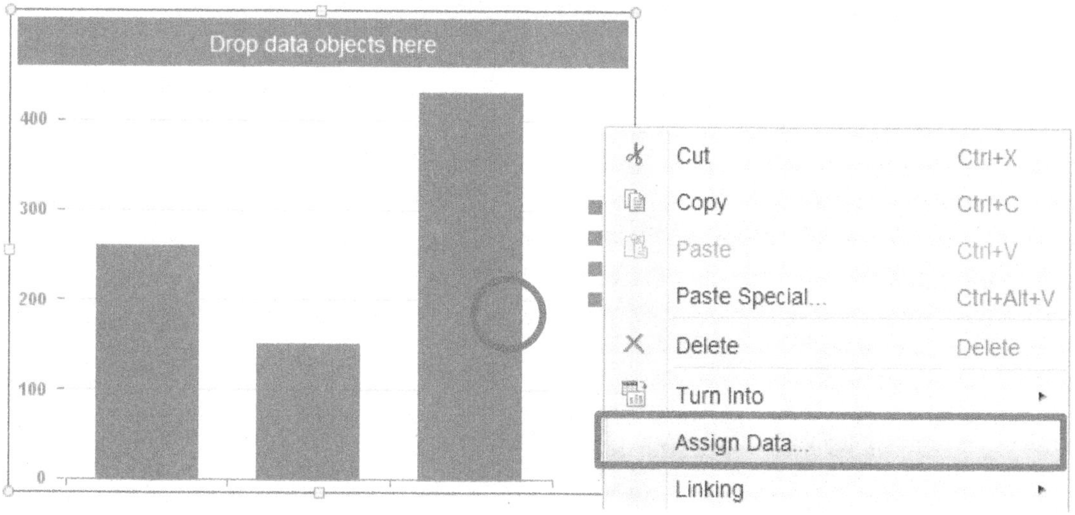
Drop data objects here
400
300
200
100
0
Cut Ctrl+X
Copy Ctrl+C
Paste Ctrl+V
Paste Special... Ctrl+Alt+V
Delete Delete
Turn Into
Assign Data...
Linking

2. We can now use the 'Assign Data' interface to select objects to be used within the chart.

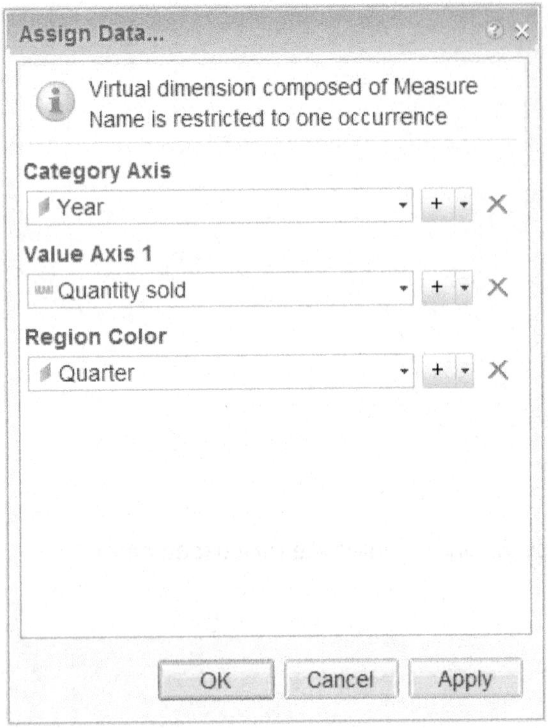
Assign Data...
Virtual dimension composed of Measure Name is restricted to one occurrence
Category Axis
Year
Value Axis 1
Quantity sold
Region Color
Quarter
OK
Cancel
Apply

3. Assign the objects as shown above and click 'OK'.

Web Intelligence will now show the chart with data.

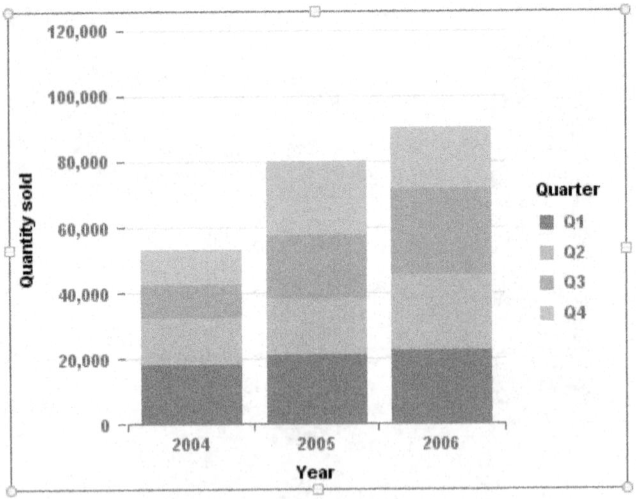
120,000
100,000
80,000
60,000
40,000
20,000
0
Quantity sold
2004
2005
2006
Year
Quarter
Q1
Q2
Q3
Q4

4. You can also assign objects to charts within the 'Turn Into…' interface.

   Right-click on a chart/table and select 'More Transformations…'

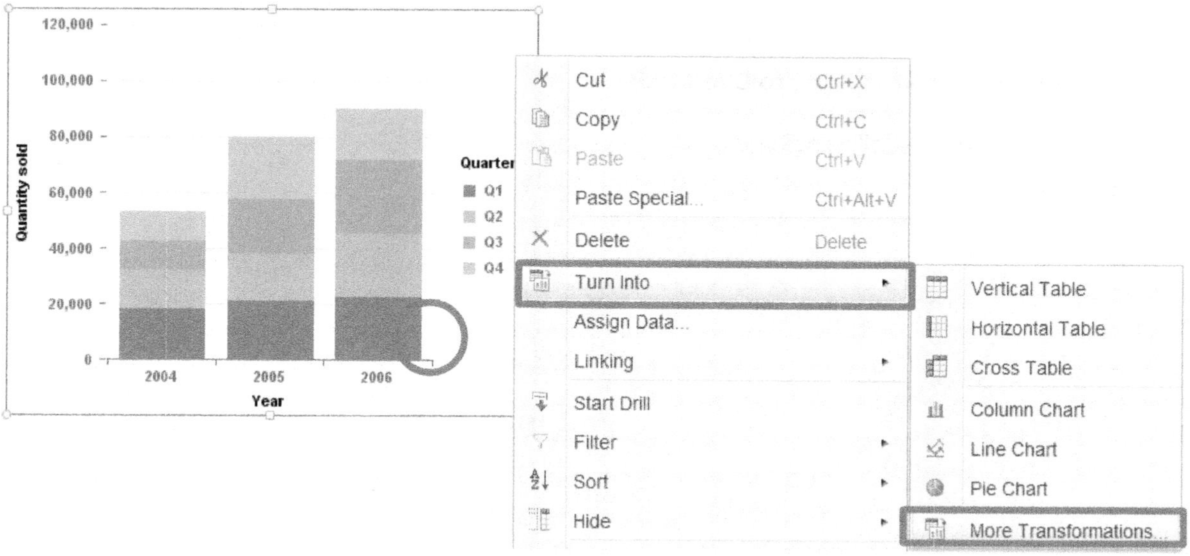
120,000
100,000
80,000
60,000
40,000
20,000
0
Quantity sold
2004
2005
2006
Year
Quarter
Q1
Q2
Q3
Q4
Cut Ctrl+X
Copy Ctrl+C
Paste Ctrl+V
Paste Special... Ctrl+Alt+V
Delete Delete
Turn Into
Assign Data...
Linking
Start Drill
Filter
Sort
Hide
Vertical Table
Horizontal Table
Cross Table
Column Chart
Line Chart
Pie Chart
More Transformations...

5. On the right hand side of the 'Turn Into…' interface you can select the objects to use for the chart (or table).

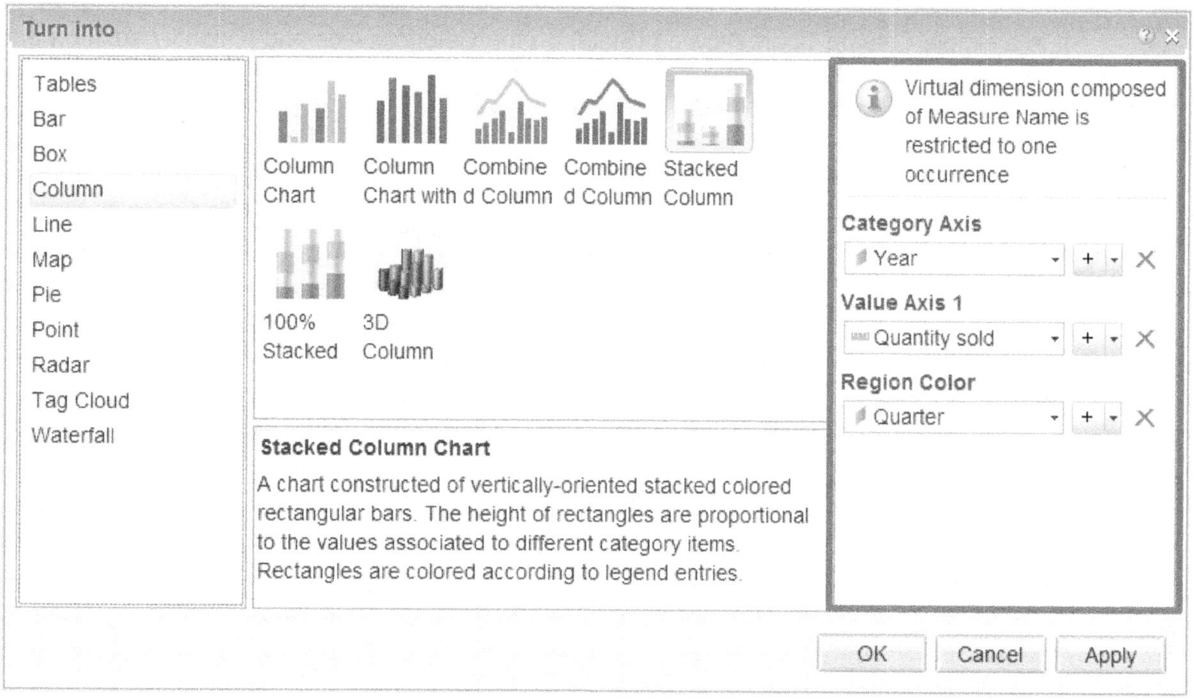
Turn Into
Tables
Bar
Box
Column
Line
Map
Pie
Point
Radar
Tag Cloud
Waterfall
Column Chart
Column Chart with
Combined Column
Combined Column
Stacked Column
100% Stacked
3D Column
Stacked Column Chart
A chart constructed of vertically-oriented stacked colored rectangular bars. The height of rectangles are proportional to the values associated to different category items. Rectangles are colored according to legend entries.
Virtual dimension composed of Measure Name is restricted to one occurrence
Category Axis
Year
Value Axis 1
Quantity sold
Region Color
Quarter
OK
Cancel
Apply

NOTE – The type of objects to assign will vary depending on the table or chart type you are working with.

15.5 Sorting Data in Charts

Data presented in charts can be sorted (Standard Sorts and/or Custom Sorts), sort priorities can be changed, and sorts can be removed.

15.5.1 Applying Sorts to Chart Data

1. Create the following chart:

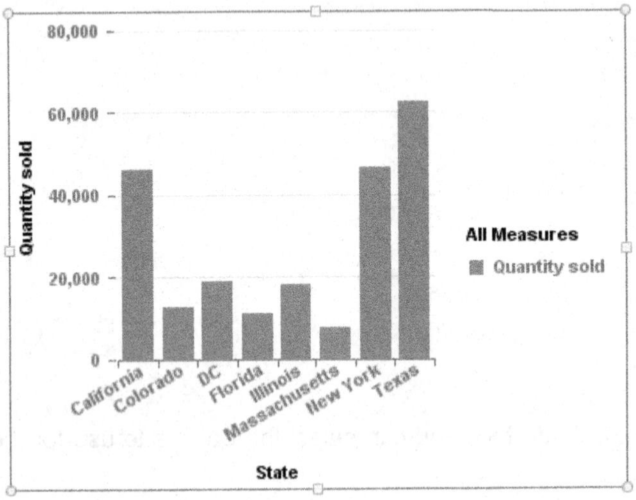
80,000
60,000
40,000
20,000
0
Quantity sold
California
Colorado
DC
Florida
Illinois
Massachusetts
New York
Texas
State
All Measures
Quantity sold

It is a simple Column Chart showing [State] on the Category Axis and [Quantity sold] on the Value Axis.

2. Right-click on the chart and select 'Sort – Quantity sold – Descending', as shown below:

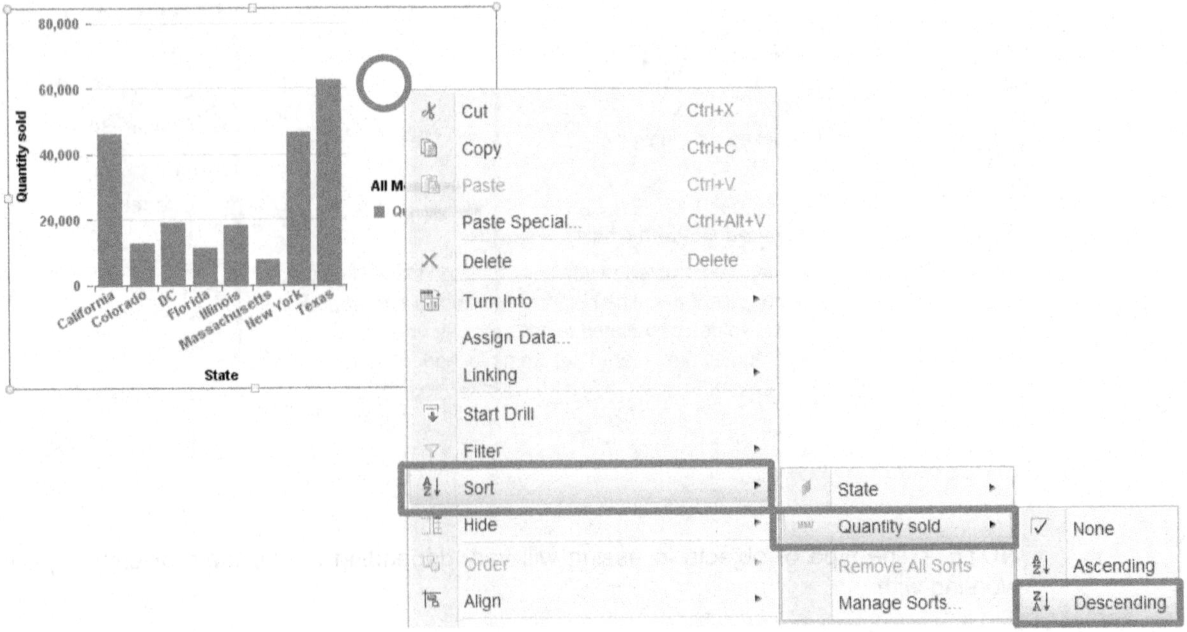
Cut Ctrl+X
Copy Ctrl+C
Paste Ctrl+V
Paste Special... Ctrl+Alt+V
Delete Delete
Turn Into
Assign Data...
Linking
Start Drill
Filter
Sort
Hide
Order
Align
State
Quantity sold
Remove All Sorts
Manage Sorts...
None
Ascending
Descending

3. The chart is now sorted on [Quantity sold] in descending order:

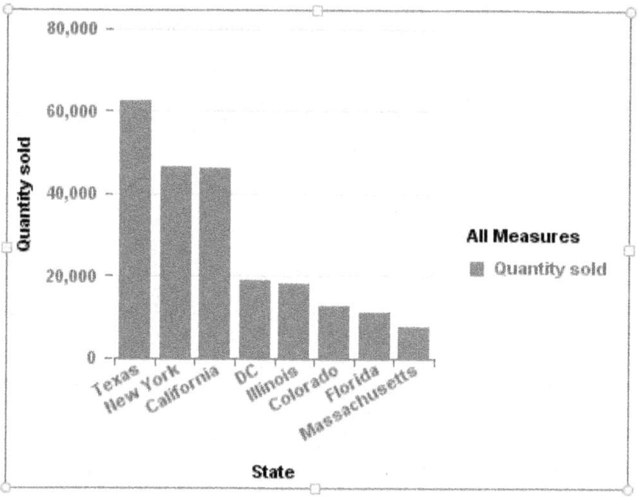
80,000
60,000
40,000
20,000
0
Quantity sold
Texas
New York
California
DC
Illinois
Colorado
Florida
Massachusetts
State
All Measures
Quantity sold

15.5.2 Managing and Removing Chart Sorts

There are a number of ways to remove sorts applied to a chart.

1. Right-click on the chart and then 'un-apply' the sort that has already been applied.

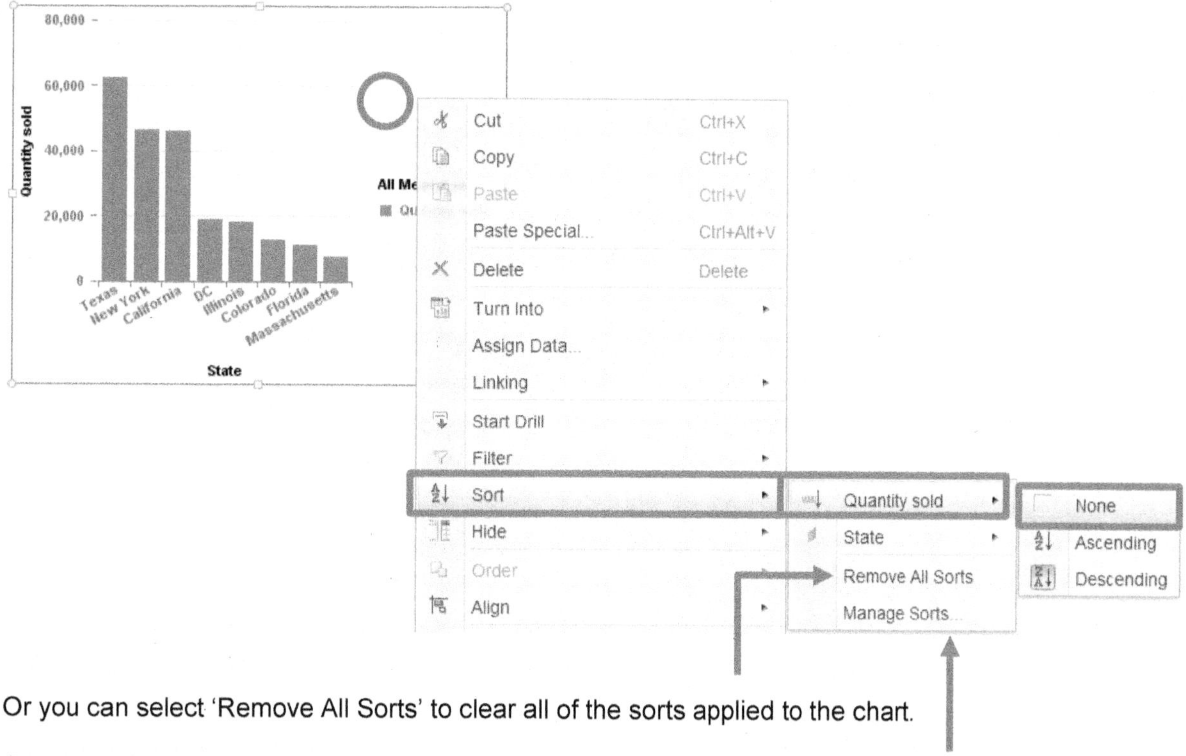
Cut Ctrl+X
Copy Ctrl+C
Paste Ctrl+V
Paste Special... Ctrl+Alt+V
Delete Delete
Turn Into
Assign Data...
Linking
Start Drill
Filter
Sort
Hide
Order
Align
Quantity sold
State
Remove All Sorts
Manage Sorts...
None
Ascending
Descending

2. Or you can select 'Remove All Sorts' to clear all of the sorts applied to the chart.

3. Or you can select 'Manage Sorts...' and use the 'Manage Sorts' interface to work with the sorts. We have already discussed the 'Manage Sorts' interface in the session 'Sorting and Hiding Data in Tables and Cross Tables'.

15.6 Hiding Data in Charts

We demonstrated how dimensions can be hidden in table type blocks. Data can be hidden in charts type blocks also.

7. Create a new document with the following query (from 'eFashion' universe).

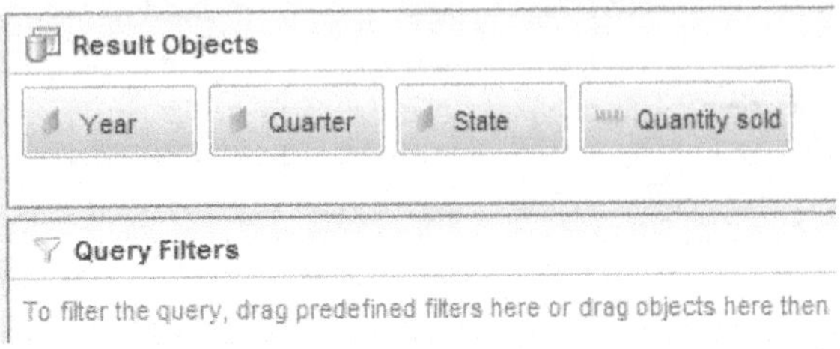
Result Objects
Year
Quarter
State
Quantity sold
Query Filters
To filter the query, drag predefined filters here or drag objects here then

8. Run the query and then delete the default Vertical Table:

9. Create a Column Chart with the following settings:

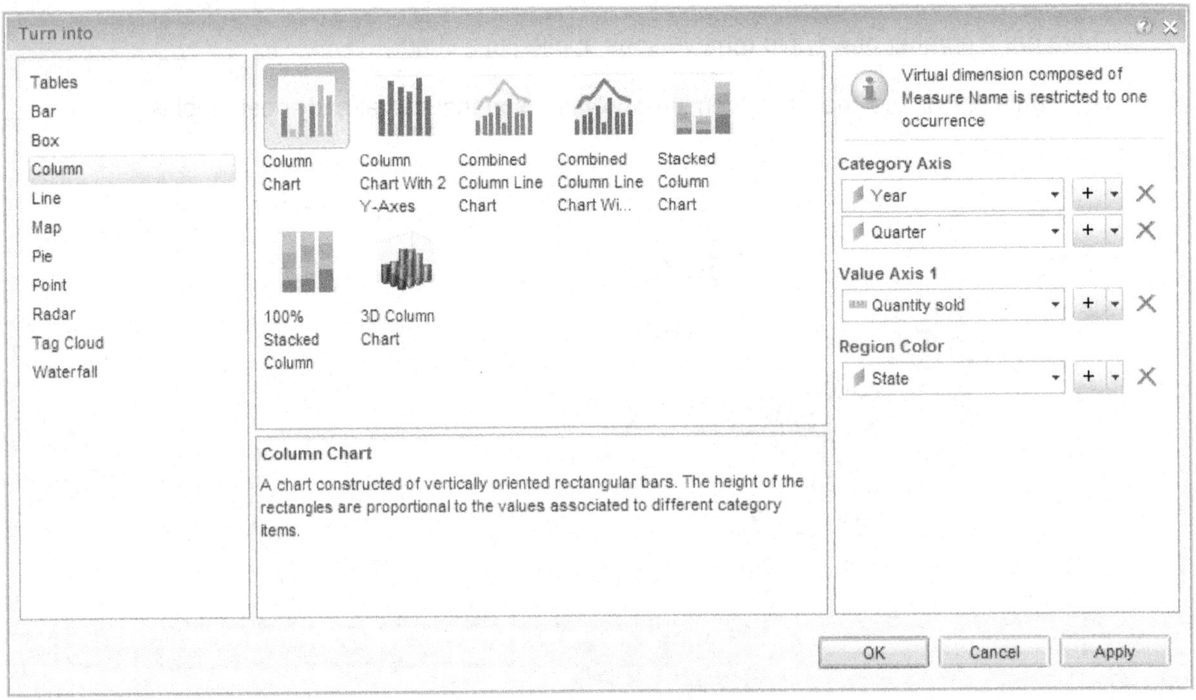
Turn into
Tables
Bar
Box
Column
Line
Map
Pie
Point
Radar
Tag Cloud
Waterfall
Column Chart
Column Chart With 2 Y-Axes
Combined Column Line Chart
Combined Column Line Chart Wi...
Stacked Column Chart
100% Stacked Column
3D Column Chart
Column Chart
A chart constructed of vertically oriented rectangular bars. The height of the rectangles are proportional to the values associated to different category items.
Virtual dimension composed of Measure Name is restricted to one occurrence
Category Axis
Year
Quarter
Value Axis 1
Quantity sold
Region Color
State
OK
Cancel
Apply

10. Click 'OK' to view the chart.

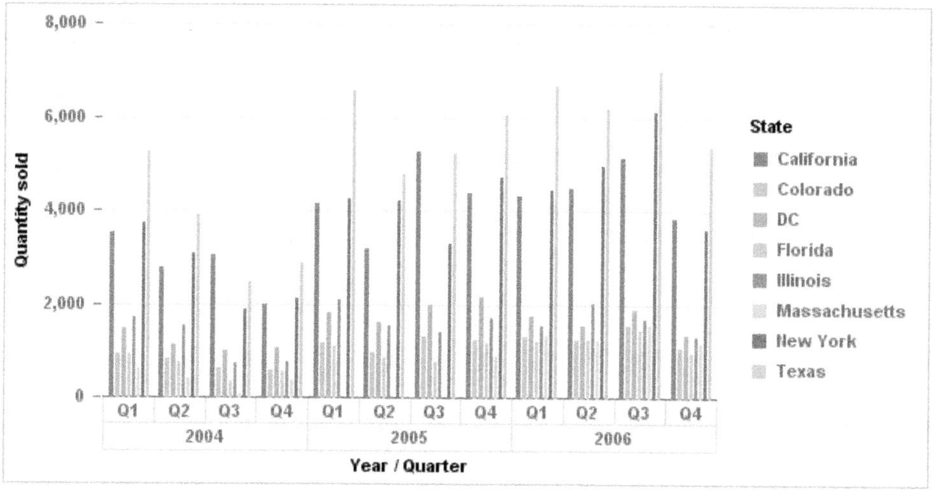
8,000
6,000
4,000
2,000
0
Quantity sold
Q1
Q2
Q3
Q4
2004
2005
2006
Year / Quarter
State
California
Colorado
DC
Florida
Illinois
Massachusetts
New York
Texas

NOTE – We have used a border on the chart.

11. Right-click on the chart and select 'Assign Data...'

12. Use the drop-down for [Quarter] and select 'Hide', i.e. tick it.

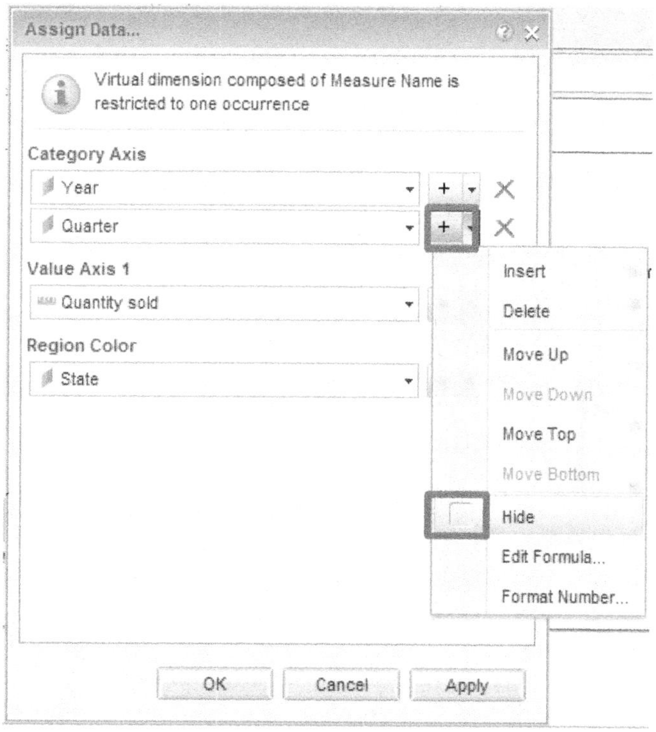
Assign Data...
Virtual dimension composed of Measure Name is restricted to one occurrence
Category Axis
Year
Quarter
Value Axis 1
Quantity sold
Region Color
State
Insert
Delete
Move Up
Move Down
Move Top
Move Bottom
Hide
Edit Formula...
Format Number...
OK
Cancel
Apply

13. Click 'OK'.

14. The [Quarter] dimension will become hidden, but the chart will continue to display data at quarterly level.

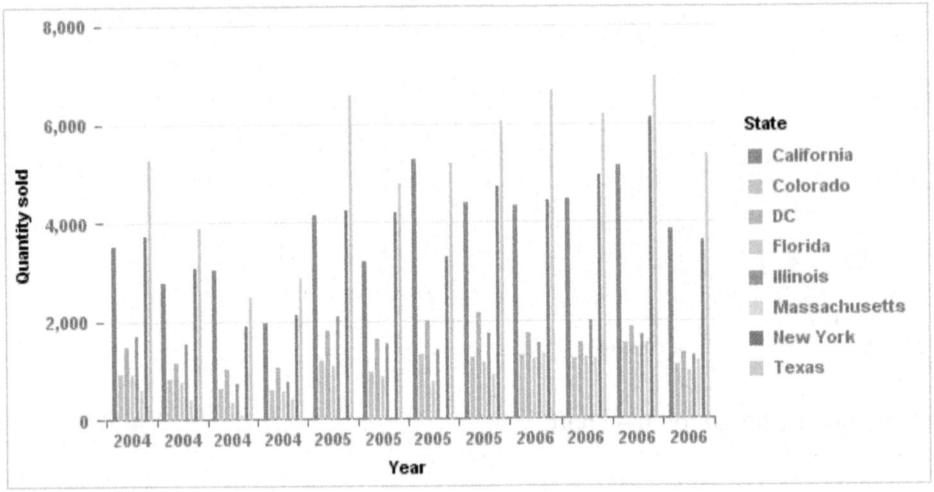
8,000
6,000
4,000
2,000
0
Quantity sold
2004 2004 2004 2004 2005 2005 2005 2005 2006 2006 2006 2006
Year
State
California
Colorado
DC
Florida
Illinois
Massachusetts
New York
Texas

i.e. the data does not aggregate like it would if we actually removed the [Quarter] column:

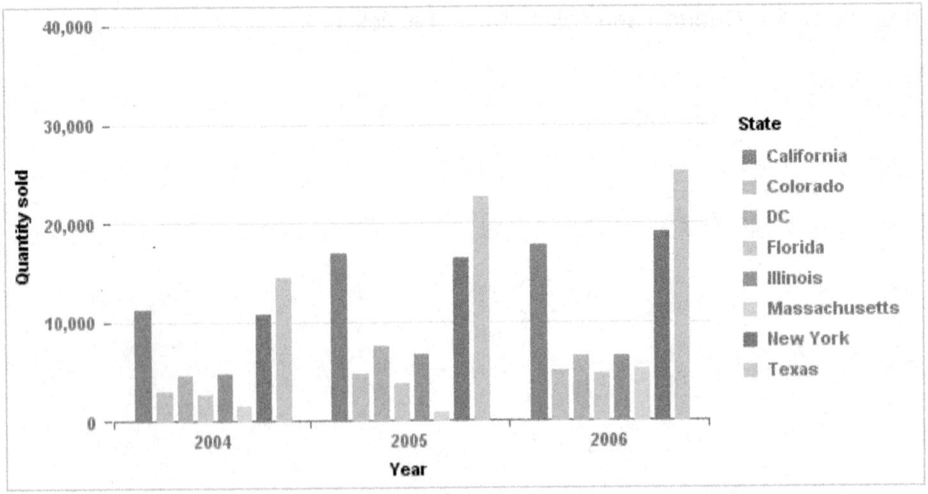
40,000
30,000
20,000
10,000
0
Quantity sold
2004
2005
2006
Year
State
California
Colorado
DC
Florida
Illinois
Massachusetts
New York
Texas

15. To unhide the dimension, simply right-click on the chart, select 'Assign Data…' and then un-tick 'Hide'.

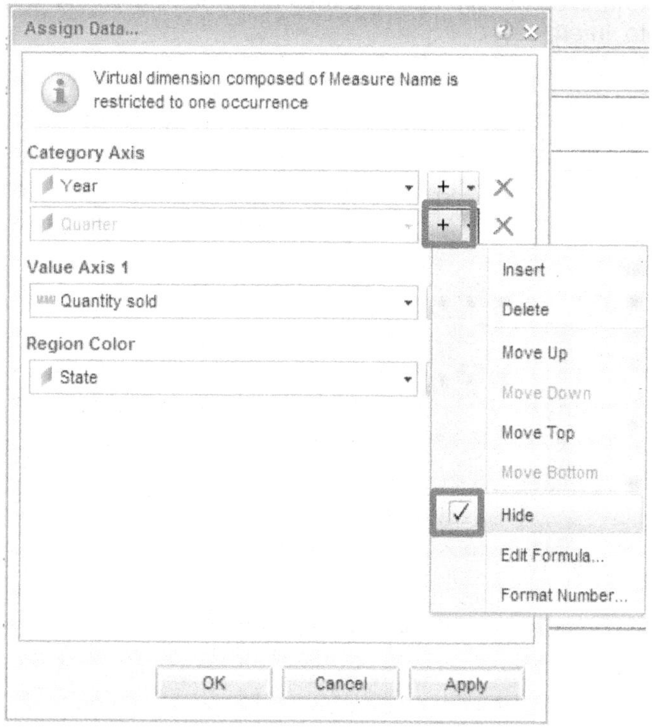
Assign Data...
Virtual dimension composed of Measure Name is restricted to one occurrence
Category Axis
Year
Quarter
Value Axis 1
Quantity sold
Region Color
State
Insert
Delete
Move Up
Move Down
Move Top
Move Bottom
Hide
Edit Formula...
Format Number...
OK
Cancel
Apply

NOTE

If you hide a dimension being used as a Region Color then it is equivalent to removing the object and Web Intelligence will automatically remove the dimension from Region Color rather than hiding it.

15.7 Chart Types in Web Intelligence

Many different charts are available for use in Web Intelligence and they have been grouped into Chart Types (as shown below using the 'Turn into' interface):

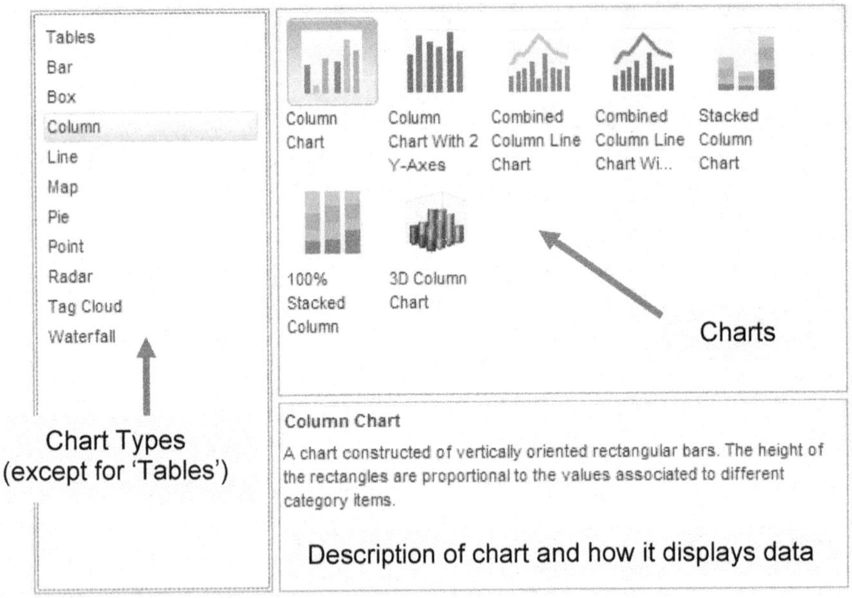
Tables
Bar
Box
Column
Line
Map
Pie
Point
Radar
Tag Cloud
Waterfall
Chart Types
(except for 'Tables')
Column Chart
Column Chart With 2 Y-Axes
Combined Column Line Chart
Combined Column Line Chart Wi...
Stacked Column Chart
100% Stacked Column
3D Column Chart
Charts
Column Chart
A chart constructed of vertically oriented rectangular bars. The height of the rectangles are proportional to the values associated to different category items.
Description of chart and how it displays data

Note

- Bar refers to Horizontal Bar charts
- Column refers to Vertical Bar charts

It is essential to use the most appropriate type of chart in your report(s) based on your data and the information/message you are trying to convey.

Experiment with the different chart types when developing reports to find the best 'fit' for the particular requirement being addressed.

16 Filtering Data in Reports

Often there is a requirement to filter the data after it has been returned by the query (or queries) within reports. This might be due to a variety of reasons such as:

1. Display data from a single data set in multiple report tabs (with each tab satisfying different requirements).

2. Display multiple blocks from a single data set in a single report tab (with each block showing a different view of the data).

Examples of this could be:

1. Data queried for 2 years (say This Year and Last Year) and then two report tabs are created to show data for each year separately.

2. Data queried for 2 states (say California and New York) but they are to be presented on a single report tab in two separate blocks (so they are side by side).

If your need is to discard unwanted data from the document then you should focus on restricting the underlying queries, but if you want to make use of selected data in certain report tabs (but still need the overall data for other report tabs) then Report Filters are better.

NOTE

Report filters are different from query filters in that report filters are applied to the data already attached to the document rather than applying conditions in the query panel. Query Filters are discussed in the session 'Restricting Query Data' (i.e. restricting the data before it is returned to the document).

16.1 Applying a Single Report Filter

In the following example we are going to run a query with no restrictions and then look at report filters.

1. Create the following query (using 'eFashion' universe).

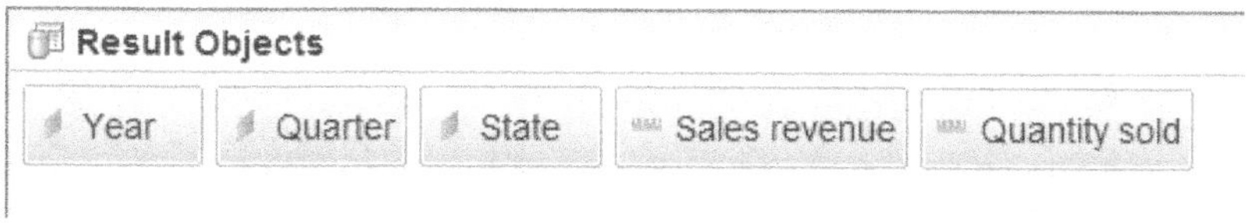
Result Objects
Year
Quarter
State
Sales revenue
Quantity sold

Some of the results of above query are shown in table below.

Year	Quarter	State	Sales revenue	Quantity sold
2004	Q1	California	$519,220	3,509
2004	Q1	Colorado	$131,797	921
2004	Q1	DC	$208,324	1,467
2004	Q1	Florida	$137,530	924
2004	Q1	Illinois	$256,454	1,711
2004	Q1	Massachusetts	$92,596	609
2004	Q1	New York	$555,983	3,717
2004	Q1	Texas	$758,796	5,278

2. Right-click in any cell of the [State] column and select 'Filter – Add Filter'.

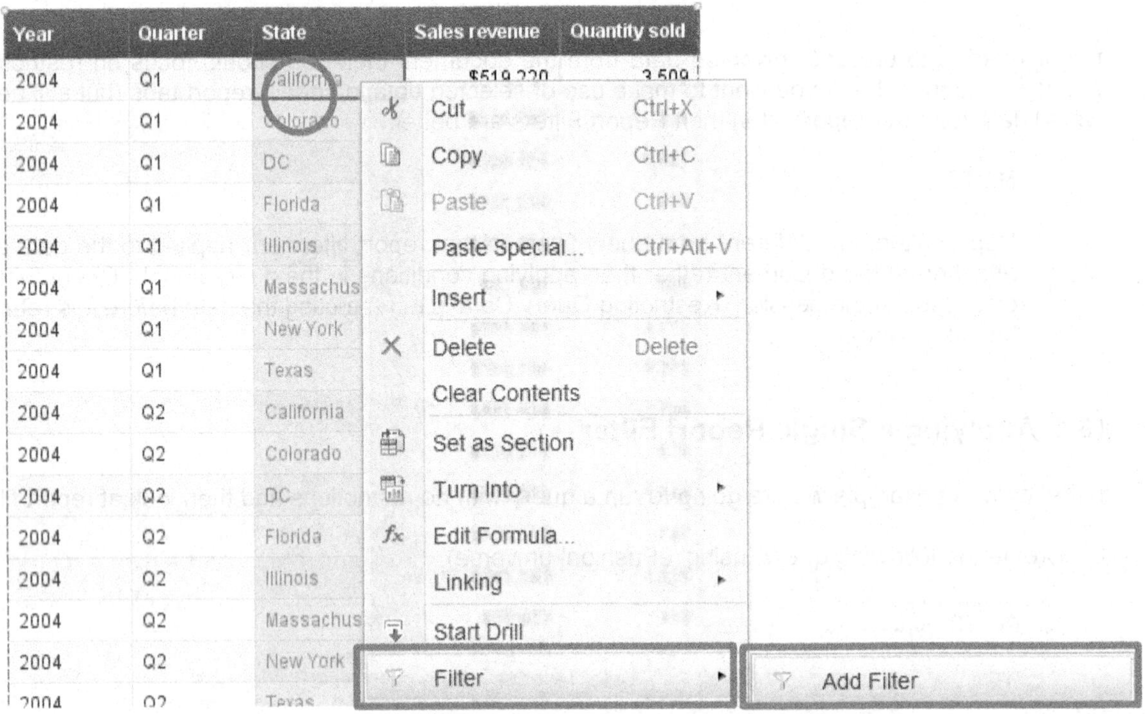
Year
Quarter
State
Sales revenue
Quantity sold
Cut
Ctrl+X
Copy
Ctrl+C
Paste
Ctrl+V
Paste Special...
Ctrl+Alt+V
Insert
Delete
Delete
Clear Contents
Set as Section
Turn Into
Edit Formula...
Linking
Start Drill
Filter
Add Filter

The 'Report Filter' interface will open:

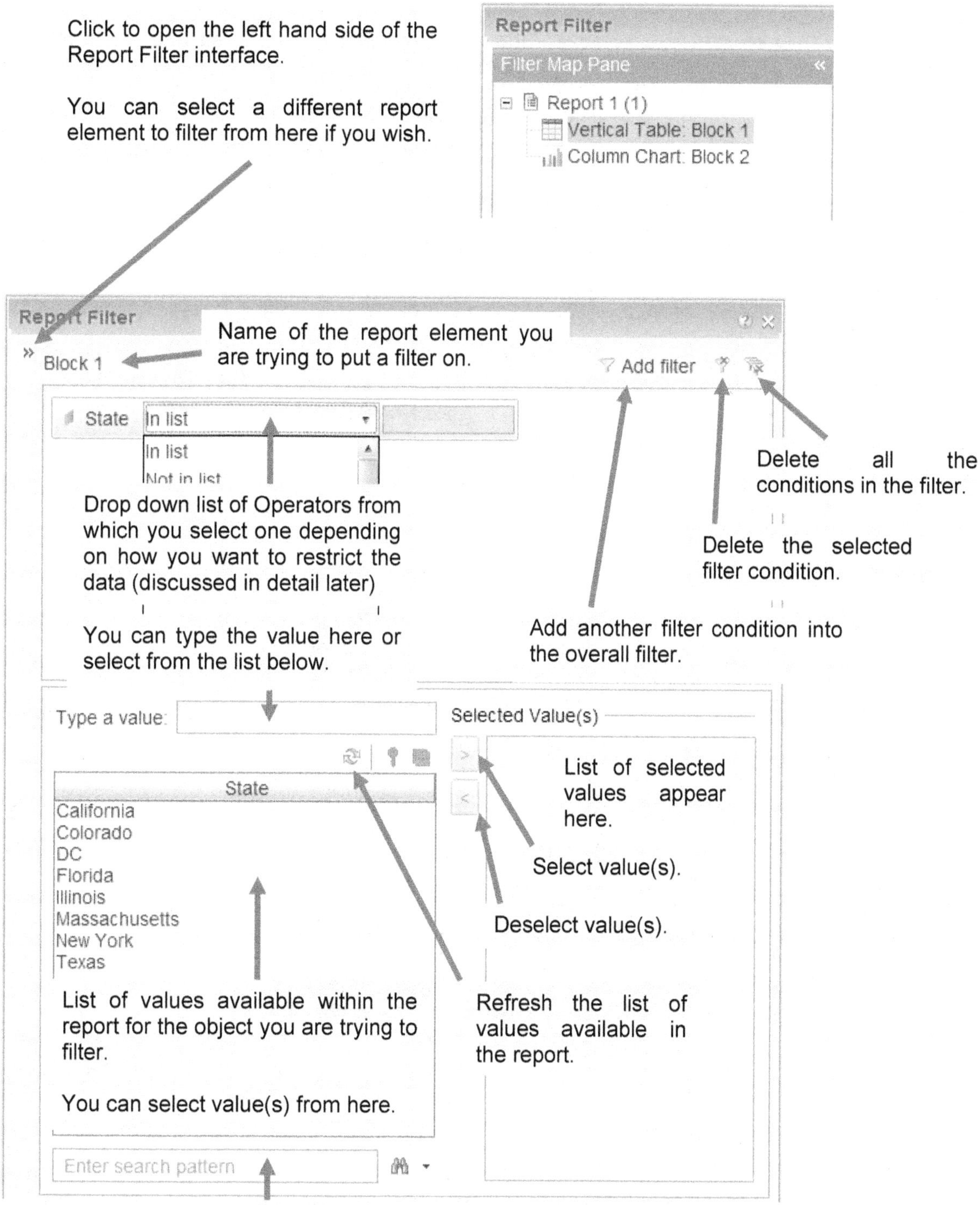
Click to open the left hand side of the Report Filter interface.
You can select a different report element to filter from here if you wish.
Report Filter
Filter Map Pane
Report 1 (1)
Vertical Table: Block 1
Column Chart: Block 2
Report Filter
Block 1
Name of the report element you are trying to put a filter on.
Add filter
State
In list
In list
Not in list
Drop down list of Operators from which you select one depending on how you want to restrict the data (discussed in detail later)
You can type the value here or select from the list below.
Delete all the conditions in the filter.
Delete the selected filter condition.
Add another filter condition into the overall filter.
Type a value:
Selected Value(s)
State
California
Colorado
DC
Florida
Illinois
Massachusetts
New York
Texas
List of selected values appear here.
Select value(s).
Deselect value(s).
List of values available within the report for the object you are trying to filter.
You can select value(s) from here.
Refresh the list of values available in the report.
Enter search pattern

You can use a search pattern when the list of values contains a lot of values to focus in on values.

After typing in the value press <Enter> to search. The default is to Ignore case but you can use Match case (via drop down arrow next to binoculars icon).

3. Set the filter condition as follows and click 'OK':

To create a report filter, you need to specify the following elements:

- the report element to be filtered (the whole report, sections, or blocks)
- a filtered object
- an operator
- filter values

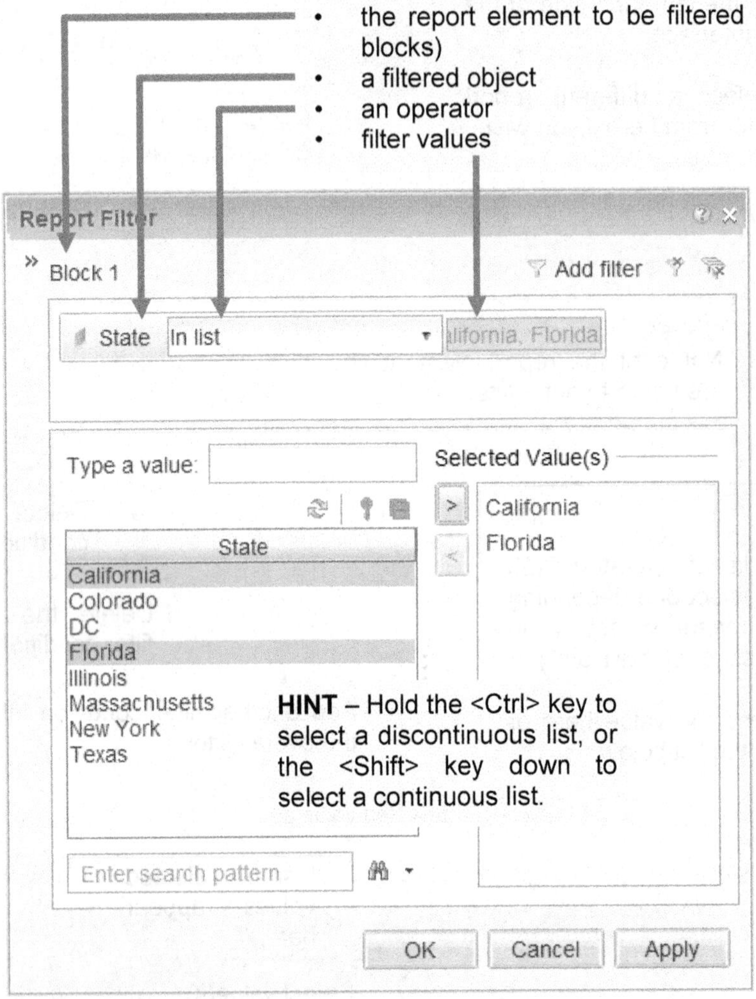
Report Filter
Block 1
Add filter
State
In list
alifornia, Florida
Type a value:
Selected Value(s)
State
California
Colorado
DC
Florida
Illinois
Massachusetts
New York
Texas
California
Florida
HINT – Hold the <Ctrl> key to select a discontinuous list, or the <Shift> key down to select a continuous list.
Enter search pattern
OK
Cancel
Apply

4. The data in the table block will now be filtered to 'California' and 'Florida'.

Year	Quarter	State	Sales revenue	Quantity sold
2004	Q1	California	$519,220	3,509
2004	Q1	Florida	$137,530	924
2004	Q2	California	$441,494	2,788
2004	Q2	Florida	$121,170	747
2004	Q3	California	$394,309	3,035
2004	Q3	Florida	$50,926	353
2004	Q4	California	$349,188	1,972
2004	Q4	Florida	$96,359	561

16.2 Viewing Filters in Reports

Sometimes there is a need to view filters that have been previously applied in reports. We have already applied a simple filter (above) so let us have a look at how we can view this filter.

Simply by looking at the data we cannot be sure how the data is filtered, so Web Intelligence offers a way of viewing applied filters.

1. On the left hand side click on the 'Document Structure and Filters' icon:

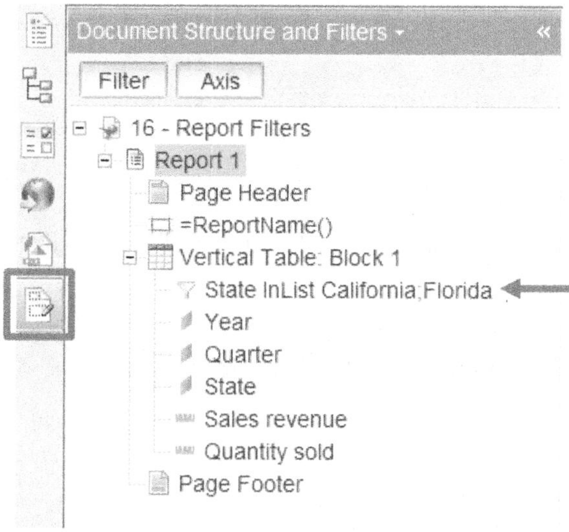
Document Structure and Filters
Filter
Axis
16 - Report Filters
Report 1
Page Header
=ReportName()
Vertical Table: Block 1
State InList California;Florida
Year
Quarter
State
Sales revenue
Quantity sold
Page Footer

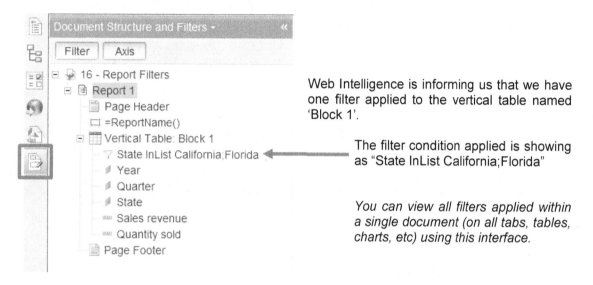

Web Intelligence is informing us that we have one filter applied to the vertical table named 'Block 1'.

The filter condition applied is showing as "State InList California;Florida"

You can view all filters applied within a single document (on all tabs, tables, charts, etc) using this interface.

16.3 Editing and Removing Filters in Reports

Sometimes there is a need to edit/delete/remove filters that have been previously applied in reports. We have already applied a simple filter so let us have a look at how we can edit/remove this filter.

Web Intelligence offers a number of ways to remove report level filters.

1. If we click into any cell within the table (but not within the [State] column) and select 'Analysis – Filters – Filter' as shown below then we see the 'Edit Filter' and 'Remove Filter' options are disabled.

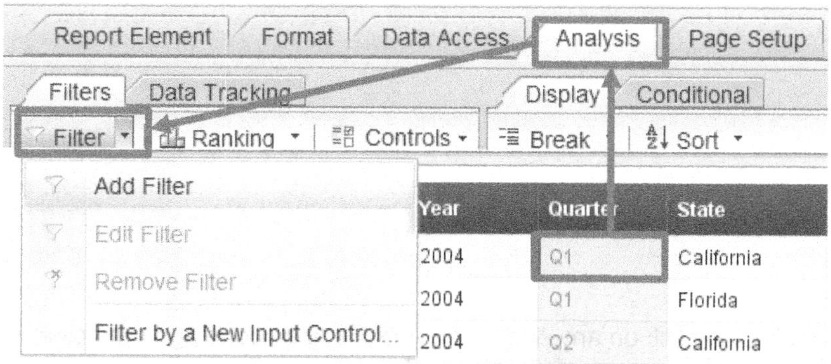
Report Element
Format
Data Access
Analysis
Page Setup
Filters
Data Tracking
Display
Conditional
Filter
Ranking
Controls
Break
Sort
Add Filter
Edit Filter
Remove Filter
Filter by a New Input Control...
Year
Quarter
State
2004
Q1
California
2004
Q1
Florida
2004
Q2
California

You get the same options if you right-click and select 'Filter'.

2. If we click into any cell within the within the [State] column and select 'Analysis – Filters – Filter' as shown below then we see the 'Edit Filter' and 'Remove Filter' options are enabled.

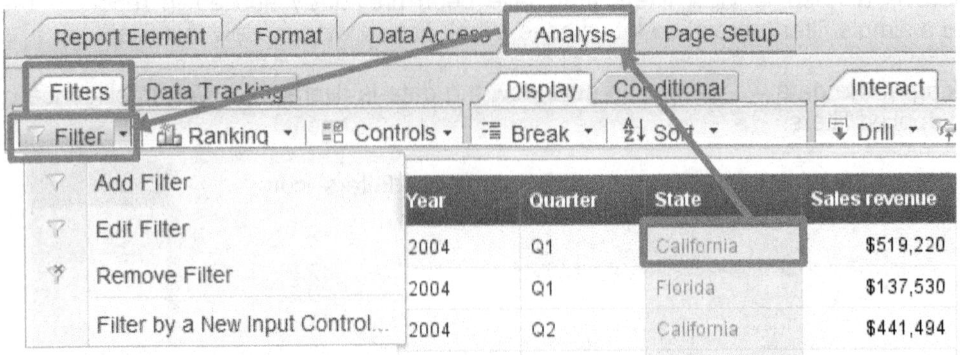
Report Element
Format
Data Access
Analysis
Page Setup
Filters
Data Tracking
Display
Conditional
Interact
Filter
Ranking
Controls
Break
Sort
Drill
Add Filter
Edit Filter
Remove Filter
Filter by a New Input Control...
Year
Quarter
State
Sales revenue
2004
Q1
California
$519,220
2004
Q1
Florida
$137,530
2004
Q2
California
$441,494

You get the same options if you right-click and select 'Filter'.

Web Intelligence recognises we have a filter applied to the [State] column and gives us the option to edit or remove it.

3. Select 'Edit Filter' but if you select 'Remove Filter' then it would be removed/deleted.

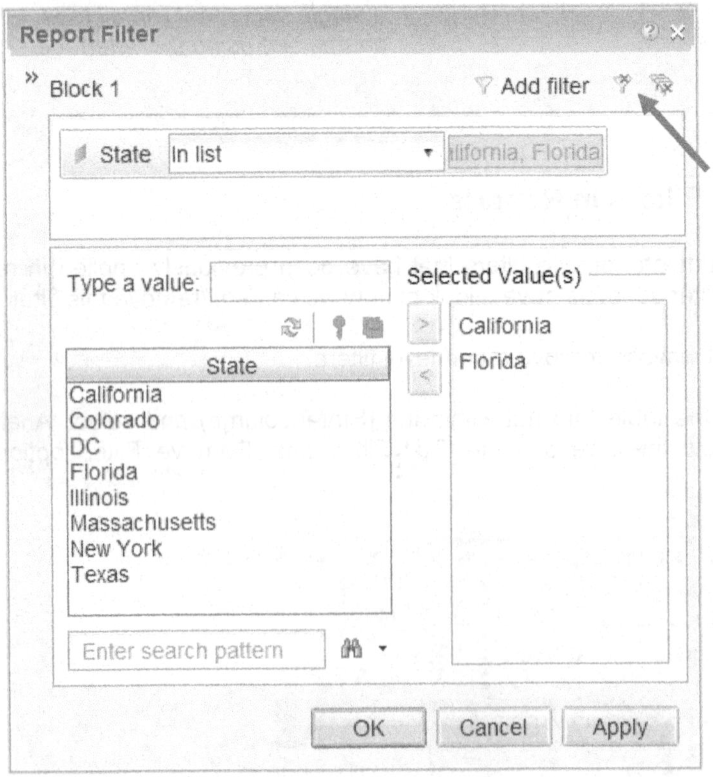
Report Filter
Block 1
Add filter
State
In list
lifornia, Florida
Type a value:
Selected Value(s)
State
California
Colorado
DC
Florida
Illinois
Massachusetts
New York
Texas
California
Florida
Enter search pattern
OK
Cancel
Apply

You can also remove filters using these icons here.

4. We only have one filter applied so click on any one of the remove filter icons and then click 'OK'.

The data in the table block will now be unfiltered.

16.4 Applying Complex Report Filters

We will now use a complex filter (made up of multiple conditions) to restrict our report in order to show data for '2005 California' and '2006 New York'.

1. Right-click in a cell of the [State] column and select 'Add Filter'.

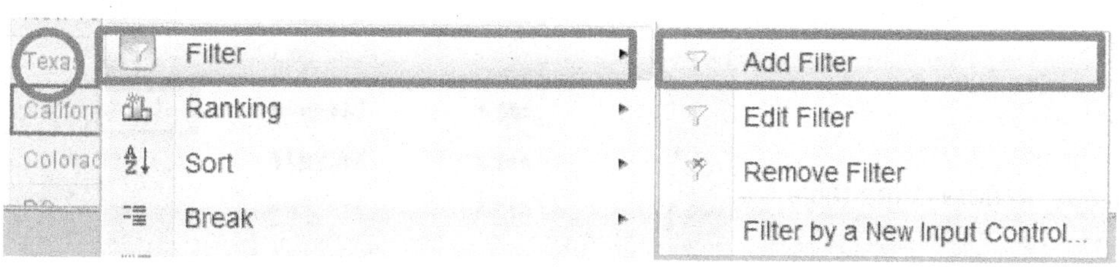
Filter
Ranking
Sort
Break
Add Filter
Edit Filter
Remove Filter
Filter by a New Input Control...

2. Set up the following condition and click 'Apply'.

Report Filter
Block 1
Add filter
State
Equal to
California

3. Click on the 'Add Filter' icon.

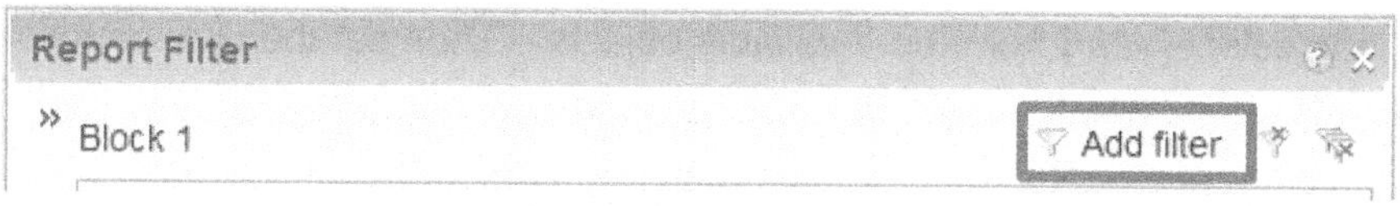
Report Filter
Block 1
Add filter

4. From the 'Available objects' interface, select [State] and click 'OK'.

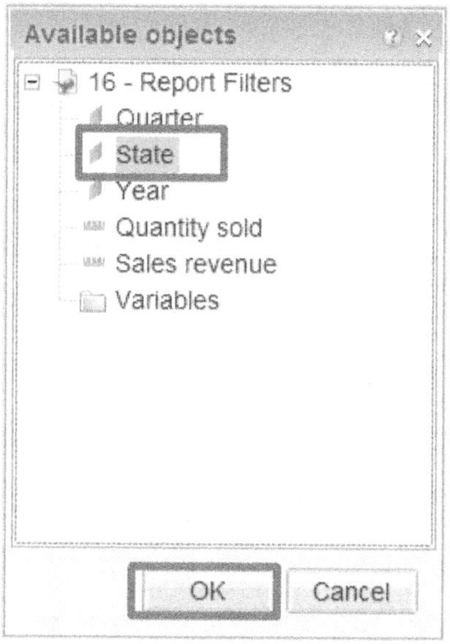
Available objects
16 - Report Filters
Quarter
State
Year
Quantity sold
Sales revenue
Variables
OK
Cancel

5. Set the new condition up as shown below and click 'Apply'.

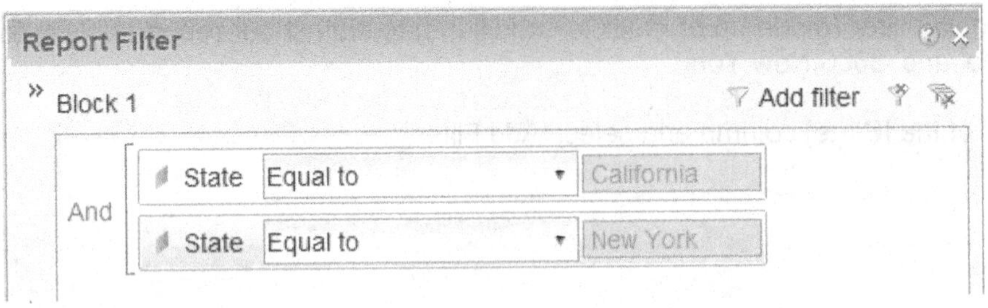
Report Filter
Block 1
Add filter
And
State
Equal to
California
State
Equal to
New York

You will see no data in the table.

6. Single-click on the 'And' and it will change to 'Or'.

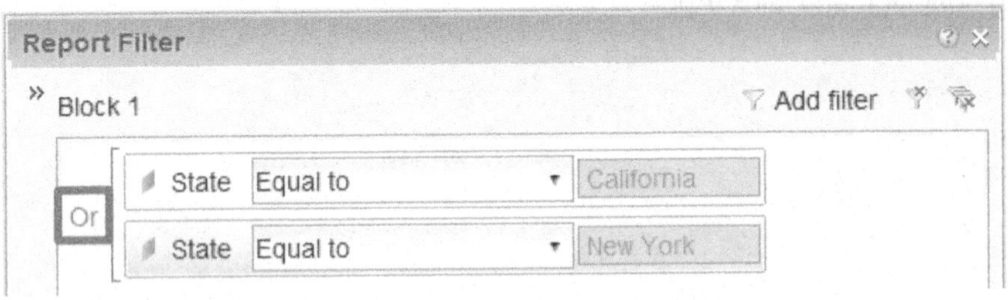
Report Filter
Block 1
Add filter
Or
State
Equal to
California
State
Equal to
New York

The table will now show data for 'California' and 'New York'.

7. Click on 'Add filter' and select [Year] from the 'Available objects'. Then set the filter as follows and click 'Apply'.

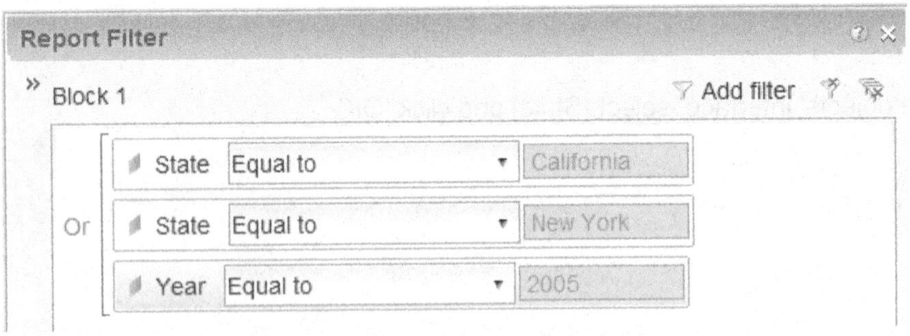
Report Filter
Block 1
Add filter
Or
State
Equal to
California
State
Equal to
New York
Year
Equal to
2005

You will see values for states other than California and New York appearing in the table. This is expected with the filter definition as it is currently set up.

Web Intelligence is interpreting the filter as show data:

- California for all years
- New York for all years
- 2005 for all states

8. Click on ‘Add filter’ and select [Year] from the ‘Available objects’. Then set the filter as follows and click ‘OK’.

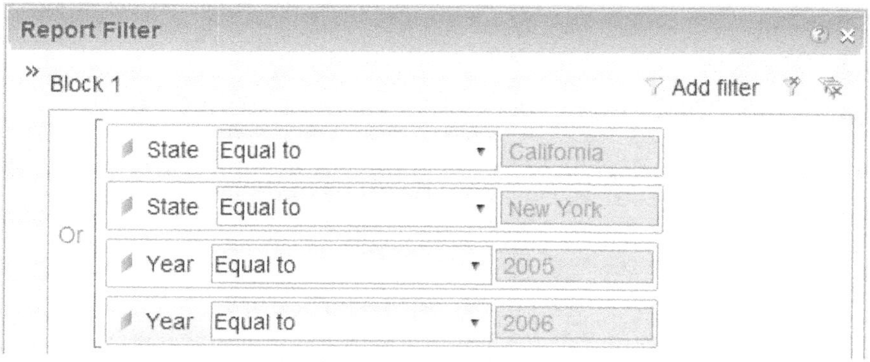
Report Filter
Block 1
Add filter
Or
State
Equal to
California
State
Equal to
New York
Year
Equal to
2005
Year
Equal to
2006

9. If we now view the data in the table we will see it showing us more data than we need.

   This is expected with the filter definition as it is currently set up.

   Web Intelligence is interpreting the filter as show data:

   - California for all years
   - New York for all years
   - 2005 for all states
   - 2006 for all states

   We need to edit the filter to set it up as 2005 California and 2006 New York.

10. Right-click in any cell of the [State] column and then select ‘Filter – Edit Filter’.

11. Drag the condition [Year] = 2005 and drop it on top of [State] = California (as shown below).

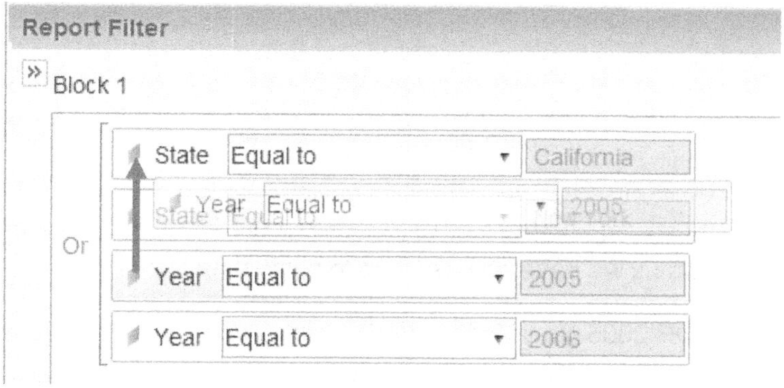
Report Filter
Block 1
Or
State
Equal to
California
Year
Equal to
2005
Year
Equal to
2005
Year
Equal to
2006

Web Intelligence will now display the filter as:

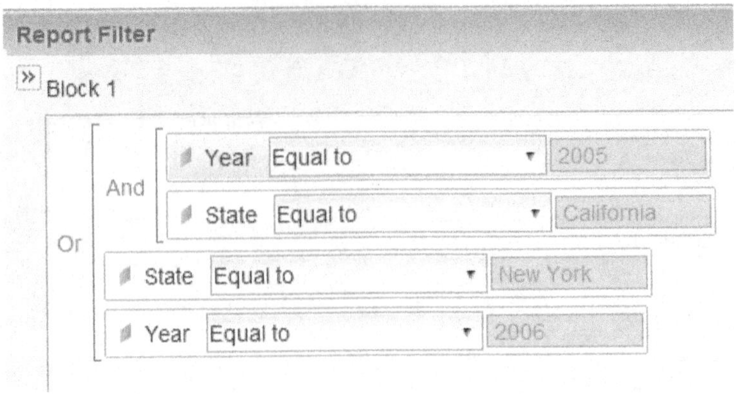
Report Filter
Block 1
Or
And
Year Equal to 2005
State Equal to California
State Equal to New York
Year Equal to 2006

12. Now drag the condition [Year] = 2006 and drop it on top of [State] = New York (as shown below).

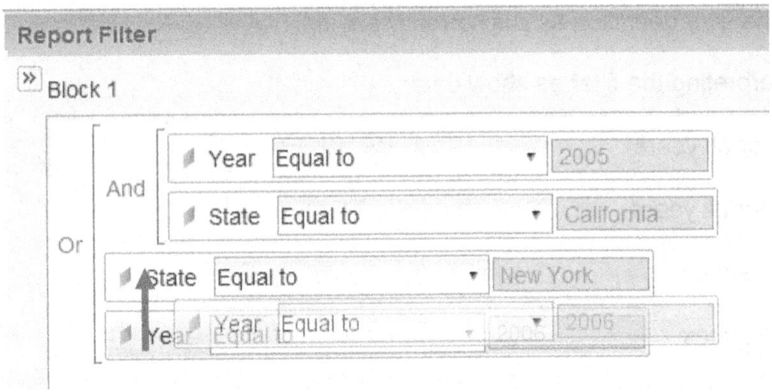
Report Filter
Block 1
Or
And
Year Equal to 2005
State Equal to California
State Equal to New York
Year Equal to 2006

Web Intelligence will now display the filter as:

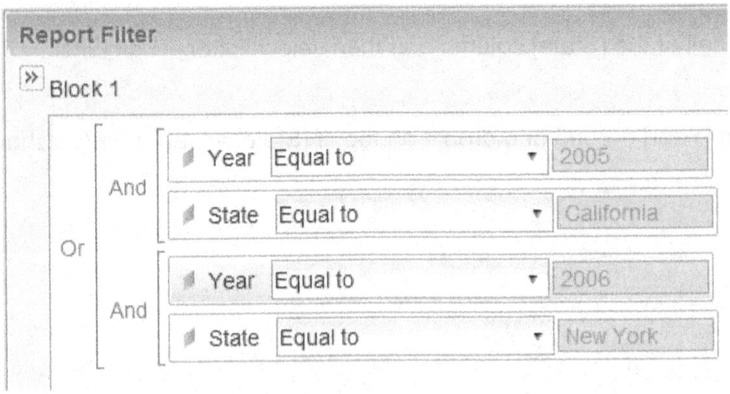
Report Filter
Block 1
Or
And
Year Equal to 2005
State Equal to California
And
Year Equal to 2006
State Equal to New York

Evaluating our filter shows us we have now set it up to show data for:

2005 California **OR** 2006 New York

This is the correct filter we need.

13. Click 'OK' and our table now displays the expected results.

Year	Quarter	State	Sales revenue	Quantity sold
2005	Q1	California	$650,715	4,145
2005	Q2	California	$529,256	3,184
2005	Q3	California	$760,442	5,280
2005	Q4	California	$842,267	4,392
2006	Q1	New York	$747,161	4,439
2006	Q2	New York	$855,617	4,944
2006	Q3	New York	$914,247	6,119
2006	Q4	New York	$633,998	3,607

We get the correct results if we re-arrange the filter definition to:

([Year] = '2005' And [State] = 'California')

Or

([Year] = '2006' And [State] = 'New York')

16.5 Use of And / Or in Report Filters

Using the previous example, in spoken (or written) English we would list the requirement as "figures for California 2005 and New York 2006", but we defined the final filter as:

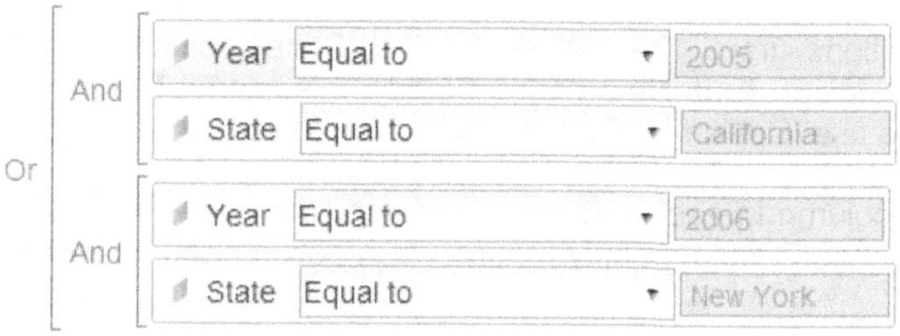
Or
And
Year
Equal to
2005
State
Equal to
California
And
Year
Equal to
2006
State
Equal to
New York

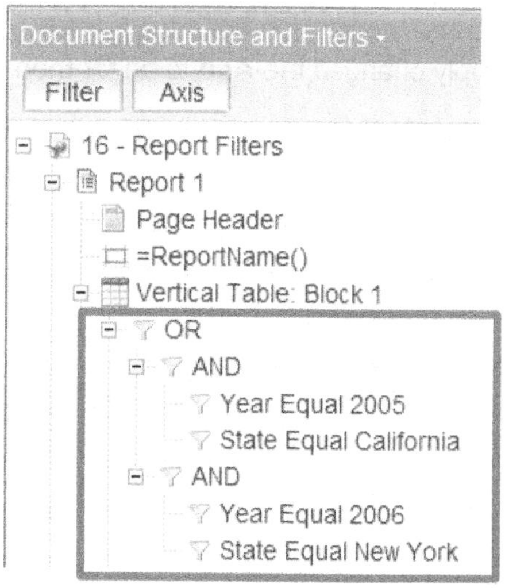
Document Structure and Filters
Filter
Axis
16 - Report Filters
Report 1
Page Header
=ReportName()
Vertical Table: Block 1
OR
AND
Year Equal 2005
State Equal California
AND
Year Equal 2006
State Equal New York

How the nested filter is conveyed in the 'Document Structure and Filters' panel.

In Web Intelligence logic (which is similar to almost all database SQL logic) we have to construct the filter using a combination of And / Or operators (as already shown).

Let us try and understand more about the use of And / Or:

And requires all conditions to be true in order to show/return any data, i.e. the conditions

[State] = 'New York' **And** [Year] = '2006'

Only rows where [State] = 'New York' and [Year] = '2006' will be shown/returned when both conditions are true.

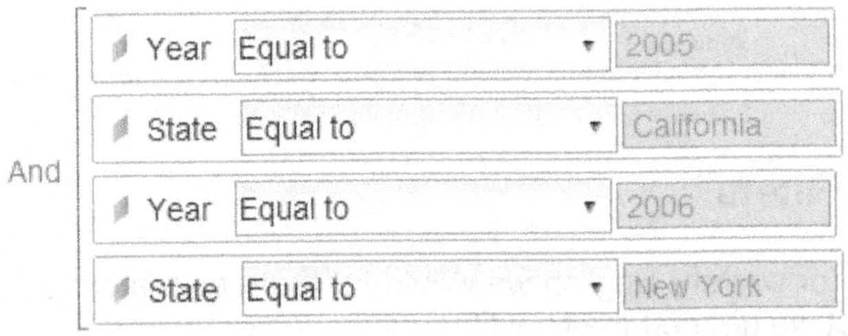

And
Year
Equal to
2005
State
Equal to
California
Year
Equal to
2006
State
Equal to
New York

When we had this filter, we were using **And** between all the conditions resulting in no data being returned. **Why?**

Well, let us take the [State] conditions first. The values for the [State] column in each row are compared first to see if they are 'California' **And** 'New York'. Clearly, this cannot be true as the [State] can only be one value so we need to use 'California' **Or** 'New York'.

Similarly, the values for the [Year] column in each row are compared to check if they are '2005' **And** '2006'. Again, this cannot be true as the [Year] can only be one value so we need to use Year = '2005' **Or** Year = '2006'.

Therefore we can see that for **And** to return any results, all conditions have to be satisfied.

If we simply changed the **And** to an **Or** then we would get too many results. **Why?**

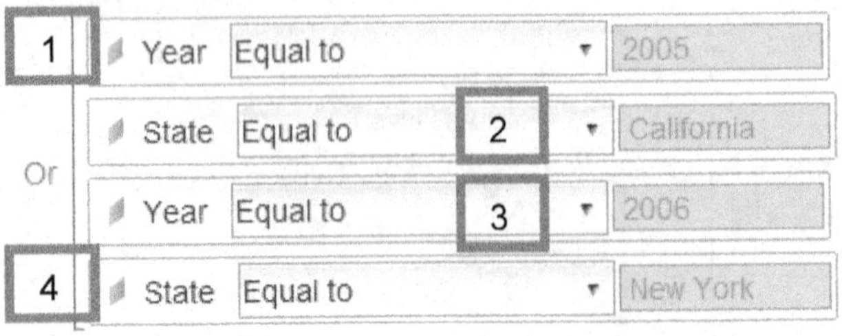

1
Year
Equal to
2005
Or
State
Equal to
2
California
Year
Equal to
3
2006
4
State
Equal to
New York

Or is almost opposite to **And**, in that if any one condition is true then data will be returned (for the true condition).

[State] = 'New York' **Or** [Year] = '2006'

Rows will be returned where the [State] = 'New York' or if the [Year] = '2006', therefore we will get all years for 'New York' and all states having data for '2006'.

Therefore, using **Or**, the filter would give:

1. 2005 (all States)
2. California (all years, 2004, 2005, 2006)
3. 2006 (all States)
4. New York (all years, 2004, 2005, 2006)

To satisfy our particular requirement "figures for California 2005 and New York 2006", we combined **And** with **Or** to group the conditions into a logical sequence to separate out the way in which the overall filter is applied.

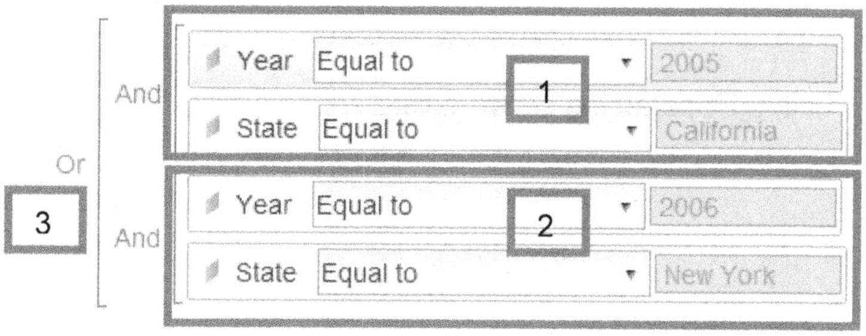

And
Or
3
And
Year
Equal to
2005
1
State
Equal to
California
Year
Equal to
2006
2
State
Equal to
New York

1. If a row contains **[Year]** = '**2005**' **and [State]** = '**California**' then it will be returned.

2. If a row contains **[Year]** = '**2006**' **and [State]** = '**New York**' then it will be returned.

3. The two sub-filters have to be nested into an overall filter using **Or**. The result is that any rows satisfying **sub-filter (1) Or sub-filter (2)** are returned.

The logic and concepts described here for **And** / **Or** in **Report Filters** can also be used for defining **Query Filters** as discussed in the session on 'Restricting Query Data'.

16.6 Using Operator Types in Report Filter Interface

The '**Report Filter**' interface is very intuitive to use and it behaves contextually depending on what is selected in the options for **Operator**.

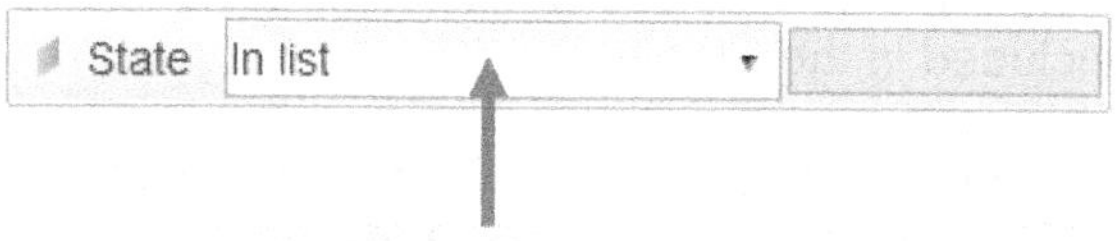

State
In list
Operator

Examples:

If Operator is **Equal to** then you can only select or specify a single value

If Operator is **In list** then you can select or specify multiple values

If Operator is **Between** then you have to specify a From and a To value

When defining filters, a range of Operators are available to restrict the data in various ways and these are listed below:

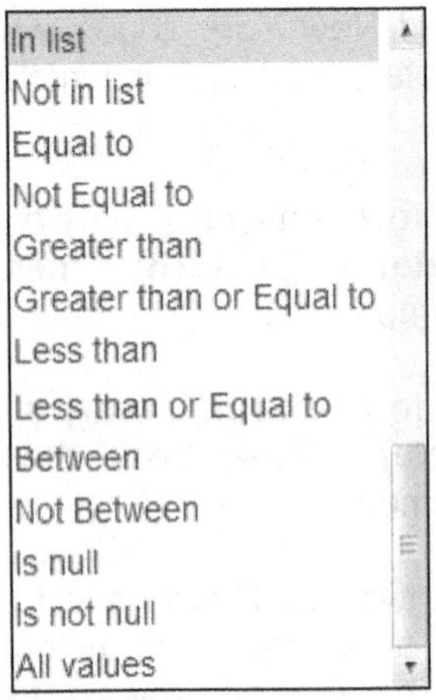
In list
Not in list
Equal to
Not Equal to
Greater than
Greater than or Equal to
Less than
Less than or Equal to
Between
Not Between
Is null
Is not null
All values

The operators are generally listed in somewhat logical opposite pairs. For instance, 'Not Equal to' is opposite of 'Equal to'.

By default, the operator is set to 'In list'.

Operator	Usage
In list	Allows you to select multiple values to filter for. Data is displayed for one or more of the filtered values, depending on how many are found in the data set. e.g. Report contains data for states California, Colorado, DC, Florida, Illinois, Massachusetts, New York, and Texas. Filter defined as [State] **In list** 'California', 'Colorado', 'Illinois', 'Texas' would display data for California, Colorado, Illinois and Texas.
Not in list	Allows you to select multiple values to filter for. Data is displayed for values not included in the filter list. e.g. Report contains data for states California, Colorado, DC, Florida, Illinois, Massachusetts, New York, and Texas. Filter defined as [State] Not in list 'California', 'Colorado', 'Illinois', 'Texas' would display data for DC, Florida, Massachusetts, and New York.
Equal to	Allows you to select a single value for the filter condition. Only data related to the filtered value will be displayed. e.g. Filter defined as [State] **Equal to** 'California' will only display data relevant to California.
Not Equal to	Allows you to select a single value for the filter condition. Data not related to the filtered value will be displayed. e.g. Filter defined as [State] **Not Equal to** 'California' will display data for states other than California.

Operator	Usage
Greater than	Allows you to select a single value for the filter condition. Values greater than the filtered value will be displayed. e.g. Report contains data for years 2004, 2005 and 2006 Filter defined as [Year] **Greater than** 2005 will result in data for 2006 to be displayed.
Greater than or Equal to	Allows you to select a single value for the filter condition. Values greater than or equal to the filtered value will be displayed. e.g. Report contains data for years 2004, 2005 and 2006 Filter defined as [Year] **Greater than or Equal to** 2005 will display data for 2005 and 2006.
Less than	Allows you to select a single value for the filter condition. Values less than the filtered value will be displayed. e.g. Report contains data for years 2004, 2005 and 2006. Filter defined as [Year] **Less than** 2005 will result in data for 2004 to be displayed.
Less than or Equal to	Allows you to select a single value for the filter condition. Values less than or equal to the filtered value will be displayed. e.g. Report contains data for years 2004, 2005 and 2006. Filter defined as [Year] **Less than or Equal to** 2005 will display data for 2004 and 2005.
Between	Specify a range of values using *value From* and *value To*. Data falling within the range (including both the upper and lower values) will be displayed. e.g. Report contains data for states California, Colorado, DC, Florida, Illinois, Massachusetts, New York, and Texas. Filter defined as [State] **Between** 'DC' and 'Massachusetts' will display data for DC, Florida, Illinois and Massachusetts.
Not Between	Specify a range of values using *value From* and *value To*. Data falling outside the range (including both the upper and lower values) will be returned. e.g. Report contains data for states California, Colorado, DC, Florida, Illinois, Massachusetts, New York, and Texas. Filter defined as [State] **Not Between** 'DC' and 'Massachusetts' will display data for California, Colorado, New York and Texas.

Operator	Usage
Is null	No value is specified for this operator as it is used to look for NULL (or blank) values. e.g. Report contains data for states California, Colorado, DC, Florida, Illinois, Massachusetts, New York, and Texas. Filter defined as [State] **Is null** will display NO DATA as all states have values.
Is not null	No value is specified for this operator as it is used to look for NON NULL (or non-blank) values. e.g. Report contains data for states California, Colorado, DC, Florida, Illinois, Massachusetts, New York, and Texas. Filter defined as [State] **Not is null** will display all data because all states have values.
All values	This is new to BI 4 and seems to be the equivalent of applying no filter. e.g. Filter defined as [State] **All values** will display all states.

16.7 Using Report (Tab) Level Filters

We have looked at applying filters to a block of data, but we can also use filters at the report level.

This type of filter is effective at the report (tab) level therefore all elements within the report (tab) will be affected by this filter, e.g. if we apply a report level filter for [Year] = '2005' then all blocks and sections within the report will be filtered automatically for [Year] = '2005'.

These can be applied in the same way as block filters, but we select the report area instead of a block.

Let us explain this using an example.

1. Create the following Vertical Table block on a new report tab.

Year	Sales revenue	Quantity sold
2004	$8,095,814	53,078
2005	$13,232,246	79,855
2006	$15,059,143	90,296

2. Right-click away from the table, i.e. on the report canvas and select 'Filter – Add Filter'

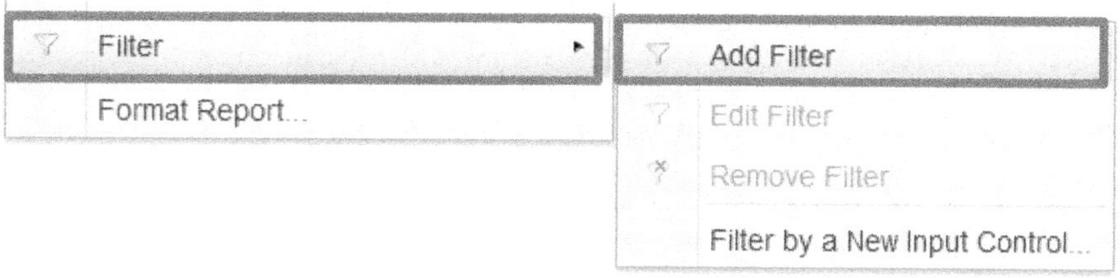
Filter
Format Report...
Add Filter
Edit Filter
Remove Filter
Filter by a New Input Control...

3. The 'Report Filter' interface will open and will inform you that the filter is going to be applied to the report tab (in this example the report tab is called 'Report 2').

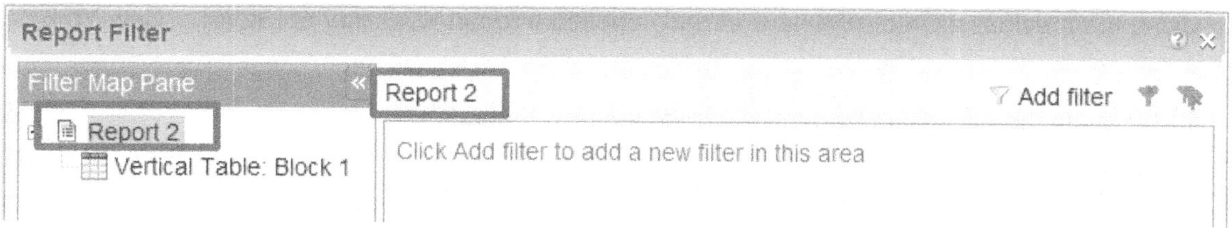
Report Filter
Filter Map Pane
Report 2
Vertical Table: Block 1
Report 2
Add filter
Click Add filter to add a new filter in this area

4. Click on 'Add Filter', create the following condition and click 'OK'.

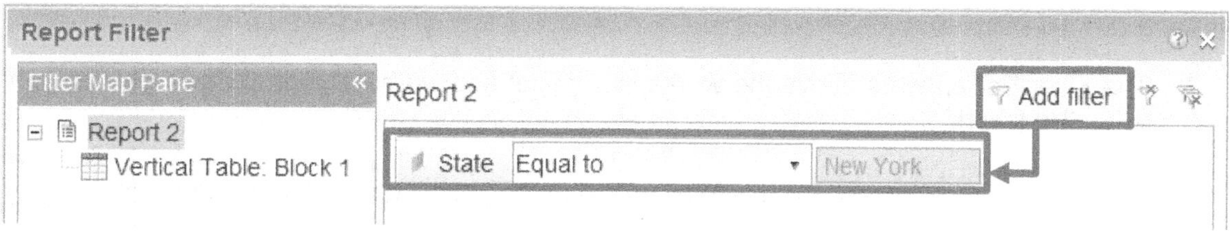
Report Filter
Filter Map Pane
Report 2
Vertical Table: Block 1
Report 2
Add filter
State
Equal to
New York

The whole report tab is now filtered to restrict data for [State] = 'New York', therefore the vertical table values are only for 'New York':

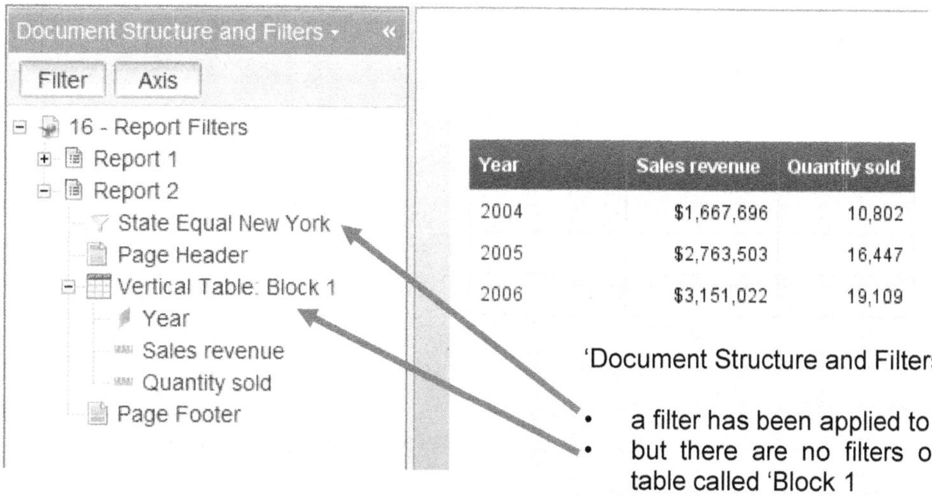
Document Structure and Filters
Filter
Axis
16 - Report Filters
Report 1
Report 2
State Equal New York
Page Header
Vertical Table: Block 1
Year
Sales revenue
Quantity sold
Page Footer

Year	Sales revenue	Quantity sold
2004	$1,667,696	10,802
2005	$2,763,503	16,447
2006	$3,151,022	19,109

'Document Structure and Filters' informs us:

- a filter has been applied to 'Report 2'
- but there are no filters on the vertical table called 'Block 1

5. If we add the [State] column into the table then we can confirm data is for 'New York' only.

Year	State	Sales revenue	Quantity sold
2004	New York	$1,667,696	10,802
2005	New York	$2,763,503	16,447
2006	New York	$3,151,022	19,109

16.7.1 Report (Tab) Level Filters using Filter Bar

Another way to apply report level filters is to use the **Filter Bar**.

Using the previous example we have already applied a report level filter of [State] = 'New York'.

1. Activate the Filter Bar using the following toolbox button:

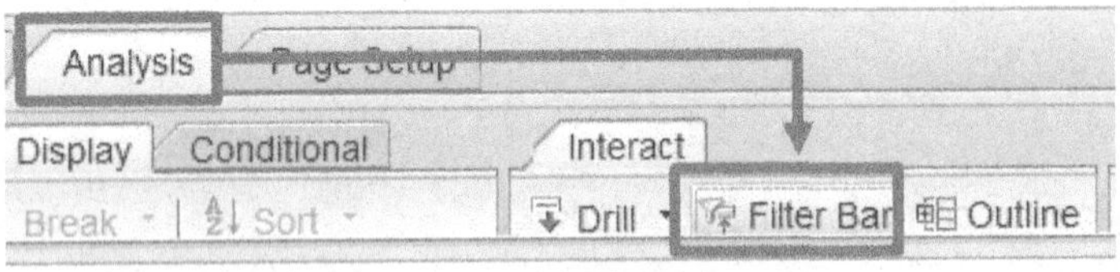
Analysis
Page Setup
Display
Conditional
Interact
Break
Sort
Drill
Filter Bar
Outline

2. The Filter Bar appears above the workspace panel and we have a drop down box containing the value 'New York'.

New York

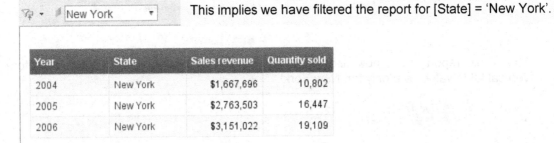

This implies we have filtered the report for [State] = 'New York'.

Year	State	Sales revenue	Quantity sold
2004	New York	$1,667,696	10,802
2005	New York	$2,763,503	16,447
2006	New York	$3,151,022	19,109

3. We can use the Filter Bar to quickly change the applied filter:

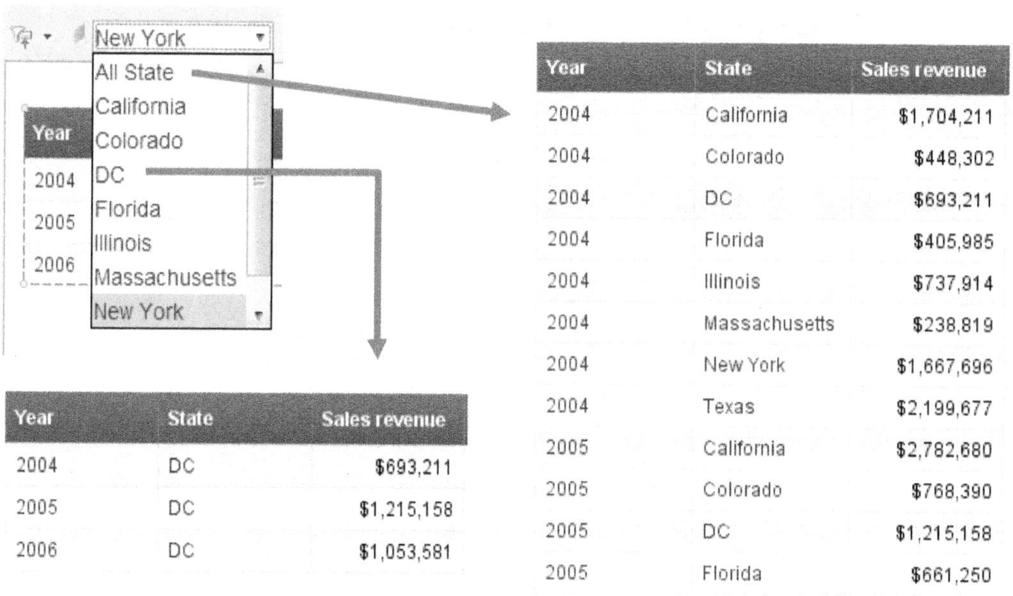
New York
All State
California
Colorado
DC
Florida
Illinois
Massachusetts
New York

Year	State	Sales revenue
2004	DC	$693,211
2005	DC	$1,215,158
2006	DC	$1,053,581

Year	State	Sales revenue
2004	California	$1,704,211
2004	Colorado	$448,302
2004	DC	$693,211
2004	Florida	$405,985
2004	Illinois	$737,914
2004	Massachusetts	$238,819
2004	New York	$1,667,696
2004	Texas	$2,199,677
2005	California	$2,782,680
2005	Colorado	$768,390
2005	DC	$1,215,158
2005	Florida	$661,250

We can also use the Filter Bar to add further conditions or to remove existing conditions.

4. You can add objects into the Filter Bar by using the drop down selector located on the left-hand side of the Filter Bar, e.g. we are going to select [Quarter] as shown below.

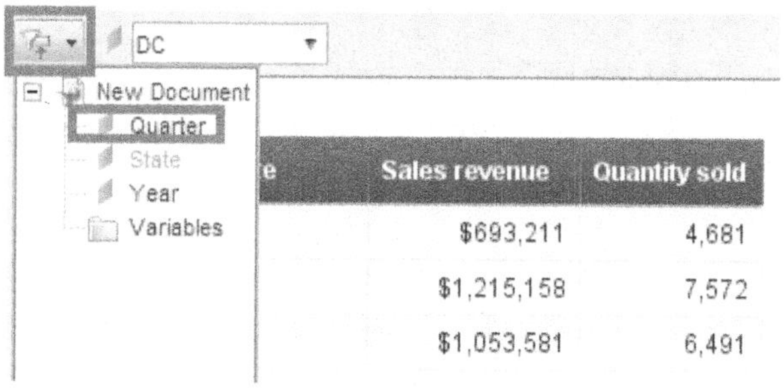
DC
New Document
Quarter
State
Year
Variables

Sales revenue	Quantity sold
$693,211	4,681
$1,215,158	7,572
$1,053,581	6,491

When an object is dropped into the Filter Bar then by default, it has no value selected:

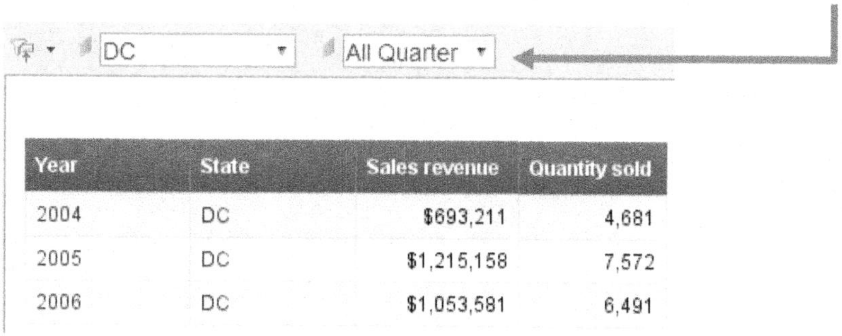
DC
All Quarter

Year	State	Sales revenue	Quantity sold
2004	DC	$693,211	4,681
2005	DC	$1,215,158	7,572
2006	DC	$1,053,581	6,491

'All' concatenated with the object name (e.g. 'All Quarter', 'All State', 'All Year') means the object is not being filtered.

5. We can only select a single value per object when using the Filter Toolbar.

   e.g. Below we have **[State] = 'DC'** and **[Quarter] = 'Q4'**.

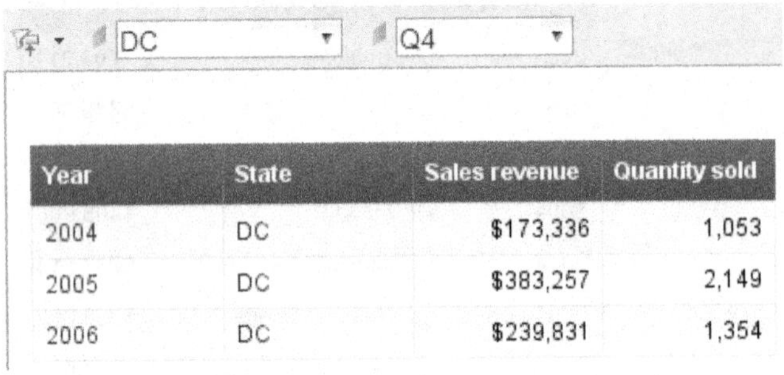
DC
Q4
Year
State
Sales revenue
Quantity sold
2004
DC
$173,336
1,053
2005
DC
$383,257
2,149
2006
DC
$239,831
1,354

6. To remove an object from the Filter Bar, simply drag and drop it out of the bar:

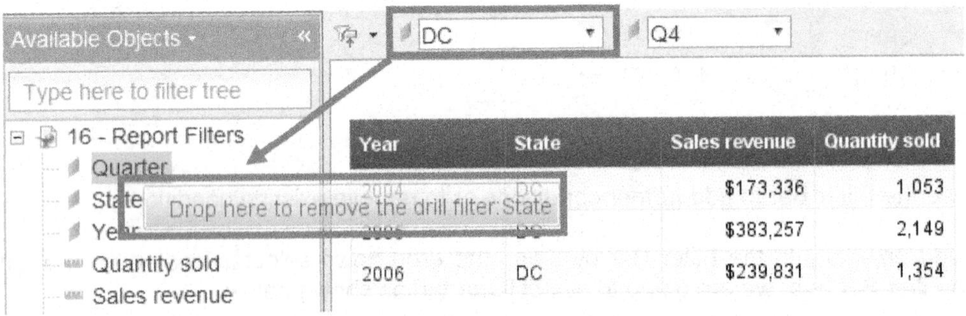
Available Objects
Type here to filter tree
16 - Report Filters
Quarter
State
Year
Quantity sold
Sales revenue
Drop here to remove the drill filter: State
DC
Q4
Year
State
Sales revenue
Quantity sold
$173,336
1,053
$383,257
2,149
2006
DC
$239,831
1,354

Or select '(Remove)' as a value from the relevant object.

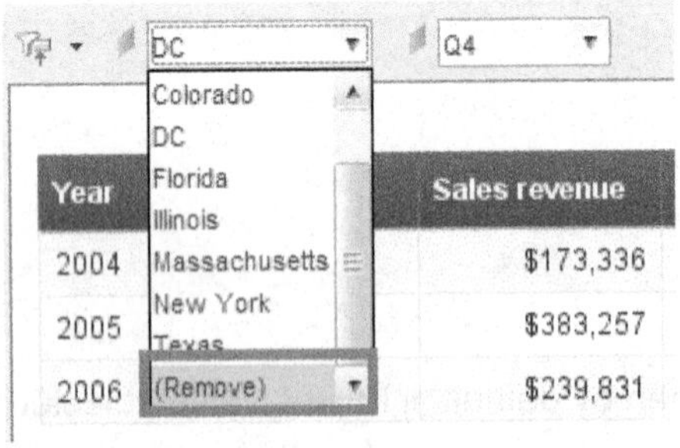
DC
Q4
Colorado
DC
Florida
Illinois
Massachusetts
New York
Texas
(Remove)
Year
Sales revenue
2004
$173,336
2005
$383,257
2006
$239,831

[State] = 'DC' has been removed from the Filter Bar, therefore data is now displayed for all states an all years, but only where:

[Quarter] = 'Q4'

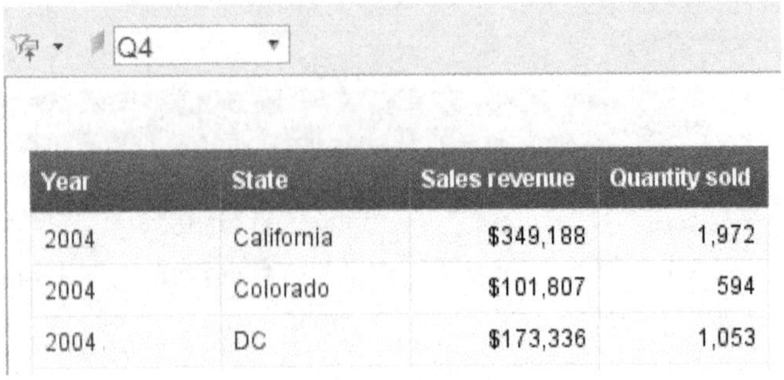
Q4
Year
State
Sales revenue
Quantity sold
2004
California
$349,188
1,972
2004
Colorado
$101,807
594
2004
DC
$173,336
1,053

16.8 Applying Filters to Sections

Sections can also be filtered if required.

1. Edit the query for the document by clicking:

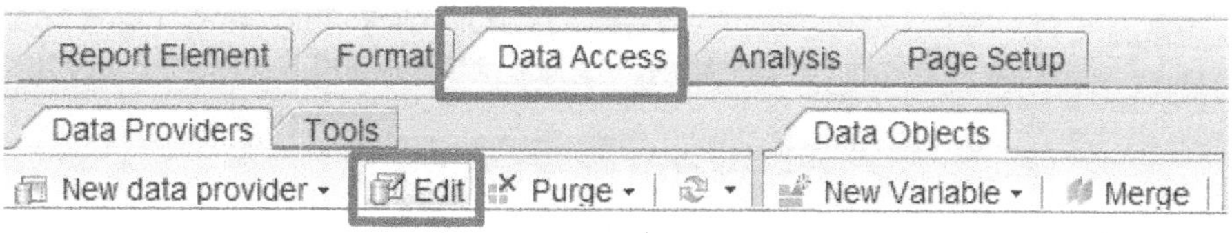
Report Element
Format
Data Access
Analysis
Page Setup
Data Providers
Tools
Data Objects
New data provider
Edit
Purge
New Variable
Merge

2. Add the [Lines] object into the query and then click 'Run query'.

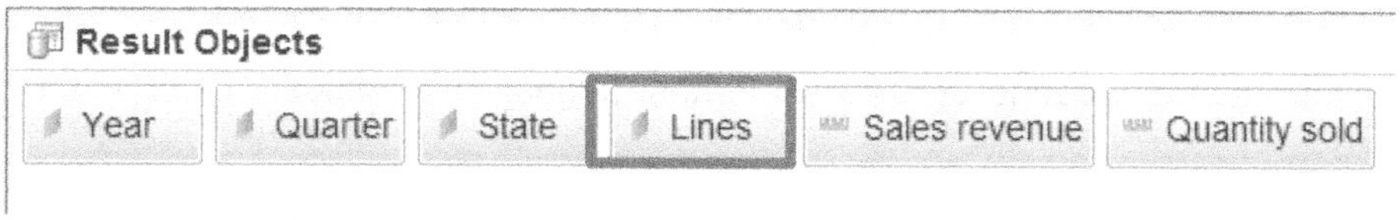
Result Objects
Year
Quarter
State
Lines
Sales revenue
Quantity sold

3. On the existing tab where we have the Filter Bar showing [Quarter] = 'Q4', insert a section on [Lines] by clicking on 'Insert Section' and then selecting [Lines].

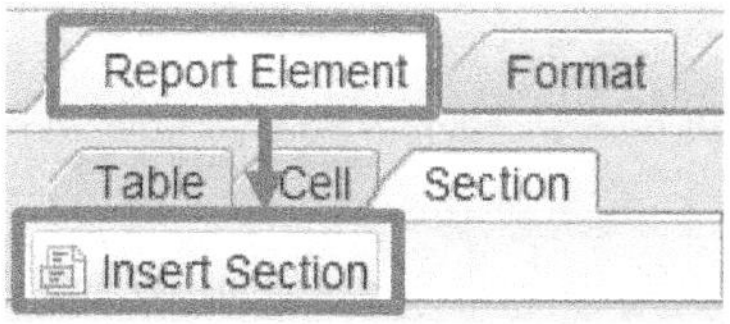
Report Element
Format
Table
Cell
Section
Insert Section

We now have a report sectioned on [Lines] as verified by the 'Report Map' tab (shown here).

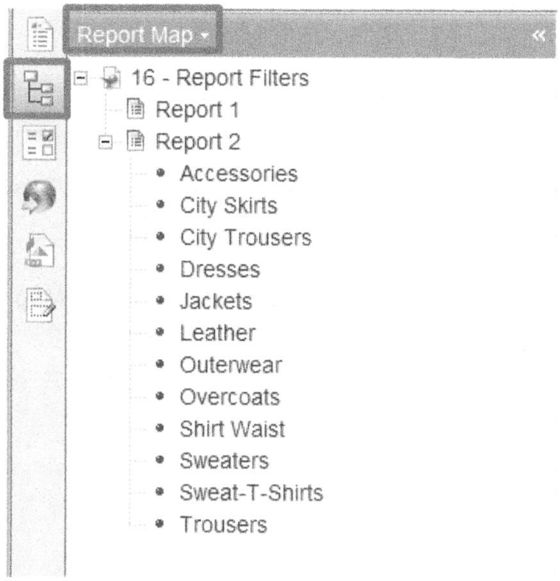
Report Map
16 - Report Filters
Report 1
Report 2
Accessories
City Skirts
City Trousers
Dresses
Jackets
Leather
Outerwear
Overcoats
Shirt Waist
Sweaters
Sweat-T-Shirts
Trousers

4. We can select the Section Header Cell and apply a restriction to it.

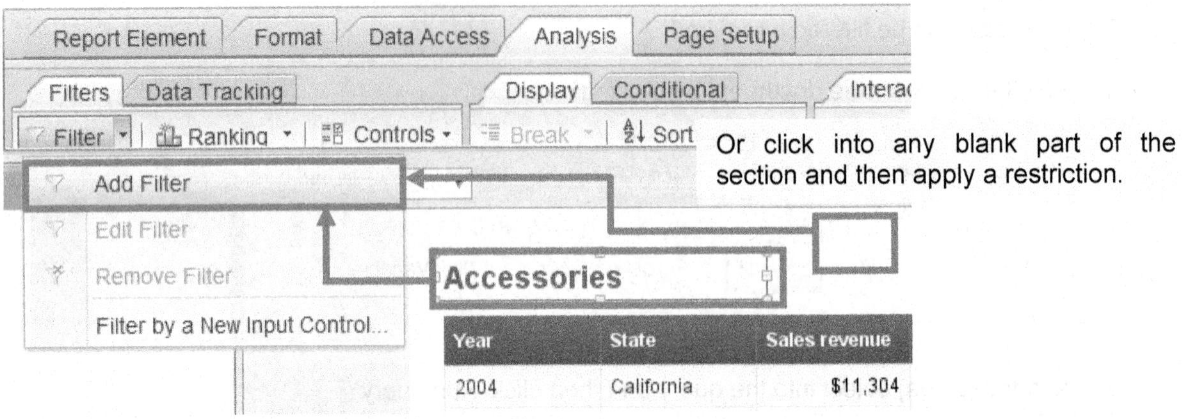
Report Element
Format
Data Access
Analysis
Page Setup
Filters
Data Tracking
Display
Conditional
Filter
Ranking
Controls
Break
Sort
Add Filter
Edit Filter
Remove Filter
Filter by a New Input Control...
Accessories
Year
State
Sales revenue
2004
California
$11,304
Or click into any blank part of the section and then apply a restriction.

5. In the 'Report Filter' interface, define the filter to restrict [Lines] to 'Dresses', 'Leather', 'Trousers' and then click 'OK'.

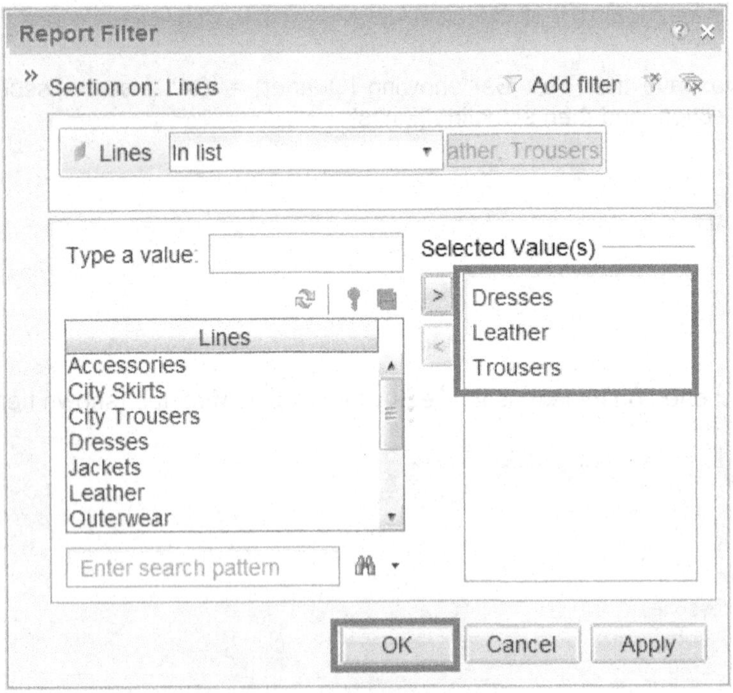
Report Filter
Section on: Lines
Add filter
Lines
In list
ather, Trousers
Type a value:
Selected Value(s)
Lines
Accessories
City Skirts
City Trousers
Dresses
Jackets
Leather
Outerwear
Dresses
Leather
Trousers
Enter search pattern
OK
Cancel
Apply

Section level filter is confirmed as we have fewer sections in the Report Map tab:

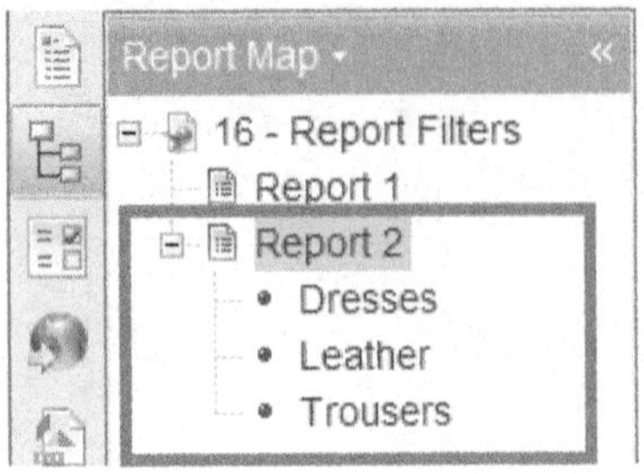
Report Map
16 - Report Filters
Report 1
Report 2
Dresses
Leather
Trousers

6. Similarly, we can select the Section Header Cell (or the section itself) and remove the filter.

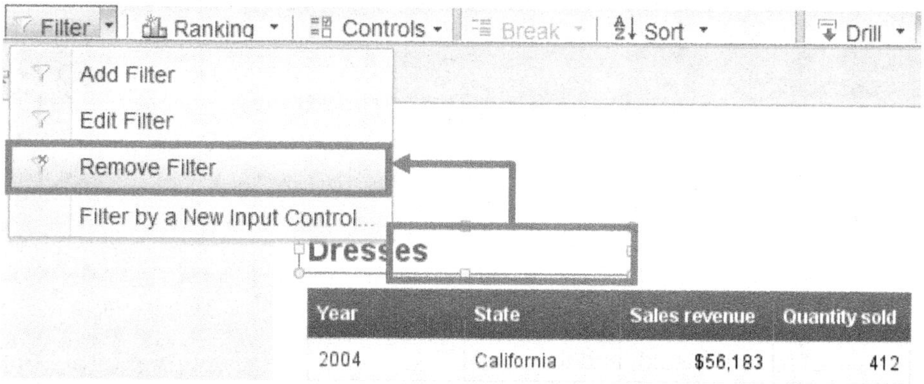
Filter
Ranking
Controls
Break
Sort
Drill
Add Filter
Edit Filter
Remove Filter
Filter by a New Input Control...
Dresses
Year
State
Sales revenue
Quantity sold
2004
California
$56,183
412

Remove the filter and we will now have all the [Lines] being reported.

7. Now remove the [Year] and [Sales revenue] columns from the vertical table, and apply a Sum calculation to the [Quantity sold] column.

Accessories

State	Quantity sold
California	645
Colorado	207
DC	245
Florida	178
Illinois	280
Massachusetts	153
New York	816
Texas	1,031
Sum:	**3,555**

City Skirts

State	Quantity sold
California	163
Colorado	34

Scroll down the report and you will see the totals for each section should be the same as the values in the following table:

Lines	Quantity sold
Accessories	3,555
City Skirts	633
City Trousers	793
Dresses	8,158
Jackets	998
Leather	265
Outerwear	174
Overcoats	1,168
Shirt Waist	9,446
Sweaters	3,389
Sweat-T-Shirts	21,698
Trousers	1,048

We can see only Dresses, Shirt Waist, and Sweat-T-Shirts have [Quantity sold] greater than 4,000 as a section total.

NOTE – If your values do not agree, please make sure you have [Quarter] = 'Q4' filter applied using the Filter Bar.

Q4

8. Right-click in a blank part of the section on [Lines] and select 'Filter – Add Filter'.

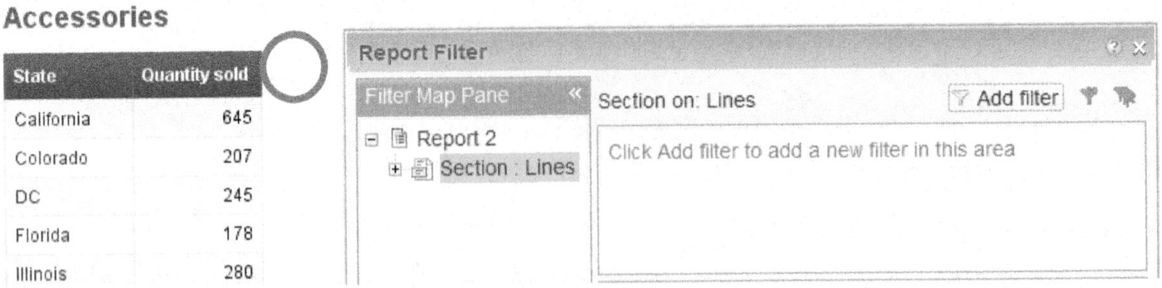
Accessories
State
Quantity sold
California 645
Colorado 207
DC 245
Florida 178
Illinois 280
Report Filter
Filter Map Pane
Section on: Lines
Add filter
Report 2
Section : Lines
Click Add filter to add a new filter in this area

9. Click 'Add Filter', select [Quantity sold] and then click 'OK'.

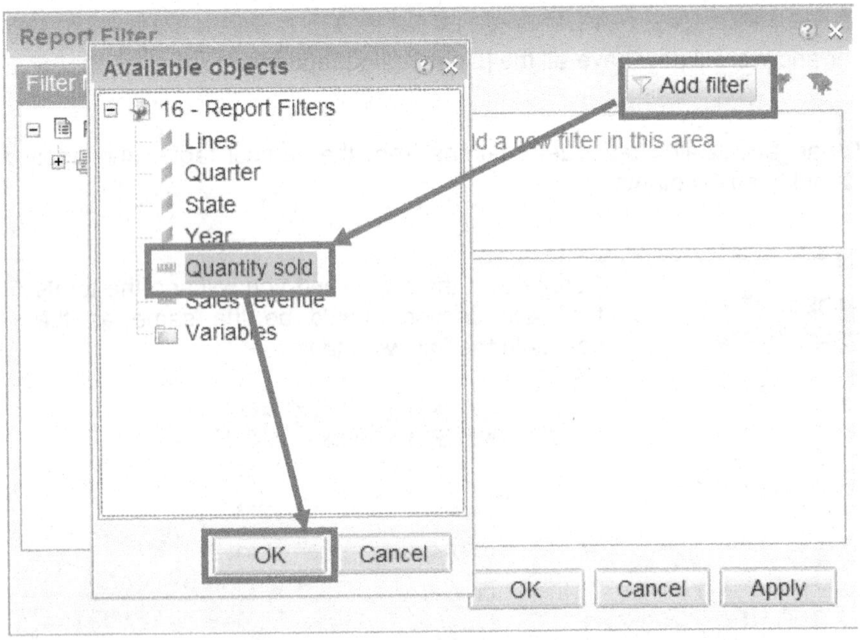
Report Filter
Available objects
16 - Report Filters
Lines
Quarter
State
Year
Quantity sold
Variables
Add filter
OK
Cancel
OK
Cancel
Apply

10. Define the condition as [Quantity sold] Greater than 4000 and click 'OK'.

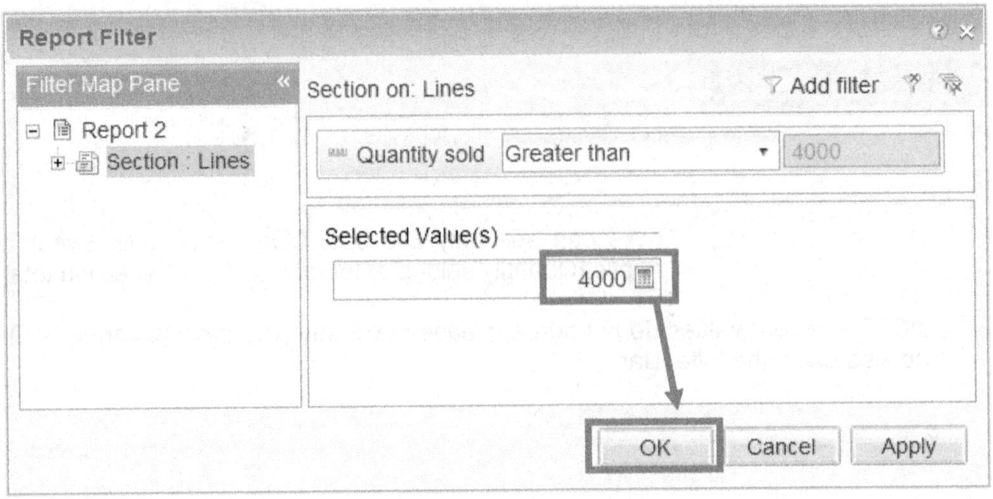
Report Filter
Filter Map Pane
Section on: Lines
Add filter
Report 2
Section : Lines
Quantity sold
Greater than
4000
Selected Value(s)
4000
OK
Cancel
Apply

Web Intelligence will now only display the sections where the [Quantity sold] is greater than 4,000 (for the whole section), as confirmed by the 'Report Map' tab.

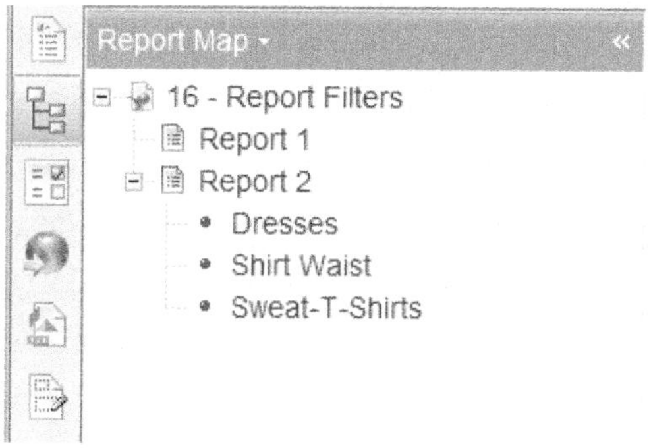
Report Map
16 - Report Filters
Report 1
Report 2
Dresses
Shirt Waist
Sweat-T-Shirts

16.9 Filtering Chart Data

Data presented in charts can be filtered if required.

We have the following chart and would like to apply a filter to present the data for 'California', 'New York' and 'Texas' only.

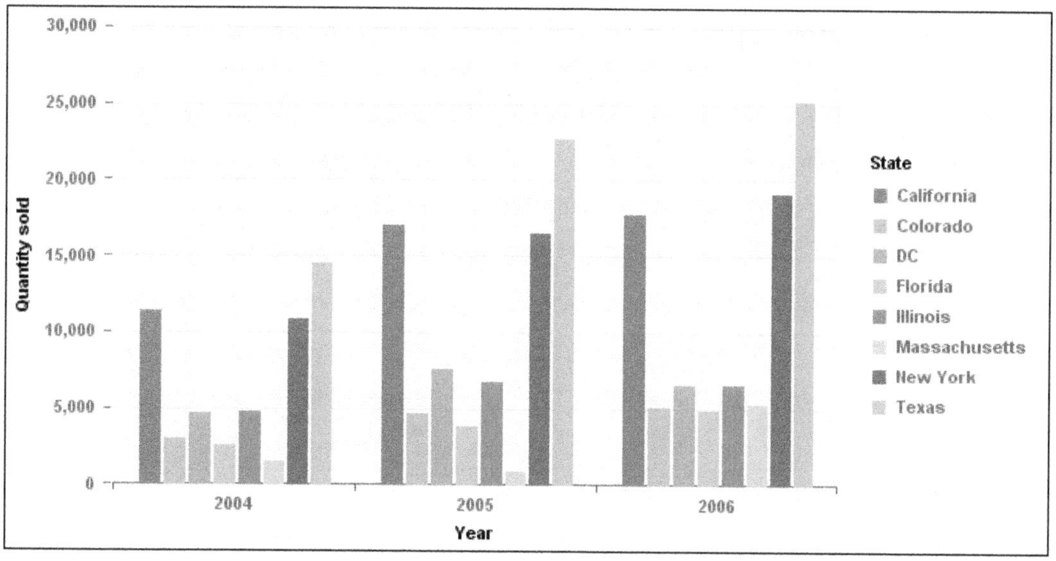
30,000
25,000
20,000
15,000
10,000
5,000
0
Quantity sold
2004
2005
2006
Year
State
California
Colorado
DC
Florida
Illinois
Massachusetts
New York
Texas

1. Right-click on the chart and select 'Filter – Add Filter':

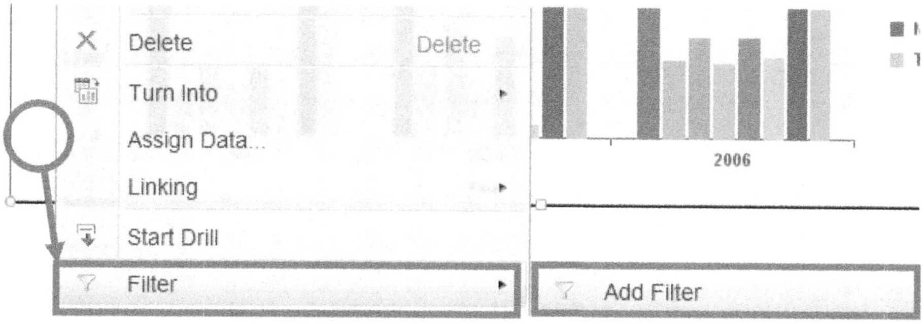
Delete
Delete
Turn Into
Assign Data...
Linking
Start Drill
Filter
Add Filter
2006

2. Click 'Add Filter', select [State] and click 'OK'.

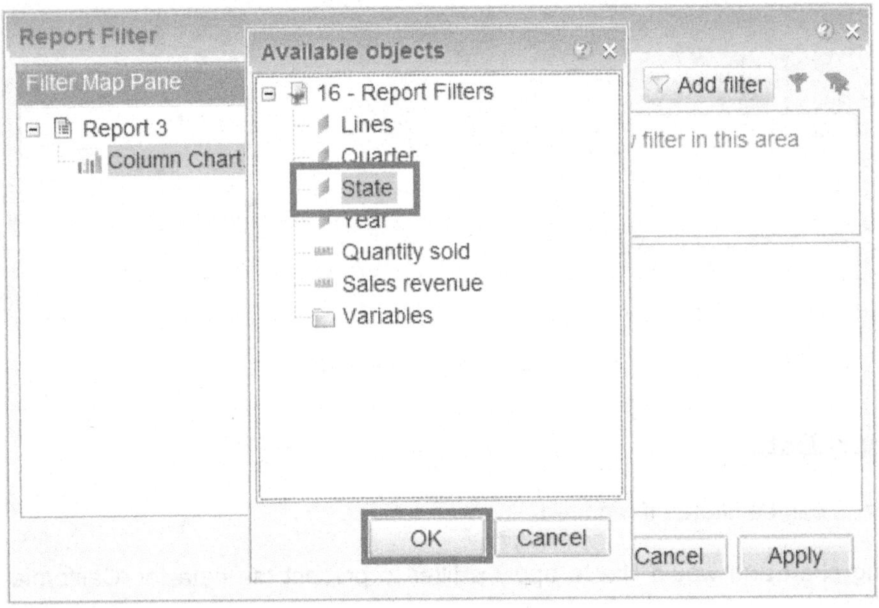
Report Filter
Filter Map Pane
Report 3
Column Chart
Available objects
16 - Report Filters
Lines
Quarter
State
Year
Quantity sold
Sales revenue
Variables
OK
Cancel
Add filter
filter in this area
Cancel
Apply

3. Define the filter condition as [State] In list California, New York, Texas and click 'OK':

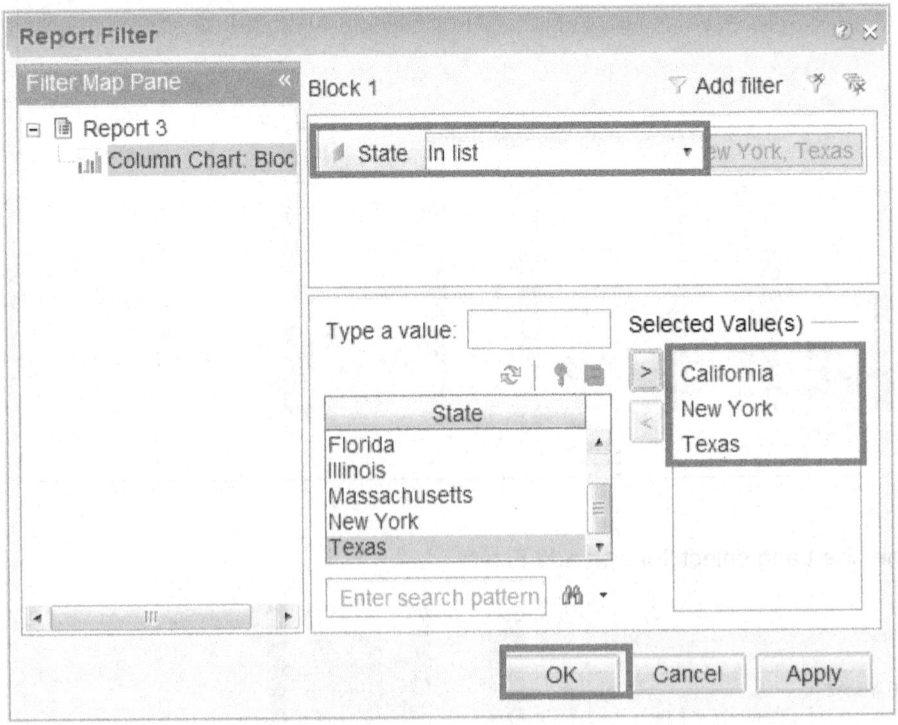
Report Filter
Filter Map Pane
Report 3
Column Chart: Bloc
Block 1
Add filter
State
In list
Type a value:
Selected Value(s)
California
New York
Texas
State
Florida
Illinois
Massachusetts
New York
Texas
Enter search pattern
OK
Cancel
Apply

4. The chart is now filtered for the three selected states.

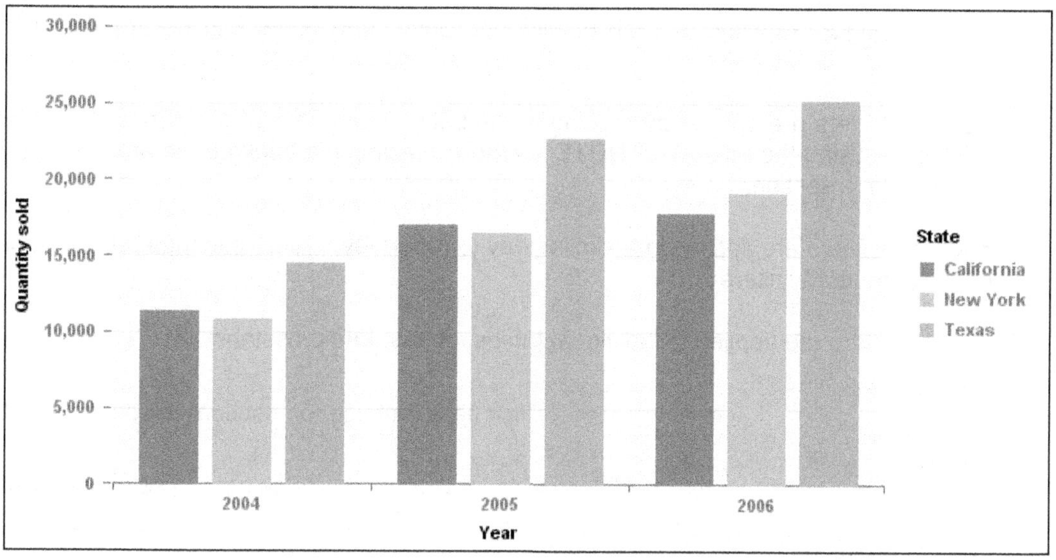
30,000
25,000
20,000
15,000
10,000
5,000
0
Quantity sold
2004
2005
2006
Year
State
California
New York
Texas

5. We can also apply a filter on the chart using an object that is not displayed in the chart. For example, let us take the above chart and add a filter condition on [Quarter] Equal to 'Q4', as shown below.

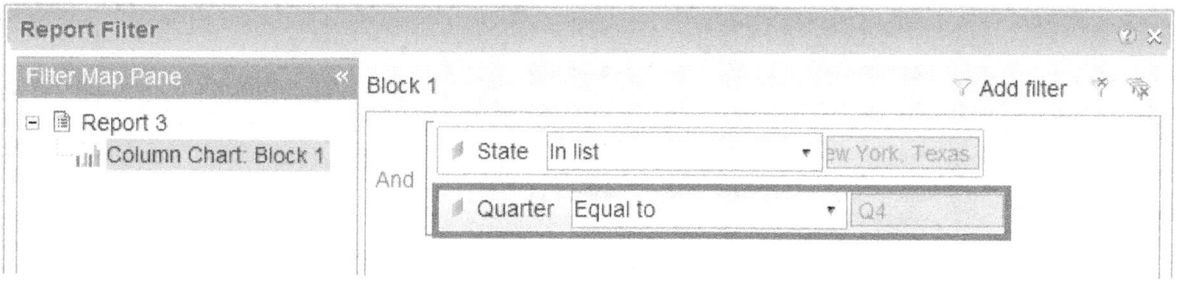
Report Filter
Filter Map Pane
Report 3
Column Chart: Block 1
Block 1
Add filter
And
State
In list
ew York, Texas
Quarter
Equal to
Q4

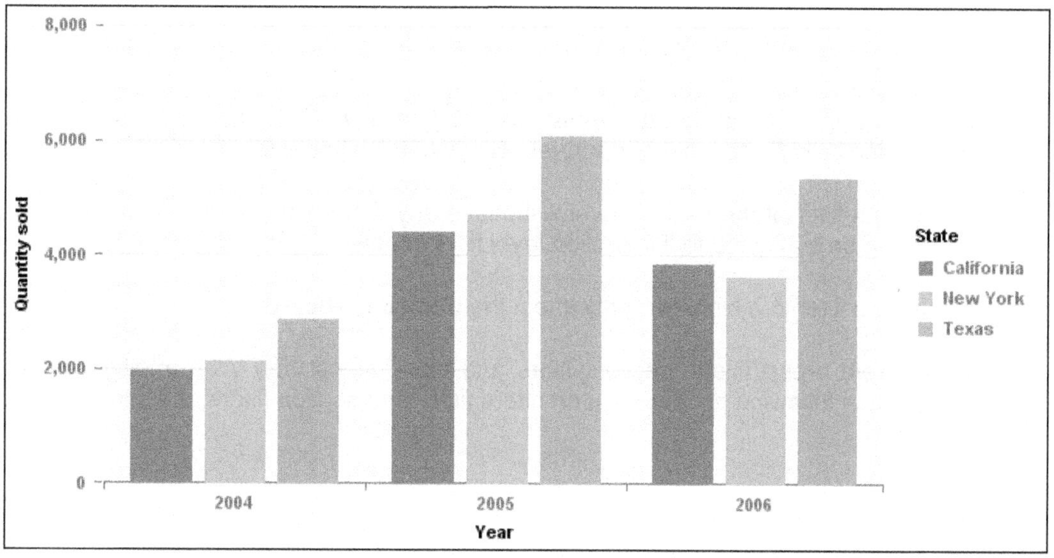
8,000
6,000
4,000
2,000
0
Quantity sold
2004
2005
2006
Year
State
California
New York
Texas

16.10 Report Filters, Section Filters and Block Filters

Within a report (a single tab within a Web Intelligence document) filters can be applied at different levels.

- Report level filters are applied by clicking in the background area of a report and then applying filter(s), or by using the Filter Bar. **NOTE** – When selecting the background area ensure it is the report and not a section.

- Section level filters are applied in a similar way to report level filters except a section is selected prior to applying any filters.

- Block level filters are applied to individual tables, charts, and crosstabs.

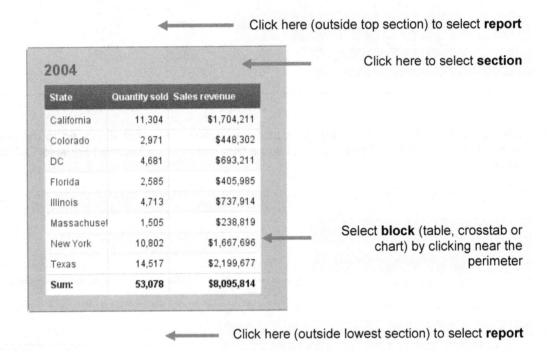

Click here (outside top section) to select **report**

Click here to select **section**

2004

State	Quantity sold	Sales revenue
California	11,304	$1,704,211
Colorado	2,971	$448,302
DC	4,681	$693,211
Florida	2,585	$405,985
Illinois	4,713	$737,914
Massachuset	1,505	$238,819
New York	10,802	$1,667,696
Texas	14,517	$2,199,677
Sum:	**53,078**	**$8,095,814**

Select **block** (table, crosstab or chart) by clicking near the perimeter

Click here (outside lowest section) to select **report**

- Applying a filter at the report level is essentially a global tab filter and therefore any sections, blocks and cells placed in the report tab will have this filter applied.

- Applying a filter at the section level will cause any sub-sections, blocks and cells placed in the section to be subjected to the section level filter condition.

- Applying a filter to a block will only affect the block it is applied to.

- If there are report filters, section filters and block filters then Web Intelligence will apply the filters in the following priority… report filters first, then section filters and finally the block filters.

17 Using Input Controls to Filter Report Data

We have had a look at restricting data in reports by applying simple report filters using the 'Add filter' button and more complex filters using the 'Report Filter' interface.

> *Usually these types of filters are applied and then fixed within reports, i.e. users request certain blocks of data to only show particular data and these filters to be 'fixed' for most purposes.*

We also looked at applying filters using the Filter Bar.

> *The end user is able to dynamically filter the report using the objects within the Filter Bar, but there is one big limitation in that for each object you can only select one value when filtering.*

Input Controls are much more interactive and offer more options for end users when dynamically filtering the reports.

17.1 Adding Input Controls in Web Intelligence

We will now use Input Controls to make the report filtering process more user-friendly.

1. Create and run the following query using the 'eFashion' universe:

Result Objects
Year
Quarter
State
Sales revenue
Quantity sold

2. Save your document.

3. From the left-hand side click on the 'New' button in the 'Input Controls' tab:

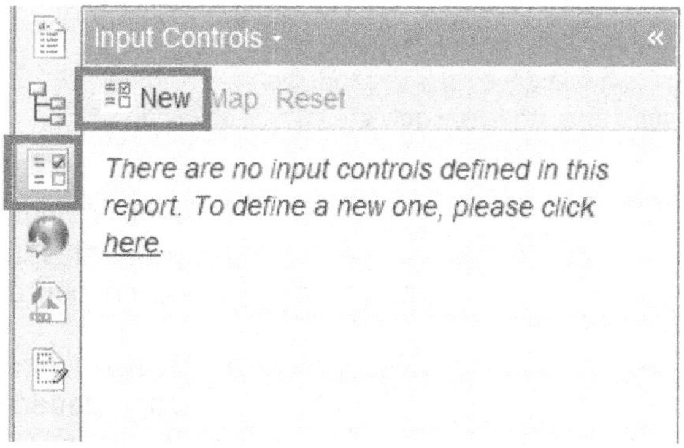
Input Controls
New
Map
Reset
There are no input controls defined in this report. To define a new one, please click here.

4. We can change the report object on which the Input Control is to be defined against. Ensure [State] is selected and click 'Next':

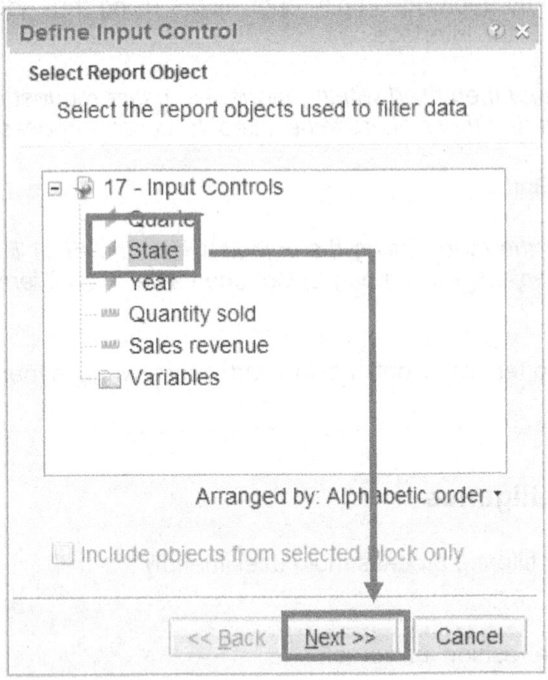
Define Input Control
Select Report Object
Select the report objects used to filter data
17 - Input Controls
State
Year
Quantity sold
Sales revenue
Variables
Arranged by: Alphabetic order
Include objects from selected block only
<< Back
Next >>
Cancel

5. The 'Define Input Control' interface will open and a list of Input Controls will be presented depending on the type of object selected (e.g. Dimension or Measure) and whether the object holds numerical values or string characters.

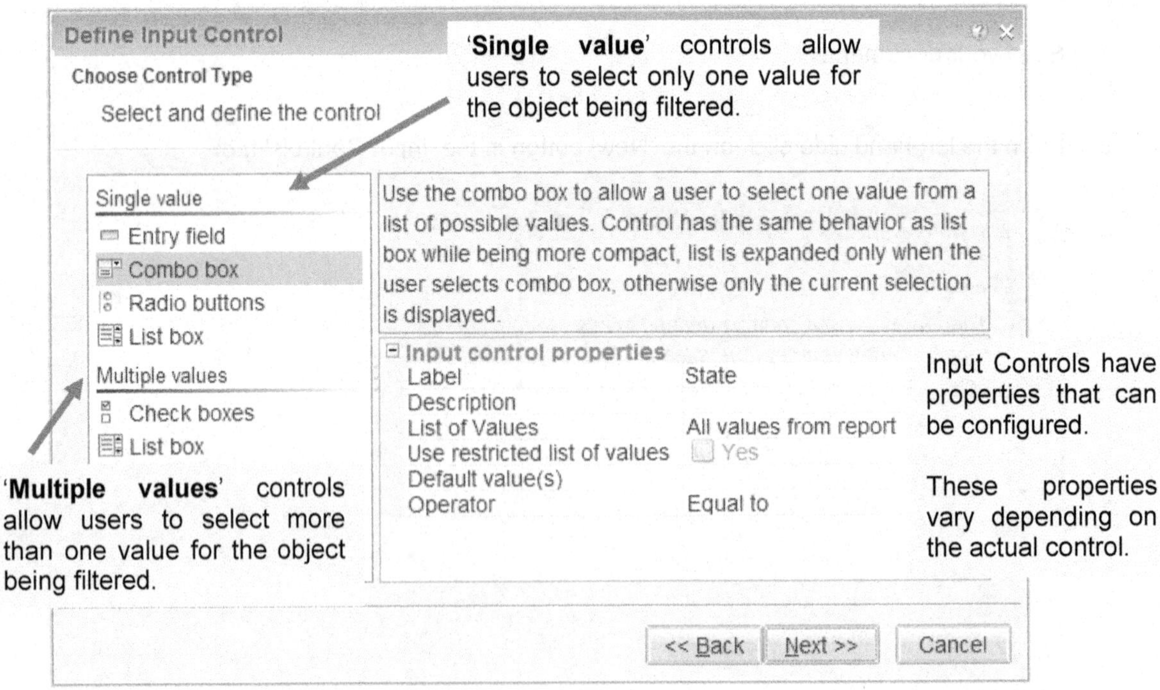
Define Input Control
'Single value' controls allow users to select only one value for the object being filtered.
Choose Control Type
Select and define the control
Single value
Entry field
Combo box
Radio buttons
List box
Multiple values
Check boxes
List box
Use the combo box to allow a user to select one value from a list of possible values. Control has the same behavior as list box while being more compact, list is expanded only when the user selects combo box, otherwise only the current selection is displayed.
Input control properties
Label
State
Description
List of Values
All values from report
Use restricted list of values
Yes
Default value(s)
Operator
Equal to
Input Controls have properties that can be configured.
These properties vary depending on the actual control.
'Multiple values' controls allow users to select more than one value for the object being filtered.
<< Back
Next >>
Cancel

6. For the time being select 'Radio buttons' and then click on 'Next'. Leave the default configuration property values.

   We will have a look at the various Input Controls and their properties later on in the session.

7. The control has to be assigned to a report element in order to filter the data within the selected element. Select 'Vertical Table: Block1' and then click on 'Finish'.

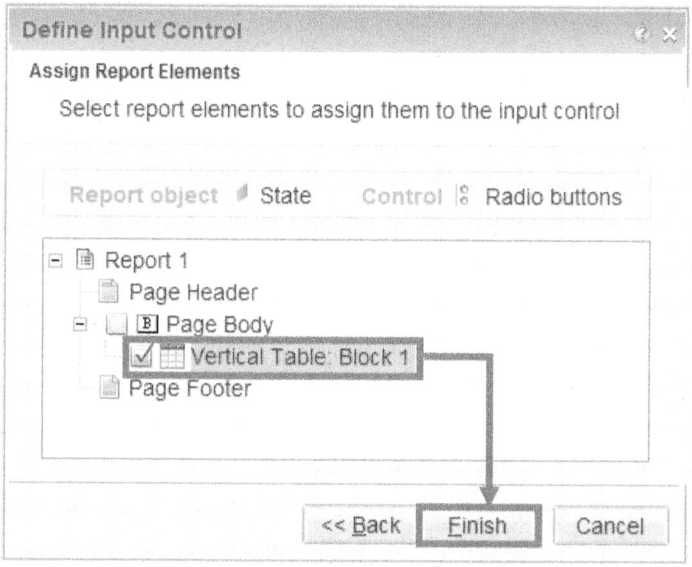
Define Input Control
Assign Report Elements
Select report elements to assign them to the input control
Report object State
Control Radio buttons
Report 1
Page Header
Page Body
Vertical Table: Block 1
Page Footer
<< Back
Finish
Cancel

Selecting an individual block (as shown here) will apply the Input Control to the table only.

If we selected 'Page Body' then all elements within the report would be affected by value(s) selected in the Input Control.

This is similar to Block level filters and Report level filters as described in the previous session on 'Filtering Data in Reports'.

8. The Input Control is now available for use in the Input Controls tab. Simply select a different value in the Input Control and the data in Block1 will be filtered.

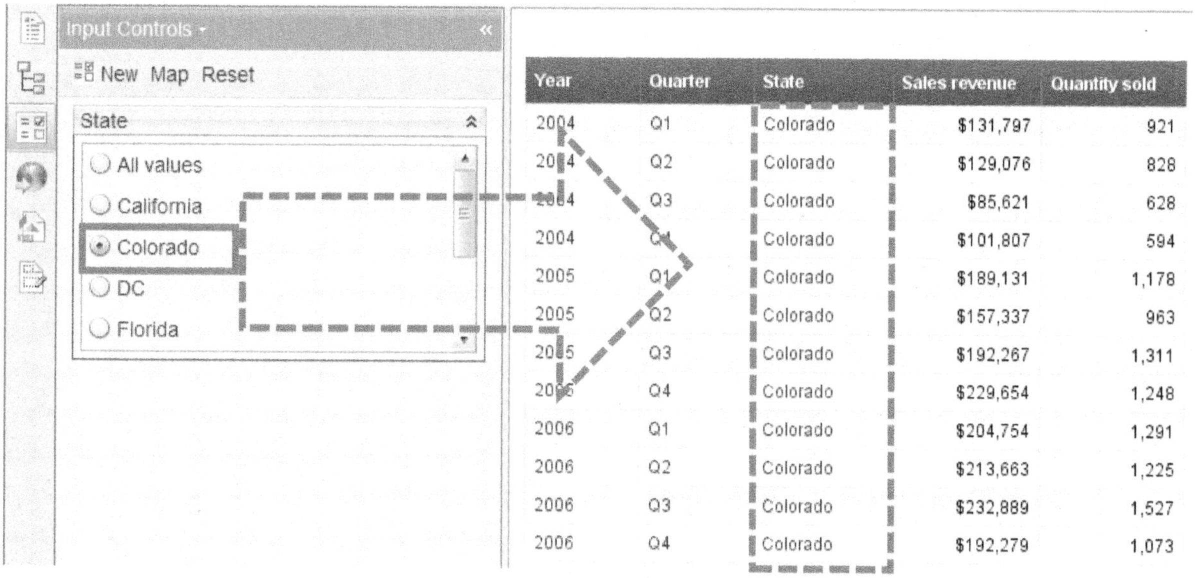
Input Controls
New Map Reset
State
All values
California
Colorado
DC
Florida
Year Quarter State Sales revenue Quantity sold
2004 Q1 Colorado $131,797 921
2004 Q2 Colorado $129,076 828
2004 Q3 Colorado $85,621 628
2004 Q4 Colorado $101,807 594
2005 Q1 Colorado $189,131 1,178
2005 Q2 Colorado $157,337 963
2005 Q3 Colorado $192,267 1,311
2005 Q4 Colorado $229,654 1,248
2006 Q1 Colorado $204,754 1,291
2006 Q2 Colorado $213,663 1,225
2006 Q3 Colorado $232,889 1,527
2006 Q4 Colorado $192,279 1,073

9. Save the document.

The input control we have used is identical to using a filter in the Filter Bar, i.e. only allows a single value to be selected, but Input Controls 'appear' more interactive compared to filters in the Filter Bar.

Let us now look at an Input Control that allows you to select multiple values.

1. Click on 'New' on the 'Input Controls' tab.

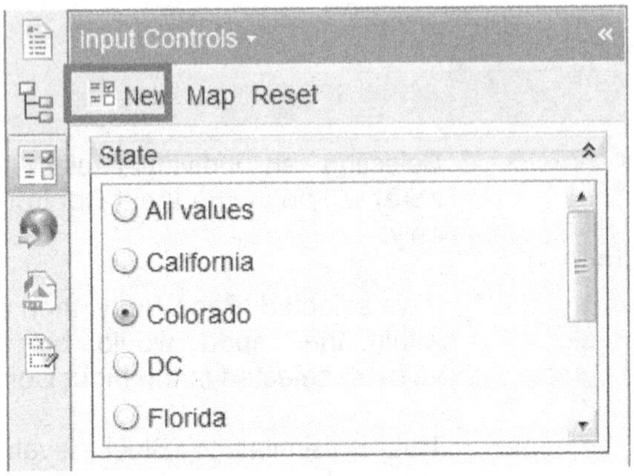
Input Controls
New
Map
Reset
State
All values
California
Colorado
DC
Florida

2. Select [Quarter] and click 'Next'.

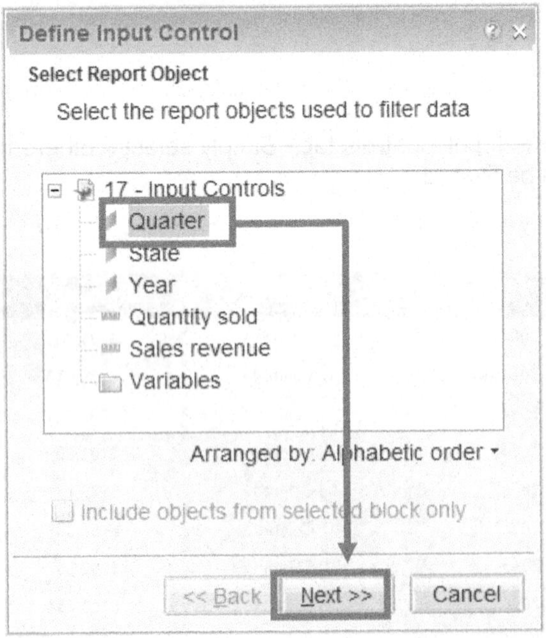
Define Input Control
Select Report Object
Select the report objects used to filter data
17 - Input Controls
Quarter
State
Year
Quantity sold
Sales revenue
Variables
Arranged by: Alphabetic order
Include objects from selected block only
<< Back
Next >>
Cancel

3. Select 'Check boxes' and click 'Next'

4. Select 'Vertical Table: Block1' and then click on 'Finish'.

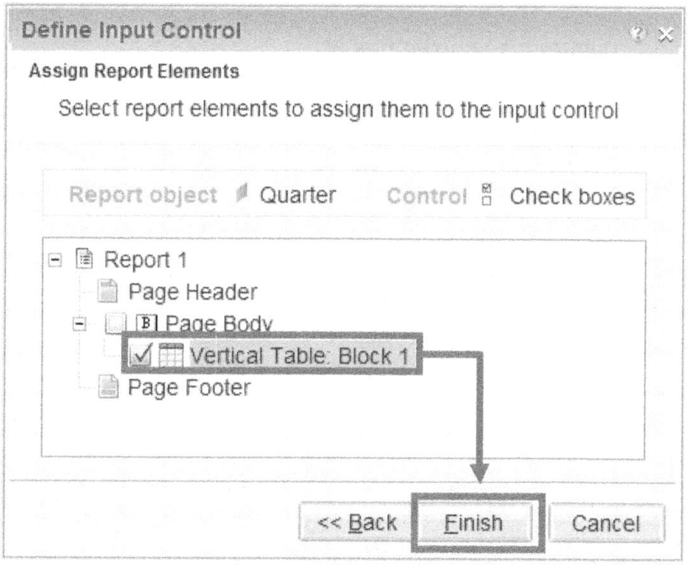
Define Input Control
Assign Report Elements
Select report elements to assign them to the input control
Report object Quarter
Control Check boxes
Report 1
Page Header
Page Body
Vertical Table: Block 1
Page Footer
<< Back
Finish
Cancel

5. Save the document.

6. The two Input Controls can be used together to filter the data in the table they are both attached to.

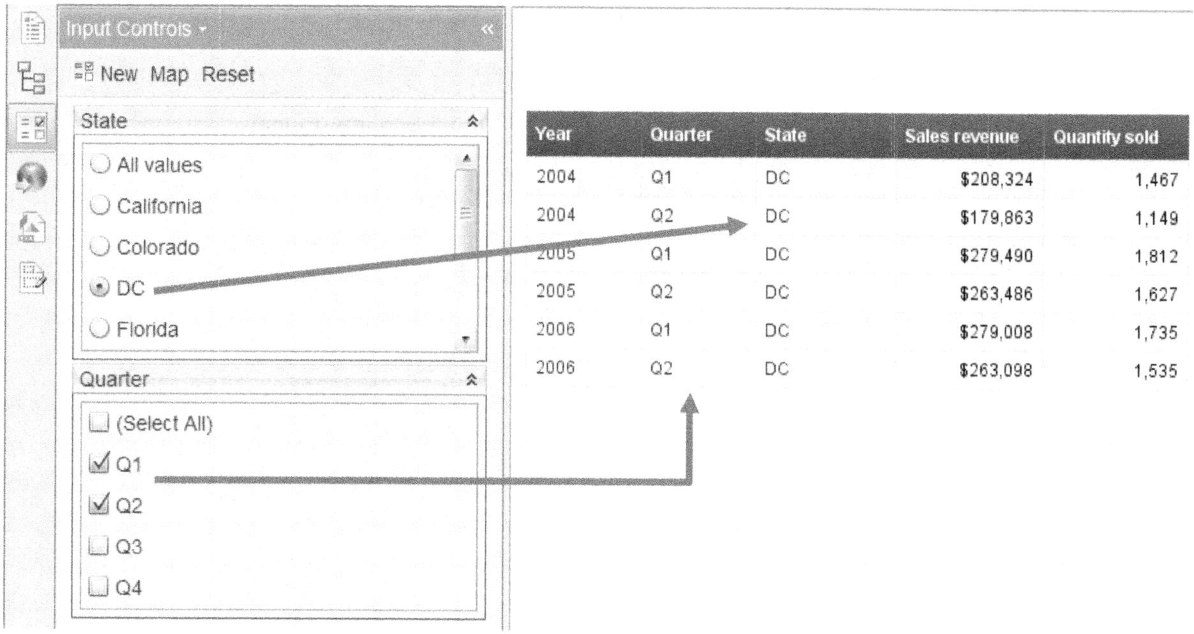
Input Controls
New Map Reset
State
All values
California
Colorado
DC
Florida
Quarter
(Select All)
Q1
Q2
Q3
Q4
Year Quarter State Sales revenue Quantity sold
2004 Q1 DC $208,324 1,467
2004 Q2 DC $179,863 1,149
2005 Q1 DC $279,490 1,812
2005 Q2 DC $263,486 1,627
2006 Q1 DC $279,008 1,735
2006 Q2 DC $263,098 1,535

7. From the 'Input Controls' tab select 'New' and then select [Quantity sold]:

8. Select the 'Double slider' control and configure it as shown below:

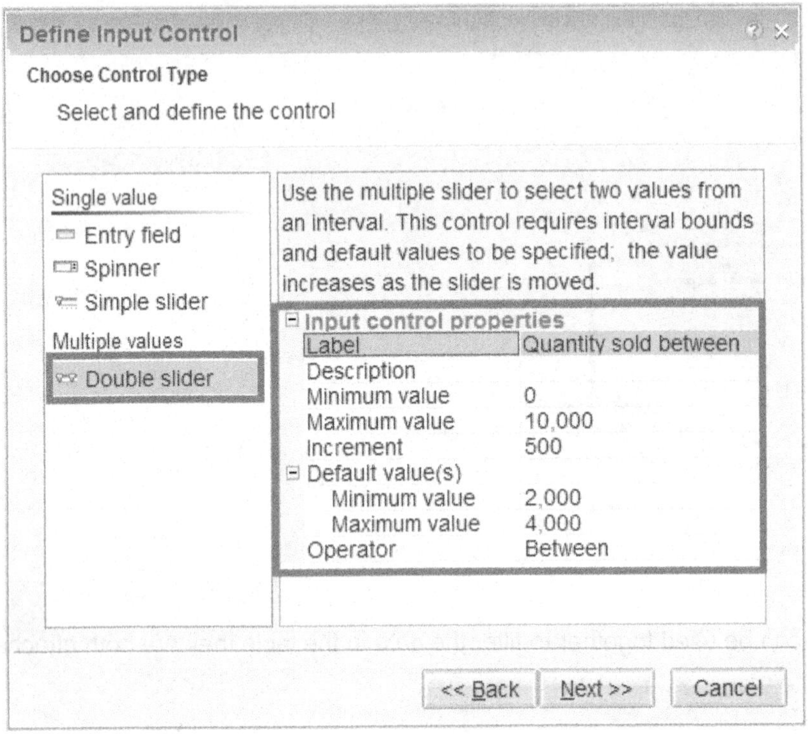
Define Input Control
Choose Control Type
Select and define the control
Single value
Entry field
Spinner
Simple slider
Multiple values
Double slider
Use the multiple slider to select two values from an interval. This control requires interval bounds and default values to be specified; the value increases as the slider is moved.
Input control properties
Label
Quantity sold between
Description
Minimum value
0
Maximum value
10,000
Increment
500
Default value(s)
Minimum value
2,000
Maximum value
4,000
Operator
Between
<< Back
Next >>
Cancel

9. Assign the Input Control to 'Vertical Table: Block1' and then click 'Finish':

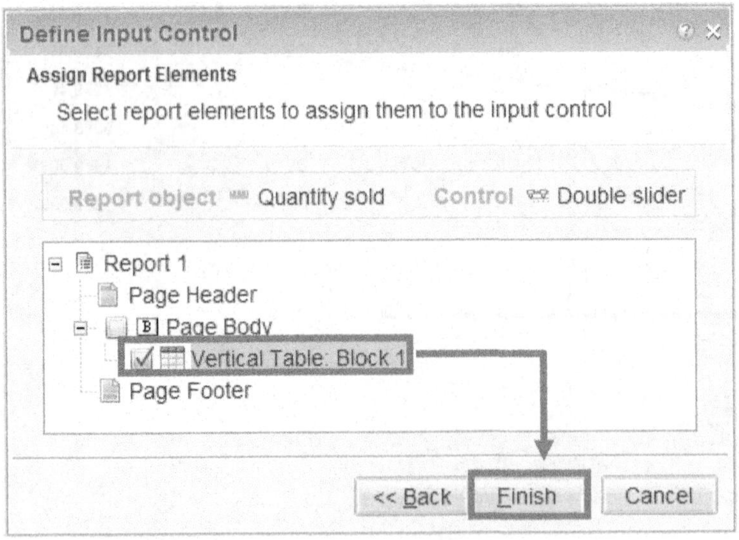
Define Input Control
Assign Report Elements
Select report elements to assign them to the input control
Report object
Quantity sold
Control
Double slider
Report 1
Page Header
Page Body
Vertical Table: Block 1
Page Footer
<< Back
Finish
Cancel

10. The new Input Control is added to the report (as shown below) and the table is showing no data.

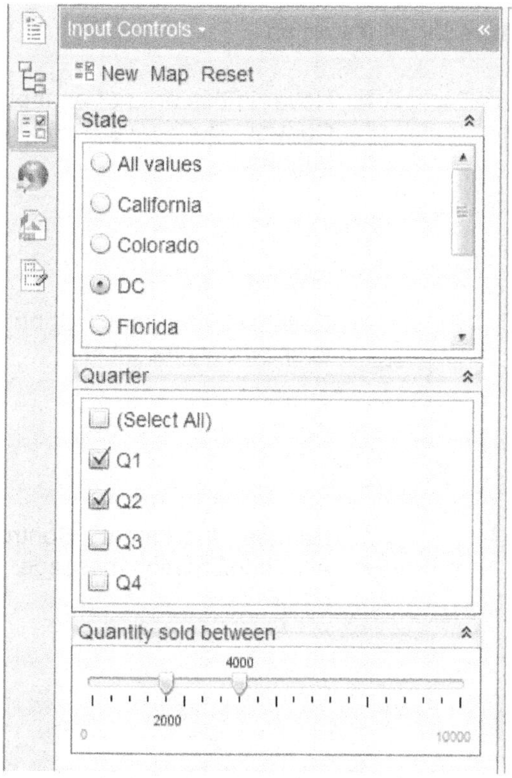
Input Controls
New Map Reset
State
All values
California
Colorado
DC
Florida
Quarter
(Select All)
Q1
Q2
Q3
Q4
Quantity sold between
4000
2000
0
10000

Year	Quarter	State	Sales revenue	Quantity sold
			Discontinued	Discontinued

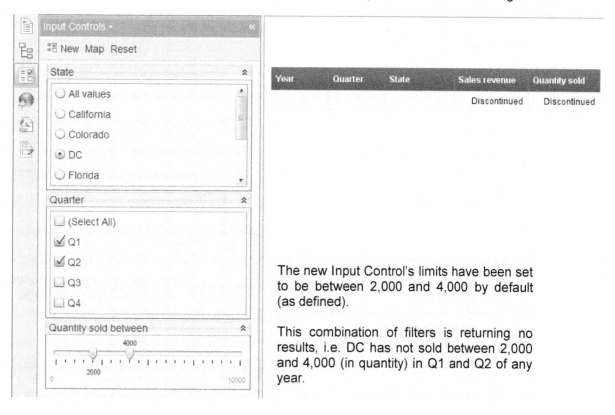

The new Input Control's limits have been set to be between 2,000 and 4,000 by default (as defined).

This combination of filters is returning no results, i.e. DC has not sold between 2,000 and 4,000 (in quantity) in Q1 and Q2 of any year.

11. Move the left-hand slider to 1500, i.e. the range becomes 1500 to 4000.

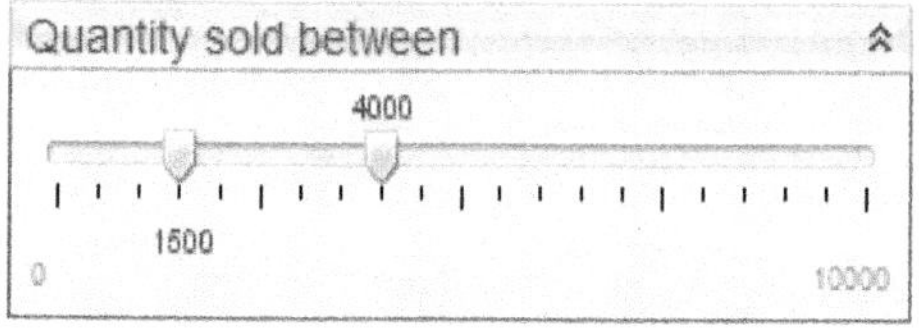
Quantity sold between
4000
1500
0
10000

We now see data in the table.

Year	Quarter	State	Sales revenue	Quantity sold
2005	Q1	DC	$279,490	1,812
2005	Q2	DC	$263,486	1,627
2006	Q1	DC	$279,008	1,735
2006	Q2	DC	$263,098	1,535

17.2 Editing and Removing Input Controls in Web Intelligence

Once defined Input Controls can then be edited or removed from the report.

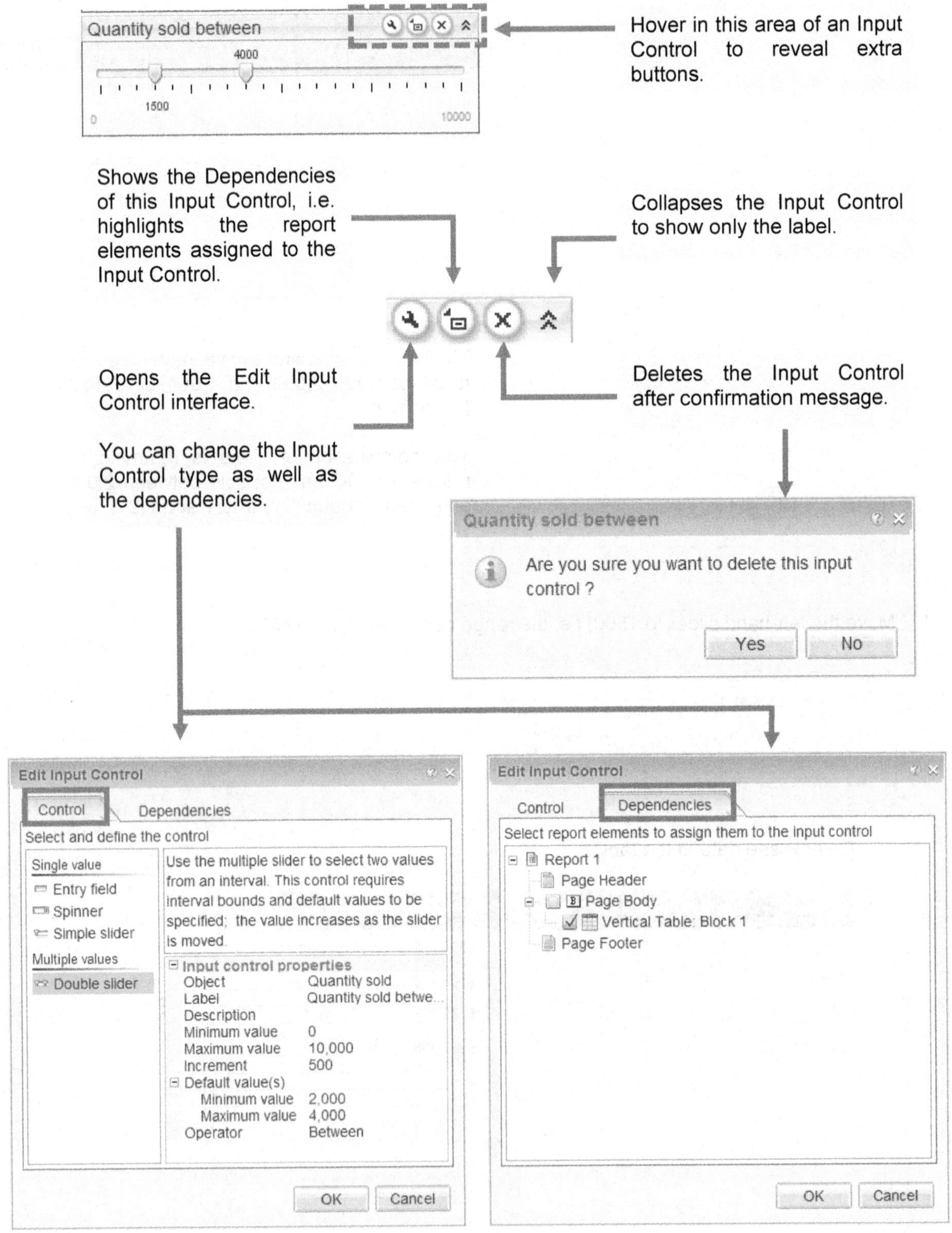
Quantity sold between
4000
1500
0
10000
Hover in this area of an Input Control to reveal extra buttons.
Shows the Dependencies of this Input Control, i.e. highlights the report elements assigned to the Input Control.
Collapses the Input Control to show only the label.
Opens the Edit Input Control interface.
You can change the Input Control type as well as the dependencies.
Deletes the Input Control after confirmation message.
Quantity sold between
Are you sure you want to delete this input control ?
Yes
No
Edit Input Control
Control
Dependencies
Select and define the control
Single value
Entry field
Spinner
Simple slider
Multiple values
Double slider
Use the multiple slider to select two values from an interval. This control requires interval bounds and default values to be specified; the value increases as the slider is moved.
Input control properties
Object Quantity sold
Label Quantity sold betwe...
Description
Minimum value 0
Maximum value 10,000
Increment 500
Default value(s)
Minimum value 2,000
Maximum value 4,000
Operator Between
OK
Cancel
Edit Input Control
Control
Dependencies
Select report elements to assign them to the input control
Report 1
Page Header
Page Body
Vertical Table: Block 1
Page Footer
OK
Cancel

17.3 Input Control Properties

The following is a list of the properties available for the various Input Controls. The actual properties used by an individual Input Control depends on its type (discussed next).

Input Control Property	Usage
Label	The name that is displayed in the Input Control tab.
Description	Extra information that is displayed in the Input Control tab when you hover over the Label.
List of Values	The default is to use all the unique values for the object from the data within the document. You can however define a custom subset of values or provide your own list using this property. For example, our data contains the values 1 to 12 for the [Month] object. We can select 3, 6, 9, 12 to use within the Input Control as shown here: Month All values All values 3 6 9 12
Use restricted list of values	Only available as a selection if you have defined a custom list for the 'List of Values' property. If set to 'Yes' then the data is automatically filtered in line with the custom list. Using the above custom list, if this property is set to 'Yes' then the data will be filtered using the values 3, 6, 9 and 12 even when the Input Control shows 'All values'. If set to 'No' then the data would not be filtered (i.e. we would see all 12 months) when 'All values' is selected, but the user would only be able to filter explicitly for months 3, 6, 9 and 12 as shown in the Input Control.
Minimum Value	Some control types require a minimum value (such as sliders).
Maximum Value	Some control types require a maximum value (such as sliders).
Default value(s)	Some control types require a single default value. Some control types require two default values (one for Minimum and the other for Maximum).
Increment	For controls that can be incremented (such as sliders and spinners) this setting specifies the step change.

Input Control Property	Usage
Number of lines	For example a list of 12 radio buttons (for the [Month] object) with 'Number of lines' set to 3 will only display three radio buttons. The other 9 radio buttons are accessed by using the scrollbar.
Operator	The operator that the input control uses to filter the data in the assigned report element(s). The operators work in the same way as already described in the previous section on 'Filtering Data in Reports'. The available operators are: Equal to, Not equal to, Less than, Less than or Equal to, Greater than, Greater than or Equal to, In list, Not in list, Between, Not Between. Not all the operators are available for every control type, for example the Between operator (and Not Between) requires a lower and upper value therefore this operator is only available for the Double Slider control.

17.4 Types of Input Controls in Web Intelligence

There are various types of Input Controls available categorised under the headings of 'Single value' and 'Multiple values'. The range of controls presented to you depends on what type of object you select (measure, dimension, etc) and the data type associated to the selected object (string, number, etc).

The following table summarises the available Input Control Types and the Object Types they can be used with.

Input Control Type		Object Type			
		Dimension *(string)*	**Dimension *(number)***	**Dimension (date)**	**Measure (number)**
Single value	Entry Field	Y	Y	Y	Y
	Combo Box	Y	Y	Y	N
	Radio Buttons	Y	Y	Y	N
	List Box	Y	Y	Y	N
	Spinner	N	Y	N	Y
	Simple Slider	N	Y	N	Y
	Calendar	N	N	Y	N
Multiple values	Check Boxes	Y	Y	Y	N
	List Box	Y	Y	Y	N
	Double Slider	N	Y	N	Y

Let us now have a brief look at each type of Input Control.

17.4.1 Entry Field

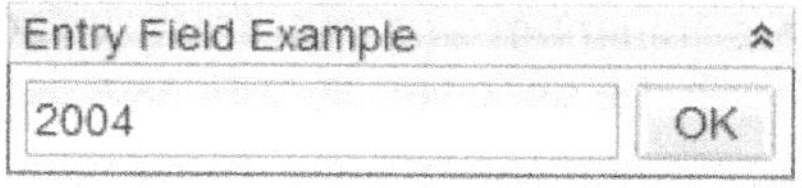
Entry Field Example
2004
OK

You input a single value directly into a text box.

There is no option to select values from a list, i.e. you simply type in the value.

17.4.2 Combo Box

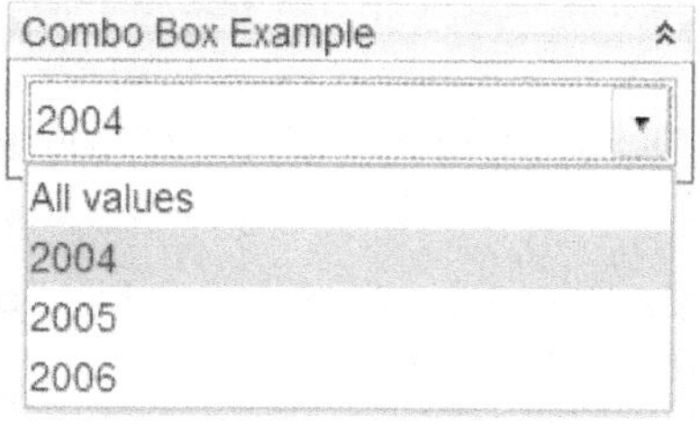
Combo Box Example
2004
All values
2004
2005
2006

A distinct list of values is presented in a drop down box for you to select a single value from.

The list is based on the values of the object within the document.

You can only select from the displayed values.

17.4.3 Radio Buttons

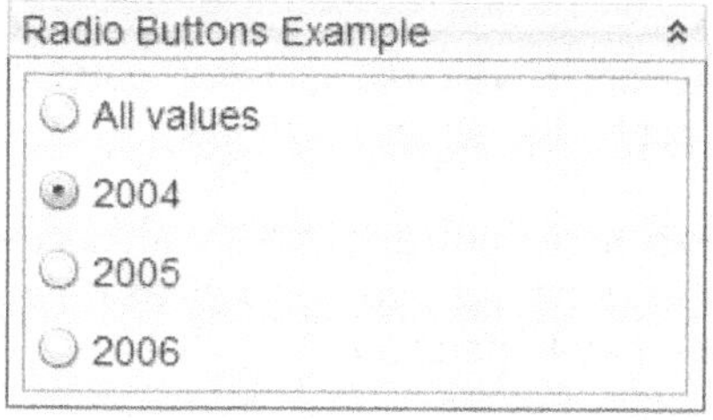
Radio Buttons Example
All values
2004
2005
2006

A distinct list of values is presented for you to select a single value from using radio buttons.

The list is based on the values of the object within the document.

You can only select from the displayed values.

17.4.4 List Box

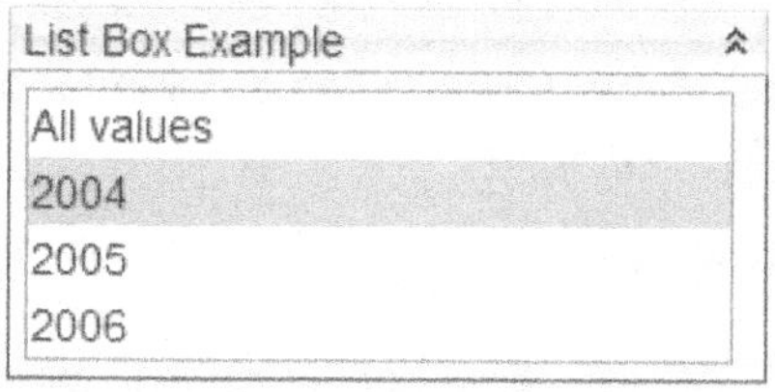
List Box Example
All values
2004
2005
2006

A distinct list of values is presented in a box for you to select a single value from.

The list is based on the values of the object within the document.

You can only select from the displayed values.

17.4.5 Spinner

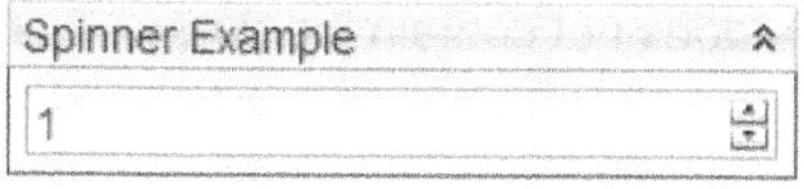
Spinner Example
1

Values are cycled using the arrow buttons.

The control needs to have a default starting point.

You can also specify the step increment, minimum and maximum values.

17.4.6 Simple Slider

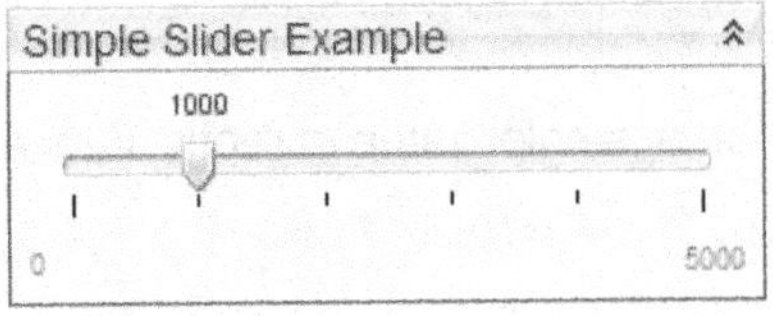
Simple Slider Example
1000
0
5000

A slider is used to filter values.

Requires minimum and maximum values for the slider to be specified as well as a default.

Here we have specified:

Min = 0, Max = 10000, Default = 2000

17.4.7 Check Boxes

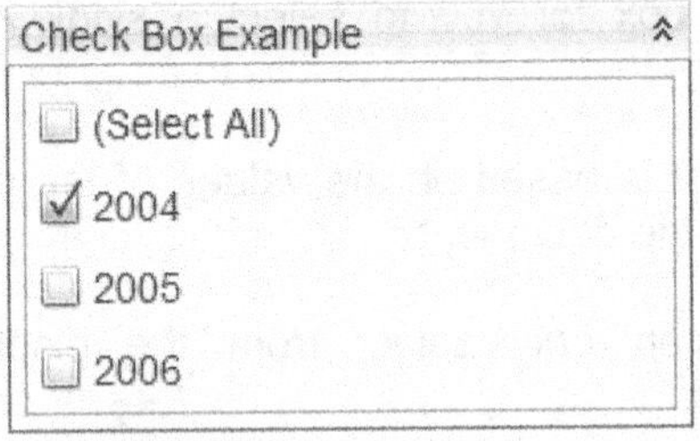
Check Box Example
(Select All)
2004
2005
2006

A distinct list of values is presented for you to select multiple values from by ticking the required values.

The list is based on the values of the object within the document.

You can only select from the displayed values.

17.4.8 Double Slider

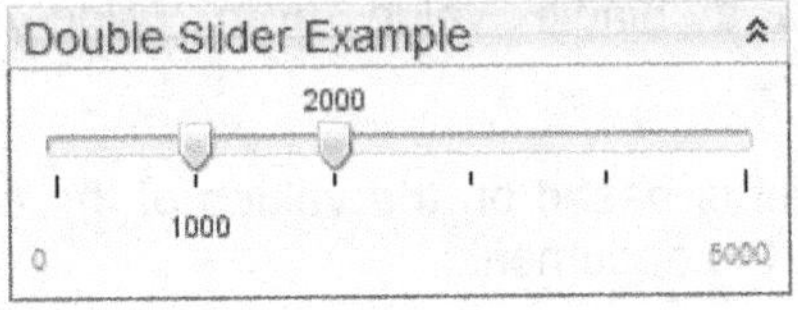
Double Slider Example
2000
1000
0
5000

Used to show values inside or outside of a range set by the slider positions.

Requires minimum and maximum values for the slider to be specified as well as defaults. Here we have specified:

Min = 0, Max = 10000,
Default Min = 4000, Default Max = 6000

17.4.9 Calendar

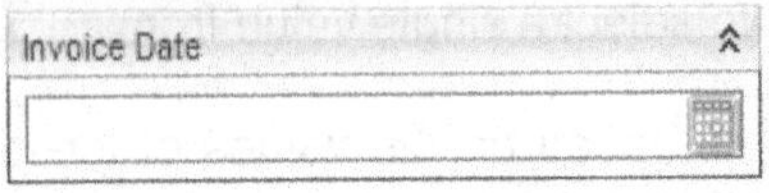
Invoice Date

December 2013
Sun Mon Tue Wed Thu Fri Sat
Today

Enables you to select using a calendar object (as shown opposite).

Note

At the time of writing it was not possible to restrict (or limit) the range of values displayed for selection, i.e. the user can select from historical and future dates, even if your report does not contain the dates.

17.5 Organising Input Controls in Web Intelligence

The order (for display purposes) of Input Controls can be re-arranged by using drag-and-drop.

Original order:

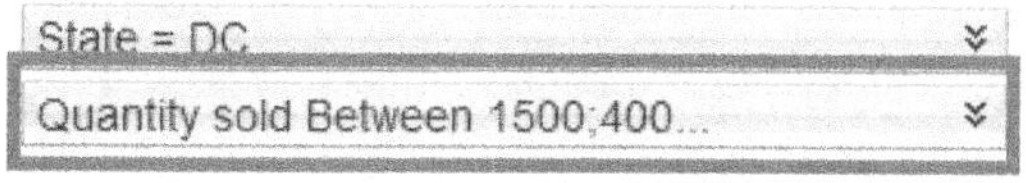
State = DC
Quantity sold Between 1500;400...

Drag ‘Quantity sold Between’ and drop
It above ‘State’:

Quantity sold Between 1500;400...

New order:

Quantity sold Between 1500;400...
State = DC

17.6 Using Tables and Charts as Input Controls

Tables and charts can be used to define Input Controls. Values selected in tables or charts are used by Web Intelligence to filter the dependant report elements.

For example, we can use a table to define an input control and then assign the control to a chart. When we select (by clicking on values) cells, rows or columns in the table then the chart will be filtered accordingly.

Practical example of using both tables and charts as Input Controls are discussed next.

17.6.1 Example of a Table Input Control

1. Modify your existing query, or create a new Web Intelligence document with the following objects (using the ‘eFashion’ universe).

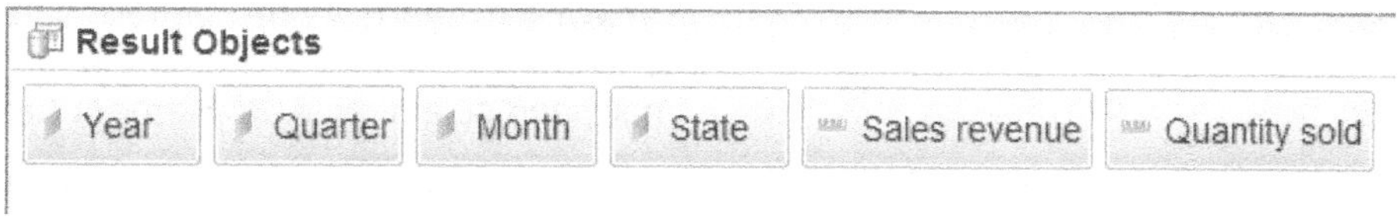
Result Objects
Year
Quarter
Month
State
Sales revenue
Quantity sold

2. Create the following table and chart (use a new report tab if you have decided not to create a new document):

   We have a vertical table (showing [Year], [State], [Quantity sold]) and a stacked column chart (showing [Year], [Month], [State], [Quantity sold]):

Year	State	Quantity sold
2004	California	11,304
2004	Colorado	2,971
2004	DC	4,681
2004	Florida	2,585
2004	Illinois	4,713
2004	Massachusetts	1,505
2004	New York	10,802
2004	Texas	14,517
2005	California	17,001
2005	Colorado	4,700
2005	DC	7,572
2005	Florida	3,852
2005	Illinois	6,744

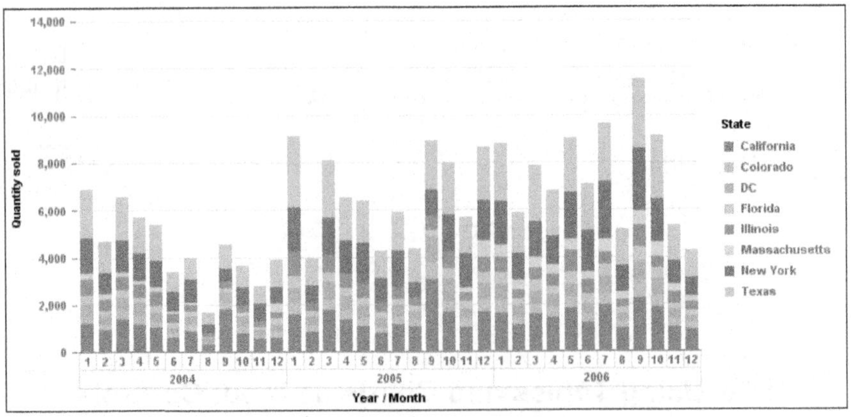

14,000
12,000
10,000
8,000
6,000
4,000
2,000
0
Quantity sold
2004
2005
2006
Year / Month
State
California
Colorado
DC
Florida
Illinois
Massachusetts
New York
Texas

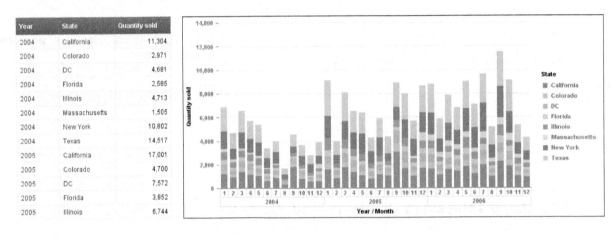

   The vertical table is named vt_YearState and the chart is named cht_YearState.

3. Right-click on the table and select 'Linking - Add Element Link...'

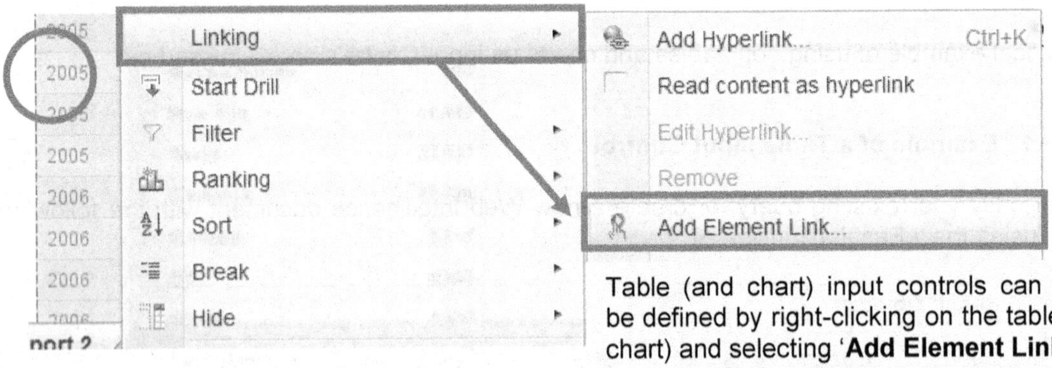

Linking
Start Drill
Filter
Ranking
Sort
Break
Hide
Add Hyperlink...
Ctrl+K
Read content as hyperlink
Edit Hyperlink...
Remove
Add Element Link...

Table (and chart) input controls can only be defined by right-clicking on the table (or chart) and selecting '**Add Element Link...**'

4. Select the dimension objects within the table that will be used to filter the data.

   You can select a 'Single object' or you can use 'All objects'.

   If you use 'All objects' then the filter will take into account the value of each dimension object in the row of data, e.g. '2004 / California'.

   If you use a single object then the filter will be based on the value of the selected object, e.g. 'California'.

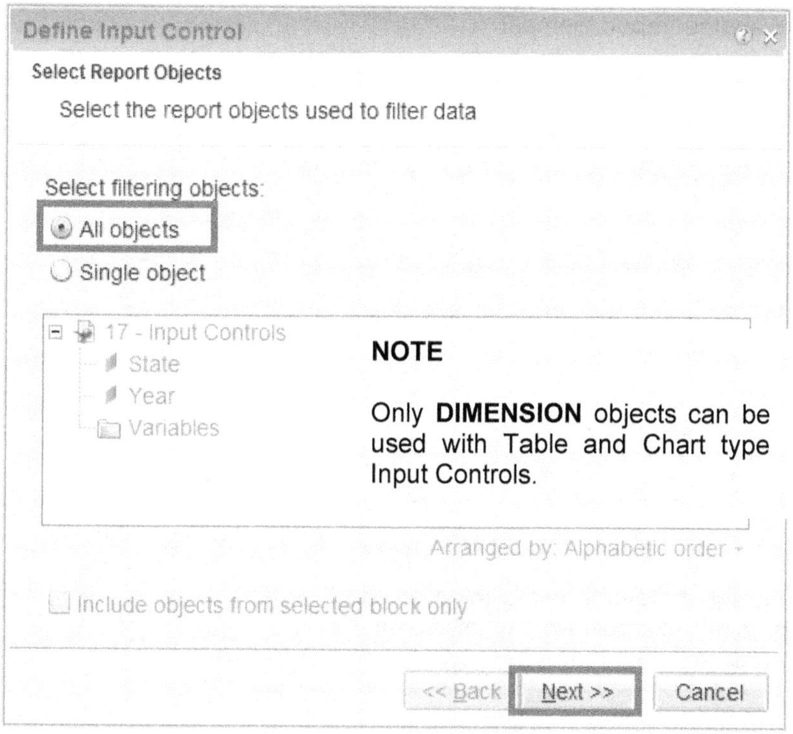
Define Input Control
Select Report Objects
Select the report objects used to filter data
Select filtering objects:
All objects
Single object
17 - Input Controls
State
Year
Variables
Arranged by: Alphabetic order
Include objects from selected block only
<< Back
Next >>
Cancel

NOTE

Only **DIMENSION** objects can be used with Table and Chart type Input Controls.

5. Set properties for the Input Control (such as Label and Description).

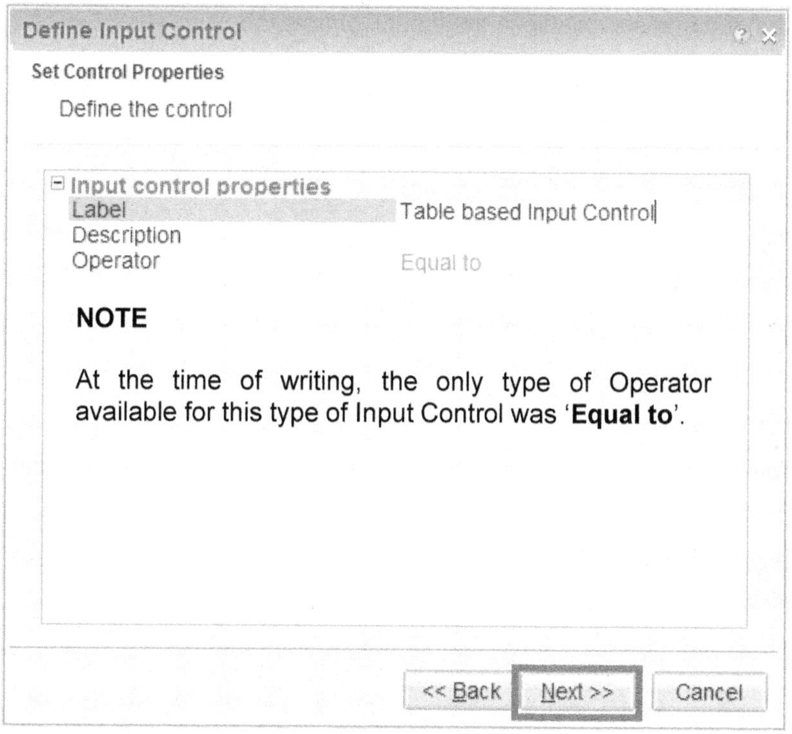
Define Input Control
Set Control Properties
Define the control
Input control properties
Label
Table based Input Control
Description
Operator
Equal to
<< Back
Next >>
Cancel

NOTE

At the time of writing, the only type of Operator available for this type of Input Control was '**Equal to**'.

6. Assign the Input Control to another report element.

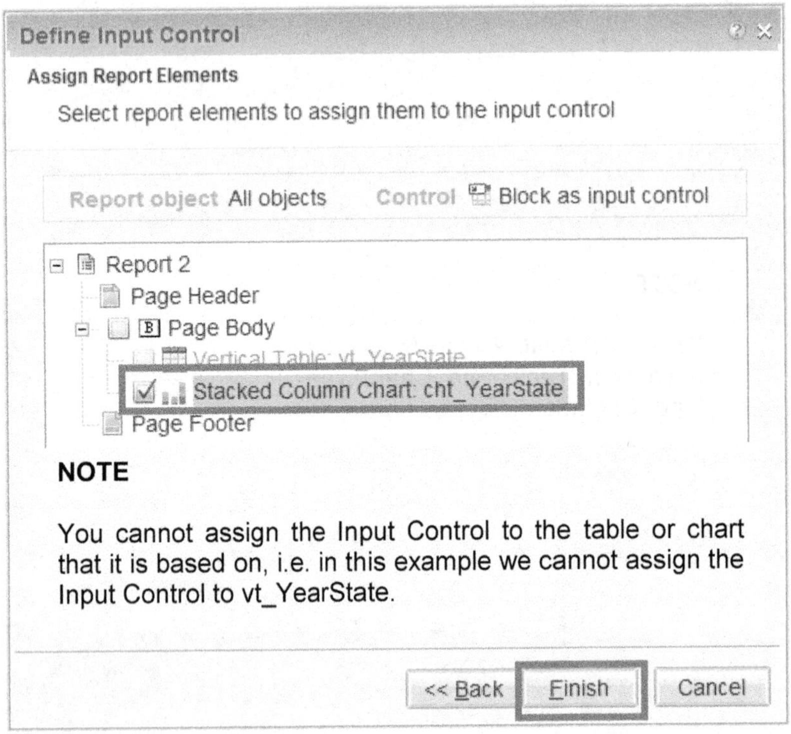
Define Input Control
Assign Report Elements
Select report elements to assign them to the input control
Report object All objects
Control Block as input control
Report 2
Page Header
Page Body
Vertical Table: vt_YearState
Stacked Column Chart: cht_YearState
Page Footer
<< Back
Finish
Cancel

NOTE

You cannot assign the Input Control to the table or chart that it is based on, i.e. in this example we cannot assign the Input Control to vt_YearState.

7. The Input Control is created and made available in the Input Controls tab.

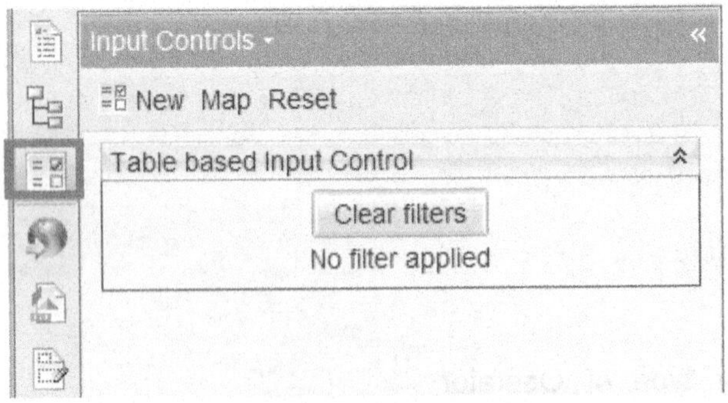
Input Controls
New
Map
Reset
Table based Input Control
Clear filters
No filter applied

8. An icon appears in the top right-hand corner of the table to indicate it is being used as a source for an Input Control.

Year	State	Quantity sold
2004	California	11,304
2004	Colorado	2,971
2004	DC	4,681
2004	Florida	2,585
2004	Illinois	4,713

9. Values appear in a pop up label when you hover over table row. Click in any cell of the row to filter the associated report element.

Year	State	Quantity sold
2004	California	11,304
2004	Colorado	2,971
2004	DC	4,681
2004	Flor[ida]	2,585
2004	Illin[ois]	4,713

Year=2004
State=DC

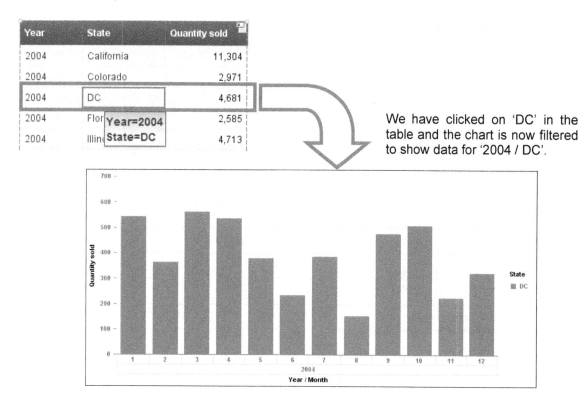

We have clicked on 'DC' in the table and the chart is now filtered to show data for '2004 / DC'.

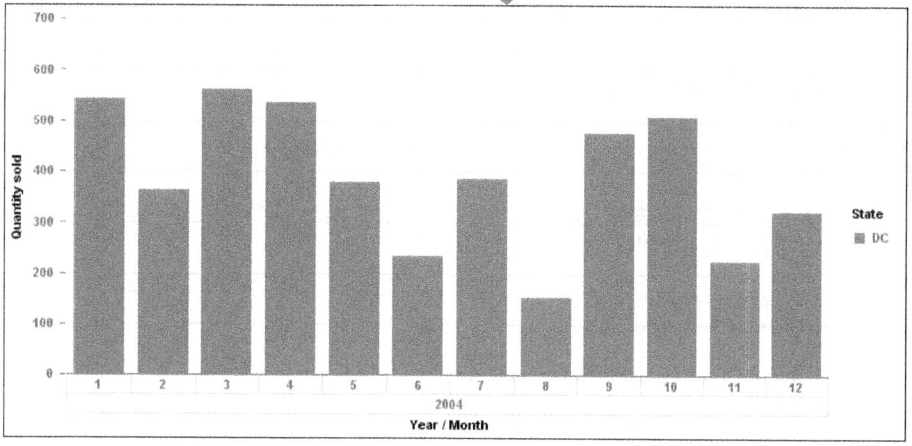
Quantity sold
700
600
500
400
300
200
100
0
1 2 3 4 5 6 7 8 9 10 11 12
2004
Year / Month
State
DC

10. The Input Control tab now shows the values being used to filter the data.

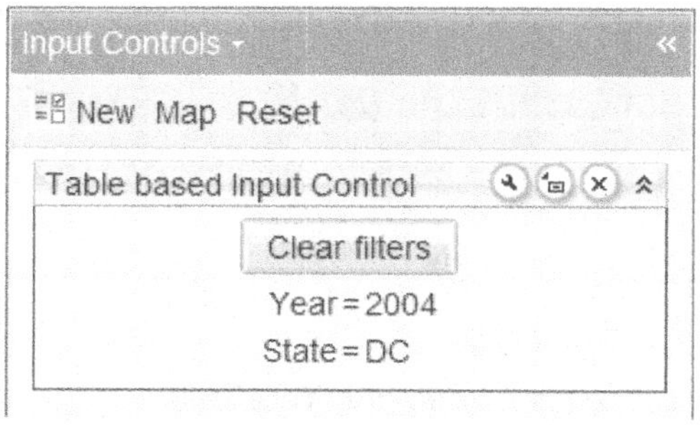
Input Controls
New Map Reset
Table based Input Control
Clear filters
Year = 2004
State = DC

'Clear filters' will reset the Input Control.

The Input Control can also be edited/removed using the other buttons, etc.

NOTE – The source table will not be filtered so you can keep clicking and the Input Control will keep using the new values to filter the assigned report element(s).

Year	State	Quantity sold
2004	California	11,304
2004	Colorado	2,971
2004	DC	4,681
2004	Florida	2,585
2004	Illinois	4,713
2004	Massachusetts	1,505
2004	New York	10,802

11. The Input Control can also be managed using right-click on the icon:

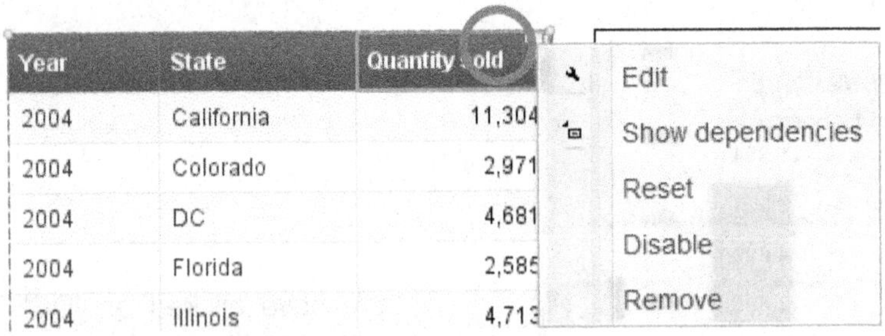
Year
State
Quantity sold
2004
California
11,304
2004
Colorado
2,971
2004
DC
4,681
2004
Florida
2,585
2004
Illinois
4,713
Edit
Show dependencies
Reset
Disable
Remove

Using the right-click menu you can 'Disable' the Input Control and the source table will then cease to act like an Input Control (until you use right-click 'Enable').

17.6.2 Example of a Chart Input Control

1. Create the following table and chart (use a new report tab):

We have a vertical table (showing [Year], [Month], [State], [Quantity sold]) and a column chart (showing [Year], [State], [Quantity sold])

Year	Month	State	Quantity sold
2004	1	California	1,185
2004	1	Colorado	309
2004	1	DC	542
2004	1	Florida	378
2004	1	Illinois	670
2004	1	Massachusetts	236
2004	1	New York	1,483
2004	1	Texas	2,094
2004	2	California	921
2004	2	Colorado	261
2004	2	DC	364
2004	2	Florida	230
2004	2	Illinois	463

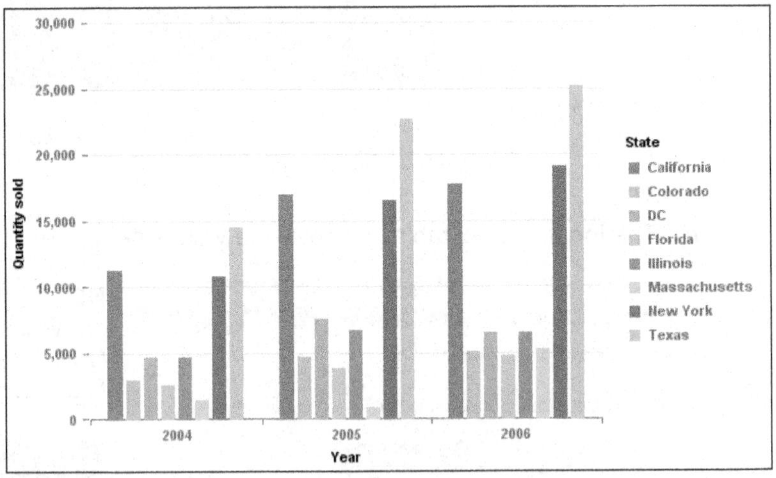
30,000
25,000
20,000
15,000
10,000
5,000
0
Quantity sold
2004
2005
2006
Year
State
California
Colorado
DC
Florida
Illinois
Massachusetts
New York
Texas

The vertical table is named vt_YearState and the chart is named cht_YearState.

2. Right-click on the chart and select 'Linking - Add Element Link...'

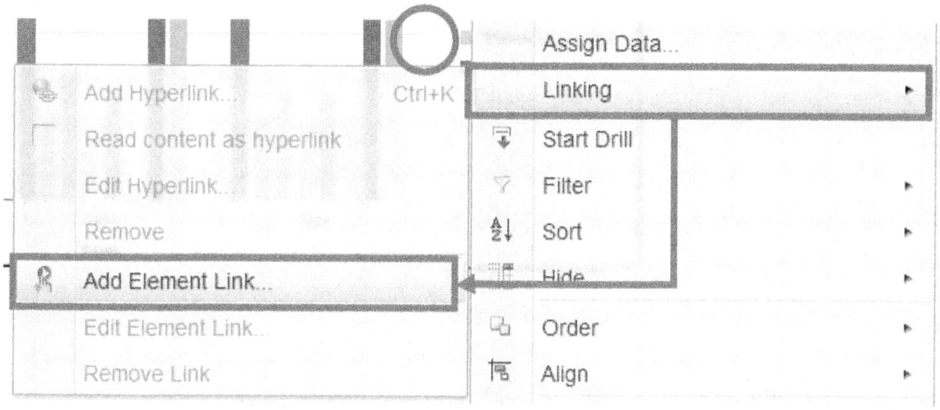
Assign Data...
Add Hyperlink...
Ctrl+K
Linking
Read content as hyperlink
Start Drill
Edit Hyperlink...
Filter
Remove
Sort
Add Element Link...
Hide
Edit Element Link...
Order
Remove Link
Align

3. Select the dimension objects within the chart that will be used to filter the data.

   You can select a 'Single object' or you can use 'All objects'. If you use 'All objects' then the filter will take into account the value of each dimension object in the row of data, e.g. 'California / 2004'. If you use a single object then the filter will be based on the value of the selected object, e.g. 'California'.

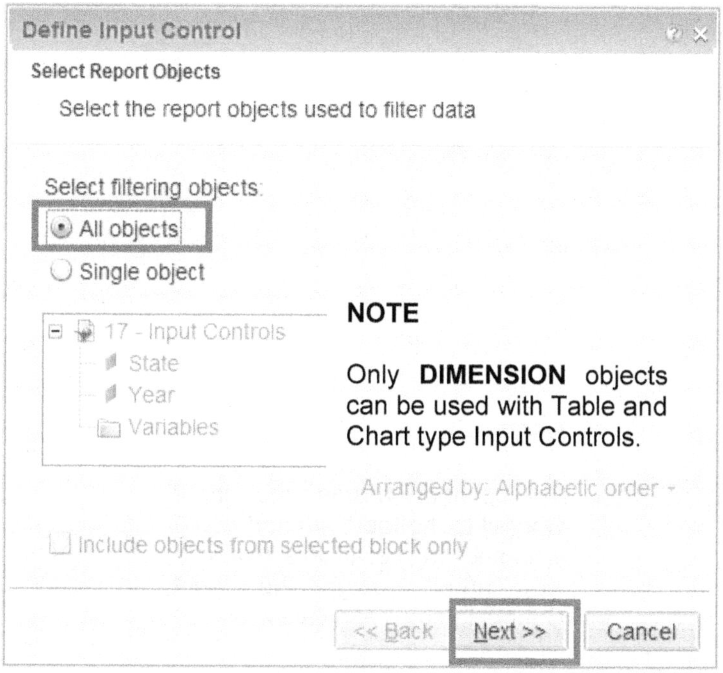
Define Input Control
Select Report Objects
Select the report objects used to filter data
Select filtering objects:
All objects
Single object
17 - Input Controls
State
Year
Variables
NOTE
Only DIMENSION objects can be used with Table and Chart type Input Controls.
Arranged by: Alphabetic order
Include objects from selected block only
<< Back
Next >>
Cancel

4. Set properties for the Input Control (such as Label and Description).

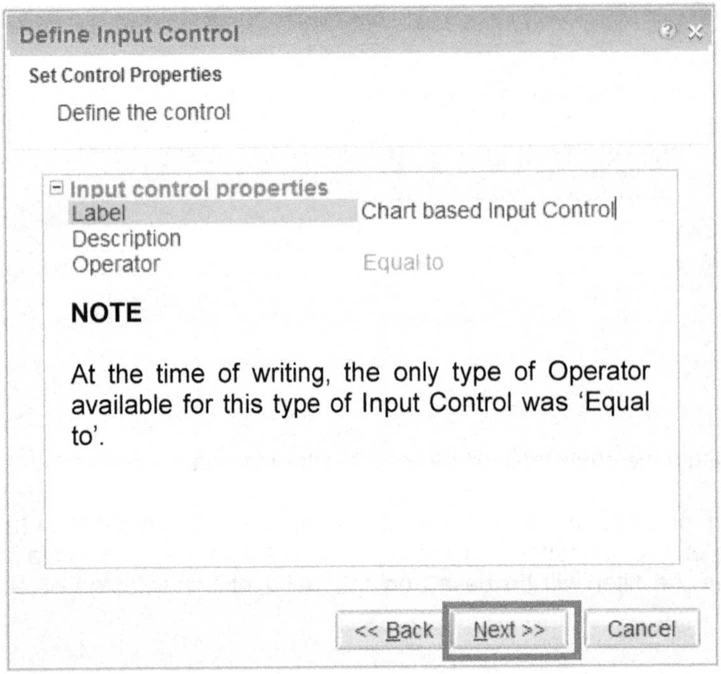
Define Input Control
Set Control Properties
Define the control
Input control properties
Label
Chart based Input Control
Description
Operator
Equal to
<< Back
Next >>
Cancel

NOTE

At the time of writing, the only type of Operator available for this type of Input Control was 'Equal to'.

5. Assign the Input Control to another report element.

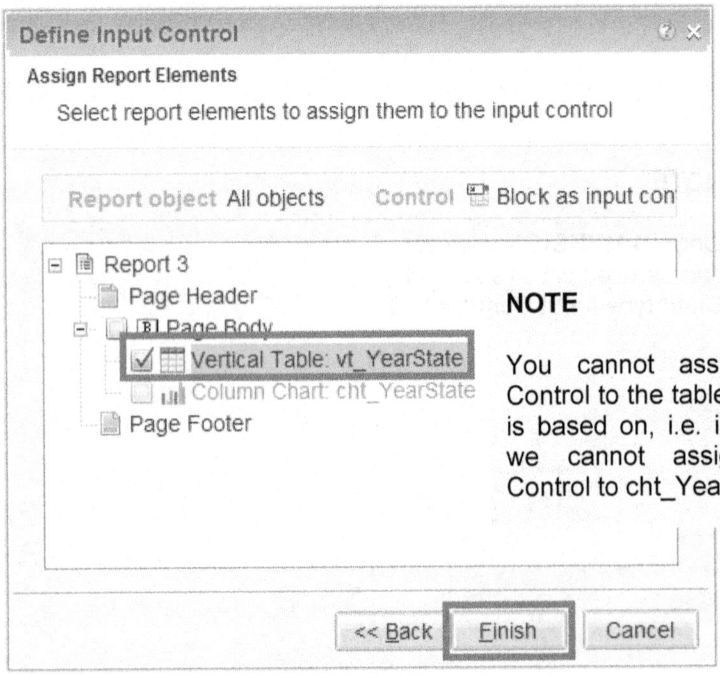
Define Input Control
Assign Report Elements
Select report elements to assign them to the input control
Report object All objects
Control Block as input con
Report 3
Page Header
Page Body
Vertical Table: vt_YearState
Column Chart: cht_YearState
Page Footer
<< Back
Finish
Cancel

NOTE

You cannot assign the Input Control to the table or chart that it is based on, i.e. in this example we cannot assign the Input Control to cht_YearState.

6. The Input Control is created and made available in the Input Controls tab.

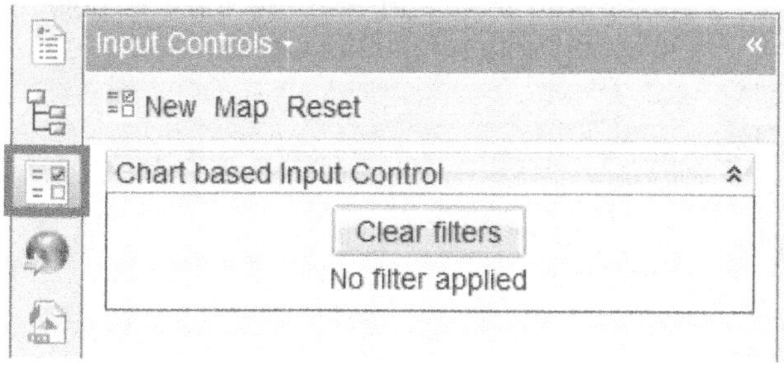
Input Controls
New Map Reset
Chart based Input Control
Clear filters
No filter applied

7. An icon appears in the top right-hand corner of the chart to indicate it is being used as a source for an Input Control.

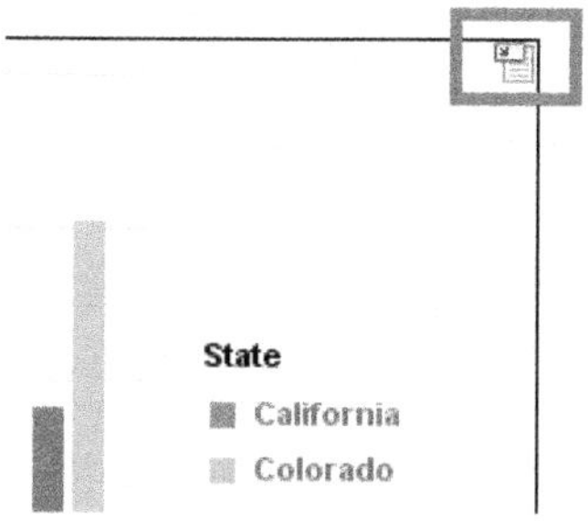
State
California
Colorado

8. Hovering over legend values and the plot area in a chart highlights the values that will be used by the Input Control to filter the data.

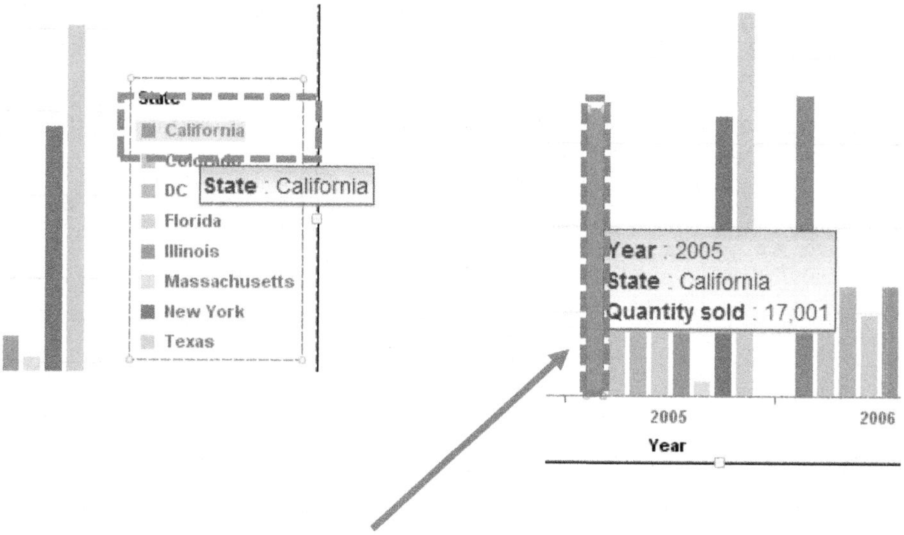
State
California
DC
State : California
Florida
Illinois
Massachusetts
New York
Texas
Year : 2005
State : California
Quantity sold : 17,001
2005
2006
Year

9. Clicking in the legend or plot area filters the associated report elements (shown below).

Year	Month	State	Quantity sold
2005	1	California	1,557
2005	2	California	842
2005	3	California	1,746
2005	4	California	1,335
2005	5	California	1,066
2005	6	California	783
2005	7	California	1,138
2005	8	California	1,086
2005	9	California	3,056
2005	10	California	1,673
2005	11	California	1,041
2005	12	California	1,678

We have clicked on ‘2005 / California’ column in the chart and the table is now showing data for ‘2005 / California’.

10. The Input Control tab now shows the values being used to filter the data.

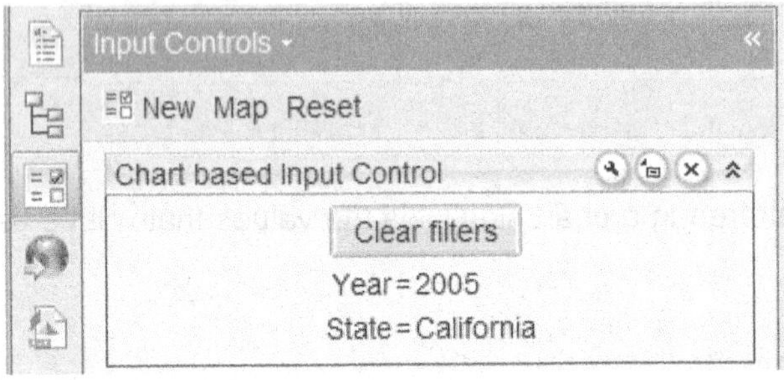
Input Controls
New Map Reset
Chart based Input Control
Clear filters
Year=2005
State=California

‘Clear filters’ will reset the Input Control.

The Input Control can also be edited/removed using the other buttons, etc.

NOTE – The source chart will not be filtered so you can keep clicking and the Input Control will keep using the new values to filter the assigned report element.

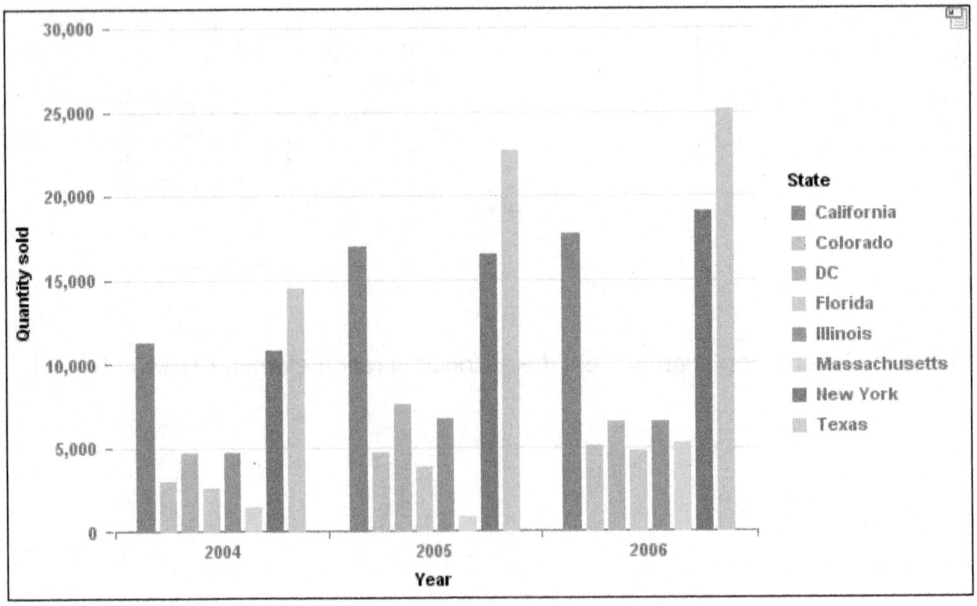
30,000
25,000
20,000
15,000
10,000
5,000
0
Quantity sold
2004
2005
2006
Year
State
California
Colorado
DC
Florida
Illinois
Massachusetts
New York
Texas

11. The Input Control can be managed using right-click on the icon:

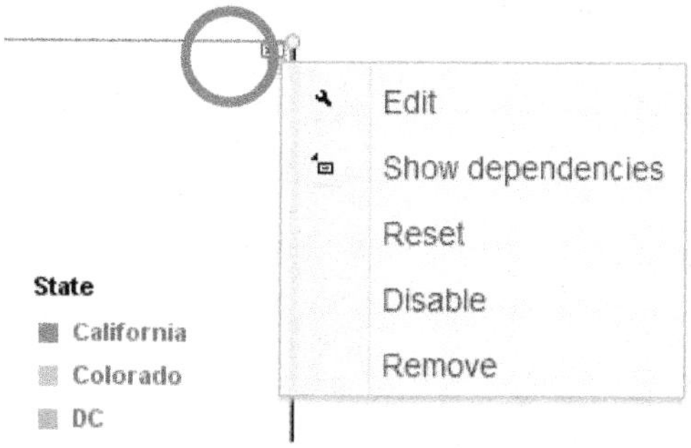
Edit
Show dependencies
Reset
Disable
Remove
State
California
Colorado
DC

Using right-click menu you can 'Disable' the Input Control and the source chart will then cease to act like an Input Control (until you use right-click 'Enable').

17.6.3 Notes on Table and Chart Type Input Controls

The following are points of note concerning the use of table and chart type Input Controls.

1. If the table or chart used for an input control is deleted then the Input Control displays the message 'The table or chart is not in the report'.

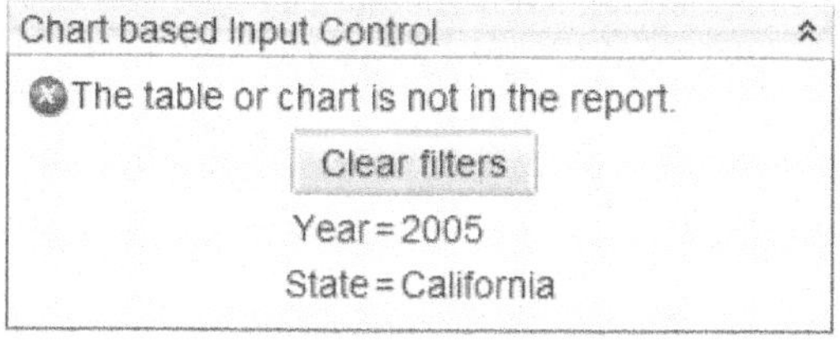
Chart based Input Control
The table or chart is not in the report.
Clear filters
Year=2005
State=California

2. The filtering dimensions used in table or chart type Input Controls must remain in the source table or chart. If the source dimension(s) are removed then the Input Control displays the message 'The filtering dimensions are not in the table or chart'.

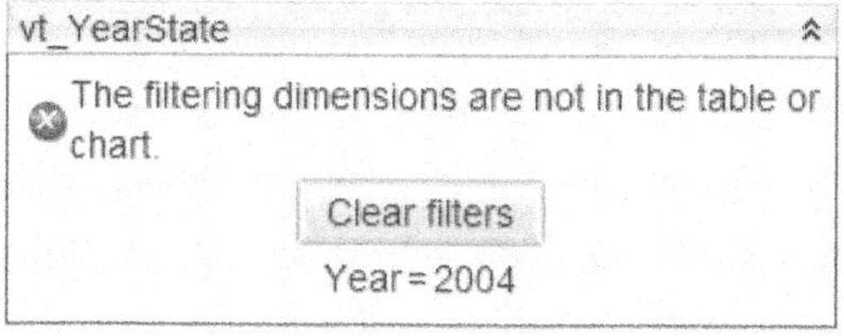
vt_YearState
The filtering dimensions are not in the table or chart.
Clear filters
Year=2004

Adding the dimensions back into the table or chart will enable the Input Control to be used again.

3. If the table or chart being used an Input Control is deleted then the 'The table or chart is not in the report' is displayed.

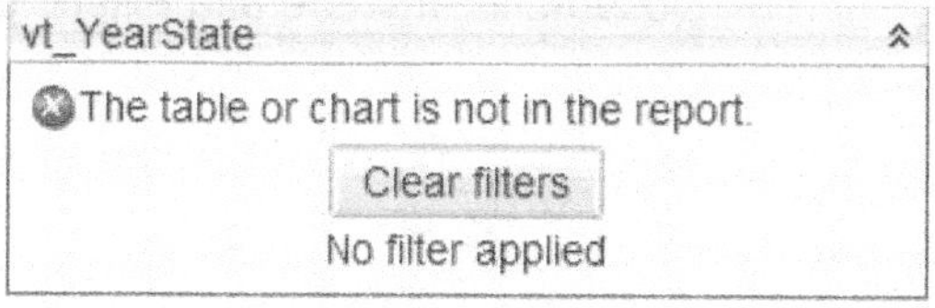
vt_YearState
The table or chart is not in the report.
Clear filters
No filter applied

4. If Drill Mode is being used on the report then drilling takes precedence over Input Controls therefore the Input Control displays the message 'Control not usable while the report is in drill mode'.

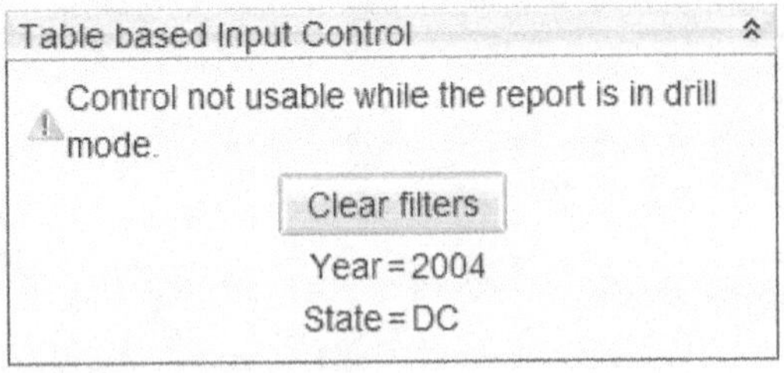
Table based Input Control
Control not usable while the report is in drill mode.
Clear filters
Year=2004
State=DC

Drill Mode is another way of filtering data within the report and is discussed in the session 'Exploring Report Data using Drill Mode'.

17.7 Map View of Input Controls

It is possible view the Input Controls used in a report by using the Input Controls tab and then clicking on 'Map' and then click on 'Input controls' as shown below.

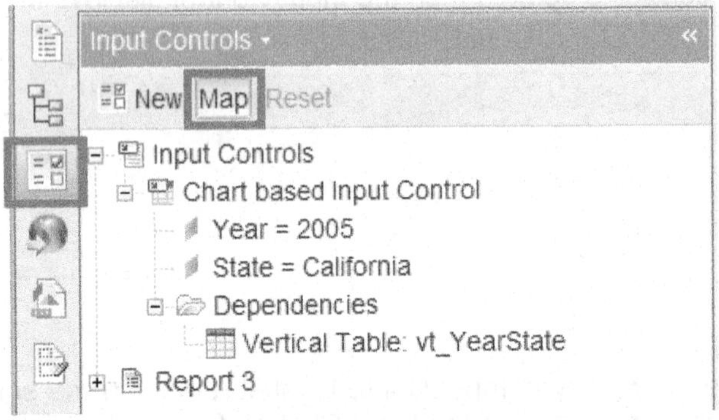
Input Controls
New
Map
Reset
Input Controls
Chart based Input Control
Year = 2005
State = California
Dependencies
Vertical Table: vt_YearState
Report 3

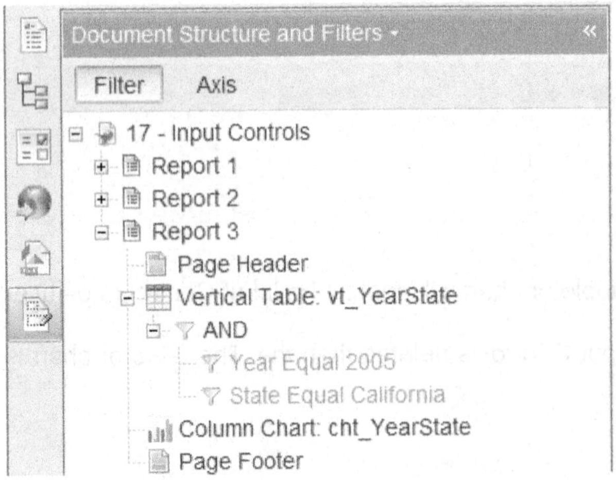
Document Structure and Filters
Filter
Axis
17 - Input Controls
Report 1
Report 2
Report 3
Page Header
Vertical Table: vt_YearState
AND
Year Equal 2005
State Equal California
Column Chart: cht_YearState
Page Footer

As previously described, Input Controls are effectively filters.

Therefore the filter(s) being applied by Input Controls also show up in the 'Document Structure and Filters' tab

17.8 General Notes on Input Controls

We have demonstrated how to define Input Controls to enable users to interactively filter data in reports. Some points of note:

1. It is not readily visible to the user that Input Controls have been defined unless the 'Input Controls' tab is used. This does not apply to table and chart type Input Controls as they have an icon in the top right-hand corner to signify an input control has been defined.

2. It is possible to define multiple Input Controls in a report using the same objects but care should be taken to ensure the different controls do not conflict with one another.

3. A table or chart can only be used as a source for one Input Control, whereas objects can be used in multiple Input Controls.

4. Input Controls are only valid for a single report (tab) that they are defined on.

5. When a report tab containing Input Controls is duplicated then the new tab is empty of Input Controls.

18 Ranking Data within Reports

This session describes ranking data in a Web Intelligence report.

Ranking allows you to isolate the top and bottom records in a data set based on a variety of criteria.

> For example, if you have a block showing countries and associated revenues, ranking allows you to rank the data in the block to show the top 3 countries only, based on the revenue they generate.
>
> Therefore, ranking is another way of filtering data within a report.

Web Intelligence allows you to rank data in many ways using the 'Ranking' button:

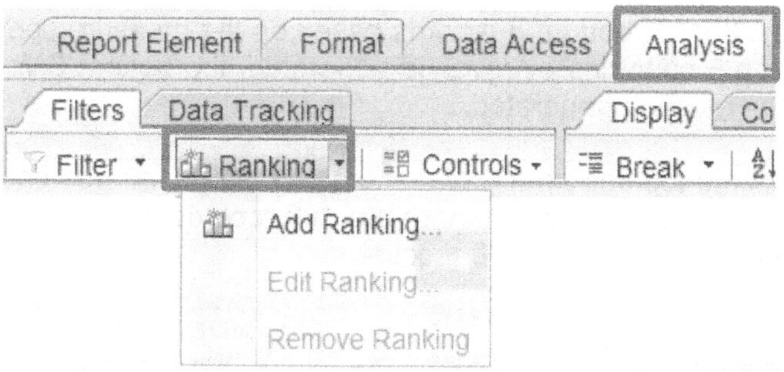
Report Element
Format
Data Access
Analysis
Filters
Data Tracking
Display
Co
Filter
Ranking
Controls
Break
Add Ranking...
Edit Ranking...
Remove Ranking

Count – the top and/or bottom *n* records based on the value of a measure.

Percentage – the top and/or bottom *n%* of the total number of records based on the value of a measure (as a percentage of the total value of the measure).

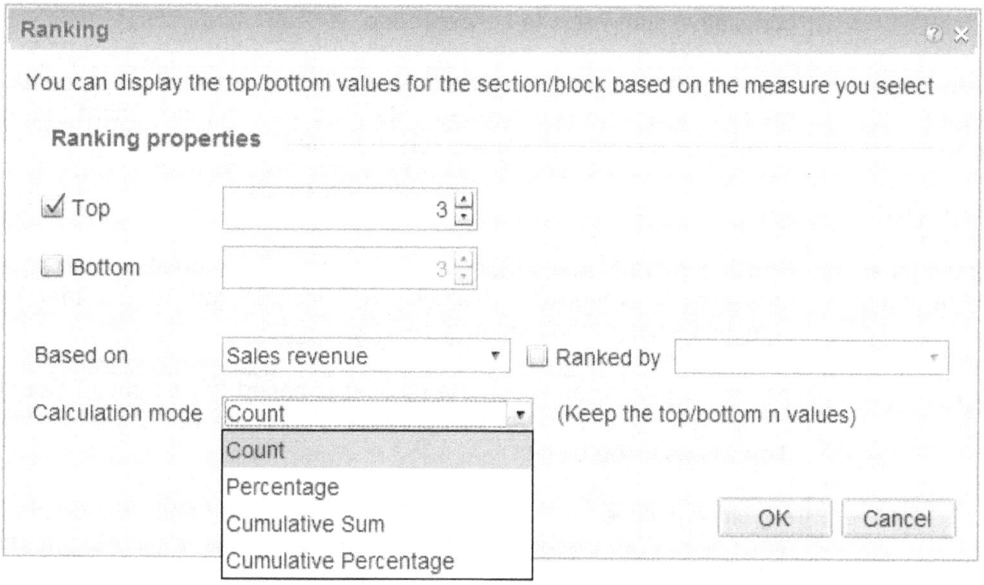
Ranking
You can display the top/bottom values for the section/block based on the measure you select
Ranking properties
Top
3
Bottom
3
Based on
Sales revenue
Ranked by
Calculation mode
Count
(Keep the top/bottom n values)
Count
Percentage
Cumulative Sum
Cumulative Percentage
OK
Cancel

Cumulative Sum – the top and/or bottom *n* records based on the cumulative sum of a measure.

Cumulative Percentage – the top and/or bottom *n* records based on the value of a measure as a cumulative percentage of the total value of the measure.

18.1 Ranking Properties

Top	Returns the top **n** records if Calculation mode is Count or Cumulative Sum. Returns the top **n%** records if Calculation mode is Percentage or Cumulative Percentage.
Bottom	Returns the bottom **n** records if Calculation mode is Count or Cumulative Sum. Returns the bottom **n%** records if Calculation mode is Percentage or Cumulative Percentage.
Based on	Measure on which the ranking is based.
Calculation mode = Count	Ranking returns the top/bottom **n** records based on the measure specified. For example, the top 3 countries by revenue generated, the bottom 3 year/quarter combinations by revenue generated.
Calculation mode = Percentage	Ranking returns the top/bottom **n%** of the total number of records based on the measure specified. For example, if there are 100 records and you rank the top 10% then ranking returns the top 10 records.
Calculation mode = Cumulative Sum	Ranking returns the top records until the cumulative sum of the measure specified is exceeded. Ranking will omit the record that causes the cumulative sum value to be exceeded. Or Ranking returns the bottom records until the cumulative sum of the measure specified is exceeded. Ranking will include the record that causes the cumulative sum value to be exceeded.
Calculation mode = Cumulative Percentage Cumulative Sum of the measure, represented as a Percentage of the Total	Ranking returns the top records until the cumulative percentage of the measure specified is exceeded. Ranking will omit the record that causes the cumulative percentage value to be exceeded. Or Ranking returns the bottom records until the cumulative percentage of the measure is exceeded. Ranking will include the record that causes the cumulative percentage value to be exceeded.
Ranked by	The dimension(s) on which the ranking is based (for example, Country). If you do not specify a value for this parameter then the ranking is based on all the dimensions in the block. e.g. If you have a block with Year and Quarter and you do not specify a dimension, Web Intelligence uses the values of the measure generated by the Year/Quarter combination. Typically, this will be left blank, but you might force the ranking to be based on a single dimension.

18.2 Ranking Examples

Let us look at an example of each type of Ranking.

18.2.1 Calculation mode = Count

You can use this ranking to find the Top/Bottom records based on the value of a measure, e.g. Top 5 and Bottom 5 rows based on Sales revenue.

1. Create the following query using the 'eFashion' universe and run it.

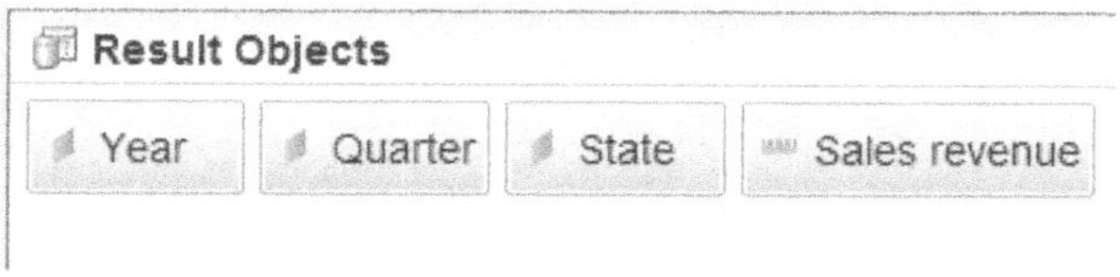
Result Objects
Year
Quarter
State
Sales revenue

2. Apply a descending sort on [Sales revenue]:

Year	Quarter	State	Sales revenue
2005	Q4	Texas	$1,138,056
2006	Q1	Texas	$1,102,481
2006	Q2	Texas	$1,088,221
2006	Q3	Texas	$1,032,629
2005	Q1	Texas	$1,014,293
2006	Q4	Texas	$961,768
2006	Q3	New York	$914,247
2005	Q4	New York	$885,800
2006	Q2	New York	$855,617
2005	Q4	California	$842,267
2005	Q2	Texas	$795,979
2006	Q2	California	$789,398
2005	Q3	Texas	$784,560

Top 10 records end here.

3. Remove the descending sort on [Sales revenue].

4. Click in any cell of the [Sales revenue] column and then click on 'Add Ranking…' as shown below.

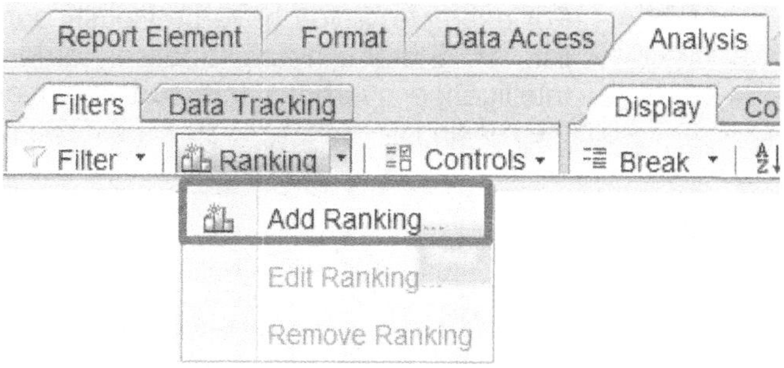
Report Element
Format
Data Access
Analysis
Filters
Data Tracking
Display
Co
Filter
Ranking
Controls
Break
Add Ranking...
Edit Ranking...
Remove Ranking

Or you can use right-click menu:

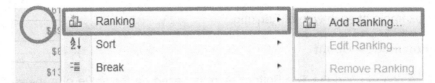
Ranking
Sort
Break
Add Ranking...
Edit Ranking...
Remove Ranking

5. Set the Ranking properties as shown below and click 'OK'.

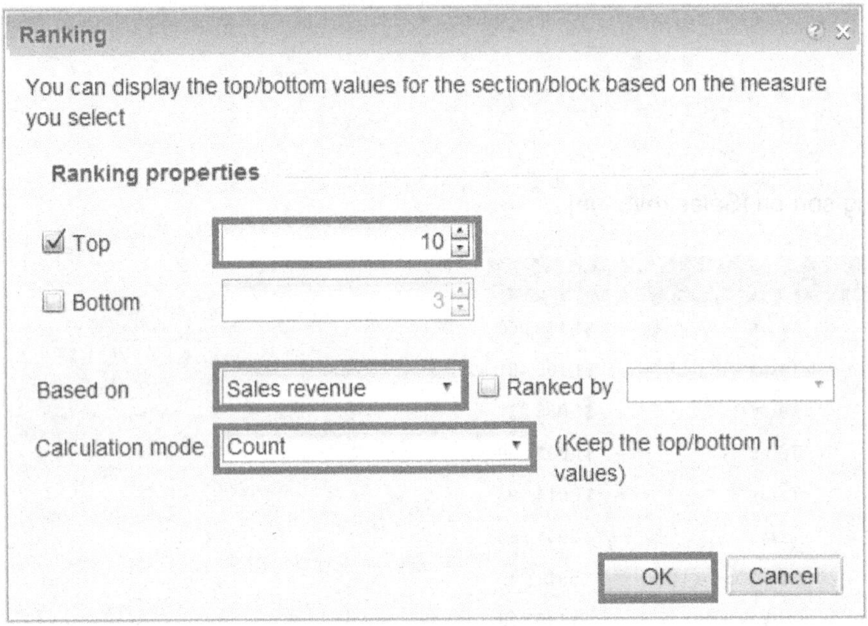
Ranking
You can display the top/bottom values for the section/block based on the measure you select
Ranking properties
Top
10
Bottom
3
Based on
Sales revenue
Ranked by
Calculation mode
Count
(Keep the top/bottom n values)
OK
Cancel

6. Block of data now only shows the top 10 rows.

Year	Quarter	State	Sales revenue
2005	Q4	Texas	$1,138,056
2006	Q1	Texas	$1,102,481
2006	Q2	Texas	$1,088,221
2006	Q3	Texas	$1,032,629
2005	Q1	Texas	$1,014,293
2006	Q4	Texas	$961,768
2006	Q3	New York	$914,247
2005	Q4	New York	$885,800
2006	Q2	New York	$855,617
2005	Q4	California	$842,267

This will always show the top 10 whenever the data changes in the underlying query.

To calculate this ranking, you can imagine Web Intelligence:

1. Sorts the records in descending order based on [Sales revenue].
2. Displays the Top 10 records.

NOTE – The sorts that Web Intelligence applies in rankings take precedence over sorts that you have previously applied to your data. For example, if you have previously sorted the list of States in alphabetical order, Web Intelligence overrides this sort when applying the ranking.

7. To edit a ranking (or remove a ranking):

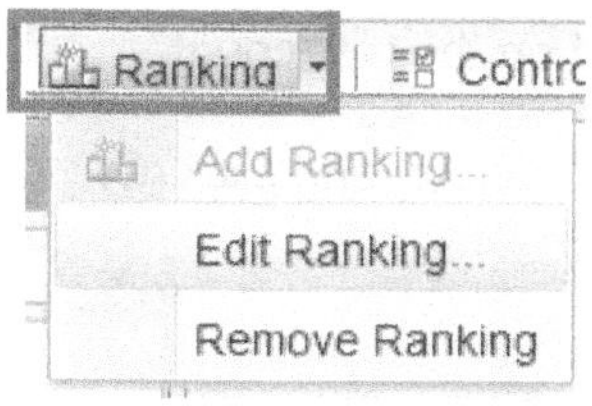
Ranking
Contrc
Add Ranking...
Edit Ranking...
Remove Ranking

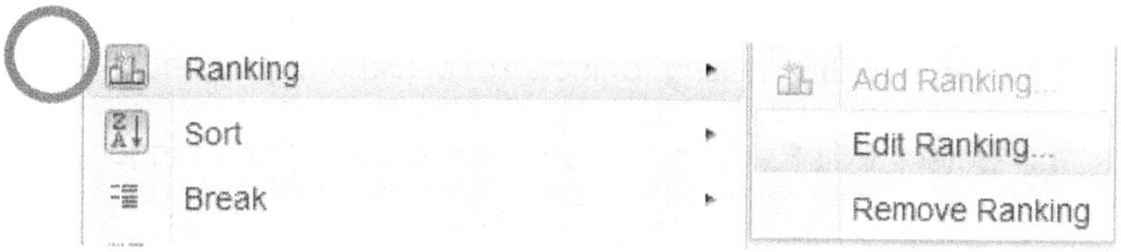
Ranking
Sort
Break
Add Ranking...
Edit Ranking...
Remove Ranking

Select 'Edit Ranking...' or 'Remove Ranking' from the toolbox

Select 'Edit Ranking...' or 'Remove Ranking' using right-click menus

8. Select 'Edit Ranking...' and then apply the following settings:

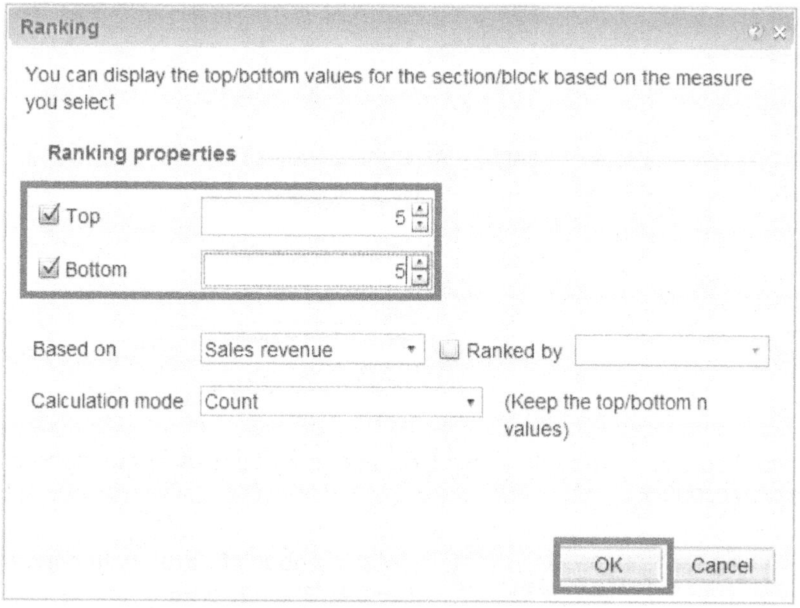
Ranking
You can display the top/bottom values for the section/block based on the measure you select
Ranking properties
Top
5
Bottom
5
Based on
Sales revenue
Ranked by
Calculation mode
Count
(Keep the top/bottom n values)
OK
Cancel

Ranking will return the Top 5 records and the Bottom 5 records within the block of data.

Year	Quarter	State	Sales revenue
2005	Q4	Texas	$1,138,056
2006	Q1	Texas	$1,102,481
2006	Q2	Texas	$1,088,221
2006	Q3	Texas	$1,032,629
2005	Q1	Texas	$1,014,293
2004	Q3	Colorado	$85,621
2004	Q2	Massachusetts	$70,903
2004	Q4	Massachusetts	$63,255
2004	Q3	Florida	$50,926
2004	Q3	Massachusetts	$12,066

To calculate this ranking, you can imagine Web Intelligence:

1. Sorts the records in descending order based on [Sales revenue].
2. Displays the Top 5 records.
3. Displays the Bottom 5 records.

18.2.2 Calculation mode = Percentage

You can use this ranking to find the Top/Bottom percent of records based on the row count.

1. Select 'Edit Ranking…' then change the ranking properties (as shown below) and click 'OK':

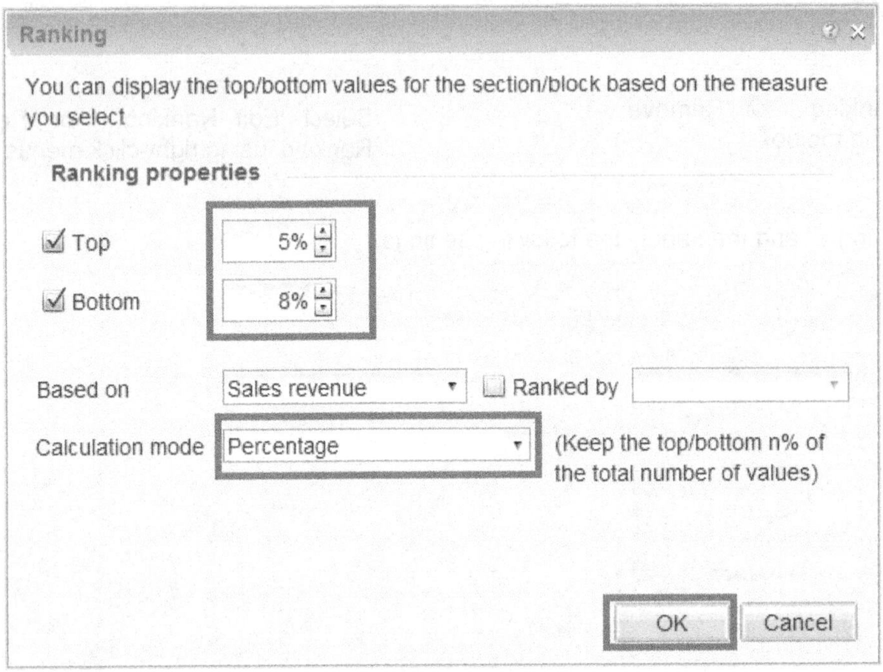
Ranking
You can display the top/bottom values for the section/block based on the measure you select
Ranking properties
Top
5%
Bottom
8%
Based on
Sales revenue
Ranked by
Calculation mode
Percentage
(Keep the top/bottom n% of the total number of values)
OK
Cancel

Ranking will return the Top 5% of records (based on the row count) and the Bottom 8% of records (based on the row count).

Year	Quarter	State	Sales revenue
2005	Q4	Texas	$1,138,056
2006	Q1	Texas	$1,102,481
2006	Q2	Texas	$1,088,221
2006	Q3	Texas	$1,032,629
2004	Q4	Florida	$96,359
2004	Q1	Massachusetts	$92,596
2004	Q3	Colorado	$85,621
2004	Q2	Massachusetts	$70,903
2004	Q4	Massachusetts	$63,255
2004	Q3	Florida	$50,926
2004	Q3	Massachusetts	$12,066

Total number of rows in this example (before ranking) is 93.

Top 5% calculated as:

(93 / 100) * 5 = 4.65

Top 4 rows are returned.

Bottom 8% calculated as:

(93 / 100) * 8 = 7.44

Bottom 7 rows are returned.

18.2.3 Calculation mode = Cumulative Sum (Top n Ranking)

You can use this ranking to find all the records until a limit is reached from the top down, e.g. Web Intelligence will apply a descending sort based on the value of a measure. The values will then be added per row until the limit you specify is breached. The rows within the limit specified will be displayed and the rest will be filtered out.

1. Select 'Edit Ranking…' then change the ranking properties (as shown below) and click 'OK':

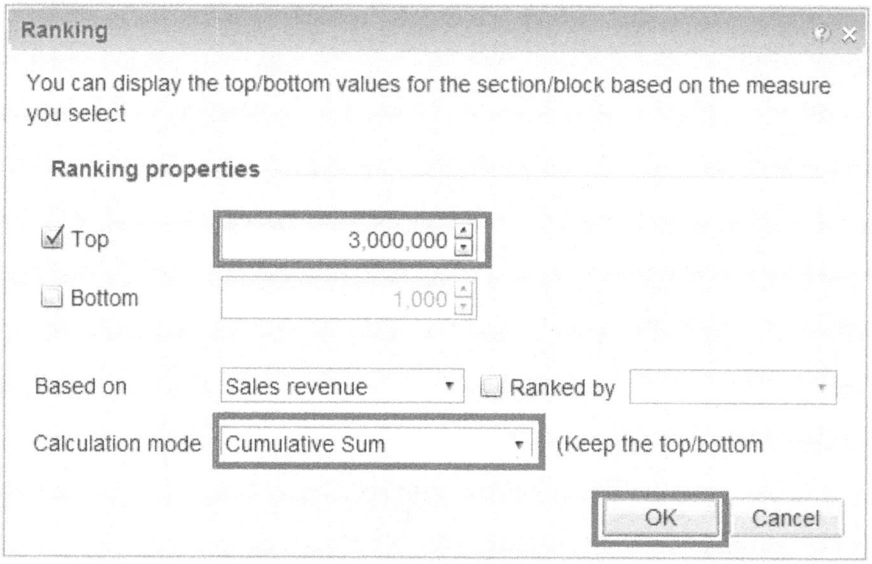
Ranking
You can display the top/bottom values for the section/block based on the measure you select
Ranking properties
Top
3,000,000
Bottom
1,000
Based on
Sales revenue
Ranked by
Calculation mode
Cumulative Sum
(Keep the top/bottom
OK
Cancel

Ranking will return the Top records until the Cumulative Sum reaches 3,000,000 (3 million).

Year	Quarter	State	Sales revenue
2005	Q4	Texas	$1,138,056
2006	Q1	Texas	$1,102,481

The third row is not shown because it causes the Cumulative Sum to exceed 3,000,000.

18.2.4 Calculation mode = Cumulative Sum (Bottom n Ranking)

You can use this ranking to find all the records until a limit is reached from the bottom up, e.g. Web Intelligence will apply an ascending sort based on the value of a measure. The values will then be added per row until the limit you specify is breached. The rows within the limit specified will be displayed and the rest will be filtered out.

1. Select 'Edit Ranking…' then change the ranking properties (as shown below) and click 'OK':

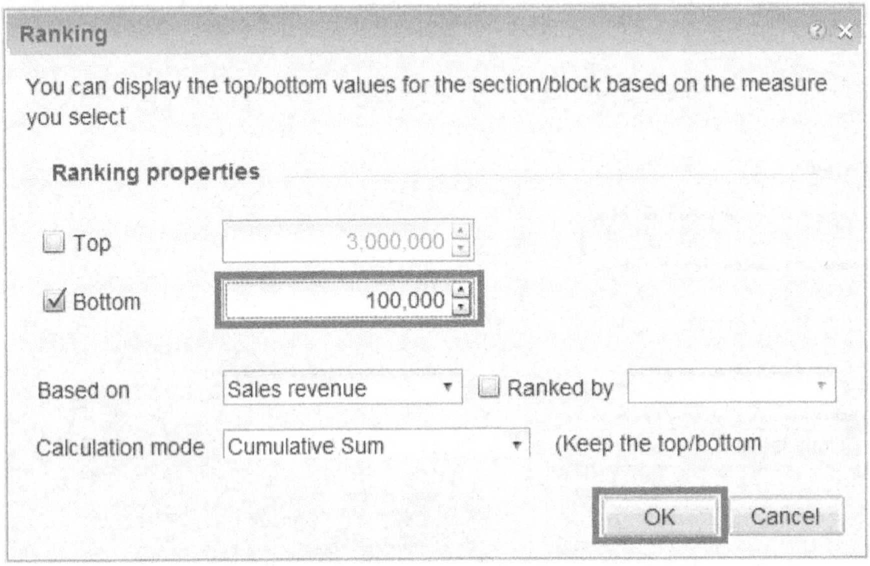
Ranking
You can display the top/bottom values for the section/block based on the measure you select
Ranking properties
Top
3,000,000
Bottom
100,000
Based on
Sales revenue
Ranked by
Calculation mode
Cumulative Sum
(Keep the top/bottom
OK
Cancel

Ranking will return the Bottom records until the Cumulative Sum reaches 100,000 (one hundred thousand).

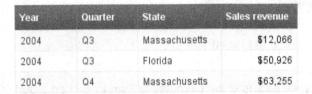

Year	Quarter	State	Sales revenue
2004	Q3	Massachusetts	$12,066
2004	Q3	Florida	$50,926
2004	Q4	Massachusetts	$63,255

The third row is shown because it causes the Cumulative Sum to exceed 100,000.

18.2.5 Calculation mode = Cumulative Percentage (Top n Ranking)

You can use this ranking to find all the records until a percentage limit is reached from the top down, e.g. Web Intelligence will apply a descending sort based on the value of a measure. The values will then be added one row at a time and after each row has been added, the sum will be divided by the total of the measure to calculate the cumulative percentage. This will continue until the percentage limit you specify is breached. The rows within the limit specified will be displayed and the rest will be filtered out.

1. Select 'Edit Ranking…' then change the ranking properties (as shown below) and click 'OK':

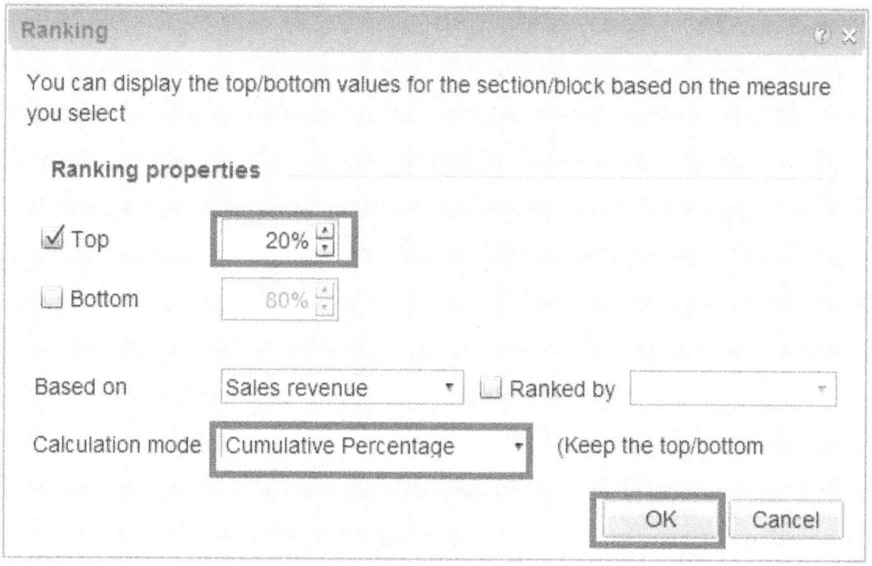
Ranking
You can display the top/bottom values for the section/block based on the measure you select
Ranking properties
Top
20%
Bottom
80%
Based on
Sales revenue
Ranked by
Calculation mode
Cumulative Percentage
(Keep the top/bottom
OK
Cancel

Ranking will return the records that contribute to the Top 20% of the Cumulative Sum.

Year	Quarter	State	Sales revenue
2005	Q4	Texas	$1,138,056
2006	Q1	Texas	$1,102,481
2006	Q2	Texas	$1,088,221
2006	Q3	Texas	$1,032,629
2005	Q1	Texas	$1,014,293
2006	Q4	Texas	$961,768
2006	Q3	New York	$914,247
		Sum:	**$7,251,694**

Total for the data within the report is 36,387,512.

20% of this total is 7,277,502.

Year	Sales revenue
2004	$8,096,124
2005	$13,232,246
2006	$15,059,143
Sum:	**$36,387,512**

In this example Web Intelligence displays the records in descending order (based on the selected measure) until the Cumulative Percentage is exceeded.

The record that causes the Cumulative Sum to be exceeded is excluded and therefore our total of 7,251,694 is lower than the 7,277,502 that makes up the 20%.

18.2.6 Calculation mode = Cumulative Percentage (Bottom n Ranking)

You can use this ranking to find all the records until a percentage limit is reached from the bottom up, e.g. Web Intelligence will apply an ascending sort based on the value of a measure. The values will then be added one row at a time and after each row has been added, the sum will be divided by the total of the measure to calculate the cumulative percentage. This will continue until the percentage limit you specify is breached. The rows within the limit specified will be displayed and the rest will be filtered out.

1. Select 'Edit Ranking…' then change the ranking properties (as shown below) and click 'OK':

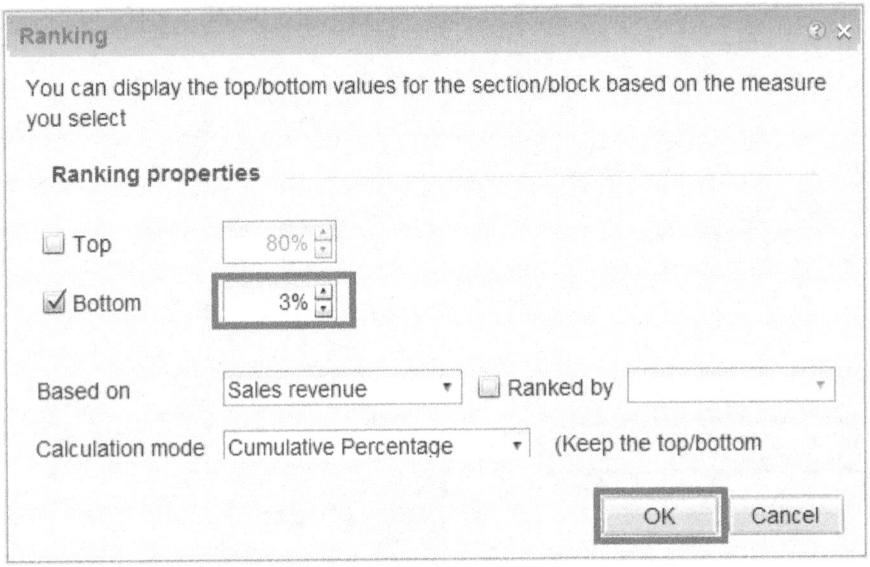
Ranking
You can display the top/bottom values for the section/block based on the measure you select
Ranking properties
Top
80%
Bottom
3%
Based on
Sales revenue
Ranked by
Calculation mode
Cumulative Percentage
(Keep the top/bottom
OK
Cancel

Ranking will return the records that contribute to the Bottom 3% of the Cumulative Sum.

Year	Quarter	State	Sales revenue
2004	Q3	Massachusetts	$12,066
2004	Q3	Florida	$50,926
2004	Q4	Massachusetts	$63,255
2004	Q2	Massachusetts	$70,903
2004	Q3	Colorado	$85,621
2004	Q1	Massachusetts	$92,596
2004	Q4	Florida	$96,359
2004	Q4	Colorado	$101,807
2004	Q3	Illinois	$107,006
2004	Q2	Florida	$121,170
2005	Q3	Florida	$121,314
2004	Q2	Colorado	$129,076
2004	Q3	DC	$131,687
		Sum:	**$1,183,785**

Total for the block is 36,387,512.

3% of this total is 1,091,625.

In this example Web Intelligence displays the records in ascending order (based on the selected measure) until the Cumulative Sum is exceeded.

Year	Sales revenue
2004	$8,096,124
2005	$13,232,246
2006	$15,059,143
Sum:	**$36,387,512**

The record that causes the Cumulative Sum to be exceeded is included and therefore our total of 1,183,785 is greater than the 1,091,625 that makes up the 3%.

18.3 Ranking using the 'Ranked by' parameter

If you do not specify this dimension, Web Intelligence calculates the values of the **Based on** measure using all the dimensions displayed in the block (in other words, Web Intelligence returns the top/bottom *n* rows in the block based on the measure selected in the **Based on** list box).

If you specify a ranking dimension, Web Intelligence aggregates the values of the **Based on** measure to the selected dimension to determine the ranking.

1. Add a new report tab and create the following block. The block contains no ranking filters or any other filters, i.e. the block is showing [Sales revenue] for [Year], [Quarter] and [State] for all three years (2004, 2005 and 2006).

Year	Quarter	State	Sales revenue
2004	Q1	California	$519,220
2004	Q1	Colorado	$131,797
2004	Q1	DC	$208,324
2004	Q1	Florida	$137,530
2004	Q1	Illinois	$256,454
2004	Q1	Massachusetts	$92,596

2. Add a Ranking as shown below and click 'OK':

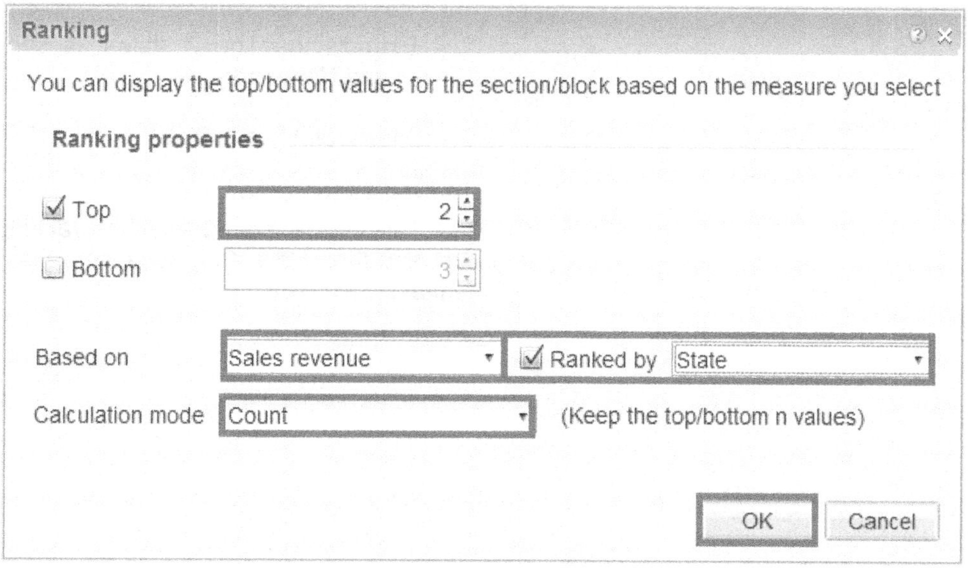
Ranking
You can display the top/bottom values for the section/block based on the measure you select
Ranking properties
Top
2
Bottom
3
Based on
Sales revenue
Ranked by
State
Calculation mode
Count
(Keep the top/bottom n values)
OK
Cancel

3. The results show:

Year	Quarter	State	Sales revenue
2004	Q1	Texas	$758,796
2004	Q2	Texas	$615,077
2004	Q3	Texas	$329,113
2004	Q4	Texas	$496,692
2005	Q1	Texas	$1,014,293
2005	Q2	Texas	$795,979
2005	Q3	Texas	$784,560
2005	Q4	Texas	$1,138,056
2006	Q1	Texas	$1,102,481
2006	Q2	Texas	$1,088,221
2006	Q3	Texas	$1,032,629
2006	Q4	Texas	$961,768
2004	Q1	New York	$555,983
2004	Q2	New York	$479,962
2004	Q3	New York	$257,114
2004	Q4	New York	$374,637
2005	Q1	New York	$683,971
2005	Q2	New York	$692,513
2005	Q3	New York	$501,220
2005	Q4	New York	$885,800
2006	Q1	New York	$747,161
2006	Q2	New York	$855,617
2006	Q3	New York	$914,247
2006	Q4	New York	$633,998

Rows shown opposite are only for Texas and New York.

Why?

Web Intelligence:

1 – Sums up the measure for each [State] as this is the dimension we have specified in the '**Ranked by**' parameter.

State	Sales revenue
Texas	$10,117,664
New York	$7,582,221
California	$7,479,569
Illinois	$3,022,968
DC	$2,961,950
Colorado	$2,060,275
Florida	$1,879,159
Massachusetts	$1,283,707

2 – Extracts the Top 2 states as shown here (Texas and New York).

3 – Shows all rows within the block for these 2 states.

4 – The data is sorted after the ranking, Texas first and then New York because Texas has the highest [Sales revenue].

4. If we apply a break on [Year] then we will see the top 2 states in each year.

Year	Quarter	State	Sales revenue
2004	Q1	Texas	$758,796
	Q2	Texas	$615,077
	Q3	Texas	$329,113
	Q4	Texas	$496,692
	Q1	California	$519,220
	Q2	California	$441,494
	Q3	California	$394,309
	Q4	California	$349,188
2004			

Year	Quarter	State	Sales revenue
2005	Q1	Texas	$1,014,293
	Q2	Texas	$795,979
	Q3	Texas	$784,560
	Q4	Texas	$1,138,056
	Q1	California	$650,715
	Q2	California	$529,256
	Q3	California	$760,442
	Q4	California	$842,267
2005			

Year	Quarter	State	Sales revenue
2006	Q1	Texas	$1,102,481
	Q2	Texas	$1,088,221
	Q3	Texas	$1,032,629
	Q4	Texas	$961,768
	Q1	New York	$747,161
	Q2	New York	$855,617
	Q3	New York	$914,247
	Q4	New York	$633,998
2006			

Web Intelligence now takes into consideration the context of [Year].

1 – Sums up the measure for each [State] within the [Year] break.

Year	State	Sales revenue
2004	Texas	$2,199,677
	California	$1,704,211
2004		

Year	State	Sales revenue
2005	Texas	$3,732,889
	California	$2,782,680
2005		

Year	State	Sales revenue
2006	Texas	$4,185,098
	New York	$3,151,022
2006		

2 – Extracts the Top 2 states per year as shown opposite.

3 – Shows data for the Top 2 states per year in the block, but we still have a row per quarter (shown opposite).

5. A sectioned report on [Year] would also show the top 2 states in each year (i.e. a Section will behave in the same way as a Break):

2004

Quarter	State	Sales revenue
Q1	Texas	$758,796
Q2	Texas	$615,077
Q3	Texas	$329,113
Q4	Texas	$496,692
Q1	California	$519,220
Q2	California	$441,494
Q3	California	$394,309
Q4	California	$349,188

2005

Quarter	State	Sales revenue
Q1	Texas	$1,014,293
Q2	Texas	$795,979
Q3	Texas	$784,560
Q4	Texas	$1,138,056
Q1	California	$650,715
Q2	California	$529,256
Q3	California	$760,442
Q4	California	$842,267

2006

Quarter	State	Sales revenue
Q1	Texas	$1,102,481
Q2	Texas	$1,088,221
Q3	Texas	$1,032,629
Q4	Texas	$961,768
Q1	New York	$747,161
Q2	New York	$855,617
Q3	New York	$914,247
Q4	New York	$633,998

Using the **Ranked by** parameter enables you to specify the dimension context on which the ranking should occur.

In Step 3 we demonstrated that without breaks and sections the calculation context was [State] only.

In Steps 4 and 5 we demonstrated the calculation context also includes the dimension used for the break or section.

6. Taking Step 3 above (i.e. we had a break on [Year]) and editing the Ranking filter to not use the **Ranked by** parameter:

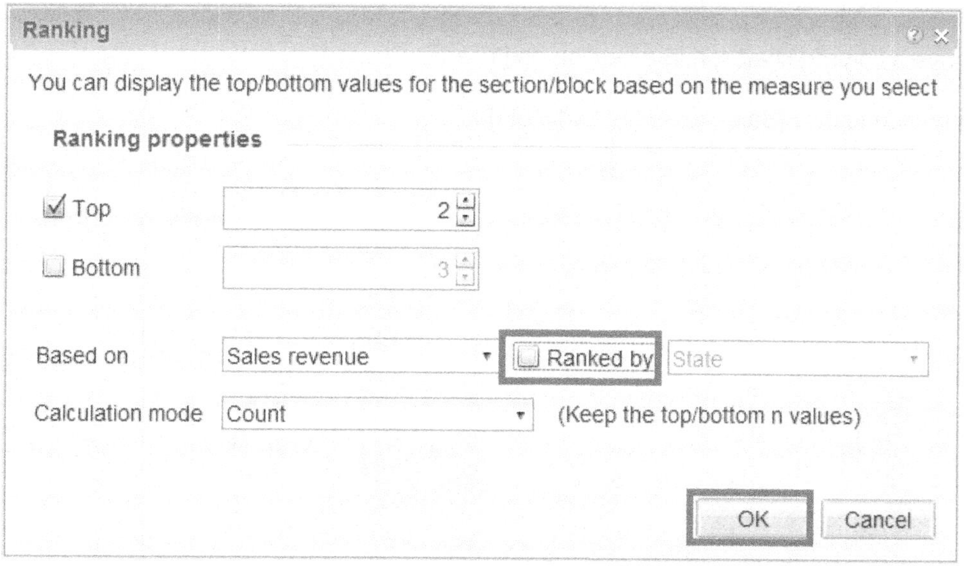
Ranking
You can display the top/bottom values for the section/block based on the measure you select
Ranking properties
Top
2
Bottom
3
Based on
Sales revenue
Ranked by
State
Calculation mode
Count
(Keep the top/bottom n values)
OK
Cancel

...results in:

Year	Quarter	State	Sales revenue
2004	Q1	Texas	$758,796
	Q2	Texas	$615,077
2004			

Year	Quarter	State	Sales revenue
2005	Q4	Texas	$1,138,056
	Q1	Texas	$1,014,293
2005			

Year	Quarter	State	Sales revenue
2006	Q1	Texas	$1,102,481
	Q2	Texas	$1,088,221
2006			

When the **Ranked by** parameter is not used then the ranking occurs using the overall dimension context being displayed in the block.

In this example the ranking context is top 2 rows per [Year] because we have a break on [Year].

7. Removing the break on [Year] results in the ranking context to be evaluated as top 2 rows in the block.

Year	Quarter	State	Sales revenue
2005	Q4	Texas	$1,138,056
2006	Q1	Texas	$1,102,481

18.4 Ranking Data in Charts and Sections

Data can also be ranked in charts and sections.

1. Here we have a column chart within a section on [Year].

   The column chart shows [Sales revenue] by [State]

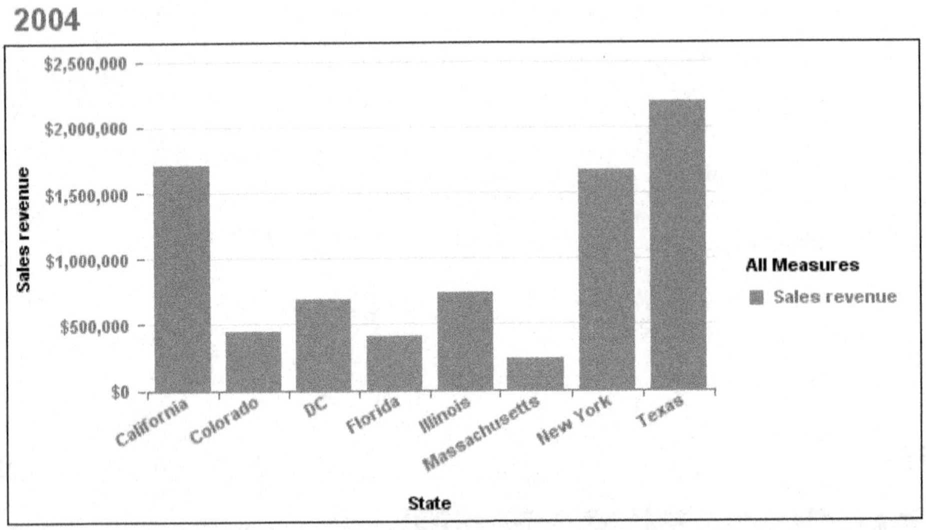
2004
$2,500,000
$2,000,000
$1,500,000
$1,000,000
$500,000
$0
Sales revenue
California
Colorado
DC
Florida
Illinois
Massachusetts
New York
Texas
State
All Measures
Sales revenue

2. We can select the chart and then apply a ranking filter to it:

At the time of writing, the 'Ranking' menu was not available using right-click on charts, but was available from the toolbox.

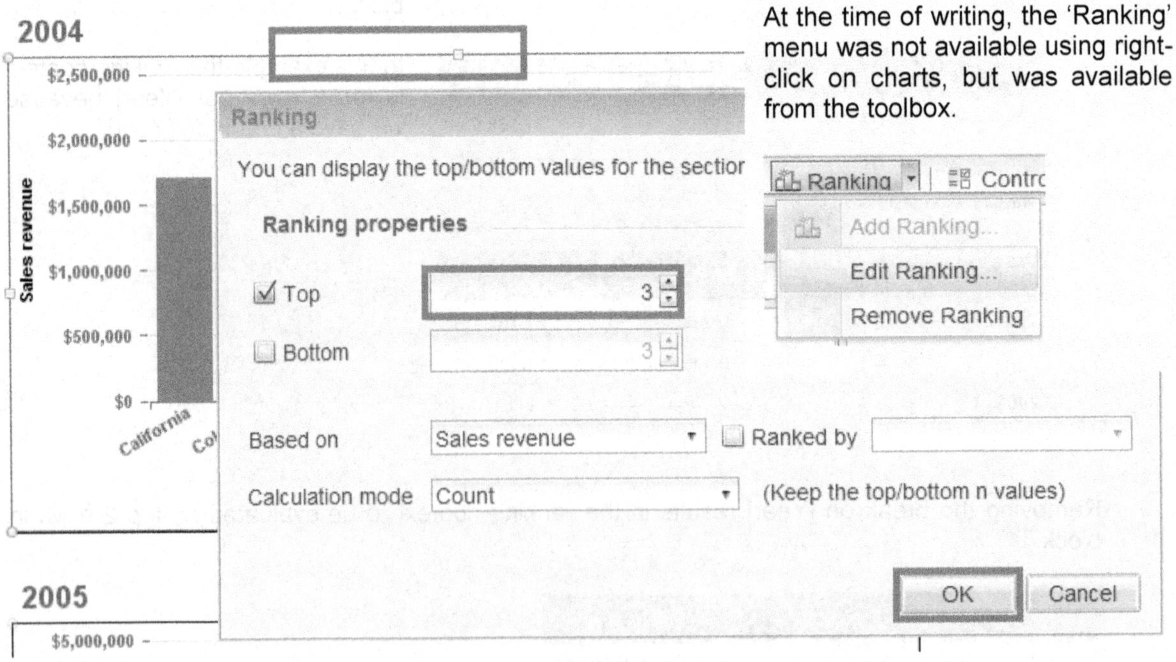
2004
Ranking
You can display the top/bottom values for the sectior
Ranking properties
Top
3
Bottom
3
Based on
Sales revenue
Ranked by
Calculation mode
Count
(Keep the top/bottom n values)
OK
Cancel
Ranking
Add Ranking...
Edit Ranking...
Remove Ranking
2005
$5,000,000

NOTE - The chart has been selected (i.e. clicked on) first as we can see in the background.

3. After applying the ranking filter the chart shows the 'Top 3 States' within each section as defined in the Rank Interface.

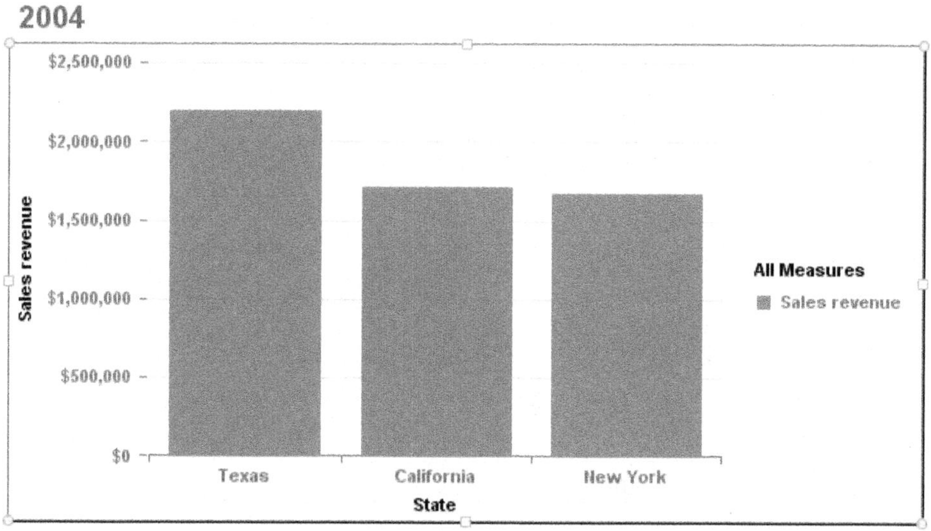
2004
$2,500,000
$2,000,000
$1,500,000
$1,000,000
$500,000
$0
Sales revenue
Texas
California
New York
State
All Measures
Sales revenue

4. Similarly we can rank data in a section by applying a ranking filter on the section master cell (highlighted below). In this example, we have removed the ranking filter on the chart (using the 'Remove Ranking' button on the toolbox, and then applied the following ranking on the section master cell.

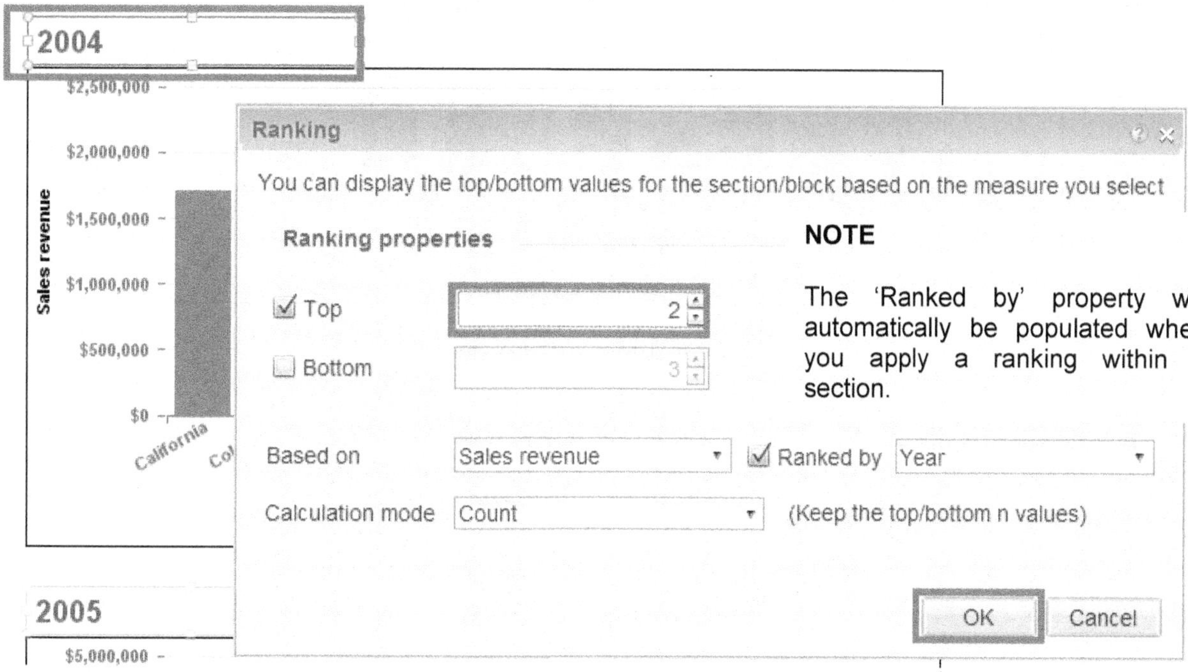
2004
Ranking
You can display the top/bottom values for the section/block based on the measure you select
Ranking properties
Top
2
Bottom
3
Based on
Sales revenue
Ranked by
Year
Calculation mode
Count
(Keep the top/bottom n values)
OK
Cancel
2005
$5,000,000

NOTE

The 'Ranked by' property will automatically be populated when you apply a ranking within a section.

5. After applying the ranking filter we now only have two sections (i.e. the Top 2 Years).

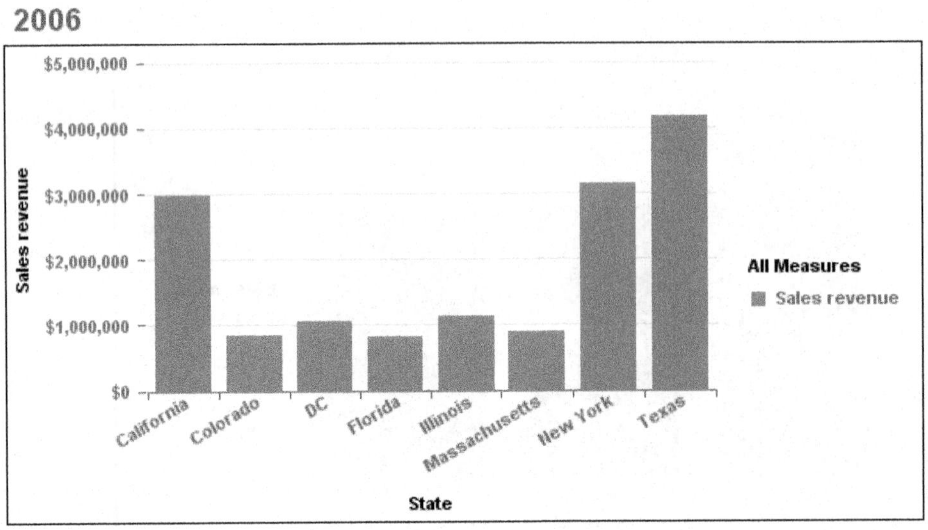
2006
$5,000,000
$4,000,000
$3,000,000
$2,000,000
$1,000,000
$0
Sales revenue
California
Colorado
DC
Florida
Illinois
Massachusetts
New York
Texas
State
All Measures
Sales revenue

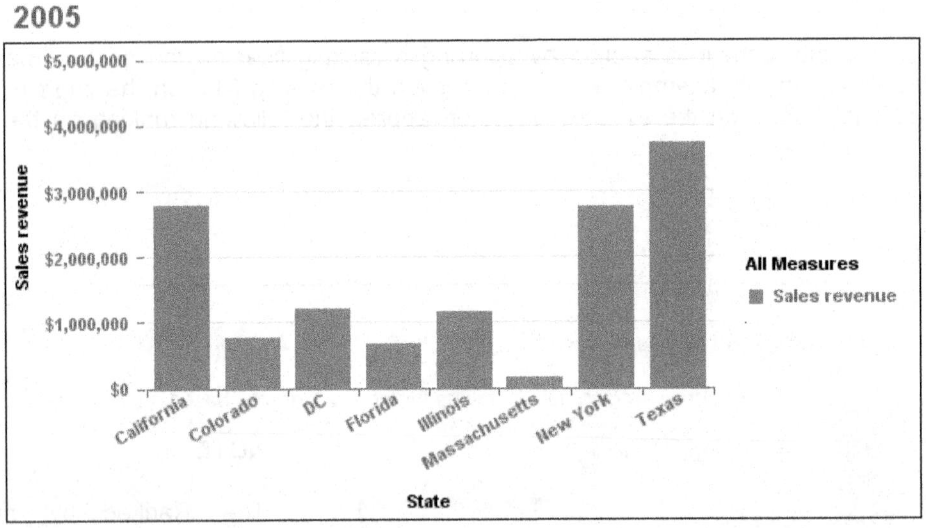
2005
$5,000,000
$4,000,000
$3,000,000
$2,000,000
$1,000,000
$0
Sales revenue
California
Colorado
DC
Florida
Illinois
Massachusetts
New York
Texas
State
All Measures
Sales revenue

19 Working in Structure Mode

We briefly saw an example of 'Structure Mode' in the sessions on 'Creating and Formatting Charts' and 'Sections'.

For example, when you select a chart template and drop it onto the canvas, Web Intelligence displays the template in Structure Mode (as shown below):

Chart Template selected and dropped onto canvas

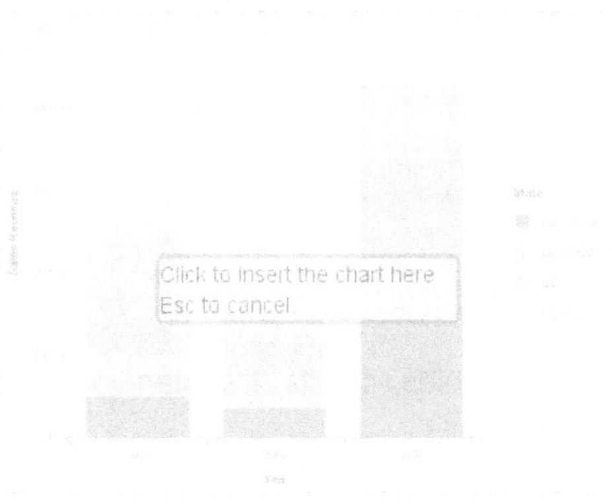
Click to insert the chart here
Esc to cancel

Chart Template is displayed in Structure Mode by default

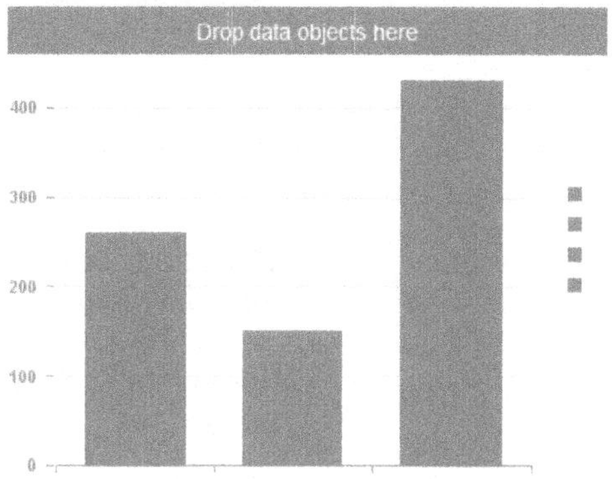
Drop data objects here
400
300
200
100
0

Structure Mode is not restricted to working with charts only and is useful for laying out report elements on the canvas (or page). In fact, some visual clues are only available in Structure Mode as we will discover.

1. Create the following query using the 'eFashion' universe and run it.

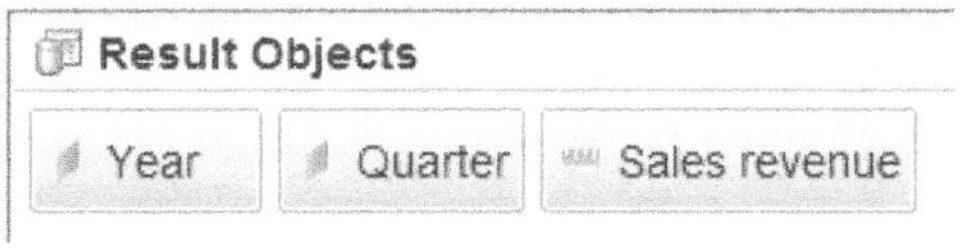
Result Objects
Year
Quarter
Sales revenue

2. Apply the Sum (Standard Calculation) on the [Sales revenue] column as shown opposite:

   This is because we are in 'Design – With Data' mode.

   In this mode, we see one header row and one footer row, but there is one body row for every row of the microcube that is displayed in this block.

Year	Quarter	Sales revenue
2004	Q1	$2,660,700
2004	Q2	$2,279,003
2004	Q3	$1,367,841
2004	Q4	$1,788,580
2005	Q1	$3,326,172
2005	Q2	$2,840,651
2005	Q3	$2,879,303
2005	Q4	$4,186,120
2006	Q1	$3,742,989
2006	Q2	$4,006,718
2006	Q3	$3,953,395
2006	Q4	$3,356,041
	Sum:	**$36,387,512**

3. From the top right-hand corner, select ‘Design – Structure Only’.

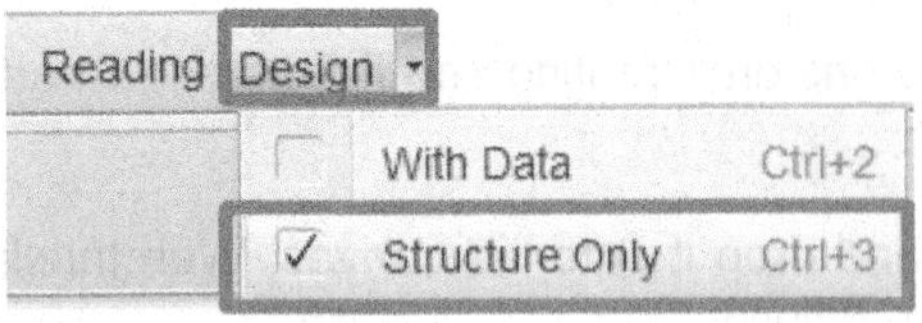
Reading
Design
With Data Ctrl+2
Structure Only Ctrl+3

4. Web Intelligence now displays the table as:

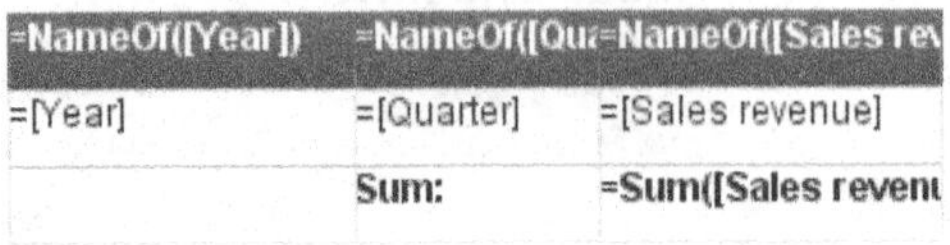
=NameOf([Year])
=NameOf([Qu
=NameOf([Sales rev
=[Year]
=[Quarter]
=[Sales revenue]
Sum:
=Sum([Sales revenu

In ‘Design – Structure Only’ mode, the block shows only 3 rows; a header row at the top, a body row in the middle and a footer row at the bottom.

Structure Only mode can be used at any time giving a different view of working with the document.

It is useful to understand the workings of tables, charts, freestanding cells, sections, breaks, etc.

5. Whilst in Structure Only mode, right-click on the [Year] column in the block and select ‘Set as Section’.

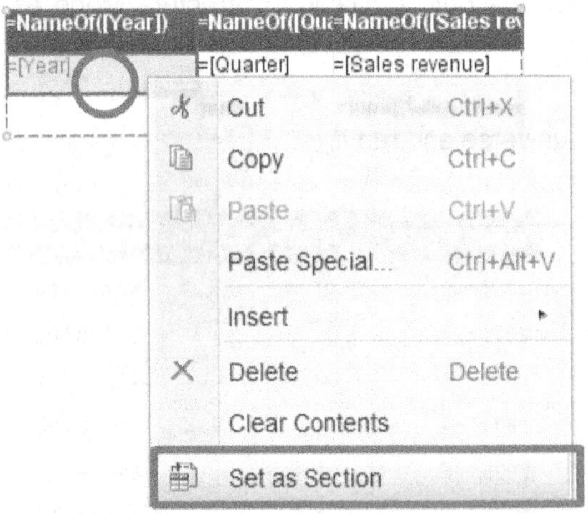
=NameOf([Year])
=NameOf([Qu
=NameOf([Sales rev
=[Year]
=[Quarter]
=[Sales revenue]
Cut Ctrl+X
Copy Ctrl+C
Paste Ctrl+V
Paste Special... Ctrl+Alt+V
Insert
Delete Delete
Clear Contents
Set as Section

6. Web Intelligence now displays:

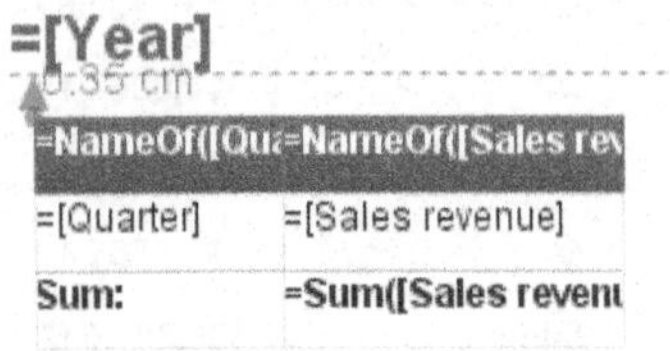
=[Year]
0.35 cm
=NameOf([Qu
=NameOf([Sales rev
=[Quarter]
=[Sales revenue]
Sum:
=Sum([Sales revenu

7. Clicking near the block (but not on the block itself) will select the section and the display will now show:

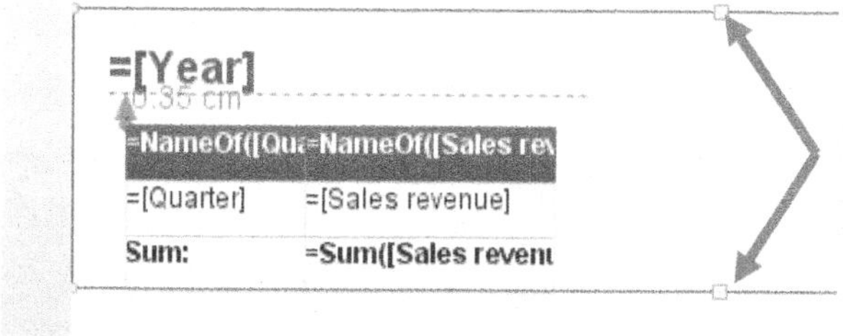
=[Year]
0.35 cm
=NameOf([Qu=NameOf([Sales re
=[Quarter]
=[Sales revenue]
Sum:
=Sum([Sales reven

In **Structure Only** mode, some report elements (such as sections) are much easier to work with.

Simply drag the section lines/margins to resize the sections within the report.

We can also see that the table is 0.35cm from the bottom of the [Year] cell.

The dashed line underneath '=[Year]' informs us of the width of the [Year] cell.

NOTE – The above can also be found from looking at the formatting properties of the table and the [Year] cell, but **Structure Only** mode gives us an overall visual picture of how the report elements have been laid out.

8. Drag the top line of the section (i.e. start of section) down a little as shown below (on the left) and this will move the start of the section further down the report page.

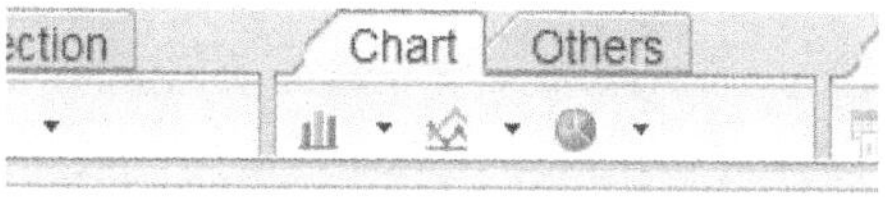
ction
Chart
Others

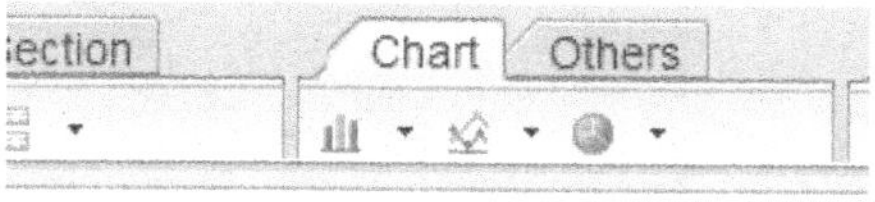
ection
Chart
Others

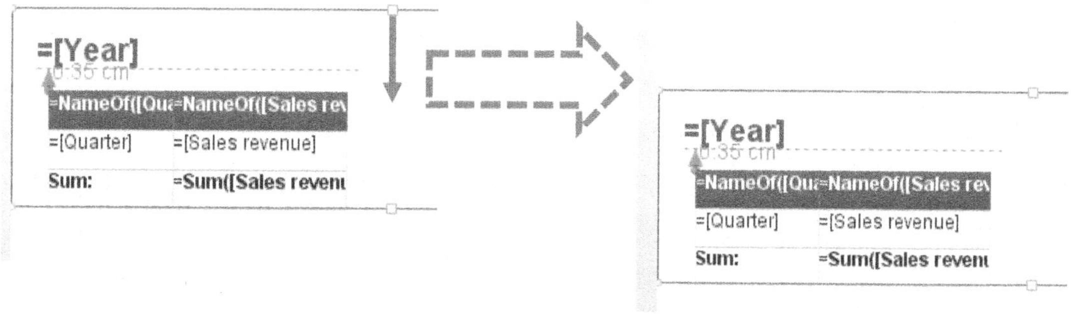
=[Year]
0.35 cm
=NameOf([Qu=NameOf([Sales re
=[Quarter]
=[Sales revenue]
Sum:
=Sum([Sales reven
=[Year]
0.35 cm
=NameOf([Qu=NameOf([Sales re
=[Quarter]
=[Sales revenue]
Sum:
=Sum([Sales reven

9. Select the Pre-Defined Cell for Document Name.

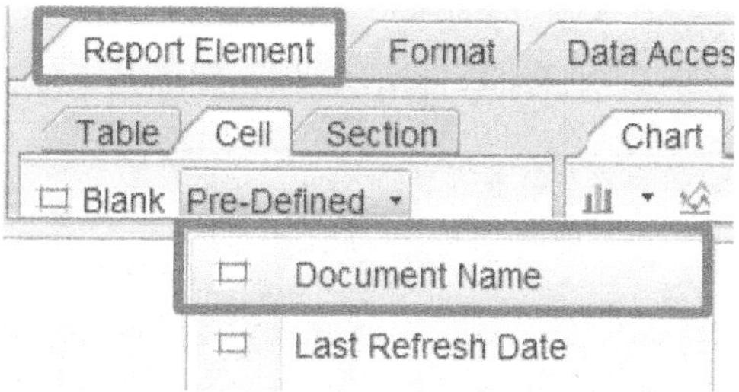
Report Element
Format
Data Acces
Table
Cell
Section
Chart
Blank
Pre-Defined
Document Name
Last Refresh Date

10. Drop the cell template into the area above the section (as shown below):

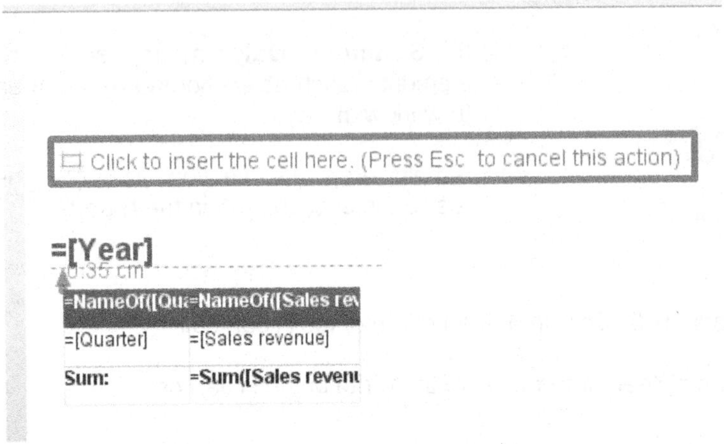
Click to insert the cell here. (Press Esc to cancel this action)
=[Year]
0.35 cm
=NameOf([Qu =NameOf([Sales re
=[Quarter] =[Sales revenue]
Sum: =Sum([Sales revenu

11. **Structure Only** mode will now show (as on the left-hand side below) and **With Data** mode (as on the right-hand side below):

Structure Only Mode

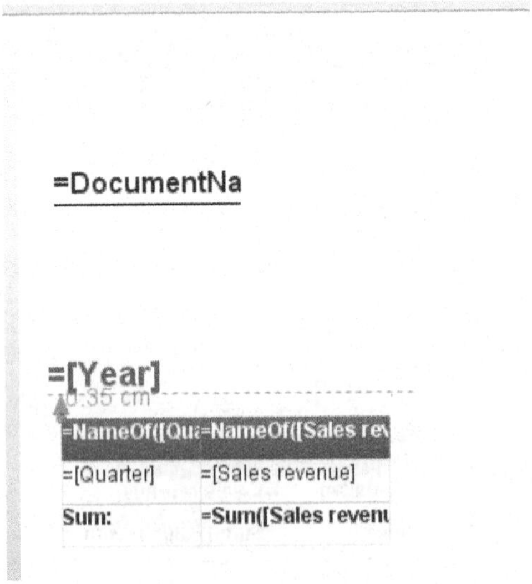
=DocumentNa
=[Year]
0.35 cm
=NameOf([Qu =NameOf([Sales re
=[Quarter] =[Sales revenue]
Sum: =Sum([Sales revenu

With Data Mode

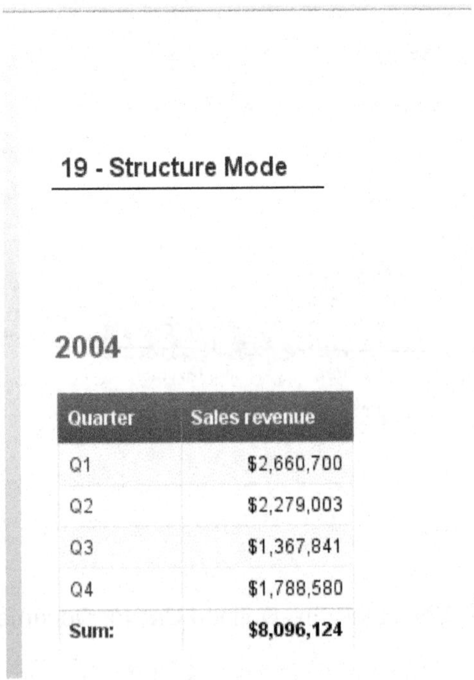
19 - Structure Mode
2004
Quarter Sales revenue
Q1 $2,660,700
Q2 $2,279,003
Q3 $1,367,841
Q4 $1,788,580
Sum: $8,096,124

12. Save your document.

19.1 Working with Report Elements using the Document Structure and Filters Tab

Sometimes it is difficult to see all the report elements being used within a report because some elements could be hidden, etc. We can use the 'Document Structure and Filters' tab to view and select report elements.

1. In the left pane, click on the 'Document Structure and Filters' tab as shown below:

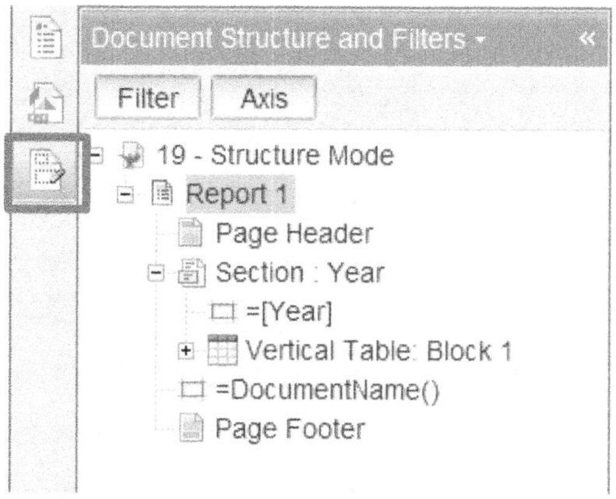
Document Structure and Filters
Filter
Axis
19 - Structure Mode
Report 1
Page Header
Section : Year
=[Year]
Vertical Table: Block 1
=DocumentName()
Page Footer

NOTE

Works in both Structure Only and With Data modes

We can now click on different report elements within the document and Web Intelligence will select the relevant element in the Workspace Panel (some examples shown below).

You can now work with the selected report element, for example right-click and format it, move it, etc.

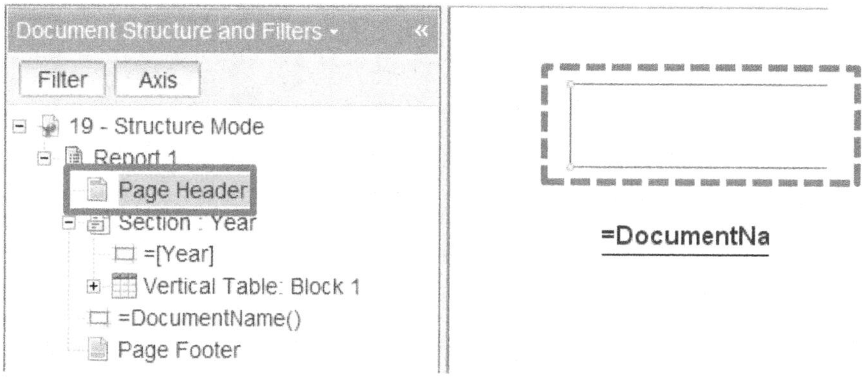
Document Structure and Filters
Filter
Axis
19 - Structure Mode
Report 1
Page Header
Section : Year
=[Year]
Vertical Table: Block 1
=DocumentName()
Page Footer
=DocumentNa

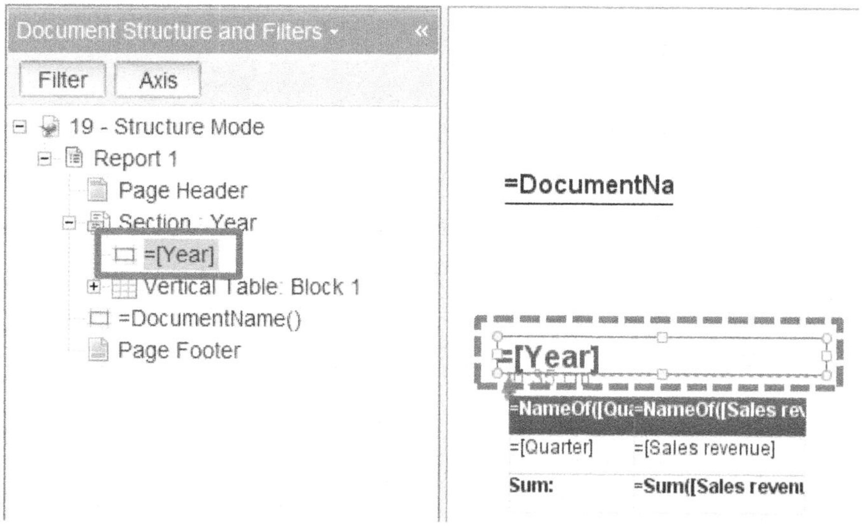
Document Structure and Filters
Filter
Axis
19 - Structure Mode
Report 1
Page Header
Section : Year
=[Year]
Vertical Table: Block 1
=DocumentName()
Page Footer
=DocumentNa
=[Year]
=[Quarter]
=[Sales revenue]
Sum:

20 Page Layouts and Alignment of Report Elements

This session looks at how report elements can be positioned and aligned using Web Intelligence functionality. We will also take a look at page layout properties for developing printable reports.

20.1 Relative Positioning

Using 'Relative Positioning' enables report elements to dynamically position themselves depending on the position of other report elements.

1. Create the following query using the 'eFashion' universe and then run the query.

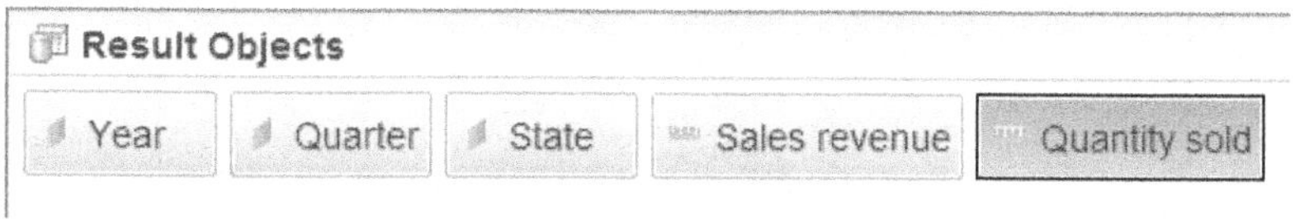
Result Objects
Year
Quarter
State
Sales revenue
Quantity sold

2. Change the default vertical table and create a chart, making sure the chart is place relatively close to the table (as shown below):

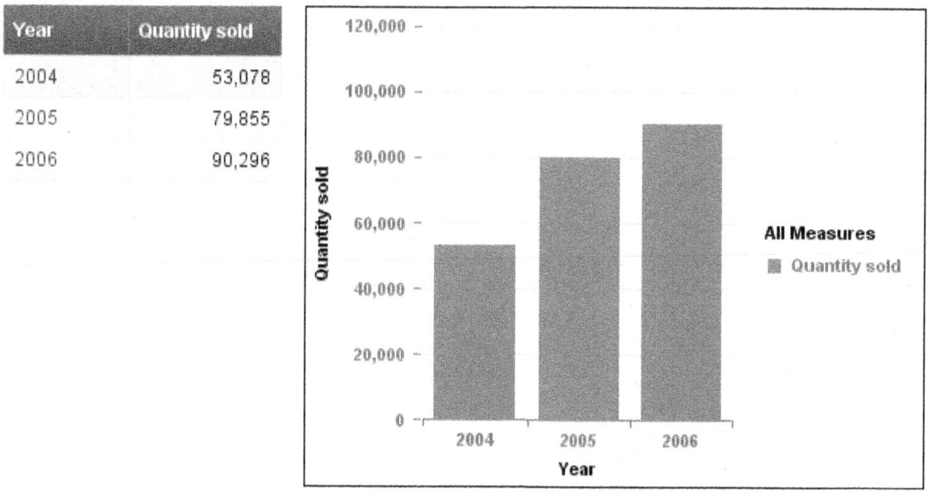
Year
Quantity sold
2004
53,078
2005
79,855
2006
90,296
120,000
100,000
80,000
60,000
40,000
20,000
0
Quantity sold
2004
2005
2006
Year
All Measures
Quantity sold

3. Save the document giving it a suitable name, e.g. 'Page Layouts and Positioning'.

4. Drop the [Quarter] object into the table so it sits between the [Year] and [Quantity sold] columns.

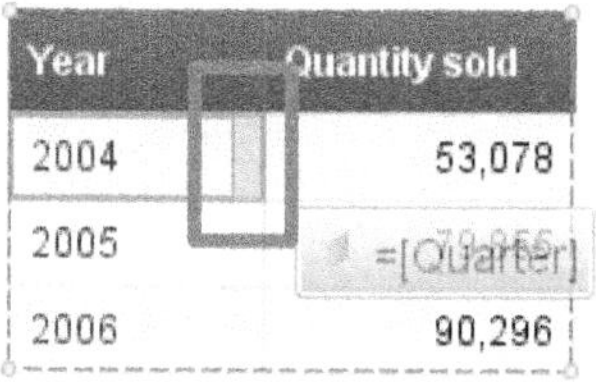
Year
Quantity sold
2004
53,078
2005
=[Quarter]
2006
90,296

The result is as follows:

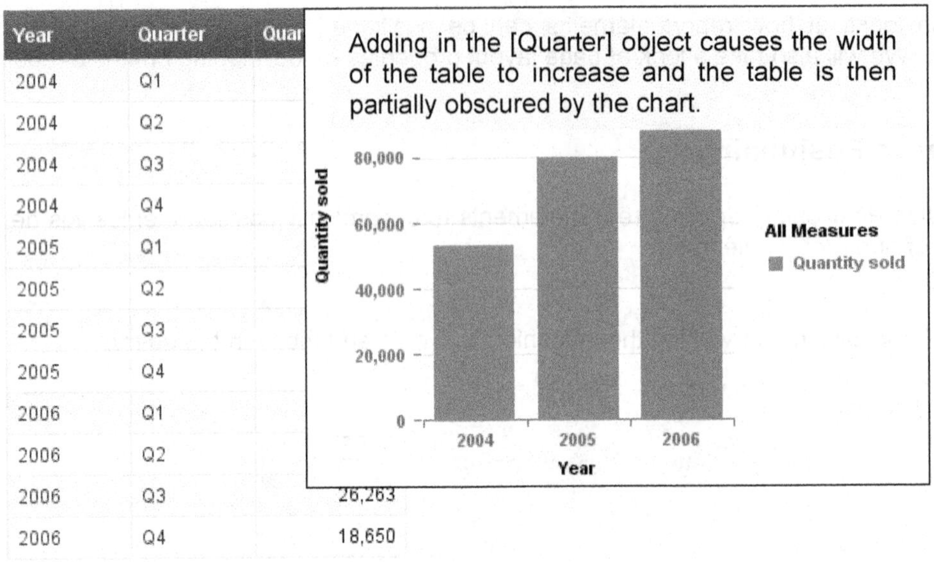

Year
Quarter
Quar
2004 Q1
2004 Q2
2004 Q3
2004 Q4
2005 Q1
2005 Q2
2005 Q3
2005 Q4
2006 Q1
2006 Q2
2006 Q3 26,263
2006 Q4 18,650
Adding in the [Quarter] object causes the width of the table to increase and the table is then partially obscured by the chart.
Quantity sold
80,000
60,000
40,000
20,000
0
2004
2005
2006
Year
All Measures
Quantity sold

Another example... the chart has been placed below the table. Adding in the [State] object causes the number of rows to increase and the table becomes partially obscured by the chart.

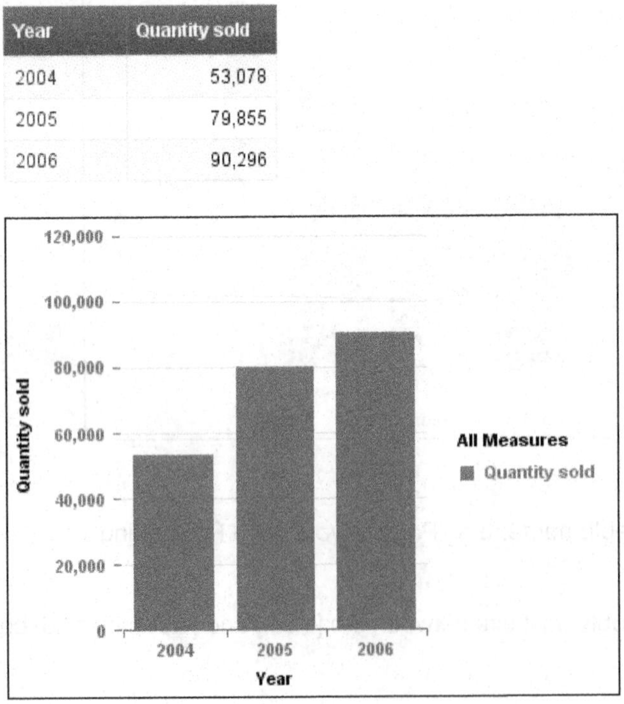

Year
Quantity sold
2004 53,078
2005 79,855
2006 90,296
120,000
100,000
80,000
60,000
40,000
20,000
0
Quantity sold
2004
2005
2006
Year
All Measures
Quantity sold

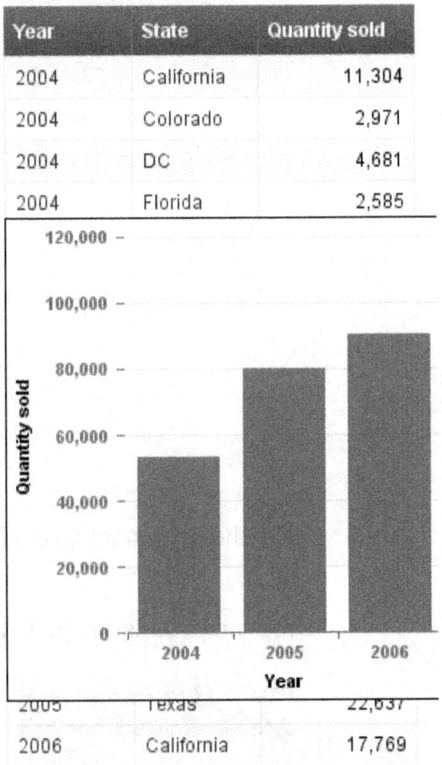

Year
State
Quantity sold
2004 California 11,304
2004 Colorado 2,971
2004 DC 4,681
2004 Florida 2,585
120,000
100,000
80,000
60,000
40,000
20,000
0
Quantity sold
2004
2005
2006
Year
2006 California 17,769

5. Select the table by clicking on its perimeter (not in any of the table cells), and then select the following option from the 'Report Element' toolbox:

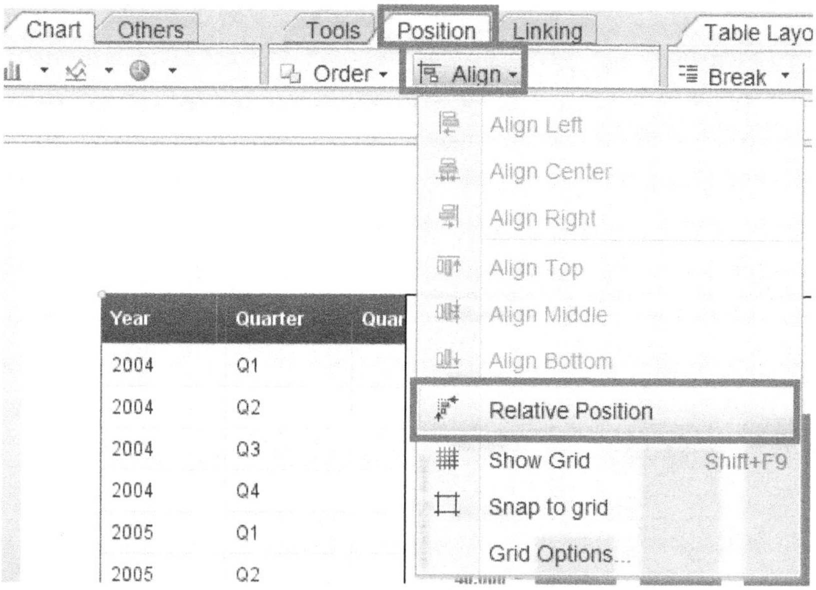
Chart
Others
Tools
Position
Linking
Table Layo
Order
Align
Break
Align Left
Align Center
Align Right
Align Top
Align Middle
Align Bottom
Relative Position
Show Grid
Shift+F9
Snap to grid
Grid Options...
Year
Quarter
Quar
2004
Q1
2004
Q2
2004
Q3
2004
Q4
2005
Q1
2005
Q2

6. Change the settings for the table as follows and click 'OK'.

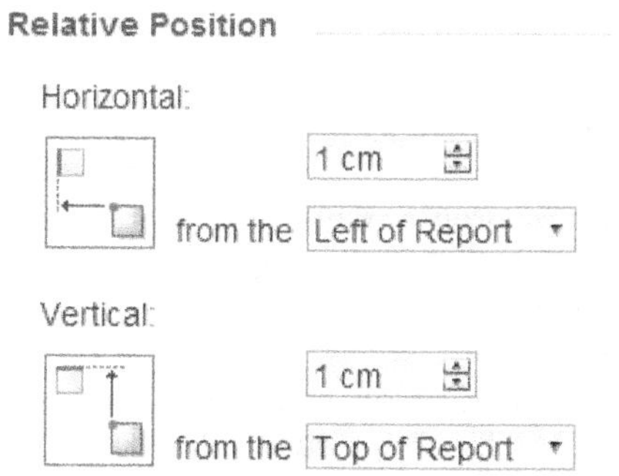
Relative Position
Horizontal:
1 cm
from the
Left of Report
Vertical:
1 cm
from the
Top of Report

7. Click on any part of the chart and then select the 'Relative Position' option from the 'Report Element' toolbox:

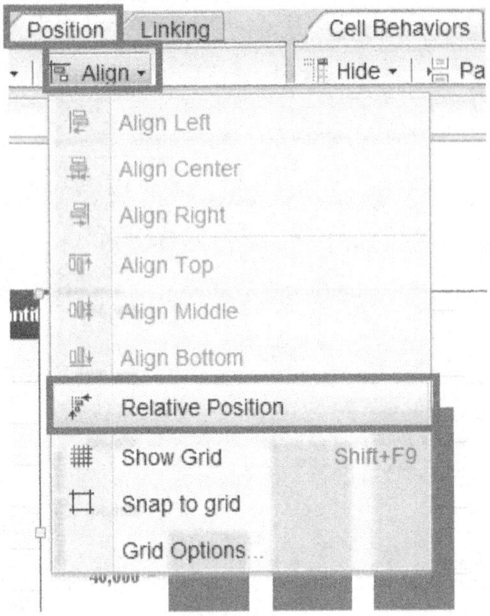
Position
Linking
Cell Behaviors
Align
Hide
Pa
Align Left
Align Center
Align Right
Align Top
Align Middle
Align Bottom
Relative Position
Show Grid
Shift+F9
Snap to grid
Grid Options...

8. Set the 'Relative Position' properties as shown below and click 'OK':

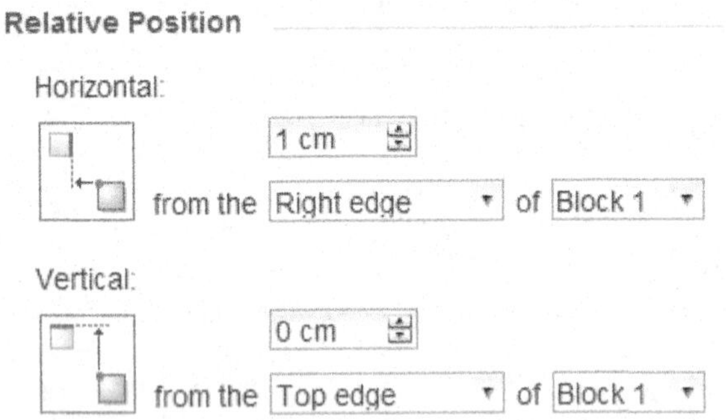
Relative Position
Horizontal:
1 cm
from the
Right edge
of
Block 1
Vertical:
0 cm
from the
Top edge
of
Block 1

NOTE

Use the drop down boxes when they appear to select the values as shown opposite.

If you have given your table a name then it will not be called 'Block 1' as shown in this example.

The result is as follows:

Year	Quarter	Quantity sold
2004	Q1	18,136
2004	Q2	14,408
2004	Q3	10,203
2004	Q4	10,331
2005	Q1	21,135
2005	Q2	17,152
2005	Q3	19,224
2005	Q4	22,344
2006	Q1	22,537
2006	Q2	22,846
2006	Q3	26,263
2006	Q4	18,650

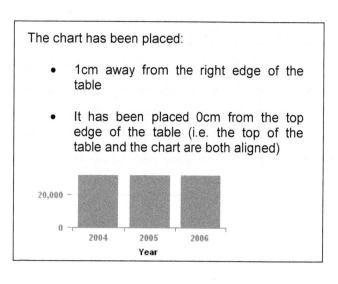

The chart has been placed:

- 1cm away from the right edge of the table
- It has been placed 0cm from the top edge of the table (i.e. the top of the table and the chart are both aligned)

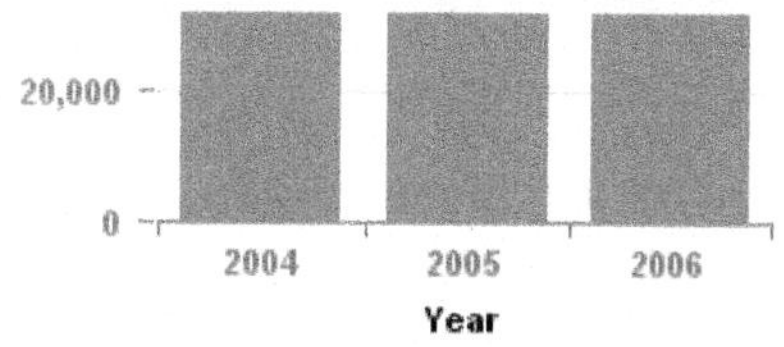
20,000
0
2004
2005
2006
Year

9. Drop the [State] object into the table between [Quarter] and [Quantity sold] as shown below:

Year	Quarter	Quantity sold
2004	Q1	18,136
2004	Q2	=[State]8
2004	Q3	10,203

The result is as follows:

Year	Quarter	State	Quantity sold
2004	Q1	California	3,509
2004	Q1	Colorado	921
2004	Q1	DC	1,467
2004	Q1	Florida	924
2004	Q1	Illinois	1,711
2004	Q1	Massachuset	609
2004	Q1	New York	3,717
2004	Q1	Texas	5,278
2004	Q2	California	2,788
2004	Q2	Colorado	828
2004	Q2	DC	1,149

The position of the chart automatically moves to satisfy the criteria:

- 1cm away from the right edge of the table
- 0cm from the top edge of the table (i.e. the top of the table and the chart are both aligned)

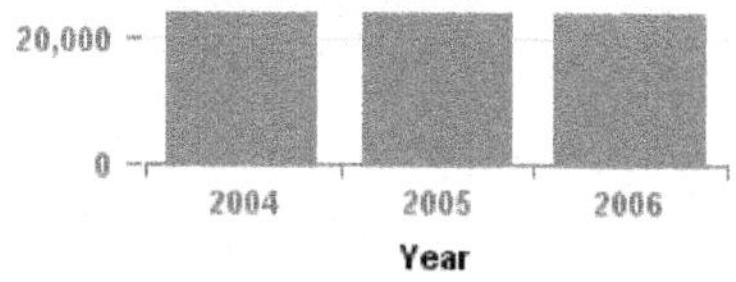
20,000
0
2004
2005
2006
Year

10. Modify the chart's position as follows and click 'OK'.

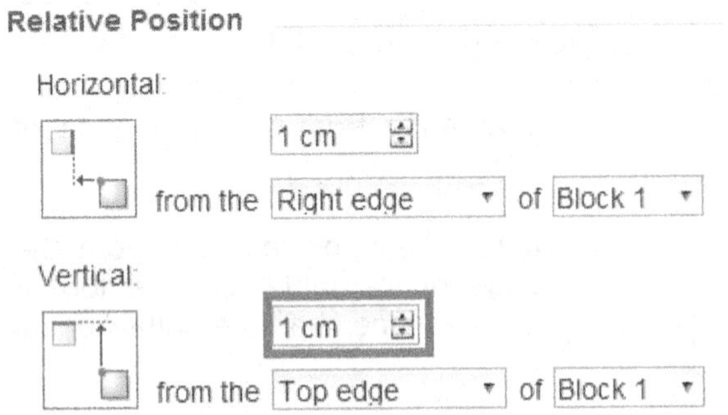
Relative Position
Horizontal:
1 cm
from the
Right edge
of
Block 1
Vertical:
1 cm
from the
Top edge
of
Block 1

11. Now switch to 'Structure Only' mode using the menus in the top right-hand corner.

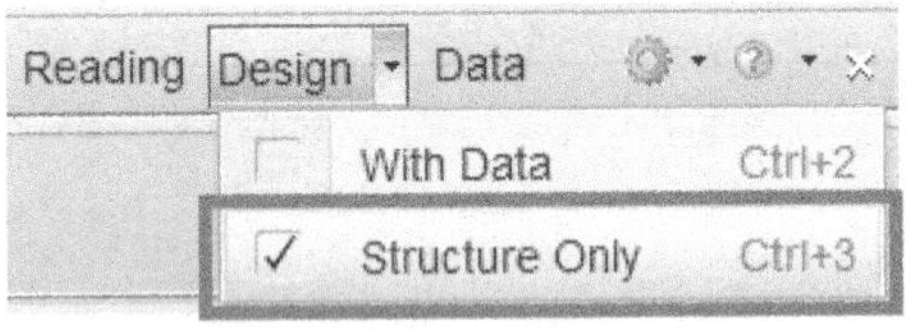
Reading
Design
Data
With Data
Ctrl+2
Structure Only
Ctrl+3

The result is as follows:

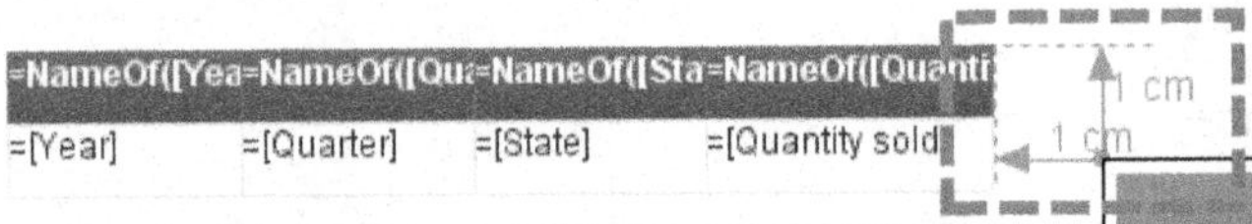
=NameOf([Yea=NameOf([Qu=NameOf([Sta=NameOf([Quanti
=[Year]
=[Quarter]
=[State]
=[Quantity sold]
1 cm
1 cm

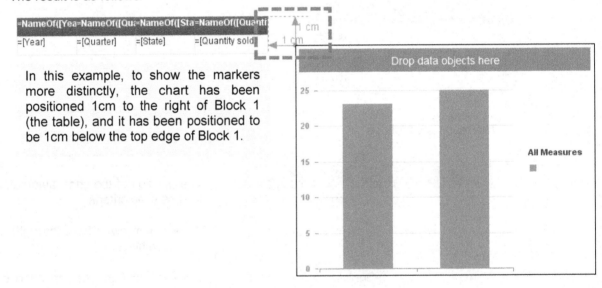

In this example, to show the markers more distinctly, the chart has been positioned 1cm to the right of Block 1 (the table), and it has been positioned to be 1cm below the top edge of Block 1.

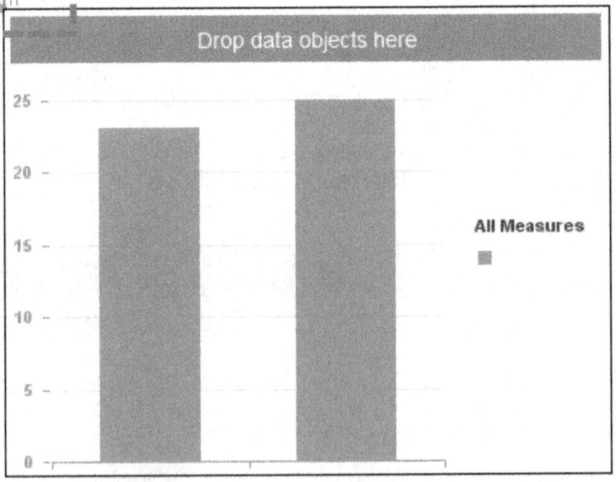
Drop data objects here
25
20
15
10
5
0
All Measures

NOTES

1. Relative Positioning can be applied to almost all report elements, such as blocks (tables, crosstabs, charts, cells, sections, etc).

2. It is good practice to use meaningful names for report elements and this becomes increasingly important when relative positioning is used and there are many report elements to arrange.

3. In 'Structure Only' mode, if a report element has been positioned relatively to another report element then this is made clearer using markers (as shown in Point 11 above).

4. Relative Positioning is especially useful on page layouts where table types are used because the number of rows/columns could vary (based on data returned or filtered). This in turn could cause the table to be obscured by nearby report elements.

20.2 Page Layouts

Web Intelligence documents are mostly created for interactive analysis (i.e. on screen) but they can also be used for printable reports (for example PDFs that can be shared and printed).

When catering for printable reports, the page layout becomes very important, for example vertical tables in printed reports work best when all the columns can be fitted horizontally on a single page.

Also, there are some properties that are only effective when a document is printed, exported into PDF, or viewed on screen in Page Mode.

Let us start with the example we already have Point 11 above.

1. Switch to 'With Data' mode.

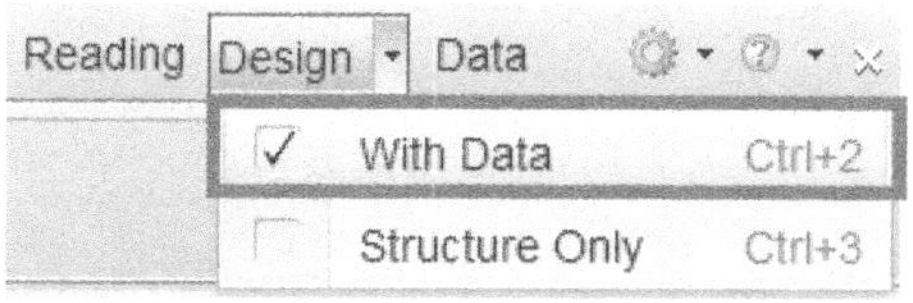
Reading
Design
Data
With Data
Ctrl+2
Structure Only
Ctrl+3

2. Make sure you are in 'Quick Display' mode (bottom right-hand side of the screen).

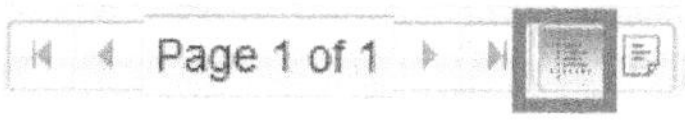
Page 1 of 1

The table and the chart will be visible on screen.

3. Now switch to 'Page' mode.

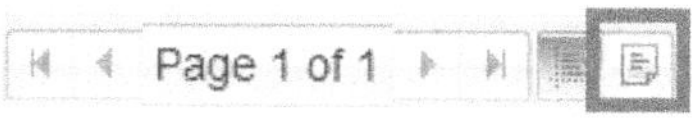
Page 1 of 1

The 'Page' mode will display the report elements as how they would appear in printed. In this particular example, our chart will be shown as being split over 2 horizontal pages.

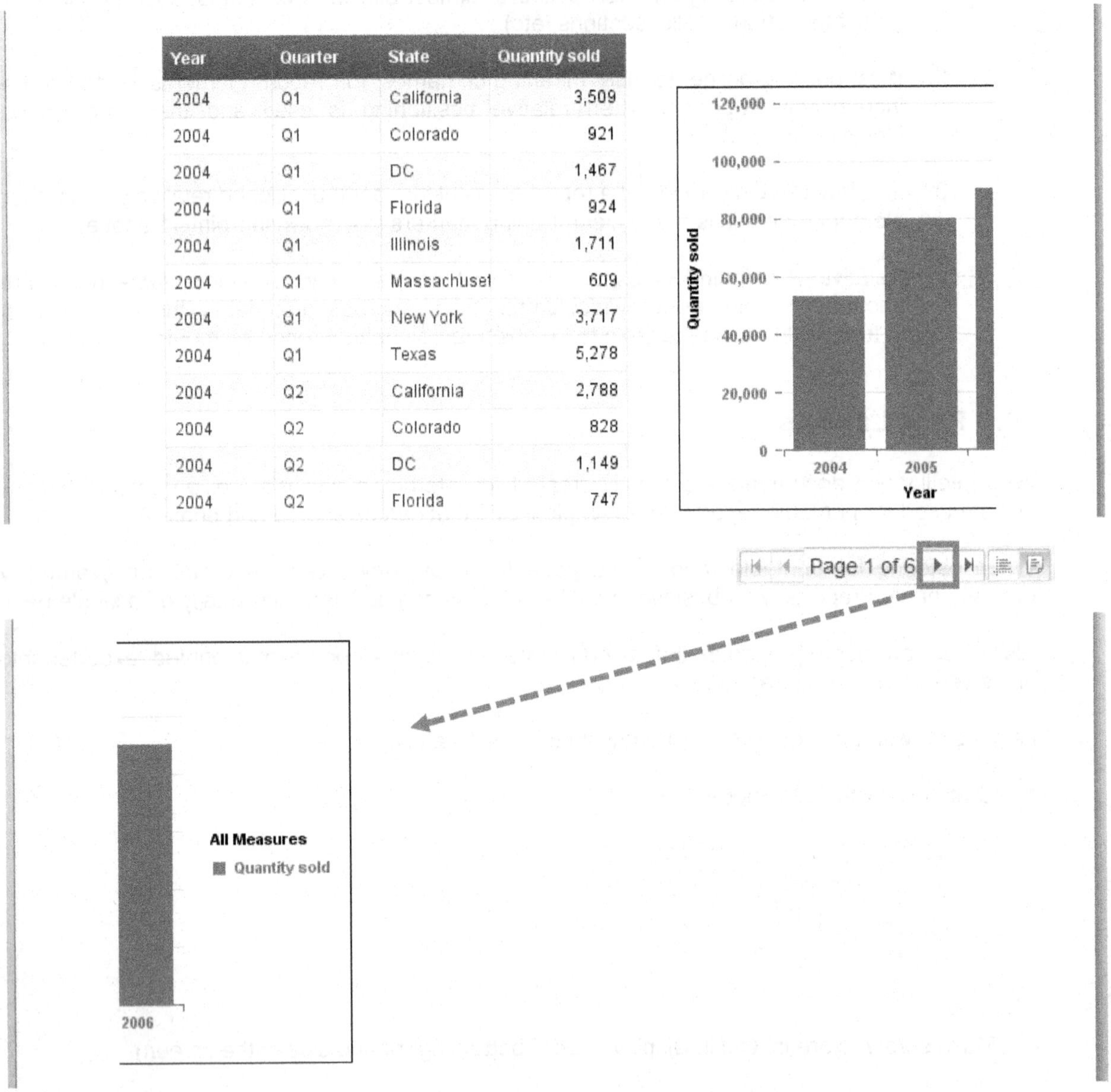

Year	Quarter	State	Quantity sold
2004	Q1	California	3,509
2004	Q1	Colorado	921
2004	Q1	DC	1,467
2004	Q1	Florida	924
2004	Q1	Illinois	1,711
2004	Q1	Massachuset	609
2004	Q1	New York	3,717
2004	Q1	Texas	5,278
2004	Q2	California	2,788
2004	Q2	Colorado	828
2004	Q2	DC	1,149
2004	Q2	Florida	747

120,000
100,000
80,000
60,000
40,000
20,000
0
Quantity sold
2004
2005
Year
Page 1 of 6
2006
All Measures
Quantity sold

4. Right-click below the chart and select 'Format Report'.

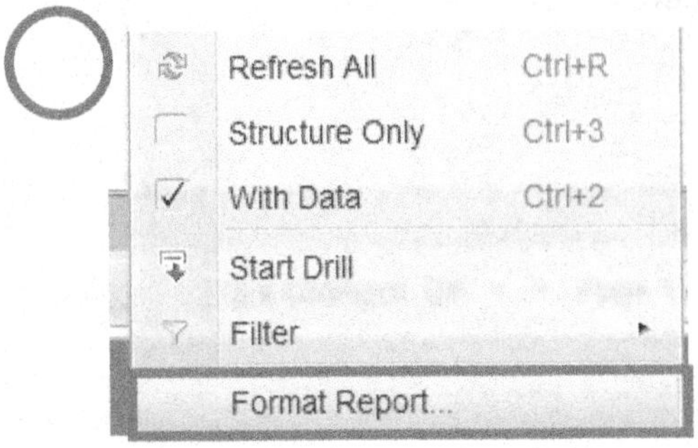
Refresh All Ctrl+R
Structure Only Ctrl+3
With Data Ctrl+2
Start Drill
Filter
Format Report...

5. Set the 'Orientation' to 'Landscape'

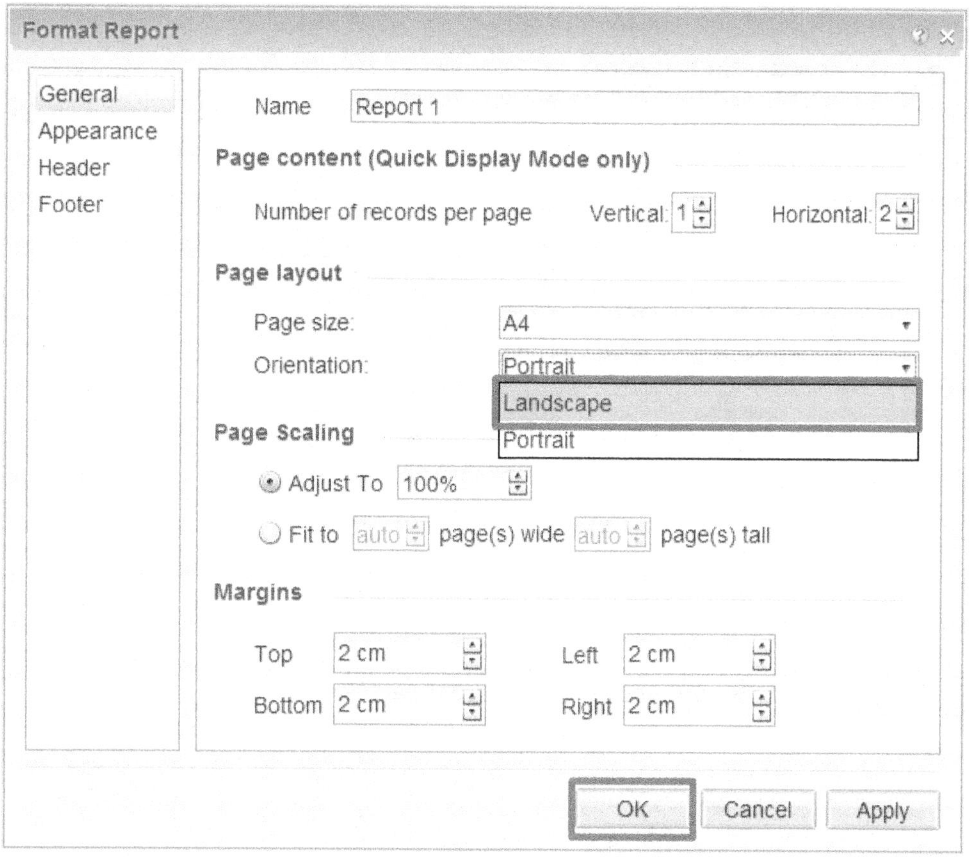
Format Report
General
Appearance
Header
Footer
Name
Report 1
Page content (Quick Display Mode only)
Number of records per page
Vertical: 1
Horizontal: 2
Page layout
Page size:
A4
Orientation:
Portrait
Landscape
Portrait
Page Scaling
Adjust To
100%
Fit to
auto
page(s) wide
auto
page(s) tall
Margins
Top
2 cm
Left
2 cm
Bottom
2 cm
Right
2 cm
OK
Cancel
Apply

NOTES

Page Scaling can be used to try and adjust the size of report elements to fit within a set number of pages when printed.

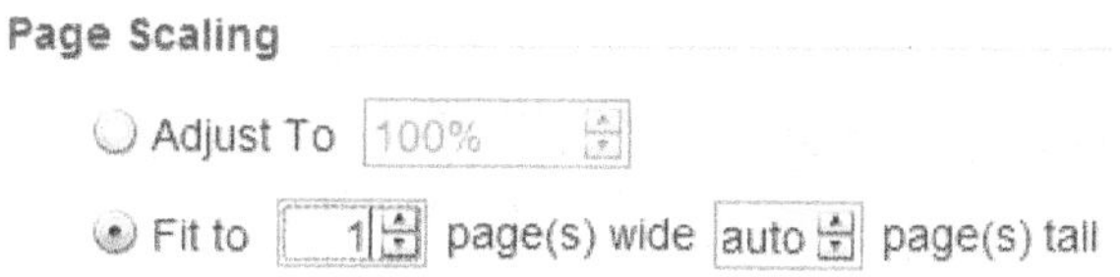
Page Scaling
Adjust To
100%
Fit to
1
page(s) wide
auto
page(s) tall

Web Intelligence will resize the report elements to fit within one page horizontally.

Margins are the effectively blank space forming a border around the page. You can reduce the margin sizes to gain more space for the report elements.

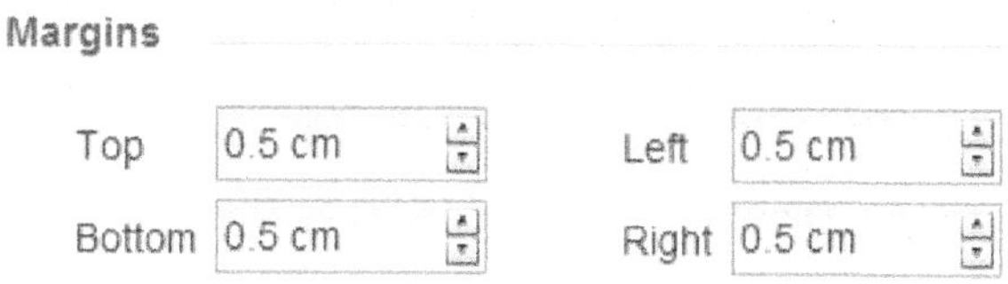
Margins
Top
0.5 cm
Left
0.5 cm
Bottom
0.5 cm
Right
0.5 cm

Keep in mind that printers might not be able print to edge of pages, so you should use some margin space, for example 0.5 cm as a minimum.

Do not use the above settings for our example.

6. Click 'OK' to close the 'Format Report' interface and the report elements will now be within a single page.

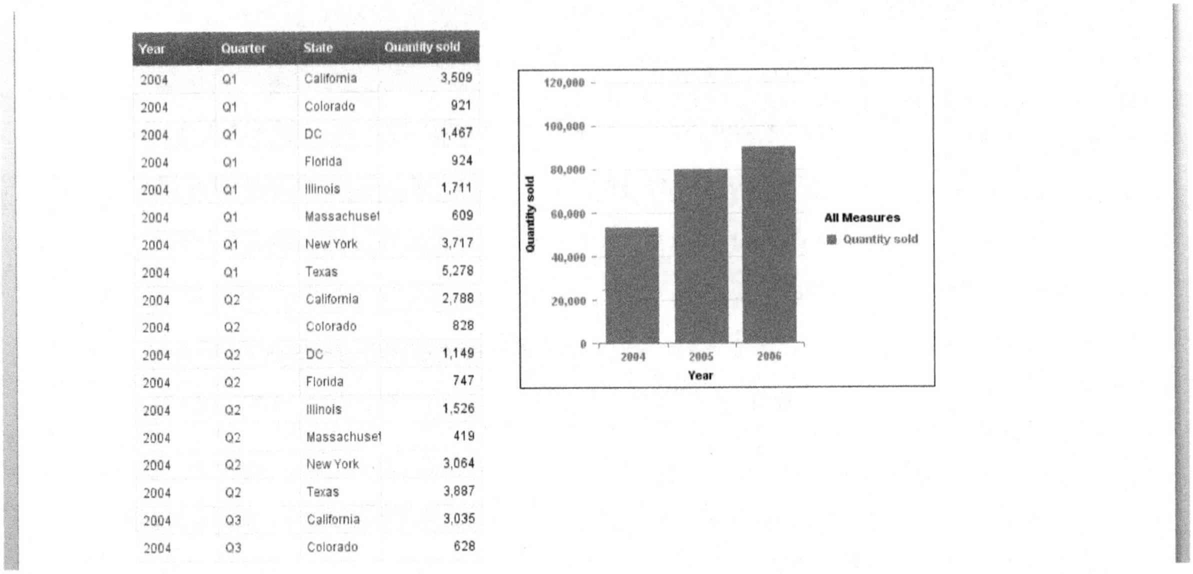

Year	Quarter	State	Quantity sold
2004	Q1	California	3,509
2004	Q1	Colorado	921
2004	Q1	DC	1,467
2004	Q1	Florida	924
2004	Q1	Illinois	1,711
2004	Q1	Massachuset	609
2004	Q1	New York	3,717
2004	Q1	Texas	5,278
2004	Q2	California	2,788
2004	Q2	Colorado	828
2004	Q2	DC	1,149
2004	Q2	Florida	747
2004	Q2	Illinois	1,526
2004	Q2	Massachuset	419
2004	Q2	New York	3,064
2004	Q2	Texas	3,887
2004	Q3	California	3,035
2004	Q3	Colorado	628

120,000
100,000
80,000
60,000
40,000
20,000
0
Quantity sold
2004
2005
2006
Year
All Measures
Quantity sold

7. Move the mouse pointer above the table (towards the top of the report canvas) and Web Intelligence will enable you to select the Report/Page Header.

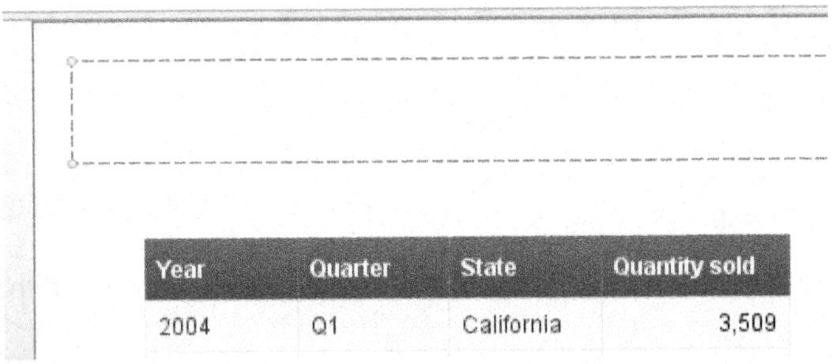

Year	Quarter	State	Quantity sold
2004	Q1	California	3,509

8. Select 'Format Header...' by right-clicking on the header.

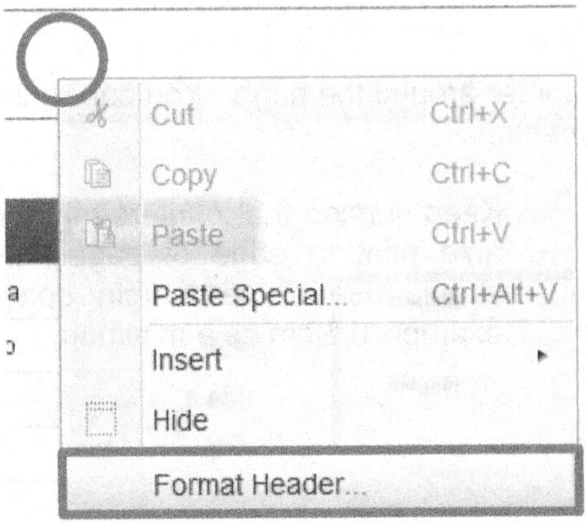
Cut Ctrl+X
Copy Ctrl+C
Paste Ctrl+V
Paste Special... Ctrl+Alt+V
Insert
Hide
Format Header...

If you select 'Format Header…' then the 'Format Report' interface will open as shown below.

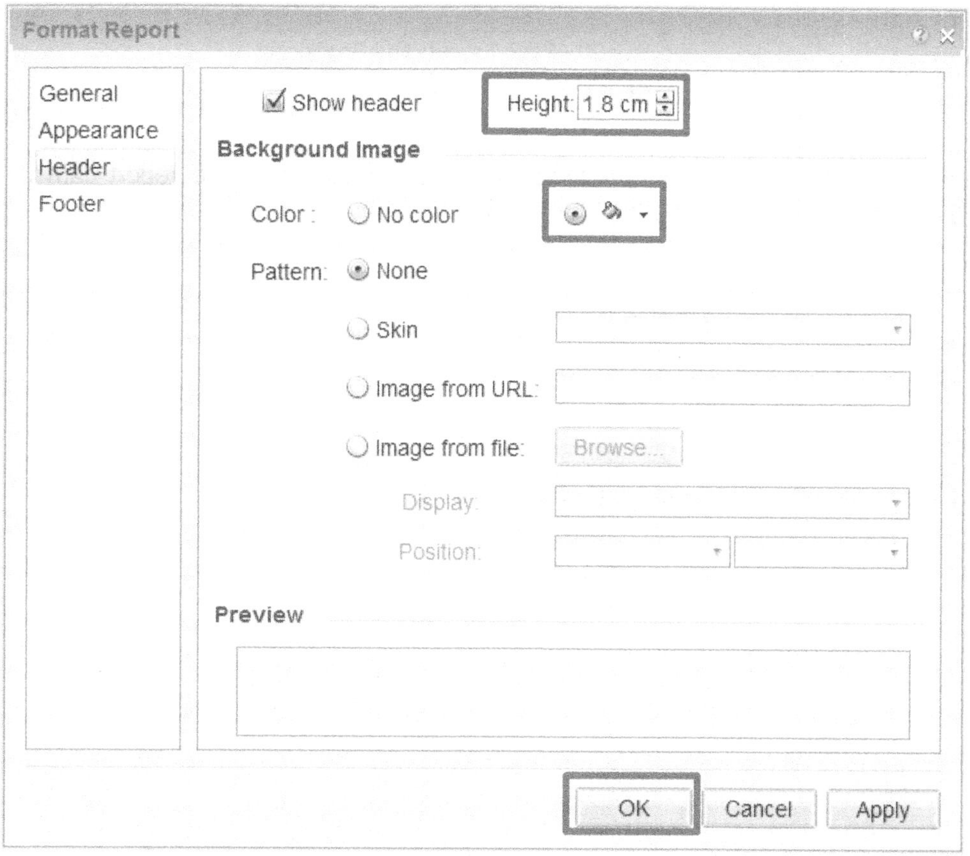
Format Report
General
Appearance
Header
Footer
Show header
Height: 1.8 cm
Background Image
Color : No color
Pattern: None
Skin
Image from URL:
Image from file:
Browse...
Display:
Position:
Preview
OK
Cancel
Apply

- You can show or hide the header and change its height.

  The width of the header will be the page width minus any space you have decided to use for the left and right margins.

- You can also apply background color to the header or use an image as the background.

9. Set the 'Height' to 1.8cm, apply a Background Color of 'Light Yellow' and click 'OK' (as shown above).

10. Select the 'Document Name' template cell and drag it into the Page Header as shown below.

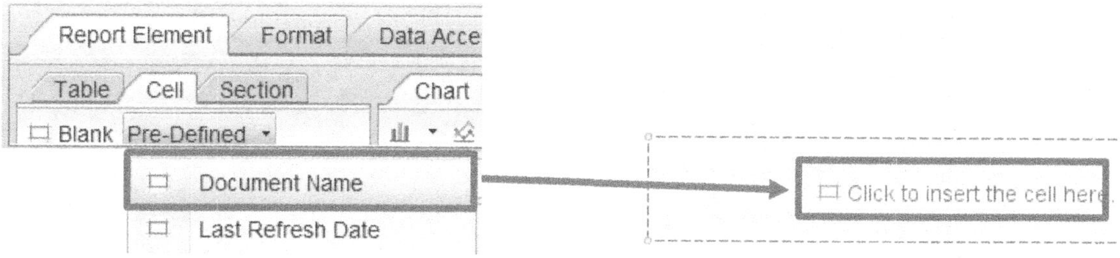
Report Element
Format
Data Acce
Table
Cell
Section
Chart
Blank
Pre-Defined
Document Name
Last Refresh Date
Click to insert the cell here

11. You can then apply further formatting to the cell if required.

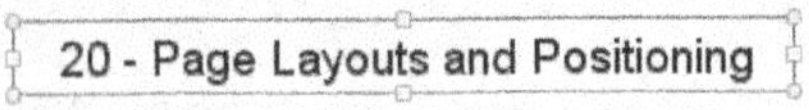
20 - Page Layouts and Positioning

12. Move the mouse pointer below the table (towards the bottom of the report canvas) and Web Intelligence will enable you to select the Report/Page Footer.

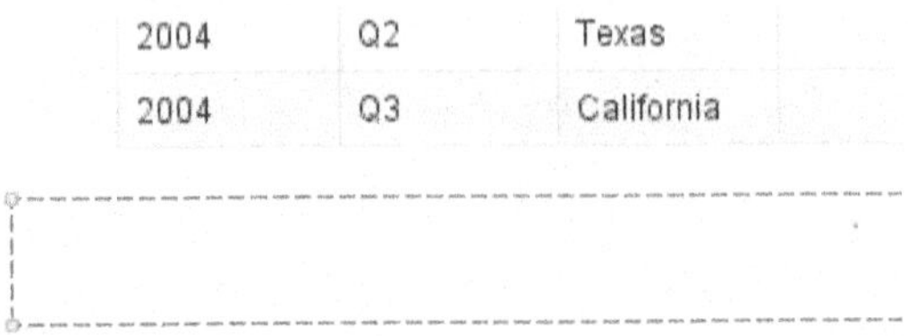
2004
Q2
Texas
2004
Q3
California

13. Select 'Format Footer…' by right-clicking on the footer.

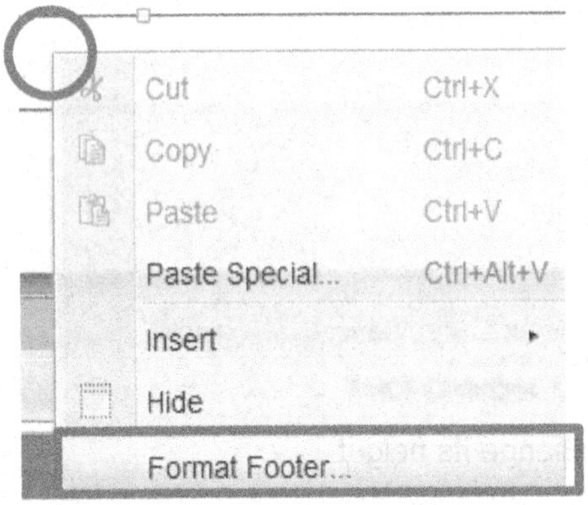
Cut
Ctrl+X
Copy
Ctrl+C
Paste
Ctrl+V
Paste Special...
Ctrl+Alt+V
Insert
Hide
Format Footer...

14. Set the 'Height' to 1.8cm, apply a Background Color of 'Light Yellow' and click 'OK'.

15. Select the 'Last Refresh Date' template cell and drag it into the Page Footer as shown below (drop into the bottom left-hand corner of the footer).

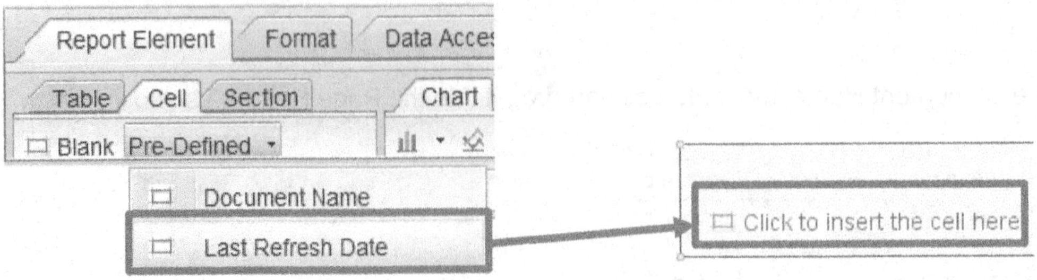
Report Element
Format
Table
Cell
Section
Chart
Blank
Pre-Defined
Document Name
Last Refresh Date
Click to insert the cell here

16. Select the 'Page Number/Total Pages' template cell and drag it into the Page Footer as shown below (drop into the top right-hand corner of the footer).

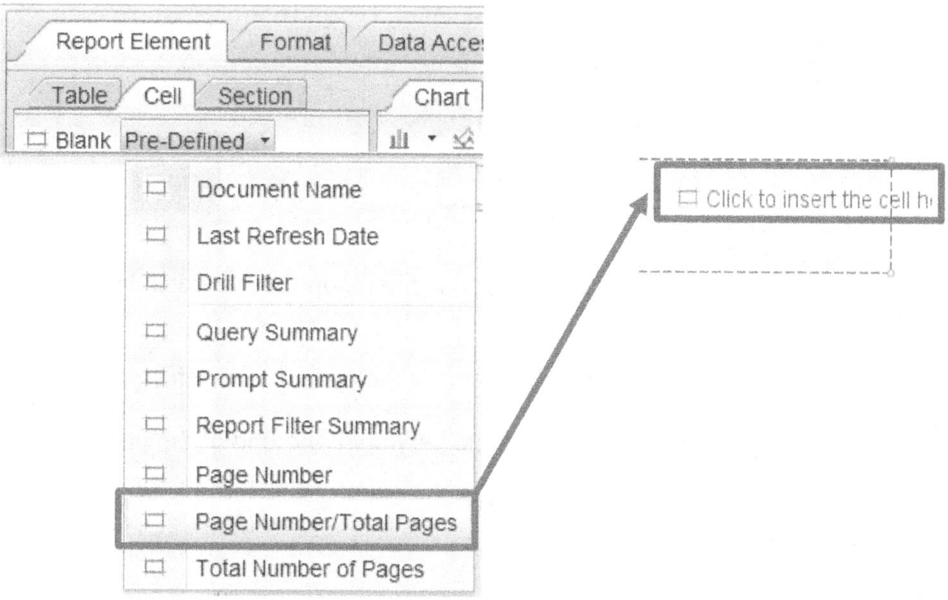
Report Element
Format
Data Acce
Table
Cell
Section
Chart
Blank
Pre-Defined
Document Name
Last Refresh Date
Drill Filter
Query Summary
Prompt Summary
Report Filter Summary
Page Number
Page Number/Total Pages
Total Number of Pages
Click to insert the cell h

17. The footer should now look something like.

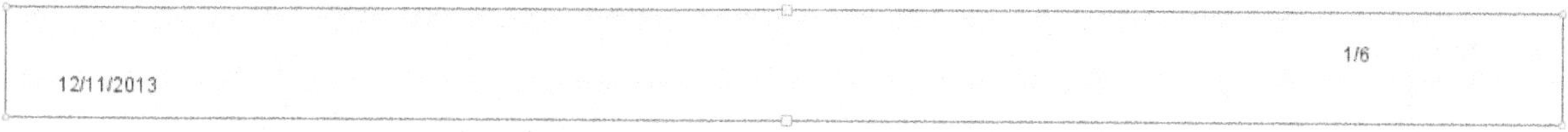
12/11/2013
1/6

18. We have 6 pages in the report and if we scroll through the pages using the page navigation buttons, we will see the Header and Footer appear on every page.

- The Header will be static, i.e. the same of every page.
- The Footer will show change depending on which page we are on, for example:

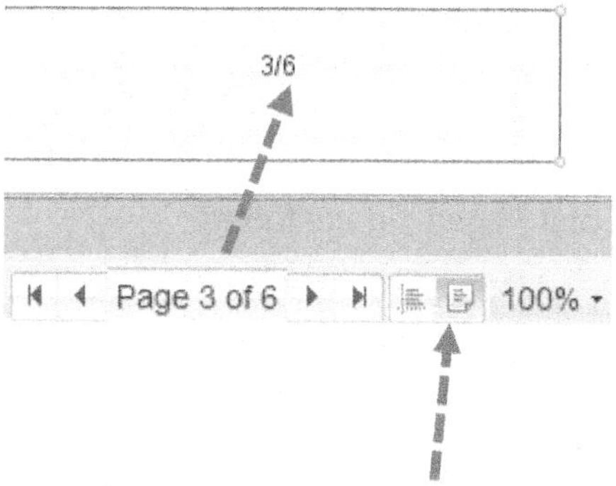
3/6
Page 3 of 6
100%

Make sure you are in 'Page' mode.

19. Switch to sure you are in 'Quick Display' mode.

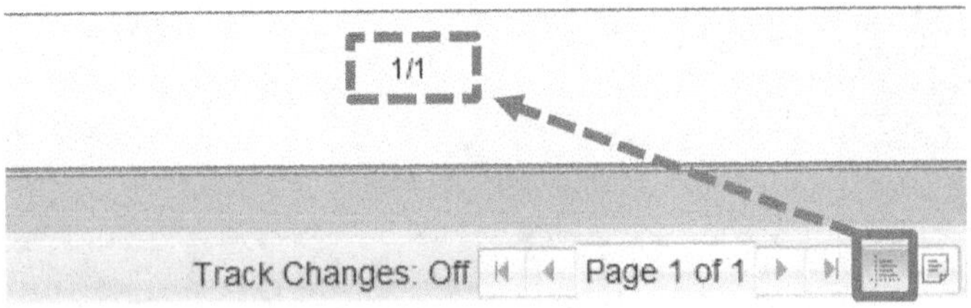
1/1
Track Changes: Off
Page 1 of 1

- In our example, we will now have only 1 page in the report (but we could have more if there were more rows in the table).
- The Header and Footer stretch all the way across the page (i.e. no left or right margins).
- The Header and Footer are positioned at the very start and end of the page (i.e. no top or bottom margins).

20. Save your document.

20.3 Alignment Functions

Other functions are available to use on multiple report elements (cells and blocks) for alignment purposes.

To demonstrate the use of these functions we will continue with our example from above.

1. Switch back to 'Page' mode.

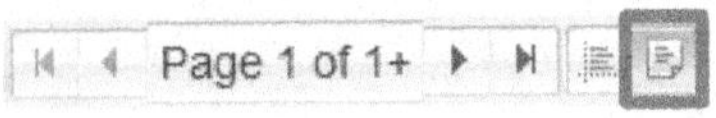
Page 1 of 1+

2. Click on the left-hand cell ('Last Refresh Date') in the footer.

3. Hold down the <CTRL> key.

4. Click on the right-hand cell ('Page Number/Total Pages') in the footer.

   Both cells will now be selected:

12/11/2013
1/6

5. Select 'Align – Middle' using the toolbox menu (or right-click menu).

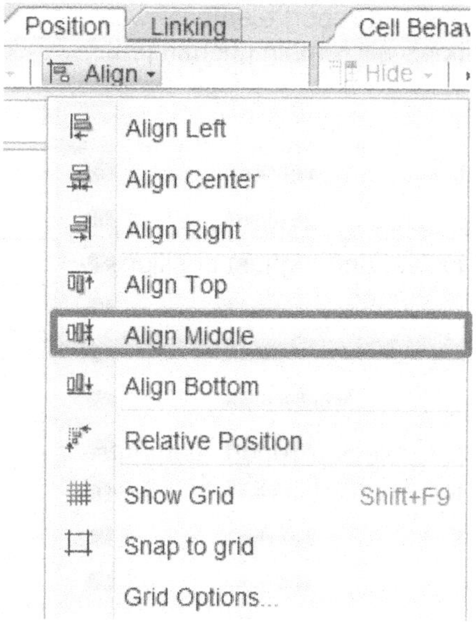
Position
Linking
Cell Behav
Align
Hide
Align Left
Align Center
Align Right
Align Top
Align Middle
Align Bottom
Relative Position
Show Grid
Shift+F9
Snap to grid
Grid Options...

The cells will now be vertically aligned in the 'Middle', based on their original positions.

12/11/2013
1/6

Alignment Function Examples

Align Left:

1/6
12/11/2013

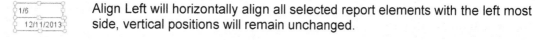

Align Left will horizontally align all selected report elements with the left most side, vertical positions will remain unchanged.

Align Center:

1/6
12/11/2013

Align Center will horizontally align all selected report elements in the center based on the original left-most and right-most positions, vertical positions will remain unchanged.

Align Right:

Align Right will horizontally align all selected report elements with the right most side, vertical positions will remain unchanged.

1/6
12/11/2013

Align Top:

12/11/2013

Align Top will vertically align all selected report elements with the top most side, horizontal positions will remain unchanged.

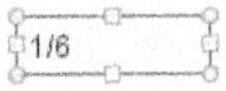
1/6

Align Middle:

12/11/2013

Align Middle will vertically align all selected report elements in the middle based on the original lowest and highest positions, horizontal positions will remain unchanged.

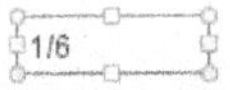
1/6

Align Bottom:

12/11/2013

Align Bottom will vertically align all selected report elements with the bottom most side, horizontal positions will remain unchanged.

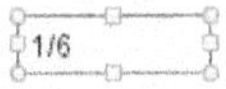
1/6

NOTES:

The purpose of using these functions is to quickly align many report elements horizontally or vertically.

After using any of these functions, each element is still individually positioned relative to the container (i.e. Page Header, Page Footer or Report) in which it is a component of, i.e. the selected elements do not get relatively positioned to one another after applying one of these functions.

20.4 Use of Grid to Align and Position Report Elements

The on-screen 'Grid' can be used to position report elements.

1. Switch on the 'Show Grid'

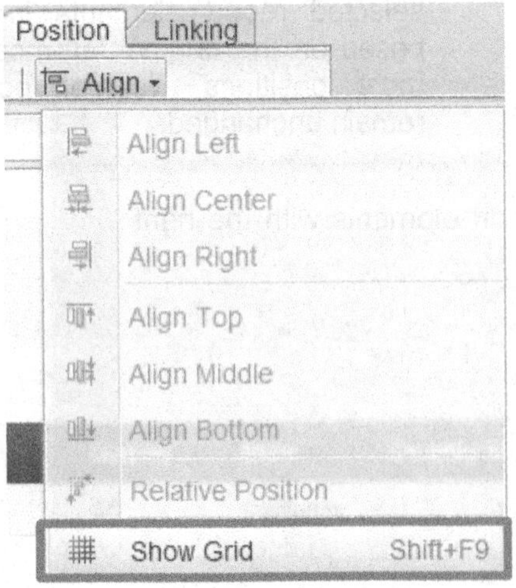
Position
Linking
Align
Align Left
Align Center
Align Right
Align Top
Align Middle
Align Bottom
Relative Position
Show Grid
Shift+F9

2. Switch on the 'Snap to grid'

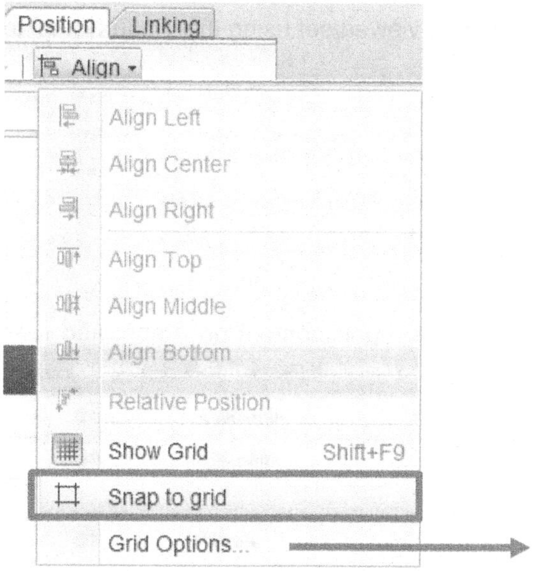
Position
Linking
Align
Align Left
Align Center
Align Right
Align Top
Align Middle
Align Bottom
Relative Position
Show Grid
Shift+F9
Snap to grid
Grid Options...

NOTE

'Grid Options...' enables you to apply all the grid settings in a single interface.

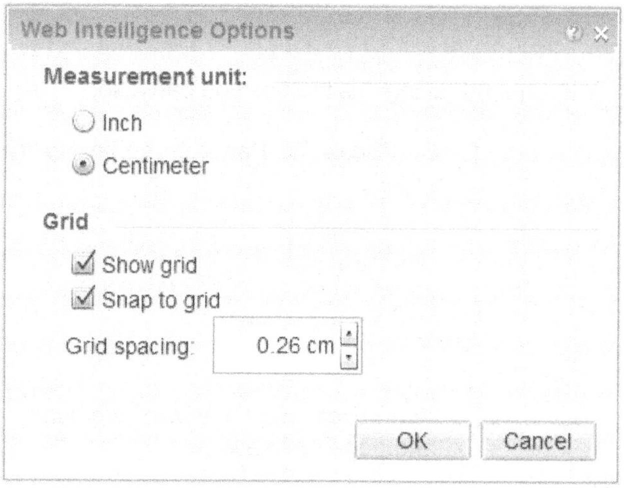
Web Intelligence Options
Measurement unit:
Inch
Centimeter
Grid
Show grid
Snap to grid
Grid spacing:
0.26 cm
OK
Cancel

3. If you move the table around then you will see its top left hand corner 'snap' to the nearest grid cell.

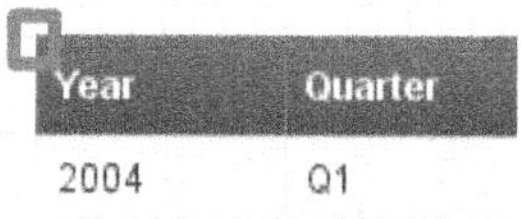
Year
Quarter
2004
Q1

4. If you move the chart then you will be given a warning because the chart has been previously positioned relative to another report element (in this case the table).

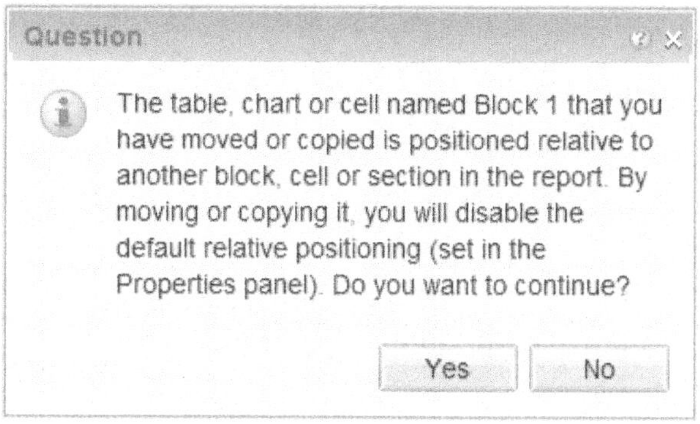
Question
The table, chart or cell named Block 1 that you have moved or copied is positioned relative to another block, cell or section in the report. By moving or copying it, you will disable the default relative positioning (set in the Properties panel). Do you want to continue?
Yes
No

20.5 Page Setup Toolbox

Some of the properties discussed in this session can also be viewed/set using the 'Page Setup' toolbox.

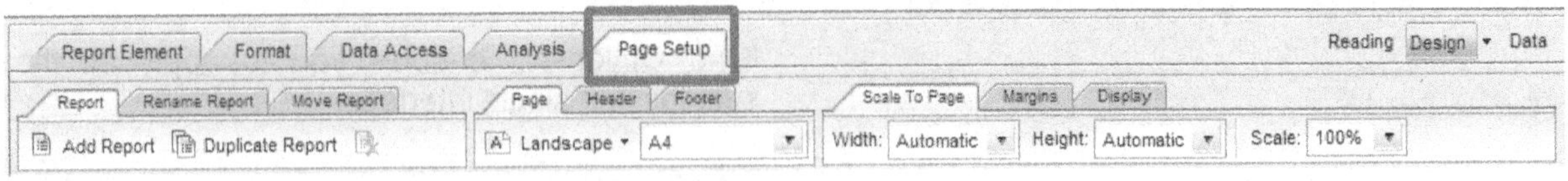
Report Element
Format
Data Access
Analysis
Page Setup
Reading
Design
Data
Report
Rename Report
Move Report
Add Report
Duplicate Report
Page
Header
Footer
Landscape
A4
Scale To Page
Margins
Display
Width:
Automatic
Height:
Automatic
Scale:
100%

If required, using this toolbox you can also:

1. Set 'Scale To Page' properties to try and fit the report content on a specified number of pages.

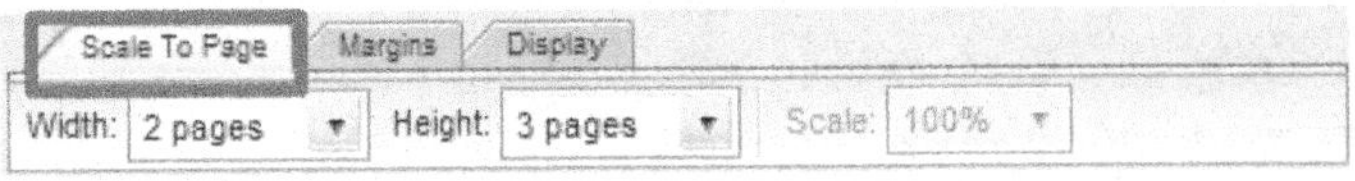
Scale To Page
Margins
Display
Width:
2 pages
Height:
3 pages
Scale:
100%

2. And specify how many rows/columns to display when viewing on-screen (to save scrolling and page navigation).

Scale To Page
Margins
Display
Page
Quick Display
Max:
100
Rows
20
Columns

21 Conditional Formatting using Rules

This session demonstrates how rules can be created and used to format displayed values (i.e. highlight results that fail or meet specific values).

Rules for conditional formatting contain 6 elements:

- A name for the Formatting Rule — More than one Formatting Rule can be created and naming them makes it easier to distinguish them.
- Description — An optional description for the Formatting Rule. This is very useful for future maintenance of the report as it enables you to explain the usage of the rule.
- An object or cell contents — The value of an object or cell to check when applying the Formatting Rule.
- An operator — How the value is to be compared (such as Equal to, Less than, Greater than, etc).
- Operand value(s) or another object — The value(s) to compare using the cell contents or another object's value.
- Conditional Formatting — The formatting to apply to the cell if the Formatting Rule is satisfied.

When you apply a Formatting Rule to a column, row or cell on a report, Web Intelligence evaluates the Formatting Rule and the cell value(s) are Conditionally Formatted based on the result of the evaluation.

Formatting Rules can be applied to tables, sections, cells, and freestanding cells but they cannot be applied to charts.

Multiple conditions can be inserted within a Formatting Rule, and advanced Formatting Rule(s) can be created using formulas.

1. Create a new Web Intelligence document and use the following query (on 'eFashion universe'):

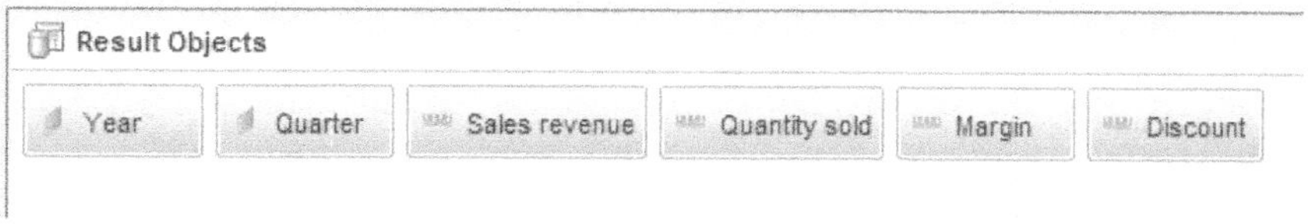
Result Objects
Year
Quarter
Sales revenue
Quantity sold
Margin
Discount

2. Run the query and save the document.

3. We will now use this document to look at a few examples of Conditional Formatting.

21.1 Creating a Formatting Rule to act on Object Values

Formatting Rules can be created to act on the value of an object.

1. Change the default table to appear as shown below, i.e. in this example, the [Sales revenue] object has been used twice.

Year	Quarter	Sales revenue	Sales revenue
2004	Q1	$2,660,700	$2,660,700
2004	Q2	$2,278,693	$2,278,693
2004	Q3	$1,367,841	$1,367,841
2004	Q4	$1,788,580	$1,788,580
2005	Q1	$3,326,172	$3,326,172
2005	Q2	$2,840,651	$2,840,651
2005	Q3	$2,879,303	$2,879,303
2005	Q4	$4,186,120	$4,186,120

The last column will be used to demonstrate conditional formatting based on the results of **[Sales revenue]**.

Repeating the values like this in a second column makes it easier to demonstrate how Conditional Formatting Rules operate.

2. Click away from the table (in the blank part of the report) and then from the 'Analysis' toolbox, click on 'Conditional – New Rule…'

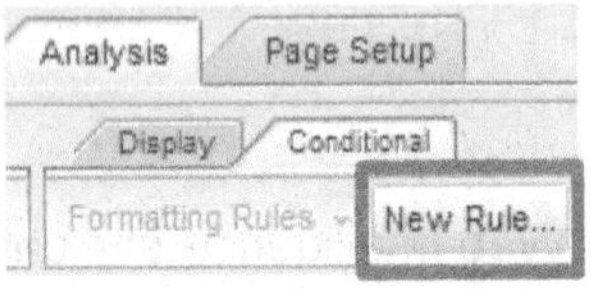
Analysis
Page Setup
Display
Conditional
Formatting Rules
New Rule...

3. This will initiate the 'Formula Rule Editor'.

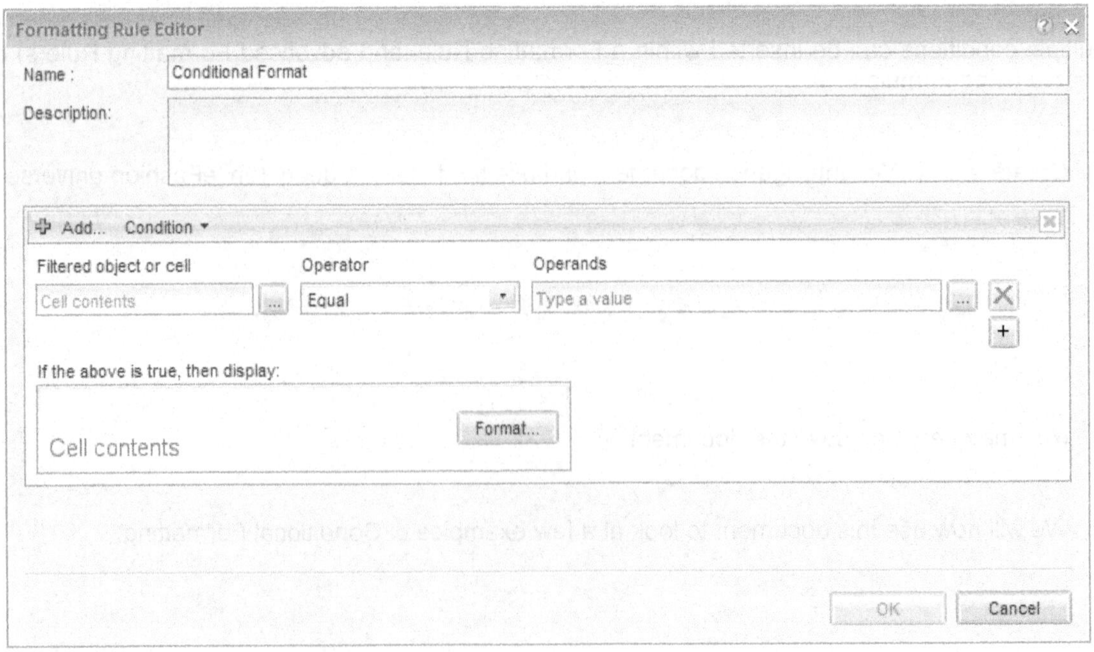
Formatting Rule Editor
Name :
Conditional Format
Description:
Add...
Condition
Filtered object or cell
Operator
Operands
Cell contents
Equal
Type a value
If the above is true, then display:
Cell contents
Format...
OK
Cancel

4. Type a name/description for the Formatting Rule, and set up the condition as shown below:

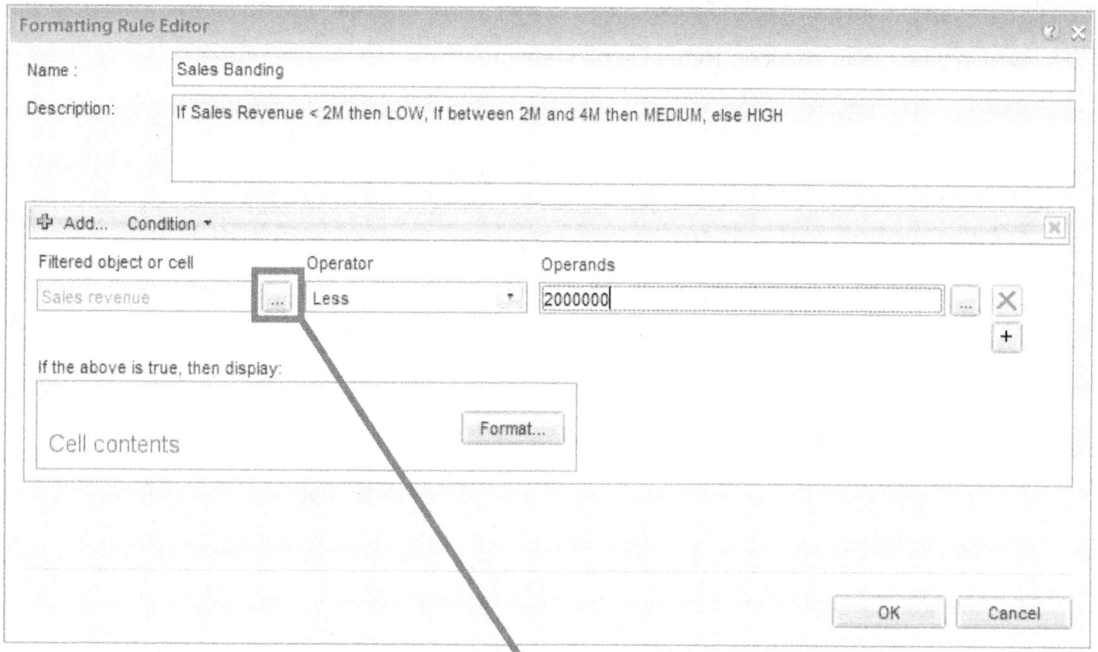
Formatting Rule Editor
Name :
Sales Banding
Description:
If Sales Revenue < 2M then LOW, If between 2M and 4M then MEDIUM, else HIGH
Add... Condition
Filtered object or cell
Operator
Operands
Sales revenue
Less
2000000
If the above is true, then display:
Cell contents
Format...
OK
Cancel

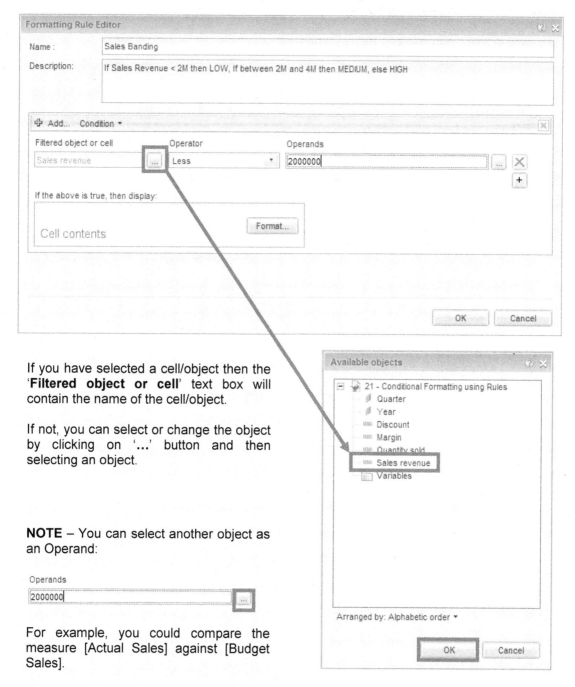

If you have selected a cell/object then the '**Filtered object or cell**' text box will contain the name of the cell/object.

If not, you can select or change the object by clicking on '**...**' button and then selecting an object.

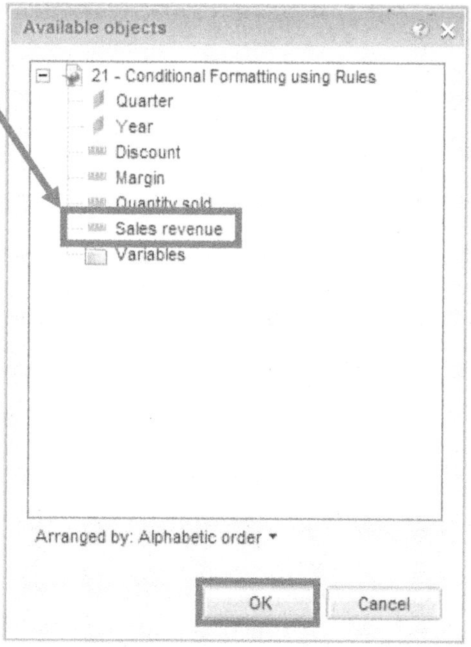
Available objects
21 - Conditional Formatting using Rules
Quarter
Year
Discount
Margin
Quantity sold
Sales revenue
Variables
Arranged by: Alphabetic order
OK
Cancel

NOTE – You can select another object as an Operand:

Operands
2000000

For example, you could compare the measure [Actual Sales] against [Budget Sales].

This has now set up the condition as when [Sales revenue] is less than 2,000,000.

NOTE – Do not type in the commas when specifying number values.

5. We now need to click on 'Format ...' in order to specify what will be displayed when this condition is met (in terms of value and formatting).

   This will initiate the Formatting Rules Display editor.

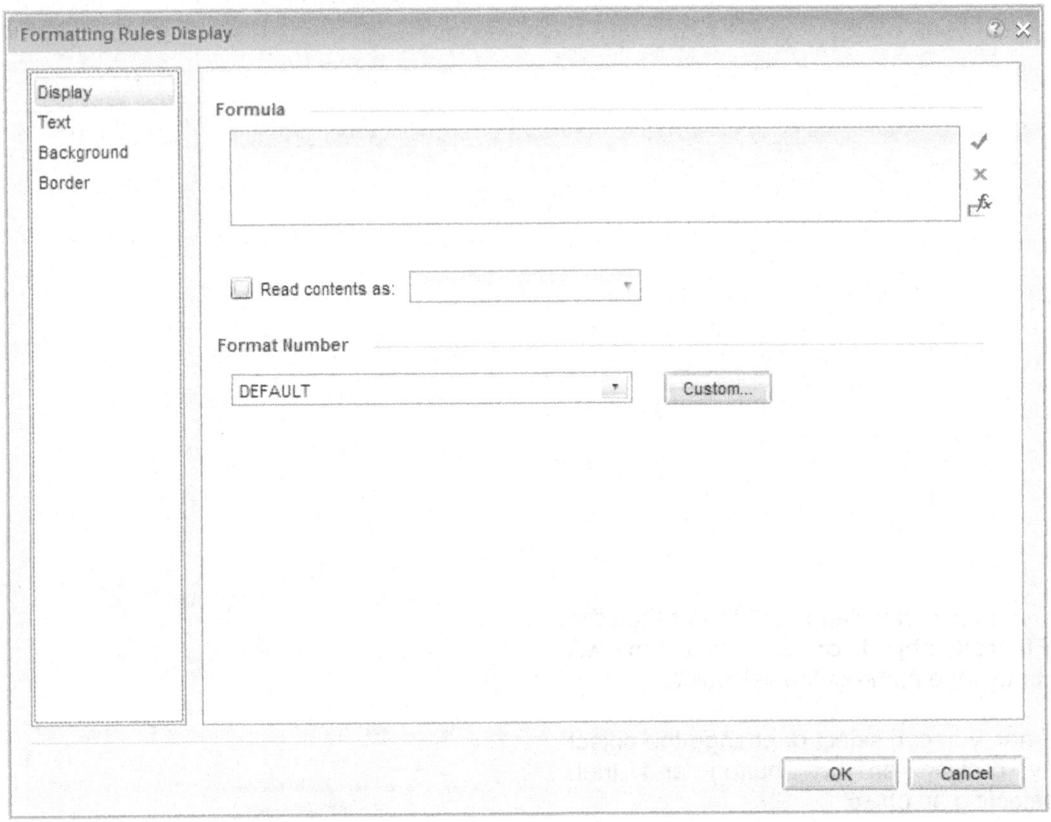
Formatting Rules Display
Display
Text
Background
Border
Formula
Read contents as:
Format Number
DEFAULT
Custom...
OK
Cancel

6. You can specify a formula to use, or value to display as shown below.

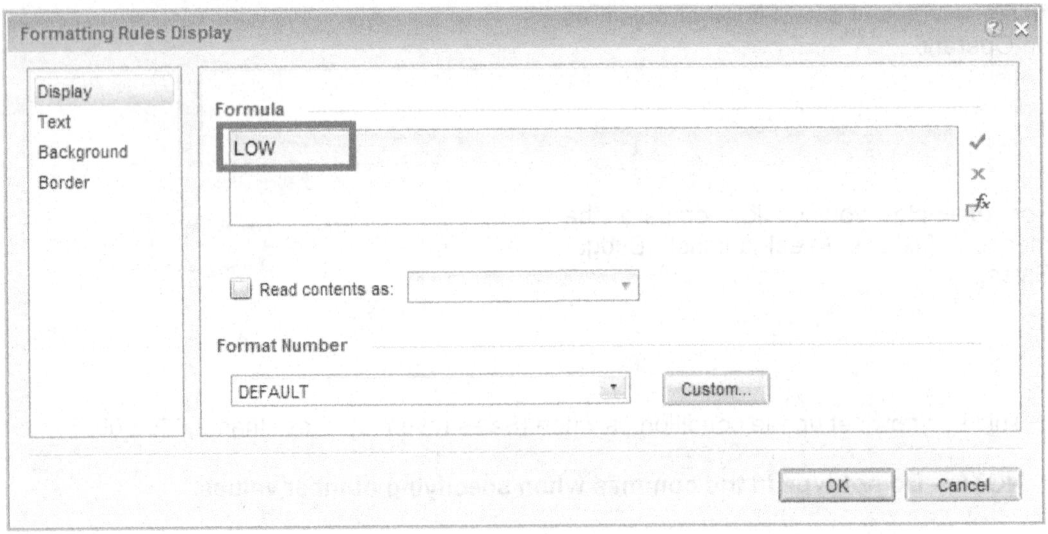
Formatting Rules Display
Display
Text
Background
Border
Formula
LOW
Read contents as:
Format Number
DEFAULT
Custom...
OK
Cancel

7. From the 'Text' options select the 'Red' color and then click 'OK'.

   We now have a Formatting Rule that will display LOW in red font color, i.e. when the [Sales revenue] is less than 2,000,000.

8. Click on the 
Add...
button and set up a sub-rule as shown below:

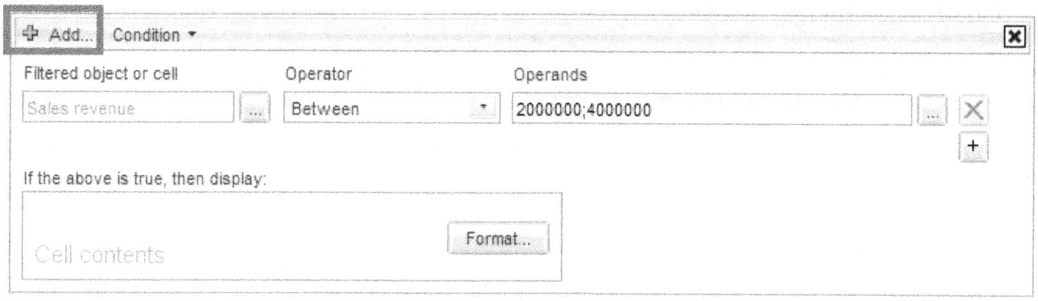
Add...
Condition
Filtered object or cell
Operator
Operands
Sales revenue
Between
2000000;4000000
If the above is true, then display:
Cell contents
Format...

Use the following settings for the sub-rule:

Filtered object or cell = [Sales revenue]

Operator = Between

Operands = 2000000;4000000

Then click 'Format...' and set:

Formula = MEDIUM

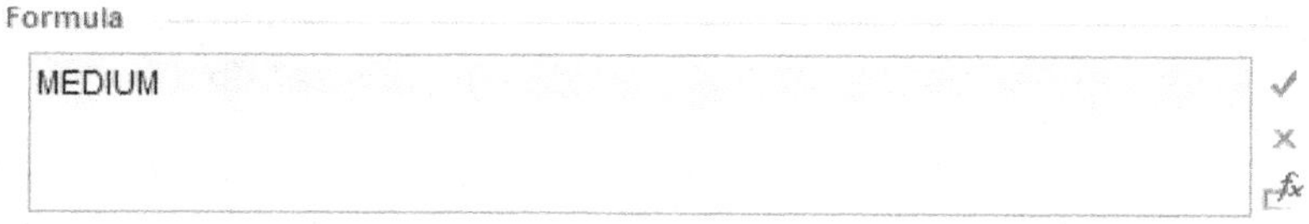
Formula
MEDIUM

Text (Font color) = 'Light Orange'

9. Click on the 
Add...
button again and set up a sub-rule as shown below:

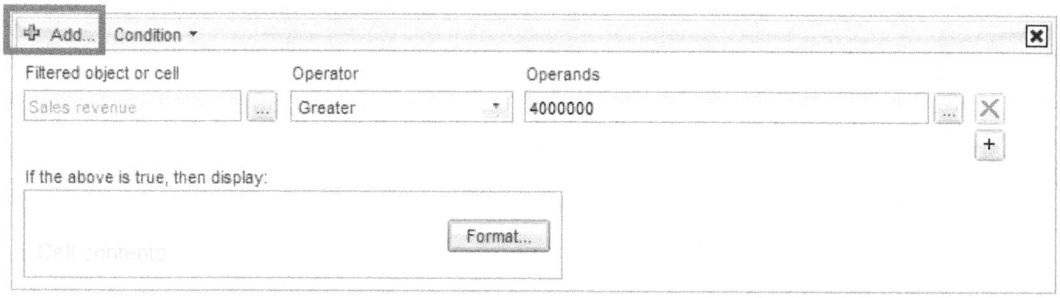
Add...
Condition
Filtered object or cell
Operator
Operands
Sales revenue
Greater
4000000
If the above is true, then display:
Cell contents
Format...

Use the following settings for the sub-rule:

Filtered object or cell = [Sales revenue]

Operator = Greater

Operands = 4000000

Then click 'Format...' and set:

Formula = HIGH

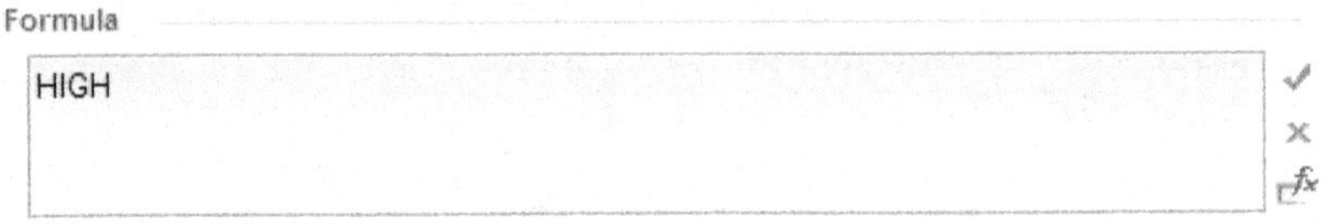
Formula
HIGH

Text (Font color) = 'Bright Green'

10. Our Formatting Rule will now appear as:

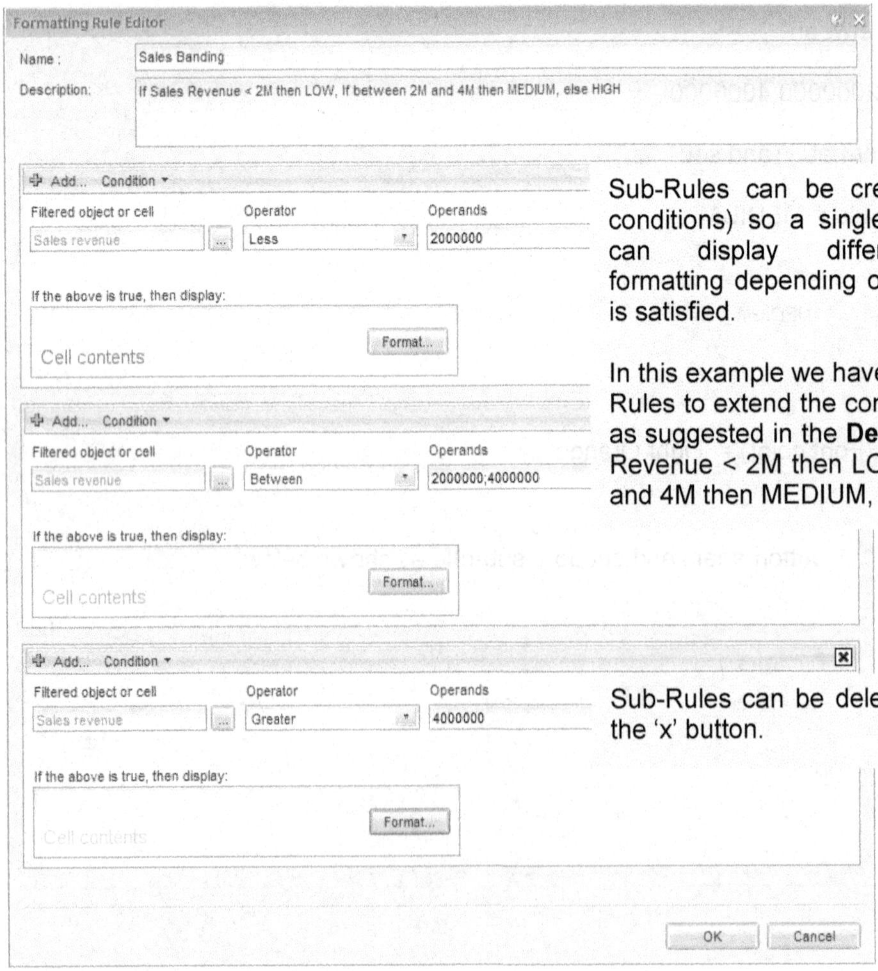
Formatting Rule Editor
Name :
Sales Banding
Description:
If Sales Revenue < 2M then LOW, If between 2M and 4M then MEDIUM, else HIGH
Add... Condition
Filtered object or cell
Operator
Operands
Sales revenue
Less
2000000
If the above is true, then display:
Format...
Cell contents
Add... Condition
Filtered object or cell
Operator
Operands
Sales revenue
Between
2000000;4000000
If the above is true, then display:
Format...
Cell contents
Add... Condition
Filtered object or cell
Operator
Operands
Sales revenue
Greater
4000000
If the above is true, then display:
Format...
Cell contents
OK
Cancel

Sub-Rules can be created (i.e. nested conditions) so a single Formatting Rule can display different conditional formatting depending on which Sub-Rule is satisfied.

In this example we have created two Sub-Rules to extend the conditional formatting as suggested in the **Description** (If Sales Revenue < 2M then LOW, If between 2M and 4M then MEDIUM, else HIGH).

Sub-Rules can be deleted by clicking on the 'x' button.

11. Click 'OK' to add the Formatting Rule to the list of Conditional Formats.

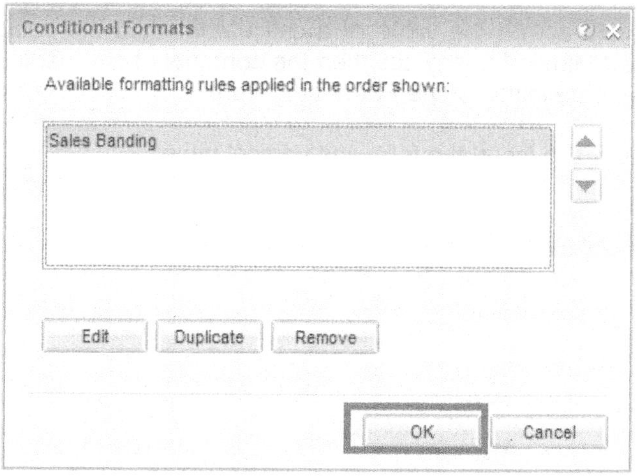
Conditional Formats
Available formatting rules applied in the order shown:
Sales Banding
Edit
Duplicate
Remove
OK
Cancel

Click 'OK' to close the 'Conditional Formats' interface.

21.2 Applying a Formatting Rule

If you had clicked into a cell within the table (before creating the Formatting Rule) then the Conditional Formatting will automatically be applied to the column cell (on exiting the Conditional Formats interface).

1. To apply a Formatting Rule, click into the table cell and then select the Formatting Rule you want to apply

In this example:

- Click into any cell of last column
- Select 'Sales Banding' from 'Formatting Rules'

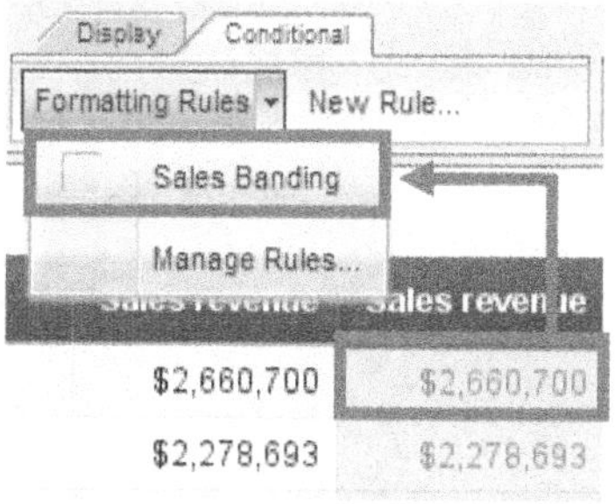
Display
Conditional
Formatting Rules
New Rule...
Sales Banding
Manage Rules...
Sales revenue
$2,660,700
$2,660,700
$2,278,693
$2,278,693

Year	Quarter	Sales revenue	Sales revenue
2004	Q1	$2,660,700	MEDIUM
2004	Q2	$2,278,693	MEDIUM
2004	Q3	$1,367,841	LOW
2004	Q4	$1,788,580	LOW
2005	Q1	$3,326,172	MEDIUM
2005	Q2	$2,840,651	MEDIUM
2005	Q3	$2,879,303	MEDIUM
2005	Q4	$4,186,120	HIGH
2006	Q1	$3,742,989	MEDIUM
2006	Q2	$4,006,718	HIGH
2006	Q3	$3,953,395	MEDIUM
2006	Q4	$3,356,041	MEDIUM

For comparison purposes the Formatting Rule conditions were created as:

Display LOW when the [Sales revenue] is less than 2,000,000.

Display MEDIUM when [Sales revenue] is between 2,000,000 and 4,000,000.

Display HIGH when [Sales revenue] is greater than 4,000,000.

21.3 Creating a Formatting Rule to act on Cell Contents

Dynamic Formatting Rules can be created to act on the value of a cell (rather than the value of an object). When this type of Formatting Rule is applied to any cell then the contents of that particular cell are evaluated against the conditions set in the definition of the Formatting Rule.

1. Create a new report tab in your document and insert the following vertical table.

Year	Quarter	Sales revenue	Discount	Margin
2004	Q1	$2,660,700	$621,461	$1,166,984
2004	Q2	$2,278,693	$-21,317	$1,086,403
2004	Q3	$1,367,841	$562,986	$552,074
2004	Q4	$1,788,580	$661,380	$926,510
2005	Q1	$3,326,172	$-393,713	$1,236,390
2005	Q2	$2,840,651	$-601,996	$1,132,666
2005	Q3	$2,879,303	$930,254	$1,026,132
2005	Q4	$4,186,120	$1,086,712	$1,792,698
2006	Q1	$3,742,989	$1,030,458	$1,384,424
2006	Q2	$4,006,718	$139,773	$1,647,660
2006	Q3	$3,953,395	$787,247	$1,344,435
2006	Q4	$3,356,041	$170,852	$1,290,564

2. Click 'New Rule' on the 'Analysis' toolbox. Then Create a rule to apply a background color of 'Light Green' if the **Cell contents** are '**Greater or equal**' to **1000000** (i.e. 1 million).

   Give the rule the name 'Cell High Low'.

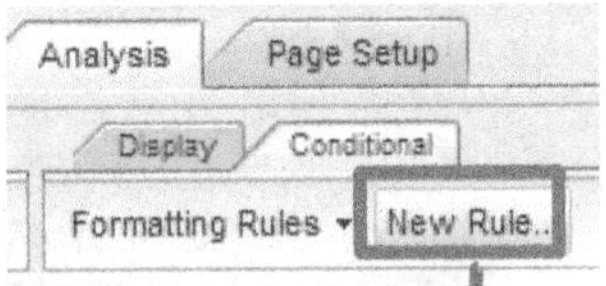
Analysis
Page Setup
Display
Conditional
Formatting Rules
New Rule..

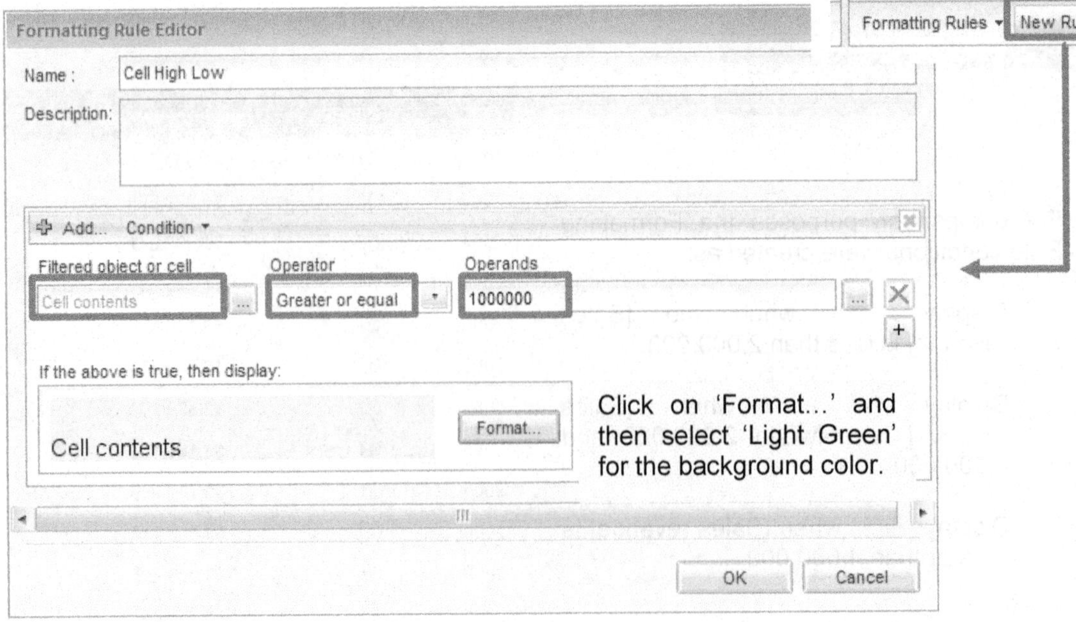
Formatting Rule Editor
Name :
Cell High Low
Description:
Add... Condition
Filtered object or cell
Cell contents
Operator
Greater or equal
Operands
1000000
If the above is true, then display:
Cell contents
Format...
Click on 'Format...' and then select 'Light Green' for the background color.
OK
Cancel

3. Click on the  button and set up a sub-rule to apply a background color of 'Light Blue' if the **Cell contents** are '**Less**' than **1000000** (i.e. 1 million).

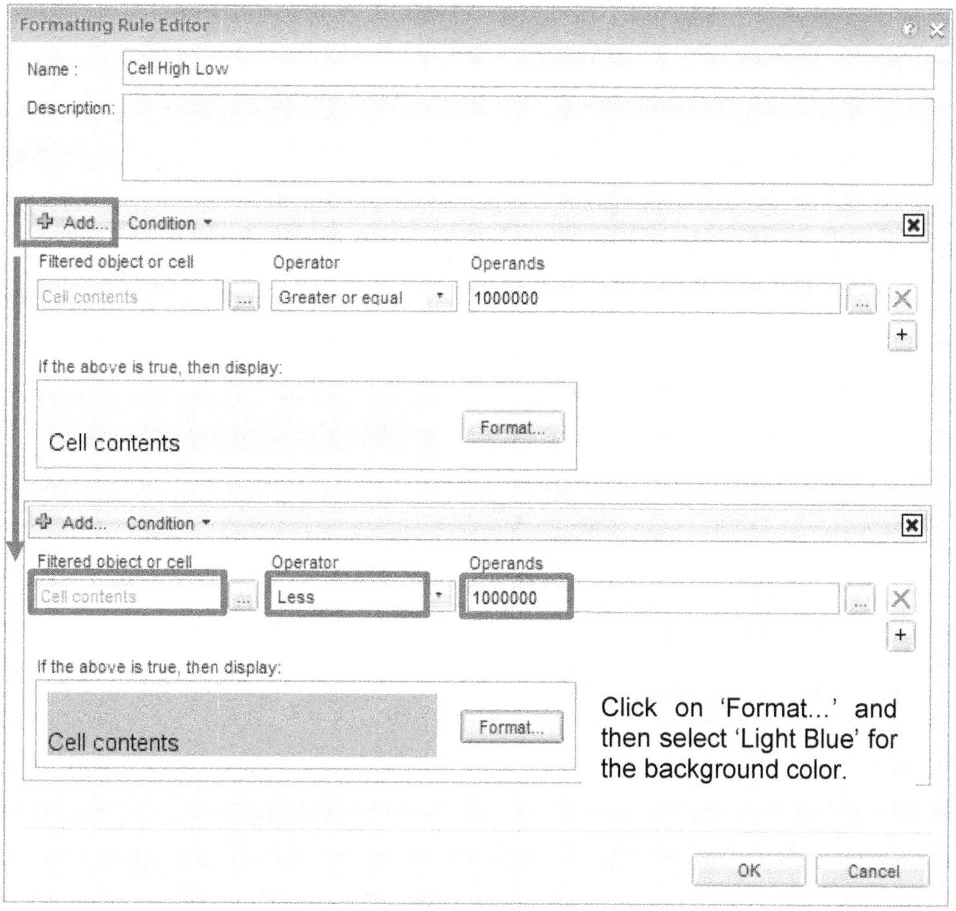
Formatting Rule Editor
Name :
Cell High Low
Description:
Add...
Condition
Filtered object or cell
Operator
Operands
Cell contents
Greater or equal
1000000
If the above is true, then display:
Cell contents
Format...
Add...
Condition
Filtered object or cell
Operator
Operands
Cell contents
Less
1000000
If the above is true, then display:
Cell contents
Format...
Click on 'Format...' and then select 'Light Blue' for the background color.
OK
Cancel

4. Click 'OK' to close the 'Formatting Rule Editor'

5. Click in any body cell of the [Sales revenue] column and then select 'Formatting Rules – Cell High Low':

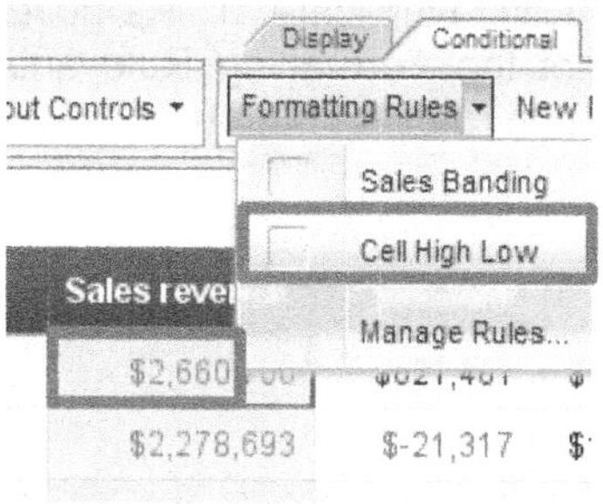
Display
Conditional
Formatting Rules
Sales Banding
Cell High Low
Manage Rules...
$2,278,693
$-21,317

6. Then apply 'Formatting Rules – Cell High Low' to [Discount] and [Margin] columns.

Year	Quarter	Sales revenue	Discount	Margin
2004	Q1	$2,660,700	$621,461	$1,166,984
2004	Q2	$2,278,693	$-21,317	$1,086,403
2004	Q3	$1,367,841	$562,986	$552,074
2004	Q4	$1,788,580	$661,380	$926,510
2005	Q1	$3,326,172	$-393,713	$1,236,390
2005	Q2	$2,840,651	$-601,996	$1,132,666
2005	Q3	$2,879,303	$930,254	$1,026,132
2005	Q4	$4,186,120	$1,086,712	$1,792,698
2006	Q1	$3,742,989	$1,030,458	$1,384,424
2006	Q2	$4,006,718	$139,773	$1,647,660
2006	Q3	$3,953,395	$787,247	$1,344,435
2006	Q4	$3,356,041	$170,852	$1,290,564

The background color of cells changes based on the value of the individual cell itself.

A single Formatting Rule is being used on multiple objects but the results are dynamic because the rule is based on 'Cell contents'.

21.4 Managing Formatting Rules

1. Once created, Formatting Rules can be edited, duplicated or deleted by using 'Manage Rules...'

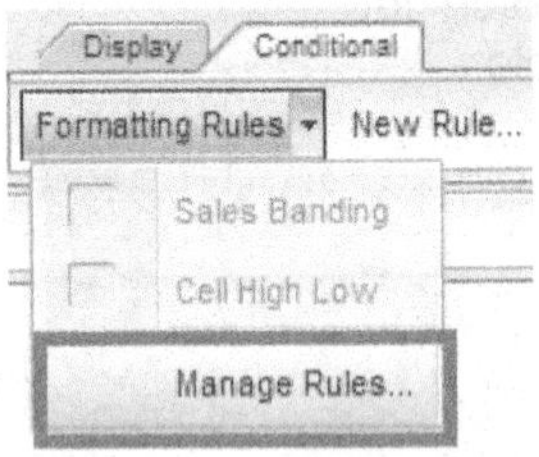
Display
Conditional
Formatting Rules
New Rule...
Sales Banding
Cell High Low
Manage Rules...

This will then open the 'Conditional Formats' interface.

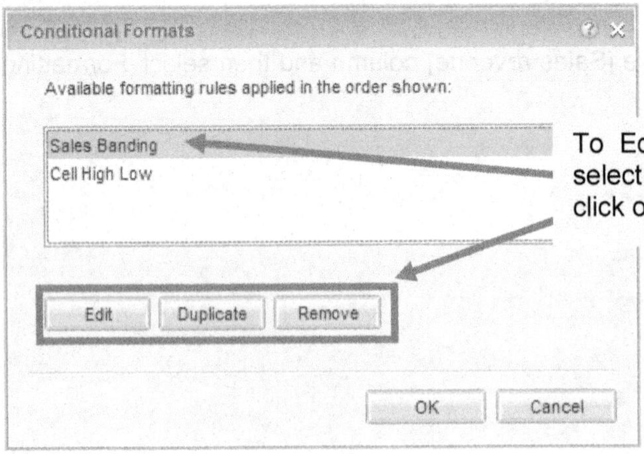
Conditional Formats
Available formatting rules applied in the order shown:
Sales Banding
Cell High Low
Edit
Duplicate
Remove
OK
Cancel

To Edit, Duplicate or Remove, first select the Formatting Rule and then click on relevant button.

2. We will make a copy of 'Sales Banding', so select 'Sales Banding' and then click 'Duplicate'. This will result in a new Formatting Rule being created called 'Sales Banding (1)'.

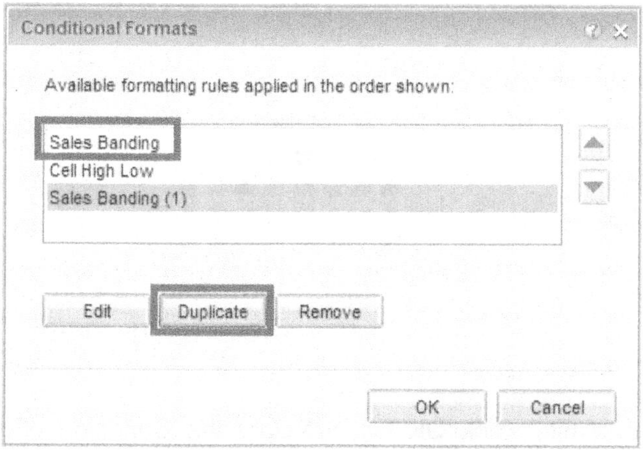
Conditional Formats
Available formatting rules applied in the order shown:
Sales Banding
Cell High Low
Sales Banding (1)
Edit
Duplicate
Remove
OK
Cancel

3. With 'Sales Banding (1)' being selected, click on 'Edit' and change the name to 'Sales Banding White BG':

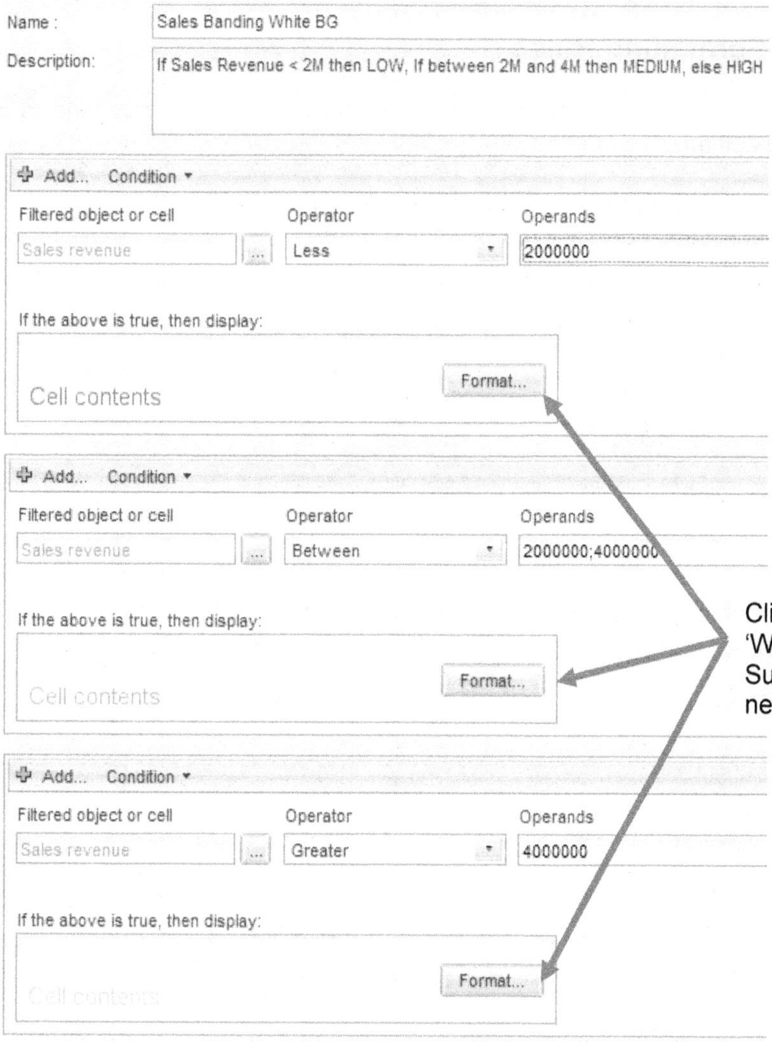
Name :
Sales Banding White BG
Description:
If Sales Revenue < 2M then LOW, If between 2M and 4M then MEDIUM, else HIGH
Add... Condition
Filtered object or cell
Operator
Operands
Sales revenue
Less
2000000
If the above is true, then display:
Cell contents
Format...
Add... Condition
Filtered object or cell
Operator
Operands
Sales revenue
Between
2000000;4000000
If the above is true, then display:
Cell contents
Format...
Add... Condition
Filtered object or cell
Operator
Operands
Sales revenue
Greater
4000000
If the above is true, then display:
Format...

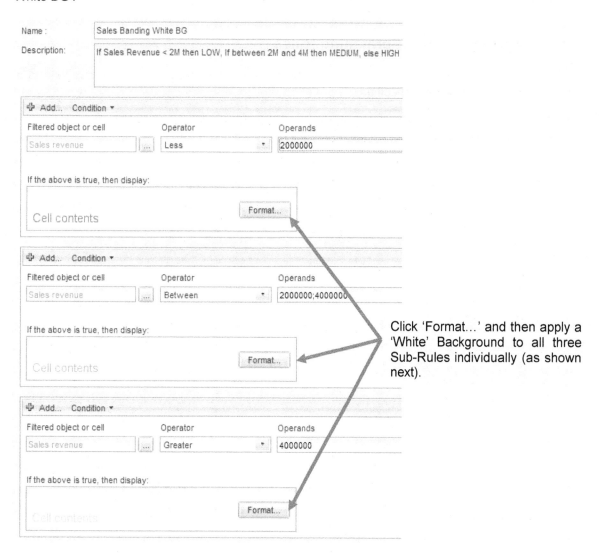

Click 'Format...' and then apply a 'White' Background to all three Sub-Rules individually (as shown next).

4. For all three conditions change the Background to 'White' as shown here:

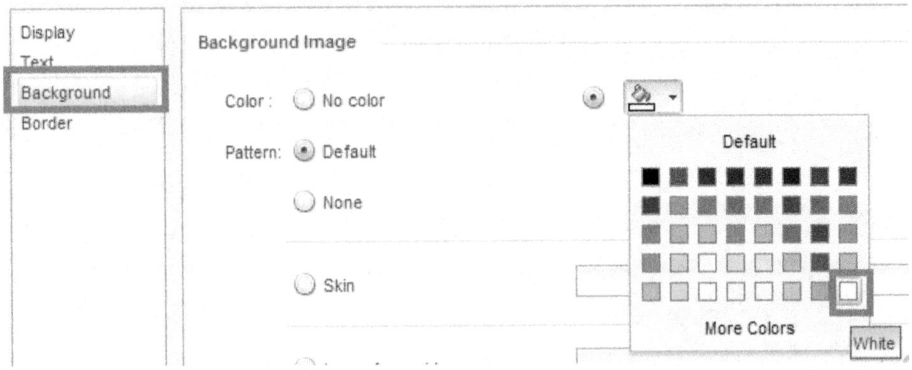
Display
Text
Background
Border
Background Image
Color :
No color
Pattern:
Default
None
Skin
Default
More Colors
White

5. After changing the three Backgrounds to 'White', click 'OK' twice to close the 'Conditional Formats' interface.

6. Save the document.

21.5 Applying Multiple Formatting Rules

Multiple Formatting Rules can be applied but the order in which they are applied can lead to different results, unless priorities are specified.

From the previous section we have 2 Formatting Rules; '**Sales Banding**' and '**Cell High Low**'. We will use these to demonstrate the application of multiple Formatting Rules.

1. Create the following block of data showing the [Sales revenue] object repeated 5 times. Simply drag [Sales revenue] in five times:

Year	Quarter	Sales revenue	Sales revenue	Sales revenue	Sales revenue	Sales revenue
2004	Q1	$2,660,700	$2,660,700	$2,660,700	$2,660,700	$2,660,700
2004	Q2	$2,278,693	$2,278,693	$2,278,693	$2,278,693	$2,278,693
2004	Q3	$1,367,841	$1,367,841	$1,367,841	$1,367,841	$1,367,841
2004	Q4	$1,788,580	$1,788,580	$1,788,580	$1,788,580	$1,788,580
2005	Q1	$3,326,172	$3,326,172	$3,326,172	$3,326,172	$3,326,172
2005	Q2	$2,840,651	$2,840,651	$2,840,651	$2,840,651	$2,840,651
2005	Q3	$2,879,303	$2,879,303	$2,879,303	$2,879,303	$2,879,303
2005	Q4	$4,186,120	$4,186,120	$4,186,120	$4,186,120	$4,186,120
2006	Q1	$3,742,989	$3,742,989	$3,742,989	$3,742,989	$3,742,989
2006	Q2	$4,006,718	$4,006,718	$4,006,718	$4,006,718	$4,006,718
2006	Q3	$3,953,395	$3,953,395	$3,953,395	$3,953,395	$3,953,395
2006	Q4	$3,356,041	$3,356,041	$3,356,041	$3,356,041	$3,356,041
		1	**2**	**3**	**4**	**5**

2. Apply the Formatting Rules to the five [Sales revenue] columns labelled above as:

Column	Formatting Rules (to be applied in order)
1	No Formatting Rules
2	Sales Banding White BG
3	Cell High Low
4	Sales Banding White BG *and then* Cell High Low
5	Cell High Low *and then* Sales Banding White BG

3. The results are as follows:

Year	Quarter	Sales revenue	Sales revenue	Sales revenue	Sales revenue	Sales revenue
2004	Q1	$2,660,700	MEDIUM	$2,660,700	MEDIUM	MEDIUM
2004	Q2	$2,278,693	MEDIUM	$2,278,693	MEDIUM	MEDIUM
2004	Q3	$1,367,841	LOW	$1,367,841	LOW	LOW
2004	Q4	$1,788,580	LOW	$1,788,580	LOW	LOW
2005	Q1	$3,326,172	MEDIUM	$3,326,172	MEDIUM	MEDIUM
2005	Q2	$2,840,651	MEDIUM	$2,840,651	MEDIUM	MEDIUM
2005	Q3	$2,879,303	MEDIUM	$2,879,303	MEDIUM	MEDIUM
2005	Q4	$4,186,120	HIGH	$4,186,120	HIGH	HIGH
2006	Q1	$3,742,989	MEDIUM	$3,742,989	MEDIUM	MEDIUM
2006	Q2	$4,006,718	HIGH	$4,006,718	HIGH	HIGH
2006	Q3	$3,953,395	MEDIUM	$3,953,395	MEDIUM	MEDIUM
2006	Q4	$3,356,041	MEDIUM	$3,356,041	MEDIUM	MEDIUM
		1	2	3	4	5

Columns 4 and 5 have the same Formatting Rules applied but they appear different. **Why?**

The priorities of the applied Formatting Rules are different as shown below:

Column 4

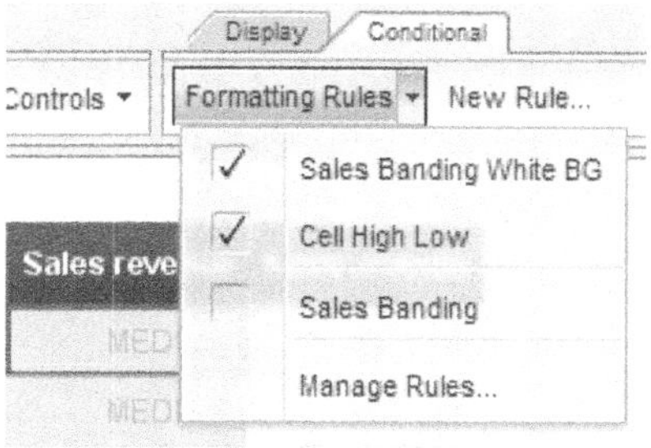
Display
Conditional
Controls
Formatting Rules
New Rule...
Sales Banding White BG
Cell High Low
Sales Banding
Manage Rules...
Sales reve
MED
MED

Column 5

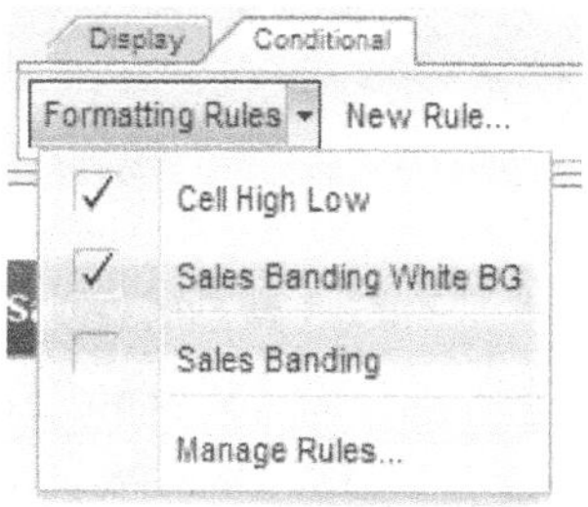
Display
Conditional
Formatting Rules
New Rule...
Cell High Low
Sales Banding White BG
Sales Banding
Manage Rules...

Priorities can be changed using 'Manage Rules…'

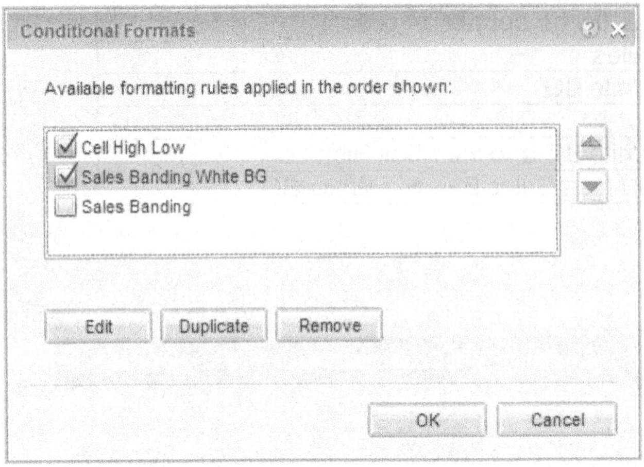
Conditional Formats
Available formatting rules applied in the order shown:
Cell High Low
Sales Banding White BG
Sales Banding
Edit
Duplicate
Remove
OK
Cancel

Select a Formatting Rule and then use the arrows to change its priority.

NOTE – When applying multiple Formatting Rules, make sure you apply them in the correct sequence to ensure the net result is as desired.

21.6 Using Multiple Conditions in Formatting Rules

We can use multiple conditions when applying formatting rules.

1. Edit 'Sales Banding' as follows:

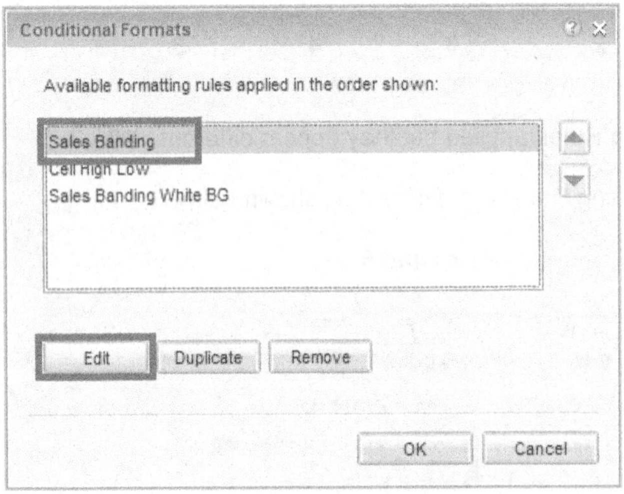
Conditional Formats
Available formatting rules applied in the order shown:
Sales Banding
Cell High Low
Sales Banding White BG
Edit
Duplicate
Remove
OK
Cancel

2. Click on the '+' button.

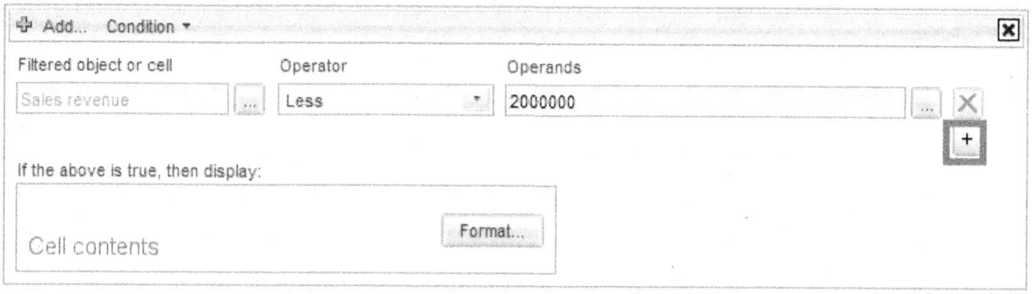
Add... Condition
Filtered object or cell
Operator
Operands
Sales revenue
Less
2000000
+
If the above is true, then display:
Cell contents
Format...

3. Click on '...' button and then 'Select an object or variable'.

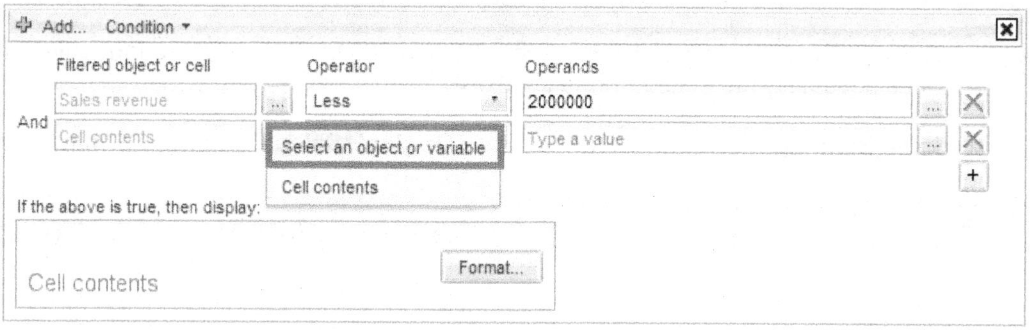
Add... Condition
Filtered object or cell
Operator
Operands
Sales revenue
Less
2000000
And
Cell contents
Select an object or variable
Type a value
Cell contents
+
If the above is true, then display:
Cell contents
Format...

4. Select [Quarter] and then click 'OK'.

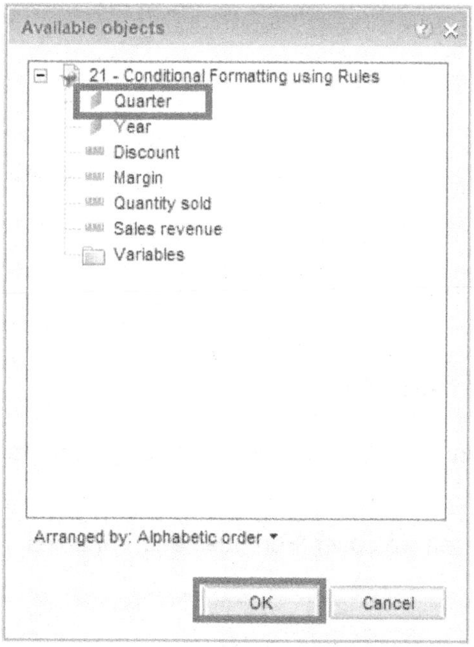
Available objects
21 - Conditional Formatting using Rules
Quarter
Year
Discount
Margin
Quantity sold
Sales revenue
Variables
Arranged by: Alphabetic order
OK
Cancel

5. Set the new condition up as [Quarter] In list Q1;Q3 as shown below.

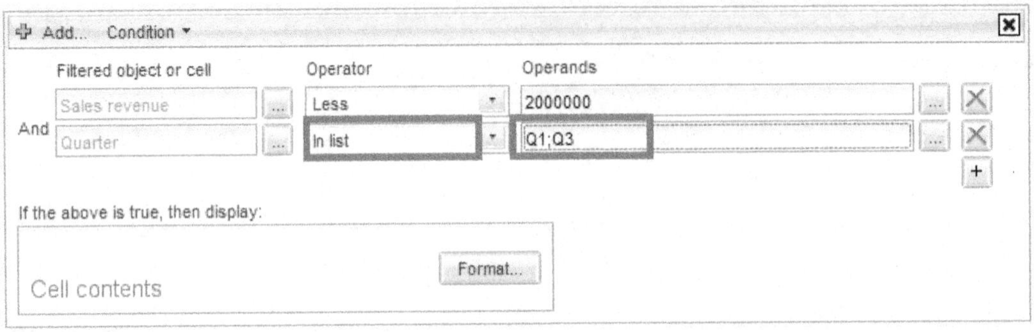
Add... Condition
Filtered object or cell
Operator
Operands
Sales revenue
Less
2000000
And
Quarter
In list
Q1;Q3
If the above is true, then display:
Cell contents
Format...

6. Click ‘OK’ twice to save the edited ‘Sales Banding’ Formatting Rule.

The example we used at the start of this session will show 2004/Q4 row with no formatting changes because it does not satisfy the edited Formatting Rule.

New ‘Sales Banding’ Formatting Rule

Year	Quarter	Sales revenue	Sales revenue
2004	Q1	$2,660,700	MEDIUM
2004	Q2	$2,278,693	MEDIUM
2004	Q3	$1,367,841	LOW
2004	Q4	$1,788,580	$1,788,580
2005	Q1	$3,326,172	MEDIUM
2005	Q2	$2,840,651	MEDIUM
2005	Q3	$2,879,303	MEDIUM
2005	Q4	$4,186,120	HIGH
2006	Q1	$3,742,989	MEDIUM
2006	Q2	$4,006,718	HIGH
2006	Q3	$3,953,395	MEDIUM
2006	Q4	$3,356,041	MEDIUM

Original ‘Sales Banding’ Formatting Rule

Year	Quarter	Sales revenue	Sales revenue
2004	Q1	$2,660,700	MEDIUM
2004	Q2	$2,278,693	MEDIUM
2004	Q3	$1,367,841	LOW
2004	Q4	$1,788,580	LOW
2005	Q1	$3,326,172	MEDIUM
2005	Q2	$2,840,651	MEDIUM
2005	Q3	$2,879,303	MEDIUM
2005	Q4	$4,186,120	HIGH
2006	Q1	$3,742,989	MEDIUM
2006	Q2	$4,006,718	HIGH
2006	Q3	$3,953,395	MEDIUM
2006	Q4	$3,356,041	MEDIUM

21.7 Using Formulas and Variables in Formatting Rules

For the time being we will mention that complex logic can be used in Formula Rules by using formulas and variables.

A formula based Formatting Rule will be demonstrated when we cover ‘Formulas and Variables’.

21.8 Un-Applying Formatting Rules

To Un-Apply Formatting Rule(s):

1. Select the cell/object on which the formatting rule has been applied.

2. Un-tick the Formatting Rule you want to un-apply.

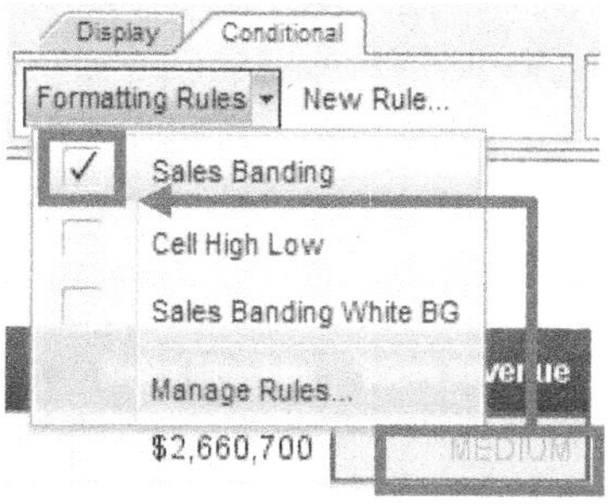
Display
Conditional
Formatting Rules
New Rule...
Sales Banding
Cell High Low
Sales Banding White BG
Manage Rules...
$2,660,700
MEDIUM

3. Or you can select 'Manage Rules...' and then un-apply rules from the 'Conditional Formats' interface by un-ticking them.

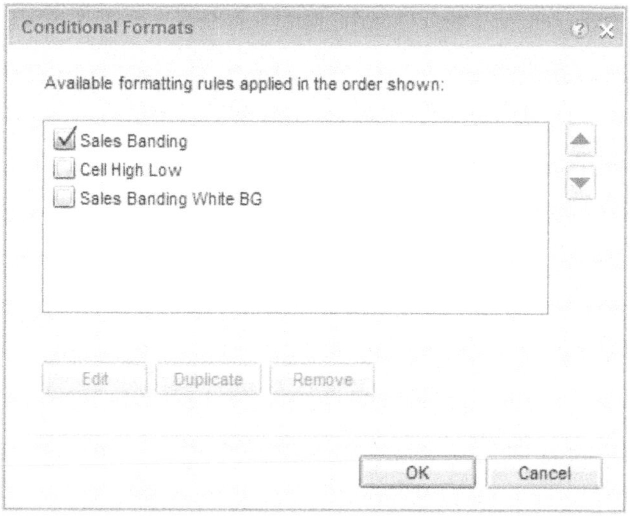
Conditional Formats
Available formatting rules applied in the order shown:
Sales Banding
Cell High Low
Sales Banding White BG
Edit
Duplicate
Remove
OK
Cancel

4. Click on 'OK' to confirm

22 Restricting Query Data

Focused queries can be created by using Query Conditions and Filters to limit the data returned by the database so the data provider does not contain unnecessary information.

Reports should only contain the relevant data to help the user to make informed decisions without having to filter the unwanted data within the report. This will make documents more efficient and responsive.

This session describes how to restrict queries by using conditions and filters within the Query Panel.

NOTE

The terms filters and conditions are interchangeable but in our case we will say:

A ***Filter*** comprises of one or more ***Conditions*** to define the overall restriction.

To apply conditions on the set of data attached to our report, we use the Query Panel to modify our query.

22.1 Using Pre-defined Conditions

The designer of the universe often sets up commonly used conditions as Pre-Defined Conditions, making them easy to apply and use.

Pre-Defined Conditions will appear as yellow funnel icons.

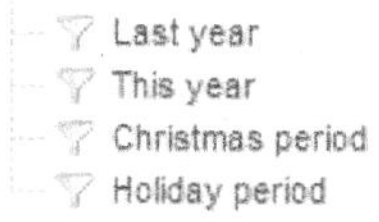
Last year
This year
Christmas period
Holiday period

To apply these to our query, we can drag and drop the Pre-Defined Conditions into the Query Filters pane of the Query Panel, or we can double-click them and they will automatically be entered into the Query Filters pane.

1. Create the following query using the 'eFashion' universe and run it:

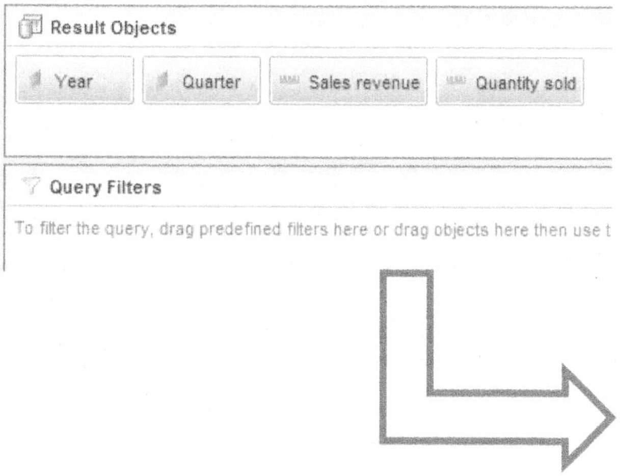
Result Objects
Year
Quarter
Sales revenue
Quantity sold
Query Filters
To filter the query, drag predefined filters here or drag objects here then use t

Year	Quarter	Sales revenu	Quantity sold
2004	Q1	$2,660,700	18,136
2004	Q2	$2,278,693	14,408
2004	Q3	$1,367,841	10,203
2004	Q4	$1,788,580	10,331
2005	Q1	$3,326,172	21,135
2005	Q2	$2,840,651	17,152
2005	Q3	$2,879,303	19,224
2005	Q4	$4,186,120	22,344
2006	Q1	$3,742,989	22,537
2006	Q2	$4,006,718	22,846
2006	Q3	$3,953,395	26,263
2006	Q4	$3,356,041	18,650

2. We will now modify the query. Click the 'Data Access – Edit' button.

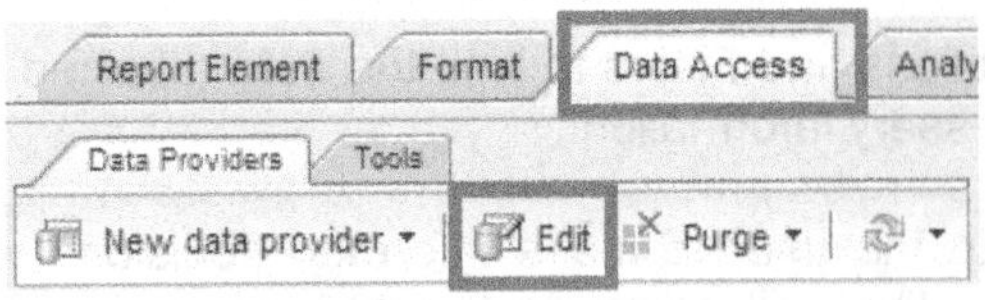
Report Element
Format
Data Access
Analy
Data Providers
Tools
New data provider
Edit
Purge

3. Add the [Last year] Pre-Defined Condition to the query. You can double click the [Last year] object, or you can drag and drop it into the 'Query Filters' pane.

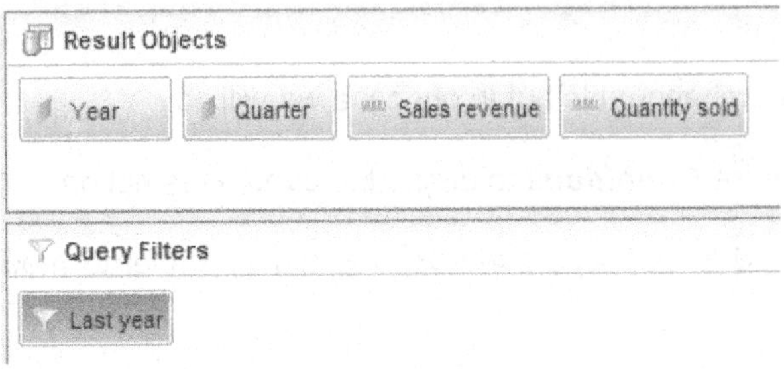
Result Objects
Year
Quarter
Sales revenue
Quantity sold
Query Filters
Last year

4. Click the 'Run Query' button to run the modified query.

Run Query
Close

Year	Quarter	Sales revenu	Quantity sold
2005	Q1	$3,326,172	21,135
2005	Q2	$2,840,651	17,152
2005	Q3	$2,879,303	19,224
2005	Q4	$4,186,120	22,344

As you can see in the above example, only data for a single year has been returned. In this case 2005 is the last year (or previous year) within our data.

5. Save the document.

NOTE

Pre-Defined Conditions are created by the Universe Designer for all to use. If there are conditions that you use in many reports then it may be more useful to have them built into the universe rather than applying the same filter(s) in each report. If the filter requirement changes then a single change in the universe will propagate the filter definition to all documents that use the Pre-Defined Condition.

22.2 Adding a Quick Filter

After placing an object in the Results Objects pane, you can apply a filter to it by selecting the object and then clicking on 'Add Quick Filter' button. In the example below, we are going to apply a quick filter to [State] object.

1. Modify the existing query and add the [State] object to the 'Result Objects' pane and remove the [Quarter] object. Also remove the [Last year] Pre-Defined Condition from the 'Query Filters' pane.

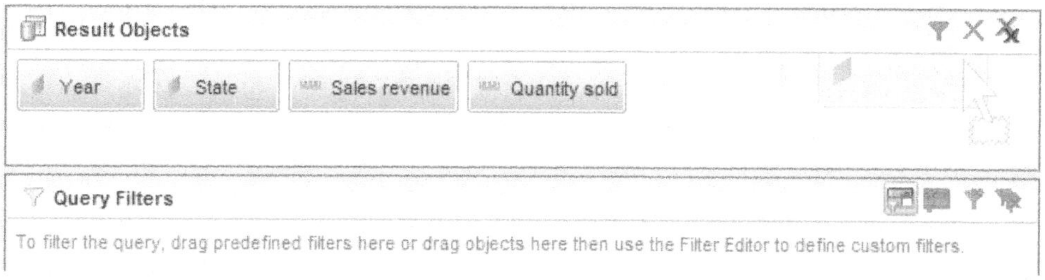
Result Objects
Year
State
Sales revenue
Quantity sold
Query Filters
To filter the query, drag predefined filters here or drag objects here then use the Filter Editor to define custom filters.

2. Select the [State] within the 'Result Objects' pane and then click on 'Add a quick filter' button.

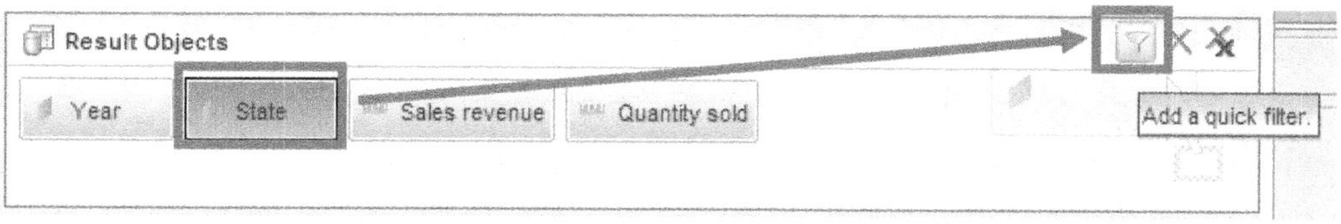
Result Objects
Year
State
Sales revenue
Quantity sold
Add a quick filter.

3. You can select one or more values from the List of Values displayed for the object (or you can type value(s) in the box labelled Type a value) and click '>' button to add value(s) into the 'Selected Value(s)' box.

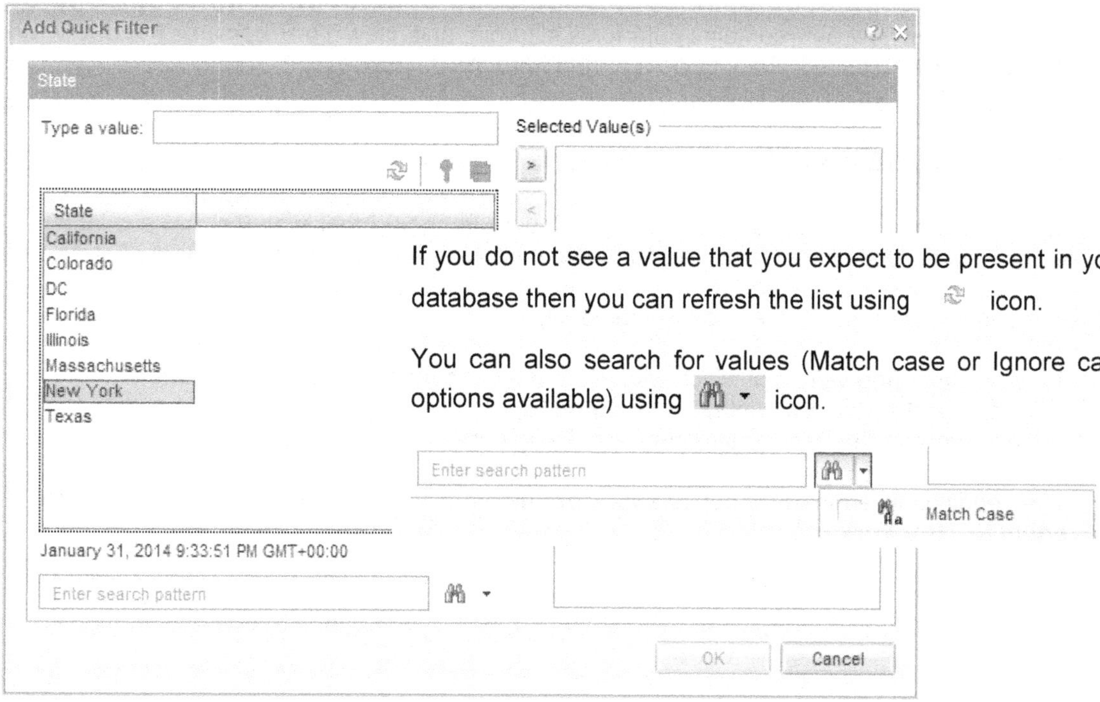
Add Quick Filter
State
Type a value:
Selected Value(s)
State
California
Colorado
DC
Florida
Illinois
Massachusetts
New York
Texas
January 31, 2014 9:33:51 PM GMT+00:00
Enter search pattern
Match Case
OK
Cancel

If you do not see a value that you expect to be present in your database then you can refresh the list using icon.

You can also search for values (Match case or Ignore case options available) using icon.

4. Click on 'California' and then hold down the <CTRL> key and click on 'New York'.

5. Click on the '>' button.

6. Click 'OK' and the Query Panel will now show:

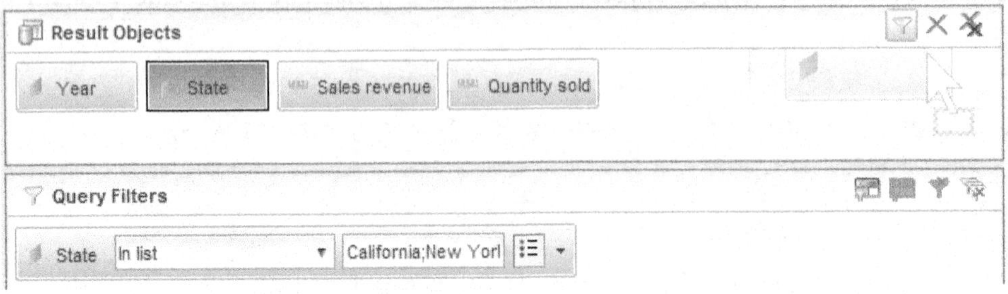
Result Objects
Year
State
Sales revenue
Quantity sold
Query Filters
State
In list
California;New Yorl

7. Run the query and then drag the [State] object into the table block:

Year	State	Sales revenu	Quantity sold
2004	California	$1,704,211	11,304
2004	New York	$1,667,696	10,802
2005	California	$2,782,680	17,001
2005	New York	$2,763,503	16,447
2006	California	$2,992,679	17,769
2006	New York	$3,151,022	19,109

The document now only contains data for 'California' and 'New York' because the query requested the data to be restricted when it was returned from the database.

22.3 Creating Custom Query Conditions

When we wish to limit the rows returned by our query in some other way (i.e. not available as one or more Pre-Defined Conditions) then we can create custom conditions within the 'Query Filters' pane.

Custom conditions require three parts to their definition:

1. An **object** (the values of which will determine the conditional test, e.g. **[State]**)
2. An **operator** (the test method, e.g. **equal to**)
3. An **operand** (the test requirement, e.g. **New York**)

The condition listed in the 3 points above evaluates to true when the value of the **[State]** object is **equal to 'New York'**.

1. Edit the existing query and clear the existing query filter(s). This can be achieved in a number of different ways:

Query Filters
State
In list
California;New Yorl

- Click on the existing filter condition and then drag it out of the 'Query Filter' pane
- Click on the existing filter condition and then press the <Del> or <delete> key
- You can also use the 'Remove' or 'Remove all' buttons located on the right-hand side of the 'Query Filters' pane

So we should now have our query looking as follows:

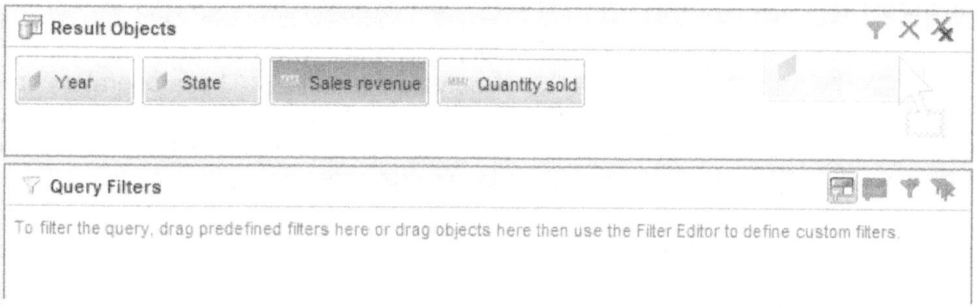
Result Objects
Year
State
Sales revenue
Quantity sold
Query Filters
To filter the query, drag predefined filters here or drag objects here then use the Filter Editor to define custom filters.

2. We begin creating a custom condition by first dragging an object into the 'Query Filters'.

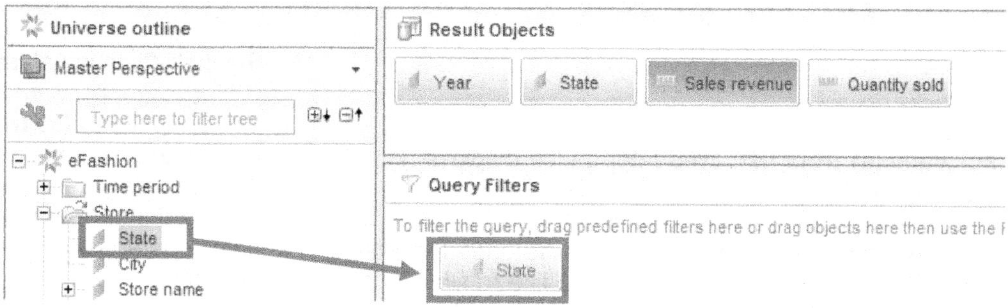
Universe outline
Master Perspective
Type here to filter tree
eFashion
Time period
Store
State
City
Store name
Result Objects
Year
State
Sales revenue
Quantity sold
Query Filters
To filter the query, drag predefined filters here or drag objects here then use the
State

Query Filters will now show:

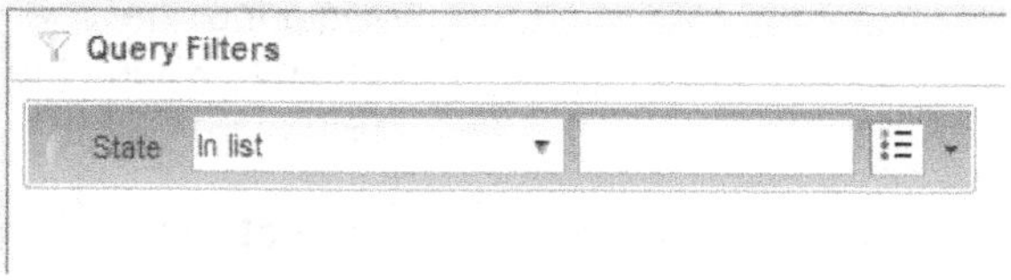
Query Filters
State
In list

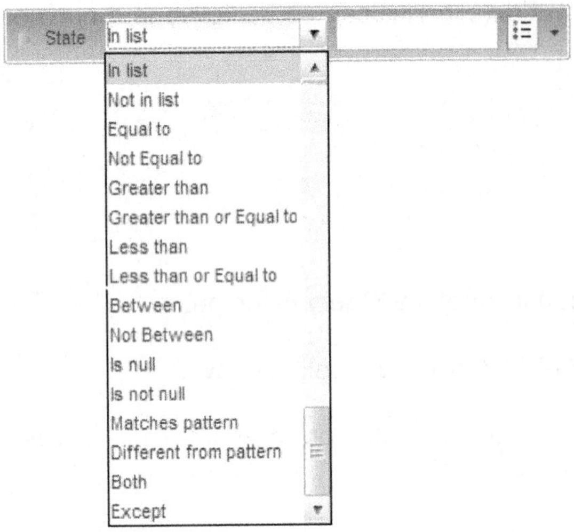
State
In list
In list
Not in list
Equal to
Not Equal to
Greater than
Greater than or Equal to
Less than
Less than or Equal to
Between
Not Between
Is null
Is not null
Matches pattern
Different from pattern
Both
Except

All **Operators** are described in detail later in the session

By default, the operator is set to 'In list' and this operator will allow multiple values to be selected for an operand.

If we wish to allow only one value to be selected then we need to use another operand, such as 'Equal to'.

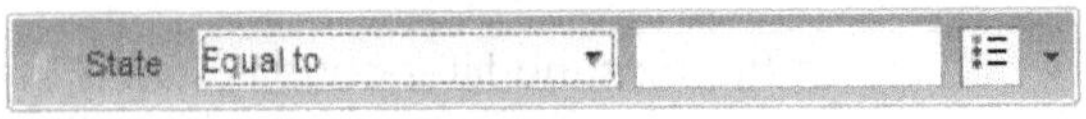
State
Equal to

A whole list of operators is available when creating custom conditions to limit a query's result.

The operators are generally listed in somewhat logical opposite pairs. For instance, 'Not Equal to' is opposite of 'Equal to'.

'Matches pattern' and 'Different from pattern' are two more operators that are only listed when working with character type objects. They perform the SQL equivalent of 'LIKE'. These operators can work with a wildcard character. The wildcard characters are **%** for multiple characters and _ (underscore) for a single character.

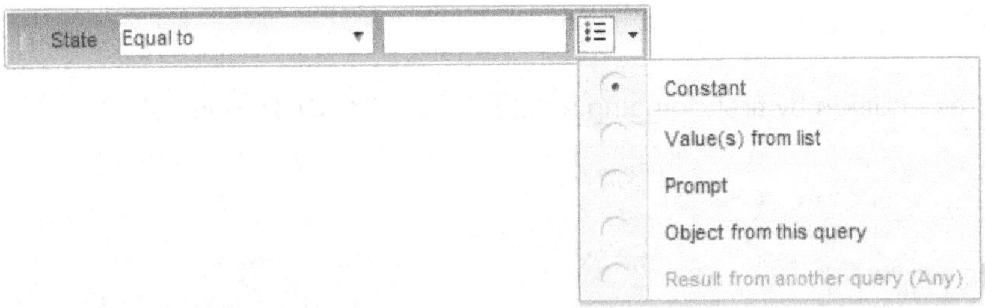
State
Equal to
Constant
Value(s) from list
Prompt
Object from this query
Result from another query (Any)

NOTE – For **Value(s) from list**, Web Intelligence displays a list for you to select value(s) from.

This can be slow if there are a lot of values in the underlying table. Due to this, if you know the value(s) you would like to filter for then it can be quicker to manually type them in by selecting **Constant**.

When typing, multiple values need to be separated by semi-colons:

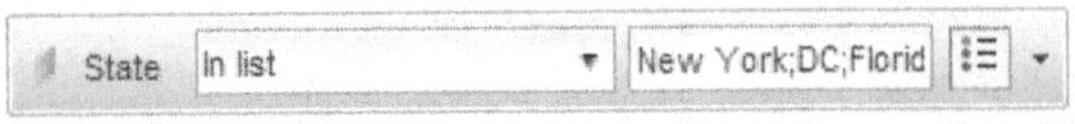
State
In list
New York;DC;Florid

Result from another query (Any) allows you to filter using values returned from another query. This will be discussed in a later session.

The simplest operands are static values. We may either type the values, or choose the values from a list.

Constant allows you to manually type in values(s).

Choosing **Value(s) from list** (rather than manually typing the value(s)) ensures you specify the correct match (as some databases are case sensitive).

Prompt is discussed later in this session and is used to create dynamic conditions requiring the user to specify values when the query is refreshed.

Object from this query allows you to select another object to compare values against.

3. Set the Operator to **In list** and then set the Operand Type to **Value(s) from list**.

4. Select 'Colorado' and 'Texas' and then click 'OK'

If you do not see a value that you expect to be present in your database then you can refresh the list using icon.

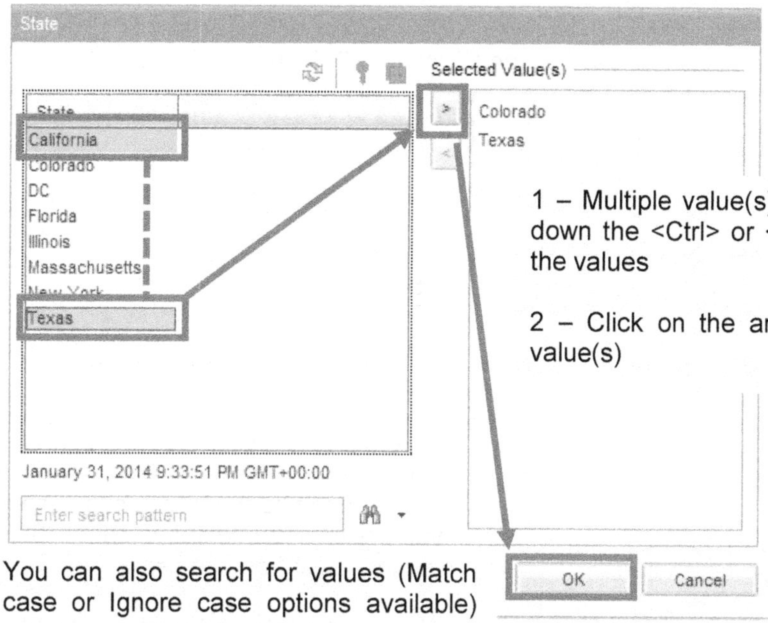
State
Selected Value(s)
State
California
Colorado
DC
Florida
Illinois
Massachusetts
Texas
Colorado
Texas
January 31, 2014 9:33:51 PM GMT+00:00
Enter search pattern
OK
Cancel

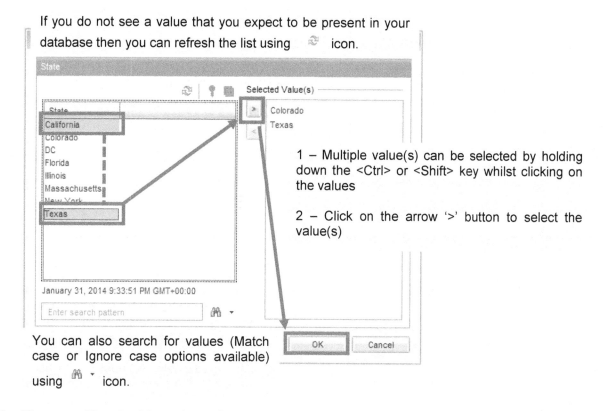

1 – Multiple value(s) can be selected by holding down the <Ctrl> or <Shift> key whilst clicking on the values

2 – Click on the arrow '>' button to select the value(s)

You can also search for values (Match case or Ignore case options available) using icon.

5. The query filter should now be as follows:

Query Filters
State
In list
Colorado;Texas

6. Run the query and the results now show:

Year	State	Sales revenu	Quantity sold
2004	Colorado	$448,302	2,971
2004	Texas	$2,199,677	14,517
2005	Colorado	$768,390	4,700
2005	Texas	$3,732,889	22,637
2006	Colorado	$843,584	5,116
2006	Texas	$4,185,098	25,193

Data returned has now been restricted to 'Colorado' and 'Texas' (as specified in the Query Filter).

7. Save the document.

22.4 Creating Dynamic Conditions using Prompts

To specify operand values at runtime, we use prompts. Prompts enable dynamic queries to be created and are especially helpful in corporate reports that are created once but reused for different values or time periods.

1. We will edit the existing query for this example.

2. To create a prompt condition, change the Operand Type to a **Prompt**.

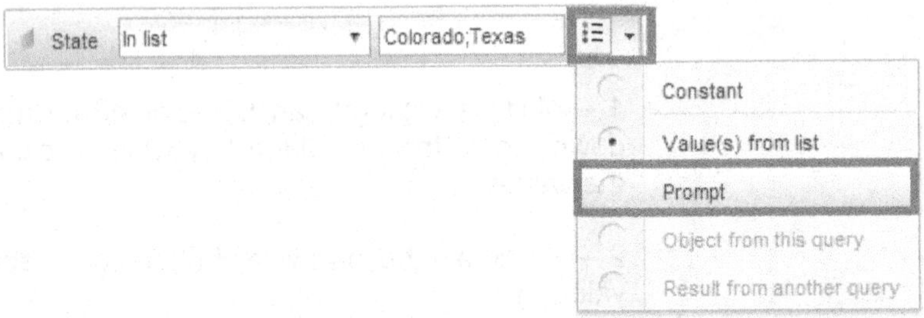
State
In list
Colorado;Texas
Constant
Value(s) from list
Prompt
Object from this query
Result from another query

3. Click the 'Prompt Properties' button.

State
In list
Enter values for St

A default prompt text based on your object will appear in the text box (e.g. we have 'Enter values for State:'), but you can change the text if you prefer. This text is used as the message to request input from the user.

The values selected/input by the user (at query refresh) are then used as the operand values.

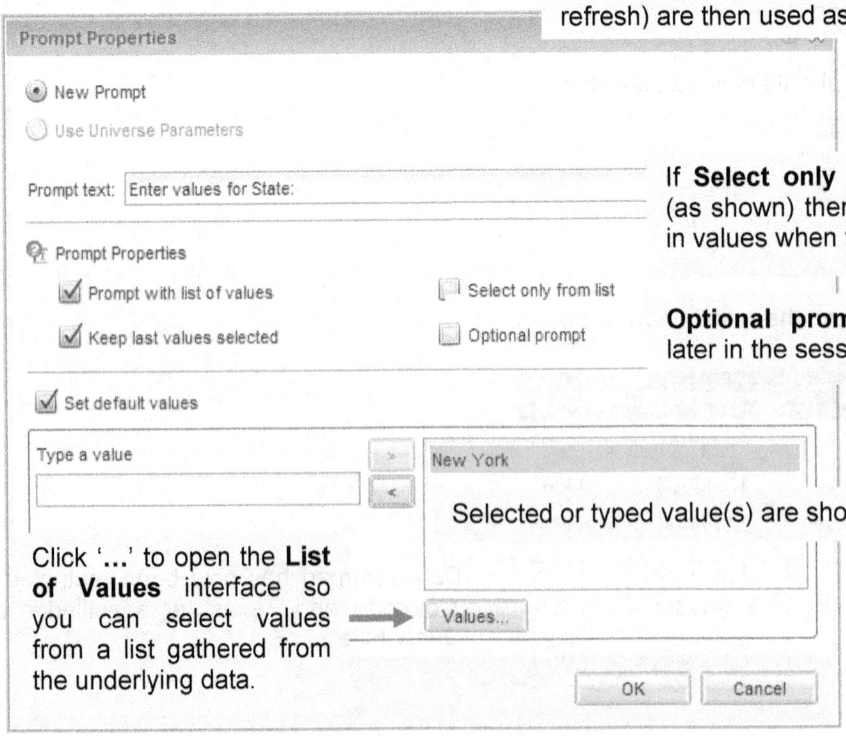
Prompt Properties
New Prompt
Use Universe Parameters
Prompt text:
Enter values for State:
Prompt Properties
Prompt with list of values
Keep last values selected
Select only from list
Optional prompt
Set default values
Type a value
New York
Values...
OK
Cancel

If **Select only from list** is deselected (as shown) then you can manually type in values when the query is run.

Optional prompt described in detail later in the session.

Selected or typed value(s) are shown here.

Click '**...**' to open the **List of Values** interface so you can select values from a list gathered from the underlying data.

Prompt with list of Values displays a list of values from the underlying data. Useful when the list is not excessively long.

Select only from list will force users to only select values that are present in the list of values retrieved from the database. Leave unchecked if you want users to be able to type values in manually.

Keep last values selected retains value(s) for next refresh.

Optional prompt makes the prompt optional so the user does not have to specify value(s) for the prompt when the query runs. If the user does not specify value(s) then effectively this condition is not applied to the query.

If using **Optional prompt** then you should inform the user the prompt is optional, for example by changing the **Prompt text**:

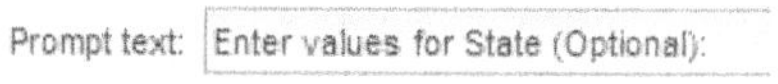
Prompt text:
Enter values for State (Optional):

Set default values allows you to specify 'pre-filled' values to use. Useful if prompts are required but most of the time the selection will not change.

Do not **Set default values** for an **Optional prompt** as the default values will be used (instead of removing the prompt).

First select **Set default values** and then specify the value(s) you want to use as default for this prompt (shown on next page):

4. Set the prompt as follows and click 'OK'.

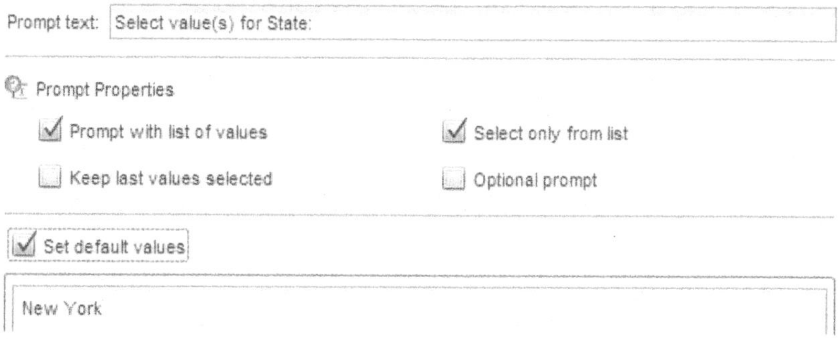
Prompt text:
Select value(s) for State:
Prompt Properties
Prompt with list of values
Select only from list
Keep last values selected
Optional prompt
Set default values
New York

5. Run the query and click 'OK' when presented with the 'Prompts' interface.

The query will return results only for 'New York' because we have specified it as a default value.

Year	State	Sales revenu	Quantity sold
2004	New York	$1,667,696	10,802
2005	New York	$2,763,503	16,447
2006	New York	$3,151,022	19,109

6. Refresh the document again using the 'Refresh' button in the Report Panel.

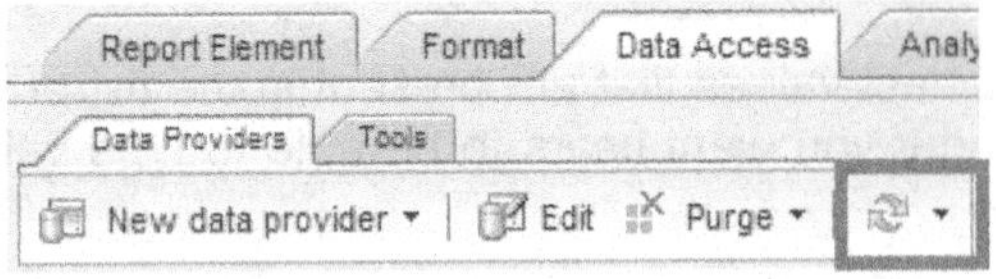
Report Element
Format
Data Access
Analy
Data Providers
Tools
New data provider
Edit
Purge

7. Select 'Florida' and 'Massachusetts' and click 'OK'.

The same query will yield different results because of user input at run time.

Year	State	Sales revenu	Quantity sold
2004	Florida	$405,985	2,585
2004	Massachusetts	$238,819	1,505
2005	Florida	$661,250	3,852
2005	Massachusetts	$157,719	902
2006	Florida	$811,924	4,830
2006	Massachusetts	$887,169	5,269

8. Save your document.

22.5 Specifying Orders for Multiple Prompts

Prompts can be ordered so they are presented to the user in a logical sequence, for example if the user has to input a start date and an end date then presenting them in the correct order is important to avoid confusion.

1. Edit the existing query to be as follows:

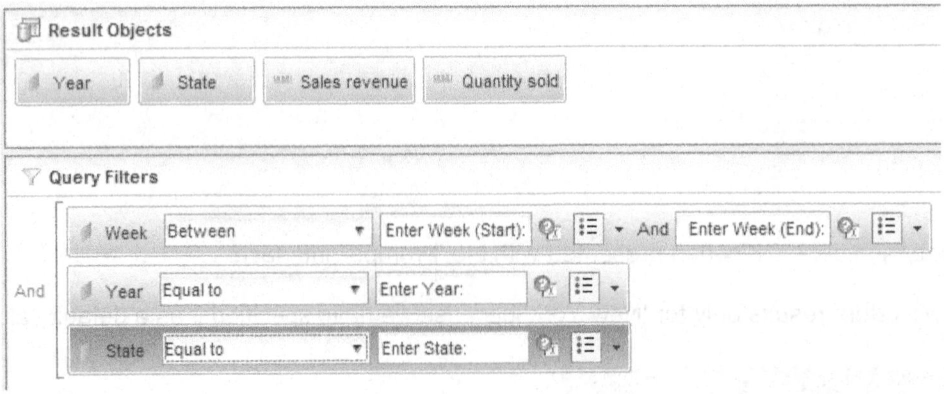
Result Objects
Year
State
Sales revenue
Quantity sold
Query Filters
Week
Between
Enter Week (Start):
And
Enter Week (End):
And
Year
Equal to
Enter Year:
State
Equal to
Enter State:

NOTE

All the conditions have been set up as prompts.

We have used two prompts for the Week condition because we have used the Operand Type 'Between'.

2. When the query is run, the order of the prompts is as follows:

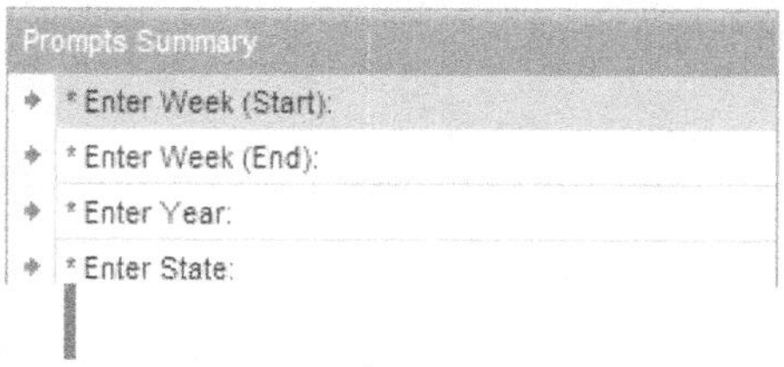
Prompts Summary
* Enter Week (Start):
* Enter Week (End):
* Enter Year:
* Enter State:

Web Intelligence places an asterisk (*) in front of the prompt text when the prompt is mandatory.

The **default Prompt Order** is based on the order in which you create the prompts in the **Query Filters** pane.

i.e. we have created the prompts in the order:

1. Enter Week (Start):
2. Enter Week (End):
3. Enter Year:
4. Enter State:

However, we would like to arrange the prompts so they are in the order [State], [Year], [Week] Start, and [Week] End.

3. Click 'Cancel' and we will be returned back to the Query Panel.

4. Click on the 'Query Properties' button:

Add Query

5. Re-arrange the prompts into the desired order and click 'OK'.

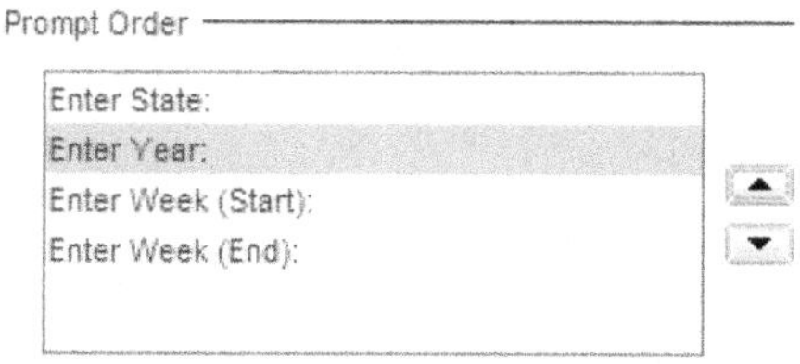
Prompt Order
Enter State:
Enter Year:
Enter Week (Start):
Enter Week (End):

Select a prompt and then use the arrow buttons to change the order of the prompt.

6. Run the query and we will now have the prompts in the correct sequence.

Select the following values and click 'OK'.

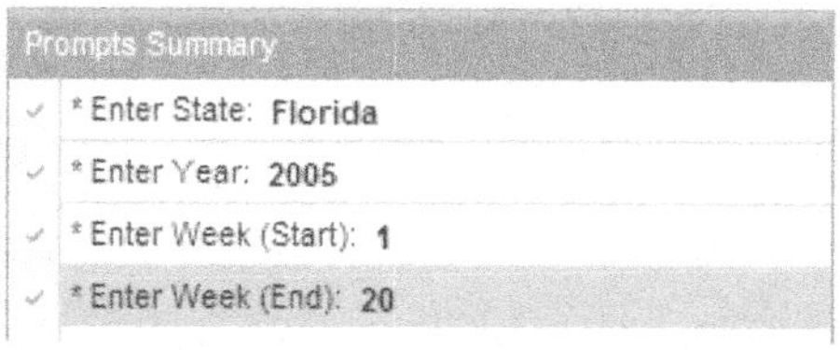
Prompts Summary
* Enter State: Florida
* Enter Year: 2005
* Enter Week (Start): 1
* Enter Week (End): 20

Year	State	Sales revenu	Quantity sold
2005	Florida	$262,514	1,604

NOTE

Re-arranging the objects in the Query Filters pane does not change the Prompt Order, unless you delete all the conditions and then recreate them in the correct sequence.

Likewise, changing the Prompt Order does not change the order of the conditions within the Query Filters pane.

9. Save your document.

22.6 Creating Query Filters using Multiple Conditions

Complex Query Filters can be applied using Drag and Drop techniques.

1. Modify the existing query by dragging in and setting up the Query Filters as follows:

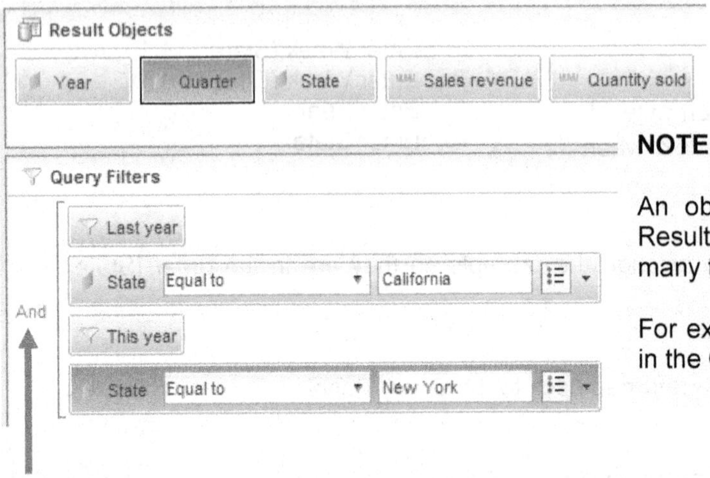
Result Objects
Year
Quarter
State
Sales revenue
Quantity sold
Query Filters
Last year
State
Equal to
California
This year
State
Equal to
New York
And

NOTE

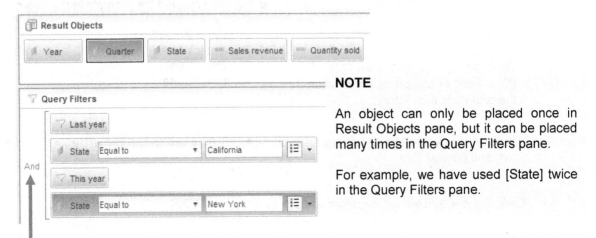

An object can only be placed once in Result Objects pane, but it can be placed many times in the Query Filters pane.

For example, we have used [State] twice in the Query Filters pane.

When two or more conditions are included in the Query Filters pane then Web Intelligence will place **And** as the default operator between multiple query conditions.

It appears we have set up the Query Filter that will request **California** data for **last year**, and **New York** data for **this year**.

2. Run the query after setting up the above Query Filter.

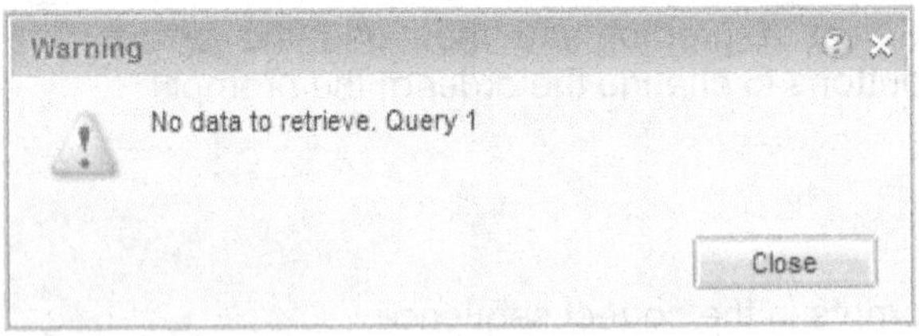
Warning
No data to retrieve. Query 1
Close

Running the query with these conditions yields no results because the filter has not been specified correctly.

3. We must re-arrange the conditions in the overall filter as shown below:

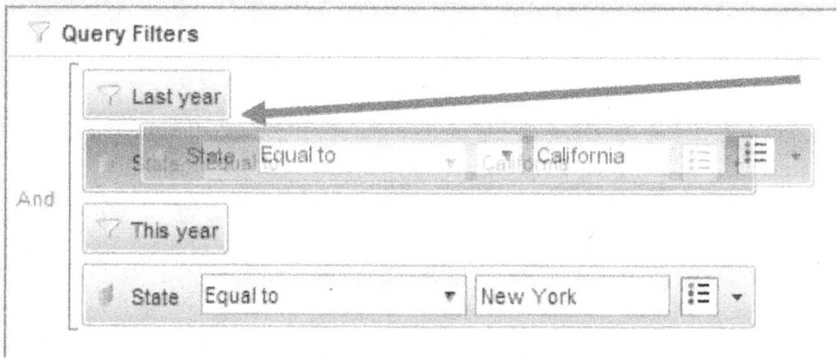
Query Filters
And
Last year
State Equal to California
This year
State Equal to New York

Drag [State] = 'California' condition onto [Last year] condition

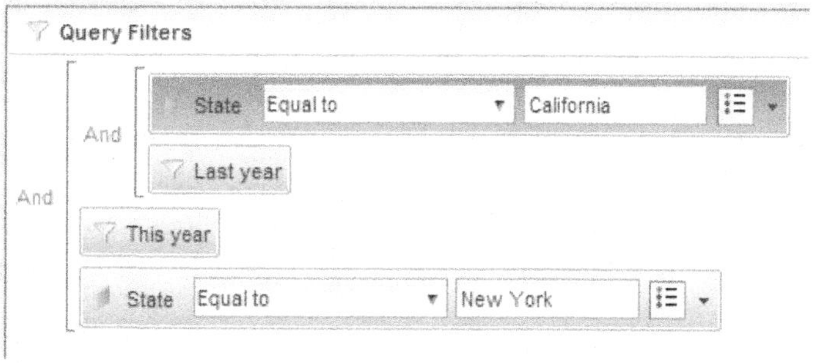
Query Filters
And
And
State Equal to California
Last year
This year
State Equal to New York

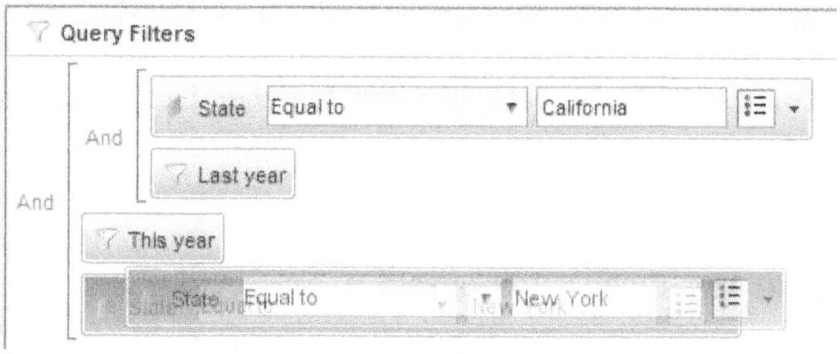
Query Filters
And
And
State Equal to California
Last year
This year
State Equal to New York

Drag [State] = 'New York' condition onto [This year] condition

NOTE – The markers indicate NESTING or GROUPING of conditions together so they can be applied at different levels.

This is similar to using parentheses (brackets) in formulas to get the correct calculation.

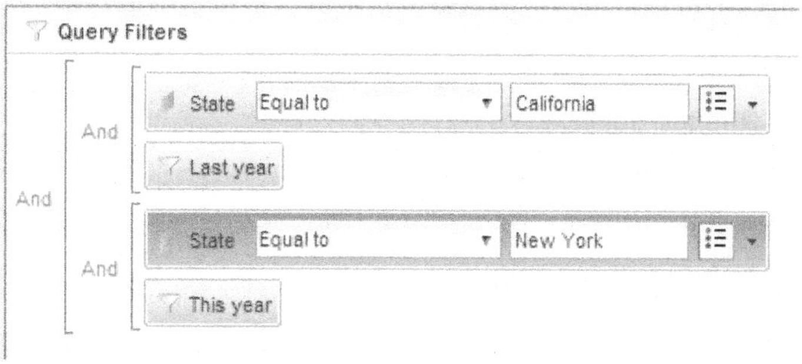
Query Filters
And
And
State Equal to California
Last year
And
State Equal to New York
This year

4. Click on the outermost 'And' and it will turn to 'Or':

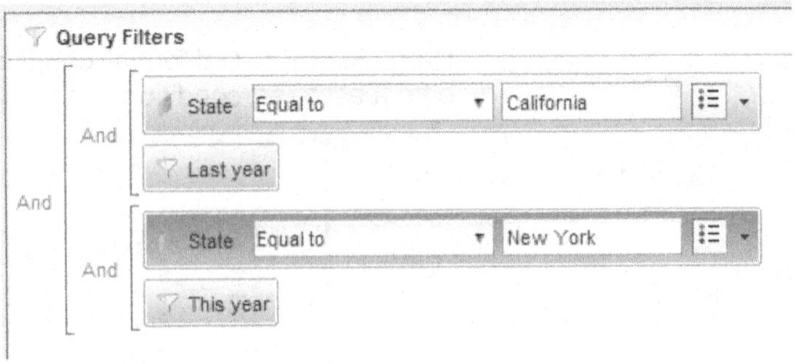
Query Filters
And
And
State
Equal to
California
Last year
And
State
Equal to
New York
This year

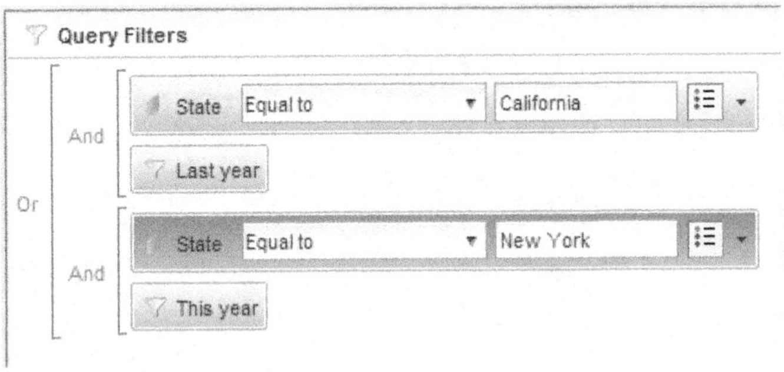
Query Filters
Or
And
State
Equal to
California
Last year
And
State
Equal to
New York
This year

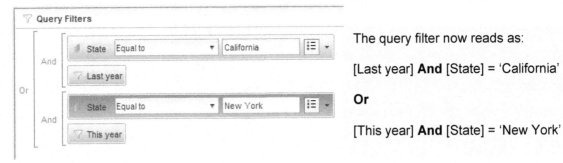

The query filter now reads as:

[Last year] **And** [State] = 'California'

Or

[This year] **And** [State] = 'New York'

Any conditions within a single marker will effectively get put together by using a pair of brackets.

(

([Last year] **And** [State] = 'California' **)**

Or

([This year] **And** [State] = 'New York' **)**

)

The visual nature of Web Intelligence makes it easier to understand complex filters.

5. Run the query.

Running this query with the re-arranged filter returns the correct results.

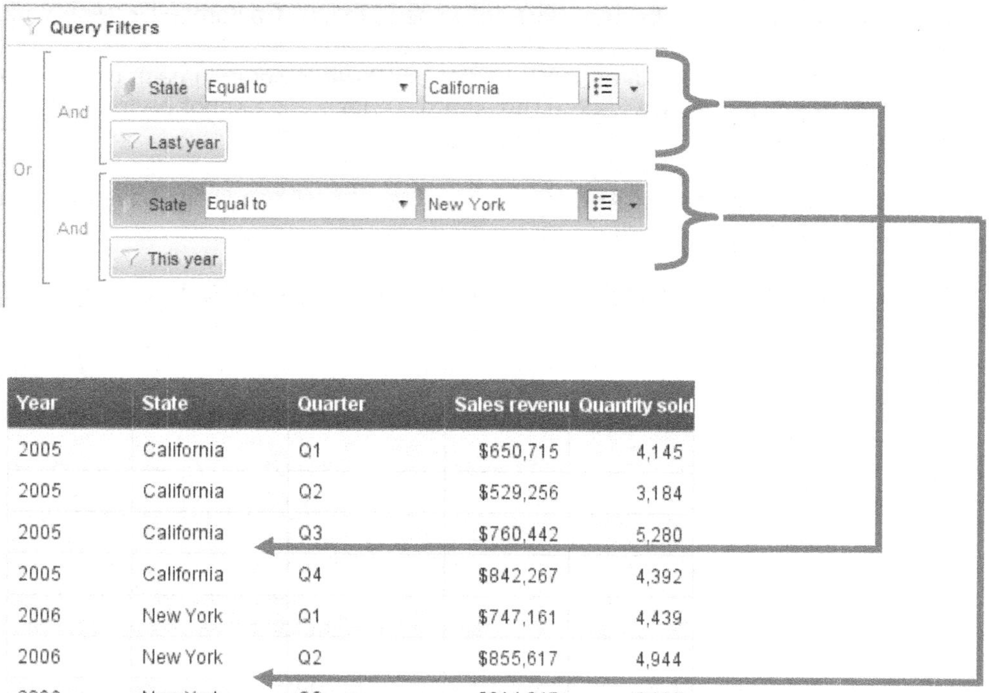
Query Filters
Or
And
State
Equal to
California
Last year
And
State
Equal to
New York
This year

Year	State	Quarter	Sales revenu	Quantity sold
2005	California	Q1	$650,715	4,145
2005	California	Q2	$529,256	3,184
2005	California	Q3	$760,442	5,280
2005	California	Q4	$842,267	4,392
2006	New York	Q1	$747,161	4,439
2006	New York	Q2	$855,617	4,944
2006	New York	Q3	$914,247	6,119
2006	New York	Q4	$633,998	3,607

6. Save your document.

22.7 Use of And / Or in Query Filters

Using the previous example, in spoken (or written) English we would list the requirement as "figures for California last year and New York this year". In database language (SQL and Web Intelligence) we have to construct the filter using a combination of And / Or operators (as already shown).

Let us try and understand more about the use of And / Or:

And requires all conditions to be true in order to return any data.

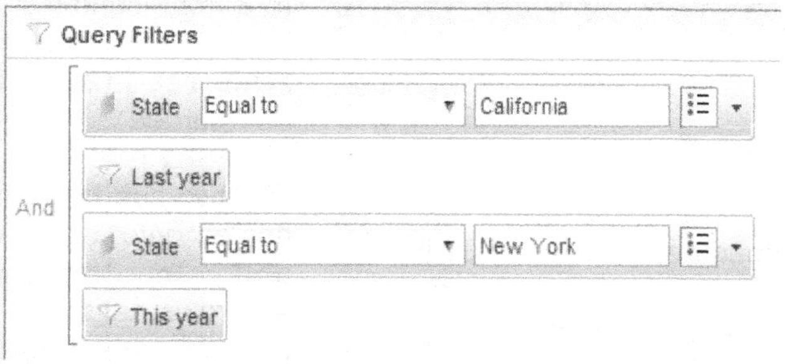
Query Filters
And
State
Equal to
California
Last year
State
Equal to
New York
This year

When we had the above filter, we were using **And** between all the conditions resulting in no data being returned.

Why?

Well, let us take the [State] conditions first. The database compares the value for the [State] column in each row and looks to see if it is 'California' **And** 'New York'. Clearly, this cannot be true as the [State] can only be one value so we need to use 'California' **Or** 'New York'.

Similarly, the database compares the value for the [Year] column in each row and looks to see if it is 2005 ([Last year]) **And** 2006 ([This year]). Again, this cannot be true as the [Year] can only be one value so we need to use [Last year] **Or** [This year].

Therefore we can see that for **And** to return any results, all conditions have to be satisfied that are '**And**ed' together.

If we simply changed the **And** to an **Or** then we would get too many results. **Why?**

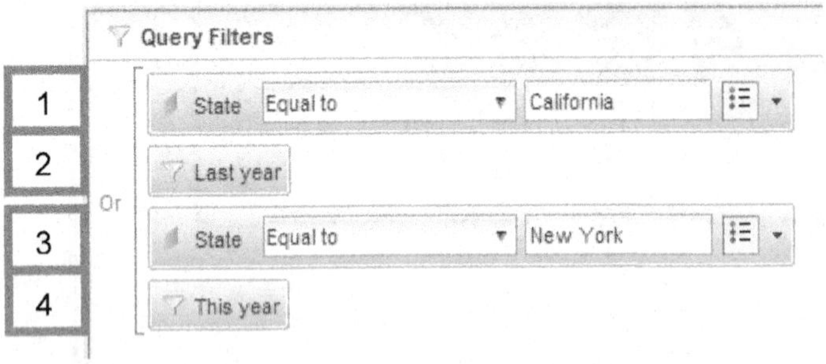
Query Filters
1
2
3
4
Or
State
Equal to
California
Last year
State
Equal to
New York
This year

Or is almost opposite to **And**, in that if any one condition is true then data will be returned (for the true condition).

[State] = 'California' **Or** [Last year] (i.e. where [Year] = 2005)

Rows will be returned where the [State] = 'California' or if the [Year] = 2005, therefore we will get all years for California and all states having data for 2005.

Our filter using **Or** would return the results:

1. California (all years, 2004, 2005, 2006)
2. Last Year (all States)
3. New York (all years, 2004, 2005, 2006)
4. This Year (all States)

To satisfy our particular requirement "figures for California last year and New York this year", we combined **And** with **Or** to group the conditions into a logical sequence to separate out the way in which the overall filter is applied.

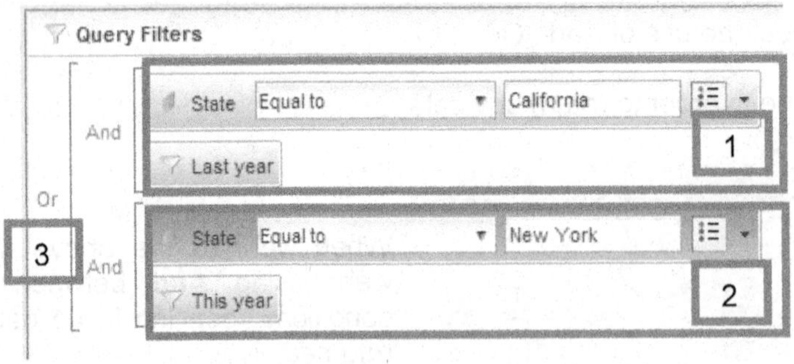
Query Filters
And
State
Equal to
California
1
Last year
Or
3
And
State
Equal to
New York
2
This year

1. If a row contains **[State] = 'California'** ***and*** **[Year] = [Last Year] (2005)** then it will be returned.
2. If a row contains **[State] = 'New York'** ***and*** **[Year] = [This Year] (2006)** then it will be returned.
3. The two sub-filters have to be nested into an overall filter using **Or**. The result is that any rows satisfying **sub-filter (1) Or sub-filter (2)** are returned.

The logic and concepts described here for **And / Or** in **Query Filters** can also be used for defining **Report Filters** as discussed previously in the session 'Filtering Data in Reports'.

22.8 Query Filter Operators

When defining filters a range of Operators are available to restrict the data in various ways and these are listed below:

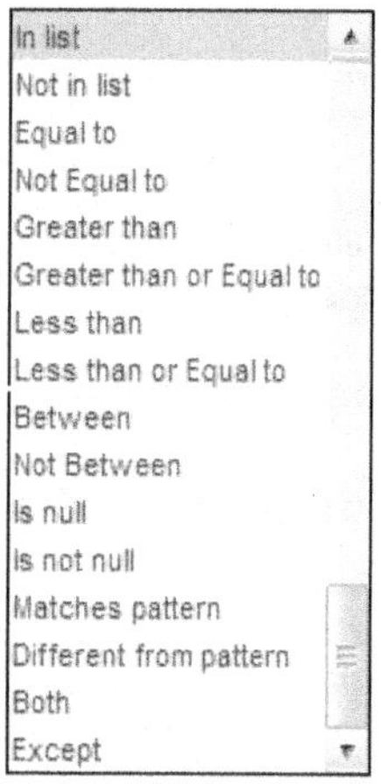
In list
Not in list
Equal to
Not Equal to
Greater than
Greater than or Equal to
Less than
Less than or Equal to
Between
Not Between
Is null
Is not null
Matches pattern
Different from pattern
Both
Except

Many operators are available when creating custom conditions to limit query data.

The operators are generally listed in somewhat logical opposite pairs. For instance, 'Not Equal to' is opposite of 'Equal to'.

By default, the operator is set to 'In list'.

Operator	Usage
Equal to	Allows you to select a single value for the filter condition. Only data related to the filtered value will be returned. e.g. Filter defined as [State] **Equal to** 'California' will only return data relevant to California.
Not Equal to	Allows you to select a single value for the filter condition. Data not related to the filtered value will be returned. e.g. Filter defined as [State] **Not Equal to** 'California' will return data for states other than California.
Greater than	Allows you to select a single value for the filter condition. Values greater than the filtered value will be displayed. e.g. Database contains data for years 2004, 2005 and 2006. Filter defined as [Year] **Greater than** 2005 will result in data for 2006 to be returned.
Greater than or Equal to	Allows you to select a single value for the filter condition. Values greater than or equal to the filtered value will be returned. e.g. Database contains data for years 2004, 2005 and 2006. Filter defined as [Year] **Greater than or Equal to** 2005 will return data for 2005 and 2006.

Operator	Usage
Less than	Allows you to select a single value for the filter condition. Values less than the filtered value will be returned. e.g. Database contains data for years 2004, 2005 and 2006. Filter defined as [Year] **Less than** 2005 will result in data for 2004 to be returned.
Less than or Equal to	Allows you to select a single value for the filter condition. Values less than or equal to the filtered value will be returned. e.g. Database contains data for years 2004, 2005 and 2006. Filter defined as [Year] **Less than or Equal to** 2005 will return data for 2004 and 2005.
Between	Specify a range of values using *value From* and *value To*. Data falling within the range (including both the upper and lower values) will be returned. e.g. Database contains data for states California, Colorado, DC, Florida, Illinois, Massachusetts, New York, and Texas. Filter defined as [State] **Between** 'DC' and 'Massachusetts' will return data for DC, Florida, Illinois and Massachusetts.
Not Between	Specify a range of values using *value From* and *value To*. Data falling outside the range (including both the upper and lower values) will be returned. e.g. Database contains data for states California, Colorado, DC, Florida, Illinois, Massachusetts, New York, and Texas. Filter defined as [State] **Not Between** 'DC' and 'Massachusetts' will return data for California, Colorado, New York and Texas.
In list	Allows you to select multiple values to filter for. Data is returned for one or more of the filtered values, depending on how many are found in the data set. e.g. Database contains data for states California, Colorado, DC, Florida, Illinois, Massachusetts, New York, and Texas. Filter defined as [State] **In list** 'California', 'Colorado', 'Illinois', 'Texas' would return data for California, Colorado, Illinois and Texas.
Not in list	Allows you to select multiple values to filter for. Data is returned for values not included in the filter list. e.g. Database contains data for states California, Colorado, DC, Florida, Illinois, Massachusetts, New York, and Texas. Filter defined as [State] **Not in list** 'California', 'Colorado', 'Illinois', 'Texas' would return data for DC, Florida, Massachusetts, and New York.

Operator	Usage
Is null	No value is specified for this operator as it is used to look for NULL (or blank) values. e.g. Database contains data for states California, Colorado, DC, Florida, Illinois, Massachusetts, New York, and Texas. Filter defined as [State] **Is null** will return NO DATA as all states have values.
Not is null	No value is specified for this operator as it is used to look for NON NULL (or non-blank) values. e.g. Database contains data for states California, Colorado, DC, Florida, Illinois, Massachusetts, New York, and Texas. Filter defined as [State] **Not is null** will return all data because all states have values.
Matches pattern	This Operator appears in the list when the object it is being applied to holds character values (i.e. is not a number or a date). A single value is specified for matching purposes and if the pattern value is matched then data is returned for the relevant rows. The wildcard characters are % for multiple characters and _ for a single character. e.g. Database contains data for states California, Colorado, DC, Florida, Illinois, Massachusetts, New York, and Texas. We would like data for [States] with names starting with 'C' (correct capitalisation is necessary for some databases): 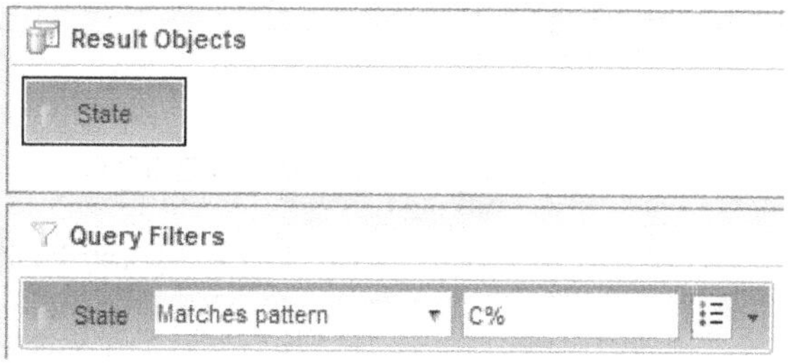Result Objects State Query Filters State Matches pattern C% Results are: State California Colorado

<table>
<tr><th>Operator</th><th>Usage</th></tr>
<tr><td></td><td>NOTE
<ul>
<li>[State] Matches pattern 'C_' would return no results as there are no states with 2 characters in their name that start with C.</li>
<li>[State] Matches pattern 'D_' would return data because DC has a two character name and starts with a D.</li>
<li>[State] Matches pattern '%C%' would return data for California, Colorado, DC and Massachusetts because they all contain a C somewhere in the name. Massachusetts would not be returned by case sensitive databases.</li>
</ul></td></tr>
<tr><td>Different from pattern</td><td>This Operator appears in the list when the object it is being applied holds character values (i.e. is not a number or a date). A single value is specified for matching purposes and if the pattern value is not matched then data is returned for the relevant rows.

The wildcard characters are % for multiple characters and _ for a single character.

e.g. Database contains data for states California, Colorado, DC, Florida, Illinois, Massachusetts, New York, and Texas.

We would like data for states with names not starting with 'C' (correct capitalisation is necessary for some databases):

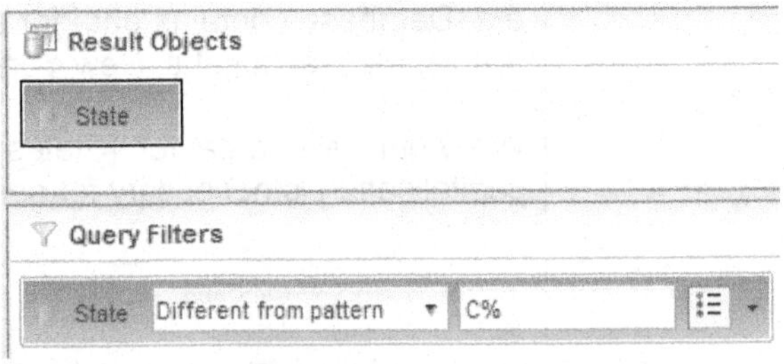
Result Objects
State
Query Filters
State
Different from pattern
C%

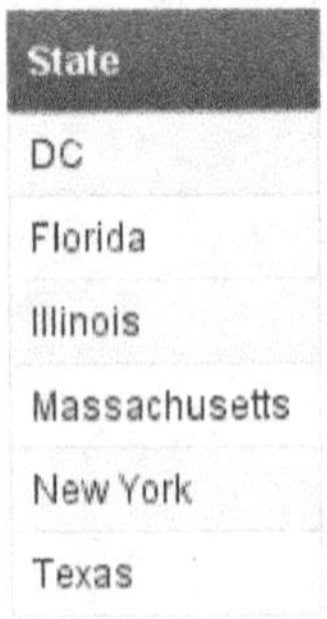
State
DC
Florida
Illinois
Massachusetts
New York
Texas

NOTE
<ul>
<li>[State] Different from pattern 'C_' would return all states as all the names are longer than 2 characters (except DC but it does not start with a C).</li>
<li>[State] Different from pattern 'D_' would return all states except DC (as DC has a two character name and starts with a D).</li>
<li>[State] Different from pattern '%C%' would return data for Florida, Illinois, New York and Texas. The other states would be filtered out because they all contain a C somewhere in the name. Massachusetts would be returned by case sensitive databases as we have specified a capital C.</li>
</ul></td></tr>
</table>

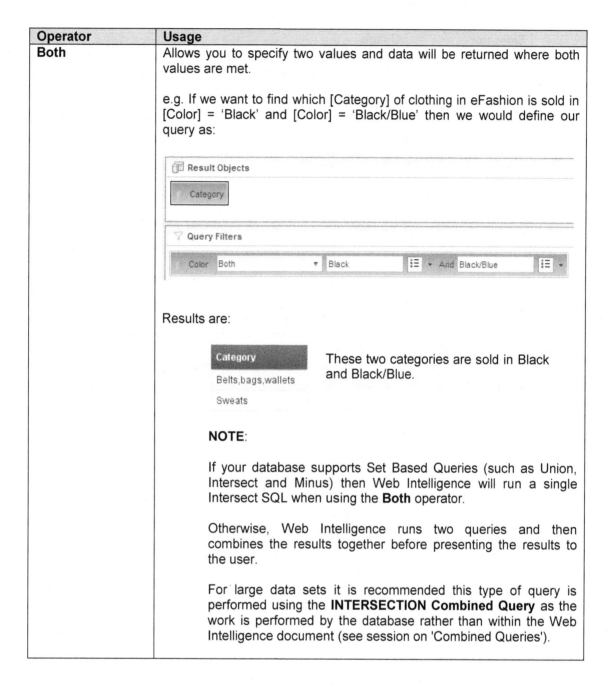

<table>
<tr><th>Operator</th><th>Usage</th></tr>
<tr><td>Both</td><td>Allows you to specify two values and data will be returned where both values are met.

e.g. If we want to find which [Category] of clothing in eFashion is sold in [Color] = ‘Black’ and [Color] = ‘Black/Blue’ then we would define our query as:

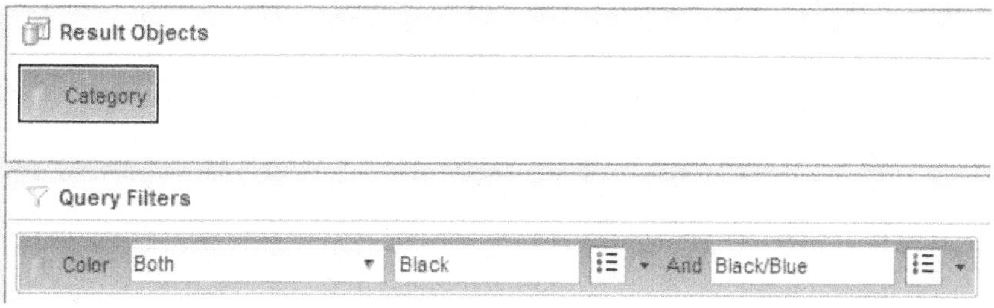
Result Objects
Category
Query Filters
Color
Both
Black
And
Black/Blue

Results are:

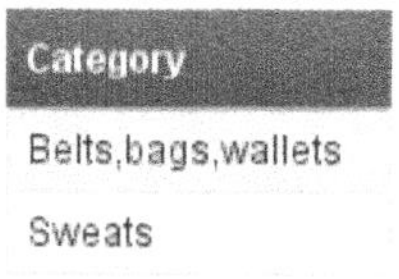
Category
Belts,bags,wallets
Sweats
These two categories are sold in Black and Black/Blue.

NOTE:

If your database supports Set Based Queries (such as Union, Intersect and Minus) then Web Intelligence will run a single Intersect SQL when using the Both operator.

Otherwise, Web Intelligence runs two queries and then combines the results together before presenting the results to the user.

For large data sets it is recommended this type of query is performed using the INTERSECTION Combined Query as the work is performed by the database rather than within the Web Intelligence document (see session on 'Combined Queries').</td></tr>
</table>

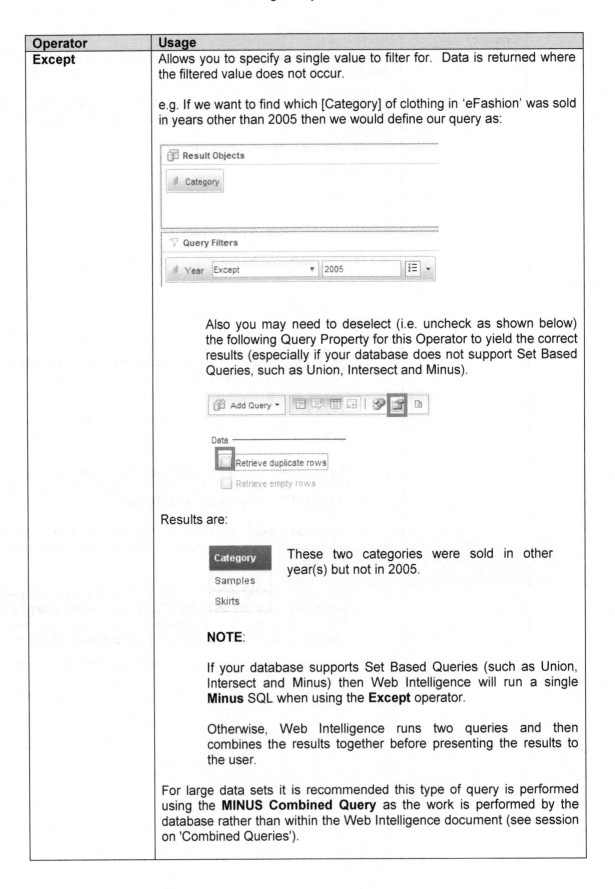

<table>
<tr><th>Operator</th><th>Usage</th></tr>
<tr><td>Except</td><td>
Allows you to specify a single value to filter for. Data is returned where the filtered value does not occur.

e.g. If we want to find which [Category] of clothing in 'eFashion' was sold in years other than 2005 then we would define our query as:

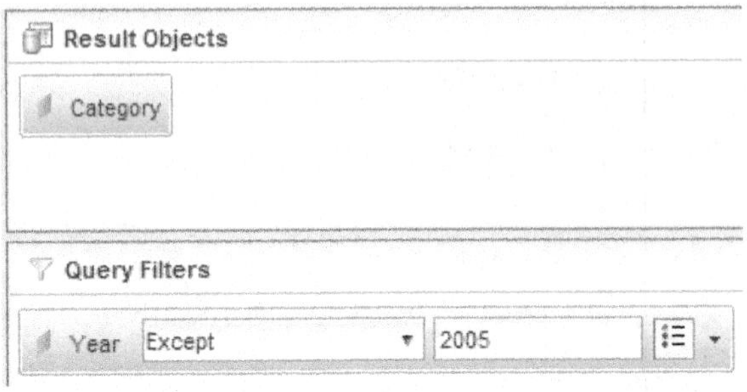
Result Objects
Category
Query Filters
Year
Except
2005

Also you may need to deselect (i.e. uncheck as shown below) the following Query Property for this Operator to yield the correct results (especially if your database does not support Set Based Queries, such as Union, Intersect and Minus).

Add Query
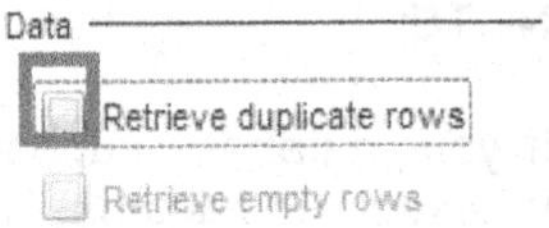
Data
Retrieve duplicate rows
Retrieve empty rows

Results are:

<table><tr><th>Category</th></tr><tr><td>Samples</td></tr><tr><td>Skirts</td></tr></table>
These two categories were sold in other year(s) but not in 2005.

NOTE:

If your database supports Set Based Queries (such as Union, Intersect and Minus) then Web Intelligence will run a single Minus SQL when using the Except operator.

Otherwise, Web Intelligence runs two queries and then combines the results together before presenting the results to the user.

For large data sets it is recommended this type of query is performed using the MINUS Combined Query as the work is performed by the database rather than within the Web Intelligence document (see session on 'Combined Queries').
</td></tr>
</table>

22.9 Optional Prompts and Operators

Earlier in the session, we mentioned you can specify prompts as 'optional' and stated the following:

> If the user does not specify value(s) then effectively this condition is not applied to the query.

> If using **Optional prompt** then you should inform the user the prompt is optional, for example by changing the **Prompt text**:

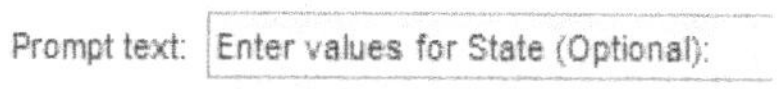
Prompt text:
Enter values for State (Optional):

1. Let us have a look at an Optional Prompt example by creating the following query using the 'eFashion; universe and running it.

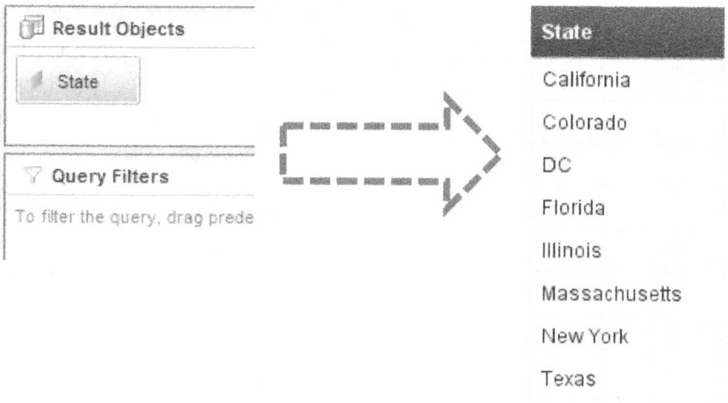
Result Objects
State
Query Filters
To filter the query, drag prede
State
California
Colorado
DC
Florida
Illinois
Massachusetts
New York
Texas

2. Edit the query and add a prompt on the [State] object as follows:

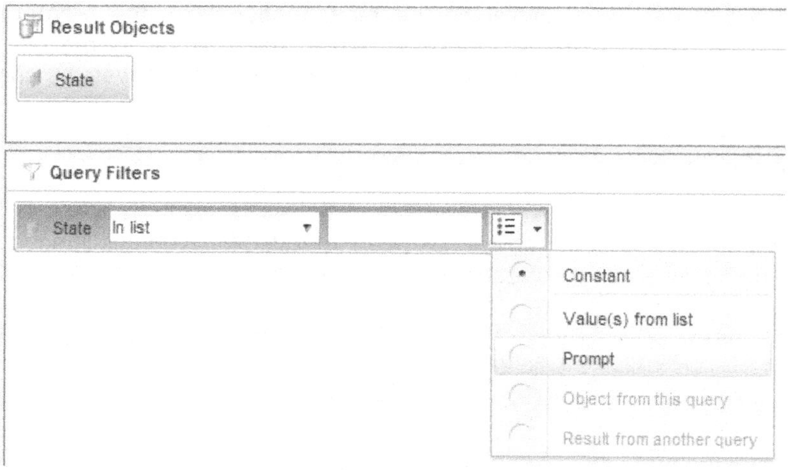
Result Objects
State
Query Filters
State
In list
Constant
Value(s) from list
Prompt
Object from this query
Result from another query

3. Click on 'Prompt Properties':

State
In list
Enter values for Sta

4. Tick the 'Optional prompt' box and click 'OK':

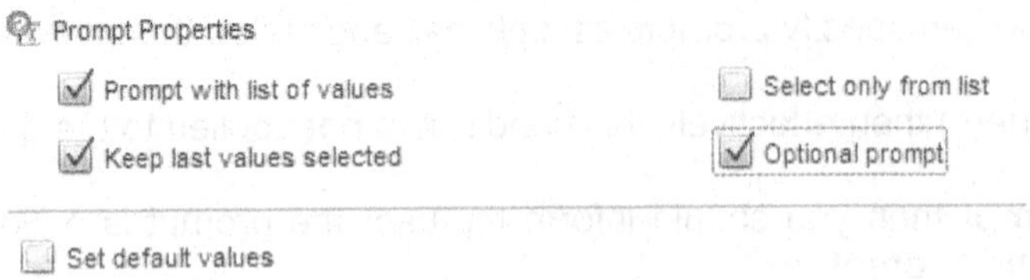
Prompt Properties
Prompt with list of values
Keep last values selected
Select only from list
Optional prompt
Set default values

NOTE

Default values can still be used with Optional Prompts.

5. Run the query and select some values for the [State] prompt and click 'OK':

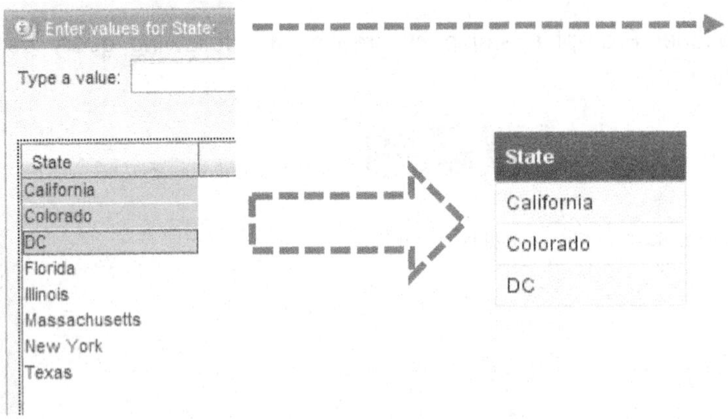
Enter values for State:
Type a value:
State
California
Colorado
DC
Florida
Illinois
Massachusetts
New York
Texas
State
California
Colorado
DC

In previous versions, Web Intelligence used to inform the user if a prompt was optional by placing the word '(optional)' at the end of your 'Prompt Text', but this feature has now been replaced by using an asterisk (*) in front of the Prompt Text to indicate mandatory prompt.

You could use the word 'optional' within your 'Prompt Text' to highlight an optional prompt.

6. Edit the query and modify the 'Prompt text' to 'Select one or more States (optional):'

7. Re-run the query, but do not select any values and simply click 'OK'.

Select one or more States (optional):
Type a value:

By placing the term '(optional)' in the prompt text, we have informed the user this prompt is ***optional*** because previously it was not obvious that this was the case.

8. The query will return a list of all the States.

State
California
Colorado
DC
Florida
Illinois
Massachusetts
New York
Texas

The prompt on the [State] object has been removed by Web Intelligence resulting in the database placing no restriction on [State] values.

The behaviour of an **Optional prompt** is affected by the **Operator** it is being used with.

The points of note are:

1. You cannot specify an Optional prompt for the operators **Is null** and **Is not null**.

2. You can specify an Optional prompt for all of the following operators: Equal to, Not Equal to, Greater than, Greater than or Equal to, Less than, Less than or Equal to, In list, Not in list, Matches pattern, Different from pattern, Except.

   These operators require a single value (or a single set of values) therefore on an optional prompt if value(s) are not specified then the condition is completely removed.

3. You can also specify Optional prompt for the following operators: Between, Not Between, Both.

   - When not used with an Optional prompt, these operators require 2 operands (values) each.

   - When used with Optional prompt, these operators can have one or both operands set to be optional.

4. When using an Optional prompt on Between, Not Between and Both then the default behaviour of each operator changes depending on which value(s) are input at query runtime.

   Let us look at each of these operators in turn:

<table>
<tr><td>Between</td><td>Optional prompt on Between where both values are specified

e.g. Database contains data for states California, Colorado, DC, Florida, Illinois, Massachusetts, New York, and Texas

Filter defined as [State] Between 'DC' and 'Massachusetts' will return data for:

<table><tr><th>State</th></tr><tr><td>DC</td></tr><tr><td>Florida</td></tr><tr><td>Illinois</td></tr><tr><td>Massachusetts</td></tr></table>
This is the default behaviour as both values have been specified therefore data falling within the range (including both the upper and lower values) is returned.</td></tr>
</table>

<table>
<tr>
<td>Between</td>
<td>
Optional prompt on Between where first value is specified only
e.g. Database contains data for states California, Colorado, DC, Florida, Illinois, Massachusetts, New York, and Texas
Filter defined as [State] Between 'DC' and '' will return data for:
<table>
<tr><th>State</th></tr>
<tr><td>DC</td></tr>
<tr><td>Florida</td></tr>
<tr><td>Illinois</td></tr>
<tr><td>Massachusetts</td></tr>
<tr><td>New York</td></tr>
<tr><td>Texas</td></tr>
</table>
When the second value is not specified then the condition behaves like Greater than or Equal to, i.e.
We end up with [State] Greater than or Equal to 'DC'.
</td>
</tr>
<tr>
<td>Between</td>
<td>
Optional prompt on Between where second value is specified only
e.g. Database contains data for states California, Colorado, DC, Florida, Illinois, Massachusetts, New York, and Texas
Filter defined as [State] Between '' and 'Massachusetts' will return data for:
<table>
<tr><th>State</th></tr>
<tr><td>California</td></tr>
<tr><td>Colorado</td></tr>
<tr><td>DC</td></tr>
<tr><td>Florida</td></tr>
<tr><td>Illinois</td></tr>
<tr><td>Massachusetts</td></tr>
</table>
When the first value is not specified then the condition behaves like Less than or Equal to, i.e.
We end up with [State] Less than or Equal to 'Massachusetts'.
</td>
</tr>
<tr>
<td>Not Between</td>
<td>
Optional prompt on Not Between where both are values specified
e.g. Database contains data for states California, Colorado, DC, Florida, Illinois, Massachusetts, New York, and Texas
Filter defined as [State] Not Between 'DC' and 'Massachusetts' will return data for:
<table>
<tr><th>State</th></tr>
<tr><td>California</td></tr>
<tr><td>Colorado</td></tr>
<tr><td>New York</td></tr>
<tr><td>Texas</td></tr>
</table>
This is the default behaviour as both values have been specified therefore data falling outside of the range (including both the upper and lower values) is returned.
</td>
</tr>
</table>

<table>
<tr>
<td>Not Between</td>
<td>Optional prompt on Not Between where first value is specified only

e.g. Database contains data for states California, Colorado, DC, Florida, Illinois, Massachusetts, New York, and Texas

Filter defined as [State] Not Between ‘DC’ and ‘’ will return data for:

<table><tr><th>State</th></tr><tr><td>California</td></tr><tr><td>Colorado</td></tr></table>
When the second value is not specified then the condition behaves like Less than or Equal to, i.e.

We end up with [State] Less than or Equal to ‘DC’.</td>
</tr>
<tr>
<td>Not Between</td>
<td>Optional prompt on Not Between where second value is specified only

e.g. Database contains data for states California, Colorado, DC, Florida, Illinois, Massachusetts, New York, and Texas

Filter defined as [State] Between ‘’ and ‘Massachusetts’ will return data for:

<table><tr><th>State</th></tr><tr><td>New York</td></tr><tr><td>Texas</td></tr></table>
When the first value is not specified then the condition behaves like Greater than or Equal to, i.e.

We end up with [State] Greater than or Equal to ‘Massachusetts’.</td>
</tr>
<tr>
<td>Both</td>
<td>Optional prompt on Both where both are values specified

Remember for the Both operator, if you specify two values then data will be returned where both values are met.

If we want to find which [Category] of clothing in eFashion is sold in [Color] = ‘Black’ and [Color] = ‘Black/Blue’ then we would specify ‘Black’ for value 1 and ‘Black/Blue’ for value 2.

<table><tr><th>Category</th></tr><tr><td>Belts,bags,wallets</td></tr><tr><td>Sweats</td></tr></table>
These two categories are sold in Black and Black/Blue Colors.

NOTE:

If you reversed the order or values, i.e. ‘Black/Blue’ for value 1 and ‘Black for value 2 then you would still get the same result.

Remember to deselect the Retrieve duplicate rows property.</td>
</tr>
</table>

Both	**Optional prompt on Both where first value is specified only** When the second value is not specified then the condition behaves like **Equal to**, i.e.: If we specified 'Black' for value 1 (on [Color] object) then results would show all Categories that are sold in [Color] = 'Black'.
Both	**Optional prompt on Both where second value is specified only** When the first value is not specified then the condition behaves like **Equal to**, i.e.: If we specified 'Black/Blue' for value 2 (on [Color] object) then results would show all Categories that are sold in [Color] = 'Black/Blue'.

NOTE:

With the Both operator if only one optional value is specified then the condition will change to **[object name] Equal to 'value specified'**, where [object name] is the object you used for the Optional prompt and 'value specified' is the value input at query run time.

22.10 Using another Object as an Operand

Another object can be used as an operand in query conditions, enabling the values of two different objects to be compared.

It is difficult to practically demonstrate this using the 'eFashion' universe but the following is possible:

1. Place [Sales revenue] in the 'Query Filters' pane and select 'Object from this query' as the Operand.

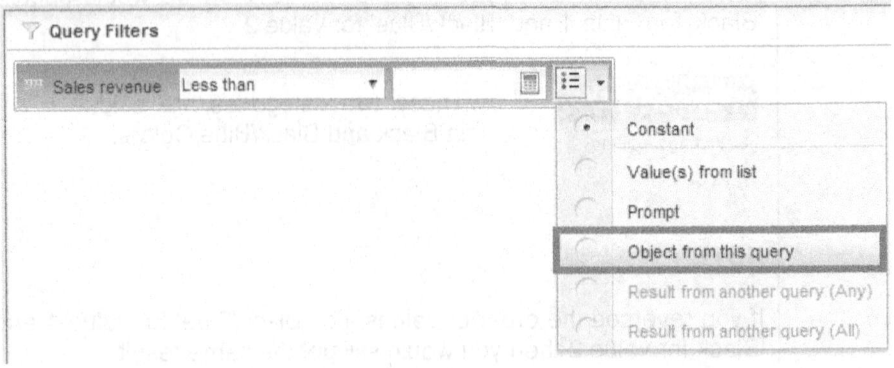
Query Filters
Sales revenue
Less than
Constant
Value(s) from list
Prompt
Object from this query
Result from another query (Any)
Result from another query (All)

2. Select the object [Margin] and click OK.

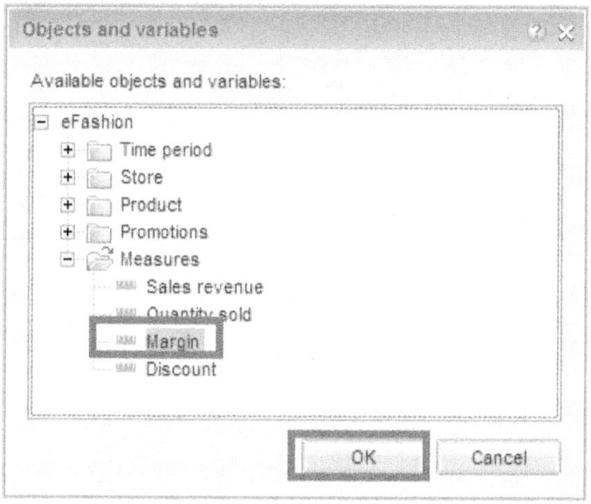
Objects and variables
Available objects and variables:
eFashion
Time period
Store
Product
Promotions
Measures
Sales revenue
Quantity sold
Margin
Discount
OK
Cancel

3. The example query filter (as shown below) returns no data because [Margin] is never greater than [Sales revenue]:

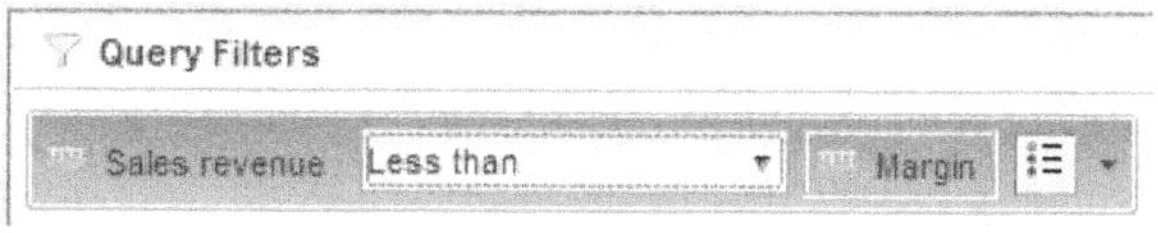
Query Filters
Sales revenue
Less than
Margin

But let's say in a real life example, our query filter was defined as:

[Sales] Less than [Commission]

Your business might pay commission to clients for sales made in previous months, therefore this filter would enable the query to return names of clients who were paid more commission in a month (for sales in previous months) than sales made in the month.

23 Query Contexts

This session describes the use of Query Contexts (which are defined in the universe) to retrieve data when queries are refreshed.

23.1 What are Query Contexts?

Broadly speaking, Query Contexts enable universe designers to specify paths that logically relate database tables together.

Not all universes contain contexts but when contexts are present:

1. They perform the job of isolating a set of tables from another set of incompatible tables.

   Example:

   If your business purchases products as well as selling products then the PRODUCT table would most likely be linked to a PURCHASE_FACT table and a SALES_FACT table.

   Without contexts there is a danger that incorrect results will occur due to the purchase rows being multiplied out by the sales rows (and vice-versa via the PRODUCT table) when objects from the three tables are all used in a query.

   The universe will be designed so that one context goes from PRODUCT to PURCHASE_FACT and the second context will go from PRODUCT to SALES_FACT. Using this approach ensures the two (or more) fact tables are isolated from row multiplication issues.

2. They enable different routes between two tables.

   Example:

   If your business hires products to customers as well as selling products to customers then a customer could be related to a product via rentals, via sales, or both.

   The universe will be designed so that one context goes from CUSTOMER to SALES_FACT to PRODUCT and the second context will go from CUSTOMER to RENTAL_FACT to PRODUCT.

23.2 Web Intelligence and Query Contexts

Contexts are used by Web Intelligence to create meaningful SQL statements to ensure integrity of the data is not violated (e.g. avoid incorrect row based multiplications).

You really do not have to be too concerned with Query Contexts other than the fact that sometimes users will be prompted to select a Query Context (names for Contexts are defined in the universe).

This will typically occur in the second scenario described above when a query is defined with an ambiguous path between two tables. Ambiguous, because Web Intelligence is unsure of what context to use, for example:

Using scenario 2, if a query is created where you select an object from CUSTOMER class and an object from PRODUCT class then the query has two possible routes to navigate for SQL generation.

Sales Context = CUSTOMER to SALES_FACT to PRODUCT

Rental Context = CUSTOMER to RENTAL_FACT to PRODUCT

In this situation, Web Intelligence will prompt the user to select a context when the query is refreshed.

NOTE

- If an object was selected from either SALES or RENTALS classes (alongside CUSTOMER and PRODUCT) then the ambiguity is removed and Web Intelligence automatically selects the correct context to use.
- If objects were selected from both SALES and RENTALS (alongside CUSTOMER and PRODUCT) then Web Intelligence creates 2 SQL statements (1 for each context) and then merges the results within the document.

23.3 Example use of Contexts in Queries

The Island Resorts Marketing universe contains 2 contexts and we will use it to describe how queries can be created and run against a context based universe.

The 2 contexts are:

Sales Context	Customer is related to Resorts/Services via actual use of Services/Resorts
Reservations Context	Customer is related to Resorts/Services via reservation of Services/Resorts

1. Create the following query using the 'Island Resorts Marketing' universe.

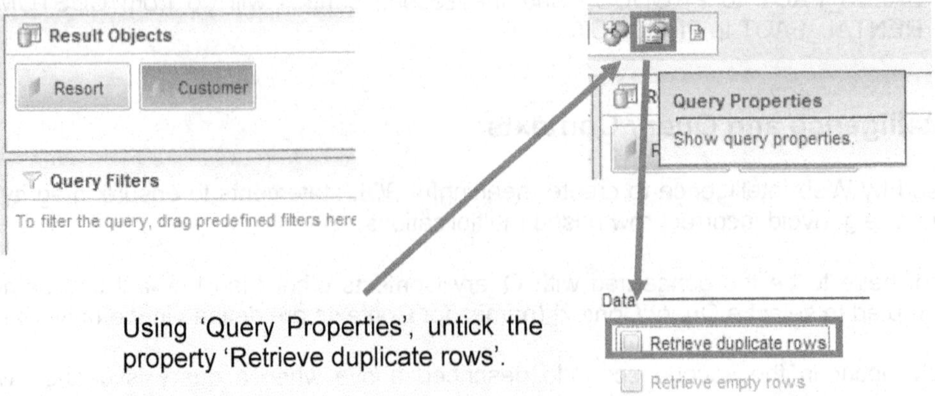
Result Objects
Resort
Customer
Query Filters
To filter the query, drag predefined filters here
Query Properties
Show query properties.
Data
Retrieve duplicate rows
Retrieve empty rows

Using 'Query Properties', untick the property 'Retrieve duplicate rows'.

The query is requesting... which customers have used which resorts?

We have a query containing only dimensions, therefore no aggregation of data will occur (as aggregation is control by properties of measure objects). We have deselected the '**Retrieve duplicate rows**' property to reduce the number of rows returned by the database because Web Intelligence will modify the SQL generated to only request for a single row per resort per customer. In SQL terminology, the SELECT statement will change to SELECT DISTINCT.

2. Run the query, and the 'Query Contexts' interface appears:

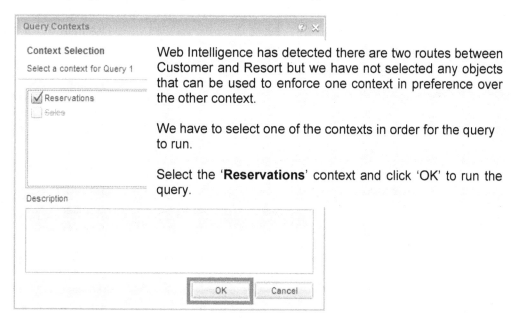

Query Contexts
Context Selection
Select a context for Query 1
Reservations
Sales
Description
OK
Cancel

Web Intelligence has detected there are two routes between Customer and Resort but we have not selected any objects that can be used to enforce one context in preference over the other context.

We have to select one of the contexts in order for the query to run.

Select the '**Reservations**' context and click 'OK' to run the query.

NOTE – We have to be careful because selecting different contexts usually means different results.

For example in our case:

- We could have customers making reservations for resorts but then have no sales for these customers

  Or

- We could have sales for customers at resorts without prior reservations

This clearly is the case as our results show overleaf, therefore users must be aware of the consequences of selecting one context over another.

Reservations Context

Resort	Customer
Bahamas Beach	Baker
	Dupont
	Durnstein
	Marlow
	Martin
	McCartney
	Piaget
	Robert
	Schultz
French Riviera	Edwards
	Gentil
	Hopkins
	Jones
	Kamimura
	Keegan
	McCartney
	Michaud
	Oneda
	Schiller
	Schultz
	Swenson
	Weimar
	Wilson
Hawaiian Club	Goldschmidt
	Mukumoto
	Reinman
	Schiller
	Titzman
	Weimar
	Wilson

Sales Context

Resort	Customer
Bahamas Beach	Arai
	Baker
	Brendt
	Diemers
	Durnstein
	Goldschmidt
	Kamata
	Kamimura
	Larson
	Makino
	McCarthy
	Mukumoto
	Okumura
	Oneda
	Reinman
	Schiller
	Schultz
	Swenson
	Titzman
	Travis
	Weimar
French Riviera	Baker
	Kamata
	Larson
	Makino
	McCarthy
	Oneda
	Schiller
	Titzman
	Weimar
Hawaiian Club	Baker
	Kamata
	Larson
	Makino
	McCarthy
	Oneda
	Schiller
	Titzman
	Weimar

3. Web Intelligence will prompt for a selection of a context on every refresh of the document/query.

   If required, you can fix the context when you develop the query so the user is not prompted. For example a particular requirement might only be fulfilled by a certain context and it makes no sense for the user to be prompted.

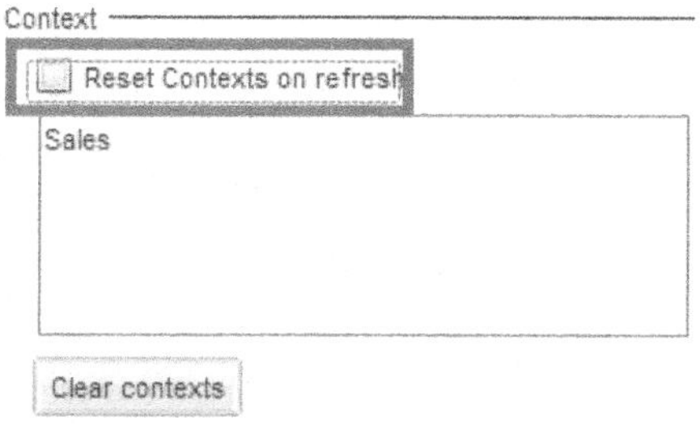
Context
Reset Contexts on refresh
Sales
Clear contexts

'**Clear Contexts**' button clears any selected context(s) and the user will be prompted to select context(s) when the query is next refreshed.

To fix a query context:

1. Run the query and select the context you want the query to use on every refresh.
2. Then edit the query and uncheck the Query Property called '**Reset contexts on refresh**'.
3. This context will now be applied every time the query is run.

NOTE – Complex or multiple queries might require the selection of multiple contexts.

24 Sub-Queries

Sub-Queries are another method of restricting data, but they use the results of one query to restrict a second query. Web Intelligence generates SQL that is processed by the database in two steps:

1. Run the sub-query and return a set of results
2. Use the results of the sub-query to restrict an outer-query
3. Return the results of the restricted outer-query back to the user

A point to note here is that only one set of results is returned to the user, although the database runs more than one query in the background.

1. Create the following query using the 'eFashion' universe and run it.

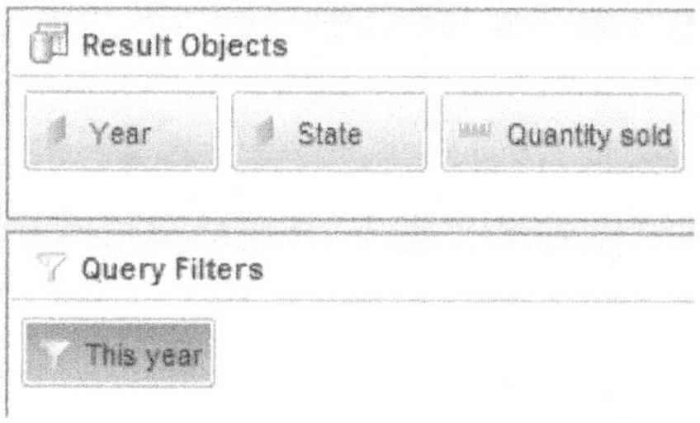

Result Objects
Year
State
Quantity sold
Query Filters
This year

Year	State	Quantity sold
2006	Texas	25,193
2006	New York	19,109
2006	California	17,769
2006	Illinois	6,519
2006	DC	6,491
2006	Massachusetts	5,269
2006	Colorado	5,116
2006	Florida	4,830

This simple query shows data for [This year] that has been sorted descending on [Quantity sold].

We have 3 States selling less than 6000.

We would like to create a query to show all years for the States that have sold less than 6000 (in quantity) in [This year], i.e. using this example we want to show data for all years for the states Massachusetts, Colorado and Florida.

To do this we edit our query to include a sub-query.

2. In the Query Panel select [State] in the Result Objects pane and then click on the 'Sub-Query' icon to start defining the sub-query:

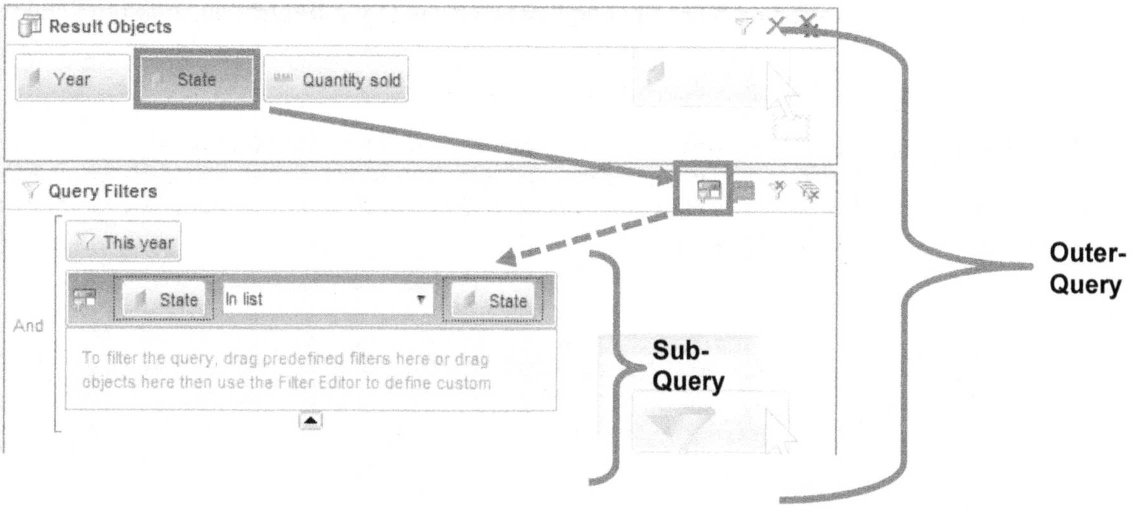

Result Objects
Year
State
Quantity sold
Query Filters
This year
State
In list
State
And
To filter the query, drag predefined filters here or drag objects here then use the Filter Editor to define custom
Sub-Query
Outer-Query

Let us first describe the actual Sub-Query Filter itself:

Object placed here will be used to restrict the outer-query by comparing the values in the database to the values returned by the sub-query object.

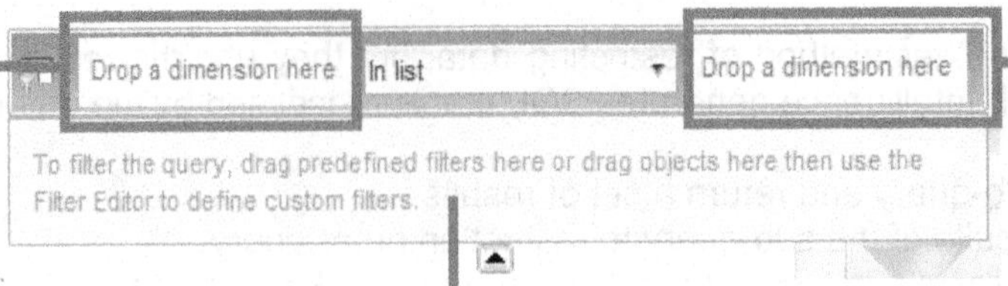
Drop a dimension here
In list
Drop a dimension here
To filter the query, drag predefined filters here or drag objects here then use the Filter Editor to define custom filters.

Object placed here will be the columns of data returned by the sub-query.

Objects placed here will be used to restrict the sub-query itself.

3. Drag and drop the objects to create the definition of the sub-query as shown below:

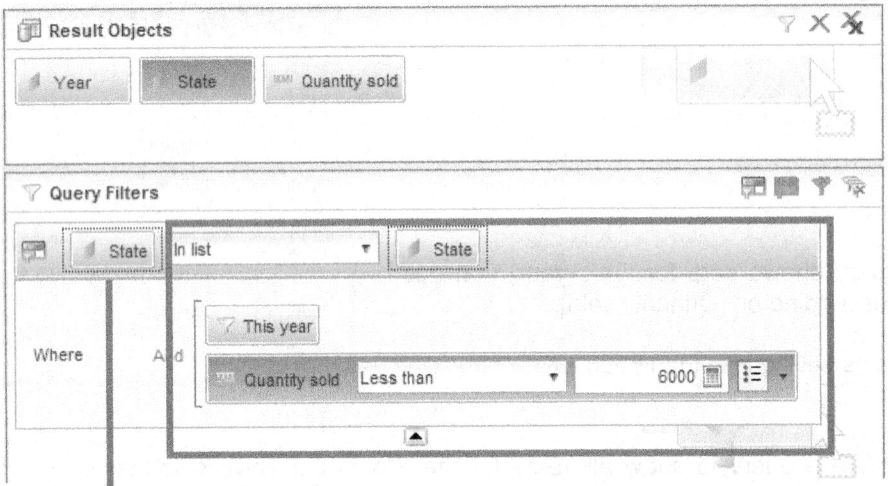
Result Objects
Year
State
Quantity sold
Query Filters
State
In list
State
Where
And
This year
Quantity sold
Less than
6000

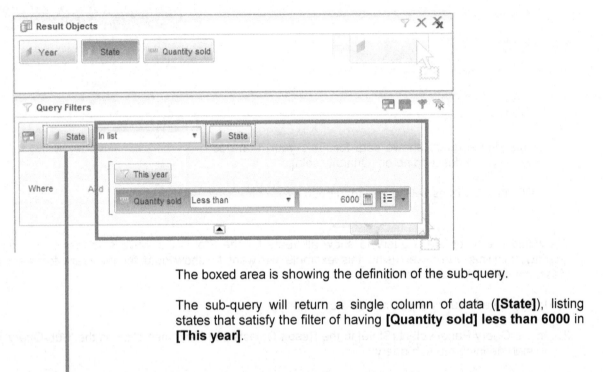

The boxed area is showing the definition of the sub-query.

The sub-query will return a single column of data (**[State]**), listing states that satisfy the filter of having **[Quantity sold] less than 6000** in **[This year]**.

The outer-query will be restricted by comparing [State] values to the [State] values returned by the sub-query.

The sub-query runs first to bring back the states that have sold less than 6000 this year.

Then its results are used to restrict the outer-query to show data for all years but only for the states that have been returned by the sub-query.

4. Run the query.

5. Create a new table as follows (or re-arrange the existing table):

State	Year	Quantity sold
Colorado	2006	5,116
	2005	4,700
	2004	2,971
Colorado		
Florida	2006	4,830
	2005	3,852
	2004	2,585
Florida		
Massachusetts	2006	5,269
	2005	902
	2004	1,505
Massachusetts		

1 – The sub-query returned three [State] values that have a [Quantity sold] of less than 6000 in [This year]. These values were Colorado, Florida and Massachusetts.

2 – These three values were then used to restrict the outer-query resulting in data being returned for all years but only for these three states.

Creating meaningful sub-queries requires an understanding of how the definition of sub-queries works.

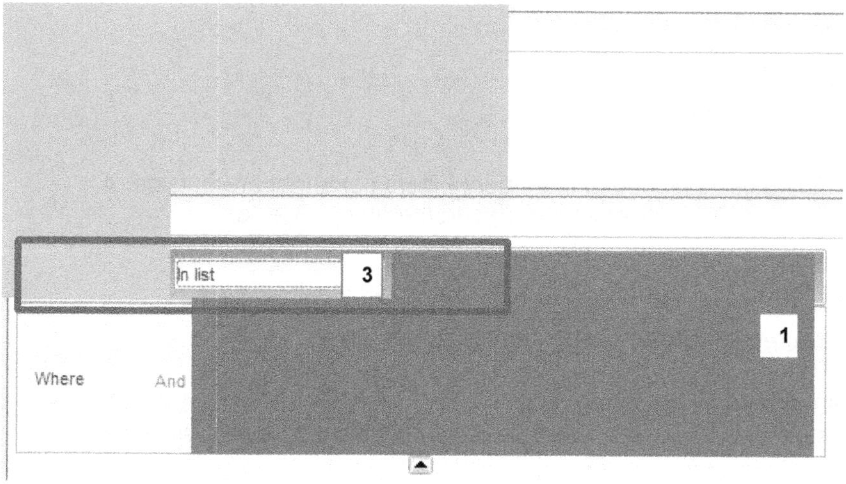
In list
3
1
Where
And

1. The red shaded area (labelled as '1') forms the definition of the sub-query:

   It is used to fetch a single column of values, i.e. States that have sold less than 6000 in quantity for this year. In other words, a sub-query effectively defines a list of values.

2. The orange shaded area (labelled as '2') can be referred to as the outer-query (in relation to the sub-query) and provides the actual data returned to use within the document:

   In this case we have 3 columns, [Year], [State] and [Quantity sold].

3. The outer-query and the sub-query are related by the area highlighted in blue (labelled as '3').

The aim is to use objects that will allow a comparison to be made to restrict the outer-query by using the values returned by the sub-query. In this case we are restricting the outer-query to fetch data for only those *states* that are returned by the sub-query.

24.1 Sub-Queries and other Query Conditions

An outer-query can have further restrictions applied to it by using other Query Filters alongside the Sub-Query filter.

Our example returned data for all years for states that sold less than 6000 in this year:

1. Edit and run the query to request only last year's data for the states that sold less than 6000 in this year:

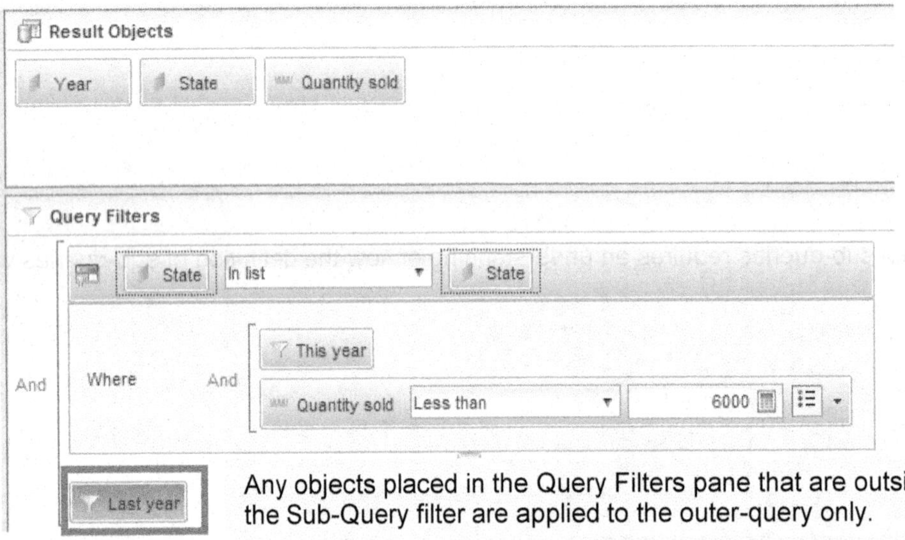
Result Objects
Year
State
Quantity sold
Query Filters
State
In list
State
And
Where
And
This year
Quantity sold
Less than
6000
Last year

Any objects placed in the Query Filters pane that are outside of the Sub-Query filter are applied to the outer-query only.

In this example we have requested the outer-query to be restricted:

- To the states returned by the sub-query.
- Then for the states satisfying the sub-query, we only want data for [Last year].

State	Year	Quantity sold
Colorado	2005	4,700
Colorado		
Florida	2005	3,852
Florida		
Massachusetts	2005	902
Massachusetts		

The results of the outer-query now show data for [Last year] only.

2. Save your document.

24.2 Sub-Queries and Query Contexts

In an earlier session it was described that 'Query Contexts' enforce data integrity by ensuring incompatible paths between tables are not used to generate SQL that yields incorrect results.

Having used the 'Island Resorts Marketing' universe, we know that sales data and reservations data are in different contexts (related to Sales and Reservations respectively). However, when using sub-queries we can use different contexts in the sub-query compared to the outer-query.

1. Create a new document with the following query using the 'Island Resorts Marketing' universe:

Result Objects
Customer
Revenue
Query Filters
Customer
In list
Customer
And
Where
Year 2007
Year 2006

[Revenue] and [Year 2006] are from Sales context therefore the outer-query is going to use the **Sales** context.

[Year 2007] is from Reservations context therefore the sub-query is going to use the **Reservations** context.

The above query definition is requesting [Revenue] for each [Customer] in '2006' where any sort of reservation was made in '2007'.

2. Run the query and the results of the above query are shown below:

Customer	Revenue
Baker	162,566
Mukumoto	16,720
Oneda	122,906
Schiller	131,282
Schultz	20,330
Titzman	126,090
Weimar	76,730

We have presented the results of the two independent queries below so we can check the results above:

Customers who generated revenue in 2006

Customer	Revenue
Baker	162,566
Goldschmidt	18,715
Kamata	112,982
Larson	101,335
Makino	89,085
McCarthy	136,989
Mukumoto	16,720
Oneda	122,906
Schiller	131,282
Schultz	20,330
Titzman	126,090
Weimar	76,730

Customers with reservations in 2007

Customer	Future guests
Baker	8
Dupont	4
Edwards	4
Jones	4
Keegan	4
Martin	2
McCartney	2
Mukumoto	6
Oneda	1
Piaget	10
Reinman	2
Robert	3
Schiller	2
Schultz	3
Titzman	4
Weimar	2
Wilson	4

3. Save your document.

24.3 Sub-Queries with Multiple Columns

We can return multiple columns in the sub-query and then use them to restrict the outer-query.

1. Let us demonstrate this by first running a query (using the 'eFashion' universe) that will be used to validate our results later on.

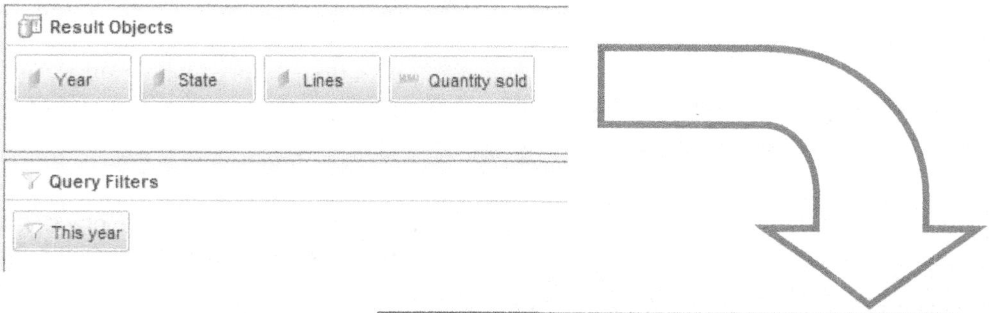
Result Objects
Year
State
Lines
Quantity sold
Query Filters
This year

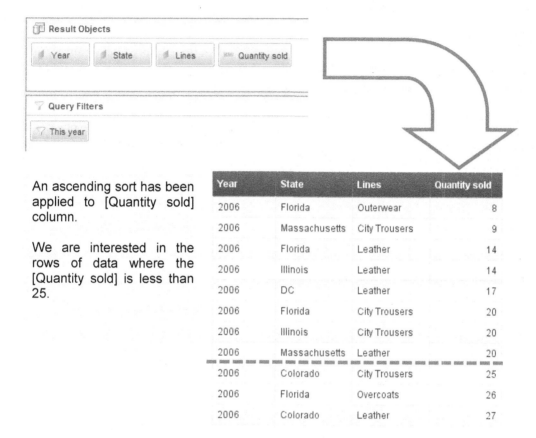

An ascending sort has been applied to [Quantity sold] column.

We are interested in the rows of data where the [Quantity sold] is less than 25.

Year	State	Lines	Quantity sold
2006	Florida	Outerwear	8
2006	Massachusetts	City Trousers	9
2006	Florida	Leather	14
2006	Illinois	Leather	14
2006	DC	Leather	17
2006	Florida	City Trousers	20
2006	Illinois	City Trousers	20
2006	Massachusetts	Leather	20
2006	Colorado	City Trousers	25
2006	Florida	Overcoats	26
2006	Colorado	Leather	27

We would like to know which lines sold less than 25 (in quantity) per state in this year and then return the data for all the years for these state/lines combination.

Breaking this down, we need to:

- Create a sub-query to return [Lines] per [State] that have a [Quantity sold] less than 25 in This Year.

- Use an outer-query to return [Year], [State], [Line] and [Quantity sold] but only for the states and lines that have been returned by the sub-query.

The sub-query we need is demonstrated next.

2. Edit the query and start defining the sub-query as:

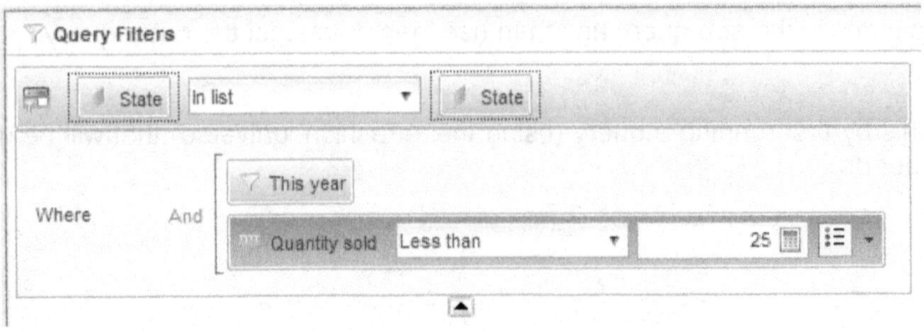
Query Filters
State
In list
State
Where
And
This year
Quantity sold
Less than
25

3. The above sub-query will return states in this year that have a total [Quantity sold] of Less than 25, but we want to expand the sub-query filter to include the [Lines]:

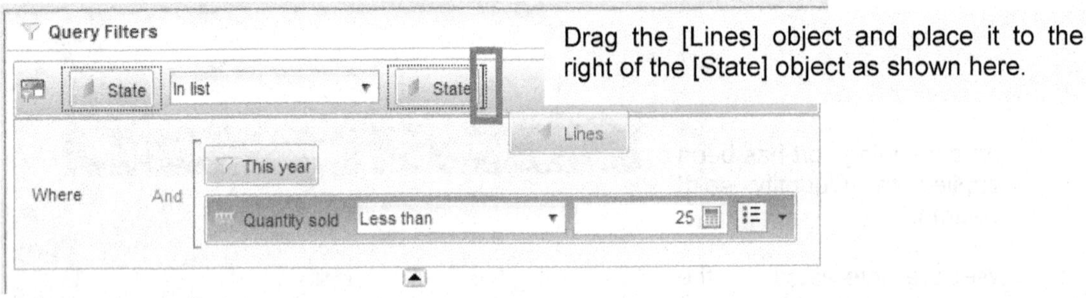
Query Filters
State
In list
State
Lines
Where
And
This year
Quantity sold
Less than
25
Drag the [Lines] object and place it to the right of the [State] object as shown here.

4. The sub-query filter should now look as follows:

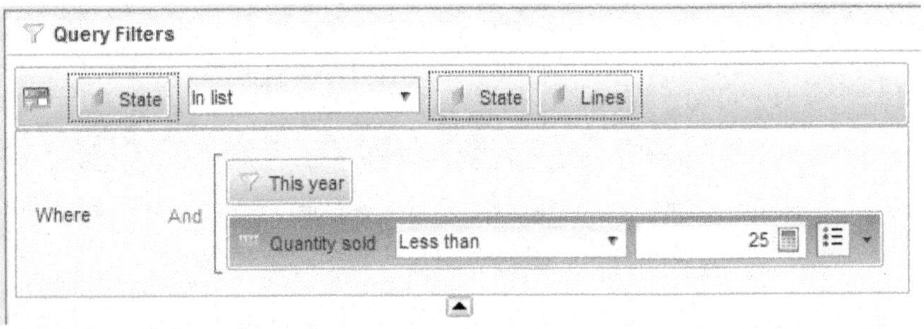
Query Filters
State
In list
State
Lines
Where
And
This year
Quantity sold
Less than
25

5. We need to expand the sub-query filter to also include [State] and [Lines] on the outer-query side for comparison purposes:

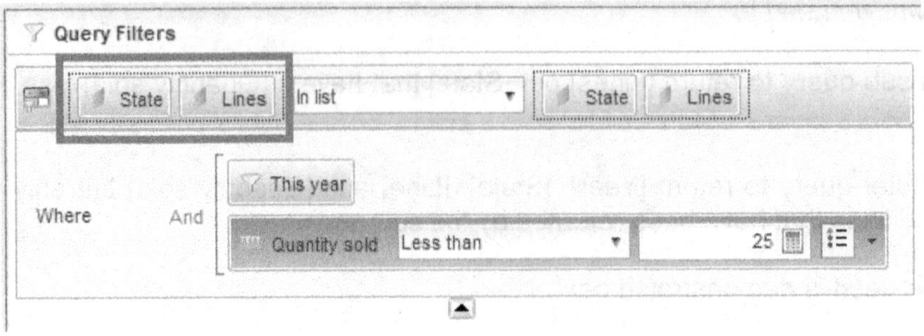
Query Filters
State
Lines
In list
State
Lines
Where
And
This year
Quantity sold
Less than
25

6. After running the query, apply a break on [Year] and then an ascending sort on [Quantity sold].

   We have data for 2004, 2005 and 2006 and this should enable further analysis to take place (e.g. trends) on the lines with low sales in 2006.

   We can also validate the results for 2006 against the original query (as shown below):

Results from sub-query

Year	State	Lines	Quantity sold
2006	Florida	Outerwear	8
	Massachusetts	City Trousers	9
	Florida	Leather	14
	Illinois	Leather	14
	DC	Leather	17
	Florida	City Trousers	20
	Illinois	City Trousers	20
	Massachusetts	Leather	20
2006			

Results from original query

Year	State	Lines	Quantity sold
2006	Florida	Outerwear	8
2006	Massachusetts	City Trousers	9
2006	Florida	Leather	14
2006	Illinois	Leather	14
2006	DC	Leather	17
2006	Florida	City Trousers	20
2006	Illinois	City Trousers	20
2006	Massachusetts	Leather	20
2006	Colorado	City Trousers	25
2006	Florida	Overcoats	26
2006	Colorado	Leather	27

A concise single query using a sub-query has been used to return the required data.

24.4 Nested Sub-Queries

Web Intelligence allows the use of sub-queries within sub-queries.

Let us demonstrate this by using the 'Island Resorts Marketing' universe to answer the following business question:

For the years 2008 and 2009, show guests per customer per resort, but only for customers who placed reservations for the first time in 2008?

In order to answer this, we need to:

I. Find the customers who placed a reservation in 2008 but exclude those that had placed a reservation in 2007 also. This would suggest these customers placed a reservation for the first time in 2008.

II. From the results of the above step we can then find out in which resorts these customers stayed, and the total number of guests.

1. Create a new document using the 'Island Resorts Marketing' universe.

2. Firstly, let us find out which customers placed reservations in 2008 and exclude those that had placed reservations in 2007.

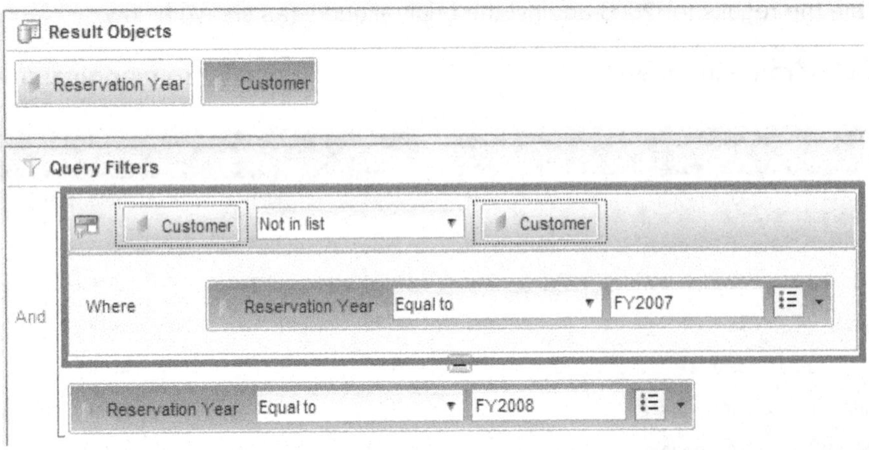
Result Objects
Reservation Year
Customer
Query Filters
Customer
Not in list
Customer
Where
Reservation Year
Equal to
FY2007
And
Reservation Year
Equal to
FY2008

The sub-query is being used to retrieve a list of customers who placed reservations in 2007.

These customers are then filtered out in the outer-query if they also placed reservations in 2008 because we are using '**Not in list**' as the operator.

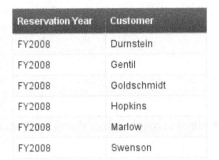

Reservation Year	Customer
FY2008	Durnstein
FY2008	Gentil
FY2008	Goldschmidt
FY2008	Hopkins
FY2008	Marlow
FY2008	Swenson

3. Edit the query then add in a second sub-query and set it to [Customer] *In list* [Customer].

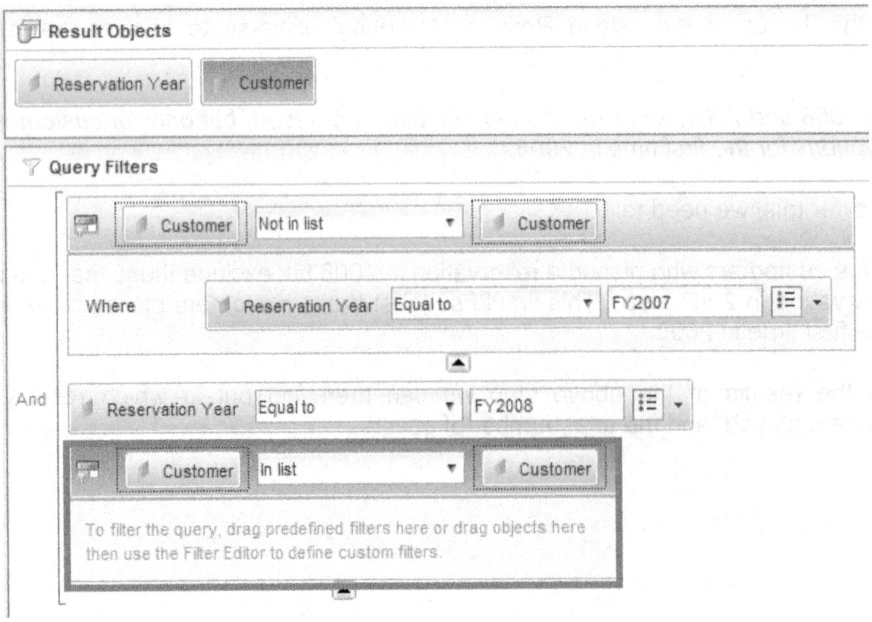
Result Objects
Reservation Year
Customer
Query Filters
Customer
Not in list
Customer
Where
Reservation Year
Equal to
FY2007
And
Reservation Year
Equal to
FY2008
Customer
In list
Customer
To filter the query, drag predefined filters here or drag objects here then use the Filter Editor to define custom filters.

4. Drag the first sub-query filter and drop into the second sub-query filter as shown below:

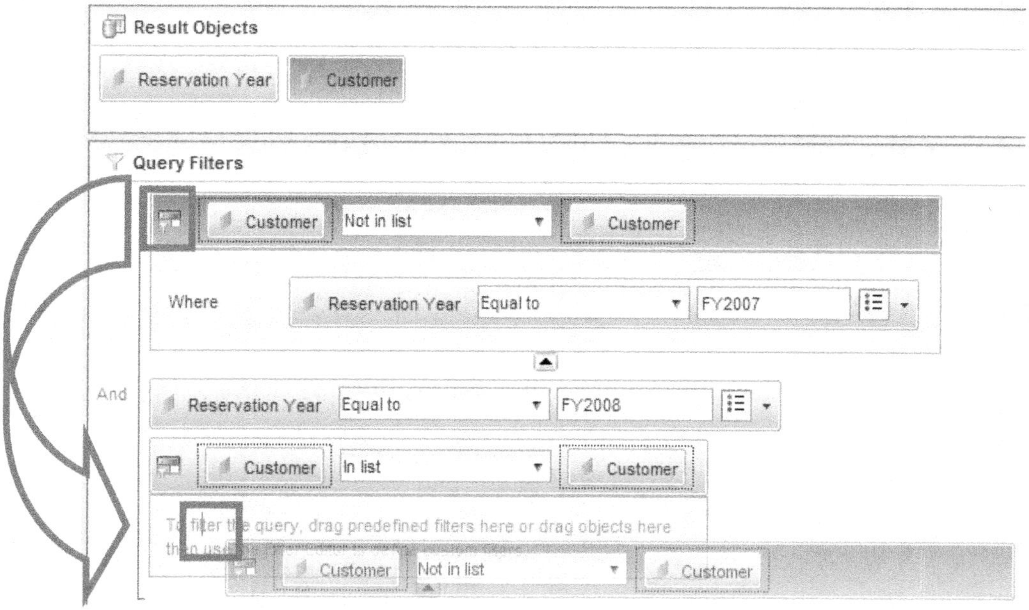
Result Objects
Reservation Year
Customer
Query Filters
Customer
Not in list
Customer
Where
Reservation Year
Equal to
FY2007
And
Reservation Year
Equal to
FY2008
Customer
In list
Customer
Customer
Not in list
Customer

The overall query should look as follows:

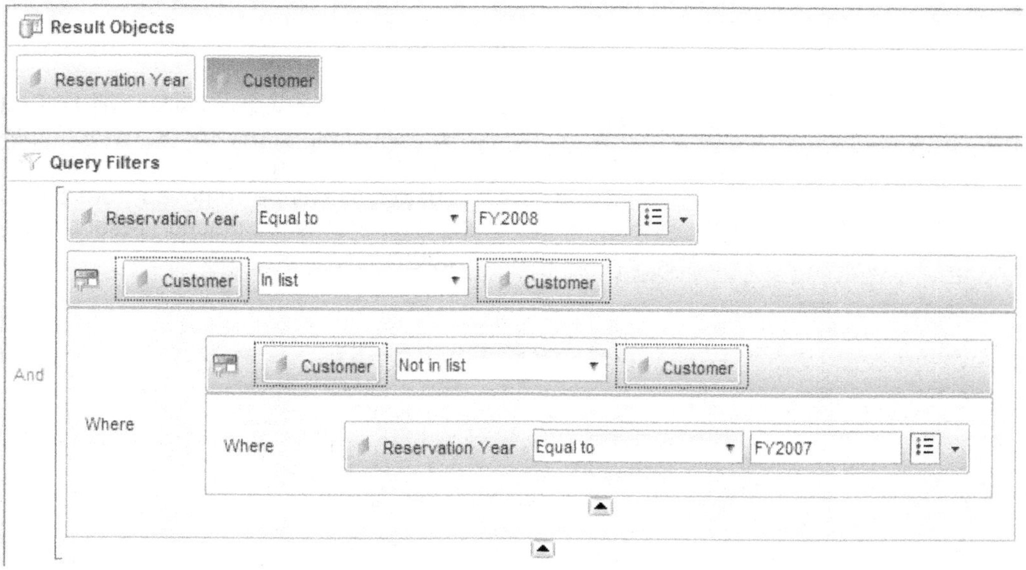
Result Objects
Reservation Year
Customer
Query Filters
Reservation Year
Equal to
FY2008
Customer
In list
Customer
And
Customer
Not in list
Customer
Where
Where
Reservation Year
Equal to
FY2007

5. Drag the condition [Reservation Year] Equal to 'FY2008' into the second sub-query filter as shown here.

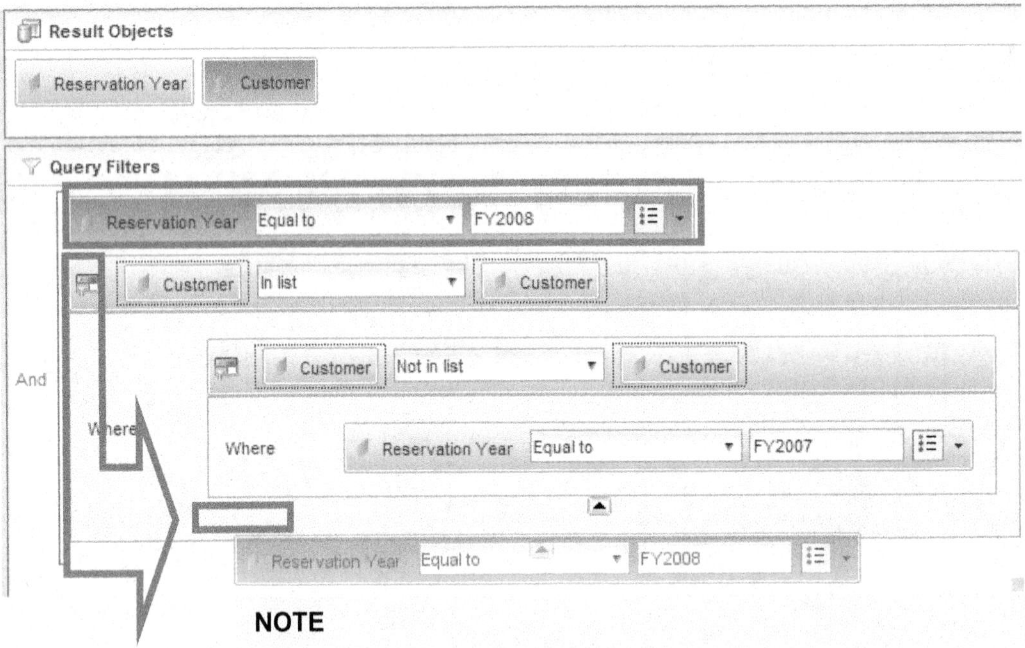
Result Objects
Reservation Year
Customer
Query Filters
Reservation Year
Equal to
FY2008
Customer
In list
Customer
And
Customer
Not in list
Customer
Where
Where
Reservation Year
Equal to
FY2007
Reservation Year
Equal to
FY2008

NOTE

Make sure to 'drop' inside (and not below) the second sub-query filter.

The overall query should look as follows:

The nested sub-query filter will first return a list of customers who placed reservations in 2007 and then these customers will be removed from the list of customers who placed reservations in 2008.

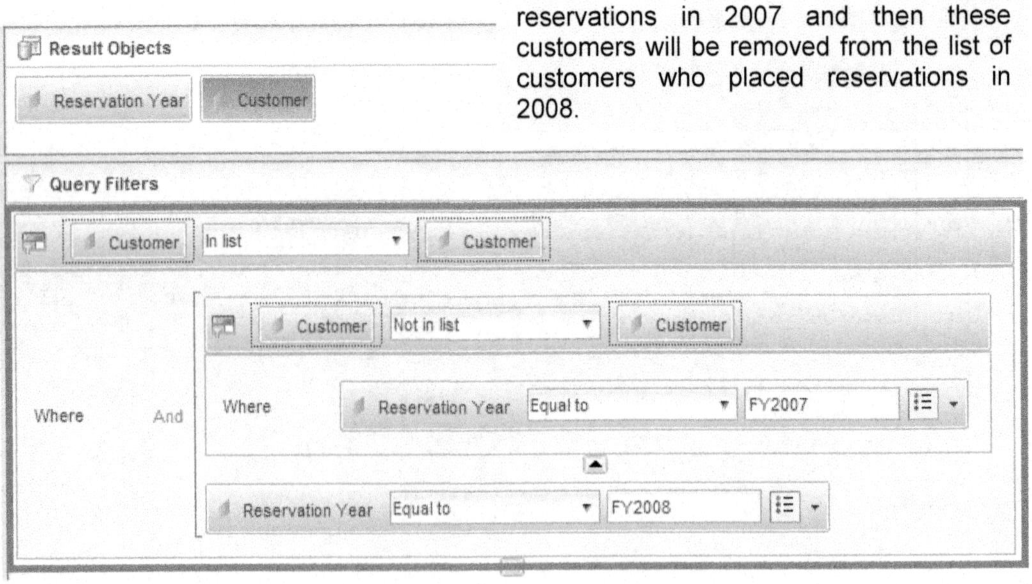
Result Objects
Reservation Year
Customer
Query Filters
Customer
In list
Customer
Customer
Not in list
Customer
Where
And
Where
Reservation Year
Equal to
FY2007
Reservation Year
Equal to
FY2008

6. Now include the extra objects required for the outer-query.

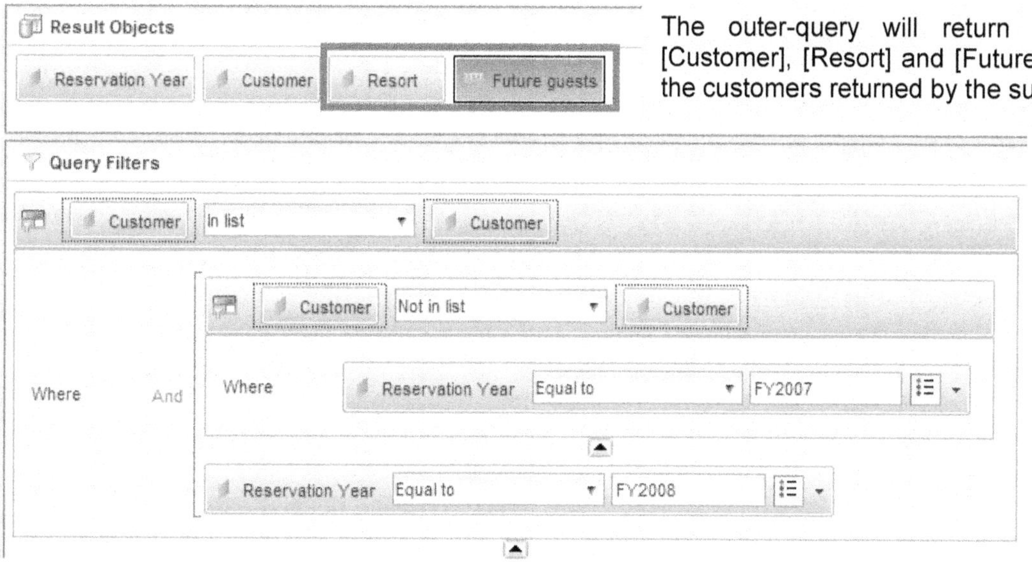
Result Objects
Reservation Year
Customer
Resort
Future guests
Query Filters
Customer
In list
Customer
Where
And
Customer
Not in list
Customer
Where
Reservation Year
Equal to
FY2007
Reservation Year
Equal to
FY2008

The outer-query will return the [Year], [Customer], [Resort] and [Future guests] for the customers returned by the sub-query.

7. Run the query and create the following cross table:

		Bahamas Beach	French Riviera	Hawaiian Club
Durnstein	FY2008	1		
Gentil	FY2008		3	
Goldschmidt	FY2008			2
Hopkins	FY2008		4	
Marlow	FY2008	2		
Swenson	FY2008		1	
Swenson	FY2009		2	

8. Save your document.

24.5 Notes on using Sub-Queries

Use of sub-queries can lead to slow refresh times and should be used with this in mind. If the document refresh times are unacceptable when a sub-query has been used then alternative methods to query the data should be investigated, including any database design changes if necessary.

However, Web Intelligence does enable you to use sub-query techniques to maybe have an interim solution whilst other options are explored.

25 Combined Queries

Combined Queries are multiple queries on the same universe but return a single data set, i.e. multiple queries are defined and run but only one set of values is returned.

Combined Queries could be used to answer questions such as:

1. Get a list of Customer Codes who purchased items in June this year **and/or** Customer Codes who purchased items in June last year.

   This would be done using a **Union** query and the results would include a single occurrence of each Customer Code (even if they purchased items in both years).

2. Get a list of Customer Codes who purchased items in June of this year **and also** June of last year.

   This would be done using an **Intersection** query and would include only those Customer Codes that had purchased items in June this year and also June last year.

3. Get a list of Customer Codes who purchased items in June last year **and did not** purchase items in June this year.

   This would be done using a **Minus** query.

   NOTE – In each of the above scenarios, 2 queries are run and the results are then 'merged' in different ways to produce a single data set.

25.1 Types of Combined Queries

There are three types of Combined Queries:

Union	Web Intelligence (or the database) combines all the data from both queries, eliminates duplicate rows, and returns the unique rows only.
Intersection	Web Intelligence (or the database) returns the data that is common to both queries.
Minus	Web Intelligence (or the database) returns the data in the first query that does not appear in the second.

Examples:

We have two queries with independent results as shown below:

	Query Results
Query 1	California New York Texas
Query 2	California Florida

Depending on the type of combined query, Web Intelligence returns the following values:

Combined Query Type	Combined Query Results
Union	California Florida New York Texas
Intersection	California
Minus	New York Texas

25.2 How does Web Intelligence generate Combined Queries?

If your database supports the type of combination specified in your query then Web Intelligence generates the relevant SQL for the database.

If your database does not support the type of combination in your query then Web Intelligence performs the Combination Query within the report, i.e. by generating multiple SQL queries and then resolving the data after retrieval from the database.

25.3 What can you do with Combined Queries?

Combined Queries allow you to answer questions that are otherwise difficult or impossible to frame in a single Web Intelligence query.

Example (using eFashion):

We want to prepare for the next Christmas period and have been given the requirement:

Produce a list of categories sold in Christmas period last year but not sold in Christmas period of this year.

Using Combined Queries we can obtain the results by using the **MINUS** operator (shown next in '**Building a Combined Query**').

25.4 Building a Combined Query

You build a combined query in the Query Panel.

1. Create the following query using the 'eFashion' universe.

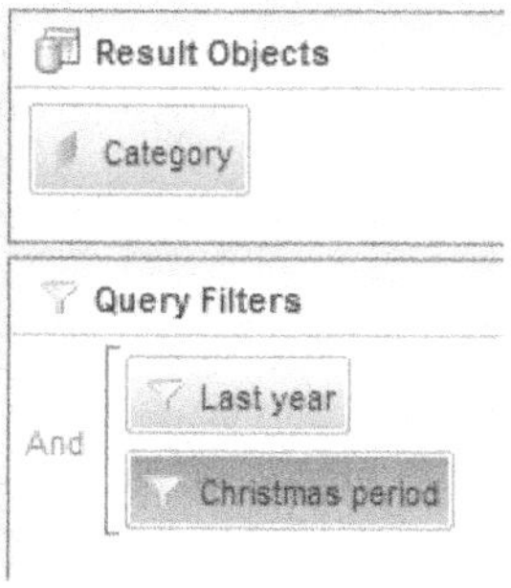
Result Objects
Category
Query Filters
And
Last year
Christmas period

NOTE

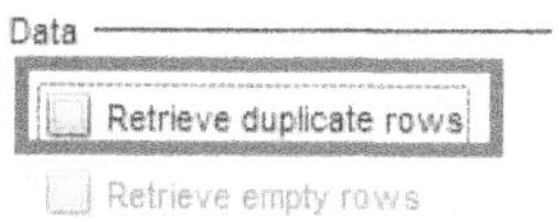
Data
Retrieve duplicate rows
Retrieve empty rows

We have found from evaluating results of queries that Oracle does not require this to be unchecked, but Microsoft Access does require it to be ticked.

If you are unsure whether your database supports Combined Queries then always uncheck this property.

2. If required, uncheck the query property 'Retrieve duplicate rows' (see **NOTE** above).

3. Click '**Add a combined query**' on the toolbar.

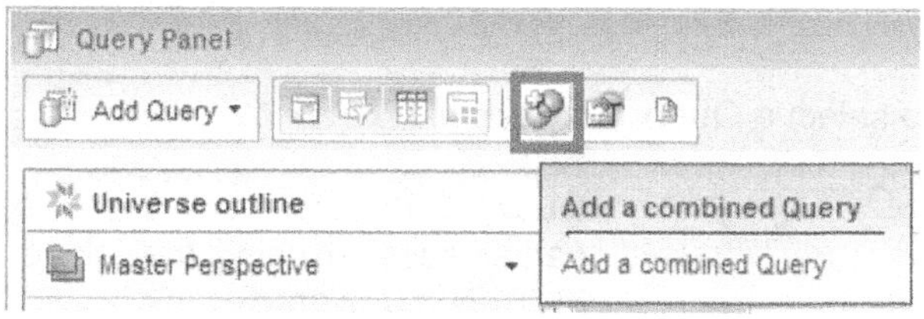
Query Panel
Add Query
Universe outline
Master Perspective
Add a combined Query
Add a combined Query

Web Intelligence adds a copy of the initial query to the data provider. The second query has the following characteristics:

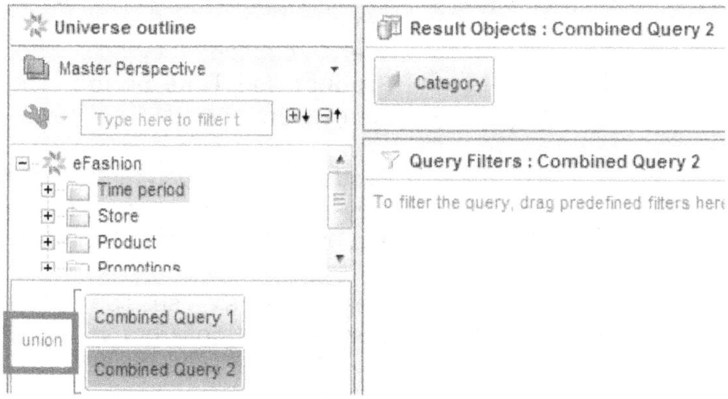
Universe outline
Master Perspective
Type here to filter t
eFashion
Time period
Store
Product
Combined Query 1
union
Combined Query 2
Result Objects : Combined Query 2
Category
Query Filters : Combined Query 2

It contains the same Result Objects as the original query.

It does not contain the filters defined on the original query.

By default, it is combined with the original query in a **UNION** relationship.

The individual queries in the combined queries will be named *Combined Query 1*, *Combined Query 2*, *Combined Query n*, etc.

4. Build up Query Filters for the second query.

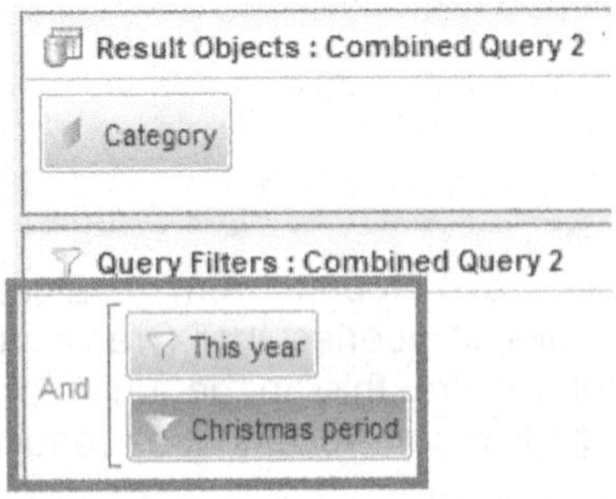
Result Objects : Combined Query 2
Category
Query Filters : Combined Query 2
And
This year
Christmas period

5. For our example we need to use a Minus query so:

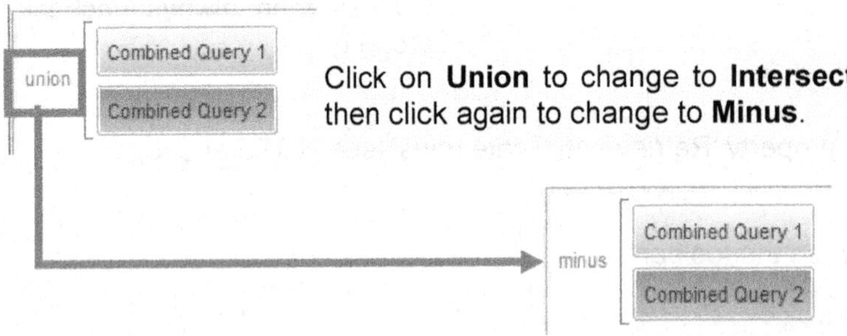
union
Combined Query 1
Combined Query 2
minus
Combined Query 1
Combined Query 2

Click on **Union** to change to **Intersect** and then click again to change to **Minus**.

6. Run the query and you will be prompted to select a Query Context:

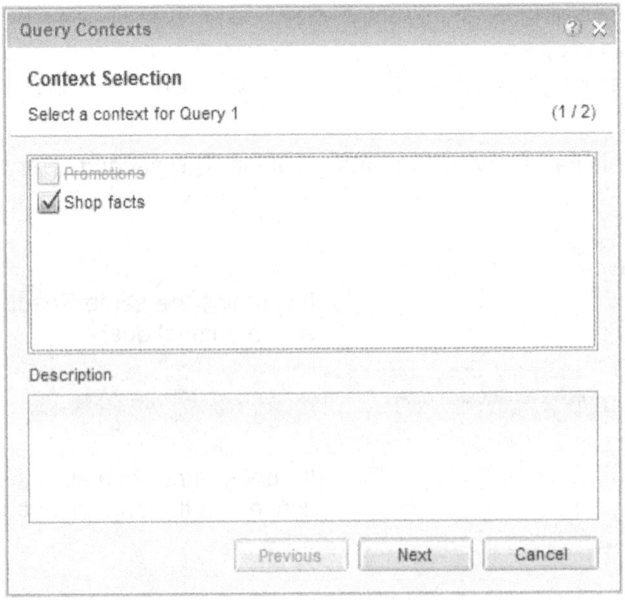
Query Contexts
Context Selection
Select a context for Query 1
(1 / 2)
Promotions
Shop facts
Description
Previous
Next
Cancel

Query Contexts were described in an earlier session using the Island Resort Marketing universe.

In this example, select '**Shop facts**' as shown opposite.

The reason we are being asked to select a Query Context is because our query contains objects from the **Product** and **Time period** classes but no measure objects.

Product is independent of **Time**, but they are related via an activity of some sort, e.g. Shop facts or Promotions.

Please revisit session on **Query Contexts** for more info.

NOTE – You will have to select '**Shop facts**' twice as we have 2 Combined Queries and they are both affected by context selection.

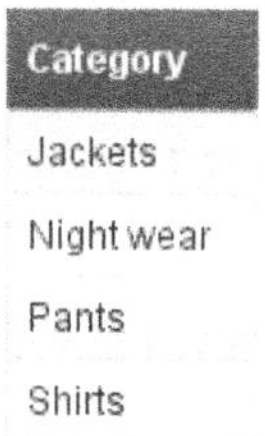
Category
Jackets
Night wear
Pants
Shirts

The results shows 4 categories were sold in the Christmas period of last year but not in the Christmas period of this year.

These results could now be used for further analysis to prepare for next year's Christmas period.

NOTE – If you do not get the results shown opposite then edit the query and make sure you have unticked the property:

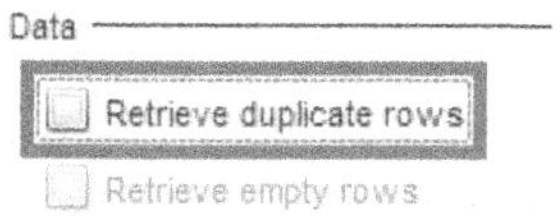
Data
Retrieve duplicate rows
Retrieve empty rows

25.5 Combined Query Structure

The queries within a Combined Query must return the same number of objects, each object must be of the same data type, and the objects must be in the same order.

You cannot combine queries when the number of objects in the query and the data types of those objects are not identical.

For example:

- You cannot combine a query that returns [Year] with a query that returns [Year] and [Sales revenue].
- You cannot combine a query that returns [State] with a query that returns [Revenue].

1. It is possible to combine a query that returns [State] with a query that returns [Category] if both dimensions are of the same data type. The result will be a mixed list of states and categories – this query is unlikely to be meaningful.
2. Typically, if your first Combined Query contains a particular dimension or detail object (e.g. [Year]), then your second Combined Query should also contain a dimension or detail object that returns a list of similar values.
3. Objects do not have to have the same name in Combined Queries, but they should be in the same order within their respective queries and return similar values, unless a mixed list is required (see point 1 above).

25.6 Using Measures in Combined Queries

Including measures in Result Objects of the Query Panel (i.e. for use in the report) usually leads to Combined Queries not working properly.

Revisiting our earlier examples, we had two queries with independent results as shown below:

	Query Results
Query 1	California New York Texas
Query 2	California Florida

Depending on the type of combined query, Web Intelligence returned the following values:

Combined Query Type	Combined Query Results
Union	California Florida New York Texas
Intersection	California
Minus	New York Texas

Let us **assume** we have included a measure in each of the queries (say **[Quantity sold]**) and the results of the two queries are now:

	Query Results (State, Qty Sold)	
Query 1	California New York Texas	20400 9050 7000
Query 2	California Florida	16700 13790

Depending on the type of combined query, Web Intelligence now returns the following values:

Combined Query Type	**Combined Query Results**	
Union	California	20400
	New York	9050
	Texas	7000
	California	16700
	Florida	13790
Intersection	No Results	
Minus	California	20400
	New York	9050
	Texas	7000

We can see that [State] = 'California' exists in both queries, but it does not appear in the results for Intersection. **Why?**

To understand this better, we can say that Combined Queries work by **comparing complete rows** of data. Initially we had one column in each row, but now we have two columns in each row.

	Query 1	**Query 2**
Initial Query Results [State]	California New York Texas	California Florida
Measure Query Results [State], [Qty Sold]	California 20400 New York 9050 Texas 7000	California 16700 Florida 13790

Remember, the Combined Query of type **Intersection**, will return results for matching rows found in both queries.

With our **Initial Query Results** we can see **California** (from Query 1) matches to **California** (from Query 2) therefore it is returned by Intersection.

But with our **Measure Query Results** the values are now matched as pairs; **California 20400** to **California 16700** and this clearly fails the criteria for Combined Query of type Intersection.

Measure values are usually different, e.g. **Revenue last year** to **Revenue this year**, so including measures as part of the output (i.e. in Results Objects) of Combined Queries can lead to the type of problem discussed above.

Make sure the output of each Combined Query produces a row of data that can be matched to another Combined Query. Typically, this means the outputs should contain only Dimension objects (Detail objects can also be included).

25.7 Adding / Deleting Combined Queries

You are not limited to two Combined Queries in Web Intelligence, so you can add more if required:

1. Edit the existing query and click 'Add a combined query':

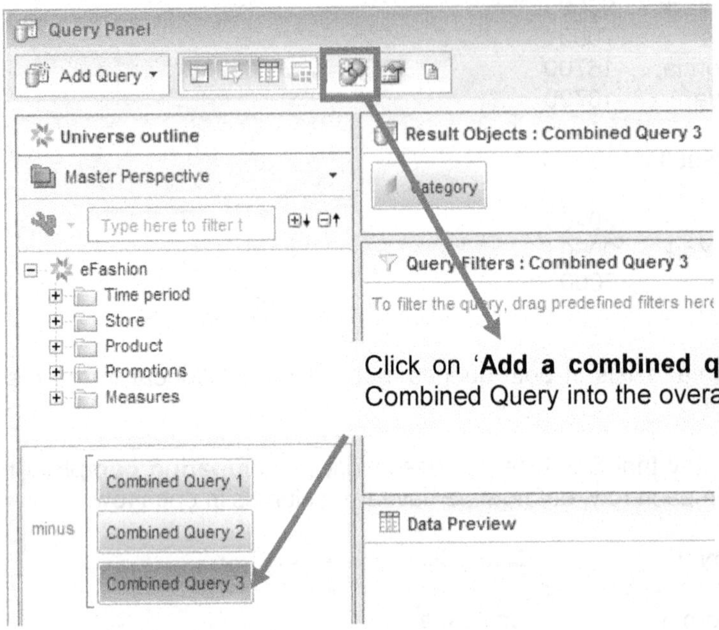
Query Panel
Add Query
Universe outline
Master Perspective
Type here to filter t
eFashion
Time period
Store
Product
Promotions
Measures
Result Objects : Combined Query 3
Category
Query Filters : Combined Query 3
To filter the query, drag predefined filters here
minus
Combined Query 1
Combined Query 2
Combined Query 3
Data Preview

Click on '**Add a combined query**' to add a new Combined Query into the overall query.

2. Combined Queries can be removed by clicking on the query name and then pressing <Del> key.

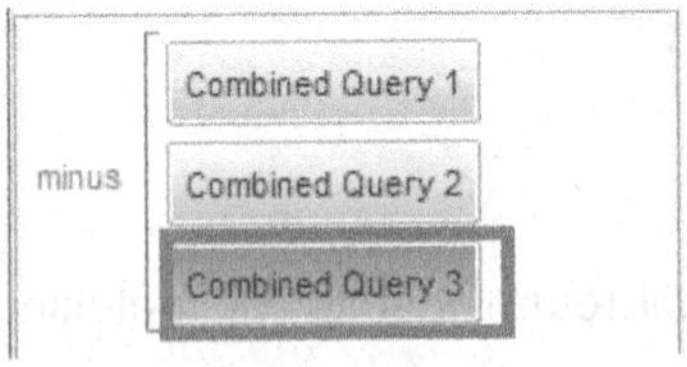
minus
Combined Query 1
Combined Query 2
Combined Query 3

1. Select the Combined Query name
2. Press <Del> key
3. Click on '**Yes**' when requested

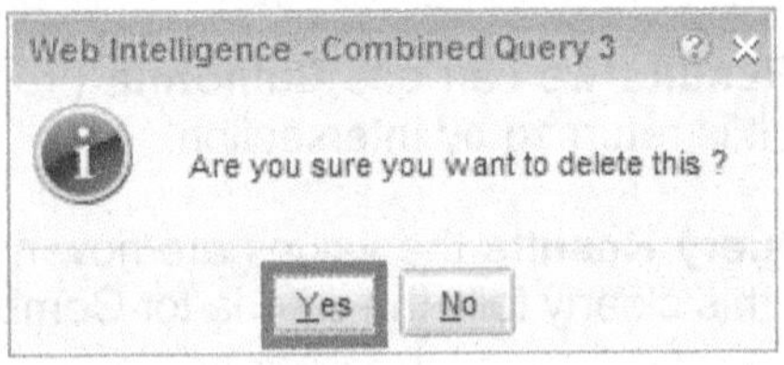
Web Intelligence - Combined Query 3
Are you sure you want to delete this ?
Yes
No

25.8 Changing Combined Query Type

The default Combined Query relationship is set to UNION. This can be changed by clicking on the relationship to cycle through the different types:

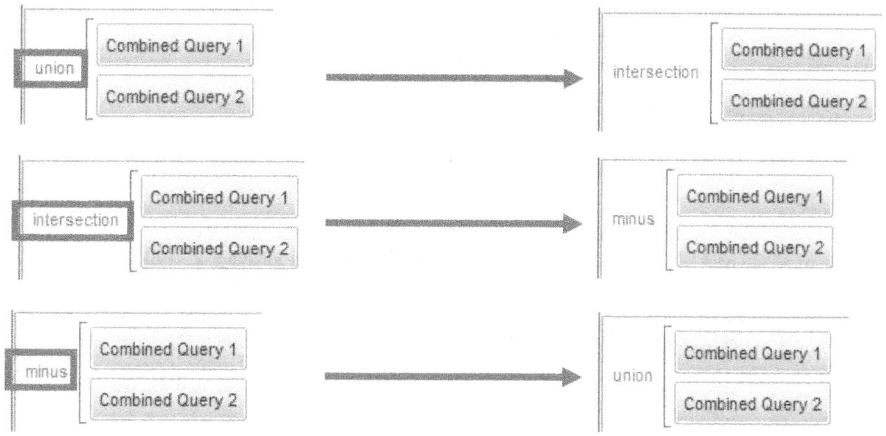
union
Combined Query 1
Combined Query 2
intersection
Combined Query 1
Combined Query 2
intersection
Combined Query 1
Combined Query 2
minus
Combined Query 1
Combined Query 2
minus
Combined Query 1
Combined Query 2
union
Combined Query 1
Combined Query 2

25.9 Combined Query Precedence

The order of execution is crucial in determining the final result of a Combined Query.

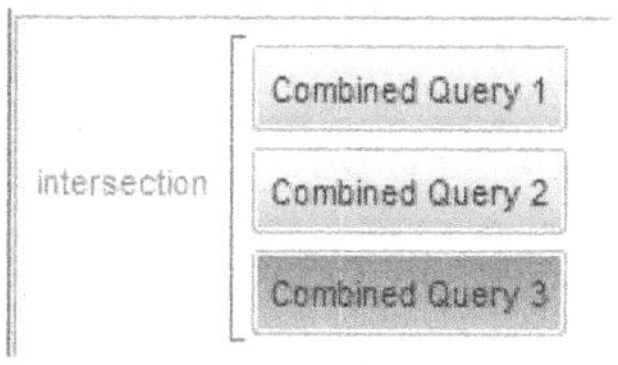
intersection
Combined Query 1
Combined Query 2
Combined Query 3

In this example Web Intelligence will:

1. Find results of Combined Query 1 and Combined Query 2 (i.e. Combined Query 1 INTERSECTION Combined Query 2)

2. Then perform Step 1 Results INTERSECTION Combined Query 3.

Web Intelligence will continue to do this for all Combined Queries in the relationship.

Example:

We have three queries with independent results as shown below:

	Query Results
Query 1	California, New York, Texas
Query 2	California, New York, Florida
Query 3	California, DC, Texas

If we were to create a Combined Query as Query 1 INTERSECTION Query 2 INTERSECTION Query 3 then the results would be:

	Results
Query 1 INTERSECTION Query 2	California, New York
Result (of above) INTERSECTION Query 3	California

How do we get the above results?

Query 1 California, New York, Texas

Intersection

Query 2 California, New York, Florida

Results in California, New York

The above result is then used to INTERSECT with Query 3 (as shown below):

Result California, New York

Intersection

Query 3 California, DC, Texas

Results in California

25.9.1 Changing Precedence of Combined Queries

Using our example from earlier in the session, our Combined Query order was:

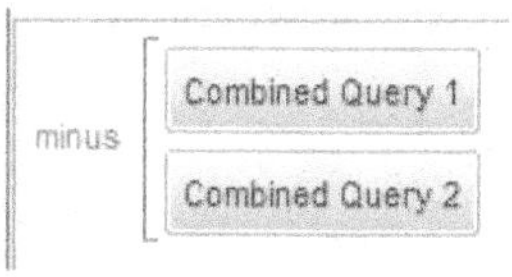
minus
Combined Query 1
Combined Query 2

The order in which the Combined Queries are run can be changed:

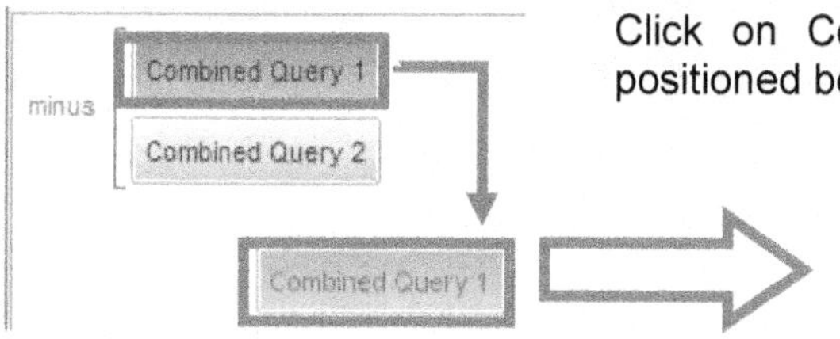
minus
Combined Query 1
Combined Query 2
Combined Query 1

Click on Combined Query 1 and drag it so it is positioned below Combined Query 2.

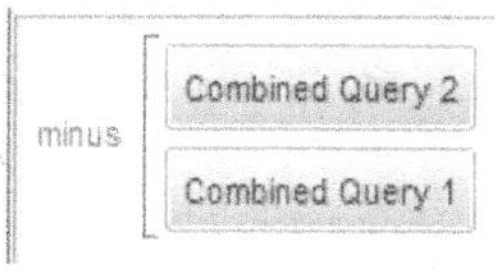
minus
Combined Query 2
Combined Query 1

This will return results from Combined Query 2 that do not exist in Combined Query 1.

Our results are now different because our overall query has changed:

FROM

Produce a list of categories sold in Christmas period of ***last year*** but not sold in Christmas period of ***this year***.

Category
Jackets
Night wear
Pants
Shirts

TO

Produce a list of categories sold in Christmas period of ***this year*** but not sold in Christmas period of ***last year***.

Category
Mini city
Samples
Skirts

25.10 Multiple Combined Queries

Complex Combined Queries can be created and the order of execution is determined by the way in which the Combined Queries are arranged:

1. If we have the following Combined Query:

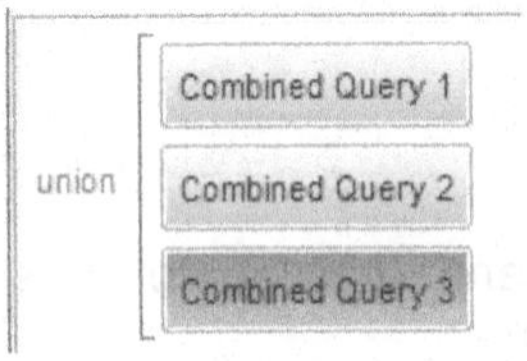
union
Combined Query 1
Combined Query 2
Combined Query 3

2. Drag 'Combined Query 2' and drop it on top of 'Combined Query 1':

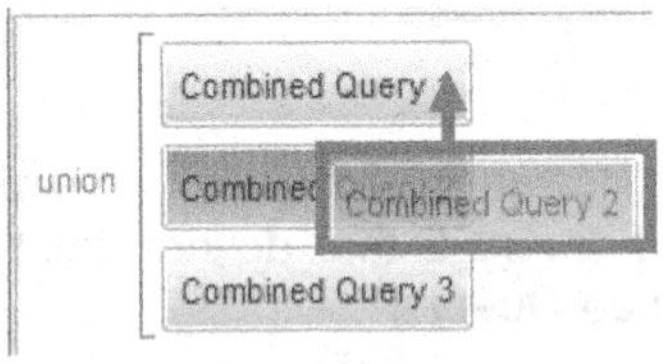
union
Combined Query
Combined Query 2
Combined Query 3

3. Then change the relationship between 'Combined Query 1' and 'Combined Query 2' to minus by clicking on it.

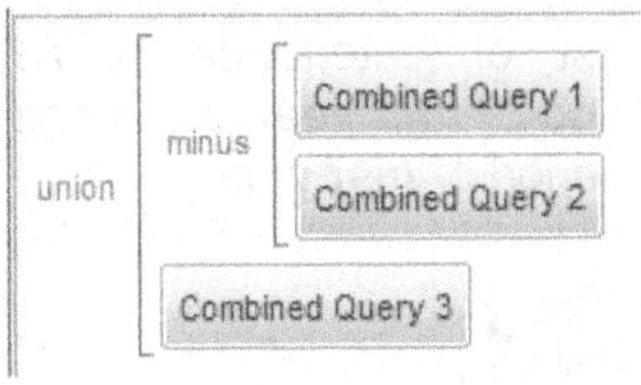
union
minus
Combined Query 1
Combined Query 2
Combined Query 3

Web Intelligence processes:

1. Groups of Combined Queries from right to left as they appear in the Query Panel
2. And from top to bottom within each group

In the query shown opposite, Web Intelligence:

1. First determines the result of the MINUS combination
2. Then finds the intersection of this result with the result of Combined Query 3

Example:

We have three queries with independent results as shown below:

	Query Results
Query 1	California, Colorado, New York, Texas
Query 2	California, New York, Florida
Query 3	California, DC, Texas

If we were to create a Combined Query as (as shown here):

Query 1
MINUS
Query 2

INTERSECTION
Query 3

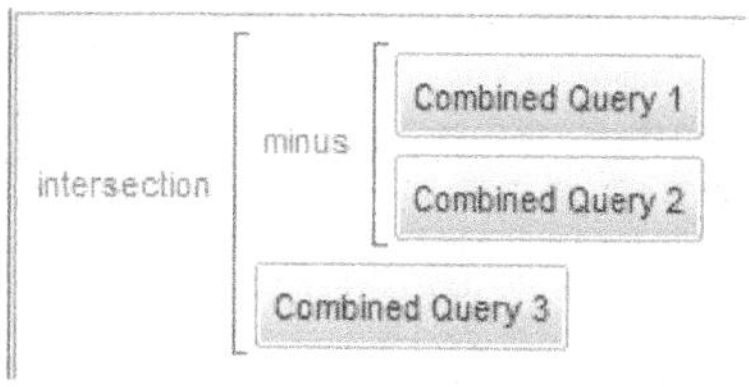
intersection
minus
Combined Query 1
Combined Query 2
Combined Query 3

Then the results would be:

	Results
Query 1 MINUS Query 2	Colorado, Texas
Above Results INTERSECTION Query 3	Texas

26 Ranking Data in Queries

This session describes how to query a database to request data such as:

Top 5 customers based on Customer Spend in this year

Bottom 10 products based on Quantity Sold in last quarter

Database Ranking calculates the ranking based on a measure and then filters the data to only return the records satisfying the request, therefore the above queries will be processed by the database as:

Top 5 customers based on Customer Spend in this year	Only the Top 5 customers are returned based on Customer Spend.
Bottom 10 products based on Quantity Sold in the last quarter	Only the Bottom 10 products are returned based on Quantity Sold.

NOTES

1. Database Ranking is only available if your database supports this type of query. If your database does not support Database Ranking then the '**Add a database ranking**' button in the Query Panel will be disabled.

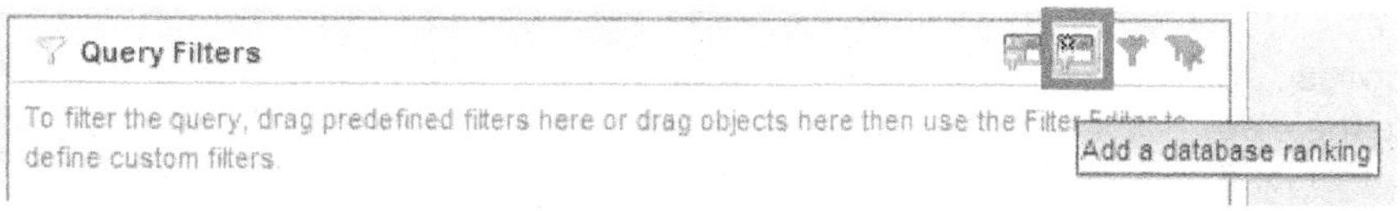
Query Filters
To filter the query, drag predefined filters here or drag objects here then use the Filte
define custom filters.
Add a database ranking

2. To demonstrate this functionality the 'eFashion' data has been migrated to Oracle and a new universe has been created to work with Oracle instead of Microsoft Access. This universe is called '**eFashion Oracle**' in our examples. If you do not have 'eFashion Oracle' available to you then hopefully you can still follow the examples shown to get an understanding of 'Database Ranking'.

3. After selecting an object and then clicking on the 'Add a database ranking' button adds the Database Ranking Filter into the Query Filters pane:

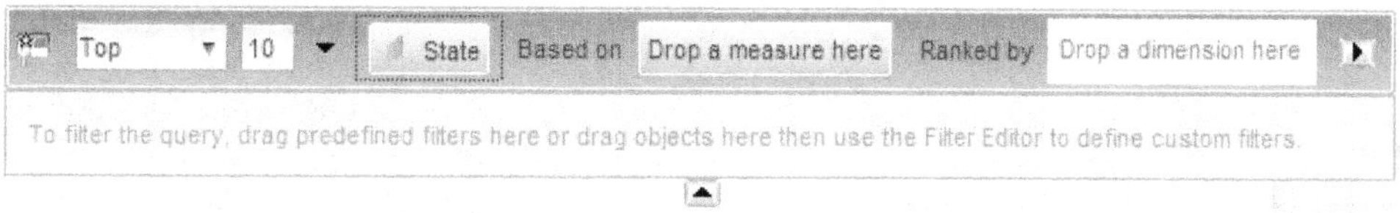
Top
10
State
Based on
Drop a measure here
Ranked by
Drop a dimension here
To filter the query, drag predefined filters here or drag objects here then use the Filter Editor to define custom filters.

For Reference, Web Intelligence uses the SQL-99 Rank function in ranking SQL.

NOTE

For 'eFashion Oracle' universe, further details and instructions can be found at www.webiworx.com**. Look for information on 'SAP BusinessObjects Web Intelligence Training Course' on the 'Downloads' page.**

26.1 Parameters for Database Ranking

The Database Ranking Filter has a number of parameters as shown below:

This is the **Ranking Order**.

You can rank based on a value (e.g. Top or Bottom 10 based on [Quantity sold]).

Or

You can rank based on a percentage of a value (e.g. Top or Bottom 20% of [Quantity sold]).

Ranking Dimension, e.g. if the dimension is [State] and the ranking is Top 10 then the Ranking Filter returns the top 10 states.

Where condition (*optional*) is used to specify additional restriction(s) on the values returned in the database ranking.

For example, a ranking for [State] with a condition of [Christmas period] restricts the ranking to use data available for the seasonal sales around Christmas.

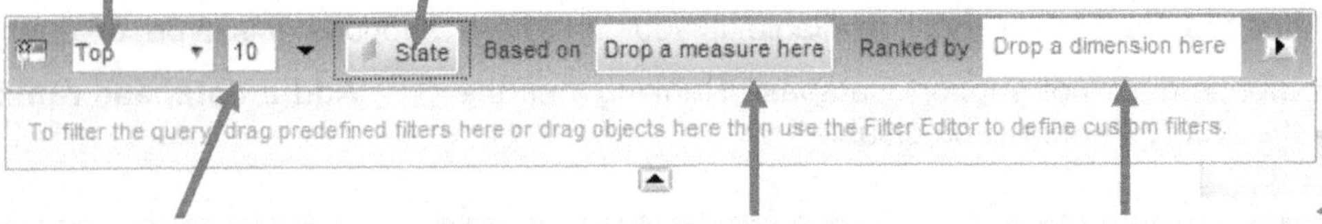
Top
10
State
Based on
Drop a measure here
Ranked by
Drop a dimension here
To filter the query, drag predefined filters here or drag objects here then use the Filter Editor to define custom filters.

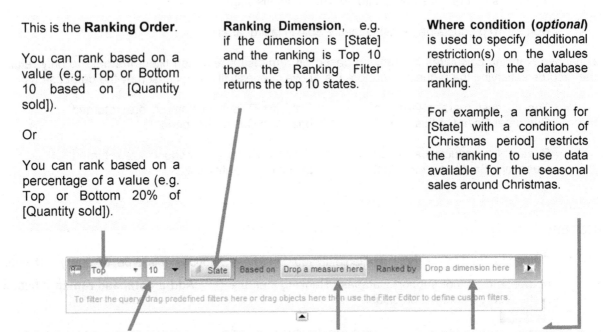

Number of records to return, for example the Top 10 records when Ranking Order is **Top** or **Bottom**.

Or

Percentage when Ranking Order is **% Top** or **% Bottom**. In this case the number of records will vary as it will be based on the records that contribute to the percentage you specify.

Based on (a Measure) by which the Ranking Dimension is ranked.

e.g. if the measure is [Quantity sold] and the dimension is [State], Web Intelligence ranks states by the quantity sold in each state.

Ranked by (*optional*) is used to specify additional calculation context for the ranking.

e.g. if the Database Ranking Filter definition is:

Top 3 [Store name] **Based on** [Quantity sold] **Ranked by** [State] **Where** [Year] = 2005

then

Web Intelligence is requesting the database to return the Top 3 stores in each state for 2005.

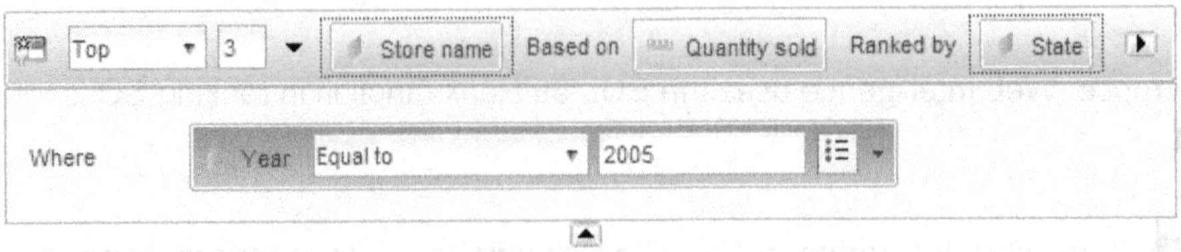
Top
3
Store name
Based on
Quantity sold
Ranked by
State
Where
Year
Equal to
2005

26.2 Using Database Ranking Filter in Queries

Let us take the example we used in Sub-Queries and adapt it to use database ranking instead.

In the Sub-Query we demonstrated how to:

> Show data for all years for the States that have sold less than 6000 (in quantity) in this year, i.e. show data for all years for the states Massachusetts, Colorado and Florida.
>
> We specified a finite limit (6000), so in the future we could run this query to find all states that have sold less than 6000 (say in January of next year) or all states have sold less than 6000 (say in September of next year). Therefore, in January we *could* get all states being reported and in September we would have no data at all!
>
> It would be better if we had a dynamic query that returned the Bottom 3 states based on the [Quantity sold] (irrespective of the actual number).

Year	State	Quantity sold
2006	Texas	25,193
2006	New York	19,109
2006	California	17,769
2006	Illinois	6,519
2006	DC	6,491
2006	Massachusetts	5,269
2006	Colorado	5,116
2006	Florida	4,830

In the Sub-Query example, we first ran a query for [This year] that was sorted descending on [Quantity sold].

From this we were able to see the 3 states that had sold less than 6000 in this year.

We then modified the query to show all years for the states that have sold less than 6000 (in quantity) in this year, i.e. show data for all years for the states Massachusetts, Colorado and Florida.

To do this we edited our query to include a Sub-Query as shown below.

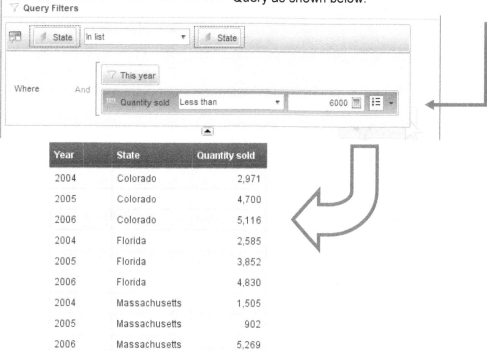

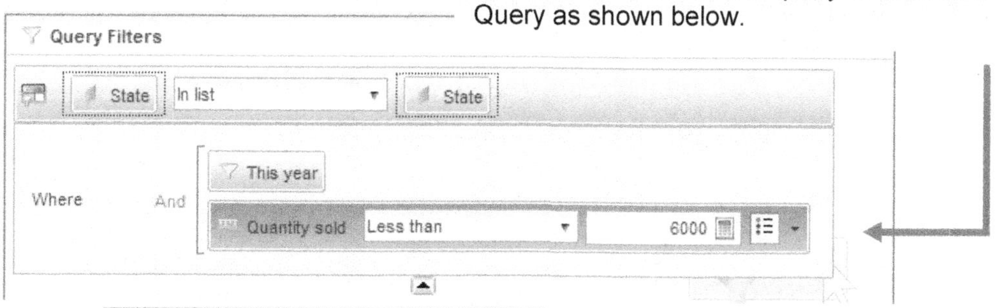
Query Filters
State
In list
State
Where
And
This year
Quantity sold
Less than
6000

Year	State	Quantity sold
2004	Colorado	2,971
2005	Colorado	4,700
2006	Colorado	5,116
2004	Florida	2,585
2005	Florida	3,852
2006	Florida	4,830
2004	Massachusetts	1,505
2005	Massachusetts	902
2006	Massachusetts	5,269

We want to keep the same result objects as the sub-query example but we will also use the Database Ranking Filter instead of the Sub-Query Filter.

NOTE – Use the '**eFashion Oracle**' universe for this example.

1. Add the following objects into the 'Result Objects' pane, then click on [State] object and then click on '**Add a database ranking**' button.

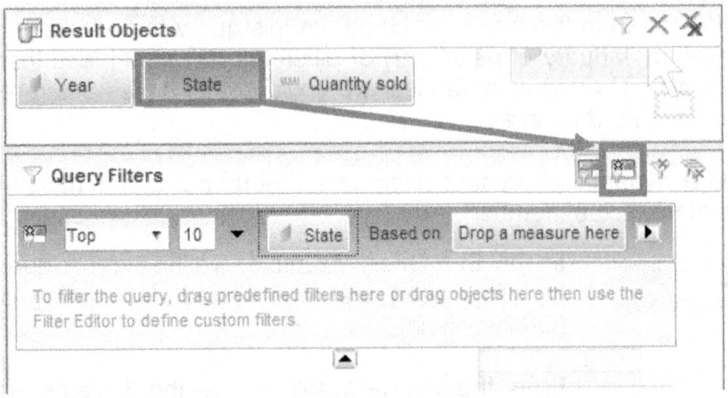
Result Objects
Year
State
Quantity sold
Query Filters
Top
10
State
Based on
Drop a measure here
To filter the query, drag predefined filters here or drag objects here then use the Filter Editor to define custom filters.

Web Intelligence will add the database ranking filter into the Query Filters pane.

2. For our example we want to specify Bottom 3.

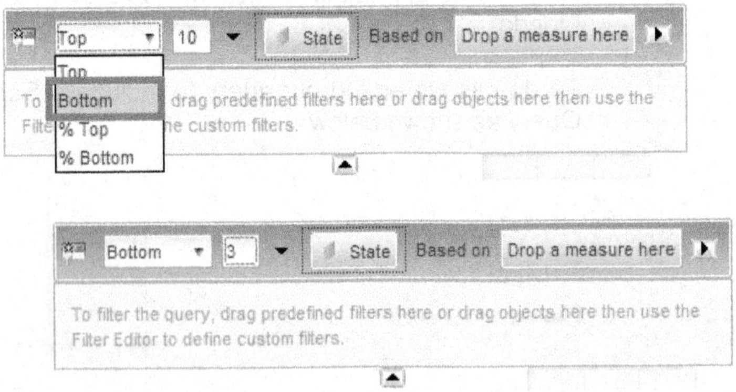
Top
10
State
Based on
Drop a measure here
Top
Bottom
% Top
% Bottom
Bottom
3
State
Based on
Drop a measure here
To filter the query, drag predefined filters here or drag objects here then use the Filter Editor to define custom filters.

3. Drag [Quantity sold] and drop into the area labelled 'Drop a measure here' in the database ranking filter.

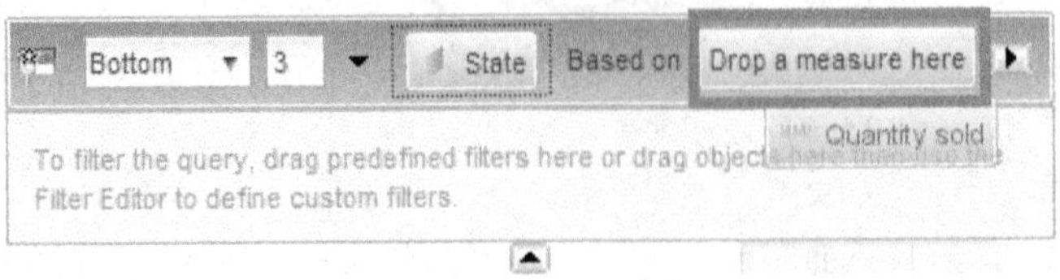
Bottom
3
State
Based on
Drop a measure here
Quantity sold
To filter the query, drag predefined filters here or drag objects here then use the Filter Editor to define custom filters.

The Database Ranking Filter is now requesting Bottom 3 [State] Based on [Quantity sold].

4. For our example we also want to add in a filter to the database ranking filter itself, so drag and drop [This year] into the database ranking filter.

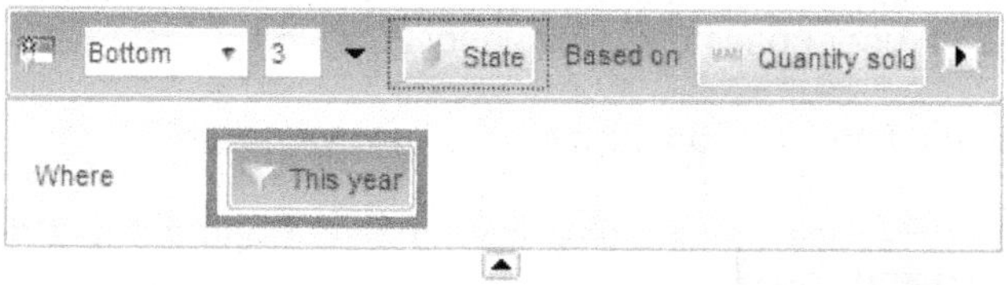
Bottom
3
State
Based on
Quantity sold
Where
This year

The Database Ranking Filter is now requesting Bottom 3 [State] Based on [Quantity sold] in [This year].

5. Running the query shows data for all years for the Bottom 3 [State] in [This year] Based on [Quantity sold].

Year	State	Quantity sold
2004	Colorado	2,971
2005	Colorado	4,700
2006	Colorado	5,116
2004	Florida	2,585
2005	Florida	3,852
2006	Florida	4,830
2004	Massachusetts	1,505
2005	Massachusetts	902
2006	Massachusetts	5,269

Our results are the same as the Sub-Query example (shown opposite), except we now have a query that is dynamic in that it will always show data for the Bottom 3 states in this year (irrespective of the values for [Quantity sold]).

State	Year	Quantity sold
Colorado	2004	2,971
	2005	4,700
	2006	5,116
Colorado		

State	Year	Quantity sold
Florida	2004	2,585
	2005	3,852
	2006	4,830
Florida		

State	Year	Quantity sold
Massachusetts	2004	1,505
	2005	902
	2006	5,269
Massachusetts		

26.3 Using Prompts in Database Ranking Filter

You can use a prompt within the database ranking filter to make the query dynamic so it will return Top ***n***, Bottom ***n***, % Top ***n*** or % Bottom ***n*** (based on user specifying a value for ***n***).

e.g. User can run the query and ask for Top 5 or Top 10, etc

Let us modify the previous query to alter the database ranking filter from a fixed Bottom 3 to a dynamic Top *n* (where *n* will be input by the user at runtime).

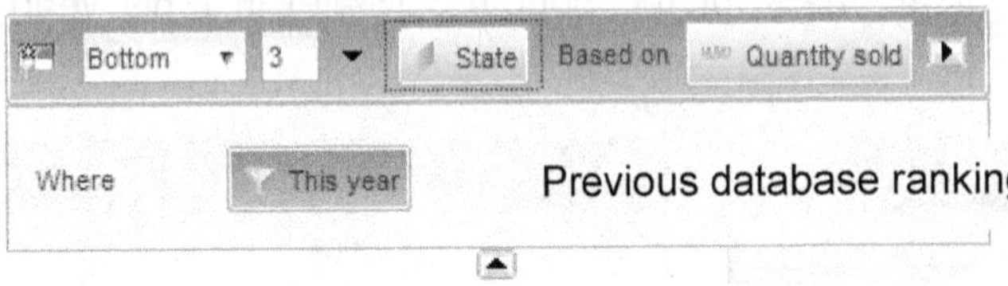
Bottom
3
State
Based on
Quantity sold
Where
This year

Previous database ranking filter.

1. Change 'Bottom' to read 'Top'.

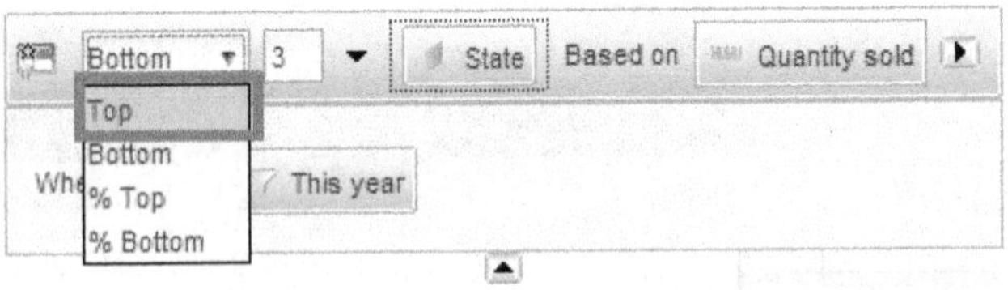
Bottom
3
State
Based on
Quantity sold
Top
Bottom
% Top
% Bottom
This year

2. Select 'Prompt' so we can specify the number of records to return at query runtime.

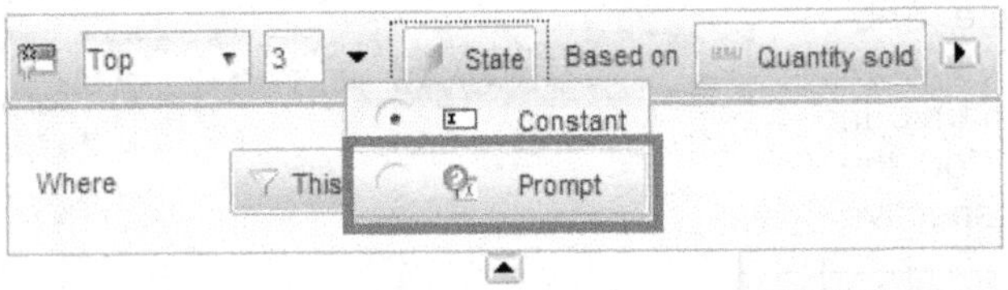
Top
3
State
Based on
Quantity sold
Constant
Where
Prompt

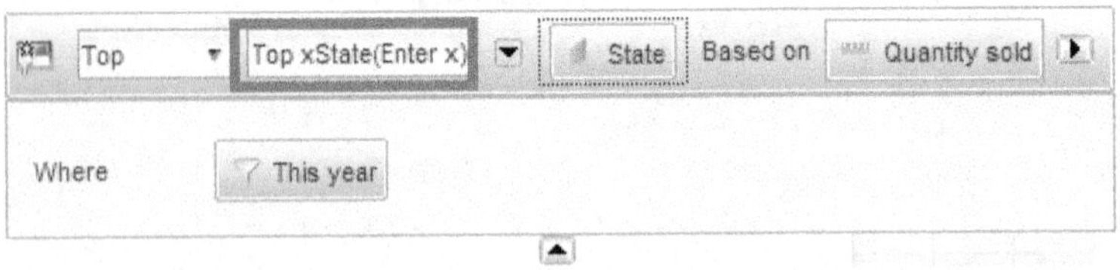
Top
Top xState(Enter x)
State
Based on
Quantity sold
Where
This year

A default prompt will be generated.

Simply click in the prompt text to change it to '**Top n States (Enter n):**'

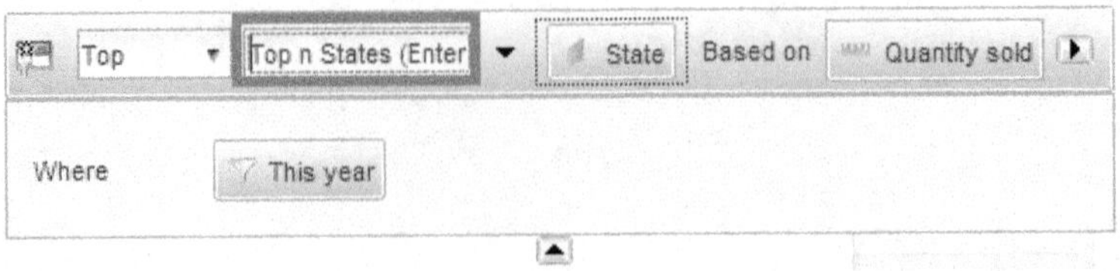
Top
Top n States (Enter
State
Based on
Quantity sold
Where
This year

3. Run the query. The prompt will appear when the query/document is refreshed.

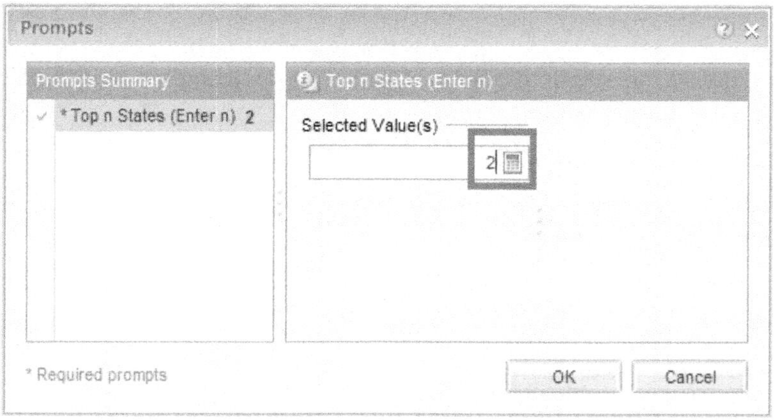
Prompts
Prompts Summary
* Top n States (Enter n) 2
Top n States (Enter n)
Selected Value(s)
2
* Required prompts
OK
Cancel

4. Results of the above query showing data for all years for the Top 2 [State] in [This year] based on [Quantity sold].

State	Year	Quantity sold
New York	2004	10,802
	2005	16,447
	2006	19,109
New York		

State	Year	Quantity sold
Texas	2004	14,517
	2005	22,637
	2006	25,193
Texas		

5. Save and close your document.

26.4 Using the Ranked by Parameter

This is an optional parameter for specifying additional calculation contexts for the database ranking query.

For example, if the Database Ranking Filter is defined as:

Top 3 [Store name] Based on [Quantity sold] **Ranked by** [State] Where [Year] = 2005

then

Web Intelligence is requesting the database to return the Top 3 stores in each state for 2005.

NOTE – In this particular example, if a state contains fewer than 3 stores then all stores for that state will be returned.

To demonstrate this functionality, we will first create a standard query and then compare its results to the results of a query that includes database ranking (with Ranked by).

1. Create a new document and define the standard query as shown below using the 'eFashion Oracle' universe.

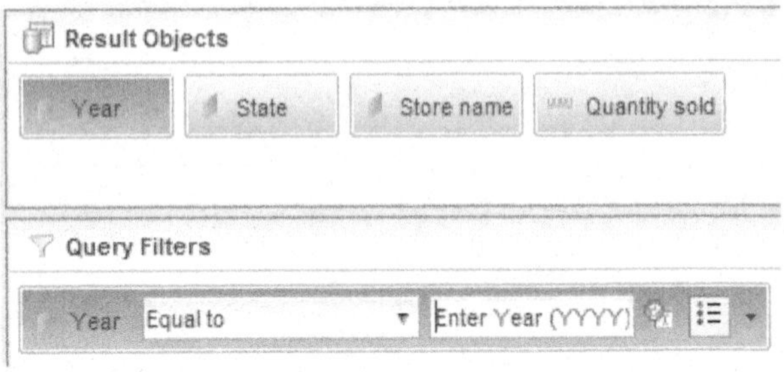
Result Objects
Year
State
Store name
Quantity sold
Query Filters
Year
Equal to
Enter Year (YYYY)

2. Run the query and select/specify 2005 for the [Year] prompt.

3. Results of this query are shown below:

Year	State	Store name	Quantity sold
[illegible]	[illegible]	[illegible]	[illegible]
2005	California	e-Fashion San Francisco	7,209
2005	Colorado	e-Fashion Colorado Springs	4,700
2005	DC	e-Fashion Washington Tolbooth	7,572
2005	Florida	e-Fashion Miami Sundance	3,852
2005	Illinois	e-Fashion Chicago 33rd	6,744
2005	Massachusetts	e-Fashion Boston Newbury	902
[illegible]	[illegible]	[illegible]	[illegible]
2005	New York	e-Fashion New York 5th	6,457
[illegible]	[illegible]	[illegible]	[illegible]
2005	Texas	e-Fashion Austin	6,335
2005	Texas	e-Fashion Houston	5,104
2005	Texas	e-Fashion Dallas	4,545

In this block the data has been first sorted by [State] (ascending) and then [Quantity sold] (ascending).

Colorado, DC, Florida, Illinois and Massachusetts have only one store each.

California, New York and Texas have more than one store each. For these 3 states, we can see that the shaded rows show the top [Store name] in each [State] based on [Quantity sold].

We have 8 states in total, therefore we would expect 8 rows of data for the Top 1 (one) [Store name] in each [State] for 2005.

4. Save your document.

5. Edit the query and define the database ranking query as shown below.

   Select the [Store name] object first and then click on the 'Add a database ranking' button.

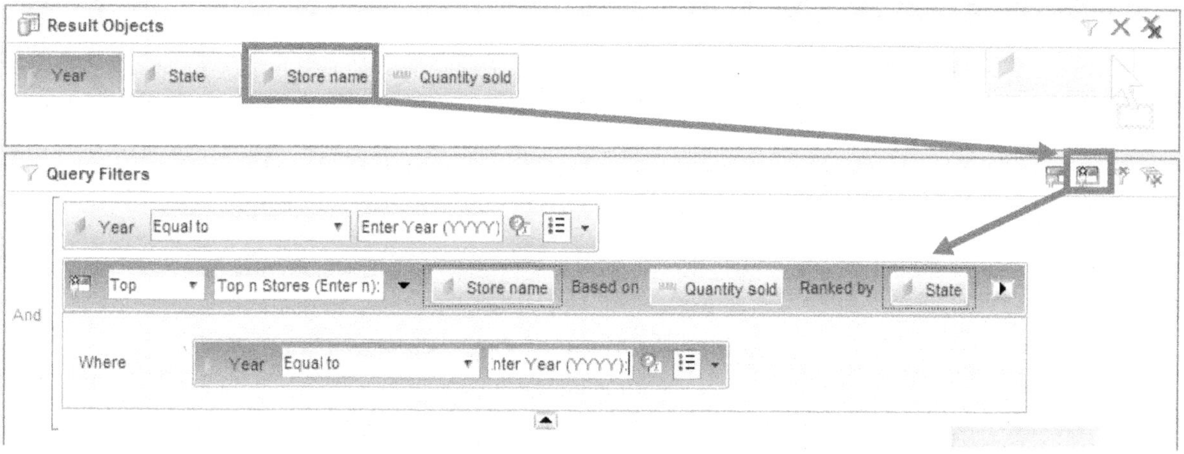

Result Objects
Year
State
Store name
Quantity sold
Query Filters
Year
Equal to
Enter Year (YYYY)
Top
Top n Stores (Enter n):
Store name
Based on
Quantity sold
Ranked by
State
And
Where
Year
Equal to
nter Year (YYYY):

   Ensure the two prompts for [Year] have the same text, e.g. **Enter Year (YYYY):**

   When this query runs it should return the Top n [Store name] per [State] based on [Quantity sold] in the [Year] = 'YYYY', where we will specify values for n and 'YYYY' in the Prompts dialog box.

6. Run the query 'Ranked Data' specifying the following prompt values:

   2005 for Enter Year (YYYY):

   and

   1 for Top n Stores (Enter n):

7. Results of 'Ranked Data' query show the Top store (i.e. Top 1) in each state for 2005:

Year	State	Store name	Quantity sold
2005	California	e-Fashion Los Angeles	9,792
2005	Colorado	e-Fashion Colorado Springs	4,700
2005	DC	e-Fashion Washington Tolbooth	7,572
2005	Florida	e-Fashion Miami Sundance	3,852
2005	Illinois	e-Fashion Chicago 33rd	6,744
2005	Massachusetts	e-Fashion Boston Newbury	902
2005	New York	e-Fashion New York Magnolia	9,990
2005	Texas	e-Fashion Houston Leighton	6,653

The values in this block can be compared to the results for the query 'All Data' (see point 3 above).

We have 8 rows of data (as expected) with California, New York and Texas correctly showing their respective top store (as they have more than one store each).

Further understanding is required of how the **Ranked by** parameters works to ensure mistakes are not made when using it.

The following query:

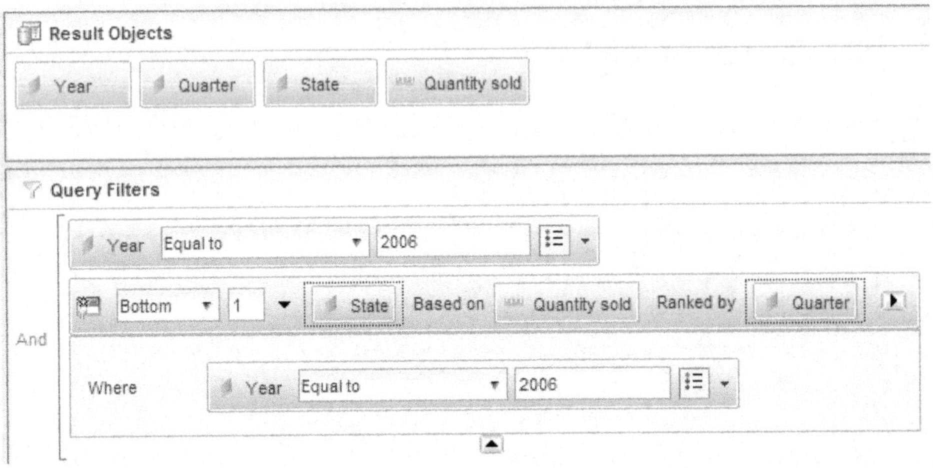
Result Objects
Year
Quarter
State
Quantity sold
Query Filters
Year
Equal to
2006
And
Bottom
1
State
Based on
Quantity sold
Ranked by
Quarter
Where
Year
Equal to
2006

It appears we are requesting in the above query (via Database Ranking Filter) to return the Bottom 1 [State] Based on [Quantity sold] Ranked by [Quarter] of [Year] = 2006, i.e. 'In each quarter of 2006 show us the state that has sold the least in quantity'.

Produces the results:

Quarter	State	Quantity sold
Q1	Colorado	1,291
	Florida	1,210
Q2	Colorado	1,225
	Florida	1,243
Q3	Colorado	1,527
	Florida	1,427
Q4	Colorado	1,073
	Florida	950

The actual results returned show 2 states per quarter and not the 1 state we expected per quarter.

Why?

To understand this further, let us take a look at the underlying data (on the next page).

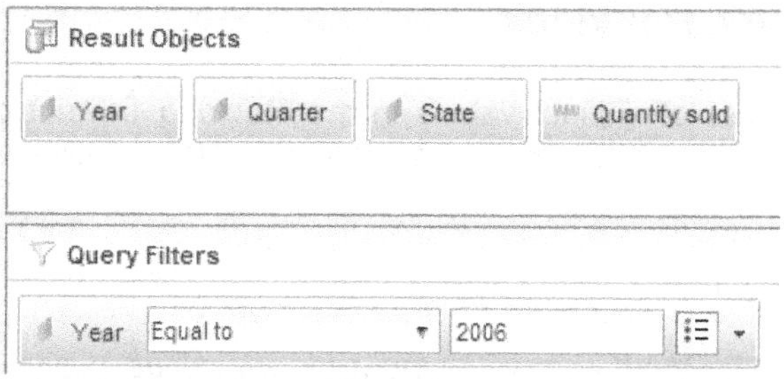
Result Objects
Year
Quarter
State
Quantity sold
Query Filters
Year
Equal to
2006

Quarter	State	Quantity sold
Q1	Texas	6,681
	New York	4,439
	California	4,317
	DC	1,735
	Illinois	1,537
	Massachusetts	1,327
	Colorado	1291
	Florida	1210
Q2	Texas	6,195
	New York	4,944
	California	4,471
	Illinois	2,005
	DC	1,535
	Florida	1,243
	Massachusetts	1228
	Colorado	1225
Q3	Texas	6,961
	New York	6,119
	California	5,134
	DC	1,867
	Illinois	1,689
	Massachusetts	1,539
	Colorado	1527
	Florida	1427
Q4	Texas	5,356
	California	3,847
	New York	3,607
	DC	1,354
	Illinois	1,288
	Massachusetts	1,175
	Colorado	1,073
	Florida	950

The above query's results (shown opposite) list the states in descending order (based on quantity sold) in each quarter of 2006.

In Q1, Q3, and Q4 we have Florida as the bottom state, but in Q2 it is Colorado. Therefore, in total we have 2 state values across the 4 quarters.

In our database ranking query (on previous page), we have these 2 state values returned by the Database Ranking Filter. These are then used for the remainder of the query as shown in the **diagram below**. A list of states is returned by '1' and these states values along with [Year] = 2006 are used to restrict '2'.

NOTE:

When generating SQL, Web Intelligence uses the Database Ranking Filter in a similar manner to the Sub-Query Filter.

The Database Ranking Filter will return a list of values depending on the **Ranking Dimension** used (e.g. we have used [State]) and these values will be used alongside other query conditions to restrict the overall (outer) query.

In the SQL statement generated, Web Intelligence automatically places a restriction on the outer query on the Ranking Dimension used in the Database Ranking Filter, whereas with the Sub-Query Filter we have the option of selecting an object to compare the returned values against.

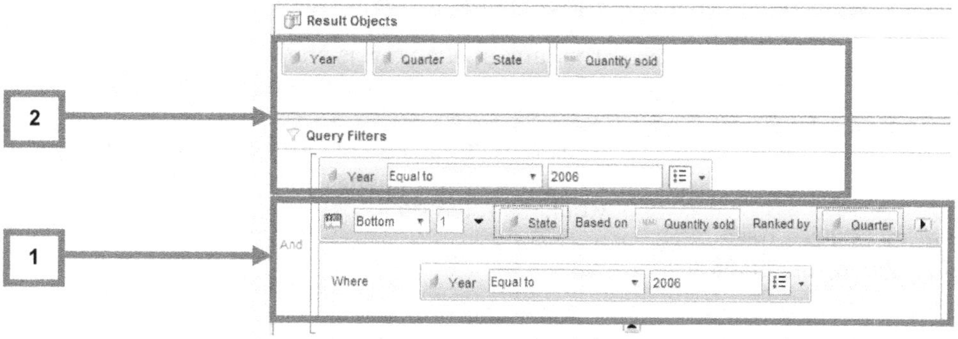
2
1
Result Objects
Year
Quarter
State
Quantity sold
Query Filters
Year
Equal to
2006
And
Bottom
1
State
Based on
Quantity sold
Ranked by
Quarter
Where
Year
Equal to
2006

26.5 Using % Top or % Bottom for Database Rankings

These parameters calculate rankings using the number of distinct values in the Ranking Dimension. For Oracle (as that is the database we are using to demonstrate these parameters), Web Intelligence uses the PERCENT_RANK analytic function.

The definition of the PERCENT_RANK analytic function in Oracle is:

As an analytic function, for a ***row r****, PERCENT_RANK calculates the rank or r minus 1, divided by 1 less than the number of rows being evaluated in the partition.*

i.e. PERCENT_RANK = ((rank of row r) – 1) / ((rows in partition) – 1)

The range of values returned by PERCENT_RANK is 0 to 1 inclusive (i.e. 0% to 100%).

To illustrate this, let us first take the query shown here and its results as shown below:

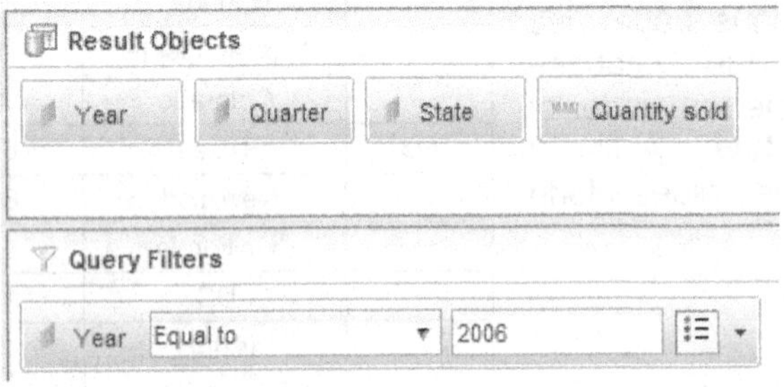
Result Objects
Year
Quarter
State
Quantity sold
Query Filters
Year
Equal to
2006

Quarter	Quantity sold
Q1	22,537
Q2	22,846
Q3	26,263
Q4	18,650
Sum:	**90,296**

The important point to note here is the number of distinct values we have for [Quarter] is 4. Therefore the PERCENT_RANK function would have 4 rows in the *partition* if we used the [Quarter] object as the Ranking Dimension.

Quarter	Quantity sold	Rank	% Rank
Q4	18,650	1	0.00%
Q1	22,537	2	33.33%
Q2	22,846	3	66.67%
Q3	26,263	4	100.00%
	90,296		

Ascending sort on [Quantity sold] shows [Quarter] in order Q4, Q1, Q2, Q3.

The rank of each row is shown along with the PERCENT_RANK that will be calculated by Oracle.

If we were to run a query for Bottom 20% with [Quarter] as the Ranking Dimension then only 'Q4' rows would be returned.

Quarter	Quantity sold	Rank	% Rank
Q3	26,263	1	0.00%
Q2	22,846	2	33.33%
Q1	22,537	3	66.67%
Q4	18,650	4	100.00%
	90,296		

Descending sort on [Quantity sold] shows [Quarter] in order Q3, Q2, Q1, Q4.

The rank of each row is shown along with the PERCENT_RANK that will be calculated by Oracle.

If we were to run a query for Top 40% with [Quarter] as the Ranking Dimension then 'Q3' and 'Q2' rows would be returned.

NOTE – 2 decimal places have been used, **66.67%** should be **66.66%** in above tables.

Now let us test our understanding of how % Bottom and % Top work with an Oracle database.

1. First, create the following query:

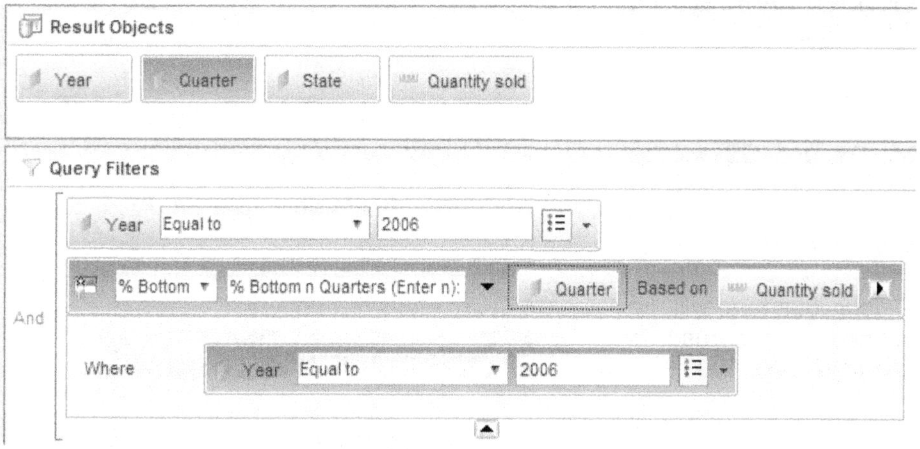
Result Objects
Year
Quarter
State
Quantity sold
Query Filters
Year
Equal to
2006
% Bottom
% Bottom n Quarters (Enter n):
Quarter
Based on
Quantity sold
And
Where
Year
Equal to
2006

We have selected **% Bottom** and used a prompt '**% Bottom n Quarters (Enter n):**'

2. Run the query and specify a value of 20 for the prompt.

   The results returned are:

Quarter	State	Quantity sold
Q4	California	3,847
	Colorado	1,073
	DC	1,354
	Florida	950
	Illinois	1,288
	Massachusetts	1,175
	New York	3,607
	Texas	5,356
Q4		

3. Refresh the query and try a prompt value of 33.33, again we will see the same results.

4. Refresh the query and try a prompt value of 33.34, this time the results will change to also include Q1.

Why?

We calculated that Q4 has the lowest PERCENT_RANK starting at 0% and then Q1 has a PERCENT_RANK starting at 33.33%.

Q4, Q1 and Q2 will be returned if we use a prompt value between 66.67 and 99.99.

All four quarters will be returned if we use a prompt value of 100.

Quarter	State	Quantity sold
Q1	California	4,317
	Colorado	1,291
	DC	1,735
	Florida	1,210
	Illinois	1,537
	Massachusetts	1,327
	New York	4,439
	Texas	6,681
Q1		

Quarter	State	Quantity sold
Q4	California	3,847
	Colorado	1,073
	DC	1,354
	Florida	950
	Illinois	1,288
	Massachusetts	1,175
	New York	3,607
	Texas	5,356
Q4		

5. Change the query from % Bottom to % Top:

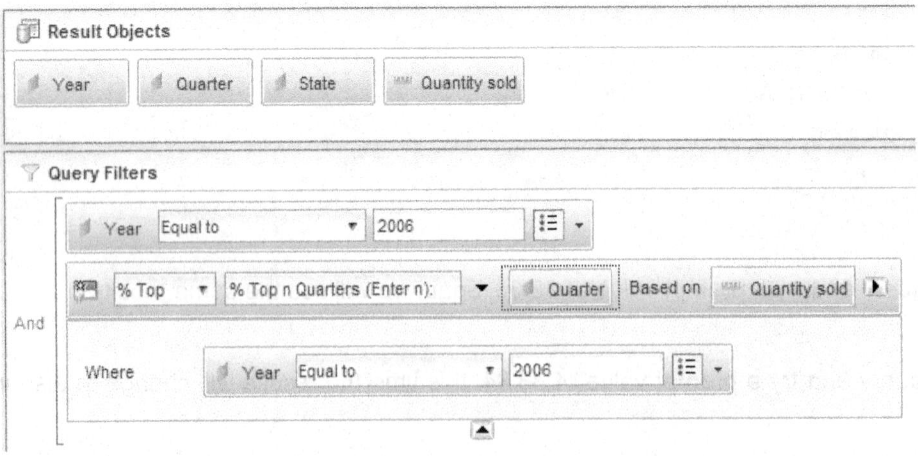

Result Objects
Year
Quarter
State
Quantity sold
Query Filters
Year
Equal to
2006
% Top
% Top n Quarters (Enter n):
Quarter
Based on
Quantity sold
And
Where
Year
Equal to
2006

6. Run the query and we will now see the data being returned in reverse order to our % Bottom query because the PERCENT_RANK function is working with the data in descending order based on [Quantity sold].

Prompt Value	Data Returned for % Bottom	Data Returned for % Top
0.00 to 33.33	Q4	Q3
33.34 to 66.66	Q4, Q1	Q3, Q2
66.67 to 99.99	Q4, Q1, Q2	Q3, Q2, Q1
100.00	Q4, Q1, Q2, Q3	Q3, Q2, Q1, Q4

The above results match our calculations (from earlier in the session):

% Bottom

Quarter	Quantity sold	Rank	% Rank
Q4	18,650	1	0.00%
Q1	22,537	2	33.33%
Q2	22,846	3	66.67%
Q3	26,263	4	100.00%
	90,296		

% Top

Quarter	Quantity sold	Rank	% Rank
Q3	26,263	1	0.00%
Q2	22,846	2	33.33%
Q1	22,537	3	66.67%
Q4	18,650	4	100.00%
	90,296		

NOTES on % TOP and % BOTTOM

The findings are based on using Web Intelligence against an Oracle database:

1. We selected % Top (or % Bottom), the Ranking Dimension [Quarter] and the Ranking Measure [Quantity sold].

2. There are 4 quarters therefore the PERCENT_RANK function calculated 4 rankings.

3. If we changed the Ranking Dimension to [State] then the PERCENT_RANK function would calculate 8 rankings because we have 8 states.

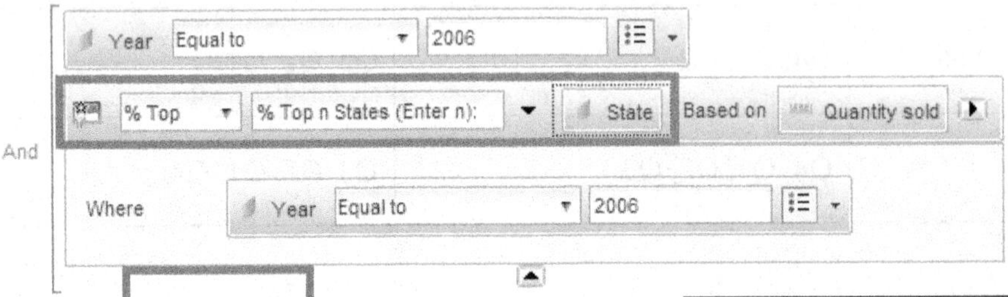
Year
Equal to
2006
% Top
% Top n States (Enter n):
State
Based on
Quantity sold
And
Where
Year
Equal to
2006

% TOP

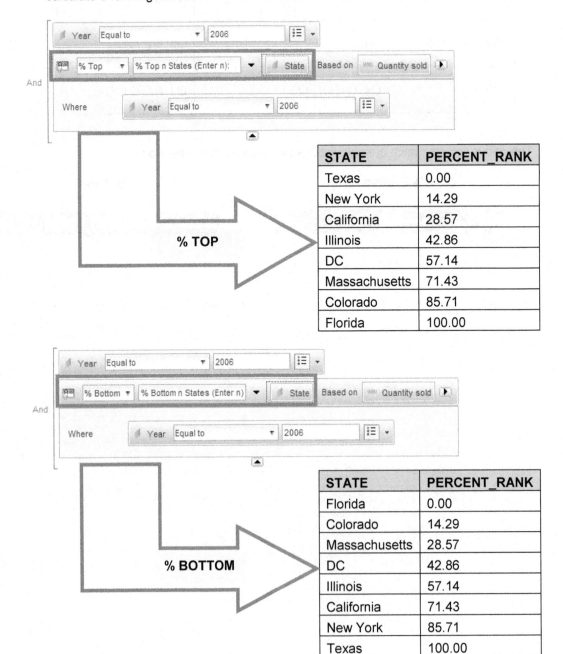

STATE	PERCENT_RANK
Texas	0.00
New York	14.29
California	28.57
Illinois	42.86
DC	57.14
Massachusetts	71.43
Colorado	85.71
Florida	100.00

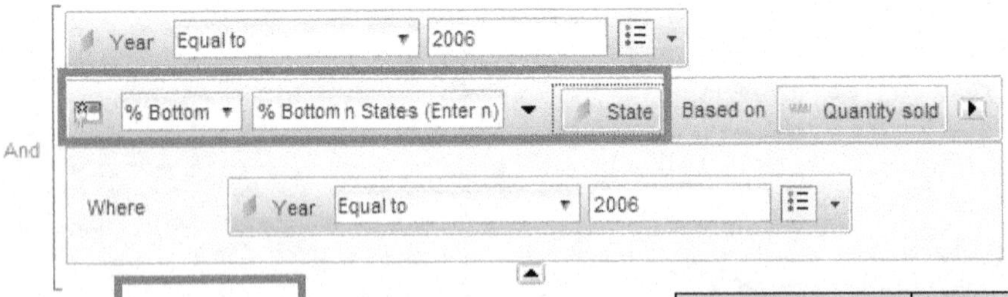
Year
Equal to
2006
% Bottom
% Bottom n States (Enter n)
State
Based on
Quantity sold
And
Where
Year
Equal to
2006

% BOTTOM

STATE	PERCENT_RANK
Florida	0.00
Colorado	14.29
Massachusetts	28.57
DC	42.86
Illinois	57.14
California	71.43
New York	85.71
Texas	100.00

27 Formulas and Variables

Formulas and variables enable you to add custom calculations within reports.

One advantage of variables is they are given a name and are re-usable across the whole document, whereas formulas need to be copied and pasted if you need to use them in multiple places.

Another advantage of variables is that if you make the change to the variable definition then the new definition will automatically be applied across the whole document, whereas with formulas you would need to modify each occurrence individually.

This session introduces custom calculations using functions and variables.

27.1 Viewing Formulas

The Formula Bar is located immediately above the report canvas area:

View and Edit formulas in this text box.

Formula Bar Buttons:

 To initiate the Formula Editor

 To take the current formula and
Create Variable from the formula definition

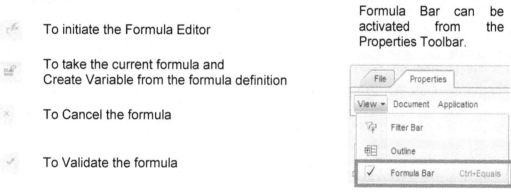

 To Cancel the formula

 To Validate the formula

Formula Bar can be activated from the Properties Toolbar.

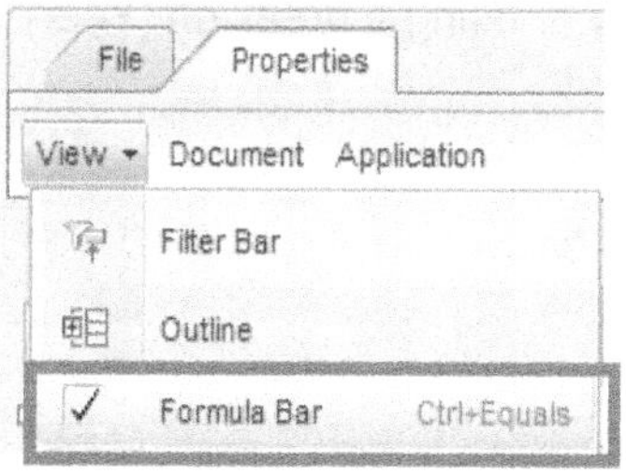
File
Properties
View
Document
Application
Filter Bar
Outline
Formula Bar
Ctrl+Equals

Formulas may be entered directly into the formula text box on the Formula Bar, but for long and/or complicated formulas, proper syntax can be best achieved using the Formula Editor.

Select a cell (within a block or free standing) and the Formula Bar will display the formula associated to the selected cell.

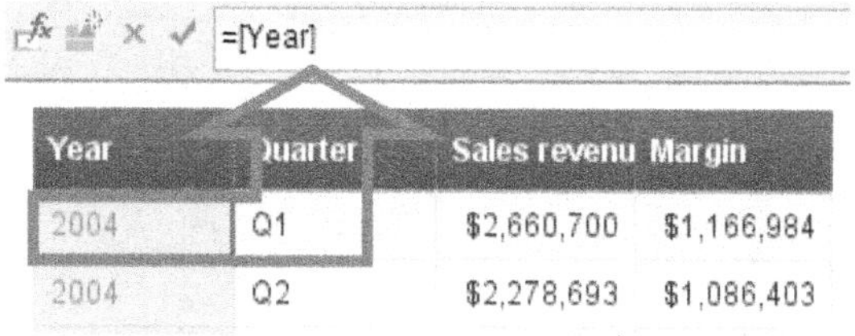
=[Year]
Year
Quarter
Sales revenu
Margin
2004
Q1
$2,660,700
$1,166,984
2004
Q2
$2,278,693
$1,086,403

IMPORTANT POINTS ON FORMULAS AND VARIABLES:

1. Formulas and variables always begin with an '=' sign, e.g. =[Year].
2. Following the '=' sign, you may use objects, other variables, functions or appropriate operators in the syntax of your formula.
3. All object and variable names should be enclosed within square brackets, e.g. [Year].

27.2 Creating Formulas using the Formula Bar

We will now take a look at how to create formulas using the Formula Bar.

1. Create the following query using the 'eFashion' universe and run it.

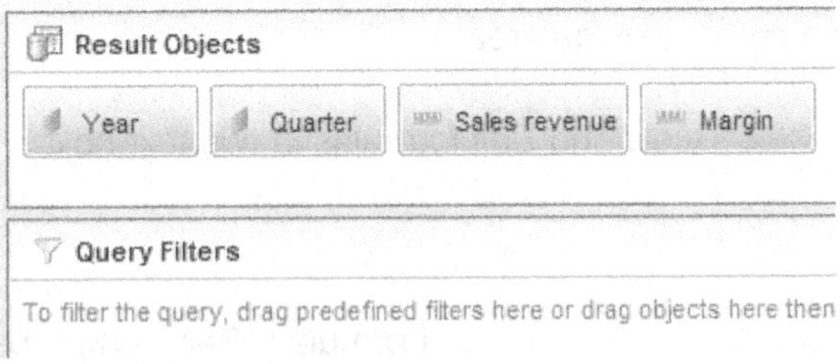
Result Objects
Year
Quarter
Sales revenue
Margin
Query Filters
To filter the query, drag predefined filters here or drag objects here then

Create the vertical table shown opposite using a break on [Year].

Year	Quarter	Sales revenue	Margin
2004	Q1	$2,660,700	$1,166,984
	Q2	$2,278,693	$1,086,403
	Q3	$1,367,841	$552,074
	Q4	$1,788,580	$926,510
2004			

Year	Quarter	Sales revenue	Margin
2005	Q1	$3,326,172	$1,236,390
	Q2	$2,840,651	$1,132,666
	Q3	$2,879,303	$1,026,132
	Q4	$4,186,120	$1,792,698
2005			

Year	Quarter	Sales revenue	Margin
2006	Q1	$3,742,989	$1,384,424
	Q2	$4,006,718	$1,647,660
	Q3	$3,953,395	$1,344,435
	Q4	$3,356,041	$1,290,564
2006			

2. We would like to add in an extra column to the right of [Margin] to show [Margin] as a percentage of [Sales revenue].

   To add in an extra column click in any cell of the [Margin] column and then use right-click menu 'Insert – Insert column on right'.

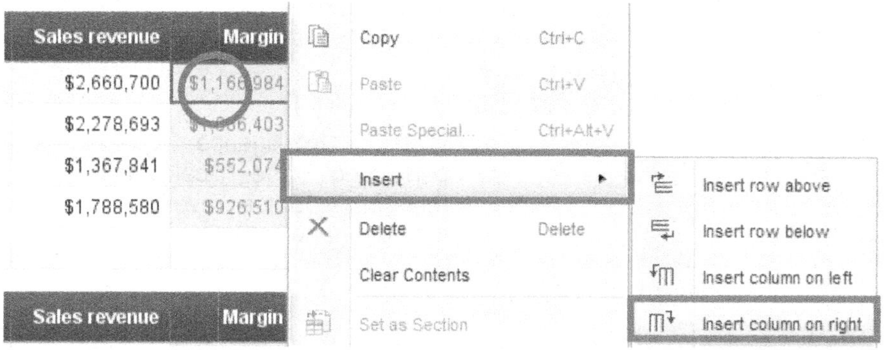
Sales revenue
Margin
$2,660,700
$2,278,693
$1,367,841
$1,788,580
Copy
Ctrl+C
Paste
Ctrl+V
Paste Special...
Ctrl+Alt+V
Insert
Delete
Delete
Clear Contents
Set as Section
Insert row above
Insert row below
Insert column on left
Insert column on right

3. After adding the new column, make sure the Formula Bar is showing.

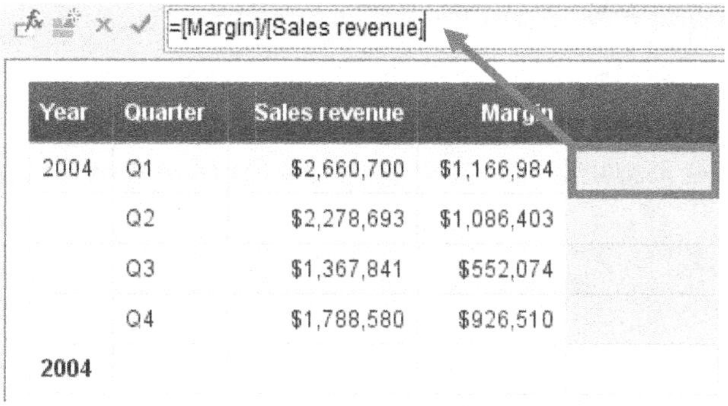
=[Margin]/[Sales revenue]
Year
Quarter
Sales revenue
2004
Q1
$2,660,700
$1,166,984
Q2
$2,278,693
$1,086,403
Q3
$1,367,841
$552,074
Q4
$1,788,580
$926,510
2004

Click in any body cell of the column and then click in the text box of the Formula Bar.

The formula we require to calculate [Margin] as a percentage of [Sales revenue] is:

1. The formula starts with an '=' sign
2. Both object names are enclosed in square brackets, e.g. [Margin]
3. Spaces (and parentheses) can be used to break formulas up for readability, e.g.

   =[Margin]/[Sales revenue] or we can use spaces

   = [Margin] / [Sales revenue]

4. Click on 'Validate' or press <Enter> and Web Intelligence will perform the calculation if there are no errors.

   If there is an error then a message will be displayed indicating where the possible error is within the formula.

=[Margin]/[Sales revenue]

Year	Quarter	Sales revenue	Margin	
2004	Q1	$2,660,700	$1,166,984	0.44
	Q2	$2,278,693	$1,086,403	0.48
	Q3	$1,367,841	$552,074	0.4
	Q4	$1,788,580	$926,510	0.52
2004				

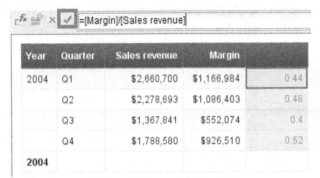

Web Intelligence has performed the calculation [Margin] / [Sales revenue] in the right hand column.

5. Change the Number Format of the body cells in the last column to show the cell contents as percentages.

Year	Quarter	Sales revenue	Margin	
2004	Q1	$2,660,700	$1,166,984	43.86%
	Q2	$2,278,693	$1,086,403	47.68%
	Q3	$1,367,841	$552,074	40.36%
	Q4	$1,788,580	$926,510	51.80%
2004				

6. Click in the column header cell and then type in the formula:

   Margin %

   Validate the formula and this will become the label for the column header.

Margin %

Year	Quarter	Sales revenue	Margin	Margin %
2004	Q1	$2,660,700	$1,166,984	43.86%
	Q2	$2,278,693	$1,086,403	47.68%
	Q3	$1,367,841	$552,074	40.36%
	Q4	$1,788,580	$926,510	51.80%
2004				

NOTE – For literal text/labels you can use following syntax:

='Margin %'

Or simply

Margin %

27.3 Creating Formulas using the Formula Editor

We will recreate the previous formula using the Formula Editor to show its ease of use.

1. Delete the formula we have previously created in the body cell of the Margin % column.

   Simply select the formula, press the <Del> key (or the <Delete> key), then press <Enter> or click on 'Validate'.

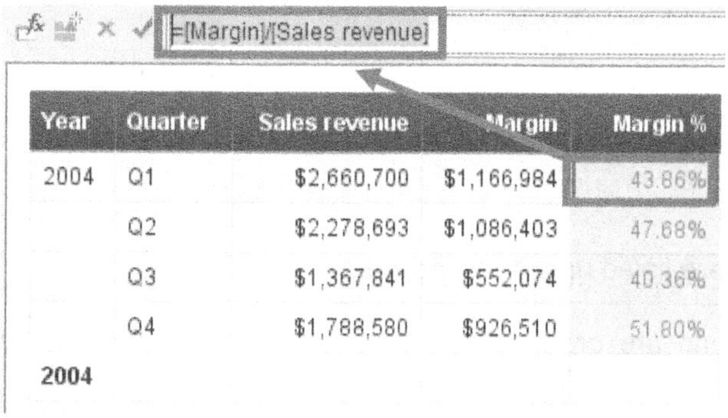
=[Margin]/[Sales revenue]
Year
Quarter
Sales revenue
Margin
Margin %
2004
Q1
$2,660,700
$1,166,984
43.86%
Q2
$2,278,693
$1,086,403
47.68%
Q3
$1,367,841
$552,074
40.36%
Q4
$1,788,580
$926,510
51.80%
2004

2. With a body cell selected in the 'Margin %' column, click on the 'Formula Editor' button that is within the Formula Bar.

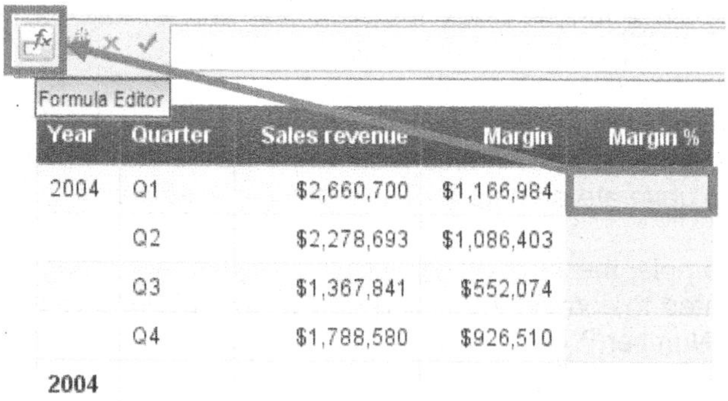
Formula Editor
Year
Quarter
Sales revenue
Margin
Margin %
2004
Q1
$2,660,700
$1,166,984
Q2
$2,278,693
$1,086,403
Q3
$1,367,841
$552,074
Q4
$1,788,580
$926,510
2004

This will activate the **Formula Editor**.

Available objects for including in formulas.

When an object is selected from the Available objects pane, or a Function from the Functions pane, or an Operator from the Operators pane then an associated Description is displayed here.

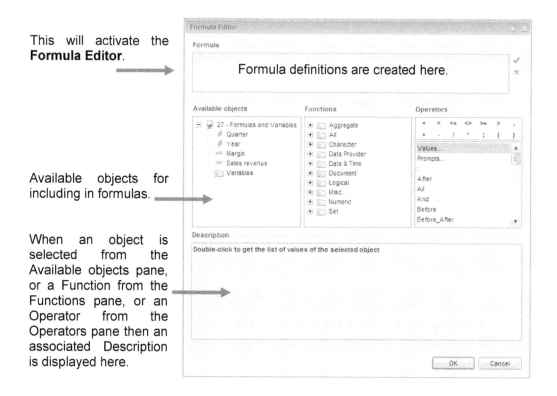

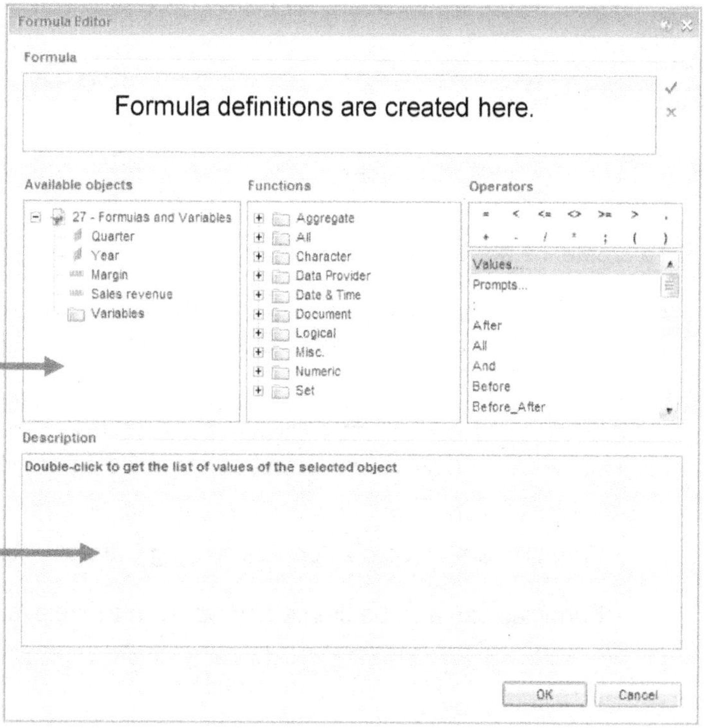
Formula Editor
Formula
Formula definitions are created here.
Available objects
27 - Formulas and Variables
Quarter
Year
Margin
Sales revenue
Variables
Functions
Aggregate
All
Character
Data Provider
Date & Time
Document
Logical
Misc.
Numeric
Set
Operators
Values...
Prompts...
After
All
And
Before
Before_After
Description
Double-click to get the list of values of the selected object
OK
Cancel

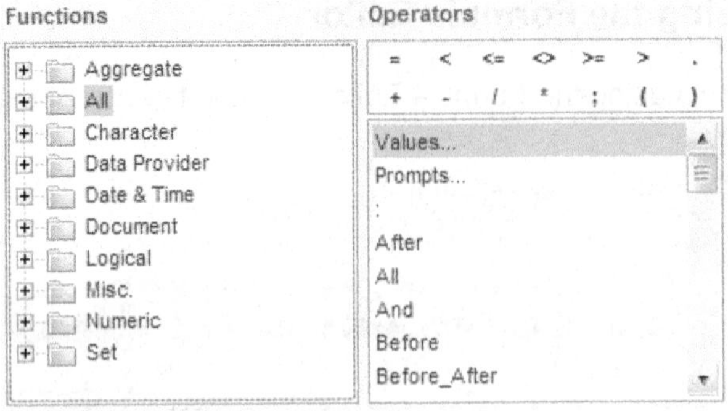
Functions
Aggregate
All
Character
Data Provider
Date & Time
Document
Logical
Misc.
Numeric
Set
Operators
= < <= <> >= > ,
+ - / * ; ( )
Values...
Prompts...
:
After
All
And
Before
Before_After

Available operators are listed under **Operators**.

Proper operational syntax can be achieved by using only the operators that appear in the operators list.

Functions are listed under **Functions**.

a) Functions are grouped into categories or they are all listed (in ascending alphabetical order) under the **All** category.

b) Clicking on a function lists the help text and syntax on how to use the function in the Descriptions area of the Formula Editor.

c) Some functions will appear with parentheses and semicolons included to aid using the correct syntax. Parentheses generally indicate that an input is required by the function in order to generate an output. The input is placed inside the parentheses.

For example, the function ToNumber() converts a string (or text) to a numeric format. If we wanted to convert the [Year] object from a string to a number then our formula would be =ToNumber([Year]).

3. Let us create the formula for [Margin] / [Sales revenue] using the Formula Editor.

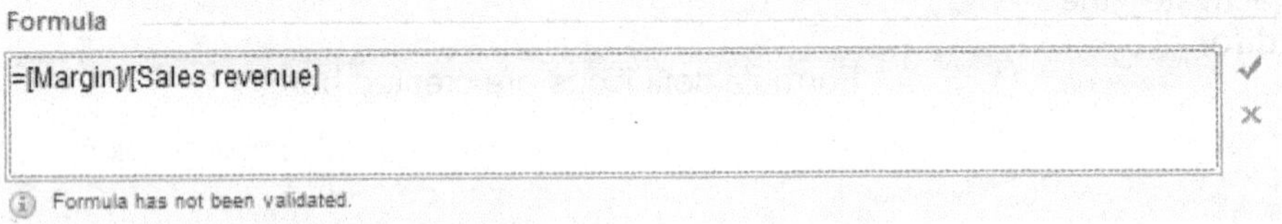
Formula
=[Margin]/[Sales revenue]
Formula has not been validated.

To create the above formula:

a) Double-click on **[Margin]** object in Data pane of Formula Editor. The '=' sign will be automatically inserted by Web Intelligence at the start of the formula.

b) Double-click on the '/' operator in Operators pane of Formula Editor.

c) Double-click on **[Sales revenue]** object in Data pane of Formula Editor.

Formulas are created by double clicking Data objects, Functions and Operators.

Formulas can also be created by typing in the relevant syntax.

d) Validate the formula to make sure the syntax is correct.

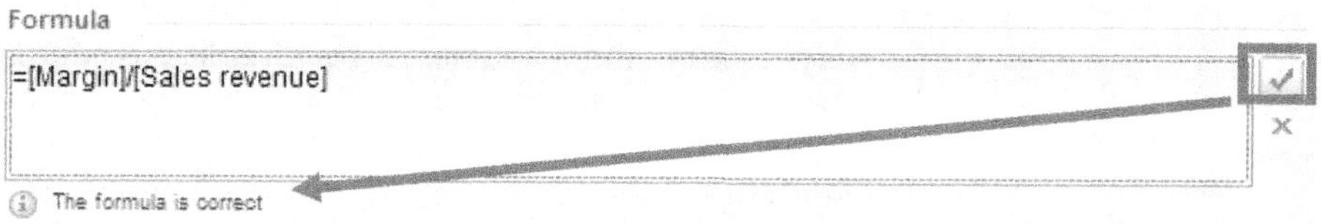
Formula
=[Margin]/[Sales revenue]
The formula is correct

e) Click 'OK' in Formula Editor to apply the formula.

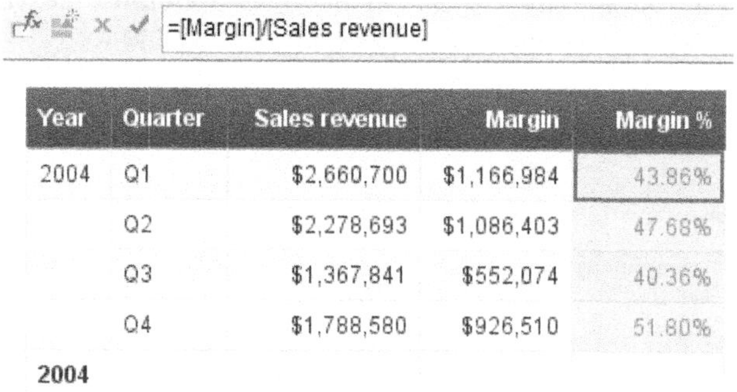
=[Margin]/[Sales revenue]
Year
Quarter
Sales revenue
Margin
Margin %
2004
Q1
$2,660,700
$1,166,984
43.86%
Q2
$2,278,693
$1,086,403
47.68%
Q3
$1,367,841
$552,074
40.36%
Q4
$1,788,580
$926,510
51.80%
2004

NOTE – The % number formatting has been retained as we applied it to the table cell in the previous example.

4. Save your document.

27.4 Creating Variables from Formulas

An existing formula can be converted into a more useable form known as a Variable.

1. Select any cell showing the relevant formula and click on '**Create Variable**' icon in the Formula Bar.

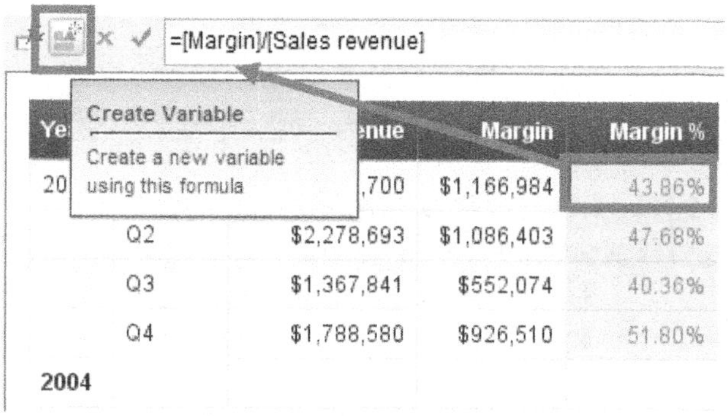
=[Margin]/[Sales revenue]
Create Variable
Create a new variable using this formula
Margin
Margin %
$1,166,984
43.86%
Q2
$2,278,693
$1,086,403
47.68%
Q3
$1,367,841
$552,074
40.36%
Q4
$1,788,580
$926,510
51.80%
2004

2. Assign a '**Name**' and '**Qualification**' to the formula to convert it into a variable.

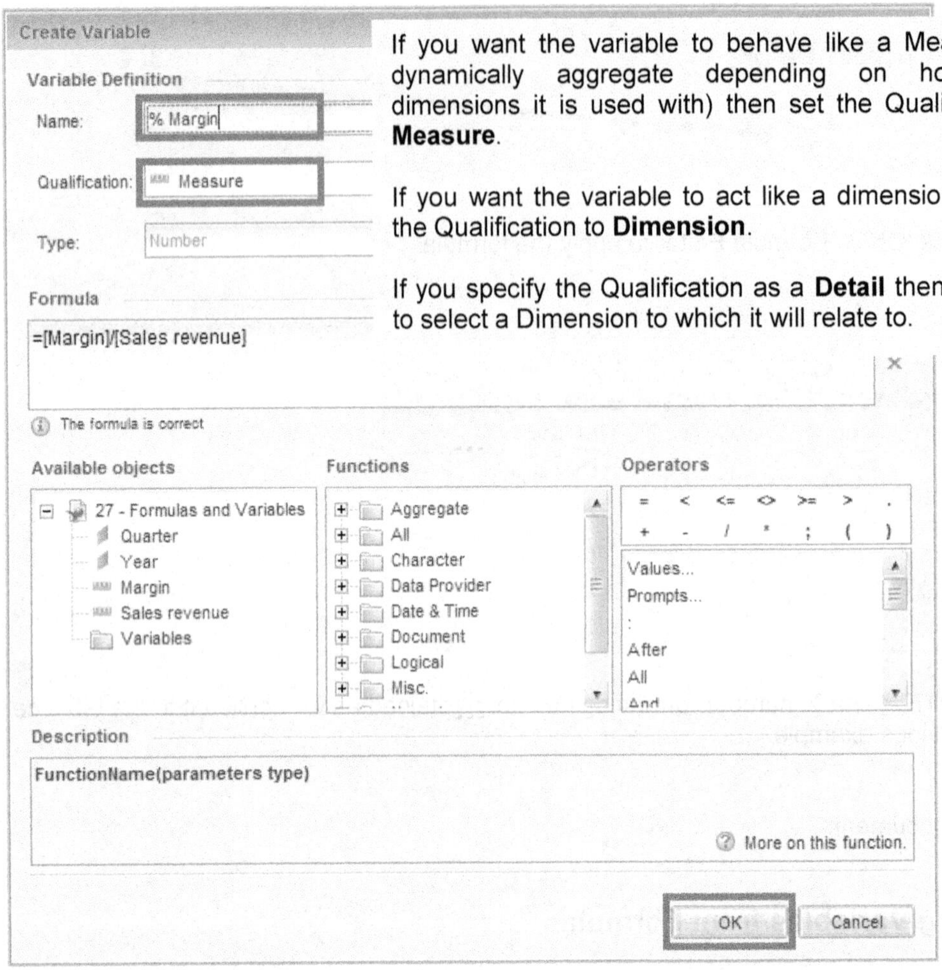
Create Variable
Variable Definition
Name: % Margin
Qualification: Measure
Type: Number
Formula
=[Margin]/[Sales revenue]
The formula is correct
Available objects
27 - Formulas and Variables
Quarter
Year
Margin
Sales revenue
Variables
Functions
Aggregate
All
Character
Data Provider
Date & Time
Document
Logical
Misc.
Operators
Values...
Prompts...
After
All
Description
FunctionName(parameters type)
More on this function.
OK
Cancel

If you want the variable to behave like a Measure (i.e. dynamically aggregate depending on how many dimensions it is used with) then set the Qualification to **Measure**.

If you want the variable to act like a dimension then set the Qualification to **Dimension**.

If you specify the Qualification as a **Detail** then you need to select a Dimension to which it will relate to.

NOTE – The 'Create Variable' editor is very much the same as the Formula Editor but with added functionality to name and qualify the formula as a variable.

3. Click 'OK' to create the variable.

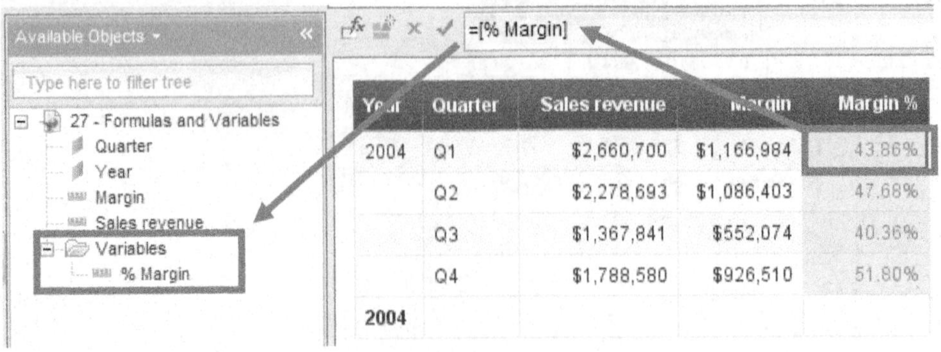
Available Objects
Type here to filter tree
27 - Formulas and Variables
Quarter
Year
Margin
Sales revenue
Variables
% Margin
=[% Margin]
Year
Quarter
Sales revenue
Margin
Margin %
2004
Q1
$2,660,700
$1,166,984
43.86%
Q2
$2,278,693
$1,086,403
47.68%
Q3
$1,367,841
$552,074
40.36%
Q4
$1,788,580
$926,510
51.80%
2004

The variable appears in the Available Objects tab as a re-useable object and the selected cell is now using the variable instead of the original formula.

27.5 Creating Variables using the Variable Editor

Variables can also be created using the Variable Editor whereby the variable is defined in one step instead of using an existing formula.

1. Edit the query and run the query after adding in the [Quantity sold] object in the Result Objects pane.

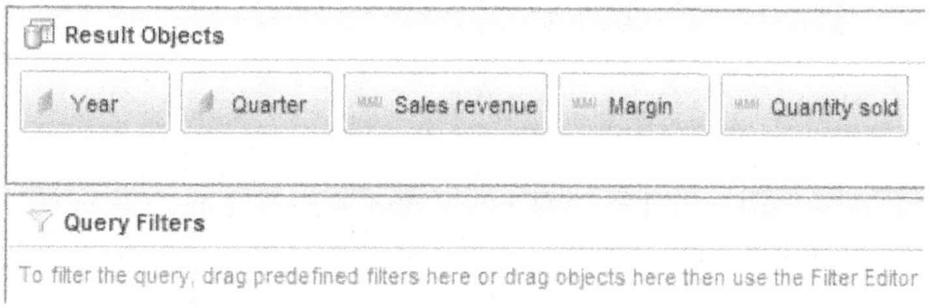
Result Objects
Year
Quarter
Sales revenue
Margin
Quantity sold
Query Filters
To filter the query, drag predefined filters here or drag objects here then use the Filter Editor

2. Clicking the 'Variable Editor' icon (on the Reporting Toolbar) activates the Variable Editor interface.

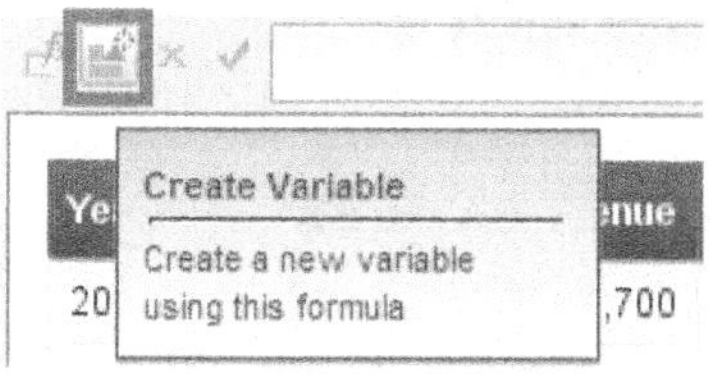
Create Variable
Create a new variable using this formula

3. Create a Measure variable called Average Sales Price with the formula:

=[Sales revenue] / [Quantity sold]

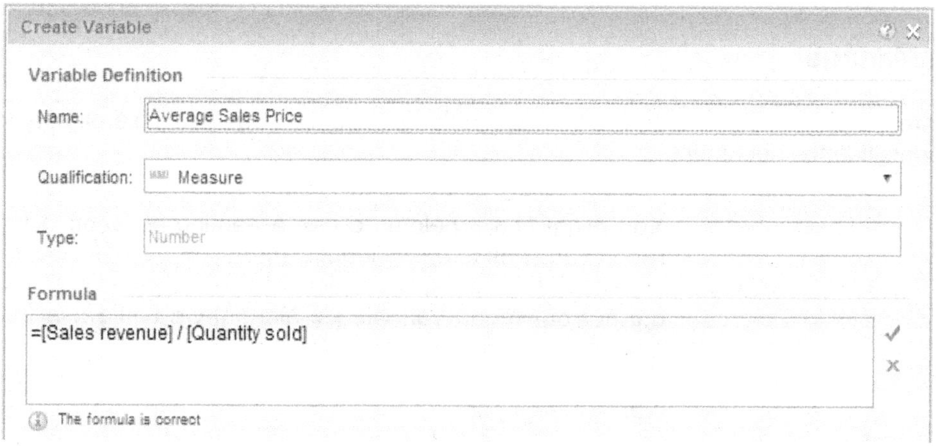
Create Variable
Variable Definition
Name:
Average Sales Price
Qualification:
Measure
Type:
Number
Formula
=[Sales revenue] / [Quantity sold]
The formula is correct

4. Validate the formula and click 'OK' to create the variable. It will now be available to use in the 'Available Objects' pane in the class called 'Variables'.

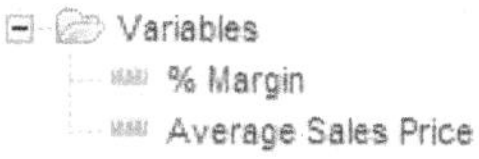
Variables
% Margin
Average Sales Price

5. Drag [Average Sales Price] and drop it into the table block:

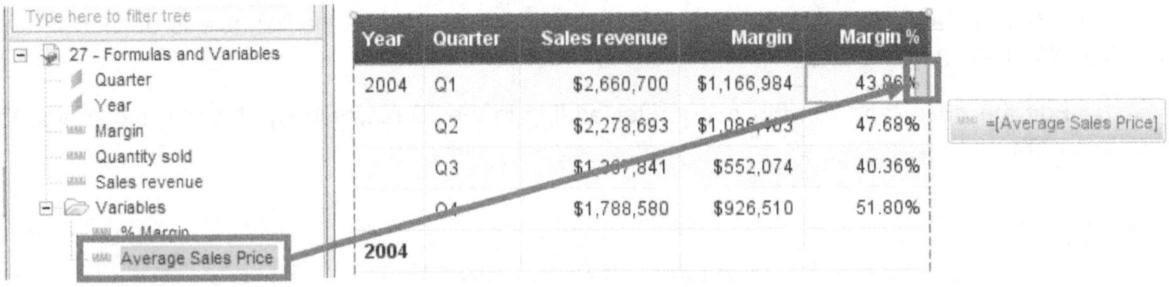
Type here to filter tree
27 - Formulas and Variables
Quarter
Year
Margin
Quantity sold
Sales revenue
Variables
Average Sales Price
Year Quarter Sales revenue Margin Margin %
2004 Q1 $2,660,700 $1,166,984
Q2 $2,278,693 47.68%
Q3 $552,074 40.36%
$1,788,580 $926,510 51.80%
2004
=[Average Sales Price]

6. The [Average Sales Price] has been added into the table block and is now available to use within the document just like the objects returned by the query.

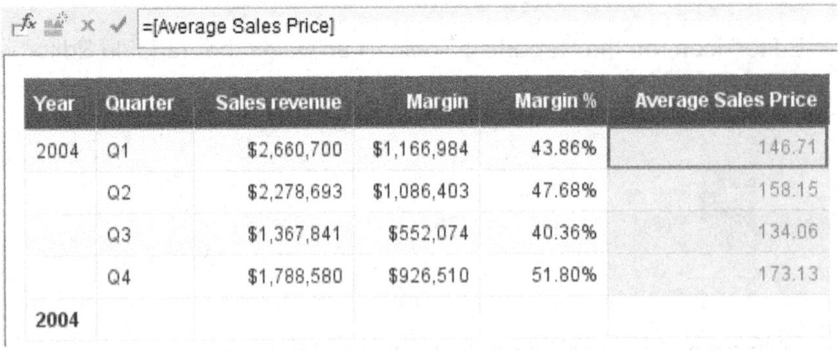
=[Average Sales Price]
Year Quarter Sales revenue Margin Margin % Average Sales Price
2004 Q1 $2,660,700 $1,166,984 43.86% 146.71
Q2 $2,278,693 $1,086,403 47.68% 158.15
Q3 $1,367,841 $552,074 40.36% 134.06
Q4 $1,788,580 $926,510 51.80% 173.13
2004

7. Save your document.

27.6 Variable Manager

When variables are created they are added to the 'Available Objects' pane as available objects for use in the entire Web Intelligence document.

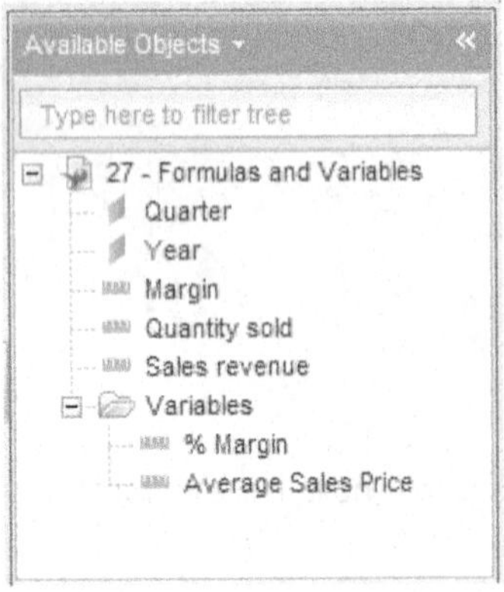
Available Objects
Type here to filter tree
27 - Formulas and Variables
Quarter
Year
Margin
Quantity sold
Sales revenue
Variables
% Margin
Average Sales Price

You might find it helpful to use a naming convention for report variables to easily identify them.

e.g. for our report variable [% Margin] we could use the names:

[var % Margin] or

[rv % Margin]

(where var or rv signify *report variable*)

1. You can edit, duplicate, or delete a variable using right-click on the variable name.

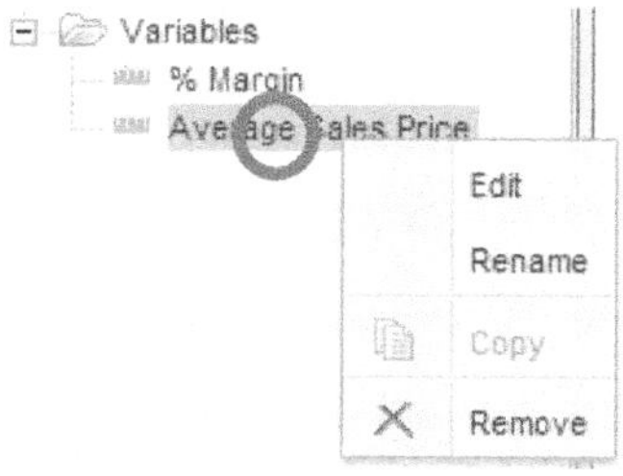
Variables
% Margin
Average Sales Price
Edit
Rename
Copy
Remove

2. Double clicking the variable will cause the 'Create Variable' editor to open with the selected variable ready to be edited.

3. Information about objects is displayed if you hover over an object:

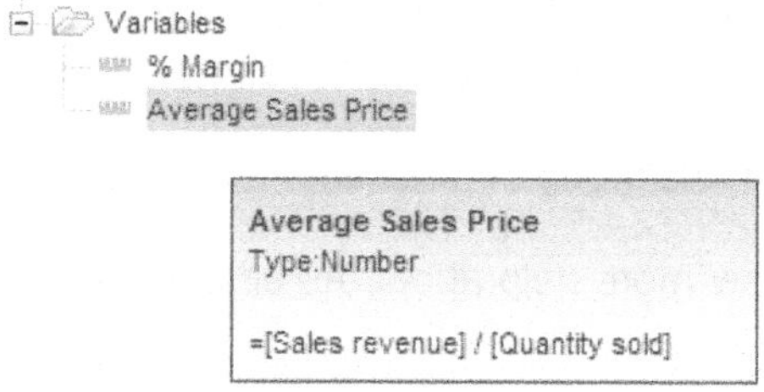
Variables
% Margin
Average Sales Price
Average Sales Price
Type:Number
=[Sales revenue] / [Quantity sold]

27.7 Using Functions in Formulas and Variables

There are many functions available that can be used in creating formulas and variables. Discussing every function is beyond the scope of this session but we will look at how you can learn more about using individual functions in formulas/variables.

We will demonstrate using the 'Create Variable' editor but the same applies to the 'Formula Editor'.

If you are unsure of what function to use then Web Intelligence assists in pointing you in the right direction by listing functions in logical groups depending on the output of each function.

- Functions available in each group are listed in alphabetic order using function names.

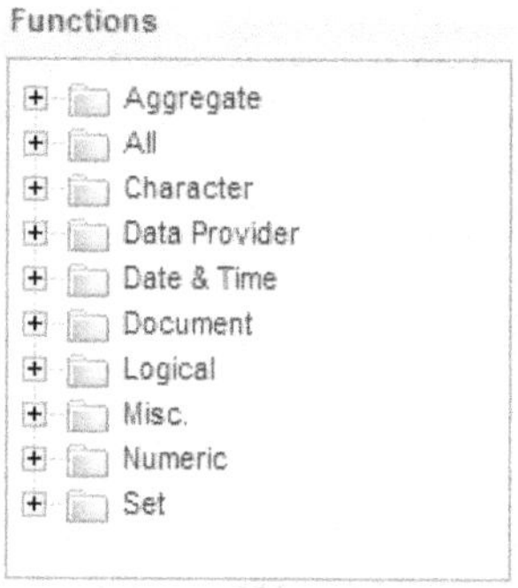
Functions
Aggregate
All
Character
Data Provider
Date & Time
Document
Logical
Misc.
Numeric
Set

- Brief information about a function is listed in the Description box when a Function is selected.

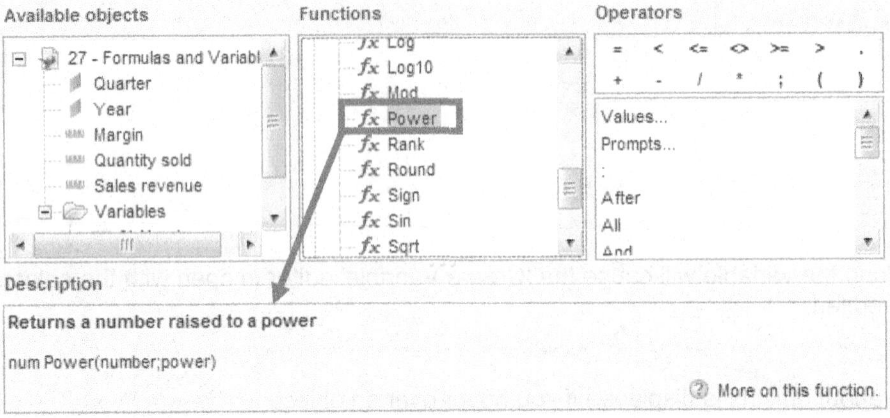
Available objects
27 - Formulas and Variabl
Quarter
Year
Margin
Quantity sold
Sales revenue
Variables
Functions
Log
Log10
Mod
Power
Rank
Round
Sign
Sin
Sqrt
Operators
= < <= <> >= > .
+ - / * ; ( )
Values...
Prompts...
After
All
Description
Returns a number raised to a power
num Power(number;power)
More on this function.

Understanding the first line of the description (**in bold**) is the most important part as it provides information about what should be provided to the function in order for it to return a value.

We have selected the function Power from the Numeric group of functions.

Clicking on the link 'More on this function.' will show more help about the selected function (as shown below).

Power

Description
Returns a number raised to a power

Function Group
Numeric

Syntax

```
num Power(number;power)
```

Input

Parameter	Description	Type	Required
number	The number to raise to a power	Number	Yes
power	The power	Number	Yes

Example
`Power(10;2)` returns 100.

The description states:

number **Power**(number **input_number**; number **power**)

We have to provide two numbers in the function and it will return a sing number back.

Example:

If we used the function as:

Power(5;2) would return 25

but

Power(2;5) would return 32

HINTS

1. The input values into a function should be separated with semicolons and not commas.

2. If the value you are passing is a string (i.e. text) then enclose it in double-quotes unless it is th name of an object, i.e.

   =Upper("Austin") would return AUSTIN

   =Upper([City]) could return AUSTIN, BOSTON, etc depending on the value of the [City] object.

NOTE ON FUNCTIONS

When using functions we usually provide other objects as values into the function.

Using the Power function as an example, we could calculate the area of a circle in a variable called **[rv Circle Area]** as:

[rv Circle Area] = [rv PI] * Power([Radius] ; 2)

Where *[rv PI]* is another variable that we have created to hold the value of π.

You can see:

1. We have created a variable called [rv PI] and set it to hold a value for the mathematical constant pi (approximate value = 3.14).
2. We have an object from the universe called [Radius] that provides the value of the radius.
3. We have created a third variable called [rv Circle Area] that uses the objects [rv PI] and [Radius] along with the function Power.

27.8 Examples of Formulas and Functions

Web Intelligence contains many functions and operators that can be used to define formulas and variables. They cannot all be covered in this session but we will have a look at some examples to become familiar with using functions.

27.8.1 If Then { Else | ElseIf } Function

If *boolean_expression* **Then** *true_expression*

{ **Else** *false_expression* | **ElseIf** *boolean_expression* **Then** *true_expression* **Else** *false_expression* }

These are four functions that are used together (in part or all together) to return a value based on whether an expression is true or false.

For example, we can use **If Then { Else | ElseIf }** to group our data within documents.

Let us assume we have a data set that includes an object called [Age]. In each row of data the value of [Age] will be based on the actual age (in years) of an individual. Within the document we want to create a variable called [Age Band] that will group together rows of data based on age bands.

We will now build up the formula in steps so we can understand how **If Then { Else | ElseIf }** works:

=If [Age] < 20 Then "Under 20" Else “Over 20”

If the age is less than 20 years **Then** it will be included in the [Age Band] of ‘Under 20’, otherwise (**Else**) it will be grouped as ‘Over 20’.

=If [Age] < 20 Then "Under 20" ElseIf [Age] < 30 Then "20 to 30" Else "Over 30"

If the age is less than 20 years **Then** it will be included in the [Age Band] of 'Under 20', but (**ElseIf**) if the age is less than 30 years **Then** it will be included in the [Age Band] of '20 to 30', otherwise (**Else**) it will be grouped as 'Over 30'.

The important point to note here is that the ages of 0-19 satisfy both conditions of being less than 20 and less than 30 so will they get included in both age bands?

No they will not because **If Then { Else | ElseIf }** stops evaluating conditions as soon as one condition is met.

> i.e. an **If Then { Else | ElseIf }** statement contains 10 conditions and a particular evaluation is satisfied on condition 4. The conditions 5 to 10 will not be applied.

=If [Age] < 20 Then "Under 20" ElseIf [Age] < 30 Then "20 to 30" ElseIf [Age] < 40 Then "30 to 40" Else "Over 40"

If the age is less than 20 years **Then** it will be included in the [Age Band] of 'Under 20', but (**ElseIf**) if the age is less than 30 years **Then** it will be included in the [Age Band] of '20 to 30', but (**ElseIf**) if the age is less than 40 years **Then** it will be included in the [Age Band] of '30 to 40',otherwise (**Else**) it will be grouped as 'Over 40'.

You can include multiple objects and use other functions within **If Then { Else | ElseIf }** statements:

=If (Lower([Gender]) = "male" And [Age] < 20) Then "Male Under 20" Else "Other"

This example, forces the value of [Gender] to lowercase and checks to see if it is 'male' And also checks if [Age] is less than 20. If both conditions are met then our return value is 'Male Under 20' otherwise the return value is 'Other'.

27.8.2 UserResponse() Function

It is useful to be able to display User Responses in documents containing Query Prompts.

This example shows how this can be achieved using variables.

1. Create the following query using the 'eFashion' universe and run it.

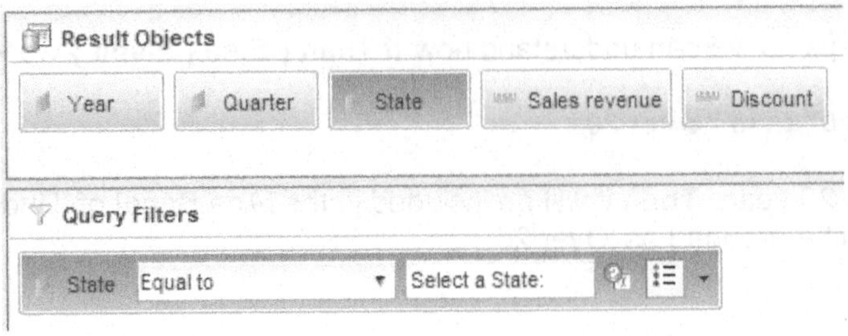
Result Objects
Year
Quarter
State
Sales revenue
Discount
Query Filters
State
Equal to
Select a State:

Query contains a Prompt **'Select a State:'**

The query will restrict the data to a single [State] due to 'Equal to' being used as the operator.

2. Data has been presented as a chart and we would like to display the [State] that has been selected by the user.

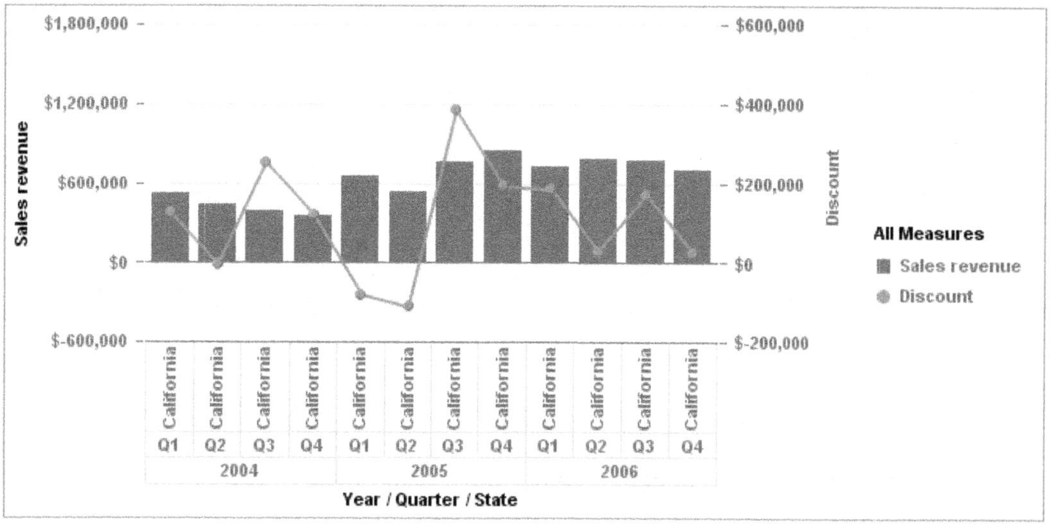
$1,800,000
$1,200,000
$600,000
$0
$-600,000
Sales revenue
$600,000
$400,000
$200,000
$0
$-200,000
Discount
All Measures
Sales revenue
Discount
California
Q1
Q2
Q3
Q4
2004
2005
2006
Year / Quarter / State

We will use the UserResponse function to display what was selected by the user when the query was refreshed. The description for UserResponse() is:

string UserResponse([dp;]prompt_string[;index])

We can provide the function UserResponse() with three parameter:

a) Name of the data_provider (i.e. name of the query), enclose the name in square brackets.

b) The prompt_text, i.e. in our case "Select a State:" enclosed in double quotes.

c) If you include the word Index as the last parameter then the database primary keys of the prompt values will be returned (*most likely you will not need to use this*).

3. Create a variable called [State Prompt Label] to display the value of the UserResponse().

="State Selected : " + UserResponse([Query 1] ; "Select a State:")

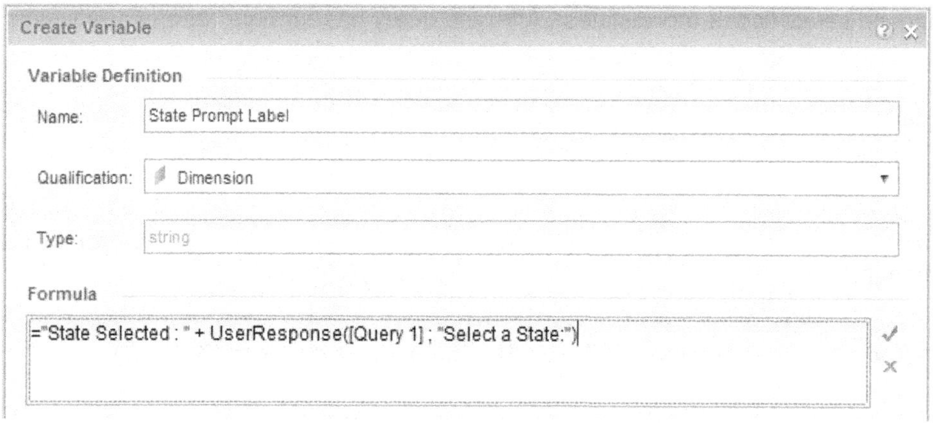
Create Variable
Variable Definition
Name:
State Prompt Label
Qualification:
Dimension
Type:
string
Formula
="State Selected : " + UserResponse([Query 1] ; "Select a State:")

4. Insert a Blank Cell above the chart:

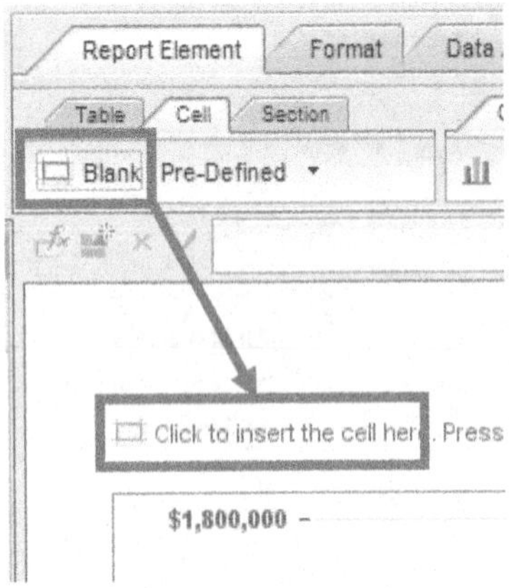
Report Element
Format
Table
Cell
Section
Blank
Pre-Defined
Click to insert the cell her
. Press
$1,800,000 -

5. Swap the Blank Cell with the variable created to show the User Response. Make sure you drop into the Blank Cell.

=[State Prompt Label]

6. Resize the cell if required:

State Selected : California

Cell now shows the value of the User Response. In our example we selected 'California' when we refreshed the query.

7. Change the prompt to allow multiple values (by using the In list operator), and also modify the prompt text to 'Select one or more States:' as shown below:

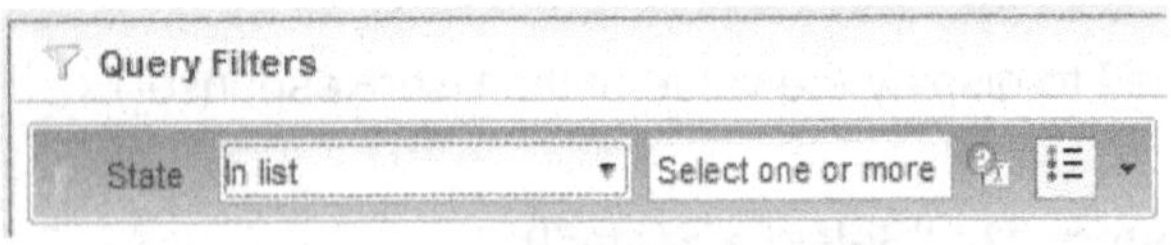
Query Filters
State
In list
Select one or more

8. Run the query and select two or more states. After the query has run, our report variable shows:

State Selected :

9. We have changed our *prompt_string* so we need to modify our variable [State Prompt Label] to reflect this change:

="State Selected : " + UserResponse([Query 1] ; "Select one or more States:")

10. Double click on the variable [State Prompt Label] and modify it to:

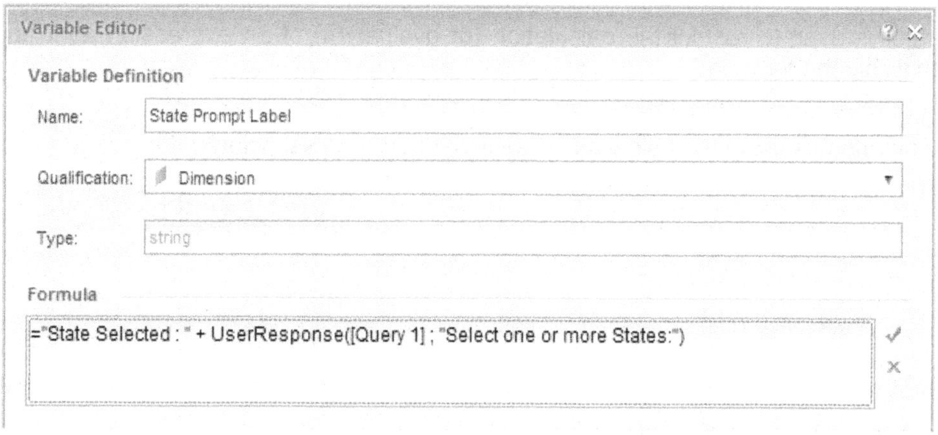
Variable Editor
Variable Definition
Name:
State Prompt Label
Qualification:
Dimension
Type:
string
Formula
="State Selected : " + UserResponse([Query 1] ; "Select one or more States:")

On changing the formula we have:

State Selected : California;New York

We selected California and New York when refreshing the query.

UserResponse() function returns the values separated by semicolons.

11. By modifying the formula of [State Prompt Label] we can show the values as:

State Selected : California / New York

="State Selected : " +

Replace(UserResponse([Query 1] ; "Select one or more States:") **; ";" ; " / ")**

We have extended the formula (as highlighted above) to use the Replace() function on the string returned by UserResponse() function.

i.e. UserResponse() returns 'DC;Texas;New York'

We have then used Replace() to take the output of UserResponse() and to replace each occurrence of the semicolon (;) with ' / '.

12. Save your document:

27.8.3 Where Operator

The Where operator is used to restrict the calculation (or evaluation) of an expression as it applies a boolean condition within the formula.

1. We will demonstrate this using the following 'eFashion' query and associated data:

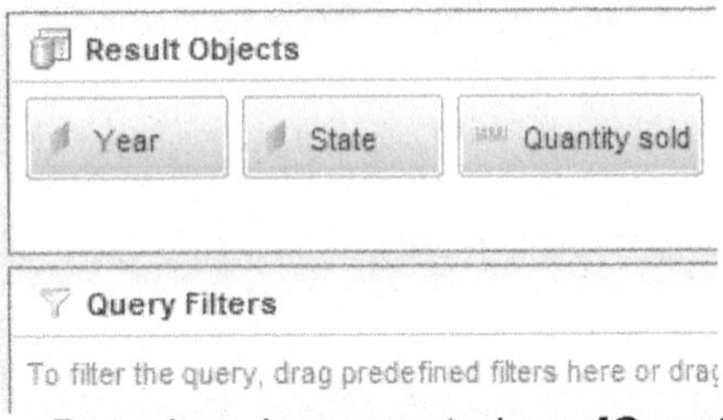
Result Objects
Year
State
Quantity sold
Query Filters
To filter the query, drag predefined filters here or drag

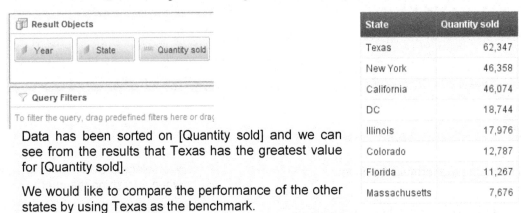

State	Quantity sold
Texas	62,347
New York	46,358
California	46,074
DC	18,744
Illinois	17,976
Colorado	12,787
Florida	11,267
Massachusetts	7,676

Data has been sorted on [Quantity sold] and we can see from the results that Texas has the greatest value for [Quantity sold].

We would like to compare the performance of the other states by using Texas as the benchmark.

2. We can create a measure variable to hold the value of [Quantity sold] for Texas using the following definition:

Variable Name	**Formula**
Benchmark	=[Quantity sold] **Where**([State]="Texas ")

Please note "Texas" is actually "Texas ", i.e. has a trailing space within the eFashion data. It would be better to use the following formula instead:

=[Quantity sold] **Where**(**Trim**([State])="Texas")

We have used the function Trim() to strip off any leading and trailing spaces found in values of states.

3. Adding the Benchmark column to the block shows the variable is being calculated as expected (i.e. every row is showing the Texas quantity sold figure).

State	Quantity sold	Benchmark
Texas	62,347	62,347
New York	46,358	62,347
California	46,074	62,347
DC	18,744	62,347
Illinois	17,976	62,347
Colorado	12,787	62,347
Florida	11,267	62,347
Massachusetts	7,676	62,347

NOTE – Hovering over the variable reveals the variable definition.

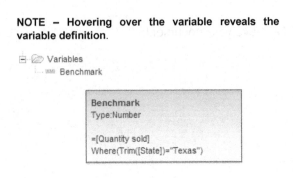

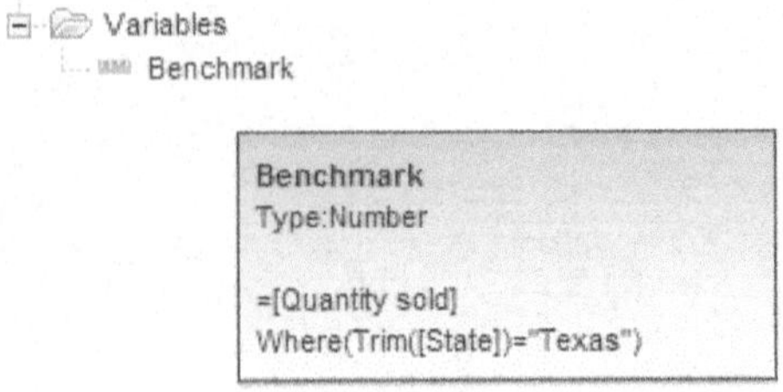
Variables
Benchmark
Benchmark
Type:Number
=[Quantity sold]
Where(Trim([State])="Texas")

4. We can create a second measure variable for comparison purposes using the following definition:

Variable Name	**Formula**
Texas Comparison	=[Quantity sold]/[Benchmark]

We have used the variable [Benchmark] as part of the definition of the second variable [Texas Comparison].

This simplifies the definition of [Texas Comparison] as it could be defined as:

=[Quantity sold]/([Quantity sold] **Where**(**Trim**([State])="Texas"))

5. Adding the [Texas Comparison] column to the block now shows the comparison of each state against Texas.

State	Quantity sold	Benchmark	Texas Comparison
Texas	62,347	62,347	1
New York	46,358	62,347	0.74
California	46,074	62,347	0.74
DC	18,744	62,347	0.3
Illinois	17,976	62,347	0.29
Colorado	12,787	62,347	0.21
Florida	11,267	62,347	0.18
Massachusetts	7,676	62,347	0.12

6. We can format the [Texas Comparison] column to a percentage and remove the Benchmark column as it is not required.

State	Quantity sold	Texas Comparison
Texas	62,347	100.00%
New York	46,358	74.35%
California	46,074	73.90%
DC	18,744	30.06%
Illinois	17,976	28.83%
Colorado	12,787	20.51%
Florida	11,267	18.07%
Massachusetts	7,676	12.31%

7. Save your document.

27.8.4 NoFilter() Function

The NoFilter function can be used to calculate values that need to include values that have been filtered out.

1. We will demonstrate this using the following 'eFashion' query and associated data:

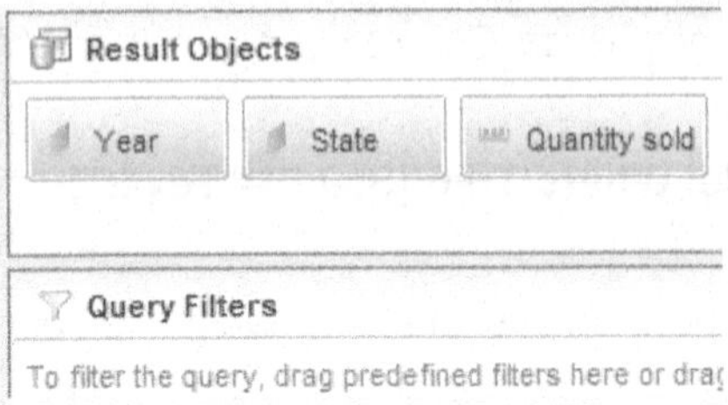
Result Objects
Year
State
Quantity sold
Query Filters
To filter the query, drag predefined filters here or drag

State	Quantity sold
Texas	62,347
New York	46,358
California	46,074
DC	18,744
Illinois	17,976
Colorado	12,787
Florida	11,267
Massachusetts	7,676

Data has been sorted on [Quantity sold] and we can see from the results that Texas has the greatest value for [Quantity sold].

We would like to compare the performance of the other states by using Texas as the benchmark.

2. We will apply a Report Filter on the block to exclude the top 3 states (i.e. do not show 'California', 'New York' and 'Texas'):

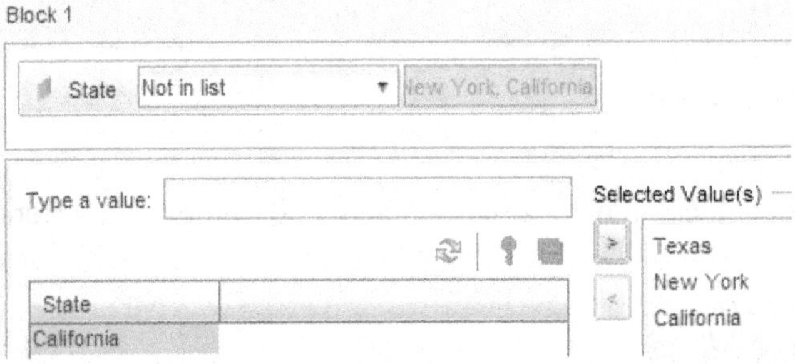
Block 1
State
Not in list
New York, California
Type a value:
Selected Value(s)
Texas
New York
California
State
California

State	Quantity sold
Colorado	12,787
DC	18,744
Florida	11,267
Illinois	17,976
Massachusetts	7,676

3. Applying a Standard Calculation of Sum to the [Quantity sold] column shows the total for the data being displayed in the block:

State	Quantity sold
Colorado	12,787
DC	18,744
Florida	11,267
Illinois	17,976
Massachusetts	7,676
Sum:	**68,450**

4. Add a row underneath our existing footer row by clicking into any of the cells in the footer row and then selecting 'Insert row below':

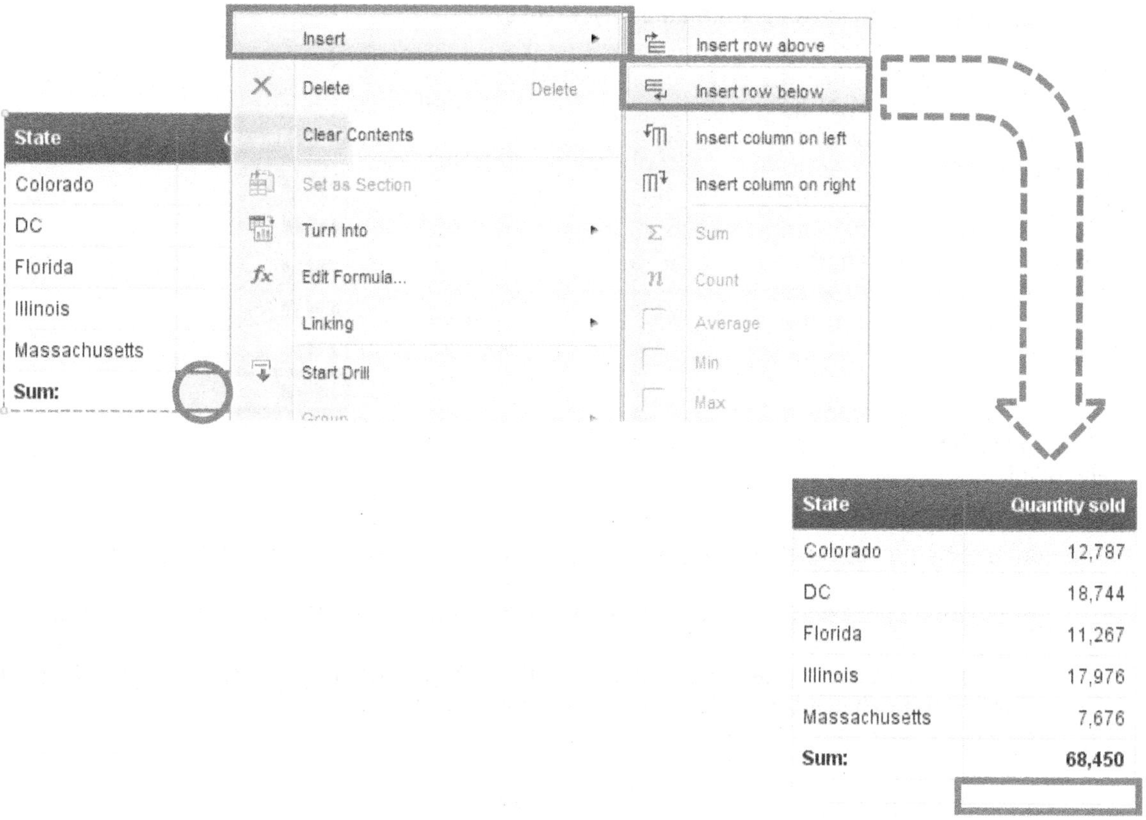
Insert
Delete
Delete
Clear Contents
Set as Section
Turn Into
Edit Formula...
Linking
Start Drill
Insert row above
Insert row below
Insert column on left
Insert column on right
Sum
Count
Average
Min
Max
State
Quantity sold
Colorado
12,787
DC
18,744
Florida
11,267
Illinois
17,976
Massachusetts
7,676
Sum:
68,450

5. Use the Formula Bar to type in the following formula for the bottom right-hand corner cell:

=NoFilter([Quantity sold]) *(as shown below)*

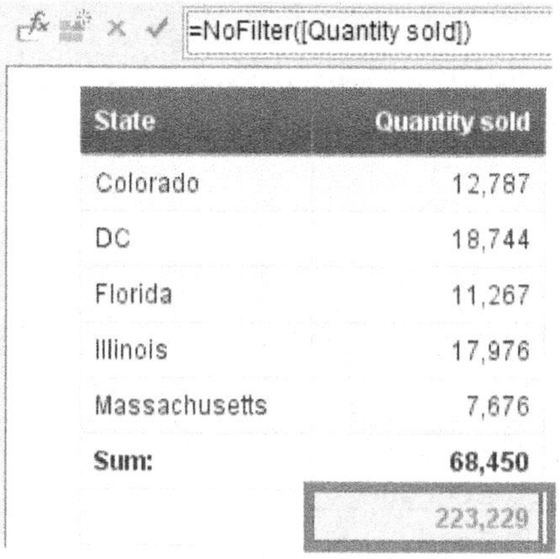
=NoFilter([Quantity sold])
State
Quantity sold
Colorado
12,787
DC
18,744
Florida
11,267
Illinois
17,976
Massachusetts
7,676
Sum:
68,450
223,229

The NoFilter() function can be used in formulas and variables to override the effects of filters.

27.9 Hyperlinks in Cells

Cells can be formatted to read contents as hyperlinks.

This can be useful for a variety of reasons, such as enabling users to jump to other sites, initiate an email inquiry concerning the report, navigate to an intranet site (or another document type) that acts as a help file concerning the report.

Simply set the property 'Read content as' to Hyperlink.

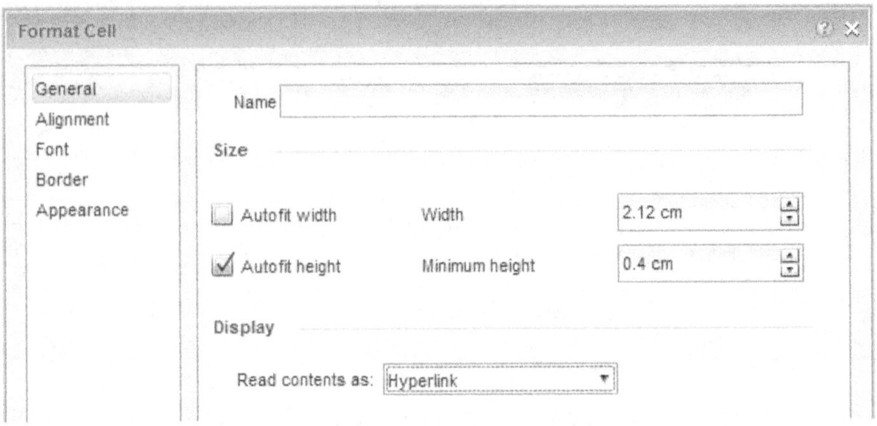
Format Cell
General
Alignment
Font
Border
Appearance
Name
Size
Autofit width
Width
2.12 cm
Autofit height
Minimum height
0.4 cm
Display
Read contents as:
Hyperlink

The contents of the cell must be of the correct syntax to ensure a valid hyperlink is created.

Example below shows two cells in a horizontal table being used to display hyperlinks.

With cell formulas, do not use an equal to character (i.e. '=') at the start of the formula when the cell content is to be read as a hyperlink.

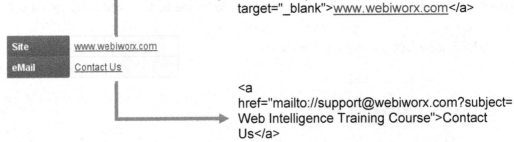

Formula Used

<a href="http://www.webiworx.com" target="_blank">www.webiworx.com</a>

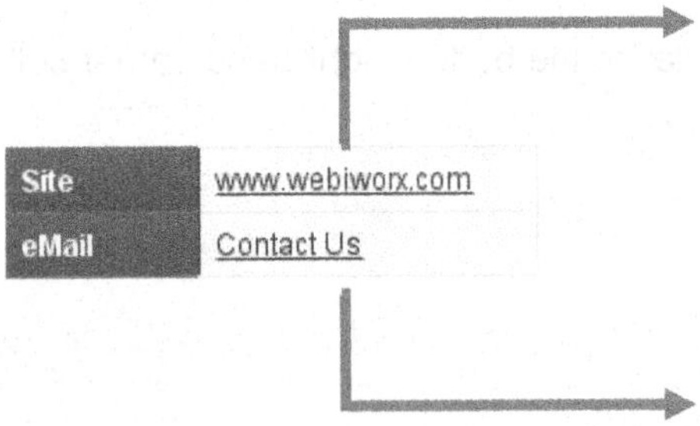
Site
www.webiworx.com
eMail
Contact Us

<a href="mailto://support@webiworx.com?subject= Web Intelligence Training Course">Contact Us</a>

We can also use variables instead of cell formulas, i.e. two variables (v_Site and v_Email) could be created:

v_Site	= <a href="http://www.webiworx.com" target="_blank">www.webiworx.com</a>
v_Email	<a href="mailto://support@webiworx.com?subject=Web Intelligence Training Course">Contact Us</a>

When using variables the equal to character (i.e. '=') at the start is necessary. So we would need to use:

=[v_Site]

=[v_Email]

The cell contents would still be read as hyperlinks if the cell property 'Read content as' is set to Hyperlink.

Hyperlinks can be used in free-standing cells as well as table cells.

27.10 Using Formulas and Variables for Conditional Formatting

In the session on 'Conditional Formatting' we mentioned rules can be created using formulas and variables.

1. Create and run the following query using the 'eFashion' universe.

Result Objects
Year
State
Quantity sold
Query Filters
To filter the query, drag predefined filters here or drag

Year	State	Quantity sold
2004	California	11,304
2004	Colorado	2,971
2004	DC	4,681
2004	Florida	2,585
2004	Illinois	4,713
2004	Massachusetts	1,505
2004	New York	10,802
2004	Texas	14,517
2005	California	17,001

2. Create a 'New Rule…' for Conditional Formatting.

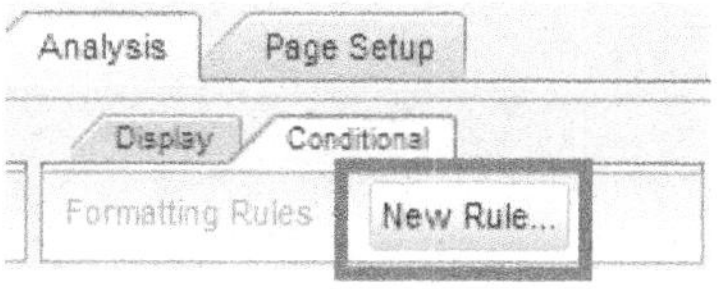
Analysis
Page Setup
Display
Conditional
Formatting Rules
New Rule...

3. Give the rule a name and then select 'Formula Editor' as shown below:

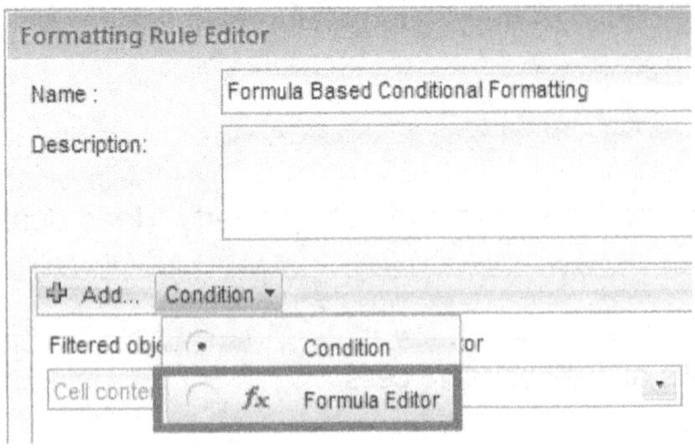
Formatting Rule Editor
Name :
Formula Based Conditional Formatting
Description:
Add...
Condition
Condition
Formula Editor

4. Type in the following formula:

   =[Year]="2005" And [Quantity sold]<5000

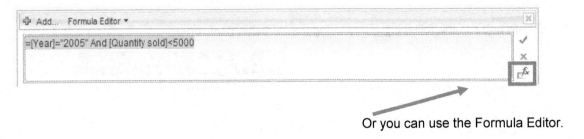
Add...
Formula Editor
=[Year]="2005" And [Quantity sold]<5000

Or you can use the Formula Editor.

5. Validate the formula and then specify a 'Red' background with 'Black' font for the formatting.

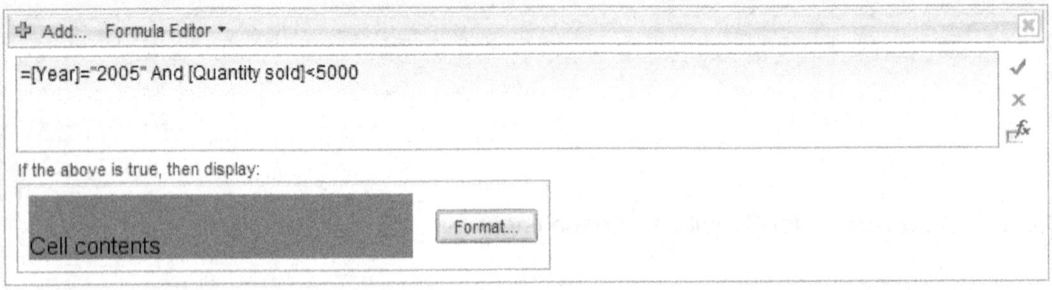
Add...
Formula Editor
=[Year]="2005" And [Quantity sold]<5000
If the above is true, then display:
Cell contents
Format...

6. Click 'OK'.

7. Apply the Formatting Rule to the [State] column.

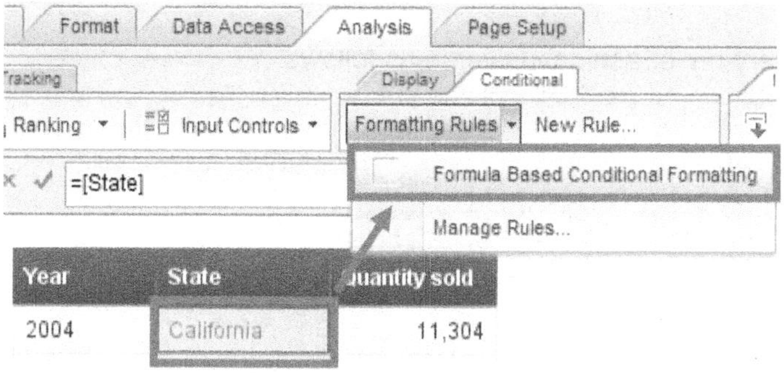
Format
Data Access
Analysis
Page Setup
Display
Conditional
Ranking
Input Controls
Formatting Rules
New Rule...
=[State]
Formula Based Conditional Formatting
Manage Rules...
Year
State
uantity sold
2004
California
11,304

8. The formatting is only being applied where the formula in the Formatting Rule is evaluated as 'True', i.e. [Quantity sold] is less than 5000 and the [Year] is 2005.

2004	Texas	14,517
2005	California	17,001
2005	Colorado	4,700
2005	DC	7,572
2005	Florida	3,852
2005	Illinois	6,744
2005	Massachusetts	902
2005	New York	16,447
2005	Texas	22,637
2006	California	17,769

9. Save your document.

NOTE

Variables can be used in Formatting Rules in the same way as objects returned by queries, both in the graphical driven conditions, or formula based expressions (as described above).

27.11 Grouping Data

We can use document level variables to 'group' data, as shown earlier using the example earlier on age:

=If [Age] < 20 Then "Under 20" ElseIf [Age] < 30 Then "20 to 30" ElseIf [Age] < 40 Then "30 to 40" Else "Over 40"

We can take this example and apply it to 'eFashion' data whereby we can attempt to group States into Regions:

1. Create a new document using a query on 'eFashion' universe as follows:

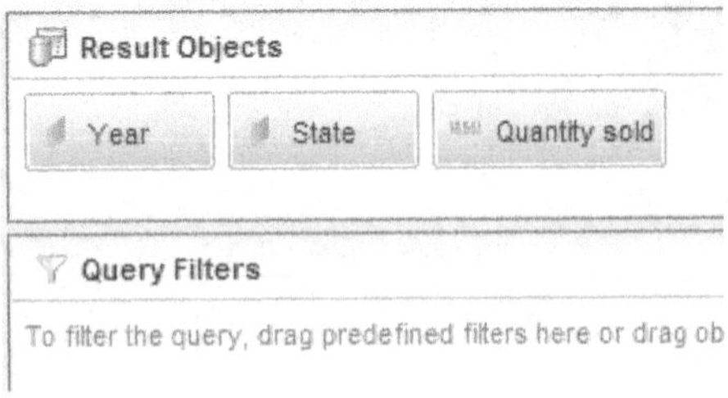
Result Objects
Year
State
Quantity sold
Query Filters
To filter the query, drag predefined filters here or drag ob

2. Run the query.

3. Create a variable called [v_Region] with the following definition:

=If Trim([State]) InList("New York";"DC") Then "North" ElseIf Trim([State]) InList("Massachusetts";"Florida") Then "East" ElseIf Trim([State]) InList("Texas";"Illinois") Then "South" ElseIf Trim([State]) InList("California";"Colorado") Then "West" Else "Others"

4. Create the following Cross Table in your report.

		2004	2005	2006
East	Florida	2,585	3,852	4,830
East	Massachusetts	1,505	902	5,269
North	DC	4,681	7,572	6,491
North	New York	10,802	16,447	19,109
South	Illinois	4,713	6,744	6,519
South	Texas	14,517	22,637	25,193
West	California	11,304	17,001	17,769
West	Colorado	2,971	4,700	5,116

5. Save your document.

We will now use an alternative and simpler method for creating the same group.

6. Click into any cell of the [State] column and then select 'Analysis – Display – Group – Manage Groups…'

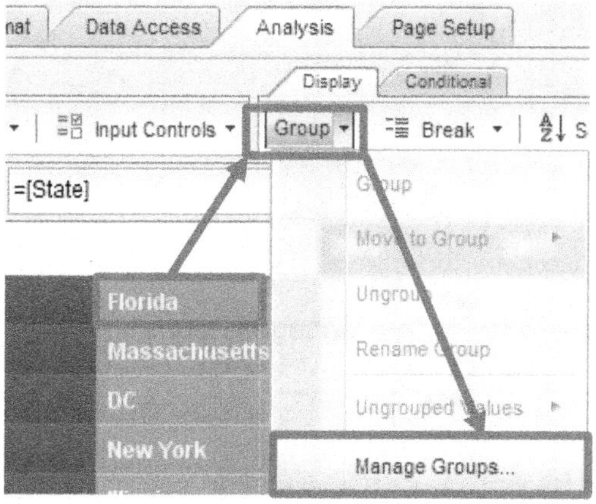
Data Access
Analysis
Page Setup
Display
Conditional
Input Controls
Group
Break
=[State]
Group
Move to Group
Ungroup
Rename Group
Ungrouped Values
Manage Groups...
Florida
Massachusetts
DC
New York

7. In the 'Manage Groups' interface, use a name of 'Region' for the Data Group:

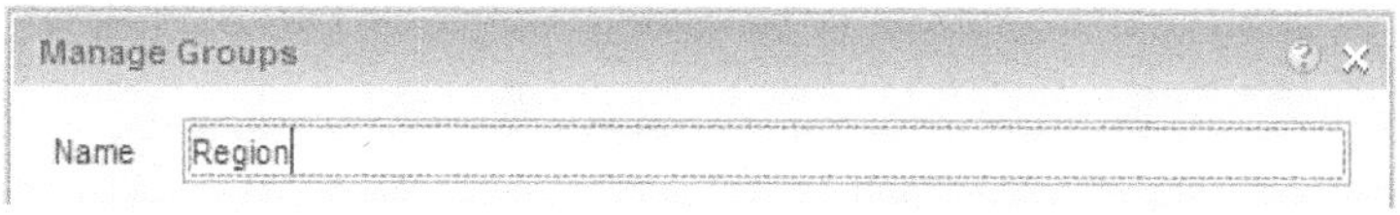
Manage Groups
Name
Region

8. Tick the boxes next to 'DC' and 'New York' and then click on 'Group'.

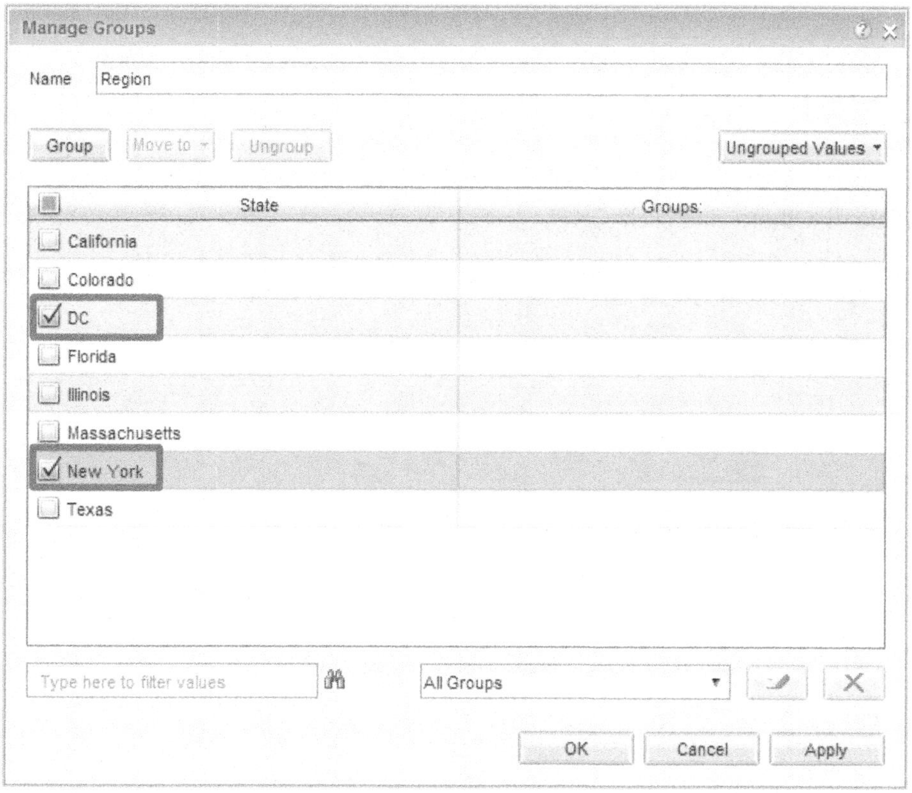
Manage Groups
Name
Region
Group
Move to
Ungroup
Ungrouped Values
State
Groups:
California
Colorado
DC
Florida
Illinois
Massachusetts
New York
Texas
Type here to filter values
All Groups
OK
Cancel
Apply

9. Give the Group a value of 'North' and click 'OK'.

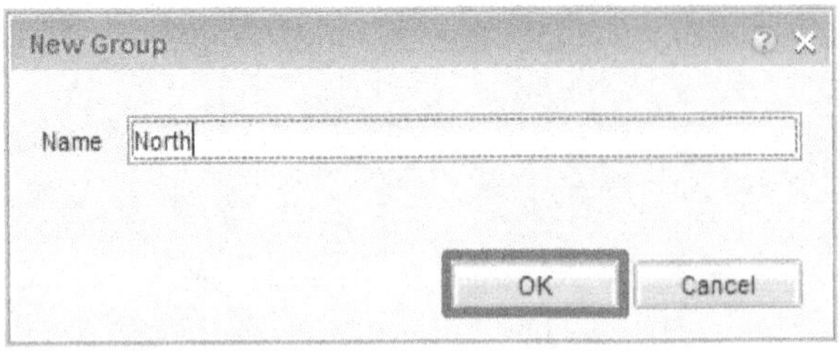
New Group
Name
North
OK
Cancel

10. We should now see 'DC' and 'New York' grouped as 'North' in the 'Manage Groups' interface.

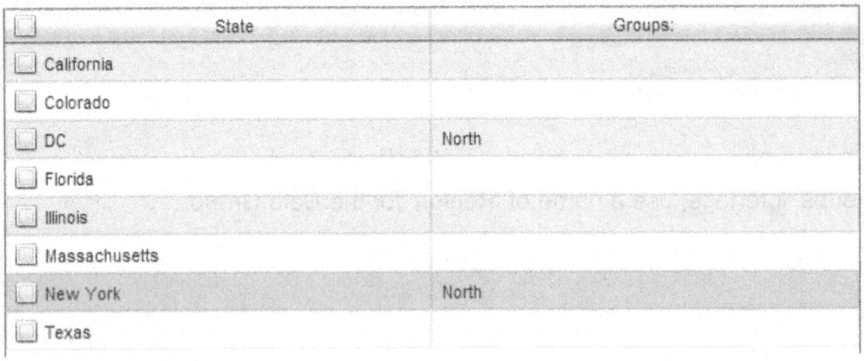
State
Groups:
California
Colorado
DC
North
Florida
Illinois
Massachusetts
New York
North
Texas

11. From the 'Ungrouped Values' dropdown, select 'Automatically grouped'.

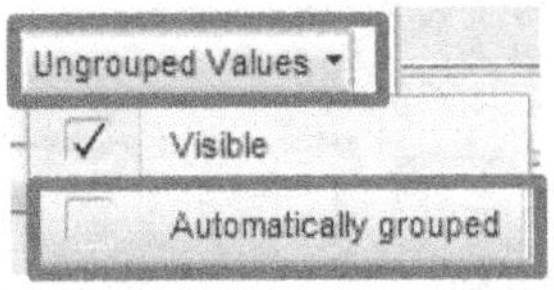
Ungrouped Values
Visible
Automatically grouped

12. Use a Group value of 'Others' and click 'OK'.

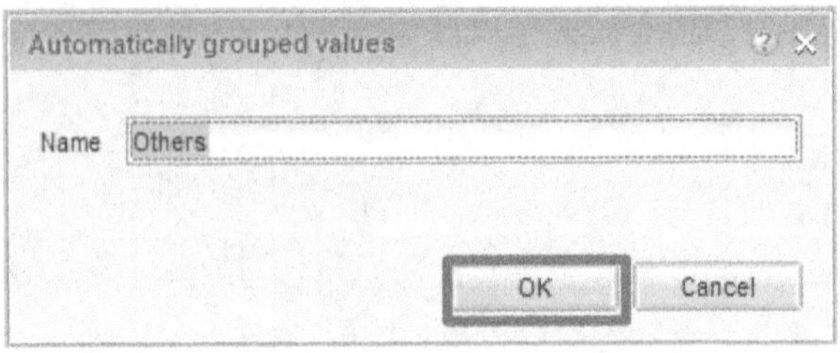
Automatically grouped values
Name
Others
OK
Cancel

13. We should now see all the remaining States being grouped as 'Others'.

	State	Groups:
☐	California	Others
☐	Colorado	Others
☐	DC	North
☐	Florida	Others
☐	Illinois	Others
☐	Massachusetts	Others
☐	New York	North
☐	Texas	Others

14. Click on 'OK' to close the 'Manage Groups' interface.

The [State] column in the Cross Table will be replaced by a new variable called [Region] that has been created automatically by Web Intelligence.

		2004	2005	2006
East	Others	4,090	4,754	10,099
North	North	15,483	24,019	25,600
South	Others	19,230	29,381	31,712
West	Others	14,275	21,701	22,885

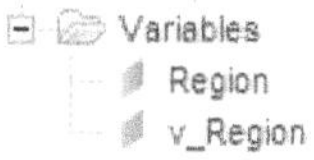

⊟ 🗁 Variables
    ── Region
    ── v_Region

15. Add [State] back into the Cross Table so we can check the assignment of the new variable [Region] is working correctly.

			2004	2005	2006
East	Others	Florida	2,585	3,852	4,830
East	Others	Massachusetts	1,505	902	5,269
North	North	DC	4,681	7,572	6,491
North	North	New York	10,802	16,447	19,109
South	Others	Illinois	4,713	6,744	6,519
South	Others	Texas	14,517	22,637	25,193
West	Others	California	11,304	17,001	17,769
West	Others	Colorado	2,971	4,700	5,116

We will now edit the [Region] variable to assign values to the other States.

16. Edit the [Region] variable by right-clicking on it and selecting 'Edit'.

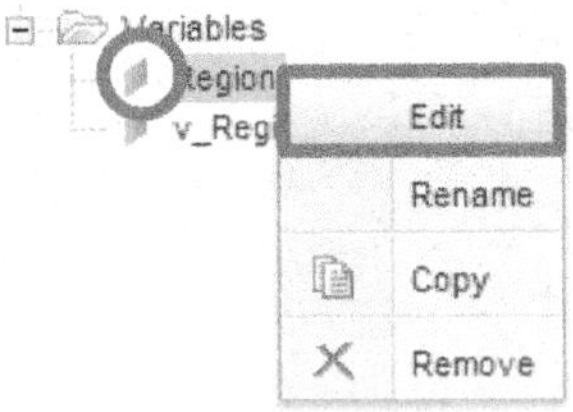
Variables
Region
v_Reg
Edit
Rename
Copy
Remove

17. Assign the groups as shown below using the 'Manage Groups' interface:

☐ State	Groups:
☐ California	West
☐ Colorado	West
☐ DC	North
☐ Florida	East
☐ Illinois	South
☐ Massachusetts	East
☐ New York	North
☐ Texas	South

18. Click 'OK' and the Cross Table will now show [Region] to be the same as [v_Region].

			2004	2005	2006
East	East	Florida	2,585	3,852	4,830
East	East	Massachusetts	1,505	902	5,269
North	North	DC	4,681	7,572	6,491
North	North	New York	10,802	16,447	19,109
South	South	Illinois	4,713	6,744	6,519
South	South	Texas	14,517	22,637	25,193
West	West	California	11,304	17,001	17,769
West	West	Colorado	2,971	4,700	5,116

We have shown grouping data using the 'Grouping' menu is more manageable than using variables, unless complex logic is required.

Web Intelligence automatically creates a variable but recognises it as a 'Grouping' variable and will display the 'Manage Groups' interface when you want to edit it.

NOTES

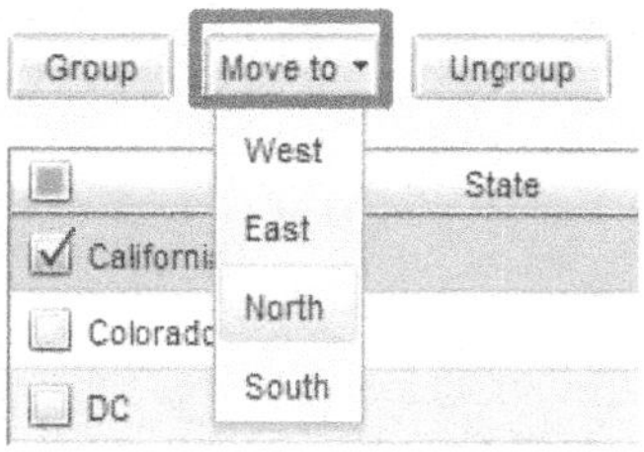
Group
Move to
Ungroup
West
East
North
South
State
Californi
Colorado
DC

You can quickly move a value from one group to another by using the 'Move' button.

Here we have selected 'California' and are moving it to the Group = 'North'.

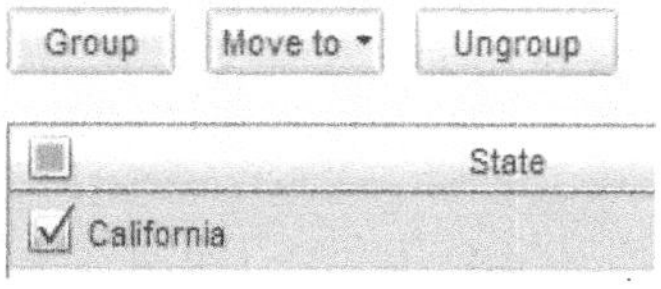
Group
Move to
Ungroup
State
California

You can remove a value from a Group by selecting it and then clicking on 'Ungroup'.

We have selected 'California' to Ungroup.

When we Ungroup, it will be automatically assigned to 'Others' because we have already assigned all ungrouped values to be assigned to 'Others'.

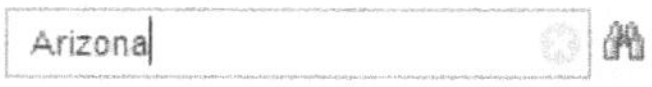
Arizona

For long lists of values you can search for values of interest.

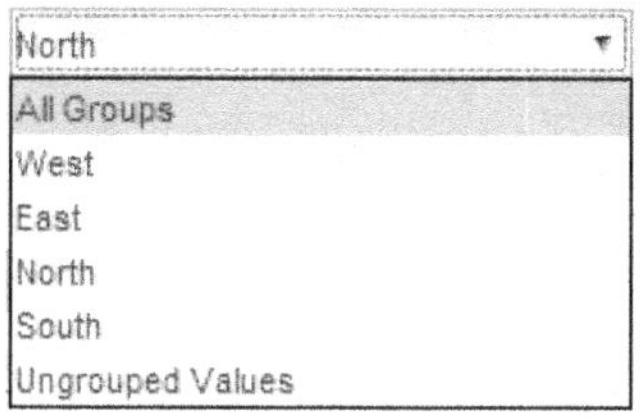
North
All Groups
West
East
North
South
Ungrouped Values

You can also filter the list by 'Group' values.

North

After filtering for a particular 'Group', you can then edit or remove the Group (similar to Ungroup).

28 Multiple Queries

A document can contain multiple queries (also known as Data Providers).

Defining multiple data providers in a single document is necessary when the data you want to include in a document is available via multiple universes, or when you want to use several focused data providers on the same universe.

It is also possible to use the results of one query to restrict a second query.

You can define multiple data providers when you create a new document or add more data providers to an existing document. You can then present the information from all of the data providers in a single report or in multiple reports in the same document.

28.1 Working with Multiple Queries

First we will take a look at creating 2 queries and using their objects in a single document. When more than 2 queries are required then the same techniques/principles apply.

For this example we start with a document containing a single query and a single report with a block presenting the data as shown below:

1. Create the following query using 'eFashion' universe:

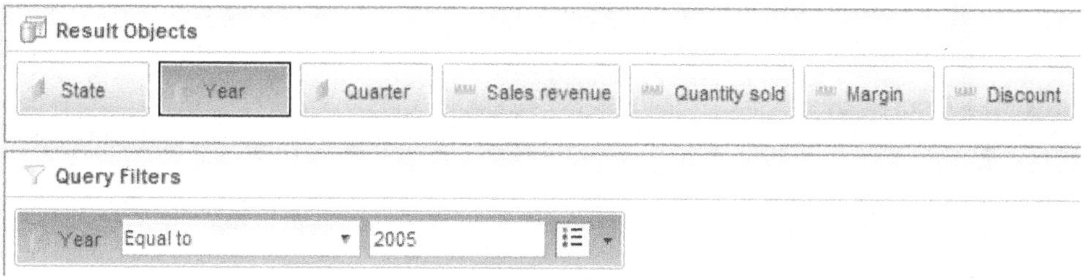
Result Objects
State
Year
Quarter
Sales revenue
Quantity sold
Margin
Discount
Query Filters
Year
Equal to
2005

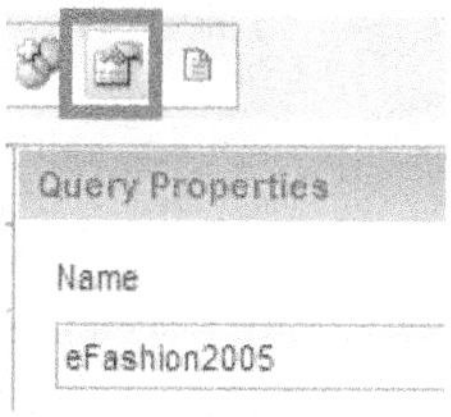
Query Properties
Name
eFashion2005

The query has been given the name '**eFashion2005**' as shown in Query Properties.

And create the following Vertical Table block.

State	Year	Quarter	Sales revenue	Quantity sold	Margin	Discount
California	2005	Q1	$650,715	4,145	$241,912	$-77,218
	2005	Q2	$529,256	3,184	$207,098	$-107,932
	2005	Q3	$760,442	5,280	$259,039	$385,204
	2005	Q4	$842,267	4,392	$368,479	$194,270
California			**$2,782,680**	**17,001**	**$1,076,528**	**$394,325**

State	Year	Quarter	Sales revenue	Quantity sold	Margin	Discount
Colorado	2005	Q1	$189,131	1,178	$71,376	$-23,247
	2005	Q2	$157,337	963	$59,764	$-38,258
	2005	Q3	$192,267	1,311	$65,016	$90,171
	2005	Q4	$229,654	1,248	$98,326	$60,349
Colorado			**$768,390**	**4,700**	**$294,483**	**$89,015**

2. Before adding a second query to the document, we will prepare our existing report.

   Double click on the report tab name 'Report 1', type 'eFashion 2005' and press <Enter>.

Report 1
eFashion 2005

Report 1
Rename Report

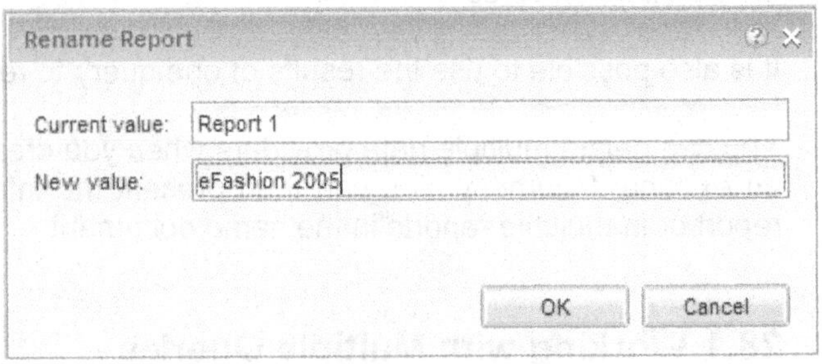
Rename Report
Current value: Report 1
New value: eFashion 2005
OK
Cancel

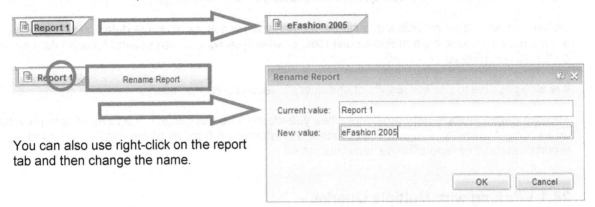

You can also use right-click on the report tab and then change the name.

3. Save your document.

We are now going to add a second query to this document.

4. Select 'New data provider – From Universe' using the Data Access toolbox.

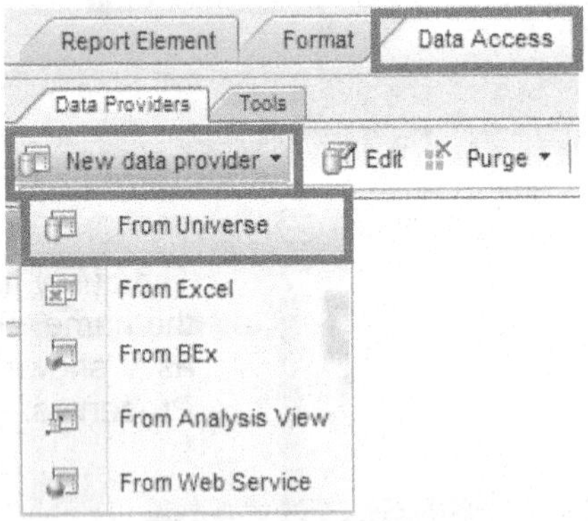
Report Element
Format
Data Access
Data Providers
Tools
New data provider
Edit
Purge
From Universe
From Excel
From BEx
From Analysis View
From Web Service

5. Select '**Island Resort Marketing**' universe for the second query.

6. Create the new query as shown below:

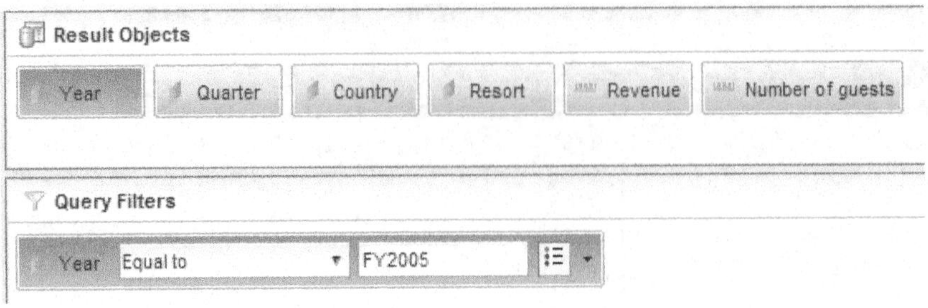
Result Objects
Year
Quarter
Country
Resort
Revenue
Number of guests
Query Filters
Year
Equal to
FY2005

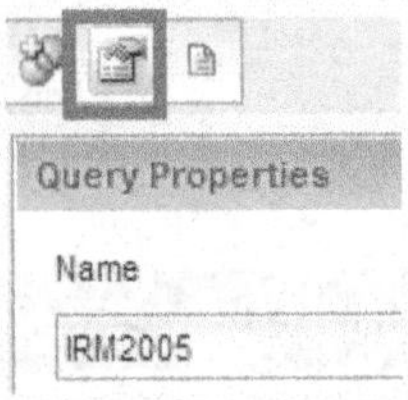
Query Properties
Name
IRM2005

Name the second query as '**IRM2005**' as shown above.

7. Run the query '**IRM2005**' only as we have already run '**eFashion2005**':

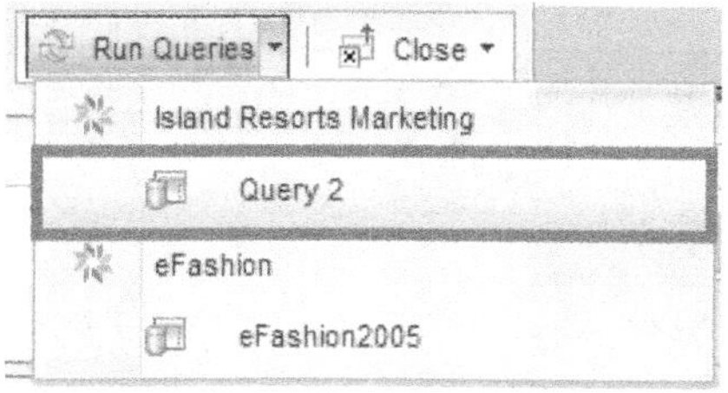
Run Queries
Close
Island Resorts Marketing
Query 2
eFashion
eFashion2005

The standard '**Run Query**' button becomes '**Run Queries**' when multiple data queries are available in the document.

If you click on '**Run Queries**' then all queries will be refreshed.

Use the drop down arrow to select the query you want to run.

NOTE

We have changed the name of the second query to 'IRM2005' but Web Intelligence is displaying it as 'Query 2'.

After running the query the new name will be applied.

When a document contains multiple data sources then all queries will be refreshed by users when using BI Launch Pad, however individual queries can be refreshed if required (both in Web Intelligence and BI Launch Pad).

8. After the second query has run, Web Intelligence might prompt to request what to do with the new data source:

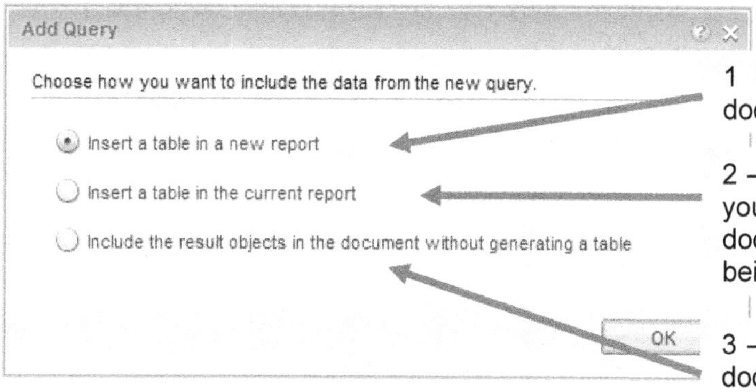
Add Query
Choose how you want to include the data from the new query.
Insert a table in a new report
Insert a table in the current report
Include the result objects in the document without generating a table
OK

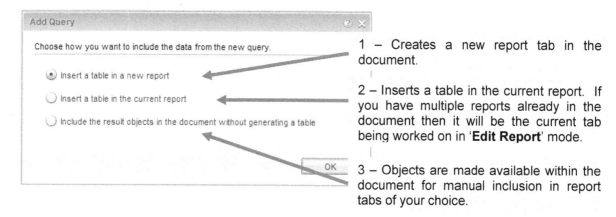

1 – Creates a new report tab in the document.

2 – Inserts a table in the current report. If you have multiple reports already in the document then it will be the current tab being worked on in '**Edit Report**' mode.

3 – Objects are made available within the document for manual inclusion in report tabs of your choice.

It all comes down to personal preference as to which option is selected.

1 and 3 are most useful as they do not interfere with any existing reports in the document.

9. Select 'Insert a table in the current report' if you are prompted. Web Intelligence will display the data for the second query in a new block on the report tab you are working on:

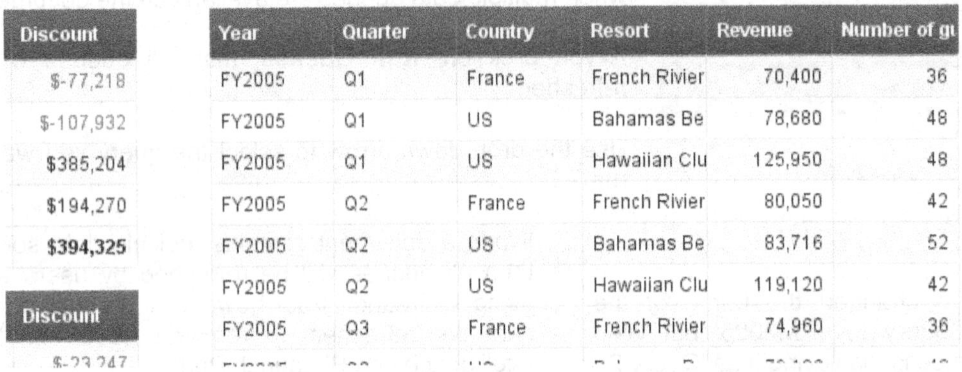
Discount
$-77,218
$-107,932
$385,204
$194,270
$394,325
Discount
Year
Quarter
Country
Resort
Revenue
Number of gu
FY2005 Q1 France French Rivier 70,400 36
FY2005 Q1 US Bahamas Be 78,680 48
FY2005 Q1 US Hawaiian Clu 125,950 48
FY2005 Q2 France French Rivier 80,050 42
FY2005 Q2 US Bahamas Be 83,716 52
FY2005 Q2 US Hawaiian Clu 119,120 42
FY2005 Q3 France French Rivier 74,960 36

10. By default the objects are listed in **Alphabetic order** as shown below.

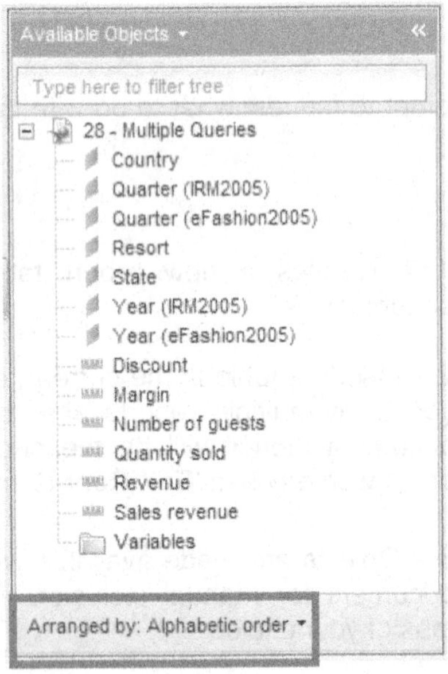
Available Objects
Type here to filter tree
28 - Multiple Queries
Country
Quarter (IRM2005)
Quarter (eFashion2005)
Resort
State
Year (IRM2005)
Year (eFashion2005)
Discount
Margin
Number of guests
Quantity sold
Revenue
Sales revenue
Variables
Arranged by: Alphabetic order

In **Alphabetic order**, any objects that have the same names also have the query name shown, e.g. Year(eFashion2005) and Year(IRM2005) are actually both called 'Year' in their respective universes, but within our document they are explicitly qualified using the query name.

Our document has been saved as '28 – Multiple Queries.

11. To view the objects in Query order use the drop down arrow to change to '**Arranged by: Query**'.

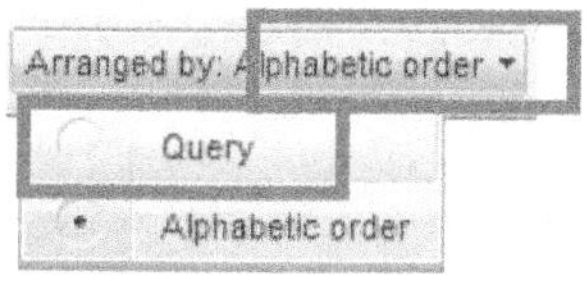
Arranged by: Alphabetic order
Query
Alphabetic order

Query order shows the objects contained in each respective query.

We now see the object names associated to their respective data source, therefore the [Year] and [Quarter] objects are no longer qualified with the query names.

NOTE – Highly recommended to use 'Arranged by: Query' at all times when working with documents containing multiple queries.

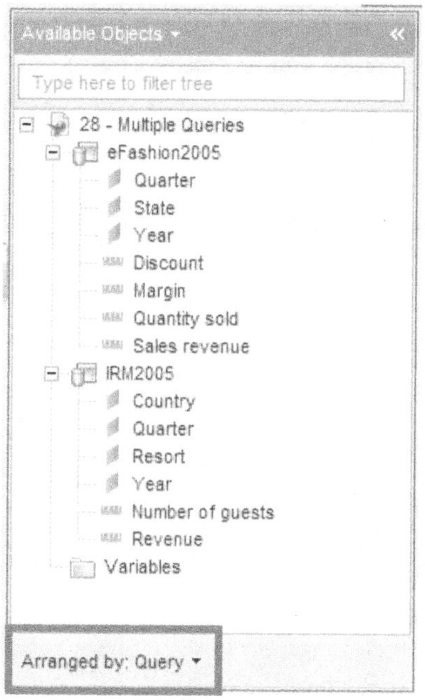
Available Objects
Type here to filter tree
28 - Multiple Queries
eFashion2005
Quarter
State
Year
Discount
Margin
Quantity sold
Sales revenue
IRM2005
Country
Quarter
Resort
Year
Number of guests
Revenue
Variables
Arranged by: Query

In the Formula Bar, when the same object name exists in multiple queries then Web Intelligence identifies the object by explicitly referring to the object name via the query name as shown below:

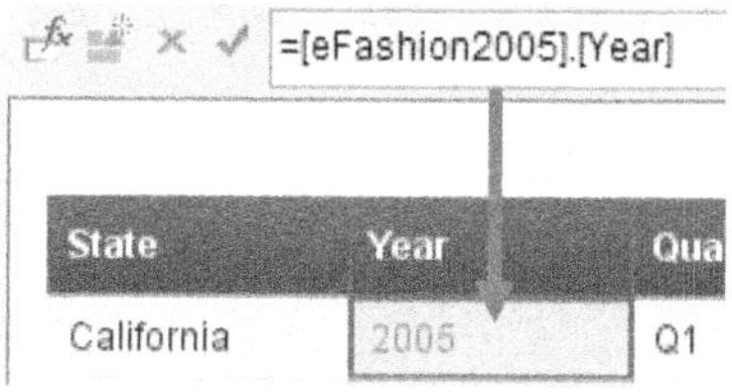
=[eFashion2005].[Year]
State
Year
Qua
California
2005
Q1

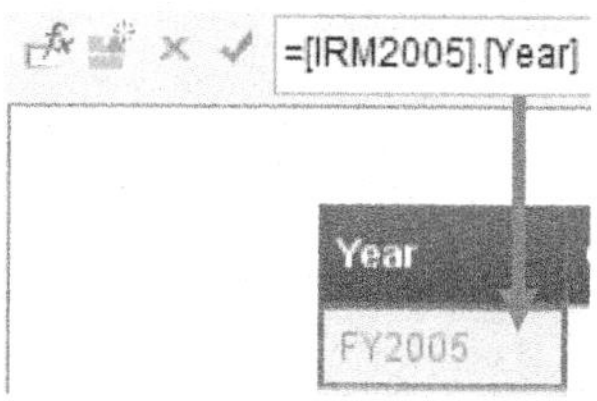
=[IRM2005].[Year]
Year
FY2005

If the same object name exists in multiple queries then you can explicitly reference an object by using the query name as follows:

[Query name].[Object name]

Any text enclosed in between **[ ]** is parsed by Web Intelligence with reference to a query name or an object name (including document variables).

12. Add a second report tab into the document by right-clicking on 'eFashion 2005' tab name and selecting 'Add Report'.

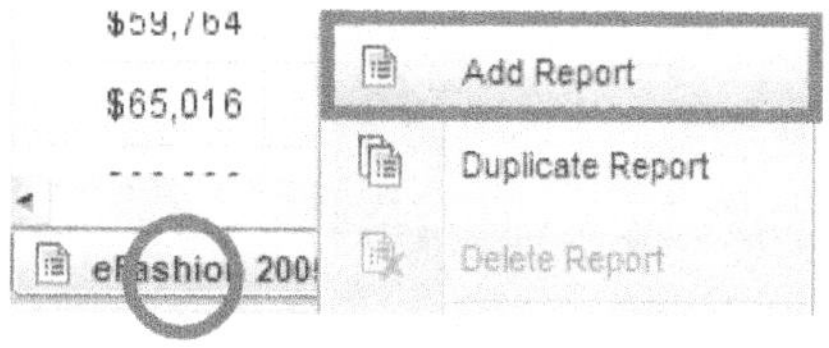
$65,016
Add Report
Duplicate Report
Delete Report

13. Rename ‘Report 2’ to ‘IRM 2005’.

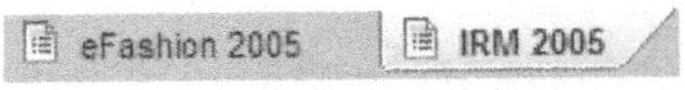
eFashion 2005
IRM 2005

14. Go back to ‘eFashion 2005’ report tab.

15. Right-click on the border/perimeter of the block containing the ‘IRM2005’ data and select ‘Cut’:

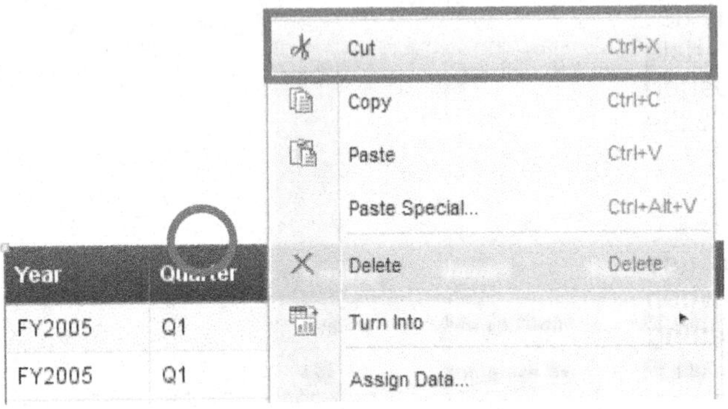
Cut Ctrl+X
Copy Ctrl+C
Paste Ctrl+V
Paste Special... Ctrl+Alt+V
Year
Delete Delete
FY2005 Q1
Turn Into
FY2005 Q1
Assign Data...

16. Go back to the ‘IRM 2005’ report tab and paste the table block by using right-click.

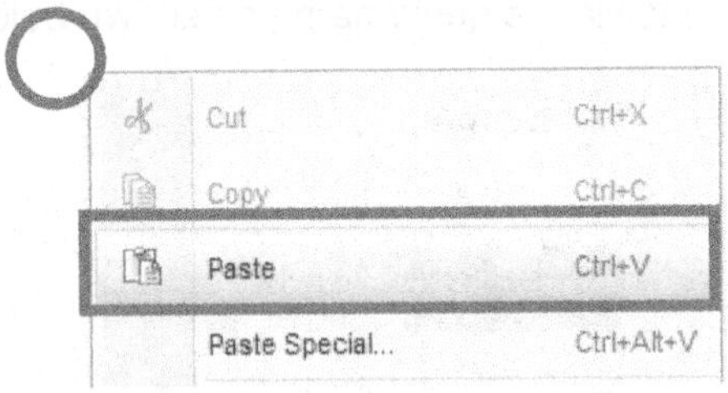
Cut Ctrl+X
Copy Ctrl+C
Paste Ctrl+V
Paste Special... Ctrl+Alt+V

17. Re-arrange and format the table as follows:

Country	Year	Quarter	Resort	Revenue	Number of guests
France	FY2005	Q1	French Riviera	70,400	36
	FY2005	Q2	French Riviera	80,050	42
	FY2005	Q3	French Riviera	74,960	36
	FY2005	Q4	French Riviera	54,900	33
France				**280,310**	**147**

Country	Year	Quarter	Resort	Revenue	Number of guests
US	FY2005	Q1	Bahamas Beach	78,680	48
	FY2005	Q1	Hawaiian Club	125,950	48
	FY2005	Q2	Bahamas Beach	83,716	52
	FY2005	Q2	Hawaiian Club	119,120	42
	FY2005	Q3	Bahamas Beach	79,180	48
	FY2005	Q3	Hawaiian Club	136,910	48
	FY2005	Q4	Bahamas Beach	65,824	43
	FY2005	Q4	Hawaiian Club	137,550	49
US				**826,930**	**378**
				1,107,240	**525**

Break has been applied to [Country] and sub-totals applied to the measures [Revenue] and [Number of guests].

18. Save your document.

We now have a Web Intelligence document containing 2 queries and showing the results of these 2 queries on individual report tabs.

We would like to keep these 2 report tabs but also create a new report that shows summarised data from the 2 queries.

19. Add a new report into the document by right-clicking on any of the existing two report tabs.

20. Name the new report as 'Summary' and create 2 separate blocks to show measures from both queries aggregated to [Year] and [Quarter] as shown below:

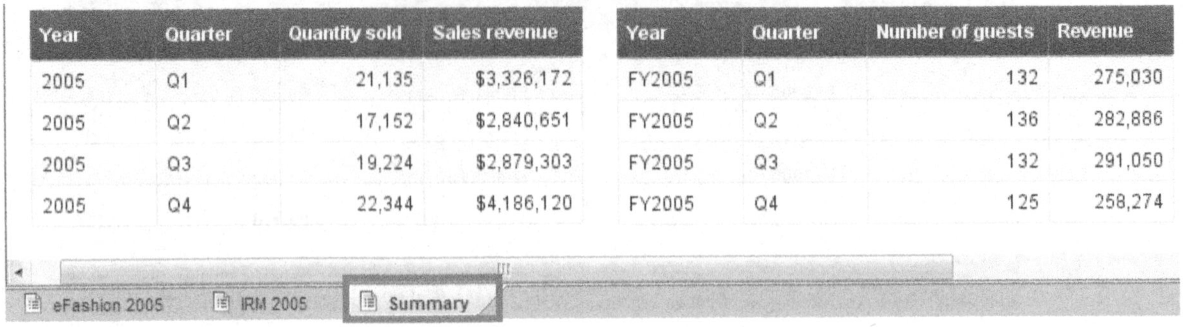

Year	Quarter	Quantity sold	Sales revenue
2005	Q1	21,135	$3,326,172
2005	Q2	17,152	$2,840,651
2005	Q3	19,224	$2,879,303
2005	Q4	22,344	$4,186,120

Year	Quarter	Number of guests	Revenue
FY2005	Q1	132	275,030
FY2005	Q2	136	282,886
FY2005	Q3	132	291,050
FY2005	Q4	125	258,274

eFashion 2005
IRM 2005
Summary

NOTES

1. The block on the left hand side has been created using [Year], [Quarter], [Quantity sold] and [Sales revenue] objects from the 'eFashion2005' query.
2. The block on the right hand side has been created using [Year], [Quarter], [Number of guests] and [Revenue] objects from the 'IRM2005' query.

21. We would like to move the 'Summary' report to be the first tab of the document.

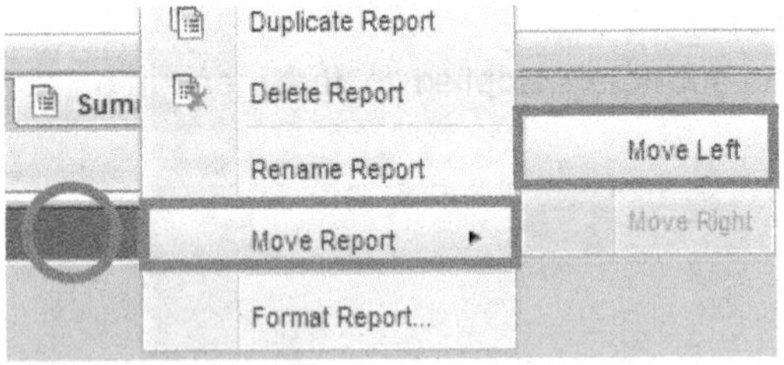
Duplicate Report
Delete Report
Rename Report
Move Report
Format Report...
Move Left
Move Right

Right-click on the 'Summary' report tab and then select '**Move Report – Move Left**'.

Perform this action **twice** to make 'Summary' the first report tab in the document.

This should have changed the report order to:

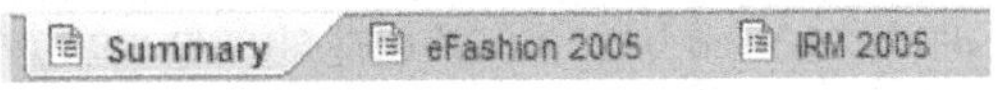
Summary
eFashion 2005
IRM 2005

We now have a document containing multiple queries and we have demonstrated how to present the data from multiple queries using individual report tabs and a combined tab. In the next session we will look at how we can define relationships between multiple queries within Web Intelligence.

22. Save and close your document.

28.2 Using a Query to Restrict another Query

It is possible to use the results from one query to restrict a second query. This is different to using Sub-Queries:

a) With Sub-Queries we create a single query but with this approach we need to create two queries and then define the restriction in the second query to use the results of the first query.

b) Sub-Queries return a single data set whereas this approach returns a dataset for each query.

c) Sub-Queries are limited to a single universe whereas with this approach we can use different universes.

The table opposite shows [Quantity sold] data from eFashion for Last Year (2005) and This Year (2006).

We have highlighted the categories 'Samples' and 'Skirts' as they were sold in 2006 and not in 2005.

We can create multiple queries:

- Query 1 to return [Quantity sold] per [Category] in 2005.
- Query 2 to return [Quantity sold] per [Category] in 2006, but only for those categories that were not sold in 2005.

  In this second query we would reference the results of the first query in our restriction.

Category	2005	2006
2 Pocket shirts	537	3,642
Belts,bags,wallets	3,677	4,348
Bermudas	253	189
Boatwear	132	1,074
Cardigan	3,824	435
Casual dresses	950	1,236
Day wear	5,005	183
Dry wear	502	317
Evening wear	5,028	2,732
Fancy fabric	292	450
Full length	368	554
Hair accessories	609	816
Hats,gloves,scarves	8,135	357
Jackets	325	27
Jeans	549	510
Jewelry	21,850	515
Long lounge pants	530	322
Long sleeve	3,056	2,857
Lounge wear	1,245	1,654
Mini city	102	617
Night wear	108	59
Outdoor	804	347
Pants	113	17
Party pants	2,047	966
Samples		**4,899**
Shirts	71	186
Short sleeve	3,823	2,724
Skirts		**3,950**
Soft fabric	213	5,329
Sweater dresses	619	1,559
Sweats	181	4,704
T-Shirts	13,970	37,076
Turtleneck	438	5,457
Wet wear	499	188

1. Create and run the first query (using 'eFashion' universe) as shown here to return [Year], [Category] and [Quantity sold] for Last Year.

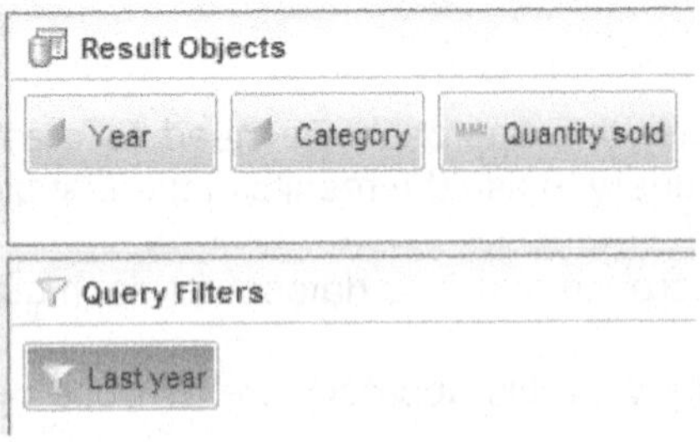
Result Objects
Year
Category
Quantity sold
Query Filters
Last year

Query Properties
Name
qryLastYear

Name the second query as '**qryLastYear**' as shown above.

2. Insert a new report by right-clicking on the report name and selecting 'Insert Report'.

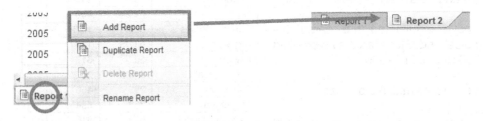
2005
2005
Add Report
Duplicate Report
Delete Report
Rename Report
Report 2

3. Edit the existing query and then 'Duplicate' the query by right-clicking on the query name and selecting 'Duplicate'.

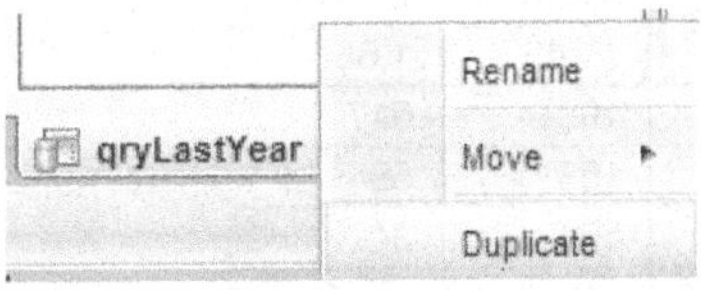
qryLastYear
Rename
Move
Duplicate

4. Rename the second query as 'qryThisYear'

qryLastYear
qryLastYear (1)

qryLastYear
qryThisYear

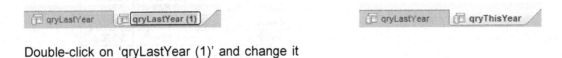

Double-click on 'qryLastYear (1)' and change it to 'qryThisYear'.

5. Modify the second query and then start to define the condition as:

   [Category] *Not in List* 'Results from another query'

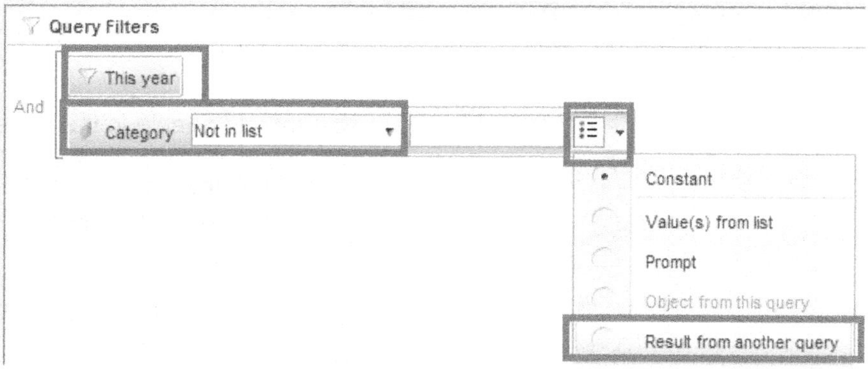
Query Filters
This year
And
Category
Not in list
Constant
Value(s) from list
Prompt
Object from this query
Result from another query

6. Select [Category] in the 'List of Data Providers' interface and click 'OK'.

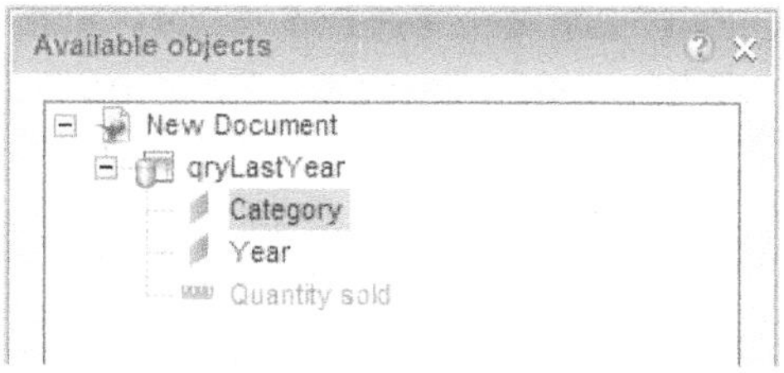
Available objects
New Document
qryLastYear
Category
Year
Quantity sold

7. Run the second query. Make sure the query filter is as shown below, i.e. uses 'And' between the two conditions.

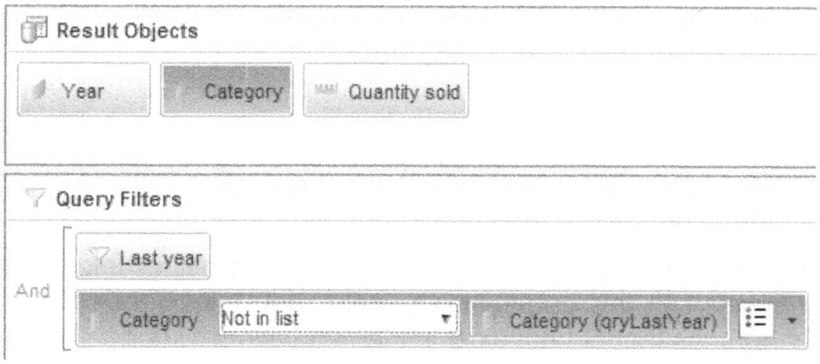
Result Objects
Year
Category
Quantity sold
Query Filters
Last year
And
Category
Not in list
Category (qryLastYear)

8. After the query has run, Web Intelligence might prompt to request what to do with the new data source:

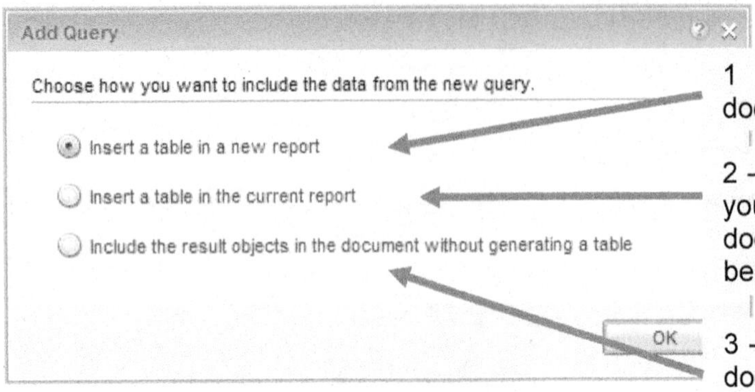
Add Query
Choose how you want to include the data from the new query.
Insert a table in a new report
Insert a table in the current report
Include the result objects in the document without generating a table
OK

1 – Creates a new report tab in the document.

2 – Inserts a table in the current report. If you have multiple reports already in the document then it will be the current tab being worked on in '**Edit Report**' mode.

3 – Objects are made available within the document for manual inclusion in report tabs of your choice.

It all comes down to personal preference as to which option is selected.

1 and 3 are most useful as they do not interfere with any existing reports in the document.

9. Select option 1 'Insert a table in a new report'.

Year	Category	Quantity sold
2006	Samples	4,899
2006	Skirts	3,950

These are the results we expect from the table shown earlier comparing categories sold in 2005 and 2006.

10. Save your document.

Web Intelligence runs the first query and then passes values from the data provider into the second query based on the query filter you create. In this particular example Web Intelligence modified the second query to request only those categories that did not exist in the first data provider:

Article_lookup.Category

NOT IN

('2 Pocket shirts', 'Belts,bags,wallets', 'Bermudas', 'Boatwear', 'Cardigan', 'Casual dresses', 'Day wear', 'Dry wear', 'Evening wear', 'Fancy fabric', 'Full length', 'Hair accessories', 'Hats,gloves,scarves', 'Jackets', 'Jeans', 'Jewelry', 'Long lounge pants', 'Long sleeve', 'Lounge wear', 'Mini city', 'Night wear', 'Outdoor', 'Pants', 'Party pants', 'Shirts', 'Short sleeve', 'Soft fabric', 'Sweater dresses', 'Sweats', 'T-Shirts', 'Turtleneck', 'Wet wear')

- Basically, the second query has been restricted to NOT return the above categories because these categories are in the first data provider.

- 'NOT IN' has been used because we selected 'Not in List' as the operator.

28.3 Managing Multiple Queries

There are a number of options available for managing multiple queries (data sources):

- Add a new query
- Run a query
- Rename a query
- Duplicate a query
- Move a query
- Delete a query
- Purge a query

28.3.1 Add Query

To add a new query to a document already containing one or more queries:

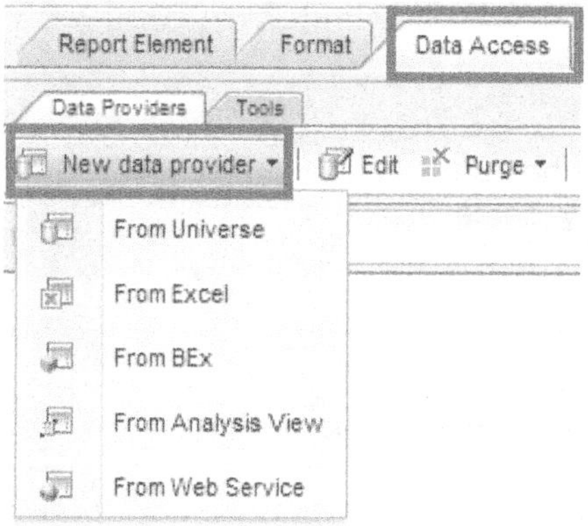
Report Element
Format
Data Access
Data Providers
Tools
New data provider
Edit
Purge
From Universe
From Excel
From BEx
From Analysis View
From Web Service

When you use 'New data provider' you have to:

1. Select the universe for the new query.

2. Proceed to create the new query as required.

3. Run the new query.

28.3.2 Duplicate Query

If you want to build a different query on a universe already included in the document, you can duplicate the existing query on that universe and then modify it, instead of starting from scratch.

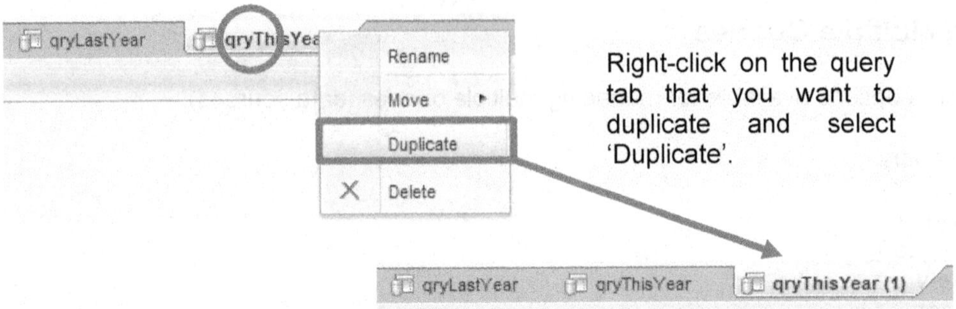
qryLastYear
qryThisYear
Rename
Move
Duplicate
Delete
qryLastYear
qryThisYear
qryThisYear (1)

Right-click on the query tab that you want to duplicate and select 'Duplicate'.

28.3.3 Run Query

You can run all queries or individual queries from within the query panel:

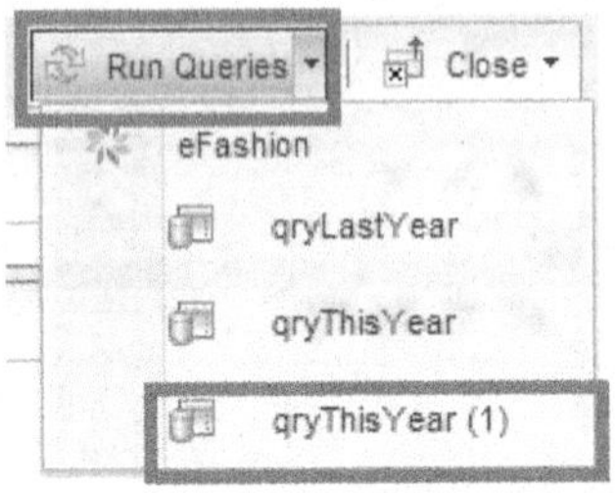
Run Queries
Close
eFashion
qryLastYear
qryThisYear
qryThisYear (1)

In the Query Panel, queries can be run individually by selecting the query name from the 'Run Queries' button.

You can also refresh all queries or individual queries from within the report panel:

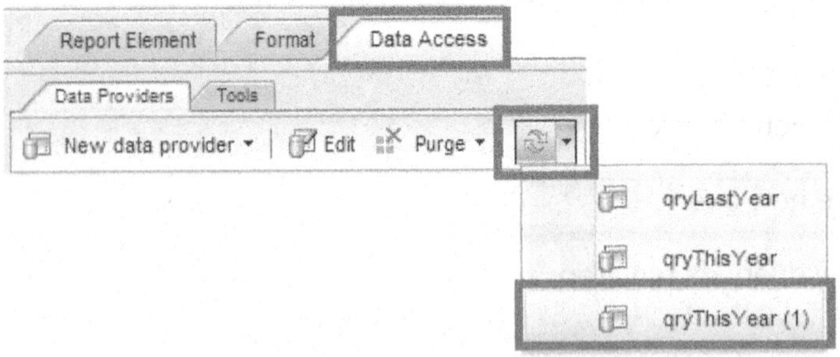
Report Element
Format
Data Access
Data Providers
Tools
New data provider
Edit
Purge
qryLastYear
qryThisYear
qryThisYear (1)

28.3.4 Rename Query

To rename a query:

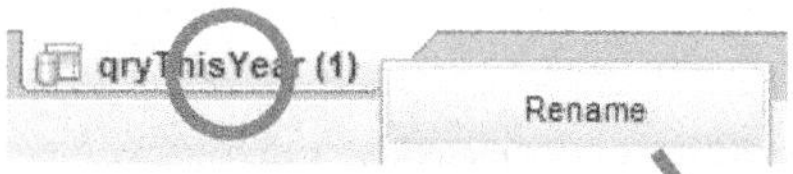
qryThisYear (1)
Rename

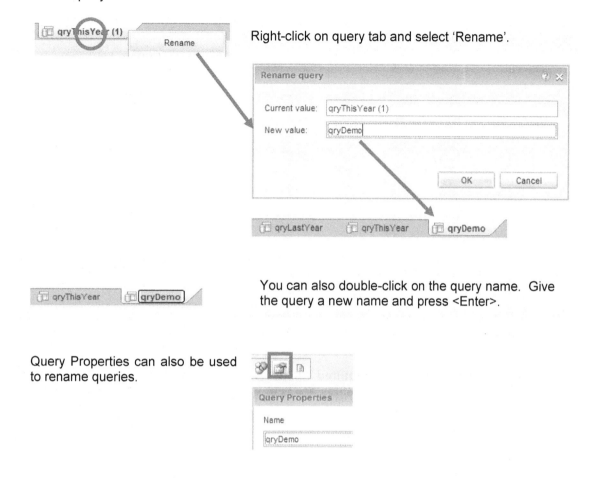

Right-click on query tab and select ‘Rename’.

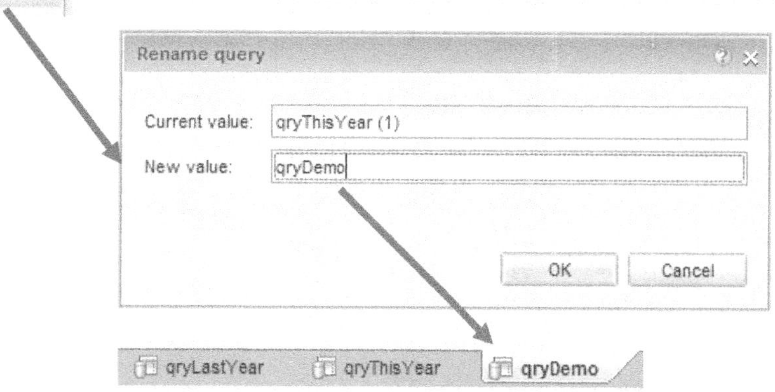
Rename query
Current value:
qryThisYear (1)
New value:
qryDemo
OK
Cancel
qryLastYear
qryThisYear
qryDemo

qryThisYear
qryDemo

You can also double-click on the query name. Give the query a new name and press <Enter>.

Query Properties can also be used to rename queries.

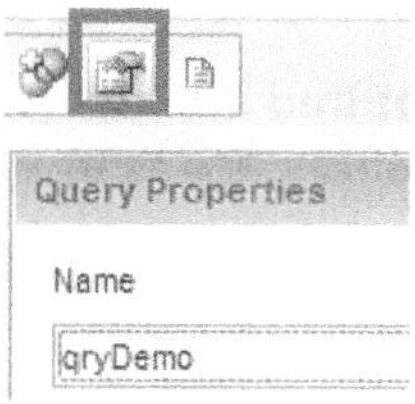
Query Properties
Name
qryDemo

Working with appropriately named queries makes referencing objects in the document much simpler than having trying to remember the difference between Query 1, Query 2, Query 3 and etc.

HINT – Where necessary (if not always) give your queries meaningful names.

28.3.5 Delete Query

Queries can be deleted from a document.

Right-click on the query tab that you want to delete and select 'Delete'.

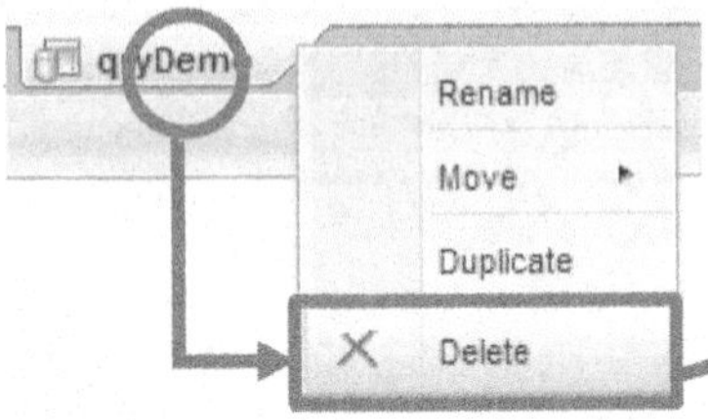
qryDem
Rename
Move
Duplicate
Delete

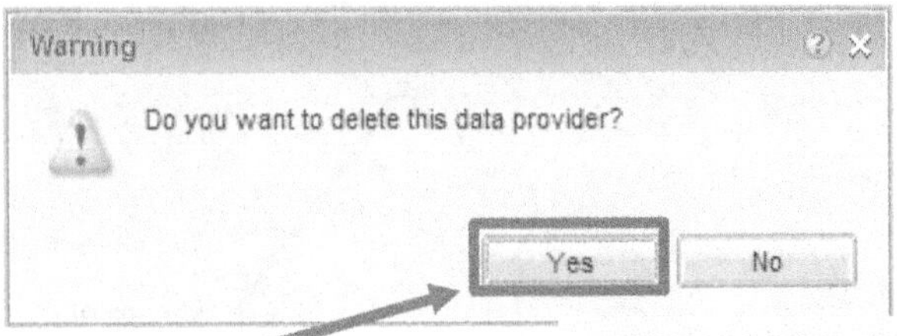
Warning
Do you want to delete this data provider?
Yes
No

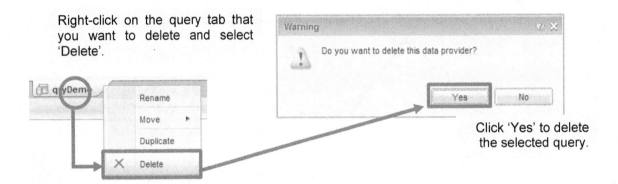

Click 'Yes' to delete the selected query.

NOTE

Web Intelligence will remove the query from the document but not will remove any report tabs associated with the deleted query.

Any reports within the document that reference objects from the deleted query (such as in tables, charts, free standing cells, report tabs, etc) will need to be deleted or changed.

All queries that are not required for use within the document should be deleted to ensure documents refresh times are kept to a minimum, and to reduce the document size.

28.3.6 Purge Query

Purging removes data from the document but retains the formatting and presentation intact, i.e. it deletes the data from the microcube. Data can be purged from all queries or individual queries within a document.

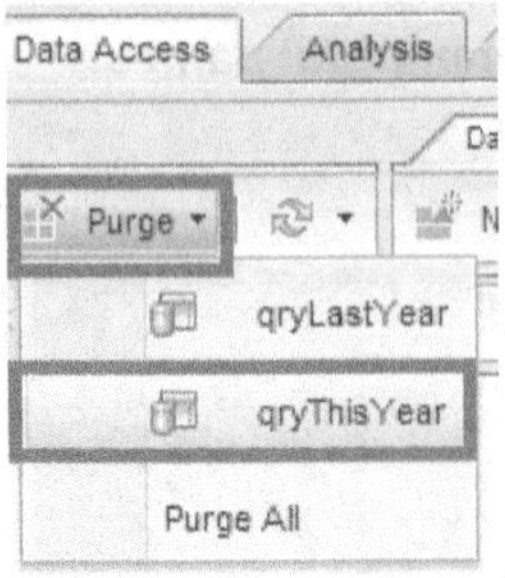
Data Access
Analysis
Purge
qryLastYear
qryThisYear
Purge All

Select an individual query to purge using 'Purge' button or 'Purge All' to purge all queries in the document.

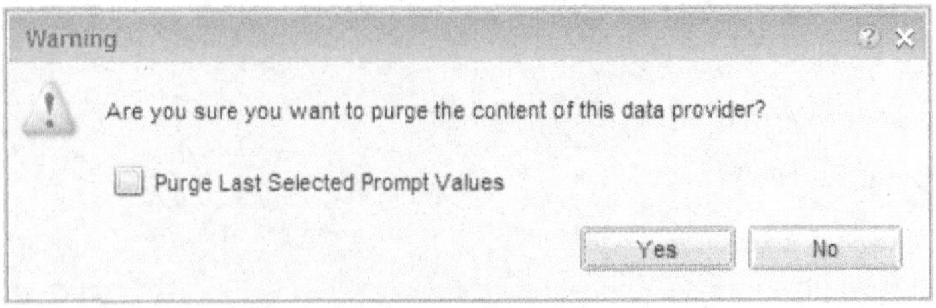
Warning
Are you sure you want to purge the content of this data provider?
Purge Last Selected Prompt Values
Yes
No

If you want to purge previously selected query prompt values then tick 'Purge Last Selected Prompt Values'.

Click 'Yes' to confirm you want to purge the data.

Click 'Close' after purging has been completed.

NOTES

1 – When all queries within the document are purged then the Purge Data button is disabled.

2 – By default charts are not visible when data is purged so it is recommended a border is used on charts so users are aware that a chart is present (but blank).

28.3.7 Move Query

Queries can be re-arranged in the query panel.

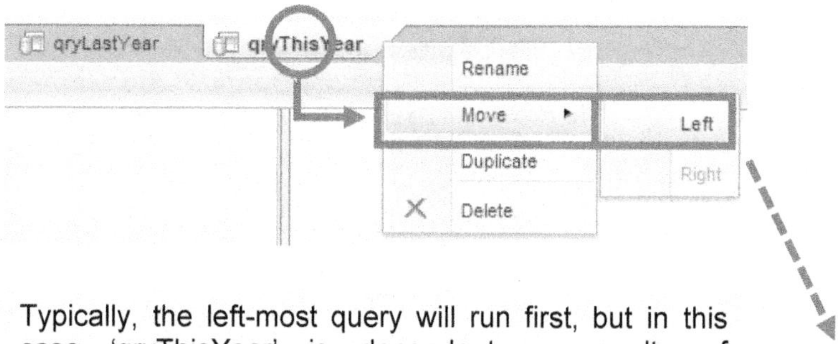
qryLastYear
qryThisYear
Rename
Move
Left
Duplicate
Right
Delete

Typically, the left-most query will run first, but in this case 'qryThisYear' is dependent on results of 'qryLastYear'.

Web Intelligence recognises this and will return the correct results even if we move 'qryThisYear' to the left of 'qryLastYear'.

qryThisYear
qryLastYear

28.3.8 Query Orders and Prompts

You can define an order for prompts that will appear when users refresh the document, by ordering the data providers accordingly.

1. Prompts can be ordered within a single query, but prompts cannot be ordered across multiple queries.

2. If you have multiple queries in a document then order the queries according to how you would like the prompts to appear.

3. All prompts of the first query will be ordered above prompts from the second query, and so on.

4. If you use the same **Prompt Text** across multiple queries then the prompt will appear only once to the user. This saves the user having to type/select the same value many times.

29 Synchronising Multiple Queries using Merged Dimensions

Web Intelligence documents can contain multiple queries from the same universe, or from different universes.

The data from the separate queries can be presented:

1. In separate reports within the document
2. In the same report as separate blocks
3. In the same report in a single block

We had a look at options 1 and 2 in the previous session. Option 3 is a powerful feature of Web Intelligence as it allows you to synchronise two or more different data providers using Merged Dimensions.

29.1 What are Merged Dimensions?

1. You can map dimensions from different data providers to create relationships (e.g. the dimension [Year] from one universe could be merged with the dimension [Year] from a second universe).

2. The names of the dimensions do not have to be the same (although quite often they are).

3. The main point to consider when merging dimensions is that they contain related data (i.e. they both contain year values such as 2001, 2002, 2003, etc).

4. The only restriction imposed by Web Intelligence on Merged Dimensions is that they have to be of the same data type, e.g. Number, Character, or Date.

29.2 When to use Merged Dimensions?

You might be requested to provide data from different universes (most likely due to different source systems) in a single table/chart for comparison/trend analysis.

An example might be:

- Actual Sales and Actual Costs are available from Sales Universe

- Budget Sales and Budget Costs are available from Budgets Universe

  SalesQuery is created on Sales Universe to return the dimension objects **[Year]** and **[Month]** with the measure object **[Actual Sales]**.

  BudgetsQuery is created on Budgets Universe to return the dimension objects **[Year No]** and **[Period]** with the measure object **[Budget Sales]**.

  The columns of the two queries are therefore:

SalesQuery (Sales Universe)		
Year	Month	Actual Sales

BudgetsQuery (Budgets Universe)		
Year No	Period	Budget Sales

Taking our example, let us assume the data for the two queries is as follows:

SalesQuery (Sales Universe)		
Year	**Month**	**Actual Sales**
2006	01	220,009
2006	02	230,105
2006	03	228,534
2006	04	190,941
2006	05	198,632
2006	06	196,842
2006	07	201,396

BudgetsQuery (Budgets Universe)		
Year No	**Period**	**Budget Sales**
2006	01	190,000
2006	02	190,000
2006	03	190,000
2006	04	195,000
2006	05	195,000
2006	06	195,000
2006	07	200,000
2006	08	200,000
2006	09	200,000
2006	10	205,000
2006	11	205,000
2006	12	205,000

NOTE – Budget data is available for 12 months but actual data is at 2006 July as this is our assumed current month

We would like to present the data in a single block and to perform a calculation as shown below:

Reporting Year	Reporting Month	Actual Sales	Budget Sales	Act to Bud Variance

Web Intelligence can do this by matching (looking up) the values found in the dimension objects of the data sources. In this example we need Web Intelligence to match values in:

[Year] (in SalesQuery) to **[Year No]** (in BudgetsQuery)

[Month] (in SalesQuery) to **[Period]** (in BudgetsQuery)

We define this relationship in Web Intelligence by creating Merged Dimensions within the document. In our example, we would have:

Merged Dimension Name	Source Dimension 01	Source Dimension 02
[Reporting Year]	[Year]	[Year No]
[Reporting Month]	[Month]	[Period]

As you can see we now have a relationship defined between the two data sources using the dimension objects contained within them.

This relationship enables us to present the measure objects from the two queries in a single block as Web Intelligence will use the dimension values to synchronise the data. So we get:

Reporting Year	Reporting Month	Actual Sales	Budget Sales
2006	01	220,009	190,000
2006	02	230,105	190,000
2006	03	228,534	190,000
2006	04	190,941	195,000
2006	05	198,632	195,000
2006	06	196,842	195,000
2006	07	201,396	200,000
2006	08		200,000
2006	09		200,000
2006	10		205,000
2006	11		205,000
2006	12		205,000
Merged Dimension Objects		**Measure from SalesQuery**	**Measure from BudgetsQuery**

Finally, we can create a variable or use a formula to calculate the [Act to Bud Variance] and display as a percentage by using number format of Percentage.

[Act to Bud Variance] =

$$\frac{\text{([SalesQuery].[Actual Sales] – [BudgetsQuery].[Budget Sales])}}{\text{[BudgetsQuery].[Budget Sales]}}$$

Reporting Year	Reporting Month	Actual Sales	Budget Sales	Act to Bud Variance
2001	01	220,009	190,000	16%
2001	02	230,105	190,000	21%
2001	03	228,534	190,000	20%
2001	04	190,941	195,000	-2%
2001	05	198,632	195,000	2%
2001	06	196,842	195,000	1%
2001	07	201,396	200,000	1%
2001	08		200,000	
2001	09		200,000	
2001	10		205,000	
2001	11		205,000	
2001	12		205,000	
Merged Dimension Objects		**Measure from SalesQuery**	**Measure from BudgetsQuery**	**Report Level Variable**

29.3 Merging Dimensions in Web Intelligence

The following is a practical example of how to merge dimensions in Web Intelligence using the example from our previous session (Multiple Queries).

The first query was given the name '**eFashion2005**' as shown below.

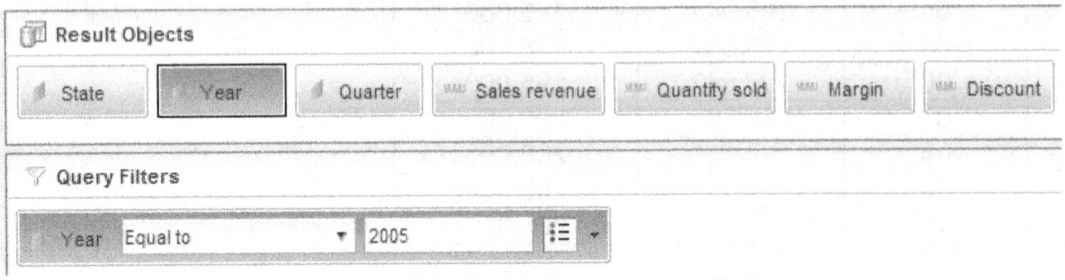
Result Objects
State
Year
Quarter
Sales revenue
Quantity sold
Margin
Discount
Query Filters
Year
Equal to
2005

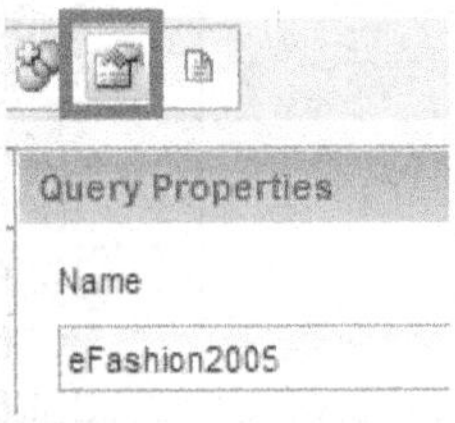
Query Properties
Name
eFashion2005

The second query was named as '**IRM2005**' as shown below.

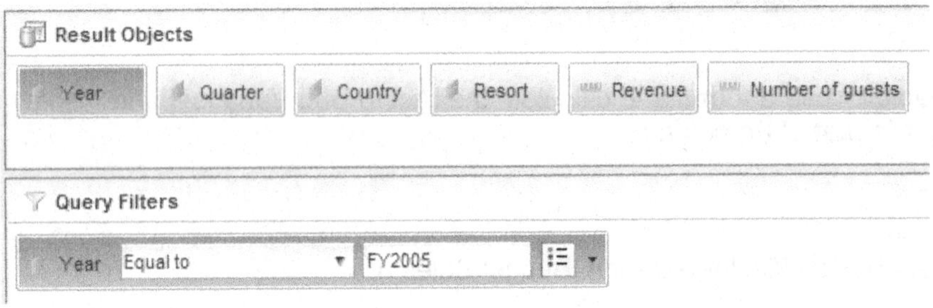
Result Objects
Year
Quarter
Country
Resort
Revenue
Number of guests
Query Filters
Year
Equal to
FY2005

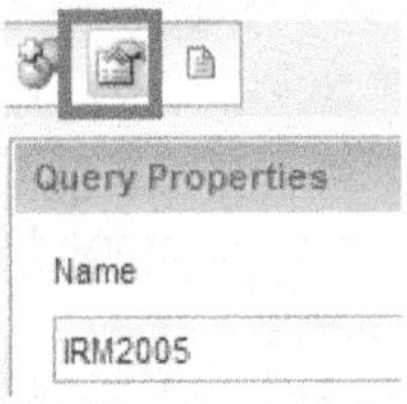
Query Properties
Name
IRM2005

Three report tabs were created:

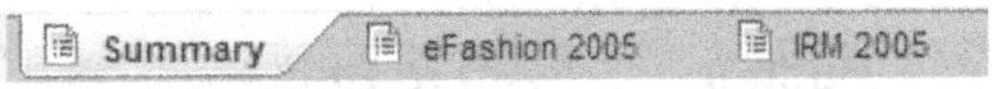
Summary
eFashion 2005
IRM 2005

1. 'eFashion 2005' displayed the data for the query 'eFashion2005' only.
2. 'IRM 2005' displayed the data for the query 'IRM2005' only.
3. 'Summary' displayed summarised data from both queries (as shown above).

The Summary tab contains 2 independent blocks but we would like to use a single block to present the data as:

Year	Quarter	Quantity sold	Sales revenue	Revenue	Number of guests

Let us attempt to create the single block.

1. Open the existing document created in the previous session for modifying.

   You can right-click on the document name in BI Launch Pad and select 'Modify'.

2. Use 'Save As' and save the document with a new name.

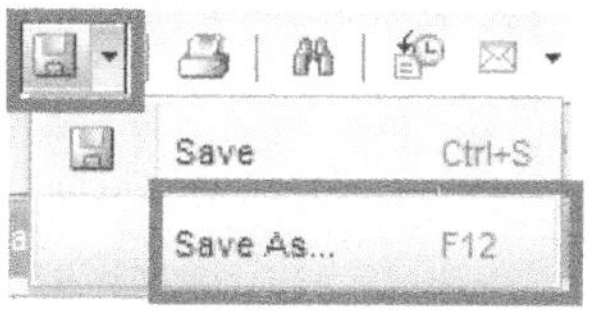
Save
Ctrl+S
Save As...
F12

3. You will now be working in your new version of the document. Create a copy of the 'Summary' tab and then rename the copied tab as 'Synchronised Data'.

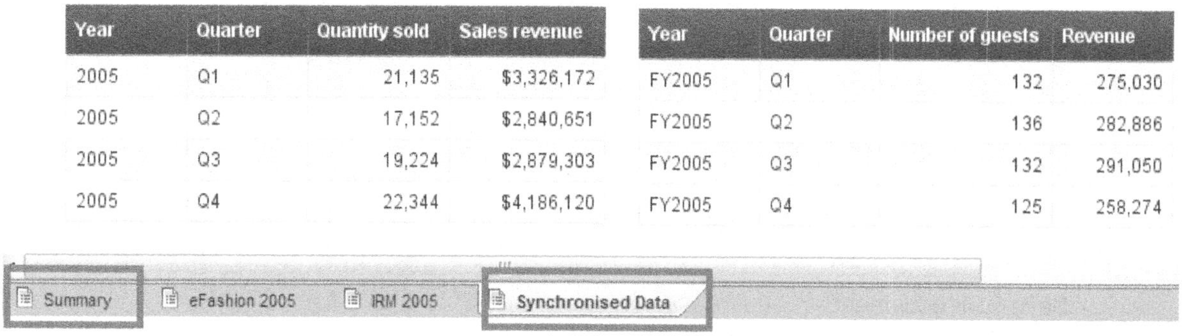

Year	Quarter	Quantity sold	Sales revenue
2005	Q1	21,135	$3,326,172
2005	Q2	17,152	$2,840,651
2005	Q3	19,224	$2,879,303
2005	Q4	22,344	$4,186,120

Year	Quarter	Number of guests	Revenue
FY2005	Q1	132	275,030
FY2005	Q2	136	282,886
FY2005	Q3	132	291,050
FY2005	Q4	125	258,274

Summary
eFashion 2005
IRM 2005
Synchronised Data

Hint – You can right-click on the 'Summary' tab and select 'Duplicate'.

4. Remove the right-hand block from 'Synchronised Data' so we only have the left-hand block.

Year	Quarter	Quantity sold	Sales revenue
2005	Q1	21,135	$3,326,172
2005	Q2	17,152	$2,840,651
2005	Q3	19,224	$2,879,303
2005	Q4	22,344	$4,186,120

Summary
eFashion 2005
IRM 2005
Synchronised Data

Hint – Right-click on the perimeter of the block and select 'Delete'.

5. Drag [Revenue] from Data tab and drop it to create a column to the right of [Sales revenue].

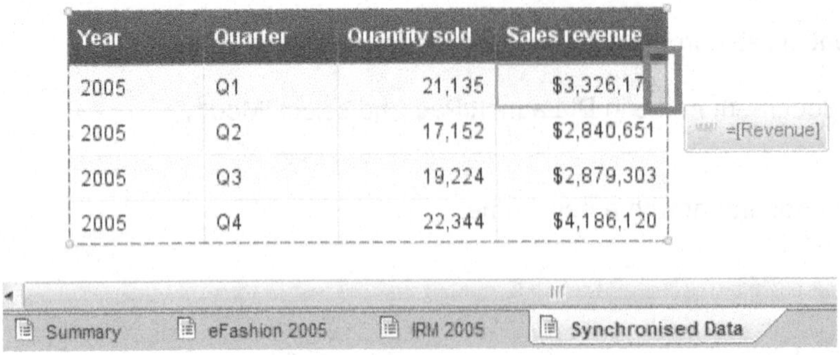

Year	Quarter	Quantity sold	Sales revenue
2005	Q1	21,135	$3,326,17
2005	Q2	17,152	$2,840,651
2005	Q3	19,224	$2,879,303
2005	Q4	22,344	$4,186,120

=[Revenue]
Summary
eFashion 2005
IRM 2005
Synchronised Data

6. Drag [Number of guests] from Data tab and drop it to create a column to the right of [Revenue].

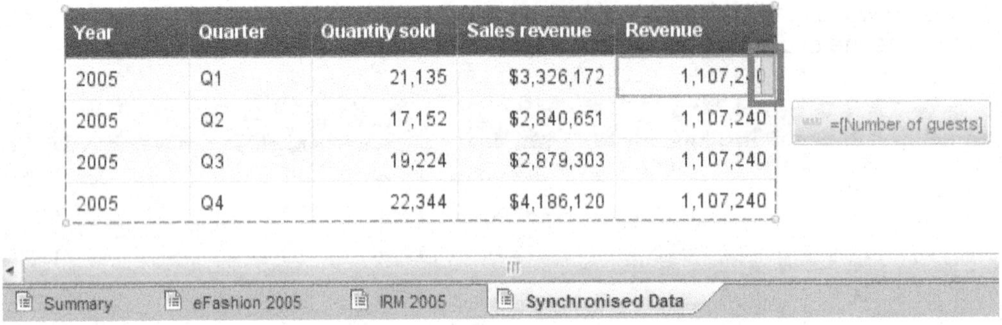

Year	Quarter	Quantity sold	Sales revenue	Revenue
2005	Q1	21,135	$3,326,172	1,107,2
2005	Q2	17,152	$2,840,651	1,107,240
2005	Q3	19,224	$2,879,303	1,107,240
2005	Q4	22,344	$4,186,120	1,107,240

=[Number of guests]
Summary
eFashion 2005
IRM 2005
Synchronised Data

7. Save your document.

8. The report 'Synchronised Data' now displays:

Year	Quarter	Quantity sold	Sales revenue	Revenue	Number of guest
2005	Q1	21,135	$3,326,172	1,107,240	525
2005	Q2	17,152	$2,840,651	1,107,240	525
2005	Q3	19,224	$2,879,303	1,107,240	525
2005	Q4	22,344	$4,186,120	1,107,240	525

The figures in [Revenue] and [Number of guests] columns are clearly not what we expected.

So what are these figures representing?

We get an idea if we go back to the 'Summary' tab and add totals to the columns as shown below:

Year	Quarter	Quantity sold	Sales revenue	Year	Quarter	Number of guests	Revenue
2005	Q1	21,135	$3,326,172	FY2005	Q1	132	275,030
2005	Q2	17,152	$2,840,651	FY2005	Q2	136	282,886
2005	Q3	19,224	$2,879,303	FY2005	Q3	132	291,050
2005	Q4	22,344	$4,186,120	FY2005	Q4	125	258,274
		79,855	**$13,232,246**			**525**	**1,107,240**

Summary | eFashion 2005 | IRM 2005 | Synchronised Data

The figures of 525 for [Number of guests] and 1,107,240 for [Revenue] are the totals for 'IRM2005' query.

In our 'Synchronised Data' tab we are trying to display these two measures against dimensions from the 'eFashion2005' query. Web Intelligence does not know how to relate the data so it is displaying the totals from IRM2005 query against the dimensions from 'eFashion2005' query.

9. We will attempt to resolve the problem by synchronising the data.

At the start of this session we mentioned the following about Merged Dimensions:

- You merge dimensions from different data providers to create relationships (e.g. the dimension [Year] from one universe could be merged with the dimension [Year] from a second universe).
- The names of the dimensions do not have to be the same (although quite often they are).
- The main point to consider when merging dimensions is that they contain related data (i.e. they both contain year values such as 2001, 2002, 2003, etc).
- The only restriction imposed by Web Intelligence on Merged Dimensions is that they have to be of the same data type, e.g. Number, Character, or Date.

In our example we have 2 dimensions in each query:

Query	Dimension 1	Dimension 2
eFashion2005	[Year]	[Quarter]
IRM2005	[Year]	[Quarter]

It would seem we can go ahead and synchronise the 2 [Year] dimensions to one another and the 2 [Quarter] objects to one another.

However, if we look at the values contained in these objects then we can see that the [Year] dimensions cannot be related because they contain different values.

Year	Quarter	Quantity sold	Sales revenue	Year	Quarter	Number of guests	Revenue
2005	Q1	21,135	$3,326,172	FY2005	Q1	132	275,030
2005	Q2	17,152	$2,840,651	FY2005	Q2	136	282,886
2005	Q3	19,224	$2,879,303	FY2005	Q3	132	291,050
2005	Q4	22,344	$4,186,120	FY2005	Q4	125	258,274
		79,855	**$13,232,246**			**525**	**1,107,240**

The [Quarter] dimensions are suitable for being merged as they contain the same values in both queries.

10. Click on 'Merge Dimensions' toolbar button.

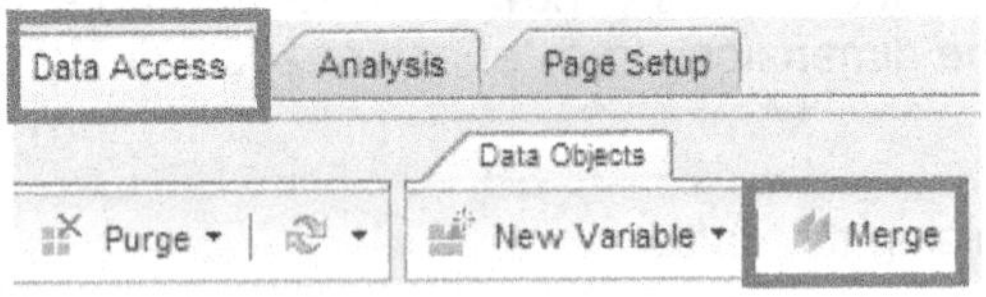
Data Access
Analysis
Page Setup
Data Objects
Purge
New Variable
Merge

11. Select the 2 [Quarter] objects and then click on the 'OK' button:

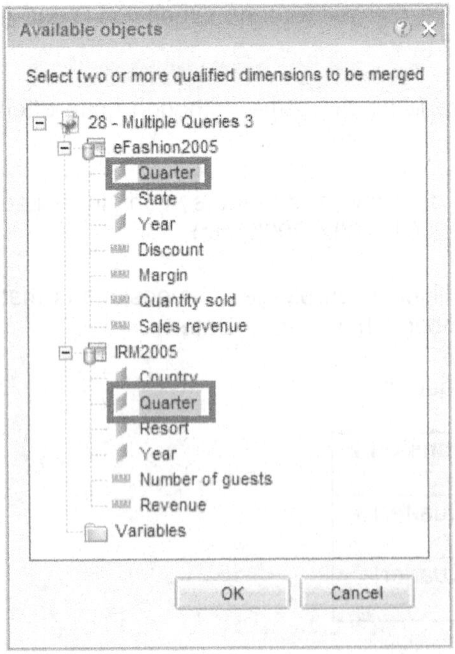
Available objects
Select two or more qualified dimensions to be merged
28 - Multiple Queries 3
eFashion2005
Quarter
State
Year
Discount
Margin
Quantity sold
Sales revenue
IRM2005
Country
Quarter
Resort
Year
Number of guests
Revenue
Variables
OK
Cancel

NOTES

1. Click on one of the [Quarter] objects and then hold down the <CTRL> key and then click on the second [Quarter] object.

2. When you select a dimension, all dimensions of different data types are disabled because you cannot merge dimensions of different data types.

12. The Merged Dimension will be automatically created and will be displayed in the 'Available Objects' pane.

Arranged by: Query

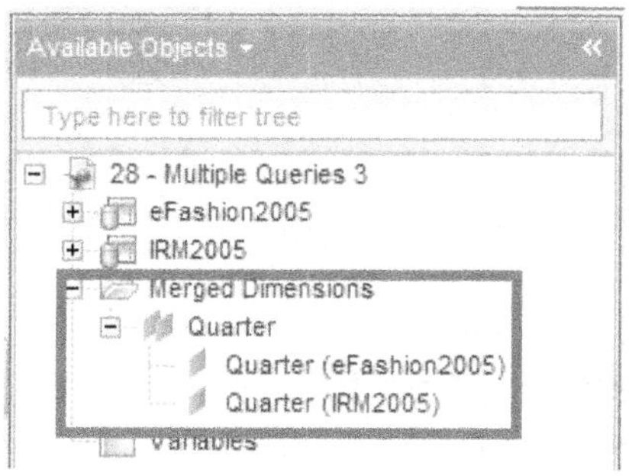
Available Objects
Type here to filter tree
28 - Multiple Queries 3
eFashion2005
IRM2005
Merged Dimensions
Quarter
Quarter (eFashion2005)
Quarter (IRM2005)
Variables

Web Intelligence adds the Merged Dimensions in the Available Objects pane within a class called 'Merged Dimensions'.

Arranged by: Alphabetic order

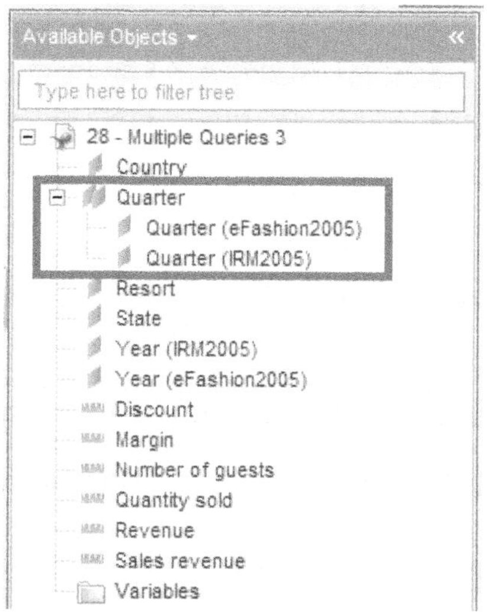
Available Objects
Type here to filter tree
28 - Multiple Queries 3
Country
Quarter
Quarter (eFashion2005)
Quarter (IRM2005)
Resort
State
Year (IRM2005)
Year (eFashion2005)
Discount
Margin
Number of guests
Quantity sold
Revenue
Sales revenue
Variables

13. Right-click on the Merged Dimension and select 'Edit Properties'.

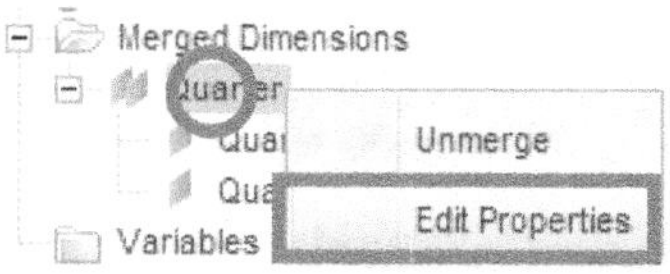
Merged Dimensions
Quarter
Variables
Unmerge
Edit Properties

14. Give the Merged Dimension a 'Name' and 'Description' (or use the default if you prefer):

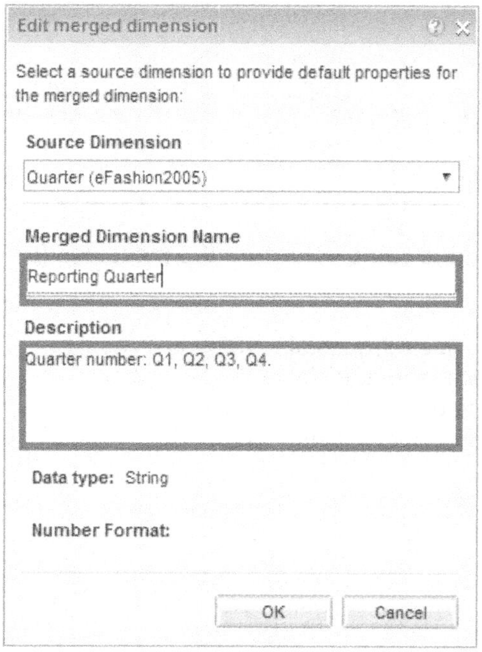
Edit merged dimension
Select a source dimension to provide default properties for the merged dimension:
Source Dimension
Quarter (eFashion2005)
Merged Dimension Name
Reporting Quarter
Description
Quarter number: Q1, Q2, Q3, Q4.
Data type: String
Number Format:
OK
Cancel

You can specify a different 'Name' and 'Description' for the Merged Dimension (as shown).

Click 'OK' to save the changes to the Merged Dimension.

15. The report tab 'Synchronised Data' now contains the correct results because Web Intelligence is synchronising the data using the values of the [Quarter] dimensions from the 2 queries.

Year	Quarter	Quantity sold	Sales revenue	Revenue	Number of guest
2005	Q1	21,135	$3,326,172	275,030	132
2005	Q2	17,152	$2,840,651	282,886	136
2005	Q3	19,224	$2,879,303	291,050	132
2005	Q4	22,344	$4,186,120	258,274	125

NOTE

If you do not see the above results after merging the [Quarter] objects... try refreshing both queries in the document.

29.4 Using Merged Dimensions with different aggregation levels

So far, our example has shown how we can use Merged Dimensions to synchronise data from different data sources, but let us now expand on this to further our understanding.

Drag the [State] object and drop it to the right of [Quarter] object in the report tab 'Synchronised Data':

Year	Quarter	State	Quantity sold	Sales revenue	Revenue	Number of guest
2005	Q1	California	4,145	$650,715	275,030	132
2005	Q1	Colorado	1,178	$189,131	275,030	132
2005	Q1	DC	1,812	$279,490	275,030	132
2005	Q1	Florida	1,095	$174,276	275,030	132
2005	Q1	Illinois	2,079	$334,297	275,030	132
2005	Q1	New York	4,248	$683,971	275,030	132
2005	Q1	Texas	6,578	$1,014,293	275,030	132
2005	Q2	California	3,184	$529,256	282,886	136
2005	Q2	Colorado	963	$157,337	282,886	136
2005	Q2	DC	1,627	$263,486	282,886	136
2005	Q2	Florida	859	$147,358	282,886	136
2005	Q2	Illinois	1,545	$254,722	282,886	136
2005	Q2	New York	4,194	$692,513	282,886	136
2005	Q2	Texas	4,780	$795,979	282,886	136

We can see that the rows in each [Quarter] are showing the same values for the measures [Revenue] and [Number of guests], i.e.:

All 'Q1' rows show [Revenue] = 275,030 and [Number of guests] = 132
All 'Q2' rows show [Revenue] = 282,886 and [Number of guests] = 136
All 'Q3' rows show [Revenue] = 291,050 and [Number of guests] = 132
All 'Q4' rows show [Revenue] = 258,274 and [Number of guests] = 125

'Q3' and 'Q4' screenshot is on next page.

2005	Q3	California	5,280	$760,442	291,050	132
2005	Q3	Colorado	1,311	$192,267	291,050	132
2005	Q3	DC	1,984	$288,926	291,050	132
2005	Q3	Florida	745	$121,314	291,050	132
2005	Q3	Illinois	1,398	$230,573	291,050	132
2005	Q3	New York	3,288	$501,220	291,050	132
2005	Q3	Texas	5,218	$784,560	291,050	132
2005	Q4	California	4,392	$842,267	258,274	125
2005	Q4	Colorado	1,248	$229,654	258,274	125
2005	Q4	DC	2,149	$383,257	258,274	125
2005	Q4	Florida	1,153	$218,301	258,274	125
2005	Q4	Illinois	1,722	$331,067	258,274	125
2005	Q4	Massachuset	902	$157,719	258,274	125
2005	Q4	New York	4,717	$885,800	258,274	125
2005	Q4	Texas	6,061	$1,138,056	258,274	125
			79,855	**$13,232,246**	**1,107,240**	**525**

In the above example, the columns [Year], [Quarter] are from 'eFashion2005' query.

So what is happening?

Well, we can see the measures [Quantity sold] and [Sales revenue] showing different values on every row because Web Intelligence knows how these values are related at the [Year], [Quarter] and [State] level. However, Web Intelligence does not know how to relate the measures [Revenue] and [Number of guests] to the combined context of [Year], [Quarter] and [State].

Therefore it uses the relationship we have defined using Merged Dimensions to display [Revenue] and [Number of guests] in the context of the dimensions being used.

In our example the defined relationship is [Quarter] only, so when we 'break' this relationship from either side then we see values from one query being repeated on multiple rows.

NOTE

In both queries, we have a single year of data (2005) and four quarters. Effectively the year is redundant, but we used it in our queries to show that we could not merge the [Year] dimensions due to the values being different.

[eFashion2005].[Year] = '2005' whereas [IRM].[Year] = 'FY2005'

The above example shows 'eFashion2005' data displayed correctly but 'IRM2005' data is repeated, whereas the next example shows 'IRM2005' data displayed correctly but 'eFashion2005' data is repeated.

Year	Quarter	Country	Quantity sold	Sales revenue	Revenue	Number of guest
FY2005	Q1	France	21,135	$3,326,172	70,400	36
FY2005	Q1	US	21,135	$3,326,172	204,630	96
FY2005	Q2	France	17,152	$2,840,651	80,050	42
FY2005	Q2	US	17,152	$2,840,651	202,836	94
FY2005	Q3	France	19,224	$2,879,303	74,960	36
FY2005	Q3	US	19,224	$2,879,303	216,090	96
FY2005	Q4	France	22,344	$4,186,120	54,900	33
FY2005	Q4	US	22,344	$4,186,120	203,374	92
			79,855	**$13,232,246**	**1,107,240**	**525**

To create the above:

1. Duplicate the report 'Synchronised Data' and rename the new report as 'Synchronised Data IRM'
2. In 'Synchronised Data IRM' remove the columns [Year], [Quarter] and [State].
3. Add in the columns [Year], [Quarter] and [Country] using the objects from 'IRM2005' query.

We now see that [Quantity sold] and [Sales revenue] cannot be displayed at [Country] level. **Why?**

Web Intelligence has no way of knowing how to distribute these measures as we have no relationship defined on the [Country] dimension between the two data providers.

If we remove the [Country] column then the data within the block corrects itself as we are at the lowest level of our relationship, i.e. at [Quarter] level.

Year	Quarter	Quantity sold	Sales revenue	Revenue	Number of guest
FY2005	Q1	21,135	$3,326,172	275,030	132
FY2005	Q2	17,152	$2,840,651	282,886	136
FY2005	Q3	19,224	$2,879,303	291,050	132
FY2005	Q4	22,344	$4,186,120	258,274	125
		79,855	**$13,232,246**	**1,107,240**	**525**

NOTE

In this example, [Year] is not having an influencing the data because we only have one year being returned in each query, and we know it is 2005 (or FY2005).

If we had multiple years being returned then we would see repeating values because the mapping should then be based on [Year] and [Quarter].

If you see repeating values when using Merged Dimensions then usually you have not 'merged' enough dimensions.

29.5 Extending Merged Dimension Values

When dimensions are merged then the defined relationships apply across the entire document. However, depending on how dimensions and measures are used will lead to different results.

1. Save the existing document with a new name.

2. Create a new report tab containing three blocks of data (as shown below). The first two blocks represent each of the two queries individually and the third block shows the combined data.

Both objects are taken from 'eFashion2005' query.

[Reporting Quarter] is the Merged Dimension.

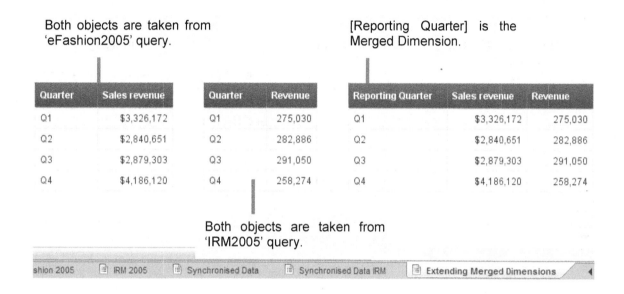

Quarter	Sales revenue
Q1	$3,326,172
Q2	$2,840,651
Q3	$2,879,303
Q4	$4,186,120

Quarter	Revenue
Q1	275,030
Q2	282,886
Q3	291,050
Q4	258,274

Reporting Quarter	Sales revenue	Revenue
Q1	$3,326,172	275,030
Q2	$2,840,651	282,886
Q3	$2,879,303	291,050
Q4	$4,186,120	258,274

Both objects are taken from 'IRM2005' query.

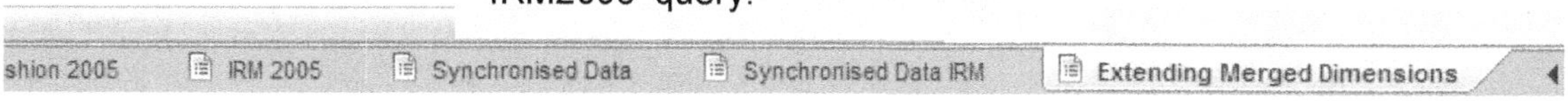
shion 2005
IRM 2005
Synchronised Data
Synchronised Data IRM
Extending Merged Dimensions

3. To demonstrate the behaviour of Merged Dimensions we will now modify our queries as follows:

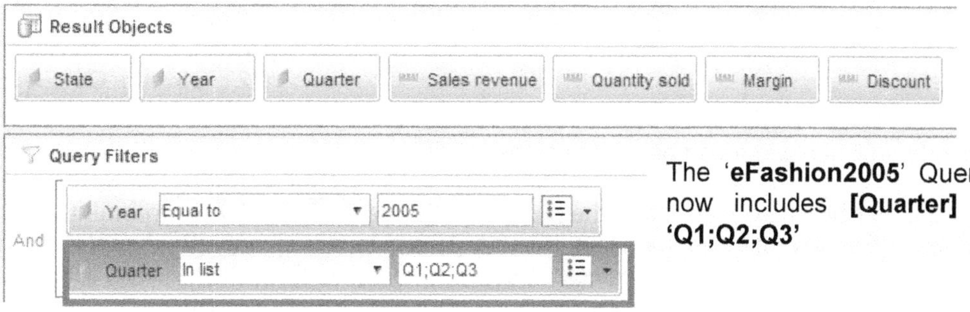
Result Objects
State
Year
Quarter
Sales revenue
Quantity sold
Margin
Discount
Query Filters
And
Year
Equal to
2005
Quarter
In list
Q1;Q2;Q3

The '**eFashion2005**' Query Filter now includes **[Quarter] In list 'Q1;Q2;Q3'**

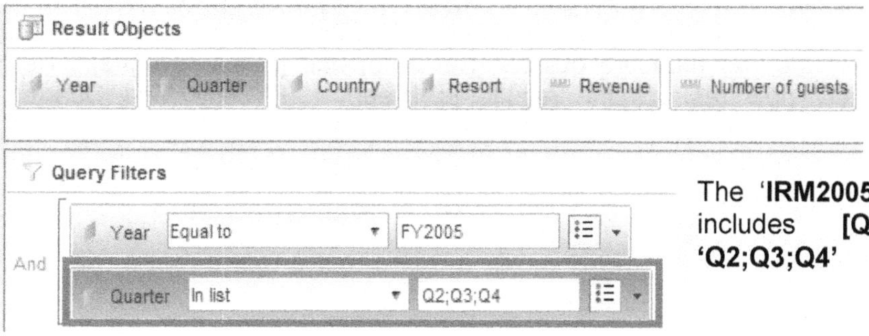
Result Objects
Year
Quarter
Country
Resort
Revenue
Number of guests
Query Filters
And
Year
Equal to
FY2005
Quarter
In list
Q2;Q3;Q4

The '**IRM2005**' Query Filter now includes **[Quarter] In list 'Q2;Q3;Q4'**

4. Run the queries and the 'Extending Merged Dimensions' report tab now displays:

Quarter	Sales revenue
Q1	$3,326,172
Q2	$2,840,651
Q3	$2,879,303

Quarter	Revenue
Q2	282,886
Q3	291,050
Q4	258,274

Reporting Quarter	Sales revenue	Revenue
Q1	$3,326,172	
Q2	$2,840,651	282,886
Q3	$2,879,303	291,050
Q4	Discontinued	258,274

The above results confirm what we expect from the two queries concerning the [Quarter] dimensions.

[eFashion2005].[Quarter] Values	[IRM2005].[Quarter] Values	[Reporting Quarter]
Q1		The Merged Dimension [Reporting Quarter] contains values from both queries therefore it shows Q1, Q2, Q3 and Q4.
Q2	Q2	
Q3	Q3	
	Q4	

5. Adding [Revenue] to the first block and [Sales revenue] to the second block gives:

Quarter	Sales revenue	Revenue
Q1	$3,326,172	
Q2	$2,840,651	282,886
Q3	$2,879,303	291,050

[Revenue] for 'Q4' is missing.

Quarter	Revenue	Sales revenue
Q2	282,886	$2,840,651
Q3	291,050	$2,879,303
Q4	258,274	Discontinued

[Sales Revenue] for 'Q1' is missing.

Reporting Quarter	Sales revenue	Revenue
Q1	$3,326,172	
Q2	$2,840,651	282,886
Q3	$2,879,303	291,050
Q4	Discontinued	258,274

[Sales revenue] is shown against 'Q1', 'Q2' and Q3'.

[Revenue] is shown against 'Q2', 'Q3' and 'Q4'.

The reason for this behaviour can be explained as

1. In the first block we have used the dimension [eFashion2005].[Quarter] and its values are used to display the two measure objects [Sales revenue] and [Revenue]. Remember 'eFashion2005' query now restricts the results to [Year] = '2005' and [Quarter] In list 'Q1;Q2;Q3'.

2. In the second block we have used the dimension [IRM2005].[Quarter] and its values are used to display the two measure objects [Revenue] and [Sales revenue]. Remember 'IRM2005' query now restricts the results to [Year] = 'FY2005' and Quarter In list 'Q2;Q3;Q4'.

We can change the behaviour of dimensions that have been merged so they always display the full range of values from the merged data providers.

6. Click on 'Properties – Document'.

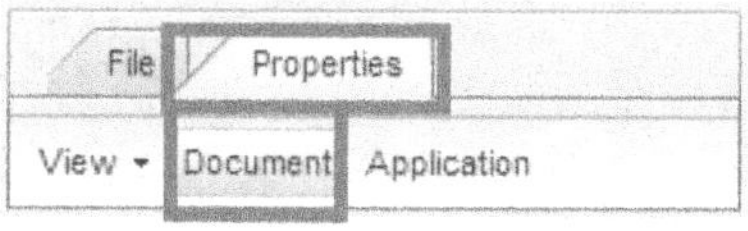
File
Properties
View
Document
Application

7. Tick 'Extend merged dimension values' and click 'OK'.

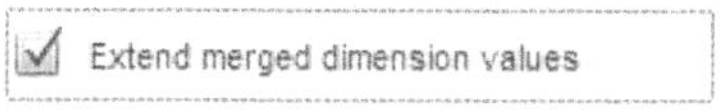
Extend merged dimension values

All three blocks now show the same results for the two measures.

Quarter	Sales revenue	Revenue
Q1	$3,326,172	
Q2	$2,840,651	282,886
Q3	$2,879,303	291,050
Q4	Discontinued	258,274

Quarter	Revenue	Sales revenue
Q1		$3,326,172
Q2	282,886	$2,840,651
Q3	291,050	$2,879,303
Q4	258,274	Discontinued

Reporting Quarter	Sales revenue	Revenue
Q1	$3,326,172	
Q2	$2,840,651	282,886
Q3	$2,879,303	291,050
Q4	Discontinued	258,274

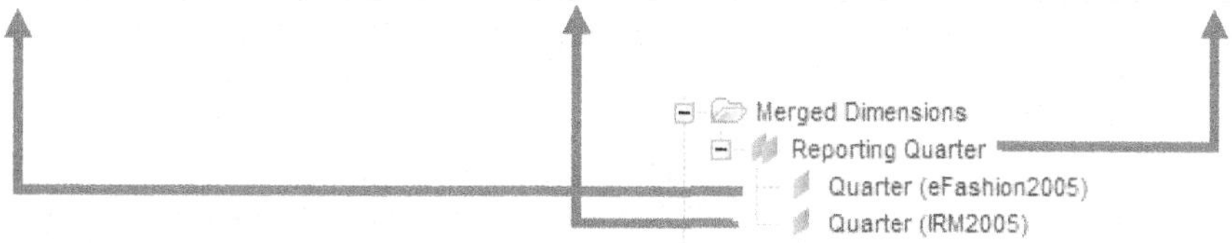
Merged Dimensions
Reporting Quarter
Quarter (eFashion2005)
Quarter (IRM2005)

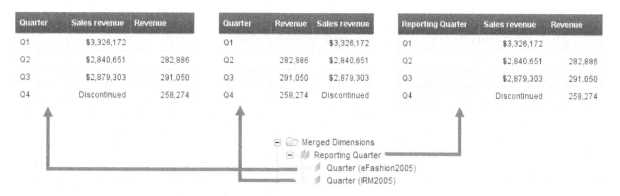

When the property 'Extend merged dimension values' is used (i.e. is ticked) then combining measures from multiple data providers will cause the source dimensions to behave like Merged Dimensions.

'Extend merged dimension values' only works with source dimensions that form part of a Merged Dimension relationship.

i.e. if we add the object [eFashion2005].[Year] into the first block then we effectively undo the 'Extend merged dimension values' (even though it is ticked) for this block

Year	Quarter	Sales revenue	Revenue
2005	Q1	$3,326,172	
2005	Q2	$2,840,651	282,886
2005	Q3	$2,879,303	291,050

Quarter	Revenue	Sales revenue
Q1		$3,326,172
Q2	282,886	$2,840,651
Q3	291,050	$2,879,303
Q4	258,274	Discontinued

Reporting Quarter	Sales revenue	Revenue
Q1	$3,326,172	
Q2	$2,840,651	282,886
Q3	$2,879,303	291,050
Q4	Discontinued	258,274

8. Save your document.

29.6 Automatic Merging of Dimensions

Web Intelligence can automatically merge dimensions under the following conditions:

1. The dimensions have the same name
2. The dimensions are of the same data type
3. The dimensions are from the same universe

If you create a second query using an existing universe in the document then **Auto-merge dimensions** will merge the dimensions.

If you want to use this functionality then **set** the 'Auto-merge dimensions' property before you create multiple queries (but after the first query).

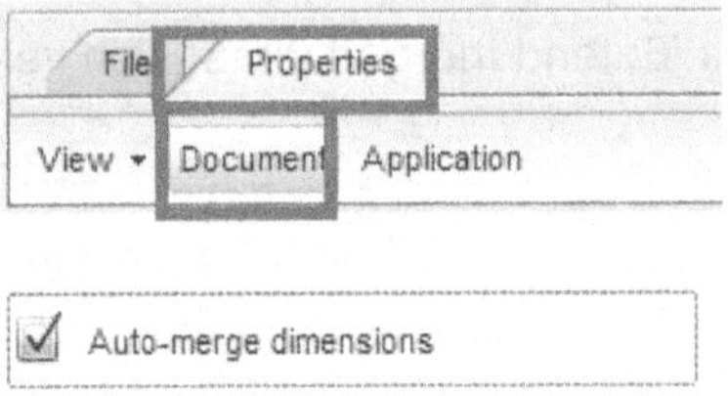
File
Properties
View
Document
Application
Auto-merge dimensions

29.7 Deleting and Editing Merged Dimensions

Merged Dimensions can be edited or deleted (unmerged) by right-clicking on the Merged Dimension and then selecting the relevant action.

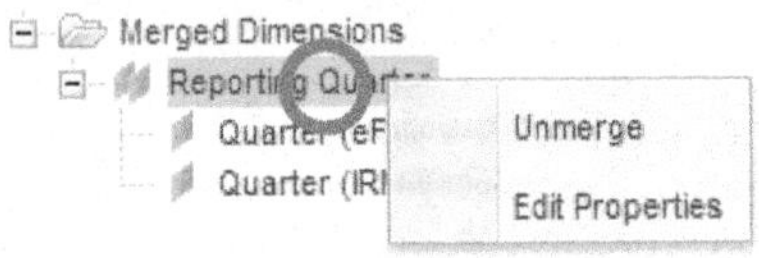
Merged Dimensions
Unmerge
Edit Properties

Selecting '**Edit Properties**' will display the 'Edit merged dimension' interface.

Selecting '**Unmerge**' will request a confirmation. If '**Yes**' is clicked then the Merged Dimension will be deleted (unmerged).

29.8 Forcing Calculations by using the ForceMerge() Function

Web Intelligence will not use merged dimension relationships in calculations if the merged dimensions do not actually appear in the calculation context.

Let us demonstrate this by creating a new document with the following two queries from the 'eFashion' universe:

1. Create the first query 'Sales' as shown below but do not run it:

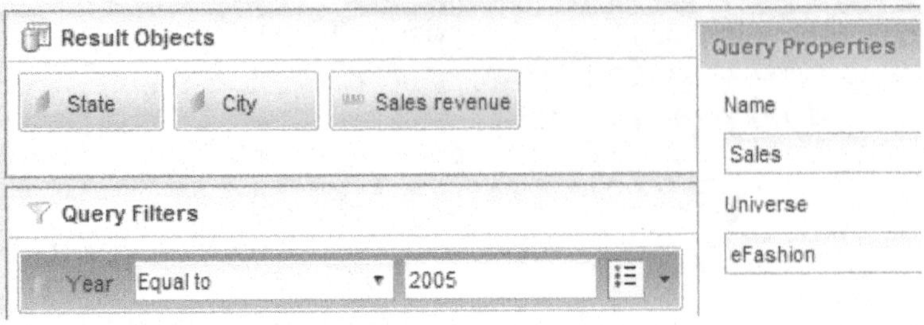
Result Objects
State
City
Sales revenue
Query Filters
Year
Equal to
2005
Query Properties
Name
Sales
Universe
eFashion

2. Select 'Add Query – From Universe'.

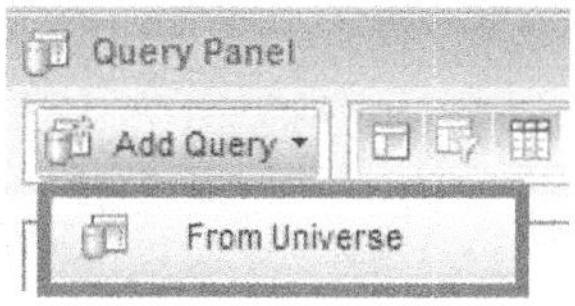
Query Panel
Add Query
From Universe

3. Create the second query 'Discounts' as shown below and run it:

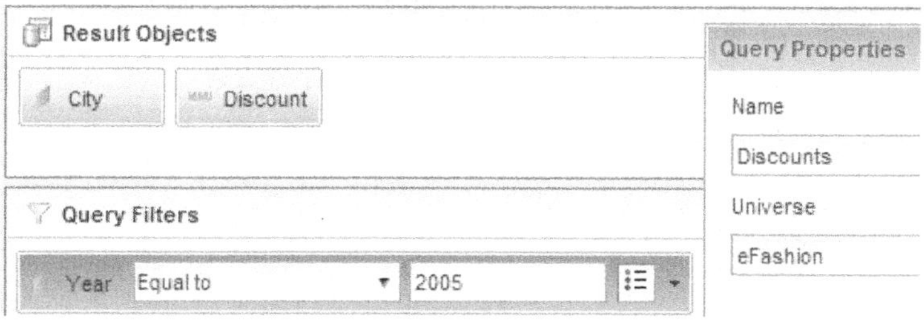
Result Objects
City
Discount
Query Filters
Year
Equal to
2005
Query Properties
Name
Discounts
Universe
eFashion

4. Run the queries and Web Intelligence will display two blocks of data (one for each query).

State	City	Sales revenu
California	Los Angeles	$1,581,616
California	San Francisc	$1,201,064
Colorado	Colorado Spr	$768,390
DC	Washington	$1,215,158
Florida	Miami	$661,250
Illinois	Chicago	$1,150,659
Massachuset	Boston	$157,719
New York	New York	$2,763,503
Texas	Austin	$1,003,071
Texas	Dallas	$739,369
Texas	Houston	$1,990,449

City	Discount
Austin	$63,825
Boston	$46,521
Chicago	$26,987
Colorado Spr	$89,015
Dallas	$100,816
Houston	$45,550
Los Angeles	$252,923
Miami	$13,989
New York	$61,577
San Francisc	$141,401
Washington	$178,653

5. Manually merge the [City] dimension from both queries as shown here:

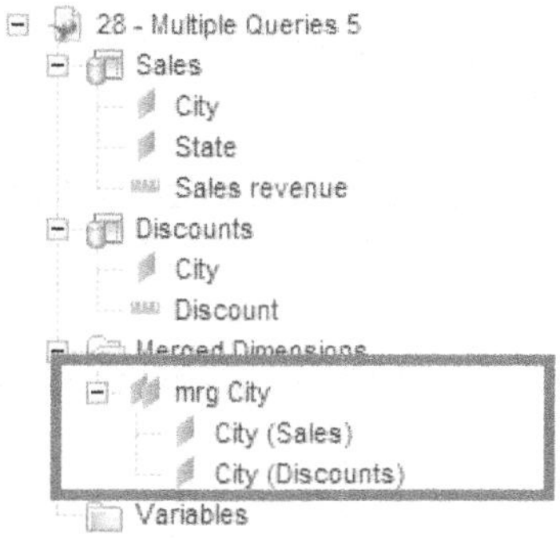
28 - Multiple Queries 5
Sales
City
State
Sales revenue
Discounts
City
Discount
Merged Dimensions
mrg City
City (Sales)
City (Discounts)
Variables

6. Create a report tab called 'Merged' to combine data for the two queries using [State], [Sales revenue] and [Discount] objects.

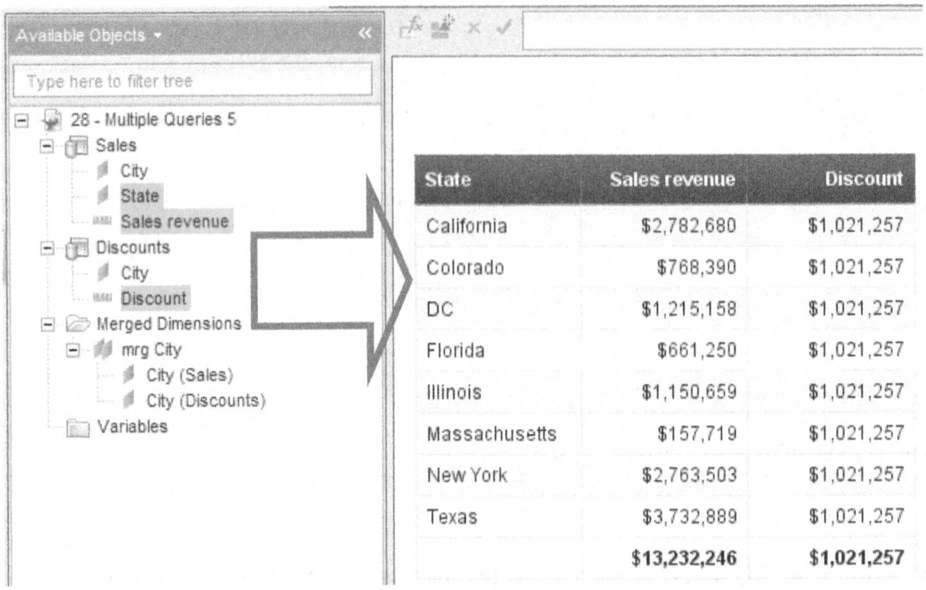
Available Objects
Type here to filter tree
28 - Multiple Queries 5
Sales
City
State
Sales revenue
Discounts
City
Discount
Merged Dimensions
mrg City
City (Sales)
City (Discounts)
Variables

State	Sales revenue	Discount
California	$2,782,680	$1,021,257
Colorado	$768,390	$1,021,257
DC	$1,215,158	$1,021,257
Florida	$661,250	$1,021,257
Illinois	$1,150,659	$1,021,257
Massachusetts	$157,719	$1,021,257
New York	$2,763,503	$1,021,257
Texas	$3,732,889	$1,021,257
	$13,232,246	**$1,021,257**

The merged dimension [City] does not appear in the table, therefore Web Intelligence does not take the relationship into account when displaying [Discount].

Web Intelligence lists the total [Discount] in the second data provider against each [State] value.

7. To display the correct result, replace [Discount] in the third column with the formula:

=ForceMerge([Discount])

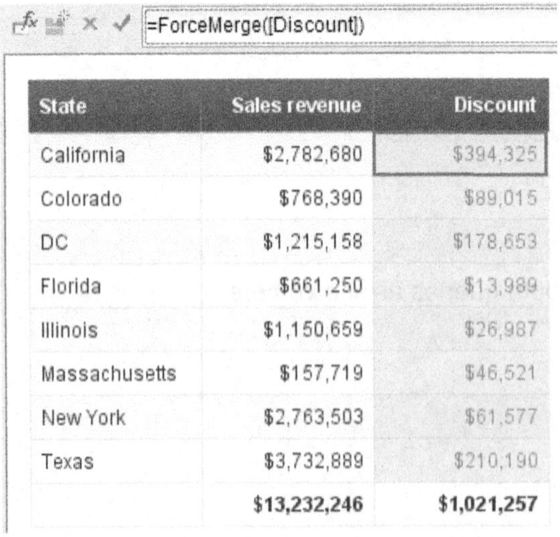
=ForceMerge([Discount])

State	Sales revenue	Discount
California	$2,782,680	$394,325
Colorado	$768,390	$89,015
DC	$1,215,158	$178,653
Florida	$661,250	$13,989
Illinois	$1,150,659	$26,987
Massachusetts	$157,719	$46,521
New York	$2,763,503	$61,577
Texas	$3,732,889	$210,190
	$13,232,246	**$1,021,257**

Discount for California = $394,325 (to zero decimal place)

This is calculated by summing up the values of [Discount] for the cities:

Los Angeles = $252,923
and
San Francisco = $141,401

Likewise other [State] values can be checked by using the 'Discounts' tab to add together [Discount] values for relevant cities.

Web Intelligence has now used the Merged Dimension [mrg City] to relate [Discounts].[City] to [Sales].[City] in order to distribute [Discount] correctly.

29.9 Other Notes on Merged Dimensions

Some other points of note when working with Merged Dimensions.

29.9.1 Incompatible Dimension Objects

28 - Multiple Queries 5
Sales
City
State
Year
Sales revenue
Discounts
City
Discount
Variables

When a dimension object is selected in a document containing multiple queries then you might see other objects becoming 'dimmed'.

i.e. we have selected the object [Discounts].[City]

and the dimensions of the query 'Sales' have become dimmed.

Web Intelligence is indicating that these objects cannot be used together in a single block because no relationship has been defined for them.

However we can select incompatible dimension objects if we want to as shown here:

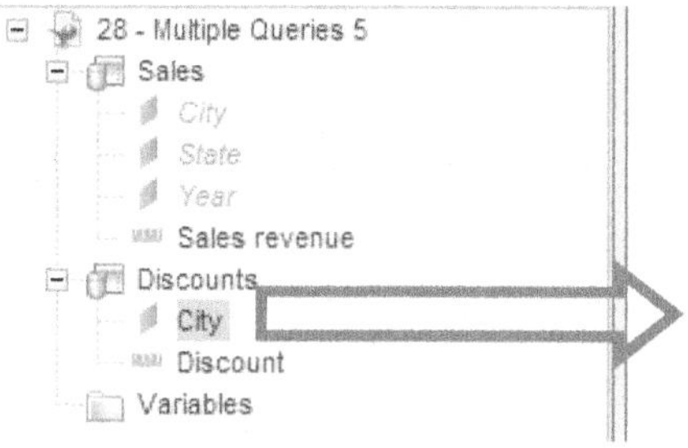
28 - Multiple Queries 5
Sales
City
State
Year
Sales revenue
Discounts
City
Discount
Variables

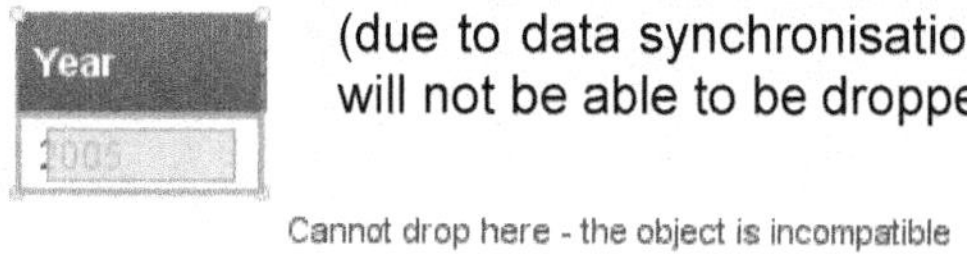
Year
Cannot drop here - the object is incompatible

If an incompatible object is dragged into an existing block and it cannot be used by Web Intelligence (due to data synchronisation issues) then the object will not be able to be dropped into place.

NOTE

Measures can generally be used anywhere in documents containing multiple queries, however without the correct use of Merged Dimensions we have seen that measures will suffer from aggregation issues.

29.9.2 Using Merged Dimensions in Documents

We have described the main purpose of Merged Dimensions, i.e. to obtain relationships between multiple data providers.

Once created, Merged Dimensions behave like normal dimension objects and you can use them very much in the same way (i.e. apply filters, create sections/breaks, use in tables, charts, cells, variables and formulas, etc).

30 Web Intelligence Rich Client

Web Intelligence Rich Client is a locally installed Microsoft Windows application. When installed it lets you work with Web Intelligence (WID) documents that are stored locally or in your SAP BusinessObjects Enterprise repository.

Web Intelligence Rich Client is based on the Web Intelligence Java Report panel and offers the same functionality in addition to being able to work with documents locally.

Some of the reasons for using Web Intelligence Rich Client to work with WID documents are:

a. You cannot connect to the repository but want to work with Web Intelligence documents (for example, whilst travelling).

b. Server response times for WID documents containing large quantities of data (and/or formulas) can be slow, but these can be overcome by using Web Intelligence Rich Client as it performs calculations locally.

c. You have a slow network and want to work with documents locally and only connect to the repository when needed (rather than be connected all the time).

d. You want to work with WID documents but you do not have an enterprise setup (i.e. do not have a repository).

30.1 Installing Web Intelligence Rich Client

The software can be installed in one of two ways:

1. Use the SAP BusinessObjects Enterprise BI 4.x CDs.

2. Install from BI Launch Pad:

   a. Using BI Launch Pad Preferences for Web Intelligence, you can install using the button below.

   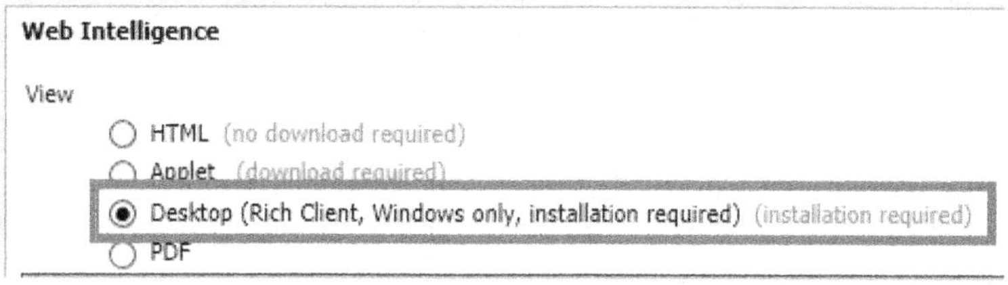
   Web Intelligence
View
HTML (no download required)
Applet (download required)
Desktop (Rich Client, Windows only, installation required) (installation required)
PDF

   If you do not have access to the '(installation required)' link then:

   b. Select 'Desktop' as the default creation/editing tool and Web Intelligence Rich Client will automatically be installed when you Web Intelligence for the first time from BI Launch Pad.

NOTE

If you install Web Intelligence Rich Client from BI Launch Pad, the Web Intelligence Rich Client online help system is not installed to your local computer.

If you work in Connected Mode (see below), Web Intelligence Rich Client can display help pages stored on the server. If you work in Offline or Standalone mode, the help pages are not available.

30.2 Working Modes of Web Intelligence Rich Client

Web Intelligence Rich Client can operate in three different modes of connectivity:

30.2.1 Connected Mode

In this mode, you specify a SAP BusinessObjects Enterprise repository to which Web Intelligence Rich Client should connect to and then you can work with repository documents or with local documents (secured and unsecured).

Depending on your security rights, you can do the following:

- import documents from the repository
- import universes from the repository
- open local documents
- create documents
- edit documents
- refresh documents
- save documents locally
- export documents to the repository

You can use Connected Mode in one of two ways:

1. When you are in BI Launch Pad and you launch 'Web Intelligence' then Web Intelligence Rich Client will be launched (only if you specify 'Desktop' as your preferred default creation/editing tool).

   In this scenario, Web Intelligence Rich Client logs into the repository using your existing session, therefore you do not have to supply any login details.

   All communication is routed through the repository therefore you do not need to have any other software installed on your local machine for communicating with databases etc.

2. When you use Web Intelligence Rich Client by opening it like any other program in Windows then you have to supply log in details. In this scenario, you need to have the relevant database client software installed on your local machine in order to communicate with the databases.

30.2.2 Offline Mode

In this mode, Web Intelligence Rich Client is not connected to the repository, but the same security rights are applied.

Before using Offline Mode you must have connected to a repository in Connected Mode at least once. This enables Web Intelligence Rich Client to download the repository security information to your local machine. You can then use Offline Mode and the security will be applied using the local security file.

Security rights in Offline Mode

As explained above, when you connect Web Intelligence Rich Client to each repository (you might have many repositories) then the security information for each repository is downloaded to your local machine.

Every document and universe downloaded from a repository also contains an access control list to identify groups and users who have access to it. In Offline Mode, Web Intelligence Rich Client applies the same security as Connected Mode by matching the access rights in each document (or universe) against the locally stored security file.

Example:

A document was downloaded to your local machine (by another user) but you do not have access to open this document in the repository. You will not be able to open the local copy of the document.

In Offline Mode, you can work with local documents and universes that are secured by the repository that you log in to, or with unsecured local documents and universes.

Depending on your security rights:

You can do the following:

- open local documents
- edit local documents
- save documents locally

You can also do the following but require local universes and a local connection server:

- refresh local documents
- create local documents

You cannot:

- import documents to a repository
- export documents to a repository

NOTE – In Offline Mode it is highly likely that access to databases will also not be possible, therefore most users would be using Offline Mode to Open, Edit and Save local documents. However, if your SAP BusinessObjects server is down but you are still able to connect to your network and your databases then working in Offline Mode could be used to refresh data.

30.2.3 Standalone Mode

In this mode, Web Intelligence Rich Client is not connected to a repository and no security is enforced. You can only work with unsecured local documents and universes.

You can do the following:

- open local documents
- create local documents
- edit local documents
- refresh local documents
- save local documents

To do the above:

- All relevant software needs to be installed on your local machine for communicating with databases, such as Oracle Client, SQL Server Client Tools, etc.
- You also need local copies of universes that must be distributed to you by Universe Designers.
- You need to have the relevant connection parameters set up in the local universes to enable retrieval of data from databases.

You cannot import or export (documents and universes) to a repository in Standalone Mode as this mode is designed to be used without a repository.

30.2.4 Recommendations on Connection Modes

The benefits of Web Intelligence and Web Intelligence Rich Client are really achieved when documents and universes are stored in a repository, i.e. security, sharing, scheduling, publishing, etc.

Therefore it is highly likely that the Standalone Mode will only be useful for very small setups where the management of documents and universes can be tracked without a central repository.

The benefits of Web Intelligence Rich Client are either:

1. Working in Connected Mode (very much like Web Intelligence) but enabling the local machine to perform the 'number crunching' instead of on the server.

2. Working in Offline Mode to Open, Edit and Save documents that have been previously imported from a repository using Connected Mode. When possible it would be best to re-establish Connected Mode and export any changes back to the repository.

We recommend either of the above two as they make use of a repository with the added flexibility of working locally when required (e.g. when travelling).

30.3 Launching Web Intelligence Rich Client

Web Intelligence Rich Client can be launched to operate in any of its three different modes of connectivity:

- Connected Mode
- Offline Mode
- Standalone Mode

Multiple instances of Web Intelligence Rich Client can be run simultaneously in any connection mode and each instance can be connected to a different repository (if required).

The repository connection status and the current working mode are displayed in the status bar in the lower right hand side of the Web Intelligence Rich Client window.

30.3.1 Launching Web Intelligence Rich Client from BI Launch Pad

This only takes place if you have specified 'Desktop' as your preferred tool for creating and editing WID documents.

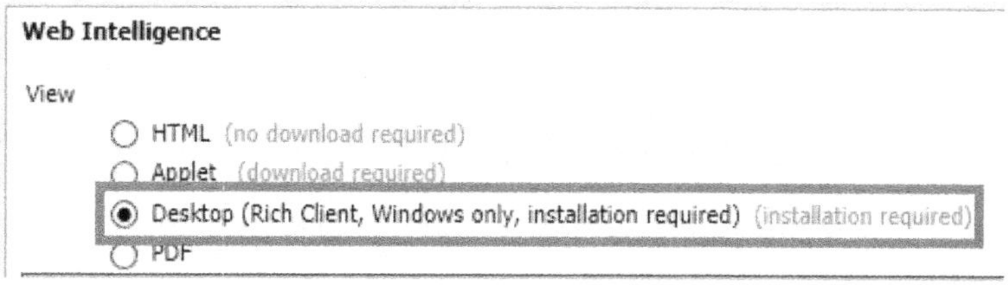
Web Intelligence
View
HTML (no download required)
Applet (download required)
Desktop (Rich Client, Windows only, installation required) (installation required)
PDF

1. Log In to BI Launch Pad.

2. Click on the Web Intelligence icon.

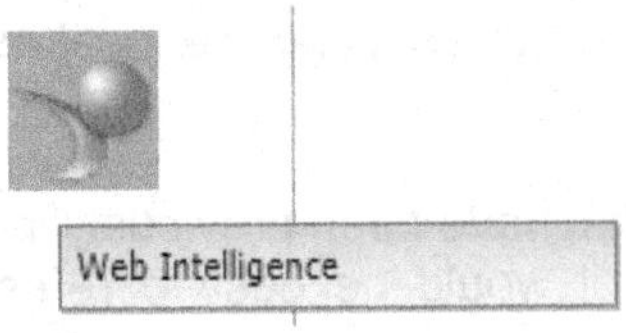
Web Intelligence

3. Web Intelligence Rich Client will be launched.

NOTES

- If Web Intelligence Rich Client is not installed on your local machine then an install will be attempted.
- If 'Desktop' is your preferred creating and editing tool then Web Intelligence Rich Client will also be launched when you edit a WID document.
- If Web Intelligence Rich Client was already running on your local machine then a new instance will be launched for the document you want to work with.

30.3.2 Launching Web Intelligence Rich Client Locally in Connected Mode

For this mode:

- Web Intelligence Rich Client needs to have already been installed on the local machine.
- You must have connected at least once to the repository you want to use via BI Launch Pad (see 'Launching Web Intelligence Rich Client from BI Launch Pad' above) or you need to specify the name of your repository server (known as the CMS) in the 'System:' box in Web Intelligence Rich Client log on screen.
- You need the relevant database client software to directly communicate with databases from the local machine.

To launch in Connected Mode locally:

1. Start the Web Intelligence Rich Client program using any of the following:

   a. Double clicking on a WID file (if you have associated the WID file to Web Intelligence Rich Client in Windows Explorer).

   b. Locating the program in Windows (under SAP Business Intelligence).

   c. Double clicking on a desktop shortcut.

2. Specify the following details:

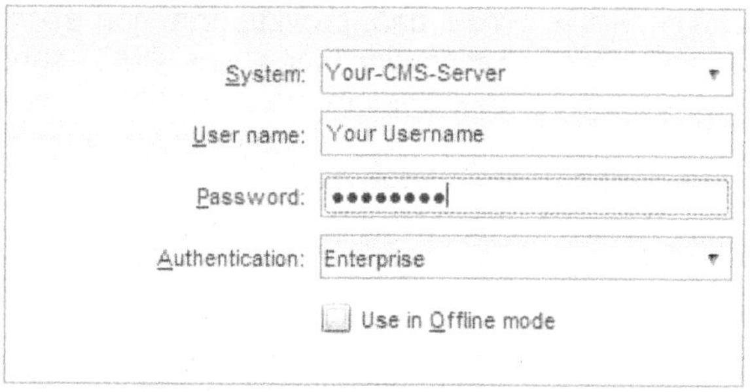
System: Your-CMS-Server
User name: Your Username
Password: ••••••••
Authentication: Enterprise
Use in Offline mode

- On the very first login to each sever you need to provide the name of your repository (known as CMS) server in the 'System' box.
- You need to provide your 'User name' and 'Password'.
- You also need to select an 'Authentication' mode used by your organisation.
- Do not select 'Standalone' when attempting to establish a Connected Mode of operation.
- Do not select 'Use in Offline Mode'.

3. Click 'Log On' after supplying your details.

4. You are now logged in to Web Intelligence Rich Client using Connected Mode.

   Status Bar shows 
Connected
 to signify Connected Mode.

30.3.3 Launching Web Intelligence Rich Client Locally in Offline Mode

For this mode:

- Web Intelligence Rich Client needs to have already been installed on the local machine.
- You must have connected at least once to the repository you want to use via BI Launch Pad because in Offline Mode you can work with previously downloaded documents and universes.
- You need the relevant database client software to directly communicate with databases from the local machine.

<u>To launch in Offline Mode locally:</u>

1. Start the Web Intelligence Rich Client program using any of the following:
   a. Double clicking on a WID file (if you have associated the WID file to Web Intelligence Rich Client in Windows Explorer).
   b. Locating the program in Windows (under SAP Business Intelligence).
   c. Double clicking on a desktop shortcut.

2. Specify the following details:

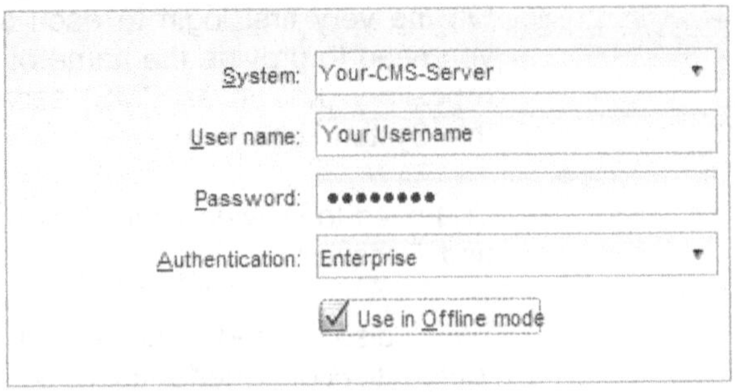
System:
Your-CMS-Server
User name:
Your Username
Password:
••••••••
Authentication:
Enterprise
Use in Offline mode

- You can provide the name of your repository (known as CMS) server in the 'System' box, or you can select a CMS you have previously logged into.
- You need to provide your 'User name' and 'Password'.
- You also need to select an 'Authentication' mode used by your organisation.
- Do not select 'Standalone' when attempting to establish an Offline Mode of operation.
- Select 'Use in Offline Mode'.

3. Click 'Log On' after supplying your details.

4. You are now logged in to Web Intelligence Rich Client using Offline Mode.

Status Bar shows 
Disconnected

Title Bar shows 
Web Intelligence Rich Client -
Disconnected (Offline)]

Offline Mode enables you to:

- Create a new document based using universes or local data sources (such as text files, excel files, etc).
- Open a local document.

But you cannot import documents from the repository as you are in Offline Mode, however the security permissions are being implemented from a local security file.

30.3.4 Launching Web Intelligence Rich Client Locally in Standalone Mode

For this mode:

- Web Intelligence Rich Client needs to have already been installed on the local machine.
- You need the relevant database client software to directly communicate with databases from the local machine.
- You cannot work with any secured documents or universes that have been previously imported from a repository using Connected Mode.

<u>To launch in Standalone Mode locally:</u>

1. Start the Web Intelligence Rich Client program using any of the following:

    a. Double clicking on a WID file (if you have associated the WID file to Web Intelligence Rich Client in Windows Explorer).

    b. Locating the program in Windows (under SAP Business Intelligence).

    c. Double clicking on a desktop shortcut.

2. Specify the following details:

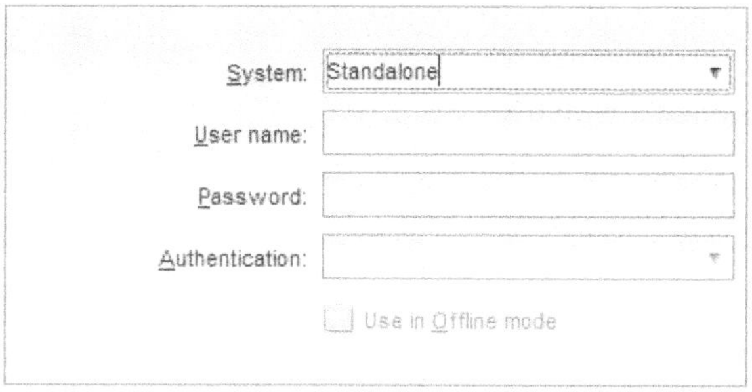
System:
Standalone
User name:
Password:
Authentication:
Use in Offline mode

- Select 'Standalone' as the 'Authentication' type.
- All other options will disable automatically when you select 'Standalone'.

3. Click 'Log On'.

4. You are now logged in to Web Intelligence Rich Client using Standalone Mode.

Status Bar shows 
Disconnected
to signify Standalone Mode.

Standalone Mode enables you to:

- Create a new document based using universes or local data sources (such as text files, excel files, etc).
- Open a local document.

But you cannot import documents from the repository as you are in Standalone Mode.

30.4 Using 'Login As…' in Web Intelligence Rich Client

If Web Intelligence Rich Client is already running then you can change the logged on user by:

1. Save any changes to current work (if necessary).

2. Select the menu 'Web Intelligence – Login as…'

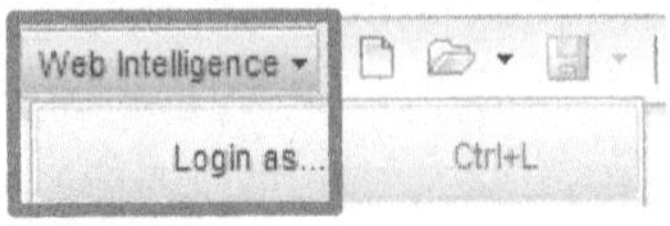
Web Intelligence
Login as...
Ctrl+L

3. Confirm you want to log off as the current user.

4. Provide details of new user and select authentication mode.

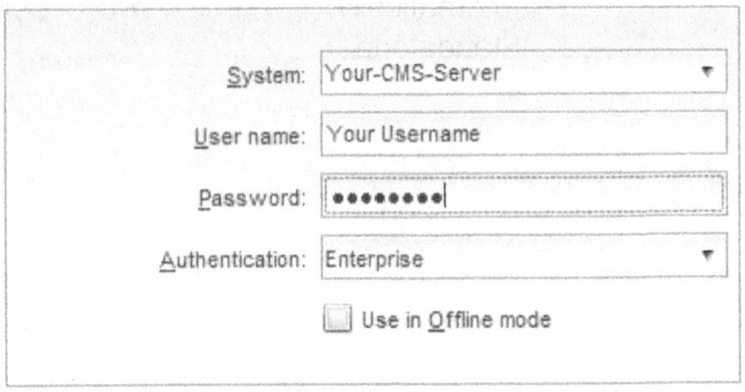
System:
Your-CMS-Server
User name:
Your Username
Password:
Authentication:
Enterprise
Use in Offline mode

5. Click 'OK' to login as the new user.

30.5 Setting User Preferences in Web Intelligence Rich Client

Web Intelligence preferences are set using BI Launch Pad preferences and are therefore stored on the server, whereas Web Intelligence Rich Client user Options are set and stored locally (per machine).

To set options use the 'Tools' menu:

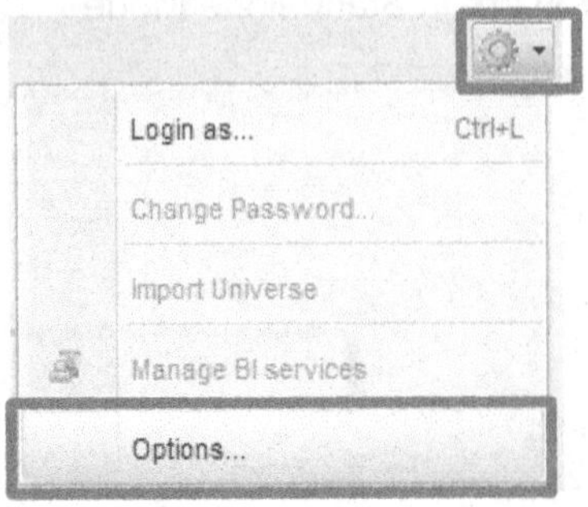
Login as...
Ctrl+L
Change Password...
Import Universe
Manage BI services
Options...

30.5.1 General Settings

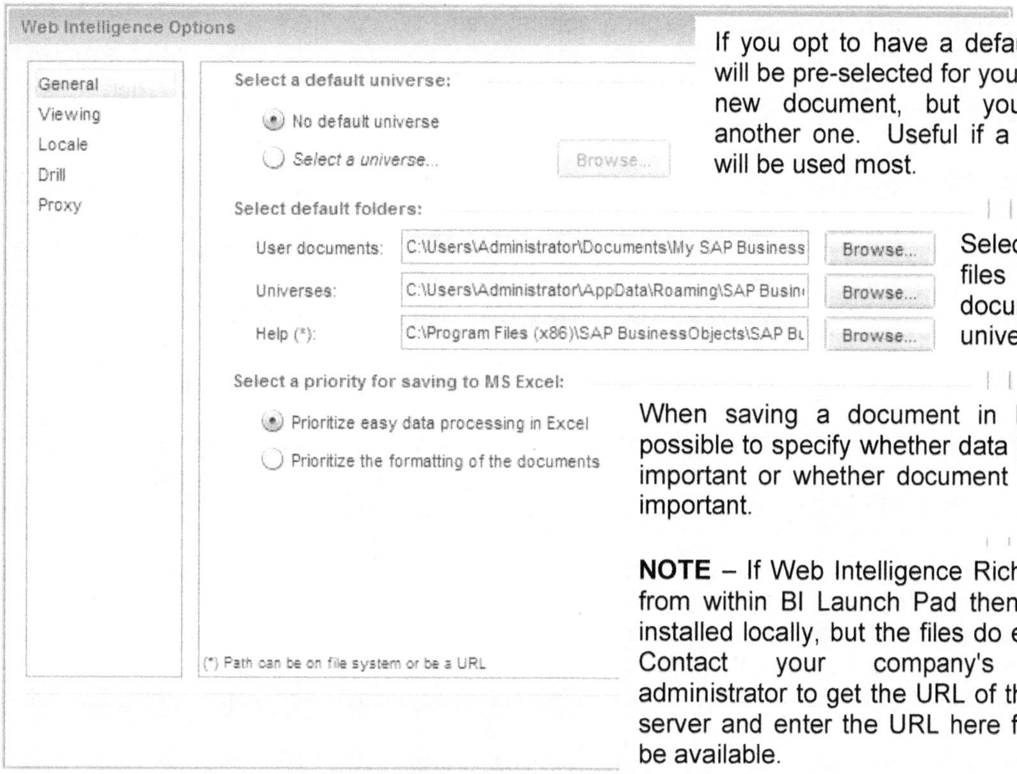
Web Intelligence Options
General
Viewing
Locale
Drill
Proxy
Select a default universe:
No default universe
Select a universe...
Browse...
Select default folders:
User documents:
C:\Users\Administrator\Documents\My SAP Business
Browse...
Universes:
C:\Users\Administrator\AppData\Roaming\SAP Busin
Browse...
Help (*):
C:\Program Files (x86)\SAP BusinessObjects\SAP Bu
Browse...
Select a priority for saving to MS Excel:
Prioritize easy data processing in Excel
Prioritize the formatting of the documents
(*) Path can be on file system or be a URL

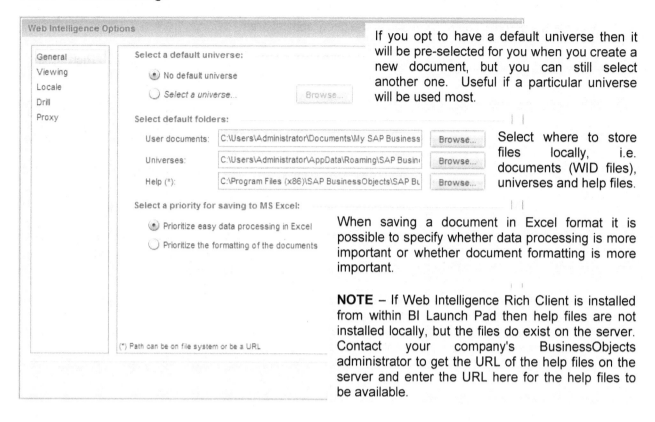

If you opt to have a default universe then it will be pre-selected for you when you create a new document, but you can still select another one. Useful if a particular universe will be used most.

Select where to store files locally, i.e. documents (WID files), universes and help files.

When saving a document in Excel format it is possible to specify whether data processing is more important or whether document formatting is more important.

NOTE – If Web Intelligence Rich Client is installed from within BI Launch Pad then help files are not installed locally, but the files do exist on the server. Contact your company's BusinessObjects administrator to get the URL of the help files on the server and enter the URL here for the help files to be available.

30.5.2 Viewing Options

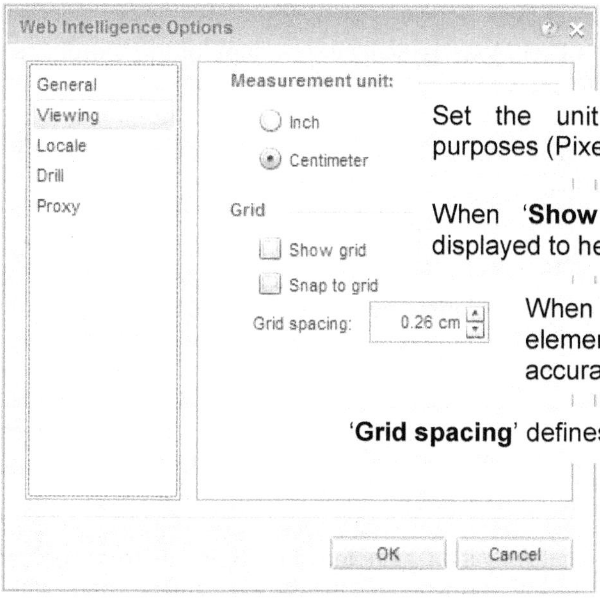
Web Intelligence Options
General
Viewing
Locale
Drill
Proxy
Measurement unit:
Inch
Centimeter
Grid
Show grid
Snap to grid
Grid spacing:
0.26 cm
OK
Cancel

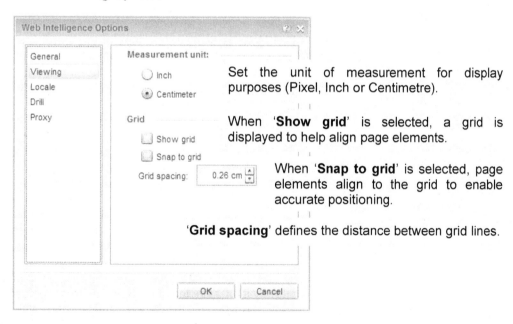

Set the unit of measurement for display purposes (Pixel, Inch or Centimetre).

When '**Show grid**' is selected, a grid is displayed to help align page elements.

When '**Snap to grid**' is selected, page elements align to the grid to enable accurate positioning.

'**Grid spacing**' defines the distance between grid lines.

30.5.3 Locale Options

A locale is a combination of language and a geographical area.

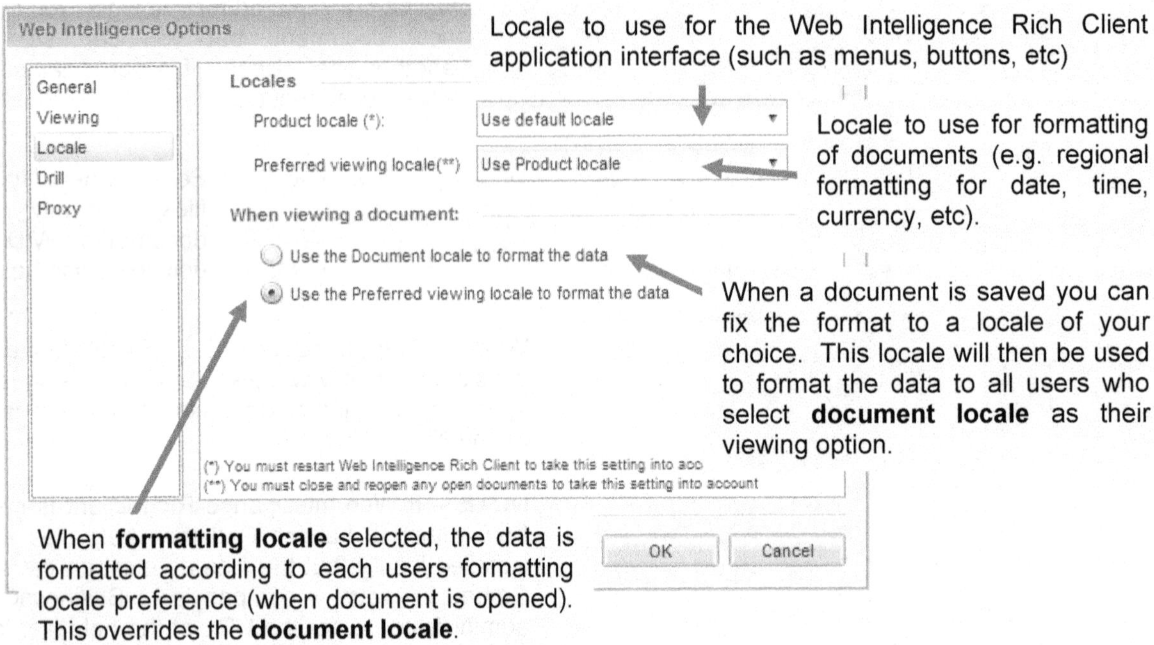
Web Intelligence Options
General
Viewing
Locale
Drill
Proxy
Locales
Product locale (*):
Use default locale
Preferred viewing locale(**)
Use Product locale
When viewing a document:
Use the Document locale to format the data
Use the Preferred viewing locale to format the data
(*) You must restart Web Intelligence Rich Client to take this setting into acc
(**) You must close and reopen any open documents to take this setting into account
OK
Cancel
Locale to use for the Web Intelligence Rich Client application interface (such as menus, buttons, etc)
Locale to use for formatting of documents (e.g. regional formatting for date, time, currency, etc).
When a document is saved you can fix the format to a locale of your choice. This locale will then be used to format the data to all users who select document locale as their viewing option.
When formatting locale selected, the data is formatted according to each users formatting locale preference (when document is opened). This overrides the document locale.

30.5.4 Drilling Options

Settings for Web Intelligence Rich Client to use when in Drill Mode.

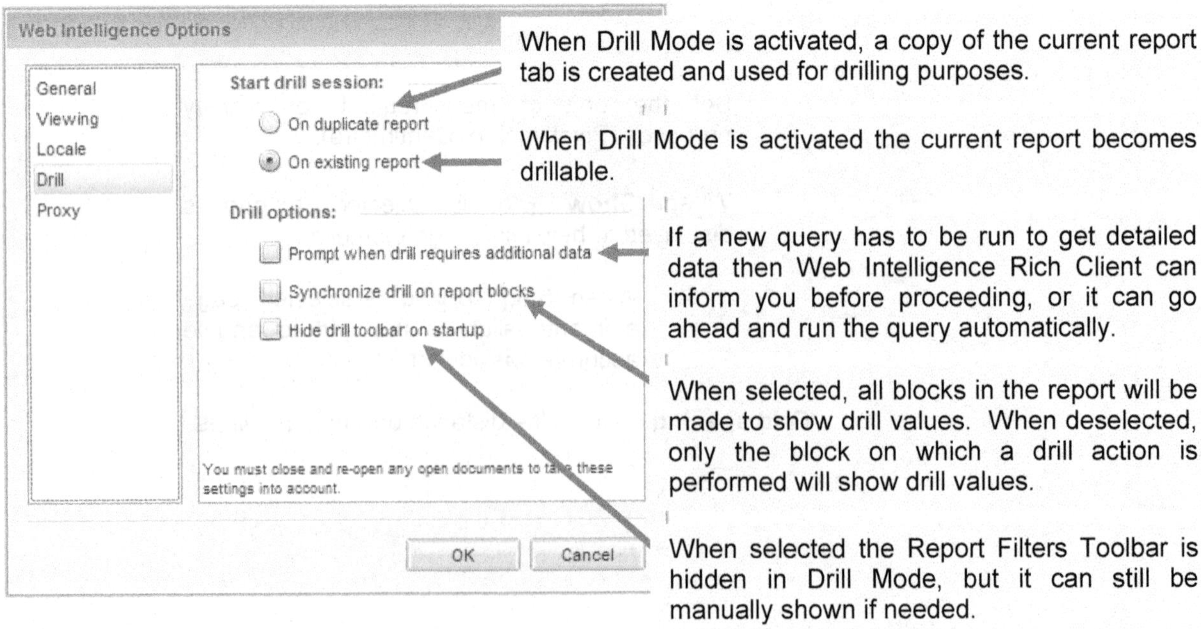
Web Intelligence Options
General
Viewing
Locale
Drill
Proxy
Start drill session:
On duplicate report
On existing report
Drill options:
Prompt when drill requires additional data
Synchronize drill on report blocks
Hide drill toolbar on startup
You must close and re-open any open documents to take these settings into account.
OK
Cancel
When Drill Mode is activated, a copy of the current report tab is created and used for drilling purposes.
When Drill Mode is activated the current report becomes drillable.
If a new query has to be run to get detailed data then Web Intelligence Rich Client can inform you before proceeding, or it can go ahead and run the query automatically.
When selected, all blocks in the report will be made to show drill values. When deselected, only the block on which a drill action is performed will show drill values.
When selected the Report Filters Toolbar is hidden in Drill Mode, but it can still be manually shown if needed.

30.5.5 Proxy Settings

Proxy Settings for Web Intelligence Rich Client to use.

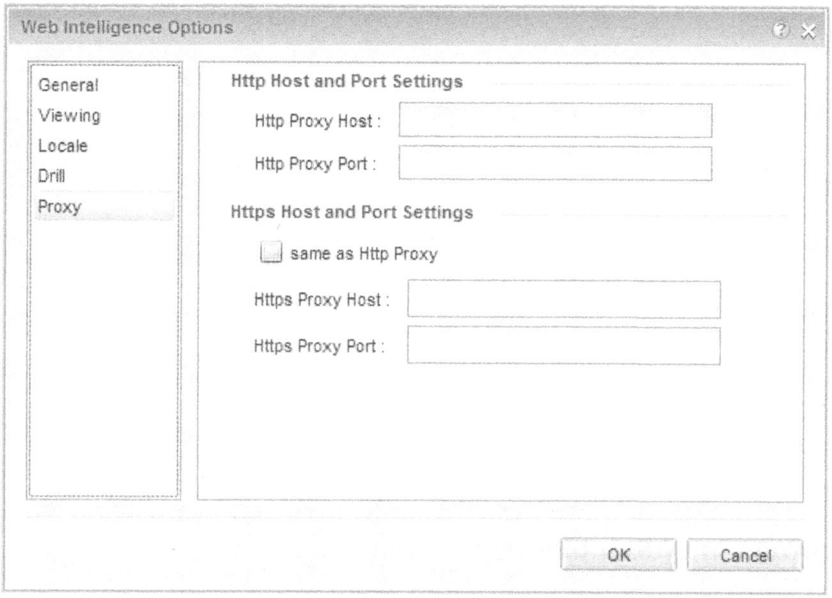
Web Intelligence Options
General
Viewing
Locale
Drill
Proxy
Http Host and Port Settings
Http Proxy Host :
Http Proxy Port :
Https Host and Port Settings
same as Http Proxy
Https Proxy Host :
Https Proxy Port :
OK
Cancel

30.6 Changing BI Launch Pad Password from Web Intelligence Rich Client

In Web Intelligence Rich Client, you can change the password you use to for BI Launch Pad and Web Intelligence Rich Client.

Use the menu '**Tools – Change Password…**'

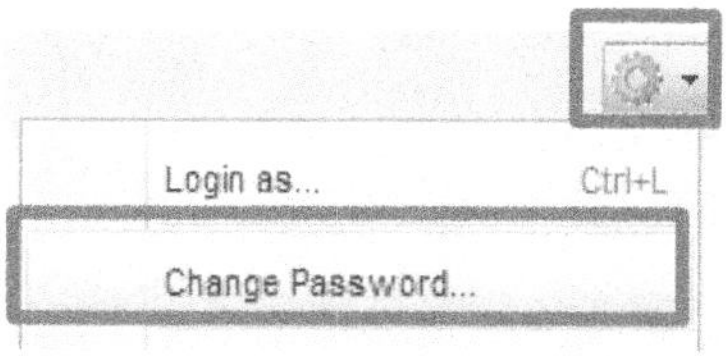
Login as...
Ctrl+L
Change Password...

NOTES:

1. You must be in Connected Mode in order to change your password.

2. You must have launched the Web Intelligence Rich Client application locally and not from within BI Launch Pad.

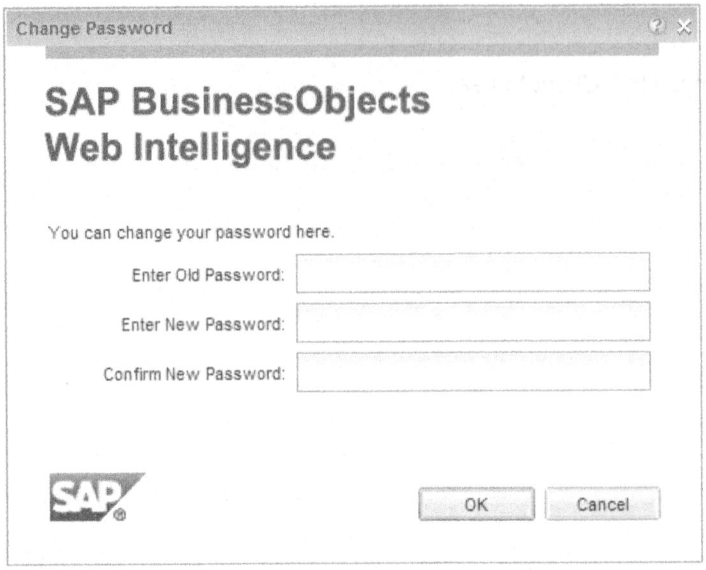
Change Password
SAP BusinessObjects
Web Intelligence
You can change your password here.
Enter Old Password:
Enter New Password:
Confirm New Password:
OK
Cancel

To change your password:

1. Provide your existing password.
2. Type a new password.
3. Type the new password again for validation purposes.
4. Click 'OK' to confirm the change of your password.

30.7 Working with Universes in Web Intelligence Rich Client

We have already discussed the purpose of universes and how they are used by Web Intelligence to generate the SQL in order to retrieve data from your databases.

Web Intelligence always uses universes from the repository you log into, but Web Intelligence Rich Client can also use local universes depending on the Connection Mode you are using.

We will describe further the use of universes in the session on 'Working with Documents in Web Intelligence Rich Client'.

31 Working with Documents in Web Intelligence Rich Client

This session demonstrates working with documents using Web Intelligence Rich Client.

31.1 Working in Connected Mode

You must have logged in using Connected Mode (per repository) at least once before Offline Mode can be used against that repository, therefore we will start with an example using Connected Mode.

1. Launch Web Intelligence Rich Client from Windows:

    a. Provide your System name (i.e. repository to connect to). Your BusinessObjects Administrator will be able to provide you with the necessary details.

    b. Provide your Log On credentials (not needed if using Single Sign-On).

    c. Select an Authentication mode.

NOTE

If you are unable to provide a System name then you can get Web Intelligence Rich Client from BI Launch Pad.

1. Log On to BI Launch Pad
2. Change your preference for '**default creation/editing tool**' to '**Desktop**'.
3. Launch Web Intelligence and this will launch Web Intelligence Rich Client.

This CMS will then be available for you to select from the drop-down box for 'System' the next time you launch Web Intelligence Rich Client.

IMPORTANT – If you will be also using Web Intelligence then change your preference for '**default creation/editing tool**' back to '**Advanced**' in order to use the Java interface. If you do not revert this setting then Web Intelligence Rich Client will be launched instead of Web Intelligence.

2. Click on 'Universe' to create a new Web Intelligence document using a Universe

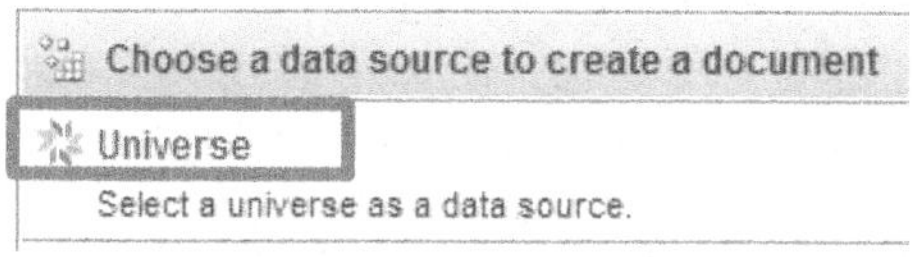
Choose a data source to create a document
Universe
Select a universe as a data source.

3. Select 'eFashion' universe.

    The universe will be imported from the repository to your local machine.

4. Create the following query (name it as '**qryActualRevenue**').

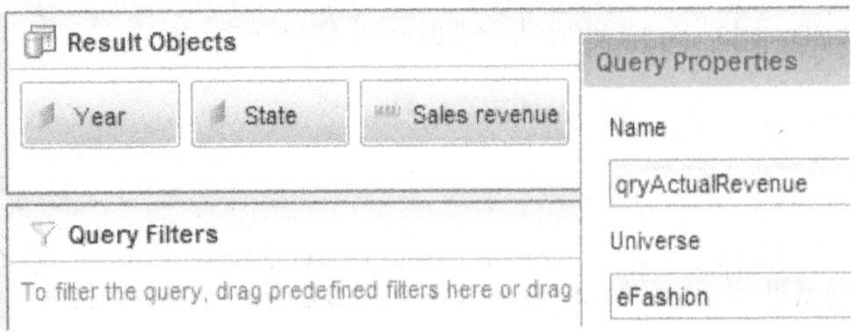
Result Objects
Year
State
Sales revenue
Query Properties
Name
qryActualRevenue
Universe
eFashion
Query Filters
To filter the query, drag predefined filters here or drag

5. Run the query and name the report tab '**Actual Sales**'.

6. Click on '**Save**' button to save the document with the name '**WIRC – Actual Sales**'.

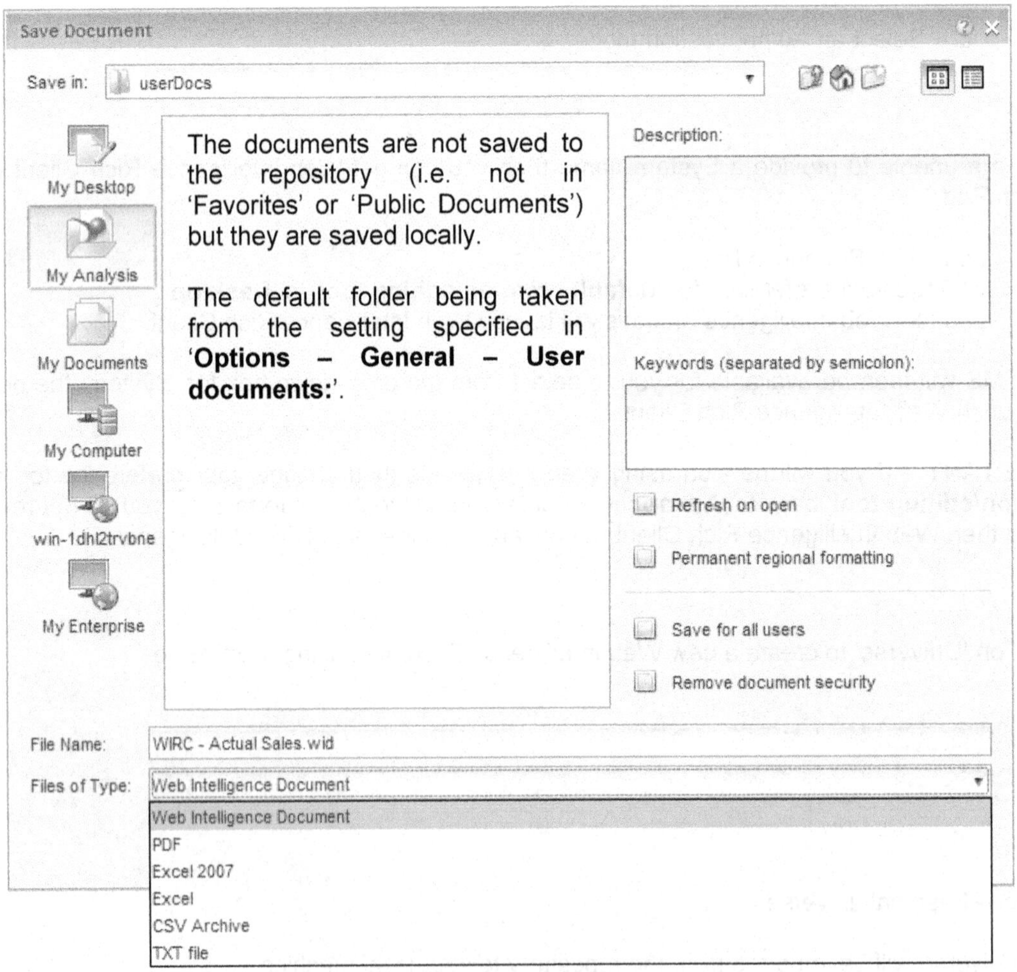
Save Document
Save in:
userDocs
My Desktop
My Analysis
My Documents
My Computer
win-1dhl2trvbne
My Enterprise
The documents are not saved to the repository (i.e. not in 'Favorites' or 'Public Documents') but they are saved locally.
The default folder being taken from the setting specified in 'Options – General – User documents:'.
Description:
Keywords (separated by semicolon):
Refresh on open
Permanent regional formatting
Save for all users
Remove document security
File Name:
WIRC - Actual Sales.wid
Files of Type:
Web Intelligence Document
Web Intelligence Document
PDF
Excel 2007
Excel
CSV Archive
TXT file

By default the documents will be saved as Web Intelligence (or WID) files but you can also save files in different formats.

The other options are:

Option	Description
Refresh on open	Document will be automatically refreshed when opened.
Permanent regional formatting	Locale of the current machine is applied to the document and will be used on any machine it is opened on.
Save for all users	All document security is removed and document can be opened in Standalone Mode.
Remove document security	If 'Save for all users' is also checked then this option is overridden. When checked only the current user can open the document in Connected or Offline modes.

7. Close your Web Intelligence Rich Client document by using 'Close' (top right-hand corner), or pressing the keys <CTRL> + <F4> together.

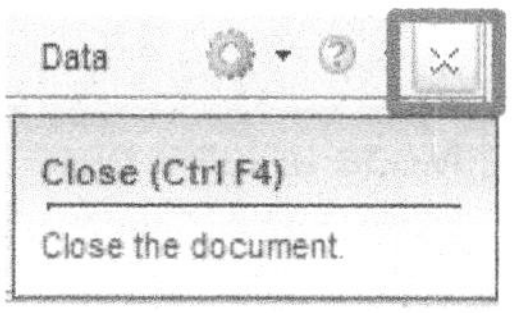
Data
Close (Ctrl F4)
Close the document.

31.2 Exiting / Closing Web Intelligence Rich Client

After you have saved your work you will want to exit/close Web Intelligence Rich Client itself.

1. Select 'Exit' from the main menu or press the keys <ALT> + <F4> together.

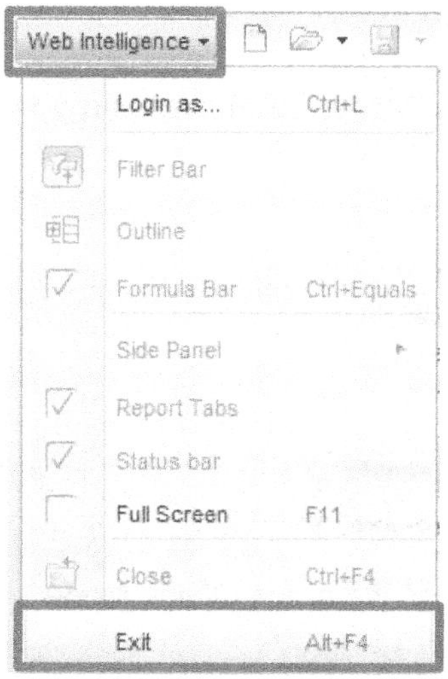
Web Intelligence
Login as... Ctrl+L
Filter Bar
Outline
Formula Bar Ctrl+Equals
Side Panel
Report Tabs
Status bar
Full Screen F11
Close Ctrl+F4
Exit Alt+F4

2. Web Intelligence Rich Client will 'close' but keep running in the 'background' as you will be given the following message:

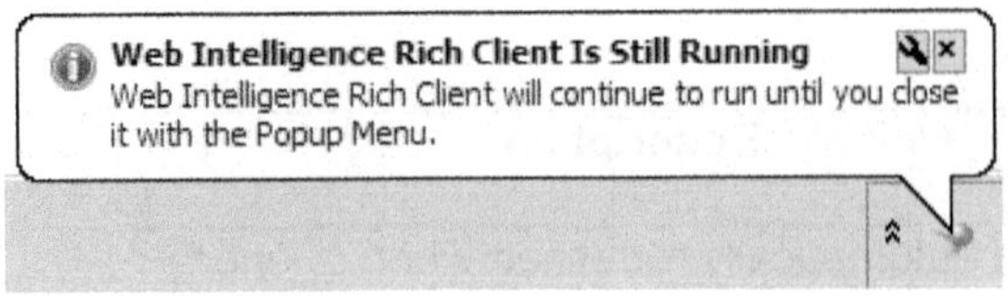
Web Intelligence Rich Client Is Still Running
Web Intelligence Rich Client will continue to run until you close it with the Popup Menu.

3. To exit Web Intelligence Rich Client completely, right-click on the Windows Notification Area Icon for Web Intelligence Rich Client and select 'Quit'.

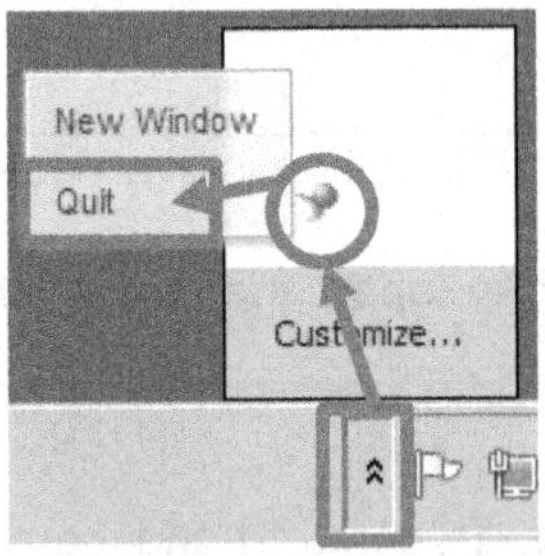
New Window
Quit

31.3 Working in Offline Mode

Offline Mode can only be used with a repository if you have used Connected Mode at least once (to the repository) in order to create a local security file from the CMS.

We have used Connected Mode and have saved a document locally, so it should now be available in Offline Mode.

1. Exit any existing sessions of Web Intelligence Rich Client completely.

2. Launch Web Intelligence Rich Client from Windows.

3. Connect against the same repository as we used for Connected Mode, but make sure you select 'Use in Offline Mode'.

   NOTE – You need to supply User Name and Password.

4. Click on the menu '**File**' to reveal:

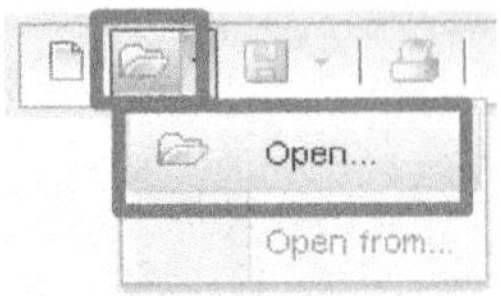
Open...
Open from...

'**Open...**' will enable you to browse for documents.

'**Open from...**' is disabled because we are in Offline Mode.

Or you can use the 'Recent Documents' list:

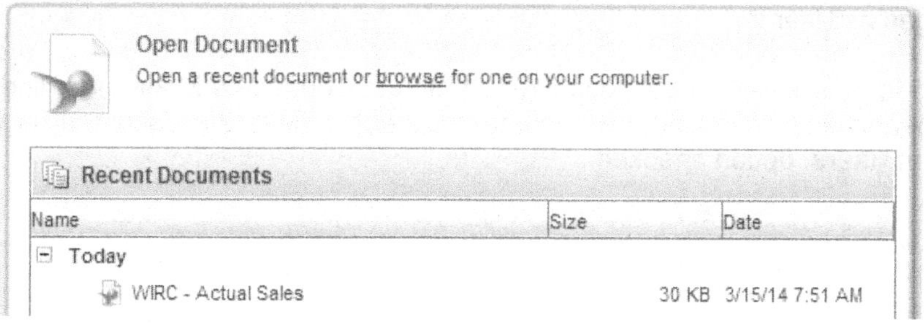
Open Document
Open a recent document or browse for one on your computer.
Recent Documents
Name
Size
Date
Today
WIRC - Actual Sales
30 KB
3/15/14 7:51 AM

5. Open the document '**WIRC – Actual Sales**' that we saved in Connected Mode.

   We have now opened a document locally using the security profile that was created on the local machine when we used Connected Mode.

6. Click on the '**Refresh Data**' button to try and refresh the document.

   If the local machine has the necessary 'middleware' installed then the document will be refreshed as Web Intelligence Rich Client will be able to communicate with the database platform you are using (such as Oracle, SQL Server, etc).

   In this case 'middleware' refers to the software programs required to communicate to your database platform (i.e. database client software, drivers, ODBC connections, etc).

   If you are totally disconnected from your network and using Web Intelligence Rich Client in Offline Mode then you will not be able to refresh documents because you will not have access to your databases.

7. You can make changes to queries and save the document. However, just like the previous point, you will only be able to refresh queries if you have the necessary middleware installed to communicate with your databases.

8. You can make formatting and other changes (variables, extra report tabs, etc) to the document and save it.

9. Close and Exit Web Intelligence Rich Client completely.

   NOTE

   If a different user logs on in Offline Mode and tries to open a local document then the document will not open until the local security file has been updated to allow access to the particular document.

   Example:

   - User 1 creates a new document in Connected Mode and saves the file locally.

- User 2 then logs on using Connected Mode and attempts to open the local document created by User 1. The document will not open, even if User 2 has the same access privileges as User 1.

The reason for this is that a new document created in Connected Mode or Offline Mode can only be opened and edited by the document creator, unless the document is saved with '**Save for all users**' option checked.

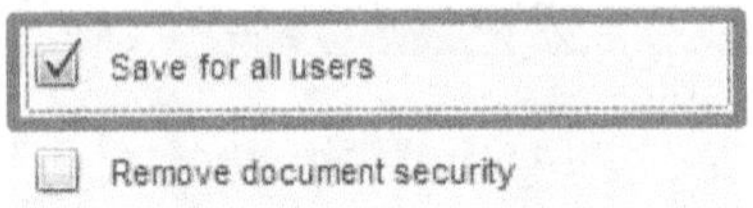
Save for all users
Remove document security

When the document is added to the repository and saved to a folder that other users have access to then those users will also be able to open the local document.

We use the '**Save to Enterprise...**' menu to move local documents into a repository (discussed later).

31.4 Working in Standalone Mode

Only unsecured documents and universes can be opened and used in Standalone Mode, therefore any documents and universes that are associated to a repository cannot be used.

31.4.1 Opening Documents in Standalone Mode

Let us demonstrate this using our example document '**WIRC – Actual Sales**'.

1. Launch Web Intelligence Rich Client in Standalone mode.

2. Try and open the document '**WIRC – Actual Sales**'.

   You will not be able to open the document as it has been saved with built-in security, due to having been created in Connected Mode (same applies to Offline Mode).

   So how do we make the document unsecured?

3. Use the menu '**Web Intelligence – Login as...**' and log on into your CMS in Connected Mode (or Offline Mode).

4. You will now be able to open the document '**WIRC – Actual Sales**' because the document security is being matched against the local security file and you have permissions to use this document (because you created it).

5. Use '**Save as...**' and resave the document but make sure the option '**Remove document security**' is checked.

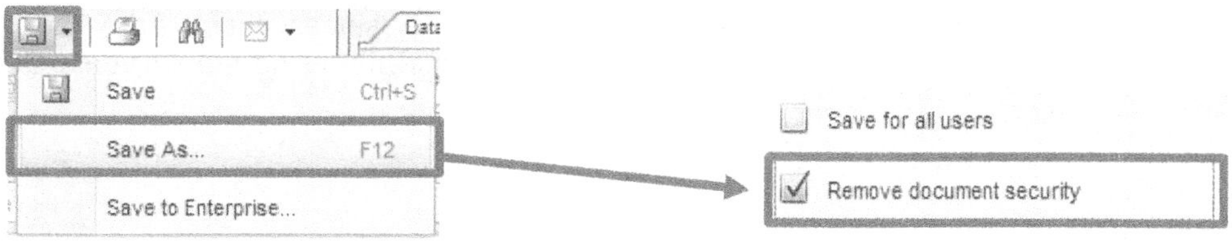
Save
Ctrl+S
Save As...
F12
Save to Enterprise...
Save for all users
Remove document security

6. Close and Exit Web Intelligence Rich Client completely.

7. Use the menu '**Web Intelligence – Login as...**' and log on into your CMS in Standalone Mode.

8. You will now be able to open the document '**WIRC – Actual Sales**' because the document security has been removed.

9. Close and Exit the application completely.

NOTE

All the necessary middleware for communicating with your database platforms needs to be installed on every machine that will be used to refresh documents in Offline Mode (i.e. database client software, drivers, ODBC connections, etc).

Security cannot exist on documents in order to open them in Standalone Mode, therefore if the documents have been created in Connected Mode or Offline Mode then the documents have to be saved with '**Save for all users**' option checked.

If the documents have been created in Standalone Mode then they will not have any built-in security.

31.4.2 Creating Documents using Universes in Standalone Mode

Let us demonstrate this using our example document '**WIRC – Actual Sales**'.

1. Launch Web Intelligence Rich Client in '**Standalone**' mode.

2. Create a new document using a Universe.

   No universes are available to use so you will be asked to connect to a repository.

3. Click on '**Cancel**' to cancel the creation of the document.

4. Close and Exit the application completely.

The only way to use universes in Standalone Mode is to have unsecured universes placed in the folder specified in the '**Options... - Universes:**' setting.

The universes can be placed in this folder by you or by your BusinessObjects Administrator, but they have to be unsecured. Universe can be made unsecure by using the Universe Designer product.

NOTES

a. If you do use Web Intelligence Rich Client in Standalone Mode then it is essential to use the latest versions of universes to ensure you are working with the latest functionality of your universes. This could prove to be a difficult task to manage if universes are stored locally per machine.

   One way to overcome this is to use a folder on your network to access unsecured universes because only one place will need to be updated (instead of many machines), but you will only have access to the universes when you are connected to your network.

b. All the necessary middleware for communicating with your database platforms needs to be installed on every machine that will be used for Web Intelligence Rich Client in Standalone Mode (i.e. database client software, drivers, ODBC connections, etc).

31.5 Exporting Local Documents to a Repository

If you are using Web Intelligence Rich Client in an enterprise implementation (i.e. use of a repository) then you will want to export documents from local machines to the repository for use in BI Launch Pad and Web Intelligence.

We have created the document '**WIRC – Actual Sales**' using Web Intelligence Rich Client and we will now use it to discuss exporting of documents.

1. Launch Web Intelligence Rich Client and make sure you are in '**Connected Mode**' because you can only export documents when you are connected to a repository.

2. Open the document 'WIRC – Actual Sales'.

3. Select '**Save to Enterprise...**'

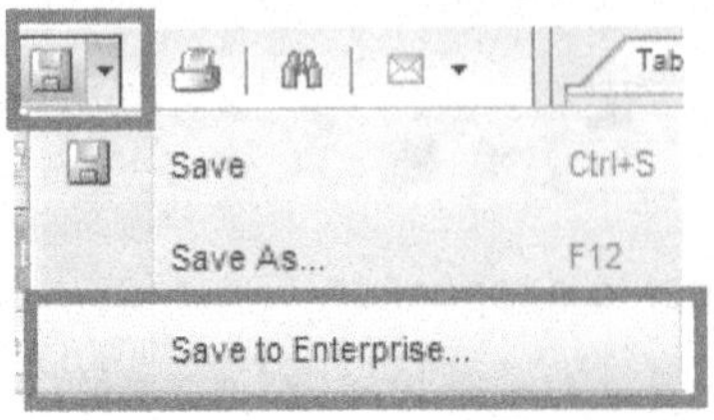
Tab
Save
Ctrl+S
Save As...
F12
Save to Enterprise...

4. The 'Save Document' interface opens:

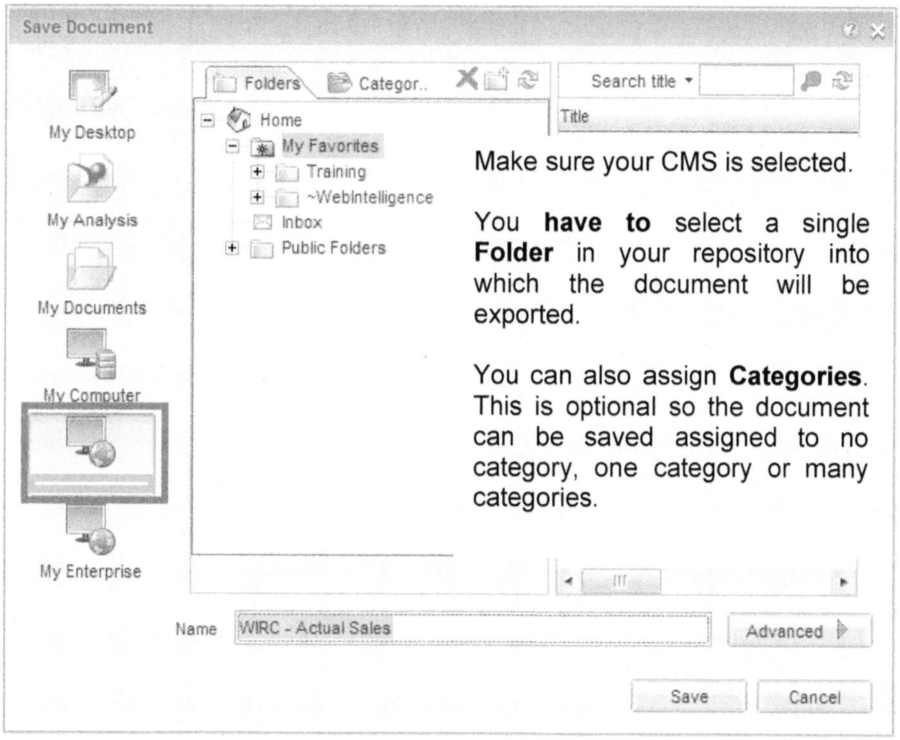
Save Document
Folders
Categor..
Search title
Title
My Desktop
My Analysis
My Documents
My Computer
My Enterprise
Home
My Favorites
Training
~WebIntelligence
Inbox
Public Folders
Name
WIRC - Actual Sales
Advanced
Save
Cancel

Make sure your CMS is selected.

You **have to** select a single **Folder** in your repository into which the document will be exported.

You can also assign **Categories**. This is optional so the document can be saved assigned to no category, one category or many categories.

5. You can create (and delete) new Folders (depending on your permissions).

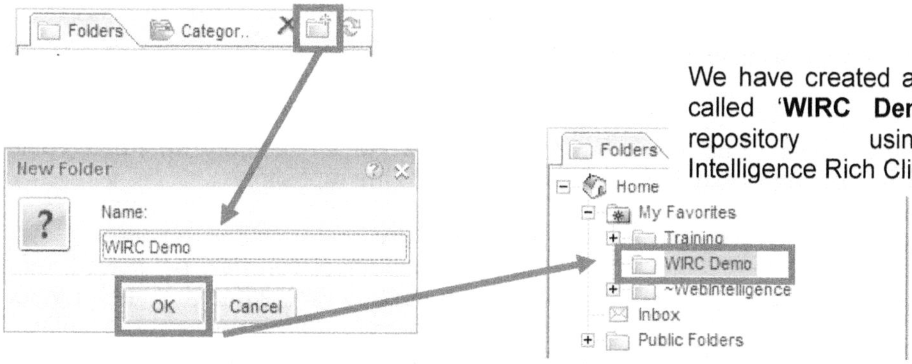
Folders
Categor..
New Folder
Name:
WIRC Demo
OK
Cancel
Home
My Favorites
Training
WIRC Demo
~WebIntelligence
Inbox
Public Folders

We have created a new folder called '**WIRC Demo**' in our repository using Web Intelligence Rich Client.

NOTE – Categories can also be created in a similar manner using the **Categories** tab.

6. You can create (and delete) Categories (depending on your permissions).

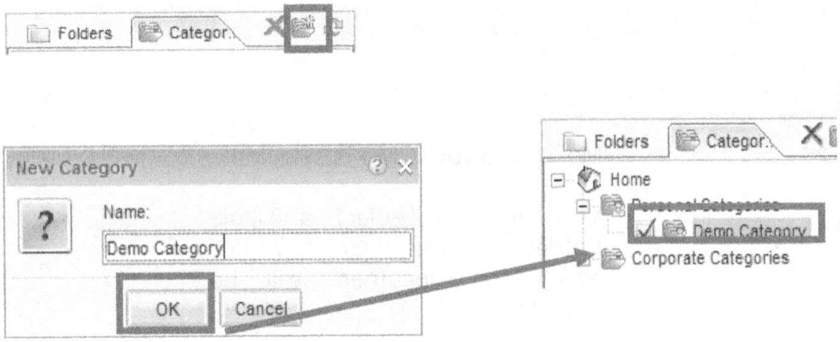
Folders
Categor
New Category
Name:
Demo Category
OK
Cancel
Home
Demo Category
Corporate Categories

We have created a new category called '**Demo Category**' in our repository using Web Intelligence Rich Client.

We have also selected it to assign it for our document

7. Click Advanced and remove the ticks we used earlier for removing security.

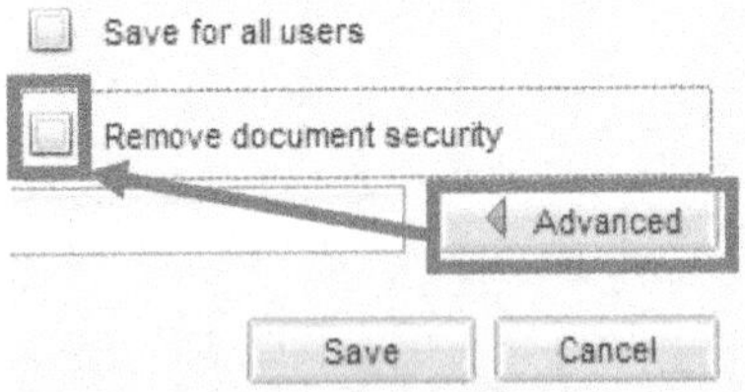
Save for all users
Remove document security
Advanced
Save
Cancel

8. Click '**Save**' to save this document into the Folder '**WIRC Demo'** assigned to the Category '**Demo Category**'.

9. Close and Exit the application completely.

10. If we Log On to BI Launch Pad then we will find the new Folder/Category we created using Web Intelligence Rich Client and the document we exported into the repository.

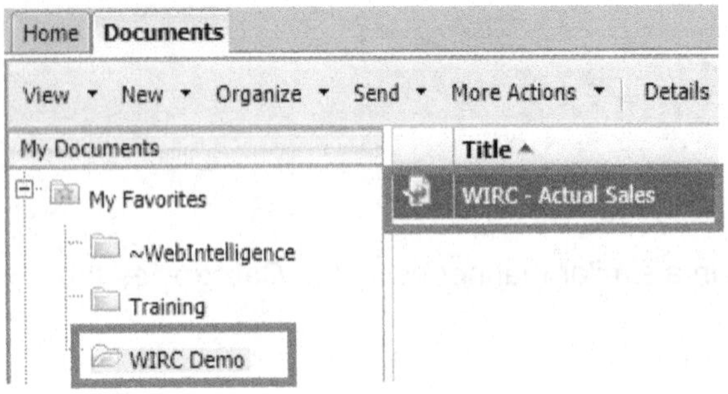
Home
Documents
View
New
Organize
Send
More Actions
Details
My Documents
Title
My Favorites
WIRC - Actual Sales
~WebIntelligence
Training
WIRC Demo

The document can now be viewed, refreshed and edited in the same manner as other Web Intelligence documents (depending on permissions).

31.6 Importing Documents from a Repository

If you are using Web Intelligence Rich Client in an enterprise implementation (i.e. use of a repository) then you will want to import documents from the repository and store them on local machines so they can be used by Web Intelligence Rich Client in Offline or Standalone modes.

We will now take a look at importing documents from a repository.

To demonstrate this we will first create a document in Web Intelligence and then import it using Web Intelligence Rich Client.

1. Log into BI Launch Pad and create the following query using the 'eFashion' universe in Web Intelligence (not Web Intelligence Rich Client).

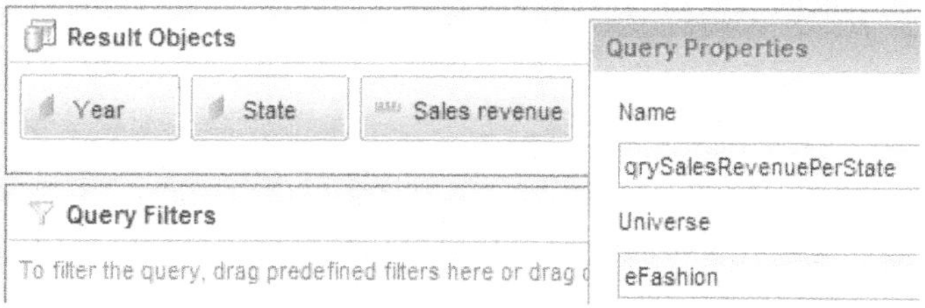
Result Objects
Year
State
Sales revenue
Query Properties
Name
qrySalesRevenuePerState
Query Filters
To filter the query, drag predefined filters here or drag
Universe
eFashion

2. Run the query and rename the report tab as 'Sales Revenue':

3. Save the document as 'Sales Revenue by State per Year' in 'My Favorites' or any other personal folder you have created for yourself.

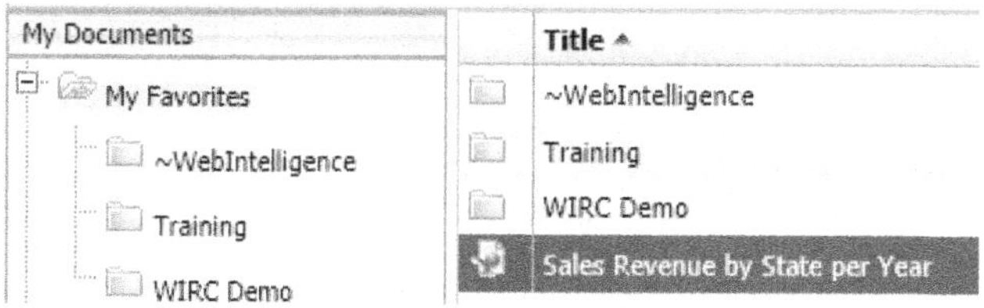
My Documents
My Favorites
~WebIntelligence
Training
WIRC Demo
Title
~WebIntelligence
Training
WIRC Demo
Sales Revenue by State per Year

4. Log Out of BI Launch Pad.

We will now use this document to demonstrate 'Open from...' functionality in Web Intelligence Rich Client.

1. Launch Web Intelligence Rich Client and make sure you are in 'Connected Mode' because you can only import documents when you are connected to a repository.

   NOTE – Points 2 and 3 do not have to be performed on every import as we are going to use these to demonstrate where local documents are stored and how you can move or delete them if you want to.

2. Check the default folder for 'User documents:' setting using the menu 'Options…':

   For example:

   'C:\Users\Administrator\Documents\My SAP BusinessObjects Documents\userDocs\'

3. Browse to this folder using Windows Explorer:

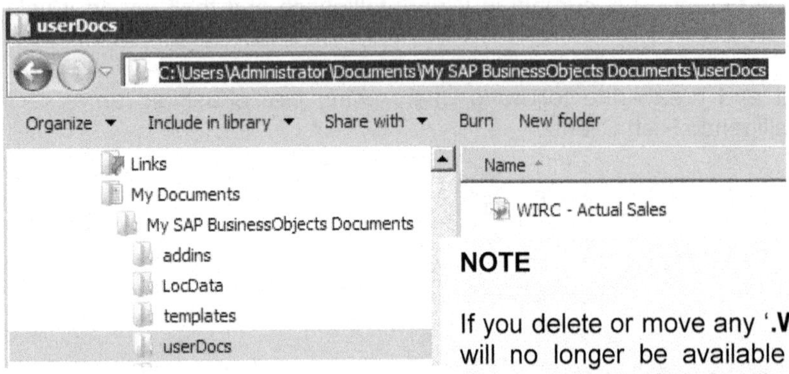
userDocs
C:\Users\Administrator\Documents\My SAP BusinessObjects Documents\userDocs
Organize
Include in library
Share with
Burn
New folder
Links
My Documents
My SAP BusinessObjects Documents
addins
LocData
templates
userDocs
Name
WIRC - Actual Sales

NOTE

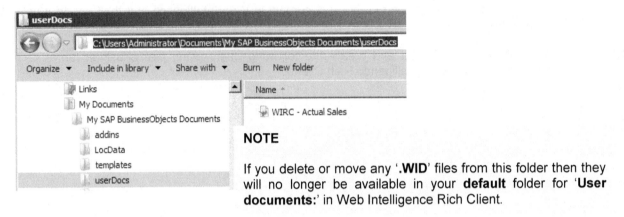

If you delete or move any '**.WID**' files from this folder then they will no longer be available in your **default** folder for '**User documents:**' in Web Intelligence Rich Client.

4. Return to Web Intelligence Rich Client and select 'Open from…'

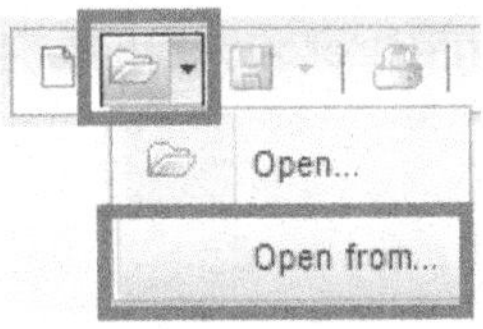
Open...
Open from...

5. The 'Open document from server' interface opens for you to select document to import:

6. Select the previously saved document 'Sales Revenue by State per Year' and click 'Open'.

7. The document will be imported and opened by Web Intelligence Rich Client.

   You can now work with the document, make changes and then save it locally or export it back to the repository.

   The Importing and Loading processes can take a while when documents contain large amounts of data, or complex formulas and variables. You can save the documents in the repository as 'Purged' documents to speed up these processes.

   This also applies to the Exporting process.

8. Close and Exit the application.

32 Using Local Data Sources in Web Intelligence Documents

We have used universes as data sources for queries created in Web Intelligence and in Web Intelligence Rich Client.

32.1 Local Data Sources in Web Intelligence Rich Client

It is also possible to use **Text** and **Excel** files (*.txt, *.csv, *.prn, *.asc, *.xls, *.xlsx) as sources of data when creating queries using Web Intelligence Rich Client.

In this example we will demonstrate using an Excel file as a data source in a document already containing a query based on a universe. We will also use Merged Dimensions to compare data between the two queries.

We will use the document 'Sales Revenue by State per Year' as the starting point as we have just imported and saved it locally. See the last few pages on 'Importing Documents from a Repository' of the previous session 'Working with Documents in Web Intelligence Rich Client'.

1. Launch Web Intelligence Rich Client in Connected Mode and browse to your local folder to open 'Sales Revenue by State per Year'.

2. Select 'Data Access – Edit' to open the Query Panel.

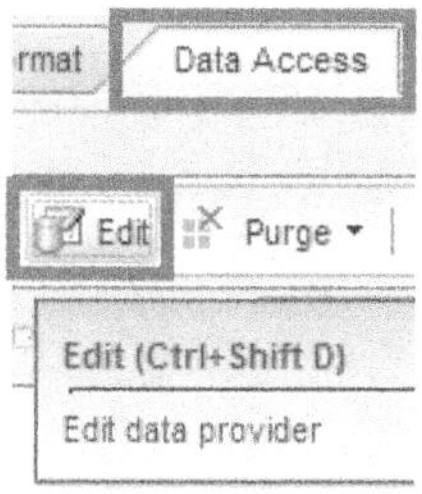
rmat
Data Access
Edit
Purge
Edit (Ctrl+Shift D)
Edit data provider

3. Select 'Add Query – From Excel'.

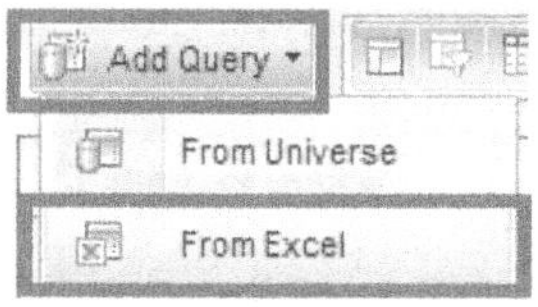
Add Query
From Universe
From Excel

4. Locate the local file you want to use:

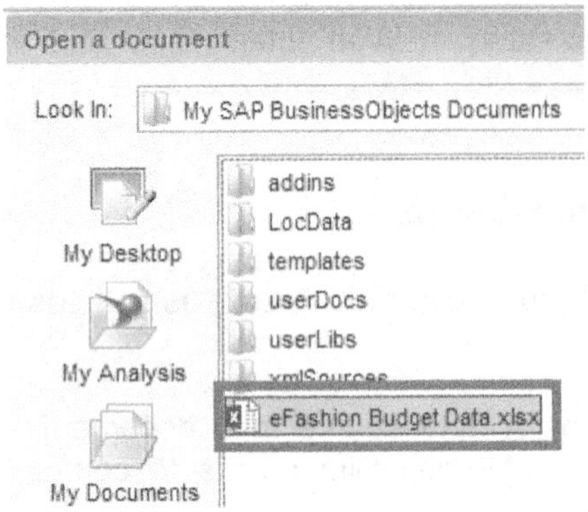
Open a document
Look In:
My SAP BusinessObjects Documents
My Desktop
My Analysis
My Documents
addins
LocData
templates
userDocs
userLibs
xmlSources
eFashion Budget Data.xlsx

NOTE – You can use files from your local machine or from other locations on your network.

'**eFashion Budget Data.xlsx**' file can be downloaded from www.webiworx.com. Look for information on 'SAP BusinessObjects Web Intelligence Training Course' on the 'Downloads' page.

The file can be placed in any location of your choice (i.e. it does not have to be in 'My BusinessObjects Documents').

5. Click on '**Open**' to use the selected file.

6. The selected file will appear in the 'Custom Data Provider' interface:

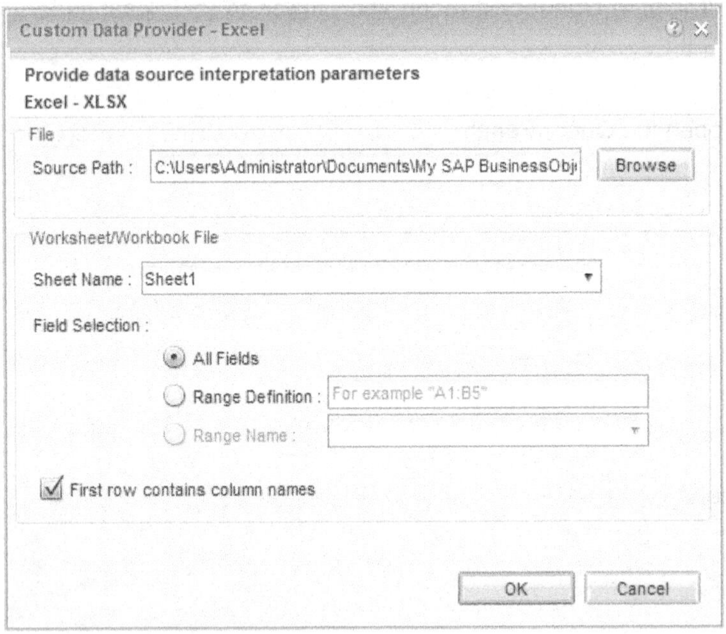
Custom Data Provider - Excel
Provide data source interpretation parameters
Excel - XLSX
File
Source Path :
C:\Users\Administrator\Documents\My SAP BusinessObj
Browse
Worksheet/Workbook File
Sheet Name :
Sheet1
Field Selection :
All Fields
Range Definition :
For example "A1:B5"
Range Name :
First row contains column names
OK
Cancel

For an Excel file, you can:

- Specify the '**Sheet Name**' to use from an Excel workbook containing more than one worksheet.

You can also specify the '**Field Selection**' (i.e. the location of the data set within the selected sheet):

- '**All Fields**' (i.e. all columns and rows containing data)
- '**Range Definition**' to manually define a range

- '**Range Name**' to select a range of cells that have already been defined in the Excel file

- Also if '**first row contains column names**' is checked then the first row of data will be used to name the objects by Web Intelligence Rich Client.

NOTE – The 'Custom Data Provider' interface will change if you select a text file (*.txt, *.csv, *.prn, *.asc) as shown below.

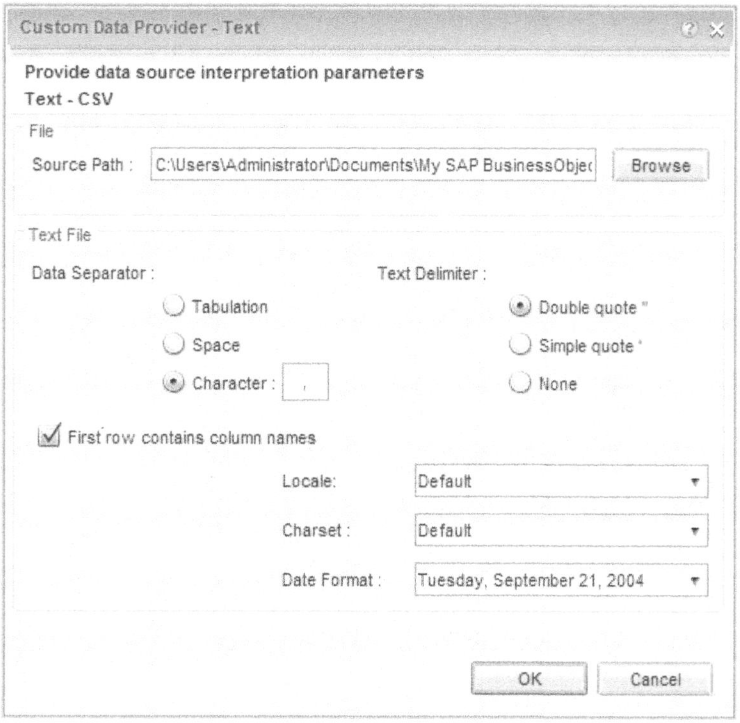
Custom Data Provider - Text
Provide data source interpretation parameters
Text - CSV
File
Source Path :
C:\Users\Administrator\Documents\My SAP BusinessObje
Browse
Text File
Data Separator :
Tabulation
Space
Character :
Text Delimiter :
Double quote "
Simple quote '
None
First row contains column names
Locale:
Default
Charset :
Default
Date Format :
Tuesday, September 21, 2004
OK
Cancel

For a text file, you have to instruct Web Intelligence Rich Client on how to parse (or process) the file contents in order to extract meaningful data:

- Specify how the data is separated using options for '**Data Separator**', i.e. in each row of data the columns are separated by Tabulation, Space or another Character.

- Specify if there is a '**Text Delimiter**' enclosing each column value.

- '**First row contains column names**' in the file.

- '**Locale**' of the data within the file.

- '**Charset**' is the Character Set in which the data has been saved within the file.

- '**Date Format**' of any date columns in the file.

7. Click 'OK' to load the data into Web Intelligence Rich Client:

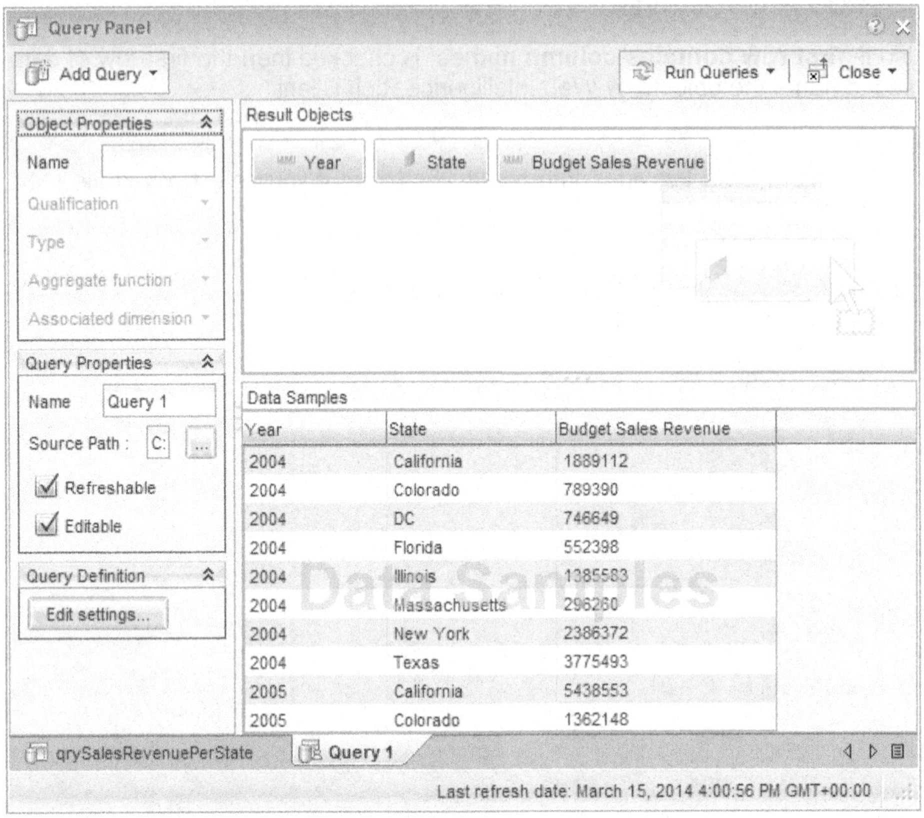
Query Panel
Add Query
Run Queries
Close
Object Properties
Name
Qualification
Type
Aggregate function
Associated dimension
Query Properties
Name
Query 1
Source Path :
Refreshable
Editable
Query Definition
Edit settings...
Result Objects
Year
State
Budget Sales Revenue
Data Samples
Year | State | Budget Sales Revenue
2004 | California | 1889112
2004 | Colorado | 789390
2004 | DC | 746649
2004 | Florida | 552398
2004 | Illinois | 1385583
2004 | Massachusetts | 296260
2004 | New York | 2386372
2004 | Texas | 3775493
2005 | California | 5438553
2005 | Colorado | 1362148
qrySalesRevenuePerState
Query 1
Last refresh date: March 15, 2014 4:00:56 PM GMT+00:00

In the example above, the Excel file has been loaded into Web Intelligence Rich Client with:

- **Name** property (of Query) set to '**Query 1**'
- The objects have been named [Year], [State] and [Budget Sales Revenue] as based on the property '**First row contains column names**' in the previous interface
- [Year] and [Budget Sales Revenue] have been created as Measures (due to values containing number formatting only)
- [State] has been created as a Dimension

8. The query '**Name**' property can be changed as shown below:

Query Properties
Name
qryBudgetData

9. The definition of each object can be changed as shown below. [Year] will be changed to a Dimension object and its '**Type**' will be changed to 'string':

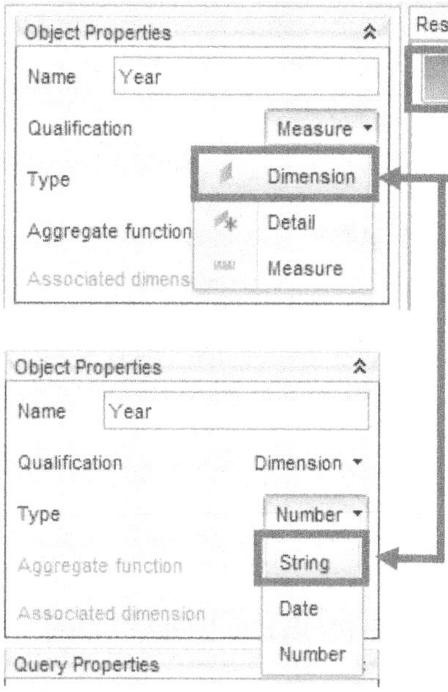
Object Properties
Name
Year
Qualification
Measure
Type
Dimension
Aggregate function
Detail
Associated dimension
Measure
Object Properties
Name
Year
Qualification
Dimension
Type
Number
Aggregate function
String
Associated dimension
Date
Number
Query Properties

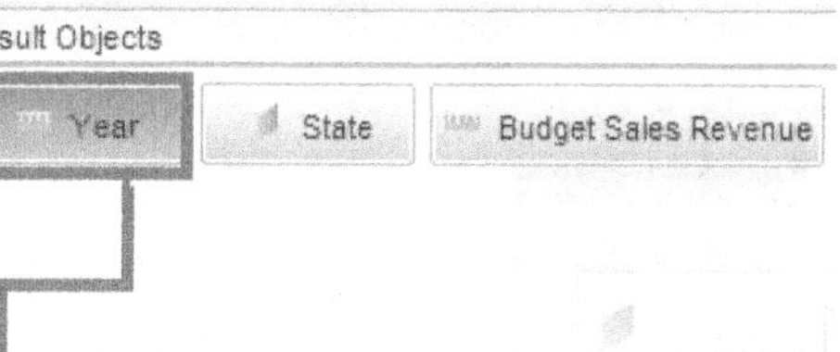
Result Objects
Year
State
Budget Sales Revenue

NOTES

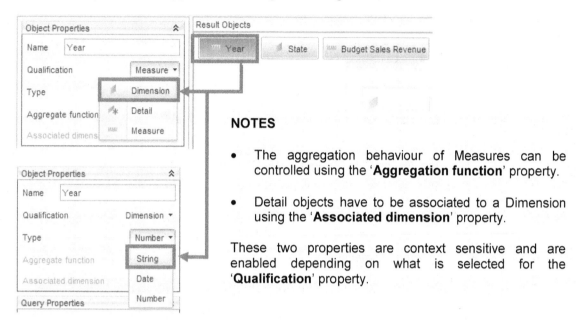

- The aggregation behaviour of Measures can be controlled using the '**Aggregation function**' property.
- Detail objects have to be associated to a Dimension using the '**Associated dimension**' property.

These two properties are context sensitive and are enabled depending on what is selected for the '**Qualification**' property.

10. Run the new query '**qryBudgetData**'...

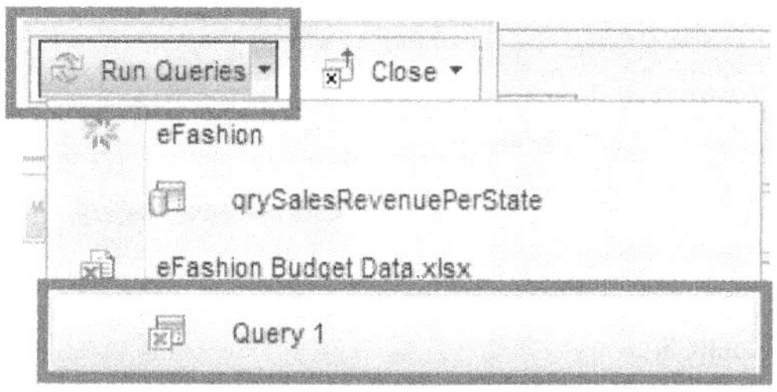
Run Queries
Close
eFashion
qrySalesRevenuePerState
eFashion Budget Data.xlsx
Query 1

and select '**Insert a table in a new report**' when prompted.

NOTE

If you choose to 'Apply changes and Close' instead of running the query then you will be able to use the objects from the new query but there will be no data within the microcube to display within the document.

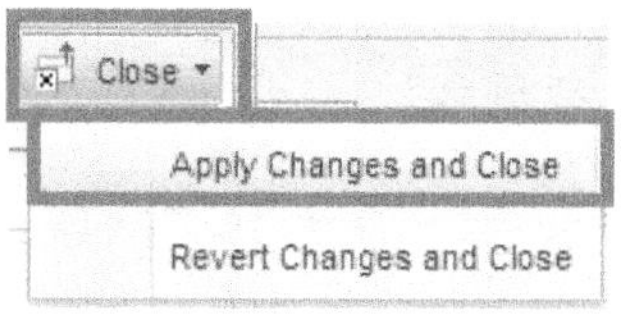
Close
Apply Changes and Close
Revert Changes and Close

11. The objects from the new query will be added to the 'Available Objects' tab and a new report will be added to the document.

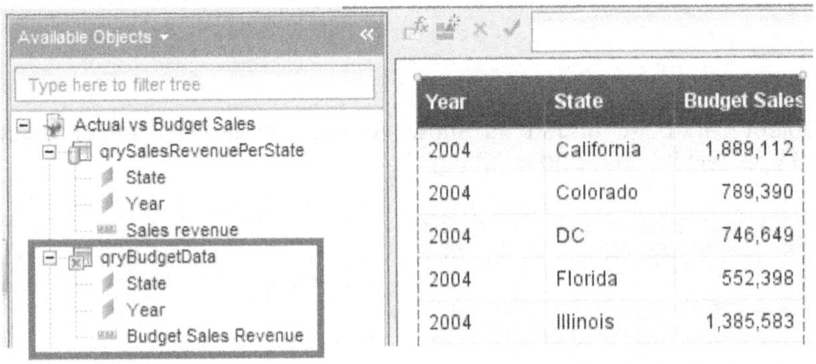

Available Objects
Type here to filter tree
Actual vs Budget Sales
qrySalesRevenuePerState
State
Year
Sales revenue
qryBudgetData
State
Year
Budget Sales Revenue
Year
State
Budget Sales
2004
California
1,889,112
2004
Colorado
789,390
2004
DC
746,649
2004
Florida
552,398
2004
Illinois
1,385,583

12. Rename the report tab 'Sales Revenue' to 'Actual Sales Revenue'.

13. Rename the report tab 'Report 2' to 'Budget Sales Revenue'.

14. Save the document as 'Actual vs Budget Sales.wid'.

15. Create the following Merged Dimensions:

- **[mrg State]** to merge [qrySalesRevenuePerState].[State] with [qryBudgetData].[State]
- **[mrg Year]** to merge [qrySalesRevenuePerState].[Year] with [qryBudgetData].[Year]

Merged Dimensions
mrg State
State (qryBudgetData)
State (qrySalesRevenuePerState)
mrg Year
Year (qrySalesRevenuePerState)
Year (qryBudgetData)

16. Insert a new report tab and rename it as 'Act vs Bud Sales'.

17. Insert a Vertical Table into 'Act vs Bud Sales' report using the objects:

    [mrg State], [mrg Year], [Sales revenue], [Bud Sales Revenue]

18. Format the [Budget Sales Revenue] column so it has the same appearance as [Sales revenue], and rename the [State] and [Year] columns as shown below:

State	Year	Sales revenue	Budget Sales Revenue
California	2004	$1,704,211	$1,889,112
California	2005	$2,782,680	$5,438,553
California	2006	$2,992,679	$3,234,724
Colorado	2004	$448,302	$789,390
Colorado	2005	$768,390	$1,362,148
Colorado	2006	$843,584	$1,169,419

19. Save the document.

20. Create a measure variable called '**Act vs Bud**' using the formula:

=([Sales revenue] - [Budget Sales Revenue]) / [Budget Sales Revenue]

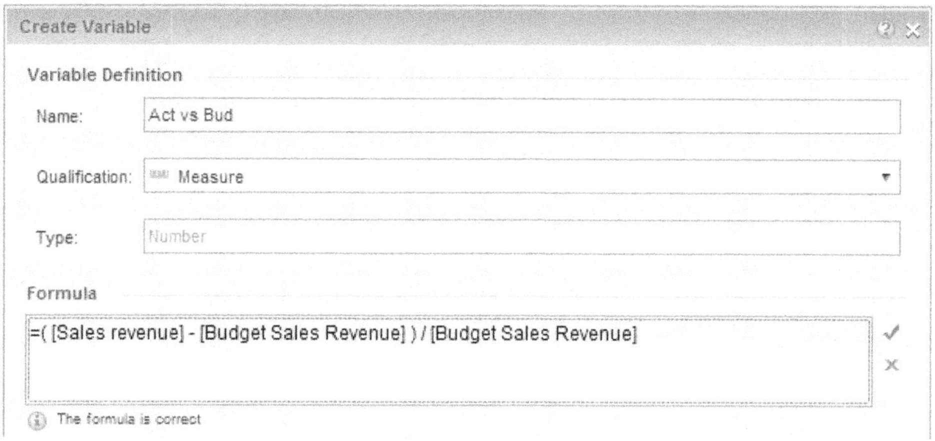

Create Variable
Variable Definition
Name:
Act vs Bud
Qualification:
Measure
Type:
Number
Formula
=([Sales revenue] - [Budget Sales Revenue]) / [Budget Sales Revenue]
The formula is correct

21. Drag and drop **[Act vs Bud]** to create a new column at the end of the table as shown below:

State	Year	Sales revenue	Budget Sales Revenue	Act vs Bud
California	2004	$1,704,211	$1,889,112	-9.79%
California	2005	$2,782,680	$5,438,553	-48.83%
California	2006	$2,992,679	$3,234,724	-7.48%
Colorado	2004	$448,302	$789,390	-43.21%
Colorado	2005	$768,390	$1,362,148	-43.59%
Colorado	2006	$843,584	$1,169,419	-27.86%

22. Format the column [Act vs Bud] as a percentage.

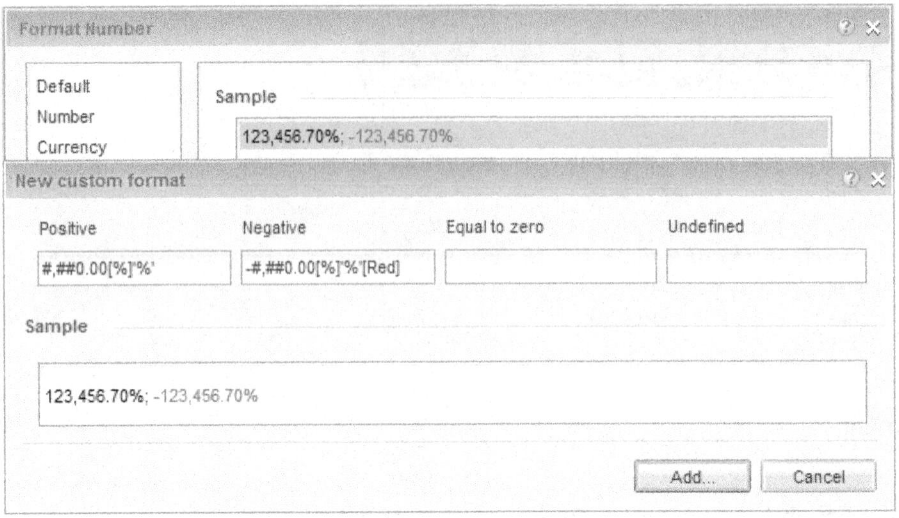
Format Number
Default
Number
Currency
Sample
123,456.70%; -123,456.70%
New custom format
Positive
Negative
Equal to zero
Undefined
#,##0.00[%]'%'
-#,##0.00[%]'%'[Red]
Sample
123,456.70%; -123,456.70%
Add...
Cancel

We have used a Custom Percentage format where negative values will be displayed in red.

23. Save the document.

24. Export the document into a folder in your repository using 'Save to Enterprise..'

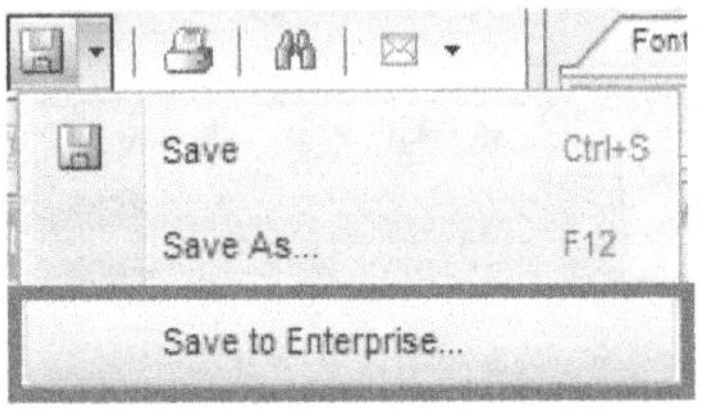
Save
Ctrl+S
Save As...
F12
Save to Enterprise...

25. Close the document and then exit Web Intelligence Rich Client.

26. Log into BI Launch Pad and open the document for editing (i.e. document opens in Web Intelligence).

27. Refresh the queries.

All universe based queries will be refreshed, i.e. in this example '**qrySalesRevenuePerState**' will be refreshed.

Local Data Source queries will only be refreshed if the BusinessObjects server has access to the source file.

28. Close your document and Log Out of BI Launch Pad.

32.2 Local Data Sources in Web Intelligence

It is also possible to use **Excel** files as sources of data when creating queries using Web Intelligence (i.e. in BI Launch Pad).

We will now look at how to use Excel based data sources.

Firstly, save a copy of the 'eFashion Budget Data' Excel file to a location on your PC or network.

We now need to load the Excel file into the repository.

1. Select the repository folder (e.g. My Favorites) into which you would like to save the Excel file into and then select 'New – Local Document' in BI Launch Pad.

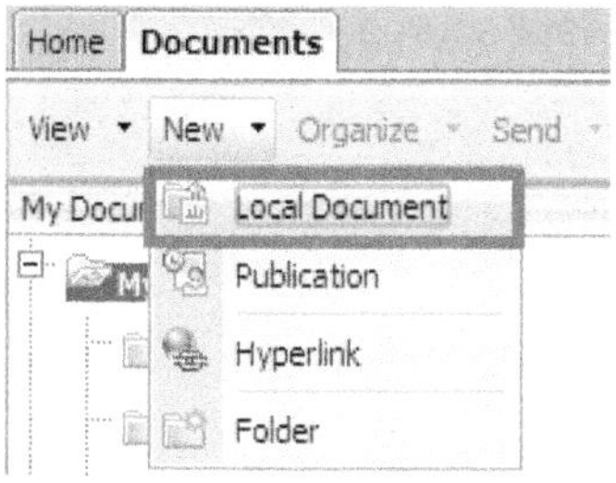
Home
Documents
View
New
Organize
Send
My Docu
Local Document
Publication
Hyperlink
Folder

2. Locate the Excel file using 'Choose File'.

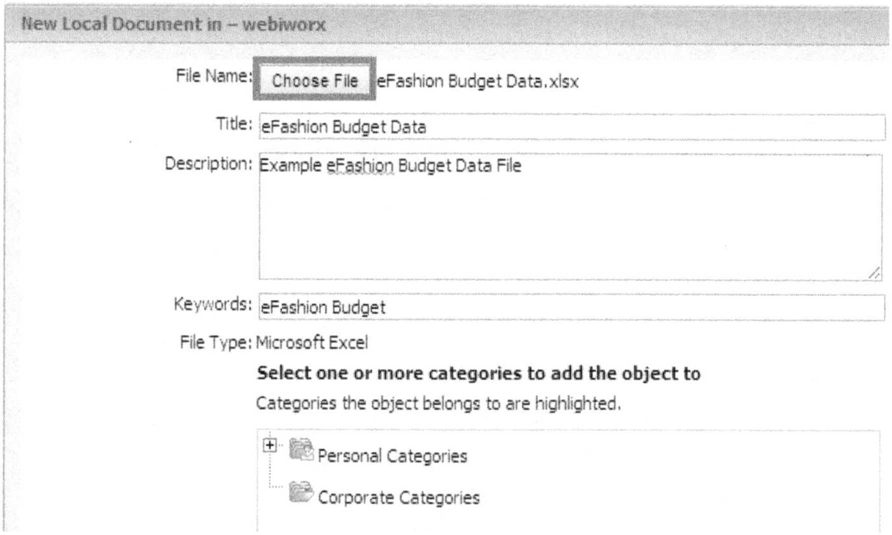
New Local Document in – webiworx
File Name:
Choose File
eFashion Budget Data.xlsx
Title:
eFashion Budget Data
Description:
Example eFashion Budget Data File
Keywords:
eFashion Budget
File Type: Microsoft Excel
Select one or more categories to add the object to
Categories the object belongs to are highlighted.
Personal Categories
Corporate Categories

You can give the file a Title, Description, and assign Keywords and Categories.

3. Click 'Add' to load the Excel file into the repository.

The Excel file will now appear in your selected folder:

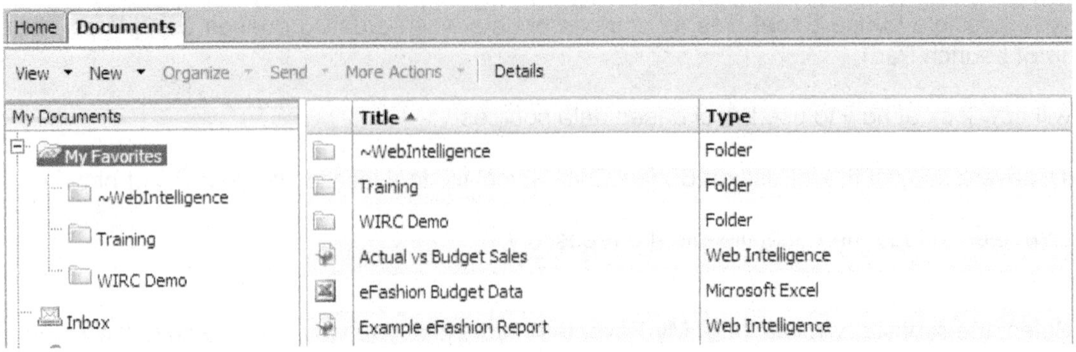
Home
Documents
View
New
Organize
Send
More Actions
Details
My Documents
My Favorites
~WebIntelligence
Training
WIRC Demo
Inbox
Title
Type
~WebIntelligence
Folder
Training
Folder
WIRC Demo
Folder
Actual vs Budget Sales
Web Intelligence
eFashion Budget Data
Microsoft Excel
Example eFashion Report
Web Intelligence

4. Create a new Web Intelligence document and select 'Excel' as a data source.

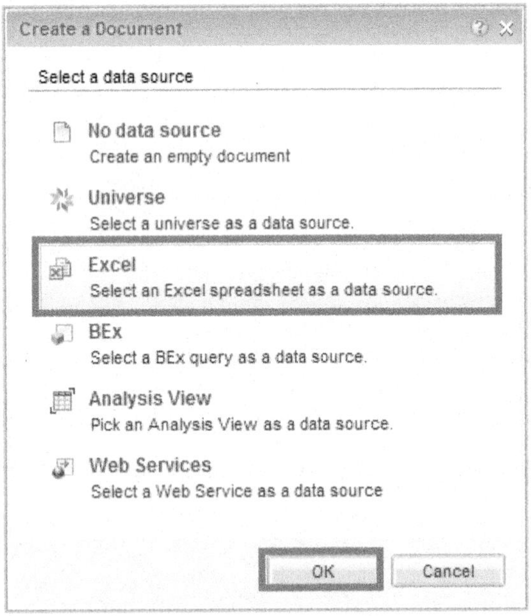
Create a Document
Select a data source
No data source
Create an empty document
Universe
Select a universe as a data source.
Excel
Select an Excel spreadsheet as a data source.
BEx
Select a BEx query as a data source.
Analysis View
Pick an Analysis View as a data source.
Web Services
Select a Web Service as a data source
OK
Cancel

5. Select the Excel file from the repository and click 'Open'.

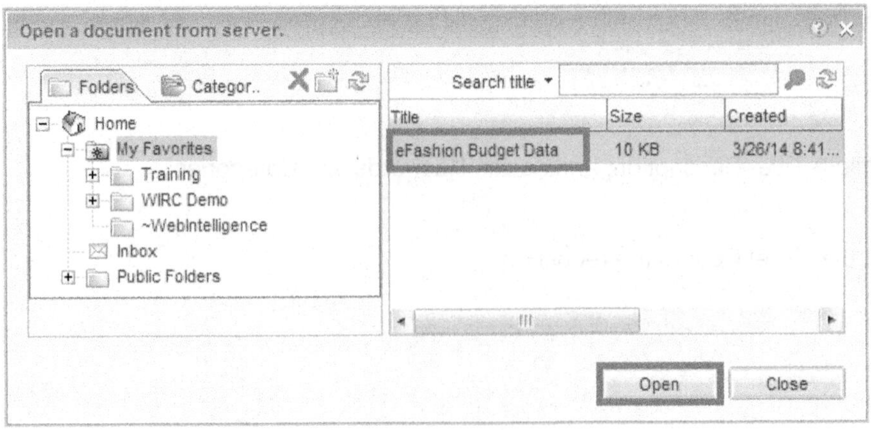
Open a document from server.
Folders
Categor..
Search title
Home
My Favorites
Training
WIRC Demo
~WebIntelligence
Inbox
Public Folders
Title
Size
Created
eFashion Budget Data
10 KB
3/26/14 8:41...
Open
Close

6. You can then specify which sheets/range, etc to use from the Excel file.

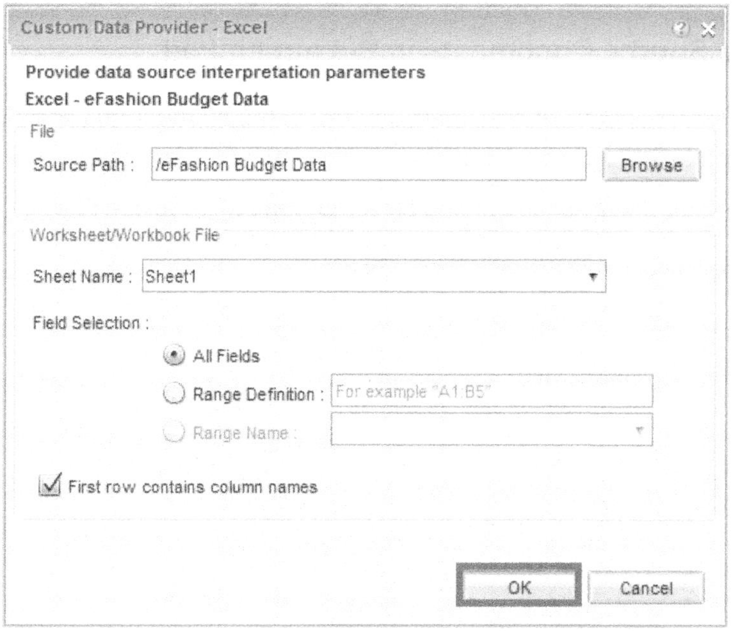
Custom Data Provider - Excel
Provide data source interpretation parameters
Excel - eFashion Budget Data
File
Source Path :
/eFashion Budget Data
Browse
Worksheet/Workbook File
Sheet Name :
Sheet1
Field Selection :
All Fields
Range Definition :
For example "A1:B5"
Range Name :
First row contains column names
OK
Cancel

7. Click 'OK' and the file will be loaded into the Query Panel, where you can make any required changes to the objects and define Query Properties.

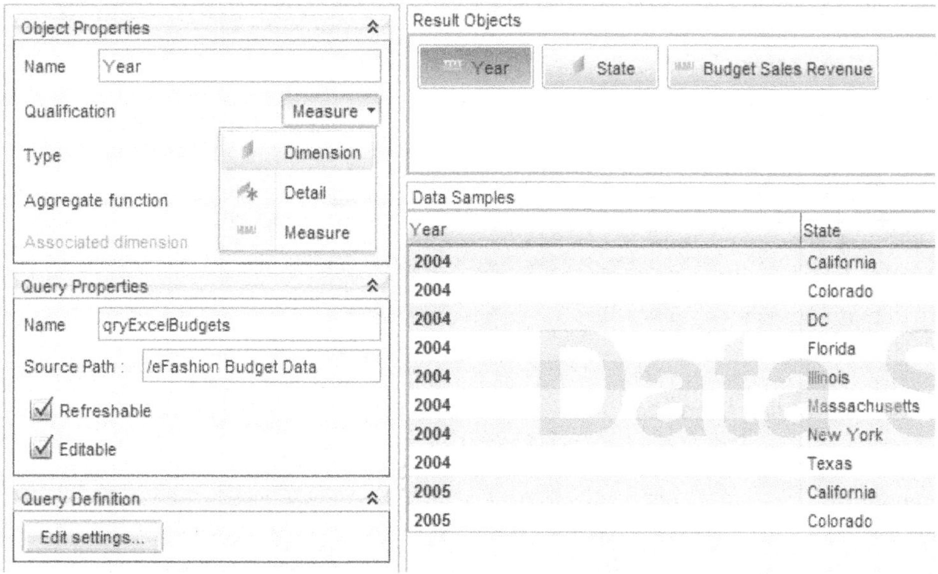
Object Properties
Name
Year
Qualification
Measure
Type
Aggregate function
Associated dimension
Dimension
Detail
Measure
Query Properties
Name
qryExcelBudgets
Source Path :
/eFashion Budget Data
Refreshable
Editable
Query Definition
Edit settings...
Result Objects
Year
State
Budget Sales Revenue
Data Samples
Year
State
2004
California
2004
Colorado
2004
DC
2004
Florida
2004
Illinois
2004
Massachusetts
2004
New York
2004
Texas
2005
California
2005
Colorado

We have changed the [Year] object to be a dimension and given the query the name 'qryExcelBudgets'.

8. Run the query and the Excel file will be loaded into Web Intelligence.

9. Save and then close your Web Intelligence document.

32.3 Refreshing Local Data Source Documents in BI Launch Pad

Your local data source files/documents might need refreshing and this can be done from the BI Launch Pad.

1. In BI Launch Pad, right-click on your local document and select 'Organize – Replace File'.

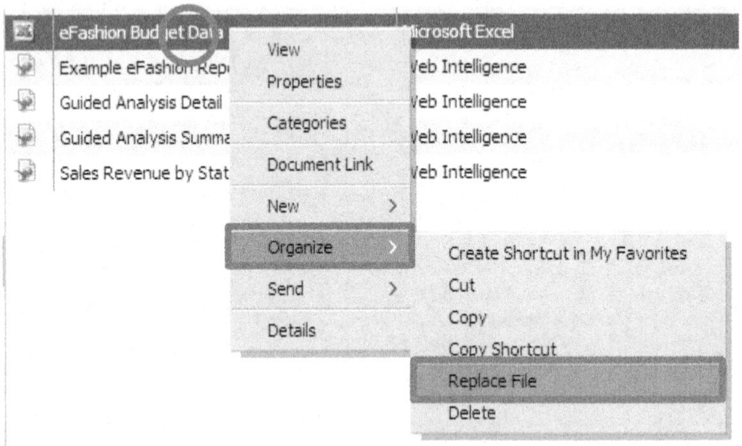
eFashion Budget Data
Microsoft Excel
Example eFashion Rep
Guided Analysis Detail
Guided Analysis Summa
Sales Revenue by Stat
Web Intelligence
View
Properties
Categories
Document Link
New
Organize
Send
Details
Create Shortcut in My Favorites
Cut
Copy
Copy Shortcut
Replace File
Delete

Or you can select the document and then select 'Organize – Replace File' from the menu.

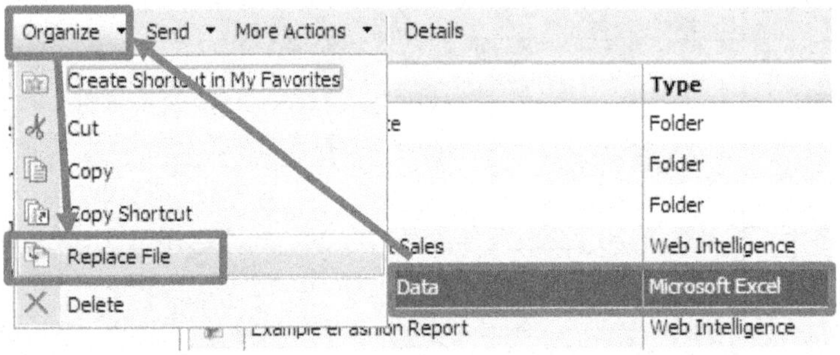
Organize
Send
More Actions
Details
Create Shortcut in My Favorites
Cut
Copy
Copy Shortcut
Replace File
Delete
Type
Folder
Web Intelligence
Data
Microsoft Excel

2. You can 'Choose File' and/or 'Replace'.

3. Click 'OK' to confirm.

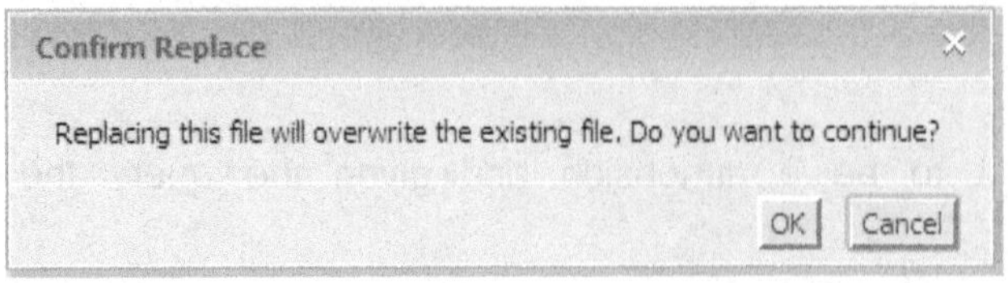
Confirm Replace
Replacing this file will overwrite the existing file. Do you want to continue?
OK
Cancel

The existing version of the file will be replaced with your chosen version.

33 Exploring Report Data using Drill Mode

Drill Functionality enables you to explore data by moving up, down and across the dataset(s) held within the document.

For example, we have the following data presented in a report (example data – not from 'eFashion'):

Year	Sales Value
2005	2,278,365
2006	2,527,743
2007	2,947,890

In Drill Analysis, if we click on '2006' then Web Intelligence would display:

Quarter	Sales Value
Q1	678,976
Q2	572,410
Q3	601,989
Q4	674,368
Total	**2,527,743**

We might then be interested in finding out why the 'Q2' [Sales Value] is lower than the other three quarters. Web Intelligence makes it simple to do this, as we can breakdown the [Sales Value] of 572,410 by [Region].

Region	Sales Value
North	150,335
East	159,354
South	98,496
West	164,225
Total	**572,410**

The drill down shows that [Sales Value] for [Region] = 'South' is lower than the other three regions. Further analysis could then be performed to delve deeper into the possible reasons, etc.

The above example illustrates how Web Intelligence uses the dynamic behaviour of measures to 'roll up' or 'break down' rows of data depending on dimension hierarchies.

33.1 Hierarchies

Hierarchies are logical drill paths following related dimensions. This simplest and most common hierarchy is a time hierarchy following Year to Quarter to Month to Day, but hierarchies may be set up (in the universe) to follow from any one dimension to another dimension.

1. Create a new document using the 'eFashion' universe.

2. To view the set of hierarchies in a universe, from the Query Panel change 'Master Perspective' to 'Display by Navigation Paths'.

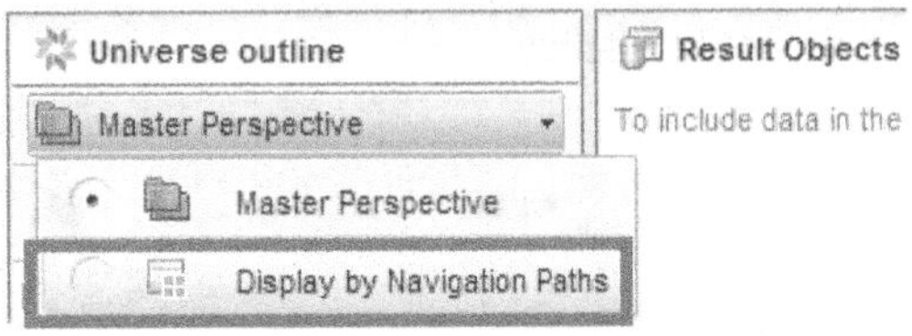
Universe outline
Result Objects
Master Perspective
To include data in the
Master Perspective
Display by Navigation Paths

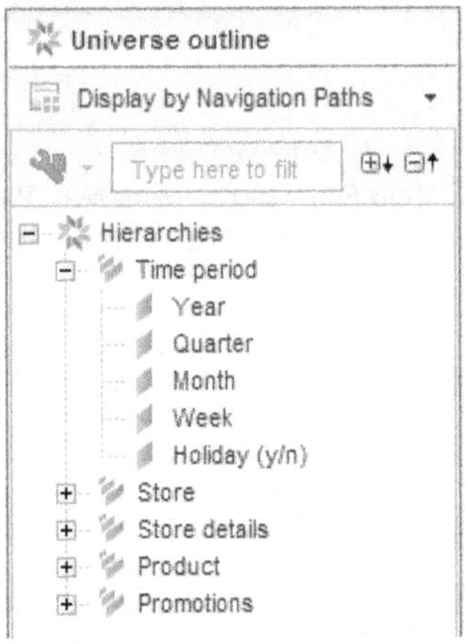
Universe outline
Display by Navigation Paths
Type here to filt
Hierarchies
Time period
Year
Quarter
Month
Week
Holiday (y/n)
Store
Store details
Product
Promotions

Hierarchies are defined in the universe according to logical drill paths, therefore hierarchies do not need to follow the order of dimension objects listed in universe classes.

A point of note is that sometimes dimensions can belong to several hierarchies. When you drill on a dimension that belongs to more than one hierarchy then Web Intelligence will prompt which hierarchy to use as the drill path.

33.2 Preparing Queries for Drill Analysis

You may drill up and down a hierarchy, or across and through the data to another hierarchy.

Typically, a query created for drilling purposes contains extra objects other than result objects. The more objects there are in the query the larger the analytical scope of data upon which to drill.

The 'Scope of Analysis' includes all the result objects, plus the list of 'extra' objects brought over from the database and are available in the microcube for drilling purposes. The scope is set according to the hierarchies in the universe.

Documents are prepared for drilling by using 'Scope of Analysis' in the Query Panel, but 'Drill Mode' has to be switched on manually in the document to begin drill analysis (unless the document is saved with 'Drill Mode' already activated). Simply using 'Scope of Analysis' in the Query Panel does not activate 'Drill Mode' in the document.

1. To prepare a query for Drill Analysis the first action should be to use define a '**Scope of Analysis**' when creating the query.

2. Make sure the 'Scope of Analysis Panel' is visible.

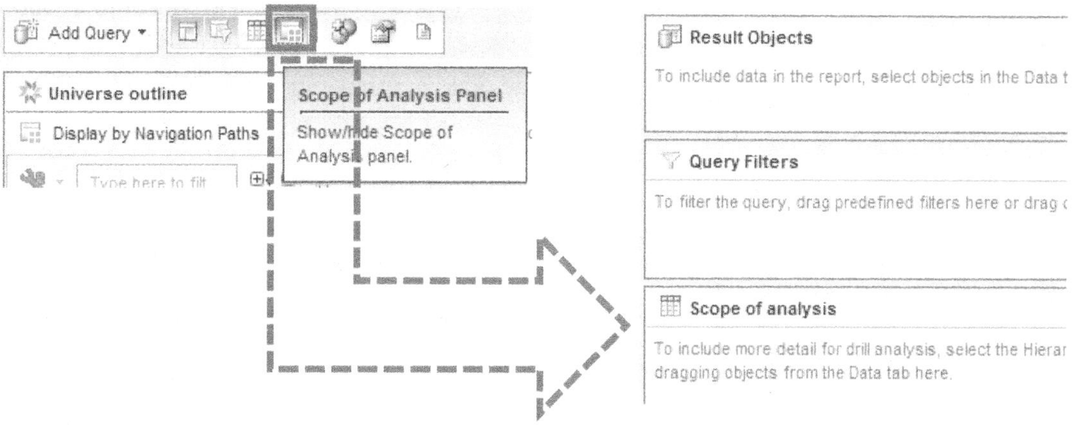
Add Query
Universe outline
Display by Navigation Paths
Scope of Analysis Panel
Show/Hide Scope of Analysis panel.
Result Objects
To include data in the report, select objects in the Data t
Query Filters
To filter the query, drag predefined filters here or drag c
Scope of analysis
To include more detail for drill analysis, select the Hierar
dragging objects from the Data tab here.

33.3 Using Scope of Analysis in the Query Panel

The 'Scope of Analysis' is the number of levels of data down in the dimension hierarchies that you wish to have available in the microcube for drilling.

The 'extra' objects will appear in the document, but not in the original table created in the report tab after running the query. The table will contain only the objects in the 'Result Objects' pane of the Query Panel, very much like the tables we have seen created by Web Intelligence in previous sessions.

The 'Scope of Analysis' is set using the 'Scope level' option which is available on the right hand side of the Scope of Analysis Pane.

Scope of Analysis pane can be activated using this button in the Query Panel.

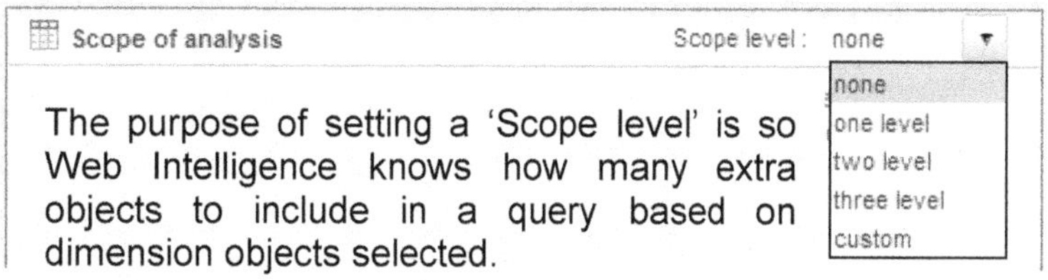
Scope of analysis
Scope level: none
none
one level
two level
three level
custom
The purpose of setting a 'Scope level' is so Web Intelligence knows how many extra objects to include in a query based on dimension objects selected.

33.3.1 Scope of Analysis Explained

1. Using the 'eFashion' universe, [Year] dimension object has been selected as a Result Object so it is automatically placed in Scope of Analysis as shown below.

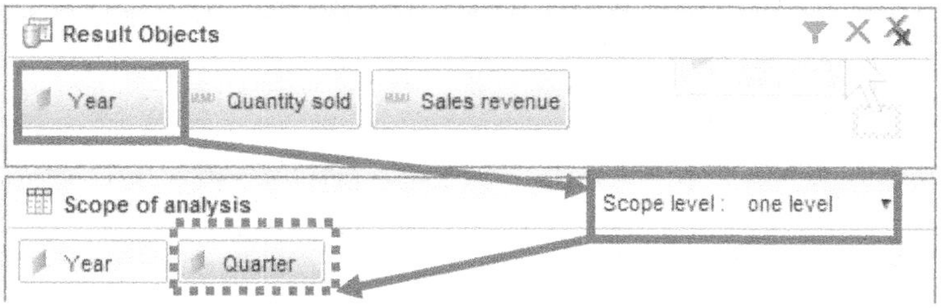
Result Objects
Year
Quantity sold
Sales revenue
Scope of analysis
Scope level: one level
Year
Quarter

Scope of Analysis set to '**One level**' so [Quarter] is the extra object placed in the query because it is the next object (after [Year]) in the 'Time period' hierarchy.

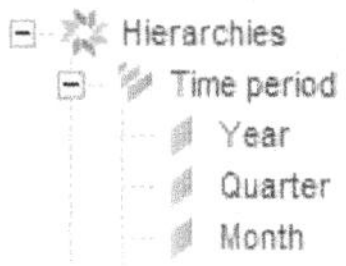
Hierarchies
Time period
Year
Quarter
Month

2. Run the query.

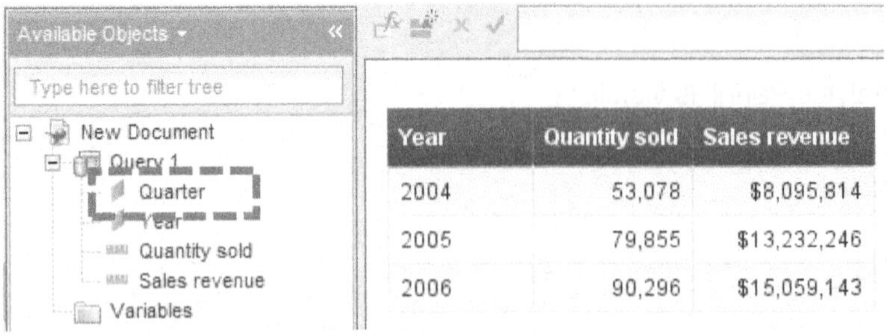

Available Objects
Type here to filter tree
New Document
Query 1
Quarter
Year
Quantity sold
Sales revenue
Variables
Year
Quantity sold
Sales revenue
2004
53,078
$8,095,814
2005
79,855
$13,232,246
2006
90,296
$15,059,143

[Quarter] object is available in the document but by default this extra object automatically selected by 'Scope of Analysis' is not displayed in the block.

3. Edit the query and change the 'Scope level' to 'two level' as shown below:

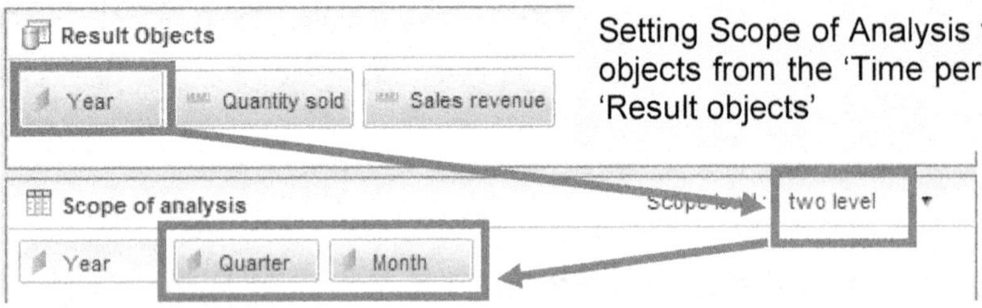

Result Objects
Year
Quantity sold
Sales revenue
Scope of analysis
two level
Year
Quarter
Month

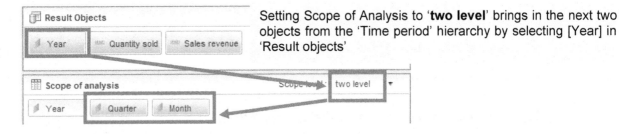

Setting Scope of Analysis to '**two level**' brings in the next two objects from the 'Time period' hierarchy by selecting [Year] in 'Result objects'

4. Drag [State] into 'Result Objects' as shown below:

Result Objects
Year
State
Quantity sold
Sales revenue
Scope of analysis
Scope level : two level
Year
Quarter
Month
State
City
Store name

'Scope of Analysis' to automatically include the two levels down from [Year] and also two levels down from [State].

NOTE

Multiple hierarchies will be used by 'Scope of Analysis' depending on the dimensions selected in Result Objects because different dimensions will belong to different hierarchies. In this example we have [Year] and [State] selected in Result Objects, and 'Scope of Analysis' is set to 'Two levels' so we are using the 'Time period' hierarchy and also the 'Store' hierarchy.

5. Expanding the query further to include [Quarter] in Result Objects causes the 'Scope of Analysis' to now go two levels down from [Quarter] instead of two levels down from [Year].

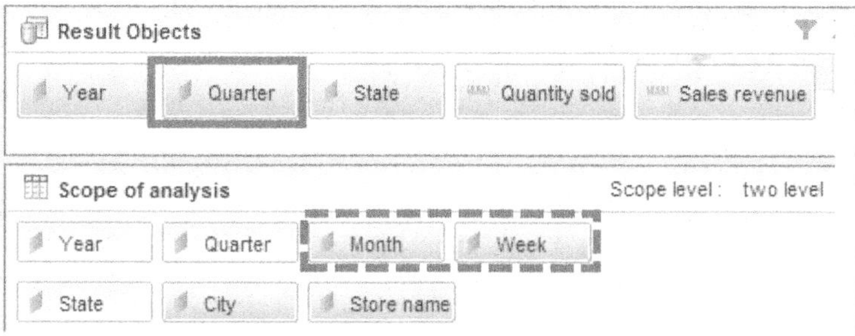
Result Objects
Year
Quarter
State
Quantity sold
Sales revenue
Scope of analysis
Scope level : two level
Year
Quarter
Month
Week
State
City
Store name

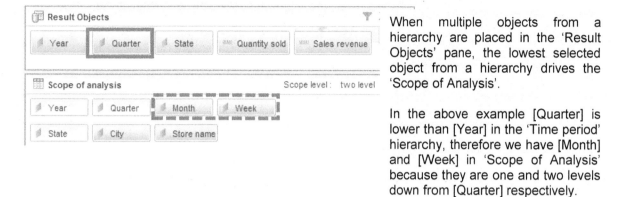

When multiple objects from a hierarchy are placed in the 'Result Objects' pane, the lowest selected object from a hierarchy drives the 'Scope of Analysis'.

In the above example [Quarter] is lower than [Year] in the 'Time period' hierarchy, therefore we have [Month] and [Week] in 'Scope of Analysis' because they are one and two levels down from [Quarter] respectively.

6. The **Custom** 'Scope of Analysis' allows levels in a hierarchy to be omitted if not required in the document. In the example below, drilling will move from [Year] down to [Week] without having to first drill on [Quarter] and [Month]. Likewise [State] will drill to [Store name] without having to drill on [City] first.

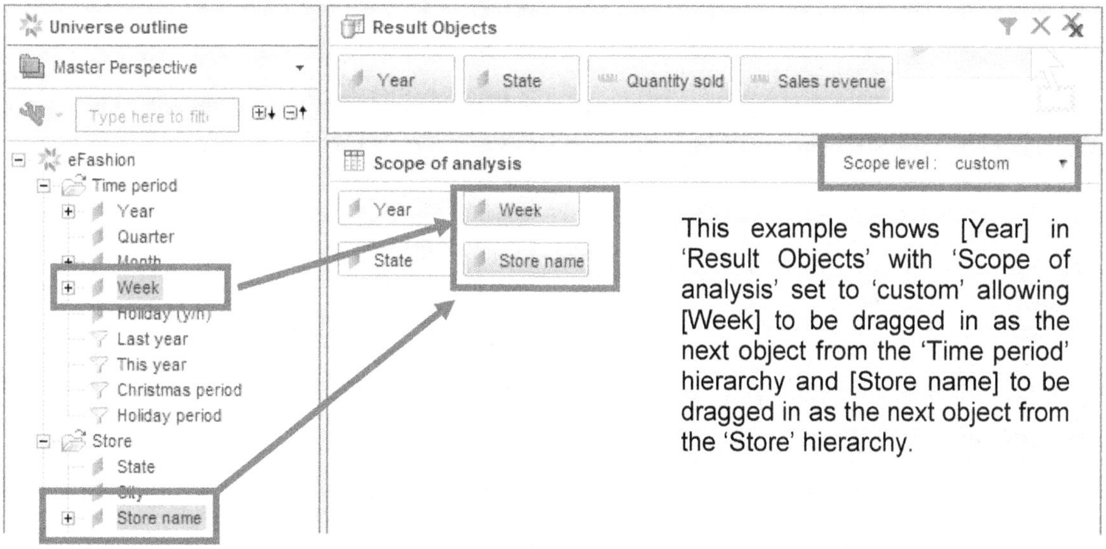
Universe outline
Master Perspective
Type here to filt
eFashion
Time period
Year
Quarter
Month
Week
Holiday (y/n)
Last year
This year
Christmas period
Holiday period
Store
State
City
Store name
Result Objects
Year
State
Quantity sold
Sales revenue
Scope of analysis
Scope level : custom
Year
Week
State
Store name

This example shows [Year] in 'Result Objects' with 'Scope of analysis' set to 'custom' allowing [Week] to be dragged in as the next object from the 'Time period' hierarchy and [Store name] to be dragged in as the next object from the 'Store' hierarchy.

NOTE

When using 'custom', you have to drag in the objects into the 'Scope of analysis' pane to define the custom drill path

7. Close the query panel and the document without saving it.

33.4 Using Drill Mode in the Java Report Panel

Actual drilling is performed in the document (or report tabs) and not the Query Panel.

1. Create the following query and run it using the 'eFashion' universe.

   NOTE – 'Scope level' has been set to 'two level'.

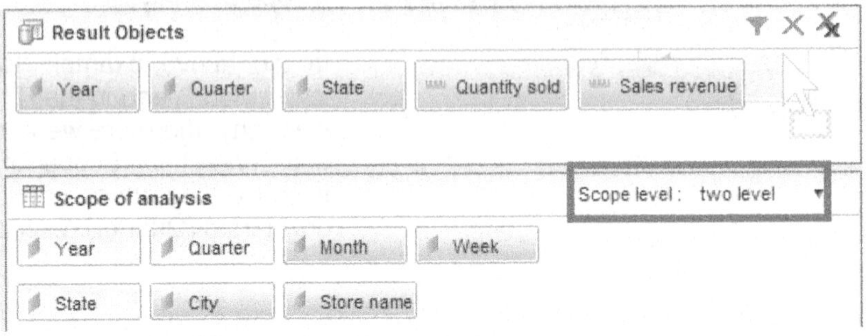
Result Objects
Year
Quarter
State
Quantity sold
Sales revenue
Scope of analysis
Scope level : two level
Year
Quarter
Month
Week
State
City
Store name

   Web Intelligence will display the following block:

Year	Quarter	State	Quantity sold	Sales revenue
2004	Q1	California	3,509	$519,220
2004	Q1	Colorado	921	$131,797
2004	Q1	DC	1,467	$208,324
2004	Q1	Florida	924	$137,530
2004	Q1	Illinois	1,711	$256,454

2. Save your document.

3. Activate Drill Mode by selecting 'Start Drill'.

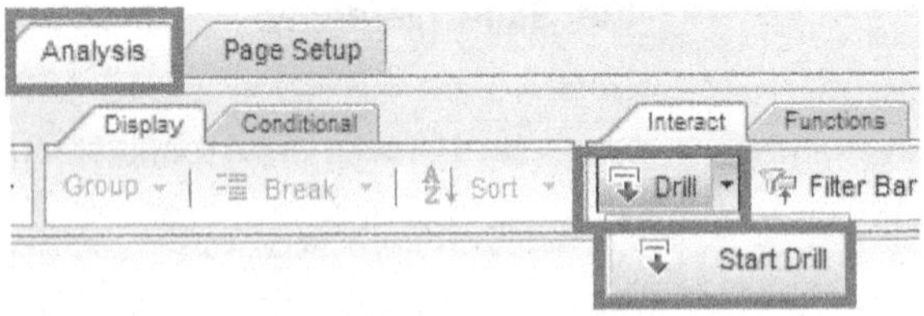
Analysis
Page Setup
Display
Conditional
Interact
Functions
Group
Break
Sort
Drill
Filter Bar
Start Drill

4. Reports in Drill Mode will have a drill icon against their name (on the report tab).

Report 1

5. The following buttons will be active:

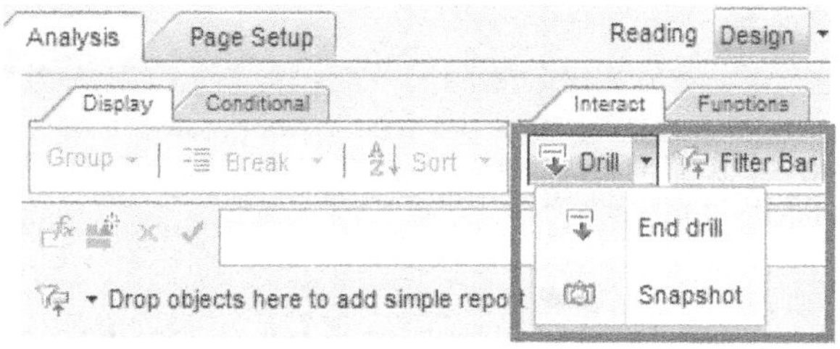
Analysis
Page Setup
Reading
Design
Display
Conditional
Interact
Functions
Group
Break
Sort
Drill
Filter Bar
End drill
Snapshot
Drop objects here to add simple repo

6. Drill Mode will change your blocks of data into drillable results.

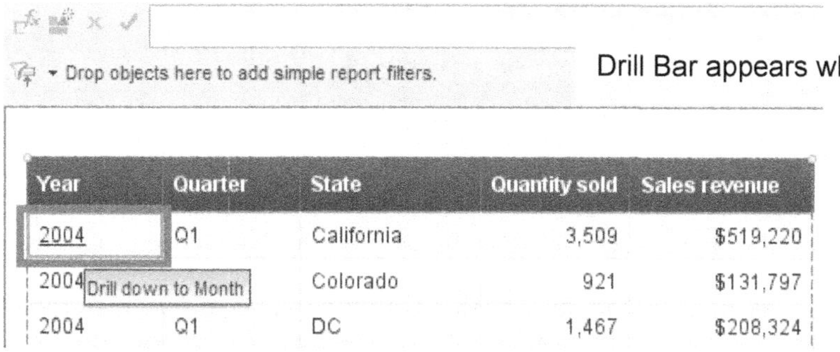
Drop objects here to add simple report filters.
Year
Quarter
State
Quantity sold
Sales revenue
2004
Q1
California
3,509
$519,220
2004
Drill down to Month
Colorado
921
$131,797
2004
Q1
DC
1,467
$208,324

Drill Bar appears when 'Drill Mode' is activated.

Hovering over values will indicate drill path.

7. Save your document.

33.5 Drill Down and Drill Up

Data can be drilled downwards (more detail) or upwards (less detail), for example:

If we have data at [Quarter] level then we have 1 row per [Quarter] value.

Drilling down on a single quarter will typically result in 3 rows if the next level is [Month].

Drilling up from [Quarter] to [Year] will aggregate 4 rows at [Quarter] level to 1 row at [Year] level.

If you hover over a dimension in which there is another drill level available down in the hierarchy, then the cursor changes to reveal 'drill tips' (i.e. which drill dimension is next in line).

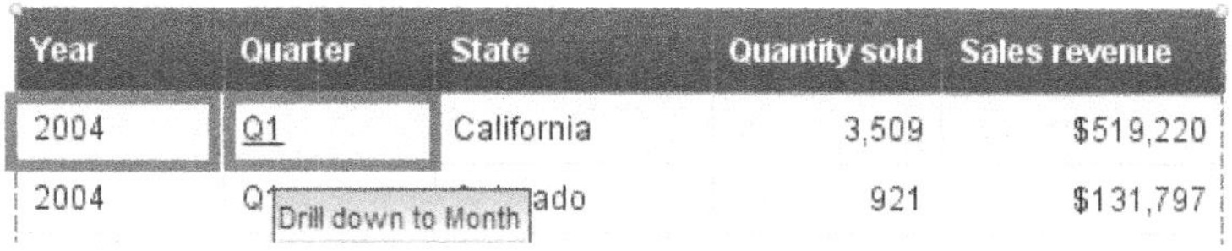
Year
Quarter
State
Quantity sold
Sales revenue
2004
Q1
California
3,509
$519,220
2004
Drill down to Month
921
$131,797

Hovering over [Year] or [Quarter] reveals the next level is 'Drill down to Month' because it is the next level down in the 'Time period' hierarchy.

Year	Quarter	State	Quantity sold	Sales revenue
2004	Q1	California	3,509	$519,220
2004	Q1	Colorado	921	$131,797

Drill down to City

Hovering over [State] reveals the next level is 'Drill down to City' because it is the next level down in the 'Store' hierarchy.

If you hover over measures then the cursor changes to reveal 'drill tips' based on the combined dimension hierarchies that are relevant to the context in which the measure is being displayed.

Year	Quarter	State	Quantity sold	Sales revenue
2004	Q1	California	3,509	$519,220
2004	Q1	Colorado	[illegible]	[illegible]
2004	Q1	DC	1,467	$208,324

Drill down to Month / Month / City

Hovering over [Quantity sold] or [Sales revenue] reveals the next level is '**Drill down to Month / Month / City**'.

This can be read as '**Drill down to Month / City**' as we have two hierarchies available because the measures are being displayed against dimensions from 'Time period' hierarchy and 'Store' hierarchy.

NOTE – The 'drill tips' text shows Month twice because we have both [Year] and [Quarter] in the block. Removing either [Year] or [Quarter] from the block would change the text to '**Drill down to Month / City**'.

33.5.1 Performing a Drill Down

1. Click in 'Q1' in the [Quarter] column on the row where [Year] = 2004 and [State] = 'Colorado' as shown below:

Year	Quarter	State	Quantity sold	Sales revenue
2004	Q1	California	3,509	$519,220
2004	Q1	Colorado	921	$131,797
2004	[illegible]	[illegible]	1,467	$208,324

Drill down to Month

Web Intelligence now displays:

Performing the action 'Drill down to Month' on [Quarter] causes [Quarter] to be placed in the Filter Bar, and [Month] replaces the [Quarter] column in the block.

An arrow appears in the header of the 'drilled' column to drill back up.

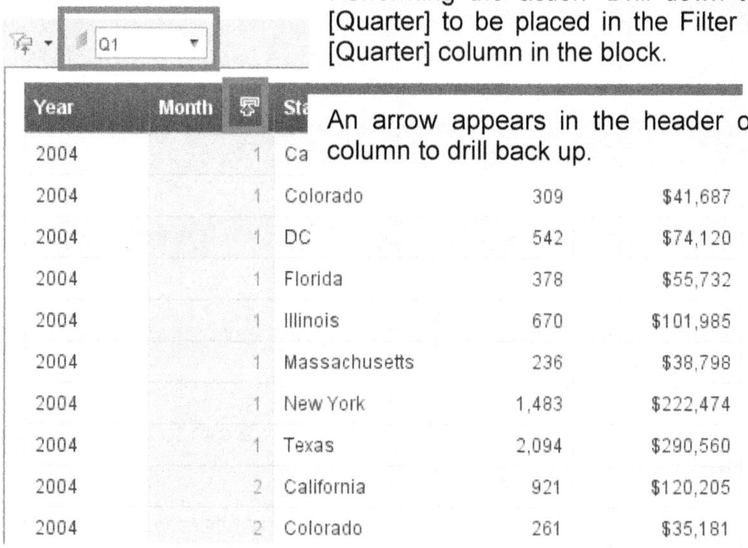

Year	Month	St...		
2004	1	Ca...		
2004	1	Colorado	309	$41,687
2004	1	DC	542	$74,120
2004	1	Florida	378	$55,732
2004	1	Illinois	670	$101,985
2004	1	Massachusetts	236	$38,798
2004	1	New York	1,483	$222,474
2004	1	Texas	2,094	$290,560
2004	2	California	921	$120,205
2004	2	Colorado	261	$35,181

We drilled on [Quarter] = 'Q1' and we now have 'Q1' automatically selected in the Filter Bar.

Scrolling down the block of data we will see only months 1, 2 and 3, but we will have all years (2004, 2005 and 2006) present in the block.

33.5.2 Performing a Drill Up

If we have already drilled down, or already are at a level where drill up is available (before 'Drill Mode' was activated) then we can drill back up:

By using the arrow in the header of the 'drilled' column.

Month
State
Drill up to Quarter

Or by using right-click on the 'drilled' column.

$55,732
Drill
Group
Drill down to Week
Drill up to Quarter

Or by using right-click on any of the measure column(s).

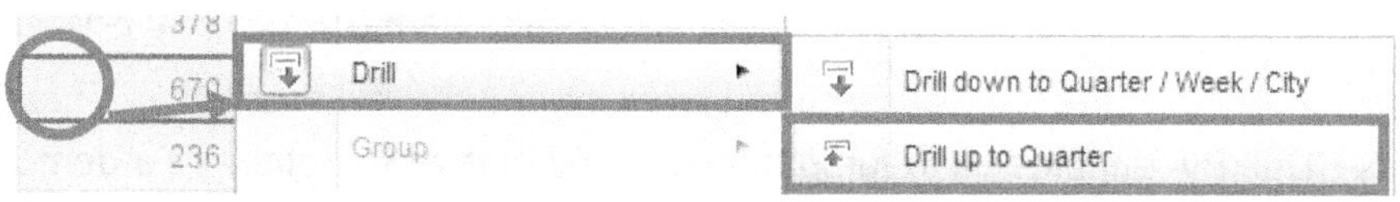
Drill
Group
Drill down to Quarter / Week / City
Drill up to Quarter

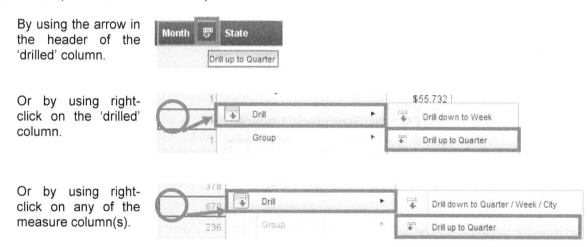

1. Use any of the above methods to 'Drill up to Quarter'.

Web Intelligence removes the [Quarter] object from the Filter Bar and places it back into the block by replacing the [Month] column.

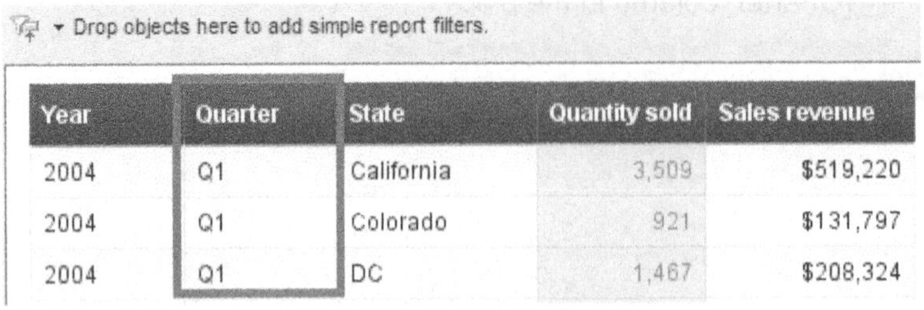
Drop objects here to add simple report filters.

Year	Quarter	State	Quantity sold	Sales revenue
2004	Q1	California	3,509	$519,220
2004	Q1	Colorado	921	$131,797
2004	Q1	DC	1,467	$208,324

NOTES

When drill has taken place (i.e. there are objects in the Filter Bar) then we can toggle these two buttons on and off without affecting the results.

Filter Bar

Will hide (or show) the Filter Bar but any filters will retain their settings.

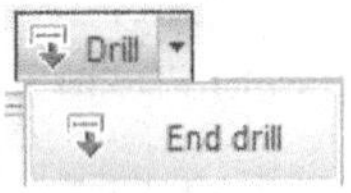
Drill
End drill

'End Drill' will switch off Drill Mode but any drilled actions will remain in place, i.e. any filters in the Filter Bar will retain their settings.

Web Intelligence will automatically display the next available dimension in the drill path.

i.e. Clicking on [Year] will automatically take us to [Month] as [Quarter] is already in the block.

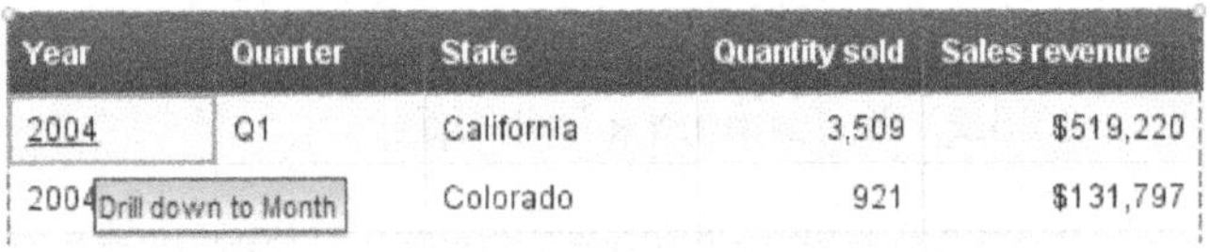
Drill down to Month

Year	Quarter	State	Quantity sold	Sales revenue
2004	Q1	California	3,509	$519,220
2004		Colorado	921	$131,797

33.6 Drill By

'Drill Down' and 'Drill Up' work in one hierarchy at a time, for example:

- We can drill down the 'Time period' hierarchy from [Year] to [Quarter] to [Month] or we can drill up this same hierarchy in the opposite direction from [Month] to [Quarter] to [Year].
- We can also drill down the 'Store' hierarchy from [State] to [City] to [Store name] or drill back up this hierarchy from [Store name] to [City] to [State].

'Drill By' enables us to jump from one hierarchy to another. To demonstrate this let us reorganise our block of data first.

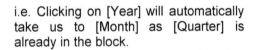

1. Remove all drilled actions so we have an empty Filter Bar, or recreate the block as shown below.

Drop objects here to add simple report filters.

Year	Quarter	State	Quantity sold	Sales revenue
2004	Q1	California	3,509	$519,220
2004	Q1	Colorado	921	$131,797
2004	Q1	DC	1,467	$208,324

2. Right-click in the [Quarter] column and delete it, and then also delete the [State] column.

Year	Quantity sold	Sales revenue
2004	53,078	$8,095,814
2005	79,855	$13,232,246
2006	90,296	$15,059,143

3. Apply 'Sum' to both measure columns.

Year	Quantity sold	Sales revenue
2004	53,078	$8,095,814
2005	79,855	$13,232,246
2006	90,296	$15,059,143
	223,229	**$36,387,203**

4. Drill down to [Quarter] on [Year] = '2005', i.e. click on '2005'.

Year	Quantity sold	Sales revenue
2004	53,078	$8,095,814
2005	79,855	$13,232,246
20 Drill down to Quarter	90,296	$15,059,143
	223,229	**$36,387,203**

2005

Quarter	Quantity sold	Sales revenue
Q1	21,135	$3,326,172
Q2	17,152	$2,840,651
Q3	19,224	$2,879,303
Q4	22,344	$4,186,120
	79,855	**$13,232,246**

Drilling down from [Year] to [Quarter] has split the yearly total into quarterly totals without any loss in values.

NOTE

For [Year] = '2005' and [Quarter] = 'Q2',

[Quantity sold] = 17,152 and [Sales revenue] = 2,840,651

5. Now right-click on 'Q2' and select 'Drill – Drill by – Store – State'.

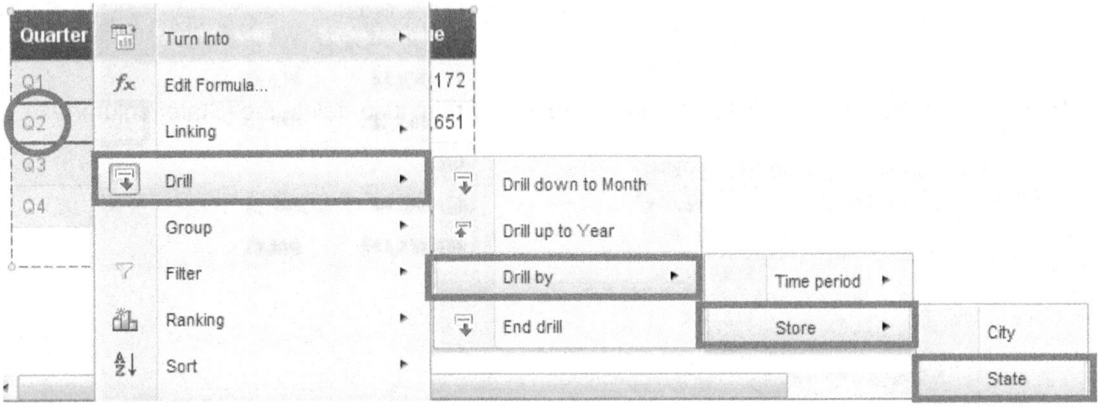
Quarter
Q1
Q2
Q3
Q4
Turn Into
Edit Formula...
Linking
Drill
Group
Filter
Ranking
Sort
Drill down to Month
Drill up to Year
Drill by
End drill
Time period
Store
City
State

6. We have now moved from the 'Time period' hierarchy to the 'Store' hierarchy and the values are now displayed by [State] in '2005' / 'Q2' as shown here.

State	Quantity sold	Sales revenue
California	3,184	$529,256
Colorado	963	$157,337
DC	1,627	$263,486
Florida	859	$147,358
Illinois	1,545	$254,722
New York	4,194	$692,513
Texas	4,780	$795,979
	17,152	**$2,840,651**

Drilling across using 'Drill by' shows how each [State] has contributed to the total '2005' / 'Q2'.

This is confirmed by the totals:

[Quantity sold] = 17,152

[Sales revenue] = 2,840,651

7. Save your document.

33.6.1 Using Filter Bar in Drill Mode

We have seen that when drilling occurs the contents of the Filter Toolbar dynamically change to reflect the drill actions performed.

When objects are in the Filter Bar we can use them to select different values and the report contents will change accordingly.

1. For example, we have changed the above filter (from '2005' / 'Q2' to '2006' / 'All Quarter') simply by using the drop down arrows to select values.

2006
All Quarter

State	Quantity sold	Sales revenue
California	17,769	$2,992,679
Colorado	5,116	$843,584
DC	6,491	$1,053,581
Florida	4,830	$811,924
Illinois	6,519	$1,134,085
Massachusett:	5,269	$887,169
New York	19,109	$3,151,022
Texas	25,193	$4,185,098
	90,296	**$15,059,143**

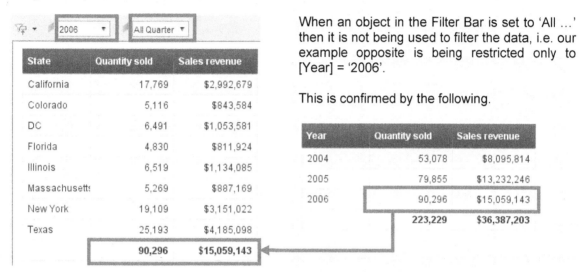

When an object in the Filter Bar is set to 'All ...' then it is not being used to filter the data, i.e. our example opposite is being restricted only to [Year] = '2006'.

This is confirmed by the following.

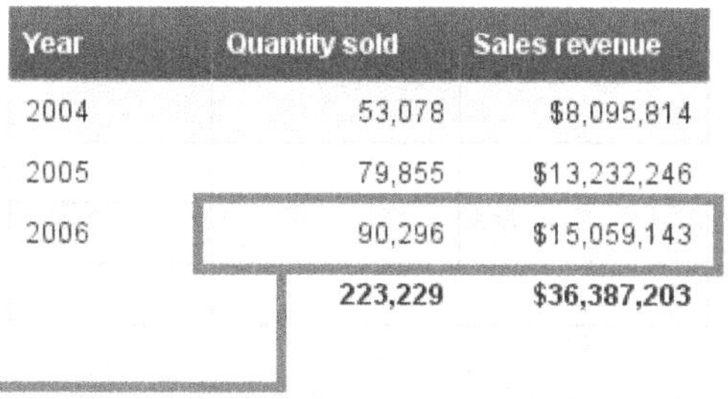

Year	Quantity sold	Sales revenue
2004	53,078	$8,095,814
2005	79,855	$13,232,246
2006	90,296	$15,059,143
	223,229	**$36,387,203**

The filter for [Quarter] is not being used because it is set to 'All Quarter', meaning use all values for [Quarter].

2. We can add new objects into the Filter Bar (without using drill actions) by selecting objects from the drop down located on the left-hand side of the Filter Bar. We are going to select the [Month] object.

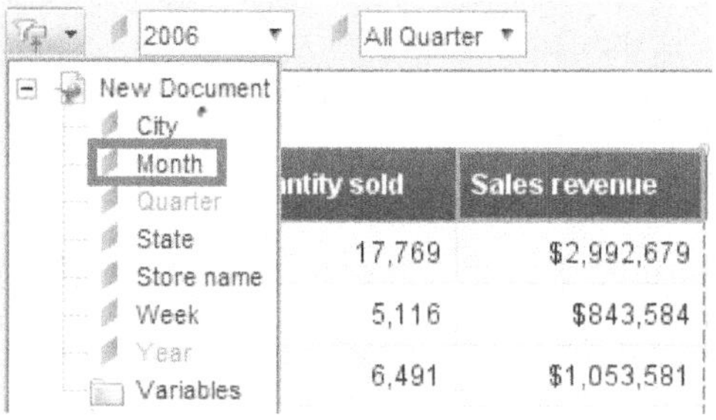
2006
All Quarter
New Document
City
Month
Quarter
State
Store name
Week
Year
Variables

...ntity sold	Sales revenue
17,769	$2,992,679
5,116	$843,584
6,491	$1,053,581

3. We can then apply a filter on the new object:

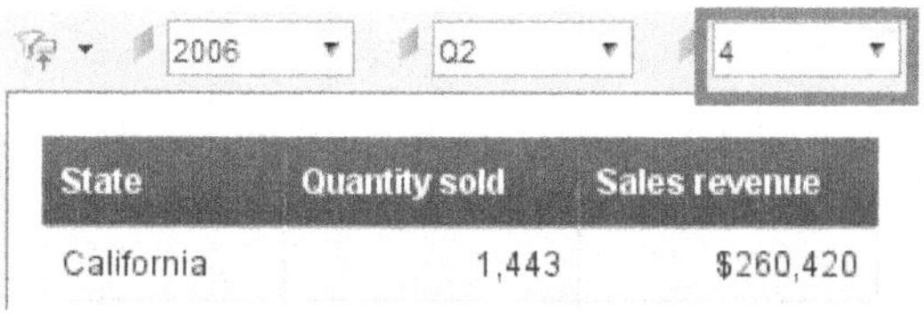
2006
Q2
4

State	Quantity sold	Sales revenue
California	1,443	$260,420

4. We can remove an object from the Filter Bar (without using drill actions) by dragging the object back into the data tab.

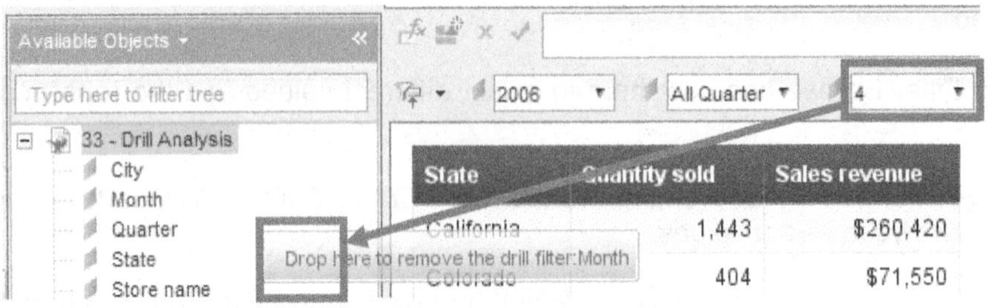
Available Objects
Type here to filter tree
33 - Drill Analysis
City
Month
Quarter
State
Store name
2006
All Quarter
4
State
Quantity sold
Sales revenue
California
1,443
$260,420
Colorado
404
$71,550
Drop here to remove the drill filter:Month

Or select 'Remove' in the object's value:

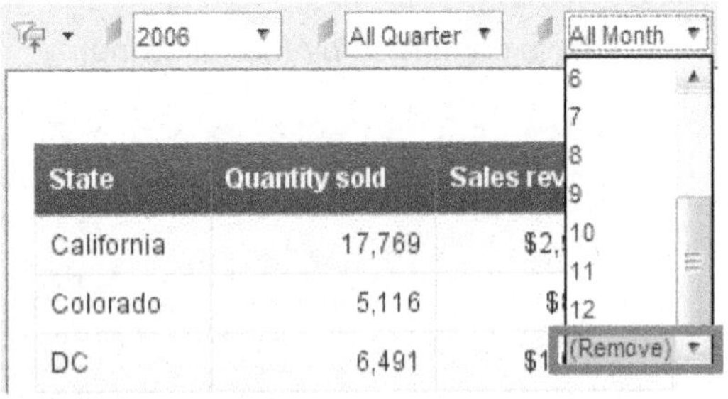
2006
All Quarter
All Month
State
Quantity sold
California
17,769
Colorado
5,116
DC
6,491
6
7
8
9
10
11
12
(Remove)

5. When using the Filter Bar to set filters, objects lower down a hierarchy will already be filtered to show only those values that are related to higher levels within the hierarchy.

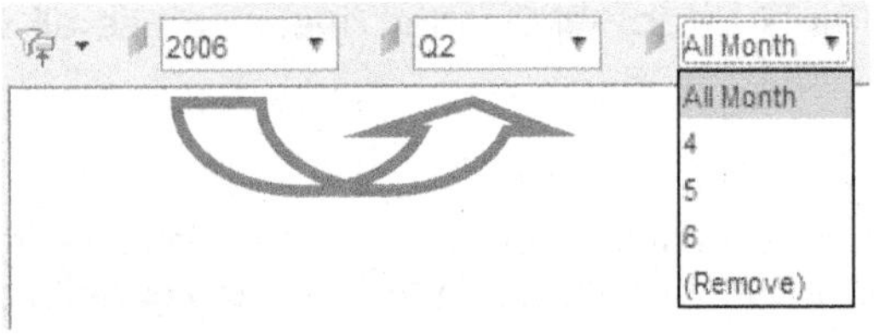
2006
Q2
All Month
All Month
4
5
6
(Remove)

We have a filter on [Year] = '2006'.

We have also filtered [Quarter] = 'Q2'.

Therefore we have the option to select [Month] = 4, 5, or 6.

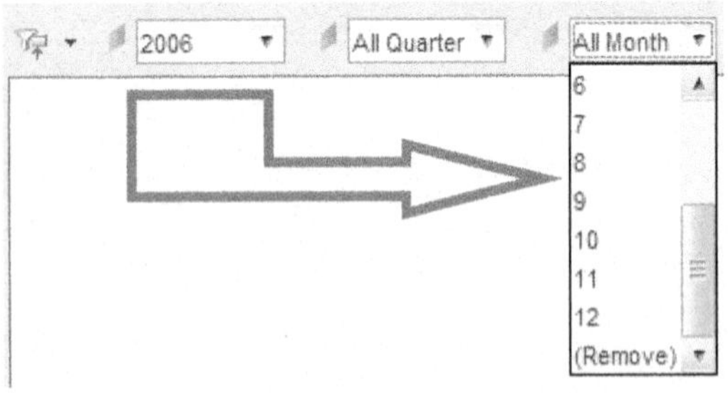
2006
All Quarter
All Month
6
7
8
9
10
11
12
(Remove)

We have a filter on [Year] = '2006'.

We have no filter on [Quarter].

Therefore we have the option to select [Month] = 1 to 12.

NOTE

Cascading occurs because Web Intelligence knows how the levels are related due to the hierarchy definition in the universe. If dimension(s) do not belong to hierarchies then cascading will not occur.

33.7 Drill Snapshots

As you move through your data, you may notice anomalies or views you wish to return to or point out as significant to others. The snapshot button is very useful for saving reports without having to quit drill mode.

1. Rename the report tab to 'Drill Example'.

2. Drill on [State]='Texas':

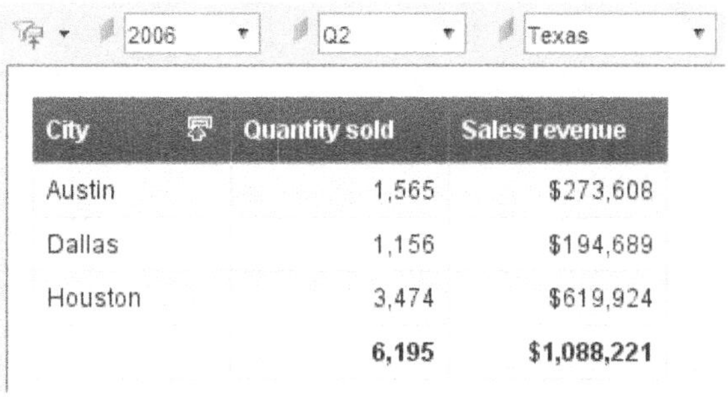
2006
Q2
Texas

City	Quantity sold	Sales revenue
Austin	1,565	$273,608
Dallas	1,156	$194,689
Houston	3,474	$619,924
	6,195	**$1,088,221**

3. To create a snapshot, just click on the snapshot button while in drill mode.

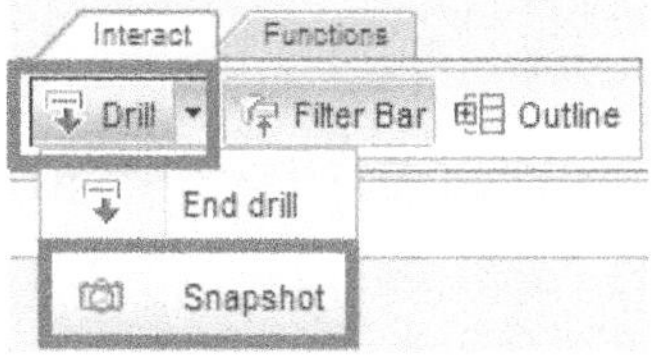
Interact
Functions
Drill
Filter Bar
Outline
End drill
Snapshot

A new report tab is created with the 'snapshot' of the current data and you are automatically moved to the new report tab.

Drill Example
Drill Example (1)

NOTE

The snapshot report is not in Drill Mode because the Drill icon is not active on the report tab name.

When simply looking at the data in the snapshot, nothing on the report indicates what values have been selected. The snapshot appears only slightly different to the report it has been created from. Drill Filters in the source report are replaced with Report Filters in the snapshot.

33.7.1 Source Report:

Right-click in the source report.

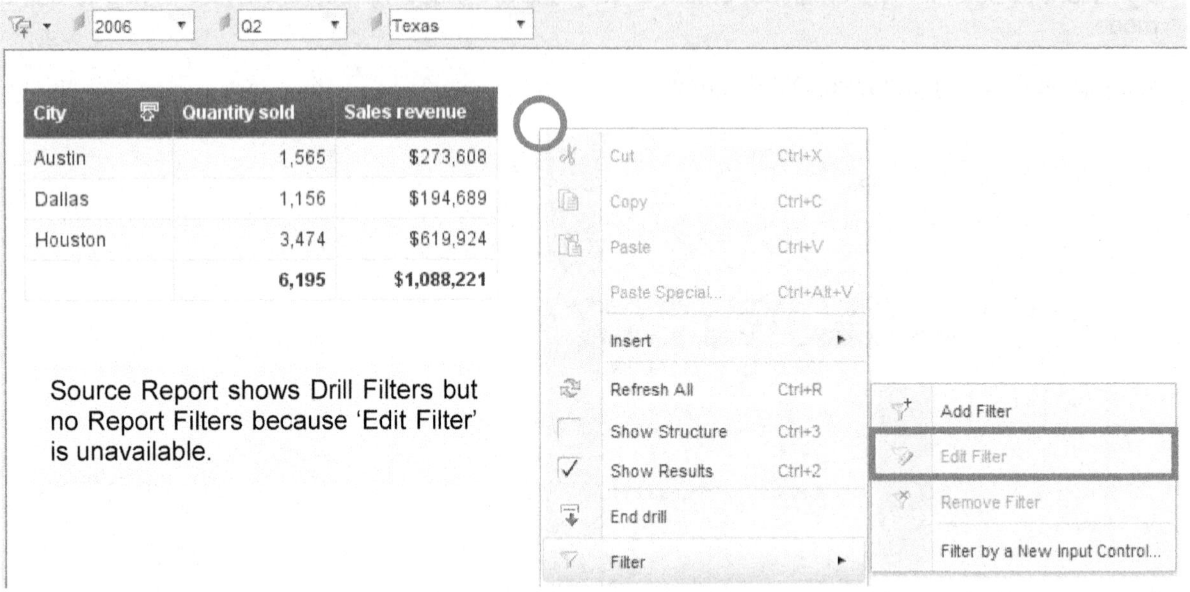
2006
Q2
Texas
City
Quantity sold
Sales revenue
Austin 1,565 $273,608
Dallas 1,156 $194,689
Houston 3,474 $619,924
6,195 $1,088,221
Source Report shows Drill Filters but no Report Filters because 'Edit Filter' is unavailable.
Cut Ctrl+X
Copy Ctrl+C
Paste Ctrl+V
Paste Special... Ctrl+Alt+V
Insert
Refresh All Ctrl+R
Show Structure Ctrl+3
Show Results Ctrl+2
End drill
Filter
Add Filter
Edit Filter
Remove Filter
Filter by a New Input Control...

33.7.2 Snapshot Report:

Right-click in the snapshot report:

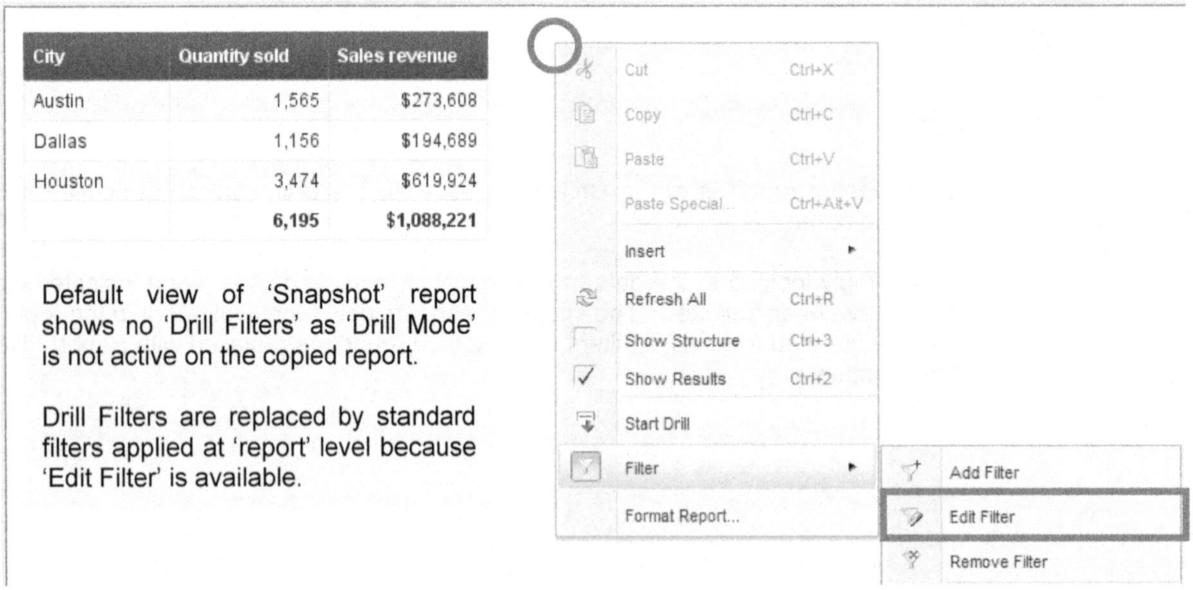
City
Quantity sold
Sales revenue
Austin 1,565 $273,608
Dallas 1,156 $194,689
Houston 3,474 $619,924
6,195 $1,088,221
Default view of 'Snapshot' report shows no 'Drill Filters' as 'Drill Mode' is not active on the copied report.
Drill Filters are replaced by standard filters applied at 'report' level because 'Edit Filter' is available.
Cut Ctrl+X
Copy Ctrl+C
Paste Ctrl+V
Paste Special... Ctrl+Alt+V
Insert
Refresh All Ctrl+R
Show Structure Ctrl+3
Show Results Ctrl+2
Start Drill
Filter
Format Report...
Add Filter
Edit Filter
Remove Filter

Switching on 'Drill Mode' in the snapshot shows the Filter Bar with the applied filters:

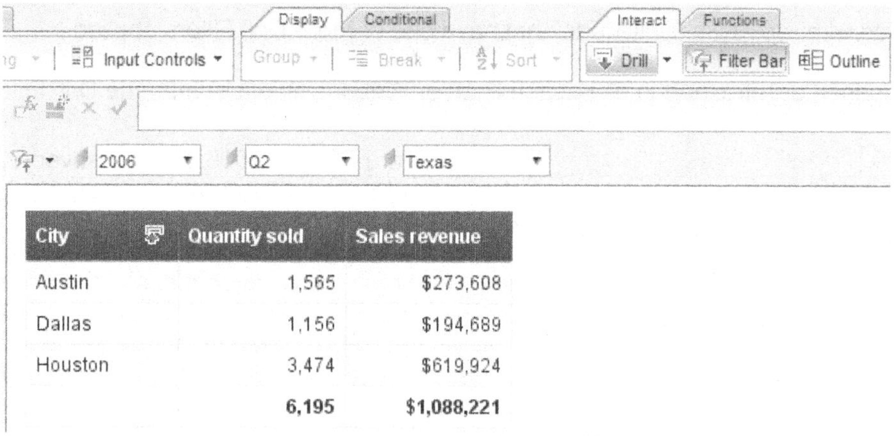
Display
Conditional
Interact
Functions
Input Controls
Group
Break
Sort
Drill
Filter Bar
Outline
2006
Q2
Texas
City
Quantity sold
Sales revenue
Austin 1,565 $273,608
Dallas 1,156 $194,689
Houston 3,474 $619,924
6,195 $1,088,221

Changing the value of a Drill Filter in the snapshot causes the Report Filters to be replaced with Drill Filters, i.e. report now starts to behave like the source report.

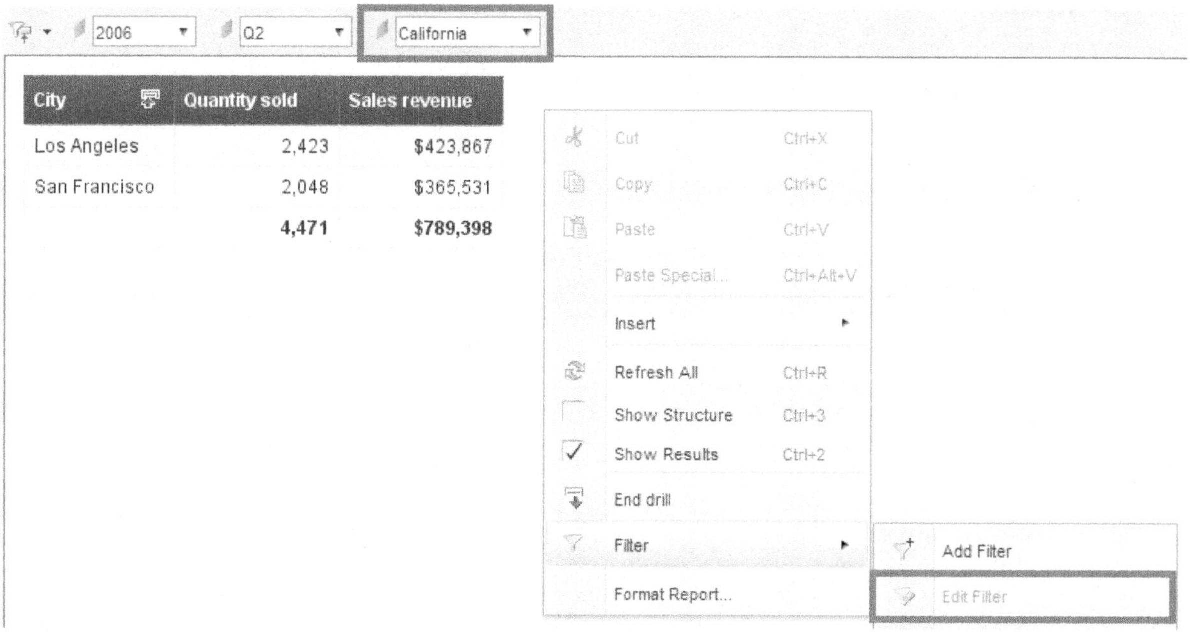
2006
Q2
California
City
Quantity sold
Sales revenue
Los Angeles 2,423 $423,867
San Francisco 2,048 $365,531
4,471 $789,398
Cut Ctrl+X
Copy Ctrl+C
Paste Ctrl+V
Paste Special... Ctrl+Alt+V
Insert
Refresh All Ctrl+R
Show Structure Ctrl+3
Show Results Ctrl+2
End drill
Filter
Format Report...
Add Filter
Edit Filter

33.8 Saving Documents with Drilled Reports

A document may be saved with reports in 'Drill Mode' that have one or more Drill Filters applied.

When the document is opened or refreshed in BI Launch Pad (or Web Intelligence) then the Drill Filters retain their settings.

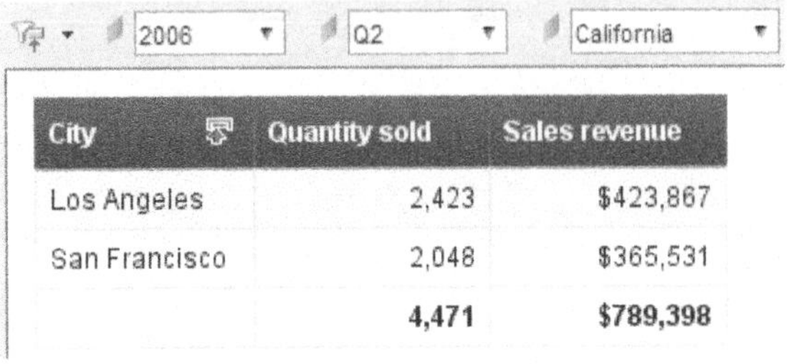
2006
Q2
California

City	Quantity sold	Sales revenue
Los Angeles	2,423	$423,867
San Francisco	2,048	$365,531
	4,471	**$789,398**

Assume we are in April 2006 and we saved the document with Drill Filters applied as shown opposite.

When we refresh the document in May and June 2006 then the Drill Filters will remain in place, but our figures should change to include the May and June 2006 values because we have [Quarter] = 'Q2'.

In July 2006 the values should not change (unless figures are restated).

NOTE

Remove Drill Filter selections before saving your reports for users, unless your users want a 'default' view of the data that can be satisfied by Drill Filters.

33.9 Extending the Scope of Analysis

Before we continue, ensure your BI Launch Pad Preferences for Web Intelligence have the following 'ticked' (as shown below):

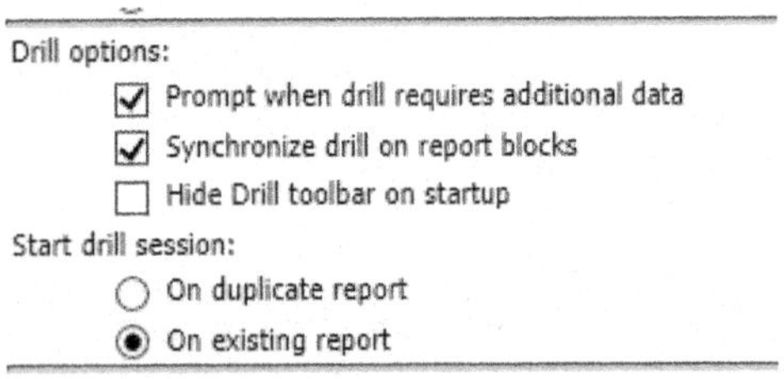
Drill options:
Prompt when drill requires additional data
Synchronize drill on report blocks
Hide Drill toolbar on startup
Start drill session:
On duplicate report
On existing report

1. Create a new document with the following query ('eFashion' universe) using a 'Scope level' of 'two level' and run it.

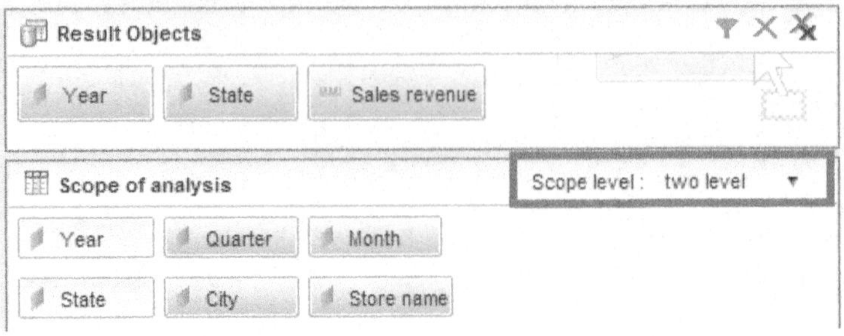
Result Objects
Year
State
Sales revenue
Scope of analysis
Scope level : two level
Year
Quarter
Month
State
City
Store name

2. Web Intelligence displays the following default block:

Year	State	Sales revenue
2004	California	$1,704,211
2004	Colorado	$448,302
2004	DC	$693,211
2004	Florida	$405,985
2004	Illinois	$737,914

From the 'Scope of analysis' we can see that we can drill down from [State] to [City] to [Store name] or we can drill down from [Year] to [Quarter] to [Month].

However the 'Time period' hierarchy also includes levels lower than [Month].

Can we drill down lower than [Month] in our document?

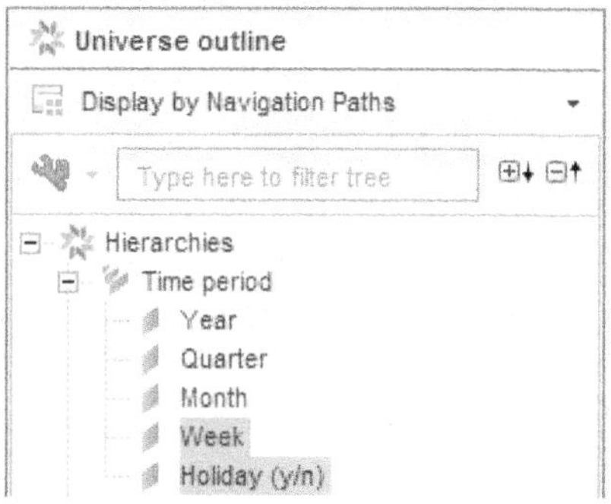
Universe outline
Display by Navigation Paths
Type here to filter tree
Hierarchies
Time period
Year
Quarter
Month
Week
Holiday (y/n)

3. Switch on 'Drill Mode' and drill down the 'Time period' hierarchy until we reach [Month] as shown below:

2004 ▾ Q1 ▾

Month	State	Sales revenue
1	California	$178,186
1	Colorado	$41,687
1	DC	$74,120

4. Hover over a [Month] value and Web Intelligence displays the tip 'Drill down to Week (new query)':

Month	State	Sales revenue
1	California	$178,186
1 Drill down to Week (new query)		$41,687

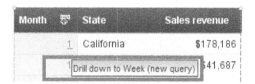

If a lower level exists in a hierarchy and it is not within the document then a new query has to be run to fetch the lower level.

5. Drill down on [Month]=1.

We now have the ability to influence what data the new query should fetch (explained on the next page).

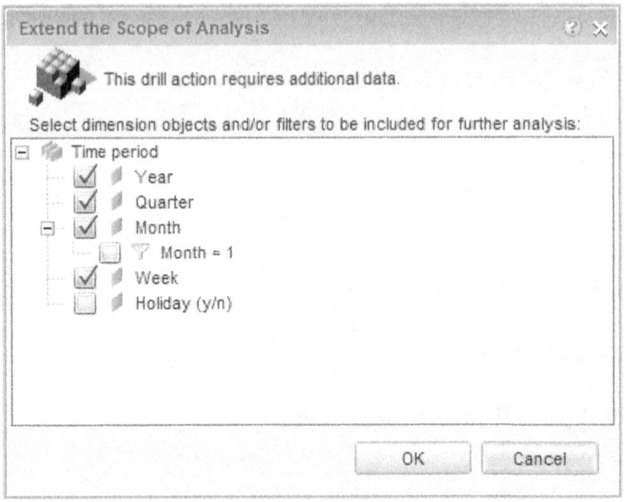
Extend the Scope of Analysis
This drill action requires additional data.
Select dimension objects and/or filters to be included for further analysis:
Time period
Year
Quarter
Month
Month = 1
Week
Holiday (y/n)
OK
Cancel

Extend the Scope of Analysis interface shows the hierarchy we are trying to extend into.

[Year], [Quarter], [Month] and [Week] are selected by default so these will be included in the new query.

We could select [Holiday (y/n)] to include it, therefore the new query would be extended by two levels rather than one.

If we leave the [Month] filter unchecked, i.e. **do not tick**:

[Month] = '1'

Then Web Intelligence will run the query at the lower level and fetch data for all weeks:

[Year] = No restriction
[Quarter] = No restriction
[Month] = No restriction

The Drill Filters will default to the drilled values (as shown below):

2004
Q1
1
Week
State
Sales revenue
2
California
$24,996
2
Colorado
$5,301
2
DC
$15,800
2
Florida
$6,040

However, we will still have data for every month and quarter for all years (in this case 2004, 2005 and 2006) that we can continue to analyse in the document.

On the other hand, if we do select the [Month] filter then the new query will be modified to include our selected filters, i.e. in the example below:

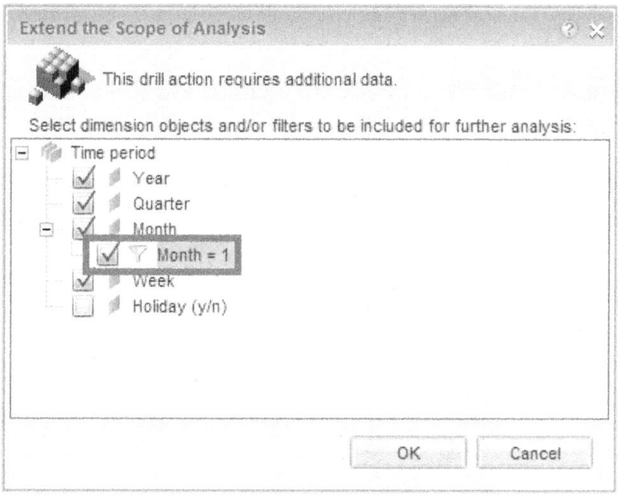
Extend the Scope of Analysis
This drill action requires additional data.
Select dimension objects and/or filters to be included for further analysis:
Time period
Year
Quarter
Month
Month = 1
Week
Holiday (y/n)
OK
Cancel

The new query would be restricted to:

[Year]	= No restriction
[Quarter]	= No restriction
[Month]	= 1

Meaning after the query has run our document would contain data for:

[Year]	= '2004', '2005', '2006'
[Quarter]	= 'Q1' (because [Month]=1)
[Month]	= 1

Further analysis will now be limited due to restriction placed on [Month]=1, i.e. we would only be able to analyse data for Month 1 across the three years.

Notes on Extending the Scope of Analysis

Running a new query could take a long time if there is a lot of data to fetch so restricting the new query using the filters can help to reduce the time it takes for the new query to run. The disadvantage of applying filters is that the document will contain less data for further analysis.

Once a new query has been run and new dimensions added to the document then drilling back up will not purge the query of the lower level dimensions.

Whether to use filters when 'Extending the Scope of Analysis' really does depend on the query and how much data is going to be returned by the document. Users of your reports should be given guidance on the advantages/disadvantages of drilling past the scope of analysis within documents you create for them.

6. Save your document.

33.10 Dynamic Drilling using Query Drill Mode

We have looked at setting a 'Scope of Analysis' in the Query Panel and then 'Extending the Scope of Analysis' in reports when drilling.

When a new query is run (due to drilling down) then Web Intelligence brings lower level dimensions into the document, but then it will retain these dimensions even if we drill back up in the report.

An alternative method of drilling is based on not using the 'Scope of Analysis' and is activated using the Document Property called 'Use query drill'.

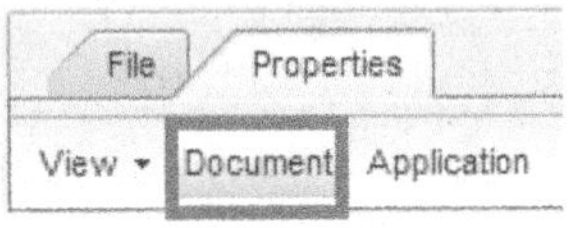
File
Properties
View
Document
Application

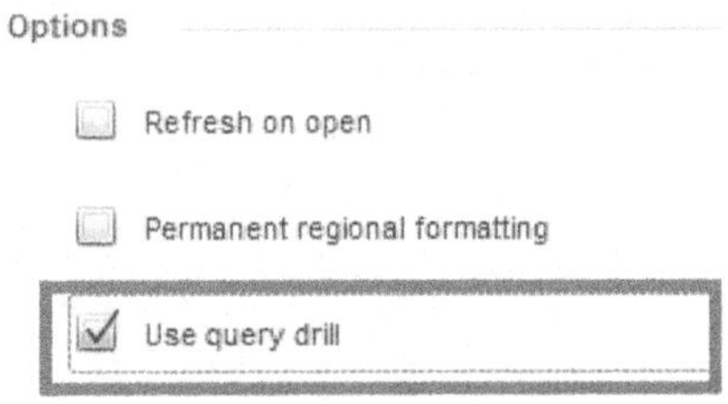
Options
Refresh on open
Permanent regional formatting
Use query drill

NOTE

Before activating 'Use query drill' you must ensure your existing queries have 'Scope of Analysis' set to:

- Drill Mode is switched off in the document
- Your existing queried have 'Scope level: None'

If you try to set 'Use query drill' and get the error message shown opposite then:

1. Uncheck 'Use query drill'.
2. Go back into the Query Panel and set 'Scope of Analysis' to:

   'Scope level: none'

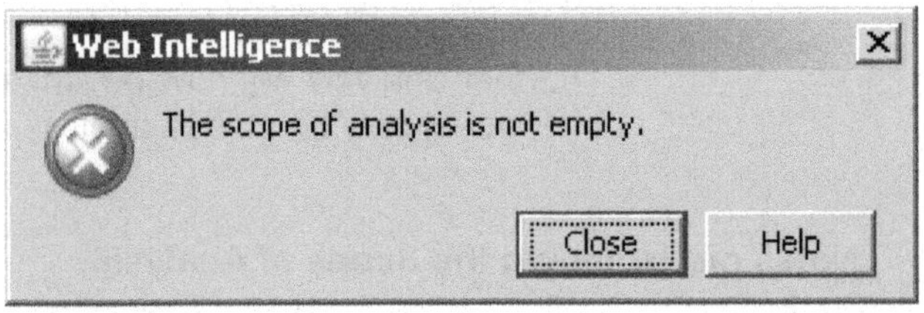
Web Intelligence
The scope of analysis is not empty.
Close
Help

NOTE

If Drill Mode is set on then you might need to switch Drill Mode off and switch it back on after setting the 'Use query drill' property.

33.10.1 What does Query Drill Mode do?

In 'Query Drill Mode', Web Intelligence drills by modifying the underlying query (by adding and removing dimensions and query filters) in addition to applying drill filters within the report.

1. Let us use the following query from 'eFashion' universe as an example:

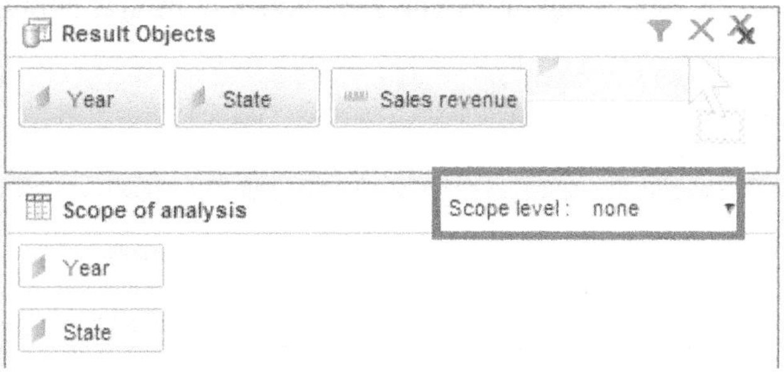
Result Objects
Year
State
Sales revenue
Scope of analysis
Scope level : none
Year
State

IMPORTANT:

'Scope of Analysis' set to '**Scope level: none**'

2. Our query is quite basic in that it has no Query Filters and has not been set up without any 'Scope Levels', therefore our default block displays:

Year	State	Sales revenue
2004	California	$1,704,211
2004	Colorado	$448,302
2004	DC	$693,211
2004	Florida	$405,985
2004	Illinois	$738,224
2004	Massachusetts	$238,819
2004	New York	$1,667,696
2004	Texas	$2,199,677
2005	California	$2,782,680

If we try and apply a filter to the [Year] column then we can see our query has returned three years of data:

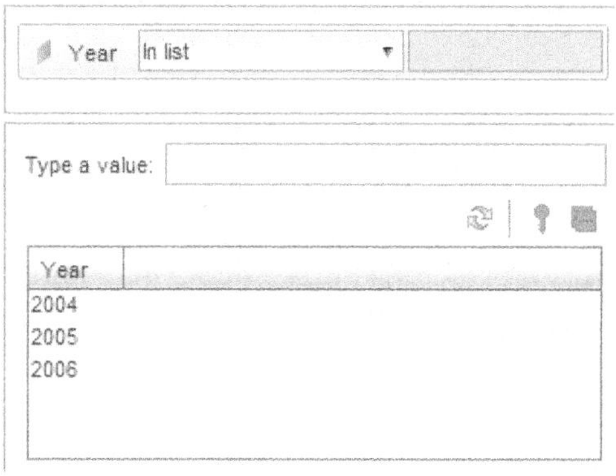
Year
In list
Type a value:
Year
2004
2005
2006

3. Set 'Use query drill' in Document Properties:

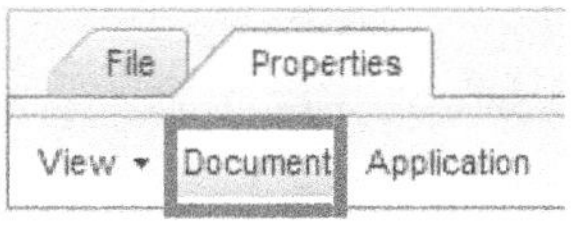
File
Properties
View
Document
Application

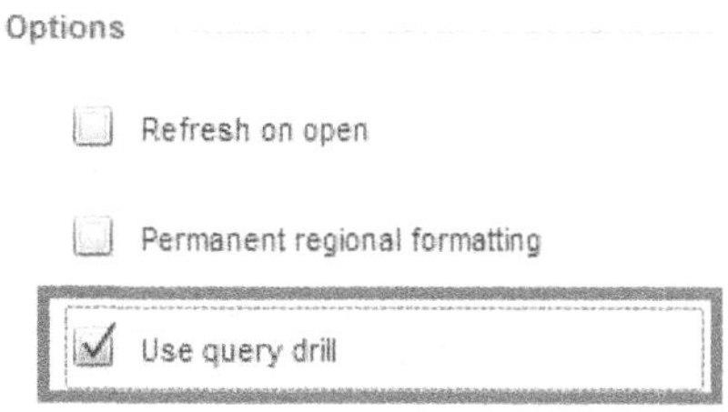
Options
Refresh on open
Permanent regional formatting
Use query drill

4. Activate 'Drill Mode' and we are presented with:

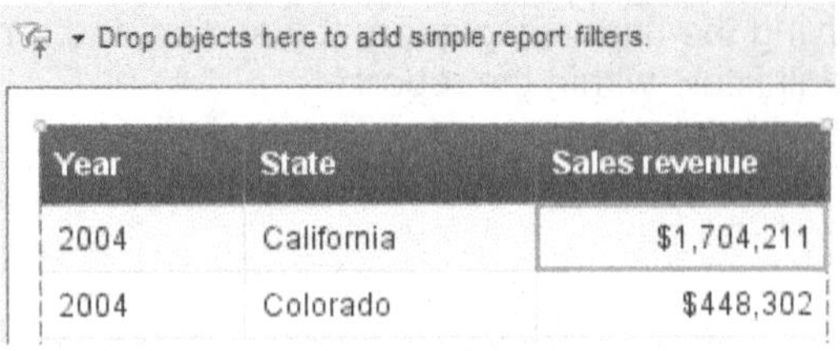
Drop objects here to add simple report filters.
Year
State
Sales revenue
2004
California
$1,704,211
2004
Colorado
$448,302

When drilling in 'Use query drill' mode, **measure** objects cannot be drilled on compared to drilling using 'Scope of Analysis'.

i.e. hovering over a measure does not show a drill path

5. Scroll down and hover over a cell where [Year] = '2005':

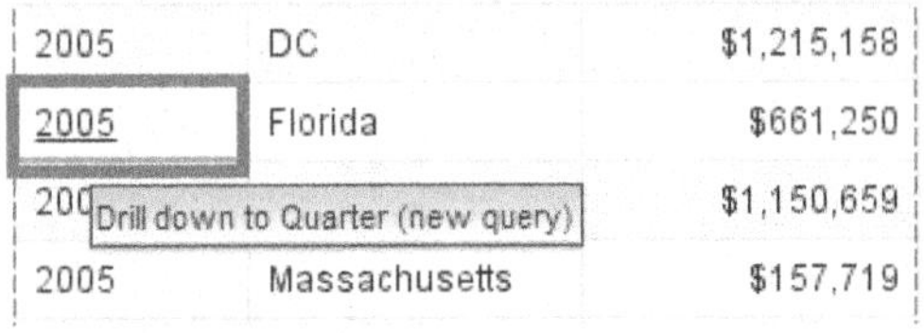
2005
DC
$1,215,158
2005
Florida
$661,250
Drill down to Quarter (new query)
$1,150,659
2005
Massachusetts
$157,719

6. Click on a cell where [Year] = '2005' to drill down to [Quarter]. The results are:

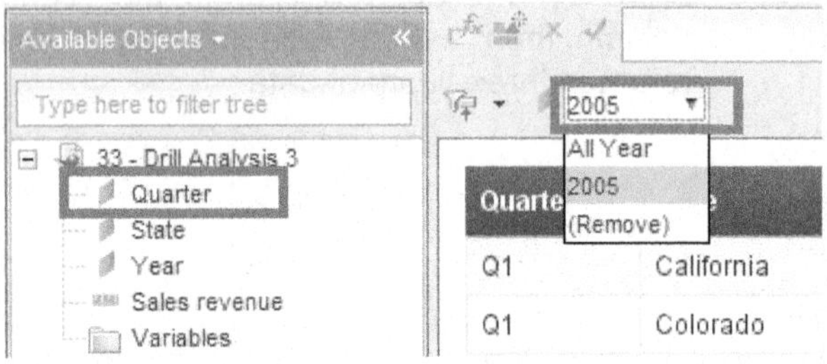
Available Objects
Type here to filter tree
33 - Drill Analysis 3
Quarter
State
Year
Sales revenue
Variables
2005
All Year
2005
(Remove)
Q1
California
Q1
Colorado

The new query has been used to fetch data at [Quarter] level, but we have only one year in Drill Filter.

This would suggest query has only returned data for one year.

Why? See below…

7. If we go into 'Edit Query' mode then we will see the original query has been modified to include the condition [Year] Equal to '2005' in the Query Filters pane.

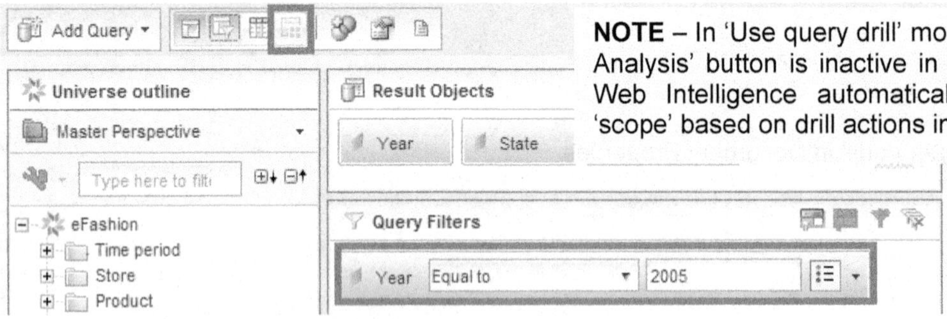
Add Query
Universe outline
Master Perspective
Type here to filt
eFashion
Time period
Store
Product
Result Objects
Year
State
Query Filters
Year
Equal to
2005

NOTE – In 'Use query drill' mode the 'Scope of Analysis' button is inactive in Query Panel as Web Intelligence automatically controls the 'scope' based on drill actions in the report.

8. Go back into the report by selecting:

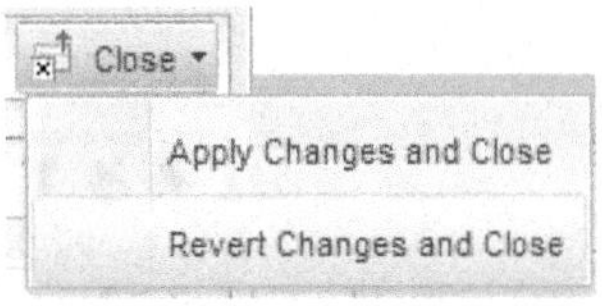
Close
Apply Changes and Close
Revert Changes and Close

9. Click to ‘Drill up to Year’:

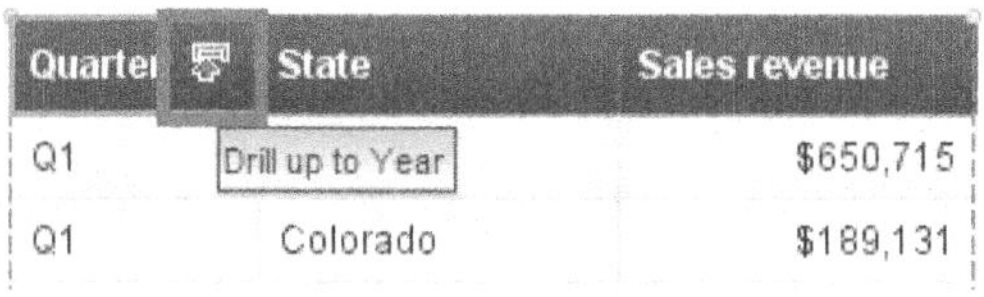
Quarter
State
Sales revenue
Q1
Drill up to Year
$650,715
Q1
Colorado
$189,131

10. Web Intelligence re-queries the database at [Year] level and the result is:

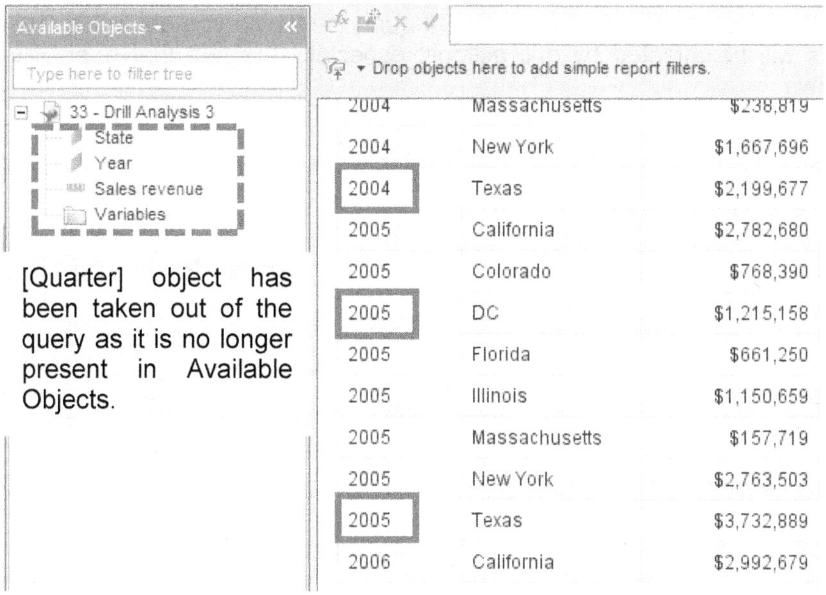
Available Objects
Type here to filter tree
33 - Drill Analysis 3
State
Year
Sales revenue
Variables
Drop objects here to add simple report filters.
2004 Massachusetts $238,819
2004 New York $1,667,696
2004 Texas $2,199,677
2005 California $2,782,680
2005 Colorado $768,390
2005 DC $1,215,158
2005 Florida $661,250
2005 Illinois $1,150,659
2005 Massachusetts $157,719
2005 New York $2,763,503
2005 Texas $3,732,889
2006 California $2,992,679

[Quarter] object has been taken out of the query as it is no longer present in Available Objects.

The query has also been modified to remove the restriction on [Year] therefore report now contains data for all three years.

NOTE

In ‘normal’ drill mode (i.e. when **not in** ‘Use query drill’ mode):

If we drill down to a new query then new objects are bought into Available Objects based on the lower level(s) of the hierarchies being drilled.

If we then drill back up within the report then the lower level objects remain in Available Objects, i.e. a new query is only run when the current ‘Scope of Analysis’ in the document needs to be extended.

In ‘dynamic’ drill mode (i.e. when **in** ‘Use query drill’ mode):

Objects are dynamically placed in Available Objects when drilling down or when drilling up because a new query is run every time to only select the required objects.

33.10.2 When to use Query Drill

As the note above explains ‘query drill’ modifies the query at each drill operation therefore it is ideal for aggregate functions such as percentages, distinct counts, ranks, standard deviations, variances, running aggregates, lead and lag functions.

33.10.3 Points of Note on Query Drill

1. Do not use snapshots when working in 'query drill' mode because snapshots cannot be guaranteed to stay the same due to the dynamic removing of dimension objects.

   As we have seen, when in 'query drill' mode, the 'drill up' action removes the dimension(s) from the underlying query. Therefore any snapshots saved at a lower level would no longer be valid as removing the dimensions from the query will also remove the dimension(s) from the snapshot.

2. If your document contains other reports based on a query on which you are using 'query drill' then these reports will be affected by drill actions, especially the fact that query filters are applied on 'drill down'.

   Example:

   We have a Web Intelligence document containing:

   - A single query with [Year], [Quarter] and [Quantity sold] as Result Objects and no Query Filters.
   - 'Summary Report' tab contains a vertical table displaying [Year], [Quarter] and [Quantity sold].

     i.e. the 'Summary Report' shows 12 rows of data due to 2004, 2005, 2006 with four quarters in each year.

   - 'Drill Report' also displays [Year], [Quarter] and [Quantity sold], but this tab is used with 'query drill'.

     If we drill down from [Quarter] to [Month], say on 'Q2' then a filter is applied to the query to restrict it to [Quarter] = 'Q2'.

     This will affect 'Summary Report' in that we will now have only 3 rows of data due to 2004, 2005 and 2006 but only for 'Q2'.

This can be avoided (at the cost of retrieving duplicate data into Web Intelligence) by creating a copy of the original query and using it to build the 'Summary Report' tab. Now when you drill in 'query drill' mode on the 'Drill Report', the 'Summary Report' will remain unaffected.

33.11 Synchronized Drilling

There are two ways to drill on a report with multiple blocks:

- Drill on only the current block of data (default mode).

  In this setting, when drilling takes place, the next dimension in the drill path replaces the previous dimension only in the current block of the report.

- Drill simultaneously on each block in the report that contains the drilled dimension.

  Drilling on two blocks at once is called 'Synchronized Drilling', however this is not the default setting and is turned on in your Preferences using **'Drill options'** under **'Web Intelligence'**.

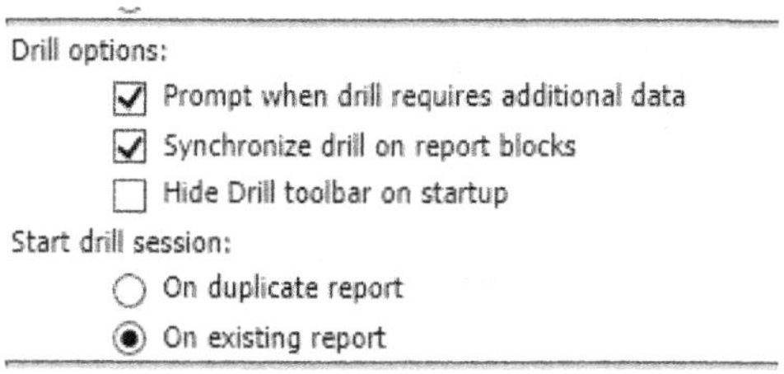
Drill options:
Prompt when drill requires additional data
Synchronize drill on report blocks
Hide Drill toolbar on startup
Start drill session:
On duplicate report
On existing report

1. Create a new document with the following 'eFashion' query.

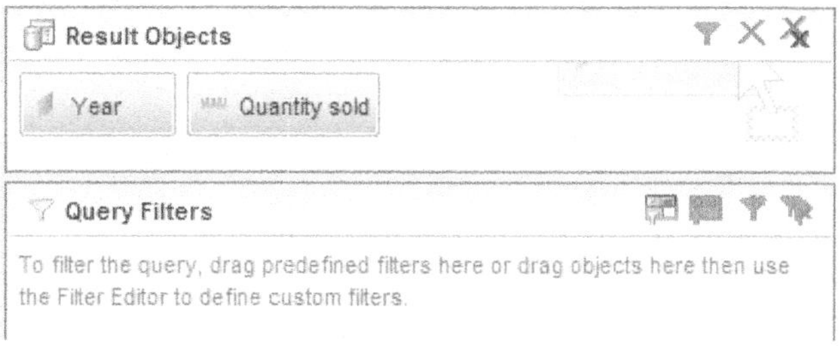
Result Objects
Year
Quantity sold
Query Filters
To filter the query, drag predefined filters here or drag objects here then use the Filter Editor to define custom filters.

2. Present the data in two blocks (a table and a chart) within a single report tab.

Year	Quantity sold
2004	53,078
2005	79,855
2006	90,296

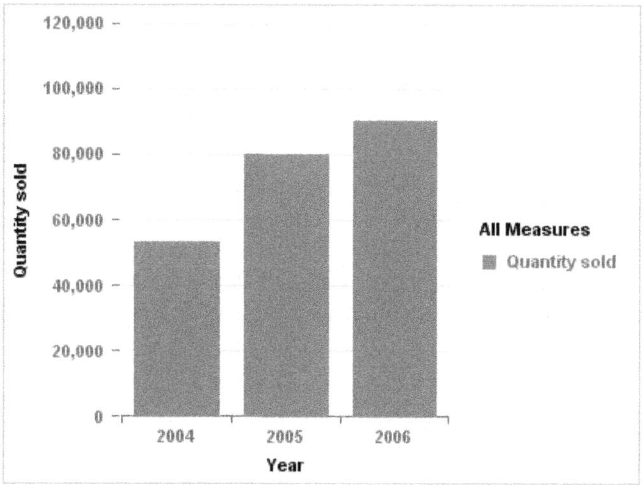
120,000
100,000
80,000
60,000
40,000
20,000
0
Quantity sold
2004
2005
2006
Year
All Measures
Quantity sold

3. Set 'Drill Mode' on and then click on the table block to drill down to [Quarter]. In this example we will click on '2005' as shown below:

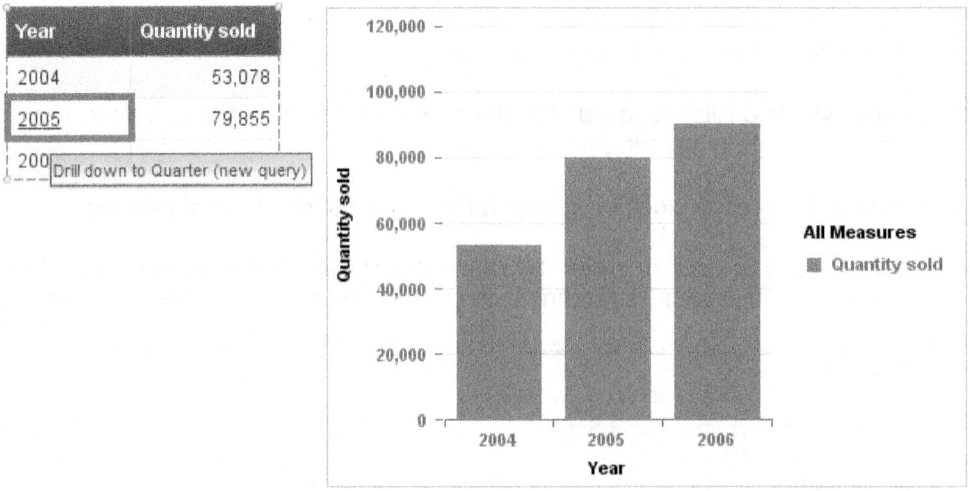
Year
Quantity sold
2004
53,078
2005
79,855
Drill down to Quarter (new query)
120,000
100,000
80,000
60,000
40,000
20,000
0
Quantity sold
2004
2005
2006
Year
All Measures
Quantity sold

4. Click 'OK' if you are presented with the 'Extend Scope of Analysis' interface.

5. Both the table and the chart synchronise to display the 'drilled' values:

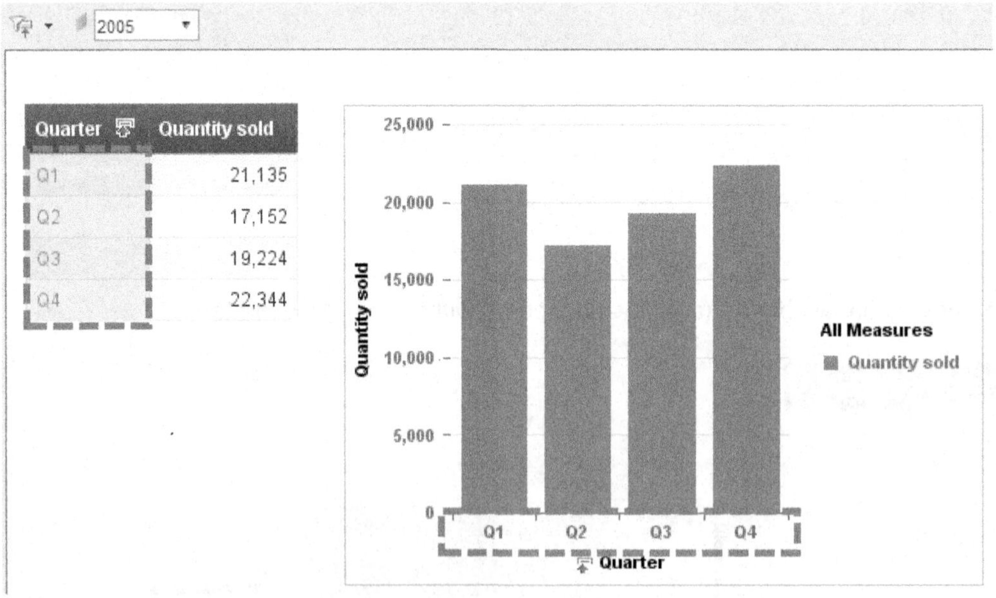
2005
Quarter
Quantity sold
Q1
21,135
Q2
17,152
Q3
19,224
Q4
22,344
25,000
20,000
15,000
10,000
5,000
0
Quantity sold
Q1
Q2
Q3
Q4
Quarter
All Measures
Quantity sold

With synchronized drilling, when you drill in one block then the next dimension in the drill path replaces the previous dimension in all blocks of the report.

6. Save your document.

33.12 Drilling on Charts

Charts can be drilled by clicking on:

- Chart axes values (for dimensions)
- Chart measures values (not available on some chart types)
- Chart legend values
- Using right-click menu

We will use the existing report to look at the above.

- Start with drilling back up to [Year] so our default view is:

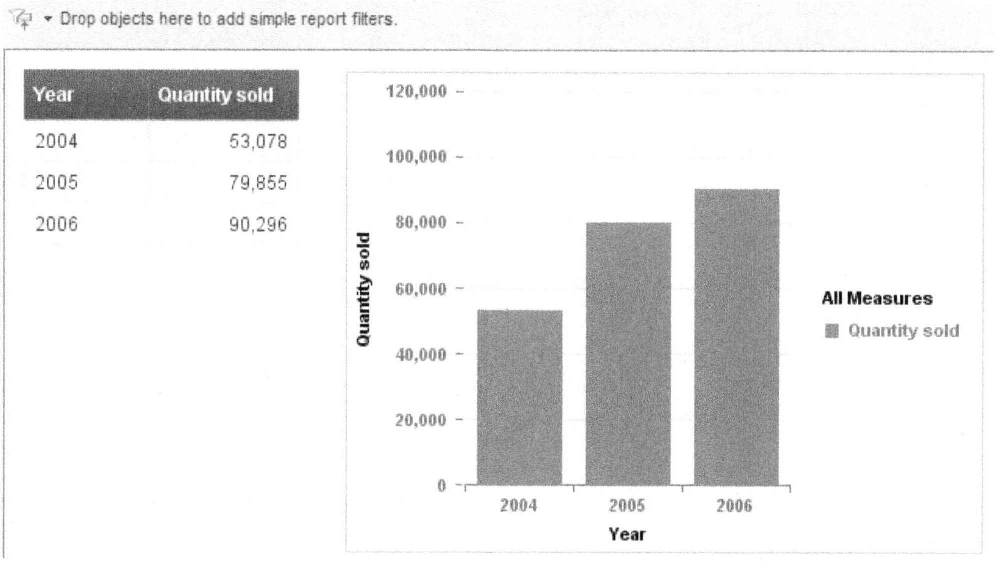
Drop objects here to add simple report filters.
Year
Quantity sold
2004
53,078
2005
79,855
2006
90,296
120,000
100,000
80,000
60,000
40,000
20,000
0
Quantity sold
2004
2005
2006
Year
All Measures
Quantity sold

33.12.1 Drilling on Chart Axes

- On 2D charts, you can drill on dimensions via the X-Axis.
- On 3D charts, you can drill on dimensions via the X-Axis and the Z-Axis.

Let us take the 2D chart (shown below) as an example to drill down and drill back up:

1. You can drill down by clicking in the highlighted areas (as shown below), i.e. the bars or the x-axis label.

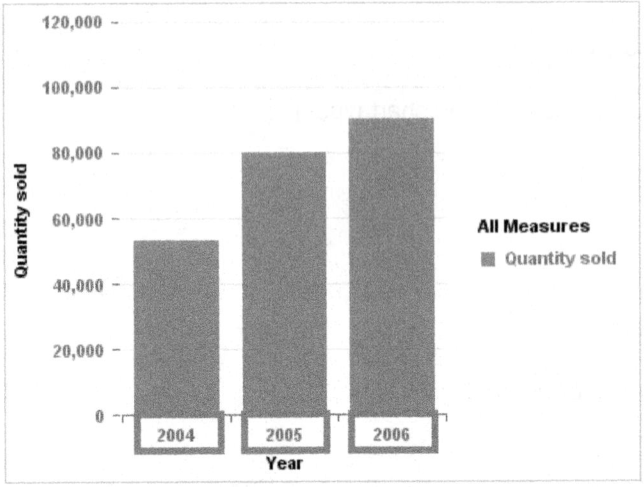
120,000
100,000
80,000
60,000
40,000
20,000
0
Quantity sold
2004
2005
2006
Year
All Measures
Quantity sold

The x-axis label '2005' has been clicked to get from example above to example below:

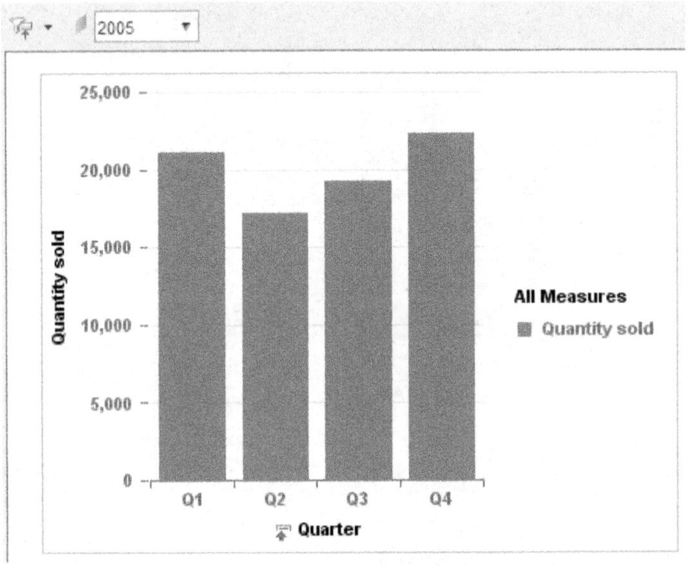
2005
25,000
20,000
15,000
10,000
5,000
0
Quantity sold
Q1
Q2
Q3
Q4
Quarter
All Measures
Quantity sold

2. There are two options available to drill up on a chart:

Click on axis labels (used for plotting dimensions)

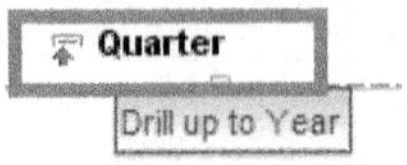
Quarter
Drill up to Year

Click in the chart body (e.g. bars, lines, etc)

Drill up to Year

Performing either of the above actions takes us from [Quarter] level for [Year] = '2005' back up to all years, i.e. no restriction on [Year].

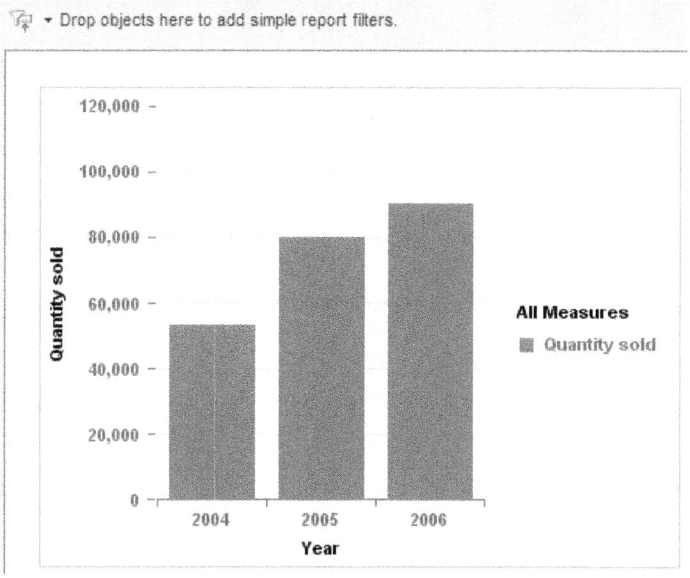
Drop objects here to add simple report filters.
120,000
100,000
80,000
60,000
40,000
20,000
0
Quantity sold
2004
2005
2006
Year
All Measures
Quantity sold

3. Remove the Drill Filter on [Year].

4. Edit the chart to display [Year] and [Quarter] on the x-axis (as shown below):

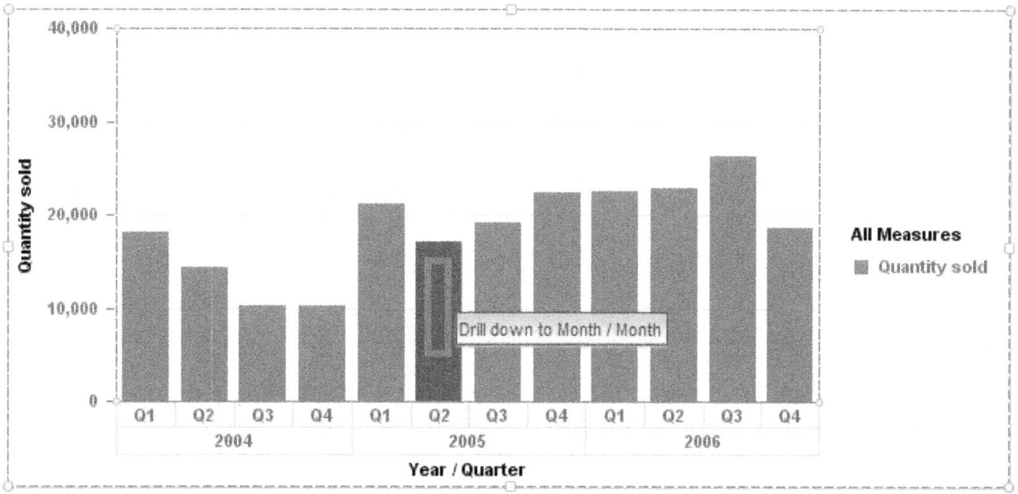
40,000
30,000
20,000
10,000
0
Quantity sold
Drill down to Month / Month
Q1
Q2
Q3
Q4
Q1
Q2
Q3
Q4
Q1
Q2
Q3
Q4
2004
2005
2006
Year / Quarter
All Measures
Quantity sold

Charts can contain one or multiple dimensions on a single axis, for example you can combine [Year] and [Quarter] on the same axis.

5. When you drill on axis labels with multiple dimensions, the drilled results are filtered by all the combined dimension values. For example, in the chart above, if you drill down on '2005/Q2' to the next level of the 'Time period' hierarchy, the results displayed on the drilled chart are those for the months in 'Q2' of '2005'.

[Year] and [Quarter] have been used to drill on the chart so they have both been added to the Report Filters Bar.

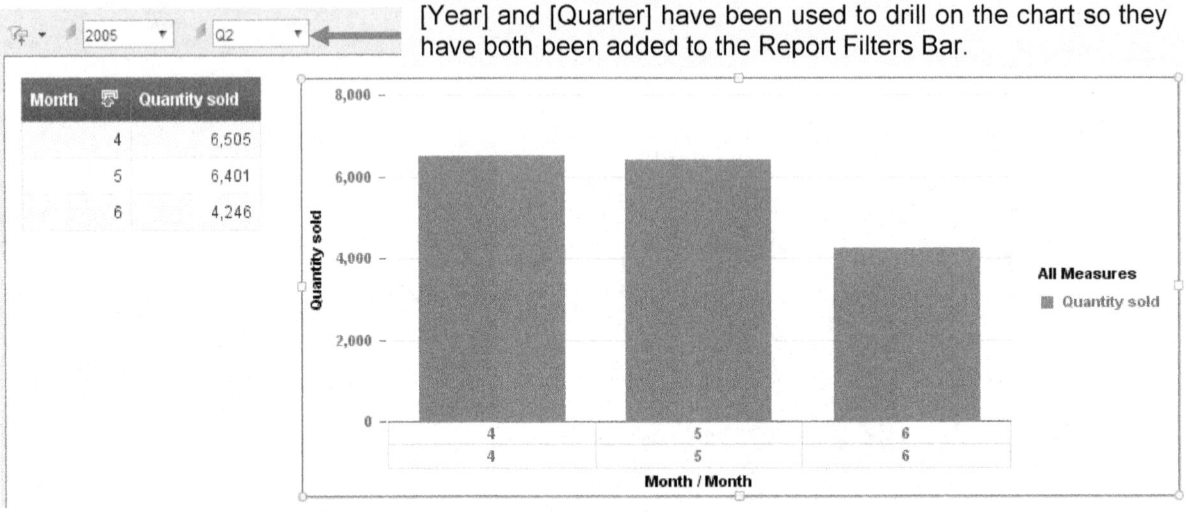
2005
Q2
Month
Quantity sold
4
6,505
5
6,401
6
4,246
8,000
6,000
4,000
2,000
0
Quantity sold
4
5
6
Month / Month
All Measures
Quantity sold

Chart x-axis has now changed from [Year]/[Quarter] to [Month]/[Month] as this is the next level down in the hierarchy for both [Year] and [Quarter].

6. If you are unsure of your drill options then use right-click and look under 'Drill'.

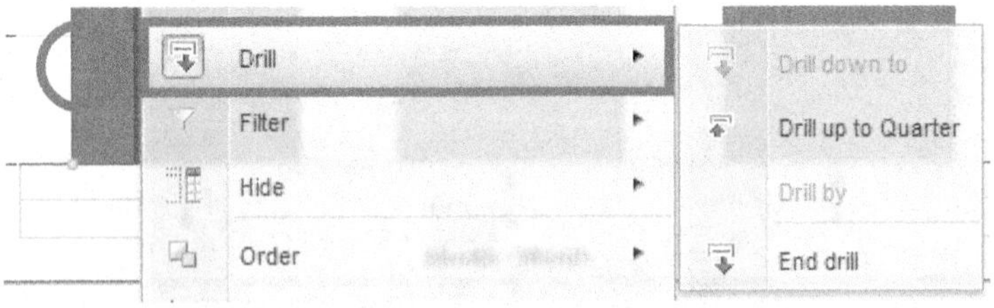
Drill
Filter
Hide
Order
Drill down to
Drill up to Quarter
Drill by
End drill

NOTE

You can use right-click on the chart body (bars, lines, etc) and also on the axes labels.

If you cannot see 'Drill up to…' on the axes labels then try right-clicking on the chart body (and vice versa).

7. Save and close your document.

33.12.2 Drilling on Chart Measures

You can drill on the measures displayed on the following types of charts:

- Bar charts by drilling on the bars
- Line and Radar Line charts by drilling on the data markers
- Pie charts by drilling on the segments

We have already used and drilled on Bar chart dimensions earlier.

When you drill on chart measures, Web Intelligence performs the drill action stated by the 'drill tip' that appears when you hover on the chart elements.

33.12.3 Drilling on Chart Legends

When the chart legend lists the measures displayed on the chart (e.g. like on a Bar chart) then drilling on the legend is not possible.

However, whenever the legend lists the dimensions displayed on the chart (e.g. like on a Pie chart) then you can drill on charts via the chart legend.

Let us take a Pie chart and have a look at drilling using the chart legend.

1. We have the following Pie chart and Drill Mode is switched on.

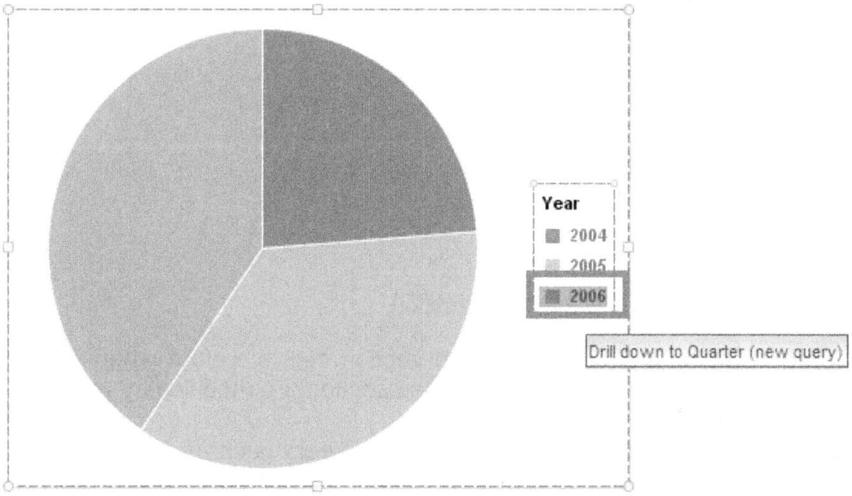
Year
2004
2005
2006
Drill down to Quarter (new query)

Pie charts do not often display the names of the dimensions represented by each pie segment therefore drilling on a pie chart legend is very useful.

2. In our example drill down on [Year] = '2006' changes the pie chart to:

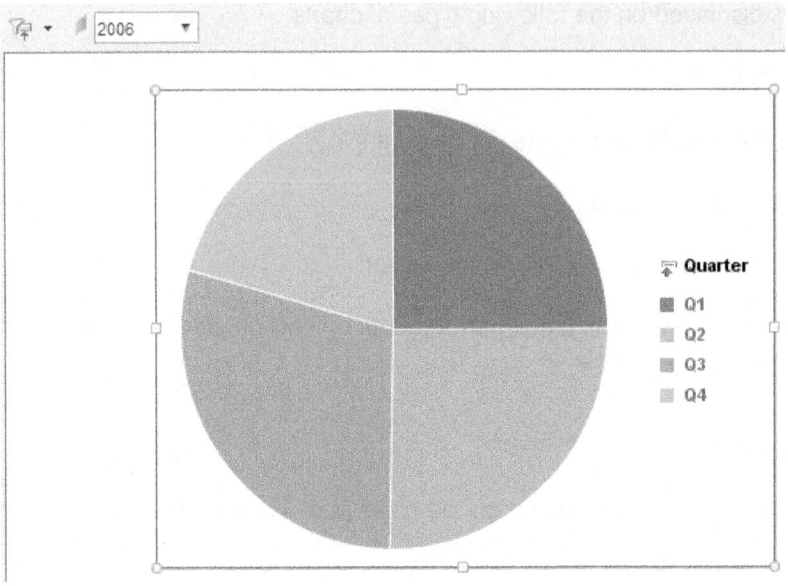
2006
Quarter
Q1
Q2
Q3
Q4

3. We can drill back up using the right-click menus:

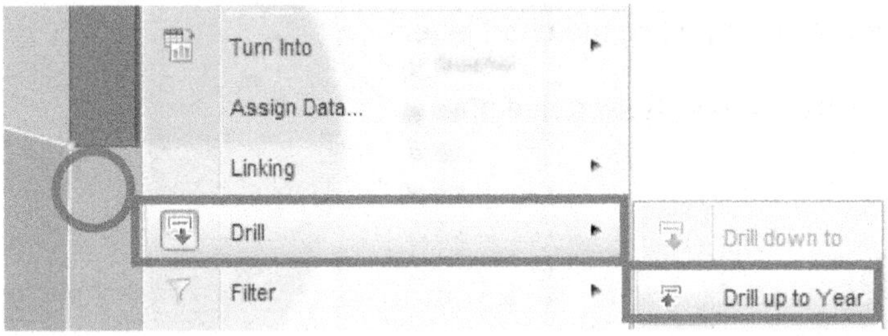
Turn Into
Assign Data...
Linking
Drill
Filter
Drill down to
Drill up to Year

33.13 Drilling on Sections

Sectioned reports can also be drilled by clicking in section cells.

The contents of a section are related to the value of the section cell, therefore when you drill on a section cell the results in all of the tables or charts in the drilled section are modified by your drill action.

For example, if you drill on a section cell that displays a value for [Year], such as '2004', the section will then change to be based on [Quarter] and the report would then display 4 section values ('Q1', 'Q2', 'Q3' and 'Q4).

Let us see this in practice.

1. Create a new document with the following 'eFashion' query and run it.

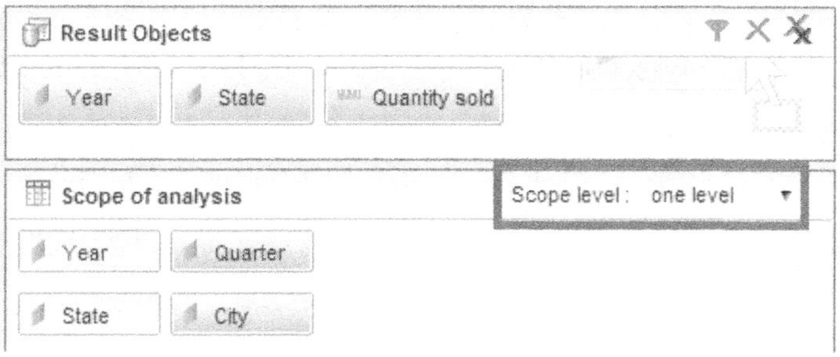
Result Objects
Year
State
Quantity sold
Scope of analysis
Scope level : one level
Year
Quarter
State
City

Modify the report to create a section on [Year] with a vertical table displaying [State] and [Quantity sold].

2. Report has been sectioned on [Year] with results for '2004' shown below and Drill Mode has been switched on.

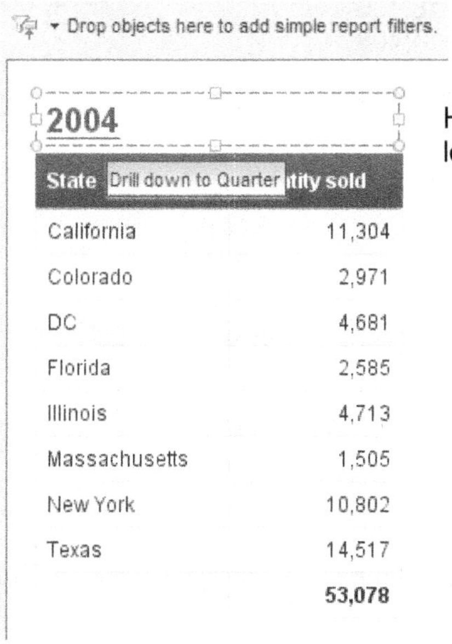
Drop objects here to add simple report filters.
2004
State
Drill down to Quarter
tity sold
California 11,304
Colorado 2,971
DC 4,681
Florida 2,585
Illinois 4,713
Massachusetts 1,505
New York 10,802
Texas 14,517
53,078

Hovering over the section cell indicates the next level down in the hierarchy.

3. Clicking on ‘2004’ results in:

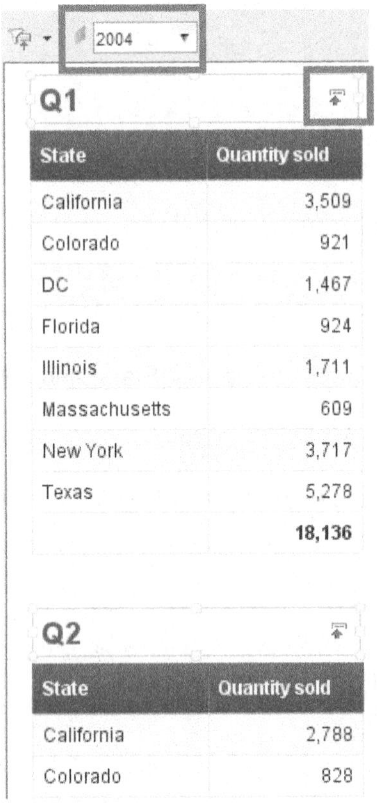
2004
Q1
State
Quantity sold
California
3,509
Colorado
921
DC
1,467
Florida
924
Illinois
1,711
Massachusetts
609
New York
3,717
Texas
5,278
18,136
Q2
State
Quantity sold
California
2,788
Colorado
828

- The single section on [Year] has been replaced by 4 sections (as there are 4 quarters with values for 2004).
- Section Cell on [Quarter] has arrow to drill back up to [Year].
- [Year] is added into the Filter Bar.

Scrolling down and summing up the totals in each section enables us to check the [Quarter] totals against the [Year] = ‘2004’ total.

Total for [Year] = ‘2004’ prior to drill = **53,078**

Sub-totals for each [Quarter] on drilling [Year] = ‘2004’:

‘Q1’	= 18,136
‘Q2’	= 14,408
‘Q3’	= 10,203
‘Q4’	= 10,331
Total	= **53,708**

4. Save and close your document.

33.14 Selecting from Multiple Drill Paths

A dimension can belong to multiple hierarchies within a single universe, for example you could have a financial year that is different to the calendar year and therefore ‘time’ objects would belong to two hierarchies, or your Sales Department might classify your products in a different way to your Marketing Department and therefore you would have two product hierarchies.

When you drill down (or up) on such a dimension, Web Intelligence does not know which drill path to follow therefore you must define the drill path to continue drilling.

> **NOTE**
>
> If the dimension value you choose to drill on is the result of a previous drill, the drill path is already known. Therefore you do not need to select a drill path.

An example is shown below.

NOTE – You will not be able to do this with the default ‘eFashion’ universe as we have modified our universe to demonstrate this particular drill behaviour.

Report block shows [Year] and [Quantity sold]. Hovering over [Year] shows a drill tip of 'Drill down to' instead of saying 'Drill down to Quarter'.

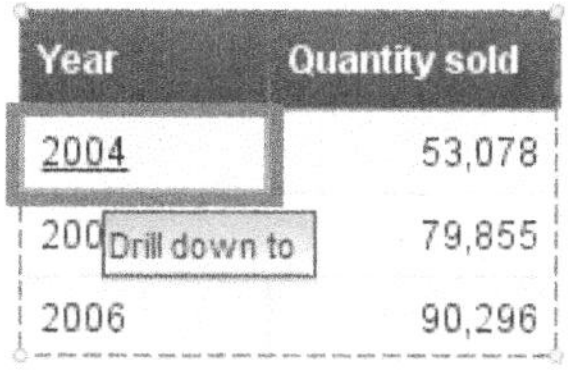
Year
Quantity sold
2004
53,078
200
Drill down to
79,855
2006
90,296

The reason for this is that we have more than one drill path available to us.

1. We have drilled on the dimension [Year].

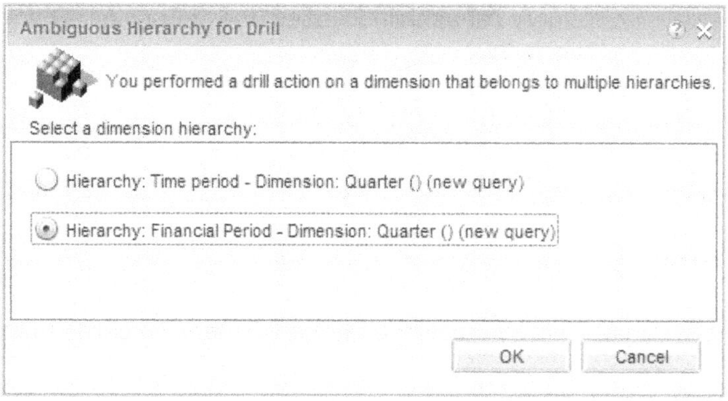
Ambiguous Hierarchy for Drill
You performed a drill action on a dimension that belongs to multiple hierarchies.
Select a dimension hierarchy:
Hierarchy: Time period - Dimension: Quarter () (new query)
Hierarchy: Financial Period - Dimension: Quarter () (new query)
OK
Cancel

The **'Ambiguous Hierarchy for Drill'** interface appears.

We now have to select which of these hierarchies we want to navigate in order to continue or drill action.

2. We have selected the 'Financial period' drill path.

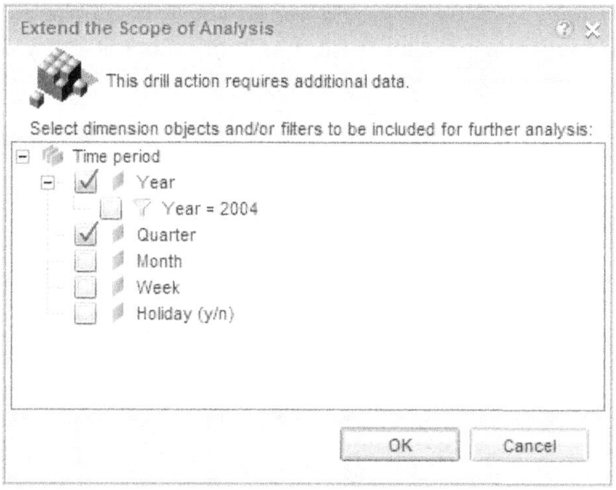
Extend the Scope of Analysis
This drill action requires additional data.
Select dimension objects and/or filters to be included for further analysis:
Time period
Year
Year = 2004
Quarter
Month
Week
Holiday (y/n)
OK
Cancel

The '**Extend the Scope of Analysis**' interface appears.

A check box appears next to each dimension below the current dimension we are drilling on so we can include them in the query.

The interface also displays filters that we can select to filter the new query.

3. We then click 'OK' to run the drilled query.

33.15 Drilling on Merged Dimensions

When a merged dimension is created then it belongs to all of the underlying source dimension hierarchies. Therefore, drilling on a merged dimension is similar to drilling on a dimension that belongs to multiple hierarchies (as described above).

1. Create a document with two queries on 'eFashion' universe:

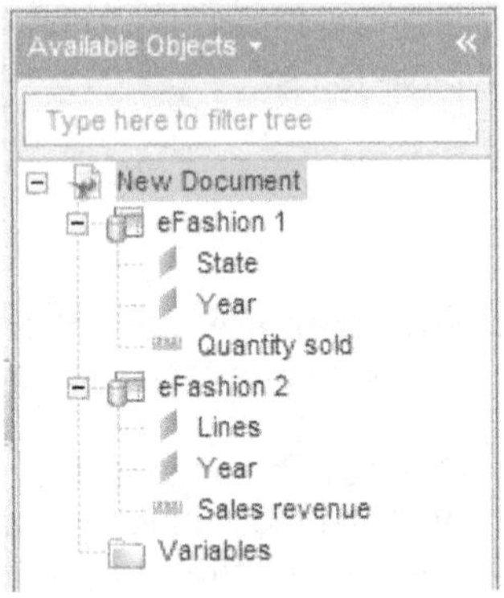
Available Objects
Type here to filter tree
New Document
eFashion 1
State
Year
Quantity sold
eFashion 2
Lines
Year
Sales revenue
Variables

We have a document containing 2 queries:

1. Query 'eFashion 1' uses the 'eFashion' universe.
2. Query 'eFashion 2' uses the 'eFashion Oracle' universe.

2. Merge the 2 queries using the [Year] objects by creating a Merged Dimension called [mrg Year].

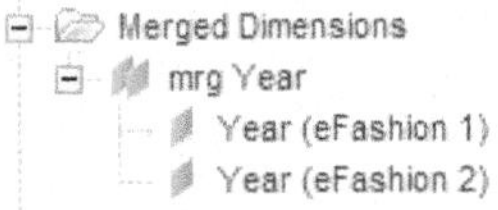
Merged Dimensions
mrg Year
Year (eFashion 1)
Year (eFashion 2)

3. The merged dimension has been used to display measures from both queries (as shown below).

mrg Year	Quantity sold	Sales revenue
2004	53,078	$8,096,124
2005	79,855	$13,232,246
2006	90,296	$15,059,143

4. Save your document.

5. Switch Drill Mode on.

6. Drill on [mrg Year]=2005.

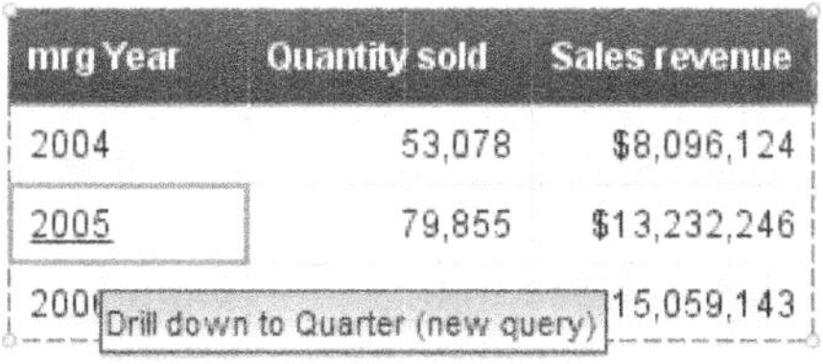
mrg Year
Quantity sold
Sales revenue
2004
53,078
$8,096,124
2005
79,855
$13,232,246
Drill down to Quarter (new query)
15,059,143

7. We now have to select which one of the underlying dimension hierarchies we want to use for our drill action.

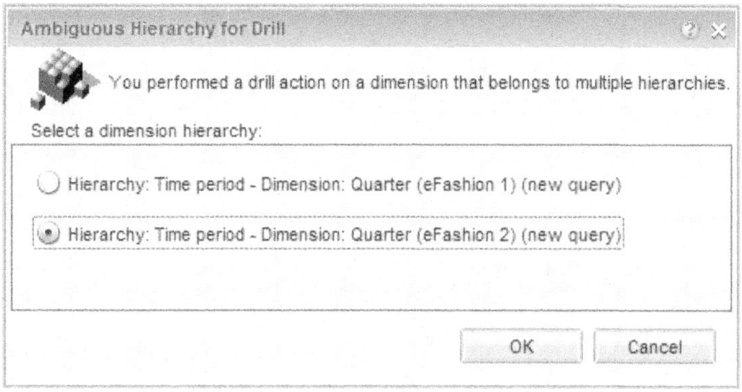
Ambiguous Hierarchy for Drill
You performed a drill action on a dimension that belongs to multiple hierarchies.
Select a dimension hierarchy:
Hierarchy: Time period - Dimension: Quarter (eFashion 1) (new query)
Hierarchy: Time period - Dimension: Quarter (eFashion 2) (new query)
OK
Cancel

You will not be prompted if you have merged dimensions from multiple queries using the same objects sourced from a single universe.

8. Select the ‘eFashion 2’ hierarchy and click ‘OK’ to confirm.

9. Select [Quarter] and click ‘OK’ for the ‘Extend the Scope of Analysis’ interface.

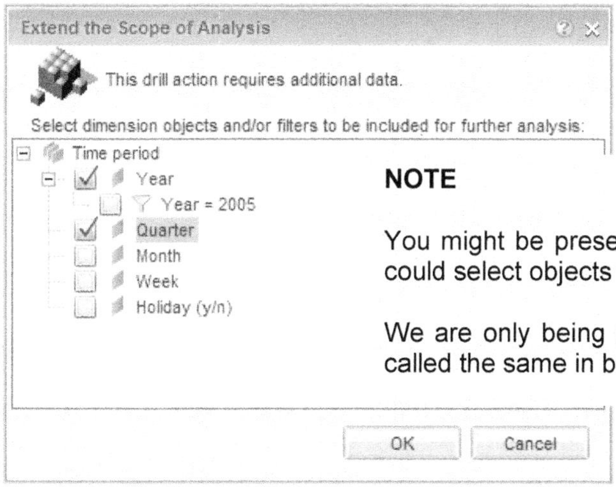
Extend the Scope of Analysis
This drill action requires additional data.
Select dimension objects and/or filters to be included for further analysis:
Time period
Year
Year = 2005
Quarter
Month
Week
Holiday (y/n)
OK
Cancel

NOTE

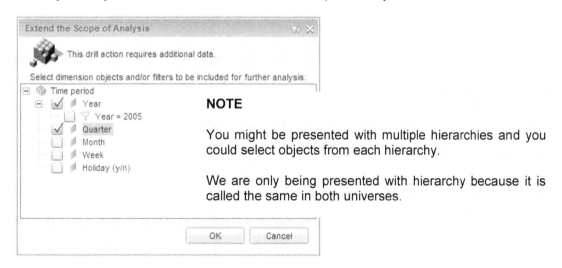

You might be presented with multiple hierarchies and you could select objects from each hierarchy.

We are only being presented with hierarchy because it is called the same in both universes.

10. Save your document.

11. The results of the drill action are shown below.

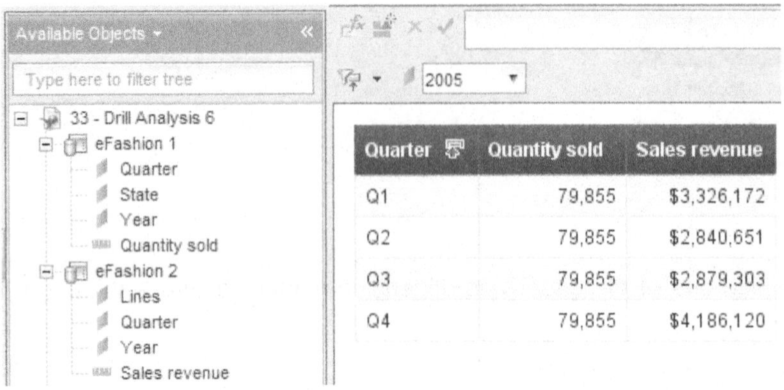
Available Objects
Type here to filter tree
33 - Drill Analysis 6
eFashion 1
Quarter
State
Year
Quantity sold
eFashion 2
Lines
Quarter
Year
Sales revenue
2005
Quarter
Quantity sold
Sales revenue
Q1
79,855
$3,326,172
Q2
79,855
$2,840,651
Q3
79,855
$2,879,303
Q4
79,855
$4,186,120

[mrg Year] in the block has been replaced with [eFashion Oracle].[Quarter].

[Sales revenue] column is showing the correct quarterly values for 2005, but [Quantity sold] is incorrect.

Why?

We have only merged the [Year] objects from the two queries, therefore Web Intelligence cannot present the [Quantity sold] at quarterly level when the [Quarter] object being used if from the 'eFashion 2' query.

12. Merge the [Quarter] objects and replace [Quarter] in the table with the merged dimension.

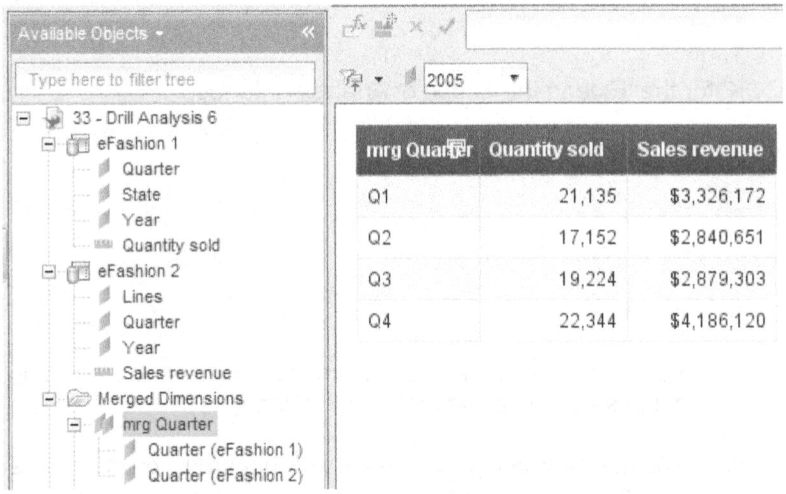
Available Objects
Type here to filter tree
33 - Drill Analysis 6
eFashion 1
Quarter
State
Year
Quantity sold
eFashion 2
Lines
Quarter
Year
Sales revenue
Merged Dimensions
mrg Quarter
Quarter (eFashion 1)
Quarter (eFashion 2)
2005
mrg Quarter
Quantity sold
Sales revenue
Q1
21,135
$3,326,172
Q2
17,152
$2,840,651
Q3
19,224
$2,879,303
Q4
22,344
$4,186,120

Both measures can be displayed correctly at [Year] and [Quarter] levels.

13. Now drill up on the merged dimension [mrg Quarter].

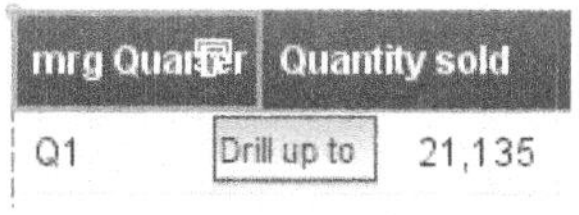
mrg Quarter
Quantity sold
Q1
Drill up to
21,135

14. If the dimension being drilled merged then we have to select which hierarchy to use for the 'drill up' action.

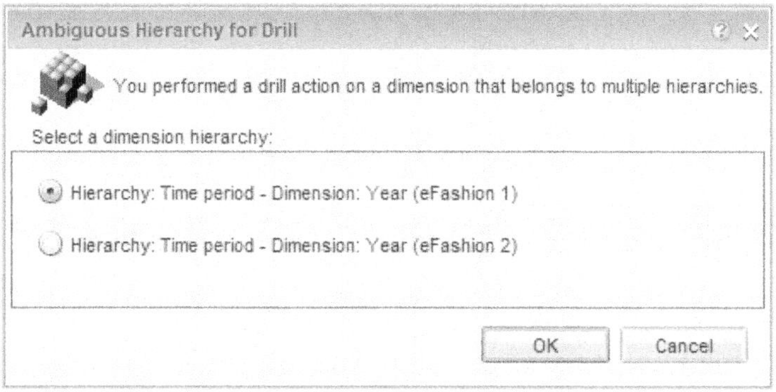
Ambiguous Hierarchy for Drill
You performed a drill action on a dimension that belongs to multiple hierarchies.
Select a dimension hierarchy:
Hierarchy: Time period - Dimension: Year (eFashion 1)
Hierarchy: Time period - Dimension: Year (eFashion 2)
OK
Cancel

You will not be prompted if you have merged dimensions from multiple queries using the same objects sourced from a single universe.

If the current dimension is not a merged dimension then Web Intelligence automatically drills up the hierarchy that we used to drill down.

15. We have selected 'eFashion 1' hierarchy and clicked 'OK'.

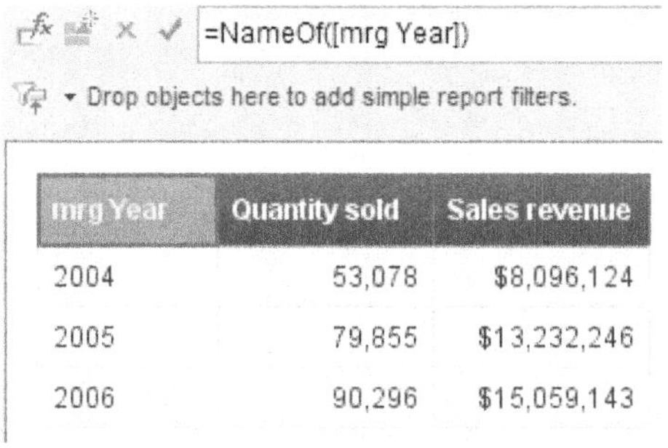
=NameOf([mrg Year])
Drop objects here to add simple report filters.
mrg Year
Quantity sold
Sales revenue
2004
53,078
$8,096,124
2005
79,855
$13,232,246
2006
90,296
$15,059,143

Web Intelligence has drilled up and used the Merged Dimension [mrg Year] to display results.

We have demonstrated drill down in one hierarchy and drill back up in a different hierarchy using the Merged Dimension relationships to correctly display the results.

16. Save and close your document.

33.16 Displaying Drill Filter Values

Printing does not printout the Filter Bar therefore it is useful to indicate what is being shown on the printed report.

1. Create the following query using the 'eFashion' universe and run it.

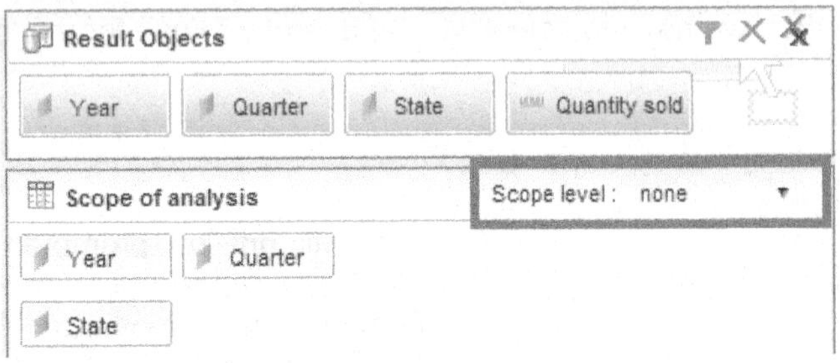
Result Objects
Year
Quarter
State
Quantity sold
Scope of analysis
Scope level : none
Year
Quarter
State

2. Remove the [Year] and [Quarter] objects from the vertical table and then apply a Sum on [Quantity sold].

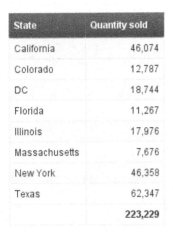

State	Quantity sold
California	46,074
Colorado	12,787
DC	18,744
Florida	11,267
Illinois	17,976
Massachusetts	7,676
New York	46,358
Texas	62,347
	223,229

3. Switch on Drill Mode and then manually add [Year] and [Quarter] into the Filter Bar.

2005
Q2

State	Quantity sold
California	3,184
Colorado	963
DC	1,627
Florida	859
Illinois	1,545
New York	4,194
Texas	4,780
	17,152

Filter the data to:

[Year]='2005'

[Quarter]='Q2'

4. Select the Pre-Defined Cell called 'Drill Filter'

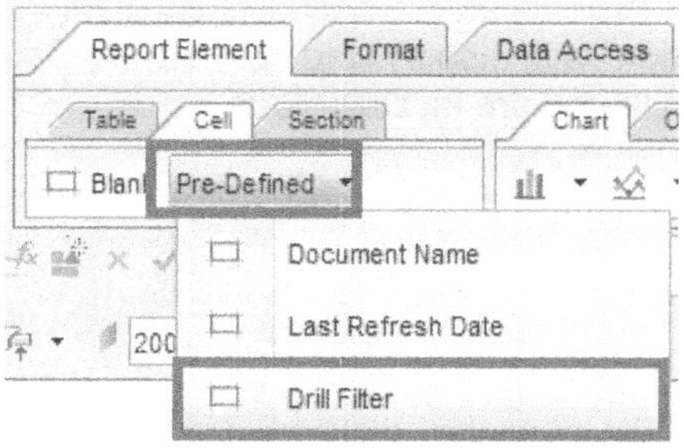
Report Element
Format
Data Access
Table
Cell
Section
Chart
Blank
Pre-Defined
Document Name
Last Refresh Date
Drill Filter

And place it above the table:

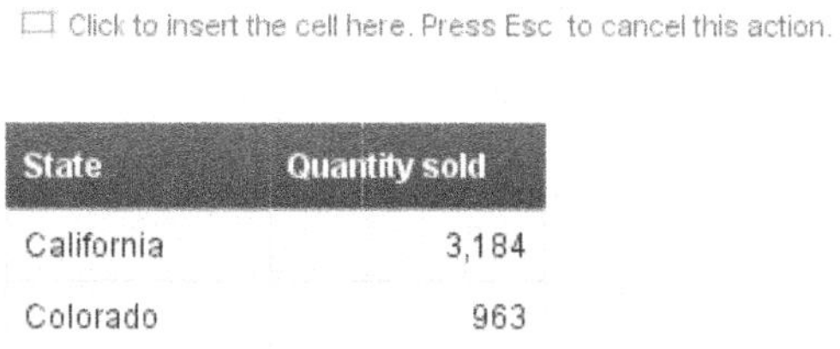
Click to insert the cell here. Press Esc to cancel this action.
State
Quantity sold
California
3,184
Colorado
963

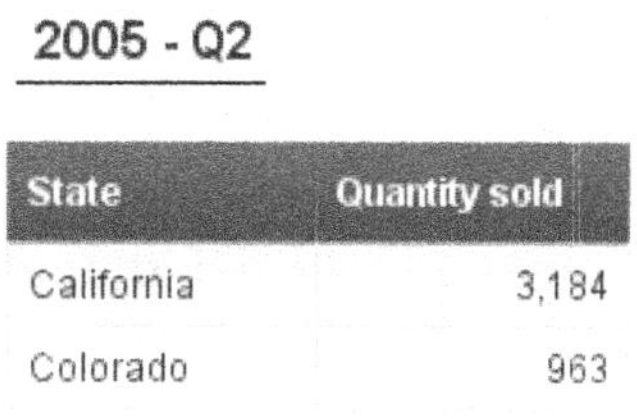
2005 - Q2
State
Quantity sold
California
3,184
Colorado
963

5. Select the new cell and view its formula:

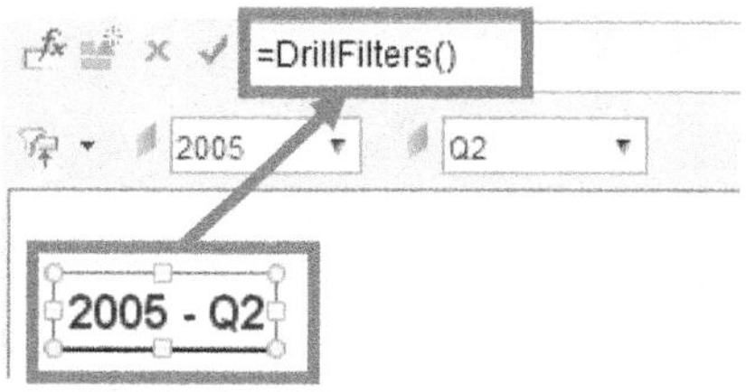
=DrillFilters()
2005
Q2
2005 - Q2

The default formula provided in Drill Filters cell = DrillFilters().

6. If a Drill Filter is set to 'All...' then it is not included in the value displayed by the DrillFilters() function.

2005
All Quarter
2005
State
Quantity sold
California
17,001

In this example [Quarter] is not included in the DrillFilters() output because it has not been filtered.

7. If we switch 'Drill Mode' off, we get:

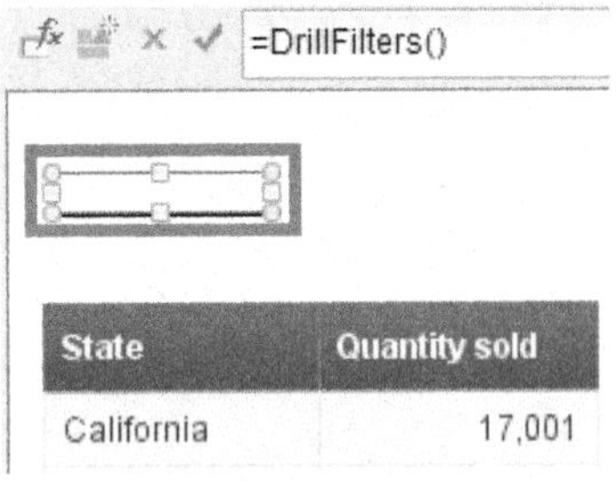
=DrillFilters()
State
Quantity sold
California
17,001

The DrillFilters() function will display the values of Drill Filters in your report while you are in 'Drill Mode'.

If you come out of 'Drill Mode' then the output of this function is Null.

A more informative drill label can be created by using the DrillFilters() function to explicitly reference individual objects within the Filter Bar.

8. Create a document variable called '**rv Drill Label**' and use the formula:

=
"Year = " + DrillFilters([Year]) + "   " +
"Quarter = " + DrillFilters([Quarter])

9. Replace the original cell containing the formula '=DrillFilters()' with the formula '=[rv Drill Label]' and then resize/format the cell to your liking:

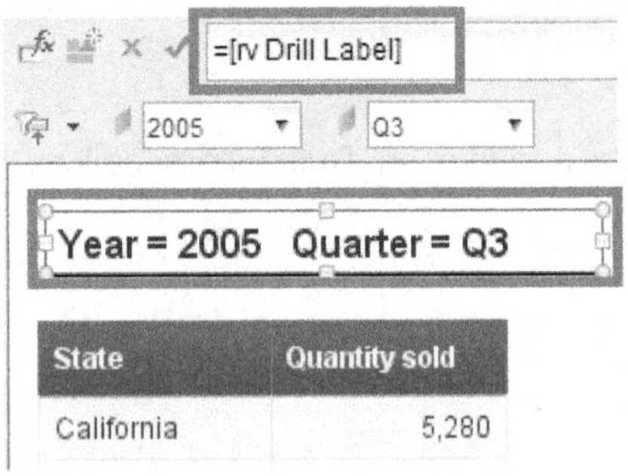
=[rv Drill Label]
2005
Q3
Year = 2005 Quarter = Q3
State
Quantity sold
California
5,280

10. With no filter value selected for [Quarter] the variable [rv Drill Label] displays:

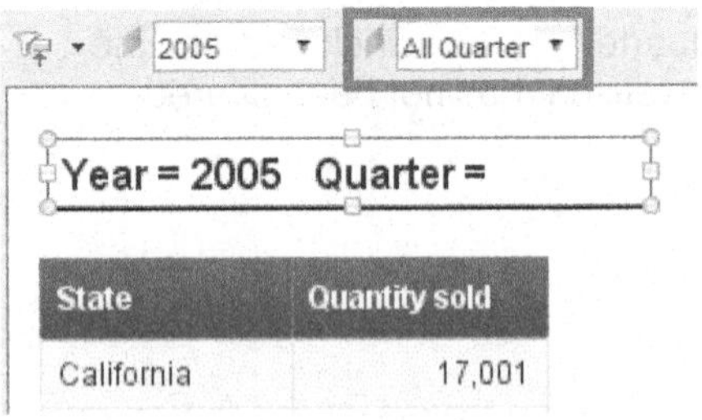
2005
All Quarter
Year = 2005 Quarter =
State
Quantity sold
California
17,001

In this example each of the Drill Filter values is prefixed with a label. [Quarter] does not have a value assigned to it because the Drill Filter for [Quarter] is showing 'All Quarter'.

The above is just an example of how the DrillFilters() function can be used. More elaborate labels could be created by using complex variables, e.g. If Then Else could be used to check Null filters, etc.

11. Save and close your document.

34 Tracking Changes in Data

Web Intelligence offers functionality to track data changes by comparing the results of the latest refresh to a previous reference point. This can aid data analysis by focusing on changes rather than on all of the data within the document.

You select a particular refresh and set it as the 'baseline' (i.e. reference). After a refresh, the current data is placed in context by showing how it relates to the reference data. Data tracking can make the current data more meaningful by placing it in context with old data.

Here are some examples of the usefulness of data tracking:

- If a product no longer appears in a list of the top products by sales, Web Intelligence displays the product as deleted from the list. You can use this information to investigate why the product is no longer a top performer.

- If sales have decreased in a territory, data tracking displays the decrease. You can then drill into the data for the territory to understand why revenue is falling.

34.1 Types of Data Changes

Web Intelligence allows you to track the following types of data change:

Data Change Type	Description
Addition	Exists in current data but was not in the reference data. Applies to DIMENSION objects.
Removal	Existed in reference data but is not in current data. Applies to DIMENSION objects.
Changes	Modification of values. Applies to DETAIL objects.
Increase	Data has increased in value compared to reference data. A percentage increase can be specified, e.g. to show a change if percentage increase is greater than or equal to 20 percent. Applies to MEASURE and DETAIL objects.
Decrease	Data has decreased in value compared to reference data A percentage decrease can be specified, e.g. to show a change if percentage decrease is greater than or equal to 20 percent. Applies to MEASURE and DETAIL objects.

34.2 Data Tracking Modes

There are two modes available for monitoring data changes.

34.2.1 Automatic Mode for Data Tracking

In automatic data tracking mode, you can think of the reference data as always being one refresh behind the current data.

1. Web Intelligence sets the current data as the reference data just before each refresh.

2. When the document is refreshed Web Intelligence compares the 'new' data with the data that was automatically assigned as reference data prior to the refresh.

34.2.2 Fixed Mode for Data Tracking

In fixed data tracking mode, you decide when you want to set the reference data.

Example:

1. Document has been refreshed in Month 1 and you set the reference point (let us term this as Reference Point 1).

2. Document is refreshed in Month 2 and comparison is made to Reference Point 1.

3. Document is refreshed in Month 6 and comparison is again made with Reference Point 1.

4. You now reset the reference data to be the data from Month 6 (let us term this as Reference Point 2).

5. Document is refreshed in Month 7 and comparison is now made against Reference Point 2.

Basically, Web Intelligence continues to use data as a reference point until you update the reference point.

34.3 Limitations of Data Tracking

Before we look at how to use Data Tracking functionality it is worth knowing about the practical limitations of this feature.

Web Intelligence will not display changes in data:

1. If the data provider behind a document is changed (for example a query is modified). In this situation the reference data is no longer compatible with the current version.

2. If the document is cleared (i.e. purged of data) then the old data will no longer exist for comparison.

As a result of the above, the following actions are incompatible with data tracking:

1. **Any modification that changes the SQL generated by a data provider**

   If a query changes then it becomes necessary to discard the results of the previous query definition, otherwise the comparisons could be made on very different queries.

   This includes any modifications to security rights that lead to query SQL changes, e.g. row-level security is applied to restrict data depending on user role.

   Basically, the definition of the query statement needs to remain constant for Web Intelligence to allow comparison of data.

   However, this does not include values you specify for prompts:

   For example, if you run a query and specify '2005' for a prompt on [Year] and on the next refresh you specify '2004' then data changes will be tracked.

2. **Purge the document.**

   If all data is removed from the document then the reference point is lost so comparisons cannot be made.

   After a purge has occurred then on the next refresh data changes will show all rows as 'Insertions' as effectively all rows are 'new' compared to an empty reference point.

   In automatic mode, on the second refresh the results of the first refresh are used as the reference point.

   In fixed mode, the reference point has to be reset by manually specifying the reference data set after a refresh.

3. **Delete a query.**

   Deleting a query effectively removes the query from the document so any previous results held within the microcube of data are no longer available for future comparisons.

4. **Drill out of scope.**

   When you drill out of scope, i.e. 'Extend the Scope of Analysis' then this modifies the underlying SQL (i.e. Point 1 above applies), therefore data history is automatically cleared from the document by Web Intelligence.

5. **Use Query drill.**

   Query Drill modifies the underlying SQL with every drill action (i.e. Point 1 above applies) therefore data history is automatically cleared from the document by Web Intelligence.

34.4 Activating and Deactivating Data Tracking

Before we look at examples of data tracking let us look at how to activate and deactivate the data tracking functionality.

34.4.1 Activating Data Tracking

An overview of how to apply data tracking is described here:

Data Tracking is activated by clicking on the 'Track' button on the 'Analysis – Data Tracking' toolbox:

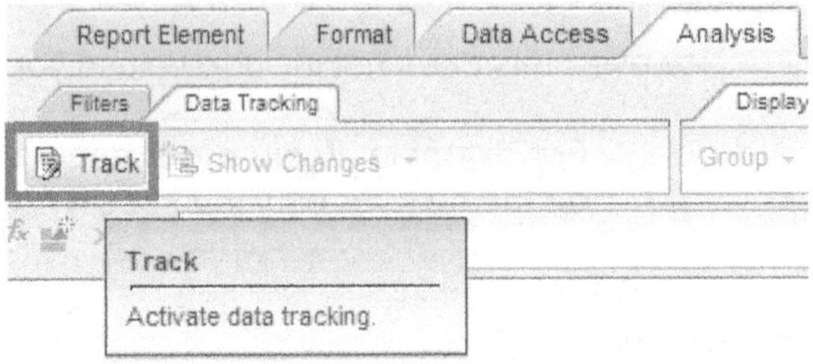
Report Element
Format
Data Access
Analysis
Filters
Data Tracking
Display
Track
Show Changes
Group
Track
Activate data tracking.

You will then be prompted to select the type of data tracking you wish to use and whether you want to refresh the document to see data changes immediately.

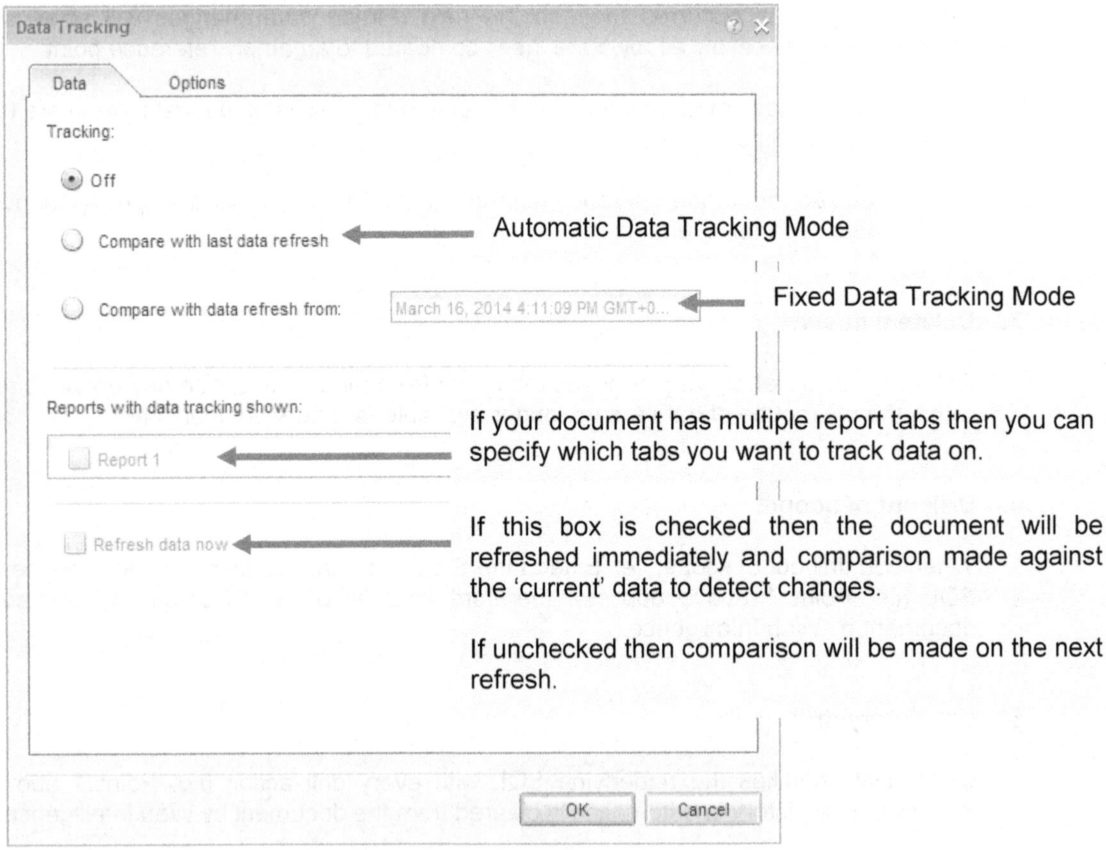
Data Tracking
Data
Options
Tracking:
Off
Compare with last data refresh
Automatic Data Tracking Mode
Compare with data refresh from:
March 16, 2014 4:11:09 PM GMT+0...
Fixed Data Tracking Mode
Reports with data tracking shown:
Report 1
If your document has multiple report tabs then you can specify which tabs you want to track data on.
Refresh data now
If this box is checked then the document will be refreshed immediately and comparison made against the 'current' data to detect changes.
If unchecked then comparison will be made on the next refresh.
OK
Cancel

After data tracking has been activated the following also occurs:

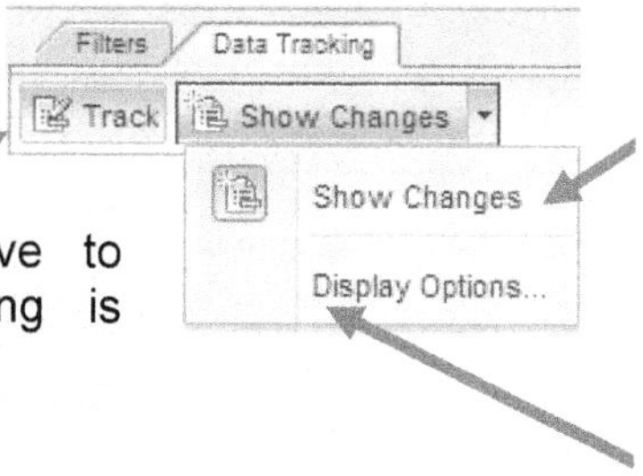
Filters
Data Tracking
Track
Show Changes
Show Changes
Display Options...

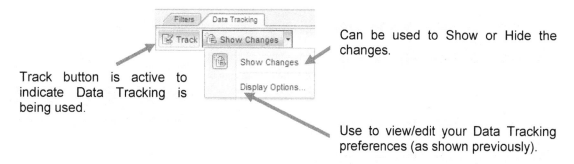

Track button is active to indicate Data Tracking is being used.

Can be used to Show or Hide the changes.

Use to view/edit your Data Tracking preferences (as shown previously).

Reports with 'Track' as active and 'Show Changes' as active have the following icon next to the report name:

Report 1

NOTE – If 'Show Changes' is inactive then this icon will not be visible.

Documents with data tracking also show a status bar message indicating on whether you are using Automatic or Fixed Data Tracking:

Track Changes: Auto-update
Track Changes: Fixed data

The 'Auto-update' text is shown in Automatic Mode and 'Fixed data' is shown for Fixed Mode.

Hover over the Status Bar text to reveal more details:

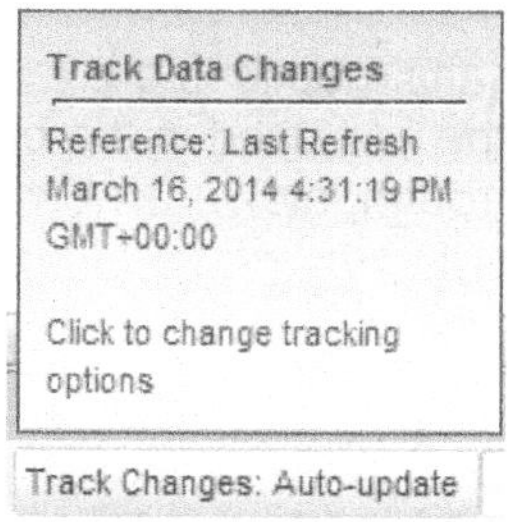
Track Data Changes
Reference: Last Refresh
March 16, 2014 4:31:19 PM
GMT+00:00
Click to change tracking options
Track Changes: Auto-update

The date and time indicate when the reference data was last updated.

Clicking on the hyperlink 'Auto update' (or 'Fixed data') initiates the 'Data Tracking' interface, i.e. same action as the 'Tracking' toolbar button.

Use the Data Tracking Options interface to select types of changes to track and formatting:

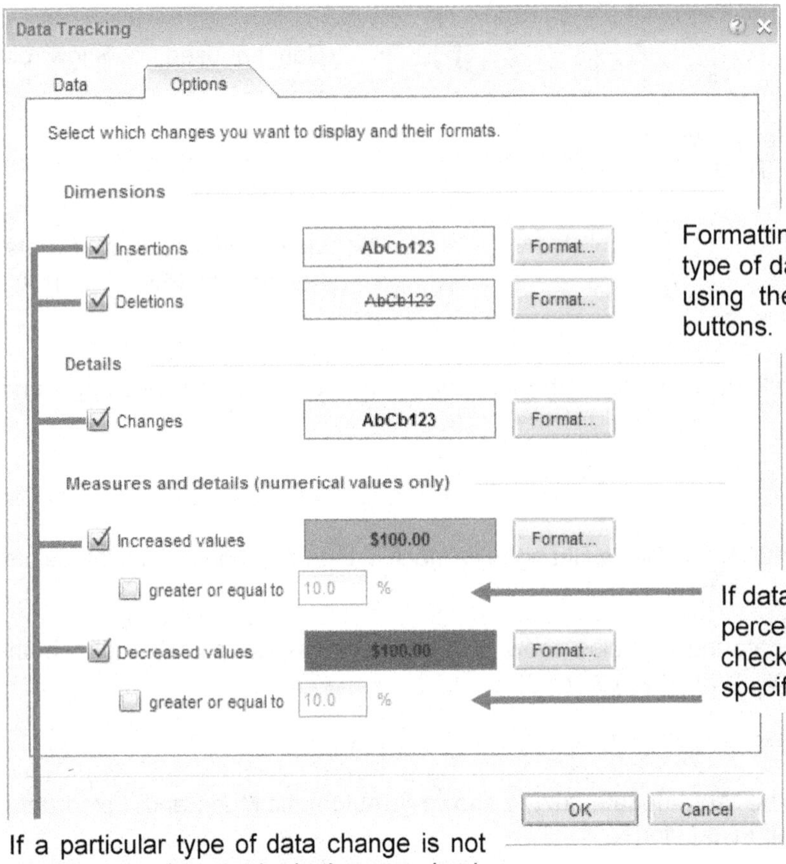
Data Tracking
Data
Options
Select which changes you want to display and their formats.
Dimensions
Insertions
AbCb123
Format...
Deletions
AbCb123
Format...
Details
Changes
AbCb123
Format...
Measures and details (numerical values only)
Increased values
$100.00
Format...
greater or equal to
10.0
%
Decreased values
$100.00
Format...
greater or equal to
10.0
%
OK
Cancel

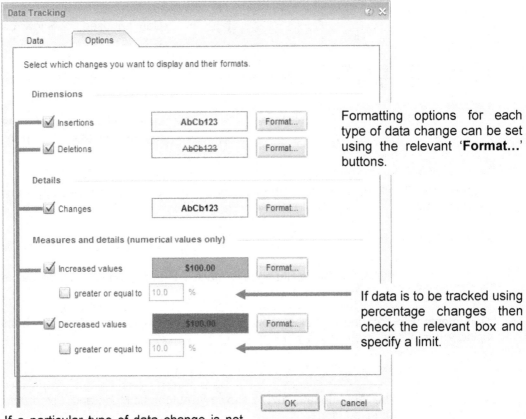

Formatting options for each type of data change can be set using the relevant '**Format...**' buttons.

If data is to be tracked using percentage changes then check the relevant box and specify a limit.

If a particular type of data change is not required to be tracked then uncheck against the relevant data change type.

Click on any of the 'Format...' buttons and formatting options are available for cell font and cell background. The font will remain the same as the font used in the block but its colour and style can be changed (Bold, Italic, Underline, Strikethrough, etc).

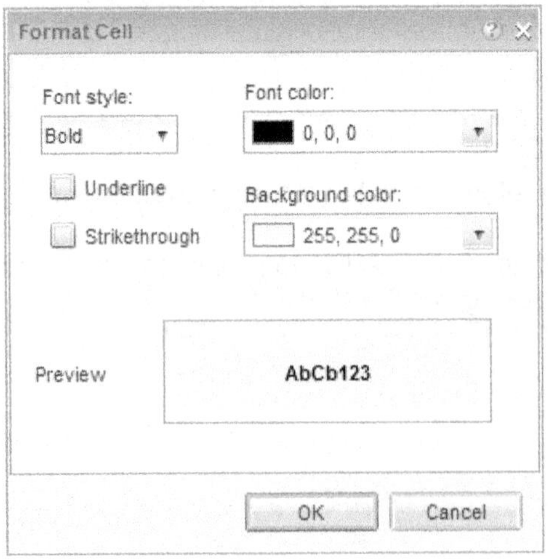
Format Cell
Font style:
Bold
Font color:
0, 0, 0
Underline
Strikethrough
Background color:
255, 255, 0
Preview
AbCb123
OK
Cancel

34.4.2 Deactivating Data Tracking

Tracking can be deactivated by using the same button as when activating:

Once activated the 'Track' button toggles to become 'Deactivate Data Tracking'.

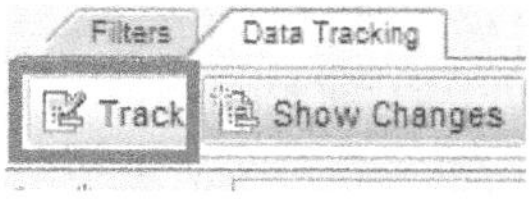
Filters
Data Tracking
Track
Show Changes

Click 'Yes' to deactivate data tracking.

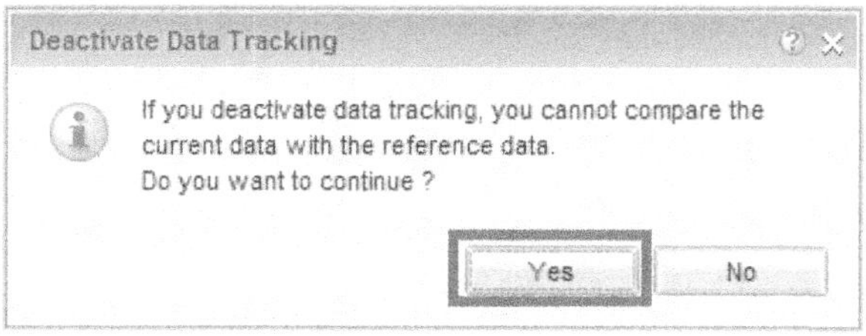
Deactivate Data Tracking
If you deactivate data tracking, you cannot compare the current data with the reference data.
Do you want to continue ?
Yes
No

NOTE

If you reactivate Data Tracking then you will have to go through the process of reselecting the mode of operation (Automatic or Fixed) but formatting changes will remain in place.

34.5 Fixed and Automatic Data Tracking

We will now look at how to use Data Tracking in Automatic and Fixed modes.

34.5.1 Query for Data Tracking Examples

Create a new document with the following query using the 'eFashion' universe:

Result Objects
Quarter
Sales revenue
Quantity sold
Query Filters
Year
Equal to
Enter Year:

Note the Query Prompt on [Year]

Run the query and select '2004' for the [Year] prompt.

Block showing all three Result Objects from the Query Panel.

Quarter	Sales revenue	Quantity sold
Q1	$2,660,700	18,136
Q2	$2,278,693	14,408
Q3	$1,367,841	10,203
Q4	$1,788,580	10,331

NOTE – We now have data in the document that can act as a start point for Reference Data.

34.5.2 Fixed Data Tracking

1. Rename the report tab to 'Data Tracking Demo'.

2. Activate data tracking by clicking on:

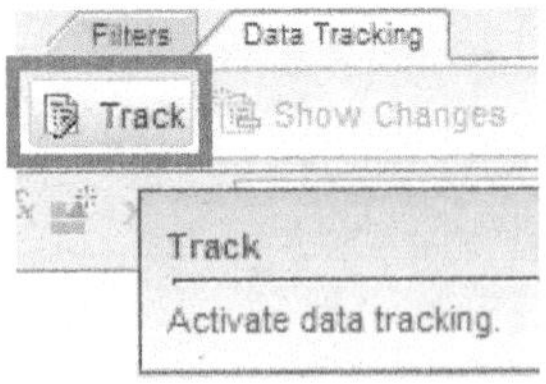
Filters
Data Tracking
Track
Show Changes
Track
Activate data tracking.

3. Select the Fixed Mode (as shown below) and click 'OK'.

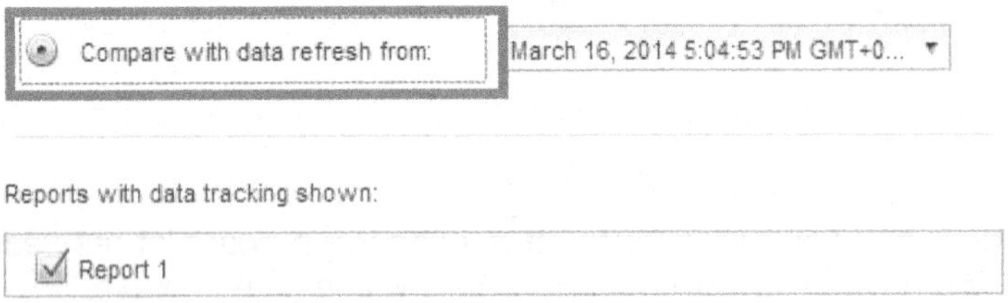
Compare with data refresh from:
March 16, 2014 5:04:53 PM GMT+0...
Reports with data tracking shown:
Report 1

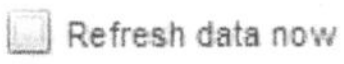
Refresh data now

NOTE – If we check the 'Refresh now' option then our query will be refreshed on clicking 'OK' and we would be prompted to select a value for [Year]. **For this example leave the 'Refresh now' unchecked.**

We now have a report with Data Tracking enabled:

Filters
Data Tracking
Track
Show Changes

Active icons on toolbar.

Data Tracking Demo

Report name has 'Show Changes' icon against it.

4. Save your document.

5. Refresh the query and select '2005' for the [Year] prompt.

The block now shows:

Quarter	Sales revenue	Quantity sold
Q1	$3,326,172	21,135
Q2	$2,840,651	17,152
Q3	$2,879,303	19,224
Q4	$4,186,120	22,344

The columns [Sales revenue] and [Quantity sold] are now coloured green to show increases in both values compared to '2004'.

You can check the formatting used by clicking on:

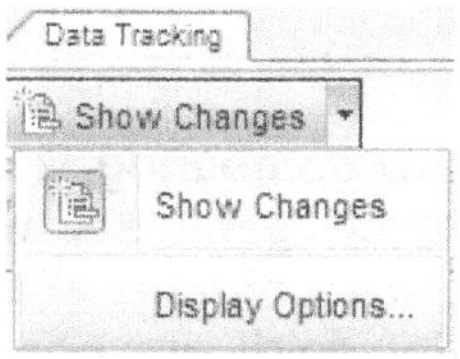
Data Tracking
Show Changes
Show Changes
Display Options...

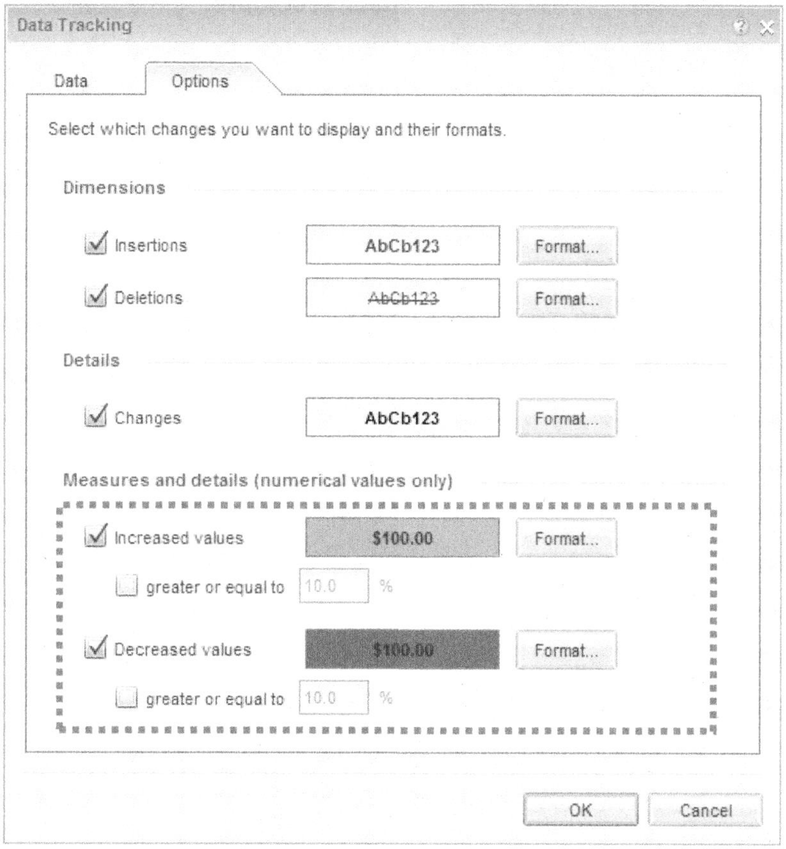
Data Tracking
Data
Options
Select which changes you want to display and their formats.
Dimensions
Insertions
AbCb123
Format...
Deletions
AbCb123
Format...
Details
Changes
AbCb123
Format...
Measures and details (numerical values only)
Increased values
$100.00
Format...
greater or equal to
10.0
%
Decreased values
$100.00
Format...
greater or equal to
10.0
%
OK
Cancel

The default colour scheme seems to be very friendly and should be sufficient for most of us, but we can change the formatting if required.

Make any formatting changes and click ‘OK’ or click ‘Cancel’ to close the interface.

6. Refresh the query again and select ‘2006’ for the [Year] prompt.

The block now shows:

Quarter	Sales revenue	Quantity sold
Q1	$3,742,989	22,537
Q2	$4,006,718	22,846
Q3	$3,953,395	26,263
Q4	$3,356,041	18,650

The columns [Sales revenue] and [Quantity sold] are again coloured green to show increases in both values compared to ‘2004’.

7. Refresh the query again and select '2004' for the [Year] prompt.

   The block now shows:

Quarter	Sales revenue	Quantity sold
Q1	$2,660,700	18,136
Q2	$2,278,693	14,408
Q3	$1,367,841	10,203
Q4	$1,788,580	10,331

Web Intelligence is now comparing '2004' data against a reference point set with '2004' data, therefore the columns [Sales revenue] and [Quantity sold] are now in default colours.

8. Save your document.

34.5.3 Automatic Data Tracking

With the last refresh (above) our latest data is for '2004'. We will now use this to set it as the reference point for the Automatic Mode.

1. Click on 'Display Options...'

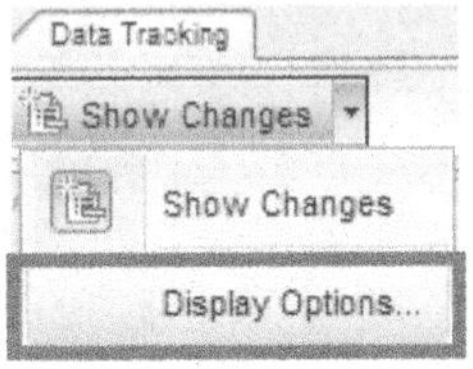
Data Tracking
Show Changes
Show Changes
Display Options...

2. Select 'Auto-update...' as shown below and click 'OK' to apply.

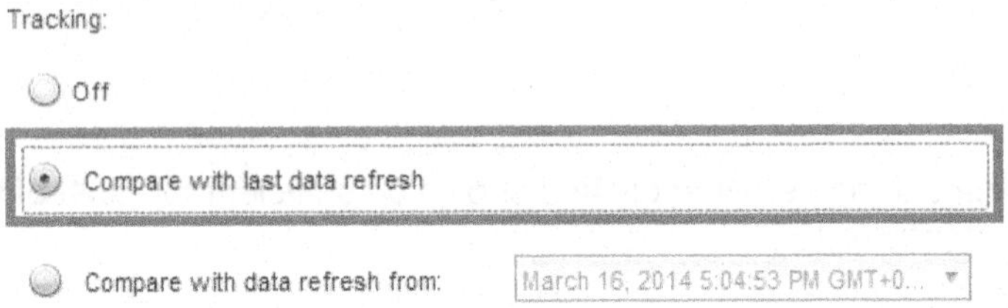
Tracking:
Off
Compare with last data refresh
Compare with data refresh from:
March 16, 2014 5:04:53 PM GMT+0...

We now have the latest data refresh selected as the reference data (i.e. for '2004').

3. Refresh the query and select '2005' for the [Year] prompt.

   The block now shows:

Quarter	Sales revenue	Quantity sold
Q1	$3,326,172	21,135
Q2	$2,840,651	17,152
Q3	$2,879,303	19,224
Q4	$4,186,120	22,344

   The columns [Sales revenue] and [Quantity sold] are now coloured green to show increases in both values compared to '2004'.

   On the next refresh our reference data will be based on this refresh (i.e. for '2005').

4. Refresh the query again and select '2006' for the [Year] prompt.

   The block now shows:

Quarter	Sales revenue	Quantity sold
Q1	$3,742,989	22,537
Q2	$4,006,718	22,846
Q3	$3,953,395	26,263
Q4	$3,356,041	18,650

   The columns [Sales revenue] and [Quantity sold] are again coloured green to show increases in both values for 'Q1', 'Q2' and 'Q3'.

   'Q4' is coloured red for both [Sales revenue] and [Quantity sold] to show decreases compared to the previous reference (i.e. '2005').

   We can see the decreases by comparing reference data based on '2005' against current data for '2006' (for 'Q4'):

Reference Data	Current Data
[Sales revenue] = $4,186,120 [Quantity sold] = 22,344	[Sales revenue] = $3,356,041 [Quantity sold] = 18.650

   On the next refresh our reference data will be based on this refresh (i.e. for '2006').

5. Refresh the query again and select '2004' for the [Year] prompt.

   The block now shows:

Quarter	Sales revenue	Quantity sold
Q1	$2,660,700	18,136
Q2	$2,278,693	14,408
Q3	$1,367,841	10,203
Q4	$1,788,580	10,331

   The columns [Sales revenue] and [Quantity sold] are now coloured red to show decreases in both values compared to '2006'.

   On the next refresh our reference data will be based on this refresh (i.e. for '2004').

6. Save your document.

34.6 Modifying Queries in Data Tracking

Having demonstrated Fixed and Automatic modes of data tracking, we will now look at some further examples and to do this we will modify our underlying query.

1. Edit the query definition to be as follows and then run the query.

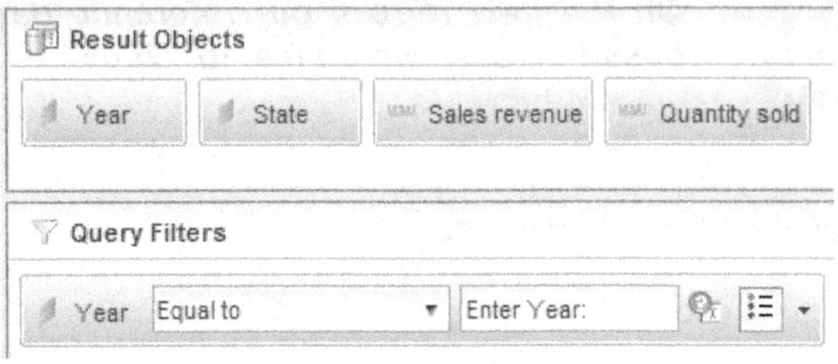
Result Objects
Year
State
Sales revenue
Quantity sold
Query Filters
Year
Equal to
Enter Year:

Select '2005' for the [Year] prompt.

2. Modify the block to include the new objects [Year] and [State] as shown below:

Year	State	Sales revenue	Quantity sold
2005	California	$2,782,680	17,001
2005	Colorado	$768,390	4,700
2005	DC	$1,215,158	7,572
2005	Florida	$661,250	3,852
2005	Illinois	$1,150,659	6,744
2005	Massachusetts	$157,719	902
2005	New York	$2,763,503	16,447
2005	Texas	$3,732,889	22,637

NOTE

Even with data tracking activated we are seeing no data change formatting.

Why?

The query has been modified so data tracking has been **reset** after this first refresh but will resume from the second refresh.

3. Refresh the query and select '2004' for the [Year] prompt.

   The block now shows:

Year	State	Sales revenue	Quantity sold
2004	**California**	**$1,704,211**	**11,304**
2004	**Colorado**	**$448,302**	**2,971**
2004	**DC**	**$693,211**	**4,681**
2004	**Florida**	**$405,985**	**2,585**
2004	**Illinois**	**$737,914**	**4,713**
2004	**Massachusetts**	**$238,819**	**1,505**
2004	**New York**	**$1,667,696**	**10,802**
2004	**Texas**	**$2,199,677**	**14,517**
~~2005~~	~~California~~	~~$2,782,680~~	~~17,001~~
~~2005~~	~~Colorado~~	~~$768,390~~	~~4,700~~
~~2005~~	~~DC~~	~~$1,215,158~~	~~7,572~~
~~2005~~	~~Florida~~	~~$661,250~~	~~3,852~~
~~2005~~	~~Illinois~~	~~$1,150,659~~	~~6,744~~
~~2005~~	~~Massachusetts~~	~~$157,719~~	~~902~~
~~2005~~	~~New York~~	~~$2,763,503~~	~~16,447~~
~~2005~~	~~Texas~~	~~$3,732,889~~	~~22,637~~

'**2004**' rows are displayed with the formatting of '**Insertions**' data change type.

The issue we have is that the [Year] column is causing the data to be split by 'Insertions' and 'Deletions'.

The [State] values are the same in both Years, so they are not driving this behaviour.

4. We have a number of options available to us by using 'Display Options…' settings:

   Deselect 'Insertions' (i.e. we do not want to see insertions) and click 'OK' to apply:

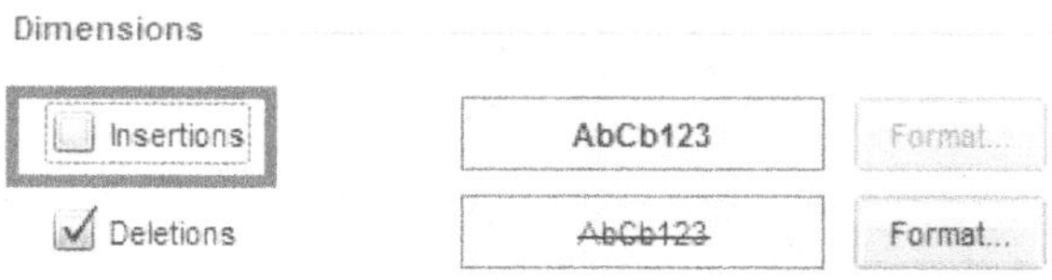
Dimensions
Insertions
AbCb123
Format...
Deletions
AbCb123
Format...

Year	State	Sales revenue	Quantity sold
2004	California	$1,704,211	11,304
2004	Colorado	$448,302	2,971
2004	DC	$693,211	4,681
2004	Florida	$405,985	2,585
2004	Illinois	$737,914	4,713
2004	Massachusetts	$238,819	1,505
2004	New York	$1,667,696	10,802
2004	Texas	$2,199,677	14,517
~~2005~~	~~California~~	~~$2,782,680~~	~~17,001~~
~~2005~~	~~Colorado~~	~~$768,390~~	~~4,700~~
~~2005~~	~~DC~~	~~$1,215,158~~	~~7,572~~
~~2005~~	~~Florida~~	~~$661,250~~	~~3,852~~
~~2005~~	~~Illinois~~	~~$1,150,659~~	~~6,744~~
~~2005~~	~~Massachusetts~~	~~$157,719~~	~~902~~
~~2005~~	~~New York~~	~~$2,763,503~~	~~16,447~~
~~2005~~	~~Texas~~	~~$3,732,889~~	~~22,637~~

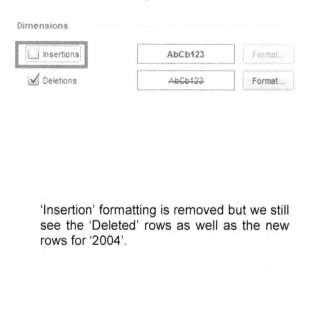

'Insertion' formatting is removed but we still see the 'Deleted' rows as well as the new rows for '2004'.

Or we can deselect 'deletions' (i.e. we do not want to see deletions) and click 'OK' to apply:

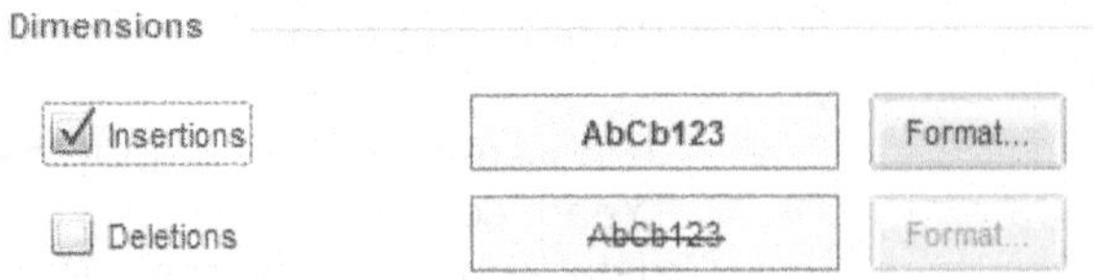
Dimensions
Insertions
AbCb123
Format...
Deletions
AbCb123
Format...

Year	State	Sales revenue	Quantity sold
2004	California	$1,704,211	11,304
2004	Colorado	$448,302	2,971
2004	DC	$693,211	4,681
2004	Florida	$405,985	2,585
2004	Illinois	$737,914	4,713
2004	Massachusetts	$238,819	1,505
2004	New York	$1,667,696	10,802
2004	Texas	$2,199,677	14,517

Results in the 'Deletion' rows to be removed and we now see the new rows with the 'Insertions' formatting applied to them.

Or we can deselect both 'insertions' and 'deletions' and click 'OK' to apply:

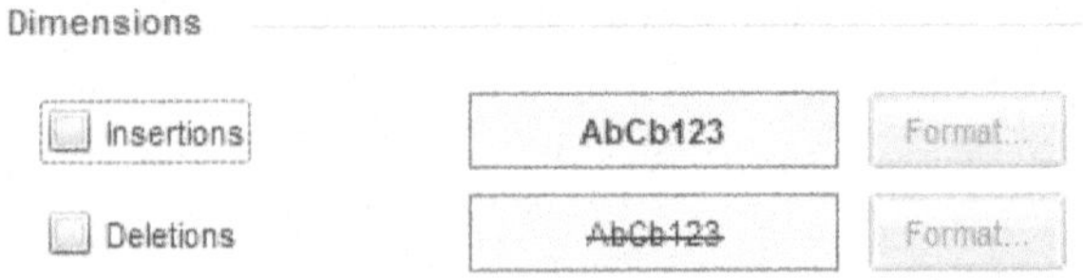
Dimensions
Insertions
AbCb123
Format...
Deletions
AbCb123
Format...

Year	State	Sales revenue	Quantity sold
2004	California	$1,704,211	11,304
2004	Colorado	$448,302	2,971
2004	DC	$693,211	4,681
2004	Florida	$405,985	2,585
2004	Illinois	$737,914	4,713
2004	Massachusetts	$238,819	1,505
2004	New York	$1,667,696	10,802
2004	Texas	$2,199,677	14,517

We now see the new rows with no data change formatting applied because we are not comparing Insertions and Deletions.

5. Save your document.

6. If we remove the [Year] column from the block then we get the following:

State	Sales revenue	Quantity sold
California	$1,704,211	11,304
Colorado	$448,302	2,971
DC	$693,211	4,681
Florida	$405,985	2,585
Illinois	$737,914	4,713
Massachusetts	$238,819	1,505
New York	$1,667,696	10,802
Texas	$2,199,677	14,517

The [Year] object is present in our query but is not displayed in the block.

Therefore, Data Tracking compares data at [State] level between the new data and the reference data without taking [Year] into context.

Relevant data change formatting is applied based on increase or decrease in measure values.

NOTE

By **removing** [Year] from the block, it does not matter whether 'Insertions' and 'Deletions' are being tracked or not, i.e. you can have them **selected** or **deselected** but the result will be as above. The reason being that all states have values in both 2004 and 2005. If a state was missing from one of the years then we would see an insertion or deletion in the above block depending on which year the state was missing.

34.7 Tracking Percentage Changes

We have seen increases and decreases of numerical values in our previous examples, whereby any increase or decrease was formatted, but it is probably more useful to track percentage changes rather than value changes.

For example, your reference date might hold the value for [Customer Spend] = $10,300 and the current data value for [Customer Spend] = $9,900.

A difference of - $400 or approx. - 4% compared to the reference data.

The requirement might be to track those customers who have shown a 25% change (positive or negative) based on [Customer Spend].

This type of data tracking can be achieved using 'greater than or equal to' in Data Tracking Options interface.

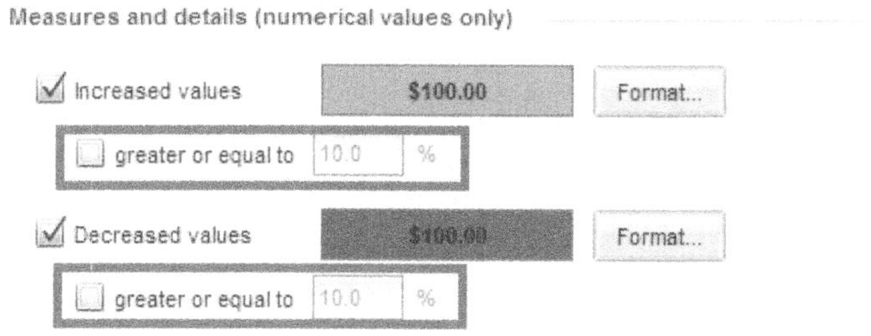
Measures and details (numerical values only)
Increased values
$100.00
Format...
greater or equal to
10.0
%
Decreased values
$100.00
Format...
greater or equal to
10.0
%

Using the results from the previous query, our document currently contains the following data:

Reference Data

Year	State	Sales revenue	Quantity sold
2005	California	$2,782,680	17,001
2005	Colorado	$768,390	4,700
2005	DC	$1,215,158	7,572
2005	Florida	$661,250	3,852
2005	Illinois	$1,150,659	6,744
2005	Massachusetts	$157,719	902
2005	New York	$2,763,503	16,447
2005	Texas	$3,732,889	22,637

Current Data

Year	State	Sales revenue	Quantity sold
2004	California	$1,704,211	11,304
2004	Colorado	$448,302	2,971
2004	DC	$693,211	4,681
2004	Florida	$405,985	2,585
2004	Illinois	$737,914	4,713
2004	Massachusetts	$238,819	1,505
2004	New York	$1,667,696	10,802
2004	Texas	$2,199,677	14,517

IMPORTANT NOTE

Percentage differences (shown below) will be calculated by Web Intelligence using the formula:

(Current Value – Reference Value) / Reference Value

State	Revenue % Change	Quantity % Change
California	-39%	-34%
Colorado	-42%	-37%
DC	-43%	-38%
Florida	-39%	-33%
Illinois	-36%	-30%
Massachusetts	51%	67%
New York	-40%	-34%
Texas	-41%	-36%

We will use these percentages to demonstrate the Data Tracking functionality for percentage changes.

We will use an increase percentage of 35% or more.

We will use a decrease percentage of 35% or more.

We expect the shaded cells to show the differences in our block of data.

1. In 'Display Options' for Data Tracking, set both % values to 35.0 as shown below and click 'OK' to apply:

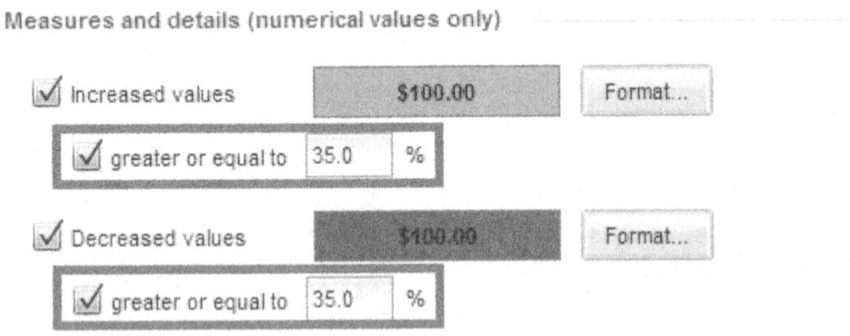
Measures and details (numerical values only)
Increased values
$100.00
Format...
greater or equal to
35.0
%
Decreased values
$100.00
Format...
greater or equal to
35.0
%

2. The results in our block now show:

State	Sales revenue	Quantity sold
California	$1,704,211	11,304
Colorado	$448,302	2,971
DC	$693,211	4,681
Florida	$405,985	2,585
Illinois	$737,914	4,713
Massachusetts	$238,819	1,505
New York	$1,667,696	10,802
Texas	$2,199,677	14,517

Massachusetts is showing an increase in both measures of more than 35% or more.

Colorado, DC and Texas are showing a decrease in both measures of 35% or more.

California, Florida, Illinois and New York are showing a decrease in [Sales revenue] of 35% or more.

State	Revenue % Change	Quantity % Change
California	-39%	-34%
Colorado	-42%	-37%
DC	-43%	-38%
Florida	-39%	-33%
Illinois	-36%	-30%
Massachusetts	51%	67%
New York	-40%	-34%
Texas	-41%	-36%

If we compare the data change formatting applied to our block with our calculated values then we find the changes to have been correctly identified by Web Intelligence.

3. If we only want to see decreases of 41% or more (i.e. no increases in this example) then we can set our Data Tracking Options as:

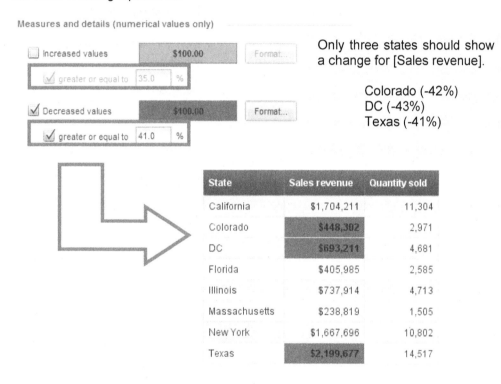

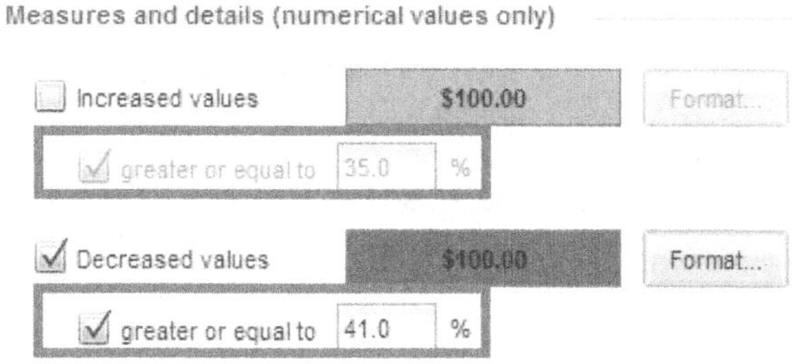
Measures and details (numerical values only)
Increased values
$100.00
Format...
greater or equal to
35.0
%
Decreased values
$100.00
Format...
greater or equal to
41.0
%

Only three states should show a change for [Sales revenue].

Colorado (-42%)
DC (-43%)
Texas (-41%)

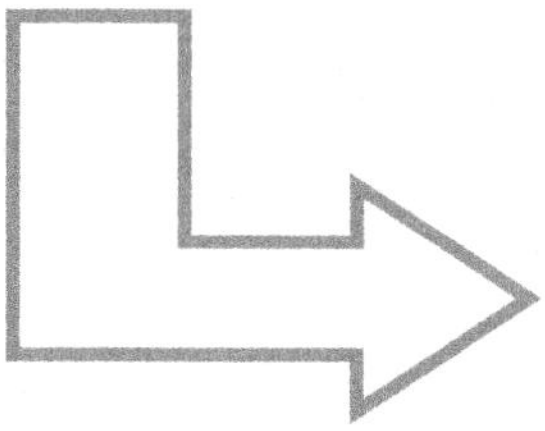

State	Sales revenue	Quantity sold
California	$1,704,211	11,304
Colorado	$448,302	2,971
DC	$693,211	4,681
Florida	$405,985	2,585
Illinois	$737,914	4,713
Massachusetts	$238,819	1,505
New York	$1,667,696	10,802
Texas	$2,199,677	14,517

4. Save and close your document.

34.8 Data Tracking in Sectioned Reports

Web Intelligence displays the data in the section header in one of two ways depending on the changes in the data contained in the section itself:

1. If all the rows in the block (within the section) have changed in the same way (i.e. Insertions, Deletions or Modifications) then the section header is displayed with the same formatting as the rows.

2. If the rows in the block (within the section) have changed in different ways, or only some rows have changed, the section header retains its default format.

1. Create a new document with the following query using 'eFashion' universe:

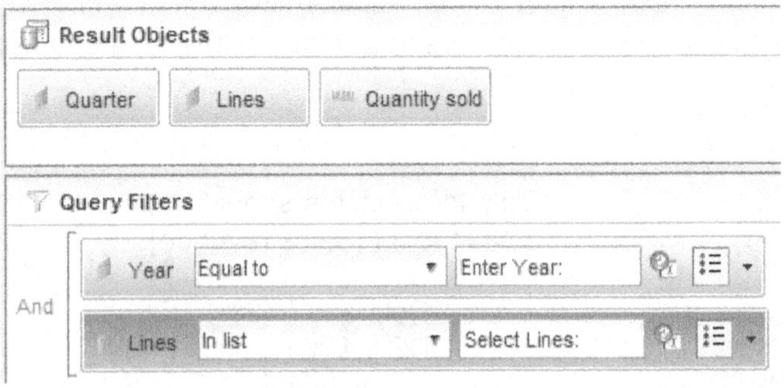
Result Objects
Quarter
Lines
Quantity sold
Query Filters
And
Year
Equal to
Enter Year:
Lines
In list
Select Lines:

Run the query and select:

'2004' for the [Year] prompt

and for the [Lines] prompt select

'Accessories;Dresses;Jackets'

2. Create a sectioned report on [Lines].

Accessories

Quarter	Quantity sold
Q1	8,074
Q2	6,541
Q3	2,555
Q4	359

Dresses

Quarter	Quantity sold
Q1	1,153
Q2	294
Q3	596
Q4	2,140

Jackets

Quarter	Quantity sold
Q1	373
Q2	224
Q3	136
Q4	177

3. Activate Data Tracking and select Automatic Mode (i.e. 'Compare with last data refresh').

4. Refresh the query again and select the prompt values as follows:

   '2006' for [Year]

   'Dresses;Jackets;Leather' for [Lines]

5. After the query has refreshed, our report shows:

~~Accessories~~

Quarter	Quantity sold
~~Q1~~	~~8,074~~
~~Q2~~	~~6,541~~
~~Q3~~	~~2,555~~
~~Q4~~	~~359~~

The section header cell for 'Accessories' is showing the same formatting as its block because it has been deleted completely, i.e. it existed in the reference data but is not in the current data.

Dresses

Quarter	Quantity sold
Q1	2,161
Q2	2,118
Q3	4,005
Q4	1,193

Jackets

Quarter	Quantity sold
Q1	700
Q2	295
Q3	449
Q4	427

Dresses and Jackets were sold in both years so only the measure formatting is being used to show data changes (i.e. on [Quantity sold]).

Leather

Quarter	Quantity sold
Q1	140
Q3	71
Q4	19

The section header cell for 'Leather' is showing the same formatting as its block because it has been inserted after the latest refresh, i.e. it is in the current data but did not exist in the reference data.

6. Save and close your document.

34.9 Data Changes in Blocks with Breaks

When a block contains a break, Web Intelligence displays the break value using rules similar to those for section header cells.

1. If all the rows in the break have changed in the same way (i.e. Insertions, Deletions or Modifications) then the break value is displayed with the same formatting as the rows.

2. If the rows have changed in different ways, or only some rows have changed, the break value retains the default formatting.

To make comparisons possible, we will use the same query as the one used to demonstrate data changes in sections to demonstrate data changes in block with breaks.

1. Create a new document with the following query using 'eFashion' universe:

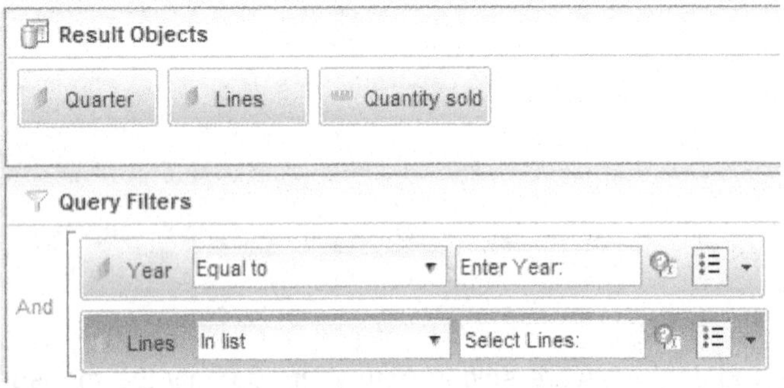
Result Objects
Quarter
Lines
Quantity sold
Query Filters
And
Year
Equal to
Enter Year:
Lines
In list
Select Lines:

Run the query and select:

'2004' for the [Year] prompt

and for the [Lines] prompt select

'Accessories;Dresses;Jackets'

2. Create a report containing a single block that has a break on [Lines] as follows:

Lines	Quarter	Quantity sold
Accessories	Q1	8,074
	Q2	6,541
	Q3	2,555
	Q4	359
Accessories		**17,529**
Dresses	Q1	1,153
	Q2	294
	Q3	596
	Q4	2,140
Dresses		**4,183**
Jackets	Q1	373
	Q2	224
	Q3	136
	Q4	177
Jackets		**910**

3. Activate Data Tracking and select Automatic Mode (i.e. 'Compare with last data refresh').

4. Refresh the query again and select the prompt values as follows:

   '2006' for [Year]

   'Dresses;Jackets;Leather' for [Lines]

5. After the query has refreshed, our report shows:

Lines	Quarter	Quantity sold
~~Accessories~~	~~Q1~~	~~8,074~~
	~~Q2~~	~~6,541~~
	~~Q3~~	~~2,555~~
	~~Q4~~	~~359~~
~~Accessories~~		**~~17,529~~**
Dresses	Q1	**2,161**
	Q2	**2,118**
	Q3	**4,005**
	Q4	**1,193**
Dresses		**9,477**
Jackets	Q1	**700**
	Q2	**295**
	Q3	**449**
	Q4	**427**
Jackets		**1,871**
Leather	**Q1**	**140**
	Q3	**71**
	Q4	**19**
Leather		**230**

The break value for 'Accessories' is showing the same formatting as all other rows associated to 'Accessories' because it has been deleted completely, i.e. it existed in the reference data but is not in the current data.

The break values for 'Dresses' and 'Jackets' have a default formatting because only the measure values have changed.

The break value for 'Leather' is showing the same formatting as all other rows associated to 'Leather' because it has been inserted after the latest refresh, i.e. it is in the current data but did not exist in the reference data.

6. Save and close your document.

34.10 Data Changes in Charts and Cross Tables

We will now look at Data Tracking on Charts and Cross Tables using two reports in a single document.

1. Create a new document with the following query using 'eFashion' universe:

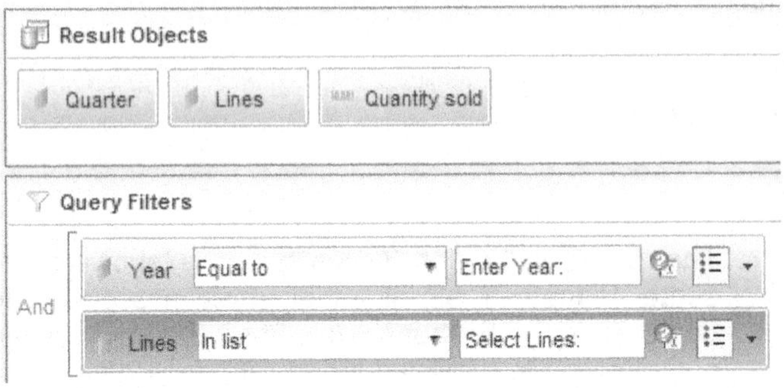
Result Objects
Quarter
Lines
Quantity sold
Query Filters
And
Year
Equal to
Enter Year:
Lines
In list
Select Lines:

Run the query and select:

'2004' for the [Year] prompt

and for the [Lines] prompt select

'Accessories;Dresses;Jackets'

2. Create a report tab showing a chart as follows:

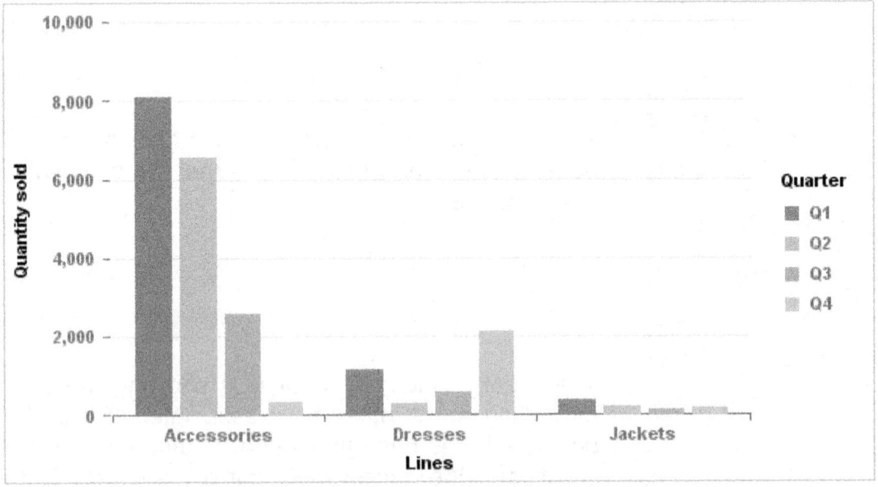
10,000
8,000
6,000
4,000
2,000
0
Quantity sold
Accessories
Dresses
Jackets
Lines
Quarter
Q1
Q2
Q3
Q4

3. Create a report tab showing a cross table as follows:

	Q1	Q2	Q3	Q4
Accessories	8,074	6,541	2,555	359
Dresses	1,153	294	596	2,140
Jackets	373	224	136	177

4. Save your document.

5. Activate Data Tracking and select Automatic Mode (i.e. 'Compare with last data refresh'). Also make sure the Data Tracking is set for all report tabs:

Reports with data tracking shown:
(Select All)
Chart
Cross Table

6. Refresh the query again and select the prompt values as follows:

   '2006' for [Year]

   'Dresses;Jackets;Leather' for [Lines]

7. After the query has refreshed, our chart shows:

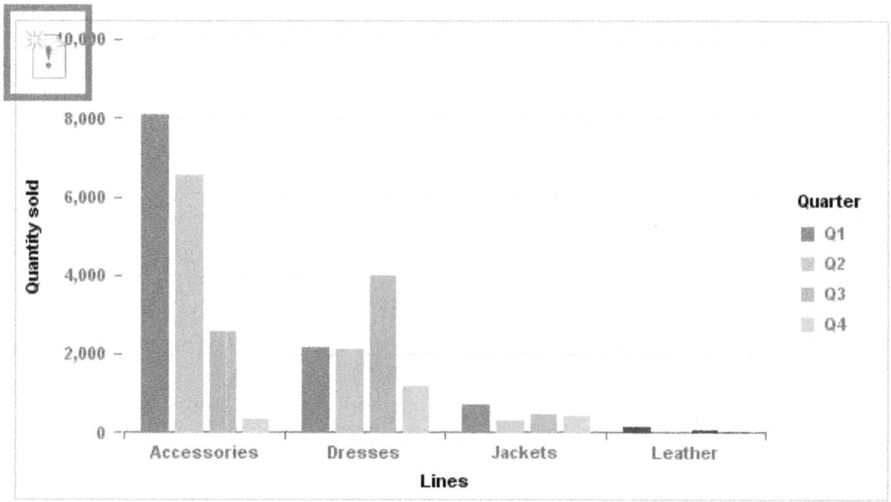
8,000
6,000
4,000
2,000
0
Quantity sold
Quarter
Q1
Q2
Q3
Q4
Accessories
Dresses
Jackets
Leather
Lines

The chart contains a 'Show Changes' icon in the top left corner. Hovering over the icon reveals the text that data in the chart has changed and we should click on the icon to see the changes in a tabular format.

   Click the icon on the chart to see the underlying data changes.

Quarter	Lines	Quantity sold
~~Q1~~	~~Accessories~~	~~8,074~~
Q1	Dresses	2,161
Q1	Jackets	700
Q1	**Leather**	**140**
~~Q2~~	~~Accessories~~	~~6,541~~
Q2	Dresses	2,118
Q2	Jackets	295
~~Q3~~	~~Accessories~~	~~2,555~~
Q3	Dresses	4,005
Q3	Jackets	449
Q3	**Leather**	**71**
~~Q4~~	~~Accessories~~	~~359~~
Q4	Dresses	1,193
Q4	Jackets	427
Q4	**Leather**	**19**

From the tabular view we can see:

- The complete row for 'Accessories' has been deleted (in reference data but not in current data)
- The complete row for 'Leather' has been inserted (in current data but not in reference data)
- 'Dresses' and 'Jackets' were present in reference data and are in current data but are affected by changes to measure values.

To revert back to chart format use the 'Undo' button :

8. Our crosstab shows:

	Q1	Q2	Q3	Q4
~~Accessories~~	~~8,074~~	~~6,541~~	~~2,555~~	~~359~~
Dresses	2,161	2,118	4,005	1,193
Jackets	700	295	449	427
Leather	140	Discontinued	71	19

From the crosstab:

- The complete row for 'Accessories' has been deleted (in the reference data but not in the current data)
- The complete row for 'Leather' has been inserted (in current data but not in reference data)
- 'Dresses' and 'Jackets' were present in reference data and are in current data but are affected by changes to measure values.

9. Save and close your document.

34.11 Data Changes and Merged Dimensions

Web Intelligence displays data changes (i.e. applies formatting changes) to a Merged Dimension only if the Merged Dimension value changes.

1. To demonstrate this create a new report and define the following two queries using the 'eFashion' universe.

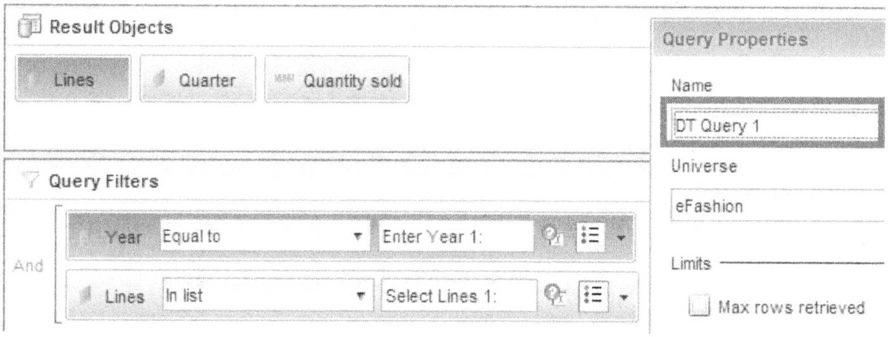
Result Objects
Lines
Quarter
Quantity sold
Query Filters
And
Year
Equal to
Enter Year 1:
Lines
In list
Select Lines 1:
Query Properties
Name
DT Query 1
Universe
eFashion
Limits
Max rows retrieved

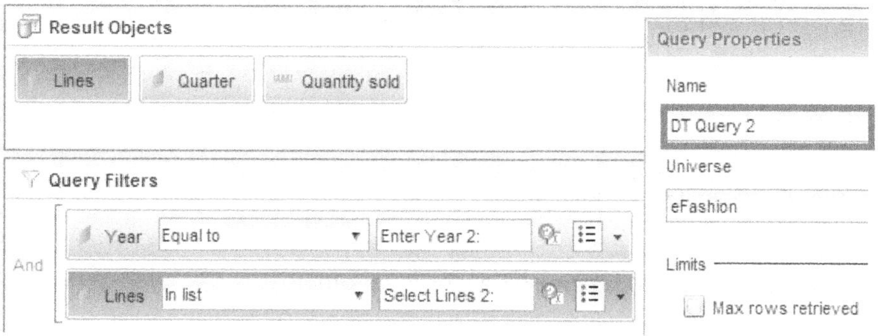
Result Objects
Lines
Quarter
Quantity sold
Query Filters
And
Year
Equal to
Enter Year 2:
Lines
In list
Select Lines 2:
Query Properties
Name
DT Query 2
Universe
eFashion
Limits
Max rows retrieved

2. Run the queries and specify the following values for the prompts:

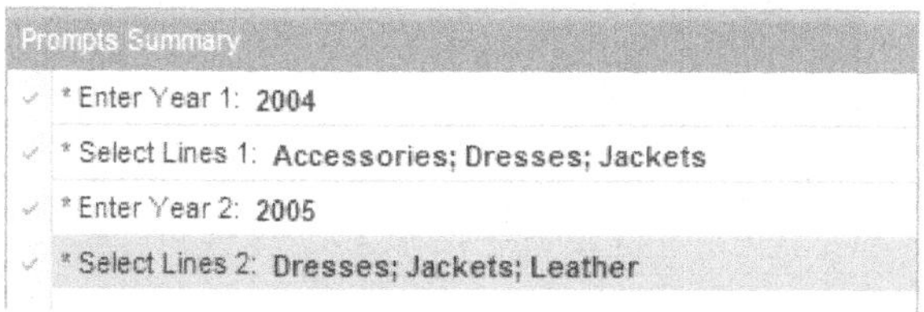
Prompts Summary
* Enter Year 1: 2004
* Select Lines 1: Accessories; Dresses; Jackets
* Enter Year 2: 2005
* Select Lines 2: Dresses; Jackets; Leather

3. Merge the dimensions as follows:

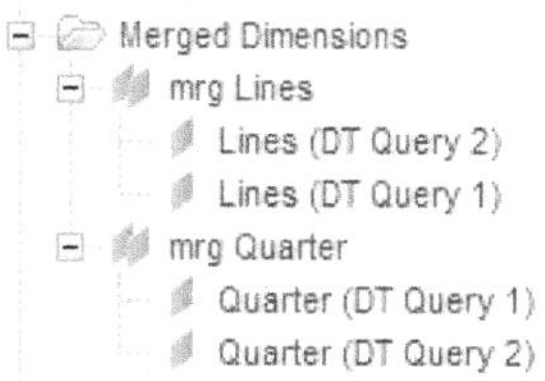
Merged Dimensions
mrg Lines
Lines (DT Query 2)
Lines (DT Query 1)
mrg Quarter
Quarter (DT Query 1)
Quarter (DT Query 2)

4. Add a new report tab and create the following vertical table using the Merged Dimensions and the measure [DT Query 2].[Quantity sold]:

mrg Lines	mrg Quarter	Quantity sold
Accessories	Q1	Discontinued
Accessories	Q2	Discontinued
Accessories	Q3	Discontinued
Accessories	Q4	Discontinued
Dresses	Q1	247
Dresses	Q2	289
Dresses	Q3	1,236
Dresses	Q4	4,825
Jackets	Q1	154
Jackets	Q2	383
Jackets	Q3	297
Jackets	Q4	394
Leather	Q3	343
Leather	Q4	166

5. Save your document.

6. Activate Data Tracking and select Automatic Mode (i.e. 'Compare with last data refresh').

7. Refresh the queries and specify the following values for the prompts:

Prompts Summary
* Enter Year 1: **2005**
* Select Lines 1: **Dresses; Jackets; Leather**
* Enter Year 2: **2006**
* Select Lines 2: **Dresses; Jackets; Overcoats**

8. Web Intelligence now displays:

mrg Lines	mrg Quarter	Quantity sold
~~Accessories~~	~~Q1~~	~~Discontinued~~
~~Accessories~~	~~Q2~~	~~Discontinued~~
~~Accessories~~	~~Q3~~	~~Discontinued~~
~~Accessories~~	~~Q4~~	~~Discontinued~~
Dresses	Q1	2,161
Dresses	Q2	2,118
Dresses	Q3	4,005
Dresses	Q4	1,193
Jackets	Q1	700
Jackets	Q2	295
Jackets	Q3	449
Jackets	Q4	427
Leather	Q3	~~343~~
Leather	Q4	~~166~~
Overcoats	**Q1**	294
Overcoats	**Q2**	6
Overcoats	**Q3**	135
Overcoats	**Q4**	70

'Accessories' existed in the reference data but it was removed from both queries in the latest refresh.

[Lines] and [Quarter] show changes for 'Accessories' as this combination of values no longer exists, therefore the 'Accessories' rows are showing as 'Deletions'.

'Dresses', 'Jackets' and 'Leather' existed in the reference data (either in [DT Query 1] or in [DT Query 2]). They also exist in the current data, therefore the dimension values are not showing changes, but are showing changes for measure values.

'Overcoats' did not exist in the reference data and is present in the current data. Therefore both [Lines] and [Quarter] show a change in value and 'Overcoats' rows are showing as 'Insertions'.

mrg Lines	Quantity sold
~~Accessories~~	~~Discontinued~~
Dresses	9,477
Jackets	1,871
Leather	~~509~~
Overcoats	505

If we remove the [Quarter] column then we can see more clearly that Data Tracking only applies formatting to Merged Dimensions if the actual Merged Dimension value changes.

'Accessories' does not exist in either of the two current result sets but it did exist in the reference data, therefore it is showing as deleted.

'Dresses' and 'Jackets' existed in the reference data and are also in one or both of the current data sets, therefore no formatting is applied to the dimension values.

'Leather' existed in the reference data in [DT Query 1] but in the current data set it exists in [DT Query 2], therefore it is showing as a deletion in terms of the measure but it has not changed in terms of a dimension value.

'Overcoats' did not exist in the reference data but is in one of the two current data sets therefore it is showing as inserted.

34.12 Data Tracking and Drill

When you drill out of scope (i.e. 'Extend the Scope of Analysis') this modifies the underlying SQL and data history is automatically cleared from the document by Web Intelligence, therefore Data Tracking does not take place.

Let us look at an example where we combine Drill and Data Tracking together.

1. Create the following query using 'eFashion' universe:

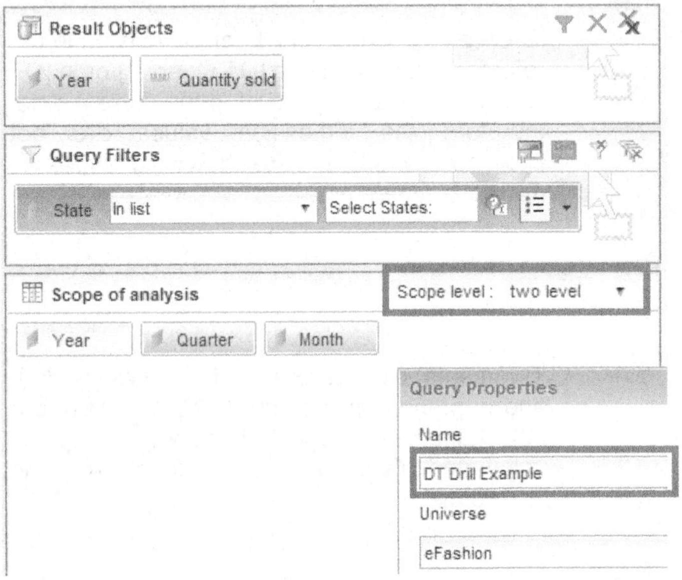
Result Objects
Year
Quantity sold
Query Filters
State
In list
Select States:
Scope of analysis
Scope level : two level
Year
Quarter
Month
Query Properties
Name
DT Drill Example
Universe
eFashion

2. Run the query and select the following [State] values:

Prompts Summary
* Select States: California; Colorado; DC; Florida

3. Display the results in a block as follows:

Year	Quantity sold
2004	21,541
2005	33,125
2006	34,206

4. Activate Data Tracking and select Automatic Mode (i.e. 'Compare with last data refresh').

5. Do not track 'Insertions' and 'Deletions':

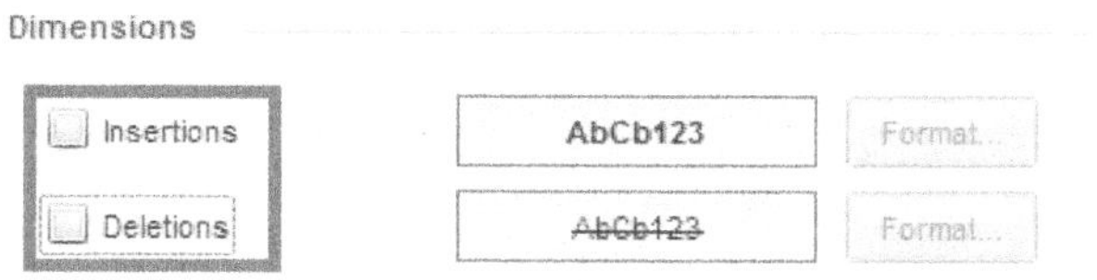
Dimensions
Insertions
AbCb123
Format...
Deletions
AbCb123
Format...

6. Activate Drill Mode.

7. Refresh the query and select the following [State] values:

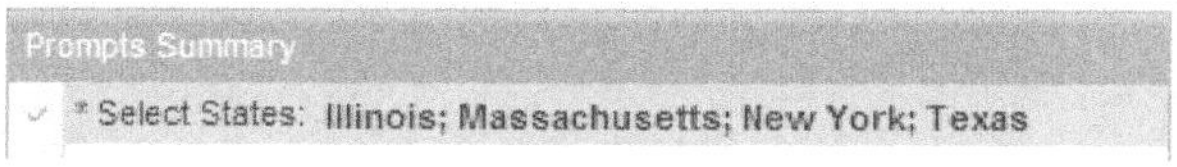
Prompts Summary
* Select States: Illinois; Massachusetts; New York; Texas

8. Report block displays:

Year	Quantity sold
2004	31,537
2005	46,730
2006	56,090

9. Drill on [Year] = '2005'.

   Report block displays:

2005

Quarter	Quantity sold
Q1	12,905
Q2	10,519
Q3	9,904
Q4	13,402

10. Drill on [Quarter] = 'Q2'.

    Report block displays:

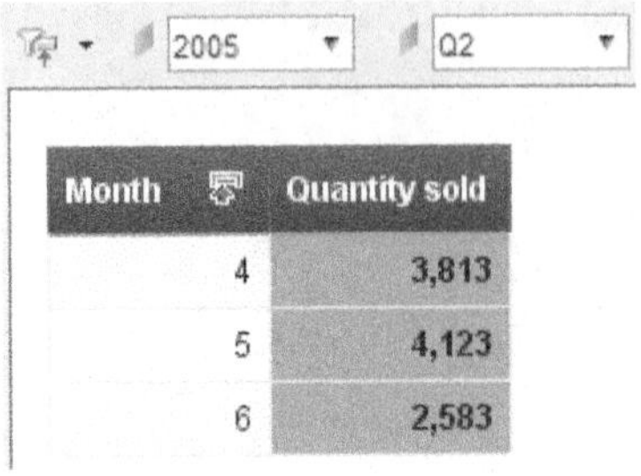
2005
Q2

Month	Quantity sold
4	3,813
5	4,123
6	2,583

11. Drill on [Month] = '5'.

    Report block displays:

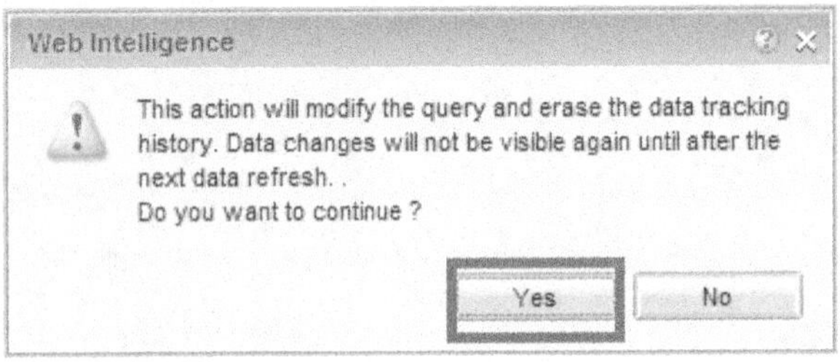
Web Intelligence
This action will modify the query and erase the data tracking history. Data changes will not be visible again until after the next data refresh. .
Do you want to continue ?
Yes
No

Click 'Yes' to continue.

12. Click 'OK' in the 'Extend the Scope of Analysis' interface.

    Report block shows no data changes because the 'Scope of Analysis' changed between the reference data and the current refresh:

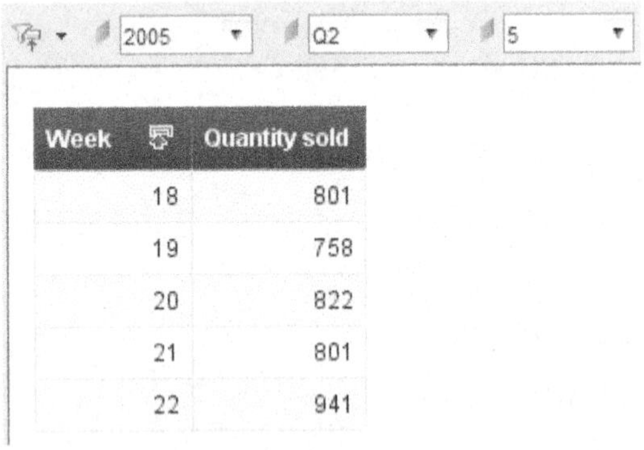
2005
Q2
5

Week	Quantity sold
18	801
19	758
20	822
21	801
22	941

13. Refresh the query and select the following [State] values:

Prompts Summary
* Select States: California; Colorado; DC; Florida

14. Report block now shows data tracking again because the 'Scope of Analysis' did not change between the reference data and the current refresh.

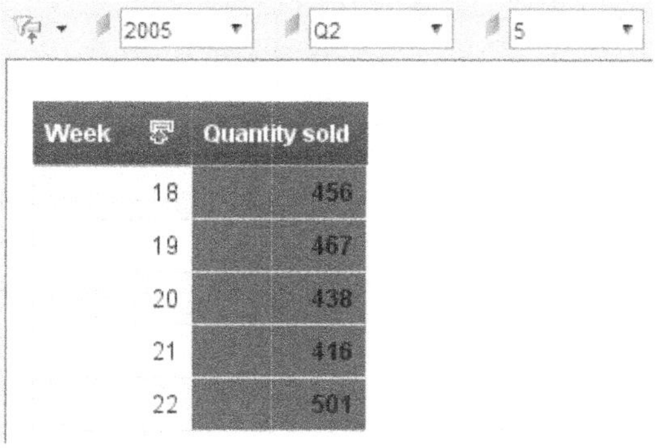
2005
Q2
5

Week	Quantity sold
18	456
19	467
20	438
21	416
22	501

NOTE

Query Drill modifies the underlying SQL with **every drill action** therefore data history is automatically cleared from the document by Web Intelligence. Data Changes will **not be tracked** once a drill action has been performed using Query Drill.

15. Save and close your document.

34.13 Data Changes and Report Level Calculation Contexts

When data tracking is activated, Web Intelligence only displays data as changed when the calculation context remains the same between query refreshes.

In other words, if a measure value changes because you change the calculation context of a block (by adding or removing dimensions) then the new value is not flagged as changed.

Let us look at an example:

1. Create the following query using the 'eFashion' universe:

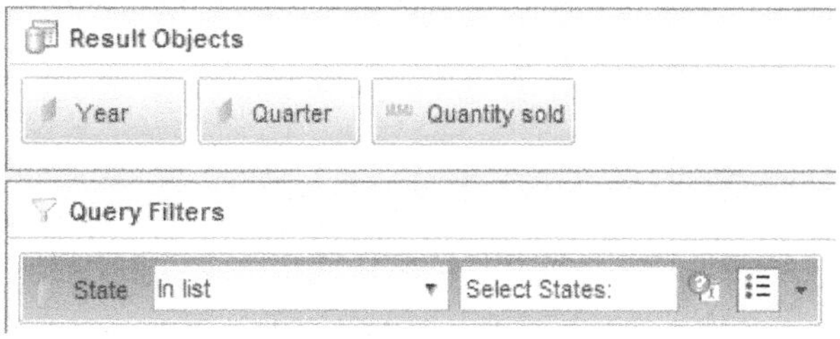
Result Objects
Year
Quarter
Quantity sold
Query Filters
State
In list
Select States:

2. Run the query and select the following [State] values:

Prompts Summary
* Select States: California; Colorado; DC; Florida

3. Report block displays:

Year	Quarter	Quantity sold
2004	Q1	6,821
2004	Q2	5,512
2004	Q3	5,028
2004	Q4	4,180
2005	Q1	8,230
2005	Q2	6,633
2005	Q3	9,320
2005	Q4	8,942
2006	Q1	8,553
2006	Q2	8,474
2006	Q3	9,955
2006	Q4	7,224

4. Activate Data Tracking and select Automatic Mode (i.e. 'Compare with last data refresh').

5. Remove [Quarter] from the block:

Year	Quantity sold
2004	21,541
2005	33,125
2006	34,206

Web Intelligence does not show [Quantity sold] as increased because the value has not changed. Only the *calculation context* has changed as [Quantity sold] is now aggregated by [Year], giving higher figures.

6. Refresh the query and select the following [State] values:

Prompts Summary
* Select States: Illinois; Massachusetts; New York; Texas

7. Report block displays:

Year	Quantity sold
2004	31,537
2005	46,730
2006	56,090

Web Intelligence now displays the data as changed because the calculation context has remained the same but the values have changed.

8. Save and close your document.

35 Detailed Analysis using Linked Documents

We have looked at providing summarised data along with detailed data in a single Web Intelligence document by using report tabs. For example:

- Run a single query at the detailed level.
- Display summarised data on one tab.
- Display more detailed data on a second tab.

We have also looked at using 'Drill Mode' to drill from aggregated data down to more detailed data. An alternative approach is to use multiple documents that are linked together to provide detailed data from a summarised view.

Using this approach it is possible to:

- Create focused documents that are navigated to by the user from other documents.
- Focused documents typically contain less data therefore they refresh quickly and response times within Web Intelligence are also quicker.
- Users can be given access to summarised data, detailed data, or both depending on security requirements, etc.
- Focused documents can be used to present the detail in many report tabs for different views of the data without cluttering high level summary documents.

In this session we will look at how to create documents for linking purposes and then link the documents together using BI Launch Pad functionality.

35.1 Considerations for Document Linking

When linking documents together we should consider what the 'linking' will achieve, for example:

1. Do we want to link documents to simply display different views of the data? Both documents use the same queries but one presents the data in tabular format whereas the second document presents the data in charts
2. Do we want to link from a summarised document to a detailed document without restricting the detailed document in any way? This is similar to 'Extending the Scope of Analysis' in Drill Mode when no filters are used to restrict the new lower level query.
3. Do we want to link to a detailed document by passing values from the summarised document? This is similar to 'Extending the Scope of Analysis' in Drill Mode when filters are used to restrict the new lower level query.
4. What part of the 'linked to' document do we want to navigate to? The 'linked to' document could contain many report tabs, or blocks within report tab(s) and we want to navigate to a particular part.

We will have look at a combination of points (3) and (4).

35.2 Creating Document for Linking Purposes

In this example we will create two documents and then link them together.

- Document 1 will show summary data (based on an unrestricted query) on a single report tab.
- Document 2 will show detailed data (based on a restricted query) on multiple report tabs.
- The two documents will be linked together by passing in parameters from Document 1 to Document 2 in order to restrict the data shown in the detailed reports of Document 2.

35.2.1 Creating the Summary Document

This document will contain very high-level aggregated/summarised data.

1. Create the query '**qrySummary**' using the 'eFashion' universe:

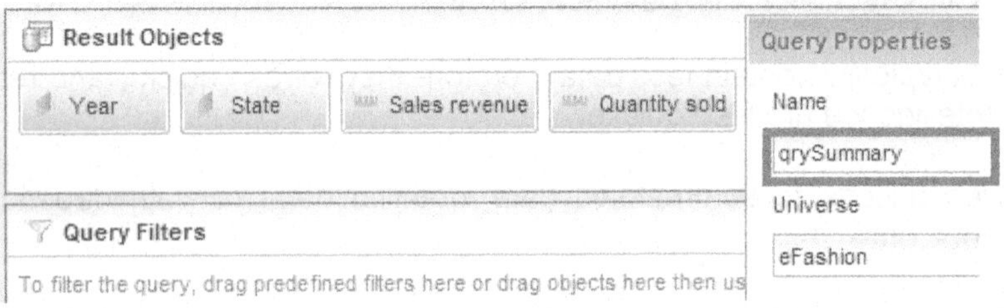
Result Objects
Year
State
Sales revenue
Quantity sold
Query Properties
Name
qrySummary
Universe
eFashion
Query Filters
To filter the query, drag predefined filters here or drag objects here then us

2. Present the data in a report tab called '**Summary**' as follows:

Year	State	Sales revenue	Quantity sold	Detailed Data Link
2004	California	$1,704,211	11,304	Click for details for 2004 / California
2004	Colorado	$448,302	2,971	Click for details for 2004 / Colorado
2004	DC	$693,211	4,681	Click for details for 2004 / DC
2004	Florida	$405,985	2,585	Click for details for 2004 / Florida
2004	Illinois	$737,914	4,713	Click for details for 2004 / Illinois

We have used a document variable called '**rv Link Text**' for the last column.

The definition of [rv Link Text] is a dimension variable with the formula:

="Click for details for " + [Year] + " / " + [State]

We have also named the block as '**table Summary**'.

3. Rename the report tab as 'Summary'.

4. Save the document as '**Guided Analysis Summary**' and then close it.

35.2.2 Creating the Detailed Document

This document will contain very detailed data for a prompted [Year] and [State].

1. Create the query '**qryDetail**' using the 'eFashion' universe. Use two prompts as shown below:

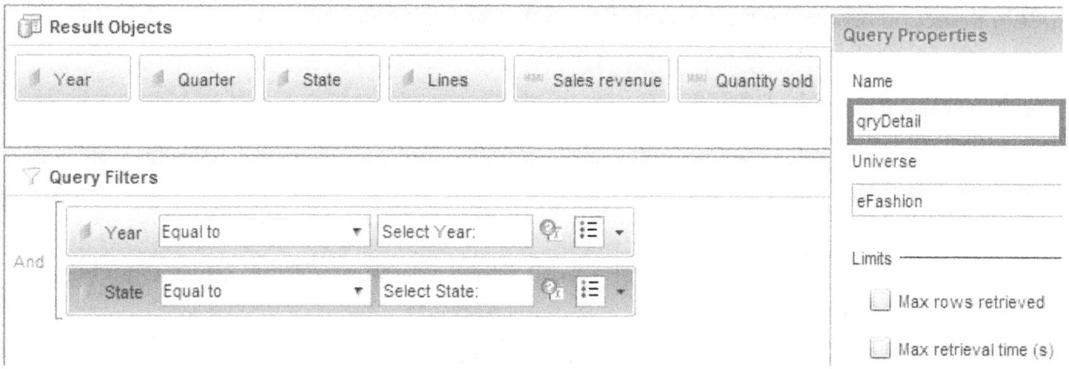
Result Objects
Year
Quarter
State
Lines
Sales revenue
Quantity sold
Query Filters
And
Year
Equal to
Select Year:
State
Equal to
Select State:
Query Properties
Name
qryDetail
Universe
eFashion
Limits
Max rows retrieved
Max retrieval time (s)

2. Run the query and select the following prompt values:

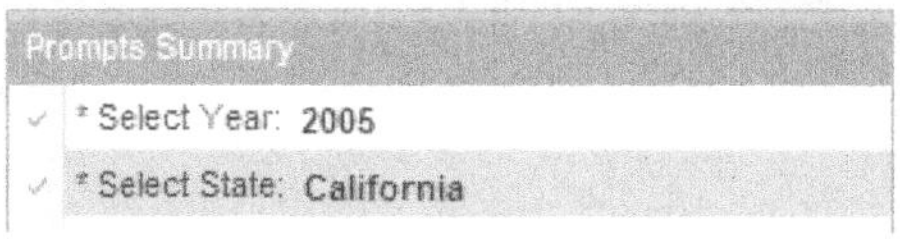
Prompts Summary
* Select Year: 2005
* Select State: California

3. Present the data in the first report tab called '**Details by Quarter**' as follows:

Year = 2005 / State = California

Quarter	Lines	Sales revenue	Quantity sold
Q1	Accessories	$528,173	3,386
	City Trousers	$207	3
	Dresses	$5,350	45
	Jackets	$8,556	44
	Outerwear	$18,908	171
	Shirt Waist	$696	4
	Sweaters	$60,637	314
	Sweat-T-Shirts	$19,533	134
	Trousers	$8,656	44
Q1		**$650,715**	**4,145**

This block is called '**table LinesPerQuarter**.

The block has had a break applied to [Quarter].

The columns [Sales revenue] and [Quantity sold] are showing sub-totals.

We have created a document variable called '**rv User Response Label**' with the definition:

="Year = " + UserResponse([qryDetail];"Select Year:") + " / " + "State = " + UserResponse([qryDetail];"Select State:")

NOTE:

To display [rv User Response Label] as a title just drag it and drop it to replace the default 'Report Title' cell and then reposition it to be above the table block.

4. Create a second report tab called '**Details wo Accessories**' as follows:

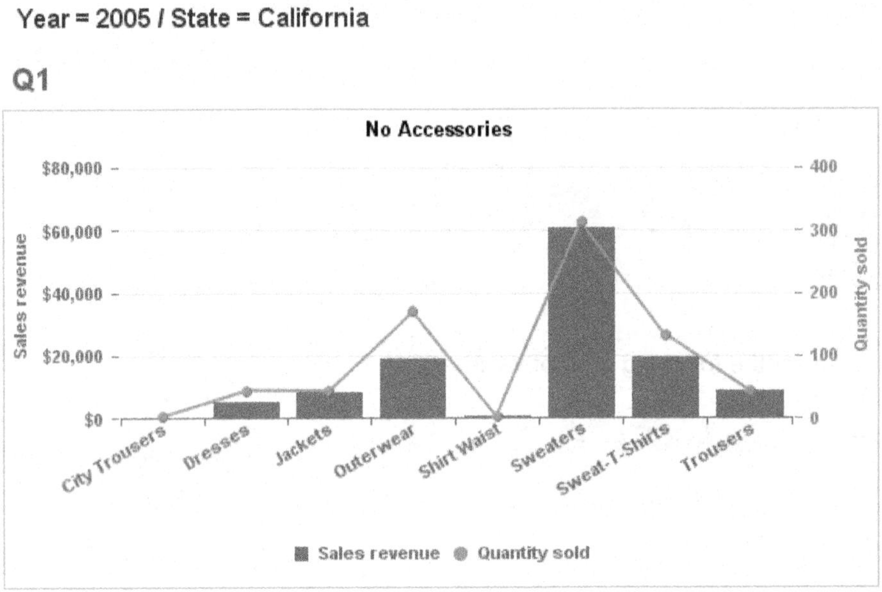
Year = 2005 / State = California
Q1
No Accessories
$80,000
$60,000
$40,000
$20,000
$0
Sales revenue
400
300
200
100
0
Quantity sold
City Trousers
Dresses
Jackets
Outerwear
Shirt Waist
Sweaters
Sweat-T-Shirts
Trousers
Sales revenue
Quantity sold

For the above, we have:

a. Created a section on [Quarter] and then used a Combined Column Line Chart with 2 Y-Axis to present [Sales revenue] and [Quantity sold] for [Lines].

b. Used a chart title of 'No Accessories' and have applied a border to the chart.

c. Applied a chart level filter of [Lines] Not Equal to 'Accessories'.

d. The chart block has been named '**chart NoAccessories**'.

5. Create a third report tab called '**Detail Accessories Only**' as follows:

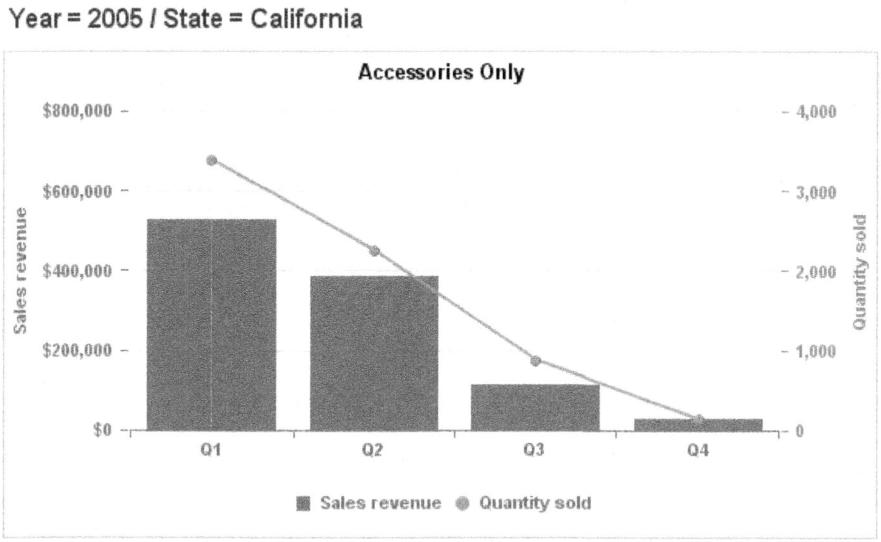
Year = 2005 / State = California
Accessories Only
$800,000
$600,000
$400,000
$200,000
$0
4,000
3,000
2,000
1,000
0
Sales revenue
Quantity sold
Q1
Q2
Q3
Q4
Sales revenue
Quantity sold

For the above, we have:

a. Created a Combined Column Line Chart with 2 Y-Axis to present [Sales revenue] and [Quantity sold] for [Quarter].

a. Used a chart title of 'Accessories Only' and have applied a border to the chart.

b. Applied a chart level filter of [Lines] Equal to 'Accessories'.

c. The chart block has been named as '**chart AccessoriesOnly**'.

6. Purge the document.

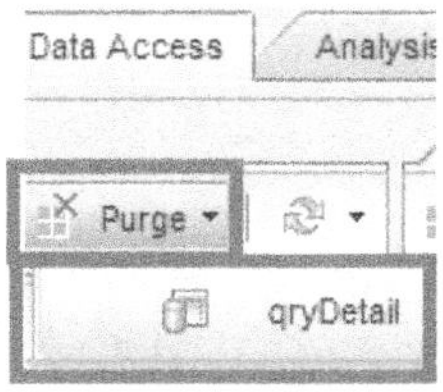
Data Access
Analysis
Purge
qryDetail

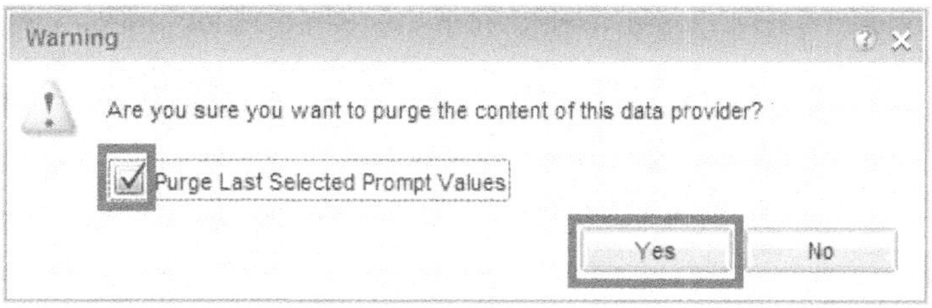
Warning
Are you sure you want to purge the content of this data provider?
Purge Last Selected Prompt Values
Yes
No

7. Click on 'Detail by Quarter' report tab to make it the default tab of the document and then save the document as '**Guided Analysis Detail**'.

8. Close the document to return to BI Launch Pad, i.e. you must not be in Web Intelligence anymore.

35.2.3 Linking Documents

Documents can be linked using an interface that is available in BI Launch Pad or you can use the formula language to achieve the same result, but we recommend the interface (except for advanced users).

IMPORTANT

To make changes to documents from within BI Launch Pad, we recommend the Preference for '**View**' to be set to 'HTML' (as shown below):

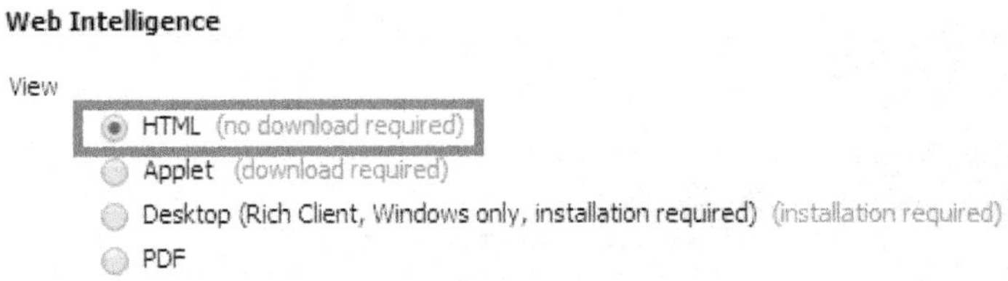
Web Intelligence
View
HTML (no download required)
Applet (download required)
Desktop (Rich Client, Windows only, installation required) (installation required)
PDF

Make sure your preference is set as stated above, Log Off and then Log On again for it to take effect.

1. Double-click on 'Guided Analysis Summary' to open in View mode, or right-click and select 'View'.

2. Change the mode to 'Design':

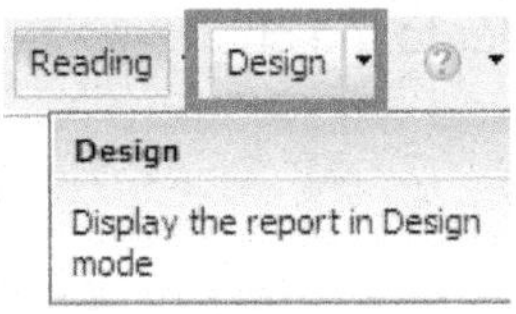
Reading
Design
Design
Display the report in Design mode

3. Click in any body-cell of the **column** 'Detailed Data Link' and select 'Add Document Link…' as shown below (it is available from the 'Report Elements – Linking' toolbox).

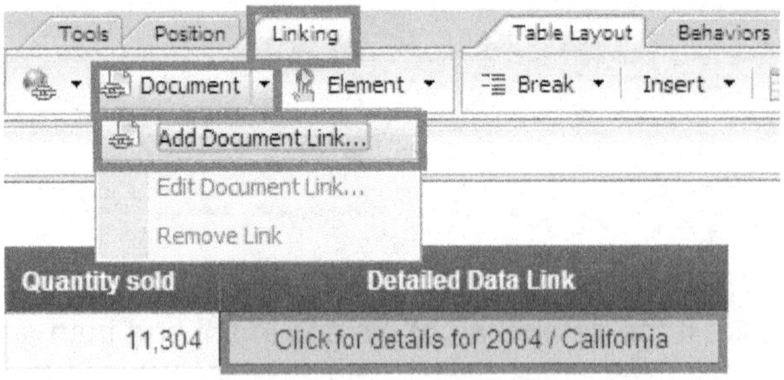
Tools
Position
Linking
Table Layout
Behaviors
Document
Element
Break
Insert
Add Document Link...
Edit Document Link...
Remove Link
Quantity sold
Detailed Data Link
11,304
Click for details for 2004 / California

This will open the 'Create Hyperlink' interface.

4. Click on 'Browse...' and select the 'Guided Analysis Detail' document from the location you saved it in.

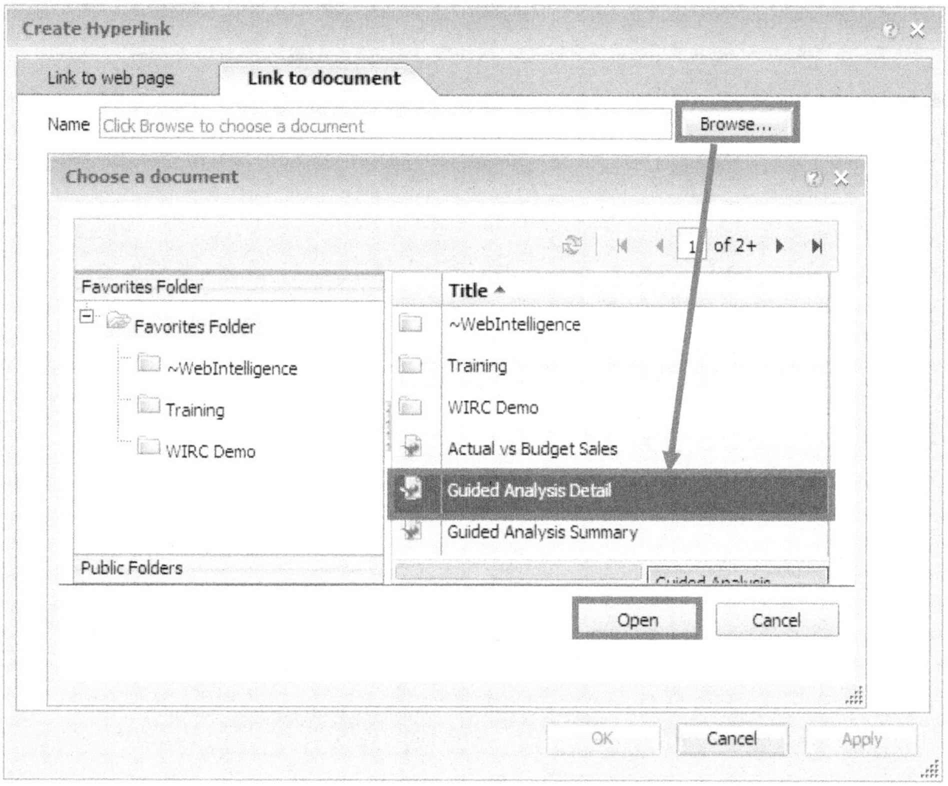
Create Hyperlink
Link to web page
Link to document
Name
Click Browse to choose a document
Browse...
Choose a document
of 2+
Favorites Folder
Favorites Folder
~WebIntelligence
Training
WIRC Demo
Public Folders
Title
~WebIntelligence
Training
WIRC Demo
Actual vs Budget Sales
Guided Analysis Detail
Guided Analysis Summary
Open
Cancel
OK
Cancel
Apply

Click 'OK' to close the 'Choose a document' interface.

5. The document will be selected and we will be presented with the 'Select Prompts' interface because our selected document contains prompts:

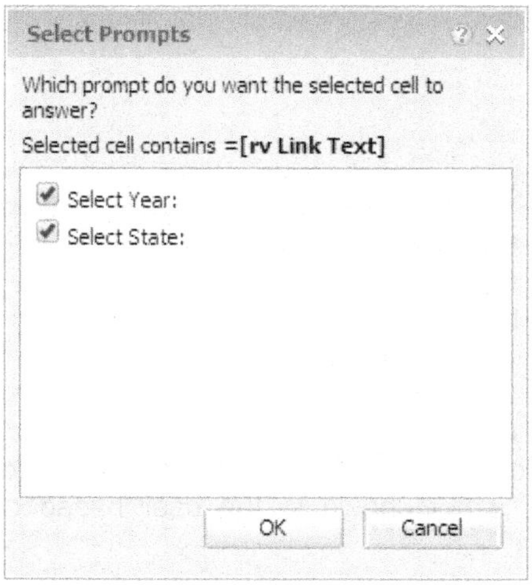
Select Prompts
Which prompt do you want the selected cell to answer?
Selected cell contains =[rv Link Text]
Select Year:
Select State:
OK
Cancel

Select both prompts as shown above and click 'OK'.

6. The 'Create Hyperlink' interface will now display:

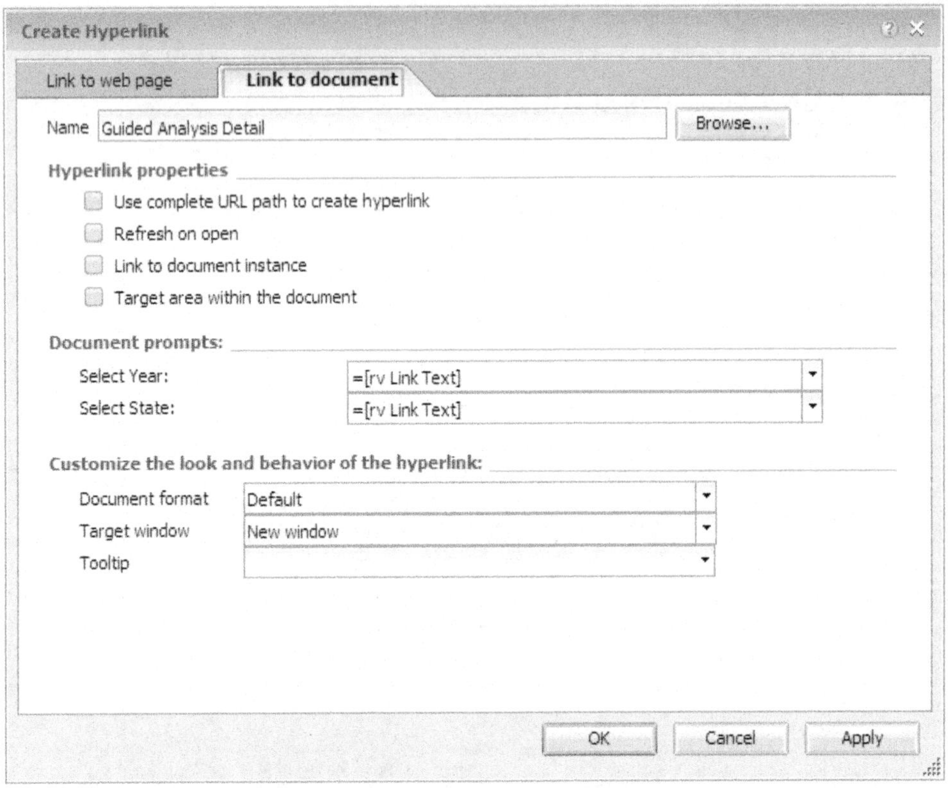
Create Hyperlink
Link to web page
Link to document
Name
Guided Analysis Detail
Browse...
Hyperlink properties
Use complete URL path to create hyperlink
Refresh on open
Link to document instance
Target area within the document
Document prompts:
Select Year:
=[rv Link Text]
Select State:
=[rv Link Text]
Customize the look and behavior of the hyperlink:
Document format
Default
Target window
New window
Tooltip
OK
Cancel
Apply

Properties for '**Link to document**':

Name

This shows the name of the selected document that will be linked to, e.g. 'Guided Analysis Detail'.

<u>Hyperlink properties:</u>

Use complete URL path to create hyperlink

If you select this property the hyperlink will contain the name of your current Web Intelligence server. If the set up changes in the future then this link will not work.

We recommend leaving this property unchecked.

Refresh on open

Selecting this property forces the 'linked to' document to refresh when navigated to. This property will also ensure any 'sensitive' data is not shown to the user based on data security that you might have implemented.

We have purged our 'Guided Analysis Detail' document so selecting this property will ensure the document displays refreshed data when it is navigated to.

Link to document instance

You can select a particular instance of the 'linked to' document.

When a document is scheduled then every run is seen as an instance in the document's history. For example:

> You might have a 'Daily History' report that is scheduled to run every day and it shows detailed data for the previous day of business. This document will be run by the scheduler every day and a snapshot (i.e. 'instance') of the data will be stored (with a date time stamp).
>
> If you want to always link to the latest snapshot then this property enables you specify this.

Target area within the document

You can select a particular report tab to navigate to within the 'linked to' document.

You can also specify if you want to select a particular area within an individual report tab, i.e. if you had a report tab containing many blocks of data (table, crosstab, charts, etc) then you can direct the link to locate a particular block.

Document prompts:

For each prompt in 'linked to' document

If the 'linked to' document contains prompts then you can specify how each prompt will be answered when the document is navigated to.

> Our example shows that both of the prompts will be answered by the contents of our report variable [rv Link Text], but this is not possible as the contents of this variable are values such as:

Detailed Data Link
Click for details for 2004 / California
Click for details for 2004 / Colorado
Click for details for 2004 / DC
Click for details for 2004 / Florida
Click for details for 2004 / Illinois

Use the dropdown selection to specify how each prompt will be answered:

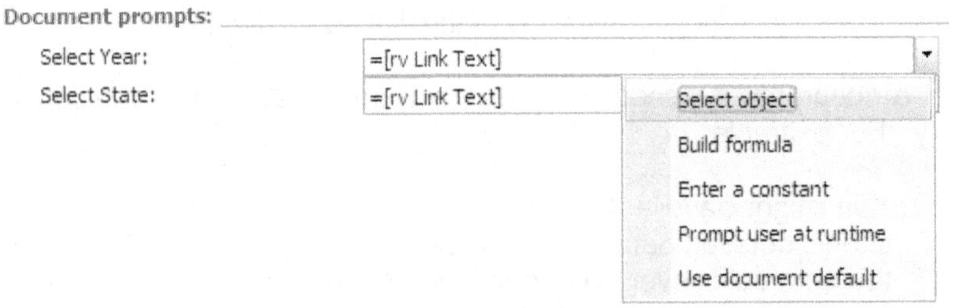
Document prompts:
Select Year:
=[rv Link Text]
Select State:
=[rv Link Text]
Select object
Build formula
Enter a constant
Prompt user at runtime
Use document default

The options are quite self-explanatory:

1. '**Select object**' enables you to select a single object from the current document whose value will be passed as an input to the selected prompt. In this example we need to select [Year] and [State] respectively.

2. '**Build formula**' initiates the Formula Editor interface from which you can create a formula to answer the selected prompt by using multiple objects, functions, operators, calculations, etc.

3. '**Enter a constant**' enables you to specify a fixed value for the selected prompt.

4. '**Prompt user at runtime**' passes in no value to the prompt but requests the user to select a value for the prompt when the 'linked to' document is refreshed on open.

5. '**Use document default**' will cause the 'linked to' document to refresh using the default value(s) assigned to the selected prompt.

Customize the look and behaviour of the hyperlink:

Document format

You can specify which format should be used to open the 'linked to' document. The options are:

Default – If the 'linked to' document is a Web Intelligence document and you select this option then the document will be opened in Web Intelligence format.

HTML – If you select this option then the 'linked to' document will be opened using the HTML panel. The HTML panel is similar to the Java Panel but has less functionality.

PDF – The 'linked to' document will be opened in PDF. You might want to use this if the purpose of the navigation is to get to an output which is to be printed, or saved for sharing, etc.

Excel – If enabled the 'linked to' document will be opened in Excel.

Word – If enabled the 'linked to' document will be opened in Word.

Target window

You can specify whether the 'linked to' document should open in a 'New window' or the 'Current window'.

If the user wants to navigate repeatedly between the 'linked to' document from the 'source document' then select 'New window' as it is more user friendly.

If the user wants to do a single navigation then 'Current window' is the more suitable option.

Tooltip

You can type in text that will be used as the 'tooltip' when the user hovers over the hyperlink.

You can also specify an object as the tooltip in which case the value of the selected object is displayed as the tooltip text.

You can also specify a formula as the tooltip in which case the result of the calculated formula is displayed as the tooltip text.

7. Select the following for our hyperlink:

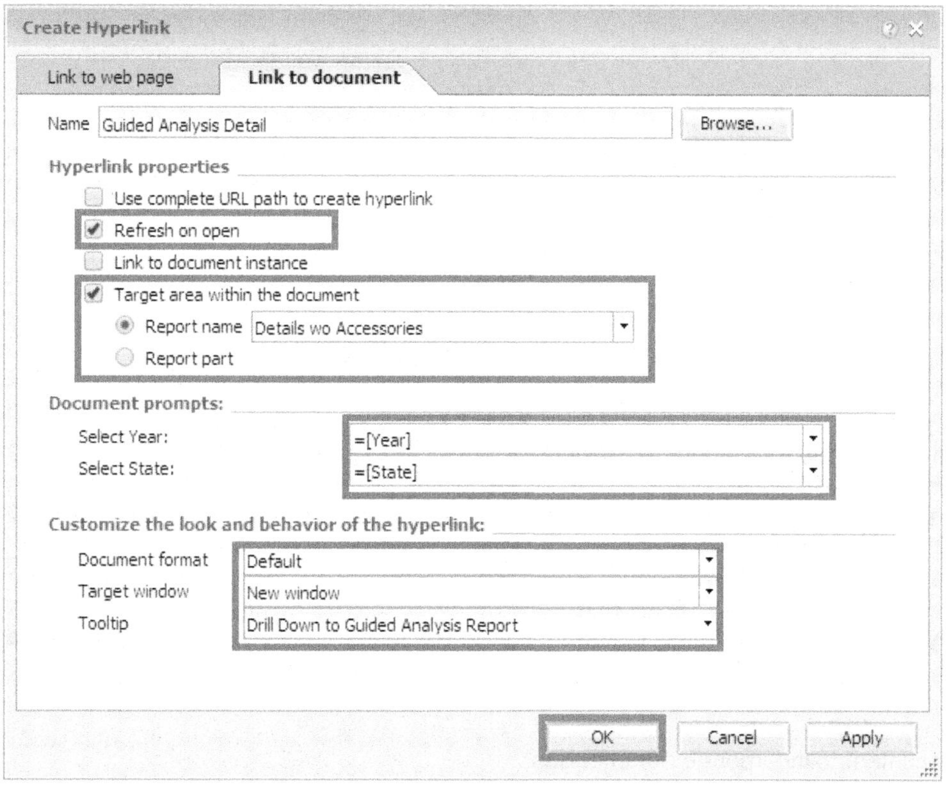

Create Hyperlink
Link to web page
Link to document
Name
Guided Analysis Detail
Browse...
Hyperlink properties
Use complete URL path to create hyperlink
Refresh on open
Link to document instance
Target area within the document
Report name
Details wo Accessories
Report part
Document prompts:
Select Year:
=[Year]
Select State:
=[State]
Customize the look and behavior of the hyperlink:
Document format
Default
Target window
New window
Tooltip
Drill Down to Guided Analysis Report
OK
Cancel
Apply

We have specified for the hyperlink:

a. Open the document 'Guided Analysis Detail'.

b. Refresh this document as it opens.

c. Navigate to the report 'Detail wo Accessories' as the default view.

d. The prompts will be answered by using the values of the objects [Year] and [State] from this document (i.e. the source).

e. Open the 'linked to' document in Web Intelligence format in a new window.

f. When we hover over the hyperlink then we will see the tooltip text 'Drill down to Guided Analysis Detail report'.

8. Click 'OK' to create the hyperlink.

The document now displays hyperlinks in the column 'Detailed Data Link'.

Year	State	Sales revenue	Quantity sold	Detailed Data Link
2004	California	$1,704,211	11,304	Click for details for 2004 / California
2004	Colorado	$448,302	2,971	Click for details for 2004 / Colorado
2004	DC	$693,211	4,681	Click for details for 2004 / DC
2004	Florida	$405,985	2,585	Click for details for 2004 / Florida
2004	Illinois	$737,914	4,713	Click for details for 2004 / Illinois
2004	Massachusetts	$238,819	1,505	Click for details for 2004 / Massachusetts
2004	New York	$1,667,696	10,802	Click for details for 2004 / New York
2004	Texas	$2,199,677	14,517	Click for details for 2004 / Texas
2005	California	$2,782,680	17,001	Click for details for 2005 / California

NOTE – The actual hyperlink formula that has been created is:

="<a href=\"../../opendoc/openDocument.jsp?iDocID=Acll6Cc5jiBKkghBEPdR41E&sIDType=CUID&sType=wid&sReportName=Details wo Accessories&sRefresh=Y&lsSSelect%20Year%3A="+URLEncode(""+[Year])+"&lsSSelect%20State%3A="+URLEncode(""+[State])+"\" title=\"Drill Down to Guided Analysis Report\" target=\"_blank\" nav=\"doc\">"+[rv Link Text]+"</a>"

This is why we recommend using the interface to generate the hyperlink rather than doing it manually.

9. Save the document to incorporate our changes.

10. Hover over any hyperlink to see our tooltip text.

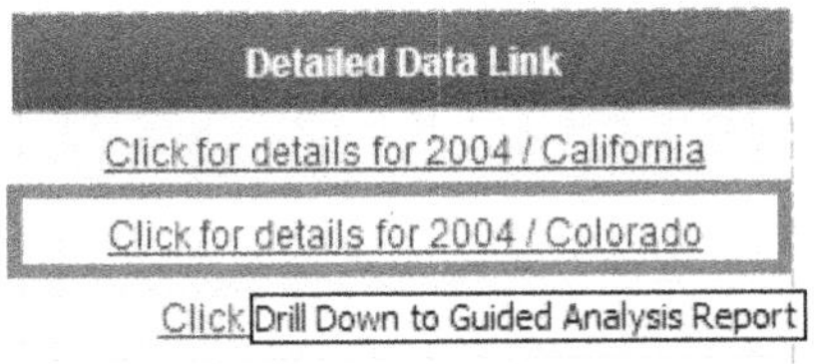
Detailed Data Link
Click for details for 2004 / California
Click for details for 2004 / Colorado
Click
Drill Down to Guided Analysis Report

11. Click on 'Click for details for 2004 / Florida'.

12. A new window opens showing the 'Guided Analysis Detail' document for [Year] = '2004' and [State] = 'Florida':

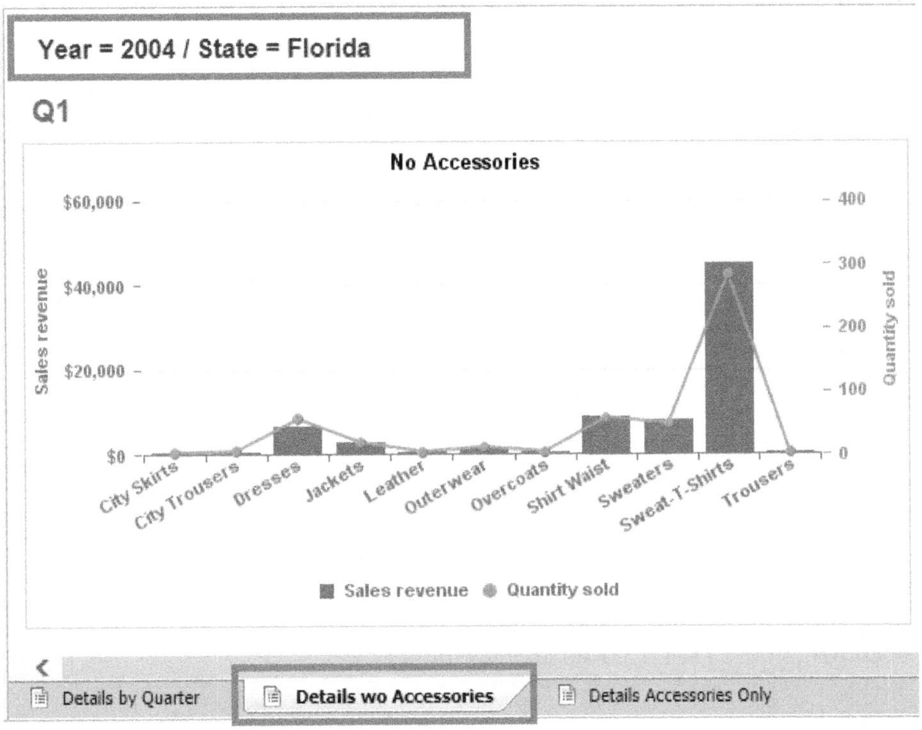
Year = 2004 / State = Florida
Q1
No Accessories
$60,000
$40,000
$20,000
$0
Sales revenue
400
300
200
100
0
Quantity sold
City Skirts
City Trousers
Dresses
Jackets
Leather
Outerwear
Overcoats
Shirt Waist
Sweaters
Sweat-T-Shirts
Trousers
Sales revenue
Quantity sold
Details by Quarter
Details wo Accessories
Details Accessories Only

NOTES

The document has opened showing the 'Detail wo Accessories' report tab as we selected this report to be the target area.

The document has been refreshed on open as we specified this action to take place.

We can view the other report tabs in the new window if we want to.

If we close the new window then we return to the 'source document' so we can navigate another hyperlink if required.

We have successfully linked together two documents.

35.2.4 Editing and Removing Document Hyperlinks

Use right-click menu options to edit or remove hyperlinks.

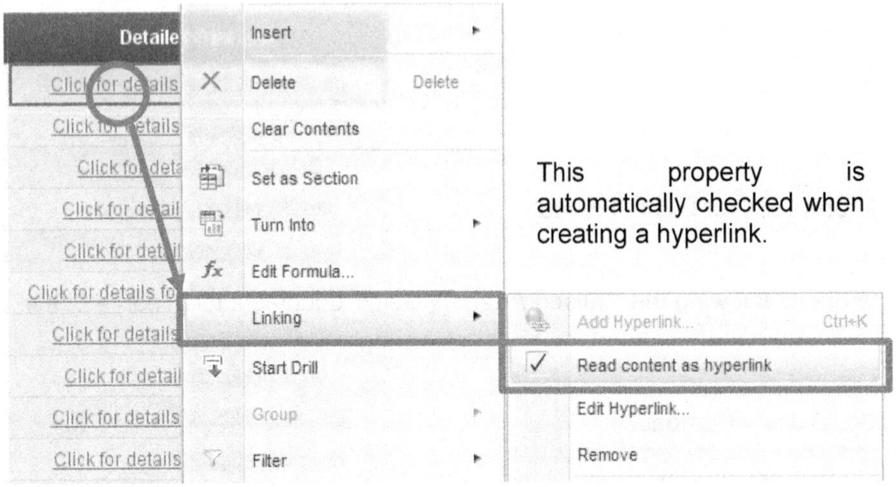
Insert
Delete
Delete
Clear Contents
Set as Section
Turn Into
Edit Formula...
Linking
Start Drill
Group
Filter
Add Hyperlink...
Ctrl+K
Read content as hyperlink
Edit Hyperlink...
Remove
This property is automatically checked when creating a hyperlink.

If we uncheck the 'Read content as hyperlink' then the hyperlink will be replaced by the underlying formula text as shown below.

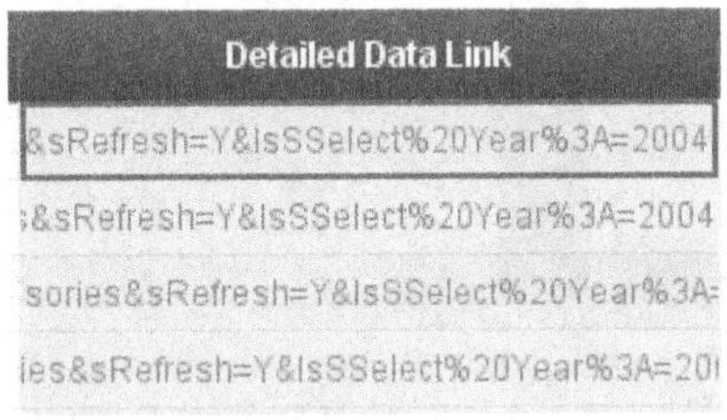
Detailed Data Link

If you want to remove the edit a document hyperlink then:

1. Open the document from BI Launch Pad in 'View' mode
2. Click on 'Design' mode
3. Select 'Edit Hyperlink…'

35.2.5 Linking to Web Pages

We can create hyperlinks to web pages if required.

For example:

You might have a requirement to show the share prices, currency rates or other information from an external site, etc.

Select your cell and then click ‘Add Document Link…’

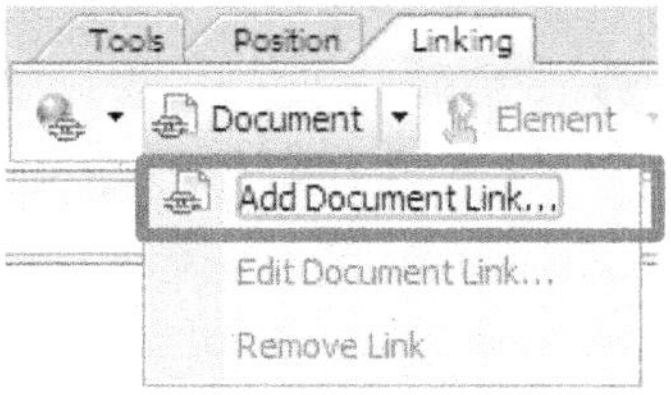
Tools
Position
Linking
Document
Element
Add Document Link...
Edit Document Link...
Remove Link

You can then specify parameters in ‘Create Hyperlink’ interface using the ‘Link to web page’ tab.

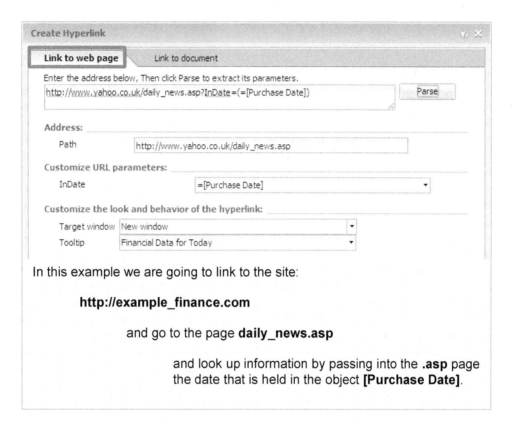

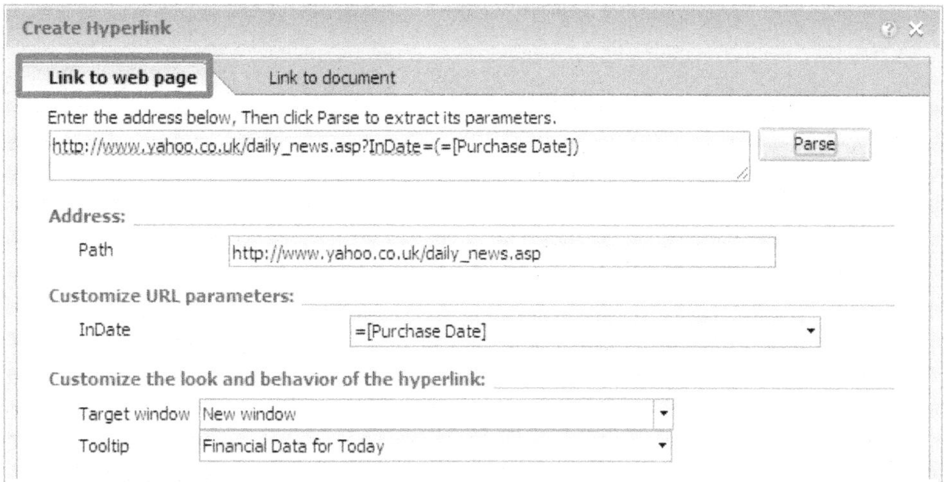
Create Hyperlink
Link to web page
Link to document
Enter the address below, Then click Parse to extract its parameters.
http://www.yahoo.co.uk/daily_news.asp?InDate=(=[Purchase Date])
Parse
Address:
Path
http://www.yahoo.co.uk/daily_news.asp
Customize URL parameters:
InDate
=[Purchase Date]
Customize the look and behavior of the hyperlink:
Target window
New window
Tooltip
Financial Data for Today

In this example we are going to link to the site:

http://example_finance.com

and go to the page **daily_news.asp**

and look up information by passing into the **.asp** page the date that is held in the object **[Purchase Date]**.

36 Using Custom SQL in Queries

This session looks at how you can use the Web Intelligence Query Panel to manually alter SQL statements generated when using universes as data sources. We will use this session to demonstrate the concepts of reading and modifying SQL statements, but it is assumed you are already familiar or experienced with SQL statements.

It is recommended that you try to get your universes and the Query Panel to generate the correct SQL, but in some instances it is not possible for this to take place. This could be due to design of the universe(s) or maybe lack of functionality in the Query Panel to generate advanced SQL statements.

36.1 Viewing and Editing Universe Generated SQL

The net result of the Query Panel is to generate SQL statement(s) that can be sent to your database(s). The database(s) process the statement(s) and return one or more sets of data that are held within the Web Intelligence document.

1. Create a simple query using 'eFashion' universe as shown below and click on the 'View Script' button:

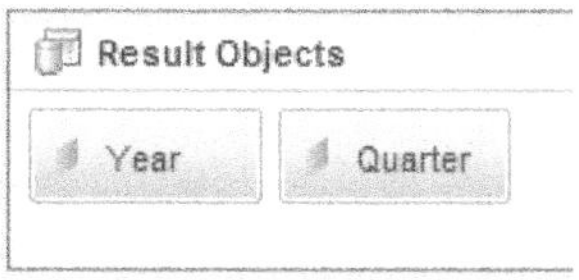
Result Objects
Year
Quarter

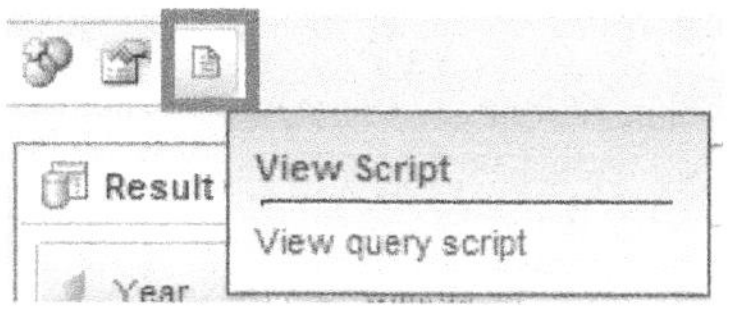
Result
View Script
View query script
Year

2. The 'Query Script Viewer' interface appears showing the generated statement:

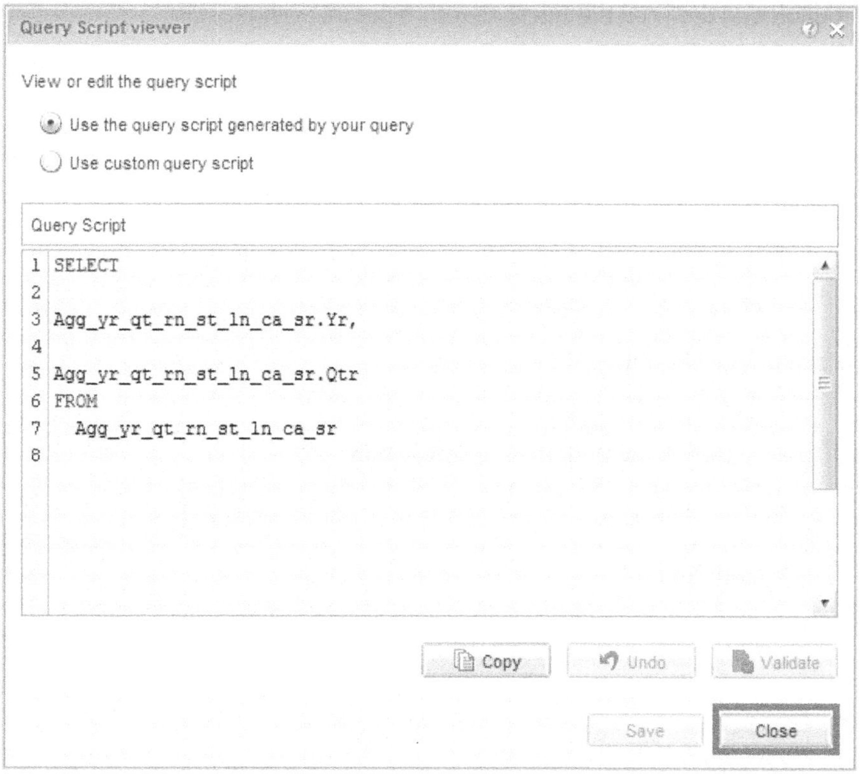
Query Script viewer
View or edit the query script
Use the query script generated by your query
Use custom query script
Query Script
SELECT
Agg_yr_qt_rn_st_ln_ca_sr.Yr,
Agg_yr_qt_rn_st_ln_ca_sr.Qtr
FROM
Agg_yr_qt_rn_st_ln_ca_sr
Copy
Undo
Validate
Save
Close

3. Click on the 'Close' button.

4. Modify the query to include the [This year] pre-defined condition:

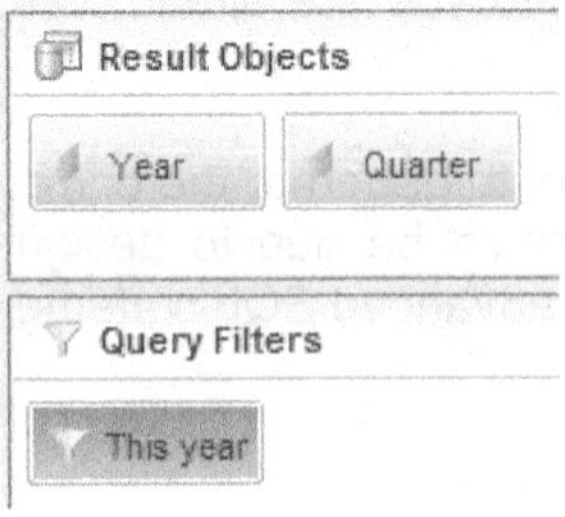
Result Objects
Year
Quarter
Query Filters
This year

5. Click on the 'View Script' button again to view the modified SQL statement:

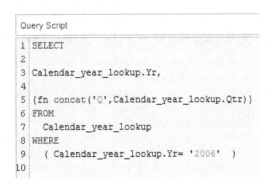

Query Script

```
SELECT

Calendar_year_lookup.Yr,

{fn concat('Q',Calendar_year_lookup.Qtr)}
FROM
  Calendar_year_lookup
WHERE
  ( Calendar_year_lookup.Yr= '2006'  )

```

6. Click on the 'Close' button and then run the query to return the following results:

Year	Quarter
2006	Q1
2006	Q2
2006	Q3
2006	Q4

7. Edit the query and click on 'View Script'.

8. Click on 'Use custom query script' radio button as shown below:

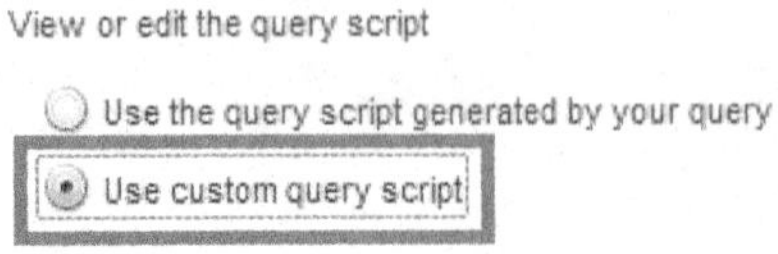
View or edit the query script
Use the query script generated by your query
Use custom query script

9. Now change the last line to read:

   (Calendar_year_lookup.Yr In ('2004','2006'))

10. Click on 'Validate':

11. Click on 'OK' if the script contains no errors, otherwise make sure the changes are as specified above.

12. Click on 'Save' in the 'Query Script Viewer' interface.

13. Run the query again to return the new results:

Year	Quarter
2004	Q1
2004	Q2
2004	Q3
2004	Q4
2006	Q1
2006	Q2
2006	Q3
2006	Q4

But the Query Panel shows the query definition as:

Result Objects
Year
Quarter
Query Filters
This year

We would expect a single year, but the results show two years due to the modified SQL statement.

36.2 Editing Existing Custom SQL Queries

From the Java Query Panel, it is not immediately obvious that a particular query has been modified to use Custom SQL.

In our example the Query Panel displays the objects to signify we have created a query to return [Year] and [Quarter] for [This year], but the underlying SQL has been modified. In the Java Report Panel and Java Query Panel, Web Intelligence does not have any property to inform you that the SQL has been modified, unless you use the 'View Script' button to see if 'Custom SQL' is being used:

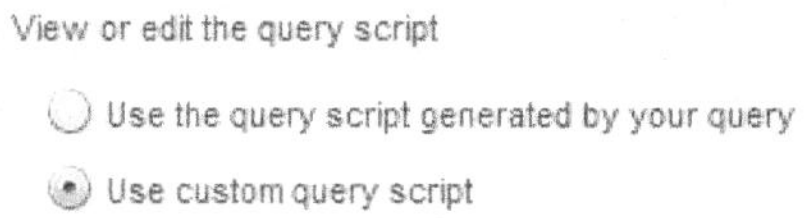
View or edit the query script
Use the query script generated by your query
Use custom query script

The default behaviour of the Query Panel is to modify the underlying SQL when objects are added, removed or edited (e.g. Filter Conditions).

NOTE – THE SQL WILL BE MODIFIED **WITHOUT WARNING.**

Previously, in our example we have modified the SQL to:

```
SELECT

Calendar_year_lookup.Yr,

{fn concat('Q',Calendar_year_lookup.Qtr)}
FROM
  Calendar_year_lookup
WHERE
  ( Calendar_year_lookup.Yr In ('2004','2006')  )
```

1. If we now simply add in the [Month] object:

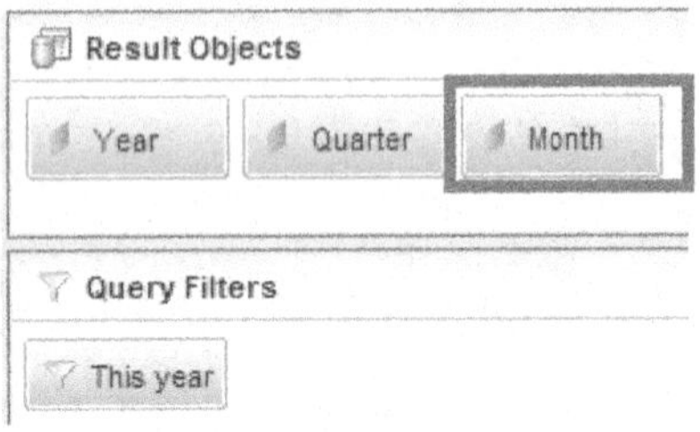
Result Objects
Year
Quarter
Month
Query Filters
This year

2. Then use 'View Script':

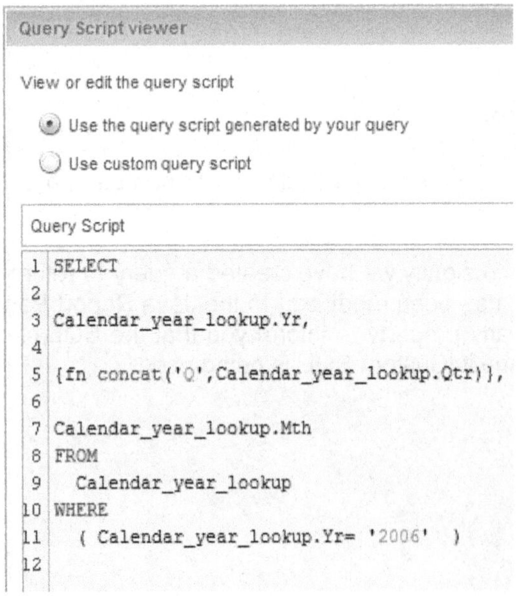
Query Script viewer
View or edit the query script
Use the query script generated by your query
Use custom query script
Query Script
SELECT
Calendar_year_lookup.Yr,
{fn concat('Q',Calendar_year_lookup.Qtr)},
Calendar_year_lookup.Mth
FROM
Calendar_year_lookup
WHERE
(Calendar_year_lookup.Yr= '2006')

The SQL has been automatically modified by the Query Panel **without warning** and we have lost the Custom SQL.

The Query Panel generated SQL is requesting [Year], [Quarter] and [Month] for [Year] = '2006'.

3. To re-include our custom 'WHERE' clause we need to change the last line of the SQL to (as shown here):

    SELECT

    Calendar_year_lookup.Yr,

    {fn concat('Q',Calendar_year_lookup.Qtr)},

    Calendar_year_lookup.Mth
    FROM
     Calendar_year_lookup
    WHERE
     (Calendar_year_lookup.Yr In ('2004','2006'))

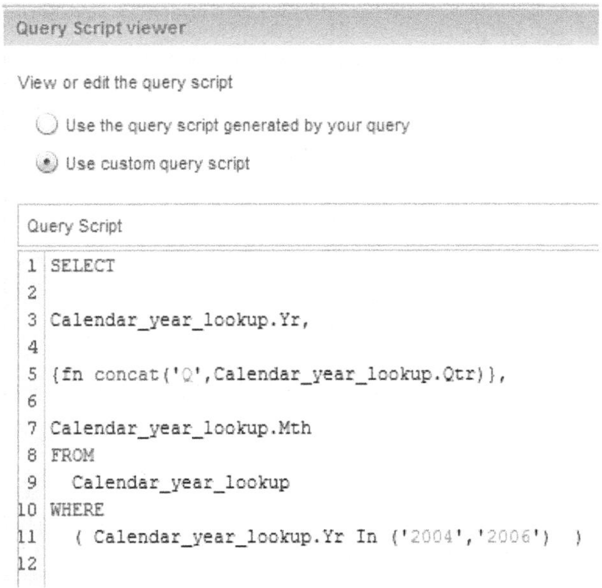

Query Script viewer
View or edit the query script
Use the query script generated by your query
Use custom query script
Query Script
SELECT
Calendar_year_lookup.Yr,
{fn concat('Q',Calendar_year_lookup.Qtr)},
Calendar_year_lookup.Mth
FROM
Calendar_year_lookup
WHERE
(Calendar_year_lookup.Yr In ('2004','2006'))

The Custom SQL is requesting [Year], [Quarter] and [Month] for years 2004 and 2006.

4. Click 'Validate' and the 'Save' after modifying the SQL statement.

5. Run the query to view the new results.

    We will now have [Year], [Quarter] and [Month] for 2004 and 2006.

6. Save and close the document.

36.3 Use of Objects in Custom SQL Queries

We can use any objects from a universe and then modify the SQL to something completely different, meaning the Query Panel display has no relation to the underlying SQL.

The points of note are:

- The number of objects placed in the Results Objects pane should match the number of columns in the SELECT clause of the Custom SQL. For example, if the Custom SQL returns 5 columns of data then we need to use 5 objects in the Query Panel.

- The sequence of the objects placed in the Results Objects pane should match the data type of each column in the SELECT clause of the Custom SQL. For example, if our Custom SQL selects the 5 objects with the following types:

  Alphanumeric, Alphanumeric, Date, Alphanumeric, Number

  Then our objects need to be sequenced in the Results Objects pane to match the above sequence otherwise the following error message will be displayed when validating the Custom SQL:

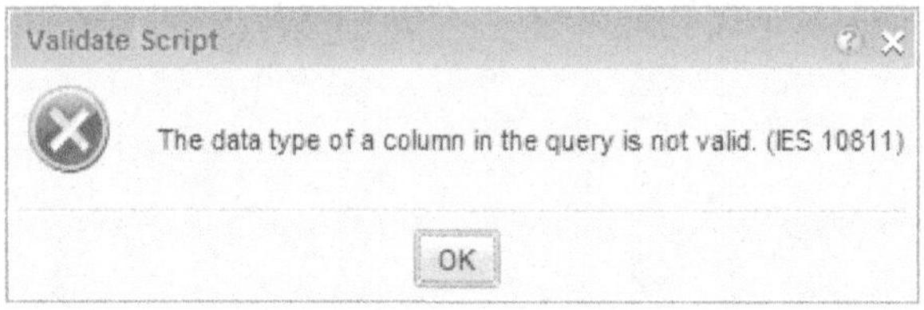
Validate Script
The data type of a column in the query is not valid. (IES 10811)
OK

  Web Intelligence is informing us that Custom SQL columns do not match the data type of columns in the Result Objects pane.

- The tables referenced in the Custom SQL should be available using the universe connection but do not have to be included in the universe itself. The objects based on the tables do not need to exist (as the Query Panel will map the universe objects to the columns in the SELECT clause of the Custom SQL).

- Restrictions can be applied to the Custom SQL without having to include any objects in the Query Filters pane.

Let us now work through a practical example.

1. Create the following query using the 'eFashion' universe:

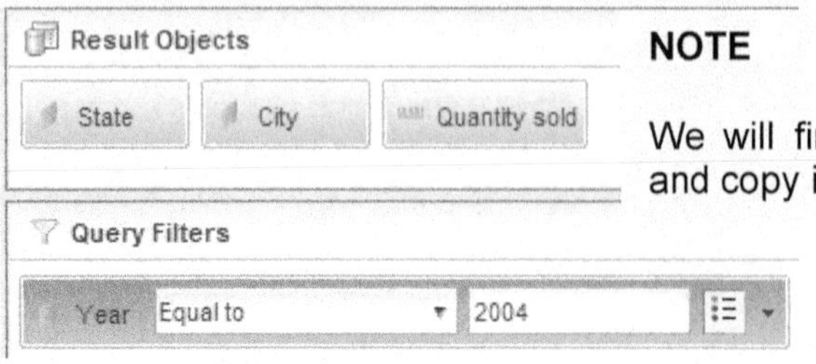
Result Objects
State
City
Quantity sold
Query Filters
Year
Equal to
2004

NOTE

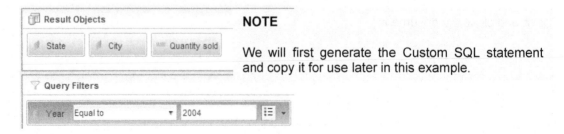

We will first generate the Custom SQL statement and copy it for use later in this example.

2. Use 'View Script' and then click on 'Copy':

Query Script viewer
View or edit the query script
Use the query script generated by your query
Use custom query script
Query Script
SELECT
Outlet_Lookup.State,
Outlet_Lookup.City,
sum(Shop_facts.Quantity_sold)
FROM
Outlet_Lookup,
Shop_facts,
Calendar_year_lookup
WHERE
(Outlet_Lookup.Shop_id=Shop_facts.Shop_id)
AND (Shop_facts.Week_id=Calendar_year_lookup.Week_id)
AND
Calendar_year_lookup.Yr = '2004'
GROUP BY
Outlet_Lookup.State,
Outlet_Lookup.City
Copy
Undo
Validate
Save
Close

3. Paste the contents into a text editor such as Microsoft Notepad.

```
SELECT

Outlet_Lookup.State,

Outlet_Lookup.City,

sum(Shop_facts.Quantity_sold)
FROM
  Outlet_Lookup,
  Shop_facts,
  Calendar_year_lookup
WHERE
  ( Outlet_Lookup.Shop_id=Shop_facts.Shop_id )
  AND ( Shop_facts.Week_id=Calendar_year_lookup.Week_id )
  AND

Calendar_year_lookup.Yr = '2004'
GROUP BY
```

Outlet_Lookup.State,

Outlet_Lookup.City

4. Click 'Close' to exit the View Script interface.

5. Do not run the query but instead modify it to be as follows, i.e. replace the objects [State], [City] and [Quantity sold] with the objects [Year], [Quarter] and [Sales revenue]:

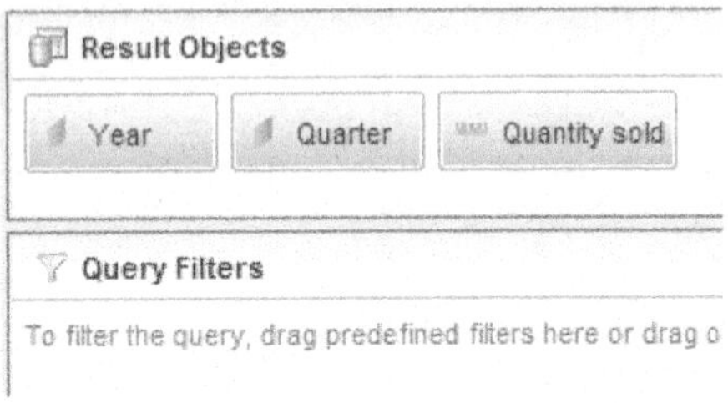
Result Objects
Year
Quarter
Quantity sold
Query Filters
To filter the query, drag predefined filters here or drag o

We have a very simple query requesting [Year], [Quarter], [Sales revenue] with no Query Filters.

6. Run the query and the results are:

Year	Quarter	Quantity sold
2004	Q1	18,136
2004	Q2	14,408
2004	Q3	10,203
2004	Q4	10,331
2005	Q1	21,135
2005	Q2	17,152
2005	Q3	19,224
2005	Q4	22,344
2006	Q1	22,537
2006	Q2	22,846
2006	Q3	26,263
2006	Q4	18,650

7. Edit the query and modify the SQL generated by the current query by overwriting it with the SQL we copied in Step 3.

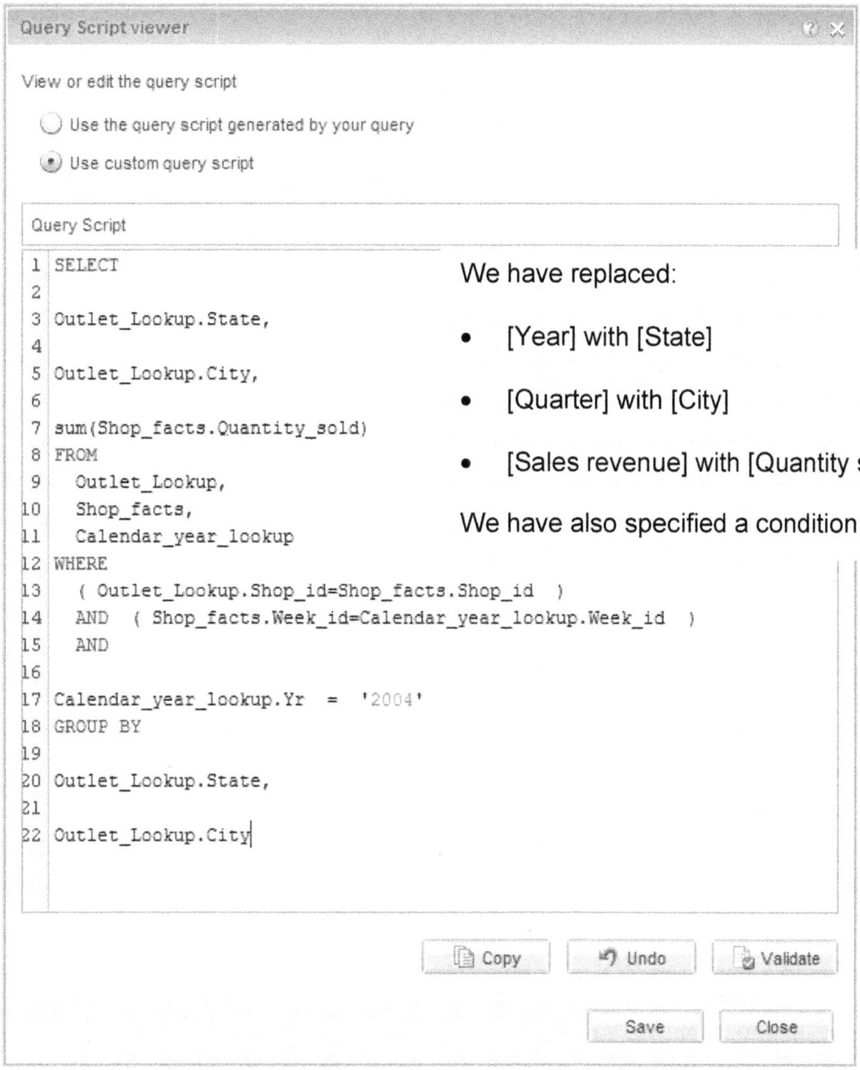
Query Script viewer
View or edit the query script
Use the query script generated by your query
Use custom query script
Query Script
SELECT
Outlet_Lookup.State,
Outlet_Lookup.City,
sum(Shop_facts.Quantity_sold)
FROM
Outlet_Lookup,
Shop_facts,
Calendar_year_lookup
WHERE
(Outlet_Lookup.Shop_id=Shop_facts.Shop_id)
AND (Shop_facts.Week_id=Calendar_year_lookup.Week_id)
AND
Calendar_year_lookup.Yr = '2004'
GROUP BY
Outlet_Lookup.State,
Outlet_Lookup.City
Copy
Undo
Validate
Save
Close

We have replaced:

- [Year] with [State]
- [Quarter] with [City]
- [Sales revenue] with [Quantity sold]

We have also specified a condition of [Year] = '2004'.

8. Click on 'Validate' to validate the Custom SQL and click 'OK'.

9. Click 'Save'.

10. Run the query again to reveal the new results:

Year	Quarter	Quantity sold
California	Los Angeles	6,583
California	San Francisco	4,721
Colorado	Colorado Springs	2,971
DC	Washington	4,681
Florida	Miami	2,585
Illinois	Chicago	4,713
Massachusetts	Boston	1,505
New York	New York	10,802
Texas	Austin	3,824
Texas	Dallas	2,888
Texas	Houston	7,805

The document and the Query Panel show the use of the objects [Year], [Quarter] and [Sales revenue].

The actual query is based on [State], [City] and [Quantity sold] for [Year] = '2004'

11. Save and close your document.

36.4 Identifying Custom SQL Queries

We have demonstrated how to use Custom SQL against universe objects in one of two ways:

1. By modifying the universe generated SQL where the objects in the Result Objects pane relate directly to the underlying Custom SQL columns.

2. By replacing the universe generated SQL with completely different SQL where the Result Objects are completely different to the Custom SQL columns.

In both cases the only way to know if the SQL has been modified is to use the 'View Script' button. We have looked at how the Custom SQL is automatically replaced (without warning) when objects in the Query Panel are altered in any way (added, removed or conditions edited). The Custom SQL is replaced with the universe generated SQL which can have no resemblance to the previously customised SQL statement.

How can we ensure documents or individual queries are easily identified as using Custom SQL?

The most visual and useful approach for is to create dummy objects in universes and then use them in Custom SQL queries. The purpose of these dummy objects is to visually indicate to the developer that the query being edited is using Custom SQL.

Your universe designer needs to create a class of objects that can be used to map Custom SQL column types to objects from this dummy class, for example:

> The class could be called 'Custom SQL Objects' and it could contain 10 character objects, 10 number objects, 10 date objects, 10 measure objects, etc.
>
> In the Query Panel, you would then select a sequence of objects from this class to match the column types in your Custom SQL and then overwrite the dummy SQL with the actual SQL you want to use.

For demonstration purposes, we have modified the 'eFashion Oracle' universe to include the following classes and objects:

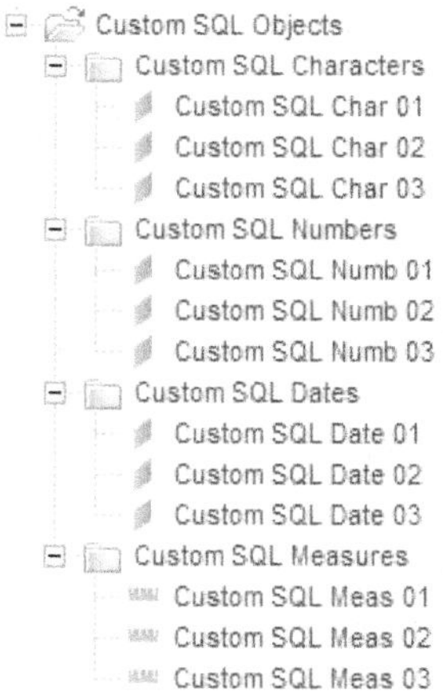
Custom SQL Objects
Custom SQL Characters
Custom SQL Char 01
Custom SQL Char 02
Custom SQL Char 03
Custom SQL Numbers
Custom SQL Numb 01
Custom SQL Numb 02
Custom SQL Numb 03
Custom SQL Dates
Custom SQL Date 01
Custom SQL Date 02
Custom SQL Date 03
Custom SQL Measures
Custom SQL Meas 01
Custom SQL Meas 02
Custom SQL Meas 03

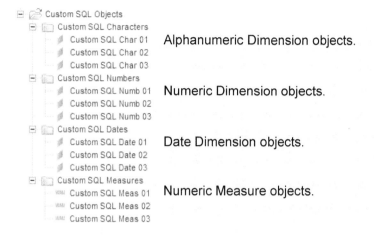

Alphanumeric Dimension objects.

Numeric Dimension objects.

Date Dimension objects.

Numeric Measure objects.

The process of using these dummy objects can be as follows:

1. If you are able to create a query from other universe objects then do that first and paste the generated SQL statement into a text editor such as Notepad.

2. In the Query Panel, replace the Result Objects with the correct sequence of Custom SQL Objects using the objects from this 'Custom SQL Objects' class.

3. Overwrite the 'dummy SQL' with the modified SQL from Step 1 above, or any other relevant SQL statement that you want to run.

4. Validate the Custom SQL statement.

5. Save the Custom SQL statement.

6. Run the query.

Let us demonstrate the above using our modified 'eFashion Oracle' universe. Please **NOTE** – this cannot be done without a modified 'eFashion Oracle' universe, but you should be able to follow the demonstration without performing the practical example.

1. Create the following query and paste the generated SQL statement into a text editor such as Notepad.

Result Objects
Year
Month
State
Quantity sold
Query Filters
And
Year
Equal to
2005
State
In list
New York;Texas

NOTE

If you do not have a modified universe with the Custom SQL Objects then please contact your BusinessObjects Administrator.

Further details and instructions can be found at www.webiworx.com. Look for information on 'SAP BusinessObjects Web Intelligence Training Course' on the 'Downloads' page.

Generated SQL Statement:

```
SELECT
 To_Char( CALENDAR_YEAR_LOOKUP.YEAR),
  CALENDAR_YEAR_LOOKUP.MONTH,
  OUTLET_LOOKUP.STATE,

sum(SHOP_FACTS.Quantity_sold)
FROM
 CALENDAR_YEAR_LOOKUP,
 OUTLET_LOOKUP,
 SHOP_FACTS
WHERE
 ( OUTLET_LOOKUP.SHOP_CODE=SHOP_FACTS.SHOP_CODE )
 AND ( CALENDAR_YEAR_LOOKUP.WEEK_KEY=SHOP_FACTS.WEEK_KEY )
 AND
 (
  To_Char( CALENDAR_YEAR_LOOKUP.YEAR) = '2005'
  AND
   OUTLET_LOOKUP.STATE IN ( 'New York','Texas ' )
 )
GROUP BY
 To_Char( CALENDAR_YEAR_LOOKUP.YEAR),
  CALENDAR_YEAR_LOOKUP.MONTH,
  OUTLET_LOOKUP.STATE
```

2. In the Query Panel, replace the Result Objects with the correct sequence of Custom SQL Objects.

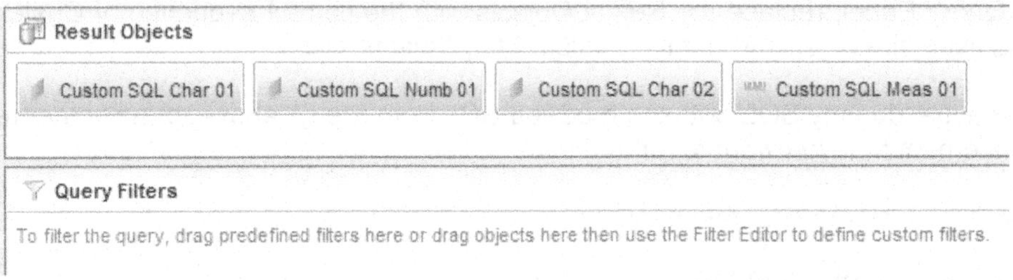
Result Objects
Custom SQL Char 01
Custom SQL Numb 01
Custom SQL Char 02
Custom SQL Meas 01
Query Filters
To filter the query, drag predefined filters here or drag objects here then use the Filter Editor to define custom filters.

NOTE – The mapping for SQL Statement from Step 1 will be:

[Custom SQL Char 01] = [Year]

[Custom SQL Numb 01] = [Month]

[Custom SQL Char 02] = [State]

[Custom SQL Meas 01] = [Quantity sold]

3. Overwrite the 'dummy SQL' with the SQL from Step 1 above. Please note we will just use the SQL statement from Step 1 without any modifications for this demonstration.

4. Validate the Custom SQL statement.

5. Save the Custom SQL statement.

6. Run the query.

7. Web Intelligence will display a default block of data based on the Result Objects:

Custom SQL	Custom SQL	Custom SQL	Custom SQL
2005	1	New York	1,918
2005	1	Texas	2,990
2005	2	New York	731
2005	2	Texas	1,140
2005	3	New York	1,599
2005	3	Texas	2,448

For this example, we could simply change the header labels and present the data in the above block but it is more useful to create document variables with meaningful names that can then be used across multiple reports tabs, tables, charts, etc.

8. Within the document, create a variable for each of the Custom SQL universe objects, i.e. in our example we need to create 4 variables.

Each variable simply points itself to a single Custom SQL object, for example:

Variable Name	Universe Object
v_Year	[Custom SQL Char 01]
n_Month	[Custom SQL Numb 01]
v_State	[Custom SQL Char 02]
n_Quantity Sold	[Custom SQL Meas 01]

9. The block can now be presented using the document variables:

Year	Month	State	Quantity Sold
2005	1	New York	1,918
2005	1	Texas	2,990
2005	2	New York	731
2005	2	Texas	1,140
2005	3	New York	1,599
2005	3	Texas	2,448

Using document variables to map to the generic Custom SQL Objects is very useful when:

- Your Custom SQL query contains many objects.
- Creating complex formula expressions.
- Using the objects in charts (for legends, etc).

10. Save and close your document.

37 Advanced Calculations using Extended Syntax

This session describes how to create reports using advanced calculation formulas by using 'extended syntax' on 'calculation contexts'.

37.1 Calculation Contexts

We have seen throughout this course how measures behave dynamically alongside dimensions, i.e. measures aggregate or break-down depending on the number of dimensions used.

A measure object has a 'calculation context' based on the dimensions used, for example:

'revenue by year', or 'revenue by store and year', or 'revenue by store, product and year', etc

Web Intelligence associates 'default contexts' based on the dimensions against which measures are being used. You can override the default calculation context by using 'extended syntax' in the definition of the variables and/or formulas.

Extended syntax is used to modify the default context of a measure in order to override the default aggregation of the measure. To use extended syntax successfully, we need to understand:

1. Default Contexts
2. Input Contexts
3. Output Contexts

37.1.1 Default Contexts

1. Create a new document with the following query using the 'eFashion' universe:

Result Objects
Year
Quarter
State
Quantity sold
Query Filters
Or
Last year
This year

2. Create a report tab as shown below:

   [Quantity] is displayed in a table alongside [Quarter].

   The table is within a section on [Year].

2005

Quarter	Quantity sold
Q1	21,135
Q2	17,152
Q3	19,224
Q4	22,344

2006

Quarter	Quantity sold
Q1	22,537
Q2	22,846
Q3	26,263
Q4	18,650

Section on [Year] containing a vertical table with the columns [Quarter] and [Quantity sold].

3. Switch to 'Structure Only' mode.

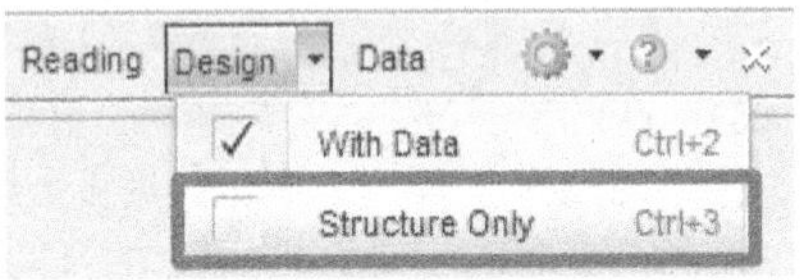

Reading
Design
Data
With Data
Ctrl+2
Structure Only
Ctrl+3

4. Drag-and-drop [Quantity sold] in positions 1, 2 and 5 shown below.

   NOTE – You can enable the property 'Show table footers' and then drag-and-drop into footer cell for position 4.

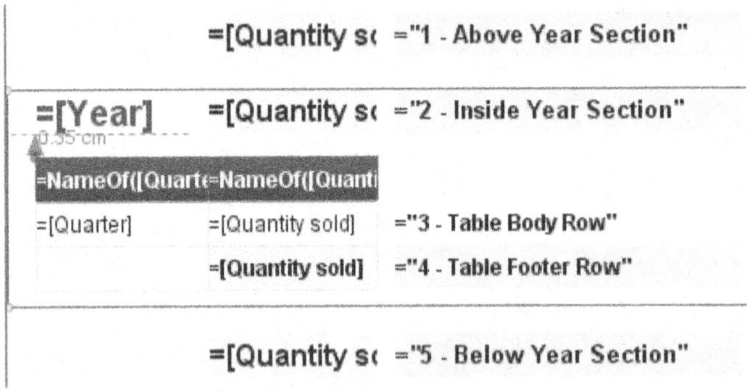

=[Quantity s(
="1 - Above Year Section"
=[Year]
=[Quantity s(
="2 - Inside Year Section"
0.55 cm
=NameOf([Quart(
=NameOf([Quanti
=[Quarter]
=[Quantity sold]
="3 - Table Body Row"
=[Quantity sold]
="4 - Table Footer Row"
=[Quantity s(
="5 - Below Year Section"

   We have 5 cells containing the formula '**=[Quantity sold]**', i.e. all the cells are being used to display the object [Quantity sold].

5. Switch back to 'Design – With Data' mode.

6. The results show examples of '**default contexts**' in a Report, Section and Vertical Table.

	170,151	1 - Above Year Section
2005	79,855	2 - Inside Year Section
Quarter	**Quantity sold**	
Q1	21,135	3 - Table Body Row
Q2	17,152	3 - Table Body Row
Q3	19,224	3 - Table Body Row
Q4	22,344	3 - Table Body Row
	79,855	4 - Table Footer Row
2006	90,296	2 - Inside Year Section
Quarter	**Quantity sold**	
Q1	22,537	3 - Table Body Row
Q2	22,846	3 - Table Body Row
Q3	26,263	3 - Table Body Row
Q4	18,650	3 - Table Body Row
	90,296	4 - Table Footer Row
	170,151	5 - Below Year Section

All the cells in the right-hand column contain the same formula, but we see different values based on which dimensions are being used to aggregate the measure for display purposes.

- In positions 1 and 5 (cells are not in a table or a section), there are no dimensions being used therefore we get the total for the report, i.e. total [Quantity sold] for 2005 and 2006.

- In position 2 (cell is in a section), we have [Quantity sold] being displayed against [Year], i.e. the position 2 cell is a free standing cell within the section on [Year]. Therefore we get a different value being shown in each of the two years.

- In position 3 (body row cells), we have [Quantity sold] being displayed against [Year] and [Quarter], i.e. section on [Year] and then further broken down by [Quarter] within the table. Therefore we get the lowest level of data (based on this query) at position 3, i.e. a different value for every quarter of the two years.

- In position 4 (footer row), we have [Quantity sold] being displayed against [Year] only because we have placed [Quantity sold] in the footer row of a table. The footer row does not use the [Quarter] dimension to aggregate [Quantity sold], but the [Year] dimension is effectively used because the footer row is within a table that is within a section on [Year].

  NOTE – You can also use a measure in the header row and the calculation context will behave exactly like the table footer row context.

Similar contexts apply to Horizontal Tables, Cross Tables and Breaks.

Cross Tables display measures in a 'pivot table' where the value of measures is determined by the intersection of horizontal and vertical dimensions.

The example below shows a Cross Table with extra columns and rows to demonstrate default contexts in a Cross Table:

			2006	2006	2006	2006	90,296	5 - Footer
			Q1	Q2	Q3	Q4	90,296	5 - Footer
	4 - Header	4 - Header	22,537	22,846	26,263	18,650		
California	17,769	1 - Cross Table Body Row	4,317	4,471	5,134	3,847	17,769	3 - HBody Footer
Colorado	5,116	1 - Cross Table Body Row	1,291	1,225	1,527	1,073	5,116	3 - HBody Footer
DC	6,491	1 - Cross Table Body Row	1,735	1,535	1,867	1,354	6,491	3 - HBody Footer
Florida	4,830	1 - Cross Table Body Row	1,210	1,243	1,427	950	4,830	3 - HBody Footer
Illinois	6,519	1 - Cross Table Body Row	1,537	2,005	1,689	1,288	6,519	3 - HBody Footer
Massachusetts	5,269	1 - Cross Table Body Row	1,327	1,228	1,539	1,175	5,269	3 - HBody Footer
New York	19,109	1 - Cross Table Body Row	4,439	4,944	6,119	3,607	19,109	3 - HBody Footer
Texas	25,193	1 - Cross Table Body Row	6,681	6,195	6,961	5,356	25,193	3 - HBody Footer
5 - Footer	90,296		22,537	22,846	26,263	18,650	90,296	
			2 - VBody Footer	2 - VBody Footer	2 - VBody Footer	2 - VBody Footer		

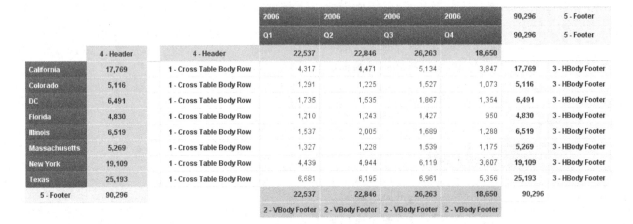

NOTE – All the non-dimension cells are set to display [Quantity sold], i.e. they all contain the formula '**=[Quantity sold]**'.

1 – Cross Table Body Row	The measures are at the lowest level as they are based on the intersection of horizontal and vertical dimensions.
2 – VBody Footer	This is a column total.
3 – HBody Footer	This is a row total.
4 – Header	Cross Tables contain horizontal and vertical headers. Placing a measure in a header cell will cause the measure to aggregate using the row dimensions for horizontal headers, or column dimensions for vertical headers. In example above, we have '4 – Header' measures being shown in the third row from the top as a sum of [Year] and [Quarter], and in the second column from the left as a sum of [State].
5 – Footer	Similarly to headers, Cross Tables contain horizontal and vertical footers.

Horizontal tables are similar to vertical tables, except rows are transposed into columns. Headers appear on the left and footers on the right (as shown below). The behaviour of measures in horizontal tables is no different to vertical tables.

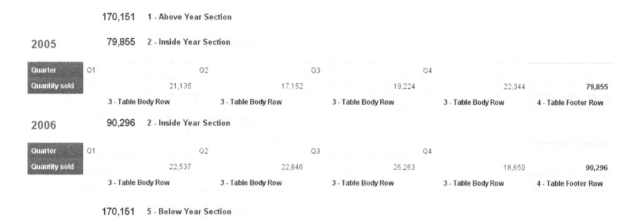

	170,151	1 - Above Year Section
2005	79,855	2 - Inside Year Section

Quarter	Q1	Q2	Q3	Q4	
Quantity sold	21,135	17,152	19,224	22,344	79,855
	3 - Table Body Row	3 - Table Body Row	3 - Table Body Row	3 - Table Body Row	4 - Table Footer Row

2006	90,296	2 - Inside Year Section

Quarter	Q1	Q2	Q3	Q4	
Quantity sold	22,537	22,846	26,263	18,650	90,296
	3 - Table Body Row	3 - Table Body Row	3 - Table Body Row	3 - Table Body Row	4 - Table Footer Row

	170,151	5 - Below Year Section

NOTE – All the non-dimension cells are set to display [Quantity sold], i.e. they all contain the formula '**=[Quantity sold]**'.

Breaks have default contexts based on the Break Header and Break Footer, as shown below:

Year	Quarter	170,151	1 - Table Header Row
Year	Quarter	79,855	2 - Break Header Row
2005	Q1	21,135	3 - Table Body Row
	Q2	17,152	3 - Table Body Row
	Q3	19,224	3 - Table Body Row
	Q4	22,344	3 - Table Body Row
2005		79,855	4 - Break Footer Row
Year	Quarter	90,296	2 - Break Header Row
2006	Q1	22,537	3 - Table Body Row
	Q2	22,846	3 - Table Body Row
	Q3	26,263	3 - Table Body Row
	Q4	18,650	3 - Table Body Row
2006		90,296	4 - Break Footer Row
		170,151	5 - Table Footer Row

NOTE – All the non-dimension cells are set to display [Quantity sold], i.e. they all contain the formula '**=[Quantity sold]**'.

In all our examples for Default Contexts, we have used '=[Quantity sold]' to demonstrate how this measure aggregates (or sums) depending on where it is being displayed.

The same results would be displayed if we used '=Sum([Quantity sold])'. We can now use this to explain input contexts.

37.1.2 Input Contexts

An 'input context' can be thought of as the list of dimensions that you want to use with a measure when the measure value is being fed into a formula (expression).

An input context is the same as the default context unless it is explicitly modified to use different dimensions than those used to display the measure. When specifying input contexts:

1. You list the required dimensions inside the parentheses of functions you want to use in your calculations.

2. The dimensions in the list need to be separated by semicolons.

3. The dimension list needs to be enclosed in its own set of parentheses, even if you only use a single dimension.

4. You use a context operator to separate the dimension list from the measure.

Taking the vertical table example from 'Default Contexts', the following shows how the default formula '=[Quantity sold]' needs to be modified in order to display the correct values using extended syntax:

	170,151	1 - Input Context = Sum([Quantity sold] In Report)
2005	79,855	2 - Input Context = Sum([Quantity sold] Section)
Quarter	**Quantity sold**	
Q1	21,135	3 - Input Context = Sum([Quantity sold] In([Year];[Quarter]))
Q2	17,152	3 - Input Context = Sum([Quantity sold] In([Year];[Quarter]))
Q3	19,224	3 - Input Context = Sum([Quantity sold] In([Year];[Quarter]))
Q4	22,344	3 - Input Context = Sum([Quantity sold] In([Year];[Quarter]))
	79,855	4 - Input Context = Sum([Quantity sold] In Block)
2006	90,296	2 - Input Context = Sum([Quantity sold] Section)
Quarter	**Quantity sold**	
Q1	22,537	3 - Input Context = Sum([Quantity sold] In([Year];[Quarter]))
Q2	22,846	3 - Input Context = Sum([Quantity sold] In([Year];[Quarter]))
Q3	26,263	3 - Input Context = Sum([Quantity sold] In([Year];[Quarter]))
Q4	18,650	3 - Input Context = Sum([Quantity sold] In([Year];[Quarter]))
	90,296	4 - Input Context = Sum([Quantity sold] In Block)
	170,151	5 - Input Context = Sum([Quantity sold] In Report)

Taking the body row example, we have used the formula:

'=Sum([Quantity sold] In ([Year];[Quarter]))'

Let us take the three points listed on the previous page and see how they have been used here:

1. You list the required dimensions inside the parentheses of functions you want to use in your calculations.

   The function used is 'Sum' and we can see that the input context has been listed inside the parentheses for this function, i.e.

   Sum**(**......**)**.

2. The dimensions in the list need to be separated by semicolons.

   The dimensions [Year] and [Quarter] have been separated by a semicolon, i.e.

   [Year]**;**[Quarter]

3. The dimension list needs to be enclosed in its own set of parentheses, even if you only use a single dimension.

   The dimensions [Year] and [Quarter] are enclosed in their own set of parentheses, i.e.

   ([Year];[Quarter]**)**

   NOTE – Do not use an extra set of parentheses unless specifying contexts using dimension objects, i.e.

   This is correct =Sum ([Quantity sold] In Section) because 'Section' is not a dimension.

   This is incorrect =Sum ([Quantity sold] In **(**Section**)**) because 'Section' has been enclosed in its own parentheses.

4. You use a context operator to separate the dimension list from the measure.

   [Quantity sold] **In** ([Year];[Quarter])

We can use input contexts in variables and formulas to define complex calculations.

Using our existing example, we can add an extra 2 columns on the right hand side of the block to show how each Quarter contributes to the Yearly total and to the Report total.

Formulas used are:

Section % column '=Sum ([Quantity sold]) / Sum ([Quantity sold] In Section)'

Report % column '=Sum ([Quantity sold]) / Sum ([Quantity sold] In Report)'

170,151

2005 79,855

Quarter	Quantity sold	Section %	Report %
Q1	21,135	26.47%	12.42%
Q2	17,152	21.48%	10.08%
Q3	19,224	24.07%	11.30%
Q4	22,344	27.98%	13.13%
	79,855	**100.00%**	**46.93%**

2006 90,296

Quarter	Quantity sold	Section %	Report %
Q1	22,537	24.96%	13.25%
Q2	22,846	25.30%	13.43%
Q3	26,263	29.09%	15.44%
Q4	18,650	20.65%	10.96%
	90,296	**100.00%**	**53.07%**

170,151

- We can see that in each [Year] section, the total for **Section %** column is 100.00% as each [Quarter] value is divided by the relevant section total.
- We can see that the **Report %** total will be 100.00% due to (46.93% + 53.07%).

37.1.3 Output Contexts

An 'output context' can be thought of as the list of dimensions that you want to use with a measure after a formula has been evaluated.

The best way to demonstrate Output Contexts is to think of an 'output context' as a formula being displayed in the footer (or header) row of a break based on the specified dimensions. Using this example of an output context, we can take the value of a break header or footer and use it elsewhere.

This is best demonstrated using a MIN or MAX example.

We have a vertical table showing [Year], [Quarter] and [Quantity sold].

There is break on [Year] and we are displaying Max([Quantity sold]) in the break footer.

Year	Quarter	Quantity sold
2005	Q1	21,135
	Q2	17,152
	Q3	19,224
	Q4	22,344
2005	**Max:**	**22,344**

Year	Quarter	Quantity sold
2006	Q1	22,537
	Q2	22,846
	Q3	26,263
	Q4	18,650
2006	**Max:**	**26,263**
	Max:	**26,263**

NOTE

We have the values for Max([Quantity sold]) in any [Quarter] for each year, i.e.:

Year 2005 = 22,344 and Year 2006 = 26,263

We also have the Max([Quantity sold]) in any [Quarter] for the report = 26,263.

1. To demonstrate output contexts, let us create the following vertical table.

Year	Quarter	Quantity sold	
2005	Q1	21,135	
2005	Q2	17,152	
2005	Q3	19,224	
2005	Q4	22,344	
2006	Q1	22,537	
2006	Q2	22,846	
2006	Q3	26,263	
2006	Q4	18,650	

We have a vertical table showing [Year], [Quarter] and [Quantity sold]. The blank column on the right hand side will be used to demonstrate output contexts.

2. Using the formula editor, type in the following formula for the body cells of the blank column:

=Max([Quantity sold]) In ([Year])

Year	Quarter	Quantity sold	
2005	Q1	21,135	22,344
2005	Q2	17,152	22,344
2005	Q3	19,224	22,344
2005	Q4	22,344	22,344
2006	Q1	22,537	26,263
2006	Q2	22,846	26,263
2006	Q3	26,263	26,263
2006	Q4	18,650	26,263

The body cells in the right hand column display the highest value of [Quantity sold] per [Year].

Yr 2005 = 22,344
Yr 2006 = 26,263

These match the values from the break example (at the top of this page).

An output context is placed after the function:

=Max([Quantity sold]) **In ([Year])**

i.e. Max([Quantity sold]) is the function and the output context is placed after the function, whereas an input context is placed within the function.

3. Modify the formula for the right column to:

=[Quantity sold] - Max([Quantity sold]) In ([Year])

Year	Quarter	Quantity sold	
2005	Q1	21,135	-1,209
2005	Q2	17,152	-5,192
2005	Q3	19,224	-3,120
2005	Q4	22,344	0
2006	Q1	22,537	-3,726
2006	Q2	22,846	-3,417
2006	Q3	26,263	0
2006	Q4	18,650	-7,613

The right-hand column now shows (per year) the variance for each quarter compared to the quarter with the highest [Quantity sold].

The two highlighted rows show the quarters in each year with the highest [Quantity sold], therefore the variance for these rows is zero.

4. We could also express the variance in percentage terms using a formula such as:

=([Quantity sold] - Max([Quantity sold]) In ([Year])) / Max([Quantity sold]) In ([Year])

Year	Quarter	Quantity sold		
2005	Q1	21,135	-1,209	-5.41%
2005	Q2	17,152	-5,192	-23.24%
2005	Q3	19,224	-3,120	-13.96%
2005	Q4	22,344	0	0.00%
2006	Q1	22,537	-3,726	-14.19%
2006	Q2	22,846	-3,417	-13.01%
2006	Q3	26,263	0	0.00%
2006	Q4	18,650	-7,613	-28.99%

5. Save and close your document.

37.2 Extended Syntax

Extended syntax is used on a formula/measure to specify a calculation context that is different to the default context in which the formula/measure is being displayed. When using extended syntax to specify calculation contexts, we use formulas/measures in conjunction with dimensions, context operators, and other keywords.

We have already used examples of extended syntax to demonstrate input and output contexts, but we will now look at other elements of extended syntax.

37.2.1 Extended Syntax Context Operators

There are three operators that are used in extended syntax to specify input and output contexts.

Context Operator	Usage
In	To explicitly define a list of dimensions to use in a calculation.
ForEach	Use the default context plus any additional dimensions that are specified using this operator.
ForAll	Use the default context but remove any dimensions that are specified using this operator.

ForEach and ForAll are very useful when the default context contains a lot of dimensions because sometimes it is easier to add/remove dimensions from the default context instead of defining an explicit list.

We have already used the 'In' operator to demonstrate input and output contexts using a defined list of dimensions, but let us use the following to demonstrate these three operators.

1. Create and run the following query using the 'eFashion' universe:

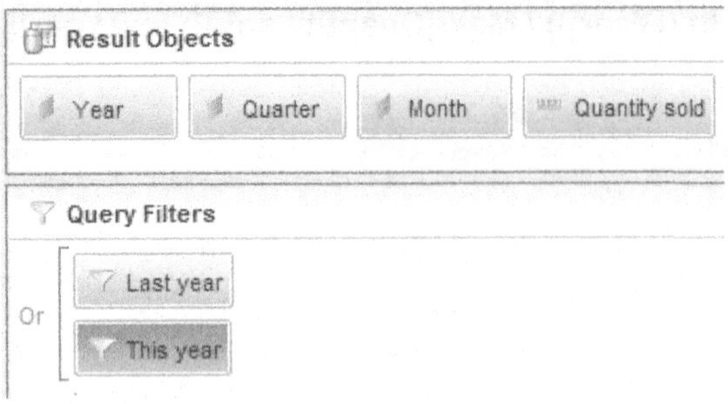
Result Objects
Year
Quarter
Month
Quantity sold
Query Filters
Or
Last year
This year

2. Display the data in a vertical table as follows:

Year	Quarter	Quantity sold	
2005	Q1	21,135	
2005	Q2	17,152	
2005	Q3	19,224	
2005	Q4	22,344	
2006	Q1	22,537	
2006	Q2	22,846	
2006	Q3	26,263	
2006	Q4	18,650	

The right-hand column will be used to demonstrate the use of the three context operators.

37.2.1.1 In Context Operator

The document contains 3 dimensions ([Year], [Quarter] and [Month]) and a single measure ([Quantity sold]), but we are not using [Month] in the vertical table.

If we use the formula:

=Max([Quantity sold] In ([Year];[Quarter];[Month]))

Then we get:

Year	Quarter	Quantity sold	
2005	Q1	21,135	9,115
2005	Q2	17,152	6,505
2005	Q3	19,224	8,939
2005	Q4	22,344	8,643
2006	Q1	22,537	8,793
2006	Q2	22,846	9,011
2006	Q3	26,263	11,494
2006	Q4	18,650	9,094

The right-hand column is displaying the highest monthly [Quantity sold] value in each quarter, based on the months within the particular quarter.

We are using a default context of [Year] and [Quarter], but we are using an extended context of [Year], [Quarter] and [Month] for the right-hand column by explicitly specifying a list of dimensions.

NOTE – The values can be checked using the [Month] object as shown below:

Year	Quarter	Month	Quantity sold
2005	Q1	1	9,115
2005	Q1	2	3,925
2005	Q1	3	8,095
2005	Q2	4	6,505
2005	Q2	5	6,401
2005	Q2	6	4,246

37.2.1.2 ForEach Context Operator

The document contains 3 dimensions ([Year], [Quarter] and [Month]) and a single measure ([Quantity sold]), but we are not using [Month] in the vertical table.

If we use the formula:

=Max([Quantity sold] ForEach ([Month]))

Then we get:

Year	Quarter	Quantity sold	
2005	Q1	21,135	9,115
2005	Q2	17,152	6,505
2005	Q3	19,224	8,939
2005	Q4	22,344	8,643
2006	Q1	22,537	8,793
2006	Q2	22,846	9,011
2006	Q3	26,263	11,494
2006	Q4	18,650	9,094

Our default context in the vertical table is [Year] and [Quarter].

The right-hand column is displaying the highest monthly [Quantity sold] value in each quarter, based on the months within the particular quarter.

By using **ForEach ([Month])** we have added an extra dimension to the default context resulting in the dimension context being [Year], [Quarter] and [Month].

This is exactly the same as **Max([Quantity sold] In ([Year];[Quarter];[Month]))** because ForEach operator works by adding extra dimensions to the default context.

37.2.1.3 ForAll Context Operator

The document contains 3 dimensions ([Year], [Quarter] and [Month]) and a single measure ([Quantity sold]) and we are going to use all the dimensions in the vertical table.

Year	Quarter	Month	Quantity sold	
2005	Q1	1	9,115	
2005	Q1	2	3,925	
2005	Q1	3	8,095	
2005	Q2	4	6,505	
2005	Q2	5	6,401	
2005	Q2	6	4,246	
2005	Q3	7	5,929	
2005	Q3	8	4,356	
2005	Q3	9	8,939	
2005	Q4	10	7,996	
2005	Q4	11	5,705	
2005	Q4	12	8,643	

If we use the formula:

=Max([Quantity sold]) ForAll ([Month])

Then we get:

Year	Quarter	Month	Quantity sold	
2005	Q1	1	9,115	9,115
2005	Q1	2	3,925	9,115
2005	Q1	3	8,095	9,115
2005	Q2	4	6,505	6,505
2005	Q2	5	6,401	6,505
2005	Q2	6	4,246	6,505
2005	Q3	7	5,929	8,939
2005	Q3	8	4,356	8,939
2005	Q3	9	8,939	8,939
2005	Q4	10	7,996	8,643
2005	Q4	11	5,705	8,643
2005	Q4	12	8,643	8,643

We have used the ForAll operator to remove [Month] from the default context, resulting in the right-hand column displaying the highest [Quantity sold] value in each quarter based on the months within the particular quarter.

Our default context in the vertical table is [Year], [Quarter] and [Month].

By using **ForAll ([Month])** we have removed a dimension from the default context resulting in the dimension context being [Year] and [Quarter].

> This is exactly the same as **Max([Quantity sold]) In ([Year];[Quarter])** because ForAll operator works by removing dimensions from the default context.

37.2.2 Extended Syntax Keywords

Extended syntax keywords can be used to reference dimension contexts without explicitly defining the dimension list, basically they are a generic or shorthand way of referencing a dimension list. Use of keywords over explicit dimension lists provides a way of ensuring calculations work even when dimensions are added or removed from a report or the overall document.

There are five keywords and we have already used these to demonstrate behaviour of default contexts.

Keyword	Usage
Report	Data is referenced on the dimension context of the entire report.
Section	Data is referenced using the dimension context within the section.
Block	Data is referenced using the dimension context within the block. If the block is within a section then the section contributes to the block dimension context.
Body	The 'Body' keyword is generic in that it references different dimension contexts depending on where it is used. • If used in a block it references data in the 'body' of the block. • If used in a section it references data in the section. • If used outside any blocks or sections then it uses data in the report.
Break	References data contained within a break. Any filters applied to the block are included when evaluating the calculation.

Examples of each keyword are given overleaf.

37.2.2.1 Report Keyword

Data is referenced on the dimension context of the entire report.

Example below shows a vertical table with a column [Quantity sold]. The total of this column is 170,151 as shown in the footer row (in bold).

We can use the Report keyword to display the total on each row of the table using the formula:

=Sum([Quantity sold]) In Report

Year	Quarter	Quantity sold	
2005	Q1	21,135	170,151
2005	Q2	17,152	170,151
2005	Q3	19,224	170,151
2005	Q4	22,344	170,151
2006	Q1	22,537	170,151
2006	Q2	22,846	170,151
2006	Q3	26,263	170,151
2006	Q4	18,650	170,151
	Sum:	**170,151**	

If we use sections on the above then the formula '**=Sum([Quantity sold]) In Report**' still evaluates correctly.

2005

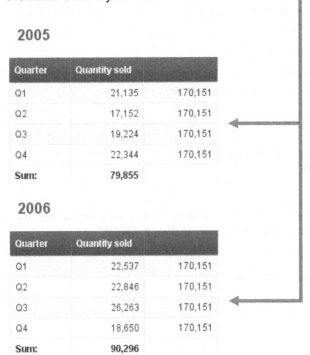

Quarter	Quantity sold	
Q1	21,135	170,151
Q2	17,152	170,151
Q3	19,224	170,151
Q4	22,344	170,151
Sum:	**79,855**	

2006

Quarter	Quantity sold	
Q1	22,537	170,151
Q2	22,846	170,151
Q3	26,263	170,151
Q4	18,650	170,151
Sum:	**90,296**	

37.2.2.2 Section Keyword

Data is referenced using the dimension context within the section.

Example below shows a sectioned report on [Year] containing a vertical table with the columns [Quarter] and [Quantity sold]. The total of [Quantity sold] column in each section is different and has been shown in the footer row (in bold).

We can use the Section keyword to display the total on **each row** of the table using the formula:

=Sum([Quantity sold]) In Section

170,151

2005 — 79,855

Quarter	Quantity sold	
Q1	21,135	79,855
Q2	17,152	79,855
Q3	19,224	79,855
Q4	22,344	79,855
Sum:	**79,855**	

2006 — 90,296

Quarter	Quantity sold	
Q1	22,537	90,296
Q2	22,846	90,296
Q3	26,263	90,296
Q4	18,650	90,296
Sum:	**90,296**	

All the highlighted cells contain the same formula but they show different results.

=Sum([Quantity sold]) In Section

The cells showing 79,855 and 90,296 are within the section on [Year], therefore they are displaying the total for each section.

The cell showing 170,151 is outside of any section therefore it is effectively displaying the report total, i.e. it is the same as:

=Sum([Quantity sold]) In Report

If the **block** is filtered and you use the Section keyword in an input context then the block filters are ignored but if you use the Section keyword in an output context then filters are included when evaluating formulas.

=Sum([Quantity sold] In Section) is an input context example

=Sum([Quantity sold]) In Section is an output context example

Examples overleaf show both of the above formulas in action.

170,151
2005
79,855
Quarter
Quantity sold
Q1
21,135
79,855
Q2
17,152
79,855
Sum:
38,287
2006
90,296
Quarter
Quantity sold
Q1
22,537
90,296
Q2
22,846
90,296
Sum:
45,383

This example shows the right-hand column using the Section keyword within an input context.

=Sum([Quantity sold] In Section)

The block has been filtered to show only 'Q1' and 'Q2', but the right-hand column still shows the actual section total.

170,151
2005
79,855
Quarter
Quantity sold
Q1
21,135
38,287
Q2
17,152
38,287
Sum:
38,287
2006
90,296
Quarter
Quantity sold
Q1
22,537
45,383
Q2
22,846
45,383
Sum:
45,383

This example shows the right-hand column using the Section keyword within an output context.

=Sum([Quantity sold]) In Section

The block has been filtered to show only 'Q1' and 'Q2', and the right-hand column now shows the filtered block total.

37.2.2.3 Block Keyword

Data is referenced using the dimension context within the block. If the block is within a section then the section contributes to the block dimension context.

We can use the Block keyword to display the total within the block on each row of the table using the formula:

=Sum([Quantity sold]) In Block

Year	Quarter	Quantity sold	
2005	Q1	21,135	83,670
2005	Q2	17,152	83,670
2006	Q1	22,537	83,670
2006	Q2	22,846	83,670
	Sum:	**83,670**	

When using 'Block', breaks on the block are ignored but filters on the block are included when evaluating calculations (above example shows block filtered for 'Q1' and 'Q2'). Therefore, a block containing filters and placed inside a section will have a dimension context encompassing both the section and block dimensions, and the result will be calculated taking into account any block level filters.

Example below shows a sectioned report on [Year] containing a vertical table with the columns [Quarter] and [Quantity sold]. The total of [Quantity sold] has been shown in the footer row (in bold).

2005

Quarter	Quantity sold	
Q1	21,135	38,287
Q2	17,152	38,287
Sum:	**38,287**	

2006

Quarter	Quantity sold	
Q1	22,537	45,383
Q2	22,846	45,383
Sum:	**45,383**	

This example shows a block within a section on [Year]. The block has been filtered for 'Q1' and 'Q2'.

The right-hand column contains a formula using the Block keyword.

=Sum([Quantity sold]) In Block

The results in the right-hand column show the formula has been evaluated in the context of [Year], [Quarter] and the filter on the block for 'Q1' and 'Q2'.

37.2.2.4 Body Keyword

The 'Body' keyword is generic in that it references different dimension contexts depending on where it is used.

1. If used in a block row it references data in the 'body' row of the block.
2. If used in a block header or footer it references data in the block.
3. If used in a section it references data in the section.
4. If used outside any blocks or sections then it uses data in the report.

Example below shows a sectioned report on [Year] containing a vertical table with the columns [Quarter] and [Quantity sold]. The total of [Quantity sold] has been shown in the footer row (in bold).

Using the Body keyword will yield different results depending on where the cell is located. The example below shows a block within a section on [Year]. The block has been filtered for 'Q1' and 'Q2'.

All the highlighted cells contain the same formula:

=Sum([Quantity sold]) In Body

170,151 [4]

2005 79,855 [3]

Quarter	Quantity sold		
Q1	21,135	21,135	1
Q2	17,152	17,152	
Sum:	**38,287**	**38,287**	2

2006 90,296 [3]

Quarter	Quantity sold		
Q1	22,537	22,537	1
Q2	22,846	22,846	
Sum:	**45,383**	**45,383**	2

1. Cell is in a block body row, therefore the value is the same as [Quantity sold] per row.
2. Cell is in a block footer row, therefore the value is the same as Sum([Quantity sold]) of the body rows.
3. Cell is within a section, therefore the value is the section total. Any block level filters will not be included in the formula evaluation, therefore in our example the section totals include 'Q1', 'Q2', Q3' and Q4' values.
4. Cell is outside any sections, therefore the value is the report total. In this example it is the sum of 79,855 and 90,296.

37.2.2.5 Break Keyword

References data contained within a break level. Any filters applied to the block are included when evaluating the calculation.

Example below shows a report containing a vertical table with the columns [Year], [Quarter] and [Quantity sold]. A break has been applied to [Year], a filter has been applied to show only 'Q1' and 'Q2', and the total of [Quantity sold] has been shown in the footer row (in bold).

We can use the Break keyword to display the break total on **each row** of the table using the formula:

=Sum([Quantity sold] In Break)

Year	Quarter	Quantity sold	
2005	Q1	21,135	38,287
	Q2	17,152	38,287
2005	**Sum:**	**38,287**	**38,287**

Year	Quarter	Quantity sold	
2006	Q1	22,537	45,383
	Q2	22,846	45,383
2006	**Sum:**	**45,383**	**45,383**
	Sum:	**83,670**	**83,670**

This is an example of using 'In Break' within an Input Context.

The values 38,287 and 45,383 are being sourced separately from each year.

The value 83,670 is sourced from the total.

=Sum([Quantity sold]) In Break

Year	Quarter	Quantity sold	
2005	Q1	21,135	83,670
	Q2	17,152	83,670
2005	**Sum:**	**38,287**	**83,670**

Year	Quarter	Quantity sold	
2006	Q1	22,537	83,670
	Q2	22,846	83,670
2006	**Sum:**	**45,383**	**83,670**
	Sum:	**83,670**	**83,670**

This is an example of using 'In Break' within an Output Context.

There is only one value of 83,670 and this is the overall value for the break on [Year], including filters on 'Q1' and 'Q2'.

Save and close your document.

38 Advanced Measures

We have seen measures dynamically aggregate based on the dimension contexts they are used in. An example we have used earlier is shown again here to illustrate this.

1 – Block of data showing **[Year]**, **[Quarter]** and **[Sales revenue]**.

Year	Quarter	Sales revenue
2004	Q1	$2,660,700
2004	Q2	$2,279,003
2004	Q3	$1,367,841
2004	Q4	$1,788,580
2005	Q1	$3,326,172
2005	Q2	$2,840,651
2005	Q3	$2,879,303
2005	Q4	$4,186,120
2006	Q1	$3,742,989
2006	Q2	$4,006,718
2006	Q3	$3,953,395
2006	Q4	$3,356,041
Sum:		**$36,387,512**

Year	Sales revenue
2004	$8,096,124
2005	$13,232,246
2006	$15,059,143
Sum:	**$36,387,512**

2 – **[Quarter]** removed leaves 3 unique values for **[Year]**. All the quarters in each year have been added together.

Quarter	Sales revenue
Q1	$9,729,861
Q2	$9,126,371
Q3	$8,200,539
Q4	$9,330,742
Sum:	**$36,387,512**

3 – **[Year]** removed leaves 4 unique values for **[Quarter]**. All the 'Q1' values have been added together and similarly all the 'Q2' values have been added together, etc.

Sales revenue
$36,387,512
$36,387,512

4 – **[Year]** and **[Quarter]** removed leaves no dimensions to be broken down by, therefore the measure rolls up to its total value.

The measure in the above example aggregates using the 'Sum' function, i.e. the measure is 'rolled' up by adding the values together, but there are other ways in which a measure can be projected depending on how the measure is defined in the universe. This session describes the projection properties of measures as you may need your Universe Designer to create new measures for you to simplify report development.

38.1 Projection Property of Measures

Measures can be defined in the universe to use one of the following functions to project (aggregate) data within Web Intelligence documents.

Projection Function	Description
Average	Average value of the measure will be displayed
Count	Count of measure values will be displayed
Delegated	This will be discussed later
Max	Maximum value of the measure will be displayed
Min	Minimum value of the measure will be displayed
None	The measure will not aggregate
Sum	Values will be added together when aggregating the measure

To demonstrate the above functions (except **Delegated**) we will use some sample data as shown below:

Year	Quarter	Month	Region	Spend
2006	Q1	1	North	8400
2006	Q1	2	North	8376
2006	Q1	3	North	8614
2006	Q2	4	North	8675
2006	Q2	5	North	8825
2006	Q2	6	North	8900
2006	Q3	7	North	8630
2006	Q3	8	North	8590
2006	Q3	9	North	8680
2006	Q4	10	North	7950
2006	Q4	11	North	8010
2006	Q4	12	North	7936
2007	Q1	1	North	8950
2007	Q1	2	North	8970
2007	Q1	3	North	8880
2007	Q2	4	North	9210
2007	Q2	5	North	9200
2007	Q2	6	North	9240
2007	Q3	7	North	9265
2007	Q3	8	North	9395
2007	Q3	9	North	9290
2007	Q4	10	North	8300
2007	Q4	11	North	8315
2007	Q4	12	North	8260
2008	Q1	1	North	8649
2008	Q1	2	North	8675
2008	Q1	3	North	8615

2006 / South has no [Spend] value (i.e. is NULL)

2006 / West has a [Spend] value of 0 (zero)

Total Rows =
4 Regions x 12 Months x 3 Years = **144 Rows**

NOTE

This data is available to download in a script format to be loaded into your database.

We have loaded the data into an Oracle database in the same place as 'eFashion' data. The 'eFashion Oracle' universe has been modified to include these extra objects.

Further details and instructions can be found at www.webiworx.com. Look for information on 'SAP BusinessObjects Web Intelligence Training Course' on the 'Downloads' page.

Instructions have been provided to load the data into Oracle or Microsoft Access.

Year	Quarter	Month	Region	Spend
2008	Q2	4	North	8820
2008	Q2	5	North	8890
2008	Q2	6	North	9035
2008	Q3	7	North	8890
2008	Q3	8	North	8875
2008	Q3	9	North	8660
2008	Q4	10	North	8905
2008	Q4	11	North	8965
2008	Q4	12	North	9005
2006	Q1	1	East	7630
2006	Q1	2	East	7620
2006	Q1	3	East	7600
2006	Q2	4	East	7400
2006	Q2	5	East	7900
2006	Q2	6	East	8205
2006	Q3	7	East	7710
2006	Q3	8	East	7605
2006	Q3	9	East	7765
2006	Q4	10	East	7701
2006	Q4	11	East	7675
2006	Q4	12	East	7744
2007	Q1	1	East	7825
2007	Q1	2	East	7867
2007	Q1	3	East	7868
2007	Q2	4	East	7910
2007	Q2	5	East	8010
2007	Q2	6	East	8055
2007	Q3	7	East	8159
2007	Q3	8	East	8220
2007	Q3	9	East	8271
2007	Q4	10	East	8330
2007	Q4	11	East	8330
2007	Q4	12	East	8373
2008	Q1	1	East	8289
2008	Q1	2	East	8331
2008	Q1	3	East	8330
2008	Q2	4	East	8560
2008	Q2	5	East	8540
2008	Q2	6	East	8600
2008	Q3	7	East	8490
2008	Q3	8	East	8510
2008	Q3	9	East	8415
2008	Q4	10	East	8560
2008	Q4	11	East	8555
2008	Q4	12	East	8563
2006	Q1	1	South	NULL
2006	Q1	2	South	NULL
2006	Q1	3	South	NULL
2006	Q2	4	South	NULL
2006	Q2	5	South	NULL
2006	Q2	6	South	NULL

Year	Quarter	Month	Region	Spend
2006	Q3	7	South	NULL
2006	Q3	8	South	NULL
2006	Q3	9	South	NULL
2006	Q4	10	South	NULL
2006	Q4	11	South	NULL
2006	Q4	12	South	NULL
2007	Q1	1	South	8770
2007	Q1	2	South	8850
2007	Q1	3	South	8915
2007	Q2	4	South	9010
2007	Q2	5	South	8990
2007	Q2	6	South	8998
2007	Q3	7	South	9230
2007	Q3	8	South	9179
2007	Q3	9	South	8984
2007	Q4	10	South	9111
2007	Q4	11	South	9245
2007	Q4	12	South	9347
2008	Q1	1	South	9201
2008	Q1	2	South	9300
2008	Q1	3	South	9299
2008	Q2	4	South	9127
2008	Q2	5	South	9339
2008	Q2	6	South	9474
2008	Q3	7	South	9410
2008	Q3	8	South	9325
2008	Q3	9	South	9186
2008	Q4	10	South	9222
2008	Q4	11	South	9233
2008	Q4	12	South	9248
2006	Q1	1	West	0
2006	Q1	2	West	0
2006	Q1	3	West	0
2006	Q2	4	West	0
2006	Q2	5	West	0
2006	Q2	6	West	0
2006	Q3	7	West	0
2006	Q3	8	West	0
2006	Q3	9	West	0
2006	Q4	10	West	0
2006	Q4	11	West	0
2006	Q4	12	West	0

Year	Quarter	Month	Region	Spend
2007	Q1	1	West	8002
2007	Q1	2	West	8120
2007	Q1	3	West	8251
2007	Q2	4	West	8230
2007	Q2	5	West	8290
2007	Q2	6	West	8162
2007	Q3	7	West	8300
2007	Q3	8	West	8330
2007	Q3	9	West	8364
2007	Q4	10	West	8310
2007	Q4	11	West	8320
2007	Q4	12	West	8277
2008	Q1	1	West	8265
2008	Q1	2	West	8468
2008	Q1	3	West	8667
2008	Q2	4	West	8429
2008	Q2	5	West	8401
2008	Q2	6	West	8471
2008	Q3	7	West	8400
2008	Q3	8	West	8420
2008	Q3	9	West	8380
2008	Q4	10	West	8590
2008	Q4	11	West	8620
2008	Q4	12	West	8632

The aggregated values at Year and Region level give us 12 rows as shown below:

Year	Region	Spend
2006	North	101586
2007	North	107275
2008	North	105984
2006	East	92555
2007	East	97218
2008	East	101743
2006	South	
2007	South	108629
2008	South	111364
2006	West	0
2007	West	98956
2008	West	101743

Points of note:

There are 12 rows in total with one duplicate [Spend] value (**2008 / East** has the same value as **2008 / West**).

There is also one row with a NULL value for [Spend] (**2006 / South**).

The following universe objects have been created (in the 'eFashion Oracle' universe) to use the above data and demonstrate the functions within Web Intelligence, but online instructions have been provided for both Oracle and Microsoft Access.

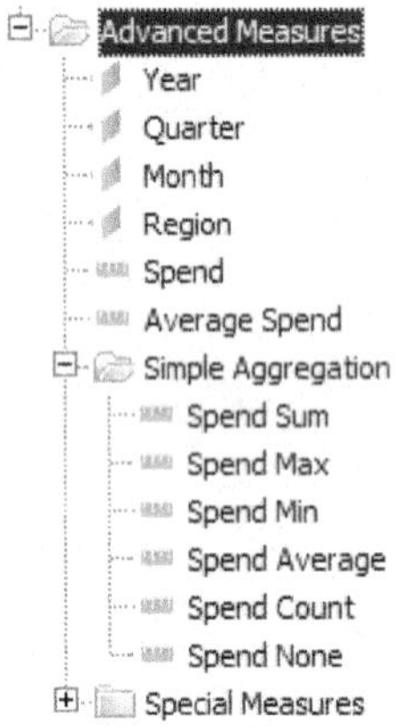
Advanced Measures
Year
Quarter
Month
Region
Spend
Average Spend
Simple Aggregation
Spend Sum
Spend Max
Spend Min
Spend Average
Spend Count
Spend None
Special Measures

Points of note:

We have 4 dimension objects (**[Year]**, **[Quarter]**, **[Month]** and **[Region]**).

The measure objects within the class **Simple Aggregation** all contain the same definition:

> **Sum(CUSTOMER_FACT.SPEND)** where the table is called ***CUSTOMER_FACT*** and ***SPEND*** is the name of the column within this table.
>
> The database will return the same value for each object within the Simple Aggregation class but Web Intelligence will aggregate the measure differently depending on the projection property of each measure (i.e. Sum, Max, Min, Average, Count, None).

1. To demonstrate projection properties, a simple query is created using the 'eFashion Oracle' universe:

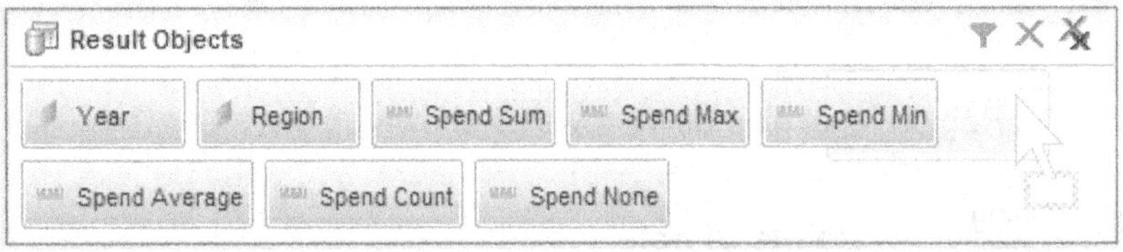
Result Objects
Year
Region
Spend Sum
Spend Max
Spend Min
Spend Average
Spend Count
Spend None

All of the result objects are displayed in a vertical table:

Year	Region	Spend Sum	Spend Max	Spend Min	Spend Average	Spend Count	Spend None
2006	East	92,555	92,555	92,555	92,555	1	92,555
2006	North	101,586	101,586	101,586	101,586	1	101,586
2006	South					0	
2006	West	0	0	0	0	1	0
2007	East	97,218	97,218	97,218	97,218	1	97,218
2007	North	107,275	107,275	107,275	107,275	1	107,275
2007	South	108,629	108,629	108,629	108,629	1	108,629
2007	West	98,956	98,956	98,956	98,956	1	98,956
2008	East	101,743	101,743	101,743	101,743	1	101,743
2008	North	105,984	105,984	105,984	105,984	1	105,984
2008	South	111,364	111,364	111,364	111,364	1	111,364
2008	West	101,743	101,743	101,743	101,743	1	101,743

All of the measure columns (within a single row) display the same values except for [Spend Count].

NOTE – For [Spend Count] a value of 0 (zero) is counted but a NULL is not counted.

2. If we display the table footer and drag each respective measure into the footer row then the table shows:

Year	Region	Spend Sum	Spend Max	Spend Min	Spend Average	Spend Count	Spend None
2006	East	92,555	92,555	92,555	92,555	1	92,555
2006	North	101,586	101,586	101,586	101,586	1	101,586
2006	South					0	
2006	West	0	0	0	0	1	0
2007	East	97,218	97,218	97,218	97,218	1	97,218
2007	North	107,275	107,275	107,275	107,275	1	107,275
2007	South	108,629	108,629	108,629	108,629	1	108,629
2007	West	98,956	98,956	98,956	98,956	1	98,956
2008	East	101,743	101,743	101,743	101,743	1	101,743
2008	North	105,984	105,984	105,984	105,984	1	105,984
2008	South	111,364	111,364	111,364	111,364	1	111,364
2008	West	101,743	101,743	101,743	101,743	1	101,743
		1,027,053	**111,364**	**0**	**93,368**	**12**	**#MULTIVALUE**

The footer row shows us how each measure is projecting as described below:

Measure	Behaviour in footer row
[Spend Sum]	The body values in this column have been summed up.
[Spend Max]	The largest body value in this column is displayed.
[Spend Min]	The lowest body value in this column is displayed (NULL is ignored).
[Spend Average]	Average of the body values = (1,027,053 / 11) = 93,368. The NULL row is ignored.
[Spend Count]	This shows the count of rows in the block.
[Spend None]	This measure's projection function has been set to None meaning it cannot project, therefore the error message '#MULTIVALUE' is shown as all of the body values in this column are trying to be displayed in a single cell.

3. Let us now take a look a further look at projection behaviour of these measures by removing the [Region] column from the block as shown below:

Year	Spend Sum	Spend Max	Spend Min	Spend Average	Spend Count	Spend None
2006	92,555	92,555	92,555	92,555	1	92,555
2006	101,586	101,586	101,586	101,586	1	101,586
2006					0	
2006	0	0	0	0	1	0
2007	97,218	97,218	97,218	97,218	1	97,218
2007	107,275	107,275	107,275	107,275	1	107,275
2007	108,629	108,629	108,629	108,629	1	108,629
2007	98,956	98,956	98,956	98,956	1	98,956
2008	101,743	101,743	101,743	101,743	1	101,743
2008	105,984	105,984	105,984	105,984	1	105,984
2008	111,364	111,364	111,364	111,364	1	111,364
2008	101,743	101,743	101,743	101,743	1	101,743
	1,027,053	**111,364**	**0**	**93,368**	**12**	**#MULTIVALUE**

By removing the [Region] object we would have expected the block to show only three rows (due to having three values for [Year] object). Instead, the block is still presenting 12 rows. **Why?**

The measure [Spend None] has been defined to use the projection function of 'None' therefore Web Intelligence cannot aggregate the values for this measure. Using one or more measures defined with a projection function of 'None' within a block will prevent other measures from aggregating.

4. Removing the [Spend None] measure from the block results in:

Year	Spend Sum	Spend Max	Spend Min	Spend Average	Spend Count
2006	194,141	101,586	0	64,714	3
2007	412,078	108,629	97,218	103,020	4
2008	420,834	111,364	101,743	105,209	4
	1,027,053	**111,364**	**0**	**90,981**	**3**

The results displayed in the table opposite can be checked using the data in the table above.

The block now displays three rows as each measure has been aggregated based on its projection function. The measures have been projected at two levels:

- Once within the block to aggregate from the context [Year], [Region] to just [Year].
- The **new** body row results are then used to project at the table footer level, i.e. the value of [Spend Average] is now calculated using the 3 body rows instead of the 11 body rows we had at quarter level. We now see a value of 90,981 instead of 93,368.

5. Save and close your document.

We can see from this example how the same measure can be defined (in the universe) to project (or aggregate) differently within Web Intelligence documents.

Based on this, it might be possible that you have a single measure available as multiple objects depending on the projection requirements.

If you do not have multiple objects then of course you can use formulas, variable and Standard Calculations (such as Sum, Min, Max, Average, Count) within documents to create the same results.

38.2 Special Measures

Some measure values can only be presented in Web Intelligence as calculated by the database, i.e. they cannot be aggregated (rolled up or broken down) within Web Intelligence using different dimension contexts. These measures typically fall into categories such as percentages and averages.

For example, if we have a query containing the dimensions [Year] and [Region] along with the measures [Spend] and [Average Spend] then we could display the following in reports:

1. **[Year], [Region], [Spend], [Average Spend]**

   This would show the total customer Spend and the Average Spend per Region per Year.

2. **[Year], [Spend]**

   This would show the total customer Spend per Year for all Regions.

3. **[Region], [Spend]**

   This would show the total customer Spend per Region across all Years.

We can confidently use [Spend] in any dimension context because its aggregation property will most likely be set to 'Sum' (in the universe) meaning that as we add/remove dimensions the value of [Spend] will dynamically aggregate using the Sum function.

However, the values of [Average Spend] will have been calculated by the database and the results sent to Web Intelligence. Meaning, within the document we do not know the source values that have contributed to each value of [Average Spend].

Using a projection function on [Average Spend] is more complex because the database will return average values based on the dimensions used in the Query Panel and Web Intelligence will then aggregate the average values within the document, i.e. in this case the [Average Spend] value will have been returned by the database at the level of [Year] and [Region].

We describe how [Average Spend] would be projected in Web Intelligence documents depending on the universe Projection Function used in its definition.

Projection Function	Description
Average	[Average Spend] from the database would be averaged within the document, meaning we would display 'an average of average values'.
Count	Count of [Average Spend] values will be displayed.
Delegated	This will be discussed later.
Max	Maximum value of [Average Spend] from the values within the document will be displayed.
Min	Minimum value of [Average Spend] from the values within the document will be displayed.
None	[Average Spend] will not aggregate. Therefore to show [Average Spend] at a higher level requires the lower level objects to be removed from the query.
Sum	[Average Spend] from the database would be summed within the document, meaning we would display 'the sum of average values'.

The following universe objects have been created (in 'eFashion Oracle' universe) to use the above data and demonstrate the functions within Web Intelligence, but online instructions have been provided for both Oracle and Microsoft Access.

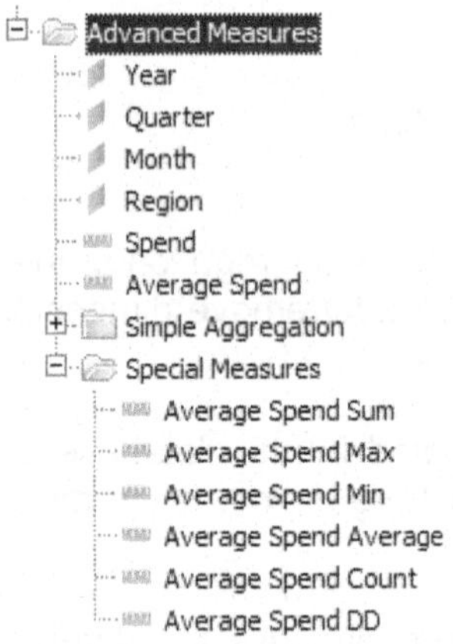
Advanced Measures
Year
Quarter
Month
Region
Spend
Average Spend
Simple Aggregation
Special Measures
Average Spend Sum
Average Spend Max
Average Spend Min
Average Spend Average
Average Spend Count
Average Spend DD

Points of note:

We have 4 dimension objects (**[Year]**, **[Quarter]**, **[Month]** and **[Region]**).

The measure objects within the class **Special Measures** all contain the same definition:

Avg(CUSTOMER_FACT.SPEND) where the table is called ***CUSTOMER_FACT*** and ***SPEND*** is the name of the column within this table.

The database will return the same value for each object within the Special Measures class but Web Intelligence will aggregate the measure differently depending on the projection property of each measure (i.e. Sum, Max, Min, Average, Count, None).

1. We can demonstrate using the following query (using 'eFashion Oracle' universe) and its results:

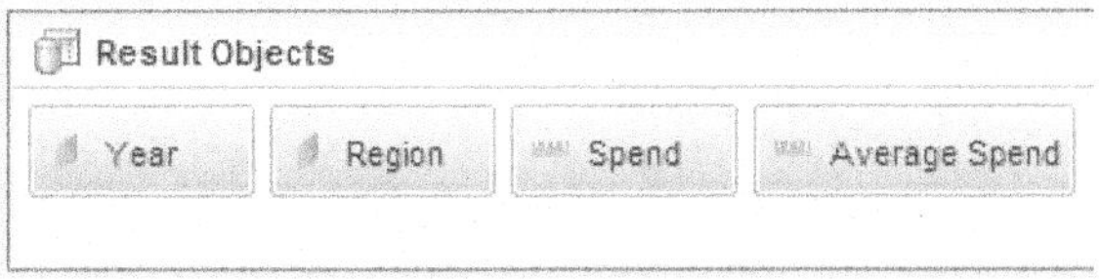
Result Objects
Year
Region
Spend
Average Spend

Year	Region	Spend	Average Spend
2006	East	92,555	7,713
2006	North	101,586	8,466
2006	South		
2006	West	0	0
2007	East	97,218	8,102
2007	North	107,275	8,940
2007	South	108,629	9,052
2007	West	98,956	8,246
2008	East	101,743	8,479
2008	North	105,984	8,832
2008	South	111,364	9,280
2008	West	101,743	8,479

This query will return for each Region and Year, the total Spend and the Average Spend.

NOTE

[Spend] is a value that can be easily aggregated, but [Average Spend] has been calculated at the level of [Year] and [Region], **so how do we correctly display [Average Spend] for [Year] or [Average Spend] for [Region] within the document?**

If we modified the query as follows:

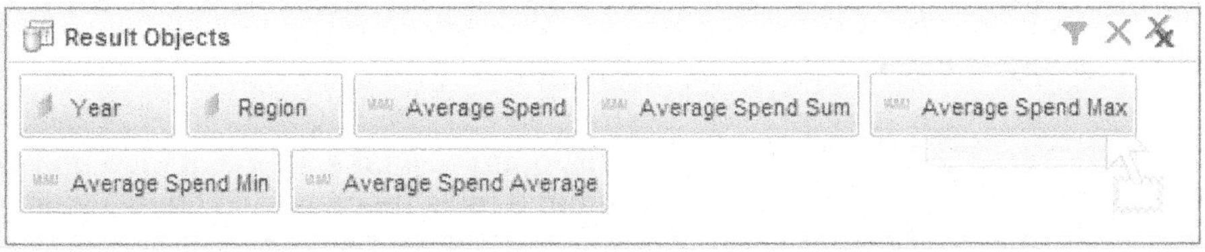
Result Objects
Year
Region
Average Spend
Average Spend Sum
Average Spend Max
Average Spend Min
Average Spend Average

Then we would get the following result on removing [Region] from the block:

Year	Average Spend Sum	Average Spend Max	Average Spend Min	Average Spend Average	Average Spend Count
2006	16,178	8,466	0	5,393	3
2007	34,340	9,052	8,102	8,585	4
2008	35,069	9,280	8,479	8,767	4

The results in this table are better understood by using the table below as it explains how each measure is being aggregated.

By removing [Region] from the block we are trying to display the 'average spend per year', therefore the values of interest are most likely to be in the column [Average Spend Average] as this column gives an indication of the average spend per region per year.

Is the measure [Average Spend Average] showing the correct values when we remove [Region] from the block?

NOTE – The measures in the query above are the same as [Average Spend] but each uses a different projection function as described below.

Measure	Projection Function Description
Average Spend Sum	[Average Spend] from the database is summed within the document, meaning we display 'the sum of average values'.
Average Spend Max	Maximum value of [Average Spend] from the values within the document is displayed.
Average Spend Min	Minimum value of [Average Spend] from the values within the document is displayed.
Average Spend Average	[Average Spend] from the database is averaged within the document, meaning 'an average of average values' is displayed.
Average Spend Count	Count of [Average Spend] values is displayed.

To find out if any of the measures are displaying the correct value at [Year] level only, we have to create the following query:

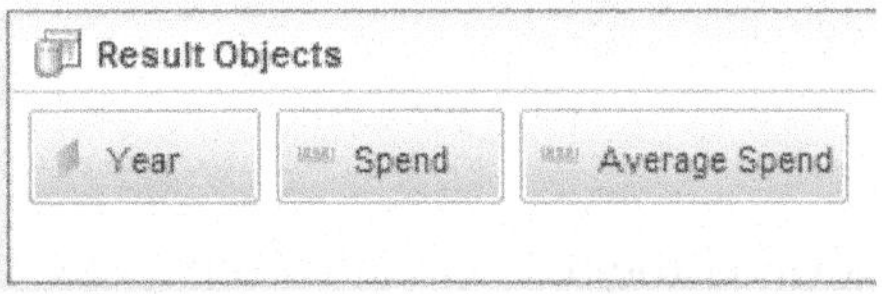
Result Objects
Year
Spend
Average Spend

This query will take the source data of 144 rows and return 3 rows (because we have 3 years of data).

For each of the 3 years the query will return a total Spend value and an Average Spend value.

Year	Spend	Average Spend
2006	194,141	5,393
2007	412,078	8,585
2008	420,834	8,767

Then compare to the 'average' measures with different projection properties:

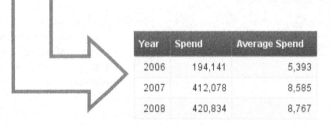

Year	Average Spend Sum	Average Spend Max	Average Spend Min	Average Spend Average	Average Spend Count
2006	16,178	8,466	0	5,393	3
2007	34,340	9,052	8,102	8,585	4
2008	35,069	9,280	8,479	8,767	4

We can see that none of the measures return the correct values at [Year] level unless we re-query the data using the correct dimensions, i.e. in this example we have removed the [Region] object from our query.

IMPORTANT – When working with Special Measures (such as percentages and averages), it might be necessary to use multiple queries within a document if data is to be presented at different dimension contexts, or retrieve the data at the lowest level and then use report level variables to calculate percentages and averages.

38.3 Smart Measures

A projection function is available that enables 'Special Measures' to behave correctly at all levels of dimensionality within documents. Like the other projection functions, 'Delegated' (or 'Database delegated') has to be assigned by the universe designer.

We will use the example used previously in 'Special Measures' to describe how database delegated measures work.

1. A new measure object has been created called [Average Spend DD] that has an SQL definition of **Avg(CUSTOMER_FACT.SPEND)** and a projection property of 'Delegated'.

2. A simple query is created as follows:

Result Objects
Year
Region
Spend
Average Spend DD

The SQL for this query is as follows:

```
SELECT
  CUSTOMER_FACT.YEAR_NO,
  CUSTOMER_FACT.REGION,
  Sum(CUSTOMER_FACT.SPEND),
  Avg(CUSTOMER_FACT.SPEND)
FROM
  CUSTOMER_FACT
GROUP BY
  CUSTOMER_FACT.YEAR_NO,
  CUSTOMER_FACT.REGION
```

3. The results of the query are displayed by default as:

Year	Region	Spend	Average Spend DD
2006	East	92,555	7,713
2006	North	101,586	8,466
2006	South		
2006	West	0	0
2007	East	97,218	8,102
2007	North	107,275	8,940
2007	South	108,629	9,052
2007	West	98,956	8,246
2008	East	101,743	8,479
2008	North	105,984	8,832
2008	South	111,364	9,280
2008	West	101,743	8,479

4. The original tab has been renamed as 'Year Region' and then this tab has been duplicated.

5. The duplicated tab has been renamed as 'Year'.

6. In the 'Year' tab, the column [Region] has been removed from the block and this results in the [Average Spend DD] object to display '#TOREFRESH':

Year	Spend	Average Spend DD
2006	194,141	#TOREFRESH
2007	412,078	#TOREFRESH
2008	420,834	#TOREFRESH

7. Clicking on 'Refresh Data' to refresh the query results in:

Year	Spend	Average Spend DD
2006	194,141	5,393
2007	412,078	8,585
2008	420,834	8,767

These are the correct values at [Year] level, but we still have the [Region] object in the document so how does Web Intelligence display the correct value?

8. Web Intelligence modifies the query to use a concept of 'Grouping Sets':

```
(
SELECT
  1 AS GID,
  CUSTOMER_FACT.YEAR_NO,
  CUSTOMER_FACT.REGION,
  Sum(CUSTOMER_FACT.SPEND),
  Avg(CUSTOMER_FACT.SPEND)
FROM
  CUSTOMER_FACT
GROUP BY
  CUSTOMER_FACT.YEAR_NO,
  CUSTOMER_FACT.REGION
UNION
SELECT
  0 AS GID,
  CUSTOMER_FACT.YEAR_NO,
  NULL,
  NULL,
  Avg(CUSTOMER_FACT.SPEND)
FROM
  CUSTOMER_FACT
GROUP BY
  CUSTOMER_FACT.YEAR_NO
)
```

We have 2 Grouping Sets within our query separated by the word '**UNION**'.

The first Grouping Set is used to fetch [Year] and [Average Spend DD] only.

The second Grouping Set is used to fetch [Year], [Region], [Spend] and [Average Spend DD].

Web Intelligence then used these Grouping Sets to display the correct values.

Web Intelligence has also included an extra column in each of the 'grouping queries' to internally reference the data. The columns 'GID' is not visible to the user within the report panel.

9. If a new tab is created ('Region') with the following block, we get:

Region	Spend	Average Spend DD
East	291,516	#TOREFRESH
North	314,845	#TOREFRESH
South	219,993	#TOREFRESH
West	200,699	#TOREFRESH

The reason for this is because the Grouping Set at [Region] does not exist within the document.

10. Refreshing the query results in the correct values to be displayed:

Region	Spend	Average Spend DD
East	291,516	8,098
North	314,845	8,746
South	219,993	9,166
West	200,699	5,575

11. The underlying query has now been modified to include 3 Grouping Sets:

```
(
SELECT
 2 AS GID,
 CUSTOMER_FACT.YEAR_NO,
 CUSTOMER_FACT.REGION,                 [Year] and [Region] level
 Sum(CUSTOMER_FACT.SPEND),
 Avg(CUSTOMER_FACT.SPEND)
FROM
 CUSTOMER_FACT
GROUP BY
 CUSTOMER_FACT.YEAR_NO,
 CUSTOMER_FACT.REGION
UNION
SELECT
 0 AS GID,
 NULL,
 CUSTOMER_FACT.REGION,
 NULL,                                 [Region] level only
 Avg(CUSTOMER_FACT.SPEND)
FROM
 CUSTOMER_FACT
GROUP BY
 CUSTOMER_FACT.REGION
UNION
SELECT
 1 AS GID,
 CUSTOMER_FACT.YEAR_NO,
 NULL,
 NULL,                                 [Year] level only
 Avg(CUSTOMER_FACT.SPEND)
FROM
 CUSTOMER_FACT
GROUP BY
 CUSTOMER_FACT.YEAR_NO
)
```

12. If we delete the 'Year' tab and click on 'Refresh Data' then our SQL changes to:

```
(
SELECT
 1 AS GID,
 CUSTOMER_FACT.YEAR_NO,
 CUSTOMER_FACT.REGION,
 Sum(CUSTOMER_FACT.SPEND),             [Year] and [Region] level
 Avg(CUSTOMER_FACT.SPEND)
FROM
 CUSTOMER_FACT
GROUP BY
 CUSTOMER_FACT.YEAR_NO,
 CUSTOMER_FACT.REGION
UNION
SELECT
 0 AS GID,
 NULL,
 CUSTOMER_FACT.REGION,
 NULL,                                 [Region] level only
 Avg(CUSTOMER_FACT.SPEND)
FROM
 CUSTOMER_FACT
GROUP BY
 CUSTOMER_FACT.REGION
)
```

NOTES

a. At every refresh the underlying query is modified (to add or remove Grouping Sets) depending on what dimension contexts are being used in the document to display 'Database delegated' measures.

b. The lowest level Grouping Set is not removed even if this level is not used within the document, i.e. it is defined by the objects placed in the 'Result Objects' pane.

38.3.1 Using Smart Measures with Document Variables

Web Intelligence might not be able to display values for Smart Measures when dimension contexts are based on one or more document level variables containing formulas. Let us take an example and then explain why this happens.

1. We have the following query using 'eFashion Oracle' universe:

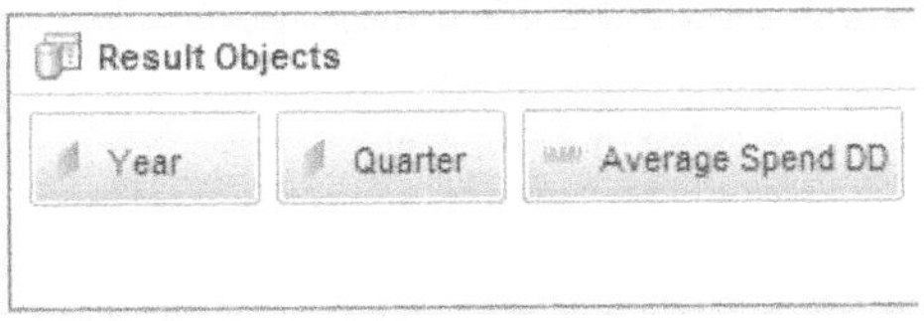
Result Objects
Year
Quarter
Average Spend DD

2. We can see the Smart Measure working correctly with the universe dimensions as shown below:

Default Block:

Year	Quarter	Average Spend DD
2006	Q1	5,360
2006	Q2	5,545
2006	Q3	5,442
2006	Q4	5,224
2007	Q1	8,439
2007	Q2	8,609
2007	Q3	8,749
2007	Q4	8,543
2008	Q1	8,674
2008	Q2	8,807
2008	Q3	8,747
2008	Q4	8,842

[Quarter] removed from block:

Year	Average Spend DD
2006	5,392.8
2007	8,585.0
2008	8,767.4

[Year] removed from block:

Quarter	Average Spend DD
Q1	7,684.8
Q2	7,845.3
Q3	7,846.3
Q4	7,746.4

3. A document variable to group the quarters into Seasons is created, 'SS' for 'Q2 and Q3' and 'AW' for 'Q4 and Q1' (where 'SS' = 'Spring/Summer' and 'AW' = 'Autumn/Winter').

[Season] =If [Quarter] InList ("Q1";"Q4") Then "AW" Else "SS"

4. Web Intelligence displays values for the Smart Measure depending on the dimension context being used:

Year	Season	Quarter	Average Spend DD
2006	AW	Q1	5,360
2006	AW	Q4	5,224
2006	SS	Q2	5,545
2006	SS	Q3	5,442
2007	AW	Q1	8,439
2007	AW	Q4	8,543
2007	SS	Q2	8,609
2007	SS	Q3	8,749
2008	AW	Q1	8,674
2008	AW	Q4	8,842
2008	SS	Q2	8,807
2008	SS	Q3	8,747

A Grouping Set exists for this dimension context.

Web Intelligence is able to display values for the Smart Measure as we are using all the dimensions from the query.

What happens if we remove [Quarter] from the block?

Year	Season	Average Spend DD
2006	AW	#MULTIVALUE
2006	SS	#MULTIVALUE
2007	AW	#MULTIVALUE
2007	SS	#MULTIVALUE
2008	AW	#MULTIVALUE
2008	SS	#MULTIVALUE

We are requesting Web Intelligence to display the average seasonal spend per year in this block.

It appears Web Intelligence is trying to use the Grouping Set [Year], [Quarter], [Average Spend DD] to calculate the values for this block.

However, for each [Year], [Season] combination there are 2 values, therefore '#MULTIVALUE' is shown because [Average Spend DD] cannot be presented within the document without a suitable Grouping Set query.

Season	Average Spend DD
AW	#MULTIVALUE
SS	#MULTIVALUE

Web Intelligence will request a Grouping Set at [Quarter], [Average Spend DD] level from the database.

However, there are 2 [Quarter] values per [Season] and Web Intelligence is unable to present the values correctly because [Quarter] is not being used in the block.

NOTE – When dimension contexts contain Web Intelligence functions then Smart Measures will either attempt relevant query Grouping Sets, or make no attempt for Grouping Sets because Web Intelligence functions might not be supported by underlying databases.

38.3.2 Using Smart Measures in Extended Syntax Formulas

Use of Extended Syntax can affect dimension contexts and Web Intelligence will generate the SQL for the relevant Grouping Set where possible.

1. We have the following query using 'eFashion Oracle' universe:

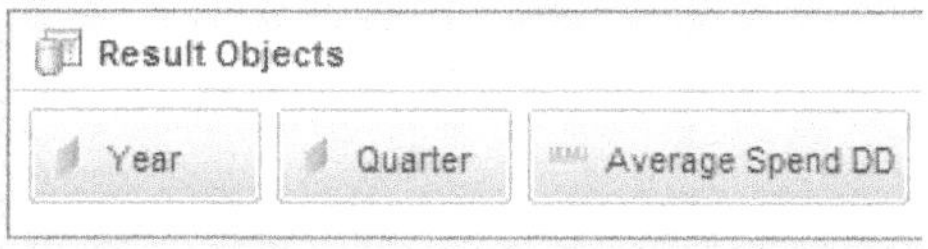
Result Objects
Year
Quarter
Average Spend DD

2. If we add an extra column into the default report block and use the following formula within this new column:

   =[Average Spend DD] ForAll ([Quarter])

3. The new column shows '#TOREFRESH', suggesting Web Intelligence has generated a new Grouping Set in order to calculate a result for this formula.

Year	Quarter	Average Spend DD	
2006	Q1	5,360	#TOREFRESH
	Q2	5,545	#TOREFRESH
	Q3	5,442	#TOREFRESH
	Q4	5,224	#TOREFRESH
2006			

4. Refreshing the query yields the following results:

Year	Quarter	Average Spend DD	
2006	Q1	5,360	5,393
	Q2	5,545	5,393
	Q3	5,442	5,393
	Q4	5,224	5,393
2006			

Year	Quarter	Average Spend DD	
2007	Q1	8,439	8,585
	Q2	8,609	8,585
	Q3	8,749	8,585
	Q4	8,543	8,585
2007			

```
(
SELECT
  1 AS GID,
  CUSTOMER_FACT.YEAR_NO,
  CUSTOMER_FACT.QUARTER,
  Avg(CUSTOMER_FACT.SPEND)
FROM
  CUSTOMER_FACT
GROUP BY
  CUSTOMER_FACT.YEAR_NO,
  CUSTOMER_FACT.QUARTER
UNION
SELECT
  0 AS GID,
  CUSTOMER_FACT.YEAR_NO,
  NULL,
  Avg(CUSTOMER_FACT.SPEND)
FROM
  CUSTOMER_FACT
GROUP BY
  CUSTOMER_FACT.YEAR_NO
)
```

In the example above, Web Intelligence has recognised a new Grouping Set is required to correctly calculate the formula '**=[Average Spend DD] ForAll ([Quarter])**'.

5. If we have the following query:

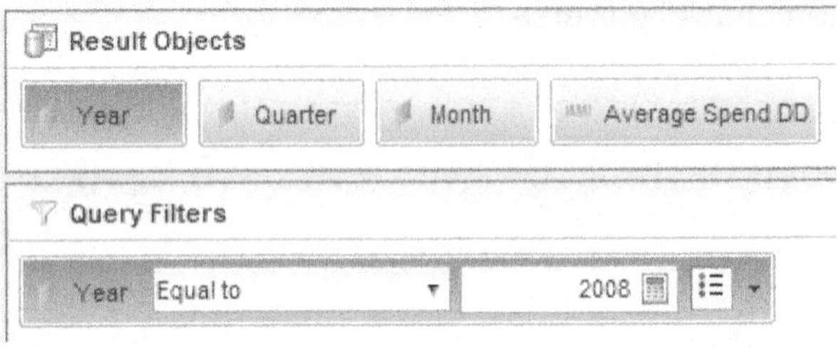
Result Objects
Year
Quarter
Month
Average Spend DD
Query Filters
Year
Equal to
2008

6. The default block contains shows:

Year	Quarter	Month	Average Spend DD
2008	Q1	1	8,601
2008	Q1	2	8,694
2008	Q1	3	8,728
2008	Q2	4	8,734
2008	Q2	5	8,793
2008	Q2	6	8,895
2008	Q3	7	8,798
2008	Q3	8	8,783
2008	Q3	9	8,660
2008	Q4	10	8,819
2008	Q4	11	8,843
2008	Q4	12	8,862

7. If we change the formula in the Average Spend DD column

   from **=[Average Spend DD]** to **=[Average Spend DD] ForEach ([Month])**

   ...then our results stay the same as Step 6, i.e. correct.

8. With the new formula in place, removing the [Month] column results in:

Year	Quarter	Average Spend DD
2008	Q1	#MULTIVALUE
2008	Q2	#MULTIVALUE
2008	Q3	#MULTIVALUE
2008	Q4	#MULTIVALUE

9. Refreshing the query does not alter the results:

   The Grouping Set being used in this example is [Year], [Quarter], [Month], [Average Spend DD] because the 'ForEach' Context Operator is trying to include the [Month] object into the block dimension context, i.e. effectively making the context [Year], [Quarter] and [Month].

   Therefore, in this example the above results are correct because we are trying to display a calculation on a Smart Measure at an aggregated level using a more detailed dimension context without showing all the required dimensions.

38.3.3 Using Filters on Smart Measures

Smart Measures can be used to filter data in reports, so let us take a look using an example.

1. We have the following query using the modified 'eFashion' universe (or the 'eFashion Oracle XI3.1' universe).

Result Objects
Year
Region
Spend
Average Spend DD

2. The default results are shown as:

Year	Region	Spend	Average Spend DD
2006	East	92,555	7,713
2006	North	101,586	8,466
2006	South		
2006	West	0	0
2007	East	97,218	8,102
2007	North	107,275	8,940
2007	South	108,629	9,052
2007	West	98,956	8,246
2008	East	101,743	8,479
2008	North	105,984	8,832
2008	South	111,364	9,280
2008	West	101,743	8,479

3. Apply the 'Default aggregation' Standard Calculation to the [Average Spend DD] column as shown below:

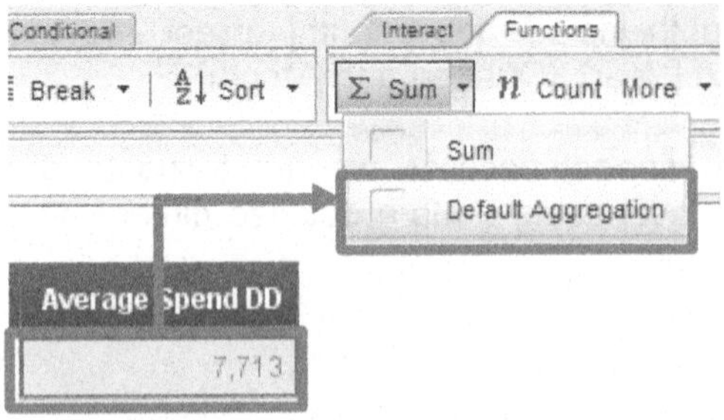
Conditional
Interact
Functions
Break
Sort
Sum
Count
More
Sum
Default Aggregation
Average Spend DD
7,713

4. This results in:

Year	Region	Spend	Average Spend DD
2006	East	92,555	7,713
2006	North	101,586	8,466
2006	South		
2006	West	0	0
2007	East	97,218	8,102
2007	North	107,275	8,940
2007	South	108,629	9,052
2007	West	98,956	8,246
2008	East	101,743	8,479
2008	North	105,984	8,832
2008	South	111,364	9,280
2008	West	101,743	8,479
		Total:	**#MULTIVALUE**

The reason for this is because we do not have a value 'average spend for all regions across all years' from the database.

5. On refreshing the query we get the correct result in the footer cell:

2008	South	111,364	9,280
2008	West	101,743	8,479
		Total:	**7,781**

6. Let us now apply a filter to the block (using the [Average Spend DD] object):

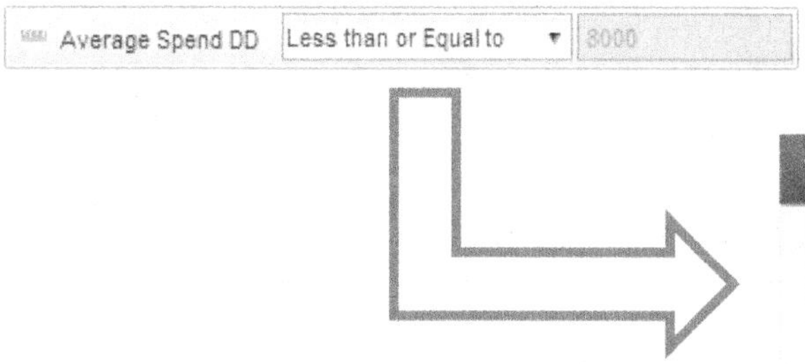
Average Spend DD
Less than or Equal to
8000

Year	Region	Spend	Average Spend DD
2006	East	92,555	7,713
2006	West	0	0
	Total:		#UNAVAILABLE

We can see our data has been reduced to only 2 body rows. These are the correct rows (can be validated against point 4 above).

The '#UNAVAILABLE' in the footer row is an indicator that filters are being used. Here we have a filter on the Smart Measure but the query is not restricted in any way to ensure we get the correct value presented in the footer row.

7. If we remove the [Region] object from the block then we get the following results because the query has no Grouping Set at [Year] level:

Year	Spend	Average Spend DD
#TOREFRESH	#TOREFRESH	#TOREFRESH
Total:		#TOREFRESH

8. Refreshing the query results in:

Year	Spend	Average Spend DD
2006	194,141	5,393
Total:		#UNAVAILABLE

The above results indicate that out of the three years (2006, 2007 and 2008) only 2006 has an average spend less than or equal to 8000.

9. This is verified if we remove the filter on [Average Spend DD]:

Year	Spend	Average Spend DD
2006	194,141	5,393
2007	412,078	8,585
2008	420,834	8,767
Total:		#TOREFRESH

10. Finally refreshing the query results in the correct value being displayed in the footer row also:

Year	Spend	Average Spend DD
2006	194,141	5,393
2007	412,078	8,585
2008	420,834	8,767
	Total:	**7,781**

We have demonstrated that Smart Measures can be used to filter data available in a grouping set. Footer rows that are effectively showing an aggregation of a filtered Smart Measure will be shown as '#UNAVAILABLE' by Web Intelligence.

38.3.4 Using Smart Measures with Filtered Dimensions

If a Smart Measure is used in a context that has a filter applied to a dimension that itself does not exist in the calculation context then Web Intelligence will display the '#UNAVAILABLE' value.

Let us see this in practice to explain further.

1. We have the following query using 'eFashion Oracle' universe:

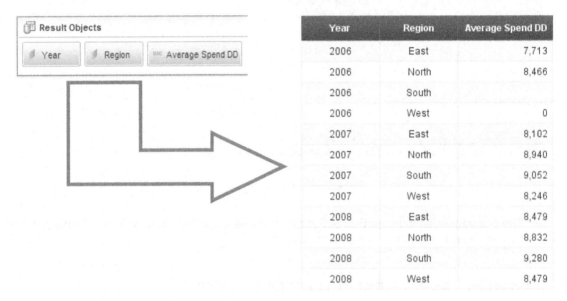

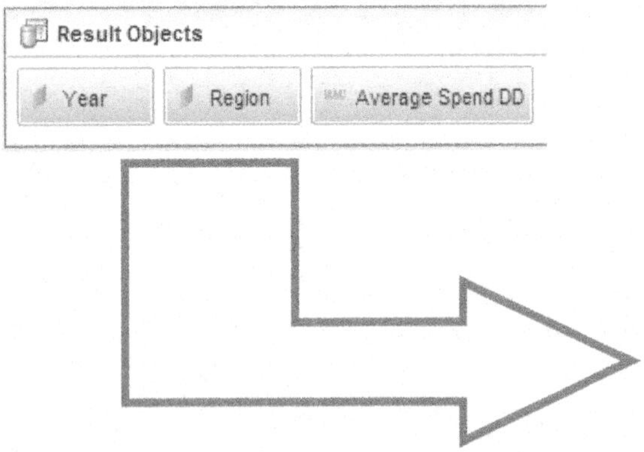
Result Objects
Year
Region
Average Spend DD

Year	Region	Average Spend DD
2006	East	7,713
2006	North	8,466
2006	South	
2006	West	0
2007	East	8,102
2007	North	8,940
2007	South	9,052
2007	West	8,246
2008	East	8,479
2008	North	8,832
2008	South	9,280
2008	West	8,479

2. Applying a Report Filter (or a Block Filter) to restrict the data to 'North' and 'South' results in:

Year	Region	Average Spend DD
2006	North	8,466
2006	South	
2007	North	8,940
2007	South	9,052
2008	North	8,832
2008	South	9,280

3. Removing the [Region] columns causes [Average Spend DD] to show:

Year	Average Spend DD
2006	#UNAVAILABLE
2007	#UNAVAILABLE
2008	#UNAVAILABLE

4. Refreshing the queries does not change the above result. **Why?**

   Web Intelligence would require a Grouping Set for [Year], [Average Spend DD] but with an added restriction on [Region] to only include 'North' and 'South'.

   We could have other report tabs that are based on the same Grouping Set but require no [Region] level query filters. As a safeguard, Web Intelligence does not take document level filters and apply them at query level when generating Grouping Sets for Smart Measures.

   '#UNAVAILABLE' is an indicator that filters are being used. Here we have a filter on a dimension that is not included in the display context.

38.3.5 Using Smart Measures with Drill Filters

Drilling with Smart Measures is not affected because Web Intelligence automatically modifies the query to include the required Grouping Sets, through setting Scope of Analysis or through drill actions within report tabs.

1. A simple query is created (using 'eFashion Oracle universe) with no Scope of Analysis:

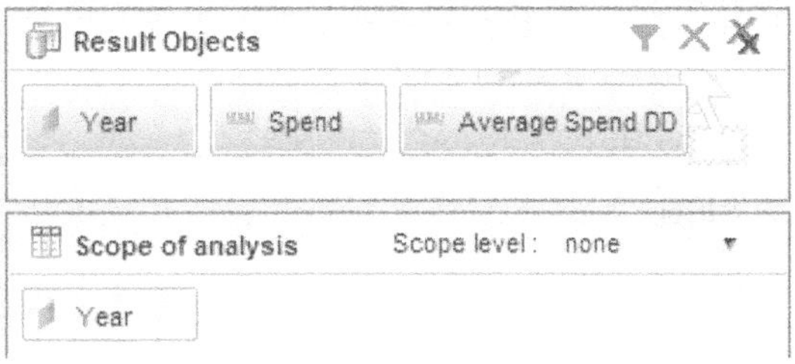
Result Objects
Year
Spend
Average Spend DD
Scope of analysis
Scope level: none
Year

SQL generated by Web Intelligence with Scope Level set to '**None**':

```
SELECT
  CUSTOMER_FACT.YEAR_NO,
  Sum(CUSTOMER_FACT.SPEND),
  Avg(CUSTOMER_FACT.SPEND)
FROM
  CUSTOMER_FACT
GROUP BY
  CUSTOMER_FACT.YEAR_NO
```

2. Setting the Scope of Analysis to 'One level' alters the generated SQL to:

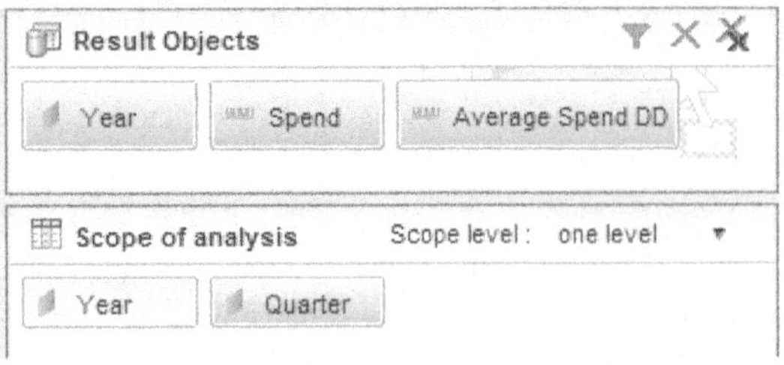
Result Objects
Year
Spend
Average Spend DD
Scope of analysis
Scope level : one level
Year
Quarter

Web Intelligence has generated SQL containing 2 Grouping Sets:

Grouping Set 1 is at the lowest level, i.e. [Year], [Quarter], [Spend] and [Average Spend DD].

Grouping Set 0 is at the highest level, i.e. [Year] and [Average Spend DD] only.

SQL generated by Web Intelligence with Scope Level set to '**One level**':

```
(
SELECT
 1 AS GID,
 CUSTOMER_FACT.YEAR_NO,
 Sum(CUSTOMER_FACT.SPEND),
 Avg(CUSTOMER_FACT.SPEND),
 CUSTOMER_FACT.QUARTER
FROM
 CUSTOMER_FACT
GROUP BY
 CUSTOMER_FACT.YEAR_NO,
 CUSTOMER_FACT.QUARTER
UNION
SELECT
 0 AS GID,
 CUSTOMER_FACT.YEAR_NO,
 NULL,
 Avg(CUSTOMER_FACT.SPEND),
 NULL
FROM
 CUSTOMER_FACT
GROUP BY
 CUSTOMER_FACT.YEAR_NO
)
```

3. Setting the Scope of Analysis to 'Two levels' alters the generated SQL to:

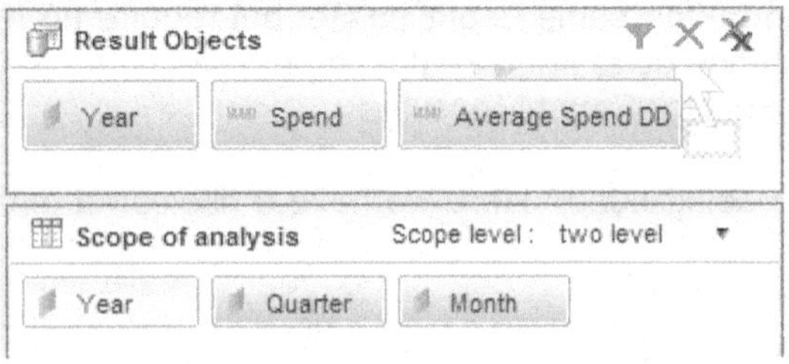
Result Objects
Year
Spend
Average Spend DD
Scope of analysis
Scope level : two level
Year
Quarter
Month

Web Intelligence has generated SQL containing 2 Grouping Sets:

Grouping Set 1 is at the lowest level, i.e. [Year], [Quarter], [Month], [Spend] and [Average Spend DD].

Grouping Set 0 is at the highest level, i.e. [Year] and [Average Spend DD] only.

There are no intermediate Grouping Sets so how will Web Intelligence display the results in Drill Mode?

SQL generated by Web Intelligence with Scope Level set to '**Two levels**':

```
(
SELECT
 1 AS GID,
 CUSTOMER_FACT.YEAR_NO,
 Sum(CUSTOMER_FACT.SPEND),
 Avg(CUSTOMER_FACT.SPEND),
 CUSTOMER_FACT.QUARTER,
 CUSTOMER_FACT.MONTH_NO
FROM
 CUSTOMER_FACT
GROUP BY
 CUSTOMER_FACT.YEAR_NO,
 CUSTOMER_FACT.QUARTER,
 CUSTOMER_FACT.MONTH_NO
UNION
SELECT
 0 AS GID,
 CUSTOMER_FACT.YEAR_NO,
 NULL,
 Avg(CUSTOMER_FACT.SPEND),
 NULL,
 NULL
FROM
 CUSTOMER_FACT
GROUP BY
 CUSTOMER_FACT.YEAR_NO
)
```

4. The query is run with Scope of Analysis set at 'Two levels' and Drill Mode is switched on as shown below:

Drop objects here to add simple report filters.

Year	Spend	Average Spend DD
2006	194,141	5,393
2007	412,078	8,585
2008	420,834	8,767

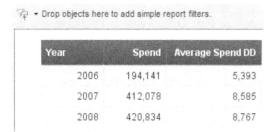

5. Drilling on [Year] = '2006' results in:

2006

Quarter	Spend	Average Spend DD
Q1	48,240	#TOREFRESH
Q2	49,905	#TOREFRESH
Q3	48,980	#TOREFRESH
Q4	47,016	#TOREFRESH

There is no Grouping Set to display the Smart Measure at [Year] and [Quarter] level so the query will have to be refreshed to retrieve the correct values.

Web Intelligence has recognised an interim drill level is being used between Scope Levels of 'None' and 'Two levels'.

6. Refreshing the query returns the results at [Year] and [Quarter] level for the Smart Measure:

2006

Quarter	Spend	Average Spend DD
Q1	48,240	5,360
Q2	49,905	5,545
Q3	48,980	5,442
Q4	47,016	5,224

7. Drilling on [Quarter] = 'Q2' results in:

2006 Q2

Month	Spend	Average Spend DD
4	16,075	5,358
5	16,725	5,575
6	17,105	5,702

Drilling down to [Month] is possible without a query refresh as the data is being filtered at [Year] and [Quarter] level.

The original Grouping Set which included all 3 dimensions ([Year], [Quarter] and [Month]) is used.

8. Drill Filter selections can be changed without any query refresh taking place:

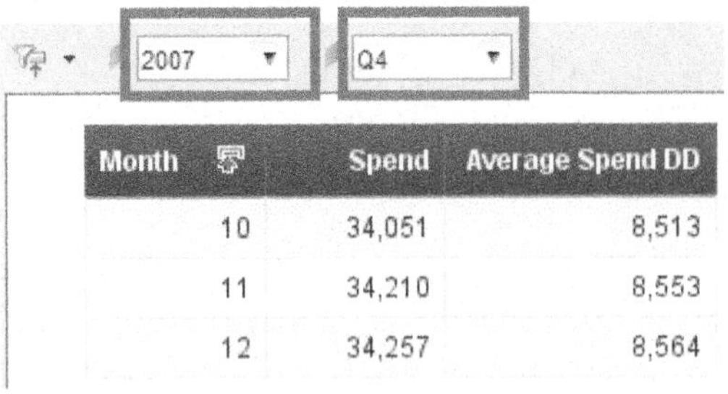
2007
Q4

Month	Spend	Average Spend DD
10	34,051	8,513
11	34,210	8,553
12	34,257	8,564

Changing the Drill Filter selections at the lowest level does not require a query refresh.

The original Grouping Set which included all 3 dimensions ([Year], [Quarter] and [Month]) is used.

9. Drilling back up to [Quarter] also requires no query refresh:

Drilling back up from [Month] to [Quarter] does not require a query refresh.

The Grouping Set created in Step 5 is used, i.e. at the level of [Quarter] and [Average Spend DD].

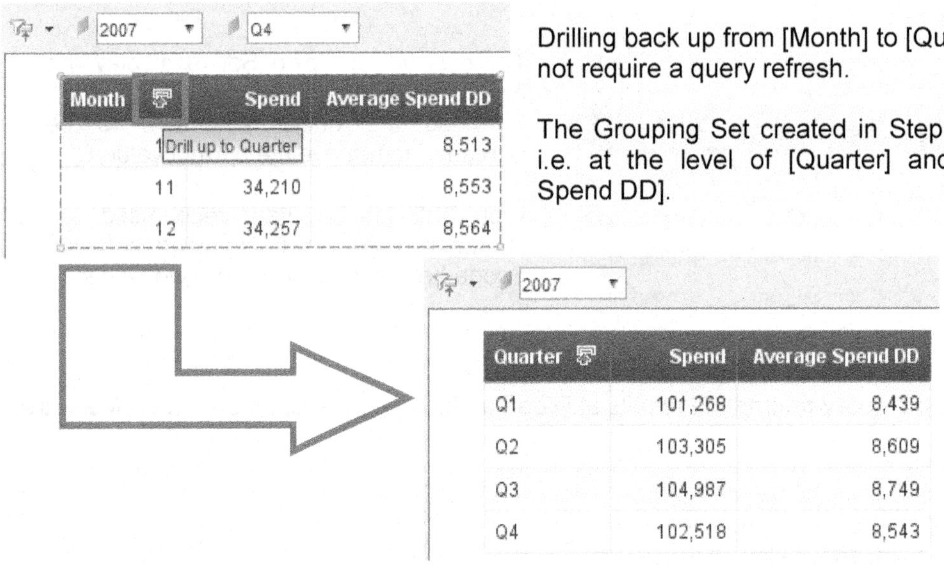
2007
Q4
Drill up to Quarter

Month	Spend	Average Spend DD
1		8,513
11	34,210	8,553
12	34,257	8,564

2007

Quarter	Spend	Average Spend DD
Q1	101,268	8,439
Q2	103,305	8,609
Q3	104,987	8,749
Q4	102,518	8,543

10. Drilling up to [Year]:

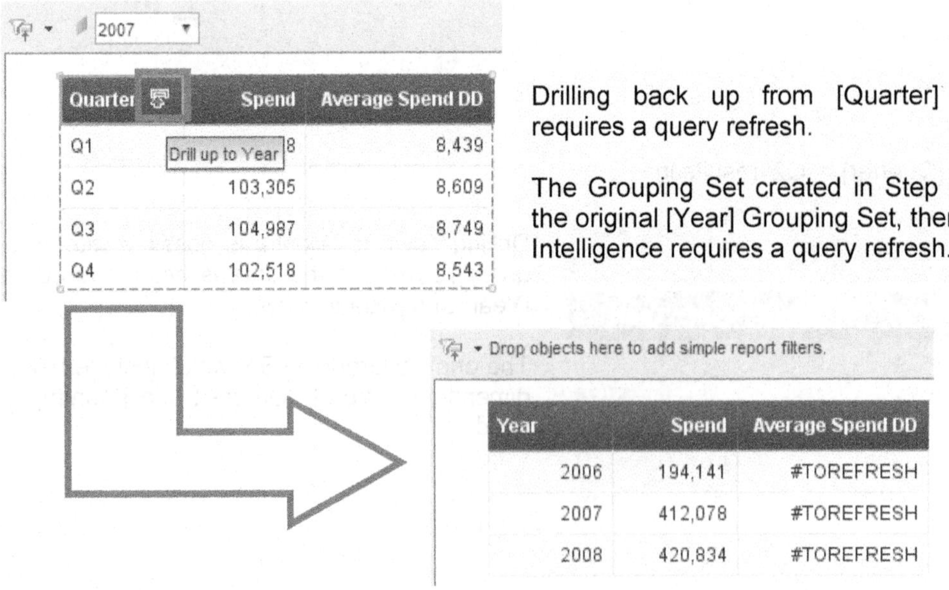
2007
Drill up to Year

Quarter	Spend	Average Spend DD
Q1	8	8,439
Q2	103,305	8,609
Q3	104,987	8,749
Q4	102,518	8,543

Drop objects here to add simple report filters.

Year	Spend	Average Spend DD
2006	194,141	#TOREFRESH
2007	412,078	#TOREFRESH
2008	420,834	#TOREFRESH

Drilling back up from [Quarter] to [Year] requires a query refresh.

The Grouping Set created in Step 5 replaced the original [Year] Grouping Set, therefore Web Intelligence requires a query refresh.

11. Refreshing the query returns the results at [Year] level for the Smart Measure:

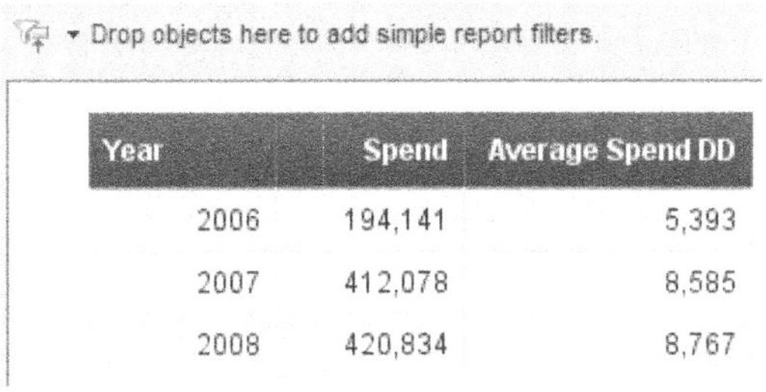

Drop objects here to add simple report filters.

Year	Spend	Average Spend DD
2006	194,141	5,393
2007	412,078	8,585
2008	420,834	8,767

Web Intelligence generates the relevant Grouping Sets when drilling with Smart Measures.

When setting the Scope of Analysis, Web Intelligence only generates 2 Grouping Sets:

1. At the highest dimensionality, based on the number of dimensions selected in the Result Objects pane.

2. At the lowest dimensionality (most detailed) based on the number of dimensions selected in the Result Objects pane plus any extra dimension objects to satisfy the Scope of Analysis setting.

Example:

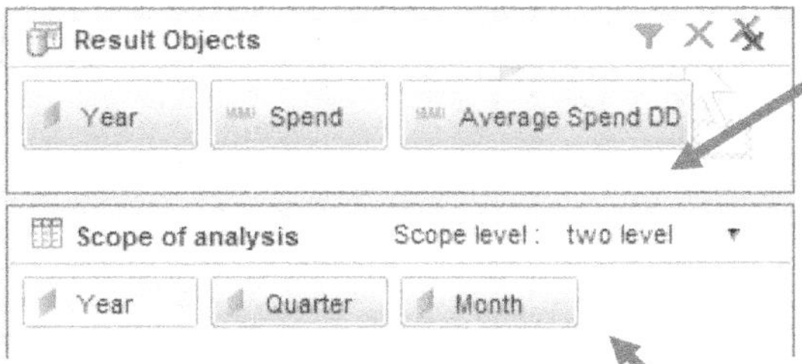
Result Objects
Year
Spend
Average Spend DD
Scope of analysis
Scope level : two level
Year
Quarter
Month

```
(
SELECT
  1 AS GID,
  CUSTOMER_FACT.YEAR_NO,
  Sum(CUSTOMER_FACT.SPEND),
  Avg(CUSTOMER_FACT.SPEND),
  CUSTOMER_FACT.QUARTER,
  CUSTOMER_FACT.MONTH_NO
FROM
  CUSTOMER_FACT
GROUP BY
  CUSTOMER_FACT.YEAR_NO,
  CUSTOMER_FACT.QUARTER,
  CUSTOMER_FACT.MONTH_NO
UNION
SELECT
  0 AS GID,
  CUSTOMER_FACT.YEAR_NO,
  NULL,
  Avg(CUSTOMER_FACT.SPEND),
  NULL,
  NULL
FROM
  CUSTOMER_FACT
GROUP BY
  CUSTOMER_FACT.YEAR_NO
  )
```

The query generated would include a Grouping Set at [Year] level (highest level based on dimension objects in Result Objects pane), plus a second Grouping Set at [Year], [Quarter] and [Month] level (lowest level based on 2 extra dimensions required due to Scope of Analysis).

When drilling is initiated then Grouping Sets for interim levels will be generated as and when required by Web Intelligence.

Web Intelligence also handles drilling on Smart Measures with the '**Use query drill**' setting. When this setting is used Web Intelligence recognises the user has explicitly opted to use this method of drilling, therefore query level filters are passed to the database to restrict the returned data.

39 Organising, Saving, Printing and Exporting Documents

Web Intelligence documents are created using Web Intelligence (including Web Intelligence Rich Client) but are organised and scheduled using the BI Launch Pad.

Some common functionality exists between Web Intelligence and BI Launch Pad (such as saving documents, exporting in different formats and printing).

39.1 Export as PDF, Excel, CSV or Text File in Design Mode

There are a number of options for sharing your work with others.

- You may save your report as a PDF or Excel, which are formats accessible by non-BusinessObjects users.
- In a typical deployment, only select users may publish documents to Public Folders, while most users may retrieve from the repository. The repository also handles documents that are scheduled for refresh and distributed to users. The right to schedule documents may also be limited to select users, but most users are typically allowed to retrieve scheduled documents after they have been refreshed.

To save your document in other formats to allow non-BusinessObjects users to view and use the data you can save your document as an Excel file, PDF file, CSV file or Text File.

1. Select a format to save the Web Intelligence document as.

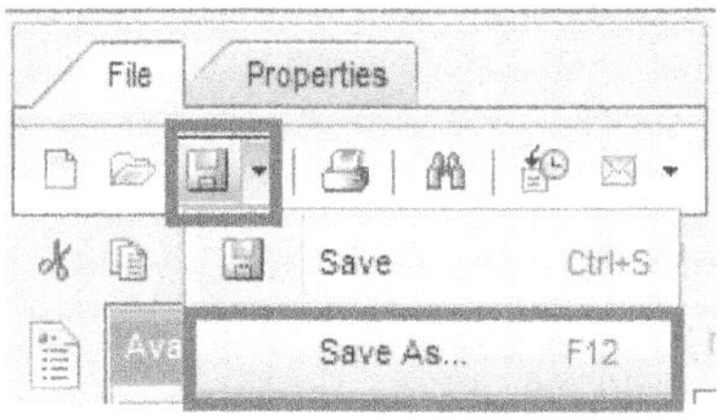
File
Properties
Save
Ctrl+S
Save As...
F12

2. In the 'Save Document' interface, select a file type.

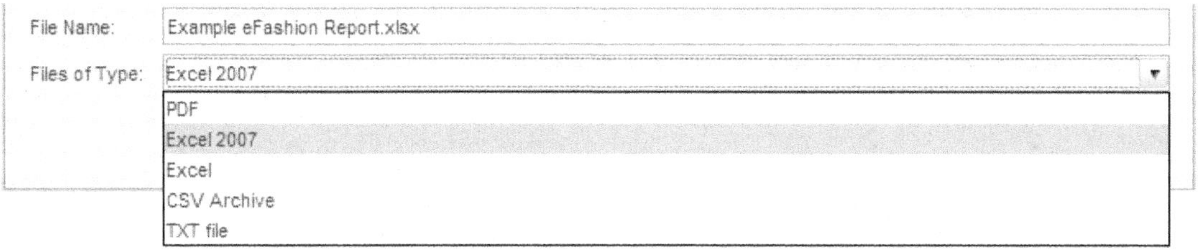
File Name:
Example eFashion Report.xlsx
Files of Type:
Excel 2007
PDF
Excel 2007
Excel
CSV Archive
TXT file

3. Browse to the location you want to save the file to and click 'Save'.

NOTE

You will be given a number of different options depending on the file type you select:

PDF

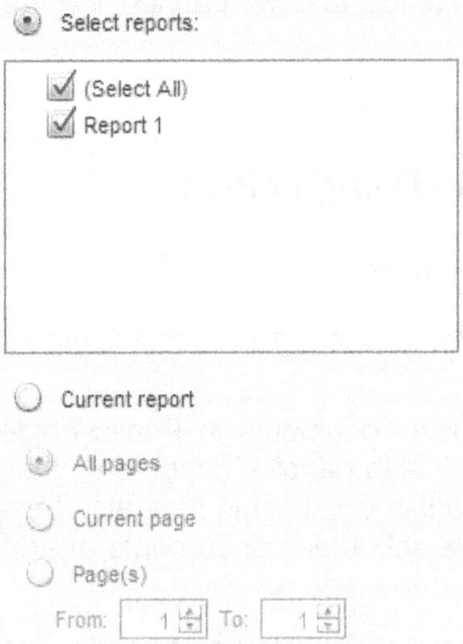
Select reports:
(Select All)
Report 1
Current report
All pages
Current page
Page(s)
From: 1 To: 1

Excel

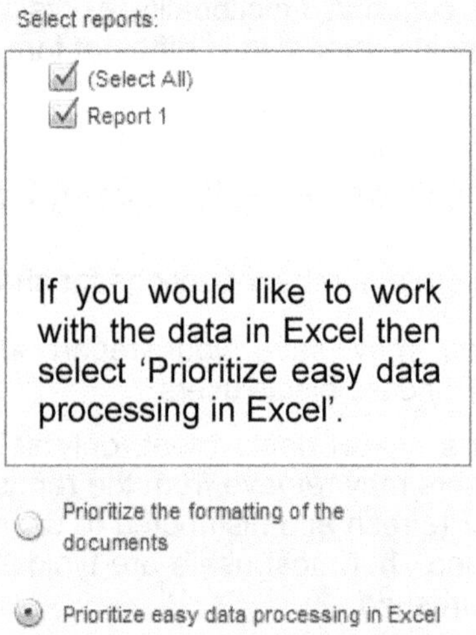
Select reports:
(Select All)
Report 1
Prioritize the formatting of the documents
Prioritize easy data processing in Excel

If you would like to work with the data in Excel then select 'Prioritize easy data processing in Excel'.

CSV

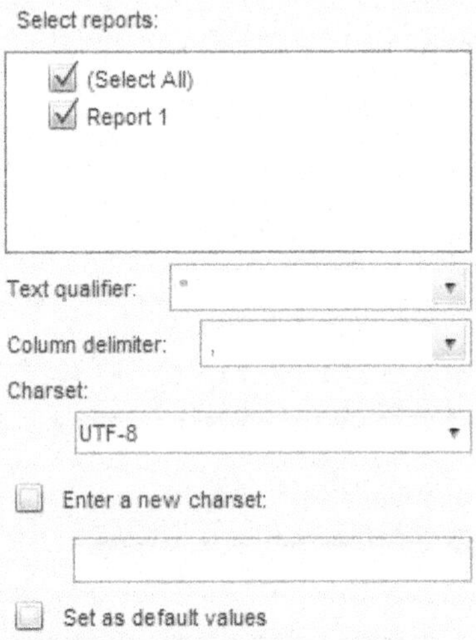
Select reports:
(Select All)
Report 1
Text qualifier:
Column delimiter:
Charset:
UTF-8
Enter a new charset:
Set as default values

TXT

Select reports:
(Select All)
Report 1

With all formats, you can save a single report tab, multiple report tabs, or all report tabs in a single 'Save As…' operation.

39.2 Export as PDF, Excel, CSV or Text File in View Mode

When documents are opened in View Mode then you can export data using the 'Export' button.

1. Export the whole document (i.e. all report tabs):

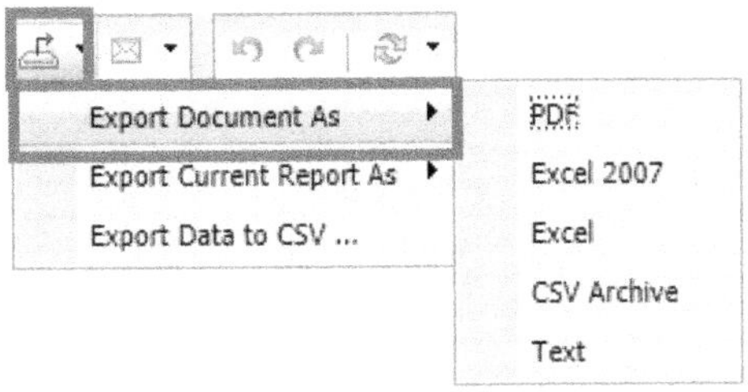
Export Document As
Export Current Report As
Export Data to CSV ...
PDF
Excel 2007
Excel
CSV Archive
Text

2. Export a single report tab (the one you are viewing):

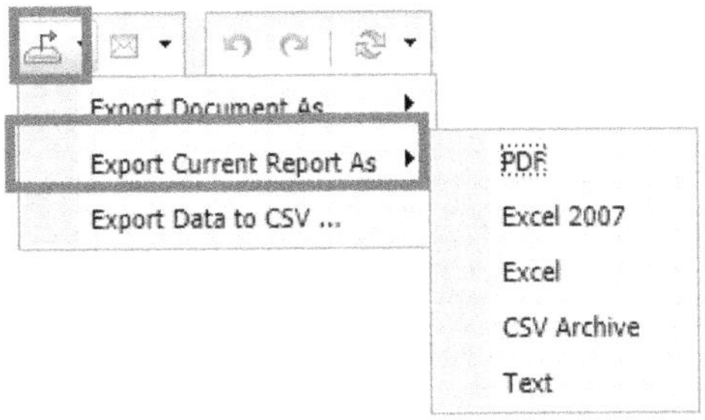
Export Document As
Export Current Report As
Export Data to CSV ...
PDF
Excel 2007
Excel
CSV Archive
Text

3. Export the query data (no tab level tables, etc):

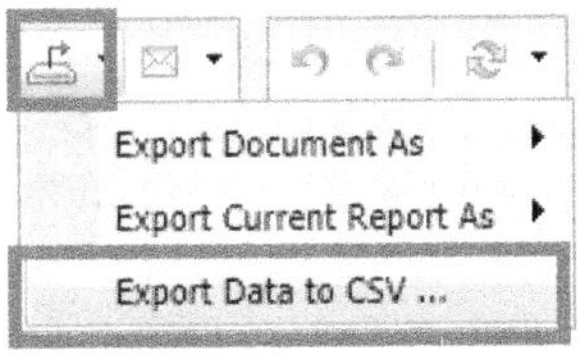
Export Document As
Export Current Report As
Export Data to CSV ...

39.3 Export as PDF, Excel, CSV or Text File in Web Intelligence Rich Client

Web Intelligence Rich Client offers similar functionality to Web Intelligence and BI Launch Pad for sharing data in different formats.

With a document open in Web Intelligence Rich Client:

1. You can use 'Save As...' to save the document in various formats.

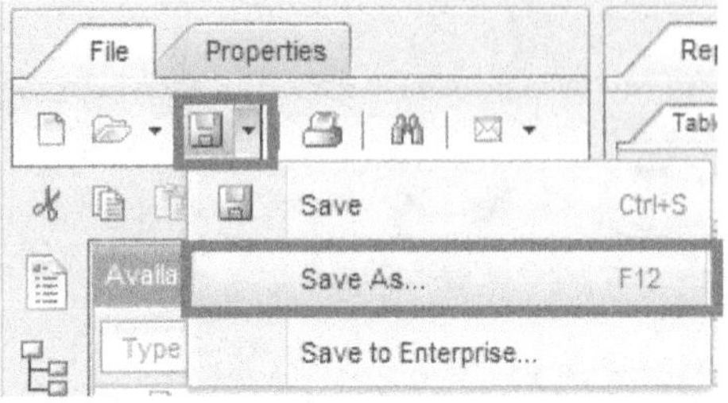
File
Properties
Save
Ctrl+S
Save As...
F12
Save to Enterprise...
Type

You can then specify a format to save as:

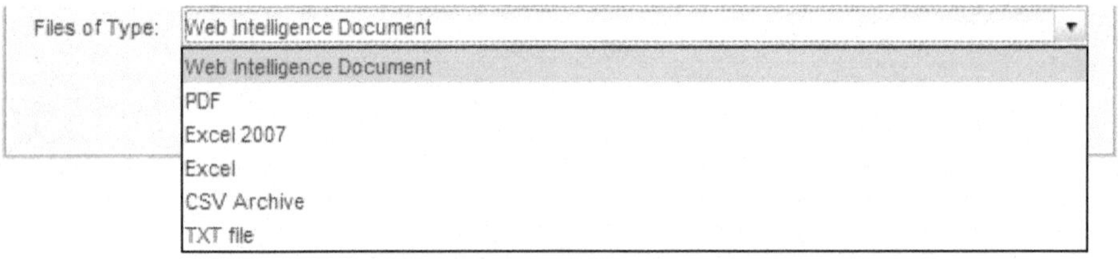
Files of Type:
Web Intelligence Document
Web Intelligence Document
PDF
Excel 2007
Excel
CSV Archive
TXT file

39.4 Printing Web Intelligence Documents

Web Intelligence documents can be printed from Web Intelligence and also from BI Launch Pad when viewing documents. The two options operate slightly differently so they will be described individually here.

39.4.1 Printing in Design Mode

Web Intelligence prints documents by converting them into PDF.

1. Use 'Print the document' in Web Intelligence

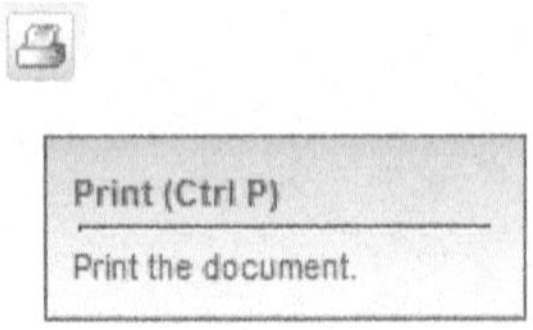
Print (Ctrl P)
Print the document.

2. Set up options for printing and click 'OK'.

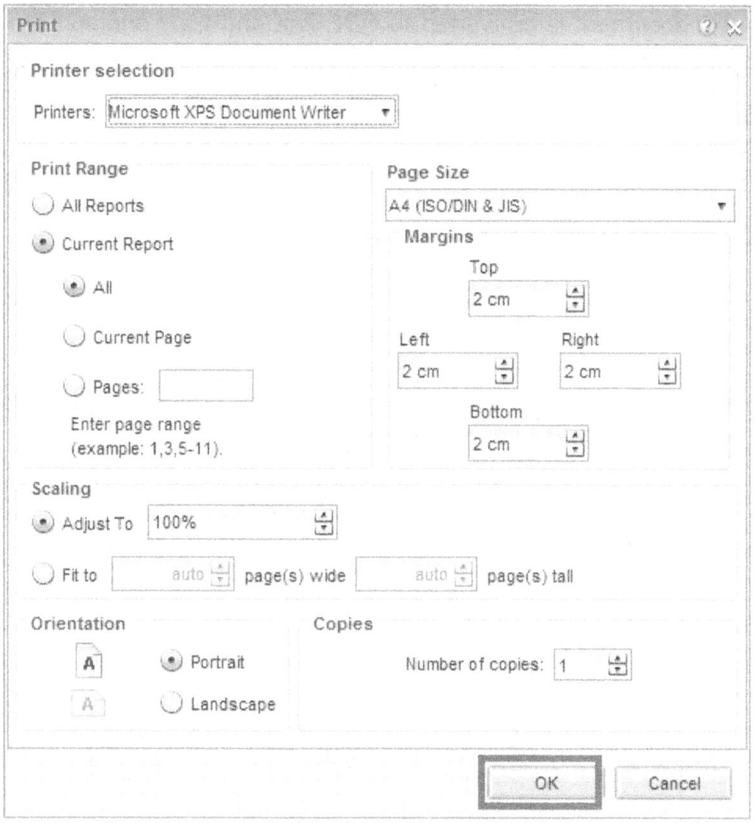
Print
Printer selection
Printers: Microsoft XPS Document Writer
Print Range
All Reports
Current Report
All
Current Page
Pages:
Enter page range
(example: 1,3,5-11).
Page Size
A4 (ISO/DIN & JIS)
Margins
Top
2 cm
Left
2 cm
Right
2 cm
Bottom
2 cm
Scaling
Adjust To
100%
Fit to
auto
page(s) wide
auto
page(s) tall
Orientation
Portrait
Landscape
Copies
Number of copies: 1
OK
Cancel

3. The document will be prepared and then sent for printing.

39.4.2 Printing in View Mode

When viewing a document, BI Launch Pad prints documents by converting them into PDF.

1. Use 'Export to PDF for Printing' in BI Launch Pad.

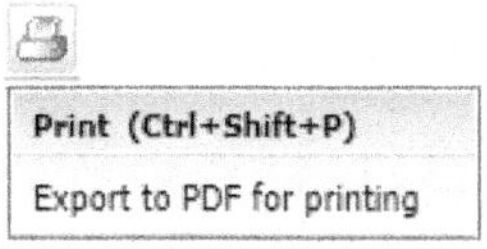
Print (Ctrl+Shift+P)
Export to PDF for printing

2. Click on 'Open' to view the document in Adobe Reader without saving it first, or click on 'Save' to first save the document to a location and then open it from the saved location for viewing/printing.

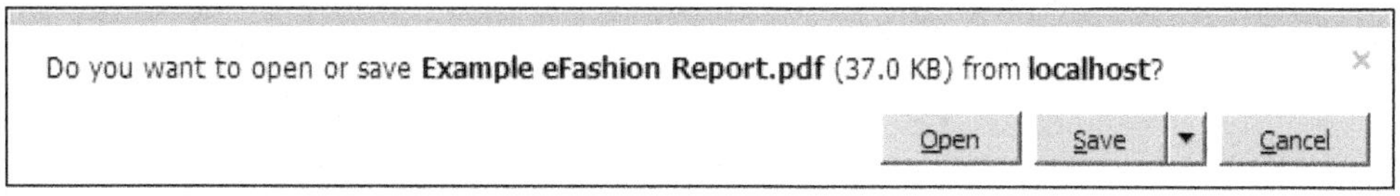
Do you want to open or save Example eFashion Report.pdf (37.0 KB) from localhost?
Open
Save
Cancel

NOTE

It is highly recommended that a document is converted to PDF first and then printed. Using the following options gives the best results:

1 – Set up page layout for each report tab using the report's properties.

2 – Save the document in PDF format using Save to my computer as PDF.

3 – Open and print the document after saving.

Using this method the whole document is converted and the layout properties are used as set up for each individual report tab.

When designing reports always consider how they will appear when printed. Amend layout properties as necessary to ensure a report is user-friendly for print purposes.

Use the Page Setup options in Web Intelligence to view how each report will look when printed.

39.4.3 Printing in View Mode

The document can be printed from Web Intelligence Rich Client in a similar fashion to Web Intelligence.

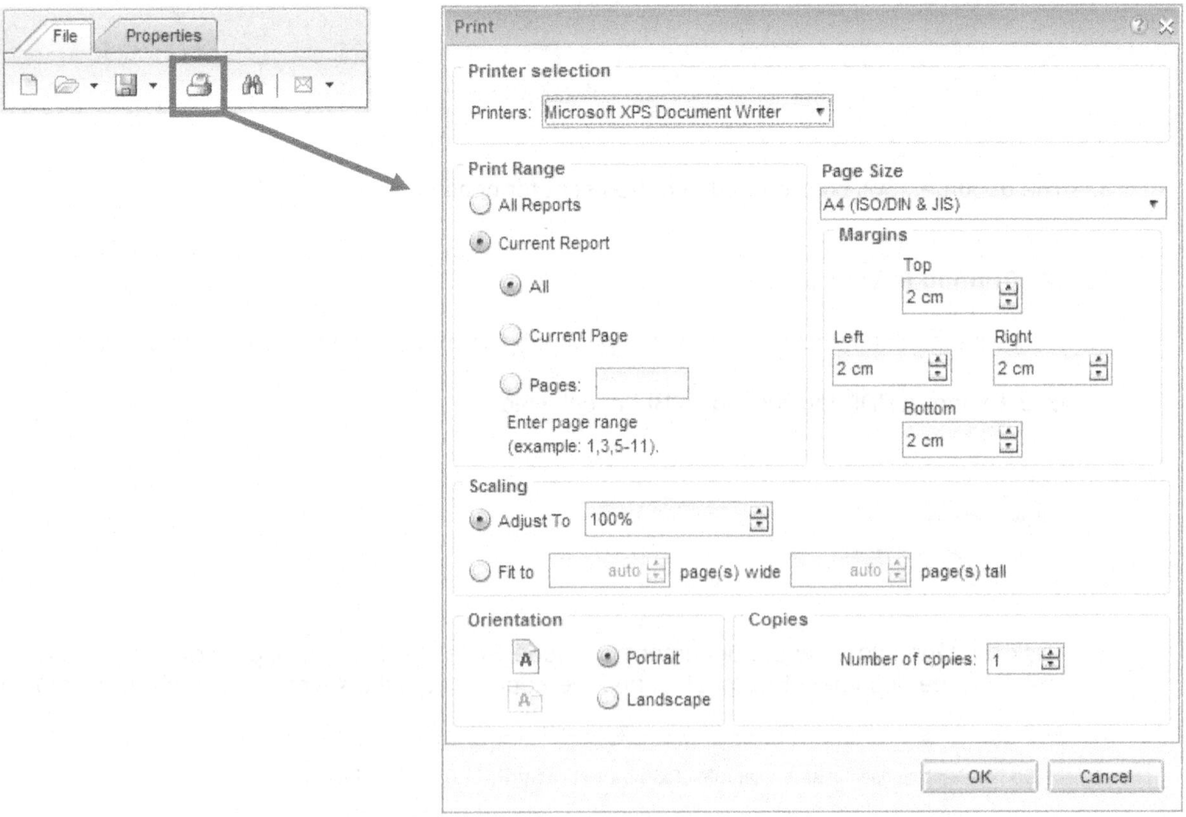
File
Properties
Print
Printer selection
Printers: Microsoft XPS Document Writer
Print Range
All Reports
Current Report
All
Current Page
Pages:
Enter page range (example: 1,3,5-11).
Page Size
A4 (ISO/DIN & JIS)
Margins
Top
2 cm
Left
2 cm
Right
2 cm
Bottom
2 cm
Scaling
Adjust To
100%
Fit to
auto
page(s) wide
auto
page(s) tall
Orientation
Portrait
Landscape
Copies
Number of copies:
1
OK
Cancel

39.5 Copying Data to other Applications

Individual cells or table blocks (vertical tables, horizontal tables, and crosstabs) can be copied to paste into other applications using 'Copy'.

1. Select the table type block and then right-click menu 'Copy' as shown below.

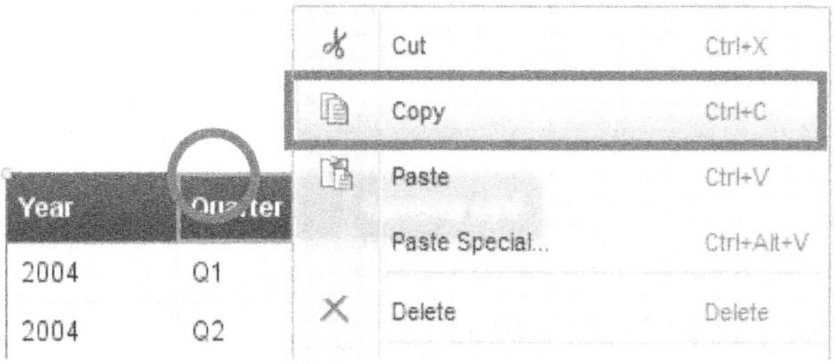
Cut
Ctrl+X
Copy
Ctrl+C
Paste
Ctrl+V
Paste Special...
Ctrl+Alt+V
Delete
Delete
Year
2004
Q1
2004
Q2

NOTE

Only available in Web Intelligence and Web Intelligence Rich Client, i.e. not available when documents are opened for View in BI Launch Pad.

2. Paste the copied contents into another application, for example, Microsoft Excel:

Pasted with formatting

	A	B	C
1	Year	Quarter	Quantity sold
2	2004	Q1	18,136
3	2004	Q2	14,408
4	2004	Q3	10,203
5	2004	Q4	10,331
6	2005	Q1	21,135
7	2005	Q2	17,152
8	2005	Q3	19,224
9	2005	Q4	22,344
10	2006	Q1	22,537
11	2006	Q2	22,846
12	2006	Q3	26,263
13	2006	Q4	18,650

Pasted without formatting

	A	B	C
1	Year	Quarter	Quantity sold
2	2004	Q1	18,136
3	2004	Q2	14,408
4	2004	Q3	10,203
5	2004	Q4	10,331
6	2005	Q1	21,135
7	2005	Q2	17,152
8	2005	Q3	19,224
9	2005	Q4	22,344
10	2006	Q1	22,537
11	2006	Q2	22,846
12	2006	Q3	26,263
13	2006	Q4	18,650

39.6 Organising Documents in BI Launch Pad

You can select one or documents and then:

- Create a Shortcut for the document(s) in My Favorites
- Cut them to paste in a different folder
- Copy them to paste in a different folder
- Copy shortcuts to these documents and paste the shortcuts in a different folder
- Delete the selected documents

1. Select the document(s) of interest.

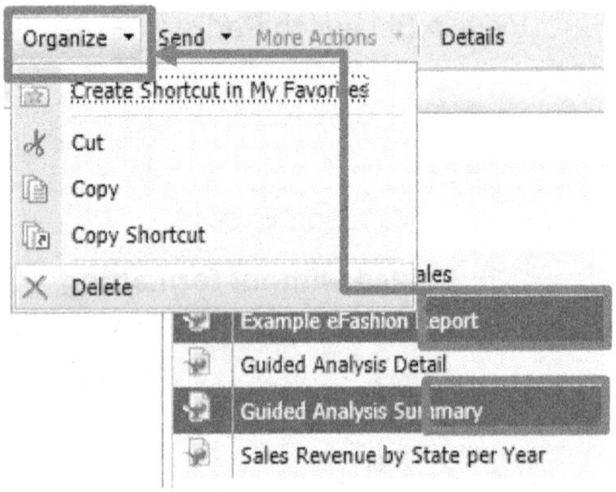
Organize
Send
More Actions
Details
Create Shortcut in My Favorites
Cut
Copy
Copy Shortcut
Delete
Example eFashion Report
Guided Analysis Detail
Guided Analysis Summary
Sales Revenue by State per Year

NOTE

To select multiple documents:

Use <Ctrl> and left-mouse button key to select a broken list.

Use <Shift> key and left-mouse button to select a continuous list.

2. Select the action you would like to perform.

3. Select a different location to Paste or confirm to delete:

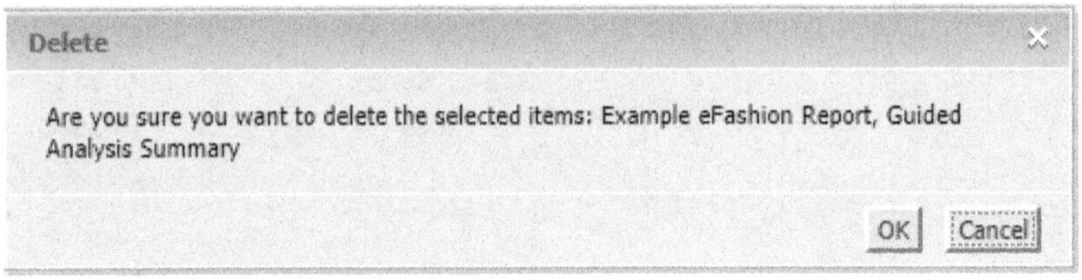
Delete
Are you sure you want to delete the selected items: Example eFashion Report, Guided Analysis Summary
OK
Cancel

NOTE - You can only delete documents from Public Folders if you have the appropriate security profile. You should always be able to delete documents saved to My Favorites.

39.7 Sending Documents to Users

You can send documents to other users in a number of different ways depending on where you perform the action. The documents will be sent to the user's Inbox within the BI Launch Pad environment.

You can send a document to other users by selecting it from a list (as shown below) or whilst a document is open.

39.7.1 Sending Documents to Users from BI Launch Pad

You can send documents from the Folder and Category view in BI Launch Pad.

1. Select document and then the menu '**Send – BI Inbox**'.

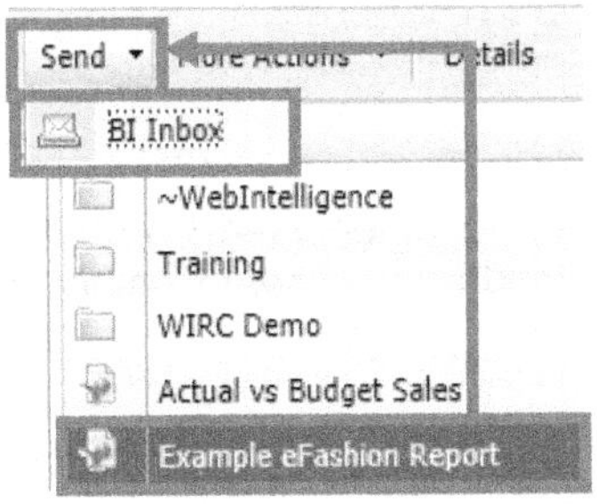
Send
BI Inbox
~WebIntelligence
Training
WIRC Demo
Actual vs Budget Sales
Example eFashion Report

You can also send documents to FTP and File Locations using 'Schedule', which is discussed next.

2. Select Users and/or Groups to send the document to.

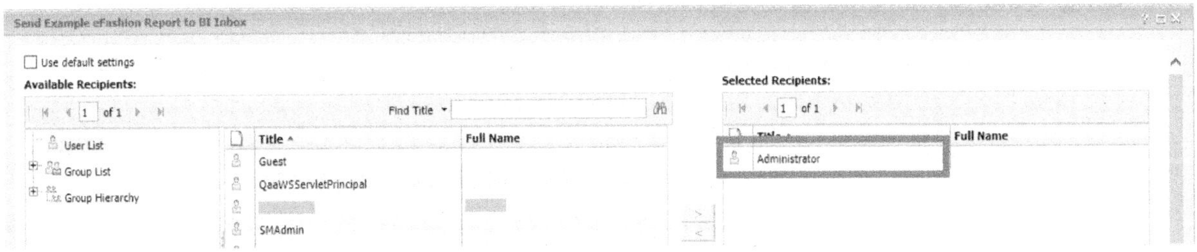
Send Example eFashion Report to BI Inbox
Use default settings
Available Recipients:
Find Title
User List
Group List
Group Hierarchy
Title
Full Name
Guest
QaaWSServletPrincipal
SMAdmin
Selected Recipients:
Full Name
Administrator

3. Specify a name to use for the sent document or let it be auto generated.

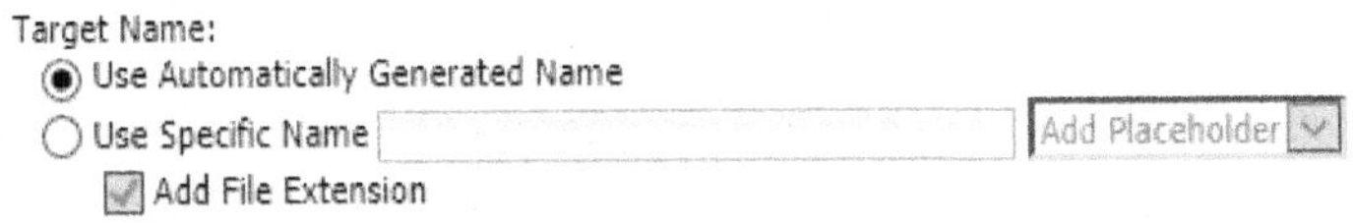
Target Name:
Use Automatically Generated Name
Use Specific Name
Add Placeholder
Add File Extension

You can give a specific name and attach a placeholder to the end of the name (selected from the drop down box).

4. **Copy** will send an actual copy of the document to the recipients, whereas a **Shortcut** is a link to the document.

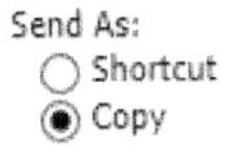
Send As:
Shortcut
Copy

For Corporate or Public documents you can send 'Shortcut' but you should send a 'Copy' if the source document is in your Personal Folders.

5. Click ‘Send’ to send the document.

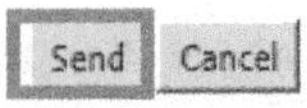
Send
Cancel

The sent document will be available in the BI Launch Pad Inbox(es) of ‘sent to’ user(s).

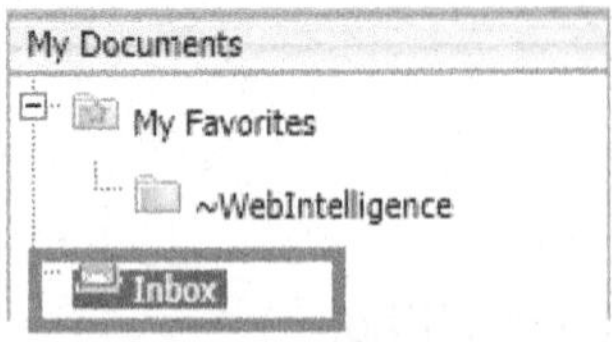
My Documents
My Favorites
~WebIntelligence
Inbox

		Title	Received On	From	Type
		Example eFashion Report : 12718	25-Mar-2014 11:27	webiworx	Web Intelligence

NOTE

Data security should be considered when sending documents to other users. For example, if you have no restrictions on data access then a document refreshed and sent to other users will contain data based on your security profile.

If other users have access to the same document but with more restrictive access to the data then you should send a purged document, preferably with the ‘Refresh On Open’ property ticked.

39.7.2 Sending Documents to Users from Web Intelligence

When a document is opened in Web Intelligence, you can use ‘Send document’ as follows:

1. Select ‘Send document’ in Web Intelligence

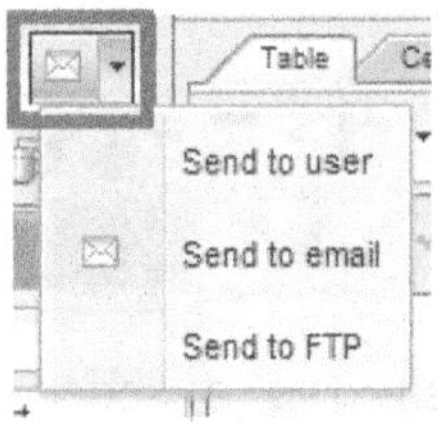
Table
Send to user
Send to email
Send to FTP

- ‘Send to user’ is the same as described above for ‘Sending Documents to Users from BI Launch Pad’, i.e. to a user’s Inbox in BI Launch Pad.
- ‘Send to email’ enables you to send the document to an email address.
- ‘Send to FTP’ enables you to post the document to an FTP location.

39.7.3 Sending Documents to Users from Web Intelligence Rich Client

In Web Intelligence Rich Client, you can send a document as an attachment.

1. With a document opened, use 'Send by email attachment' to send your document as an email attachment:

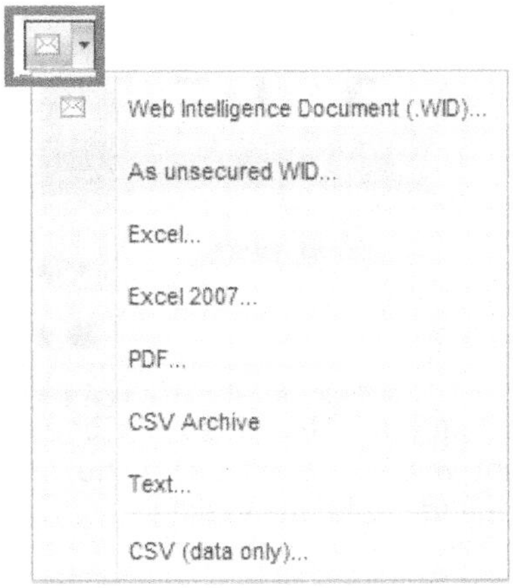
Web Intelligence Document (.WID)...
As unsecured WID...
Excel...
Excel 2007...
PDF...
CSV Archive
Text...
CSV (data only)...

If you send the document as 'Web Intelligence Document (.WID)...' then security permissions will be used when the user receiving the document attempts to open the document.

If you send the document using 'As unsecured WID...' then security will not be used when the document is opened.

In 'CSV (data only)...' format only the raw 'query' data will be saved, i.e. no tables, etc.

39.8 Using BI Launch Pad to Schedule Documents

Scheduling enables you to specify when a document should be refreshed (including the setup of recurring refreshes such as daily, weekly, etc), what format the refresh should be saved as, and where the document should be sent or saved.

Scheduling and distributing documents (together known as Publishing) is a subject area in its own right that cannot be discussed in great detail here. However, we will briefly discuss how documents can be scheduled to illustrate the concepts.

1. First select a document and then select 'Schedule' from the Actions toolbar button (or from right-click menus).

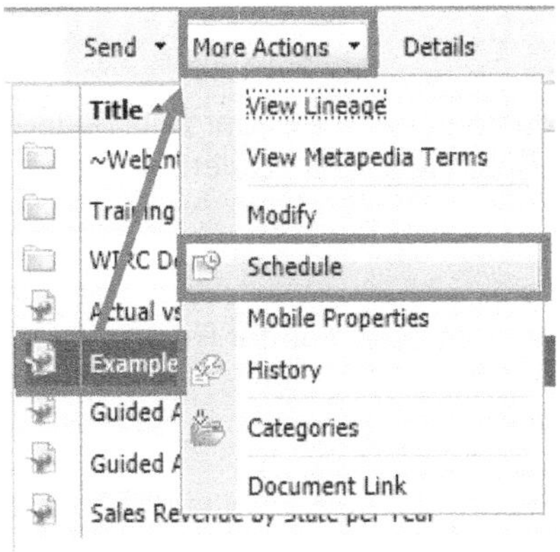
Send
More Actions
Details
Title
View Lineage
View Metapedia Terms
Modify
Schedule
Mobile Properties
History
Categories
Document Link

2. Scheduling requires the configuration of a number of different settings (shown below).

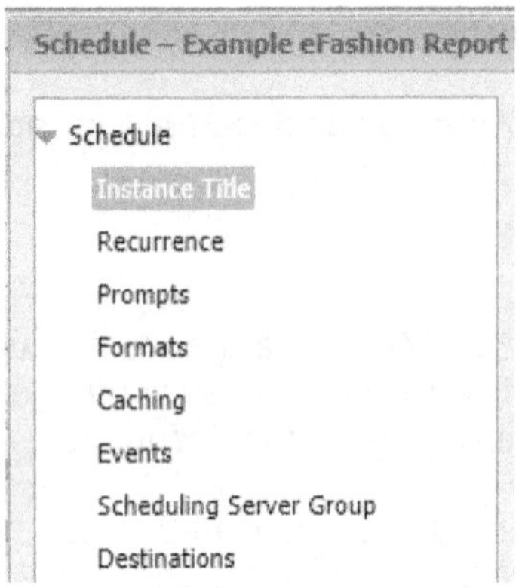
Schedule – Example eFashion Report
Schedule
Instance Title
Recurrence
Prompts
Formats
Caching
Events
Scheduling Server Group
Destinations

We will take each setting in turn as we proceed to schedule the selected document.

3. You can change the name for the scheduled document if required. This does not change the original name of the document, but the scheduled document will be saved using the specified name. If you want to use the original name then keep the default value in this setting.

Instance Title
Scheduling Demo

4. Specify the 'Recurrence' of the schedule.

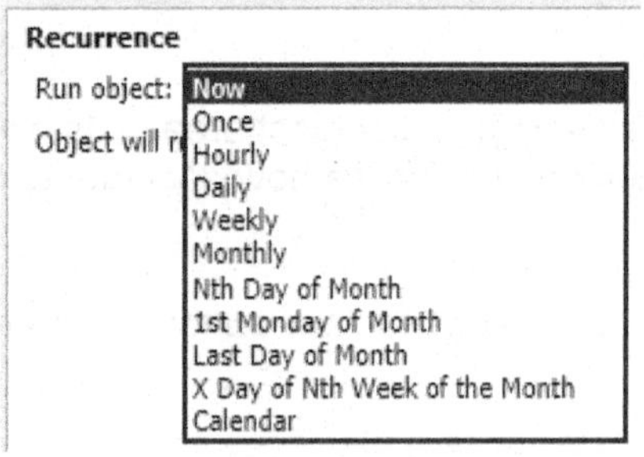
Recurrence
Run object:
Now
Once
Hourly
Daily
Weekly
Monthly
Nth Day of Month
1st Monday of Month
Last Day of Month
X Day of Nth Week of the Month
Calendar

The 'Now' option refreshes the document immediately (with no repeat), therefore you do not need to specify any more details for the recurring schedule

The 'Once' option refreshes the document with no repeats, but you specify when the single refresh should take place.

The 'Calendar' option enables you to select customised calendars if defined by your BusinessObjects Administrator, for example, a Financial Year Calendar specific to your business.

Further configuration could be required depending on your selection for Recurrence.

Here we have selected 'Once' so we are required to specify when the document should be refreshed.

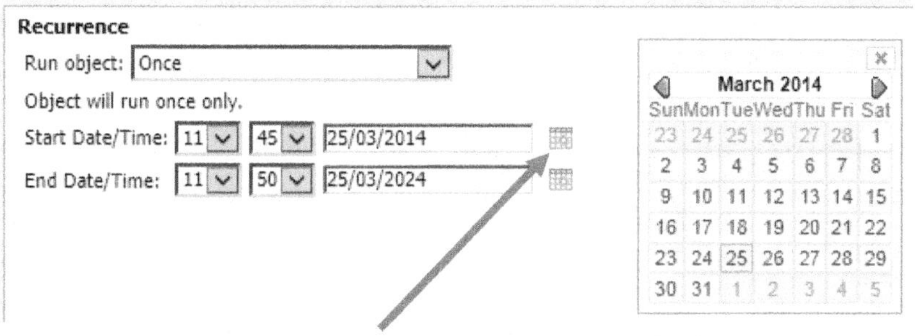
Recurrence
Run object: Once
Object will run once only.
Start Date/Time: 11 45 25/03/2014
End Date/Time: 11 50 25/03/2024
March 2014
Sun Mon Tue Wed Thu Fri Sat

Click the calendar icon to navigate dates using a calendar display, or simply type in the date(s).

5. If any queries within the document to be scheduled contain prompts then you can specify the prompt values for this particular schedule.

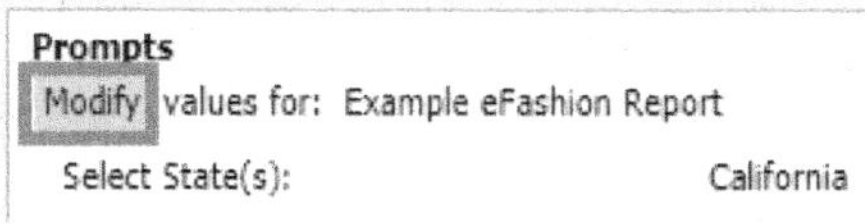
Prompts
Modify values for: Example eFashion Report
Select State(s): California

If you need to, click on 'Modify' to specify prompt values.

6. You can select a single 'Format' for the schedule, i.e. Web Intelligence, Microsoft Excel, Adobe Acrobat.

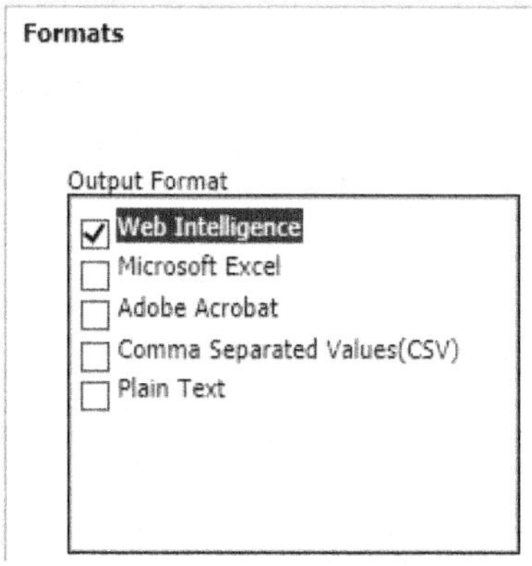
Formats
Output Format
Web Intelligence
Microsoft Excel
Adobe Acrobat
Comma Separated Values(CSV)
Plain Text

7. Scheduled documents can also be cached in other formats when the 'Output Format' is selected as Web Intelligence. You can also select locales to use for the cached files.

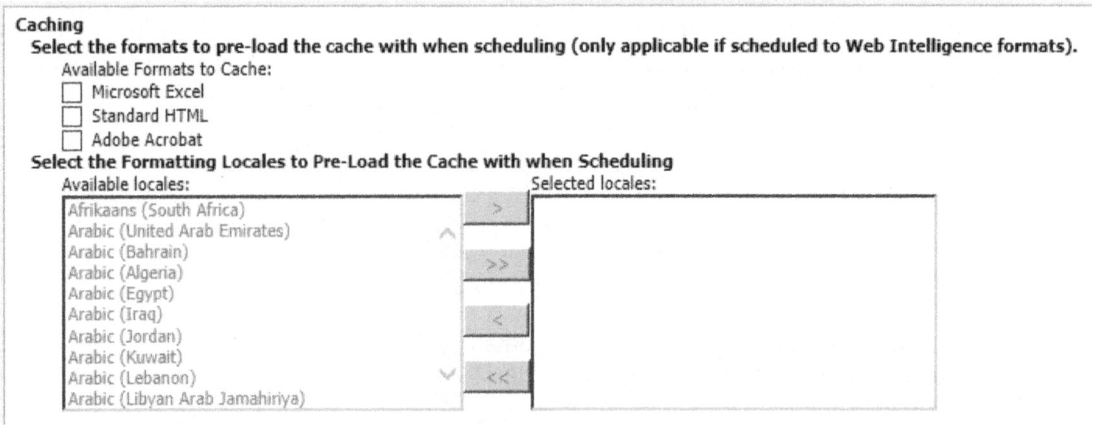
Caching
Select the formats to pre-load the cache with when scheduling (only applicable if scheduled to Web Intelligence formats).
Available Formats to Cache:
Microsoft Excel
Standard HTML
Adobe Acrobat
Select the Formatting Locales to Pre-Load the Cache with when Scheduling
Available locales:
Selected locales:
Afrikaans (South Africa)
Arabic (United Arab Emirates)
Arabic (Bahrain)
Arabic (Algeria)
Arabic (Egypt)
Arabic (Iraq)
Arabic (Jordan)
Arabic (Kuwait)
Arabic (Lebanon)
Arabic (Libyan Arab Jamahiriya)

If you have documents that will be opened in BI Launch Pad and then converted into Excel or PDF by users (with no interactive filtering, etc) then caching the documents helps to speed up the 'Save As…' process because the cached copies will be used.

8. Documents can be scheduled to use 'Events'. These Events have to be already defined by your BusinessObjects Administrator before they can be used in schedules.

   For example, an Event might exist for 'Daily Sales Loaded' and you can use this in '**Events to wait for:**' to trigger the refresh of your document.

   After your document has been refreshed, you could use a second event as '**Events to trigger on completion:**' and this could then be used in a schedule of another document, etc.

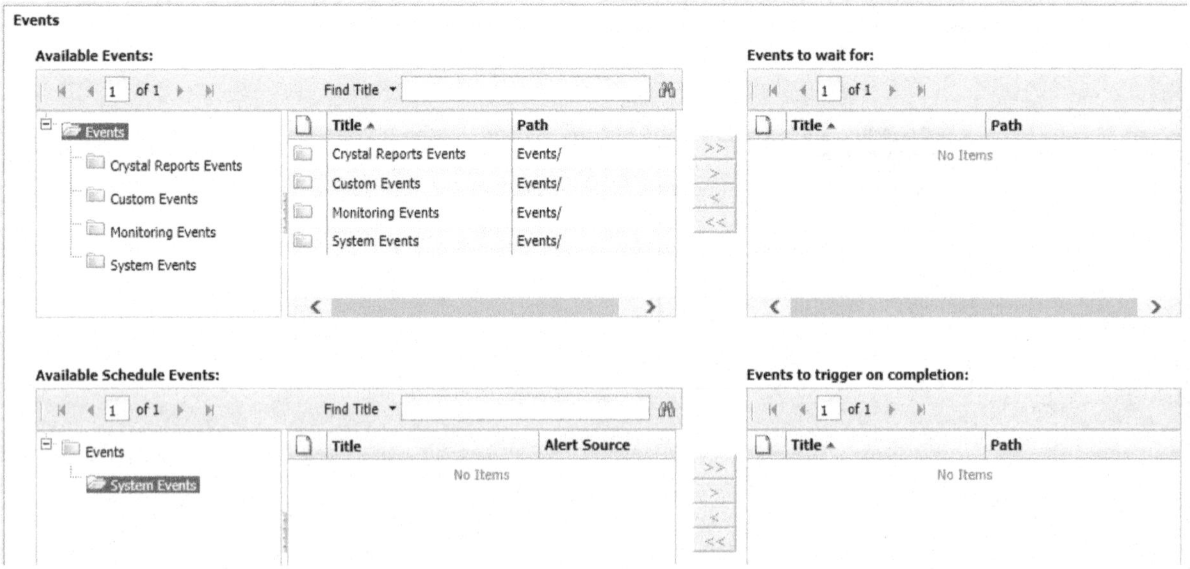
Events
Available Events:
Events to wait for:
Find Title
Events
Crystal Reports Events
Custom Events
Monitoring Events
System Events
Title
Path
Events/
No Items
Available Schedule Events:
Events to trigger on completion:
Alert Source

NOTE – Events are extremely useful if you have 'timing' issues with your data, for example if you schedule a document to refresh at 07:00AM everyday then the refreshed document might not contain the latest information if your overnight data loads have not completed.

If you schedule the document to refresh at 07:00AM and wait for the Event 'Data Load Completed' then attempts will start at 07:00AM to refresh the document, but the actual refresh will not take place until the Event being waited for actually occurs.

9. There is also the capability to specify on which servers the schedule should actually run on. Please see your BusinessObjects Administrator before changing these settings.

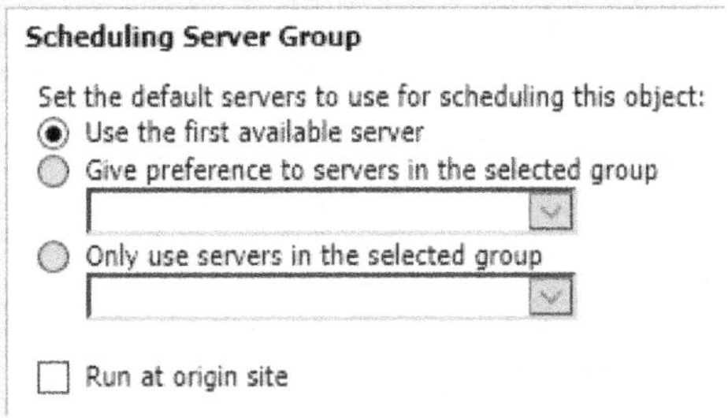
Scheduling Server Group
Set the default servers to use for scheduling this object:
Use the first available server
Give preference to servers in the selected group
Only use servers in the selected group
Run at origin site

10. You can also specify a destination for the scheduled document to be saved to.

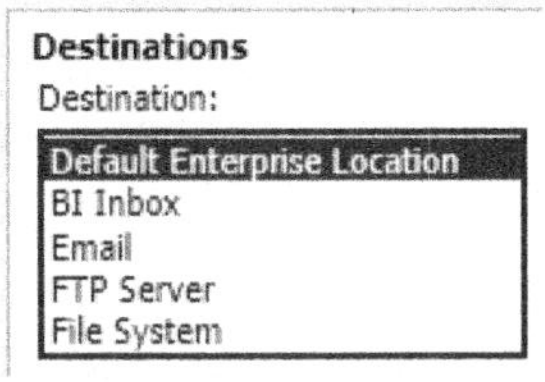
Destinations
Destination:
Default Enterprise Location
BI Inbox
Email
FTP Server
File System

NOTE – If you do not specify a destination then the scheduled document will be saved in the same location as the original document but in the chosen 'Format' (i.e. Web Intelligence, Microsoft Excel, Adobe Acrobat).

Default Enterprise Location	If you do not specify a destination then the scheduled document will be saved in the same location as the original document but in the chosen 'Format' (i.e. Web Intelligence, Microsoft Excel, Adobe Acrobat).
BI Inbox	You will be required to specify further settings such as Groups and/or Users to send the scheduled document to (i.e. to BI Launch Pad Inbox).
Email	You will need to specify email addresses.
FTP Server	Server and Account settings will be needed to post the file using FTP.
File System	Account settings and a Directory to post the file to will be required.

For all Destinations (except Default Enterprise Location), you can specify if you want to retain a copy (or instance). A copy is automatically retained when using Default Enterprise Location.

11. Click on 'Schedule' to set up the actual schedule.

Schedule
Cancel

NOTES ON SCHEDULING AND DOCUMENT INSTANCES

1. When a document is refreshed via a schedule then a new instance of the document is created in the document's history.

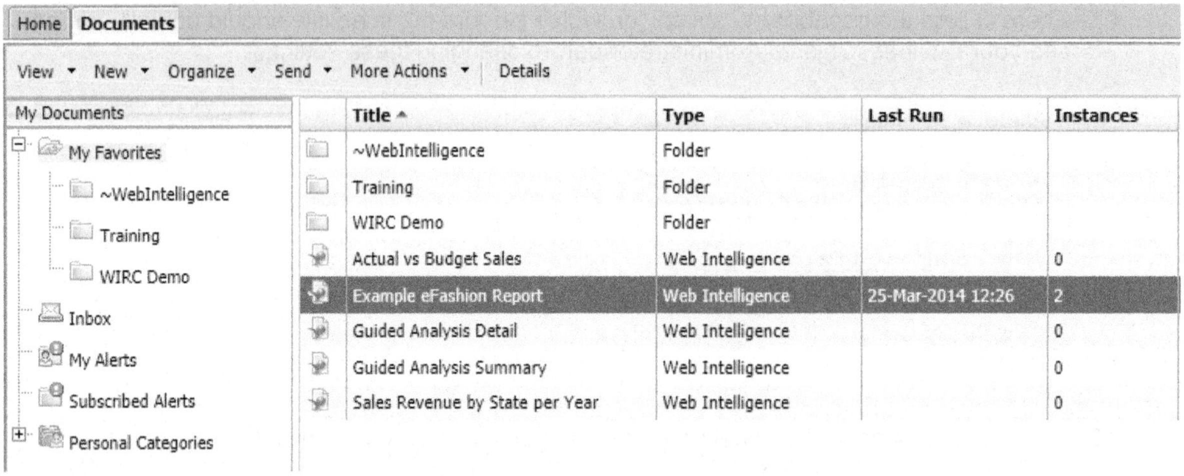
Home
Documents
View
New
Organize
Send
More Actions
Details
My Documents
My Favorites
~WebIntelligence
Training
WIRC Demo
Inbox
My Alerts
Subscribed Alerts
Personal Categories
Title
Type
Last Run
Instances
~WebIntelligence
Folder
Training
Folder
WIRC Demo
Folder
Actual vs Budget Sales
Web Intelligence
0
Example eFashion Report
Web Intelligence
25-Mar-2014 12:26
2
Guided Analysis Detail
Web Intelligence
0
Guided Analysis Summary
Web Intelligence
0
Sales Revenue by State per Year
Web Intelligence
0

Each instance is time stamped enabling you to retain snapshots of the document (i.e. data). You can manage each document's history manually by deleting unwanted instances, or they can be managed by a default setting (for example, retain the latest 10 instances).

2. The History of a document can be viewed by selecting a document in BI Launch Pad and then using right-click menu or 'More Actions' menu.

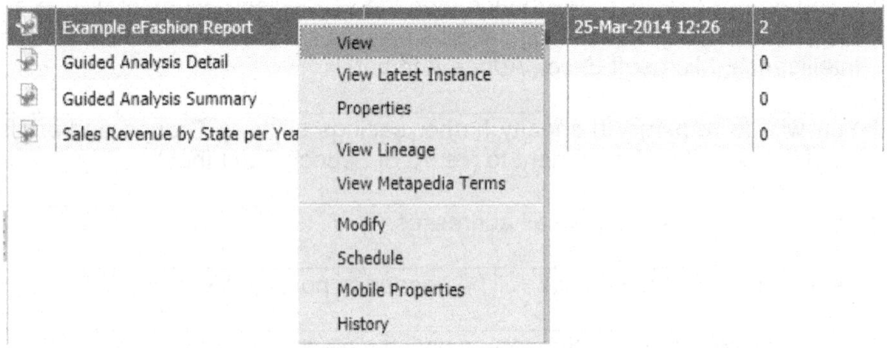
Example eFashion Report
25-Mar-2014 12:26
2
Guided Analysis Detail
0
Guided Analysis Summary
0
Sales Revenue by State per Yea
0
View
View Latest Instance
Properties
View Lineage
View Metapedia Terms
Modify
Schedule
Mobile Properties
History

- View will open the master document, not a scheduled instance.
- View Latest Instance will open the most recent instance.
- History will open a 'History' window from which you can select a particular instance and manage the instances (like deleting and rescheduling).

3. When the schedule has been created, but not yet run it will show as 'Pending':

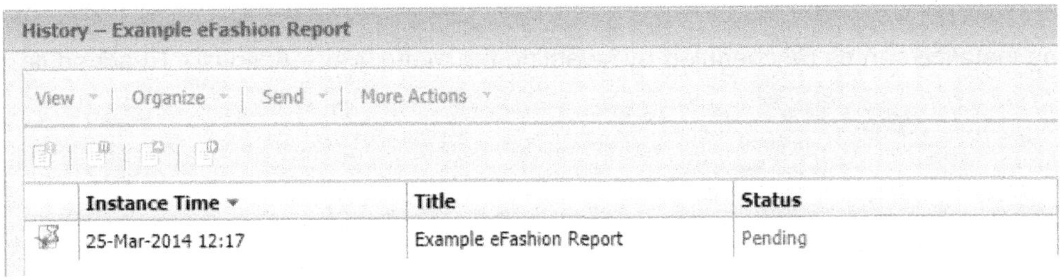
History – Example eFashion Report
View
Organize
Send
More Actions
Instance Time
Title
Status
25-Mar-2014 12:17
Example eFashion Report
Pending

4. When the schedule is running then the 'Status' will indicate 'Running'.

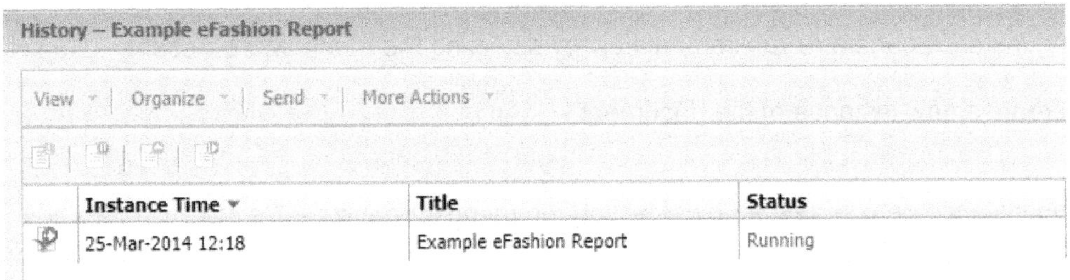
History – Example eFashion Report
View
Organize
Send
More Actions
Instance Time
Title
Status
25-Mar-2014 12:18
Example eFashion Report
Running

5. When the schedule has completed then the 'Status' will indicate 'Success' or 'Failed'.

History – Example eFashion Report
View
Organize
Send
More Actions
Instance Time
Title
Status
25-Mar-2014 12:18
Example eFashion Report
Success

You can use the 'Refresh' button to view the latest 'History Status'.

6. Click on the actual 'Status' value for detailed information about the instance.

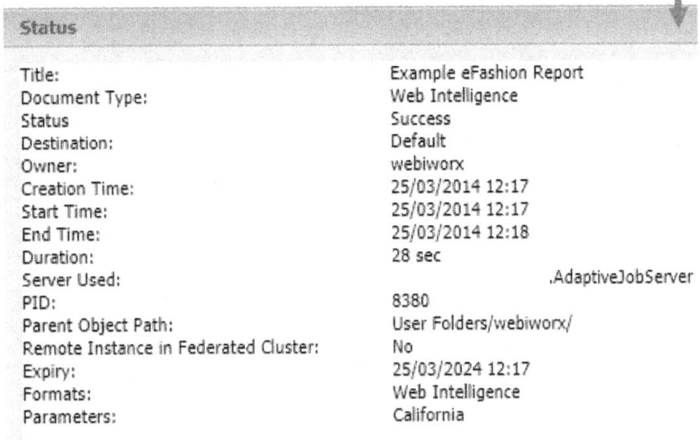
Status
Title: Example eFashion Report
Document Type: Web Intelligence
Status Success
Destination: Default
Owner: webiworx
Creation Time: 25/03/2014 12:17
Start Time: 25/03/2014 12:17
End Time: 25/03/2014 12:18
Duration: 28 sec
Server Used: .AdaptiveJobServer
PID: 8380
Parent Object Path: User Folders/webiworx/
Remote Instance in Federated Cluster: No
Expiry: 25/03/2024 12:17
Formats: Web Intelligence
Parameters: California

7. Click on the 'Instance Time' or 'Title' to open the relevant instance of the document.

8. An existing instance can be rescheduled by selecting the menu 'More Actions – Reschedule'.

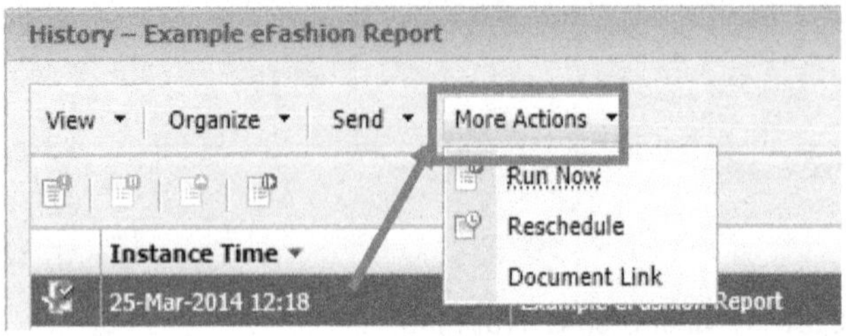
History – Example eFashion Report
View
Organize
Send
More Actions
Run Now
Reschedule
Document Link
Instance Time
25-Mar-2014 12:18

9. An existing instance can be re-run immediately by selecting the menu 'More Actions – Run Now'.

   This will create a new instance of the document.

10. An existing instance can be deleted by selecting the menu 'Organize – Delete'.

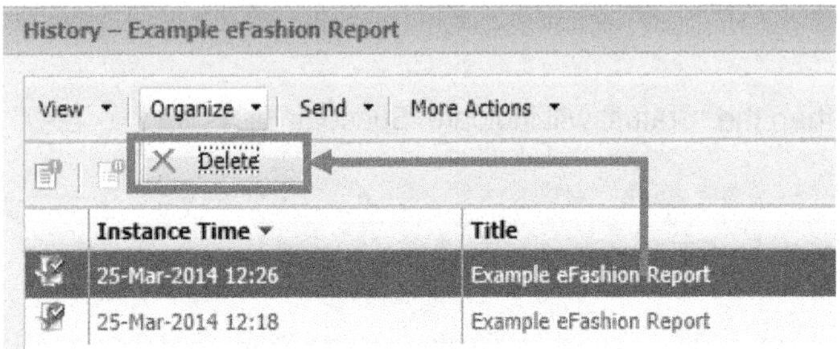
History – Example eFashion Report
View
Organize
Send
More Actions
Delete
Instance Time
Title
25-Mar-2014 12:26
Example eFashion Report
25-Mar-2014 12:18
Example eFashion Report

11. You can send a copy of an instance to a 'BI Inbox'.

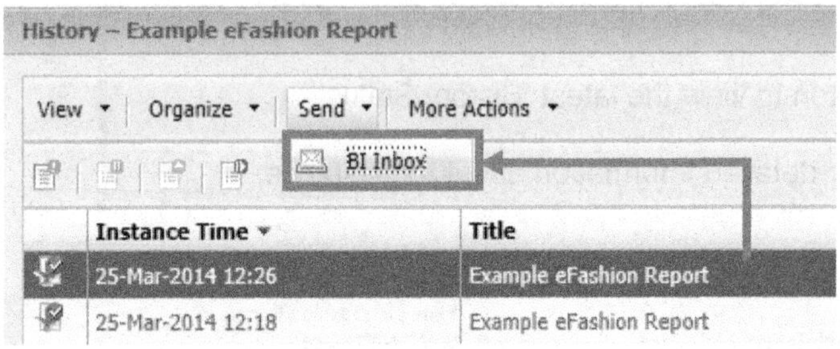
History – Example eFashion Report
View
Organize
Send
More Actions
BI Inbox
Instance Time
Title
25-Mar-2014 12:26
Example eFashion Report
25-Mar-2014 12:18
Example eFashion Report

12. You can send an external link to the document instance by copying and pasting the 'Document Link'.

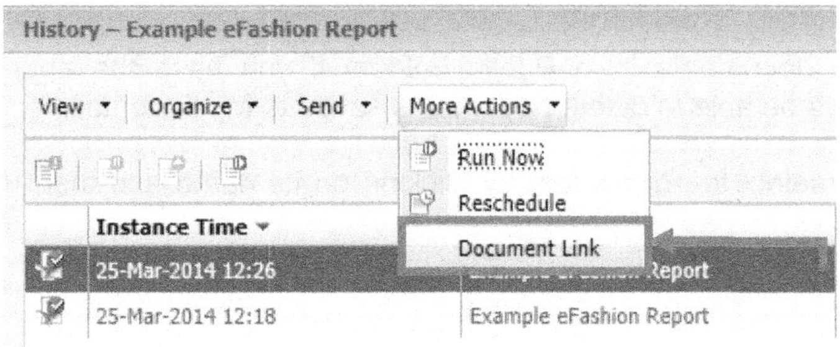
History – Example eFashion Report
View
Organize
Send
More Actions
Run Now
Reschedule
Document Link
Instance Time
25-Mar-2014 12:26
25-Mar-2014 12:18
Example eFashion Report

39.9 Saving Web Intelligence Documents in View Mode

Web Intelligence documents can be saved when being viewed in BI Launch Pad. Typically, users will want to save versions of Public Documents to their own My Favorites folder.

NOTE – Your permissions might restrict you from saving to Public Folders.

1. With a document open select '**Save As**'.

Example eFashion Re...
Save
Ctrl+S
Save As

NOTE – If you select '**Save**' then the document will be saved without allowing you to specify a new name, etc. Also, if you have opened a Public Document and you do not have access to save the document then you need to use '**Save as**' in order to specify a **Personal Folder**.

You can then save the document:

- Give the document a new **name** if you want to.
- Select a **single folder** to save the document into.
- Select **one or more categories** you want to assign to the document.
- Make the document **Refresh on open** if required.
- Apply **Permanent Regional Formatting** if necessary.

39.10 Deleting Documents in BI Launch Pad

You can delete Web Intelligence documents you save to BI Launch Pad.

> **NOTE** - You can only delete documents from Public Folders if you have the appropriate permissions. You should always be able to delete documents saved to My Favorites.

1. To delete a single document, first select the document by clicking on its name and then use the menu 'Organize – Delete'.

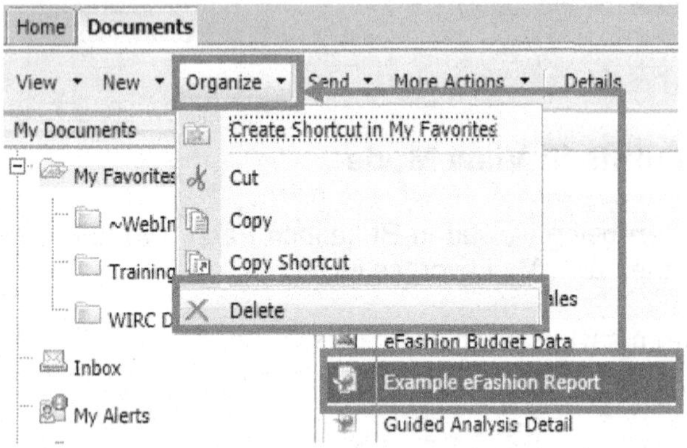
Home
Documents
View
New
Organize
Send
More Actions
Details
My Documents
My Favorites
~WebIn
Training
WIRC D
Inbox
My Alerts
Create Shortcut in My Favorites
Cut
Copy
Copy Shortcut
Delete
eFashion Budget Data
Example eFashion Report
Guided Analysis Detail

Or use the right-click menu '**Organize – Delete**' and then confirm to delete the document.

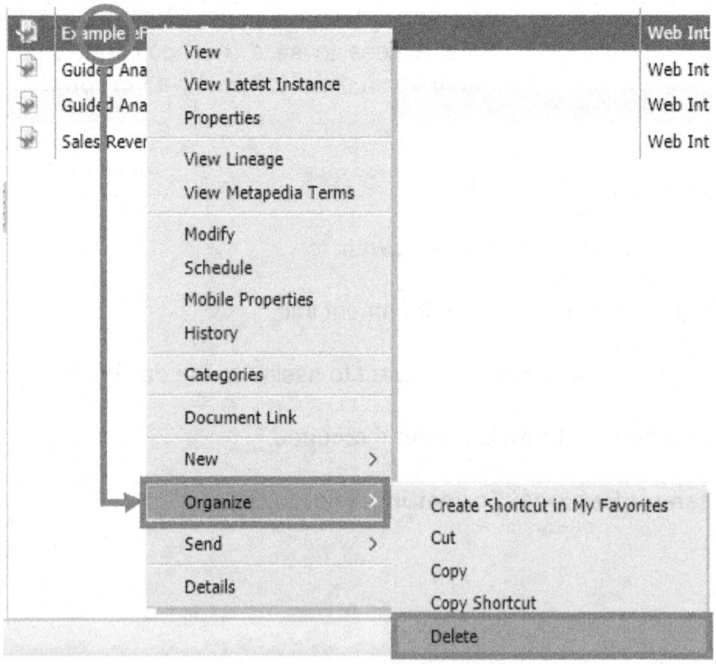
View
View Latest Instance
Properties
View Lineage
View Metapedia Terms
Modify
Schedule
Mobile Properties
History
Categories
Document Link
New
Organize
Send
Details
Create Shortcut in My Favorites
Cut
Copy
Copy Shortcut
Delete

NOTE:

Multiple documents can be deleted in the same manner after selecting the documents first.

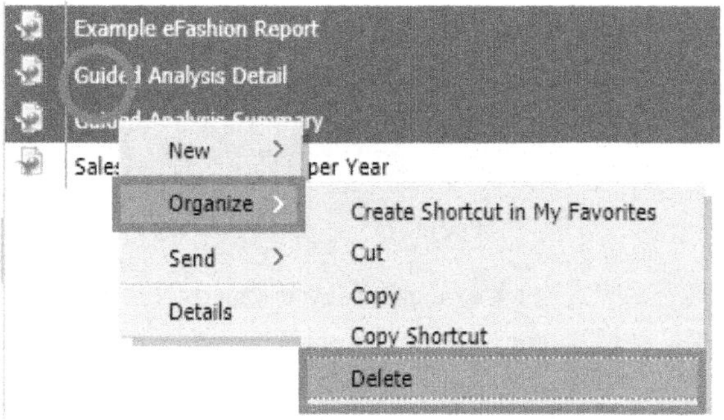
Example eFashion Report
New
Organize
Send
Details
per Year
Create Shortcut in My Favorites
Cut
Copy
Copy Shortcut
Delete

To select a continuous list of documents click on the first document name, then hold down the <Shift> key and click on the last document name.

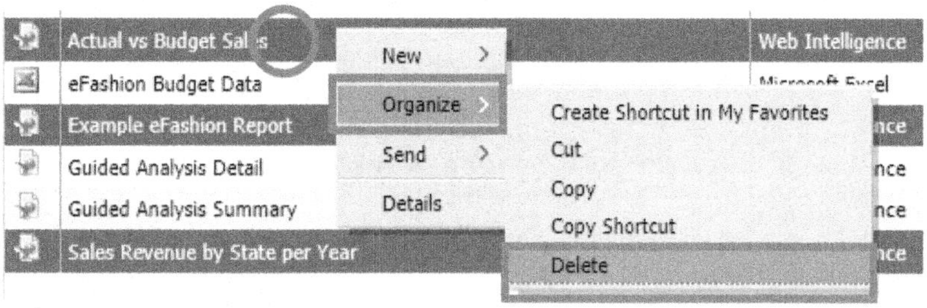
Web Intelligence
eFashion Budget Data
Example eFashion Report
Guided Analysis Detail
Guided Analysis Summary
Sales Revenue by State per Year
New
Organize
Send
Details
Create Shortcut in My Favorites
Cut
Copy
Copy Shortcut
Delete

To select a discontinuous list of documents click on the first document name, then hold down the <Ctrl> key and click on other document names to include in the list.

39.11 Web Intelligence Document Properties

Document Properties can be viewed and changed in a variety of ways.

39.11.1 Viewing Document Properties

1. With the document open, select the 'Document Summary' tab in the Left Panel.

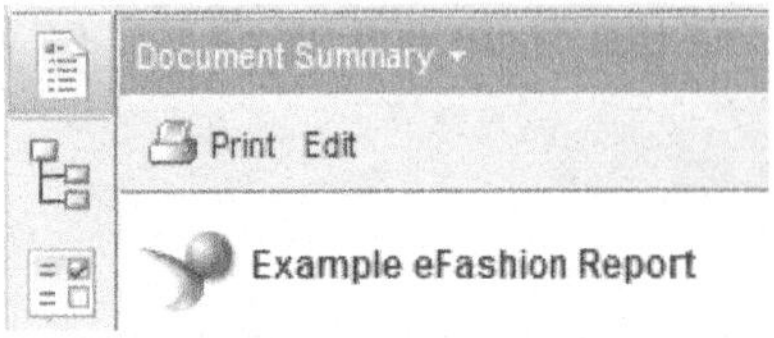
Document Summary
Print Edit
Example eFashion Report

You can then view the different types of Document Properties.

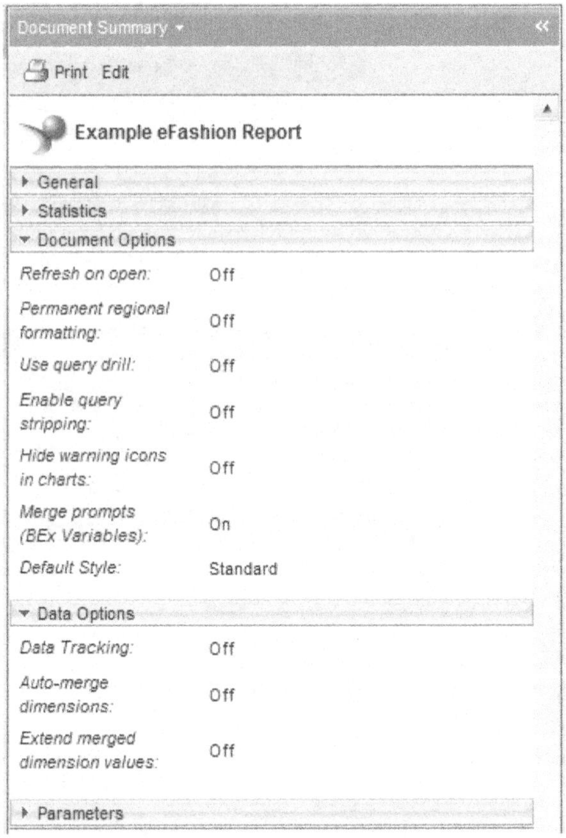
Document Summary
Print Edit
Example eFashion Report
General
Statistics
Document Options
Refresh on open: Off
Permanent regional formatting: Off
Use query drill: Off
Enable query stripping: Off
Hide warning icons in charts: Off
Merge prompts (BEx Variables): On
Default Style: Standard
Data Options
Data Tracking: Off
Auto-merge dimensions: Off
Extend merged dimension values: Off
Parameters

2. An alternative is to use right-click in BI Launch Pad after selecting the document name.

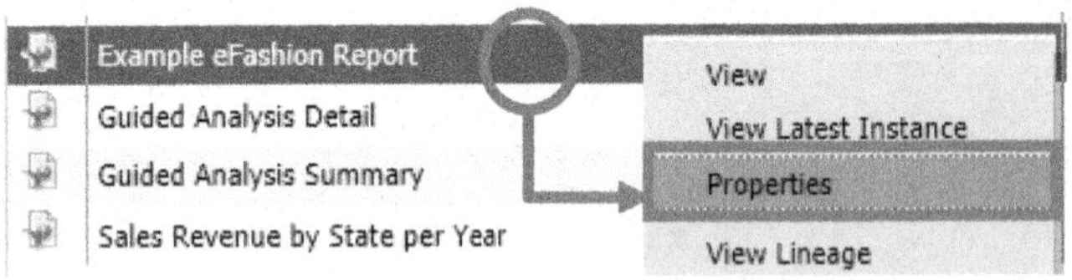
Example eFashion Report
Guided Analysis Detail
Guided Analysis Summary
Sales Revenue by State per Year
View
View Latest Instance
Properties
View Lineage

Or select the document name and then use the menu 'View – Properties'.

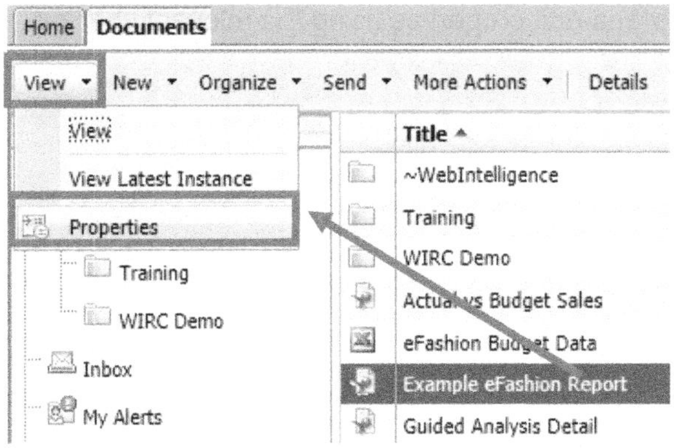
Home
Documents
View
New
Organize
Send
More Actions
Details
View
View Latest Instance
Properties
Training
WIRC Demo
Inbox
My Alerts
Title
~WebIntelligence
Training
WIRC Demo
Actuals vs Budget Sales
eFashion Budget Data
Example eFashion Report
Guided Analysis Detail

This will open the '**Properties**' window showing the Title, Description and Keywords associated with the document. These three properties can be changed and saved. The other properties are view only and cannot be modified.

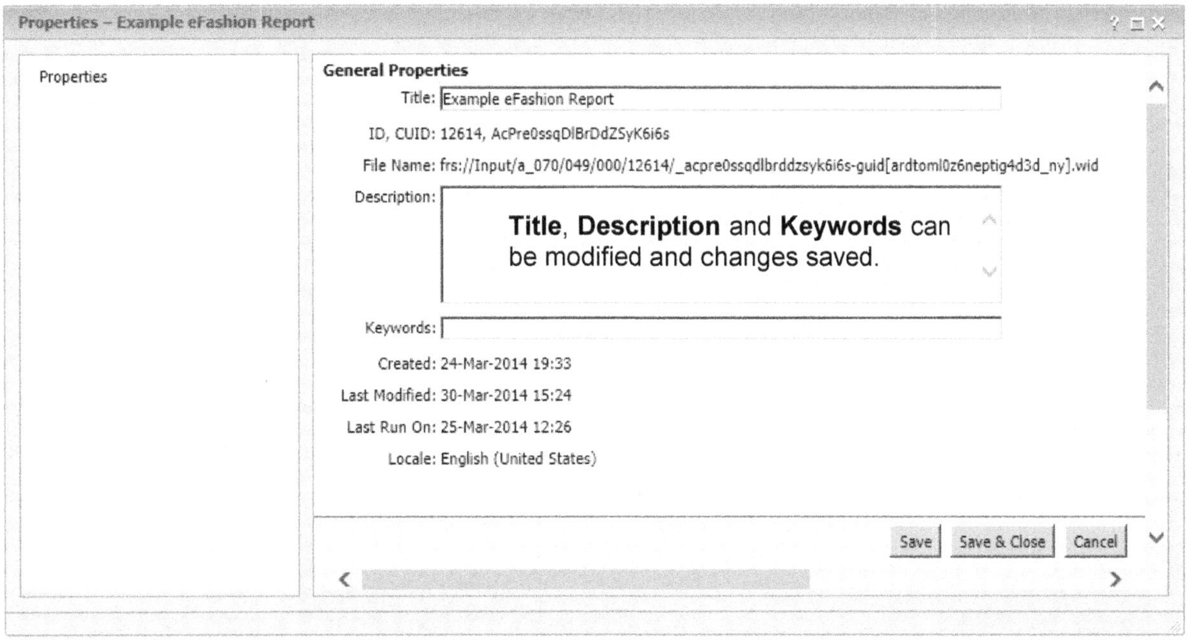
Properties – Example eFashion Report
Properties
General Properties
Title: Example eFashion Report
ID, CUID: 12614, AcPre0ssqDlBrDdZSyK6i6s
File Name: frs://Input/a_070/049/000/12614/_acpre0ssqdlbrddzsyk6i6s-guid[ardtoml0z6neptig4d3d_ny].wid
Description:
Title, **Description** and **Keywords** can be modified and changes saved.
Keywords:
Created: 24-Mar-2014 19:33
Last Modified: 30-Mar-2014 15:24
Last Run On: 25-Mar-2014 12:26
Locale: English (United States)
Save
Save & Close
Cancel

39.11.2 Modifying Document Properties

1. With the document open, use the menu '**Properties – Document**'.

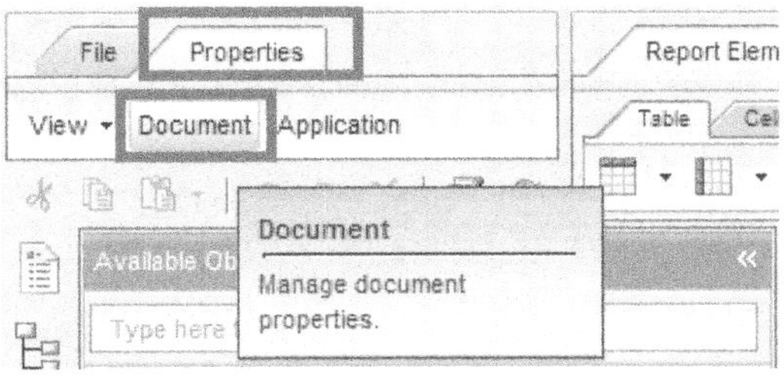
File
Properties
Report Elem
View
Document
Application
Table
Available Ob
Type here
Document
Manage document properties.

Properties can then be changed using this 'Document Summary' interface.

This interface allows the user to view and edit properties using the relevant check boxes.

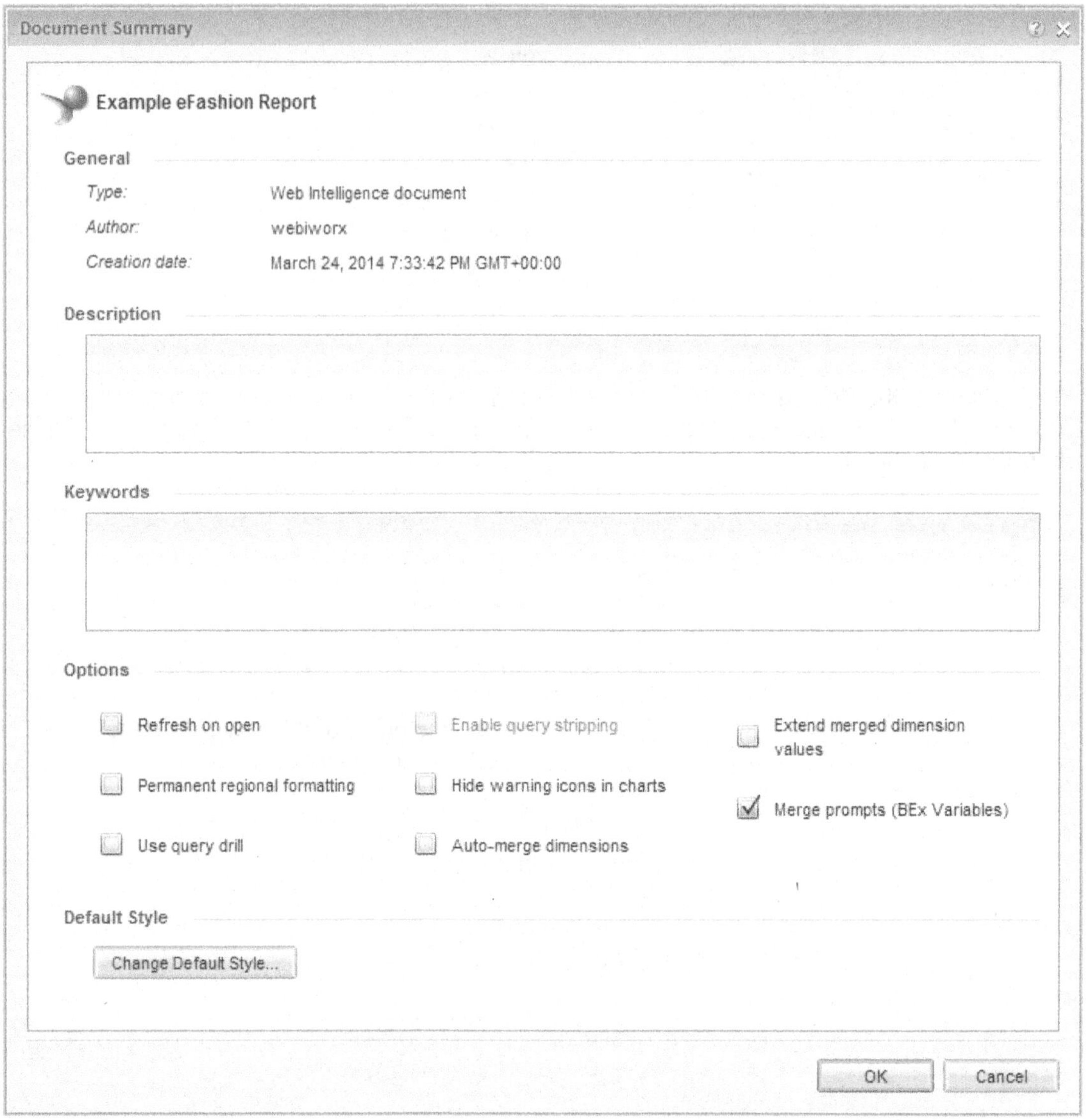
Document Summary
Example eFashion Report
General
Type:
Web Intelligence document
Author:
webiworx
Creation date:
March 24, 2014 7:33:42 PM GMT+00:00
Description
Keywords
Options
Refresh on open
Enable query stripping
Extend merged dimension values
Permanent regional formatting
Hide warning icons in charts
Merge prompts (BEx Variables)
Use query drill
Auto-merge dimensions
Default Style
Change Default Style...
OK
Cancel

After making a change the document needs to be saved if the properties are to be retained for future use. Saving to Public Folders for some users might not be possible depending on permissions.

39.12 Viewing and Assigning Categories from BI Launch Pad

Categories assigned to documents (when saving documents) can be viewed and edited using the following method:

1. Right-click on document name and select '**Categories**' or use the menu '**Actions – Categories**' as shown above.

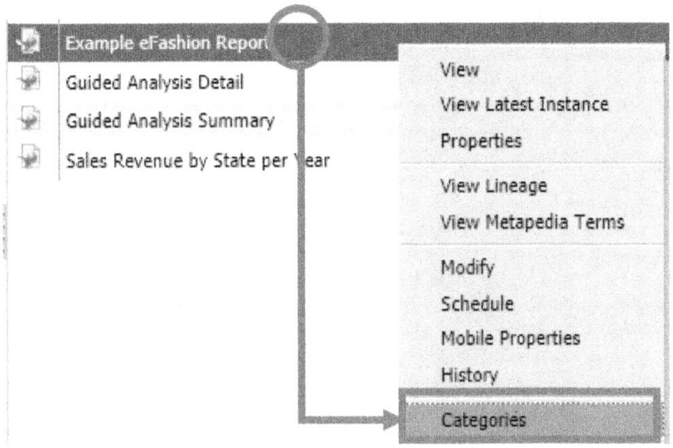
Example eFashion Report
Guided Analysis Detail
Guided Analysis Summary
View
View Latest Instance
Properties
View Lineage
View Metapedia Terms
Modify
Schedule
Mobile Properties
History
Categories

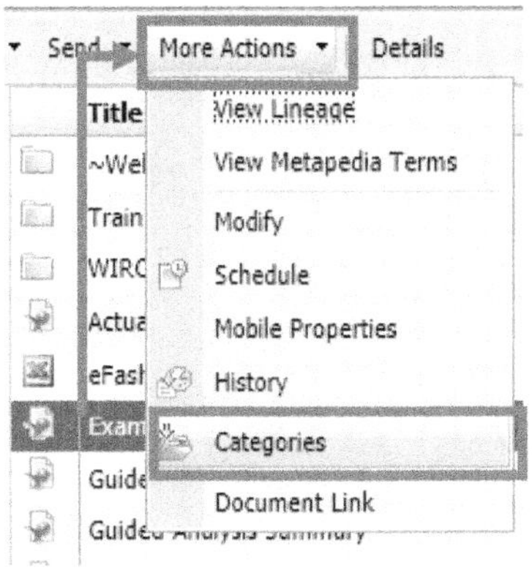
More Actions
Details
Title
View Lineage
View Metapedia Terms
Modify
Schedule
Mobile Properties
History
Categories
Document Link

2. Assigned categories will be highlighted:

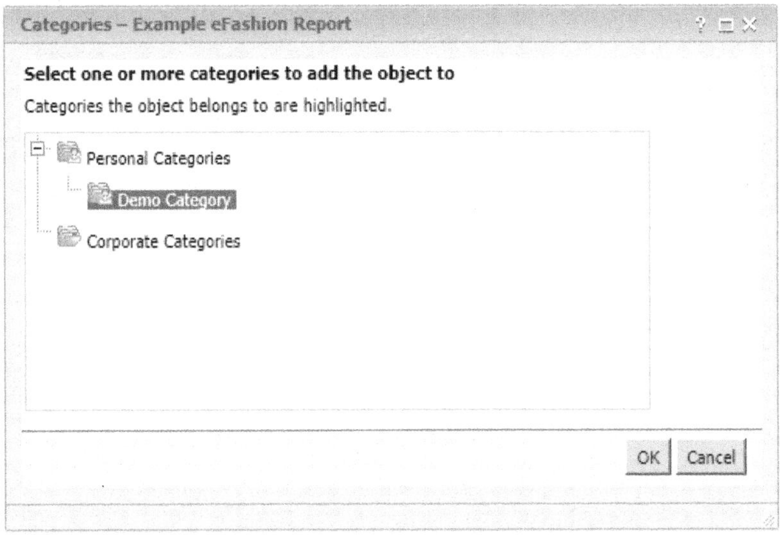
Categories – Example eFashion Report
Select one or more categories to add the object to
Categories the object belongs to are highlighted.
Personal Categories
Demo Category
Corporate Categories
OK
Cancel

Other categories can be assigned by clicking on them and clicking 'OK'.

NOTE

You can also assign and remove categories when performing a save operation on a document at any time.